FOOTBALL
LEAGUE CLUB
DIRECTORY
1987

Editor: Tony Williams

Sponsored by **COMPOSITE GRANDSTANDS**

The publisher wishes to thank Mei Lim
for ground drawings, and the AA for
'how to get there' directions

Published by Tony Williams
and distributed by
The Hamlyn Publishing Group Limited
Rushden, Northants, England

© Tony Williams 1986

This edition first published 1986

ISBN 1 869833 01 5 (softback)
ISBN 1 869833 00 7 (hardback)

Phototypeset by Orchard Typesetting, Weston-super-Mare
Printed by Sovereign Print Works, Sidmouth
Paper supplied by St Regis Paper Mill, Watchet

Front cover photo: Liverpool's goalscoring hero Ian Rush is
seen in colourful action as challenged by Queens Park
Rangers captain Terry Fenwick.

Photo: Bob Thomas

CONTENTS

ACKNOWLEDGEMENTS

The League Club Directory is now in its third year and it is heartening to report that the help and co-operation from all League clubs' administrative staff has been quite superb. My very sincere thanks go to them all.

Acting as my right hand man this year has been George Brown and my particular thanks go to him for the hours of patient research and painstaking logging of statistics that have seen him miss many a beer!

Tony Pullein has again been loyally available to help at a moment's notice as has Bill Mitchell and this year the talents of Ray Spiller's Association of Statisticians have been particularly useful as we have tried to create time in which the club statisticians for the Directory could run through their club pages. My thanks also to Duncan Hoskins for his club sequence figures.

Week by week compilation of the club match by match details was shouldered by a brave team 'bullied' by George Brown and consisting of Stan Clements (Uncle Clem), Mike Fairbairn and Robin Ryall.

The co-operation received from The Football League staff at a time when they were at their busiest was greatly appreciated and our thanks go especially to the registration department.

It has been a pleasure working with Orchard Typesetting of Weston-super-Mare and Jon Codd's team has excelled itself throughout the operation while the quiet support and encouragement from The Sovereign Print Works at Sidmouth and the St Regis Paper Mill at Watchet have been greatly appreciated.

Indeed the efficiency of P.H.M. the integrated Direct Marketing company from Penn near High Wycombe and the enthusiasm of W. H. Smiths and the sales force from Hamlyn Publishing Company have all made the Directory a 'fun' publication this year.

Thank you one and all—your support has been appreciated.

Tony Williams

Editor: Tony Williams

Editorial Committee: Tony Williams, George Brown (Assistant Editor) and Tony Pullein

Editorial Office: Football Directories, 2 Elder Cottages, Hatch Beauchamp, Taunton, Somerset TA3 6TH

EDITORIAL

The 1985-86 season couldn't possibly have started under a blacker cloud. The aftermath of Brussels and Bradford wasn't helped by the wrangling over television contracts and then we had to endure the tug of war between the elite clubs and the rest, who were frightened of being cut off from a possible 'Super League'.

So what happened?

Some superb football was played in the early season as Manchester United, Everton and Liverpool all sparkled, albeit without television showing us the special fare we were only able to read about, but the quality was there and the incentive was there for us to go and see for ourselves.

Those of us touring the grounds found an amazing spirit within the clubs (both League and strangely, non-League). It was as if the 'game' had closed ranks and was determined to show its 'real heart' having been hurt by so much that often had very little direct link with the actual game itself.

There was suddenly a welcome at the grounds.

Polite and smartly dressed officially were available to help visitors.

Obviously the supporters were better behaved at matches, and the rabble that had infiltrated into the popular areas of all grounds realised there was little point in taking on the police, when not fortified by alcohol.

A different sort of supporter was coming back to the game. Family areas multiplied.

Managers realised that supporters would not cross the road to see boring and destructive tactics and they also drew up their own code of conduct for their players so in general we saw less of those desperately petty and irritating actions such as:

Kicking the ball away when throws and free kicks have been conceded;

Petty dissent;

Obvious time wasting;

Petulant retaliation.

Players, it appeared, were being encouraged to enjoy themselves and how that helped the rest of us. Football was certainly very much more fun for us all!

Yes, by the time television brought the game back to the firesides a new spirit was apparent although there hadn't realistically been time for it to influence the waning attendances.

Happily the World Cup reminded us all of the excitement caused when skilful players are encouraged to take on the opposition and let's hope that our manager's reactions to this is positive.

Having seen the most superb skills from some of our own English lads (from the GM FA School) who had been encouraged to perfect AND USE a fine repertoire of tricks in a Wembley schoolboy international, a well known expert stated it wouldn't be long before those skills would be 'kicked out of him in our game'. Sadly a true reflection of our attitudes *in the past.*

Could we possibly hope that managers will now be looking for fast, brave and skillful players to lift us all out of our seats? I'm sure we all hope so!.

Tony Williams

FOOTBALL'S 'GOOD NEWS' AWARDS

Although I accept it is now a fact of modern sporting life that good news is no news, I am pleased to say 'The League Club Directory' will continue to feature individuals, clubs or organisations who have produced happy football stories during the year.

We felt it was unfair to ask **Bobby Robson** to give time to our awards this year with all the responsibilities of the World Cup, although knowing him he would probably have joined us again. The views expressed in the editorial and this 'Good News summary' are not of course necessarily the views of all of the panel.

When **Bob Wilson** or **Brian Moore** comment on the game in their Television programmes you know that an honest appraisal will be given and be presented in such a way that their love for the game is quite obvious. It hurts them if they are covering stories that bring the game into disrepute but I have never heard them being vindictive or bitchy. Honest and positive comment has brought them both the respect of their colleagues in the media and the players.

Because of this I am particularly pleased that they have once again contributed to the selection of this year's awards. Last season we read all sorts of views on the subject of 'super leagues' and re-organisation of the game. As some opinions became heated and certainly went 'over the top' one steady and sensible voice stood out—the voice of The Professional Footballers Association. **Gordon Taylor** expressed the Association's views in an articulate manner based on common sense and I am sure the game has a great deal to thank the PFA for, as the whole emotive subject was brought to a reasonably amicable conclusion. We are pleased that Gordon and his colleague **Brendan Batson** have again put forward some names for this season's awards.

I am also very pleased that **Graham Taylor** has again helped us with our selections as he has stood up for standards within the game during his whole football life and the pressures of First Division managership hasn't diverted him from his principles.

When the 1985-86 season kicked off, the game could hardly have been in a worse state. Because of the Brussels disaster, the consistent presence of the thugs attaching themselves to the professional clubs and the terrible tragedy at Bradford, everyone was watching how the game would react and of course a lot of regular supporters sadly drifted away from the grounds.

Luckily the game is blessed with a very high standard of young manager who brings nothing but credit to the profession. Those regularly impressing us through the media were **Howard Kendall, Kenny Dalglish, Graham Taylor** and **John Lyall** amongst a host of others. Even the biggest critic of the game would find it difficult to find any fault in the principles of these men whose attitude and sense of humour was just what the public needed if football was to remain credible to its faithful followers.

It was good to see that the majority of clubs had obviously attempted to 'educate' their players into realising what petty apologies of professional sportsmen they looked when kicking the ball away, after decisions had gone against them, arguing with referees and wasting time blatantly. We suddenly saw a few smiles, pleasant sportsmanship and an atmosphere in which we could realise that however much the management, players and supporters wanted to win, the game really was of little consequence compared with the loss of life at Brussels and Bradford. Perhaps we were getting our attitude to the game into perspective again.

We have always known that the Liverpool citizens whether 'red' or 'blue' were usually the most amusing and happy of supporters and it was great for the country that the two clubs qualified to give their supporters the stage on which they could show the world their real character and the two games at Wembley once again proved that **Merseyside supporters are Special.**

Two very different characters, who at the time of writing are not completely in harmony at West Bromwich Albion have in their own ways provided a fine example to society. **Ron Saunders** took it upon himself to launch an attack on the tragic scourge of modern youngsters—the trafficking of drugs. Ron introduced a 'Save our Society' campaign in which he encouraged many well known personalities to provide the inspiration to the young people of the Midlands (and indeed the country) to give them the belief in themselves and strength to kick the drug habit.

FOOTBALL'S 'GOOD NEWS' AWARDS

Garth Crooks meanwhile dedicated himself to helping the black community by raising money for research into the causes of sickle cell desease.

Valuable time given by personalities in this way is obviously of great value to society and is greatly appreciated throughout the country.

The World Cup gave us all a chance to see the very best of our wonderful game. It also produced some British heroes who became prominent in many homes throughout the country.

Bobby Robson who kept his head when having prepared a very sound and confident side which was favoured by many respected pundits, saw them dominate their first game, and lose, then fail to beat unfashionable opposition. The media prepared to 'bury' the manager and all credit to 'the boss' for steering the team to the quarter finals under severe pressure.

With a lovely smile and a naturally modest and pleasant attitude **Gary Lineker** captured the hearts and admiration of the nation. No parent could wish for a better hero on which their children could model themselves. Just as popular and a great deal more experienced was **Pat Jennings** who of course conducted himself with great dignity as he broke all sorts of records and carried on producing quality performances despite his 41 years. Hopefully these characters will be the ones that inspire our youngsters to copy them and not only work at their game but also at their attitude.

Back home on the television panels a lot of publicity was given to personality clashes but the man to impress most with positive attitudes, given with that tell tale glisten of the eye, that showed an emotional involvement, was **Andy Gray**. To be fair, the majority of experts gave us an excellent back-up to the games themselves and we are certainly lucky that our television 'teams' are so professional.

As some famous clubs struggled to survive, one such situation provided the chance for sterling service to be put in. At Swansea City, having also served another famous but waning club Burnley with incredible enthusiasm for his age, **Tommy Hutchinson** battled impressively. Small clubs were certainly producing their share of heroes as **Oxford United** won the Milk Cup and **Wimbledon** won promotion to the First Division. Their managers, **Maurice Evans** and **David Bassett** respectively brought smiles to many faces as they described their enjoyment and satisfaction at their achievements which no-one would have forecast. The interview with Maurice after Oxford's semi-final win was a 'gem'.

The founder of 'Supporters United' **Tony Russell** spent three months raising money for cancer research and his efforts have been rewarded by excellent Good News publicity for the game. While Blackpool striker **Eamonn O'Keefe** also showed what can be done with dedication and effort when he organised a 'fun run' in Blackpool to raise funds for the club. His efforts were so successful that 1,400 people took part, including all his playing colleagues. Eamonn himself managed to obtain most of the sponsorship for the runners and in the end the event raised £20,000!

Congratulations also to **Sheffield Wednesday** who organise the pre-match distribution of sweets thrown to supporters at Hillsborough (both home and away) and have created an atmosphere which has inspired their supporters to win awards last season for good behaviour at both home and away matches.

I know that there must be many more praiseworthy stories concerning football and footballers that we have missed and we would like to hear about any happy stories this season and whether they are 'newsworthy' or not we will continue to publicise them with our thanks.

Tony Williams

The whole Football World was saddened by the news of the death of Sir Stanley Rous earlier this year. He was probably the most loved and admired of football administrators and he was able to continue attending matches regularly, at the age of ninety, until last season. We were thrilled that Sir Stanley attended our little meeting at Watford Football Club last October when he received one of our first Good News Awards. Sir Stanley had always given me encouragement and help with my different publications over the years and I felt very priviledged to have known him. He will be sorely missed.

'GOOD NEWS' AWARD WINNERS

LIVERPOOL FOOTBALL CLUB and SUPPORTERS: At a time when a lunatic few had in one evening ruined the previously excellent reputation of the club and its supporters, Liverpool Football Club rose to their biggest ever challenge by winning the League and FA Cup double with a smile and the best disciplinary record in the First Division while their supporters backed by their neighbours across the park also proved that the majority of Merseyside had their priorities right. **Kenny Dalglish** went on record by committing himself to sportsmanship on and off the field and he was given excellent support by **Bruce Grobbelaar** who accepted criticism during a bad spell in the right spirit and their captain Alan Hansen who, when ommitted from the Scottish World Cup squad to the admiration of the football world, wished the team good luck and got on with the job of getting fully fit for the next season. Obviously, Chairman John Smith and his directors have built a club with thier priorities (from the boot room to the boardroom) just right for all other clubs to emulate. Congratulations and thanks to you all!

PETER SMITH: There is no doubt that hundreds of football-loving fanatics are giving time, help, money and care to causes within the game every week of the season. We will probably never hear about them unless someone writes in to tell us. So it was good to receive a letter about **Peter Smith** a 21-year-old ex-postman who devotes hours of his spare time bringing football to patients in Burnley hospitals. His match commentaries, star interviews and chat programmes with colleague Francis Ryan all bring great pleasure to hundreds and he also regularly visits the wards to talk football with the patients. Peter used to start his round at 5a.m. six days of the week and also found time to visit all 92 League grounds. His totally voluntary football work has been undertaken since he was seventeen and I am sure is typical of many fine unsung heroes throughout the country. Graham Taylor, who has been interviewed by Peter is also tremendously impressed with the work Peter does to promote the good in the game.

TONY RUSSELL founded 'Supporters United', an organization which dedicated itself to bringing rival fans together in a spirit of fellowship which used to be prevelent throughout the professional game and now can very rarely be realistically found outside 'Non-League' football. Tony set out on a walk around the 92 League grounds from last season's Cup Final and for three months, while losing two stone, he raised a substantial sum for cancer research before arriving back at Wembley Stadium at the Charity Shield match in August. Hopefully his belief that the vast majority of supporters are dedicated to creating a happy and sporting atmosphere at most grounds will be proved correct and his example will prove an inspiration.

JOHN LYALL: It has been said that John Lyall has never been heard to say a bad word about anyone in the game and at the same time you will never hear anyone in football running John down. In a highly competitive professional sport, that really is an incredible reputation to have and of course it says a lot for the man himself. John has been able to introduce an acceptable degree of 'steel' to go with the traditional attractive football that has always been associated with West Ham. And his team's challenge for the championship last season brought great pleasure to all those football followers who believe that quality pays off in the end.

WIMBLEDON FOOTBALL CLUB: I will admit I am biased with this award. I played my best ever game of football in a 3-0 win for Corinthian Casuals in the Isthmian League at Wimbledon against 'The Dons' who were then the champions. About 3,000 watched and the Wimbledon club went through the Southern League and the Football League to the First Division. The magic of their run cannot really be described. It is a fairytale and is being enjoyed by many people who were involved in the club in those Non-League days. Oxford United have proved the same point and I am sure that the new entries into the League via the G M Vauxhall Conference over the next few years will also do well. Perhaps attendances won't be much better than on that day on the 3rd September 1960 but the club has performed miracles and I for one have enjoyed all their 'Good News Stories'.

SPECTATOR SAFETY IS PERHAPS THE GREATEST CHALLENGE FACING BRITISH FOOTBALL. BUT HOW CAN CLUBS ADDRESS THE PROBLEM WITHIN A SENSIBLE BUDGET?

COMPOSITE GRANDSTANDS IS A SPECIALIST COMPANY OFFERING AN ECONOMICAL SOLUTION.

MAKING A STAND FOR SAFETY

Building a stand is a major commitment for any football club...

Of course safety is important, but so too is overall cost. There's also the sheer scale of the project in terms of paper-work, organisation and planning.

After extensive research, Composite Grandstands has designed a complete package to provide safe and flexible spectator accommodation at lower cost than traditional 'one-off' stands.

Moreover, the company can handle the entire operation from planning permission and stand erection to electrics, plumbing and the installation of under-stand facilities. Clubs may choose as much or as little of this package as they require.

CONCRETE FOR SAFETY

All Composite Grandstands accommo-dation is built around a frame of pre-cast reinforced concrete.

In tests, the Composite Grandstands System was shown to exceed the requirements set out in the Home

Office's 'Guide to Safety at Sports Grounds.'

ECONOMY WITHOUT COMPROMISE

Composite Grandstands facilities are constructed from a wide range of proven standard components.

The large-scale pre-casting of these components ensures an economical solution. In addition, there are none of the costs and delays associated with on-site casting.

Yet the system provides so many options that the end result is tailored to the needs of the individual club.

In this way, Composite Grandstands ensures an economical solution without compromise on safety, appearance or long-term flexibility.

DESIGNED TO GROW

The 'components' approach also means that it's a simple matter to extend facilities when finance permits or additional accommodation is required. ▶

MAKING A STAND FOR SAFETY (continued)

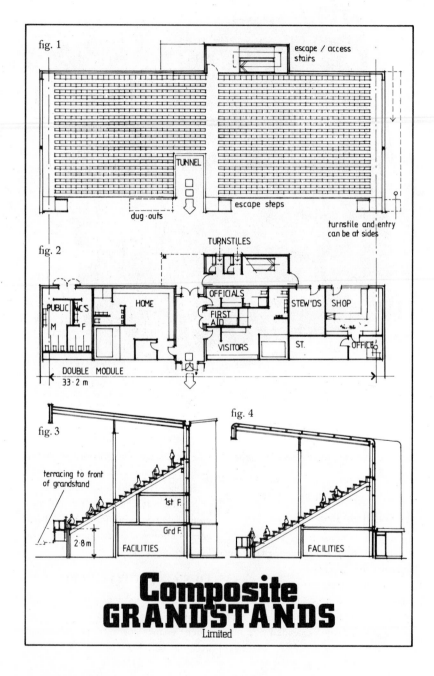

fig. 1

escape / access stairs

TUNNEL

dug·outs

escape steps

turnstile and entry can be at sides

fig. 2

TURNSTILES

OFFICIALS

STEW'DS SHOP

PUBLIC WC'S

HOME

M F

FIRST AID

VISITORS

ST.

OFFICE

DOUBLE MODULE
33·2 m

fig. 3

terracing to front of grandstand

1st F.

Grd F.

2·8 m

FACILITIES

fig. 4

FACILITIES

Composite
GRANDSTANDS
Limited

FLEXIBILITY. THE KEY TO ALL THE BEST PLANS

The basic unit of the versatile Composite Grandstands system is a stand with seating for 196 people. The illustration left (fig. 1) shows how such units can be combined.

The under-stand area can be used for changing facilities, officials accommodation and so on (fig. 2).

Alternatively, the space could be used for shops or offices; or left empty and fitted out at a later date.

Units can also provide two-storey accommodation (fig. 3), or be adjusted to suit the club's requirements (fig. 4).

A WINNING APPEARANCE

For most clubs, looks are important. Composite Grandstands can provide glazing, seating and coloured cladding. The company can also install fully-fitted under-stand facilities.

A COMPLETE SERVICE

Composite Grandstands is a subsidiary of Composite Holdings Limited, set up specifically to serve the sports and leisure market.

Composite Grandstands offers a complete building package, including site work, assistance with grants, planning permission and building regulations.

Clubs can choose as much or as little of this package as they wish. For a full consultation – without obligation – call Ted Langford on 0703 616712.

Or write to:
Composite Grandstands Limited, Omega House, Southampton Road, Eastleigh, Hants., SO5 5PB.

INTRODUCTION TO CLUB PAGES

Hopefully the Directory will now have started to pick up regular readers so gradually more football fans will be finding their way around the book with reasonable ease.

However if each club page is introduced individually then I hope the book will become that much more enjoyable.

Page One: A short revue is supplied either by the club statistician for the Directory or a member of staff. We obviously have to rely on the club secretary for supplying the changes in club personnel and a team photo for the current season. As we go to print after the first day of the season this is extremely difficult at times when clubs often have to wait for new kit with new sponsors names.

Page Two and Three Last season's match by match details include the following interesting statistics:

1. Season's achievements in each competition (i.e. the final position in the League and the Round of each cup that was reached).
2. Every score, half-time score, League position, scorer, attendance, player's position, substitute introduction, dismissal (indicated by †) and referee.
3. Also featured in dark print are the best and worst results, scorers of three or more goals in a match, 'ever present' players in their club's League programme and the best, worst and average home attendances of the season with a comparison with last season.
4. Players end of season goal and appearance totals for each competition (including penalties scored and substitute appearances), No 12, with * indicating player substituted.
5. Details of players on loan and those who have since left the club.
6. Letters behind players names on club page three are: L =On Loan, NC =Non-contract, M =Monthly Contract, A =Apprentice and S =Schoolboy.

Page Four: An extended club history and records page is included this year.

Page Five: Players details should be self explanatory except for * indicating the club captain and † showing 'Player of the Year'. Also in the player's honours column the following abbreviations are given: Div 1 80 means Division One Championship 1979-80; FAC —FA Cup winners; Lg.C —League Cup winners; EC —European Cup winners; ECWC —European Cup Winners Cup winners; ES — European Super Cup winners; EF —European Fairs Cup winners, SPD —Scottish Premier Division champions; S Div 1—Scottish Division One champions; etc. International honours for England (E), Scotland (S), Northern Ireland (NI), Wales (W), Eire (E) and overseas countries are shown thus: E (10) B (2) U21 Y,S. This indicates that the player has won ten full caps, made two 'B' international appearances, two for the Under 21 team and was a Youth and Schoolboy International.

Other initials used are AS for Anglo-Scottish; Tex for Texaco; D for Dryborough Cup; FAYC for FA Youth Cup. FA Cup appearances for 'Non-League' clubs do not refer to the qualifying rounds

We have not included players appearances and goals in the Full Members Cup and the Super Cup. These can be checked on the double page match by match details.

Page Six: This year we have omitted the ground photo but hopefully, with an increase in pages in the future, this can return. Ground details are self explanatory but the small programme feature unfortunately has to show THE PREVIOUS SEASON'S PUBLICATION because the delay in waiting for the current issues for this season forces the Directory to go to print very late indeed.

We are probably being too ambitious once again and as we attempt to include many of the last minute transfer fees and club changes that occur just before the season starts there may be omissions. However, we do appreciate letters from any readers who possess missing statistics that maybe even the club or club statistician do not know: such as the oldest and youngest players to represent the club.

Hopefully you will find all the information stimulating and enjoyable to read, we know we are not infallible, but we are working on it!

Tony Williams

KEY TO GROUND PLANS

Open Terrace		◗ Turnstile	
Covered Terrace		◀ Main Entrance/Exit	
Open Seats		PE Players'/Officials' Entrance	
		PR Press Entrance	
Covered Seats		RLY Railway	

Acting Chairman
C Hancock

Directors
R R Potter (Vice-Chairman)
T Lewis
C Hancock
R J Driver

Manager
Len Walker

Coach
Ian Gillard

Administrative Director
R J Driver

Trainer
J Anderson

Commercial Manager
Mrs K Carver

Two late wins at the Recreation Ground against Hereford United and Preston led to a final 4th Division position of 16th which meant another very modest season in every respect for Aldershot. Apart from a brief ninth position after the second match the team hovered between 14th and a dreadful 23rd (on April 5th) during the season and the team should need no reminder that if ever they drop to bottom place non-League football will be the penalty in future.

In fact, there were few redeeming features of the season which began badly enough with Orient ending the Milk Cup challenge in the 1st Round — 5-3 on aggregate. League form continued in the same vein and by October the club were in the re-election region, which was relieved by an astonishing six-clear goal win at home to Wrexham. Such high scoring was to be repeated once more — on April 19th a home to Stockport County (6-1) — but in general the strikers were none too successful with the inconsistent form bringing the expected penalties in the other cup competitions. Both brought swift exits involving FA Cup elimination at Plymouth (0-1) and Freight Rover Trophy disaster at home to Cambridge United (0-1). A subsequent fixture in the latter competition away to Peterborough saw 'the Shots' take the field with several players who may have been making their sole appearances in senior football! This lack of interest spread to the public — the crowd was 279!

In such a situation it is not easy to deal out praise to individual players, but Johnson's 15 League goals (four against Wrexham) were a good effort. Mazzon — mainly in central defence — and McDonald were other consistent players, but newcomers are urgently needed if the club is to remain in the League, because from this coming season there will be an intense effort by all clubs to avoid extinction and survival will not be easy.   WLM

Back Row L to R: John Anderson (Trainer), Andy King, Mike Ring, Martin Foyle, Tony Lange, Darrren Anderson, Colin Smith, Tommy Langley, Len Walker (Team Manager), Ian Gillard (Coach). **Front Row:** Barry Blankley, Glen Burvill, Paul Shrubb, Ian McDonald, Colin Fielder, Paul Friar, Giorgio Mazzon.

ALDERSHOT

DIVISION FOUR: 16th   **FA CUP:** 1st ROUND   **MILK CUP:** 1st ROUND

MATCH	DATE	COMPE-TITION	VENUE	OPPONENTS	RESULT		HALF TIME	L'GUE POS'N	GOALSCORERS/GOAL TIMES	ATTEN-DANCE
1	A 17	CL	A	Rochdale	L	0-2	0-1			(1,069)
2	20	MC1/1	H	Orient	L	1-3	1-2		Massey 36	1,423
3	24	CL	H	Exeter City	W	4-0	2-0	9	Foyle 10, 45, Staff 87, 88	1,411
4	27	CL	A	Colchester United	L	0-4	0-1	15		(1,928)
5	31	CL	H	Burnley	L	0-2	0-0	20		1,744
6	S 3	MC1/2	A	Orient	D	2-2	0-1		Foyle 46, 68	(1,761)
7	7	CL	A	Cambridge United	W	2-0	1-0	14	Massey 28, Johnson 72	(1,504)
8	14	CL	H	Mansfield Town	L	1-2	0-1	19	Johnson 48	1,307
9	17	CL	H	Port Vale	D	0-0	0-0	19		1,027
10	21	CL	A	Tranmere Rovers	L	0-3	0-2	20		(1,249)
11	28	CL	H	Scunthorpe United	W	2-1	2-1	20	Foyle 2, 10	1,056
12	O 2	CL	A	Hereford United	L	1-4	0-2	22	Johnson 58	(2,256)
13	5	CL	A	Halifax Town	D	1-1	1-1	22	Johnson 39	(1,066)
14	12	CL	H	Southend United	L	1-3	0-1	22	Foyle 67	1,816
15	19	CL	H	Wrexham	W	6-0	2-0	16	Johnson 4 (25, 32, 53, 86) Foyle 6, Macdonald 78	1,165
16	22	CL	A	Orient	D	1-1	0-1	16	Foyle 84	(2,833)
17	26	CL	H	Crewe Alexandra	W	3-2	0-0	15	Johnson 54, 73, Foyle 90	1,457
18	N 2	CL	A	Chester City	L	0-1	0-0	17		(2,180)
19	6	CL	A	Hartlepool United	L	1-2	0-1	18	Fern 60	(3,329)
20	9	CL	H	Northampton Town	W	1-0	0-0	17	Massey (pen) 58	1,556
21	16	FAC 1	A	Plymouth Argyle	L	0-1	0-1			(7,209)
22	23	CL	A	Stockport County	L	2-3	1-2	17	Foyle 7, Fielder 79	(1,354)
23	30	CL	H	Peterborough United	W	1-0	1-0	17	McDonald 1	1,375
24	D 7	CL	A	Chester City	D	1-1	0-0	16	Johnson 65	1,528
25	14	CL	A	Preston North End	W	3-1	1-1	15	Shrubb 37, Staff 80, Fielder 85	(2,774)
26	21	CL	A	Exeter City	L	0-2	0-1	15		(1,954)
27	28	CL	H	Colchester United	D	1-1	1-1	15	Coleman 35	1,757
28	J 14	FRT	H	Cambridge United	L	0-1	0-1			826
29	18	CL	H	Rochdale	W	2-1	1-0	15	Ferns (pen) 35, Butler 47	1,375
30	25	CL	A	Mansfield Town	L	0-2	0-2	15		(3,097)
31	F 1	CL	H	Cambridge United	W	2-1	1-0	15	Fielder 45, Stein 50	1,131
32	4	CL	H	Orient	D	1-1	1-1	15	Fielder 9	1,248
33	M 1	CL	A	Scunthorpe United	L	0-1	0-0	16		(1,270)
34	8	CL	H	Halifax Town	L	1-2	1-0	18	Staff 15	1,340
35	11	CL	A	Burnley	W	2-1	0-1	16	Johnson 51, Staff 72	(2,650)
36	15	CL	A	Southend United	L	0-2	0-2	16		(1,505)
37	18	CL	A	Port Vale	L	1-3	0-2	18	Staff 49	(2,461)
38	22	CL	A	Crewe Alexandra	L	0-2	0-0	20		(1,701)
39	25	CL	A	Wrexham	L	1-4	0-1	21	Fielder 84	(1,090)
40	29	CL	H	Torquay United	D	1-1	0-1	21	Fielder 22	1,396
41	31	CL	A	Swindon Town	L	1-4	1-3	21	Fielder 45	(8,437)
42	A 5	CL	H	Hartlepool United	L	0-1	0-1	23		1,277
43	8	CL	A	Torquay United	W	2-1	1-1	22	Barnes (pen) 30, McMenemy 66	(1,245)
44	12	CL	A	Northampton Town	W	3-2	0-1	21	Johnson 48, Barnes 58, 83	(2,049)
45	15	CL	H	Tranmere Rovers	W	3-1	0-0	19	Fadida 58, 85, Johnson 65	1,067
46	17	FRT	A	Peterborough United	L	0-2	0-1			(279)
47	19	CL	H	Stockport County	W	6-1	2-0	17	Fielder 15, Smith 41, Johnson 54, Barnes 3 (pen 66, 72, pen 75)	1,369
48	22	CL	H	Swindon Town	L	2-4	1-3		Barnes 31, McMenemy 50	3,723
49	26	CL	A	Peterborough United	L	0-3	0-2	20		(1,942)
50	29	CL	H	Hereford United	W	2-0	1-0	16	Fadida 6, McMenemy 76	1,164
51	M 3	CL	H	Preston North End	W	4-0	0-0	16	McMenemy 57, 69, Barnes 67, Fadida 75	1,866

Best Home League Attendance: 1,866 v Preston N E 3/5   **Smallest:** 1,027 v Port Vale 17/9   **Av Home Att:** 1,484

Goal Scorers:

Compared with 84-85: −525

League (66): Johnson 15, Foyle 9, Barnes 8 (3 pen), Fielder 8, Staff 6, McMenemy 5, Fadida 4, Fern 2 (1 pen), MacDonald 2, Massey 2, Butler 1, Coleman 1, Shrubb 1, Smith 1, Stein 1

Milk Cup (3): Foyle 2, Massey 1

FA CUP (Nil):

FRT (Nil):

Cox (N-C)	Blankley	Gillard	Massey	Smith	Mazzon	Staff	Johnson	Foyle	Ferns	McDonald	Fielder	Shrubb	Lange (L)	Coles	Duncan (M)	Morris (L)	McNeil	Coleman	Butler (L)	Stein	Fadida (M)	Barnes	Rigby	McMenemy (L)	Lunn (NC)	Referee	
1	2	3	4	5	6	7	8	9	10*	11	12															D Phillips	1
1	2	3	4	5	6	7	8	9*		11	10	12														**M Bodenham**	2
	2	3	4	5	6	7	8	9		11	10		1													B Hill	3
	2	3*	4	5	6	7	8	9		11	10	12	1													J Baker	4
	2		4	5	6	7*	8	10	3	11	9	12	1													K Hamer	5
	2		4	5	6	7	8	10		11		3		1	9											**J Ashworth**	6
	2		4	5	6		8	10		11		3		1	9		7									P Vanes r'd V Wood	7
	2		4*	5	6	12	8	10		11		3		1	9		7									M Dimblebee	8
	2		4	5	6	12	8	10		11		3		1	9*		7									K Miller	9
	2		4*	5	6	12	8	10		11		3		1	9		7									D Scott	10
			4	5	3		8	10		11	12	2		1	9		7	6*								A Buksh	11
			4	5	3		8	10		11	2	6		1	9	7										J Deakin	12
		3	4	5	2		8	10		11		6		1	9	7										T Fitzharris	13
		3	4	5	2		8	10		11		7		1	9	6										R Milford	14
	2		4	5	3		8	10		11		7		1	9	6										T Ward	15
	2		4	5	3		8	10		11		7		1	9	6										D Axcell	16
	2		4	5	3		8	10		11		7		1	9	6										I Hemley	17
	2		4	5	3*	12	8	10	9	11		7		1			6									I Hendrick	18
	2		4	5	3		8	10	9	11		7		1			6									N Wilson	19
	2		4	5	3*	12	8	10	9	11		7		1			6									A Gunn	20
	2	3*		5		7	8	10	4	11	12			1	9		6									**B Stevens**	21
	2			5	3	7	8	10	9	11	4			1			6									D Hutchinson	22
	2			5	6	7	8	10	3	11	4			1			9									R Groves	23
	2	9			6		8		3	11	4			1			10	5								M Robinson	24
	2	9			6		8		3	11	4	7*		1			10	5								K Redfearn	25
	2	9			6	7	8		3	11	4			1			10	5								A Seville	26
	2		4	5	10		8		3	11	7			4				6	9							K Cooper	27
			4*	5	2	9	8		3	11	10	7		1				6								M Bodenham	28
			4	5	2*	12	8		3	11	10	7		1				6	9							J Moules	29
			4	5	2	9	8		3	11	17	7		1				6								J Worrall	30
			4	5	2		8		3	11	10	7		1				6	9							J Bray	31
			4	5	2	12	8*		3	11	10	7		1				6	9							G Ashby	32
			4	5			8		3	11		7		1	9			10	6							C Trussell	33
	2		4	5	10		8		3	11*		7		1	9			6†			12					D Axcell	34
	2		4	5	10		8		3	11	7	9		1				6								M Heath	35
	2	3*	4	5	12		8		3	11	10	9		1				6				7				M Robinson	36
	2		4	5	9		8		3	11	10	3		1				6				7				A Robinson	37
	2			4	5	9	8		3	11	10	3		1								7	6			D Allison	38
	2			5	4		8		3	11	10	7		1				12			9*	6				N Glover	39
	2			5			8		3	11	4	10		1				6				9		7		J Borrett	40
	2	12		5			8		3	11	10	9		1*				6			7†		4			P Tyldesley	41
	2			5			8		3*	11	10	4						6			12	7		9	1	K Barratt	42
	2			5			8		3	11	10	4						6				7		9	1	R Gifford	43
	2	9	3	5			8		3	11	10							6				7		9	1	N Midgley	44
	2		4	5			8		3	11	10							6				7		9	1	V Callow	45
		3						11				1		5			7				8					**J Key**	46
	2		4	5			8*			11	10	3						6			12	7		9	1	A Seville	47
	2		4	5			8*			11	10	3						6			12	7		9	1	C Downey	48
	2		4	5	8					11	10*	3						6			12	7		9	1	D Vickers	49
	2	10	5	4						11		3						6			8	7		9	1	D Hedges	50
	2	10	5	4						11		3						6			8	7		9	1	M Scott	51
1	38	6	38	34	44	12	43	20	24	46	28	36	7	29	15	14	5	24	2	2	4	14	1	10	9	League Appearances	
		1				9					2	2						1			5					Substitute Appearances	
1	2	1	2	2	2	2	2			2	1	1+1		1	1											Milk Cup Appearances	
1	1		1				1	1	1	1	0-1			1	1											FA Cup Appearances	
	1	1	1	1	2	1	1		1	2	2	1	1	0-1	1			1								FR Trophy Appearances	

Also Played: Position(Game): Knight (NC) 2(46), Chinyol (A) 4(46), Mortara (NC) 6(46), Halsgrove (NC) 9(46), Pope 10 (46), Roberts (NC) 12(46), Yeomans (NC) 13(46)

Players on Loan: Lange (Charlton), Butler (York City), Morris (Wimbledon), Stein (Luton), McMenemy (West Ham)

'THE SHOTS'

Formed: 1926
Turned Professional: 1927 **Ltd Co:** 1927

Previous Managers: 1932-7 Angus Seed   1937-49 Bill McCracken   1950-5 Gordon Clark
1955-9 Harry Evans   1959-67 Dave Smith   1967-8 Tom McAnearney   1968 Dick Connor
1968-72 Jimmy Melia   1972 Cliff Huxford   1972-81 Tom McAnearney
Honours: None
League Career: Elected to Div 3 (S) 1932   Joined Div 4 1958
Promoted to Div 3 1972-3   Relegated to Div 4 1975-6
Colours: Red and blue striped shirts, blue trim on collar and cuffs, blue shorts, red stockings with two blue hoops
Change Colours: White shirt, red trim on collar and cuffs, white shorts with blue stripe, white stockings with two blue hoops
Aldershot's only other side is the Youth Team who play in the FA Youth Cup and County Youth Cup

---

CLUB RECORDS

Most Appearances for Club: Murray Brodie: Football League 461 + FA Cup 32 + League Cup 18 **Total 511** (1970-83)
Most Capped Player: Peter Scott, 1, N. Ireland 1979   **For England:** None
Record Goalscorer in a Match: Harry Brooks, 5 v Reading, 7-3, FA Cup 24.11.1945
Harry Brooks, 5 v Newport (IOW), 7-0, FA Cup, 08.12.45   Charlie Mortimore, 5 v Orient, 7-2, Div 3 (S), 25.02.1950
Dale Banton, 5 v Halifax Town, Div 4, 07.05.1983
Tommy Lawton scored 6 on two occasions for Aldershot in Football League South games during the war
Record League Goalscorer in a Season: John Dungworth, 26, Div 4, 1978-9   **In All Competitions:** John Dungworth, 34 (League 26 + FA Cup 8), 1978-9
Record League Goalscorer in a Career: Jack Howarth, 171, 1965-71, 1972-77   **In All Competitions:** Jack Howarth, 196 (League 171 + FA Cup 19 + League Cup 6) 1965-71
Record Transfer Fee Received: £100,000 from Shrewsbury Town for John Dungworth, Nov 1979
Record Transfer Fee Paid: £54,000 to Portsmouth for Colin Garwood, Feb 1980
Best Performances: League: 8th Div 3 1973-4   **FA Cup:** 5th Round Replay   **League/Milk Cup:** 3rd Round Replay
Most League Points: 75, Div 4, 1983-4   **Most League Goals:** 83, Div 4, 1963-4
Record League Victory: 8-1 v Gateshead, Div 4, 13 Sept 1958
Most Goals Scored in a Senior Competition: 11 v Kingstonian, FA Cup Qual Rnd, 16 Nov 1929
Record League Defeat: 0-9 v Bristol City, Div 3 (S), 28 Dec 1946
Oldest Player in League Match:
Youngest Player in League Match: Paul Hampshire, 17 yrs
Most Consecutive Undefeated League Matches: 13 1966, 1978
Longest Run of Undefeated Home League Matches: 26 1977-78
Longest Run Without Home League Win: 9 1936-37 & 1947
Most Consecutive League Wins: 6 1961
Most Consecutive League Defeats: 9 1965-66

League Matches Without a Win: 17 1936-37
Away League Matches: 9 1949-50, 1968
Away League Win: 26 1965-66
Home League Wins: 8 1962
Away League Wins: 4 1968

Club Statistician for the Directory: Patrick Worrall

ALDERSHOT

PLAYERS NAME Ht Wt Birthdate	Honours	Birthplace Transfers	Clubs	League	Milk Cup	FA Cup	Other Comps	League	Milk Cup	FA Cup	Other Comps
GOALKEEPERS											
David Coles		Wandsworth	Birmingham City (A)								
5.10 12.0 15.6.64			Mansfield Town (L)	3							
		F	Aldershot	108	11	6	2				
Tony Lange		London	Charlton Athletic (A)	12			1				
6.1 12.12 10.12.64		F	Aldershot	7							
DEFENDERS											
Barry Blanckley		Farnborough	Southampton (A)	7+1			4				
5.11 11.6 27.10.64		F	Aldershot	66	2	1	2				
Georgio Mazzon		Cheshunt	Hertford Town								
5.11 12.2 4.9.60		F	Tottenham Hotspur	3+1	0+2	1					
		F	Aldershot	122	12	3	3	4			
Colin Smith		Ruddington	Nottingham Forest								
6.0 12.0 3.11.58		Hong Kong	Norwich City	2+2	2						
		Hong Kong	Cardiff City	60	3			2			
		F	Aldershot	44	2	1	2	12			
MIDFIELD											
Glen Burvill	FAYC 81	Camden Town	West Ham U (A)								
5.9 10.10 26.10.52		F	Aldershot	57+8	7+1	1	2	15	2		
		F	Reading	24+5	0+1	5	2				
			Fulham (L)	9							
		F	Aldershot								
Colin Fielder		London	Aldershot	48+8	1	0+1	3	8			
5.9 11.0 5.1.64											
Ian McDonald*	Div. 3, 77	Barrow	Barrow (A)	30+5	1	2		1			
5.9 11.9 10.5.53		£3,000	Workington	42	2	1		4	1		
		£35,000	Liverpool								
			Colchester Utd (L)	5							
		£19,000	Mansfield Town	47+9	6+1	6		4	3	1	
		F	York City	175	9	11		29	1	1	
		F	Aldershot	210	14	12	4	30	2	2	
Paul Shrubb		Guildford	Fulham (A)	1							
5.8 10.8 1.8.55			Hellenic (S.A.)								
			Brentford	170+12	9	6+1		8			: *
			Aldershot	146+8	10+1	6+1	5	4			
Darren Anderson		Merton	Coventry City (A)								
6.1 12.5 6.9.66			Charlton Athletic	10							
			Crewe Alexandra (L)	5		1					
			Aldershot								
Andy King	EU21(2)	Luton	Luton Town (A)	30+3	1	2		9			
5.9 10.10 14.8.56		£35,000	Everton	150+1	21	11		38	8	2	
		£425,000	QPR	28+2	1	2		9			
		£400,000	WBA	21+4	8+1			4	1	1	
		Player Exch.	Everton	43+1	8+1	5		9	3	2	
		Cambour (Hol)	Wolverhampton W.	48	4			20			
		Orebro Sweden	Luton Town	3		3					
			Aldershot								
FORWARDS											
'Bobby' Barnes	E.Y.	K'ston-on-T	West Ham U (A)	31+12	2+2	5+1	0+1	5		1	
5.7 11.0 17.12.62			Scunthorpe U (L)	6							
			Aldershot								
Martin Foyle		Salisbury	Southampton (A)	6+6	0+2			1	2		
5.10 11.2 2.5.62		£10,000	Aldershot	64	8	4	2	25	5	2	
Garry Johnson		Peckham	Chelsea (A)	16+3				9			
5.11¾ 11.8 14.9.49			Brentford	55+5		3	1	13			1
			P.G. Rangers (SA)								
			Aldershot								
Tommy Langley	EU21(1) B(3)	Lambeth	Chelsea (A)	129+13	4	6		40	1	2	
5.11 10.7 8.2.58	Y.S		QPR	24+1	3			8	1		
			Crystal Palace	54+5	5+1	5+1		9	1	1	
		A.E.K. Athens	Coventry City (L)	2							
			Wolverhampton W.	22+1	2+1	2		4			
		Hong Kong	Aldershot								
Jon Rigby	FAYC 83	Bury St Edmunds	Norwich City (A)	7+3							
6.2 11.2 31.1.65			Aldershot	1							
Mike Ring	Irish Cup	Brighton	Brighton	15	1+1						
5.10 11.7 13.2.61			Morton	6							
			Ballymena	2	1						
			Hull City	17+7	2+1	3+1	1+1	1	1	1	
			Aldershot								

ADDITIONAL CONTRACT PROFESSIONALS

APPRENTICES

Tony Chinyou

NON-CONTRACT PLAYERS

Mark Cameron, Graham Cox, Jason Eade, Mark Frampton, Stephen Hagart, Paul Holsgrove (1L), Steve Killick, Carl Knight (1FRT), Grant Lynn, Darren Mortora (1FRT), Chris Peters, Neil Roberts (0+1FRT), Derek Traymen, Darren Yeomans (0+1FRT)

RECREATION GROUND

High Street, Aldershot GU11 1TW   **Capacity:** 16,000

Record Attendance: 19,138 v Carlisle United, FA Cup 4th Round Replay, 28 Jan 1970

Smallest Home Attendance for a First Class Match: 1,027 v Port Vale, Div 4, 17 Sept 1985

Record Receipts: £21,275.30 v Norwich City, Milk Cup 3rd Round Replay, 6 Nov 1984

Season Tickets: Stand: £57.50, £62.20 (£29.50 juveniles/OAP); Ground: £45.50 (£19.00 juveniles/OAP)

Executive Box Season Tickets: VIP Club (Members Only)

Cost of Stand Tickets: £3.60, £3.50, £3.40; Terraces: £2.80 (juveniles/OAP £1.10)

Match and Ticket Information: Telephone ground two weeks before match

Car Parking: Multi-Storey within ¾ mile of ground

Nearest Railway Station: Aldershot (04862 65251)

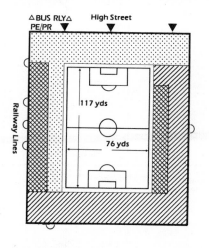

How to get to the ground

From London: Leave M3 at junction 4, then follow signs Aldershot A325. In 5 miles at roundabout take 1st exit A323 into Wellington Avenue. In 0.8m at roundabout take 2nd exit into High Street for Recreation Ground (on left)
From East: From Guildford follow signs Aldershot and enter via A323 High Street for Recreation Ground (on right)
From South & West: From Farnham follow signs Farnborough A325. Then at roundabout take 2nd exit into Wellington Avenue A323. In 0.8m at roundabout take 2nd exit into High Street for Recreation Ground (on left)

Price of 1986-7 Programme: 40p
Number of Pages: 16
Subscriptions: £14.00 per season for home matches (postage included)

Local Newspapers: The Aldershot News, The Farnham Herald, The Surrey Advertiser

Local Radio Stations: County Sound Radio, Radio 210 (Thames Valley)

Chairman
P D Hill-Wood

Directors
D Dein (Vice-Chairman)
Sir Robert Bellinger CBE, DSC
S C McIntyre MBE, FCIS
A Wood
R G Gibbs
C E B L Carr
R C L Carr

Secretary/Managing Director
K J Friar (01-226 0304)

Assistant Secretary
D Miles

Commercial Manager
A J Kelsey (01-226 9562)

Manager
George Graham

First Team Coach
T Foley

Youth Team Coach
P Rice

Chief Scout
S Burtenshaw

Physiotherapist
R Johnson

Groundsman
D Farrell

Many clubs would be happy with seventh place in the 1st Division but of course Arsenal supporters and indeed their staff do expect the club to be among the honours and in this context last season was a disappointment.

By mid September a run of four consecutive victories saw Don Howe's squad reach an encouraging third place and hopes were high. However an injury to the very impressive Stewart Robson unsettled the side and it wasn't until the youngsters David Rocastle, Niall Quinn and Martin Keown were drafted in that consistent form was achieved again. In a highly emotive spell Arsenal beat Liverpool (home) and Manchester United (away) in consecutive weeks and played nine matches without defeat. Senior players Tommy Caton, Steve Williams and Tony Woodcock must have wondered what the future held for them at Highbury but Don Howe must have felt particularly happy as his youngsters proved themselves and the reserves and youth team led their divisions.

There were no cup runs to set the club alight although having drawn at Aston Villa in the Milk Cup quarter-final a semi-final place seemed to be there for the taking. It wasn't to be and as Luton Town put paid to 'The Gunners' FA Cup hopes in the second replay of their 5th Round tie, the season went a little flat.

There was no lack of controversy however as the board, having apparently privately warned Don Howe that they were approaching Terry Venables to discuss his manager's job, decided to make the matter public and gave their manager very little option but to stand down.

Sadly another honest professional appeared to be treated shabbily and once again the public's image of the game of professional football took another knock. To most people who follow football, Arsenal had always stood for everything that was good, but even they had appeared to be losing their standards.

Steve Burtenshaw valiantly tried to keep heads up and an interest in the run in at the end of the season but the team looked a dejected outfit and only three victories were managed in the last 11 games.

Stewart Robson won the Player of the Year award and forced his way into the reckoning for the Senior England squad while Charlie Nicholas produced his flashes of class more often and won his place back in Scotland's World Cup team. The dependable Kenny Sansom was an ever present and his inspirational qualities could be of great importance if George Graham is going to lift Arsenal back to their rightful place, challenging for honours at the top of the League. T W

Standing L to R: Theo Foley (First Team Coach), Viv Anderson, David O'Leary, Tommy Caton, Niall Quinn, John Lukic, Rhys Wilmot, Tony Adams, Ian Allinson, Steve Williams, Roy Johnson (Physiotherapist). **Seated:** Gus Caesar, Stewart Robson, Charlie Nicholas, Paul Davis, George Graham (Manager), David Rocastle, Martin Hayes, Graham Rix, Kenny Sansom.

ARSENAL

DIVISION ONE: 7th   **FA CUP:** 5th ROUND   **MILK CUP:** QUARTER-FINAL

MATCH	DATE	COMPE-TITION	VENUE	OPPONENTS	RESULT	HALF TIME	L'GUE POS'N	GOALSCORERS/GOAL TIMES	ATTEN-DANCE
1	A 17	CL	A	Liverpool	L 0-2	0-1			(38,261)
2	20	CL	H	Southampton	W 3-2	1-0		Caton 6, Robson 47, Woodcock 67	21,895
3	24	CL	H	Manchester United	L 1-2	0-1	16	Allinson (pen) 89	37,145
4	27	CL	A	Luton Town	D 2-2	0-1	15	Donaghy (og) 53, Woodcock 71	(10,012)
5	31	CL	H	Leicester City	W 1-0	1-0	10	Woodcock 15	18,027
6	S 3	CL	A	Q.P.R.	W 1-0	0-0	7	Allinson 62	(15,993)
7	7	CL	A	Coventry City	W 2-0	1-0	5	Woodcock 31, Nicholas 90	(12,189)
8	14	CL	H	Sheffield Wednesday	W 1-0	1-0	3	Allinson (pen) 30	23,108
9	21	CL	A	Chelsea	L 1-2	0-0	7	Nicholas 72	(33,241)
10	25	MC2	A	Hereford United	D 0-0	0-0			(6,049)
11	28	CL	H	Newcastle United	D 0-0	0-0	6		24,104
12	O 5	CL	H	Aston Villa	W 3-2	2-1	5	Woodcock 4, Anderson 18, Whyte 87	18,881
13	8	MC2	H	Hereford United	W 2-1*	1-1		Anderson 26, Nicholas 114	15,789
14	12	CL	A	West Ham United	D 0-0	0-0	4		(24,057)
15	19	CL	H	Ipswich Town	W 1-0	1-0	4	Davis 5	19,552
16	26	CL	A	Nottingham Forest	L 2-3	0-1	6	Rix 89, Davis 90	(17,756)
17	30	MC3	A	Manchester City	W 2-1	0-1		Nicholas 5, Allinson 75	(18,279)
18	N 2	CL	H	Manchester City	W 1-0	0-0	5	Davis 71	22,264
19	9	CL	A	Everton	L 1-6	0-2	7	Nicholas 46	(28,620)
20	16	CL	H	Oxford United	W 2-1	2-0	7	Davis 14, Woodcock 34	19,632
21	19	MC4	H	Southampton	D 0-0	0-0			18,244
22	23	CL	A	W.B.A.	D 0-0	0-0	7		(9,165)
23	26	MC4R	A	Southampton	W 3-1	0-0		Hayes 56, Nicholas 71, Robson 76	(14,010)
24	30	CL	H	Birmingham City	D 0-0	0-0	7		16,673
25	D 7	CL	A	Southampton	L 0-3	0-1	8		(15,052)
26	14	CL	H	Liverpool	W 2-0	2-0	7	Nicholas 4, Quinn 25	35,048
27	21	CL	A	Manchester United	W 1-0	0-0	7	Nicholas 75	(44,386)
28	28	CL	H	Q.P.R.	W 3-1	1-0	7	Rix 12, Nicholas 67, Woodcock 82	25,770
29	J 1	CL	H	Tottenham Hotspur	D 0-0	0-0	7		45,109
30	4	FAC3	A	Grimsby Town	W 4-3	2-1		Rix 13, Nicholas 3 (30, 51, 58)	(12,829)
31	18	CL	A	Leicester City	D 2-2	1-0	9	Robson 44, Nicholas 59	(11,246)
32	22	MC QF	A	Aston Villa	D 1-1	1-0		Nicholas 33	(26,093)
33	25	FAC4	H	Rotherham United	W 5-1	2-0		Allinson (pen) 1, 81, Robson 19, Nicholas 49, Rix 62	28,490
34	F 1	CL	H	Luton Town	W 2-1	1-1	7	Allinson (pen) 4, Rix 58	22,473
35	4	MC QFR	H	Aston Villa	L 1-2	0-1		Mariner 78	33,091
36	15	FAC 5	A	Luton Town	D 2-2	2-2		Allinson 16, Rocastle 27	(15,799)
37	M 1	CL	A	Newcastle United	L 0-1	0-0	8		(21,860)
38	3	FAC5R	H	Luton Town	D 0-0*	0-0			26,547
39	5	FAC5R	A	Luton Town	L 0-3	0-1			(13,251)
40	8	CL	A	Aston Villa	W 4-1	0-0	7	Elliot (og) 58, Nicholas 72, Hayes 81, Rocastle 89	(10,584)
41	11	CL	A	Ipswich Town	W 2-1	1-1	5	Nicholas 15, Woodcock 49	(13,967)
42	15	CL	H	West Ham United	W 1-0	0-0	5	Woodcock 76	31,240
43	22	CL	H	Coventry City	W 3-0	1-0	5	McInally (og) 32, Woodcock 50, Hayes 89	17,189
44	29	CL	A	Tottenham Hotspur	L 0-1	0-1	5		(33,427)
45	31	CL	A	Watford	L 0-2	0-1	6		19,599
46	A 1	CL	A	Watford	L 0-3	0-2	7		(18,635)
47	5	CL	A	Manchester City	W 1-0	0-0	5	Robson 67	(19,590)
48	8	CL	H	Nottingham Forest	D 1-1	1-0	6	Allinson (pen) 19	15,098
49	12	CL	H	Everton	L 0-1	0-0	7		28,251
50	16	CL	A	Sheffield Wednesday	L 0-2	0-1	8		(16,344)
51	26	CL	H	W.B.A.	D 2-2	2-0	9	Robson 18, Allinson (pen) 26	14,843
52	29	CL	H	Chelsea	W 2-0	0-0	7	Anderson 67, Nicholas 77	24,025
53	M 3	CL	A	Birmingham City	W 1-0	0-0	7	Woodcock 84	(6,234)
54	5	CL	A	Oxford United	L 0-3	0-1	7		(13,651)

Best Home League Attendance: 45,109 v Tottenham H. 29/12   **Smallest: 14,843 v W.B.A. 26/4**   **Av Home Att: 23,813**

Goal Scorers:

*After Extra-time   Compared with 84-85: −7,872

League (49): Woodcock 11, Nicholas 10, Allinson 6, Davis 4, Robson 4, Rix 3, Opponents 3, Anderson 2, Hayes 2, Caton 1, Rocastle 1, Quinn 1, Whyte 1

Milk Cup (9): Nicholas 4, Allinson 1, Anderson 1, Hayes 1, Mariner 1, Robson 1

FA Cup (11): Nicholas 4, Allinson 3 (1 pen), Rix 2, Robson 1, Rocastle 1

Lukic	Anderson	Sansom	Williams	O'Leary	Caton	Allinson	Robson	Nicholas	Woodcock	Rix	Davis	Mariner	Rocastle	Whyte	Hayes	Keown	Quinn	Caesar	Wilmot	Adams	Referee	#
1	2	3	4	5	6	7	8	9	10	11											D Hutchinson	1
1	2	3	4	5	6	7	8	9	10	11											G Napthine	2
1	2	3	4*	5	6	7	8	9	10	11		12									B Stevens	3
1	2	3		5*	6	8	7	9	10	11	4	12									A Seville	4
1	2	3			6	8	7	9	10	11	4	5									J Martin	5
1	2	3		5	6	8	7	9	10	11	4										K Baker	6
1	2	3		5	6	8	7	9	10	11	4										I Hendrick	7
1	2	3		5	6	8	7	9	10	11	4										A Gunn	8
1	2	3		5	6	8	7	9	10	11	4										J Bray	9
1	**2**	**3**		**5**	**6**	**8**	**7***	**9**	**10**	**11**	**4**	**12**									**H Taylor**	**10**
1	2	3		5	6	8		9	10	11	4		7	12							K Barratt	11
1	2	3		5	6	8		9	10	11	4			7							D Axcell	12
1	**2**	**3**		**5**	**6**	**8**		**9**	**10**	**11**	**4***		**12**	**7**							**I Borrsti**	**13**
1	2	3		5*	6	8		9	10	11	4		12	7							Alan Robinson	14
1	2	3		5	6	8		9*	10	11	4		12	7							J Milford	15
1	2	3		5	6	8*		9	10	11	4		12	7							J McAvlay	16
1	**2**	**3**	**7**	**5**	**6**	**8**		**9**	**10**	**11**	**4**										**R Bridges**	**17**
1	2	3	7	5	6	8*		9	10	11	4	12									J Ashworth	18
1	2	3	7	5	6	8		9	10	11	4										L Robinson	19
1	2	3	7	5	6	12	8	9	10*		4				11						M Bodenham	20
1	**2**	**3**	**7**	**5**	**6**	**12**	**8**	**9**	**10**		**4**				**11***						**A Gunn**	**21**
1	2	3	7		6		8	9	10		4		12		11*	5					J Deakin	22
1	**2**	**3**	**7***	**5**	**6**		**8**	**9**	**10**		**4**				**11**						**R Gifford**	**23**
1	2	3	7*	5	6	12	8	9	10		4				11						M James	24
1	2	3	7	5	6	12	8	9	10		4				11*						B Hill	25
1	2	3		5		7	8	9		11	4					6	10				D Hedges	26
1		3		5		7	8	9		11	4					6	10	2			T Holbrook	27
1		3		5		7	8*	9	12	11	4					6	10	2			R Lewis	28
1	2	3		5		7		9	12	11	4	8				6	10*				J Moules	29
1	**2**	**3**		**5**		**7**		**9**		**11**	**4**	**8**				**6**	**10**				**J Bray**	**30**
1	2	3		5		7	8	9		11	4					6	10				T Fitzharris	31
	2	**3**		**5**	**6**	**7**	**8***	**9**	**12**	**11**	**4**					**10**		**1**			**R Milford**	**32**
1	2	3		5		7	8*	9	12	11	4					6	10				A Seville	33
1	2	3		5		7		9		11	8			4		6	10				H Taylor	34
1	**2**	**3**		**5**	**6**	**7***		**9**	**12**	**11**	**8**			**4**			**10**				**B Hill**	**35**
1	2	3	4	5		7		9*	10	11	8		12			6					A Gunn	36
1	2	3	4	5		7		9	10*	11	8		12			6					N Midgley	37
1	**2**	**3**	**4**	**5**		**7**		**9**		**11**	**8**		**10**			**6**					**A Gunn**	**38**
1	**2**	**3**	**4**	**5**		**7**		**9**	**10**		**8**				**11***	**6**	**12**				**D Scott**	**39**
	2	3	4	5				9	10	11	8			7		6		1			J Worrall	40
	2	3	4	5*				9	10	11	8			7		6		1			D Axcell	41
1	2	3	4	5				9	10	11	8			7		6					J Borrett	42
1		3	4	5				9	10	11	8			7		6			2		L Shapter	43
1	2	3	4	5				9		11	8		12	7		6	10*				P Vanes	44
1	2	3	4	5		12		9		11	8		10	7*		6					J Martin	45
1	2	3	4*		12	7		9	10	11	8					6				5	K Cooper	46
1	2	3	4			7		9		11	8		12			6†	10*			5	K Lupton	47
1	2	3	4			7		9		11	8*		12			6	10			5	L Robinson	48
1	2	3	4			7		9		11	8					6	10			5	G Napthine	49
1	2	3	4			7		9	10	11	8					6				5	J Lovatt	50
1	2	3		5		7		9	10*	11	8			4			12			6	B Stevens	51
1	2	3		5		7		9	10	11*	8			4			12			6	Alan Robinson	52
1	2	3		5		7		9	10	11	8			4						6	D Phillips	53
1	2	3		5*	12	7		9	10	11	8			4						6	D Axcell	54
40	39	**42**	17	35	20	28	26	41	31	38	28	3	13	4	11	22	10	2	2	10	League Appearances	
						5	1		2			1	6	3	3		2				Substitute Appearances	
6	7	7	3	7	7	5+1	4	7	5+2	5	5	1+1	2+1	1	2	2	1				Milk Cup Appearances	
5	5	5	3	5	5	5	1	5	1+1	4	1	2+1	5		1	5	2+1				FA Cup Appearances	

Also Played:

Players on Loan:

Departures: Tony Woodcock (FC Cologne), Paul Mariner (Portsmouth), Martin Keown (Aston Villa)

'THE GUNNERS'

Formed: 1886
Turned Professional: 1891   **Ltd Co:** 1893

Previous Names: Royal Arsenal 1886-91, Woolwich Arsenal 1891-1914
Previous Managers: 1897-8 T B Mitchell   1898-9 Mr Ellcoat   1899-1904 H Bradshaw
1904-8 P Kelso   1908-15 G Morrell   1919-25 A L Knighton   1925-34 Herbert Chapman
1934-47 George Allison   1947-56 Tom Whittaker   1956-58 Jack Crayston   1958-62 George Swindin
1962-6 Billy Wright   1966-76 Bertie Mee   1976-83 Terry Neill   1983-1986 D Howe

Honours: Champions Div 1 (8),   FA Cup Winners (5)   League + Cup 'Double' 1970-71   European Fairs
Cup Winners 1969-70
League Career: Elected to Div 2 1893   Promoted to Div 1 1904-13
Relegated to Div 2 1913   Promoted to Div 1 1919
Colours: Red shirts, white sleeves, white shorts with red and white stockings
Change Colours: Yellow shirts, blue shorts, yellow stockings
Reserves League: Football Combination   **Youth League:** S E Counties

---

CLUB RECORDS

Most Appearances for Club: George Armstrong: Football League 490 + 10 subs = 500 + FA Cup 58 + 2
subs = 60 + League/Milk Cup 35 + European Cup 5 + Fairs Cup 19 + 2 subs = 21 **Total 621** (1960-77)
Most Capped Player: Pat Rice, 49, N Ireland   **For England:** Kenny Sansom 35
Record Goalscorer in a Match: Ted Drake, 7 v Aston Villa, (a), Div 1, 7-1, 14.12.1935
Record League Goalscorer in a Season: Ted Drake, 42, Div 1, 1934-35   **In All Competitions:** Ted Drake, 43 (League
42 + FA Cup 1), 1934-5
Record League Goalscorer in a Career: Cliff Bastin, 150, 1929-46   **In All Competitions:** Cliff Bastin, 176 (League
150 + FA Cup 26) 1929-46
Record Transfer Fee Received: £1,250,000 from Crystal Palace for Clive Allen, Aug 1980
Record Transfer Fee Paid: £1,250,000 to Queens Park Rangers for Clive Allen, June 1980
Best Performances: League: Champions Div 1 1931, 1933, 1934, 1935, 1938, 1948, 1953, 1971   **FA Cup:** Winners
1930, 1936, 1950, 1971, 1979   **League/Milk Cup:** Runners-Up 1968, 1969
Most League Points: 71, Div 1, 1981-2   **Most League Goals:** 127, Div 1, 1930-31
Record League Victory: 12-0 v Loughborough Town, Div 2, 12 March 1900
Most Goals Scored in a Cup Tie: 12-0 v Ashford United, 1st Round FA Cup, 14 Oct 1893-4
Record League Defeat: 0-8 v Loughborough Town, Div 2, 12 Dec 1896
European Competitions Entered: European Cup 1971-2   European Cup Winners Cup 1979-80 (Runners-Up)   Fairs Cup
1963-4, 1969-70 (winners), 1970-1   UEFA Cup 1978-9, 1981-2, 1982-3
Oldest Player in League Match: Pat Jennings 39 yrs
Youngest Player in League Match: Gerry Ward 16 yrs
Most Consecutive Undefeated League Matches: 17 1947
Longest Run of Undefeated Home League Matches: 33 1902-04
Longest Run Without Home League Win: 16 1912-13
Most Consecutive League Wins: 9 1971
Most Consecutive League Defeats: 7 1977

League Matches Without a Win: 23 1912-13
Away League Matches: 10 1930-31
Away League Win: 15 1928
Home League Wins: 15 1903-04
Away League Wins: 6 1977

During the years 1930-31 Arsenal scored in 40 successive away League games

Club Statistician for the Directory: J A S Waters

ARSENAL

PLAYERS NAME Ht Wt Birthdate	Honours	Birthplace Transfers	Clubs	APPEARANCES				GOALS			
				League	Milk Cup	FA Cup	Other Comps	League	Milk Cup	FA Cup	Other Comps
GOALKEEPERS											
John Lukic	EU21 (7)Y	Chesterfield	Leeds United (A)	146	7	9					
6.4 13.7 11.12.60			Arsenal	71	6	8					
Rhys Wilmot	WU21 (3)	Newport	Arsenal (A)	2	1						
6.1 12.0 21.2.62			Herford United (L)	9							
			Orient (L)	46	4	4	3				
DEFENDERS											
Tony Adams	EU21 (3), Y	Romford	Arsenal (A)	28+1	0+1	1					
6.1 12.01 10.10.66											
Viv Anderson	EU21, B(7)	Nottingham	Nottingham For. (A)	328+5	39	23+1	28+1	15	5	1	1
6.0 11.01 28.8.56	U21(1), Div.1, 78	£200,000	Arsenal	80	10	8		5	2	1	
	EC 80, ESC 79,										
	LgC 78										
Tommy Caton	EU21 (14), YS	Kirby	Manchester City (A)	165+1	21	12		8			
6.2 13.0 6.10.62		£500,000	Arsenal	81	10	4		2			
Gus Caesar		London	Arsenal (A)	2							
6.0 12.0 5.3.66											
David O'Leary	EI (40), FAC 79	London	Arsenal (A)	382	47	46	20	8	1	3	
5.11 11.3 2.5.58											
Kenny Sansom*	E (70), B (2)	Camberwell	Crystal Palace (A)	172	11	17		3		1	
5.6 11.8 26.9.58	U21(8), YS, Div.	£800,000	Arsenal	245	27	17	6	5			
	2, 79, FAYC 77										
MIDFIELD											
Paul Davis	EU21 (6)	London	Arsenal (A)	166+12	19+2	8+1	3+1	14	2	2	
5.8 9.7 9.12.61											
Martin Hayes		Walthamstow	Arsenal (A)	11	2	1		2	1		
6.0 11.8 21.3.66											
Graham Rix	E (16), B (3)	Doncaster	Arsenal (A)	318+5	42	41+1	21	39	2	6	1
5.9 11.0 23.10.57	EU21 (1), FAC 79										
Stewart Robson†	EU21 (6), Y	Billericay	Arsenal (A)	145+1	20	13	2	16	3		1
5.11 11.13 6.11.64											
David Rocastle		Stockwell (Lon.)	Arsenal (A)	13+3	2+1	5		1		1	
5.9 11.1 2.5.67											
Steve Williams	E (6), B (4)	London	Southampton (A)	278+1	28+1	27	12	18	3	3	3
5.11 10.11 12.7.58	EU21 14	£550,000	Arsenal	31+1	3	6		1			
FORWARDS											
Ian Allinson		Hitchin	Colchester U. (A)	308				69			
5.10 11.0 1.10.57		F	Arsenal	55+14	7+1	5+2		10+1	2	1	
Charlie Nicholas	S (17), U21 (6),	Glasgow	Celtic	74+3	15+4	8	8+1	48	22	7	5
5.10 11.0 30.12.61	YS, SPD (1),	£750,000	Arsenal	117+3	14	9		30+2	7	6	
	SLC (1)										
Niall Quinn	EI (2), Y	Dublin	Arsenal	10+2	2	2+1		1			
6.4 12.4 6.10.66											

CONTRACT PLAYERS WITH NO FIRST TEAM APPEARANCES

Mike Thomas (A), Greg Allen (A), Nick Hammond (A), Lawrie Osborne (A), Paul Smith (A)

APPRENTICES

Jason Ball, Paul Birch, Scott McGregor, Russell Milton, Adrian Pennington, Danny Rebuck, Paul Turner

NON-CONTRACT PLAYERS

Westley Reid, Francisco Rivero, Roger Stanislaus

Record Attendance: 73,295 v Sunderland, Div 1, 9 Mar 1935

Smallest Home Attendance for a First Class Match: 4,554 v Leeds United, Div 1, 5 May 1966

Record Receipts: £116,498 v Juventus, Cup Winners Cup Semi-Final 1st Leg, 9 Apr 1980

Season Tickets: Stands: £104.00, £117.00, £143.00, £195.00; Ground: £50.00

Executive Box Season Tickets: £700 with Private Restaurant & Bars

Cost of Stand Tickets: £4.50, £5.00, £6.00, £8.50; **Terraces:** £3.00

Match and Ticket Information: Ansafone Service, 01-359 0131, Dial-a-seat 226 4050

Car Parking: Parking is permitted in adjacent streets

Nearest Underground Railway Station: Arsenal (Piccadilly Line)

Nearest Railway Stations: Drayton Park and Finsbury Park

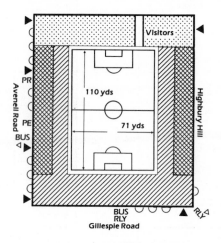

How to get to the ground

From North: Leave Motorway M1 at junction 2 and follow signs City. In 6.2m pass Holloway Road Station and then take 3rd turning on left into Drayton Park Road. In 0.7m to right into Avenell Road for Arsenal FC

From South: From London Bridge follow signs, to Bank of England, then follow signs to Angel (Islington). At traffic signals turn right (S.P. The North) and in 1m at Highbury roundabout forward into Holloway Road. Then take 3rd turning on right into Drayton Park Road. In 0.7m turn right into Avenell Road for Arsenal FC

From West: Leave Motorway M4 at junction 1 Chiswick and follow A315 (S.P. Chiswick). In 0.9m turn left A40 then follow signs City to join Motorway M41, then A40(m) at end forward into Ring Road A501. At Angel (Islington) turn left to Highbury roundabout, keep forward into Holloway Road. Then take 3rd turning on right into Drayton Park Road. In 0.7m turn right into Avenell Road for Arsenal FC

Programme Editor: Kevin Connolly
Price of 1986-7 Programme: 60p
Number of Pages: 24
Subscriptions: Subscription price on application to club shop

Local Newspaper: Islington Gazette

Local Radio Stations: Capital Radio, LBC, BBC Radio London

ASTON VILLA

Chairman
H D Ellis

Directors
J A Alderson
T Alderson
Dr D Targett
P D Ellis

Secretary
Steven Stride (021-327 6604)

Assistant Secretary
Arthur Moseley

Manager
Graham Turner

First Team Coach
Ron Wylie

Youth Team Coach
Colin Dobson

Commercial Manager
Tony Stephens (021-327 5399)

Physiotherapist
Jim Williams

Groundsman
Tony Eden

Aston Villa had an equivocal season but for a club with the talent (on paper) that they had available they should have done better. The high spot was a semi-final appearance in the Milk Cup where defeat was suffered on aggregate against the eventual winners, Oxford United. That apart it was pretty ordinary stuff at Villa Park with an ultimate League position of 16th — and that could have been a great deal worse — and cup elimination after a replay against Millwall at the Den.

The season started fairly well for Villa, but League form soon slumped and a defeat at home by Manchester United in December saw the club slip dangerously towards the relegation zone from which escape was only achieved in April with home wins over Watford, Ipswich (relegated) and Chelsea allowing fans to relax.

The cups produced a mixed bag with an excellent Milk Cup run the high point. To reach the semi-finals it was necessary to dispose of Exeter City (12-3 on aggregate), Leeds United (3-0 away), West Bromwich (2-1 in an away replay) and Arsenal (in the same manner as the previous round); this brought a two-legged semi-final against Oxford United and defeat on a 4-3 aggregate. The FA Cup was, however, a bad disappointment with the elimination of Portsmouth (3-2 in a Villa Park replay) being followed by another replay at Millwall being necessary and an early departure from the competition. As English clubs are still banned from Europe it can be said that a poor season at least did no come at the wrong time! But when European competition is restored the fans will want to see Villa thereabouts.

Manager Graham Turner must know this and he has spent money during the close season (and before) in strengthening the team, so there will be such new men at Villa Park as Martin Keown, the Arsenal defender, Andy Blair, midfield from Sheffield Wednesday, Neale Cooper, the versatile Aberdeen man, Steve Hodge from Forest, Simon Stainrod, the striker from Wednesday and Gary Thompson, another striker from the same club. If others such as the goalkeepers Poole and Spink, Paul Elliott, Allan Evans (now almost a veteran but still good), Paul Birch and the brilliant Mark Walters can 'do the business', things could be made to happen, but whither Graham Turner if there is no success? And where goes Andy Gray with that influx of new players?

Back Row L to R: Martin Keown, Paul Elliott, Nigel Spink, Kevin Poole, Garry Thompson, Simon Stainrod. **Middle Row:** Paul Birch, Gary Williams, Tony Dorigo, Andy Blair, Steve Hunt, Steve Hodge. **Front Row:** Neale Cooper, Allan Evans, Graham Turner (Manager), Ron Wylie (Coach), Andy Gray, Tony Daley.

ASTON VILLA

DIVISION ONE: 16th   **FA CUP:** 4th ROUND   **MILK CUP:** SEMI-FINAL

MATCH	DATE		COMPE-TITION	VENUE	OPPONENTS	RESULT		HALF TIME	L'GUE POS'N	GOALSCORERS/GOAL TIMES	ATTEN-DANCE
1	A	17	CL	A	Manchester United	L	0-4	0-0			(49,743)
2		21	CL	H	Liverpool	D	2-2	1-1		Shaw 8, Walters 77	20,197
3		24	CL	H	Q.P.R.	L	1-2	0-1	21	Walters 68	11,896
4		27	CL	A	Southampton	D	0-0	0-0	18		(14,220)
5		31	CL	H	Luton Town	W	3-1	3-0	14	Walters 3, Hodge 16, Norton 34	10,524
6	S	4	CL	H	W.B.A.	W	3-0	2-0	12	Evans (pen) 23, Daley 40, Walters 81	(17,800)
7		7	CL	A	Birmingham City	D	0-0	0-0	12		(24,971)
8		14	CL	H	Coventry City	D	1-1	1-1	12	Hodge 10	12,198
9		21	CL	H	Ipswich Town	W	3-0	2-0	11	Walters 14, Hodge 45, Birch 47	(11,598)
10		25	MC2	A	Exeter City	W	4-1	2-0		Stainrod 4 (11, 16, 56, 70)	(5,325)
11		28	CL	H	Everton	D	0-0	0-0	12		22,048
12	O	5	CL	A	Arsenal	L	2-3	1-2	13	Stainrod 5, Walters 72	(18,881)
13		9	MC2	H	Exeter City	W	8-1	6-0		Gray 16, 19, Stainrod 29, Ormsby 36, 84, Williams 37, 42, Birch 85	7,678
14		12	CL	H	Nottingham Forest	L	1-2	0-0	16	Gibson 67	15,315
15		19	CL	A	West Ham United	L	1-4	1-2	16	Stainrod 6	(15,034)
16		26	CL	H	Newcastle United	L	1-2	1-1	17	Gray 15	12,033
17		30	MC3	A	Leeds United	W	3-0	1-0		Walters 14, Stainrod 63, 71	(15,444)
18	N	2	CL	H	Oxford United	W	2-0	1-0	15	Evans (pen) 42, Stainrod 56	12,922
19		9	CL	A	Watford	D	1-1	1-0	17	Gray 40	(14,085)
20		16	CL	H	Sheffield Wednesday	D	1-1	1-1	16	Gibson 37	13,849
21		20	MC4	H	W.B.A.	D	2-2	0-1		Evans (pen) 58, Stainrod 63	20,204
22		23	CL	A	Chelsea	L	1-2	1-1	16	Gray 34	(17,509)
23		27	MC4R	A	W.B.A.	W	2-1	1-0		Hodge 25, Walters 60	(19,800)
24		30	CL	H	Tottenham Hotspur	L	1-2	0-0	16	Walters 88	14,099
25	D	7	CL	A	Liverpool	L	0-3	0-1	16		(29,418)
26		14	CL	H	Manchester United	L	1-3	1-1	19	Hodge 29	27,626
27		17	CL	A	Q.P.R.	W	1-0	1-0	17	Birch 3	(11,237)
28		26	CL	A	Leicester City	L	1-3	1-2	17	Walters 31	(13,752)
29		28	CL	H	W.B.A.	D	1-1	1-0	18	Kerr 44	18,796
30	J	1	CL	H	Manchester City	L	0-1	0-0	18		14,215
31		4	FAC3	A	Portsmouth	D	2-2	1-0		Kerr 40, Birch 89	(17,732)
32		11	CL	H	Coventry City	D	3-3	1-3	18	Stainrod 2, Gray 61, Elliot 79	(10,328)
33		13	FAC3R	H	Portsmouth	W	3-2†	1-0		Evans (pen) 40, Stainrod 92, 99	14,958
34		18	CL	A	Luton Town	L	0-2	0-0	18		(10,217)
35		22	MC QF	H	Arsenal	D	1-1	0-1		Glover 75	26,093
36		25	FAC4	H	Millwall	D	1-1	1-1		Hodge 25	12,205
37		29	FAC4R	A	Millwall	L	0-1	0-0			(10,273)
38	F	1	CL	A	Southampton	D	0-0	0-0	19		8,456
39		4	MC QFR	A	Arsenal	W	2-1	1-0		Birch 32, Evans 57	(33,091)
40	M	1	CL	A	Everton	L	0-2	0-0	20		(32,133)
41		4	MC SF1	H	Oxford United	D	2-2	1-1		Birch 33, Stainrod 55	23,098
42		8	CL	H	Arsenal	L	1-4	0-0	20	Walters 49	10,584
43		12	MC SF2	A	Oxford United	L	1-2	0-0		Walters 87	(13,989)
44		15	CL	A	Nottingham Forest	D	1-1	0-0	20	Walters 72	(12,933)
45		19	CL	H	West Ham United	W	2-1	1-1		Hodge 38, 78	11,567
46		22	CL	H	Birmingham City	L	0-3	0-2	20		26,694
47		29	CL	A	Manchester City	D	2-2	1-0	20	Hodge 37, Stainrod 88	(20,935)
48		31	CL	H	Leicester City	W	1-0	0-0	20	Stainrod 50	12,200
49	A	5	CL	A	Oxford United	D	1-1	0-0	20	Stainrod 53	(11,406)
50		9	CL	A	Newcastle United	D	2-2	1-1	20	Daley 33, Hunt 87	(20,107)
51		12	CL	H	Watford	W	4-1	0-1	17	Dorigo 47, Evans (pen) 65, Gray 67, Stainrod 79	12,781
52		16	CL	H	Ipswich Town	W	1-0	0-0		Hodge 62	13,611
53		19	CL	A	Sheffield Wednesday	L	0-2	0-1	16		(19,782)
54		26	CL	H	Chelsea	W	3-1	1-0	16	Norton 43, Hunt 84, Stainrod 89	17,770
55	M	3	CL	A	Tottenham Hotspur	L	2-4	1-1	16	Stainrod 2, Elliot 70	(14,854)

Best Home League Attendance: 27,626 v Man Utd 14/12   **Smallest:** 8,456 v Southampton 1/2   **Av Home Att:** 15,208

Goal Scorers: **Compared with 85-85:** −3,080

League (51): Stainrod 10, Walters 10, Hodge 8, Gray 5, Evans 3 (pens), Birch 2, Daley 2, Elliot 2, Gibson 2, Hunt 2, Norton 2, Dorigo 1, Kerr 1, Shaw 1

Milk Cup (25): Stainrod 9, Birch 3, Walters 3, Evans 2 (1 pen), Gray 2, Ormsby 2, Williams 2, Glover 1, Hodge 1

FA Cup (4): Stainrod 2, Evans 1 (pen), Hodge 1

Spink	Williams	Dorigo	Evans	Ormsby	McMahon	Birch	Shaw	Gray	Gibson	Walters	Bradley	Glover	Daley	Walker	Norton	Hodge	Stainrod	Elliot	Poole	Kerr	Hunt	Blair	Referee	No.
1	2	3	4	5	6	7	8	9	10*	11	12												C Steel	1
1	2*	3		5	6	7	8	9		11		4	12	10									K Cooper	2
1		3		5	6	7	8	9		11		4	12	10*	2								N Midgley	3
1		3		5		7		9*		8	6	4	11	12	2	10							A Ward	4
1		3		5		7				8	6	4	11	9	2	10							D Shaw	5
1	2	3	4	5		7		10		9	6		11			8							J Hough	6
1	2	3	4	5		7		9		8	6*		11	12		10							N Wilson	7
1	2	3	4	5		7		9	6	8			11			10							R Nixon	8
1	2	3	4	5		7		9*	6	8	12		11			10							K Miller	9
1	2	3	4	5		7				11	6*	9				10	8						**M Cotton**	10
1	2	3	4	5		7		9		11	6					10	8						R Groves	11
1	2	3	4	5		7		9		11	6					10	8						D Axcell	12
1	2	3	4*	5		7		9	6	11		12				10	8						**P Tyldesley**	13
1	2	3	4	5		7*		9	6	11		12				10	8						A Buksh	14
1	2*	3	4	5		7		9		11	12		6			10	8						M Bodenham	15
1		3	4	5*		7		9		11		12	6		2	10	8						N Glover	16
1	2	3	4					9	6	11		5	7			10	8						**K Redfern**	17
1	2	3	4					9	6	11		5	7			10	8						R Guy	18
1	2	3	4					9	6	11		5	7			10	8						J Martin	19
1	2	3	4					9	6	11		5	7			10	8						I Hendrick	20
1	2	3	4				12	9	6*	11		5	7			10	8						**K Hackett**	21
1	2	3	4				12	9		11	6	5	7*			10	8						A Gunn	22
1	2	3	4			7	12	9*		11	6	5				10	8						**J Worrall**	23
1		3	4			7		9*		11	6	5	12		2	10	8						F Roberts	24
1	2	3					12	9		11	6	4	7			10	8*	5					G Courtney	25
1	2	3	4					9		11	6		7			10	8	5					D Reeves	26
	2	3				7		9		11	6	4				10	8	5	1				A Robinson	27
	2	3				7	8			11	6*	4	12			10	9	5	1				L Dilkes	28
1		3	4			6				11			7		2	10	9	5		8			A King	29
1		3	4			6		9		11			7*		2	10	8	5		12			N Ashley	30
1		3	4			6	8			11					2	10	9	5		7			**C Downey**	31
1		3	4			6		9		11					2	10	8	5		7			D Shaw	32
1		3	4			6		9		11					2	10	8	5		7			**A Ward**	33
		3	4			6	12	9		11			10		2		8*	5		7			**R Lewis**	34
1	2	3	4			7		9				6	11			10	8	5					**R Milford**	35
1	2	3	4			7		9		11		6				10	8	5					**K Hackett**	36
	2	3	4			7		9		11*		6			12	10	8	5	1				**K Hackett**	37
	3	4					8	9			7*	6			2	10	12	5	1	11			R Bridges	38
	3	4				7		9		11*		6			2	10	12	5	1	8			**B Hill**	39
1		3*	4			7				11		6	12		2	10	9	5		8			G Aplin	40
1			4			7				11		6	3		2	10	9	5		8			**J Worrall**	41
1			4			7		9		11		6	3		2	10	8	5		7			J Worrall	42
1	2	3	4			7		9		11		6				10		5		8			**Alan Robinson**	43
1	2	3	4			12	8*	9		11						10		5			6	7	J Moules	44
1	2	3	4				8	9		11						10		5			6	7	K Walmsley	45
1	2	3	4				8	9		11						10		5			6	7	K Hackett	46
1	2*	3	4					9				12	11			10	8	5	1		6	7	J Lloyd	47
		3	4					9		11					2	10	8	5	1		6	7	N Midgley	48
		3	4					9		11					2	10	8	5	1		6	7	T Jones	49
		3†	4							11		9			2	10	8	5	1		6	7	D Scott	50
		3	4							11					2	10	8	5	1		6	7	L Shapter	51
		3	4					9		11*		12			2	10	8	5	1		6	7	K Breen	52
1		3	4					9*		11	12				2	10	8	5	1		6	7	G Courtney	53
		3	4			10		9		11					2		8	5	1		6	7	R Nixon	54
		3	4			10	9			11					2		8	5	1		6	7	M Bodenham	55
31	25	38	35	14	3	25	10	35	7	40	15	15	16	5	20	36	29	23	11	5	12	12	League Appearances	
				2	2						3	3	7	2			1		1				Substitute Appearances	
8	7	8	9	2		7-1	0-1	7	3	8	3	7	2-1	2	3	8	7-1	4	1	3			Milk Cup Appearances	
3	2	4	4			4		3		4	2				3	4	4	4	1	2			FA Cup Appearances	

Also Played:
Players on Loan:
Departures: McMahon (Liverpool), Gibson (Manchester Utd), Ormsby (Leeds Utd)

'THE VILLA'

Formed: 1874
Turned Professional: 1885   **Ltd Co:** 1896

Previous Managers: 1934-6 Jimmy McMullen   1936-9 Jimmy Hogan   1945-50 Alex Massie
1950-3 George Martin   1953-8 Eric Houghton   1958-64 Joe Mercer   1964-7 Dick Taylor
1967-8 Tommy Cummings   1968 Arthur Cox   1968-70 Tommy Docherty   1970-4 Vic Crowe
1974-82 Ron Saunders   1982-4 Tony Barton
Honours: Champions Div 1 (7), 1893-4, 1895-6, 1896-7, 1898-9, 1899-1900, 1909-10,
1980-1   Champions Div 2, 1937-8, 1959-60,   Champions Div 3 1971-2   FA Cup Winners (7) 1887,
1895, 1897, 1905, 1913, 1920, 1957 (joint Record Holders)   Football League Cup Winners (3) 1961,
1975, 1977   European Cup Winners 1981-2   European Super Cup 1982-3
League Career: Original Members of Football League 1888   Relegated to Div 2 1935-6
Promoted to Div 1 1937-8   Relegated to Div 2 1958-9   Promoted to Div 1 1959-60
Relegated to Div 2 1966-7   Relegated to Div 3 1969-70   Promoted to Div 2 1971-2
Promoted to Div 1 1974-5
Colours: Claret shirts with light blue sleeves and trim, white shorts with light blue trim, blue stockings
Change Colours: White shirt with faint yellow/claret hoops, white shorts with yellow/claret stripe, white
stockings with yellow/claret hoops
Reserves League: Central League   **Youth Team:** Midland Intermediate

CLUB RECORDS

Most Appearances for Club: Charlie Aitken: Football League 559 + 2 + FA Cup 33 + League Cup 59 + UEFA Cup 2
Total 653 + 2 subs (1961-76)
Most Capped Player: Peter McParland, 33, N Ireland 1954-61   **For England:** Billy Walker, 18, 1921-33
Record Goalscorer in a Match: Harry Hampton, 5 v Sheffield Wednesday, 10-0, 05.10.1912   Len Capwell, 5 v Burnley
10-0, 29.08.1925   George Brown, 5 v Leicester City 8-3 (a), 02.01.1932   Gerry Hitchens, 5 v Charlton Athletic, 11-1,
14.11.1959
Record League Goalscorer in a Season: Pongo Waring, 49, Div 1, 1930-1   **In All Competitions:** Pongo Waring, 50
(League 49 + FA Cup 1), 1930-1
Record League Goalscorer in a Career: Harry Hampton (1904-20) and Billy Walker (1919-34), 213   **In All**
Competitions: Harry Hampton, 247 (League 213 + FA Cup 34) 1904-20
Record Transfer Fee Received: £1,469,000 (£1,175,000 basic fee) from Wolverhampton W. for Andy Gray, Sept 1979
Record Transfer Fee Paid: £500,000 to Newcastle United for Peter Withe, May 1980
Best Performances: League: As in Honours
Most League Points: (2pts for win) 70, Div 3, 1971-2   **Most League Goals:** 128, Div 1, 1930-1
Record League Victory: 12-2 v Accrington Stanley, Div 1, 12 March 1892; 11-1 v Charlton Athletic, Div 2, 24 Nov 1959;
10-0 v Sheffield Wednesday, Div 1, 5 Oct 1912; 10-0 v Burnley, Div 1, 29 Aug 1925
Record Victory in Any Senior Competition: 13-1 v London Casuals (h) FA Cup 1st Round, 17 Jan
1891   13-0 v Wednesbury Old Athletic (h), FA Cup 1st Round, 30 Oct 1886
Record League Defeat: 0-7 v Blackburn Rovers, (a), Div 1, 19 Oct 1889; 0-7 v Everton (a), Div 1, 4 March 1890;
0-7 v WBA (h), Div 1, 19 Oct 1935; 0-7 v Manchester Utd (a), Div 1, 8 March 1950; 0-7 v Manchester United (a), Div 1, 24
Oct 1964
European Competitions Entered: European Cup 1981-2, 1982-3   UEFA Cup 1975-6, 1977-8   World Club Championship
1982-3   European Super Cup 1982-3
Oldest Player in League Match: Mush Callaghan 37 yrs
Youngest Player in League Match: Jimmy Brown 16 yrs

Most Consecutive Undefeated League Matches: 15 1897	**League Matches Without a Win:** 13 1973-74
Longest Run of Undefeated Home League Matches: 37 1909-11	**Away League Matches:** 8 1896
Longest Run Without Home League Win: 8 1920-21	**Away League Win:** 27 1963-64
Most Consecutive League Wins: 9 1897, 1910	**Home League Wins:** 14 1903, 1930-31
Most Consecutive League Defeats: 11 1963	**Away League Wins:** 6 1897

Aston Villa scored two or more goals in a record 23 successive home games between 1930-1931. They also hold the record
of scoring three or more in 15 games during that period. Between 1894-95 Villa scored in 35 consecutive matches

ASTON VILLA

PLAYERS NAME Ht Wt Birthdate	Honours	Birthplace Transfers	Clubs	APPEARANCES				GOALS			
				League	Milk Cup	FA Cup	Other Comps	League	Milk Cup	FA Cup	Other Comps
GOALKEEPERS											
Kevin Poole 5.10 11.10¾ 21.7.63		Bromsgrove	Aston Villa (A)	18	1	2					
			Northampton T. (L)	3							
Nigel Spink 6.1½ 14.6 8.8.58	E (1), EC 82, ESC 82	Chelmsford £4,000	Chelmsford								
			Aston Villa	101	15	10	8+1				
DEFENDERS											
Tony Dorigo† 5.10 11.0 31.12.65		Australia	Aston Villa (A)								
			Aston Villa	65+5	9+1	5		1			
Paul Elliot 6.1½ 12.8 18.3.64	EU21 (3), Y	London £145,000	Charlton Athletic (A)	61+2	2	1		1			
			Luton Town	54+3	5	2		5			
			Aston Villa	23	4	4		2			
Allan Evans 6.1½ 13.2 12.10.56	S(4), Y, Div.1, 81 EC 82, ESC 82	Dunfermline	Dunfermline (A)	94+4	20+2	2		14			
			Aston Villa	305+2	35	20	21+1	41	5	3	
Dean Glover 5.10¼ 12.0 29.12.63		Birmingham	Aston Villa (A)								
			Aston Villa	20+3	7	3		1			
Martin Keown 6.0 12.9 24.7.66		Oxford	Arsenal (A)	22		5					
		£150,000	Brighton (L)	21+2	2		2	1	1		
David Norton 5.7½ 11.8½ 3.3.65		Cannock	Aston Villa (A)								
			Aston Villa	22	3	3		2			
Ray Walker 5.10 11.9 28.9.63	EY, FAYC 80, ESC 82	North Shields	Aston Villa (A)	15+8	2+1	2					
			Port Vale (L)	15				1			
Gary Williams 5.9 11.1 17.6.60	Div.1 81, EC 82, ESC 82	Wolverhampton	Aston Villa (A)	209+5	28	12	17		2		
			Walsall (L)	9							
MIDFIELD											
Paul Birch 5.6 10.6 20.11.62	FAYC 80, ESC 82	Birmingham	Aston Villa (A)								
			Aston Villa	71+3	12+1	7	0+1	7	3		
Andy Blair 5.9 10.9 18.12.59	SU21 (5), ESC 82	Bedworth £300,000	Coventy (A)	90+3	11	8		6	1	7	
			Aston Villa	24+10	0+2	3					
			W'hampton W. (L)	10							
			Sheffield Wed.	58	10	7		3	3	4	
			Aston Villa	12							
Neale Cooper 6.1 12.3 24.11.63	SU21 (13), SL 84, 85, SC 82, 83, 84, 86, Skol Cup 86, ECWC 83	India	Aberdeen (A)	123		26		9		4	
			Aston Villa	126+19	26+3	24+3	28+3	4	1	3	
No details		£400,000	Aston Villa								
Steve Hodge 5.8 10.8 25.10.62	E (8), U21 (8)	Nottingham	Nottingham F. (A)	122+1	9	5	11	30	1	1	4
			Aston Villa	36	8	4		8	1	1	
Steve Hunt 5.7 10.10 8.7.56	E (2)	Birmingham New York C.	Aston Villa (A)	4+3				1			
			Coventry City	178+7	17	14		26	3	4	
			WBA	68	11	2	3	15	3	1	1
			Aston Villa	12				2			
FORWARDS											
Tony Daley 5.6¾ 9.12 18.10.67		Birmingham	Aston Villa (A)								
			Aston Villa	20+8	2+1			2			
Andy Gray 5.11 11.7 30.11.55	S (20), U23 (4), YS, LgC 77, 80, FAC 84, Div. 1 85, ECWC 85	Glasgow £110,000 £1,525,000 £200,000 £150,000	Dundee United	61+1	6	8		36	5	3	
			Aston Villa	112+1	18	6		54	10	3	
			Wolverhampton W.	130+3	13	13		38	3	3	
			Everton	44+5	0+1	14+1	3	14		3	5
			Aston Villa	35	7	3		5	2		
Paul Kerr 5.8½ 11.3½ 9.6.64		Portsmouth	Aston Villa (A)								
			Aston Villa	11+5	5	2		1			
Gary Shaw 5.10 11.9 12.1.62	EU21 (7), YS, Div.1, 81, EC 82, ESC 82	Birmingham	Aston Villa (A)								
			Aston Villa	156+4	16+2	11	16		5	4	9
Simon Stainrod 6.1½ 11.11 1.2.59	EY Div. 2, 83	Sheffield £60,000 £275,000 £250,000	Sheffield United	59+8	1+1	1+1		14			
			Oldham Athletic	69	3	1		21	1		
			QPR	143+2	17	12	3	43	2	6	3
			Sheffield Wed.	8+7				2			
			Aston Villa								
Gary Thompson 6.0 12.9 7.10.59	EU21 (6)	Birmingham £225,000 £450,000 £430,000	Coventry City (A)	127+7	12+1	11		38	7	4	
			WBA	91	9	5		39	5	1	
			Sheffield Wed.	35+1	2+1	5		6		1	
			Aston Villa								
Mark Walters 5.9 11.5 2.6.64	EU21 (9), YS, FAYC 80, ESC 82 ESC 82	Birmingham Aston Villa	Aston Villa (A)	126+10	15	9+1	4+3	28	5	1	2
Stuart Ritchie (M) 5.10 11.0 20.5.68		Southampton									

ADDITIONAL CONTRACT PROFESSIONALS
Bernard Gallacher (D), Phillip Robinson (D), Peter Howell (F)

APPRENTICES

NON-CONTRACT PLAYERS

VILLA PARK Trinity Road, Birmingham B6 6HE

Record Attendance: 76,588 v Derby County, FA Cup Round 6, 2 Mar 1946

Record Receipts: £165,481 v Juventus, European Cup Semi-Final, 2 Mar 1983

Season Tickets: Trinity Road Stand: £80, £88 or £104, Shareholders £76, £83.60, £98.80 (Juveniles £40, £44 or £52, OAPs £40)
Witton Lane Stand: £80 or £88, Shareholders £76 or £83.60 (Juveniles £40 or £44 OAPs £40.00)
North Stand Family Area: £80, other entrances £88, Shareholders £76 or £83.60 (Juveniles and OAPs £40 or £44)
Trinity Road Enclosure: £80, Shareholders £76, (Juveniles and OAPs £40)
Holte End Terrace: £48, Shareholders £45.60 (Juveniles and OAPs £24)

Executive Box Season Tickets: 57 boxes leased on three year basis. Information can be obtained from Commercial Manager

Cost of Stand Tickets: £5.00, £5.50, £6.50
Terraces: £3.00 (£1.50 juveniles)

Match and Ticket Information: By post or in person, applications accepted anytime during season

Car Parking: Asda Park in Aston Hall Road. Street parking also available

Nearest Railway Station: Witton and Aston

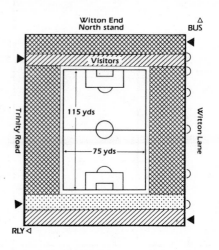

How to get to the ground

From North, East, South and West: Use Motorway M6 with Junction 6. Leave motorway and follow signs Birmingham (NE). Shortly at roundabout take 4th exit A38 (S.P. Aston). In 0.5m turn right into Aston Hall Road for Aston Villa FC

Price of 1986-7 Programme: 50p
Number of Pages: 24
Subscriptions: Please apply to Commercial Department

Local Newspapers: Birmingham Post & Mail, Sports Argus (Sat Football Special), Express & Star, Daily News

Local Radio Stations: BRMB, BBC Radio Birmingham

BARNSLEY

Chairman
G Buckle LLB

Directors
J A Dennis
M Hayselden
R F Potter
C B Taylor

Secretary
M J Spinks (0226 295353)

Manager
A J Clarke

Coach
E Winstanley

Commercial Manager
G Whewall (0226 286718)

Groundsman
R Hatton

Physiotherapist
N Rimmington

There's not much one can say about a season that is spent practically permanently in mid-table and when no progress is made in the two major cup competitions.

In a move that was surprising to the rest of the country, Bobby Collins was replaced after two very solid seasons of team building and replaced as manager by Allan Clarke who hadn't exactly set the town alight in his last spell in charge.

Certainly the defence were again consistent with Clive Baker an 'ever present' in goal and Joyce, Futcher, May and Gray forming a very solid rearguard.

Ian Walsh finished the season as top scorer and Gordon Owen again featured as a strong attacking player down the right and was as sure as ever from the penalty spot.

One of the bright spots of the season was the emergence of ex-apprentice David Hirst who scored nine League goals but it was strange that old favourite Trevor Aylott failed to score in nine games when on loan from Crystal Palace.

The two best victories of the season must have given the fans a special boost however as 3-0 scorelines against Leeds United and Blackburn Rovers (away), came either side of a victory against Oldham Athletic and provided the club's best spell of the season. It was around this time that Hirst scored eight times in ten matches but he only managed one more in the new year. In a first full season this is understandable but with a solid defence and hard working midfield, Barnsley's success next season will probably depend on the youngsters consistency in front of goal.

With attractive local crowd-pulling games against Leeds, Huddersfield, Bradford and Sheffield United there will be plenty of spice again next season so hopefully Allan Clarke will be able to inspire some finishing reminiscent of the great goals he scored for Leeds and England. If he does 'The Reds' should be challenging back at the top of Division Two again.

Back Row L to R: Gwyn Thomas, Calvin Plummer, Clive Baker, Stuart Gray.
Middle Row: Eric Winstanley (Coach), David Hirst (Now with Sheffield Wednesday), Larry May, Paul Malcolm, Rodger Wylde, Paul Futcher, Norman Rimmington (Physiotherapist). **Front Row:** Wayne Goodison, Paul Cross, Gordon Owen, Allan Clarke (Manager, Joe Joyce, Chris Hedworth, John Beresford.

BARNSLEY

DIVISION TWO: 12th   **FA CUP:** 3rd ROUND   **MILK CUP:** 2nd ROUND

MATCH	DATE	COMPE-TITION	VENUE	OPPONENTS	RESULT		HALF TIME	L'GUE POS'N	GOALSCORERS/GOAL TIMES	ATTEN-DANCE
1	A 17	CL	A	Charlton Athletic	L	1-2	0-1		Gray 63	(4,178)
2	20	CL	H	Brighton & H.A.	W	3-2	2-1		Thomas 8, 49, Walsh 15	5,051
3	24	CL	H	Stoke City	D	0-0	0-0	9		6,598
4	26	CL	A	Norwich City	D	1-1	0-0	9	Owen 55	(13,510
5	31	CL	H	Fulham	W	2-0	1-0	7	Walsh 4, Owen 46	5,197
6	S 3	CL	A	Wimbledon	L	1-2	0-1	7		(2,351)
7	7	CL	A	Carlisle United	D	1-1	0-0	8	Owen (pen) 68	(2,418)
8	14	CL	H	Shrewsbury Town	W	2-0	1-0	8	Campbell 4, Walsh 47	4,516
9	21	CL	H	Grimsby Town	W	1-0	1-0	6	Walsh 36	5,365
10	25	MC2/1	A	**Newcastle United**	D	0-0	0-0			(18,544)
11	28	CL	A	Middlesborough	D	0-0	0-0	7		(5,589)
12	O 5	CL	H	Portsmouth	L	0-1	0-1	8		7,064
13	8	MC2/2	H	**Newcastle United**	L	1-1*	0-1		Gray (pen) 50	10,084
14	12	CL	A	Bradford City	L	0-2	0-1	11		(5,707)
15	19	CL	A	Sheffield United	L	1-3	0-2	13	Owen (pen) 78	(11,167)
16	27	CL	H	Leeds United	**W**	3-0	1-0	13	Owen 6, Hirst 60, Walsh 75	8,302
17	N 2	CL	H	Oldham Athletic	W	1-0	0-0	9	Donachie (og) 89	7,118
18	9	CL	A	Blackburn Rovers	**W**	3-0	1-0	9	Hirst 43, 70, Walsh 60	(5,927)
19	16	CL	H	Sunderland	D	1-1	1-0	9	Hirst 34	9,410
20	23	CL	A	Crystal Palace	L	0-1	0-0	9		(5,625)
21	30	CL	H	Millwall	W	2-1	1-0	7	Owen (pen) 32, Gray 61	4,340
22	D 7	CL	A	Brighton & H.A.	W	1-0	0-0	7	Hirst 77	(8,819)
23	14	CL	H	Charlton Athletic	W	2-1	2-0	4	Hirst 6, 39	6,231
24	21	CL	A	Stoke City	D	0-0	0-0	4		(9,856)
25	26	CL	A	Huddersfield Town	D	1-1	1-1	5	Hirst 23	(10,575)
26	28	CL	H	Wimbledon	L	0-1	0-1	6		8,949
27	J 1	CL	H	Hull City	**L**	1-4	1-1	7	Owen (pen) 39	8,363
28	11	CL	A	Shrewsbury Town	L	0-3	0-2	9		(2,756)
29	13	FAC3	A	**Bury**	L	0-2	0-1			(3,676)
30	18	CL	A	Fulham	L	0-2	0-0	10		(3,580)
31	F 1	CL	H	Norwich City	D	2-2	1-2	10	Hirst 26, Thomas 86	5,608
32	15	CL	H	Leeds United	W	2-0	0-0	9	Walsh 61, 89	(11,765)
33	M 8	CL	A	Portsmouth	D	1-1	1-1	9	Walsh 25	(10,426)
34	15	CL	H	Bradford City	D	2-2	1-1	10	Thomas 44, Owen (pen) 54	7,512
35	22	CL	H	Carlisle United	L	1-2	1-0	11	Walsh 44	4,400
36	25	CL	H	Middlesbrough	D	0-0	0-0			3,827
37	29	CL	A	Hull City	W	1-0	1-0	11	Plummer 18	(7,903)
38	31	CL	H	Huddersfield Town	L	1-3	1-1	11	Plummer 23	5,746
39	A 6	CL	A	Oldham Athletic	D	1-1	1-0	12	Thomas 23	(3,971)
40	8	CL	H	Sheffield United	W	2-1	0-1	9	Walsh 51, 65	5,451
41	12	CL	H	Blackburn Rovers	D	1-1	1-1	9	Walsh 43	4,256
42	19	CL	A	Sunderland	L	0-2	0-1	11		(12,349)
43	22	CL	A	Grimsby Town	W	2-1	1-1	10	Walsh 5, Owen 66	(4,009)
44	26	CL	H	Crystal Palace	L	2-4	1-2	11	Owen 8, Walsh 57	3,862
45	M 3	CL	A	Millwall	D	2-2	0-1	12	Plummer 44, Owen (pen) 80	(4,230)

Best Home League Attendance: 8,302 v Leeds 27/10   **Smallest:** 3,862 v Crystal Palace 26/4   **Av Home Att:** 6,055

Goal Scorers: **Compared with 84-85:** −1,169

League (47): Walsh 15, Owen 11 (7 pens), Hirst 9, Thomas 5, Plummer 3, Gray 2, Campbell 1, Opponents 1
Milk Cup (1): Gray 1
FA Cup (Nil):

1985-86

Baker	Joyce	Law	Thomas	Burns (N-C)	Jeffels	Goodison	Hirst	Walsh	Gray	Campbell	Ronson	Futcher	Glavin (N-C)	Owen	Plummer	May	Cross	Agnew	Ogley	Mackenzie (NC)	Jonsson (L)	Aylott (L)	Kiwonya (NC)	Referee	
1	2	3*	4	5	6	7	8	9	10	11	12													R Milford	1
1	2		4	5	7	3	8	9	10*	11		6	12											R Nixon	2
1	2		4	5	10	3	8	9*		11		6		7	12									M Peck	3
1	2		8	5	10	3		9		11		6	4	7										E Scales	4
1	2			5	8*	3	12	9	10	11		6	4	7										D Scott	5
1	2			5	8	3		9	10	11		6	4	7										B Hill	6
1	2			5		3		9	10	11		6	4*	7	12	8								N Glover	7
1	2		8	5				9	3	11		6		7		4	10							J Holigh	8
1	2		8	5				9	3	11		6		7		4	10							D Allison	9
1	2		8	5		3		9		11		6		7		4	10							C Seel	10
1	2		8	5				9*	3	11		6				4	10							K Walmsley	11
1	2		8	5			7	9	3	11		6				4	10							M Heath	12
1	2		10	5			8*		3	11		6	4	7	12			9						M Dimblebee	13
1	2		10	5			8*		3	11		6	4	7	12			9						P Tydesley	14
1	2		10	5			8	9	3	11		6	4	7										N Ashley	15
1	2		8			4	10	9	3	11		6		7		5								R Bridges	16
1	2		8			4	10	9	3	11		6		7		5								G Courtney	17
1	2		8			4	10	9	3	11		6		7		5								P Vanes	18
1	2		8			4	10	9	3	11		6		7		5								R Guy	19
1	2		8			4	10	9	3			6		7*		5			11					J Moules	20
1	2		8			4	10	9	3	11		6		7		5								J Lloyd	21
1	2		8			4	10		3	9		6		7		5								J Martin	22
1	2		8			4	10	9	3	11		6		7		5								J Worrall	23
1	2		8			4	10	9	3	11		6		7		5								A Robinson	24
1	2		8			4	10	9	3	11		6		7		5								M Scott	25
1	2		8		12	4	10		3	9		6		7		5	11*							K Breen	26
1	2		8			4	10	9	3	11		6		7		5								T Fitzharris	27
1	2		8				10	9	3	11†		6		7		5			4					R Gifford	28
1	2		8	10*			4	9	3			6		7	12	5	11							J Lovatt	29
1	2		8				12	9*	3	11		6		7	10	5	4							D Axcell	30
1	2		4				10	9	3			6		7		5	11				8			I Hendrick	31
1	2		4				10*	9	3	12		6		7		5	11				8			L Dilkes	32
1	2		4					9	3			6		7		5	11				8	10		C Downey	33
1	2		4					9	3			6		7*	12	5	11				8	10		N Midgley	34
1	2		4					9	3			6		7	12	5	11*				8	10		G Napthine	35
1	2		4				10		3	8		6		7		5	11					9		P Vanes	36
1	2		4		6		10		3	11				7		5	8					9		A Seville	37
1	2		4			3	10			11		6		7		5	8					9		D Hutchinson	38
1	2		4	12	8		10			11*		6		7		5	3					9		J Lovatt	39
1	2		4		8		10			11		6		7		5	3					9		C Trussell	40
1	2		4	12	8		10			11		6		7		5	3					9*		B Hill	41
1	2		4				9	10		8		6		7	11	5	3							C Seel	42
1	2		4		6*		12	9	10	8				7		5	3						11	P Willis	43
1	2		4	12	6	11		9	10*	8				7		5	3							K Redfern	44
1	2		4				11	9		8		6		7	10	5	3		6					T Holbrook	45
42	40	1	39	19	10	19	26	33	36	28	1	37	5	32	18	36	20	2	2	1	5	9	1	League Appearances	
			3	1	2	2				1	1	1			5									Substitute Appearances	
2	2	2	2	1	1	1	1	1	2	2		1		1	1+1	2	1					1		Milk Cup Appearances	
1	1	1	1	1	1	1		1	1	1					0-1	1	1							FA Cup Appearances	

Players on Loan: Jonsson (Sheffield Wednesday), Aylott (Crystal Palace)
Departures: Law (Blackpool), Rhodes (Doncaster R), Walsh (Grimsby Town)

'THE TYKES'

Formed: 1887
Turned Professional: 1888 **Ltd Co:** 1899

Previous Names: Barnsley St. Peter's
Previous Managers: 1901-4 John McCartney 1904-12 Arthur Fairclough 1912-4 John Hastie
1914-9 Harry Percy Lewis 1919-26 Peter Sant 1926-9 John Commins 1929-30 Arthur Fairclough
1930-7 Brough Fletcher 1937-53 Angus Seed 1953-60 Tim Ward 1960-71 Johnny Steel
1971-72 John McSeveney 1972-3 Johnny Steel (caretaker) 1973-8 Jim Iley 1978-80 Allan Clarke
1980-84 Norman Hunter 1984-85 Bobby Collins
Honours: Champions Div 3 (N) 1933-4, 1938-9, 1954-5 FA Cup Winners 1912
League Career: Elected to Div 2 1898 Moved to Div 3 (N) 1932
Promoted to Div 2 1933-4 Relegated to Div 3 (N) 1937-8 Promoted to Div 2 1938-9
Relegated to Div 3 (N) 1952-3 Promoted to Div 2 1954-5 Relegated to Div 3 1958-9
Relegated to Div 4 1964-5 Promoted to Div 3 1967-8 Relegated to Div 4 1971-2
Promoted to Div 3 1980-1 Promoted to Div 2 1981-2
Colours: Red shirts, white shorts, white stockings
Change Colours: Yellow shirts, black shorts, yellow stockings
Reserves League: Central League **Youth League:** Northern Intermediate

---

CLUB RECORDS

Most Appearances for Club: Barry Murphy: Football League 509 + FA Cup 26 + League Cup 29 **Total 564** (1962-78)
Most Capped Player: Eddie McMorran 9, N Ireland 1950-52 **For England:** G Utley 1
Record Goalscorer in a Match: P Cunningham, 5 v Darlington 6-2 (h), Div 3 (N) 4.2.1933 B Asquith 5 v Darlington 7-1 (h) Div 3 (N), 12.11.1938 C McCormack 5 v Luton Town 6-1 (h), Div 2 9.9.1950
Record League Goalscorer in a Season: Cecil McCormack 33, Div 2, 1950-1 **In All Competitions:** Cecil McCormack, 34 (League 33 + FA Cup 1), 1950-1
Record League Goalscorer in a Career: Ernie Hine, 122, 1921-6 and 1934-5 **In All Competitions:** Ernie Hine, (League 80 + FA Cup 2 in 1921-6 and League 42 + FA Cup 5 in 1934-5)
Record Transfer Fee Received: £200,000 from Manchester City for Mick McCarthy, Dec 1983
Record Transfer Fee Paid: £110,000 to Leicester City for Larry May, Aug 1983
Best Performances: League: 3rd Div 2 1914-15, 1921-2 **FA Cup:** Winners 1912 **League/Milk Cup:** 5th Round 1981-2
Most League Points: (2pts for win) 67, Div 3 (N) 1938-9 (3pts for win) 67 Div 2, 1981-2
Most League Goals: 118, Div 3 (N), 1933-4
Record League Victory and Most Goals Scored in a League Match: 9-0 v Loughborough Town, Div 2, 28 Jan 1899 9-0 v Accrington Stanley (a) Div 3 (N) 3 Feb 1934
Most Goals Scored in a Cup Tie: 8-0 v Leeds City (h) 2nd Qualifying Round FA Cup, 1894-5
Record League Defeat: 0-9 v Notts County, Div 2, 19 Nov 1927
Oldest Player in League Match: Beaumont Asquith, 37 yrs 3 months v Coventry City, Div 2, 27.12.47
Youngest Player in League Match: Eric Brooks, 16 yrs 7 months v Bradford City, Div 3, 24.9.60

Most Consecutive Undefeated League Matches: 21 1933-34	**League Matches Without a Win:** 26 1952-53
Longest Run of Undefeated Home League Matches: 36 1933-34	**Away League Matches:** 15 1938-39 1946
Longest Run Without Home League Win: 11 1952-53	**Away League Win:** 29 1908-09
Most Consecutive League Wins: 10 1955	**Home League Wins:** 12 1914-15
Most Consecutive League Defeats: 9 1953	**Away League Wins:** 5 1938-39, 1955

Barnsley scored in a record 44 successive League games between 1926-27 and also in 35 successive games in the 1926-27 season

Club Statistician for the Directory: Arthur Bower

PLAYERS NAME Ht Wt Birthdate	Honours	Birthplace Transfers	Clubs	APPEARANCES				GOALS			
				League	Milk Cup	FA Cup	Other Comps	League	Milk Cup	FA Cup	Other Comps
GOALKEEPERS											
Clive Baker† 5.9 11.0 14.3.59		North Walsham F	Norwich City Barnsley	14 79	4	2 5					
Paul Malcolm 6.4½ 14.6 11.12.64		Gateshead F F	Rochdale Shrewsbury Barnsley	24	1	1	3				
DEFENDERS											
Paul Cross 5.7 9.6 31.10.65		Barnsley	Barnsley (A)	21	2	1					
Paul Futcher 6.0 12.3 25.9.56	EU21 (11)	Chester £100,000 £350,000 £150,000 £44,000 £30,000	Chester (A) Luton Town Manchester City Oldham Athletic Derby County Barnsley	20 131 36+1 98 35 83	4 3+1 9 1 4	1 6 3 4 4 4		1 1			
Wayne Goddison 5.8 11.7 23.9.64		Wakefield	Barnsley (A)	31+5	1	3					
Simon Jeffers 6.1 11.8 18.1.61	EY	Darton	Barnsley (A)	31+1	0+1	1+1					
Joe Joyce* 5.9 10.5 18.3.61		Consett	Barnsley	212+2	1+1	24		2	1	1	
Larry May 6.0 12.6 26.12.58	Div. 2, 80	Sutton C'ldfield	Leicester City (A) Barnsley	180+7 100	8 4	12 5		12 2	3		
Mark Ogley 5.10 11.7 10.3.67		Barnsley	Barnsley (A)	2							
Chris Hedworth 6.1 10.11 5.1.64		Wallsend	Newcastle U. (A)	8+1	1						
MIDFIELD											
Winston Campbell 5.8 11.6 17.10.62		Sheffield	Barnsley (A)	122+5	9+1	5+1		9	1	3	
Andy Kynomya 5.9½ 10.5 1.10.67		Huddersfield	Barnsley	1							
Gwyn Thomas 5.8 11.0 26.9.57	WU23 (3)	Swansea £40,000	Leeds United (A) Barnsley	79+10 92	9+1 4	4+1 5		3 6			
Calvin Plummer 5.8 10.7 14.2.63		Nottingham Player exch. £10,000 £10,000	Nottingham F. Chesterfield Derby County Barnsley	10+2 28 23+4 41+10	2 2	3+1 0+1		2 7 3 7			
John Beresford 5.6 10.12 4.9.66		Sheffield F	Manchester City (A) Barnsley								
Mark Hine 5.8½ 9.0 18.5.64		Middlesbrough F	Grimsby Town Barnsley	8+1							
FORWARDS											
Stuart Gray 5.9 11.10 19.4.60		Withernsea £40,000	Nottingham F. Bolton W. (L) Barnsley	48+1 7 57+3	5+1 1	3 1		3 10	1		
Alan Semley 6.0½ 11.0 21.2.66		Barnsley	Barnsley (A)	1+3		1					
Roger Wylde 6.1½ 12.0 6.3.54		Sheffield £180,000 Sporting Lisbon £15,000	Sheffield Wed. (A) Oldham Athletic Sunderland Barnsley	157+12 109+4 8+2 16+1	10 8 4	15 4 2		54 51 3 4	8 1 2	4	

ADDITIONAL CONTRACT PROFESSIONALS

APPRENTICES

Mark Johnson

NON-CONTRACT PLAYERS

Ian MacKenzie, Bobby Jones

Record Attendance: 40,255 v Stoke City, FA Cup 5th Round, 15 Feb 1936

Smallest Home Attendance for a First Class Match: 1,972 v Wrexham, Div 3, 8 March 1972

Record Receipts: (not given) v Manchester City, Milk Cup, 2 Dec 1981

Season Tickets: Stand: £72.00 (juveniles/OAP £55.00); Ground: £42.00 (juveniles/OAP £26)

Cost of Stand Tickets: £5.00 (all seats); Terraces: £2.70 (£1.70 juveniles/OAP)

Match and Ticket Information: Phone ground. Available two weeks in advance

Car Parking: Two official club parks adjacent ground for 1,200 vehicles (fee 50p). Visiting supporters should use Queens Road free park — two minutes from ground in side streets and at the Molyneux Hotel

Nearest Railway Station: Exchange Station, Barnsley (0226-5681/2)

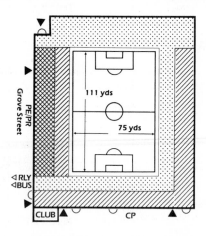

How to get to the ground

From North: Leave Motorway M1 at junction 37 and follow signs into Barnsley A628. Then follow signs Pontefract into Pontefract Road. In 0.3m turn left into Grove Street for Barnsley FC

From East: From A1(M) and Doncaster, follow signs Barnsley A635, then 10·7m after Ardsley turn right into Pontefract Road. In 0.3m turn left into Grove Street for Barnsley FC

From South: Leave Motorway M1 at junction 36 and follow signs into Barnsley A628. Then follow signs Pontefract into Pontefract Road. In 0.3m turn left into Grove Street for Barnsley FC

From West: Follow signs Barnsley to enter via A628 or A635 then follow signs Pontefract into Pontefract Road. In 0.3m turn left into Grove Street for Barnsley FC

Price of 1986-7 Programme: 50p
Number of Pages: 32
Subscriptions: Rates on request

Local Newspapers: Barnsley Chronicle (weekly), Barnsley Star (daily), Morning Telegraph, Yorkshire Post

Local Radio Stations: Radio Sheffield, Radio Hallam

Chairman
K Wheldon

Directors
J F Wiseman
H Parkes
N B A Bosworth
R Homden (Vice-Chairman)

Secretary
A R Waterhouse (021-772 0101/2689)

Manager
John Bond

Assistant Manager
Fred Davies

Youth Coach
Kevin Reeves

Commercial Manager
T Edmunds (021-772 0101)

Physiotherapist
G Doig

Groundsman
J Hindle

Back Row L to R: Brian Roberts, Jim Hagan, Stuart Storer, Tom Williams, **Middle Row:** Fred Davies (Assistant Manager), Ian Handysides, Dave Gedddis, Andy Kennedy, Roger Hansbury, Vince Overson, Nicky Platnauer, Wayne Clarke, John Bond (Manager), **Front Row:** Martin Kuhl, Des Bremner, Julian Dicks, Robert Hopkins.

D espite having clinched promotion at the first attempt it was plainly obvious that the team was not strong enough to cope with the more arduous demands of the First Division. Therefore if the club was to make any impression in the top flight team strengthening was a priority. The necessary cash was not available however and the club thus started the season without any new signings.

The frustration that manager Ron Saunders felt about this situation was evident when following a pre-season friendly at Bristol Rovers he declared that 'we will be relegated by Christmas'. Although the accuracy of this prophecy was slightly exaggerated it signalled the start of one of the most disastrous First Division campaigns in the club's history.

Surprisingly the season began well with five victories in the first nine games and by the end of September Birmingham were lying 8th in the table.

During the next four months a catastrophic run of 17 League games without a win sent them plummeting into the relegation zone from which there was to be no escape. This terrible sequence included ten consecutive home defeats, eight consecutive games without scoring (just five goals being scored in that time) and a decisive exit from the Milk Cup at Southampton.

In December changes at boardroom level took place, when chairman Keith Coombes resigned and former Walsall chairman Ken Wheldon took over. It has been said that prior to the takeover the club was within days of almost certain bankruptcy.

The one chance of salvaging anything from the wretched season was the prospect of a lucrative run in the FA Cup but hopes of that were shattered by an embarrassing third round defeat at the hands of non-league Altrincham and the aftermath of that result saw the end of Ron Saunders reign as manager.

He was replaced by John Bond whose first game in charge realised the first League victory since September and as the team began to play more positive and attacking football, hopes began to rise that the dreaded drop might be avoided after all.

Unfortunately the problems proved insurmountable and as the initial confidence drained away so the goals once again dried up and the defence began conceding goals at an alarming rate. By now most supporters had accepted the inevitable and just 5,833 fans, the lowest 1st Division attendance for 78 years witnessed the home defeat by Southampton which sealed their fate. This is the second time in the club's history that relegation has been suffered after just one season in Division 1.

Clearly John Bond faces a massive task to pull the club round and, as last year, new signings are essential if they are to create any impression in the promotion race next season. Failure to do so this time could mean a very bleak future indeed.

Dave Drage

BIRMINGHAM CITY

DIVISION ONE: 21st   **FA CUP:** 3rd ROUND   **MILK CUP:** 3rd ROUND

MATCH	DATE		COMPE-TITION	VENUE	OPPONENTS	RESULT		HALF TIME	L'GUE POS'N	GOALSCORERS/GOAL TIMES	ATTEN-DANCE
1	A	17	CL	H	West Ham United	W	1-0	0-0		Hopkins 65	11,164
2		20	CL	A	Watford	L	0-3	0-2			(14,278)
3		24	CL	A	Chelsea	L	0-2	0-1	17		(16,534)
4		26	CL	H	Oxford United	W	3-1	2-1	11	Kennedy 33, Briggs (og) 42, Hopkins 58	10,568
5		31	CL	A	Everton	L	1-4	1-2	12	Kennedy 25	(28,066)
6	S	3	CL	A	Manchester City	W	1-0	0-0	11	Geddis 67	11,706
7		7	CL	H	Aston Villa	D	0-0	0-0	11		24,971
8		14	CL	A	Ipswich Town	W	1-0	0-0	10	Geddis 74	(11,616)
9		21	CL	H	Leicester City	W	2-1	0-1	8	Geddis 78, 89	9,864
10		24	MC2/1	A	Bristol Rovers	W	3-2	1-1		Wright 37, 56 (pen), Geddis 80	(4,332)
11		28	CL	A	Q.P.R.	L	1-3	1-2	10	Armstrong 17	(10,911)
12	O	5	CL	H	Sheffield Wednesday	L	0-2	0-1	12		11,708
13		8	MC2/2	H	Bristol Rovers	W	2-1	0-1		Kennedy 72, Tanner (og) 76	3,686
14		19	CL	A	W.B.A.	L	2-1	1-2	14	Kennedy 4	(14,747)
15		26	CL	H	Coventry City	L	0-1	0-1	15		9,267
16		29	MC3	H	Southampton	D	1-1	1-1		Kennedy 34	4,832
17	N	2	CL	A	Luton Town	L	0-2	0-0	17		(8,550)
18		6	MC3R	A	Southampton	L	0-3	0-2			(9,085)
19		9	CL	H	Newcastle United	L	0-1	0-1	17		8,162
20		16	CL	A	Southampton	L	0-1	0-0	17		(13,167)
21		23	CL	H	Liverpool	L	0-2	0-2	20		15,062
22		30	CL	A	Arsenal	D	0-0	0-0	20		(16,637)
23	D	7	CL	H	Watford	L	1-2	1-0	20	Wright 45	7,043
24		14	CL	A	West Ham United	L	0-2	0-2	20		(17,481)
25		21	CL	H	Chelsea	L	1-2	0-1	20	Platnauer 81	10,594
26		26	CL	H	Nottingham Forest	L	0-1	0-1	21		10,378
27		28	CL	A	Manchester City	D	1-1	1-0	21	Geddis 15	(24,955)
28	J	1	CL	A	Manchester United	L	0-1	0-0	21		(43,095)
29		11	CL	H	Ipswich Town	L	0-1	0-1	21		6,856
30		14	FAC3	H	Altrincham	L	1-2	0-0		Hopkins 67	6,636
31		18	CL	H	Everton	L	0-2	0-1	21		10,502
32	F	1	CL	A	Oxford United	W	1-0	0-0	21	Clarke 78	(9,068)
33		8	CL	H	W.B.A.	L	0-1	0-0	21		11,514
34		16	CL	A	Coventry City	D	4-4	2-0	21	Kennedy 2, 83, Whitton 16, Kuhl 58	(14,271)
35	M	1	CL	H	Q.P.R.	W	2-0	0-0	21	Clarke (pen) 52, Hopkins 85	7,093
36		8	CL	A	Sheffield Wednesday	L	1-5	0-3	21	Geddis 81	(17,491)
37		12	CL	A	Leicester City	L	2-4	2-3	21	Clarke 2, Kennedy 10	(8,458)
38		15	CL	H	Tottenham Hotspur	L	1-2	0-2	21	Kennedy 58	9,394
39		22	CL	A	Aston Villa	W	3-0	2-0	21	Clarke 31, 38, Whitton 61	(26,694)
40		29	CL	H	Manchester United	D	1-1	0-0	21	Handysides 66	22,551
41		31	CL	A	Nottingham Forest	L	0-3	0-1	21		(12,134)
42	A	6	CL	H	Luton Town	L	0-2	0-0	21		8,836
43		12	CL	A	Newcastle United	L	1-4	0-1	21	Hopkins 77	(19,981)
44		16	CL	A	Tottenham Hotspur	L	0-1	0-1	21		(9,359)
45		19	CL	H	Southampton	L	0-2	0-1	21		5,833
46		26	CL	A	Liverpool	L	0-5	0-1	21		(42,021)
47	M	3	CL	H	Arsenal	L	0-1	0-0	21		6,234

Best Home League Attendance: 24,971 v Aston Villa 7/9   **Smallest:** 5,833 v Southampton 19/4   **Av Home Att:** 10,917

Goal Scorers:

                                                            Compared with 84-85: −1,604

League (30):   Geddis 6, Kennedy 7, Clarke 5 (1 pen), Hopkins 4, Whitton 2, Armstrong 1, Handysides 1, Kuhl 1, Platnauer 1, Wright 1, Opponents 1

Milk Cup (6):   Kennedy 2, Wright 2 (1 pen), Geddis 1, Opponents 1

FA Cup (1):   Hopkins 1

1985-86

Seaman	Ransom	Roberts	Wright	Armstrong	Daly	Bremner	Clarke	Jones	Geddis	Hopkins	Kuhl	Hagan	Kennedy	Dicks (A)	Platnauer	Jenkins	Ronson (L)	Rees	Russell (NC)	Whitton (L)	Garton (L)	Smalley (L)	Handysides	Frain	Storer	Referee	
1	2	3	4	5*	6	7	8	9	10	11	12															N Glover	1
1	2	3	4		6	7	8	9*	10	11	12	5														B Hill	2
1	2		4	5		7	8	3	10*	11	6	9	12													D Hedges	3
1	2		4	5		7	8	3	10	11	6	9	12													J Lovatt	4
1	2		4	5*		7	8	3	10	11	6	9	12													J McAulay	5
1	2*	12	4	5		7	8	3	10	11	6	9														H Taylor	6
1	2		4	5			8	3	10	11	6	9	7													N Wilson	7
1	2	8	4					3	10	11	6*	5	9	7	12											E Scales	8
1	2	8	4	5		7		3	10	11	6	9														M Heath	9
1	2*	8	4	5		7		3	10	11		12	9	6												J Deakin	10
1	2		4	5		7	8	3	10	11	9	6*	12													M Bodenham	11
1	2		4	5		7	3*		10	11	8	6	9	12												R Nixon	12
1	2		4	5		7				11	6	3	9	8												A Ward	13
1	2		4	5		7		3		11	6	9	12	10	8*											J Key	14
1	2	7	4	5*				3	10	11	6	8	9	12												K Hackett	15
1	2	7	4					3	10*	11	6	5	9	12	8											T Fitzharris	16
1	2	8	5			7		3	10	11	6	4	9													K Miller	17
1	2	8	12	5		7		3*	10	11	6	4	9													A Buksh	18
1	2	3		5		7	8*		10		4	9	6				11	12								R Bridges	19
1	2	3	7	5			8		10		6*	4	9	12			11									M Dimblebee	20
1	2	3	8	5		7			10	11	6*	4	9	12												H King	21
1	2	3	6	5		7	8	9*		11	4	12	10													M James	22
1	2	3	6	5		7			10*	11	12	4	9	8												J Lloyd	23
1	2	3	6			7			10	5	4	8	11		9											L Shapter	24
1	2	3	4			7				11	6	5	9	8*	12			10								D Scott	25
1	2	3	4			7				11	6	5		8*	12			10								K Walmsley	26
1	2		4			7			10*	11	6	5	9	3	8			12								F Roberts	27
1	2	12	4	5			8*			11	6	7	9	3	10											D Hutchinson	28
1	2		5			7			10*	11	6	4	9	3	8			12								J Worrall	29
1	2	8	12	5		7				11	6*	4	9	3	10											K Hackett	30
1	2	3	6*	5		7	8			11	4	12	10					9								J Deakin	31
1	2	3	5*			7	8		10	11	6	4	12							9						M Heath	32
1	2	3	5			7	8		10	11	6	4								9						H Taylor	33
1	2	3				7	8		10	11	6	4	9*							5						K Lupton	34
1	2	3				7	8		10	11	6	4	9*		12					5						N Ashley	35
1	2	3				7	8		10	11	6	4*	12							9	5					D Scott	36
1	2	3				7	8	12		11	6	4	9*							10	5					F Roberts	37
1	2	3				7	8*			11	6	4	9	12						10	5					D Allison	38
1	2	3	9			7	8			11	6	4								10	5					K Hackett	39
1	2	3	9			7	8			11	6	4										5	10			A Ward	40
1	2	3*	9			7	8			11	6	12									4	5	10			J Worrall	41
1	2	5				7	8			11	6	9		3							4		10			K Breen	42
1	2	5					8			11	6	7		3								4	10	9		N Glover	43
1	2						8	9*		11	6	4	12	3	7							5	10			I Borrett	44
1	2						8	9*		11	6	4		3	7							5	10		12	R Guy	45
1	6	2*	10				8			11	12	5		3	9							4			7	G Tyson	46
1	2						8			11	6	5	10*	3	9							4	12		7	D Phillips	47
42	37	31	29	22	2	32	28	19	25	38	33	31	27	18	12	1	2	4		8	5	7	6	1	2	League Appearances	
	2								1				4	5	6	5		2		4	1		3			Substitute Appearances	
4	3	4	3-1	3		3		3	3	4	3	3-1	4	1-1	3											Milk Cup Appearances	
1	1	1	0-1	1		1		1	1	1	1	1	1	1												FA Cup Appearances	

Also Played:

Players on Loan: Garton (Manchester Utd), Ronson (Barnsley), Smalley (Nottm Forest), Whitton (West Ham)

Departures: Armstrong (Walsall), Daly (Shrewsbury, Prudhoe (Walsall), Broadhurst (Retired injured), Wright, Jenkins , Shearer

'THE BLUES'

Formed: 1875
Turned Professional: 1885   **Ltd Co:** 1888

Previous Names: Small Heath Alliance (1875-88), Small Heath (1888), Birmingham (1905-45)
Previous Managers: Since 1946: Ted Goodier   Harry Storer   Bob Brocklebank   Arthur Turner
Pat Beasley   Gil Merrick   Joe Mallett   Stan Cullis   Fred Goodwin   Willie Bell   Sir Alf Ramsey
Jim Smith   Ron Saunders
Honours: Champions Div 2, 1892-3, 1920-1, 1947-8, 1954-5   Football League Cup Winners 1962-3
League Career: Elected to Div 2 1892   Promoted to Div 1 1894
Relegated to Div 2 1896   Promoted to Div 1 1901   Relegated to Div 2 1902
Promoted to Div 1 1903   Relegated to Div 2 1908   Promoted to Div 1 1921
Relegated to Div 2 1939   Promoted to Div 1 1948   Relegated to Div 2 1950
Promoted to Div 1 1955   Relegated to Div 2 1965   Promoted to Div 1 1972
Relegated to Div 2 1979   Promoted to Div 1 1980   Relegated to Div 2 1984
Promoted to Div 1 1985   Relegated to Div 2 1986
Colours: Royal blue shirts with white and red trim, white shorts with blue trim and red stockings
Change Colours: Red shirts and shorts, white stockings
Reserves League: Midland Intermediate

CLUB RECORDS

Most Appearances for Club: Gil Merrick: Football League 485 + FA Cup 56 + IC Fairs Cup 10 **Total 551** (1946-60)
Most Capped Player: Malcolm Page, 28, Wales 1971-79   **For England:** Harry Hibbs, 25
Record Goalscorer in a Match: Walter Abbott, 5 v Darwen (H), Div 2 (8-0), 26.11.1898   John McMillan, 5 v Blackpool,
(H), Div 2, (10-1), 2.3.1901   Ben Green, 5 v Middlesbrough, (H), Div 1, (7-0), 26.12.1905   Jimmy Windridge, 5 v Glossop
(H) Div 2 (11-1), 23.1.1915
Record League Goalscorer in a Season: Walter Abbott, 34, Div 2, 1898-99   **In All Competitions:** Walter Abbott, 50
(League 42 + Cup 8), 1898-99
Record League Goalscorer in a Career: Joe Bradford, 249   **In All Competitions:** Joe Bradford, 267 (League 249 + FA
Cup 18) 1920-35
Record Transfer Fee Received: £975,000 from Nottingham Forest for Trevor Francis, Feb 1979
Record Transfer Fee Paid: £350,000 to Derby Co. for David Langan, June 1980
Best Performances: League: 6th Div 1 1955-6   **FA Cup:** Finalists (2)   **League/Milk Cup:** Winners (1)   **European Fairs
Cup:** Finalists
Most League Points: 82, Div 2, 1984-5   **Most League Goals:** 103, Div 2, 1893-4
Record League Victory and Most Goals Scored in a League Match: 12-0 v Walsall Town Swifts, Div 2, 17.12.1892
12-0 v Doncaster Rovers, Div 2, 11.4.1903
Most Goals Scored in a Cup Tie: 10-0 v Druids (H), FA Cup, 19.11.1898   10-0 v Oswestry T. (H), FA Cup, 30.10.1899
Record League Defeat: 1-9 v Sheffield Wednesday, Div 1, 13.12.30   1-9 v Blackburn Rovers, Div 1 5.1.1895
European Competitions Entered: European Fairs Cup 1955-8, 1958-60, 1960-1, 1960-2
Oldest Player in League Match:
Youngest Player in League Match:

Most Consecutive Undefeated League Matches: 18 1972	**League Matches Without a Win:** 17 1985-86
Longest Run of Undefeated Home League Matches: 36 1971-72	**Away League Matches:** 15 1947-48
Longest Run Without Home League Win: 11 1962-63	**Away League Win:** 32 1980-82
Most Consecutive League Wins: 13 1892-93 ('Test' matches lost)	**Home League Wins:** 17 1902-03
Most Consecutive League Defeats: 8 1978-79, 1985	**Away League Wins:** 9 1897

Club Statistician for the Directory: Dave Drage

BIRMINGHAM

PLAYERS NAME Ht Wt Birthdate	Honours	Birthplace Transfers	Clubs	APPEARANCES League	Milk Cup	FA Cup	Other Comps	GOALS League	Milk Cup	FA Cup	Other Comps
GOALKEEPERS											
Roger Hansbury 5.11 12.0 26.1.55		Barnsley	Norwich City	78	4						
		F	Cambridge United	11							
		Hong Kong	Burnley	83	6	8	6				
		F	Cambridge United	37	1	1	3				
		F	Birmingham City								
DEFENDERS											
Julian Dicks 5.7 10.5 8.8.68		Bristol	Birmingham (A)	18+5	1+1	1					
Jim Hagan 5.11 11.9 10.8.56	NI, Y	Monkstown	Larne								
			Coventry City	12+1							
			Detroit & H. Kong (L)								
			Torquay United	7							
		F	Birmingham City	122+13	17+1	2+1					
Mark Jones 5.6 10.1 22.10.61	ESC 82 FAYC 80	Warley £50,000 Player exch.	Aston Villa (A)	24	2	1	3+1				
			Brighton	9							
			Birmingham City	28+1	4+1						
Ray Ranson 5.9½ 12.1 12.6.60	EU21 (11), YS	St. Helens £15,000	Manchester City (A)	181+2	22	13		1			
			Birmingham City	65	3	5					
Brian Roberts 5.8 11.3 6.11.55		Manchester	Coventry City (A)	209+6	19+2	13					
			Hereford United	5							
		£10,000	Birmingham City	83+2	8	5					
Tommy Williams 5.10 10.12 18.12.57	Div. 2, 80	Leicester F	Leicester City (A)	236+5	12	18		10		1	
			Birmingham City								
Vince Overson 6.0 13.0 15.5.62	EY, Div. 3, 82	Kettering F	Burnley (A)	207+4	9	19	8	6	1		
			Birmingham City								
MIDFIELD											
Des Bremmer 5.10 11.11 17.9.52	S (1), U23 (9), Y S Div. 1, 81, EC 81, ESC 82	Aberchider	Hibernian	198	26+2	26	1+1	18	2	2	
			Aston Villa	170+4	13	14	19	9	1		
			Birmingham City	62	6	5					
Martin Kuhl 5.11 11.9 10.1.65		Frimley	Birmingham City (A)	80+8	10	6		4			
Dennis Mortimer 5.10 12.0 5.4.52	E B (3), U23 (6), Y, LgC 77, Div.1 81, EC 82, ESC 82	Liverpool	Coventry City (A)	179+14	18	8+1		10			
			Aston Villa	316+1	38	21	28	31	2	1	
			Sheffield United (L)	7							
			Brighton & H.A.	40	3	4		2			
			Birmingham								
Nicky Platnauer 5.11 12.10 10.6.61		Leicester F	Bedford Town			1					
		£50,000	Bristol Rovers	21+3	1	0+1		7	1		
		£60,000	Coventry City	38+5	5	4		6			
			Birmingham City	23+5	3	5		2			
			Reading (L)	6			1				
Steve Whitton 6.0 12.7 4.12.60		East Ham	Coventry City (A)	64+10	2+2	3		21			
			West Ham United	35+4	6	1		6	2		
			Birmingham City	8				3			
FORWARDS											
Wayne Clarke 5.11¼ 10.6 28.2.61		Wolverhampton £80,000	W'hampton W. (A)	129+19	8+2	9+2	0+1	30	2	1	
			Birmingham City	68	3	4		22	2		
David Geddis 5.10½ 12.2 12.3.58	E B (1), Y, FAYC 75, FAC 78	Carlisle	Ipswich Town (A)	26+17	0+1	2+1	2+5	5		1	
			Luton Town (L)	9+4				4			
		£300,000	Aston Villa	43+4	4	4+1		12		4	
			Luton Town (L)	4							
		£50,000	Barnsley	45	2			24		1	
		£50,000	Birmingham City	43+1	3	4		18	1	1	
Robert Hopkins 5.7 10.5 25.10.61	FAYC 80	Birmingham	Aston Villa (A)	1+2							
			Birmingham City	120	12	10		20	3	2	
Andy Kennedy 6.1 11.10 8.10.64		Stirling F	Glasgow Rangers								
			Birmingham City	31+6	4	1		9	2		
Robert Hopkins 5.7 10.5 25.10.61	FAYC 80	Birmingham	Aston Villa (A)	1+2							
			Birmingham City	120	12	10		20	3	2	
Tony Rees 5.8½ 11.0 1.8.64	W (1), U21 (1), S FAYC 80	Merthyr Tydfil F	Aston Villa (A)								
			Birmingham City	31+11	1+1	3		4	1	1	
			Peterborough U. (L)	5				2			
			Shrewsbury (L)								
Stuart Storer 5.10 11.0 16.1.67		Coventry	Birmingham City	2							

ADDITIONAL CONTRACT PROFESSIONALS
Ian Gore, Guy Russell (0+1 Lg)

APPRENTICES
Kevin Ashley, John Frain, David Smith, Martin Weir

NON-CONTRACT PLAYERS
Adrian Bird, Dean Peer, Nigel Thomas

Record Attendance: 66,844 v Everton, FA Cup Round 5, 11 Feb 1939

Smallest Home Attendance for a First Class Match: 1,500 v Chesterfield, Div 2, 17 Apr 1909

Record Receipts: £110,450.72 v Watford, FA Cup Round 6, 10 Mar 1984

Season Tickets: Centre Stand: £105.00 (adults), £52.50 (OAP or child); Wing Stand: £90.00 (adults), £45.00 (OAP or child); Family City Stand: £65.00 (adults), £32.50 (OAP or child); Terracing: £37.50 (adult), £18.75 (OAP or child)

Executive Club: £275.00

Cost of Stand Tickets: £4.50, £6.00
Terraces: £3.00 (reductions for juniors & OAPs)

Match and Ticket Information: (021-772 0101)

Car Parking: Public car park in Coventry Road and Cattell Road. Passes for Kingston Road park £25

Nearest Railway Station: Buses from Birmingham New Street or Snow Hill, or walk from Bordesley Station from Birmingham Moor Street

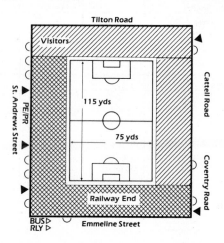

How to get to the ground

From North and East: Use Motorway M6 until junction 6. Leave motorway and follow signs Birmingham Central A38M. In 1.9m branch left and at roundabout take 1st exit A45 along Dartmouth Middleway. In 1.2m turn left A45 into St Andrews Road for Birmingham City FC
From South: Leave M5 at Junction 4 or use A435 or A41 to enter Birmingham. Then follow signs Coventry A45 to enter Coventry Road, then in 0.3m turn left into St Andrews Road for Birmingham City FC
From West: Follow signs Birmingham A456, then follow signs The South A41 then Coventry A45 to enter Coventry Road, then in 0.3m turn left into St Andrews Road for Birmingham City FC

Price of 1986-7 Programme: 60p
Number of Pages: 32
Subscriptions:

Local Newspapers: Birmingham Post and Evening Mail, Sports Argus (Saturday Football Special)

Local Radio Stations: Radio West Midlands, BRMB, BBC Radio Birmingham

President
W H Bancroft

Chairman
W Fox

Directors
R D Coar, BSc (Vice-Chairman)
Dr M Jeffries TD
T W Ibbotson LLB
L Neale
K C Lee
I R Stanners
G R Root FCRA

Secretary
J W Howarth FAAI (0254 55432)

Commercial Department
(0254 55432)

Manager
Bobby Saxton

Reserve Team Manager
Jim Furnell

Coach
T Parkes

Physiotherapist
J M Walker

Groundsman
T Wilkin

On 5th May Blackburn Rovers went into their final game against Grimsby in the knowledge that a win would ensure they retained their Second Division status. It was an ignominious if ultimately successful end to a season that had commenced with a challenge for promotion. In 1986 the team took 15 of the 57 points played for, and six of these came in the last three games. Included in the spell were five consecutive home defeats, the worst spell for 20 years — though they managed to beat Nottingham Forest in the FA Cup — yet the deterioration was surprising only in its speed. Virtually unchanged for seasons, the blend was stale and the style predictable. The manager Bobby Saxton had placed his trust in honest journeymen players and remained faithful to them even when they were off form. This policy was made easier to enforce because of financial constraints that ruled out the acquisition of new players. Two squad players Randell and Glenn left the club in the close season, leaving only sixteen men. The only recruitment came at the turn of the year when Alan Ainscow of Wolves was taken on trial, and even he was used sparingly. But a show of adrenalin came from the introduction of Simon Barker and Mark Patterson. It is sad that a brilliant youngster like Franz Carr decided his future lay elsewhere. Indeed the failure to provide new faces was puzzling at Christmas when the team was down to less than a dozen fit players the only loan signing was a Sunderland youngster. Even before the transfer deadline, when relegation was a possibility, no loan player was taken on. It would be disloyal to criticise veteran players who have served the club well. The rock solid back four of Branagan, Keeley, Fazackerley and Rathbone disintegrated to surrender goals with alarming ease. Even Gennoe behind them lost form and ended in the reserves with O'Keefe preferred. Simon Garner ended as top scorer, just in front of young Patterson whose ten league goals were a sound return considering that he was absent for four months. Permutations between Northern Irish international Jimmy Quinn and the more industrious Chris Thompson failed to find a striking partner for Garner. However complete reliance on orthodox crosses from Miller on the right and Rathbone on the left was possibly too predictable.

On a happier note it was nice to see Derek Fazackerley beat the club record of League appearances, previously held by Ronnie Clayton. It is no coincidence that the defence has suffered from the decline of Fazackerley's speed, for he has been the unsung mainstay of the team for a decade. Harry Berry

Back Row L to R: Jim Branagan, Ian Miller, Jimmy Quinn, Glen Keeley, David Mail, **Middle Row:** Jim Walker (Physio), Bob Saxton (Manager), Chris Price, Tony Diamond, Terry Gennoe, Vince O'Keefe, Michael Rathbone, Noel Brotherstone, Jim Furnell (Reserve Team Manager), Tony Parkes (First Team Coach), **Front Row:** Scott Sellars, Mark Patterson, Derek Fazackerley, William Fox (Chairman), John Haworth (Secretary), Simon Barker, Alan Ainscow, Simon Garner, **Seated:** Ray Driver, Alex Binnie, Keith Hill, David Fantom, Leonard Johnrose, David May, Paul Taylor, Gary Brown.

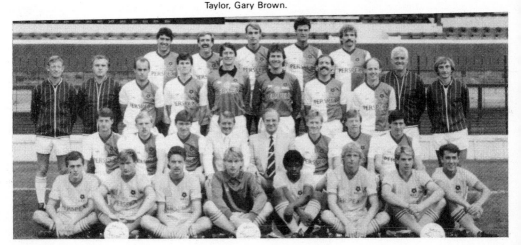

BLACKBURN ROVERS

DIVISION TWO: 19th   **FA CUP:** 4th ROUND   **MILK CUP:** 2nd ROUND

MATCH	DATE		COMPE-TITION	VENUE	OPPONENTS	RESULT		HALF TIME	L'GUE POS'N	GOALSCORERS/GOAL TIMES	ATTEN-DANCE
1	A	17	CL	A	Sunderland	W	2-0	0-0		Patterson 67, Quinn 87	(21,202)
2		20	CL	H	Norwich City	W	2-1	0-1		Fazackerley (pen) 63, Garner 87	6,567
3		24	CL	H	Shrewsbury Town	D	1-1	0-0	2	Garner 73	6,071
4		26	CL	A	Hull City	D	2-2	0-2	2	Barker 53, Patterson 63	(7,288)
5		31	CL	H	Carlisle United	W	2-0	0-0	2	Garner 57, Patterson 67	5,956
6	S	3	CL	A	Huddersfield Town	D	0-0	0-0	2		(9,060)
7		7	CL	A	Brighton H. A.	L	1-3	1-1	5	Keeley 35	(8,159)
8		14	CL	H	Wimbledon	W	2-0	1-0	2	Patterson 31, 47	5,006
9		21	CL	H	Fulham	W	1-0	0-0	2	Patterson 83	5,241
10		**24**	**MC2/1**	**A**	**Wimbledon**	**L**	**0-5**	**0-3**			**(2,072)**
11		28	CL	A	Portsmouth	L	0-3	0-1	3		(16,870)
12	O	5	CL	H	Bradford City	W	3-0	1-0	3	Quinn 35, Keeley 52, Garner 89	7,728
13		**8**	**MC2/2**	**H**	**Wimbledon**	**W**	**2-1**	**1-1**		**Patterson 30, Quinn 65**	**2,160**
14		12	CL	A	Millwall	W	1-0	1-0	2	Garner 12	(6,050)
15		19	CL	H	Oldham Athletic	D	0-0	0-0	2		9,666
16		26	CL	A	Crystal Palace	L	0-2	0-0	3		(5,408)
17	N	2	CL	A	Middlesbrough	D	0-0	0-0	4		(5,126)
18		9	CL	H	Barnsley	L	0-3	0-1	5		5,927
19		16	CL	A	Sheffield United	D	3-3	2-2	8	Keeley 12, Barker 21, Lowey 76	(13,610)
20		23	CL	H	Charlton Athletic	D	0-0	0-0	7		5,321
21		30	CL	A	Grimsby Town	L	2-5	0-3	10	Lowey 56, 59	(5,016)
22	D	7	CL	A	Norwich City	L	0-3	0-2	10		(12,820)
23		14	CL	H	Sunderland	W	2-0	1-0	9	Barker (pen) 11, Garner 85	6,045
24		20	CL	A	Shrewsbury Town	L	0-2	0-0	9		(3,174)
25		26	CL	H	Leeds United	W	2-0	2-0	9	Brotherston 3, Barker 70	8,666
26	J	1	CL	A	Stoke City	D	2-2	1-2	10	Garner 20, Barker (pen) 48	(11,875)
27		**4**	**FAC3**	**A**	**Nottingham Forest**	**D**	**1-1**	**1-0**	**10**	**Thompson 43**	**(15,772)**
28		**13**	**FAC3R**	**H**	**Nottingham Forest**	**W**	**3-2**	**3-1**		**Lowey 17, Brotherston 42, Thompson 44**	**11,710**
29		18	CL	A	Carlisle United	L	1-2	0-1	11	Garner 70	(4,076)
30		**25**	**FAC4**	**A**	**Everton**	**L**	**1-3**	**0-2**		**Van den Hauwe (og) 53**	**(41,831)**
31	F	1	CL	H	Hull City	D	2-2	0-1	11	Ainscow 73, 74	5,414
32		8	CL	A	Oldham Athletic	L	1-3	0-3	21	Barker 48	(5,314)
33		15	CL	H	Crystal Palace	L	1-2	0-1	12	Keeley 72	4,825
34	M	1	CL	H	Portsmouth	W	1-0	0-0	13	Garner 59	4,980
35		8	CL	A	Bradford City	L	2-3	1-1	13	Quinn 22, Hamilton 50	(5,263)
36		11	CL	A	Fulham	D	3-3	0-1	13	Patterson 54, Garner 58, Quinn 75	(2,555)
37		15	CL	H	Millwall	L	1-2	0-1	14	Barker 66	4,336
38		18	CL	H	Brighton & H.A.	L	1-4	0-1		Barker (pen) 90	3,616
39		22	CL	A	Wimbledon	D	1-1	1-1	15	Miller 11	(3,261)
40		29	CL	H	Stoke City	L	0-1	0-0	15		5,408
41		31	CL	A	Leeds Utd	D	1-1	0-0	16	Mail 52	(9,919)
42	A	5	CL	H	Middlesbrough	L	0-1	0-0	18		4,049
43		12	CL	A	Barnsley	D	1-1	1-1	18	Hamilton 26	(4,256)
44		15	CL	H	Huddersfield Town	L	0-1	0-1	18		5,183
45		19	CL	H	Sheffield United	W	6-1	2-0	18	Garner 1, Patterson 3 29, 75, 86, Thompson 54, Barker 57	4,736
46		26	CL	A	Charlton Athletic	L	0-3	0-2	18		(5,766)
47	M	5	CL	H	Grimsby Town	W	3-1	2-1	19	Garner 1, Hamilton 32, Barker (pen) 74	7,600

Best Home League Attendance: 9,666 v Oldham 19/10   **Smallest:** 3,616 v Brighton 18/3   **Av Home Att:** 5,826

Goal Scorers: **Compared with 84-85:** −3,839

League (53): Garner 12, Barker 10 (4 pens), Patterson 10, Keeley 4, Quinn 4, Hamilton 3, Lowey 3, Ainscow 2, Brotherston 1, Fazackerley 1 (pen) Mail 1, Miller 1, Thompson 1

Milk Cup (2): Patterson 1, Quinn 1

FA Cup (4): Brotherston 1, Lowey 1, Thompson 1, Opponents 1

Gennoe	Hamilton	Rathbone	Barker	Mail	Fazackerley	Miller	Patterson	Quinn	Garner	Brotherston	Keeley	Lowey	Branagan	O'Keefe	Thompson	Ainscow	Referee	
1	2	3	4	5	6	7	8	9	10	11							T Mills	1
1	2	3	4	5	6	7	8	9	10	11							M Scott	2
1	2	3	4	5	6	7	8	9	10	11							D Aplin	3
1	2	3	4	5	6	7	8	9	10	11							H Taylor	4
1	2	3	4		6	7	8	9	10	11	5						L Robinson	5
1	2	3	4		6		8	9	10*	11	5	7	12				N Ashley	6
1	2	3	4		6	7	8	9	10	11	5						D Vickers	7
1	2	3	4		6		8	9	10	11	5	7					T Holbrook	8
1	2	3	4		6		8	9	10	11	5	7					D Hutchinson	9
1	2	3	4†		6		8	9	10	11	5	7					**R Milford**	10
1	2	11	4		6	7		9	10		5	8	3				K Cooper	11
1		3	4		6	7	11	9	10		5	8	2				D Shaw	12
	4	3			6	7	11	9	10		5	8	2	1			**A Saunders**	13
	4	3	12		6	7	11*	9	10		5	8	2	1			B Hill	14
1		3	4		6	7		9	10	11	5	8	2				C Seel	15
1		3	4		6	7		9	10	11	5	8	2				R Gifford	16
1	12	3*	4		6	7		9	10	11	5	8	2				M Peck	17
1	12	3	4		6	7		9	10*	11	5	8	2				P Vanes	18
1	11	3	4		6	7		9			5	8	2		10		M Reed	19
1	11	3	4	5	6	7		9	12			8	2		10*		D Phillips	20
1	11	3	4	5	6	7		9	10			8	2				G Tyson	21
1	11	3	4	6	12	7		9			5*	8	2		10		M Dimblebee	22
1	11	3	4	6	5	7			10			8	2		9		M McAulay	23
1	11	3	4	6	5	7*		9	12			8	2		10		G Ashby	24
1	11	3	4	6	5	7		9				8	2		10		J Lovatt	25
1		3	4		6	7			10	11		8	2		9		K Baker	26
1		3	4	5	6	7			10	11		8	2		9		**G Courtney**	27
1		3	4	5	6	7			10	11		8	2		9		**G Courtney**	28
1		3	4	5	6	7			10	11		8	2		9		P Willis	29
1		3	4		6	7			10	11	5	8	2		9		**A Saunders**	30
1		3	4		6	7	12		10		5	8	2		9*	11	T Holbrook	31
1		3	4		6	7		9			5	8	2		10	11	K Hackett	32
1	8	3	4		6*	7	12	9	10		5		2			11	G Aplin	33
1	8	3	4		6	7	11	9	10		5		2				K Barratt	34
1	8	3	4		6	7	11	9	10		5		2				M Robinson	35
1	8	3	4		6	7	11	9	10		5		2				I Hemley	36
1	2	3	4		6	7	11	9	10		5	8					R Bridges	37
1	11	3	4		6	7	12	9	10		5	8*	2				M Heath	38
	8	3	4		6	7	10	9		11	5		2	1			J Bray	39
	8	3	4		6	7	10	9*	12	11	5		2	1			R Guy	40
		3	4		6	7	11		10		5		2	1	9	8	K Redfern	41
		3	4		6	7	11	12	10		5		2	1	9	8*	N Ashley	42
	8	3	4		6	7	11		10		5		2	1	9		B Hill	43
	8	3	4		6	7	11		10		5		2	1	9		R Nixon	44
	8	3	4		6	7	11		10		5		2	1	9		D Shaw	45
	8	3	4		6	7	11		10		5		2	1	9		I Borrett	46
	8	3	4		6	7	11		10		5		2	1	9		J Lovatt	47
32	31	**42**	41	17	36	38	24	29	36	18	31	23	32	10	17	5	League Appearances	
	2		1	1			2	2	2	1				1			Substitute Appearances	
1	2	2	1		2	1	2	2	2	1	2	2	1	1			Milk Cup Appearances	
2		2	2	1	2	2			2	2	1	2	2		2		FA Cup Appearances	

Players on Loan:
Departures:

'THE ROVERS'

Formed: 1875
Turned Professional: 1880   **Ltd Co:** 1897

Previous Names: Blackburn Grammar School O.B.
Previous Managers: (Since 1946) Eddie Hapgood   Will Scott   Jack Bruton   Jackie Bestall   John Carey
Dally Duncan   Jack Marshall   Eddie Quigley   John Carey   Ken Furphy   Gordon Lee   Jim Smith
Jim Iley   Howard Kendall
Honours: Div 1 Champions 1911-12, 1913-14   Div 2 Champions 1938-9   Div 3 Champions
1974-5   FA Cup Winners 1884, 1885, 1886, 1890, 1891, 1928
League Career: Original Members of League 1888   Relegated to Div 2 1935-6
Promoted to Div 1 1938-9   Relegated to Div 2 1946-7   Promoted to Div 1 1956-7
Relegated to Div 2 1965-6   Relegated to Div 3 1970-1   Promoted to Div 2 1974-5
Relegated to Div 3 1978-9   Promoted to Div 2 1979-80
Colours: Blue and white halved shirts, white shorts, blue stockings with red and white tops
Reserves League: Central Div 1   **'A' Team:** Lancashire Div 2

CLUB RECORDS

Most Appearances for Club: Derek Fazackerley: 586 + 3 subs
Most Capped Player: Bob Crompton, 41, England 1902-14
Record Goalscorer in a Match: Tommy Briggs, 7 v Bristol Rovers (Div 2 record), 5 Feb 1955
Record League Goalscorer in a Season: Ted Harper, 43, Div 1, 1925-6   **In All Competitions:** Ted Harper, 45 (League
43 + FA Cup 2), 1925-6
Record League Goalscorer in a Career: Tommy Briggs, 140, 1952-8   **In All Competitions:** Tommy Briggs, 150 (League
140 + FA Cup 10)
Record Transfer Fee Received: £357,000 from Leeds United for Kevin Hird, Feb 1979
Record Transfer Fee Paid: £100,000 to Chelsea for Duncan McKenzie, March 1979
Best Performances: League: Champions (2)   **FA Cup:** Winners (6)   **League/Milk Cup:** Semi-Final 1961-2
Most League Points: (3pts for win) 71, Div 2,   (2pts for win) 60, Div 3, 1974-5
Most League Goals: 114, Div 2, 1954-5
Record League Victory and Most Goals in a League Match: 9 v Middlesbrough (9-0) Div 2, 6 Nov
1954   9 v Nottingham Forest (9-1) Div 2, 10 April 1937
Record League Defeat: 0-8 v Arsenal, Div 1, 25.2.33
Most Goals Scored in a Senior Competition: 11-0 v Rossendale, FA Cup, 1884-5
Oldest Player in League Match:
Youngest Player in League Match:
Most Consecutive Undefeated League Matches: 19 1972-73 | **League Matches Without a Win:** 16 1978-79
Longest Run of Undefeated Home League Matches: 30 1911-12 | **Away League Matches:** 11 1913
Longest Run Without Home League Win: 11 1978-79 | **Away League Win:** 24 1910-11
Most Consecutive League Wins: 8 1980 | **Home League Wins:** 13 1954
Most Consecutive League Defeats: 7 1966 | **Away League Wins:** 7 1980

Club Statistician for the Directory: Harry Berry

BLACKBURN ROVERS

PLAYERS NAME Ht Wt Birthdate	Honours	Birthplace Transfers	Clubs	Appearances League	Milk Cup	FA Cup	Other Comps	Goals League	Milk Cup	FA Cup	Other Comps
GOALKEEPERS											
Vince O'Keefe		Birmingham	A. P. Leamington				4				
6.0 11.0 2.4.57			Exeter City	53	11	3					
		£30,000	Torquay United	108	4	6					
		£15,000	Blackburn Rovers	36	2						
			Bury (L)	2							
DEFENDERS											
Jim Branagan		Barton	Oldham Ath.	24+3	2						
5.10 11.6 3.7.55		F	Cape Town								
		F	Huddersfield Town	37+1		0+1					
		£20,000	Blackburn Rovers	262+2	13	19		4			
David Fazackerly*	Div. 3, 75	Preston	Blackburn R. (A)	586+3	34	38		23	1	1	
5.11 11.6 5.11.51											
Glen Keeley	EY	Basildon	Ipswich Town (A)	4							
6.0 12.0 1.9.54		£70,000	Newcastle U.	43+1	12	8+1		2	2		
		£30,000	Blackburn Rovers	330+5	18	18+1		22		1	
			Everton (L)	1							
David Mail	FAYC 80	Bristol	Aston Villa (A)								
5.11 11.12 12.9.62		F	Blackburn Rovers	63+4	2+1	5		2			
Mike Rathbone	EY	Birmingham	Birmingham City (A)	17+3	1	2					
5.10 11.13 12.9.62		£40,000	Blackburn Rovers	246+2	9	13		2			
Chris Price	EY	Bridgnorth	Hereford United (A)	327+3	17	18	7+1	27	1	1	
5.7 10.2 30.3.60											
MIDFIELD											
Simon Barker	EU21 (4)	Farnworth	Blackburn R. (A)	107	1	8		12			
5.9 11.0 4.11.64											
David Hamilton	EY	South Shields	Sunderland (A)								
5.8 9.12 7.11.60		F	Blackburn Rovers	106+2	8	1+1		7			
			Cardiff City (L)	10							
Ian Miller†		Perth	Bury								
5.9 11.7 13.5.55		F	Nottingham F.								
		Player exch.	Doncaster Rovers	124	10	4		14			
		£25,000 & P/E	Swindon Town	123+4	19+1	12		9	2	2	
		£67,000	Blackburn Rovers	183+2	8+1	9		15	1		
Scott Sellars		Sheffield	Leeds United (A)	72+4	4	3		12	1		
5.8 10.0 27.11.65			Blackburn Rovers								
FORWARDS											
Alan Ainscow	EY	Bolton	Blackpool (A)	178+14	9	6+1		28			
5.6½ 9.4 15.7.53		£40,000	Birmingham City	104+4	9	6		16	4	1	
		£250,000	Everton	24+4				3			
			Barnsley (L)	2							
		F	Wolverhampton W.	56+2	3+1	3		5		1	
			Blackburn Rovers	5				2			
Noel Brotherston	NI (27), U21 (1),	Belfast	Tottenham H. (A)	1							
5.9 10.8 18.11.56	YS, FAYC 74	F	Blackburn Rovers	291+8	18	22+1		39	2	3	
Simon Garner		Boston	Blackburn R. (A)	267+13	18+2	12+3		100	8	5	
5.8 11.3 23.11.59											
Mark Patterson		Darwen	Blackburn R. (A)	60+4	4			17			
5.6 10.10 24.5.65											
Jimmy Quinn	NI (11)	Belfast	Oswestry Town								
6.0½ 11.6 24.1.60		£10,000	Swindon Town	34+15	1+1	5+2		10		2	
		£32,500	Blackburn Rovers	43+13	2+1	4		14	1	3	

ADDITIONAL CONTRACT PROFESSIONALS

APPRENTICES

NON-CONTRACT PLAYERS

Ian Arthur, John Binnie, Gary Brown, Paul Byrom, Tony Diamond, Keith Hill, Gareth Mather, Peter Rigby

EWOOD PARK Blackburn BB2 4JF

Record Attendance: 61,783 v Bolton Wanderers, FA Cup Round 6, 2 Mar 1929

Smallest Home Attendance for a First Class Match: 2,161 v Wimbledon, Milk Cup, 8.10.85

Record Receipts: £60,612 v Liverpool, FA Cup 3rd Round, 8 Jan 1983

Season Tickets: £63 (Stand) (£37 juniors/OAP), £37 (Enclosure) (£23 juniors/OAP), £34 (Ground) (£23 juniors/OAP)

Private Box Season Tickets: £125 which includes admission into '100 Club' lounge & bar facilities

Cost of Stand Tickets: £5.00, (£2.50 juniors/OAP), £2.50 (Ground) (£2.00 juniors/OAPS), £2.80 (Enclosure) (£2.00 juniors/OAP)

Match and Ticket Information:

Car Parking: Ewood Car Park within walking distance of ground

Nearest Railway Station: Blackburn Central (0254 662537/8)

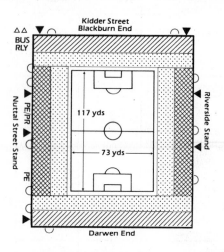

How to get to the ground

From North and West: Leave Motorway M6 at junction 31, and follow signs Blackburn, or use A666 into Blackburn. Then follow signs Bolton A666 into Bolton Road. In 1.5m turn left into Kidder Street for Blackburn Rovers FC

From East: Follow signs Blackburn A679 or A677. Then follow signs Bolton A666 into Bolton Road. In 1.5m turn left into Kidder Street for Blackburn Rovers FC

From South: Use M6, junction 31 as route from North or via Bolton and A666, then follow signs Blackburn, 2.7m after Darwen turn right into Kidder Street for Blackburn Rovers FC

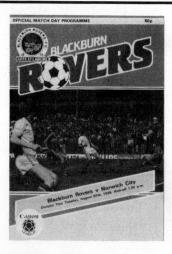

Price of 1986-7 Programme: 50p
Number of Pages: 24
Subscriptions: Not available

Local Newspaper: Lancashire Evening Telegraph

Local Radio Stations: Red Rose Radio, BBC Radio Lancashire

Chairman
K Chadwick, LLB

Directors
G Bloor
M H Melling
R P Gibrail
T White

Secretary
D Johnson (0253 404331)

Manager
Sam Ellis

Physiotherapist
B Haydock

Commercial Manager
Geoff Warburton (0253 404331)

Back in Division 3 Blackpool ended with a respectable mid-table position which, if nothing else, was a step in the right direction. After a modest start form improved and four consecutive League wins from October 19th took the team into second place and a promotion challenging position, which was maintained on and off until the New Year, when the bad weather came and form slumped accordingly with some bad losses in February making sure that another season in the 3rd Division would be necessary. Even so there were good performances such as a five-goal home win over Bury and an excellent match at Bolton (won 3-1). With interest in the League evaporating after the poor spell a final position of twelfth was no surprise.

The cups brought little to cheer with a Milk Cup exit coming at the first hurdle — on an aggregate of 2-5 against Preston North End. The FA Cup started in the 1st Round with a single goal win at Lincoln, but then the non-League giants Altrincham arrived at Bloomfield Road and won well (2-1). The Freight Rover Trophy followed a similar path with an early partial success against Wrexham followed by elimination at Port Vale (1-3).

Seventy-three goals in all competitions would suggest that the attack was reasonable with O'Keefe's 15 goals in only 24 games a fine effort; his absence through injury was a major handicap. Goalkeeper O'Rourke was very consistent and played in every game and other good performers were Moore, Deary, Greenall, Stewart, Dyer and Law. The basis for a promotion challenge is certainly there.

Blackpool fans demand a return to better days, but in Sam Ellis they have one of the most promising and shrewd managers in the business so the way ahead should be upwards.

Back Row L to R: Colin Methven, Nicky Law, Alex Dyer, Kevin Stonehouse, Colin Greenall, Bobby Thomson, Steve Morgan, **Middle Row:** Bob Ward (Physio), Paul Stewart, David Moore, Barry Siddall, Phil Harrington, Billy O'Rourke, Richard Sendall, Pat McGinley, Bobby Downes (Coach), **Front Row:** Mike Davies, Eamon O'Keefe, Mike Walsh, Sam Ellis (Manager), John Deary, Brian Butler, Neil Matthews.

BLACKPOOL

DIVISION THREE: 12th   **FA CUP:** 2nd ROUND   **MILK CUP:** 1st ROUND

MATCH	DATE	COMPE-TITION	VENUE	OPPONENTS	RESULT	HALF TIME	L'GUE POS'N	GOALSCORERS/GOAL TIMES	ATTEN-DANCE
1	A 17	CL	A	Reading	L 0-1	0-0			(3,190)
2	20	MC1/1	A	Preston N. E.	L 1-2	0-1		Davies 80	(4,704)
3	24	CL	H	Notts County	L 1-3	1-3	21	O'Keefe 14	4,011
4	26	CL	A	Darlington	L 1-2	0-1	21	O'Keefe 55	(3,548)
5	31	CL	H	Swansea City	W 2-0	0-0	18	Deary (pen) 55, Dyer 76	3,085
6	S 3	MC1/2	H	Preston N. E.	L 1-3	1-0		Greenall 18	5,043
7	7	CL	A	Derby County	W 2-1	0-0	16	O'Keefe (2 pen) 68, 83	(10,702)
8	14	CL	H	York City	L 0-2	0-0	19		4,053
9	17	CL	A	Bournemouth	W 4-1	2-1	12	Dyer 6, 83, O'Keefe 33, Nightingale og 50	(3,039)
10	21	CL	H	Cardiff City	W 3-0	0-0	7	Davies 55, O'Keefe 83, Deary 87	3,783
11	28	CL	A	Bristol City	L 1-2	1-1	12	O'Keefe 16	(6,570)
12	O 1	CL	H	Doncaster Rovers	W 4-0	3-0	9	Dyer 21, O'Keefe 3 42, 45, 68 (pen)	4,121
13	5	CL	H	Gillingham	D 2-2	1-2	10	Deary 5, O'Keefe (pen) 76	4,571
14	12	CL	A	Wigan Athletic	D 1-1	1-0	11	O'Keefe 3	(5,993)
15	19	CL	H	Bury	W 5-0	2-0	9	Davies 5, O'Keefe 7, 86 (pen), Deary 75, Hetzke 85	5,496
16	22	CL	A	Chesterfield	W 2-1	0-0	5	Windridge 71, Davies 77	(3,720)
17	26	CL	H	Brentford	W 4-0	0-0	2	Hetzke 49, Stewart 72, 79, Windridge 83	5,548
18	N 2	CL	A	Lincoln City	W 3-0	0-0	2	Hetzke 51, Stonehouse 80, Deary 83	(2,373)
19	5	CL	A	Wolverhampton W.	L 1-2	1-1	3	Dyer 15	(3,690)
20	9	CL	H	Bristol Rovers	W 4-2	3-1	2	Hetzke 3, Dyer 12, 56, Windridge 19	4,707
21	16	FAC1	A	Lincoln City	W 1-0	0-0		West (og) 84	(2,596)
22	23	CL	A	Walsall	D 1-1	1-1	3	Greenall 22	(5,161)
23	30	CL	H	Plymouth Argyle	D 1-1	1-0	6	Stonehouse (pen) 28	6,184
24	D 7	FAC2	H	Altrincham	L 1-2	0-1		Stewart 60	5,037
25	14	CL	A	Newport County	D 1-1	1-1	6	Stewart 53	(1,991)
26	22	CL	A	Notts County	W 2-1	1-0	3	Stonehouse 39, Dyer 67	(5,926)
27	26	CL	H	Bolton Wanderers	D 1-1	0-0	3	Stewart 89	9,473
28	28	CL	H	Darlington	D 0-0	0-0	4		5,595
29	J 1	CL	A	Rotherham United	L 1-4	0-4	5	Walsh 72	(4,200)
30	11	CL	A	Swansea City	L 0-2	0-1	8		(5,705)
31	18	CL	H	Reading	D 0-0	0-0	10		5,295
32	23	FRT	H	Wrexham	D 2-2	0-0		Davies 81, Thompson 89	1,611
33	F 1	CL	H	Derby County	L 0-1	0-1	11		6,732
34	4	CL	H	Chesterfield	L 0-1	0-1	12		2,988
35	10	FRT	A	Port Vale	L 1-3	1-0		Thompson 22	(1,569)
36	22	CL	A	Cardiff City	L 0-1	0-0	13		(2,430)
37	25	CL	H	Lincoln City	W 2-0	1-0		Hodson (og) 15, Deary 58	1,995
38	M 1	CL	H	Bristol City	W 2-1	1-0	8	Butler 8, Deary (pen) 63	3,366
39	4	CL	A	Doncaster Rovers	D 0-0	0-0			(2,316)
40	8	CL	A	Gillingham	D 2-2	1-1	10	O'Keefe (pen) 40, Oakes (og) 61	(4,537)
41	15	CL	H	Wigan Athletic	L 1-2	0-0	12	O'Keefe (pen) 76	6,218
42	22	CL	H	Brentford	D 1-1	0-0	12	Britton 53	(3,528)
43	29	CL	H	Rotherham United	W 2-1	0-0	12	Thompson 63, Davies 81	4,007
44	31	CL	A	Bolton Wanderers	W 3-1	0-1	9	Thompson 48, Stewart 87, O'Keefe 88	(7,878)
45	A 5	CL	H	Wolverhampton W.	L 0-1	0-1	12		4,563
46	12	CL	A	Bristol Rovers	L 0-1	0-1	12		(3,472)
47	19	CL	H	Walsall	W 2-1	1-0	12	Stewart (pen) 19, Hawker (og) 88	2,964
48	22	CL	A	Bury	L 1-4	0-2	12	Stewart (pen) 65	(2,738)
49	26	CL	A	Plymouth Argyle	L 1-3	1-0	12	Stewart 30	(14,975)
50	29	CL	H	Bournemouth	W 2-0	0-0	11	Law 49, Davies 68	2,259
51	M 3	CL	H	Newport County	D 0-0	0-0	11		3,407
52	6	CL	A	York City	L 0-3	0-1	12		(3,370)

Best Home League Attendance: 6,184 v Plymouth 30/11   **Smallest:** 1,995 v Lincoln City 25/2   **Av Home Att:** 4,540

Goal Scorers: **Compared with 84-85:** – 366

League (66):	O'Keefe 15 (5 pen), Deary 9 (3 pen), Dyer 8, Stewart 8 (2 pen), Davies 5, Hetzke 4, Stonehouse 3 (1 pen), Windridge 3, Thompson 2, Britton 1, Butler 1, Law 1, Thompson 1, Greenham 1, Opponents 4
Milk Cup (2):	Davies 1, Greenall 1
FA Cup (2):	Stewart 1, Opponent 1
FRT (3):	Thompson 2, Davies 1

O'Rourke	Moore	Walsh	Deary	Hetzke	Greenall	Britton	O'Keefe	Stewart	Windridge	Dyer	Conroy	Davies	Matthews (A)	Butler	Law	Stonehouse	Thompson	Sendell	Ronson (M)	Price (NC)	Morgan (A)	Referee	#
1	2	3	4	5	6	7	8	9	10	11												M Dimblebee	1
1	2	3	4		6	7	10	5		11	8	9										P Tyldesley	2
1	2	3	4	5*	6	7	10	9	12	11	8											T Jones	3
1	2	3*	8		6	7	10				9	4	12	5	11							J Key	4
1	2		8		6	7	10	9		11	4				3	5						P Willis	5
1	2		8		6	7*	10	9		11	4			5	3	12						R Nixon	6
1	2		8		6		10	9		11	4	7			3	5						J Ashworth	7
1	2	3	8		6		10	9		11	4	7			5							J Lloyd	8
1	2	3	8		6		10	9		11	4	7			5	12						M Cotton	9
1	2	3	8		6		10	9		11	4	7			5							G Aplin	10
1	2	3	8		6		10	9		11	4	7			5							Alan Robinson	11
1	2		8	5	6		10*	9		11	4	7			3	12						J Lovatt	12
1	2		8	5	6		10	9		11	4	7			3							G Courtney	13
1	2		8	5	6		10	9		11	4	7			3							T Mills	14
1	2		8	5	6		10	9		11	4*	7			3	12						G Tyson	15
1	2		8	5	6		10*	9	12	11		7			3	4						N Ashley	16
1	2		8	5	6	12		9	10	11		7*			3	4						D Hutchinson	17
1	2		8	5	6			9	10	11		7			3	4						K Hackett	18
1	2			5	6		8	9	10	11		7			3	4						B Hill	19
1	2			5	6		8	9	10	11		7			3	4						C Steel	20
1	2			5	6		8	9	10	11		7			3	4						J Ashworth	21
1	2			5	6		8	9	10	11		7			3	4						R Gifford	22
1	2			5	6		8	9	10	11		7			3	4						J Key	23
1	2	3	8	5	6			9	10	11		7				4						T Simpson	24
1	2	3	4	5	6	7		9	10	11						8						G Ashby	25
1		3	4	5	6	7	9*	8		11				2		10	12					I Borrett	26
1		3	8	5	6	7*		9	10	11				2	4	12						M Peck	27
1		3	8	5	6			9*	10	11		7		2	4	12						J McAulay	28
1		3	8	5	6				10	11		7		2	4	9						V Callow	29
1	2		8	5	6			9		11		7			3	10	4					K Barratt	30
1	2			5	6	7		9	10*	11		12			3	4	8					M Heath	31
1	2	6	5					9		11	4	12				10	7	8*	3*		12	C Seel	32
1	2	4	5	6	7*			9		11				8	3	12	10					R Guy	33
1	2	4	5	6	12			9		11				8*	3	10	7					G Aplin	34
1	2	4	5†	6				9		11		7			3	10	8					J Key	35
1	2	4	5	6	7			9		11		12		8*	3		10					T Ward	36
1	2		8				10	9		11*	4	7			3	5	6		12			T Holbrook	37
1	2	3	8		6	7	12	9		11	4					10*	5					J Lloyd	38
1	2	3	8		6		12	9		11	4	7*				10	5					K Baker	39
1	2	5	8		6		12	9		11	4	7*			3		10					J Ashworth	40
1	2	5	8		6	12	10	9		11	4*				3		7					I Hendrick	41
1		3*			6		8	9	10	11	4	12		2		5	7					J Deakin	42
1	2	9			6	7	10			11	4*	12			3	5	8					M Ashley	43
1	2*	4			6	7	10	9		11	3	12				5	8					K Breen	44
1	2	6	4			7	10	9		11*		12			3	5	8					R Nixon	45
1	2	6	4			7		9				10			3*	5	8		12		11	D Axcell	46
1	2	3	8		6	7		9			4				5	10*		12		11		R Bridges	47
1	2	3	4		6	7*		9						8		5	10		12		11	J Bray	48
1	2	3	4		6			9				7		8		5	10		11			J Martin	49
1	2	3	4		6		12	9				7		8		5	10*		11			T Mills	50
1	2*	3	4		6		10	9				7		8		5			11		12	K Lupton	51
1	2	3	4		6*		10	9						8		5	7		11		12	T Jones	52
46	41	25	40	23	43	25	19	42	14	39	25	30	1	18	37	14	14	4	3		3	League Appearances	
				4		3			2			6		1	2	2	2		4		2	Substitute Appearances	
2	2	1	2		2		2	2			1	1		0-1								Milk Cup Appearances	
2	2	1	2	1	2	1	2	2			2	2			1		2					FA Cup Appearances	
2	2	1	1	2	1		2	2	1	1-1		1		2	1	2	1		2	1	0-1	FR Trophy Appearances	

Players on Loan:

Departures: Hetzke (Sunderland)

'THE SEASIDERS'

Formed: 1887
Turned Professional: 1887   **Ltd Co:** 1896

Previous Names: In 1899 South Shore amalgamated with Blackpool who had been formed when Blackpool St John disbanded in 1887
Previous Managers: (Since 1946)   Joe Smith   Ron Stuart   Stan Mortensen   Les Shannon   Jimmy Meadows   Bob Stokoe   Harry Potts   Allan Brown   Jimmy Meadows   Bob Stokoe   Stan Ternent   Alan Ball (jnr)   Allan Brown
Honours: Div 2 Champions 1929-30   FA Cup Winners 1953   Anglo-Italian Cup Winners 1971
League Career: Elected to Div 2 1896   Failed to gain re-election 1899
Re-elected to Div 2 1900   Promoted to Div 1 1929-30   Relegated to Div 2 1932-3
Promoted to Div 1 1936-7   Relegated to Div 2 1966-7   Promoted to Div 1 1969-70
Relegated to Div 2 1970-1   Relegated to Div 3 1977-8   Relegated to Div 4 1980-1
Promotion to Div 3 1984-5
Colours: Tangerine shirts with blue and white trim, white shorts, tangerine stockings with blue and white tops
Change Colours: All blue
Reserves League: Central Div 2   **Youth League:** Lancashire

---

CLUB RECORDS

Most Appearances for Club: Jimmy Armfield: Football League 568 + Cup ties 101 **Total 659** (1952-71)
Most Capped Player: Jimmy Armfield, 43, England
Record League Goalscorer in a Season: Jimmy Hampson, 45, Div 2   **In All Competitions:** Jimmy Hampson, 50 (League 45 + FA Cup 5), 1929-30
Record League Goalscorer in a Career: Jimmy Hampson, 247, 1927-38   **In All Competitions:** Jimmy Hampson, 271 (League 247, FA Cup 24) 1927-38
Record Transfer Fee Received: £325,000 from Everton for Mickey Walsh, Aug 1978
Record Transfer Fee Paid: £110,000 to Peterborough United for Bobby Doyle, July 1979
Best Performances: League: 2nd Div 1 1955-6   **FA Cup:** Winners (1)   **League/Milk Cup:** Semi-Final 1962
Most League Points: (3pts for win) 72, Div 4, 1983-4   (2pts for win) 58, Div 2, 1929-30   58, Div 2, 1967-8
Most League Goals: 98, Div 2, 1929-30
Record League Victory: 7-0 v Preston, Div 1, 1 May 1948
Record League Defeat: 1-10 v Small Heath, Div 2, 2.3.01   1-10 v Huddersfield Town, Div 1, 13.12.30
Oldest Player in League Match: Sir Stanley Matthews 46
Youngest Player in League Match: Colin Greenhall
Most Consecutive Undefeated League Matches: 17 1968
Longest Run of Undefeated Home League Matches: 21 1925-26
Longest Run Without Home League Win: 16 1966-67
Most Consecutive League Wins: 9 1936-37
Most Consecutive League Defeats: 8 1898-99

League Matches Without a Win: 19 1970-71
Away League Matches: 10 1973-74
Away League Win: 41 1907-09
Home League Wins: 11 1951-52
Away League Wins: 6 1936-37

Club Statistician for the Directory: Roger Harrison

BLACKPOOL

				APPEARANCES				GOALS			
PLAYERS NAME Ht Wt Birthdate	Honours	Birthplace Transfers	Clubs	League	Milk Cup	FA Cup	Other Comps	League	Milk Cup	FA Cup	Other Comps
GOALKEEPERS											
Billy O'Rourke		Nottingham	Burnley (A)	14							
6.0 12.7 2.4.60		F	Chester	5							
		F	Blackpool	98	8	3	4				
DEFENDERS											
Bryan Butler		Salford	Blackpool (A)	18+3	1				1		
5.6½ 10.6 4.7.66											
Colin Greenhall	EY	Billinge	Blackpool (A)	176+4	10	8	3	8	2		
5.11 11.10 30.12.63											
Nicky Law		Greenwich	Arsenal (A)								
6.0 13.5 8.9.61		F	Barnsley	113+1	6	6					
		F	Blackpool	37+2		1	1		1		
Neil Matthews		Manchester	Blackpool (A)	1+2	1						
5.10 10.11 3.12.67											
Colin Methven	FRT 85	India	East Fife	144	16	8		14			
6.2 12.7 10.12.55		£30,000	Wigan Athletic	295+1	20	23	14				
			Blackpool								
Dave Moore		Grimsby	Grimsby Town (A)	136	9	8		2			
5.10 13.0 14.10.56		F	Carlisle United	13	2			1			
		£3,500	Blackpool	113	6	5	2	1			
Mick Walsh	EI (5)	Manchester	Bolton Wanderers	169+8	13	10+1		4	1		
6.0 12.0 20.6.56			Everton	20	2						
			Norwich City (L)	5							
			Burnley (L)	3							
		Fort Lauderdale	Manchester City	3+1							
		£6,000	Blackpool	80	4	2	4	3			
MIDFIELD											
Ian Britton		Dundee	Chelsea (A)	253+10	11	14		33			
5.5 9.7 19.5.54		F	Dundee United	7+3	6			1	1		
		F	Blackpool	66	6	1	1	1			
Mike Conroy	SPD 81, 82	Glasgow	Celtic	58+9	8+5	5+1	2	9	3	1	
5.9½ 11.2 31.7.57	SC 80	F	Hibernian	31+1	6	1		2	2		
		F	Blackpool	66	6	1	1	1			
John Deary		Ormskirk	Blackpool (A)	17+13	8	9+2	4	21	16	1	1
5.10 11.11 18.10.62											
Alex Dyer		West Ham	Watford (A)								
5.11 11.12 14.11.65		F	Blackpool	77+7	7	4+1	5	16	1		
Bobby Thomson		Glasgow	Morton	90	14	11		25	10	5	
5.10 11.6 21.3.55			Middlesbrough	18+2				2			
			Hibernian	55+7	14	2		12	1		
			Morton (L)	11				2			
			Blackpool								
FORWARDS											
Mike Davies		Stretford	Blackpool (A)	48+8	4	3	2+2	5	1	1	
5.7 10.7 19.1.66											
Eamonn O'Keefe	EI (3), ESP (2)	Manchester	Stalybridge Celtic								
5.7 11.5 13.10.53			Plymouth Argyle								
			Mossley			1					
		£25,000	Everton	26+14	1	4		6	1	1	
		£65,000	Wigan Athletic	56+2	3			25	1		
		£40,000	Port Vale	50+9	5	4	2	17			
		£20,000	Blackpool	31+3	2			20			
Richard Sendall		Stamford	Watford (A)								
5.10 11.6 10.7.67			Blackpool	4+4		1					
Paul Stewart	EY	Manchester	Blackpool (A)	156+13	10	6	4	28	4	1	
5.11 11.10 7.10.64											
David Windridge		Atherstone	Sheffield United								
5.9 11.0 7.12.61		F	Chesterfield	66+12	1+1	3+1		14	1		
		F	Blackpool	82+7	5	6	3	17	1		

ADDITIONAL CONTRACT PROFESSIONALS

APPRENTICES
Stephen Morgan

NON-CONTRACT PLAYERS
Craig Bell, Ian Boyle, Martin Clarke, Bobby Downes, Tony Duckworth, Carl Lancashire, Richard Powell.

BLOOMFIELD ROAD Blackpool FY1 6JJ

Capacity: 12,000 est.

Record Attendance: 39,118 v Manchester United, Div 1, 19 Apr 1952

Record Receipts: £28,986 v Everton, League Cup Round 2, 2nd Leg, 3 Sept 1980

Season Tickets: Stand: £79.00 (adults), £64.50 (Juniors) (West & South); Paddock: £51.40 (adults), £28.40 (Juniors/OAP); Ground: £37.90, £19 (Juniors/OAP)
Family Season Tickets: 1 + 1 = £95.50; 1 + 2 = £107.00; 1 + 3 = £118.50; 2 + 1 = £187.50; 2 + 2 = £199.00; 2 + 3 = £210.00

Executive Box Season Tickets: £130.00

Cost of Stand Tickets: £4.00 South West; £3.50 North West; £3.50 (New Stand).
Terraces: £2.80, £1.80 (Junior/OAP). **Kop:** £2.30 (Adults), £1.30 (Juniors). **West Paddock:** Admission by Membership only. Season Membership £5.00. Admission for Members £2.30
Family Tickets Match Day: 1 + 1 = £4.50; 1 + 2 = £5.00; 1 + 3 = £5.50; 2 + 1 = £8.50; 2 + 2 = £9.00; 2 + 3 = £9.50; 3 + 1 = £12.50; 3 + 2 = £13.00; 3 + 3 = £13.50; 3 + 4 = £14.00

Match and Ticket Information: Bookable four weeks prior to match

Car Parking: Parking for 1,000 cars. Street parking available

Nearest Railway Station: Blackpool North (0772 59439)

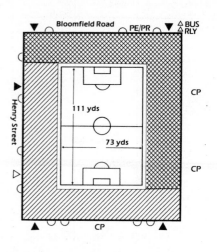

How to get to the ground

From North, East and South: Leave M6 Motorway at junction 32 and follow signs Blackpool M55. At end of Motorway join A583. In 2m at traffic signals turn left into Waterloo Road (S.P. South Shore). In 0.7m turn right into Central Drive. Then take 3rd turning on left into Bloomfield Road for Blackpool FC

Price of 1986-7 Programme: 40p
Number of Pages: 16
Subscriptions: Apply to club for details

Local Newspapers: Blackpool Evening Gazette, Lancashire Evening Post

Local Radio Stations: Red Rose Radio, Radio Lancashire

BOLTON WANDERERS — Division 3

<table>
</table>

President
J Battersby

Senior Vice-President
Nat Lofthouse

Chairman
G Warburton

Directors
G Ball
G Hargreaves
S Jones
G Seymour
B Clayton

Secretary
D McBain (0204 389200)

Assistant Secretary
K Gardiner

Manager
Phil Neal

Assistant Manager
Colin Irwin

Reserve & Youth Team Manager
Steve Carrolle

Commercial Manager
A Davies (0204 389200)

Physiotherapist
P Nightingale

Groundsman
A Whittle

Back Row L to R: Mark Came, Mike Salmon, Kevin Mailey, Simon Farnworth, Jimmy Phillips, **Middle Row:** Steve Carroll (Youth Team Coach), Steve Thompson, Mark Winstanley, George Oghani, Steve Elliott, Dave Sutton, Warren Joyce, Paul Clarke, Colin Irwin (Coach), Peter Nightingale (Physio), **Front Row:** Paul Allen, Julian Darby, Mark Gavin, Phil Neale (Player/Manager), Derek Scott, Tony Caldwell, Asa Hartford.

Bolton Wanderers ended a traumatic season in their worst ever League position with the possibility of relegation only fading away in the final week.

Things looked optimistic in August with manager Charlie Wright signing new faces with plenty of experience in the shape of David Cross, Sam Allardyce and Asa Hartford. Unfortunately only Hartford proved to be a success, playing in every game, and winning the Player of the Year Award. Cross started well but suffered with injury as did Allardyce and by the end of November the Wanderers found themselves in the bottom four.

The bonfire night game against Darlington at Burnden attracted the lowest recorded League gate of 2,902, and the club were also knocked out of the FA Cup by 4th Division Wrexham, and Charlie Wright paid the price with his job.

Bolton signed Phil Neal as player manager along with his ex-Liverpool team mate Colin Irwin as assistant. The New Year opened with three successive defeats and Bolton's Freight Rover Trophy interests were only kept alive thanks to two goals in the final three minutes that earned a 2-2 draw at Stockport County.

A shameful performance in a 3-1 defeat at Swansea brought matters to a head and for the next game Neal signed keeper Dave Felgate, an ex-Wanderers youth player, and Stuart Ripley on loan from Grimsby and Middlesbrough respectively. The Wanderers then defeated Newport 4-0 at Burnden with Ripley setting up the first goal for Tony Caldwell who again topped Bolton's scoring chart, after only 13 seconds. Ripley also got onto the scoresheet himself and it was this victory that turned the tide as only two losses were incurred in nine games during March.

Runaway League leaders Reading were beaten 2-0 at Burnden; the first point in London was won since April 1980 with a 1-1 draw at Brentford; a northern semi-final place in the Freight Rover Trophy was won and the Wanderers defeated relegation rivals Cardiff City 5-0 for their biggest win of the season. On Easter Saturday the Wanderers ended Wigan's 33-game unbeaten home run with new signing Mark Gavin scoring the second goal in a 3-1 win.

Two League victories in April virtually assured Bolton of 3rd Division football for 1986/87, providing other results went for them. A 1-0 win at Darlington were the last points of the season to be won but it was Wembley fever that was now taking over. A week after the League win at Darlington, Bolton again visited for the Freight Rover Northern area semi-final and won 3-0 before a crowd twice that of the League game.

This brought Bolton face to face with local rivals Wigan Athletic in a two-legged northern final and with League pressures out of the way Wembley was the goal. Tony Caldwell scored a last minute winner at Wigan to take a lead back home and the best crowd of the season was at Burnden to see Bolton come from behind to win 2-1 on the night and 3-1 on aggregate, everyone was going to Wembley.

Over 22,000 Bolton supporters were at Wembley for the first time since 1958 but bogey side Bristol City proved to be too good on the day but it brought plenty of cheer to a season that looked full of gloom three month's previous.   S M

BOLTON WANDERERS

DIVISION THREE: 18th   **FA CUP:** 1st ROUND   **MILK CUP:** 2nd ROUND   **FRT:** RUNNERS-UP

MATCH	DATE	COMPE-TITION	VENUE	OPPONENTS	RESULT		HALF TIME	L'GUE POS'N	GOALSCORERS/GOAL TIMES	ATTEN-DANCE
1	A 17	CL	H	Rotherham United	D	1-1	1-0		Caldwell 17	5,129
2	20	MC1/1	H	Stockport County	W	4-1	0-1		Hartford 53, Cross 59, 87, Bell 82	3,311
3	24	CL	A	Doncaster Rovers	D	1-1	0-0	17	Cross 68	(3,414)
4	26	CL	H	Bury	L	1-4	0-1	19	Cross 88	8,772
5	31	CL	A	Gillingham	L	1-2	0-0	22	Cross 82	(2,773)
6	S 3	MC1/2	A	Stockport County	D	1-1	0-1		Caldwell 89	(2,573)
7	7	CL	H	Wolverhampton W.	W	4-1	0-0	18	Thompson 48, 61 (pen), Cross 64, 89	4,986
8	14	CL	A	Walsall	L	0-2	0-1	21		(4,532)
9	17	CL	H	Lincoln City	D	1-1	1-1	20	Thompson 17	3,928
10	21	CL	A	Newport County	W	1-0	0-0	17	Oghani 71	(2,212)
11	25	MC2/1	A	Nottingham Forest	L	0-4	0-0			(10,530)
12	28	CL	H	Plymouth Argyle	W	3-1	3-0	13	Joyce 13, Caldwell 39, Rudge 44	4,270
13	O 1	CL	A	York City	L	0-3	0-1	17		(4,680)
14	5	CL	A	Reading	L	0-1	0-1	19		8,000
15	8	MC2/2	H	Nottingham Forest	L	0-3	0-0			4,010
16	12	CL	H	Brentford	L	1-2	1-1	20	Joyce 16	4,106
17	19	CL	H	Swansea City	D	1-1	0-0	20	Thompson (pen) 85	3,558
18	22	CL	A	Bristol Rovers	L	1-2	1-1	20	Caldwell 40	(4,308)
19	26	CL	A	Cardiff City	W	1-0	1-0	20	Bell 20	(2,502)
20	N 2	CL	H	Bournemouth	W	1-0	0-0	16	Thompson 85	3,800
21	5	CL	H	Darlington	L	0-3	0-0	17		2,902
22	9	CL	A	Notts County	L	0-1	0-0	17		(4,497)
23	16	FAC1	A	Wrexham	L	1-3	0-2		Thompson (pen) 61	(2,738)
24	23	CL	H	Derby County	L	0-1	0-1	18		5,887
25	30	CL	A	Bristol City	L	0-2	0-1	18		(6,253)
26	D 14	CL	H	Chesterfield	W	2-1	0-0	18	Thompson 49, Hartford 64	3,621
27	21	CL	A	Doncaster Rovers	W	2-0	1-0	18	Cross 42, 65	4,546
28	26	CL	A	Blackpool	D	1-1	0-0	18	Cross 60	(9,473)
29	J 1	CL	H	Wigan Athletic	L	1-2	1-1	18	Thompson (pen) 33	9,252
30	11	CL	H	Gillingham	L	0-1	0-0	20		5,232
31	18	CL	A	Rotherham United	L	0-4	0-2	20		(3,821)
32	20	FRT	A	Stockport County	D	2-2	0-1		Came 87, Caldwell 88	(1,874)
33	25	CL	H	Walsall	W	3-1	1-1	19	Caldwell 24, Bell 67, Oghani 75	4,088
34	28	FRT	H	Crewe Alexandra	W	1-0	0-0		Oghani 64	2,428
35	F 1	CL	A	Wolverhampton W.	W	2-0	1-0	16	Rudge 40, Oghani 67	(3,110)
36	4	CL	H	Bristol Rovers	L	0-2	0-2	17		3,672
37	8	CL	A	Swansea City	L	1-3	1-2	18	Hartford 21	(4,242)
38	22	CL	H	Newport County	W	4-0	3-0	18	Caldwell 14secs, 22, Oghani 27, Ripley 53	4,063
39	25	CL	A	Bury	L	1-2	0-1	18	Caldwell (pen) 62	(6,006)
40	M 4	CL	H	York City	D	1-1	0-1	17	Hartford 54	3,589
41	8	CL	H	Reading	W	2-0	0-0	16	Caldwell (pen) 58, Joyce 65	4,903
42	11	FRT QF N	H	Tranmere Rovers	W	2-1	1-1		Oghani , Caldwell	3,865
43	14	CL	A	Brentford	D	1-1	0-0	15	Sutton 84	(3,284)
44	18	CL	A	Bournemouth	L	1-2	1-1	16	Oghani 4	(2,063)
45	22	CL	H	Cardiff City	W	5-0	1-0	15	Neal 45, Came 46, Joyce 56, Caldwell 62, Oghani 80	4,114
46	25	CL	A	Lincoln City	D	1-1	1-1	15	Neal 17	(2,329)
47	29	CL	A	Wigan Athletic	W	3-1	0-0	15	Hartford 55, Gavin 64, Caldwell 71	(8,009)
48	31	CL	H	Blackpool	L	1-3	0-0	15	Thompson 53	7,878
49	A 12	CL	H	Notts County	W	1-0	0-0	16	Phillips 73	4,688
50	19	CL	A	Derby County	L	1-2	0-1	16	Hartford 57	(12,232)
51	22	CL	A	Plymouth Argyle	L	1-4	1-0	18	Sutton 17	(12,183)
52	24	CL	A	Darlington	W	1-0	0-0	15	Oghani	(1,870)
53	26	CL	H	Bristol City	L	0-4	0-1	16		4,493
54	M 1	FRT SF N	A	Darlington	W	3-0	2-0		Oghani 8, Caldwell 25, Hartford 47	(3,771)
55	3	CL	A	Chesterfield	L	0-3	0-0	18		(3,183)
56	6	FRT F1 N	A	Wigan Athletic	W	1-0	0-0		Caldwell 89	(6,975)
57	9	FRT F2 N	H	Wigan Athletic	W	2-1	0-1		Oghani 61, Caldwell 88	12,120
58	24	FRT F	N	Bristol City	L	0-3	0-1			54,502

Best Home League Attendance: 9,252 Wigan 1/1/86   **Smallest:** 2,902 Darlington 5/11   **Av Home Att:** 4,847

Goal Scorers: **Compared with 84-85:** +256

League (54): Caldwell 10 (2 pen), Cross 8, Thompson 8 (3 pen), Oghani 7, Hartford 5, Joyce 4, Bell 2, Neal 2, Rudge 2, Sutton 2, Came 1, Gavin 1, Phillips 1, Ripley 1

Milk Cup (5): Cross 2, Bell 1, Caldwell 1, Hartford 1

FA CUP (1): Thompson 1 (pen)

FRT (11): Caldwell 5, Oghani 4, Came 1, Hartford 1

1985-86

Farnworth	Joyce	Phillips	Rudge	Sutton	Carne	Thompson	Caldwell	Cross	Hartford	Bell	Walker (NC)	Scott	Oghani	Allardyce	Fitzpatrick	Entwistle	Neal	Roberts	Ripley (L)	Felgate (L)	Winstanley (NC)	Gavin	Darby (NC)	Ring (L)	Referee	No
1	2	3	4*	5	6	7	8	9	10	11	12														J Hough	1
1	4	3		5	6*	7	8	9	10	11		2	12												C Seel	2
1	4	3		5		7	8*	9	10	11		2	12	6											K Redfearn	3
1	4	3		5		7	8	9	10	11*		2	12	6											D Allison	4
1	2		4	5		7*	8	9	10	11		3	12	6											M Bodenham	5
1	4*			5		7	12	9	10		11	3	8	6	2										T Holbrook	6
1	4			5		7	8*	9	10		12	3	11	6	2										D Phillips	7
1	4			5		7	8	9†	10			3	11†	6	2										J Ball	8
1				5	4		8	9	10	11	7	3		6	2										G Tyson	9
1		8		5	4			9	10	7		3	11	6	2										A Seville	10
1	12	8*		5	4			9	10	7		3	11	6	2										P Vanes	11
1	7	9		5	4		8		10	11		3		6	2										G Aplin	12
1	7	9*		5.	4		8		10	12		3	11	6	2										K Lupton	13
1	4	3		5		7	8	9	10	12		2*	11	6											G Ashby	14
1	4	3		5		7	8	9	10				11	6	2										D Hutchinson	15
1	4	3		5		7*		9	10	11	12		8	6	2										J Lloyd	16
1	2	3		5	4		8*	9	10	7	12	6	11												G Courtney	17
1	2	3		5	4		8	9*	10	11	7	6				12									M Reed	18
1	2	3			4		8		10	11	7	5		6		9									M Cotton	19
1	2	3			4		8	12	10	11	7	5		6		9*									J Key	20
1	2	3			4*	12	8		10	11	7	5		6		9									H Taylor	21
1	2	3		5	4		8		10	7		6	11			9									D Reeves	22
1	4	3	12	5		7			10	11		6	8		2	9*									K Breen	23
1	4	3	9	6	5		12		10	11		2	8				7*								A Saunders	24
1	2	4	6	5			8		10	11	12	3	9†				7								D Delaney r'd N Butler	25
1	4		6	5		7	8	9	10	11		2					3								J Lovatt	26
1	4	12	6	5		7	8	9*	10	11		2					3								M Heath	27
1	6			5	4	7	8	9	10	11		2					3								M Peck	28
1	6			5	4	7	8†	9	10	11*		2	12				3								K Walmsley	29
1	6	3		5		7	8*	9	10	11		2	12				4								N Ashley	30
1		3	6	5		7		9	10	11		2	8				4								J Bray	31
1		3	6	5		7*		9	10	11		2	8	12			4								J Lloyd	32
1		3	6	5	4	7		9	10	11		2	8												P Willis	33
1		3	6	5	4	7		9	10			2	8	12							11*				R Bridges	34
1	11	3*	6	5	4			9	10			2	8												B Stevens	35
1	11	3*	6	5	4	7		9	10			2	8	12											F Roberts	36
1			6	5	4*	7		9	10	11		2	8	12				3							K Baker	37
	6	3		4	5			9	10	11		2	8						7	1					G Courtney	38
	6	3		4	5			9	10	11		2	8						7	1					T Mills	39
	6	3		4	5			9	10			2	8						7	1	11				R Bridges	40
	6	3		4	5			9	10	12		2	8						7	1	11*				T Jones	41
	6	3		4	5			9	10	11		2	8	13					7	1	12					42
		3		4	5			9	10	11		2	8						7	1					M James	43
	6	3		4				9*	10	11		2	8	12					7	1		5			J Deakin	44
	6*	3	12	4	5			9	10	11		2	8						7	1					C Seel	45
	6*	3	12	4	5		11	9	10			2	8						7	1					K Milller	46
	6	3		4				9	10	12		2*	8						7	1	11	5			N Wilson	47
	6	3		4				9	10				8*						7	1	11	5	2	12	K Breen	48
	6	3		4	5			9*	10			2	8						7	1	11			12	G Tyson	49
	6	3		4	5				10			2	8						7	1	11			9	J Key	50
	6	3		4	5			9*	10	12		2	8						7	1	11				Alan Robinson	51
	6	3		4	5			9	10			2	8						7	1	11				A Saunders	52
1	6	3		4	5			9	10			2	8						7		11				J Ashworth	53
	6	3		4	5			9	10			2	8						7	1	11				V Callow	54
	6	3		4	5			9	10	12		2	8						7	1	11*				J Lloyd	55
	6	3		4	5			9	10			2	8						7	1	11				N Ashley	56
	6	3		4	5			9	10			2	8						7	1	11				N Wilson	57
1	6*	3		4	5			9	10	12		2	8						7	1	11				G Tyson	58
31	31	33	13	32	35	35	39	19	46	30	6	43	31	14	10	5	20	5	15	3	8	2	1		League Appearances	
			3				2	1		6	5		5			1	3						2		Substitute Appearances	
4	3·1	2	1	1	4	4	2·1	4	4	2	1	3	3·1	3	3										Milk Cup Appearances	
1	1	0·1	1	1		1	1		1	1		1	1	1		1									FA Cup Appearances	
3	1	7	2	7	7	5	7	7	2·1	7	7	0·1					0·2	6	1	0·1	4			4	FR Trophy Appearances	

Players on Loan: Ripley (Middlesbrough), Felgate (Grimsby), Ring (Hull)

Departures:

'THE TROTTERS'

Formed: 1874
Turned Professional: 1880 **Ltd Co:** 1895

Previous Names: Christ Church FC from 1874-1877
Previous Managers: 1910-5 Will Settle   1915-9 Tom Mather   1919-45 Charles Foweraker
1945-50 Walter Rowley   1950-68 Bill Ridding   1968-70 Nat Lofthouse   1970-71 Jimmy McIlroy
1971 Jimmy Meadows   1971 Nat Lofthouse   1971-4 Jimmy Armfield   1974-80 Ian Greaves
1980-1 Stan Anderson   1981-2 George Mulhall   1982-5 John McGovern   1985 Charlie Wright
Honours: Champions Div 2, 1908-9, 1977-8   Champions Div 3, 1972-3
FA Cup Winners 1923, 1926, 1929, 1958
League Career: Founder Members of Football League 1888   Relegated to Div 2 1898-9
Promoted to Div 1 1899-1900   Relegated to Div 2 1902-3   Promoted to Div 1 1904-5
Relegated to Div 2 1907-8   Promoted to Div 1 1908-9   Relegated to Div 2 1909-10
Promoted to Div 1 1910-1   Relegated to Div 2 1932-3   Promoted to Div 1 1934-5
Relegated to Div 2 1963-4   Relegated to Div 3 1970-1   Promoted to Div 2 1972-3
Promoted to Div 1 1977-8   Relegated to Div 2 1979-80   Relegated to Div 3 1982-3
Colours: White shirts, navy blue shorts, white stockings
Change Colours: Red shirts, white shorts, red stockings
Reserves League: Central League   **'A' Team:** Lancashire

CLUB RECORDS

Most Appearances for Club: Eddie Hopkinson: Football League 519 + FA Cup 59 **Total 578** (1956-70)
Most Capped Player: Nat Lofthouse, 33, England (1951-58)
Record Goalscorer in a Match: J Cassidy, 5 v Sheffield United, 13-0, 2nd round FA Cup 1890
Tony Caldwell, 5 v Walsall, 8-1, Div 3 1983
Record League Goalscorer in a Season: Joe Smith, 38, Div 1, 1920-1   **In All Competitions:** Joe Smith, 38, 1,920-1
Record League Goalscorer in a Career: Nat Lofthouse, 255, 1946-61   **In All Competitions:** Nat Lofthouse, 285 (League
255 + FA Cup 30)
Record Transfer Fee Received: £340,000 from Birmingham City for Neil Whatmore, Aug 1974
Record Transfer Fee Paid: £350,000 to West Bromwich Albion for Len Cantello, May 1979
Best Performances: League: 3rd, 1891-2, 1920-1, 1924-5   **FA Cup:** Winners 1923, 1926, 1929, 1958   **League/Milk
Cup:** Semi-Final 1976-7
Most League Points: 61, Div 3, 1974-5   **Most League Goals:** 96, Div 2, 1934-5
Record League Victory: 8-0 v Barnsley, Div 2, 6 Oct 1934
Most Goals Scored in a First Class Match: 13-0 v Sheffield United, FA Cup 2nd Round, Feb 1890
Record League Defeat: 0-7 v Manchester City, Div 1, 21.3.36
Oldest Player in League Match: Stan Hanson 40 yrs 11 days
Youngest Player in League Match: Ray Parry, 15 yrs 267 days
Most Consecutive Undefeated League Matches: 19 1934   **League Matches Without a Win:** 24 1979-80
Longest Run of Undefeated Home League Matches: 27 1920-21   **Away League Matches:** 11 1904-05
Longest Run Without Home League Win: 11 1902-03   **Away League Win:** 36 1948-50
Most Consecutive League Wins: 11 1904   **Home League Wins:** 17 1924-25
Most Consecutive League Defeats: 10 1902-03   **Away League Wins:** 5 1904-05

Club Statistician for the Directory: Simon Marland

BOLTON WANDERERS

PLAYERS NAME Ht Wt Birthdate	Honours	Birthplace Transfers	Clubs	League	Milk Cup	FA Cup	Other Comps	League	Milk Cup	FA Cup	Other Comps
GOALKEEPERS											
Simon Farnworth 5.11 10.11 28.10.63	ES	Chorley	Bolton Wanderers	113	11	6	8				
Mike Salmon 6.2 12.12 14.7.64		Leyland F F	Blackburn Rovers Chester (L) Stockport County Bolton Wanderers	1 10 118	10	2 3	3				
DEFENDERS											
Sam Allardyce 6.1½ 14.0 14.10.54		Huddersfield	Bolton W. (A) Sunderland Millwall Coventry City Huddersfield Town Bolton Wanderers	180+4 24+1 63 28 37 14	15 2 3 3 2 3	14+1 5 1 3	0+1	21 2 2 1	1 1	2	
Phil Neal 5.11 12.2 20.2.51	E (50), B (1), FLg (1), EC (4), Div.1 (7), LgC (4), ESC (1)	Irchester £65,000 F	Northampton T. (A) Liverpool Bolton Wanderers	182+4 454+2 20	9 54	8+2 49 5	71	29 41 2	1 3	1 3	12
Jim Phillips 6.0 11.12 8.2.66		Bolton	Bolton W. (A)	70+4	6	2	9	2			
David Sutton 6.1 12.2 21.2.57	Div. 4, 80	Tarleton	Plymouth Argyle (A) Reading (L) Huddersfield Town Bolton Wanderers	60+1 9 242 32	2+1 23 1	3 19	6	11 2	1	3	
MIDFIELD											
Mark Came 6.1 13.0 14.9.61		Exeter	Bolton Wanderers	57+1	5+1	2	19	2			1
Asa Hartford† 5.5½ 11.2 24.10.50	S (50), U23 (5), U21 (1), MC 85	Clydebank £225,000 £450,000 £400,000 £350,000 USA F	WBA Manchester City Nottingham Forest Everton Manchester City Norwich City Bolton Wanderers	206+7 184+1 3 81 75 28 46	15 21 6 8 8 4	9 12 11 5 4 1	6 12 7	18 22 6 7 2 5	2 2 1 1	2 1 1	3 2 1
Warren Joyce 5.8½ 11.5 20.1.65		Oldham	Bolton Wanderers	126+3	10+1	6	6	12	1	1	2
Derek Scott 5.8 11.12 8.2.58	ES	Gateshead F	Burnley (A) Bolton Wanderers	277+8 43	21 3	23 1	4 6	24	3		
Steve Thompson 5.8½ 11.0 2.11.64		Oldham	Bolton W. (A)	112	9	6	10	15	1	1	
FORWARDS											
Tony Caldwell 5.9 11.7 21.3.58		Salford	Horwich RMI Bolton Wanderers	99+5	7+1	1 9	6	47	2	1	9
Wayne Entwistle 5.11 11.8 6.8.58	EY	Bury £30,000 £60,000 F F F	Bury (A) Sunderland Leeds United Blackpool Wimbledon Bury Carlisle United Bolton Wanderers	25+6 43+2 7+4 27+5 4+5 80+3 8+1	4+2 1 5 2	0+2 4 0+1 2+1 2 2	1+1 0+1	7 12 2 6 3 32 2	2 1	2 1 3	
Mark Gavin 5.9 11.4 10.12.63		Holytown F F	Leeds United Hartlepool Utd (L) Carlisle United Bolton Wanderers	12+6 7 21+1 8	4+1 2	0+1		3 1 1	1 1		
George Oghani 5.10½ 12.3 2.9.60		Manchester F F	Bury Hyde United Bolton Wanderers	69+9	8+1	2	10	23			4
Steve Elliott 5.11½ 11.10 15.9.58		Haltwhistle £95,000 Player exch. £25,000	Nottingham Forest (A) PNE Luton Town Walsall Bolton Wanderers	4 202+6 12 68+1	2 11+1 3 4	5 4	3 5	70 2 21	2 1	3	3 2

ADDITIONAL CONTRACT PROFESSIONALS
Paul Allen (monthly), Paul Clarke (monthly), Kevin Mailey (monthly), Mark Winstanley

APPRENTICES

NON-CONTRACT PLAYERS
Paul Allen, Julian Darby, Kevin Mailey, Mark Winstanley

Record Attendance: 69,912 v Manchester City, FA Cup Round 5, 18 Feb 1933

Smallest Home Attendance for a First Class Match: Approx 700 v Aston Villa, Div 1, 18 Nov 1893 or 2,902 v Darlington, Div 3, 5 Nov, 1985

Record Receipts: £53,931 v Everton, League Cup Semi-Final 2nd Leg, 15 Feb 1977

Season Tickets: Stand: £50 (Great Lever), £86 (Burnden), £60 (Block 'A' Wing), £86 (Manchester Road), Juveniles/OAP £30, £46, £35, £46 respectively. Manchester Road Terrace/Burnden Terrace £50 (juveniles/OAP £30)

Executive Box Season Tickets: £330

Cost of Stand Tickets: Manchester Road & Burnden £4.50 (OAP/juveniles £2.80), Block A £3.50 (£2.00), Great Lever £3.00 (£1.80); **Terraces:** £3.00 (£1.80), Visitors (Embankment) £3.00

Match and Ticket Information: (0204 21101)

Car Parking: Private car parking only in forecourt. Large car park 200 yards from ground. Limited street parking nearby. Multi-storey car parks are in town centre

Nearest Railway Station: Bolton (0204 28216)

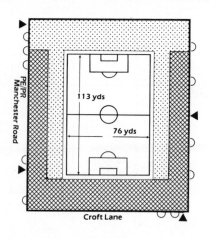

How to get to the ground

From North: Leave M61 at junction 5 or enter Bolton via A666 or A676. Then follow signs Farnworth B653 into Manchester Road. In 0.6m turn left into Croft Lane to Bolton Wanderers FC
From South, East and West: Use M62 until junction 14 then join M61. In 2.1m leave Motorway and at roundabout take 1st exit B6536. In 2.1m turn right into Croft Lane for Bolton Wanderers FC

Price of 1986-7 Programme: 50p
Number of Pages: 20
Subscriptions: No subscriptions

Local Newspaper: Bolton Evening News

Local Radio Station: Piccadilly Radio

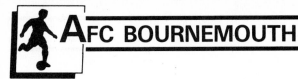

AFC BOURNEMOUTH
Division 3

A very undistinguished season for Bournemouth had one main consolation, which was retention of 3rd Division status. That apart it was uninspiring stuff and the end of season report could read 'must do better next time.'

The League programme was completed with the team in 15th position, which from the end of September was approximately the spot which seemed likely for them to achieve. In all matches the attack, spearheaded by the Nothern Irishman Clarke, managed 84 goals, but the defence was less satisfactory and silly goals conceded cost points. Only one of the last seven matches was won which contributed to the final modest achievement. Earlier there had been large wins over the two Bristol clubs at home—Rovers by 6-1 and City by 5-0.

Moderate League form was only partially offset by good cup performances with the Milk Cup ending honourably against Everton (2-5 on aggregate after a good match at Goodison Park); a first round aggregate thrashing of Reading (5-1) preceeded this. The FA Cup campaign started poorly with a scoreless draw at home to Dartford, but no mistake was made in the replay (2-0) and the second round brought home success over Dagenham (4-1) so that yet again the club reached the 3rd Round and an away tie at Wigan, who had no troubles in winning (3-0). The Freight Rover Trophy this time was a sad affair with early elimination.

The team's star was Clarke, who scored 35 goals in all matches and made his Northern Ireland debut in the Mexico World Cup, but he will not be available this coming season and will be difficult to replace. Russell and Thompson also managed a few goals but not on the Clarke scale and elsewhere in the team consistency was really only seen from Smeulders in goal, Heffernan, Sulley, Newson, Brown, O'Driscoll and Morrell.

With consistency, and someone to take over the mantle of Clarke, Harry Redknapp could cause a few surprises with his team in the new season. Not too much is ever expected from the seaside club, but they have a pleasant habit of creating shocks and long may they continue to do so.   WLM

Back Row L to R: Billy Clark, Gary Howlett, Mark Whitlock, David Coleman, Tony Pulis.
Middle Row: Keith Williams (Player/Youth Team Coach), Carl Richards, Trevor Aylott, Gerry Peyton, Tommy Heffernan, Paul Morrell, Roger Brown (Player/Coach). **Front Row:** Mark O'Connor, Robbie Savage, Sean O'Driscoll, Harry Redknapp (Manager), John Kirk (Trainer), Mark Newson (Captain), David Puckett, Morgan Lewis.

BOURNEMOUTH

DIVISION THREE: 15th   **FA CUP:** 3rd ROUND   **MILK CUP:** 2nd ROUND

MATCH	DATE		COMPE-TITION	VENUE	OPPONENTS	RESULT		HALF TIME	L'GUE POS'N	GOALSCORERS/GOAL TIMES	ATTEN-DANCE
1	A	17	CL	A	Derby County	L	0-3	0-1			(11,324)
2		21	MC1/1	A	Reading	W	3-1	0-0		Clarke 55, 62, Thompson 58	(2,614)
3		24	CL	H	Bristol City	W	5-0	4-0	8	Clarke 3 (1, 9, 89) Russell 7, 40	4,969
4		26	CL	A	Brentford	L	0-1	0-0	14		(4,283)
5		31	CL	H	Newport County	L	0-1	0-0	17		3,381
6	S	3	MC1/2	H	Reading	W	2-0	0-0		Thompson 51, Russell (pen) 82	2,590
7		7	CL	A	Chesterfield	W	1-0	0-0	15	Clarke 61	(3,207)
8		14	CL	H	Notts County	D	0-0	0-0	14		4,235
9		17	CL	H	Blackpool	L	1-4	1-2	17	Morrell 16	3,039
10		21	CL	A	Wigan Athletic	L	0-3	0-0	21		(3,057)
11		25	MC2/1	A	Everton	L	2-3	2-2		Clarke 1, Russell 11	(13,930)
12		28	CL	H	Darlington	W	4-2	3-0	19	Newson 10, 65, Clarke 35, Thompson 44	2,755
13	O	2	CL	A	Lincoln City	L	2-3	0-0	21	Clarke 80, Shaw 83	(1,962)
14		5	CL	A	Cardiff City	W	1-0	1-0	17	Shaw 8	(2,156)
15		8	MC2/2	H	Everton	L	0-2	0-1			8,081
16		12	CL	H	Bury	W	2-1	1-0	15	Russell (pen) 3, Heffernan 48	3,122
17		19	CL	H	Gillingham	L	2-3	1-1	16	Russell 1, Clarke 61	3,561
18		22	CL	A	York City	L	1-2	1-1	17	Russell 40	(4,194)
19		26	CL	H	Bristol Rovers	W	6-1	4-1	14	Russell 12, 38, Clarke 25, 48, Beck 27, O'Driscoll 62	3,798
20	N	2	CL	A	Bolton Wanderers	L	0-1	0-0	15		(3,800)
21		5	CL	A	Plymouth Argyle	L	1-2	1-1	16	Newson 30	(6,816)
22		9	CL	H	Wolverhampton W.	W	3-2	2-1	14	Heffernan 4, Clarke 12, Beck 48	4,126
23		16	FAC1	H	Dartford	D	0-0	0-0			3,499
24		19	FAC1R	A	Dartford	W	2-0	2-0		Clarke 20, Newson 30	(2,555)
25	2	23	CL	A	Doncaster Rovers	D	1-1	1-1	16	Russell 17	(2,390)
26	D	7	FAC2	H	Dagenham	W	4-1	2-1		O'Driscoll 16, Thompson 37, Brown 61, Clarke 66	3,336
27		14	CL	A	Walsall	L	2-4	0-1	17	O'Driscoll 69, Clarke 73	(4,460)
28		17	CL	H	Rotherham United	L	1-2	0-2	18	Brown 77	2,489
29		21	CL	A	Bristol City	W	3-1	0-1	16	Heffernan 65, Howlett 73, Newson 78	(5,691)
30		26	CL	H	Reading	L	0-1	0-1	16		6,105
31		28	CL	H	Brentford	D	0-0	0-0	17		4,006
32	J	1	CL	A	Swansea City	D	1-1	1-0	16	Clarke 10	(6,989)
33		4	FAC3	A	Wigan Athletic	L	0-3	0-0			(4,185)
34		11	CL	A	Newport County	L	1-2	0-0	16	Thompson 67	(2,333)
35		14	FRT	A	Orient	L	1-3	0-2		Shinners (og) 51	(947)
36		18	CL	H	Derby County	D	1-1	1-1	18	Howlett 19	4,223
37		21	FRT	H	Reading	W	5-0	2-0		Clarke 4 (pen 8, pen 40, 85, 87) O'Driscoll 46	1,974
38		31	CL	H	Chesterfield	W	3-2	1-0	15	Clarke 18, Newson 56, Heffernan 66	2,347
39	F	4	CL	A	York City	W	2-0	2-0	15	Clarke 16, 37	2,476
40		8	CL	A	Gillingham	L	0-2	0-1	15		(3,895)
41		22	CL	H	Wigan Athletic	L	0-2	0-0	16		2,949
42	M	1	CL	A	Darlington	D	0-0	0-0	16		(2,576)
43		4	CL	H	Lincoln City	D	2-2	2-0	16	O'Driscoll 5, Clarke (pen) 36	1,873
44		8	CL	H	Cardiff City	D	1-1	1-0	17	Clarke 21	2,707
45		15	CL	A	Bury	L	0-3	0-0	17		(2,097)
46		18	CL	H	Bolton Wanderers	W	2-1	1-1	15	Clarke 21, 71	2,063
47		22	CL	A	Bristol Rovers	W	3-2	1-1	14	Thompson 26, Clarke 78, 88	(3,296)
48		29	CL	H	Swansea City	W	4-0	1-0	14	Clarke 3, Thompson 57, Beck 75, O'Driscoll 85	3,328
49		31	CL	A	Reading	W	2-1	0-1	14	Clarke 47, Beck 81	(7,122)
50	A	5	CL	H	Plymouth Argyle	L	1-3	0-2	14	Beck 72	5,351
51		12	CL	A	Wolverhampton W.	W	3-0	1-0	14	O'Driscoll 40, Thompson 56, Clarke 61	(3,382)
52		15	CL	A	Notts County	L	1-3	0-2	14	O'Connell 46	(2,423)
53		19	CL	H	Doncaster Rovers	D	1-1	0-0	14	Clarke 51	2,796
54		26	CL	A	Rotherham United	L	1-4	1-3	14	Clarke 18	(2,101)
55		29	CL	A	Blackpool	L	0-2	0-0	15		(2,259)
56	M	3	CL	H	Walsall	L	0-1	0-1	15		3,047

Best Home League Attendance: 6,105 Reading 26/12   **Smallest:** 1,873 v Lincoln 4/3   **Av Home Att:** 3,424

Goal Scorers: **Compared with 84-85:** −342

League (65):	Clarke 16 (1 pen), Russell 8 (1 pen), Beck 5, Newson 5, O'Driscoll 5, Thompson 5, Heffernan 4, Howlett 2, Shaw 2, Brown 1, Morrell 1, O'Connell 1
Milk Cup (7):	Clarke 3, Russell 2 (1 pen), Thompson 2
FA Cup (6):	Clarke 2, Brown 1, Newson 1, O'Driscoll 1, Thompson 1
FRT (6):	Clarke 4 (2 pen), O'Driscoll 1, Opponents 1

Smeulders	Heffernan	Sulley	Newson	Brown	Nightingale	O'Driscoll	Howlett	Clarke	Thompson	Beck	Russell	Morrell	Shaw	Lewis	Claridge	Leigh	Randall A	Williams	O'Connor	Clark (NC)	White (NC)	Coleman (NC)	Keane (A)	Referee	
1	2	3	4	5	6	7*	8	9	10	11	12													L Dilkes	1
1	2	3	4	5	6	7		9	10		8	11												**E Scales**	2
1	2	3	4	5	6	7		9	10	12	8*	11												A Ward	3
1	2	3	4	5	6	7		9	10	12	8	11*												J Ashworth	4
1	2	3	4	5	6	7		9	10*	12	8	11												M James	5
1	2	3	4	5	6	7		9	10		8	11												**K Cooper**	6
1	2	3	4	5	6	7		9	10		8	11												K Breen	7
1			4	5	6	7		9	10	2	8	11	3											R Gifford	8
1	2		4	5	6	7		9	10	3	8	11												M Cotton	9
1	2	3	4	5	6*	7		9	10	12	8	11												D Phillips	10
1	2	3	4	5		7		9	10	6	8	11												**M Heath**	11
1	2	3	4	5	12	7		9	10*	6	8	11												G Ashby	12
1	2*	3†	4	5	12	7		9		6	8	11	10											J McAulay	13
1	2	3	4	5		7		9		6	8	11	10											M Reed	14
1	2	3	4	5		7		9		6	8	11	10											**E Butler**	15
1	2	3	4	5		7		9		6	8	11	10											M Dimblebee	16
1	2		4	5	3	7	12	9		6	8	11	10*											J Martin	17
1	2		4	5		7	10	9		6	8			11										N Glover	18
1	2	3	4	5		7	10	9		6	8*			11	12									M Bodenham	19
1	2	3	4	5		7	10	9		6†	8			11										J Key	20
1	2	3	4	5		7	10	9		6	8	12		11*										P Vanes	21
1	2	3	4	5		7	10	9		6	8	11												R Hamer	22
1	2	3	4	5		7	10	9			8	11	6											**C Downey**	23
1	2	3	4	5	6	7		9	10		8	11												**C Downey**	24
1	2	3	4	5	6	7		9	10*	12	8	11												D Allinson	25
1	2	3	4	5		7		9	10	6	8	11												**D Reeves**	26
1	2	3	4	5		7		9	10	6	8	11												I Hendrick	27
1	2	3	4	5		7		9	10	6	8	11												J Moules	28
	2	3	4	5		7	8	9	10	6		11				1								R Lewis	29
	2	3	4	5		7		9	10	6	8	11				1								K Miller	30
1	2	3	4	5		7		9	10	6	8	11												R Groves	31
1	2	3	4	5		7		9	10	6	8	11												B Stevens	32
1	2	3	4	5		7		9	12	6	8*	11	10											**J Ball**	33
1	2	3	4	5*	12	7		9	10	6	8	11												J Bray	34
	2	3*	4		5	7	8*	9	10	6		11	12			1		12						**K Barratt**	35
	2	3	4		5	7	8	9	10	6		11				1								M Bodenham	36
	2	3	4		5	7	8	9	10	6		11				1								**D Reeves**	37
	2*	3	4		5	7	8	9	10	6		11	12			1								A Gunn	38
	2	3	4		5	7	8	9	10	6		11				1								L Shapter	39
	2	3	4		5	7	8	9	10	6		11				1								T Ward	40
	2	3	4		5	7	8*	9	10	6	12	11				1								M James	41
	2	3	4	5	8	7	12	9	10	6		11*				1								R Nixon	42
	2	3	4	5	8	7	11	9	10	6						1								C Downey	43
		3	4	5	2	7	11	9	10	6	8*		12			1								N Butler	44
		3	4	5	2	7	11	9	10	6	8					1								K Lupton	45
1	2	3	4	5	8	7		9	10	6								11						J Deakin	46
1	2	3	4		8	7	12	9	10	6		5						11*						E Scales	47
1	2	3	4			7		9	10	6		5						8	11					D Hedges	48
1	2	3	4			7		9	10	6		5						8	11					J Ashworth	49
1	2	3	4		12	7*		9	10	6		5						8	11					J Moules	50
1		3	4	2		7		9	10	6		5						8	11					H King	51
1			4	5	2	7		9	10*	6	12	3						8	11					N Wilson	52
			4		2	7		9		8		3				1	6	10	11	5				R Milford	53
			4		2	7	10	9		6	8								11		3			D Allison	54
			4	5	2	7	10	9			8	3							11			6		T Mills	55
1			4	5	2	7		9			8	3					6	10*	11				12	T Ward	56
34	37	37	46	34	28	46	17	46	33	37	29	37	6	4		12	2	9	9	1	1	1		League Appearances	
					4		3			4	3	1	2		1								1	Substitute Appearances	
4	4	4	4	4		4	3	4	3	2+1	4	4	1											Milk Cup Appearances	
4	4	4	4	4	1	4	1	4		2+1	4	4	2											FA Cup Appearances	
2	2	2			2	2	2	2	2	2		2		0+1			2	0+1						FR Trophy Appearances	

Departures: Claridge (Weymouth), Shaw (Bristol City), Leigh, Clark & Coleman (Poole Town), Clarke (Southampton) Smeulders (Torquay Utd), Sully (Dundee Utd), Russell (Doncaster R), White (Doncaster R)

'THE CHERRIES'

Formed: 1899
Turned Professional: 1912 **Ltd Co:** 1914

Previous Names: Boscombe St Johns 1890-9   Boscombe FC 1899-1923   Bournemouth & Boscombe Athletic FC 1923-72

Previous Managers: -1925 Harry Kinghorn   1925-8 Leslie Knighton   1928-30 Frank Richards   1930-5 Billy Birrell   1935-6 Bob Crompton   1936-9 Charles Bell   1939-47 Harry Kinghorn   1947-50 Harry Lowe   1950-6 Jack Bruton   1956-8 Freddie Cox   1958-61 Don Welsh   1961-3 Bill McGarry   1963-5 Reg Flewin   1965-70 Freddie Cox   1970-3 John Bond   1973-5 Trevor Hartley   1975-9 John Benson   1979-80 Alec Stock   1980-2 David Webb   1983 Don Megson

Honours: Associate Members Cup Winners 1983-4

League Career: Elected to Div 3 (S) 1923   Transferred to Div 3 1958   Relegated to Div 4 1969-70   Promoted to Div 3 1970-1   Relegated to Div 4 1974-5   Promoted to Div 3 1981-2

Bournemouth's stay in the Third Division from 1923 until 1970 is a record for consecutive years membership of that Division

Colours: All red with single white stripe under arm and down side

Change Colours: All white with red trim

Reserves League: Macbar South West Counties   **Youth Team:** S E Counties

---

CLUB RECORDS

Most Appearances for Club: Ray Bumstead: Football League **Total 511** (1958-70)

Most Capped Player: Tommy Godwin, 4 Eire 1956-58   **For England:** None

Record Goalscorer in a Match: Ted MacDougall, 9 v Margate, FA Cup 1st Round, 20.11.71

Record League Goalscorer in a Season: Ted MacDougall, 42, Div 4, 1970-1   **In All Competitions:** Ted MacDougall, 49 (League 42 + FA Cup 7)

Record League Goalscorer in a Career: Ron Eyre, 202 (Cup goals not known), 1924-33

Record Transfer Fee Received: £195,000 from Manchester United for Ted MacDougall, Sept 1972

Record Transfer Fee Paid: £70,000 to Cardiff City for Brian Clark, Oct 1972

Best Performances: League: 3rd Div 3 1961-2   2nd Div 3 (S) 1947-8   **FA Cup:** 6th Round, 1956-7   **League/Milk Cup:** 4th Round, 1962, 1964

Most League Points: (3pts for win) 88, Div 4, 1981-2   (2pts for win) 62, Div 3, 1971-2

Most League Goals: 88, Div 3 (S), 1956-57

Record League Victory: 10-0 v Northampton Town, Div 3 (S), Sept 1939

Most Goals Scored in a Cup Tie: 11-0 v Margate, 1st Round FA Cup, 1971-2

Record League Defeat: 0-9 v Lincoln City, Div 3, 1 Dec 1982

Oldest Player in League Match: Harry Kinghorn 48, 11.3.29 v Brentford

Youngest Player in League Match: Jimmy White 15, 30.4.58 v Brentford

Most Consecutive Undefeated League Matches: 18 1982

Longest Run of Undefeated Home League Matches: 33 1962-63

Longest Run Without Home League Win: 10 1931-32

Most Consecutive League Wins: 7 1970

Most Consecutive League Defeats: 7 1955

League Matches Without a Win: 14 1973-74
Away League Matches: 13 1961
Away League Win: 26 1976-77
Home League Wins: 12 1968, 1971
Away League Wins: 5 1948

Club Statistician for the Directory: John Treleven

BOURNEMOUTH

PLAYERS NAME Ht Wt Birthdate	Honours	Birthplace Transfers	Clubs	APPEARANCES League	Milk Cup	FA Cup	Other Comps	GOALS League	Milk Cup	FA Cup	Other Comps
GOALKEEPERS											
Gerry Peyton	EI (20)	Birmingham	Atherstone United								
6.2 13.11 20.5.56			Burnley	30	1	1					
		£40,000	Fulham	309	22	19					
			Southend United (L)	10							
		F	Bournemouth								
DEFENDERS											
Roger Brown*	AMC 84	Tamworth	A.P. Leamington			6					
6.1 11.10 12.12.52		£5,000	Bournemouth	63	2	3		3	1		
		£85,000	Norwich City	16	2	3					
		£100,000	Fulham	141	8	8		18	1		
		£40,000	Bournemouth	57	6	12	6	5		1	
Morgan Lewis		Bournemouth	Bournemouth	8							
5.9 11.4 8.9.65											
Mark Newson	ESP (4)	Stepney	Maidstone United			11					
5.11 12.0 7.12.60		F	Bournemouth	46	4	4	2	5		1	
Chris Sulley	AMC 84	Camberwell	Chelsea (A)								
5.8 10.0 3.12.59		F	Bournemouth	205+1	14	17	8	3			
Mark Whitlock		Portsmouth	Southampton (A)	55+6	5		3	1			
5.11½ 12.2 14.3.61			Grimsby Town (L)	7+2							
			Aldershot (L)	14		2					
		Player exch.	Bournemouth								
MIDFIELD											
Tom Heffernan		Dublin	Dunleary								
6.2 12.7 30.4.55			Tottenham H								
		F	Bournemouth	154	8	6		21			
		£20,000	Sheffield United	82	7	6	3	5			
		F	Bournemouth	37	4	4	2				
Gary Howlett	EY	Dublin	Home Farm								
5.8 10.4 2.4.63			Coventry City								
			Brighton	30+2	2	3		1	2		
			Bournemouth	34+3		1	5	4			
Paul Morrell	AMC 84	Poole	Weymouth			5					
5.11 13.5 23.3.61			Bournemouth	100+4	7	12	12	4			1
Sean O'Driscoll†	EI (3), AMC 84	Wolverhampton	Alvechurch								
5.8 10.6 1.7.57			Fulham	141+7	13+1	11+1		13			
			Bournemouth	109	6	9	13	7		1	1
Bob Savage	AMC 84	Liverpool	Liverpool (A)								
5.7 11.1 8.1.60			Wrexham (L)	27		2		10	1		
			Stoke City	5+2							
			Bournemouth	65+1	1	5	10	14		3	3
Tony Pulis		Newport	Bristol Rovers	78+7	7+1	5		3		1	
5.10 11.8 16.1.58		Hong Kong (F)	Bristol Rovers	44+1	3						
		£8,000	Newport County	75+2	2	5	5			1	
Keith Williams	YT	Burntwood	Aston Villa								
5.9 11.10 12.4.57			Wolverhampton W.	128+3	8	2+1		6			
		F	Bournemouth	93+3	8	9	2	1			
FORWARDS											
Mark O'Connor	EU21	Basildon	QPR (A)	2+1							
5.6 9.10 10.3.66			Exeter City (L)	38							
		£20,000	Bristol Rovers	80+1	8	7	4	12	1	1	1
			Bournemouth	9				1			
Carl Richards		St. Marys, Jam.	Enfield								
6.1 13.6 12.1.60		£10,000	Bournemouth								
Ian Thompson	AMC 84	Dartford	Salisbury								
6.1 11.0 8.5.58		£18,000	Bournemouth	119+2	6	11+1	12	30	2	4	4
David Puckett		Southampton	Southampton (A)	42+43	5+6	2+1	0+1	14	1		
5.7 10.5 29.10.60											

ADDITIONAL CONTRACT PROFESSIONALS

APPRENTICES
Tom Keane, Adrian Randall

NON-CONTRACT PLAYERS
Billy Clark, David Coleman

DEAN COURT Bournemouth

Record Attendance: 28,799 v Manchester United, FA Cup Round 6, 2 Mar 1957

Smallest Home Attendance for a First Class Match: 1,706 v Aldershot AM Cup 1983-4   1,873 v Lincoln, Div 3, 1985-6

Record Receipts: £33,723 v Manchester United, FA Cup Round 3, 7 Jan 1984

Season Tickets: Centre Stand: £90.00, B or E Block £80.00

Executive Box Season Tickets: None

Cost of Stand Tickets: Centre Stand £4.50, B or E Block £4.00, F Block (Wing Stand) £3.50 (juveniles/OAP £2.00), A Block (visiting supporters) £4.00; **Terraces:** £3.00, (juveniles/OAP £1.50)

Match and Ticket Information: Phone Club

Car Parking: Adequate for 1,500 vehicles

Nearest Railway Station: Bournemouth (0202 28216)

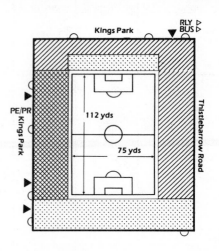

How to get to the ground

From North and East: Use A338 (S.P. Bournemouth) and at roundabout junction with A3060 take 2nd exit. At next roundabout take 1st exit into Littledown Avenue, then turn right into Thistlebarrow Road for AFC Bournemouth
From West: Follow signs Bournemouth A3049, 0.7m after Wallisdown (traffic signals) turn left into Talbot Road. In 2m at roundabout take 1st exit into Queens Park South Drive then at roundabout take 2nd exit into Littledown Ave., then turn right into Thistlebarrow Road for AFC Bournemouth

Price of 1986-7 Programme: 50p
Number of Pages: 20
Subscriptions: £15

Local Newspaper: Evening Echo

Local Radio Stations: Two Counties Radio, BBC Radio Solent

BRADFORD CITY   Division 2

Chairman
Stafford Heginbotham

Directors
Jack Tordoff
Peter Flesher, FCA

Secretary
Terry Newman (0274 306062)

Manager
Trevor Cherry

Chief Scout
Maurice Lindley

Commercial Manager
Tony Thornton (0274 306062)

Physiotherapist
Brian Edwards

Stadium Manager
Alan Gilliver

Back Row L to R: Terry Dolan (Coach), Don Goodman, Ian Olmondroyd, Gavin Oliver, Peter Litchfield, Dave Evans, Tony Clegg, Steve O'Shaughnessy, Brian Edwards (Physio). **Middle Row:** Mark Ellis, John Hendrie, Peter Jackson, Trevor Cherry (Manager), Bobby Campbell, Stuart McCall, Arthur Graham. **Front Row:** Andy Thorpe, Nigel Beaumont, Carl Goddard, Chris Withe, Martin Singleton, Greg Abbott.

A standing ovation after their last match of the campaign against fairytale club Wimbledon spoke volumes for the feelings of the Bradford supporting public towards the achievements of their nomadic heroes. A 1-1 draw, whilst denying next season's First Division newcomers the runners-up spot in Division Two, also meant 'The Paraders' had ended their incredible season — 42 games away from Valley Parade — as self-styled "Champions of Yorkshire", with a mid-table position which for so long had looked unlikely, especially considering their dismal away record.

Their first season in Division Two for 48 years began with a daunting task of obligatory away fixtures (9 of their first 12 games), and perhaps understandably only one victory was registered, that coming on the opening day of the season at Carlisle, although there were creditable draws at Charlton Athletic's "new" home at Selhurst Park, and at Middlesbrough.

However, fixtures played on their adopted grounds at Leeds Road (Huddersfield), Elland Road (Leeds) and Odsal Stadium (Bradford) reaped the requisite rewards. Just one defeat — a 1-4 reversal against Sheffield United at Leeds up to the beginning of March 1986 when Grimsby Town were 1-0 victors — saw them healthily placed for an assault on the top half of the table.

A spell of inactivity caused by the arctic freeze-up brought the customary back-log of fixtures which had to be fitted in, the club found themselves close to the relegation area. In fact, only a 3-1 "home" victory over struggling Shrewsbury Town made them mathematically safe.

During this frenetic spell, two local youngsters made their mark — Tony Clegg, who after a lengthy stay on the sub's bench made the number 6 jersey his own, and the gangling 6'4" striker Ian Ormondroyd weighed in with some important goals in his first season out of local league soccer. Special praise has to be afforded to goalkeeper Peter Litchfield, who has performed heroics between the sticks after being plunged into immediate League action following the injury to first team choice Eric McManus.

Their cup exploits were short, but sweet. Defeat at the hands of Brighton on a 7-2 aggregate of the 2nd Round stage of the Milk Cup, followed an extra-time decider at Chesterfield in the previous round. The club also made its FA Cup exit at the first hurdle against Ipswich Town, but only after an extra-time winner in the replay, after an eight-goal thriller at Portman Road.

The management team of Trevor Cherry and Terry Yorath considered actually staying in the 2nd Division a bigger achievement than clinching the 3rd Division championship, but with the promise of a new ultra-modern ground by the latter half of next season, it is important that the Board strengthens the squad.

Terry Frost

NB. When Bradford City meet relegated Ipswich Town in their Division 2 fixture, they will join the select band of Football League teams who have met all the other current sides in a League game.

BRADFORD CITY

DIVISION TWO: 13th   **FA CUP:** 3rd ROUND   **MILK CUP:** 2nd ROUND

MATCH	DATE	COMPE-TITION	VENUE	OPPONENTS	RESULT	HALF TIME	L'GUE POS'N	GOALSCORERS/GOAL TIMES	ATTEN-DANCE
1	A 17	CL	A	Carlisle United	W 2-1	0-0		Campbell 62, 72	(5,086)
2	21	MC1/1	H¹	Chesterfield	D 2-2	2-1		Campbell 22, McCall 42	2,980
3	24	CL	A	Brighton & H. A.	L 1-2	1-1	14	Thorpe 7	(9,263)
4	26	CL	A	Wimbledon	L 0-1	0-0	18		(3,205)
5	S 1	CL	H²	Stoke City	W 3-1	1-1	15	Abbott (2 pen) 10, 50, Singleton 56	6,999
6	3	MC1/2	A	Chesterfield	W 4-3*	0-1		Abbott pen 48, Campbell 74, Jackson 83, McCall 115	(4,326)
7	7	CL	A	Huddersfield Town	L 0-2	0-1	18		(11,667)
8	14	CL	H¹	Hull City	W 4-2	1-0	10	McCall 29, Goodman 56, Graham 59, Campbell 75	4,930
9	21	CL	A	Leeds United	L 1-2	0-0	17	Hendrie 70	(21,104)
10	25	MC2/1	A	Brighton & H. A.	L 2-5	1-3		Hendrie 22, 75	(6,664)
11	28	CL	A	Grimsby Town	L 0-2	0-1	18		(5,158)
12	O 5	CL	A	Blackburn Rovers	L 0-3	0-1	19		(7,728)
13	8	MC2/2	H³	Brighton & H. A.	L 0-1	0-1			5,368
14	12	CL	H¹	Barnsley	W 2-0	1-0	15	Campbell 26, McCall 73	5,707
15	15	CL	A	Charlton Athletic	D 1-1	0-1	15	Hendrie 55	(3,141)
16	19	CL	A	Middlesbrough	D 1-1	0-1	15	McCall 67	(6,130)
17	23	FMC	A	Hull	L 1-4	1-1		Thorpe 9	(2,177)
18	26	CL	H²	Sheffield Utd	L 1-4	0-2	18	Abbott 76	7,448
19	N 2	CL	H³	Crystal Palace	W 1-0	1-0	16	Hendrie 1	5,604
20	9	CL	A	Norwich City	D 0-0	0-0	15		(13,939)
21	23	CL	A	Shrewsbury Town	L 0-2	0-1	18		(3,148)
22	D 3	CL	H³	Portsmouth	W 2-1	1-1	16	Campbell 9, Graham 85	4,701
23	7	CL	A	Fulham	L 1-4	0-1	18	Abbott (pen) 55	(3,724)
24	13	CL	H	Carlisle United	W 1-0	0-0	17	Hendrie 85	5,212
25	20	CL	H³	Brighton & H. A.	W 3-2	2-0	14	Abbott 3 (2 pen) 16, 18, 65	4,318
26	26	CL	A	Oldham Athletic	W 1-0	0-0	12	Campbell 78	(6,680)
27	J 1	CL	H¹	Sunderland	W 2-0	1-0	11	Singleton 5, Hendrie 85	8,369
28	4	FAC3	A	Ipswich Town	D 4-4	3-3		Goodman 9, Abbott 13, pen 79, Hendrie 27	(13,003)
29	11	CL	A	Hull City	L 0-1	0-0	12		(9,333)
30	13	FAC3R	H²	Ipswich Town	L 0-1	0-0			10,108
31	18	CL	A	Stoke City	L 1-3	0-1	13	Oliver 68	(8,808)
32	M 1	CL	H²	Grimsby Town	L 0-1	0-0	19		5,158
33	4	CL	H²	Oldham Athletic	W 1-0	0-0	16	Campbell (pen) 80	3,964
34	8	CL	H¹	Blackburn Rovers	W 3-2	1-1	14	Goodman 21, Campbell 65, Abbott pen 67	5,263
35	11	CL	A	Sheffield United	L 1-3	1-1	15	Goodman 37	(8,405)
36	15	CL	A	Barnsley	D 2-2	1-1	15	Goodman 34, Abbott (pen) 80	(7,512)
37	19	CL	H³	Charlton Athletic	L 1-2	1-1	17	Abbott 33	5,645
38	22	CL	H³	Huddersfield Town	W 3-0	1-0	13	Ellis 26, Campbell 53, Ormondroyd 83	9,058
39	29	CL	A	Sunderland	D 1-1	0-0	13	Ellis 57	(14,870)
40	A 2	CL	H³	Fulham	W 3-1	1-1	11	Campbell 44, McCall 67, Ellis 87	5,564
41	5	CL	A	Crystal Palace	L 1-2	0-0	13	Hendrie 48	(5,079)
42	9	CL	H³	Leeds United	L 0-1	0-1	14		10,751
43	12	CL	H³	Norwich City	L 0-2	0-1	15		7,190
44	19	CL	A	Millwall	L 1-2	0-1	17	Ormondroyd 59	(3,763)
45	23	CL	H¹	Middlesbrough	W 2-1	2-0	15	Clegg 15, Hendrie 42	3,426
46	26	CL	H¹	Shrewsbury Town	W 3-1	3-0	13	Ormondroyd 10, Hendrie 29, 37	4,663
47	30	CL	H³	Millwall	L 0-2	0-1	13		3,826
48	M 3	CL	A	Portsmouth	L 0-4	0-1	13		(9,568)
49	8	CL	H³	Wimbledon	D 1-1	0-1	13	Hendrie 34	4,316

Best Home League Attendance: 10,751 v Leeds Utd² 9/4   **Smallest:** 3,426 v Middlesbrough   **Av Home Att:** 5,816

Goal Scorers: **Compared with 84-85:** −235

League (51): Abbott 10 (7 pen), Campbell 10 (1 pen), Hendrie 10, Goodman 4, McCall 4, Ellis 3, Ormondroyd 3, Graham 2, Singleton 2, Clegg 1, Oliver 1, Thorpe 1

Milk Cup (8): Campbell 2, Hendrie 2, McCall 2, Abbott 1 (1 pen), Jackson 1

FA Cup (4): Abbott 2 (1 pen), Goodman 1, Hendrie 1

FM Cup (1): Thorpe 1   **Key:** ¹Leeds Rd, Huddersfield Town, ²Elland Rd, Leeds Utd, ³Odsal Stadium, Bradford

Litchfield	Abbott	Withe	McCall	Jackson	Evans	Hendrie	Thorpe	Campbell	Singleton	Graham	Ellis	Clegg	Goodman	Ormondroyd	Beaumont (NC)	Oliver	Chalmers (L)	Referee	
1	2	3	4	5	6	7	8	9	10	11								A Saunders	1
1	2	3	4	5	6*	7	8	9	10	11	12							R Guy	2
1	2	3	4	5	6	7*	8	9	10	11		12						N Butler	3
1	2	3	4	5	6	7	8	9	10	11								D Axcell	4
1	2	3	4	5	6	7	8	9	10	11								G Tyson	5
1	2	3	4	5	6	7	8*	9	10	11	12							L Robinson	6
1	2	3	4	5	6	7	8*	9	10	11	12							K Redfern	7
1	2	3	4	5	6	7		9	10	11*	12		8					N Wilson	8
1	2	3	4	5	6	7		9	10	11			8					R Nixon	9
1	2	3	4	5	6	7		9	10		11*	12	8					C Downey	10
1	2	3	4	5	6	7		9	10		11*	12	8					G Napthine	11
1	2	3	4	5	6	7		9	10*	11		12	8					D Shaw	12
1	2	3	4	5	6	7	8*	9	10	11†	12							J Hough	13
1	2	3	4	5	6		8	9	10	11	7							P Tyldesley	14
1	2	3	4	5	6		8	9	10	11	7							J Ashworth	15
1	2	3	4	5	6		8	9	10	11	7*	12						G Aplin	16
1	2	3	4	5	6		8*		10	11	7		9	12				M Scott	17
1	2	3	4	5	6	7		9	10	11	12		8*					D Allison	18
1	8	3	4	5	6	7		9	10	11	2							J Lovatt	19
1	8	3	4	5	6	7		9	10*	11	2							K Miller	20
1	8	3	4	5	6	7		9	10*	11				12		2		R Hamer	21
1	8	3	4	5	6	7		9	10	11						2		J Worrall	22
1	8	3*	4	5	6	7		9	10	11	12					2		J Deakin	23
1	8*	3	4	5	6	7		9	10	11		12				2		R Bridges	24
1	4	3		5	6	7		9	10	11			8			2		K Walmsley	25
1	4	3		5	6	7		9	10	11	12		8*			2		M Heath	26
1	4	3		5	6	7		9	10	11			8			2		K Breen	27
1	4	3		5	6	7		9	10	11	12		8*			2		R Lewis	28
1	4	3		5	6	7		9	10	11	12		8*			2		A Saunders	29
1	4	3		5	6	7		9	10*	11	8		12			2		N Wilson	30
1	8	3*	4	5	6	7		9	10	11	12					2		R Groves	31
1		3	4	5	6	7		9	10	11*	12					2	8	M Reed	32
1		3	4	5	6	7		9	10	11						2	8	G Tyson	33
1	12	3	4	5	6	7		9	10	11*		8				2		M Robinson	34
1	11	3	4	5	6	7		9	10*	12		8				2		P Willis	35
1	11		4	5		7		9	10*		12	6	8		3	2		N Midgley	36
1	11		4	5		7		9	10		12	6	8		3*	2		D Scott	37
1	10	3	4	5		7		9			11	6	8*	12		2		J Key	38
1	10	3	4	5		7		9			11	6	8*	12		2		T Jones	39
1	10	3	4	5		7		9	12	11		6		8*		2		I Hendrick	40
1	10	3	4	5		7		9	12	11*		6		8		2		J Ashworth	41
1	10	3	4	5		7	12	9			11	6		8*		2		K Barratt	42
1	10		4	5	3	7	12	9			11*	6	8			2		T Fitzharris	43
1	10		4	5	3	7		9	11			6	8*	12		2		M James	44
1	10		4	5	3	7		9	11	12		6	8*			2		R Guy	45
1	10		4	5	3	7	12	9*	11			6	8			2		D Shaw	46
1	10		4	5	3	7	11*		12			6	8			2		T Jones	47
1			4	5	3	7	11*		12			6	9	8		2		B Stevens	48
1			4	5	3	7		9	10*		12	6	8	11		2		K Lupton	49
42	38	33	38	42	35	42	6	41	35	23	13	16	19	8	2	27	2	League Appearances	
	1						4	1	2	12	5	1	4					Substitute Appearances	
4	4	4	4	4	4	4	3	4	4	3	1-3	0-1	1					Milk Cup Appearances	
2	2	2		2	2	2		2	2	2	1-1		1-1			2		FA Cup Appearances	
1	1	1	1	1	1		1			1		1	1			1	0-1	FM Cup Appearances	

Players on Loan: Charlmers (Glasgow Celtic)
Departures: McManus (Tramere Rovers), Hudson (Rochdale), Beeby (Preston North End)

'THE BANTAMS'

Formed: 1903
Turned Professional: 1903   **Ltd Co:** 1908

Previous Managers: 1903-5 Robert Campbell   1905-21 Peter O'Rourke   1921-6 David L Menzies   1926-8 Colin Campbell McKechnie Veitch   1928-30 Peter O'Rourke   1930-5 Jack G Peart   1935-8 Richard Ray   1938-43 Fred Westgarth   1943-6 Councillor Robert Sharp   1946-7 Jack Barker   1947-8 John Milburn   1948-52 David M Steele   1952 Albert V Harris   1952-5 Ivor V Powell   1955-61 Peter Jackson   1961-4 Robert Brocklebank   1965-6 William Harris   1966-8 William Watson   1968 Grenville Hair   1968-71 Jimmy Wheeler   1971-5 Bryan Edwards   1975-8 Robert Kennedy   1978 John Napier   1978-81 George Mulhall   1981-2 Roy McFarland

Honours: Div 2 Champions, 1907-8   Div 3 (N) Champions 1928-9   FA Cup Winners 1911

League Career: Elected to Div 2 1903   Promoted to Div 1 1907-8   Relegated to Div 2 1921-2   Relegated to Div 3 (N) 1926-7   Promoted to Div 2 1928-9   Relegated to Div 3 1936-7   Relegated to Div 4 1960-1   Promoted to Div 3 1968-9   Relegated to Div 4 1971-2   Promoted to Div 3 1976-7   Relegated to Div 4 1977-8   Promoted to Div 3 1981-2   Promoted to Div 2 1985

Colours: Claret and amber striped shirts, claret shorts, amber stockings

Change Colours: Amber shirts with white and claret shoulders, amber shorts and stockings

Reserves League: Central Div 2   **'A' Team:** N/A   **Youth:** North Intermediate

---

CLUB RECORDS

Most Appearances for Club: Cyril Podd: Football League 494 + 8   + FA Cup 30 + 1   + League Cup 33 + 1 **Total 557   + 9 subs**

Most Capped Player: Harry Hampton, 9, N Ireland 1914-18   **For England:** Evelyn Lintott 4

Record Goalscorer in a Match: Albert Whitehurst, 7 v Tranmere Rovers, (8-0) (H), Div 3 (N), 6 March 1929

Record League Goalscorer in a Season: David Layne 34, Div 4, 1961-62   **In All Competitions:** David Layne 36 (League 34   + FA Cup 2), 1961-2

Record League Goalscorer in a Career: Bobby Campbell, 88, 1906-13   **In All Competitions:** Bobby Campbell, 96 (League 85   + FA Cup 2   + League Cup 9) 1979-83, 1984-

Record Transfer Fee Received: £50,000 from Walsall for Steve Baines, July 1980

Record Transfer Fee Paid: £31,000 to Burnley for Billy Ingham, August 1980

Best Performances: League: 5th Div 1 1910-1   **FA Cup:** Winners   **League/Milk Cup:** 5th Round 1965

Most League Points: (3pts for win) 91, Div 4, 1981-2   (2pts for win) 63, Div 3 (S), 1971-2

Most League Goals: 128, Div 3 (N), 1928-9

Record League Victory and Most Goals Scored in a League Match: 11-1 v Rotherham United, Div 3 (N), 25 Sept 1928

Most Goals Scored in a First Class Match: 11-1 v Rotherham United, Div 3 (N), 28 Sept 1928   11-3 v Walker Celtic FA Cup 1st Round Replay, 1 Dec 1937

Record League Defeat: 1-9 v Colchester United, Div 4, 30 Dec 1961

Oldest Player in League Match:

Youngest Player in League Match:

Most Consecutive Undefeated League Matches: 21 1969

Longest Run of Undefeated Home League Matches: 25 1976-77

Longest Run Without Home League Win: 10 1963

Most Consecutive League Wins: 10 1983-84

Most Consecutive League Defeats: 8 1933

League Matches Without a Win: 16 1948

Away League Matches: 10 1969

Away League Win: 29 1926-27

Home League Wins: 9 1953, 1962

Away League Wins: 5 1929, 1981, 1984-85

Club Statistician for the Directory: Terry Frost

BRADFORD CITY

PLAYERS NAME Ht Wt Birthdate	Honours	Birthplace Transfers	Clubs	APPEARANCES				GOALS			
				League	Milk Cup	FA Cup	Other Comps	League	Milk Cup	FA Cup	Other Comps
GOALKEEPERS											
Peter Litchfield 6.1 13.9 27.7.56		Manchester £10,000	Droylsden PNE	 149	 16	2 8	 1				
DEFENDERS											
Greg Abbott 5.9 10.7 14.12.63		Coventry	Coventry City (A) Bradford City	 119+8	 8+1	 7	 3+1	 19	 1	 3	 1
Tony Clegg 6.0 11.5 8.11.65		Bradford	Bradford City (A)	25+5		1	4	1			
David Evans 5.11 12.6 6.5.61		Solihull £25,000 F	Aston Villa (A) Halifax Town Bradford City	2 18 80	 8 8	 11 4	 1 4	 9 1	 1 		
Gavin Oliver 5.11 12.10 6.4.61		Felling £20,000	Sheffield Wed. Brighton (L) Tranmere Rovers (L) Bradford City	14+6 15+1 17 27	1+3	1	 1 2	 1			
Peter Jackson* 6.1 12.6 6.4.61		Bradford	Bradford City (A)	257+11	25	10+1	3	24	1		
Chris Withe 5.10 11.3 25.9.62		Liverpool F	Newcastle U. (A) Bradford City	2 123	 9	 7	 4	 1			
Nigel Beaumont 6.1 13.5 11.2.67		Hemsworth	Bradford City	2		2+2					
MIDFIELD											
John Hendrie 5.8½ 10.11 24.10.63	SY	Lennoxtown F	Coventry City (A) Hereford United (L) Bradford City	15+6 6 88	2 8	 5	 3	2 19	 2	 2	 2
Stuart McCall† 5.6 10.2 10.6.44		Leeds	Bradford City (A)	155+3	12	5	6	21	2	1	1
Martin Singleton 5.9 10.0 2.8.63	EY	Banbury £20,000	Coventry City (A) Bradford City	20+3 52+1	4+1 4	 2	 1	 2			
Steve O'Shaughnessy 6.2 13.1 15.10.67	WY	Wrexham F	Leeds United Bradford City								
Carl Goddard 10.7 5.7 29.12.67	EY	Leeds F	Manchester U. (A) Bradford City								
FORWARDS											
Bobby Campbell 6.0 12.7 13.4.56	NI (2), Y	Belfast F £10,000 F F Brisbane City F £70,000 £20,000	Aston Villa (A) Halifax Town (L) Huddersfield Town Sheffield United Huddersfield Town Halifax Town Bradford City Derby County Bradford City	7+3 14+1 30+1 35+2 7 19+3 147+1 11 142	1 3 1 15 8	 6 6	 2	1 9 11 3 76 4 19	 1 9 2	 2 3	 1
Mark Ellis 5.9 10.5 6.1.62		Bradford	Bradford City	137+16	11+4	8+1	5	13	1		
Don Goodman 5.9 10.8 9.5.66		Leeds	Bradford City	42+5	1+1	2+2	1+1	9		4	1
Arthur Graham 5.8 11.10 26.10.52	S (10), U23 (3), SC (1), SLC (1)	Glasgow £125,000 £45,000 F	Aberdeen Leeds United Manchester United Bradford City	217+7 222+1 33+4 24+2	41 22 6 4	16+1 12 1 2	9 3 6+1	32 37 7	5 4 1	 3	2 3 1
Ian Ormondroyd 6.4 13.7 22.9.64		Bradford	Thackley Bradford City	 8+4		 1		 3			
Adrian Thorpe 5.7 10.10 25.11.63		Chesterfield £250	Heanor Town Bradford City	 6+4	 3		 1	 1			 1

ADDITIONAL CONTRACT PROFESSIONALS

APPRENTICES

NON-CONTRACT PLAYERS

Phil Kitching, Russ Latapy, Robert Moverly, Bobby Whellans

VALLEY PARADE GROUND   Bradford BD8 7DY   Capacity: 16,000 seats

Record Attendance: 39,146 v Burnley, FA Cup Round 4, 11 Mar 1911

Smallest Home Attendance for a First Class Match: 1,249 v Hereford United, Div 4, 15 May 1981

Record Receipts: £27,000 v Southampton, FA Cup Round 6, 6 Mar 1976

Season Tickets: Stand: £100.00 (juvenile/OAP £60.00); Ground: £50.00 (juvenile/OAP £30.00)

Cost of Stand Tickets: £5.00 (juvenile/OAP £3.00) **Ground:** £3.00 (juvenile/OAP £1.50)

Match and Ticket Information: Bradford 306062 (2 weeks prior)

Car Parking: Street parking in nearby side streets. None at Valley Parade or South Parade

Nearest Railway Station: Bradford Exchange (0274 733994/8)

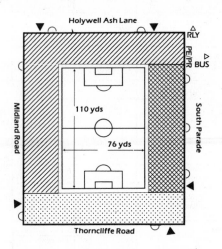

How to get to the ground

From North: Follow signs Bradford A650. 0.3m after junction with A6036 (Ring Road) turn left into Valley Parade for Bradford City FC

From East: Follow signs Bradford A647 then at cross roads turn right A6036 (S.P. Keighley). In 2.2m at cross roads turn left A650. In 0.3m turn left into Valley Parade for Bradford City FC

From South, West: Use M62 and A606(M) (S.P. Bradford) then at roundabout take 4th exit into Ring Road A6036 (S.P. Keighley). In 4.8m at crossroads turn left A650. In 0.3m turn left into Valley Parade for Bradford City FC

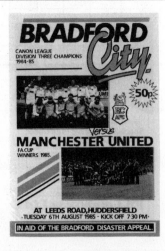

Price of 1986-7 Programme: 50p
Number of Pages: 12
Subscriptions: Subscriptions on request to club

Local Newspapers: Telegraph and Argus Bradford Star

Local Radio Stations: Pennine Radio (235 medium wave), BBC Radio Leeds (388 medium wave)

 # BRENTFORD

The 1985/86 season saw Brentford finish in their usual middle of table position but it could have been so different. At Christmas 'The Bees' were challenging for promotion with the defence in excellent form. It was rather surprising considering the loss of some of the club's more influential players. Chris Kamara (to Swindon and Keith Cassells to Mansfield) had left the club while injury curtailed the career of Gary Roberts and Francis Joseph took longer to recover than was expected.

The New Year saw the challenge fade as they went ten home games without a win only breaking the sequence in the final match of the season. Away from home meanwhile the good form continued and Brentford ended the season with the third best away record in the division. Amazingly this was the third time in this decade the Bees had a better away than home record.

Brentford didn't last long in the Cup competitions. After beating Cambridge in the Milk Cup they held Sheffield Wednesday in an exciting match at Griffin Park and were unlucky to lose the second leg. The FA Cup saw immediate elimination at the hands of Bristol Rovers while the Freight Rover Trophy saw draws against Derby and Gillingham which wasn't enough to see the Bees progress.

Player of the Year Gary Phillips (in goal), Jamie Murray and Danis Salman (in defence), the ever-reliable Bob Booker (mainly in midfield) and Robbie Cooke (the top scorer who toiled away with little support up front) were the mainstays of the team, all making forty-plus appearances. Terry Hurlock looked likely to join them until his club record transfer to Reading in February while Roger Joseph was the find of the season, improving with every game.

If the quality close season signings promised by Frank McLintock, especially a big centre forward, materialise then there is every reason to believe that the 1986/87 season will see Brentford promoted to Division 2.   Frank Coumbe and Graham Haynes

Back Row L to R: Brent Hills (Youth Team Manager), Sid Rudgley (Youth Coach), Gary Stevens, Keith Millen, Terry Evans, Bob Booker, Jamie Bates, Paul Maddy, Ron Woolnough (Physiotherapist). **Middle Row:** Robbie Cooke, Richard Key, Gary Phillips, Jamie Murray. **Front Row:** Terry Mancini (Coach), Phil Bater, Andy Sinton, Roger Joseph, Martin Lange (Chairman), Steve Wignall, Barry Evans (KLM Marketing Manager), Francis Joseph, Ian Holoway, Steve Allen, Frank McLintock (Manager).

BRENTFORD

DIVISION THREE: 10th   **FA CUP:** 1st ROUND   **MILK CUP:** 2nd ROUND

MATCH	DATE	COMPE-TITION	VENUE	OPPONENTS	RESULT	HALF TIME	L'GUE POS'N	GOALSCORERS/GOAL TIMES	ATTEN-DANCE
1	A 17	CL	H	Wolverhampton W.	W	2-1	0-0		Bullivant 46, Murray 86	5,576
2	20	MC1/1	A	Cambridge United	D	1-1	0-1		Evans 89	(1,794)
3	24	CL	A	Bristol Rovers	W	1-0	1-0	3	Lynch 8	(4,140)
4	26	CL	H	Bournemouth	W	1-0	0-0	3	Cooke 49	4,238
5	31	CL	A	Wigan Athletic	L	0-4	0-3	6		(2,871)
6	S 3	MC1/2	H	Cambridge United	W	2-0	0-0		Cooke (pen) 56, Hurlock 57	2,512
7	7	CL	H	Plymouth Argyle	D	1-1	1-0	3	Lynch 25	3,927
8	13	CL	A	Doncaster Rovers	L	0-1	0-0	9		(2,831)
9	17	CL	H	Reading	L	1-2	1-1	12	Booker 33	6,351
10	21	CL	A	Lincoln City	L	0-3	0-1	16		(1,856)
11	25	MC2/1	H	Sheffield Wednesday	D	2-2	1-0		Alexander 45, 88	5,352
12	28	CL	A	Rotherham United	D	1-1	1-0	17	Alexander 34	3,257
13	O 1	CL	A	Darlington	W	5-3	3-0	12	Alexander 2, 59, Lynch 14, 78, Booker 23	(2,477)
14	5	CL	H	Swansea City	W	1-0	1-0	8	Alexander 6	3,508
15	12	CL	A	Bolton Wanderers	W	2-1	1-1	6	Wignall 35, Cooke 63	(4,106)
16	15	MC2/2	A	Sheffield Wednesday	L	0-2	0-1			(11,132)
17	19	CL	H	Newport County	D	0-0	0-0	7		3,646
18	22	CL	A	Walsall	W	2-1	1-0	7	Wignall 41, Hurlock 65	(4,318)
19	26	CL	A	Blackpool	L	0-4	0-0	8		(5,548)
20	N 2	CL	H	Cardiff City	W	3-0	3-0	6	Hurlock 3, Cooke 15, Lynch 16	3,934
21	6	CL	H	Derby County	D	3-3	1-1	9	Murray 28, Cooke 68, Butler 83	4,707
22	9	CL	A	Bristol City	D	0-0	0-0	10		(6,596)
23	16	FAC1	H	Bristol Rovers	L	1-3	1-1		Evans 41	4,716
24	23	CL	H	Chesterfield	W	1-0	1-0	7	Roberts 18	3,502
25	30	CL	A	York City	L	0-1	0-0	9		(3,674)
26	D 14	CL	H	Bury	W	1-0	0-0	7	Sinton (pen) 89	4,038
27	22	CL	H	Bristol Rovers	W	1-0	0-0	5	Cooke 61	5,742
28	28	CL	A	Bournemouth	D	0-0	0-0	6		(4,006)
29	J 4	CL	A	Cardiff City	L	0-1	0-0	10		(3,398)
30	11	CL	H	Wigan Athletic	L	1-3	0-0	11	Booker 46	4,048
31	15	FRT	H	Derby County	D	0-0	0-0			2,531
32	18	CL	A	Wolverhampton W.	W	4-1	3-0	8	Cooke 16, 37, Sinton 25, 51	(3,420)
33	21	CL	H	Notts County	D	1-1	0-1	8	Evans 50	4,002
34	24	CL	H	Doncaster Rovers	L	1-3	0-1	9	Cooke 77	3,678
35	29	FRT	A	Gillingham	D	1-1	1-0		Murray 23	(1,464)
36	F 1	CL	A	Plymouth Argyle	L	0-2	0-1	9		(4,873)
37	4	CL	H	Walsall	L	1-3	1-0	10	Alexander 15	3,015
38	M 1	CL	A	Rotherham United	W	2-1	1-0	11	Booker 44, Cooke 56	(3,268)
39	8	CL	A	Swansea City	L	0-2	0-0	12		(3,683)
40	11	CL	H	Newport County	W	2-1	1-1	10	Lynch 22, Cooke 87	(1,508)
41	14	CL	H	Bolton Wanderers	D	1-1	0-0	11	Booker 57	3,284
42	18	CL	A	Gillingham	W	2-1	0-0	8	Booker 50, Cooke 76	(3,582)
43	22	CL	H	Blackpool	D	1-1	0-0	9	Cooke 80	3,528
44	29	CL	H	Notts County	W	4-0	3-0	7	Burke 5, Cooke 27, 42, Holloway 80	(3,857)
45	31	CL	H	Gillingham	L	1-2	1-1	8	Cooke 20	4,702
46	A 5	CL	A	Derby County	D	1-1	0-0	10	Holloway 82	(1,026)
47	13	CL	H	Bristol City	L	1-2	1-2	10	Millen 17	3,702
48	16	CL	H	Reading	L	1-3	0-1	12	Murray 78	(6,635)
49	19	CL	A	Chesterfield	W	3-1	0-1	10	Cooke 75, Butler 78, Booker 87	(2,344)
50	22	CL	H	Lincoln City	L	0-1	0-1	11		3,011
51	26	CL	H	York City	D	3-3	1-0	11	Hood og 14, Joseph R 52, Joseph F 57	2,864
52	M 3	CL	A	Bury	D	0-0	0-0	12		(2,953)
53	5	CL	H	Darlington	W	2-1	1-1	10	Millen 43, Cooke 77	2,824

Best Home League Attendance: 6,351 v Reading 17/9   **Smallest: 2,824 v Darlington 5/5**   **Av Home Att: 3,962**

Goal Scorers: **Compared with 84-85: −86**

League (58): Cooke 17, Booker 7, Lynch 6, Alexander 5, Murray 3, Sinton 3 (1 pen), Butler 2, Holloway 2, Hurlock 2, Millen 2, Wignall 2, Bullivant 1, Burke 1, Evans 1, Joseph F 1, Joseph R 1, Roberts 1, Opponents 1
Milk Cup (5): Alexander 2, Cooke 1 (pen), Evans 1, Hurlock 1
FA Cup (1): Evans 1
FRT (1): Murray 1

74

Phillips	Salman	Murray	Millen	Wignall	Hurlock	Lynch	Cooke	Booker	Butler	Bullivant	Evans	Joseph R	Torrance (NC)	Alexander	Cooper (L)	Roberts	Sinton	Key (NC)	Holloway (L)	Burke (L)	Joseph F	Referee	
1	2	3	4	5	6	7*	8	9	10	11†	12											D Axcell	1
1		3	4		6	7	8	9		10	5	2	11									**H Taylor**	2
1	2	3		5	6	7	8	9		10	4		11									K Cooper	3
1	2	3		4	6	7	8	9		10	5		11									J Ashworth	4
1	2	3	10*	4	6	12	8	9			5	7	11									J Lovatt	5
1	10	3	4	5	6	7	8	9				2*	11	12								**K Miller**	6
1	2	3	4	5	6	7	8	9					12	10	11*							K Baker	7
1	2	3	4	5	6	7	8	9				10		11								G Napthine	8
1	2	3	4	5	6	7	8	9				10*	12	11								J Moules	9
1	2	3	4	5	6†	7	8*	9				10	12	11								T Fitzharris	10
1	2	3	4	5	6	7	8	9				11	10									**M James**	11
1	2	3	4	5	6	7	8	9					12	10	11*							I Borrett	12
1	2	3	4	5	6	7	12	9*		8			10	11								D Phillips	13
1	2*	3	4	5	7	6	9			8			12	10	11							D Hedges	14
1		3	4	5	6	7	8	9				2		10	11							J Lloyd	15
1		3	4	5	6	7	8	9				2		10	11							**K Walmsley**	16
1	7	3	4	5	6	12	8	9				2		10	11*							K Barratt	17
1	4	3		5	6	7	8	9				2	11	10								D Shaw	18
1	4	3		5	6	7	8	9				2	11	10								D Hutchinson	19
1	2	3		5	6	7	8	9	12		4			11	10*							M Bodenham	20
1	2	3		5	6	7	8	9	10		4			11								A Gunn	21
1	2	3		5	6	7	8†	9	10		4			11								M Scott	22
1	2	3		5		7	8	9		6	4			11	10							**Alan Robinson**	23
1	2	3		5				9	8	6	4			11	10	7						B Stevens	24
1	2	3		5*	6	12		9	8		4			11	10	7						N Midgley	25
1	2	3	4		6		11	9	10		5					7	8					P Vanes	26
1	4	3			6		10	11			5	2	7	9			8					B Hill	27
1	4	3			6		10	11			5	2	7	9			8					R Groves	28
1	4	3	12		6		10	11			5	2*	7	9			8					A Seville	29
1	4	3	12				10	11*	9		5	2	7	6			8					L Robinson	30
1	4	3	6				11	10	9*		5	2	7	12			8					**D Hedges**	31
	4	3			6		11	10			5	2	7	9			8	1				K Breen	32
	4	3			6	7	10				5	2	11	9			8	1				K Miller	33
	4	3			6	7	10	11	9*		5	2		12			8	1				K Cooper	34
1	4	3			6	7	10	11			5	2		9			8					**D Axcell**	35
1	4	3*	9		6	7	10	11			5	2		12			8					R Groves	36
1	4		3		6	7	10	11			5	2		9			8					M Bodenham	37
1	2	3	4	5		7	10	11		6				9			8					K Lupton	38
1	2	3	4	5		7*	10	11		6†		12		9			8					A Gunn	39
1	2	3	4			7	10	11		6	5			9			8					T Jones	40
1	5	3	4			7	10	6				2		9			8		11			M James	41
1	5	3	4				10	11		12		2	6*	9			8		7			M Scott	42
1	5	3	4			7	10	6	12			2		9*			8		11			J Deakin	43
1	5	3	4				10	6	9			2					8		11	7		N Glover	44
1	2	3	4	5			10	6	9								8		7	11		I Borrett	45
1	2	3	4	5		12	10	6	9*								8		7	11		J Deakin	46
1	2	3	4	5		12	10	6	9								8		7	11*		M Heath	47
1		3	4	5			10	6	9			2					8		11	7*	12	T Holbrook	48
1		3	4	5			10	6	9			2					8		7	11*	12	I Hendrick	49
1	5*	3	4				10	6	9			2					8		11	7	12	L Robinson	50
1		3	4	5			10	6				2					8		11	7	9	V Callow	51
1		3	4			7	10	6	12			2					8		11	5	9*	T Mills	52
1		3	4			5	10	6				2					8		11	7	9	J Ashworth	53
43	40	45	29	28	27	28	43	44	15	7	18	29	18	25	9	3	26	3	13	10	3	League Appearances	
	2			5	1		3	1	1	1	1	3	4								3	Substitute Appearances	
4	2	4	4	3	4	4	4	4			1	1	3	3	2	1						Milk Cup Appearances	
1	1		1		1	1	1	1			1	1		1	1							FA Cup Appearances	
2	2	2	1		1	2	2	1	1			2	2	1	1-1		2					FR Trophy Appearances	

Players on Loan: Cooper (Q.P.R.), Holloway (Wimbledon), Burke (Q.P.R.)
Departures: Hurlock (Reading), Salman (Millwall), Butler, Torrance (Maidstone Utd)

Brentford FC

Sponsored by
KLM

'THE BEES'

Formed: 1889
Turned Professional: 1899   **Ltd Co:** 1901

Previous Managers: A committee handled team matters until 1903
1903-6 Richard Molyneux (Secretary/Manager)   1906-8 W G Brown (Secretary/Manager)
1908-12 Fred Halliday (Secretary/Manager)   1912-5 Ephraim 'Dusty' Rhodes (Player/Manager)
1915-21 Fred Halliday (Secretary/Manager)   1921-4 Archie Mitchell (Player/Manager 1921/22 then
Secretary/Manager)   1924-6 Fred Halliday (Secretary/Manager)   1926-49 Harry Curtis (Secretary/Manager)
1949-52 A H 'Jackie' Gibbons (Secretary/Manager)   1952-3 Jim Bain   1953 Tommy Lawton
(Player/Manager)   1953/7 Bill Dodgin (Senior)   1957-65 Malcolm McDonald   1965-6 Tommy Cavanagh
1966-7 Billy Gray   1967-9 Jimmy Sirrel   1969-73 Frank Blunstone   1973-5 Mike Everitt
1975-6 John Docherty   1976-80 Bill Dodgin (Junior)   1980-4 Fred Callaghan
Honours: Champions Div 2, 1934-5   Champions Div 3 (S), 1932-3   Champions Div 4 1962-3
League Career: Founder Members of Div 3 1920   Div (S) 1921-33
Promoted to Div 2 1932-3   Promoted to Div 1 1934-5   Relegated to Div 2 1946-7
Relegated to Div 3 (S) 1953-4   Relegated to Div 4 1962   Promoted to Div 3 1962-3
Relegated to Div 4 1965-6   Promoted to Div 3 1971-2   Relegated to Div 4 1972-3
Promoted to Div 3 1977-8
Colours: Red and white striped shirts, black shorts, red stockings with white turnover
Change Colours: Navy/shadow pin stripe shirts, navy shorts and sky stockings with 3 white stripes
Reserves League: Capital League   **Youth League:** S E Counties

---

CLUB RECORDS

Most Appearances for Club: Ken Coote: Football League 514 + FA Cup 35 + League Cup 10 **Total 559**
Most Capped Player: Idris Hopkins, 12, Wales   **For England:** Billy Scott and Leslie Smith, one each
Record Goalscorer in a Match: Jack Holliday, 5 v Luton Town 5-5, Div3 (S) (A) 28.01.33   Billy Scott, 5 v Barnsley 8-1,
Div 2, (h), 15.12.34   Peter McKennan 5 v Bury 8-2, Div 2 (h), 18.02.49
Record League Goalscorer in a Season: Jack Holliday, 38, Div 3 (S), 1932-3   **In All Competitions:** Jack Holliday, 39
(League 38 + FA Cup 1), 1932-3
Record League Goalscorer in a Career: Jim Towers, 153, 1954-61   **In All Competitions:** Jim Towers, 163 (League
153 + FA Cup 9 + League Cup 1) 1954-61
Record Transfer Fee Received: £95,000 from Reading for Terry Hurlock, Feb 1986
Record Transfer Fee Paid: £78,000 to Bury for Alan Whitehead, July 1981
Best Performances: League: 5th Div 1 1935-6   **FA Cup:** 6th Round, 1938, 1946, 1949   **League/Milk Cup:** 4th Round
1982-3
Most League Points: (2pts for a win): 62, Div 3 (S), 1932-3   62, Div 4, 1962-3   (3pts for a win): 68, Div 3, 1981-2
Record League Victory and Most Goals Scored in a League Match: 9-0 v Wrexham, Div 3, 15 Oct 1963
Most Goals Scored in a Cup Tie: 8-0 v Uxbridge, 1st Qualifying Round, 31 Oct 1903
Record League Defeat: 0-7 v Swansea, Div 3 (S), 8 Nov 1924
Oldest Player in League Match: Dai Hopkins 39 yrs 7 months 13 days
Youngest Player in League Match: Danis Salman, 15 yrs 8 months 3 days

Most Consecutive Undefeated League Matches: 16 1932 1967	**League Matches Without a Win:** 14 1925, 1928, 1947
Longest Run of Undefeated Home League Matches: 24 1934-35	**Away League Matches:** 9 1936
Longest Run Without Home League Win: 11 1947	**Away League Win:** 21 1965-66
Most Consecutive League Wins: 9 1932	**Home League Wins:** 21 1929-30
Most Consecutive League Defeats: 9 1925, 1928	**Away League Wins:** 5 1956, 1981

Brentford won all 21 home games in season 1929-30, they also played 44 away League games without a draw between 1923-25.

Club Statisticians for the Directory: Graham Haynes and Frank Coumbe

BRENTFORD

PLAYERS NAME Ht Wt Birthdate	Honours	Birthplace Transfers	Clubs	League	Milk Cup	FA Cup	Other Comps	League	Milk Cup	FA Cup	Other Comps
GOALKEEPERS											
Gary Phillips† 5.11 14.5 20.9.61	ESP (1)	St Albans £5,000	Barnet Brentford	 64	 4	9 1	 9				
DEFENDERS											
Terry Evans 6.4 12.7 12.4.65		London Small fee	Hillingdon Brentford	 18+1	 1	 1	 2	 1	 1	 1	
Roger Joseph 5.10 9.3 24.2.65		Paddington F	Southall Brentford	 30+1	 3		 2	 1			
Jamie Murray 5.9 10.12 27.12.58		Glasgow Small fee £27,500	Rivet Sports Cambridge United Sunderland (L) Brentford	 213+16 1 91	 11+2 8	 10+2 5	 7	 3 			 1
Danis Salman 5.10 11.8 12.3.60	EY	Famagusta	Brentford (A)	316+9	16+1	16+1	10	8			
Steve Wignall 5.11 11.11 17.9.54		Liverpool F £20,000 £12,000	Liverpool (NC) Doncaster Rovers Colchester United Brentford	 127+3 279+2 64	 3+1 21 5	 8+1 26 4	 2 8	 1 22 	 3 	 3 	 2
MIDFIELD											
Phil Bater 5.10½ 12.12 26.10.55	WU21 (2)	Cardiff £50,000 £10,000 F	Bristol Rovers (A) Wrexham Bristol Rovers Brentford	211+1 73 63+7	13 5 1+1	13 6 6	 2				
Paul Maddy 5.10 10.9 17.8.62	WU21 (2), Y	Cwmcam F £10,000 F	Cardiff City (A) Hereford United (L) Swansea City Hereford United Brentford	35+8 9 18+2 75+2	 5	3 2	 8	3 3 16			 1
Keith Millen 6.1 12.0 26.9.66		Croydon	Brentford	45+3	4		6	2			
Andy Sinton 5.7 10.7 19.3.66	ES	Newcastle Small fee	Cambridge U. (A) Brentford	90+3	16	13	2	13	1		1
FORWARDS											
Robbie Cooke 5.9 10.8 16.2.57		Rotherham F £12,000 £13,000 £20,000	Mansfield Town Grantham Peterborough U. Cambridge U. Brentford	7+8 115 62+3 67+1	 9 4 4	1 13 2 1	 2	1 51 14 29	 7 3 1	 10 	 4
Bob Booker* 6.2 12.4 25.1.58		Watford F	Bedmund Social Brentford	 199+30	 16+1	 10+3	 9	 31		 1	 2
Francis Joseph 5.10 12.0 6.3.60		London £1,000 £40,000	Hillingdon Borough Wimbledon Brentford	 42+9 91+4	 2 13	 1 7	 2	 14 43	 3	 3	 2
Gary Stevens 6.2 12.0 30.8.54		Birmingham £14,000 £20,000	Evesham United Cardiff City Shrewsbury Town Brentford	 138+12 144+6	 9 8	 4+2 4	 2	 44 30	 3 2	 1	
Ian Holloway 5.7 9.12 12.3.63		Kingswood £35,000	Bristol Rovers Wimbledon Brentford	104+7 19	10 3	8 1	5	14 2		2	

ADDITIONAL CONTRACT PROFESSIONALS
Richard Key (G)

APPRENTICES

NON-CONTRACT PLAYERS

GRIFFIN PARK
Braemar Road, Brentford, Middx TW8 0NT

Record Attendance: 39,626 v Preston North End, FA Cup Round 6, 5 Mar 1938

Smallest Home Attendance for a First Class Match: 2,024 v Walsall, Div 3 (S), 5 Dec 1927

Record Receipts: £55,002 v Liverpool, Milk Cup Round 2, 4 Oct 1983

Season Tickets: Stand: £90; Ground: £54

Cost of Stand Tickets: £4.30, £4.80; **Terraces:** £2.80 (£1.00 Juveniles/OAPs, under 12's free subject to identity card) (50p extra for non-members)

Match and Ticket Information: Postal applications with sae and remittance by post or by personal application. Latest information on the Club ring Bee-line on 01-571 5888

Car Parking: Street parking available

Nearest Railway Station: Brentford or South Ealing (Tube) Piccadilly Line.

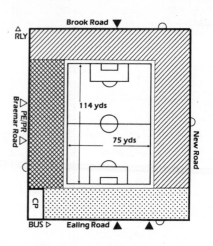

How to get to the ground

From North: Use M1 or A1 then A406 North Circular Road to Chiswick then follow signs South Circular Road. In 0.3m turn right A315 (S.P. Brentford). In 0.5m turn right into Ealing Road for Brentford FC
From East: Use either A406 North Circular Road then as above or South Circular Road A205. Cross Kew Bridge and turn left A315 (S.P. Brentford). In 0.5m turn right into Ealing Road for Brentford FC
From South: Use A240/A3/M3/ or A316 to junction with South Circular Road A205. Cross Kew Bridge and turn left A315 (S.P. Brentford). In 0.5m turn right into Ealing Road for Brentford FC
From West: Use M4 until junction 1, leave Motorway and follow signs South Circular Road. In 0.3m turn right A315 (S.P. Brentford). In 0.5m turn right into Ealing Road for Brentford FC

Price of 1986-7 Programme: 60p
Number of Pages: 24
Subscriptions: Apply to club for details

Local Newspapers: Brentford & Chiswick Times, Ealing Gazette, Middlesex Chronicle, Hounslow Informer, Weekend Recorder

BRIGHTON & HOVE ALBION Division 2

Chairman
B Bedson

Directors
T Appleby
J Campbell
F Shannon
D Sizen
G Stanley
P Kent
R Bloom

Secretary/Chief Executive
R A Pavey (0273 739535)

Manager
Alan Mullery MBE

Club Coach
Peter Suddaby

Youth Development Officer
Barry Lloyd

Commercial Department
(0273 778230)

A season that started quietly, and promised much in the New Year, eventually fizzled out and ended in uproar.

The lowest crowds for twenty-two years watched the home league games in which too many points were dropped for a serious promotion challenge. The heights were rarely reached; Carlisle were knocked for six but perhaps the best football was played in the nil-all draw with Sheffield United; the depths were reached against Shrewsbury. Seventy-two goals were scored at the Goldstone but 30 of them landed in Albion's net. Away from home, the team often performed well, particularly at Grimsby, Leeds and Portsmouth in December, and Charlton and Blackburn in the New Year.

The disappointing end to the season began at Easter. Lying on the fringe of the promotion race, Albion lost vital games against Crystal Palace and Portsmouth, won only one of the last ten games, and eventually finished eleventh. The only consolation was that Charlton and Wimbledon proved to be consistent enough anyway.

In the FA Cup, there were excellent performances at Newcastle and Hull with a fighting comeback at snow-bound Peterborough. Reaching the quarter-finals for only the second time ever, Albion were prevented from performing before their highest crowd for three years by well-organised Southampton. In the Milk Cup, Brighton cruised past Bradford City but were outclassed by Liverpool.

Player of the year was Dean Saunders who hit 19 goals in his first Goldstone season. Of the two other signings, Dennis Mortimer's thoughtful play was appreciated, but Justin Fashanu, injured for most of the season, managed only two goals. The most consistent performer was Terry Connor.

The season suddenly ended in controversy. Chris Cattlin, who had no money to spend all season, was sacked and predictably replaced by former boss Alan Mullery. There can be no denying that Cattlin was popular with many supporters. There can also be no denying that the Mullery years were the club's most successful. Whether he can repeat that success on much more limited resources remains to be seen.

Tim Carder

Back Row L to R: Daren Newman, Steve Gatting, Gerry Armstrong, Gary O'Reilly, Franco Massimo, David Gipp. **Middle Row:** Peter Suddaby (Coach), Dale Jasper, Terry Connor, Perry Digweed, Eric Young, Sean Edwards, Mike Yaxley (Physiotherapist), Barry Lloyd (Coach)
Front Row: Kieran O'Regan, Steve Penney, Dean Saunders, Alan Mullery (Manager), Danny Wilson Dennis Mortimer (now with Birmingham), Chris Hutchings.

BRIGHTON & HOVE ALBION

DIVISION TWO: 11th   **FA CUP:** 6th ROUND   **MILK CUP:** 3rd ROUND

MATCH	DATE		COMPE-TITION	VENUE	OPPONENTS	RESULT			HALF TIME	L'GUE POS'N	GOALSCORERS/GOAL TIMES	ATTEN-DANCE
1	A	17	CL	H	Grimsby Town	D	2-2		0-1		Biley 74, Connor 80	9,787
2		20	CL	A	Barnsley	L	2-3		1-2		Connor 18, Saunders 48	(5,051)
3		24	CL	H	Bradford City	W	2-1		1-1	7	Wilson (pen) 23, Connor 51	9,263
4		27	CL	H	Sheffield United	D	0-0		0-0	8		10,128
5		31	CL	A	Middlesbrough	W	1-0		1-0	9	Wilson (pen) 11	(5,543)
6	S	4	CL	H	Leeds United	L	0-1		0-0	9		9,798
7		7	CL	H	Blackburn Rovers	W	3-1		1-1	7	Biley 21, Ferguson 65, Saunders 77	8,159
8		14	CL	A	Millwall	W	1-0		0-0	4	Ferguson 68	(8,013)
9		21	CL	A	Wimbledon	W	2-0		1-0	4	Wilson 2, Ferguson 47	9,973
10		25	MC2/1	H	**Bradford City**	W	5-2		3-1		**Wilson 3 (5,10,42), Keown 58, Penney 83**	6,664
11		28	CL	A	Fulham	L	0-1		0-0	4		(5,861)
12	O	2	FMC	H	W.B.A.	L	1-2		1-2		**Wilson (pen) 36**	4,649
13		5	CL	H	Carlisle United	W	6-1		2-0	4	Ferguson 9, Biley 24, Wilson 51, Jacobs 54, Saunders 67, Mortimer 79	8,608
14		7	MC2/2	A	**Bradford City**	W	2-0		1-0		**Biley 19, Ferguson 70**	(5,368)
15		12	CL	A	Stoke City	D	1-1		1-0	5	Hutchings 24	(7,662)
16		16	FMC	A	**Crystal Palace**	W	3-1		2-0		**O'Regan 1, Wilson 25, Keown 69**	(2,207)
17		19	CL	H	Charlton Athletic	L	3-5		1-1	7	Saunders 44, Keown 47, Wilson (pen) 78	11,546
18		26	CL	A	Oldham Athletic	L	0-4		0-1	8		(4,970)
19		29	MC3	A	**Liverpool**	L	0-4		0-1			(15,291)
20	N	2	CL	H	Norwich City	D	1-1		0-0	8	Saunders 54	10,423
21		9	CL	A	Shrewsbury Town	L	1-2		1-2	11	Fashanu	(2,942)
22		16	CL	H	Huddersfield Town	W	4-3		2-1	10	Ferguson 20, Biley (pen) 33, Young 64, Saunders 73	7,952
23		23	CL	A	Sunderland	L	1-2		0-1	11	Connor 59	(14,712)
24		30	CL	H	Hull City	W	3-1		2-1	8	Connor 36, Wilson 43, Fashanu 47	8,487
25	D	7	CL	H	Barnsley	L	0-1		0-0	8		8,819
26		14	CL	A	Grimsby Town	W	2-0		2-0	8	Connor 10, 21	(5,320)
27		20	CL	A	Bradford City	L	2-3		0-2	8	Wilson (pen) 63, Saunders 69	(4,318)
28		26	CL	H	Portsmouth	W	2-1		1-1	8	Saunders 18, Connor 72	15,265
29		28	CL	A	Leeds United	W	3-2		1-0	7	Connor 21, Snodin (og) 54, Pearce 89	13,110
30	J	1	CL	H	Crystal Palace	W	2-0		1-0	5	Saunders 28, Wilson (pen) 57	15,469
31		4	FAC3	A	**Newcastle United**	W	2-0		1-0		**Young 1, Saunders 82**	(24,643)
32		18	CL	H	Middlesbrough	D	3-3		1-2	5	Connor 39, 74, Saunders 86	10,106
33		25	FAC4	A	**Hull City**	W	3-2		2-1		**Saunders 19, Connor 20, 78**	(12,228)
34	F	1	CL	A	Sheffield United	L	0-3		0-0	7		(7,367)
35		4	CL	A	Charlton Athletic	D	2-2		1-0	8	Penney 39, Saunders 67	(5,932)
36		15	FAC5	A	**Peterborough United**	D	2-2		0-0		**Saunders 75, Jacobs 82**	(15,812)
37		22	CL	A	Wimbledon	D	0-0		0-0	6		(5,797)
38	M	3	FAC5R	H	**Peterborough United**	W	1-0		0-0		**Saunders 79**	19,010
39		8	FAC6	H	**Southampton**	L	0-2		0-2			25,069
40		15	CL	H	Stoke City	W	2-0		1-0	7	Wilson 38, Mortimer 88	8,783
41		18	CL	A	Blackburn Rovers	W	4-1		1-0	6	Connor 44, 82, Wilson 49, Saunders 53	(3,616)
42		22	CL	H	Millwall	W	1-0		0-0	5	Young 62	9,370
43		29	CL	A	Crystal Palace	L	0-1		0-1	5		(9,124)
44		31	CL	H	Portsmouth	L	2-3		0-3	6	Saunders 54, O'Regan 87	16,640
45	A	2	CL	H	Oldham Athletic	D	1-1		0-0	7	Saunders 62	8,200
46		5	CL	A	Norwich City	L	0-3		0-0	8		(15,155)
47		12	CL	H	Shrewsbury Town	L	0-2		0-0	8		7,210
48		16	CL	H	Fulham	L	2-3		1-1	9	Wilson 3, Connor 49	6,225
49		19	CL	A	Huddersfield Town	L	0-1		0-0	9		(5,469)
50		26	CL	H	Sunderland	W	3-1		1-0	9	Venison (og) 19, Saunders 78, Penney 79	9,189
51		29	CL	A	Carlisle United	L	0-2		0-1	10		(4,854)
52	M	2	CL	A	Hull City	L	0-2		0-0	11		(5,459)

Best Home League Attendance: 16,640 v Portsmouth 13/3   **Smallest:** 6,255 v Fulham 16/4   **Av Home Att:** 9,772

Goal Scorers: Compared with 84-85: −1,876

League (64): Saunders 15, Connor 14, Wilson 11 (5 pen), Ferguson 5, Biley 4 (1 pen), Fashanu 2, Mortimer 2, Penney 2, Young 2, Hutchings 1, Jacobs 1, Keown 1, O'Regan 1, Pearce 1, Opponents 2

Milk Cup (7): Wilson 3, Biley 1, Ferguson 1, Keown 1, Penney 1

FA Cup (8): Saunders 4, Connor 2, Jacobs 1, Young 1

FM Cup (4): Wilson 2, O'Regan 1, Keown 1

Moseley	Keown (L)	Hutchings	Wilson	Oliver (L)	O'Reilly	Penney	Biley	Fashanu	Connor	Mortimer	Saunders	O'Regan	Digweed	Pearce	Young	Jacobs	Ferguson	Edwards	Gatting	Newman (A)	Massimo (A)	Referee	
1	2	3*	4	5	6	7	8	9	10	11	12											K Miller	1
1	2		4	5	6	7	8*	9	10	11	12	3										R Nixon	2
			4	2	6	12	8*	9†	10	11	7		1	3	5							N Butler	3
	12		4	2	6	7		9	10	11	8		1	3	5*							A Buksh	4
			4	5	6	7		9*	10	11	12	2	1	3		8						A Banks	5
	2		5	6		7	9		10*	11	8	12	1	3		4						J Moules	6
	2		4	5	6	10				11	8		1	3		7	9					D Vickers	7
			4	6	2	12	10*			11	8		1	3	5	7	9					R Milford	8
			4	6	2		10			11	8		1	3	5	7	9					D Hedges	9
	2		4		6	8	10*			11	12		1	3	5	7	9					C Downey	10
			4	6	2*	8				11	10	12	1	3	5	7	9					J Bray	11
	9	12	4		2*	6	8			11*	10	12	1	3	5	7						D Reeves	12
	2		4		6	5	12	10*		11	8		1	3		7	9					A Ward	13
	2		4		6	10				11	8		1	3	5	7	9					J Hough	14
	2		4	12	6	10*				11	8		1	3	5	7	9					T Simpson	15
1	9	2*	4		6				10	11	8			3	5	7		12				I Borrett	16
	9	2	4	5	6	10				11*	8	12	1	3		7						Alan Robinson	17
1		2*	4	10	6	12				11	8			3	5	7†	9					T Holbrook	18
1	2		4			7*	12	9		11	8	10		3	5	6						K Barratt	19
1	12	7	4	2	6	10*	9			11	8			3	5							D Axcell	20
1	2		4		6		8	10	9	11		7*	12	3	5							T Fitzharris	21
1	2						8	10	4	11	7			3	5	6	9†					R Groves	22
1	2		4		6†		8	9	10	11	7*			3	5	12						D Scott	23
1	2		4				8	9	10	11	7			3	5	6†						E Scales	24
1	2		4				8	9	10	11	7			3	5	6						J Martin	25
	2		4		6		8	9	10	11	7	12	1	3	5*							T Mills	26
			4		6		8	9	10	11	7		1	3	5	2						K Walmsley	27
			4		6		8	9	10	11	7		1	3	5	2						L Shapter	28
			4		6		8	9	10	11	7		1	3	5	2						D Allison	29
			4		6		8	9	10*	11	7		1	3	5	2			12			Alan Robinson	30
			4		6		8	9	10	11	7		1	3	5	2						J Key	31
	2		4		6		8	9	10	11	7		1	3	5							M Dimblebee	32
	2		4		6		8	9	10	11	7		1	3	5							P Tyldesley	33
	2		4		6		8		10	11*	7		1	3	5		9		12			P Vanes	34
	2		4		6		9		10	11	7		1	3†	5				8			R Lewis	35
	2		4		6		8	9*	10	11	7		1	3	5				12			J Worrall	36
	2		4		6		8		10		7		1		5	11			3			D Axcell	37
	2		4		6		8	12	10	9	7		1	3	5				11*			C Downey	38
			4		6		8	12	10	11	7		1	3	5	2*		9				N Midgley	39
	3		4		6		8	9	10	11	7		1		5*	2			12			D Reeves	40
	2		4		6		12	9	10	11	7		1		5	8*			3			M Heath	41
	2*		4		6		12	9	10	11	7		1		5	8			3			R Groves	42
	2		4		6		12	9	10	11	7		1		5	8*			3			J Ball	43
	2		4*		6		8	9	10	11	7	12	1		5				3			E Scales/P Alcock	44
	2						8	9	10	11	7	4	1	3	5				6			I Hemley	45
	2						8	9*	10	11	7	12	1	3	5	4			6			K Baker	46
	2						8	9*	10	11	7	4	1	3					6	5	12	H Taylor	47
	2		4		6		8		10	11	9		1		5	7			3			J Moules	48
	2		4*		6		8		10	11	9	12	1		5	7			3			K Walmsley	49
	2				6		8		10	11	9	12	1	4	5*	7			3			M Scott	50
	2				6		8		10	11	9	5	1	4		7			3			P Tyldesley	51
	2				6		8		10	11	9	4	1			7			5			N Glover	52
9	5	29	33	15	35	30	22	16	33	40	39	6	33	32	32	29	9		14	1		League Appearances	
	2		1			7					3	9							3	1		Substitute Appearances	
1	2	1	3		2	2	2+1	1		3	2	1+1	2	3	3	3	2					Milk Cup Appearances	
	3	5		5	5	0+2	3	5	4	5		5	5	5	3+1	1			1			FA Cup Appearances	
1	2	1+1	2	1	2	1			2	2	1+1	1	2	2	2			0+1				FM Cup Appearances	

Players on Loan: Keown (Arsenal), Oliver (Sheffield Wednesday)

Departures: Ferguson (Colchester Utd), Pearce (Gillingham), Fashanu (Retired injured), Moseley (Cardiff City), Biley (New York Cosmos)

'THE SEAGULLS'

Formed: 1900
Turned Professional: 1901 **Ltd Co:** 1904

Previous Names: Brighton & Hove Rangers 1900-01
Previous Managers: John Jackson   Frank Scott-Walford   John Robson   Charles Webb
Tommy Cook   Don Walsh   Billy Lane   George Curtis   Archie MacAulay   Freddie Goodwin
Pat Saward   Brian Clough   Peter Taylor   Alan Mullery MBE   Mike Bailey   Jimmy Melia
Honours: Southern League Champions 1909-10   FA Charity Shield Winners 1910   Div 3 (S)
Champions 1957-8   Div 4 Champions 1964-5
League Career: Original Members of Div 3 1920   Transferred to Div 3 (S) 1921
Promoted to Div 2 1958-9   Relegated to Div 3 1961-2
Relegated to Div 4 1962-3   Promoted to Div 3 1964-5
Promoted to Div 2 1971-2   Relegated to Div 3 1972-3
Promoted to Div 2 1976-7   Promoted to Div 1 1978-9
Relegated to Div 2 1982-3
Colours: Blue shirts with red and white trim, white shorts with blue trim, blue stockings with white tops
Change Colours: Red shirts and shorts with white trim and stockings
Reserves League: Football Combination   **Youth League:** SE Counties

CLUB RECORDS

Most Appearances for Club: 'Tug' Wilson: Football League 510 + FA Cup 49 + Div 3 (S) Cup 8, 1922-36 **Total 567**
Most Capped Player: Gerry Ryan, 16, Eire   **For England:** Steve Foster, 3
Record Goalscorer in a Match: Arthur Attwood, 6 v Shoreham, 12-0, 1st Qualifying Round, FA Cup, 1.10.33
Adrian Thorne, 5 v Watford (6-0), Div 3 (S), 30.4.58   Jack Doran, 5 v Northampton Town (7-0), Div 3 (S), 05.11.21
Record League Goalscorer in a Season: Peter Ward, 32, Div 3, 1976-7   **In All Competitions:** Peter Ward, 36 (League
32 + FA Cup 1 + League Cup 3)
Record League Goalscorer in a Career: Tommy Cook, 114, 1922-9   **In All Competitions:** Tommy Cook 123 (League
114 + FA Cup 9) 1922-29
Record Transfer Fee Received: £900,000 from Liverpool for Mark Lawrenson, August 1981
Record Transfer Fee Paid: £500,000 to Manchester United for Andy Ritchie, October 1980
Best Performances: League: 13th Div 1 1981-2   **FA Cup:** Finalists 1982-3   **League/Milk Cup:** 5th Round 1978-9
Most League Points: 72 in Div 2, 1984-5   **Most League Goals:** 112, Div 3 (S), 1955-56
Record League Victory: 9-1 v Newport County, Div 3 (S), 18 April 1951, 9-1 v Southend United, Div 3 27 Nov 1965
Most Goals Scored in a League Match: Record Victory (as above) and 9-3 v Swindon Town, Div 3 (S), 18 Sept 1926
Most Goals Scored in a Cup Tie: 10-1 v Wisbech Town 1st Round FA Cup, 13 Nov 1965
Record League Defeat: 0-9 v Middlesbrough, Div 2, 23 Aug 1958
Oldest Player in League Match: Frank Worthington 36 yrs 169 days (11.5.1985)
Youngest Player in League Match: Micky Coway 17 yrs 48 days (28.4.1973)

Most Consecutive Undefeated League Matches: 16 1930-31	**League Matches Without a Win:** 15 1947-48 1972-73
Longest Run of Undefeated Home League Matches: 27 1975-76	**Away League Matches:** 8 1948-49
Longest Run Without Home League Win: 10 1972-73	**Away League Win:** 21 1982-83
Most Consecutive League Wins: 9 1926	**Home League Wins:** 14 1955-56, 1975-76
Most Consecutive League Defeats: 12 1972-73	**Away League Wins:** 4 1926, 1936 (twice)

Club Statistician for the Directory: Tim Carder

BRIGHTON

PLAYERS NAME Ht Wt Birthdate	Honours	Birthplace Transfers	Clubs	APPEARANCES				GOALS			
				League	Milk Cup	FA Cup	Other Comps	League	Milk Cup	FA Cup	Other Comps
GOALKEEPERS											
Perry Digwood 6.0 11.4 26.10.59		London £150,000	Fulham (A) Brighton	15 79	 2	 5	 1				
John Keeley 6.0 12.3 27.7.61		Plaistow £120,000 F	Southend United (A) Chelmsford City Brighton & H.A. Brighton Cardiff	63 189	4 17	5 17	3 1				
DEFENDERS											
Les Berry 6.2 11.13 4.5.56		Plumstead F	Charlton Athletic (A) Brighton & H.A.	352+6		19+1	18			11	
Steve Gatting 5.11 11.11 25.9.59		Willesden £200,000	Arsenal (A) Brighton	50+8 136+3	3 9	9 14		5 11	 1	1	
Chris Hutchings 5.10 11.0 5.7.57		Winchester £10,000 £50,000	Harrow Borough Chelsea Brighton	 83+4 97	 7 3	 7 8	 1+1	 3 3		 1	
Eric Young 6.3 12.6 25.3.60		Singapore £10,000	Slough Brighton	 97	 8	2 9	 2	 9		 1	
MIDFIELD											
Kieran O'Reagan 5.7 10.8 9.11.63	EI (4)	Cork	Tramore Athletic Brighton	 48+14	 4+1	 2	 1+1	 2			
Gary O'Reilly 6.0 12.12 21.3.61	E1, YS	Isleworth £45,000	Tottenham Hotspur Brighton	39+6 71	4 4	2 7	2+2 2	 3			
Danny Wilson* 5.7 10.3 1.1.60	ASC 81	Wigan F £100,000 Player exch. £45,000	Wigan Athletic Bury Chesterfield Nottingham Forest Scunthorpe U. (L) Brighton	 87+3 100 9+1 6 97	 4 8 5	 11 9 7	 0+1 2	 8 13 1 3 26	 3		 2
FORWARDS											
Gerry Armstrong 5.11 13.2 23.5.54	NI (62)	Belfast Mallorca F F	Tottenham Hotspur Watford WBA Chesterfield Brighton	69+19 50+36 7+1 12	3+1 5+2 2	6+4 12	 3	10 12 1	3 3	3 2	
Terry Connor 5.7 10.8 9.11.62	EY	Leeds Player exch.	Leeds United Brighton	83+13 115+3	4+2 5	5 9		19 42	1 4	1 4	
Steve Penny 5.9 10.4 16.1.64	NI (9)	Ballymena	Ballymena Brighton	 70+12	 4	 7		 6	 1		
Dean Saunders† 5.8½ 10.0 21.6.64	W (1)	Swansea F	Swansea City (A) Brighton	42+7 39+3	2+1 2	1 5	1+8 2	12 15		 4	

ADDITIONAL CONTRACT PROFESSIONALS
Andy Rollings, David Gipp

APPRENTICES
Darren Carter, Paul Dobinson, David Gipp, Phil Lovell, Franco Massimo (0+1Lg)

NON-CONTRACT PLAYERS

Record Attendance: 36,747 v Fulham, Div 2, 27 Dec 1958

Smallest Home Attendance for a First Class Match: 1,758 v Walsall, Div 3 (S), 22 Oct 1927

Record Receipts: £66,000 v Norwich City, FA Cup Round 6, 12 Mar 1983

Season Tickets: Stand: seats up to £200. Family season tickets: £42

Executive Club Season Tickets: £500.00

Cost of Stand Tickets: £5.50, £4.50 (£3.00 Family Stand) **Terraces:** £3.00

Match and Ticket Information: Postal bookings depending on availability four weeks before each match

Car Parking: Available at the Greyhound Stadium (Nevill Road). Limited parking adjacent to ground

Nearest Railway Station: Hove (0273 25476)

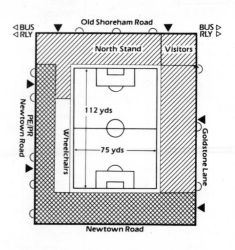

How to get to the ground

From North: Use A23 with Pyecombe, then in 2m turn right (S.P. Hove). In 1.1m bear left into Nevill Road A2023. In 0.9m at cross roads turn left A27 into Old Shoreham Road for Brighton and Hove Albion
From East: From Lewes use A27 to Brighton then follow signs Worthing A27 along Old Shoreham Road for Brighton and Hove Albion
From West: Use A27 (S.P. Brighton) along Old Shoreham Road for Brighton and Hove Albion

Price of 1986-7 Programme: 50p
Number of Pages: 32
Subscriptions: £17.50

Local Newspapers:

Local Radio Stations:

Chairman
D Williams

Directors
L J Kew (Vice-Chairman)
O Newland
D Russe
P Manning
M Fricker
T Cooper
W Williams

Secretary
Miss J Harrison (0272 632812)

Commercial Manager
J Hillier

Manager
Terry Cooper

Assistant Manager
Clive Middlemass

Reserve Team Manager
Mike Gibson

Physiotherapist
Alex Lockhart

Chief Scout
Jock Rae

Take a squad which provided the nucleus of the previous season's success in finishing 6th in Division 3. Add a couple of close season signings of proven players at this level. Include a strike force (Riley, Neville and Walsh), who contributed 55 goals the previous term and it is no wonder that Bristol City were second favourites with the bookmakers for promotion in 85/86.

Take a disastrous start in which the first five games were lost with a goals aggregate of 4-17 and it's no wonder that City were constantly just out of the frame once the effects of that poor start had been overcome.

The habit of giving away late goals, picked up the previous season, was still evident and was to cause manager Terry Cooper much frustration. And yet proof of the team's ability as a unit can be seen in a final goal difference of +9 and a final league record of 13 clean sheets.

All in all a position of 9th, although disappointing, was no mean achievement given that awful August.

Both the Milk Cup (aggregate 3-5 v Hereford United), and the FA Cup (a home defeat by Exeter City), were non-starters but the much maligned (by this writer too!) Freight Rover Trophy was to provide City with the stage that players of the calibre of Neville (just pipping Curle for consistency this season), 'keeper Waugh, skipper Hutchinson and the unselfish Riley deserved.

Cooper fielded first teamers throughout believing that they could go all the way in the competition and realising what a welcome source of finance this competition could be. Despite defeat in the Area Final 1st Leg 0-2 v Hereford United the return at Ashton Gate brought a 3-0 win in an epic tie — the winner (fittingly scored by Neville), coming in the last minute of extra-time!

And so to Wembley and a highly professional performance to outplay Bolton Wanderers 3-0 (Riley (2) and Pritchard) after an uncomfortable first half-hour in front of a crowd of 54,500. What a day for those connected with the club in any capacity!

For the forthcoming season, manager Terry Cooper has the finance available to strengthen where necessary. More importantly he has proven his ability in the transfer market and at motivating his players. William Hill's certainly won't be getting my money this season by way of a prediction but I don't think that I'd be sticking my neck out in saying that it won't be dull.

Watch this space!

                        David Peacey

Back Row L to R: Paul Fitzpatrick, Keith Curle, John McPhail, Lee Rogers.
Middle Row: Steve Neville, Gary Marshall, Mike Tanner, David Moyes, Keith Waugh, Rob Newman, Alan Walsh, Chris Honor, Graham Underhill.
Front Row: Gordon Owen, Andy Llewellyn, David Harle, Bobby Hutchinson, Brian Williams, Glyn Riley, Gary Hamson, Gordon Moore.

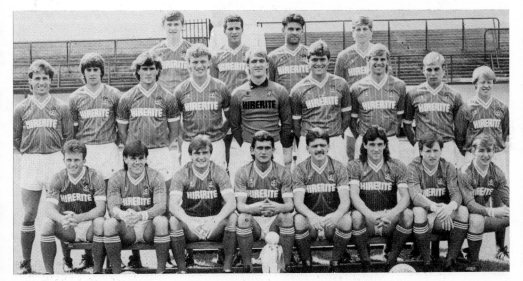

BRISTOL CITY

DIVISION THREE: 9th　　　　**FA CUP:** 2nd ROUND　　　　**MILK CUP:** 1st ROUND　　　　**FRT:** WINNERS

MATCH	DATE		COMPE-TITION	VENUE	OPPONENTS	RESULT		HALF TIME	L'GUE POS'N	GOALSCORERS/GOAL TIMES	ATTEN-DANCE
1	A	17	CL	H	Walsall	L	2-3	1-1		Walsh (pen) 7, Neville 86	7,196
2		21	MC1/1	A	Hereford United	L	1-5	0-3		Johnson 76	(2,449)
3		24	CL	A	Bournemouth	L	0-5	0-4	24		(4,969)
4		26	CL	H	Gillingham	L	1-2	1-0	24	Hutchinson 41	6,052
5		31	CL	A	Rotherham United	L	0-2	0-1	24		(3,134)
6	S	3	MC1/2	H	Hereford United	W	2-0	1-0		Johnson 6, Hutchinson 83	2,273
7		7	CL	H	Wigan Athletic	W	1-0	0-0	23	Pritchard 68	5,663
8		14	CL	A	Cardiff City	W	3-1	1-0	20	Walsh 44, 78, Pritchard 86	(4,412)
9		17	CL	H	Derby County	D	1-1	1-0	21	Newman 36	7,750
10		21	CL	A	York City	D	1-1	0-1	19	Pritchard 74	(3,904)
11		28	CL	H	Blackpool	W	2-1	1-1	16	Neville 24, Pritchard 73	6,570
12	O	1	CL	A	Newport County	D	1-1	0-0	17	Neville 72	(3,776)
13		5	CL	H	Chesterfield	D	0-0	0-0	18		6,416
14		12	CL	A	Notts County	L	0-4	0-2	19		(4,332)
15		19	CL	H	Darlington	W	1-0	0-0	17	Walsh 64	5,878
16		22	CL	A	Bury	L	3-6	0-1	18	Walsh (pen) 47, Neville 58, Riley 60	(2,460)
17		26	CL	H	Wolverhampton W.	W	3-0	2-0	16	Riley 2, Hutchinson 40, Walsh (pen) 85	7,138
18	N	2	CL	A	Doncaster Rovers	D	1-1	0-0	14	Riley 7	(2,871)
19		6	CL	A	Lincoln City	D	1-1	1-1	15	Neville 35	(1,379)
20		9	CL	H	Brentford	D	0-0	0-0	16		6,596
21		17	FAC1	A	Swindon Town	D	0-0	0-0			(10,468)
22		20	FAC1R	H	Swindon Town	W	4-2	1-0		Neville 3 (25, 57, 60), Riley 77	8,979
23		23	CL	A	Swansea City	W	3-1	2-1	14	Hutchinson 38, 40, Walsh 50	(4,414)
24		30	CL	H	Bolton Wanderers	W	2-0	1-0	12	Riley 9, Neville 85	6,253
25	D	7	FAC2	H	Exeter City	L	1-2	1-1		Walsh (pen) 17	8,052
26		14	CL	A	Reading	L	0-1	0-0	13		(5,565)
27		21	CL	H	Bournemouth	L	1-3	0-0	14	Hutchinson 10	5,691
28		26	CL	H	Plymouth Argyle	W	2-0	2-0	12	Walsh (pen) 8, Neville 37	8,298
29		28	CL	A	Gillingham	D	1-1	0-0	12	Newman 78	(4,672)
30	J	7	CL	H	Doncaster Rovers	W	4-1	1-0	12	Pritchard 6, Walsh (pen) 52, 70, Neville 73	5,385
31		11	CL	H	Rotherham United	W	3-1	2-0	12	Williams 34, Walsh 38, Neville 49	6,672
32		14	FRT	H	Plymouth Argyle	D	0-0	0-0			2,402
33		18	CL	A	Walsall	L	1-2	1-0	12	Neville 35	(4,952)
34		25	CL	H	Cardiff City	W	2-1	2-1	12	Neville 23, Marshall 37	7,541
35		28	FRT	A	Walsall	W	2-1	2-1		Walsh 14, Gunn (og) 22	(2,625)
36	F	1	CL	A	Wigan Athletic	D	1-1	0-1	10	Newman 68	(3,402)
37		4	CL	H	Bury	W	4-1	1-1	9	Riley 26, 68, Neville 47, Walsh 48	5,074
38		22	CL	H	York City	D	2-2	1-1	9	Moyes 2, Neville 69	6,409
39	M	1	CL	A	Blackpool	L	1-2	0-1	10	Bryant 66	(3,366)
40		4	CL	H	Newport County	W	3-1	1-0	9	Walsh 12, Marshall 83, Curle 89	4,395
41		8	CL	A	Chesterfield	D	0-0	0-0	9		(2,547)
42		15	CL	H	Notts County	W	3-0	1-0	7	Walsh 44, Moyes 71, Riley 88	5,701
43		19	CL	A	Derby County	L	0-2	0-2	9		(11,113)
44		22	CL	A	Wolverhampton W.	L	1-2	0-0	10	Walsh 63	(3,696)
45		27	FRT S QF	H	Northampton Town	W	3-2	1-1		Riley 34, Hutchinson 54, Neville 81	3,038
46		29	CL	H	Bristol Rovers	W	2-0	1-0	9	Neville 26, Walsh 70	12,171
47	A	5	CL	H	Lincoln City	D	1-1	0-1	11	Neville 48	5,385
48		13	CL	A	Brentford	W	2-1	2-1	11	Riley 32, Pritchard 39	(3,702)
49		16	FRT S SF	H	Gillingham	W	3-0	0-0		Neville 57, Walsh (pen) 73, Riley 88	5,707
50		19	CL	H	Swansea City	L	0-1	0-0	11		6,013
51		22	CL	A	Bristol Rovers	D	1-1	0-0	11	Neville 74	(9,926)
52		26	CL	A	Bolton Wanderers	W	4-0	1-0	9	Riley 19, Neville 51, 55, Llewellyn 67	(4,493)
53		29	CL	A	Plymouth Argyle	L	0-4	0-1	10		(19,900)
54	M	3	CL	H	Reading	W	3-0	3-0	9	Neville 7, Walsh (pen) 33, (pen) 40	7,814
55		6	FRT S F1	A	Hereford United	L	0-2	0-2			(7,608)
56		9	FRT S F2	H	Hereford United	W	3-0†	0-0		Riley 63, Pejic (og) 66, Neville 120	11,558
57		15	CL	A	Darlington	D	1-1	0-1	9	Riley 60	(1,615)
58		24	FRT F	N	Bolton Wanderers	W	3-0	1-0		Riley 44, 84, Pritchard 73	54,000

Best Home League Attendance: 12,171 v Bristol Rovers 29/3　　　　**Smallest:** 4,395 v Newport C. 4/3　　　　**Av Home Att:** 6,612

Goal Scorers:　　　　　　　　　　　　　　　　　　　　　　　　　　　　**Compared with 84-85:** −1,859

League (69):　Neville 19, Walsh 18 (7 pen), Riley 10, Pritchard 6, Hutchinson 5, Newman 3, Marshall 2, Moyes 2, Bryant 1, Curle 1, Llewellyn 1, Williams 1

Milk Cup (3):　Johnson 2, Hutchinson 1

FA Cup (14):　Neville 3, Riley 1, Walsh 1 (pen)

FRT (14):　Riley 5, Neville 3, Walsh 2 (1 pen), Hutchinson 1, Pritchard 1, Opponents 2

†After extra time

1985-86

Waugh	Llewellyn	Curle	Hughes	Williams	Emmanuel (M)	Hutchinson	Marshall	Walsh	Riley	Neville	Johnson	Newman	Rogers	Pritchard	Hirst	Moyes	Tong	Tanner	Bryant	Vaughan (L)	Underhill	Harle (L)	Moore	Honour (A)	Referee	
1	2	3	4	5†	6	7	8	9	10	11	12														J Deakin	1
1	2	3	4	5	9	7	8	11	6	10	12														**K Barratt**	2
1	2	4		5		8	7	10	6	11	9	3													A Ward	3
1	2	3		6		7	8	12	9*	10	5	4		11											L Robinson	4
1	2	4					8	10	12	11	9	3	5	7	6*										R Nixon	5
1	2	3		7*		8		12	6	11	10	5	4	9											**R Gifford**	6
1	2	4		6		8	7		12	11*	10	3	5	9											M Read	7
1	2	4		6				10	12	11	9*	3	5	7											V Callow	8
1	2	3		7			8	9	10	11*		5	4	6											D Hedges	9
1	2	4		6			8	12	10	9*		3	5	7											J Hough	10
1	2	3		7			8	9	10*	11	12	5	4	6											Alan Robinson	11
1	2	4		6			8	10	12	11	9*	3	5	7											H Taylor	12
1	2*	3		6		7	8		12	11	10	5	4	9											M James	13
1		4		6†			8	10	12	11	9*	3	2	7		5									C Trussell	14
1	7	5		8				9	10	11		2	3	6		4									M Cotton	15
1		4		6			8	10	9	11	12	3*	2	7		5									F Roberts	16
1	2	4		7			11	9	10			5	3	8			6								A Buksh	17
1	2	4		8				10	6	11		3	5	7			9								A Robinson	18
1	2	4		8				10	6	11		3	5	7			9								L Dilkes	19
1	2	4		8				9*	11	10	12	5	3	6			7								M Scott	20
1	2	4		8				10	6	11		3	5	7			9								**K Miller**	21
1	2	3		7				9	10	11		5	4	6			8								**K Miller**	22
1	2	4		8				10	6	11		3	5	7			9								A Seville	23
1	2	3		8				9	11	10		5	4	6			7								D Delaney r'd N Butler	24
1	2*	3		8				9	10	11		5	4	6			7								**H King**	25
1	2	3		8				10	6†	11		5	4			7	9								I Hemley	26
1	2	4		8				10	6	11		3		7		5	9								R Lewis	27
1	2	4		8				10		11		2	6	7		5	9								J Carter r'd D Vickers	28
1		4		3		8		10		11		2	6	7		5	9								D Reeves	29
1		4		3		8		10	6	11		2		7		5	9								G Ashby	30
1		4		3		8		10	6	11		2		7		5	9								H King r'd L Loosemoore	31
1		4		3		8		10	6	11	12	2		7*		5	9								**J Bray**	32
1	6	4		3		8		10		11	12	2		7*		5	9								D Scott	33
1		4		3		8	7	10	6	11		2				5	9								T Holbrook	34
1	7	4		3		8		10	6	11*		2		12		5	9								**M Dimblebee**	35
1	7	4		3		12		10	6	11		2				5	9	8*							K Redfern	36
1		4		3		8	7	10	6	11		2				5	9								C Downey	37
1	2	4		3		8	7	10	6	11						5	9								J Deakin	38
1*	2	4		3		8	12	10	6	11						5	9	7							J Lloyd	39
	2	4		3		8	7	10	6	11	12					5	9			1					J Moules	40
	2	4		3		8	7	10	6	11		9				5				1					I Hemley	41
1	2	4		3		8	7	10	6	11		9				5									R Gifford	42
1	2	4		3		7*		10†	6	11*		9		12		5									M Reed	43
1	2			3		8	7	10	6	11*		9		12		5					4				P Willis	44
1	2	4		3		8	7*	10	6	11		9		12		5						9*			**T Ward**	45
1	2	4		3		8		10	6	11		12		7		5						9*			K Cooper	46
1	2	4		3		8	10		6	11				7					5			9			R Bridges	47
1	2	4		3		8	10*		6	11		12		7		5						9			M Heath	48
1	2	4		3		8		10	6	11				7		5						9			**J Martin**	49
1	2	4		3				10	6*	11				7		5						9	12		D Vickers	50
1	2	4		3				10	6	11				7		5						9			L Shapter	51
1	2	4		3				10	6	11		8		7		5						9			J Ashworth	52
1	2	4		3				10	6	11		8		7		5						9			J Deakin	53
1	2			3		8		10	6	11		4		7		5						9			M James	54
1	2	4		3		8		10	6*	11		7		12		5						9			**G Napthine**	55
1	12	4		3		12		10	6	11		2		7*		5						9*			**R Lewis**	56
1	2	4		3			7	10	12	11*		9				5	8							6	M Peck	57
1		4		3		8		10	6	11		2		7		5						9			**G Tyson**	58
44	38	44	2	36	2	42	14	44	33	46	8	37	21	32	1	27	19	2	2	2	1	8		1	League Appearances	
				5					8		5	2		2									1		Substitute Appearances	
2	2	2	1	2	1	2	1+1	2	1	2	1+1	1	1	1											Milk Cup Appearances	
3	3	3		3		0+1	3	3	3	3		3	3	3		3									FA Cup Appearances	
7	4+1	7		7		7	2+1	7	6+1	7		6		4+3		7	2					4			FR Trophy Appearances	

Players on Loan: Vaughan (West Ham)

Departures: Emmanuel (Swansea), Hughes (Tranmere), Johnson (Scunthorpe), Pritchard (Gillingham), Hirst (Torquay), Tong (Gillingham), Bryant (Robinsons DRG)

FC

'THE ROBINS'

Formed: 1894
Turned Professional: 1897   **Ltd Co:** 1897

Previous Names: Bristol South End 1894-7
Previous Managers: Sam Hollis   Bob Hewison   Bob Wright   Pat Beasley   Peter Doherty
Fred Ford   Alan Dicks   Bob Houghton   Roy Hodgson
Honours: Champions Div 2, 1905-6   Champions Div 3 (S) 1922-3, 1926-7, 1954-5   Welsh Cup
Winners   Anglo-Scottish Cup Winners 1977-8   Freight Rover Trophy Winners 1985/86
League Career: Elected to Div 2 1901   Promoted to Div 1 1905-6   Relegated to Div 2 1910-11
Relegated to Div 3 (S) 1921-2   Promoted to Div 2 1922-3   Relegated to Div 3 (S) 1923-4
Promoted to Div 2 1926-7   Relegated to Div 3 (S) 1931-2   Promoted to Div 2 1954-5
Relegated to Div 3 1959-60   Promoted to Div 2 1964-5   Promoted to Div 1 1979-80
Relegated to Div 2 1980-1   Relegated to Div 3 1981-2   Relegated to Div 4 1982-3
Promoted to Div 3 1983-4
Colours: Red shirts, white shorts, red and white stockings
Change Colours: White shirts, black shorts, white stockings
Reserves League: Macbar South West   **Youth League:** Gloucestershire Youth

---

CLUB RECORDS

Most Appearances for Club: John Atyeo, 1951-66: Football League 597 + FA Cup 42 + League Cup 6 **Total 645**
Most Capped Player: Billy Wedlock, 26, England
Record Goalscorer in a Match: "Tot" Walsh, 6 v Gillingham (H), 9-4, Div 3 (S), 15 Jan 1927
Record League Goalscorer in a Season: In All Competitions: Don Clark, 41 (League 36 + Fairs Cup 5), 1946-7
Record League Goalscorer in a Career: In All Competitions: John Atyeo, 350 (League 315 + Fairs Cup 30 + League Cup 5) 1951-66
Record Transfer Fee Received: £325,000 from Coventry City for Gary Collier, July 1979
Record Transfer Fee Paid: £235,000 to St. Mirren for Tony Fitzpatrick, July 1979
Best Performances: League: 2nd Div 1 1906-7   **FA Cup:** Finalists 1909   **League/Milk Cup:** Semi-Final 1970-1
Most League Points: 82, Div 4, 1983-4   **Most League Goals:** 104, Div 3 (S), 1926-7
Record League Victory: 9-0 v Aldershot, Div 3 (S), 28 April 1946
Record League Defeat: 0-9 v Coventry City, Div 3 (S), 28 Dec 1946
Oldest Player in League Match: Terry Cooper 40 yrs 3 mnts
Youngest Player in League Match: Nyrere Kelly, 16 yrs 8 mnts

Most Consecutive Undefeated League Matches: 24 1905-06	**League Matches Without a Win:** 15 1933
Longest Run of Undefeated Home League Matches: 25 1953-54	**Away League Matches:** 21 1905-06
Longest Run Without Home League Win: 10 1931-32	**Away League Win:** 23 1932-33
Most Consecutive League Wins: 14 1905	**Home League Wins:** 12 1926-27
Most Consecutive League Defeats: 7 1931, 1970	**Away League Wins:** 6 1905

Bristol City played 18 consecutive away League games without defeat in 1905-06

Club Statistician for the Directory: David Woods

BRISTOL CITY

				APPEARANCES				GOALS			
PLAYERS NAME Ht Wt Birthdate	Honours	Birthplace Transfers	Clubs	League	Milk Cup	FA Cup	Other Comps	League	Milk Cup	FA Cup	Other Comps
GOALKEEPERS											
Keith Waugh		Sunderland	Sunderland (A)								
6.1 12.0 27.10.56		F	Peterborough United	195	22	10					
		£90,000	Sheffield United	99	12	6	1				
			Cambridge United (L)	4							
		F	Bristol City	48	2	3	7				
DEFENDERS											
Keith Curle		Bristol	Bristol Rovers (A)	21+11	3	1		4			
6.0 11.9 14.11.63		£5,000	Torquay United	16				5			
		£10,000	Bristol City	21+1	1		3				
Paul Fitzpatrick		Liverpool	Bolton Wanderers	13+1	3	1	1				
6.4 11.10 5.10.65		F	Bristol City								
Gary Hamson		Nottingham	Sheffield United (A)	107+1	3	5+1		8	1		
5.9 11.11 24.8.59		£140,000	Leeds United	126+8	4	10+1	3+1	3		1	
		F	Bristol City								
Andy Llewellyn	EY	Bristol	Bristol City (A)	65+2	2	5	6+2	1			
5.7 11.4 26.2.66											
John McPhail	Div. 4, 82	Dundee	Dundee	64+4	11	5					
6.0½ 12.3 7.12.55	Div. 4, 84		Sheffield United	135	9	8		7		1	
			York City	141+1	10	16	5	17	2		1
		£14,000	Bristol City								
David Moyes	SS	Blythswood	Celtic	19+8	7+1		2+1				
6.1 11.5 25.4.63	SP Div. 82	F	Cambridge United	79	3	1	3				
		£10,000	Bristol City	27				2			
Rob Newman		Bradford-on-Avon	Bristol City (A)	156+10	10	6	10	13	1		
6.2 12.0 13.12.63											
Lee Rogers		Bristol	Bristol City (A)	27	3	3					
5.11 11.8 8.4.67											
Brian Williams		Salford	Bury (A)	148+11	11	12		19			
5.8 12.12 5.11.55		£70,000	QPR	9+10	1+1	0+2					
		£50,000	Swindon Town	81+10	14	9		8			
		F	Bristol Rovers	172+2	13	10	6	14	2		1
		F	Bristol City	36	2	0+1	7	1			
MIDFIELD											
David Harle	EY	Denaby	Doncaster Rovers (A)	48+13	4	1		3			
5.9 10.7 15.8.63		F	Exeter City	42+1	4	1		6			
			Doncaster Rovers	80+3	3	5	5	17		2	1
			Leeds United	3							
		£5,000	Bristol City (L)	8							
Bobby Hutchinson+*		Glasgow	Hibernian								
5.9 11.4 19.6.57			Wigan Athletic	34+1	4	2		3	1		
			Tranmere Rovers	42+3	7	2		6	3		
			Mansfield Town	25		3					
			Tranmere Rovers	21			5				
		F	Bristol City	71+2	2	4	11	9	1	1	
Steve Neville	Div. 4, 82	Walthamstow	Southampton (A)								
5.9½ 11.0 18.9.57			Exeter City	90+3	9	3		22	3	1	
		£80,000	Sheffield United	40+9	4	5+1		6			
		£40,000	Exeter City	89+3	4	5		27		2	
		£20,000	Bristol City	72+2	2	3	11	26		3	3
Michael Tanner		Bristol	Bristol City	2							
5.11½ 10.12½ 28.10.64											
FORWARDS											
Gary Marshall		Shepton Mallet	Bristol City	17+8	1+1		2+1	4			
5.11½ 10.10 20.4.64			Torquay United (L)	7				2			
Glyn Riley		Barnsley	Barnsley (A)	31+7	1	5+1		2		2	
5.10 11.1 24.7.58		F	Doncaster Rovers	59+6	2+1	8		11			
		F	Bristol City	162+8	11	9	10+1	60	3	3	6
Graham Underhill		Bristol	Bristol City	1							
No details											
Alan Walsh		Hartlepool	Horden CW								
6.0 12.8 9.12.56		F	Middlesbrough	0+3							
		F	Darlington	245+6	12	14+1		87	7	6	
		£18,000	Bristol City	89	6	5	11	38	2	1	6

ADDITIONAL CONTRACT PROFESSIONALS
Gordon Moore, Chris Honor (1Lge)

APPRENTICES

NON-CONTRACT PLAYERS

Record Attendance: 43,335 v Preston North End, FA Cup Round 5, 16 Feb 1935

Record Receipts: £45,300 v Bristol Rovers, FA Cup Round 2, 8 Dec 1984

Season Tickets: £80 adults (£40 juveniles/OAP), £65 (£35 juveniles/OAP) (Stands); Family (2 adults, 2 children) £200, £130

Executive Box Season Tickets: Six boxes to be installed

Cost of Stand Tickets: £4.50 (Grand Stand) (£2.50 juveniles/OAP); £4.00 (£2.00 juveniles/OAP); **Enclosure:** £2.50 (£1.20 juveniles/OAP); **Covered standing:** £2.20 (£1.00 juveniles/OAP); **Uncovered standing:** £2.20 (£1.00 juveniles/OAP)

Match and Ticket Information: Any time before match applications by post (with sae) are accepted. Personal applications four weeks prior to each match

Car Parking: Season car park tickets for season ticket holders. Coaches park at Cannons Marsh. There is limited street parking around ground

Nearest Railway Station: Temple Meads (0272 294255)

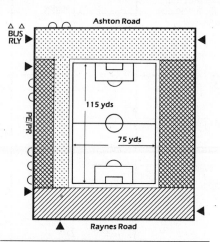

How to get to the ground

From North and West: Use Motorway M5 until junction 16, leave motorway and follow signs Bristol A38. Follow signs to City Centre then follow signs Taunton A38. In 1.2m cross Cumberland Basin swing bridge, then branch left into Winterstoke Road for Bristol City FC

From East: Use Motorway M4, then M32 and follow signs to City Centre, then follow signs Taunton A38. In 1.2m cross Cumberland Basin swing bridge, then branch left into Winterstoke Road for Bristol City FC

From South: Use Motorway M5 until junction 18. Leave motorway and follow signs Bristol A4 along Portway then turn right and follow signs Taunton over Cumberland Basin swing bridge, then branch left into Winterstoke Road for Bristol City FC. To use Bristol City FC park and ride scheme follow AA signs to "Bristol City FC Car Park", which is in Anchor Road

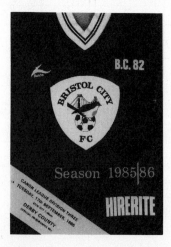

Price of 1986-7 Programme: 50p
Number of Pages: 32
Subscriptions: Rates obtainable from club

Local Newspapers: Bristol Evening Post, Western Daily Press, Sunday Independent

Local Radio Stations:

President
Marquis of Worcester

Vice-Presidents
H E L Brown
Dr W T Cussen
G A W Holmes
A I Seager

Chairman
Denis M H Dunford

Directors
R C Redman (Vice-Chairman)
R Craig
G H M Dunford
M D Ross
G J Bennett (Managing)

Honorary Company Secretary
A E Hill FCA, MBA

Manager
Bobby Gould

Trainer
Roy Dolling

Club Coach
Harold Jarman

Commercial Manager
Tony Wood (0272 510363)

Groundsman
Jackie Pitt

The re-appointment of former manager Bobby Gould was a surprise to many of Rovers fans. However, the exodus of eight experienced players to reduce the club's wage bill was predictable. Gould acted promptly by replacing his squad with free transfer signings including Welsh international defender Byron Stevenson. The remainder were primarily youngsters like Andy Spring, John Scales and David Mehew. The only transfer fees paid were for goalkeeper Ron Green and striker Trevor Morgan. Throughout the season 28 different players were tried albeit some with more success than others. The experience was provided by former England Skipper, Gerry Francis, whose contribution together with the vital goals of Morgan did more to stop the club being relegated.

While the League form was inconsistent the highlights of a disappointing season was undoubtedly confined to the FA Cup. Fine away wins at Brentford and Swansea were followed by a convincing 3-1 defeat over 1st Division Leicester City. The artificial pitch at Luton where Rovers were outclassed ended the cup run.

Besides the major personnel changes to the playing staff, joint chairmen Martin Flook and Barry Bradshaw, who had provided vital financial support over the last few years for the club, both resigned in March. This coincided with their joint proposal for planning permission for a multi-sports complex at Stoke Gifford being rejected. The scheme was to incorporate a 10,000 capacity rent-free new stadium for Rovers.

A new but inexperienced Board of Directors have now made a move from Eastville (Rovers home since 1897) to share Twerton Park with Bath City, and the immediate future of the club looks decidedly bleak.

Rovers League form with just two wins in their final 20 matches underlined the major task facing manager Bobby Gould next season. With part-time players and severe financial constraints and the move to Bath, Rovers will do well to retain their 3rd Division status.
                                                    Mike Jay

Back Row L to R: Wayne Noble, Ian Weston, David Mehew, Lee Portch, Phil Purnell. **Second Row:** Roy Dolling (Trainer), Martin Boyle, John Scales, Darren Carr, Tim Carter, Trevor Morgan, Nick Tanner, Kenny Hibbitt, Ray Kendall (Kit Manager). **Third Row:** Gary Penrice, Vaughan Jones, Geoff Dunford (Director), Bobby Gould (Manager), Denis Dunford (Chairman), Ron Craig (Director), Ian Alexander, Gary Smart. **Front Row:** Jon Gould, Gary Eyles, Steve Yates, Marco Corota, Martin Davidson, Lee Howells, Richard Dryden.

BRISTOL ROVERS

DIVISION THREE: 16th   **FA CUP:** 4th ROUND   **MILK CUP:** 2nd ROUND

MATCH	DATE		COMPE-TITION	VENUE	OPPONENTS	RESULT		HALF TIME	L'GUE POS'N	GOALSCORERS/GOAL TIMES	ATTEN-DANCE
1	A	18	CL	A	Darlington	D	3-3	1-3		Badock 3, Stevenson (pen) 34, White 85	(4,196)
2		20	MC1/1	H	Newport County	W	2-0	1-0		Randall 26, Badock 84	2,777
3		24	CL	H	Brentford	L	0-1	0-1	18		4,140
4		26	CL	A	Reading	L	2-3	1-1	23	Davies 19, Penrice 47	(3,529)
5		31	CL	H	Derby County	D	0-0	0-0	21		4,961
6	S	3	MC1/2	A	Newport County	L	0-1	0-1			(2,012)
7		7	CL	A	Newport County	L	0-3	0-1	22		(2,775)
8		14	CL	H	Lincoln City	D	0-0	0-0	23		3,077
9		17	CL	A	Wolverhampton W.	W	4-3	1-2	22	Randall 30, Badock 50, 85, White 83	(3,244)
10		21	CL	H	Walsall	L	0-1	0-1	22		3,787
11		24	MC2/1	H	Birmingham City	L	2-3	2-1		O'Connor 8, Randall 25	4,332
12		28	CL	A	Swansea City	W	1-0	0-0	20	Morgan 83	(4,008)
13	O	1	CL	H	Notts County	D	1-1	0-1	20	Penrice 65	3,549
14		5	CL	H	Plymouth Argyle	L	2-4	0-3	20	Morgan 78, 81	(5,662)
15		8	MC2/2	A	Birmingham City	L	1-2	1-0		Randall 5	(3,686)
16		12	CL	H	Rotherham United	W	5-2	3-1	17	White 7, Morgan 3 (11, 18, 89), Parkin 77	3,499
17		19	CL	A	Doncaster Rovers	W	2-0	2-0	15	Morgan 24, 33	(3,032)
18		22	CL	H	Bolton Wanderers	W	2-1	1-1	13	White 38, Stevenson 73	(4,308)
19		26	CL	A	Bournemouth	L	1-6	1-4	15	Randall 40	(3,798)
20	N	2	CL	H	York City	L	0-1	0-1	17		4,274
21		5	CL	H	Bury	W	2-1	1-0	14	Tanner 16, White 68	2,959
22		9	CL	A	Blackpool	L	2-4	1-3	15	Tanner 36, Morgan 38	(4,707)
23		16	FAC1	A	Brentford	W	3-1	1-1		Penrice 9, White 55, Francis 57	(4,716)
24		23	CL	H	Cardiff City	W	2-1	2-1	13	O'Connor 2, Penrice 20	4,563
25	D	7	FAC2	A	Swansea City	W	2-1	2-0		Morgan (pen) 1, White 45	(4,230)
26		14	CL	H	Gillingham	W	1-0	0-0	12	Morgan 52	4,224
27		22	CL	A	Brentford	L	0-1	0-0	13		(5,742)
28		26	CL	A	Wigan Athletic	L	0-4	0-1	15		(3,711)
29		28	CL	H	Reading	L	0-2	0-1	16		7,555
30	J	4	FAC3	H	Leicester City	W	3-1	0-0		Stevenson 50, Morgan 53, 74	9,392
31		15	FRT	A	Hereford United	L	0-2	0-1			(1,770)
32		18	CL	H	Darlington	W	3-1	2-0	14	White 3 (7, 31, 88)	3,395
33		21	FRT	H	Swindon Town	W	2-1	2-0		O'Connor 7, White 30	2,335
34		24	FAC4	A	Luton Town	L	0-4	0-2			(12,463)
35	F	1	CL	H	Newport County	W	2-0	0-0	14	O'Connor 84, Morgan 87	3,284
36		4	CL	H	Bolton Wanderers	W	2-0	1-0	13	Parkin 15, White 35	(3,672)
37		8	CL	A	Doncaster Rovers	W	1-0	1-0	13	White 37	3,894
38	M	1	CL	H	Swansea City	D	0-0	0-0	14		3,098
39		4	CL	A	Notts County	D	0-0	0-0	14		(3,183)
40		8	CL	H	Plymouth Argyle	L	1-2	0-1	14	Morgan 75	4,667
41		12	CL	A	York City	L	0-4	0-1	14		(2,857)
42		15	CL	A	Rotherham United	L	0-2	0-1	14		(2,734)
43		18	CL	A	Walsall	L	0-6	0-3	15		(3,734)
44		22	CL	H	Bournemouth	L	1-2	0-1	16	Penrice 3, White 67	3,296
45		25	CL	H	Wolverhampton W.	D	1-1	1-1	16	Morgan (pen) 36	3,378
46		29	CL	A	Bristol City	L	0-2	0-1	16		(12,171)
47	A	1	CL	H	Wigan Athletic	D	1-1	0-0	17	Stevenson 56	3,428
48		5	CL	A	Bury	D	1-1	0-0	18	Morgan 75	(1,866)
49		9	CL	A	Derby County	W	2-0	0-0	16	White 56, Morgan 60	(11,033)
50		12	CL	H	Blackpool	W	1-0	1-0	15	Penrice 12	3,472
51		15	CL	A	Chesterfield	L	0-2	0-0	15		(1,911)
52		19	CL	A	Cardiff City	L	0-2	0-2	15		(2,735)
53		22	CL	H	Bristol City	D	1-1	0-0	16	Scales 80	9,926
54		26	CL	H	Chesterfield	D	1-1	1-0	17	Morgan 21	3,576
55		30	CL	A	Lincoln City	D	2-2	2-1	17	Purnell 8, 10	(2,233)
56	M	3	CL	A	Gillingham	L	0-2	0-2	16		(2,050)

Best Home League Attendance: 9,926 v Bristol City 22/4   **Smallest:** 2,959 Bury 5/11   **Av Home Att:** 4,187

Goal Scorers: **Compared with 84-85:** −776

League (51):	Morgan 16 (1 pen), White 12, Penrice 5, Badock 3, Stevenson 3 (1 pen), O'Connor 2, Parkin 2, Purnell 2, Randall 2, Tanner 2, Davies 1, Scales 1
Milk Cup (5):	Randall 3, Badock 1, O'Connor 1
FA Cup (8):	Morgan 3 (1 pen), White 2, Francis 1, Penrice 1, Stevenson 1
FRT (2):	O'Connor 1, White 1

1985-86

Green	Spring	Davies (M)	Stevenson	Parkin	Jones	Badock	O'Connor	Randall	Penrice	Tanner	White	Bater	Cockram (N.C.)	Vaughan (L)	Obi (M)	Scales	Francis (N.C.)	Morgan	England	Smart	Mehew	Carter	Porter	Noble	Purnell	Referee	
1	2	3	4	5	6	7	8	9	10	11*	12															D Scott	1
1	2	3	4	5	6	7	8	9	10	11																**K Baker**	2
1	2*	3	4	5	6	7	8	9	10	11	12															K Cooper	3
1	2	3	4	5	6	7	8		10		9	11														A Gunn	4
1	2	3		5	6	7	8		10		9	11	4													N Butler	5
1	2			5	6	8	7		10	3	9	11	4													**V Callow**	6
	2			5	6	7	8		10	3	9	11		1	4*	12										C Downey	7
	7*			5	6	11	8	9	10	12		3		1		2	4									G Ashby	8
				5	6	7	8	9	10		11	3		1		2	4									D Shaw	9
	2*			5	6	7		11	9	10	8	3		1		4		12								H King	10
1		7		5	6	12	11	9	10		8	3				2	4*									**J Deakin**	11
	12	4	5					11	9	10	7	3		1		2		8	6							T Holbrook	12
	2	8	5					12	11	10*	7	4	3	1				9	6							R Lewis	13
1	8	2	4	5		7*			11	10	12	3						9	6							L Robinson	14
1		3	4	5	6*	2			11	10	7					8		12								**A Ward**	15
1		3	4	5			11	10*	12	7						2	8	9	6							D Vickers	16
1		3	4	5			11	10*		12	7	2				8*		9	6							T Fitzharris	17
1		3	4	5			11	10		2	7							9	6	8						M Reed	18
1		3	4	5			11	10		2	7							9	6	8*	12					M Bodenham	19
1		3	4*	5	6		11	12	10	2	7	8						9								D Reeves	20
1		3	4	5	6		11		7	8	10	2						9								M James	21
1		3	4	5	6		11		7	8	10	2						9								C Seel	22
1				5	6	11			4	8	10	3				2	7	9								**Alan Robinson**	23
1				5	6	11			7	8	10	3				2	4	9								K Miller	24
1				5	6	11			4	8	10	3				2	7	9								**G Ashby**	25
1				5	6	11			4†	8	10	3				2	7	9								M Cotton	26
1				5	6	11			4	8	10	3				2	7	9								B Hill	27
1				5	6*	11	12		4	8	10	3				2	7	9								J Lloyd	28
				5		11			4	8	10	3				2	7	9	6			1				R Gifford	29
1		4		5	6	7*	11			8	10					2		9	12	3						A Gunn	30
1		4		5	6	7*	11			8	10					2		9	12			3				**K Vanes**	31
1	2	4		5	6		11			8	10	3					7	9								R Bridges	32
1	6	4	5			11	12		8	7*	10	3*				2		9					12			**D Reed**	33
1	6	4	5			11	12		3	8	10					2*	7	9								**J Moules**	34
1	6	4	5			11				8	10	3				2	7	9								J Martin	35
1	6	4	5			11				8	10	3				2	7*	9						12		F Roberts	36
1	6	4	5*			11				8	10	3	12			2	7	9								M James	37
1	6	4	5			11	9*			8	10	3				2	7							12		K Miller	38
1	6	4	5			11	9			8	10	3				2	7									V Callow	39
1	6	4	5			11				8	10	3				2	7	9								M Scott	40
1	12	4	5	6		11				8	10*	3				2	7	9								C Trussell	41
1	4			5	6	12				8	10	3				2	7*	9						11		A Saunders	42
1	6			5	7	11				8	10	3	4			2		9						12		P Tyldesley	43
1	6			5	2	11				8	10	3						9					7			E Scales	44
1	6*			5	2	11				8	4	10	3			12	7	9								Alan Robinson	45
1		11		5	6					8	4	10	3			2	7*	9						12		K Cooper	46
1		10	5	6	7					8	4					2		9	3	12					11*	K Barrett	47
1		10	5	6	7					8	4					2		9	3						11	K Redfern	48
1		11	5	6						8	3	7				2		9	4						10	K Walmsley	49
1		10	5		7*					8	4					2		9	3	12					11	D Axcell	50
		11	5	6						8	3	7				2	9		4	12		1			10*	J Bray	51
1		10	5	6		11*				8	4					2	3	9							12	M Robinson	52
1				5	6					8	4*	10				2	7	9	3					12	11	L Shapter	53
1		12	5*	6						8		10	2				7	9	3				4		11	J Moules	54
1			5		6					8		10	2			4	7	9	3						11	I Hemley	55
1		4			6	12						10	3			2	7	9	8						11*	D Vickers	56
38	18	13	30	43	32	14	34	15	39	35	37	26	1	6	1	27	27	35	17	2		2		3	9	League Appearances	
	1	1	1			3		2			2	3	1				1		2	1	4			4	2	Substitute Appearances	
4	2	2	3	4	4	2+1	4	4	3	3	3	2	1			1	2	0+1								Milk Cup Appearances	
4	1		2	4	3		4	0+1	3	4	4	3				4	4	4								FA Cup Appearances	
2	1		2	2	1	1	2	0+1	2	1	2	1				2		2				0+1		1+1		FR Trophy Appearances	

Also Played: Position (Game): Iles (NC) 6(50), Carr (NC) 5(56)   Players on Loan: Vaughan (West Ham)

Departures: Cockram (Cambridge Utd N.C.), Bater (Brentford), White, Parkin (Swindon Town), Spring (Cardiff Citt), Randall (Yeovil Town), O'Connor (Bournemouth), Stevenson (F), Green (F)

'THE PIRATES'

Formed: 1883
Turned Professional: 1897   **Ltd Co:** 1896

Previous Managers: 1889-1920 Alf Homer (Secretary-Manager)   1920-1 Ben Hall
1921-6 Andrew Wilson   1926-9 Joe Palmer   1929-30 David McLean   1930-6 Captain Albert Prince-Cox
1936-7 Percy Smith   1938-49 Brough Fletcher   1950-8 Bert Tann   1968-9 Fred Ford
1969-72 Bill Dodgin (Snr)   1972-7 Don Megson   1978-9 Bobby Campbell   1979-80 Harold Jarman
1980-1 Terry Cooper   1981-3 Bobby Gould   1983-5 David Williams
Honours: Champions Div 3 (S)
League Career: Original Members of Div 3 1920   Transferred to Div 3 (S) 1921
Promoted to Div 2 1952-3   Relegated to Div 3 1961-2   Promoted to Div 2 1973-4
Relegated to Div 3 1980-1
Colours: Blue shirts with blue and white quartered fronts and white trim, blue shorts and blue stockings
with white trim
Change Colours: Yellow and orange quarters, yellow shorts and stockings
Reserves League: **'A' Team:**

CLUB RECORDS

Most Appearances for Club: Stuart Taylor, 1965-80: Football League 548 + FA Cup 16 + League Cup 36 **Total 600**
Most Capped Player: Matt O'Mahoney, 6, Eire and 1 N Ireland   **For England:** Geoff Bradford 1
Record Goalscorer in a Match: A player has scored 4 on 11 occasions
Record League Goalscorer in a Season: Geoff Bradford, 33, Div 3 (S), 1952-3   **In All Competitions:** Geoff Bradford, 34
(League 33 + FA Cup 1)
Record League Goalscorer in a Career: Geoff Bradford, 245, 1949-64   **In All Competitions:** Geoff Bradford, 260
(League 245 + FA Cup 12 + League Cup 3)
Record Transfer Fee Received: £200,000 from Luton Town for Steve White, Dec 1979
Record Transfer Fee Paid: £100,000 to Birmingham City for Stewart Barrowclough, July 1979
Best Performances: League: 6th Div 2 1955-6, 1958-9   **FA Cup:** 6th Round, 1950-1, 1957-8   **League/Milk Cup:** 5th
Round 1970-1, 1971-2
Most League Points: (3pts for win) 79, Div 3, 1983-4   (2pts for win) 64, Div 3 (S), 1952-3
Most League Goals: 92, Div 3 (S), 1952-3
Record League Victory: 7-0 v Swansea Town, Div 2, 2 Oct 1954   7-0 v Brighton & Hove Albion, Div 3 (S), 29 Nov 1952
7-0 v Shrewsbury Town, Div 3, 21 March 1964
Most Goals Scored in a League Match: 8-2 v Brighton (a)
Most Goals Scored in a Cup Tie: 15-1 v Weymouth (h), 4th Qualifying Round FA Cup, 17 Nov 1900
Record League Defeat: 0-12 v Luton Town, Div 3 (S), 13 April 1936
Oldest Player in League Match: Bill Culley, 43 yrs, 1928
Youngest Player in League Match: Ronnie Dix, 15 yrs 180 days — Youngest player to score in Football League (in his
second match)

Most Consecutive Undefeated League Matches: 32 1973-74	**League Matches Without a Win:** 20 1980
Longest Run of Undefeated Home League Matches: 27 1952-53	**Away League Matches:** 17 1973-74
Longest Run Without Home League Win: 10 1980	**Away League Win:** 29 1929-30
Most Consecutive League Wins: 12 1952-53	**Home League Wins:** 10 1935
Most Consecutive League Defeats: 8 1961	**Away League Wins:** 5 1952-53, 1964

In both their promotion campaigns in 1952-53 and 1973-74 Bristol Rovers played 27 consecutive games without defeat

Club Statistician for the Directory: Mike Jay

BRISTOL ROVERS

PLAYERS NAME Ht Wt Birthdate	Honours	Birthplace Transfers	Clubs	APPEARANCES				GOALS			
				League	Milk Cup	FA Cup	Other Comps	League	Milk Cup	FA Cup	Other Comps
GOALKEEPERS											
Tim Carter 6.2 13.8 5.10.67		Bristol	Bristol Rovers (A)								
DEFENDERS											
Darren Carr 6.2 12.5 4.9.68		Bristol	Bristol Rovers								
Vaughan Jones* 5.6 10.8 5.3.61	WU21 (2)	Tunirefail	Bristol Rovers (A) Newport County Cardiff City Bristol Rovers	93+8 67+1 11 32	5+3 10 4 4	11 10 3	 1 1	3 4			
Wayne Noble 5.9 11.9 11.6.67		Bristol	Bristol Rovers	3+4			0+1				
Lee Portch 5.11 12.10 11.10.66		Bristol	Bristol Rovers (A)								
John Scales 6.2 12.7 4.7.66		Harrogate	Bristol Rovers	27+2	1	4	2	1			
Nick Tanner 5.10 13.12 24.5.65		Bristol	Bristol Rovers	35+2	3	4	1	2			
MIDFIELD											
Kenny Hibbitt 5.10 12.0 3.1.51	EU23 (1) Div. 2, 77 LgC 74, 80	Bradford P.A.	Bradford Wolverhampton W. Coventry City Bristol Rovers	13+2 446+19 20+4	1 34+1 0+1	 46 	 16+1 1	 88	 12	 10	 3
Gary Smart 5.8 11.2 8.12.63		Bristol	Bristol Rovers	2+1			0+1	1			
Tarki Micallef 5.5 11.5 24.1.61		Cardiff	Cardiff City (A) Newport County Cardiff City Bristol Rovers	67+14 22+2	2	1+1 5		11 2			
Ian Weston 5.9 11.0 6.5.68		Bristol	Bristol Rovers (A)								
FORWARDS											
Ian Alexander 5.9 9.12 26.1.63		Glasgow F F Cyprus F	Rotherham United Motherwell Morton Bristol Rovers	5+6 19+5 6+1	1+1 4	1 1		 2 1	 1		
David Mehew 5.11 11.8 29.10.67		Surrey	Leeds United (NC) Bristol Rovers	 0+4							
Trevor Morgan** 6.1 13.1 30.9.56		Forest Gate £3,000 £10,000 £10,000 £12,000 Player exch.	Leytonstone Bournemouth Mansfield Town Bournemouth Bristol City Exeter City Bristol Rovers	 53 12 88 32 30 35+1	 2 1 8 4 2	 2 7 1 4	 1 2	 13 6 33 11 9 16	 3 3	 3	 1
Gary Penrice 5.7 9.11 23.3.64			Bristol Rovers (A)	43+1	3	3	2+2	6		1	
Philip Purnell 5.7 9.12 12.6.64		Bristol	Bristol Rovers (P/T)	9+2				2			

ADDITIONAL CONTRACT PROFESSIONALS

APPRENTICES
Lee Howels

NON-CONTRACT PLAYERS

Martin, Boyle, Jason Eaton, Nick Hendy, Ian Macdonald

Record Attendance: (Eastville): 38,472 v Preston North End, FA Cup Round 4, 30 Jan 1960

Record Receipts: (Eastville): £31,809 v Bristol City, FA Cup Round 2, 2 Dec 1983

Season Tickets: £90 (£65 Juveniles/OAP); £195 (Family of 3), £260 (Family of 4); Terrace seats: £70 (£35 Juveniles/OAP) £145 (Family of 3) £180 (Family of 4); Standing: £45 Adults, £22.50 Juveniles/OAP, £85 (Family of 3), £110 (Family of 4)

Executive Box Season Tickets: Presidents Club. Adults £200, OAP £160, Juveniles £160

Cost of Stand Tickets: Seats: £5 (£3 Juveniles/OAP); Terrace Seats: £4 (£2 Juveniles/OAP); Standing: £2.50 (£1.25 Juveniles/OAP)

Match and Ticket Information: Stand tickets available two weeks before each match

Car Parking: Restricted to season ticket holders only

Nearest Railway Station: Bath Spa (1 mile from ground)

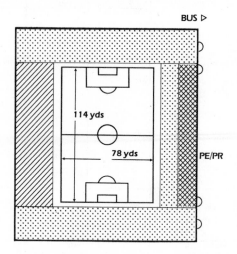

BUS ▷

114 yds

78 yds

PE/PR

How to get to the ground

From North, East, South & West: Use M4 & M5. Leave M5 at Junction 18 via A46 to Bath, follow ring road to Twerton for Bristol Rovers FC

Price of 1986-7 Programme: 50p
Number of Pages: 16
Subscriptions: £18.25

Local Newspapers: Western Daily Press, Bristol Evening Post

Local Radio Stations: Radio West, Radio Bristol

BURNLEY

Chairman
F J Teasdale

Directors
D R D Iven (Vice-Chairman)
MRCS(Eng), LRCOP(Lond), MRCGP
B Blakeborough
B M Rothwell JP
C Holt
B Dearing
J Simmons

Secretary
R Bradshaw (0282 27777)

Manager
Brian Miller

Assistant Manager
Arthur Bellamy

Youth Team Coach
George Bray

Physiotherapist
J Holland

Commercial Manager
J Thomson (0282 27777)

Groundsman
George Oldfield

In the 4th Division for the first time in their history Burnley started the season optimistically with a new manager in Martin Buchan and a good spirit in the club in spite of the disasters of recent seasons. Immediate promotion was the aim and when it became clear that this could not happen there was a state of disillusionment in the team and Buchan resigned to be replaced by former captain, Brian Miller. A final position of 14th was the worst in the club's history and League defeats by the likes of Stockport County, Crewe Alexandra, Colchester United, Aldershot, Halifax and Scunthorpe United were an indication of the depths to which the club had slumped. There were some satisfactory wins, but not enough of them.

One always looks for cup form to provide consolation, but this was not forthcoming. The Milk Cup programme began and ended in the 1st Round — on aggregate against Bury (5-6) — and although the FA Cup lasted a little longer it was still pitifully short as a campaign with a narrow away win at Nuneaton being followed by heavy defeat at Rotherham. The Freight Rover Trophy ended as soon as it had started.

So this once great club faces a bleak future unless it can reverse the downward trend. The scoring form of Taylor was one piece of encouragement, whilst Joe Neenan in goal continued to be a consistent performer. Hampton, the ever-present Deakin, Hird and Malley were the other people who earned good marks, but new players (if they can be afforded) are badly needed if Brian Miller is to deliver some cheer to the loyal fans. They have waited long enough and they deserve to have their patience rewarded, so it is now the responsibility of the players to lift themselves to promotion as the start of a revival.   WLM

Back Row L to R: Joe Gallagher, Tony Woodworth, Jim Heggarty, Joe Neenan, Steve Kennedy, Wayne Entwistle, Ray Deakin. **Second Row:** George Bray (Coach), Leighton James, Peter Devine, Peter Hampton, Phil Malley, Darren Heesom, Robert Regis, Neil Grewcock, Ashley Hoskin, Ian Britton, Jim Thomson (Commercial Manager), Jimmy Holland (Physio). **Third Row:** Billy Rodaway, Brian Miller (Manager), Bob Blakeborough (Director), Basil Dearing (Director), Frank Teasdale (Chairman), Dr David Iven (Vice-Chairman), Bernard Rothwell (Director), Clive Holt (Director), Arthur Bellamy (Assistant Manager), Derrick Parker. **Front Row:** Jason Hardy, Jason Harris, John Mercer, Phil Devaney, Peter Leebrook, Stuart Darley, Micky Southern, Mark Hazeldene.

BURNLEY

DIVISION FOUR: 14th   **FA CUP:** 2nd ROUND   **MILK CUP:** 1st ROUND

MATCH	DATE		COMPE-TITION	VENUE	OPPONENTS	RESULT		HALF TIME	L'GUE POS'N	GOALSCORERS/GOAL TIMES	ATTEN-DANCE
1	A	17	CL	H	Northampton Town	W	3-2	3-0		Hird 12, Biggins 28, Mundee (og) 44	4,214
2		20	MC1/1	H	Bury	W	2-1	1-1		Taylor 10, Biggins 82	3,298
3		23	CL	H	Stockport County	L	0-1	0-0	12		3,966
4		26	CL	H	Port Vale	L	1-2	1-1	15		3,940
5		31	CL	A	Aldershot	W	2-0	0-0	9	Taylor 62, 68	(1,744)
6	S	3	MC1/2	A	Bury	L	3-5	2-2		Taylor 25, 84, Hird 41	(3,762)
7		7	CL	H	Hartlepool United	W	2-0	1-0	7	Biggins 37, Heggarty 89	3,154
8		14	CL	A	Hereford United	D	2-2	1-0	8	Malley 17, Hird (pen) 65	(3,411)
9		17	CL	A	Preston N. E.	L	0-1	0-1	10		(5,585)
10		21	CL	H	Rochdale	W	1-0	1-0	8	Biggins 1	4,177
11		28	CL	A	Peterborough United	D	0-0	0-0	8		(3,700)
12	O	1	CL	H	Colchester United	L	0-2	0-0	10		3,375
13		5	CL	A	Chester City	L	0-4	0-2	12		(3,005)
14		12	CL	H	Swindon Town	L	0-2	0-1	14		2,979
15		19	CL	A	Crewe Alexandra	L	1-3	0-2	17	Taylor 48	(1,998)
16		22	CL	H	Torquay United	W	3-0	2-0	15	Hird (pen) 15, Taylor 30, 88	2,235
17		26	CL	A	Halifax Town	D	2-2	1-0	16	Parker 17, Grewcock 87	(2,334)
18	N	2	CL	H	Southend United	L	1-3	1-0	18	Robinson 44	2,641
19		5	CL	H	Mansfield Town	W	2-1	1-0	14	Taylor 44, Hird 66	2,200
20		9	CL	A	Cambridge United	W	4-0	4-0	12	Hird 1, Parker 28, Devine 29, Taylor 35	(1,917)
21		16	FAC1	A	Nuneaton Borough	W	3-2	2-0		Malley 15, Devine 43, 89	(4,500)
22		23	CL	H	Exeter City	W	3-1	1-0	11	McNicol (og) 14, Hird (pen) 50 (pen) 81	2,874
23		30	CL	A	Scunthorpe United	D	1-1	1-0	13	Hoskin 7	(2,001)
24	D	7	FAC2	A	Rotherham United	L	1-4	0-1		Parker 50	(4,264)
25		14	CL	H	Orient	W	1-0	1-0	10	Taylor 23	3,007
26		20	CL	A	Stockport County	D	1-1	0-0	12	Heesom 79	(3,472)
27		26	CL	A	Tranmere Rovers	L	1-2	1-0	12	Taylor 45	(3,188)
28	J	1	CL	H	Wrexham	W	5-2	2-2	11	Taylor 27, Deakin 32, Grewcock 50, Parker 58, 75	4,037
29		3	CL	A	Southend United	W	3-2	0-1	9	Taylor 65, 77, Deakin 66	(2,619)
30		18	CL	A	Northampton Town	L	0-2	0-1	11		(3,095)
31		21	FRT	A	Chesterfield	W	2-1	1-1		Lawrence 23, Taylor 46	(1,053)
32		25	CL	H	Hereford United	W	3-2	1-2	8	Taylor 5, 56, Lawrence 72	3,920
33	F	1	CL	A	Hartlepool United	L	1-3	0-0	9	Lawrence 56	(3,336)
34		4	CL	A	Torquay United	L	0-2	0-1	10		(1,430)
35		24	CL	A	Port Vale	D	1-1	0-1	10	Lawrence 86	(3,030)
36	M	1	CL	H	Peterborough United	D	1-1	0-0	10	Paris (og) 50	2,686
37		8	CL	H	Chester City	W	1-0	0-0	9	Lawrence 70	3,690
38		11	CL	H	Aldershot	L	1-2	1-0	10	Grewcock 19	2,650
39		13	FRT	H	Darlington	D	1-1	1-1		Taylor 13	1,138
40		15	CL	A	Swindon Town	L	1-3	1-1	10	Lawrence 45	(7,212)
41		18	CL	A	Rochdale	L	0-1	0-0	11		(2,597)
42		22	CL	H	Halifax Town	L	1-3	1-2	12	Hampton 15	3,321
43		29	CL	A	Wrexham	W	1-0	1-0	11	Hoskin 42	(2,057)
44		31	CL	H	Tranmere Rovers	W	3-1	1-1	9	Grewcock 34, 90, Malley 66	3,099
45	A	5	CL	A	Mansfield Town	D	0-0	0-0	10		(3,671)
46		12	CL	H	Cambridge United	D	1-1	0-1	11	Grewcock 88	2,705
47		15	CL	H	Crewe Alexandra	L	0-1	0-0	13		1,961
48		19	CL	A	Exeter City	W	2-0	1-0	12	Taylor 20, Parker 48	(2,019)
49		22	CL	H	Preston North End	D	1-1	0-0	12	Deakin 49	3,783
50		26	CL	H	Scunthorpe United	L	1-2	1-1	12	Grewcock 20	2,563
51	M	3	CL	A	Orient	L	0-3	0-1	15		(1,955)
52		6	CL	A	Colchester United	D	2-2	0-1	14	Lawrence 62, Devine 89	(2,726)

Best Home League Attendance: 4,214 v Northampton 17/8   **Smallest: 1,961 Crewe Alex. 15/4**   **Av Home Att: 3,182**

Goal Scorers: Compared with 84-85: −1,038

League (60):	Taylor 16, Grewcock 7, Hird 7 (4 pen), Lawrence 6, Parker 5, Biggins 3, Deakin 3, Devine 2, Hoskin 2, Malley 2, Hampton 1, Heesom 1, Heggarty 1, Robinson 1, Opponents 3
Milk Cup (5):	Taylor 3, Biggins 1, Hird 1
FA Cup (4):	Devine 2, Malley 1, Parker 1
FRT (3):	Taylor 2, Lawrence 1

Neenan	Palmer	Hampton	Heggarty	Overson	Deakin	Hird	Malley	Taylor	Biggins	Grewcock	Chippendale	Devine	Peacock (L)	Rhodes (M)	Robinson (L)	Parker	Heesom	Hoskin	Harrington (L)	Lawrence	Haddock (L)	Kilner	Holden (NC)	Referee	
1	2	3	4	5	6	7	8	9	10	11														J Lloyd	1
1	2	3	6	5	11	4	8	9	10	7														N Wilson	2
1	2	3	6	5	11	4	8	9	10	7														P Willis	3
1	2	3	6	5	11	4	8	9	10	7*	12													C Trussel	4
1	2	3	6	5	11	4	8	9*	10	7		12												K Hamer	5
1	2	3	6	5	11	4	8	9	10*	7		12												G Aplin	6
1	2	3	6	5	11	4	8	9	10*	7		12												R Bridges	7
1	2	3	6	5	11	4	8	9	10		7													D Hedges	8
1	2	3	6	5	11	4	8	9*	10		7	12												C Seel	9
1	2	3	6	5	11	4	8		10	7*	12	9												N Ashley	10
	2	3	6		5		8	9*	10	7	4	12	1		11									R Lewis	11
	2	3	6		5		8	12	10	7	4*	9	1		11									A Saunders	12
	2	3	6		5		8	9	10	7*	12		1		11									H King	13
	5	3		4	6*	2	9		11			8	1	12		7	10							D Phillips	14
	2	6			5	4	10*	9			12	11	1		7	8	3							J Ball	15
	2	5			6	4	8	9				11	1		7	10	3							R Nixon	16
	2	5			6	4*	8	9			12	11	1		7	10	3							J Worrall	17
			3*	4		2	7	10			6	9	1		8	11	5	12						G Tyson	18
	2*	5			6	4	8	9		7		11				10	3	12	1					T Jones	19
		5			6	2	8	9		7		4				10	3	11	1					A Buksh	20
1		5			6	2	8	9		7		4				10	3	11						B Hill	21
1		5			6	2	8	9*		7		4				10	3	11		12				J Lloyd	22
1		5			6	2	8	9		7		4				10	3	11						K Hackett	23
1	2	5			6	4	8	9		7						10	3	11						R Bridges	24
1	12	5			6	2	8	9		7		4				10	3	11*						K Lupton	25
1	11	5			6	2	8	9		7		4				10	3							L Robinson	26
1	11*	4		5	6	2	8	9		7						10	3			12				F Roberts	27
1	4	5			6	2	8	9		7		11*				10	3	12						G Courtney	28
1	4	5			6	2		9		7		8				10	3	11						I Hemley	29
1	4	5			6	2		9		7		8				10*	3	12		11				V Callow	30
1	11	5			6	2	4	9				8					3			10				J Ashworth	31
1	11	5			6	2	4	9		7		8					3			10				J Key	32
1	11	5			6	2	4	9		7		8					3*			10		12		D Phillips	33
1	11	5			6	2	4	9*		7		8					3			10		12		K Cooper	34
1	11	5			6	2	4	9		7		8					3			10				G Ashby	35
1	11	5			6	2	4	9		7		8					3			10				J Lovatt	36
1	11	5	12		6	2	4	9		7		8*					3			10				C Seel	37
1	11	5	12		6	2	4	9		7		8*					3			10				M Heath	38
1	3	6	5		8	2	4	9		7*		12						11		10				C Trussell	39
1	3	6	5		8	2	4	9		7								11		10				Alan Robinson	40
1	3	6	5		8	2	4*	9		7		12						11		10				D Allinson	41
1	3	6	5		7	2	4	10*		9		12					8	11						M Peck	42
1	3				6	2	4	9		7		8						11		10	5			D Shaw	43
1	3				6	2*	4	9		7		8				12		11		10	5			J McAulay	44
1	2		4		6			9		7		8					3	11		10	5			I Borrett	45
1	2	12			6		4	9		7		8					3*	11		10	5			F Roberts	46
1	3	2			6	8	4	9		7*						10		11		12	5			T Holbrook	47
1	3	2			6	8	4	9		7						10		11			5			M Dimblebee	48
1	3	2			6	8	4	9		7						10		11			5			K Breen	49
1	6	3	5		8	2	4	9		7						10		11						D Phillips	50
1	3	5			6	2	4	9		7		8						11*		10		12		J Deakin	51
1	3	5			6	2	4	9		7		8						11		10				M Cotton	52
36	11	39	33	28	46	39	43	44	12	36	6	31	8	3	5	19	23	17	2	16	7	2		League Appearances	
		3					1		2	2		6		1		2	2			4		3	1	Substitute Appearances	
2	2	2	2	2	2	2	2	2	0+1			1				2	2							Milk Cup Appearances	
2	1		2		2	2	2		2			1				2	2	2						FA Cup Appearances	
2		2	1	2	2	2		2				1+1					1	1		2				FR Trophy Appearances	

Players on Loan: Peacock (Doncaster), Robinson (Man Utd), Harrington (Blackpool), Haddock (Newcastle Utd)

Departures: Palmer (Wolverhampton W), Overson (Birmingham C), Biggins (Norwich C)

'CLARETS'

Formed: 1882
Turned Professional: 1883　**Ltd Co:** 1897

Previous Names: Burnley Rovers 1881-2
Previous Managers: 1945-9 Cliff Britton　1949-54 Frank Hill　1954-7 Alan Brown　1957-8 Billy Dougal
1958-70 Harry Potts　1970-6 Jimmy Adamson　1976-7 Joe Brown　1977-9 Harry Potts
1979-83 Brian Miller　1983 Frank Casper (Caretaker)　1983-4 John Bond　1984-5 John Benson
1985-6 Martin Buchan
Honours: Champions Div 1, 1920-1, 1959-60　Champions Div 2, 1897-8, 1972-3　Champions Div 3
1981-2　FA Cup Winners 1913-4　Anglo-Scottish Cup Winners 1978-9　FA Charity Shield Winners
1973; Joint Winners 1960
League Career: Founder Members of Football League 1888　Relegated to Div 2 1896-7
Promoted to Div 1 1897-8　Relegated to Div 2 1899-1900　Promoted to Div 1 1912-3
Relegated to Div 2 1929-30　Promoted to Div 1 1946-7　Relegated to Div 2 1970-1
Promoted to Div 1 1972-3　Relegated to Div 2 1975-6　Relegated to Div 3 1979-80
Promoted to Div 2 1982-3　Relegated to Div 4 1984-5
Colours: Claret shirts with light blue sleeves, white shorts and stockings
Change Colours: All yellow
Reserves League:　　　　　　'A' Team:

CLUB RECORDS

Most Appearances for Club: Jerry Dawson: 1907-28, Football League 522 + FA Cup 45 + Charity Shield 1 **Total 568**
Most Capped Player: Jimmy McIlroy, 51, N Ireland　**For England:** Bob Kelly 11
Record Goalscorer in a Match: Louis Page, 6 v Birmingham City (a), 7-1, Div 1, 10.04.1926
Record League Goalscorer in a Season: George Beel, 35, Div 1, 1927-8　**In All Competitions:** Jimmy Robson, 37
(League 25 + FA Cup 5 + League Cup 4 + European Cup 3), 1960-1　Willie Irvine, 37 (League 29, FA Cup 5, League Cup
3) 1965-6
Record League Goalscorer in a Career: George Beel, 178, 1923-4　**In All Competitions:** George Beel, 187 (League
178 + FA Cup 9)
Record Transfer Fee Received: £325,000 from Everton for Trevor Steven, July 1983
Record Transfer Fee Paid: £165,000 to Queen's Park Rangers for Leighton James, Sept 1978
Best Performances: League: Champions (2)　**FA Cup:** Winners　**League/Milk Cup:** Semi-Finalists 1960-1, 1968-9,
1982-3　**European Cup:** Quarter-Final　**European Fairs Cup:** Quarter-Final
Most League Points: (3pts for win) 80, Div 3, 1981-2　(2pts for win) 62, Div 2, 1972-3
Most League Goals: 102, Div 1, 1960-1
Record League Victory and Most Goals Scored in a League Match: 9-0 v Darwen, Div 1, 9 Jan 1892
Most Goals Scored in a Cup Tie: 9-0 v Crystal Palace, 2nd Round FA Cup, 10 Feb 1909
9-0 v New Brighton, 4th Round FA Cup, 26 Jan 1957　9-0 Penrith, 1st Round FA Cup, 17 Nov 1984
Record League Defeat: 0-10 v Aston Villa, Div 1, 29 Aug 1925　0-10 v Sheffield United, Div 1, 19 Jan 1957
European Competitions Entered: European Cup 1960-1　European Fairs Cup 1966-7
Oldest Player in League Match:
Youngest Player in League Match:

Most Consecutive Undefeated League Matches: 30 1920-21	**League Matches Without a Win:** 24 1979
Longest Run of Undefeated Home League Matches: 34 1911-13	**Away League Matches:** 15 1972-73
Longest Run Without Home League Win: 11 1979	**Away League Win:** 31 1901-03
Most Consecutive League Wins: 10 1912-13	**Home League Wins:** 17 1920-21
Most Consecutive League Defeats: 8 1889-90, 1895	**Away League Wins:** 6 1919

Club Statistician for the Directory: W G Chadwick

BURNLEY

PLAYERS NAME Ht Wt Birthdate	Honours	Birthplace Transfers	Clubs	APPEARANCES				GOALS			
				League	Milk Cup	FA Cup	Other Comps	League	Milk Cup	FA Cup	Other Comps
GOALKEEPERS											
Joe Neenan 6.3 11.3 17.3.59		Manchester Player exch.	York City (A)	56	5	3					
			Scunthorpe United	172	12	20	3				
			Burnley	59	2	2	2				
DEFENDERS											
Joe Gallagher 6.1 12.0 11.1.55	E B (1)	Liverpool £350,000 F £25,000	Birmingham City (A)	281+5	16	21		17	4	3	
			Wolverhampton W.	31	2	1					
			West Ham United	8+1	1	1					
			Burnley	5+1			2				
			Halifax Town (L)	4							
Peter Hampton 5.7½ 10.9 12.9.54	EY	Oldham £165,000 F	Leeds United (A)	63+5	5+1	5	3+1	2			
			Stoke City	144+4	11	7		4			
			Burnley	84+1	6	3	2	2			
Phil Malley 5.7½ 11.2 1.11.65		Felling F F	Sunderland (A)								
			Hartlepool United	0+1							
			Burnley	52+2	2	2	4+1	2		1	
			Stockport Country (L)	3							
Steve Kennedy 6.0¼ 11.11 22.7.65		Aydenshaw	Burnley (A)	15	0+1	1+1	2				
Jim Hoggarty 6.2 13.10 4.8.65		Larne	Burnley	33+3	2	2	1	1			
Darren Heesom 5.8 11.4 8.5.68		Warrington	Burnley (A)	23+2		2	1				
MIDFIELD											
Ray Deakin 5.8 10.11 29.10.64		Liverpool F F F	Everton (A)								
			Port Vale	21+2	4			6			
			Bolton Wanderers	104+1	5	6	5	2			
			Burnley	46	2	2	2	3			
Peter Devine 5.7½ 12.0 20.11.60		Chorley	Leeds United (a)								
			Bristol City	19+2	1+1	5		1			
			Blackburn Rovers	8				2			
			Burnley	46+10	0+1	3	4+2	4		2	
Ashley Hoskins 5.2 8.5 27.3.68		Accrington	Burnley (A)	17+2		2	1				
Billy Rodaway 5.10 13.2 26.9.54	ES	Liverpool F F F	Burnley (A)	207+2	16	11					
			Peterborough United	80+1	6	6					
			Blackpool	41	2	5					
			Tranmere Rovers	55+3	3	6	3	5		1	
FORWARDS											
Leighton James 5.9½ 12.6 16.2.53	W (34), U23 (2)	Llwchwyr £140,000 £180,000 £165,000 £130,000 F F F F	Burnley (A)	180+1	14	10		44	6	1	
			Derby County	67+1	7	1		4			
			QPR	27+1		5		7			
			Burnley	76	3	5		4			
			Swansea City	88+10	6	1		27			
			Sunderland	50+2	11	1		4			
			Bury	46	2	1		4			
			Newport County	21+7	2	4		2		1	
			Burnley								
Neil Grewcock 5.6 11.11 26.4.62		Leicester F F	Leicester City (A)	7+1				1			
			Gillingham	30+4				4			
			Shepshed C'terhouse								
			Burnley	80+4	6	5	6	13	2	1	
Les Lawrence 6.3 12.0 18.5.57		Wolverhampton F £15,000	Stourbridge								
			Shrewsbury Town	10+4							
			Torquay United	170+9	11+4	9+1		45	4	4	
			Telford United								
			Weymouth		15						
			Port Vale	5+3	0+1						
			Aldershot	39	4	2	1	23	2		
			Rochdale	15	2	1		4	1		
			Burnley	22+9			2+2	8			1
Derrick Parker 5.9½ 11.8 7.2.57		Wallsend F F £40,000	Burnley (A)	5+1				2			
			Southend United	129	8	12		43	1	7	
			Barnsley	104+3	15	6		33	4	3	
			Oldham Athletic	54+3	4	1		11	2		
			Doncaster Rovers (L)					1			
			Burnley								

ADDITIONAL CONTRACT PROFESSIONALS

APPRENTICES
Phil Devaney

NON-CONTRACT PLAYERS

Chris Conway, Stuart Darley, Steven Eagleton, Richard Holden, Peter Leebrook, John Mercer, Mike Southern

Record Attendance: 54,775 v Huddersfield Town, FA Cup Round 3, 23 Feb 1924

Smallest Home Attendance for a First Class Match: 2,655 v Bournemouth, Div 3, 23 March 1985

Season Tickets:

Executive Box Season Tickets:

Cost of Stand Tickets: £5.00, £3.50 (£2.50/£2.00 OAP/juveniles) **Terraces:** £2.50 (£1.20 juveniles/OAP)

Match and Ticket Information: As for club

Car Parking: Parks in Church Street and Fulledge Recreation Ground for approx 500 vehicles each (chargeable). Both are 5 minutes walk from ground

Nearest Railway Station: Burnley Central

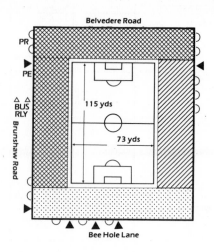

How to get to the ground

From North: Follow signs Burnley A56 into Town Centre, then at roundabout take 1st exit into Yorkshire Street, shortly over crossroads into Brunshaw Road for Burnley FC

From East: Follow signs Burnley A646 then join A671 enter city centre by Todmorden Road and at end at crossroads turn right into Brunshaw Road for Burnley FC

From South: (or use route from west). Use M62, M66 and A56 signposted Burnley into town centre, then at roundabout take 3rd exit into Yorkshire Street, shortly at crossroads forward into Brunshaw Road for Burnley FC

From West and South: Use M6 to junction 31, then Blackburn bypass and A679 into Burnley town centre and at roundabout take 3rd exit into Yorkshire Street, shortly over crossroads into Brunshaw Road for Burnley FC

Price of 1986-7 Programme: 50p
Number of Pages: 24
Subscriptions: No subscription

Local Newspapers: Lancashire Evening Telegraph, Burnley Express

Local Radio Station: Radio Lancashire

BURY

Division 3

The season began well with goals flowing freely from the new strike partnership of Craig Madden and John Kerr, 14 from the first 7 games. The 4-1 demolition of neighbours Bolton being the finest performance. This was to be however the only away win of the season. Indeed the record of one win and six draws constituting the worst away record for 75 years. Third Division survival was therefore founded on a very good home record.

October saw runaway leaders Reading visit Gigg Lane but again Bury proved to be their bogey side as their thirteenth match unbeaten run ended with a 3-1 loss. November was a disastrous month with four defeats in five games. The only bright spot was Craig Madden's goal against Walsall which equalled the club record. Nine matches without a win and only three goals scored plunged the Shakers into the relegation zone.

In an attempt to improve the scoring rate David Cross was loaned from Bolton. The move failed as he did not score in any of his 14 games. The transfer deadline passed and no players were signed. The only movement was Craig Madden to WBA for £60,000, a strange move as he was Bury's only scoring player and WBA were already doomed to Division 2. Goals did however come from the defence. In April three wins and a draw in four home games lifted the team out of the relegation zone. Other teams however had games in hand. The final match against Brentford at home was a tense affair. Whatever the result Bury could be relegated or stay up, destiny was not in their hands. Lincoln's defeat by Cardiff coupled with a draw ensured another Third division campaign.

Bury proved that league form and cup form are usually completely opposite. Following two highly entertaining ties against Burnley in the Milk Cup and a 6-5 aggregate win the draw paired Bury with Manchester City. What should have been a great day for the club was spoilt. Following the Council's decision to impose a totally unrealistic crowd limit of 8,000 on the ground the tie was switched to Old Trafford. Two very competent performances by the team were not enough to prevent a 4-2 aggregate defeat. The team progressed even further in the FA Cup however. Two second-half goals from Kevin Young and John Kerr removed high-flying Chester and earned a tie at Tranmere. The tie was settled by a Trevor Ross penalty after a replay. This success brought Second Division Barnsley to Gigg Lane with the reputation of a tight defence. They opened this up however with an own goal. The Bury defence held out until a Joe Jakub goal confirmed a fourth round tie at Reading. Hardly the glamour tie they'd hoped for! A repeat of the League victory finally meant a big match. After umpteen postponements a good contingent of Bury fans saw a match which will live long in the memory. The equaliser five minutes from time followed a second half of sustained pressure. The replay was a televised anti-climax with three second half goals making Watford the first FA Cup visitors to win a tie at Gigg Lane since 1975.

The season ended with goalkeeper Phil Hughes travelling to Mexico as Pat Jenning's understudy. The Player of the Season Award was presented to Lee Dixon the attacking right-back. Paul Greenlees

Back Row L to R: Jamie Hoyland, Peter Valentine, Phil Hughes, Andy Hill, John Kerr. **Middle Row:** Martin Dobson (Manager), Trevor Ross, Terry Pashley, Kevin Young, Peter Butler. **Front Row:** Andy Robinson, Liam Robinson, Alan Taylor, Joe Jakub, Brian Flynn, Carl Harris, Winston White.

BURY

DIVISION THREE: 20th   **FA CUP:** 5th ROUND   **MILK CUP:** 2nd ROUND

MATCH	DATE		COMPE-TITION	VENUE	OPPONENTS	RESULT		HALF TIME	L'GUE POS'N	GOALSCORERS/GOAL TIMES	ATTEN-DANCE
1	A	17	CL	A	Chesterfield	L	3-4	1-2		Dobson 44, Kerr 57, 60	(3,835)
2		20	MC1/1	A	Burnley	L	1-2	1-1		Madden 13	(3,298)
3		24	CL	H	York City	W	4-2	2-0	10	Madden 14, 33, Ross (pen) 79, White 89	2,782
4		26	CL	A	Bolton Wanderers	W	4-1	1-0	6	Young 29, Madden 63, 64, Jakub 69	(8,772)
5		30	CL	H	Lincoln City	W	4-0	1-0	2	Madden 3 (9, 75, 78), Kerr 67	2,888
6	S	3	MC1/2	H	Burnley	W	5-2	2-2		Jakub 22,35, Young 46, Kerr 55, Madden 90	3,762
7		14	CL	H	Derby County	D	1-1	0-0	4	Kerr 49	3,684
8		17	CL	A	Cardiff City	D	0-0	0-0	7		(2,011)
9		21	CL	H	Gillingham	L	1-2	1-1	10	Jones 25	2,802
10		25	MC2/1	H*	Manchester City	L	1-2	0-2		Ross (pen) 60	11,377
11		28	CL	A	Notts County	D	2-2	0-1	11	Valentine 66, Young 85	(4,662)
12	O	1	CL	H	Wolverhampton W	W	3-1	0-1	9	Young 46, Madden 74, Dixon 76	3,220
13		5	CL	H	Wigan Athletic	D	0-0	0-0	9		4,610
14		8	MC2/2	A	Manchester City	L	1-2	0-1		Madden 69	(9,799)
15		12	CL	A	Bournemouth	L	1-2	0-1	14	Beckford 82	(3,122)
16		19	CL	A	Blackpool	L	0-5	0-2	14		(5,496)
17		22	CL	H	Bristol City	W	6-3	1-0	12	Dobson pen 36,81, Beckford 46 White 59, Young 72, Madden 90	2,460
18		26	CL	H	Reading	W	3-1	2-0	12	Dobson (pen) 41, Beckford 45, 70	3,967
19		30	CL	A	Darlington	D	1-1	1-1	12	Young 32	(2,334)
20	N	2	CL	A	Swansea City	L	0-1	0-0	12		(3,530)
21		5	CL	A	Bristol Rovers	L	1-2	0-1	13	White 90	(2,959)
22		9	CL	H	Plymouth Argyle	L	0-1	0-1	13		2,975
23		16	FAC1	H	Chester City	W	2-0	0-0		Young 73, Kerr 87	3,424
24		23	CL	A	Rotherham United	L	0-2	0-1	15		(3,335)
25		30	CL	H	Walsall	W	2-1	1-0	13	Madden 26, Beckford 73	2,559
26	D	7	FAC2	A	Tranmere Rovers	D	1-1	1-0		Madden 26	(3,398)
27		10	FAC2R	H	Tranmere Rovers	W	2-1	1-0		Valentine 38, Ross (pen) 58	3,210
28		14	CL	A	Brentford	L	0-1	0-0	14		(4,038)
29		20	CL	A	York City	D	0-0	0-0	15		(3,645)
30		26	CL	H	Newport County	D	1-1	1-0	14	Dixon 29	3,013
31	J	1	CL	A	Doncaster Rovers	L	0-1	0-0	15		(3,283)
32		11	CL	A	Lincoln City	L	0-2	0-1	15		(2,226)
33		13	FAC3	H	Barnsley	W	2-0	1-0		Owen (og) 26, Jackub 74	3,676
34		18	CL	H	Chesterfield	D	1-1	0-0	16	Harris 90	2,614
35		25	FAC4	A	Reading	D	1-1	1-0		Young 12	(9,495)
36		28	FAC4R	H	Reading	W	3-0	2-0		Madden 23, 33, Dixon 76	5,527
37		29	FRT	A	Preston North End	L	0-2	0-0			(751)
38	F	1	CL	H	Darlington	L	0-1	0-0	20		2,613
39		4	CL	A	Bristol City	L	1-4	1-1	20	Madden 35	(5,074)
40		22	CL	A	Gillingham	L	0-1	0-1	21		(4,212)
41		25	CL	H	Bolton Wanderers	W	2-1	1-0	19	Madden 4, 90	6,006
42		26	FRT	H	Tranmere Rovers	L	1-2	1-1		Cross 3	461
43	M	1	CL	A	Notts County	L	2-4	2-2	20	Madden 27, Jakub 44	2,379
44		5	FAC5	A	Watford	D	1-1	0-1		Bramhall 84	(13,316)
45		8	FAC5R	H	Watford	L	0-3	0-0			7,501
46		11	CL	A	Wigan Athletic	L	0-1	0-0	20		(3,521)
47		15	CL	H	Bournemouth	W	3-0	0-0	18	Bramhall 46, Jakub 70, 83	2,097
48		18	CL	A	Wolverhampton W	D	1-1	1-0	18	Valentine 56	(2,205)
49		22	CL	A	Reading	L	0-2	0-1	19		(5,347)
50		25	CL	H	Swansea City	D	2-2	1-0	19	Ross 26, White 68	2,049
51		29	CL	H	Doncaster Rovers	L	1-2	0-1	19	Dixon 86	2,294
52		31	CL	A	Newport County	L	0-1	0-0	22		(1,983)
53	A	5	CL	H	Bristol Rovers	D	1-1	0-0	21	Valentine 90	1,866
54		8	CL	H	Cardiff City	W	3-0	0-0	19	Dixon 53, Harris 56, Hill 77	1,720
55		12	CL	A	Plymouth Argyle	L	0-3	0-2	19		(13,626)
56		19	CL	H	Rotherham United	W	2-0	1-0	19	Dixon 44, Jakub 59	2,166
57		22	CL	H	Blackpool	W	4-1	2-0	19	Hill 25, White 35, Harris 51, Dixon 67	2,738
58		26	CL	A	Walsall	L	2-3	0-2	19	Jakub 54, Pashley 64	(3,454)
59		30	CL	A	Derby County	D	1-1	1-1	20	Ross 39	(11,790)
60	M	3	CL	H	Brentford	D	0-0	0-0	20		2,953

Best Home League Attendance: 6,006 v Bolton Wanderers 25/2   **Smallest:** 1,720 v Cardiff City 8/4   **Av Home Att:** 2,889

Goal Scorers: **Compared with 84-85:** −572

League (63): Madden 14, Dixon 6, Jakub 6, Harris 5, White 5, Young 5, Dobson 4 (1 pen), Kerr 4, Beckford 3, Ross 3 (1 pen), Valentine 3, Hill 2, Bramhall 1, Jones 1, Pashley 1
Milk Cup (8): Madden 3, Jakub 2, Kerr 1, Ross 1 (pen), Young 1
FA CUP (12): Madden 3, Young 2, Bramhall 1, Dixon 1, Jakub 1, Kerr 1, Opponents 1, Ross 1 (pen), Valentine 1
FRT (1): Cross 1

* Played at Old Trafford

Hughes	Dixon	Pashley	Dobson	Valentine	Hill	White	Madden	Kerr	Jakub	Grimshaw	Lee	Ross	Young	Buckley	Bramhall	Beckford (L)	Butcher (L)	Lowe (N.C.)	Welsh (N.C.)	Harris (M)	Robinson	Harrison	Cross (L)	Brown	Referee	
1	2	3	4	5	6	7	8	9	10	11*	12														M Heath	1
1	2	3	4	5	6	7	8	9	10	11															N Wilson	2
1	2	5		3	4	10	11	9	7			6	8												D Shaw	3
1	2	3		5	6	7	8	9	10			4	11												D Allison	4
1	2	5		4	3	9	11	10	7			6	8												A Saunders	5
1	2	3	12	5*	6	7	8	9	10			4	11												G Aplin	6
1	2	5		4	3	9	11	10	7			6	8												K Lupton	7
1	2	3		5	6	7	9	8	10			4	11												G Ashby	8
1	2	5		3	4	9	11	10	7			6	8												J Lloyd	9
1	2	3		5	6	7	8	9*	10			4	11	12											K Barratt	10
1	2	3		5	6	7	8	9	10			4	11												E Scales	11
1	2	3		5	6*	7	8	9	10			4	11	12											C Seel	12
1	2	5		3	4	9	11	10*	7			6	8	12											K Walmsley	13
1	2	3	9	5	6		8		10				11		4										J McAulay	14
1	2	3	12	5	6*		7		8				11		4	9									M Dimblebee	15
1	2	3	6	5			7		8				11		4†	9									G Tyson	16
	2	3	6	5			7		8				11		4	9	1								F Roberts	17
	2	5	6	3	4	9	11		7				8			10	1								J Lovatt	18
	2	3	6	5			7		8				11			9	1								D Hutchinson	19
	2	3*	4	5	6	7	8		10				11			9	1	12							J Bray	20
	2	3*	4	5	6	7	8		10				11		12	9	1								M James	21
1	2		7	4	5	6	10*	12	8				9		3	11									D Phillips	22
1	2	5	6	4	3	9	11	10	7				8												G Aplin	23
1		3*	4	5	6	7	8	2	10	12			11		9										M Scott	24
1	2			4	5	6	11	3	8			7	9			10*		12							K Redfern	25
1	2	3*		5	6	7	8	9	10			4	11	12											M Heath	26
1	2		3	5	6	7	8	9	10			4	11												M Heath	27
1	2		6	5		7	8	9	10			4	11	3†											P Vanes	28
1	2		6	5		7	8	12	10			4*	11		9		3								G Courtney	29
1	2	3	6	5		7	8		10				11		9		4								J Key	30
1	2*	3		5		7	8	9	10				11		6		4			12					J Ball	31
1	2	3		5		7*	8	9	10			4			6					12					B Hill	32
1	2	3		5		7	8	9	10			4	11		6										J Lovatt	33
1	2	3		5		9	11	10*	7			4	8		6					12					M Peck	34
1	2	3		5		7	8		10			4	11		6					9	4				K Baker	35
1	2	3		5		7	8		10			4	11		6					9	4				K Baker	36
1			7		5		9	10	8	12					6			3	11	4*	2				J Lovatt	37
1	2	3		5		7	11		8				9		6					10*	4				M Robinson	38
1	2	3		5	6		8		10				11		12					7*			9		C Downey	39
1	2			5	3	7	8	12				10	11		6					4*			9		K Baker	40
1	2			5	3	7	8					4	11		6					9	10				T Mills	41
	2	3	4		6	7		5	10									11	8			9		1	G Aplin	42
1	2			4	5	9	11		7			6	8		3					10					G Ashby	43
1	2			5	3		8		10			4	11		6					7			9		R Lewis	44
1	2			4	5		11		7			6	8		3					9			10		L Shapter	45
1	2	12		5*	3		8		10			4	11		6					7			9		R Dilkes	46
1	2	12		4	5	9	11		7			6	8		3					10*					K Lupton	47
1	2	12		5	3	7*	8		10			4	11		6								9		D Vickers	48
1	2	8		5	3	7		12	10			4	11		6								9*		B Stevens	49
1	2	8		5	3	7			10			4	11		6							12	9*		J Lloyd	50
1	2	8		5	3		9		10			4	11		6										K Barratt	51
1	2	8		5	3		9		10			4	11		6										D Reeves	52
1	2	8		5	3	7			10			4	11*		6					9	12				K Redfern	53
1	2	8		5	3	7			10			4*			6					11	12		9		M Scott	54
1	2	8		5	3	7			10				12		6*					11	4		9		R Gifford	55
1	2	5		3*	4	9			7			6	8							11			10		C Trussell	56
1	2	3		5	6	7			10			4	11							9			8		J Bray	57
1	2	3		5	6*	7			10			4	11							9	12		8		K Cooper	58
1	2	3		5		7			10			4	11		6					9			8		R Lewis	59
1	2	3		5		7		8	10			4	11		6					9					T Mills	60
41	45	36	12	46	35	44	34	19	44	1		31	43	1	23	12	5	3		14	5		12		League Appearances	
	3	1					4		1	1	1		1	2	2			1	1	3	4				Substitute Appearances	
4	4	4	2+1	4	4	4	4	3	4	1		2	3		1										Milk Cup Appearances	
8	8	5	2	8	5	6	8	4	8			5	8	0-1	5					4	2		2		FA Cup Appearances	
1	1	1	2	1			2		2			1	0+1		1			1	2	1	1	1	1	1	FR Trophy Appearances	

Players on Loan: Beckford (Manchester City), Butcher (Chester), Cross (Bolton)
Departures: Madden (W.B.A.)

'THE SHAKERS'

Formed: 1885
Turned Professional: 1885   **Ltd Co:** 1897

Previous Managers: Since 1946
Norman Bullock   John McNeil   Dave Russell   Bob Stokoe   Bert Head   Les Shannon   Jack Marshall
Les Hart   Colin McDonald   Tommy McAnearney   Allan Brown   Bobby Smith   Bob Stokoe
Dave Hatton   Dave Connor   Jim Iley
Honours: Champions Div 2, 1894-5   Champions Div 3, 1960-1   FA Cup Winners 1900, 1903
League Career: Elected to Div 2 1894   Promoted to Div 1 1894-5
Relegated to Div 2 1911-2   Promoted to Div 1 1923-4   Relegated to Div 2 1928-9
Relegated to Div 3 1956-7   Promoted to Div 2 1960-1   Relegated to Div 3 1966-7
Promoted to Div 2 1967-8   Relegated to Div 3 1968-9   Relegated to Div 4 1970-1
Promoted to Div 3 1973-4   Relegated to Div 4 1979-80
Colours: White shirts, royal blue shorts, blue stockings
Change Colours: All yellow
Reserves League: Lancashire Div 1

CLUB RECORDS

Most Appearances for Club: Norman Bullock, 1920-35: Football League 506 + FA Cup 33 **Total 539**
Most Capped Player: Bill Gorman, 11, Northern Ireland and Eire
Record Goalscorer in a Match: Ray Pointer, 5 v Rotherham United, Div 2, 02.10.65
Eddie Quigley, 5 v Millwall (h), 5-2, Div 2, 15.02.47
Record League Goalscorer in a Season: Craig Madden, 35, Div 4, 1981-2   **In All Competitions:** Craig Madden, 42
(League 35 + FA Cup 4 + League Cup 3)
Record League Goalscorer in a Career: Norman Bullock, 124, Div 4, 1920-35   **In All Competitions:** Wally Amos 130
(League 121 + FA Cup 9) 1921-35
Record Transfer Fee Received: £150,000 from Chesterfield for Danny Wilson, July 1980   £150,000 from Everton for
Neville Southall, July 1981
Record Transfer Fee Paid: £30,000 to Port Vale for Ken Beamish, Sept 1978   £30,000 to Stoke City for David Gregory,
Sept 1978
Best Performances: League: 4th Div 1 1925-6   **FA Cup:** Winners (2)   **League/Milk Cup:** Semi-Final 1963
Most League Points: 81, Div 4, 1982-3   **Most League Goals:** 108, Div 3, 1960-1
Record League Victory: 8-0 v Burnley, Div 3, 10 Jan 1970 (Bury have scored eight goals four times in the League)
Most Goals Scored in a League Match: 12-1 v Stockton, 1st Rnd Replay FA Cup, 2 Feb 1897
Record League Defeat: 0-8 v Sheffield United, Div 1, 6 April 1896   0-8 v Swindon Town, Div 3, 8 Dec 1979
Oldest Player in League Match:
Youngest Player in League Match:
Most Consecutive Undefeated League Matches: 18 1961   **League Matches Without a Win:** 19 1911
Longest Run of Undefeated Home League Matches: 25 1967-68   **Away League Matches:** 8 1961
Longest Run Without Home League Win: 13 1937, 1978   **Away League Win:** 42 1910-12
Most Consecutive League Wins: 9 1960   **Home League Wins:** 15 1894-95
Most Consecutive League Defeats: 6 1953, 1967   **Away League Wins:** 6 1960

Club Statistician for the Directory: Paul Greenlees

BURY

PLAYERS NAME Ht Wt Birthdate	Honours	Birthplace Transfers	Clubs	League	Milk Cup	FA Cup	Other Comps	League	Milk Cup	FA Cup	Other Comps
GOALKEEPERS											
Phil Hughes	NI, Y	Belfast	Manchester United (A)								
5.11½ 11.11 19.11.64		F	Leeds United			1					
		F	Bury	6							
DEFENDERS											
Andy Hill		Ilkeston	Kimberley Town								
6.1 12.0 10.11.60		F	Carlisle United	26	2	0+1		3			
			Derby County (L)	19+3	3	3		2	1	1	
		F	Bury	78	6	6	3	5			
Terry Pashley	ES	Chesterfield	Burnley (A)	16+2							
5.8 12.0 11.10.56			Blackpool	201	19	15	1	7	2	1	
			Bury	99+8	9	8	1	2			
Peter Valentine		Huddersfield	Huddersfield Town (A)	19	2		1		1		
5.10 12.0 16.4.63		F	Bolton Wanderers	66	4	4	5				
		F	Bury	46	4	8		3		1	
Kevin Young	Div. 3, 82	Sunderland	Burnley (A)	114+6	10+7	17+1		11	1		
5.9 10.9 12.8.61			Port Vale (L)	28				8			
			Torquay United (L)	4							
			Bury	73+3	4	9		5	1	2	
MIDFIELD											
Peter Butler		Halifax	Huddersfield Town (A)	0+5							
5.7 11.3 27.8.66			Bury								
Joe Jakub*		Falkirk	Burnley (A)	42	2						
5.6 9.6 7.12.56		£19,000	Bury	252+3	13	21	4	26	4	2	
Gary Lowe		Prescot	Bury	3+1			1				
21.2.67											
Trevor Ross	SU21 (1)	Ashton-u-Lyme	Arsenal (A)	57+1	6	3		5	3	1	
5.9½ 11.10 16.1.57		£150,000	Everton	120+6	8	13		16	3	1	
Jamie Hoyland	EY	Sheffield	Manchester City (A)	2							
6.0 12.8½ 23.1.66			Portsmouth (L)	5							
			Sheffield United (L)	4							
		AEK Athens	Sheffield United (L)	4							
		F	Bury	76	4	6		9	1	2	
Winston White		Leicester	Leicester City (A)	10+2				1			
5.8 11.2 26.10.58		F	Hereford United	169+6							
		Hong Kong	Chesterfield	0+1							
		F	Port Vale	0+1							
			Stockport County	4							
			Bury	118	6	7	3	11			
FORWARDS											
Nigel Greenwood		Preston	PNE (A)	36+0	3+3	0+1	1+2	14			1
5.11 12.0 27.11.66		F	Bury								
Liam Robinson		Bradford	Huddersfield Town	17+4		2		1			
5.7 11.5 29.12.65		F	Bury								
John Kerr		Birkenhead	Tranmere Rovers (A)	145+9	10	6+2		38	4	1	
5.11 12.5 23.11.59		F	Stockport County	48	2	2	2	16			
		F	Bury	21+10	3	4	3	4	1	1	
Alan Taylor	FAC 75	Hinckley	Morecambe			1					
5.9¼ 10.12 14.11.53			Rochdale	55	3	3		7	1	1	
			West Ham United	88	8	7	6+1	25	2	6	3
			Norwich City	20				5			
		USA	Cambridge United	8	2			2			
			Hull City	13+1				3			
			Burnley	60+4	5	3	3	22	3	3	3
			Bury								

ADDITIONAL CONTRACT PROFESSIONALS

David Lee MF (0+1Lg)

APPRENTICES

NON-CONTRACT PLAYERS

Record Attendance: 35,000 v Bolton Wanderers, FA Cup Round 3, 9 Jan 1960

Smallest Home Attendance for a First Class Match: 1,096 v Northampton Town, Div 4, 5 May 1984

Record Receipts: £22,000 v Nottingham Forest, League Cup Quarter-Final, 17 Jan 1978

Season Tickets: Reserved Chairs £82, Ground £52 (£32 juveniles/OAP)

Executive Box Season Tickets: £150 per season

Cost of Stand Tickets: £4.00, £3.50; **Terraces:** £2.50 (£1.50 juveniles/OAP)

Match and Ticket Information: 500 seats in reserved chair section bookable two weeks before each match
Re: Family Tickets: A number of tickets are available on the day of the match only. These tickets are for 'A' stand which is also open to the public. So it is not strictly a family only area

Car Parking: Available for use of season ticket holders only. Ample side-street parking is avaialable

Nearest Railway Station: Bury Metro Interchange

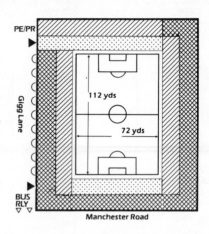

How to get to the ground

From North: Use Motorway M66 until junction 2, then leave motorway and follow signs Bury A58. In 0.5m turn left into Heywood Street and at end forward into Parkhills Road. At end turn left A56 into Manchester Road, then shortly turn left into Gigg Lane for Bury FC
From East, South and West: Use Motorway M62 until junction 17. Leave Motorway and follow signs Bury A56. In 3.1m turn right into Gigg Lane for Bury FC

Price of 1986-7 Programme: 50p
Number of Pages: 16
Subscriptions: Apply to club for details

Local Radio Stations: Piccadilly Radio, Radio Manchester

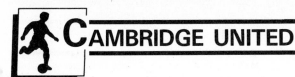 **C**AMBRIDGE UNITED  Division 4

Chairman
D A Ruston

Directors
C R Brett, (Vice-Chairman)
J E K Barnes
R H Smart
S G Line
G E Taylor

Company Secretary
Philip Mark Hough (0223 241237)

Manager
Chris Turner

Assistant Manager
Malcolm Webster

Youth Team Coach
Micky Lambert

Commercial Manager
John Carter (0233 241237)

Physiotherapist
Peter Melville

Stadium Manager
I Darler

At the end of the season, Cambridge United had to apply for re-election to the Canon League for the first time in their League history. This was disappointing but the season ended on a high note with only one defeat in the last 11 games, and the club were only one point away from avoiding the bottom four.

The season started on a bright note with a 4-2 win in the first game, against Hartlepool, and a hat-trick by Steven Pyle the first for the club for 5½ years. After this, results went against the club and a series of defeats saw United rapidly slide down the table to hit bottom place by the end of September. Results picked up in October, but heavy home defeats in November by Burnley (0-4), Northampton (2-5) and an FA Cup defeat at the hands of non-league Dagenham eventually saw manager Ken Shellito leave the club in early December.

A week later, a surprise choice as the new manager was former player Chris Turner who brought new life into the club and in the first few weeks of his reign they recorded good wins against Chester (the top club) and Tranmere. However, injuries were to leave him short of experienced players at key points during the remainder of the season, with the loss of players such as Steve Fallon, Steve Spriggs and central defender Geoff Scott who was forced to quit the game through injury.

On the bright side, the club scored 65 goals in the League and David Crown broke the club goalscoring record (previously held by Alan Biley) with 24 League goals and 27 in all competitions. A fine achievement as this was achieved in a team that spent most of the season in the bottom half of the division.

In cup competitions the club continued its poor from and were knocked out in the first round of the Milk Cup and the FA Cup. Their only success was in the Freight Rover Trophy beating Aldershot and Peterborough, before losing to Gillingham in the southern area quarter-finals.

The outlook for next season is much brighter as the club has a good mix of young and old players, and loyal support, and as long as key players such as Crown, Spriggs, Fallon, Tom Finney and Steve Dowman can steer clear of injury, there is every hope of the side challenging for promotion in 1986/87.

Colin Faiers

Back Row L to R: Mark Cooper, Andrew Beattie, Keith Branagan, Steve Dowman, Lindsay Smith. **Middle Row:** Malcolm Webster (Assistant Manager), Patrick Rayment, John Beck, Ian Meesham, Steve Fallon, Chris Turner (Manager). **Front Row:** Brian Mundee, Steve Spriggs, David Crown, David Tong, Tony Towner.

CAMBRIDGE UNITED

DIVISION FOUR: 22nd　　　**FA CUP: 1st ROUND**　　　**MILK CUP: 1st ROUND**　　　**FRT: QUARTER-FINAL (South)**

MATCH	DATE		COMPE-TITION	VENUE	OPPONENTS	RESULT		HALF TIME	L'GUE POS'N	GOALSCORERS/GOAL TIMES	ATTEN-DANCE
1	A	17	CL	H	Hartlepool United	W	4-2	0-1		Pyle 3 (49, 57, 60) Spriggs 83	1,821
2		20	MC1/1	H	Brentford	D	1-1	1-0		Sinton (pen) 12	1,794
3		23	CL	A	Tranmere Rovers	L	2-6	2-3	15	Pyle 13, Massey 28	(1,642)
4		27	CL	H	Southend United	L	1-2	0-1	17	Finney 70	2,038
5		31	CL	H	Hereford United	L	0-1	0-1	19		(2,924)
6	S	3	MC1/2	A	Brentford	L	0-2	0-0			(2,512)
7		7	CL	H	Aldershot	L	0-2	0-1	22		1,504
8		14	CL	A	Port Vale	L	1-4	1-1	23	Spriggs 40	(2,674)
9		17	CL	A	Colchester United	L	1-4	0-2	23	Adcock (og) 78	(2,574)
10		20	CL	H	Exeter City	D	1-1	1-0	23	Crown 2	1,479
11		27	CL	A	Halifax Town	D	1-1	1-0	22	Crown 44	(1,409)
12	O	2	CL	H	Preston North End	W	2-0	1-0	21	McPherson 44, Spriggs 78	1,543
13		5	CL	H	Mansfield Town	W	4-2	1-0	21	Massey (pen) 44, Graham (og) 81, Spriggs 84, Crown 87	1,957
14		11	CL	A	Scunthorpe United	D	0-0	0-0	20		(1,496)
15		15	CL	A	Wrexham	L	2-6	0-3	22	Comfort 84, Crown 86	(1,651)
16		19	CL	H	Orient	L	1-2	0-1	22	Crown 79	2,743
17		26	CL	H	Peterborough United	W	3-1	0-0	21	Crown 56, 65, Massey (pen) 61	3,234
18	N	1	CL	A	Stockport County	L	1-3	1-3	21	Massey (pen) 20	(1,734)
19		6	CL	A	Swindon Town	L	0-1	0-0	22		(5,489)
20		9	CL	H	Burnley	L	0-4	0-4	23		1,917
21		16	FAC1	A	Dagenham	L	1-2	0-0		Crown 80	(1,351)
22		23	CL	A	Crewe Alexandra	W	1-0	1-0	21	Crown 3	(1,312)
23		30	CL	H	Northampton Town	L	2-5	1-2	22	Crown 38, Fallow 61	2,235
24	D	6	CL	H	Stockport County	L	1-2	1-2	23	Massey 2	1,535
25		14	CL	A	Torquay United	D	1-1	1-0	21	Comfort 40	(1,066)
26		20	CL	H	Tranmere Rovers	W	3-2	2-1	21	Crown 30, Spriggs 44, Massey (pen) 72	1,499
27		26	CL	A	Chester City	W	3-2	2-1	19	Lockhart 23, Cooper 34, Massey 58	2,395
28		28	CL	A	Southend United	L	0-1	0-0	19		(2,528)
29	J	1	CL	A	Rochdale	L	1-2	1-1	19	Massey (pen) 9	(2,046)
30		11	CL	H	Hereford United	W	4-0	2-0	19	Massey pen 1, 47, Crown 36, Lockhart 52	2,144
31		14	FRT	A	Aldershot	W	1-0	1-0		Comfort 40	(826)
32		18	CL	A	Hartlepool United	L	1-2	0-1	19	Massey (pen) 80	(3,300)
33		21	FRT	H	Peterborough United	W	4-1	0-1		Crown 46, 88, Dowman 78, Rayment 86	2,253
34		25	CL	H	Port Vale	L	1-3	0-1	20	Walker 86	(2,437)
35	F	1	CL	A	Aldershot	L	1-2	0-1	20	Rayment (pen) 83	(1,131)
36		4	CL	H	Wrexham	W	4-3	3-1	20	Comfort 10, Salathiel og 37, Crown 45 63	1,503
37		8	CL	A	Orient	L	1-3	0-1	20	Massey 81	(2,727)
38		21	CL	A	Exeter City	D	0-0	0-0	20		(1,369)
39		24	FRT QF S	A	Gillingham	L	0-2	0-1			(1,812)
40	M	8	L	A	Mansfield Town	L	0-2	0-0	22		(3,373)
41		15	CL	H	Scunthorpe United	L	0-1	0-0	22		1,785
42		18	CL	A	Preston North End	W	2-1	1-1	22	Butler 27, Crown 46	(2,840)
43		22	CL	A	Peterborough United	D	0-0	0-0	22		(2,894)
44		28	CL	H	Rochdale	W	1-0	1-0	22	Dowman 11	1,992
45		31	CL	A	Chester City	D	1-1	0-0	22	Dowman 60	(2,893)
46	A	5	CL	H	Swindon Town	D	1-1	1-1	21	Crown 18	3,128
47		8	CL	H	Halifax Town	W	4-0	2-0	22	Crown 3 (15, 72, pen 89), Finney 27	1,909
48		12	CL	A	Burnley	D	1-1	1-0	22	Crown 25	(2,705)
49		19	CL	H	Crewe Alexandra	W	1-0	0-0	22	Crown 56	2,225
50		26	CL	A	Northampton Town	W	2-0	0-0	22	Crown 46, Mundee 47	(2,100)
51		29	CL	H	Colchester United	L	1-3	0-3	22	Crown pen 89	3,115
52	M	3	CL	H	Torquay United	W	3-0	2-0	22	Richards S 24, 47, Crown pen 40	2,209

Best Home League Attendance: 3,234 v Peterborough Utd 26/10　　　**Smallest: 1,479 v Exeter City 20/9**　　　**Av Home Att: 2,102**

Goal Scorers:　　　　　　　　　　　　　　　　　　　　　　　　　　　　　**Compared with 84-85:**

League (65):	Crown 23 (2 pen), Massey 12 (7 pen), Spriggs 5, Pyle 4, Comfort 3, Dowman 2, Finney 2, Lockhart 2, Richards S 2, Butler 1, Cooper 1, Fallow 1, McPherson 1, Mundee 1, Rayment 1 (pen), Walker 1, Opponents 3
Milk Cup (1):	Sinton (pen) 1
FA Cup (1):	Crown 1
FRT Cup (5):	Crown 2, Comfort 1, Dowman 1, Rayment 1

1985-86

Hansbury	Mundee	Bennett	Finney	Beattie	Scott	Sinton	Spriggs	Pyle	Comfort	Crown	Branagan	Richards G (NC)	Moyes	Rayment	Lee (M)	Steve Massey	Clarke	McPherson (L)	Cooper (NC)	Dowman	Butler (L)	Fallon	Lockhart	Philliben (L)	Walker (NC)	Referee	No.
1		3	4	5	6	7	8	9	10	11																J Ball	1
		3	4		6	7	8	9	10	11	1															**H Taylor**	2
1		3	4	5	6†	7	8	9	10	11																N Glover	3
1		3	4	5	6	7	8	9	10*	11			2													D Hedges	4
1		3	4		6	7	8	9	10	11					5		2									M Reed	5
1		3	4		6	7*	8	9	10	11					5	12	2									**K Miller**	6
1		3	4	5		7	8*	9	10	11			6			12	2									V Wood r'd P Vanes	7
1		3	4		6†	7	8		10	11					5		2									I Hendrick	8
1		3	4		6	7	8	9	10	11					5		2									N Butler	9
1		3	4		6	7	8	12	10	11					5	9*	2									M Bodenham	10
1		3	4		6	7	8		10	11					5	9	2									C Trussell	11
1		3	4			7	8		10	11					5	9	2	6								A Gunn	12
1		3	4			7	8		10	11					5	9*	2	6	12							C Downey	13
1		3	4		6	7	8		10	11				2		9				5						L Dilkes	14
1		3	4		6	7	8		10	11			12	2*		9				5						A Robinson	15
1		4		3	7	8	12		10	11				2		9*		6		5						T Holbrook	16
1		4		3	7	8			10	11				2		9		6		5						A Vickers	17
1		4		3	7	8*			10	11				2		9		6		5						T Simpson	18
1		5	4	3	7		8		11	9				2		10				6						R Gifford	19
1		4		3	7		8		11	9				2		10		6		5						A Buksh	20
1		6	4	3	7*		8		10	11						12	2		9	5						**P Vanes**	21
1		3	4†	11			8			9						12	2	6	10*	5		7				T Fitzharris	22
1		4	8	3*	9				10							11	2	6	12	5		7				D Reeves	23
1		4	8	3*	12	9				11						10	2	6		5		7				M Cotton	24
1		3	5		6*		8		11	9			12			10	2				7	4				H King	25
1		3	5				8		11	9			6			10	2				7	4				J Moules	26
1		3	5				8		11	9*			6			10	2		12		7	4				A Ward	27
1		3	5				8		11				6			10	2*		9		4	7				M James	28
1		3	12				8		11				6			10	2*		9	5	4	7				M Heath	29
1		3	7†				8		11	9						10				5	4	6	2			D Axcell	30
1		3	7				8		11	9						10	2			5	4	6				**M Bodenham**	31
1		3	7				8		11							10	12			5	4	6*	2	9		C Seel	32
1		3	7				8		11	9			6			10*				5	4		2	12		**J Hemley**	33
1		3					8		11	9			6						8	5	7	4	2	10		D Hedges	34
1		3					8		11	9			6				8			5	7	4	2	10		J Bray	35
1		3	6†				8		11	9				2		10				5	7	4				K Miller	36
1		3	6				8		11	9						12	2	10*		5	7	4				R Milford	37
1		3	6				8		11	9						10	2		11	5	7	4				V Callow	38
1		3	8	6			12			9						10	2		11	5	7	4*				**A Gunn**	39
1		3	8	6						9						10	2			5	7	4	11			M Heath	40
1		3	6	4			8			9						10	2			5	7		11			M Reed	41
1	3	8	6	4						9						10	2		11	5	7					G Courtney	42
1	3	7	4				8			9						10	2		11	5		6				A Robinson	43
	3	6	4				8			9	1					10	2		11	5	7					N Butler	44
	3	6	4							9	1	8				10*	2		11							B Stevens	45
	3	6	4							9	1	7					2		11							M Cotton	46
	3	6	4							9	1	8					2		11	5	7					C Downey	47
	3	6	4							9	1	8					2		11	5	7					F Roberts	48
	3	6	4							9	1	8							11	5	7	2				K Baker	49
	3	6	4							9	1	8				7			11	5						D Axcell	50
	3	6	4							9	1	8					2		11	5						G Napthine	51
	3	6	4							9	1	8				10	7			5						K Barratt	52
37	**11**	**31**	**38**	**22**	**19**	**19**	**29**	**12**	**30**	**43**	**9**	**8**	**9**	**12**	**8**	**28**	**25**	**11**	**15**	**28**	**14**	**15**	**9**	**6**	**3**	League Appearances	
			1			1	2									1	1	3		1					3	Substitute Appearances	
1		2	2	2	2	2	2	2	2	1			1	1		0-1										Milk Cup Appearances	
1		1	1		1	1	1		1	1						0-1	1		1	1						FA Cup Appearances	
3		3	3	1			2	2+1	3					1		3	2			3	1	3	1	1	0-1	FR Trophy Appearances	

Also Played: Position(Game): Osgood 2(1,2,3), Massey K 12(3,4), 9(8), Galloway (L) 12(45), Richards S. (NC) 5(46), 2(50, 52), 7(51), Littlejohns (NC) 8(46), Towner (NC) 10(46, 47, 48, 49, 50, 51), Conway (NC) 11(52)

Players on Loan: McPherson (West Ham), Philliben (Doncaster R), Galloway (Crystal Palace), Butler (Huddersfield)

Departures: Greygoose (Orient), Pyle (Torquay U), Sinton (Brentford) Moyes (Bristol C), Comfort (Orient), Finney (F)

'UNITED'

Formed: 1919
Turned Professional: 1946   **Ltd Co:** 1948

Previous Name: Until 1949 Abbey United
Previous Managers: From 1951: 1951-5 Bill Whittaker   1955 Gerald Williams   1955-9 Bert Johnson   1959 Bill Craig   1960-3 Alan Moore (was player coach from 1959-60)   1963-4 Roy Kirk (Caretaker)   1964-6 Roy Kirk   1966-7 Matt Wynn (Caretaker)   1967-74 Bill Leivers   1974 Ray Freeman (Caretaker)   1974-8 Ron Atkinson   1978-83 John Docherty   1984-85 John Ryan   John Cozens (Caretaker)   1985-6 Ken Shellito   1986 Chris Turner
Honours: Champions Div 4, 1976-7
League Career: Elected to Div 4 1970   Promoted to Div 3 1972-3   Relegated to Div 4 1973-4   Promoted to Div 3 1976-7   Promoted to Div 2 1977-8   Relegated to Div 3 1983-4   Relegated to Div 4 1984-85
Colours: Amber shirts with black pin stripe, black shorts with amber stockings with black trim
Change Colours: All sky blue

CLUB RECORDS

Most Appearances for Club: Steve Fallon: Football League 390 + 5 subs + FA Cup 16 + League/Milk Cup 21 **Total 427 + 5 subs**
Most Capped Player: Tom Finney, 7, N Ireland   **For England:** None
Record Goalscorer in a Match: Brian Greenhalgh, 4 v Darlington, 6-0, Div 4, 18.09.1971
Record League Goalscorer in a Season: Alan Biley, 21, 1977-8   **In All Competitions:** Alan Biley, 24 (League 21 + FA Cup 2 + League/Milk Cup 1) 1977-8
Record League Goalscorer in a Career: Alan Biley, 74   **In All Competitions:** Alan Biley, 81 (League 74 + FA Cup 3 + League/Milk Cup 4)
Record Transfer Fee Received: £350,000 from Derby County for Alan Biley, Jan 1980
Record Transfer Fee Paid: £140,000 to Northampton Town for George Riley, Nov 1979
Best Performances: League: 8th Div 2 1979-80   **FA Cup:** 5th Round 1982-3   **League/Milk Cup:** 4th Round, 1980-1
Most League Points: 65, Div 4, 1976-7   **Most League Goals:** 87, Div 4, 1976-7
Record League Victory and Most Goals Scored in a League Match: 6-0 v Darlington, Div 4, 18 Sept 1971
Most Goals Scored in a Cup Tie: 3 (3rd Round FA Cup, 4th Leg Milk Cup Ties)
Record League Defeat: 0-6 v Aldershot, (a), Div 3, 13 April 1974   0-6 v Darlington (a), Div 4, 28 Sept 1974   0-6 v Chelsea, Div 2 (a), 15 Jan 1983
Oldest Player in League Match:
Youngest Player in League Match:

Most Consecutive Undefeated League Matches: 14 1972	**League Matches Without a Win:** 31 1983-84 (A League Record)
Longest Run of Undefeated Home League Matches: 22 1977-78	**Away League Matches:** 7 1972, 1975
Longest Run Without Home League Win: 16 1983-84 (A League Record)	
	Away League Win: 32 1981-83
Most Consecutive League Wins: 7 1977	**Home League Wins:** 10 1977-78
Most Consecutive League Defeats: 7 1983, 1984, 1984-85, 1985	**Away League Wins:** 3 1971, 1975, 1977

Club Statistician for the Directory: Colin Faiers

CAMBRIDGE UNITED

PLAYERS NAME Ht Wt Birthdate	Honours	Birthplace Transfers	Clubs	APPEARANCES				GOALS			
				League	Milk Cup	FA Cup	Other Comps	League	Milk Cup	FA Cup	Other Comps
GOALKEEPERS											
Keith Branagan 6.0 11.0 10.7.66		Fulham	Cambridge United	29	2						
DEFENDERS											
John Beck 5.10½ 11.9 25.5.54	AMC 84	Edmonton	QPR (A)	32+8	2	4		1			
			Coventry City	60+9	5	3		6			
			Fulham	113+1	6	6		13			
			Bournemouth	132+5	6+1	5+1	12+1	14		2	3
		F	Cambridge United								
Steve Dowman 5.11 12.4 15.4.58		Manor Park £75,000 £20,000 F	Colchester United (A)	150+4	10+1	21		21	2	3	
			Wrexham	87	7	6		2			
			Charlton Athletic	60+1		0+1		5			
			Newport County	9	2			1			
			Cambridge United								
Steve Fallon 6.1 12.7 3.8.56	Div. 4, 77	Whittlesey F	Kettering Town								
			Cambridge	464+5	21	16	5	28	2	1	
Brian Mundee 5.10 10.12 12.1.66		London F F F	Hungerford Town								
			Bournemouth	3+1	1	3					
			Northampton Town	46+4	6	8	4	3		1	
			Cambridge United								
Pat Rayment 5.11 12.3 11.4.65		Peterborough F	Peterborough U. (A)	24+6	1+2		0+1	3			
			Cambridge United	38+6	1	1	1	12			1
Lindsay Smith 5.11 12.0 18.9.54		Enfield	Colchester United (A)	185+27	8+2	12+1		16			
			Charlton Ath. (L)	1							
			Millwall (L)	5							
			Cambridge United	173+1	9	7+1		7			
			Lincoln City (L)	5							
			Plymouth Argyle	76	4	14	3	5		1	1
			Millwall	54+1	2		2	5			
			Cambridge United								
MIDFIELD											
Andy Beattie 6.2 11.6 9.2.64		Lincoln	Cambridge United (A)	60+3	3						
Steve Spriggs 5.3 10.2 16.2.56	Div. 4, 77	Doncaster F	Huddersfield Town (A)	2+2	1						
			Cambridge United	377+5	24	14	4	53	2	1	
David Tong 5.9 11.7 21.9.55	Div. 3, 79	Blackpool £25,000 F	Blackpool (A)	70+8	5	1		7			
			Shrewsbury Town	156+4	8	16		8			
			Cardiff City	119+1	10	5					
			Rochdale	0+2							
			Bristol City	19		3	2				
			Gillingham	5							
FORWARDS											
David Crown 5.10 11.4 16.2.58		Enfield £15,000 Player exch. F F	Walthamstow Avenue								
			Brentford	44+2	4	3	1	8	1	1	
			Portsmouth	25+3		2		2			
			Exeter City (L)	6+1				3			
			Reading	87+1	4	6	2+1	14	2	1	
			Cambridge United	43	2	1	3	23	1	2	
Steve Massey 5.11 11.5 28.3.58		Denton	Stockport Co. (A)	87+14	8	5		20	3	1	
			Bournemouth	85+12	5	3+1		19	1	2	
			Peterborough United	13+5		1+1		2			
			Northampton Town	60	4	5		26	3	1	
			Hull City	62+11	4+2	3+1	4+2	21	1	1	

ADDITIONAL CONTRACT PROFESSIONALS

Mark Cooper, Tony Towner (monthly), Ian Mersham

APPRENTICES

NON-CONTRACT PLAYERS

Paul Casey, Mervyn Cawston, Pat Conway, Mark Cooper, Jason Cowling, Aidan Dobson, David Hedley, Colin Littlejohn, Tony Towner

Record Attendance: 14,000 v Chelsea
(friendly), 1 May 1970

**Smallest Home Attendance for a First Class
Match:** 1,361 v Newport County, Div 4, 6 April
1976

Record Receipts: £25,134 v Chelsea, 11 Feb
1984

Season Tickets: Seats: C,D,E £75; B,F £65; A
£55 (OAP) £30 (juvenile with adult £19;
Terraces: £40 (juvenile/OAP £19)

Cost of Stand Tickets: C,D,E £4.75; B,F
£4.00; A £3.50, OAPs/juveniles £2.25, £1.85,
£1.60; **Terraces:** £2.50, (juveniles/OAP £1.10)

Match and Ticket Information: Cambridge
241237 (Postal applications with payment &
SAE two weeks in advance)

Car Parking: Limited parking at main entrance.
Off-street parking permitted. Also at Coldhams
Common

Nearest Railway Station: Cambridge (0223
311999)

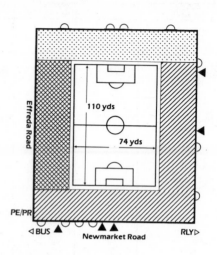

How to get to the ground

From North: Use A1 and A604 S.P. Cambridge
into City Centre, then follow signs Newmarket
A45 into Newmarket Road for Cambridge United
FC
From East: Follow signs Cambridge A45 into
Newmarket Road for Cambridge United FC
From South: Use A10 or A130 into Cambridge,
then follow signs Newmarket A45 into
Newmarket Road for Cambridge United FC
From West: Follow signs Cambridge A422, into
Cambridge via A45 then keep forward S.P.
Newmarket into Newmarket Road for Cambridge
United FC

Price of 1986-7 Programme: 50p
Number of Pages: 16
Subscriptions: Please apply to club

Local Newspaper: Cambridge Evening News

Local Radio Station: BBC Radio
Cambridgeshire

 # CARDIFF CITY

Chairman
J A Clemo Dip PE

Director
B Proctor

Managing Director/Secretary
R Jones

Commercial Manager
Mrs Susan Wynne

Manager
Frank Burrows

Coach
Bobby Smith

Chief Scout
Stan Montgomery

Physiotherapist
J Hemmerman

ardiff City's efforts to maintain a record of returning to the Second Division immediately failed and they dropped for the second year running, with the humiliation of playing in the Fourth Division for the first time.

On the opening day of the season the side inflicted a 4-1 defeat on Notts County at Meadow Lane. But from then on Cardiff's fortunes took a tumble that continued, through to the end of the season. The only real glimpse of hope came when the team hit a purple patch around Christmas time when they managed to score four goals in each of three games, winning 4-0 at Lincoln City, 4-3 at Chesterfield and drawing 4-4 at Plymouth on New Year's Day. During this period they collected 16 points in 8 games while remaining undefeated, but only four wins in the remaining 20 fixtures sealed their fate.

Their Cup fortunes followed those of previous seasons as they tumbled out of the Milk Cup and FA Cup at the first hurdle (against Swansea City and Exeter City respectively). There was a concerted effort to salvage something out of the season by qualifying for the European Cup Winners Cup by winning the Welsh Cup for the first time in a decade, but after poor performances against local non-league sides Caerleon, Mold Alexandra and Barry Town they were bundled out of the competition by Wrexham who won both legs of the semi-final.

The squad, which had proved itself inadequate during the previous campaign, had not been strengthened to any degree. A staggering total of 33 players were fielded in first team games, and although the youth side found some success by winning the Macbar South West Counties League Cup, the South Wales Youth Cup and the Welsh Youth Cup it came as no surprise when Alan Durban was relieved of his duties as manager. Just prior to this move the owners of the club, Kenton Utilities based in the North-East of England, decided to terminate their association with the club as from June 2nd, 1986. Although there were three separate offers put on the table that of the current Vice-Chairman, Tony Clemo, was successful. Thanks to Kenton Utilities support over the previous eight years, and the fact that they sold the club for a figure well below a 'reasonable sum', most of the club's overdraft at the bank has been wiped out and soccer at Ninian Park is guaranteed for the foreseeable future. Indeed, the club are on a sounder footing now financially than for many years.

What sort of standard of football can be expected over the coming seasons remains to be seen. Unless new, experienced, quality players can be found who wish to come to Cardiff their chances of climbing out of the 4th Division will be slim. The new manager Frank Burrows has been promised that money will be made available for team strengthening, but it must be spent wisely. The loss of team captain Jimmy Mullen, who has accepted the position of player-manager at neighbours Newport County, is a blow with the lack of any suitable replacement among the current first-team players.

With promotion and relegation between the 4th Division and the Gola League possible non-League football at Ninian Park is now a threat. Steps must be taken to ensure that the rot is halted.   Alan Jenkins

Back Row L to R: Chris Marustik, Mike Ford, Andy Kerr, Alan Rodgers, Graham Moseley, Mel Rees, Robert Turner, Paul Wheeler, Steve Shorlock, Phil Brignull.
Front Row: Nigel Vaughan, Paul Wimbeton, Alan Curtis, Terry Boyle, Wayne Curtis, Jason Gummer, David Giles.

CARDIFF CITY

DIVISION THREE: 22nd   **FA CUP:** 1st ROUND   **MILK CUP:** 1st ROUND

MATCH	DATE	COMPE-TITION	VENUE	OPPONENTS	RESULT		HALF TIME	L'GUE POS'N	GOALSCORERS/GOAL TIMES	ATTEN-DANCE
1	A 17	CL	A	Notts County	W	4-1	3-0		McLoughlin 8, Farrington 22, Vaughan 37 Mullen 60	(5,436)
2	20	MC1/1	H	Swansea City	W	2-1	1-0		Flynn 20, 86	4,218
3	24	CL	H	Chesterfield	L	0-2	0-1	11		3,601
4	26	CL	A	Newport County	W	2-1	1-0	9	Mullen (pen) 25, Vaughan 89	(5,027)
5	31	CL	H	Reading	L	1-3	0-1	14	McLoughlin 60	3,539
6	S 3	MC1/2	A	Swansea City	L	1-3	1-1		Farrington 40	(4,621)
7	7	CL	A	York City	D	1-1	0-1	12	Ford 86	(3,760)
8	14	CL	H	Bristol City	L	1-3	0-1	17	Withey 75	4,412
9	17	CL	H	Bury	D	0-0	0-0	17		2,011
10	21	CL	A	Blackpool	L	0-3	0-0	18		(3,783)
11	28	CL	H	Derby County	L	0-2	0-1	21		3,435
12	O 1	CL	A	Rotherham United	L	0-3	0-2	21		(2,906)
13	5	CL	H	Bournemouth	L	0-1	0-1	21		2,156
14	12	CL	A	Gillingham	L	0-2	0-2	22		(3,367)
15	19	CL	H	Wigan Athletic	W	3-1	1-0	22	Marustik 40, Turner 78, Vaughan 87	2,020
16	22	CL	A	Darlington	L	1-4	0-0	22	McLoughlin 80	(2,446)
17	26	CL	H	Bolton Wanderers	L	0-1	0-1	22		2,502
18	N 2	CL	A	Brentford	L	0-3	0-3	23		(3,934)
19	5	CL	A	Walsall	L	3-6	0-3	23	Mullen 48, Christie 50, Vaughan 72	(3,282)
20	8	CL	H	Doncaster Rovers	L	0-1	0-0	24		2,015
21	16	FAC1	A	Exeter City	L	1-2	0-1		Stevenson 79	(2,772)
22	23	CL	H	Bristol Rovers	L	1-2	1-2	24	Mullen (pen) 3	(4,563)
23	30	CL	H	Wolverhampton W.	D	1-1	1-0	24	Curtis 35	2,453
24	D 14	CL	A	Lincoln City	W	4-0	0-0	24	Vaughan 50, Turner 81, Mullen (pen) 88, Farrington 89	(2,127)
25	20	CL	A	Chesterfield	W	4-3	2-2	22	Turner 15, Christie 21, Vaughan 80, Farrington 82	(1,773)
26	26	CL	H	Swansea City	W	1-0	0-0	21	Vaughan 88	9,375
27	28	CL	H	Newport County	D	1-1	0-0	21	Ford 65	7,450
28	J 1	CL	A	Plymouth Argyle	D	4-4	2-2	21	Turner 35, Ford 39, Vaughan 53, Mullen (pen) 59	(8,920)
29	4	CL	H	Brentford	W	1-0	0-0	19	Vaughan 78	3,398
30	11	CL	A	Reading	D	1-1	0-0	19	Ford 51	(6,784)
31	18	CL	H	Notts County	L	1-3	1-1	19	Mullen (pen) 45	2,410
32	21	FRT	A	Newport County	L	0-1	0-0			(1,863)
33	25	CL	A	Bristol City	L	1-2	1-2	20	Vaughan 34	(7,541)
34	28	FRT	H	Swansea City	L	0-2	0-1			1,006
35	31	CL	H	York City	W	2-1	0-1	19	Vaughan 72, Wheeler 81	2,051
36	F 4	CL	H	Darlington	L	0-1	0-0			2,222
37	8	CL	A	Wigan Athletic	L	0-2	0-1	20		(3,428)
38	22	CL	H	Blackpool	W	1-0	0-0	19	Curtis 60	2,430
39	M 1	CL	A	Derby County	L	1-2	0-0	19	Vaughan 57	(11,014)
40	8	CL	A	Bournemouth	D	1-1	0-1	19	Turner 78	(2,707)
41	15	CL	H	Gillingham	D	1-1	1-1	21	Gummer 33	2,505
42	22	CL	A	Bolton Wanderers	L	0-5	0-1	22		(4,114)
43	25	CL	H	Rotherham United	L	2-3	0-1	22	McLoughlin 6, Mullen (pen) 90	1,863
44	28	CL	H	Plymouth Argyle	L	1-2	0-2	22	Nardiello 50	3,834
45	31	CL	A	Swansea City	L	0-2	0-0	23		(6,643)
46	A 5	CL	H	Walsall	D	1-1	1-1	24	Foley 4	1,777
47	8	CL	A	Bury	L	0-3	0-0	24		(1,720)
48	12	CL	A	Doncaster Rovers	W	2-0	2-0	22	Nardiello 12, 25	(2,051)
49	19	CL	H	Bristol Rovers	W	2-0	2-0	21	Tanner (og) 21, Vaughan 33	2,735
50	26	CL	A	Wolverhampton W.	L	1-3	0-2	23	Nardiello 51	(3,353)
51	M 3	CL	H	Lincoln City	W	2-1	2-1	22	Turner 32, 40	1,904

Best Home League Attendance: 9,375 v Swansea 26/12   **Smallest:** 1,777 v Walsall 5/4   **Av Home Att:** 3,135

Goal Scorers: **Compared with 84-85:** −854

League (53): Vaughan 13, Mullen 8 (6 pen), Turner 7, Ford 4, McLoughlin 4, Nardiello 4, Farrington 3, Christie 2, Curtis 2, Foley 1, Gummer 1, Marustik 1, Wheeler 1, Withey 1, Opponents 1

Milk Cup (3): Flynn 2, Farrington 1

FA CUP (1): Stevenson 1

FRT (Nil):

Sander (NC)	King	Carver (MC)	Gibbins	Ford	Mullen	Flynn	Farrington	Turner	Vaughan	McLoughlin	Micallef (NC)	Stevenson (L)	Rees	Leonard (NC)	Meacock	Gummer	Giles (NC)	Withey	Curtis (NC)	Corner (L)	Wheeler (NC)	Christie	Marustik	Smelt	Brignull	Referee	
1	2	3	4	5	6	7	8	9	10	11																P Tyldesley	1
1	**2**	**3**	**4**	**5**	**6**	**7**	**8**	**9**	**10**	**11***	**12**															**A Seville**	**2**
1	2	3	4	5	6	7†	8	9	10	11																R Groves	3
1	2	3	4	5	6	7	8*	9	10	11	12															J Martin	4
1		3	4	5	6	7		9*	10	11	12															P Vanes	5
		3	**4**	**5**	**6**	**7***	**8**		**9**		**11**		**1**	**2**	**10**											**R Milford**	**6**
		3	4	5	6		8		9	2	12		1		10*	7	11									A Robinson	7
		3	4	5	6		8		9	2	12		1			7	11*	10								V Callow	8
		3	4	5	6		8		9	2	11*		1			12		10								G Ashby	9
		3	4	5	6	7	8		9*	2	11		1					10	12							G Aplin	10
		3	4	11	6	7	8		9*	2	11		1					10	12	5	10					D Reeves	11
		3	4	11	6	7*	8			2	12		1					9	5	10						C Trussell	12
		3	2	4	6	7	8		10		12		1					9*		5	11					M Reed	13
				4	6	7	8*	9		12		1	3			11			5			10				A Gunn	14
1		3		4	6			9	8	7					12	11			5			10				B Stevens	15
1		2*		5	6			9	8	3					11	7		12	4			10				T Simpson	16
1	5			4	6		11	9	8	2		3									7	10				M Cotton	17
1	5			4	6			9	8	2	11	3				10					7					M Bodenham	18
1	2			4	6		10*	9	8	12		5	3								7	11				J Ashworth	19
	2			4	6		9†	8	10			5	3								7	11	1			K Barratt	20
	2			**4**	**6**			**9**	**8**	**12**	**10**	**5**	**3**								**7***	**11**	**1**			**R Hamer**	**21**
					6		12		8		11	5				3	9	2			7	4	.1			K Miller	22
					6		12	9	8			5		2		3		11		10	7*	4	1			C Downey	23
				11	6		12	9	8			5			4	3		2		10*	7		1			H Taylor	24
				10	6		12	9	8		11	5			4*	3		2		7			1			J Worrall	25
				4	6		10	9	8		11	5				3		2			7		1			R Lewis	26
				4	6		10	9	8		11	5				3		2	12	7*			1			G Napthine	27
				4	6		10	9	8		11	5				3		2		7			1			R Hamer	28
				4	6		12	9	8		11	5				3		2	10*	7			1			A Seville	29
				4	6		12	9	8		11	5				3		2	10*	7			1			M Reed	30
				5	6		10*	9	8		11					3		2	12	7	4		1			L Shapter	31
				5	**6**			**10**	**9**	**8**	**7**	**11**				**3**		**12**		**4***		**2**	**1**			**E Scales**	**32**
				4	6		10		8	12	11	5				3			9	7*	2	1			T Holbrook	33
				5	**6**				**8**	**10**	**11**					**3**		**2**	**9**	**7**	**4**	**1**			**R Gifford**	**34**
				5	6		7	9	8	12	11					3		2*	10		4	1			K Baker	35
				11	6		7	9	8	12						3		2*	10	12	4	1	5			R Groves	36
				11	6		7	9	8							3		2*	10	7	4	1	5			R Bridges	37
				11	6			9	8							3		2	10	7*	4	1	5			T Ward	38
				11			12	9	8	6						3		2	10	7*	4	1	5			D Phillips	39
				11	6		10*	9	8	5	7					3		2	12		4	1	5			N Butler	40
				9	6			8	7				10			3		2	11*		4	1	5			G Ashby	41
				4	6		10	9	8	7						3		2	11*		4	1	5			C Seel	42
				11	6			9		7	10					3		2	12		4*	1	5			R Milford/J Connock	43
				4	6			12	8	7	10*					3					2	1	5			M Dimblebee	44
1				10	6			9	12	7	11*					3		2			4		5			J Bray	45
1				11	6			12	4	7	10					3					2	1	5			R Guy	46
				11	6			12	4	7	10					3					2	1	5			M Scott	47
				11				8	12	10						3		2		7*	4	1	5			D Allison	48
				11	6			8	7	10						3		2			4	1	5			M Robinson	49
1				11	6			10	8	2						3				7*	4		5			T Simpson	50
1				11	6			10	8	12						3		2		7*	4		5			D Reeves	51
12	7	13	11	44	44	10	24	31	42	26	21	14	9	4	2	5	34	5	24	6	17	18	26	25	15	League Appearances	
							7	3											6	7	2		3	4	1	Substitute Appearances	
1	1	2	2	2	2		2	1	2	2	0-1		1	1	1											Milk Cup Appearances	
	1			1	1			1	1	0-1	1	1		1								1	1	1		FA Cup Appearances	
		2	2		1		1	2	2	2	2							2	0-1	1		2	1	2	2	FR Trophy Appearances	

Also Played: Tong 2(5), Spring (L) 2(14), Price (NC) 2(15), 6(48), O'Connor (NC) 10(22), 12(41), Foley (NC) 12(42,50) 8(43), 11(44), 9(46*, 47*, 51), Nardiello (L) 9(44, 48, 49, 50), 8(45, 46, 47)

Players on Loan: Corner (Sunderland), Stevenson (Swansea), Spring (Bristol Rovers), Nardiello (Shrewsbury)

Departures: Tong (Bristol C), Gibbins (F), Meacock (F), Flynn (Doncaster), Witney (F), Christie (P/boro), John King (Retired injury), Lee Smelt (Welsh Lge), Powey (Frickley)

'THE BLUEBIRDS'

Formed: 1899
Turned Professional: 1910   **Ltd Co:** 1910

Previous Name: Riverside FC (1899-1902), Riverside Albion (1902-1906), Cardiff City (1906-)
Previous Managers: 1910-1 Davy McDougall   1911-33 Fred Stewart   1933-4 Bartley Wilson
1934-7 B Watts Jones   1937-9 Bill Jennings   1939-46 Cyril Spiers   1946-8 Billy McCandless
1948-54 Cyril Spiers   1954-8 Trevor Morris   1958-62 Bill Jones   1962-4 George Swindin
1964-73 Jimmy Scoular   1973-4 Frank O'Farrell   1974-8 Jimmy Andrews   1978-81 Richie Morgan
1981-2 Graham Williams   1982-4 Len Ashurst   1984 to date Jimmy Goodfellow & Jimmy Mullen
(Caretakers)
Honours: Champions Div 3 (S), 1946-7   FA Cup Winners 1926-7   Welsh FA Cup Winners (19)
League Career: Elected to Div 2 1920   Promoted to Div 1 1920-1
Relegated to Div 2 1928-9   Relegated to Div 3 (S) 1930-1   Promoted to Div 2 1946-7
Promoted to Div 1 1951-2   Relegated to Div 2 1956-7   Promoted to Div 1 1959-60
Relegated to Div 2 1961-2   Relegated to Div 3 1974-5   Promoted to Div 2 1975-6
Relegated to Div 3 1981-2   Promoted to Div 2 1982-3   Relegated to Div 3 1984-5
Relegated to Div 4 1985-6
Colours: Royal blue shirts and shorts, blue stockings
Change Colours: All red
Reserves League: Macbar S W Counties

CLUB RECORDS

Most Appearances for Club: Phil Dwyer: Football League 471 + FA Cup 23 + League/Milk Cup 28 + Welsh Cup 43 + Anglo Scottish Cup 3 + European Cup Winners Cup 5 **Total 573**
Most Capped Player: Alf Sherwood, 39, Wales   **For England:** None
Record Goalscorer in a Match: Derek Tapscott, 6 v Knighton Town (Welsh FA Cup) 20.01.61
Record League Goalscorer in a Season: Stan Richards, 30, 1946-7   **In All Competitions:** John Toshack, 31, 1968-9
Record League Goalscorer in a Career: Len Davies, 127, 1920-31
Record Transfer Fee Received: £110,000 from Liverpool for John Toshack, Nov 1970
Record Transfer Fee Paid: £200,000 to San Jose Earthquakes for Godfrey Ingram, Sept 1982
Best Performances: League: Runners-Up Div 1 1923-4   **FA Cup:** Winners 1926-7   **League/Milk Cup:** Semi-Final 1965-66   **Welsh Cup:** Winners (19)   **European Cup Winners Cup:** Semi-Final 1967-8
Most League Points: 86, Div 3, 1982-3
Record League Victory and Most Goals Scored in a League Match: 9-2 v Thames, Div 3 (S), 6 Feb 1932
Most Goals Scored in a Cup Tie: 16 v Knighton, Welsh Cup, 28 Jan 1961
Record League Defeat: 2-11 v Sheffield United, Div 1, 1 Jan 1926
European Competitions Entered: European Cup Winners Cup 1964-5, 1965-6, 1967-8, 1968-9, 1969-70, 1970-1, 1971-2, 1973-4, 1974-5, 1976-7, 1977-8
Oldest Player in League Match: George Latham 42 v Blackburn (Div 1) 2.1.22
Youngest Player in League Match: John Toshack, 16 v Leyton Orient (Div 2) 13.11.65
Most Consecutive Undefeated League Matches: 21 1946-47   **League Matches Without a Win:** 15 1936-37
Longest Run of Undefeated Home League Matches: 27 1939-46-47   **Away League Matches:** 10 1946-47
Longest Run Without Home League Win: 9 1981   **Away League Win:** 44 1971-73
Most Consecutive League Wins: 9 1946   **Home League Wins:** 9 1922-23, 1951-52
Most Consecutive League Defeats: 7 1933   **Away League Wins:** 8 1946

Cardiff missed promotion in an incredibly close finish in 1923-24. When Davies missed a penalty with 15 minutes to go the score remained at 0-0 at Birmingham. So as Huddersfield beat Nottingham Forest 3-0, any lesser win would have made Cardiff Champions and City would also have won the League if decided on goal difference.

Club Statistician for the Directory: Richard Shepherd (BBC Radio Wales)

CARDIFF CITY

119

PLAYERS NAME Ht Wt Birthdate	Honours	Birthplace Transfers	Clubs	APPEARANCES				GOALS			
				League	Milk Cup	FA Cup	Other Comps	League	Milk Cup	FA Cup	Other Comps
GOALKEEPERS											
Graham Moseley 6.0 11.8 16.11.53	EY	Manchester	Blackburn Rovers (A)								
			Derby County	32	4	4					
			Aston Villa (L)	3							
			Walsall (L)	3							
		£120,000	Brighton	189	17	17	1				
			Cardiff City								
Mel Rees 6.2 12.12 25.1.67		Cardiff	Cardiff City (A)	9	1						
DEFENDERS											
Terry Boyle* 5.10 12.4 29.10.58	W (2), U21 (1)	Ammanford F	Tottenham Hotspur (A)								
			Crystal Palace	24+2							
			Wimbledon (L)	5							
		Player exch.	Bristol City	36+1	4	8				2	
		F	Newport County	165+1	4	10	6	11	1	1	1
		F	Cardiff City								
Phil Brignull 6.0 11.2 2.10.60		Stratford	West Ham United (A)	10+1							
			Bournemouth	128+1	7	7	4+1	11	2		
			Wrexham (L)	5					1		
			Cardiff City	15							
Mark Curtis 5.4 12.2 22.2.67		Port Talbot	Cardiff City	24+3							
Mike Ford 6.0 11.6 9.2.66		Bristol	Cardiff City	64	3	2	2	4			
Andy Kerr 5.11½ 12.0 7.4.66		WBA	Shrewsbury Town	9+1	1+1		2				
			Port Vale (L)								
		F	Cardiff City								
Chris Marustik 5.8¾ 11.5 10.8.61	W (6), U21 (7) YS	Swansea F	Swansea City (A)	143+10	11	9	5	11	1	1	
			Cardiff City								
Steve Sherlock 5.9 11.8 10.5.59		Birmingham	Manchester City (A)								
			Luton Town	2							
		F	Stockport County	237+8	18+1	6	2	7			
		F	Cardiff City								
MIDFIELD											
David Giles 5.7 10.4 21.9.56	W (12), U21 (4) YS	Cardiff	Cardiff City (A)	51+8	6	4	1+1	3	1	1	
			Wrexham	38	3	3	2	2			
			Swansea City	49+5	2	5+1	0+2	13		4	
			Orient (L)	3							
		Player exch.	Crystal Palace	83+5	5	5		6			
			Birmingham City								
		F	Newport County	28+4	1	2	5	1			
			Cardiff City								
Jason Gummer 5.8 10.11 27.10.67		Pontllanfraith	Cardiff City								
Chris Wilder No details		F	Southampton (A)								
			Cardiff City								
Paul Wimbleton 5.8 10.6 13.11.64		Havant F	Portsmouth (A)	5+5							
			Cardiff City								
FORWARDS											
Alan Curtis 5.11 12.5 16.5.54	W (32), U23 (1), U21 (1)	Rhondda	Swansea City	244+4	12	14	5	72	6	7	
		£350,000	Leeds United	28	2	1	4	5			
		£165,000	Swansea City	82+8	5	3	2	21	1		
		£75,000	Southampton	43+2	12	3	1	16	1	1	
			Cardiff City								
Rob Turner 6.3 13.2 18.9.66		Peterlee F	Huddersfield Town (A)	0+2	1						
			Cardiff City	31+3	1	1	1	7			
Alan Rogers 5.10 10.7 6.7.54	Div. 3, 84	Plymouth	Plymouth Argyle (A)	107+10	13	7		5			
		£15,000	Portsmouth	154+8	13+1	9+2		15	2		
		£20,000	Southend United	85+2	4	3	1+2	4			
		F	Cardiff City								
Nigel Vaughan 	W (9), U21 (2), Y, W. Cup (1)	Newport Player exch.	Newport County (A)	215+9	13+1	15+1	6	32	3		
			Cardiff City	113+4	6	2	2	37			

ADDITIONAL CONTRACT PROFESSIONALS

APPRENTICES

NON-CONTRACT PLAYERS

Con Micallef, Allen Price, Paul Wheeler

Record Attendance: 61,566 v
Wales v England, 14 Oct
1961   57,893 v Arsenal, Div 1, 22 Apr 1953

**Smallest Home Attendance for a First Class
Match:** 1,006 v Swansea City, Freight Rover
Trophy, 28 Jan 1986   604 v Molel (Welsh Cup)
Jan 8th 1986

Record Receipts: £33,164.01 v Sheffield
Wednesday, Div 2, 12 May 1984

Season Tickets: Stand: £75 Grandstand:
(£42.50 OAP/juveniles); Canton Stand & Family
Enclosure £50.00 (£28.00 OAP/juveniles),
£75.00 (adult, 1 child); £80.00 (1 adult, 2
children); £90.00 (1 adult, 3 children); Ground:
£45.00 (£24.00 OAP/juveniles)

Executive Box Season Tickets: None available

Cost of Stand Tickets: £4.00 (£3.00
OAP/juveniles) Grandstand; Canyon Stand &
Family Enclosure £3.00 (adult), £4.50 (adult & 1
child), £6.00 (adult & 2 children), £7.50 (adult
and 3 children; **Standing:** £2.50 (£2.00
OAP/juveniles)

Match and Ticket Information: Bookable in
advance

Car Parking: Surrounding streets and opposite
stadium

Nearest Railway Station: Cardiff Central
(0222 28000)

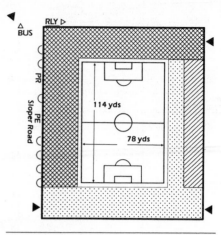

How to get to the ground

From North: Follow signs Cardiff A470 until
junction with Cardiff bypass. At roundabout take
3rd exit A48 (S.P. Port Talbot). In 2m at
roundabout take 1st exit A4161 into Cowbridge
Road. In 0.5m turn right along Lansdowne Road.
At end at crossroads turn right A4055 into
Leckwith Road. In 0.2m turn left into Sloper
Road to Cardiff City FC

From East: Use Motorway M4, then A48 into
Cardiff bypass. Follow signs Port Talbot then in
2m at roundabout take 1st exit A4161 into
Cowbridge Road. In 0.5m turn right along
Lansdowne Road. At end at crossroads turn right
A4055 into Leckwith Road. In 0.2m turn left into
Sloper Road for Cardiff City FC

From West: Follow signs Cardiff City Centre
A4161 into Cowbridge Road. In 0.5m turn right
along Lansdowne Road. At end at crossroads
turn right A4055 into Leckwith Road. In 0.2m
turn left into Sloper Road for Cardiff City FC

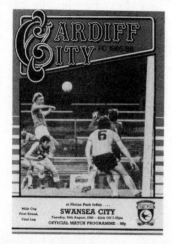

Price of 1986-7 Programme: 50p
Number of Pages: 20
Subscriptions: £22.00 per season (postage
included for UK) for home matches

Local Newspapers: South Wales Echo,
Western Mail

Local Radio Stations: BBC Radio Wales, Red
Rose Radios (ILR)

CARLISLE UNITED

Chairman
H A Jenkins

Vice-Chairman
J R Sheffield

Directors
R S Liddell
J B Lloyd
C J Vasey
Dr T Gardner
T A Bingley

Club Secretary
Mrs L Allan

Commercial Manager
G Butterfield (0228 24014)

Administrator
Miss A Moore

Manager
Harry Gregg

Groundsman
Bill Hullock

Though by November the Cumbrians' position looked utterly hopeless, they made a spirited recovery and in the end were decidedly unlucky not to avoid the drop.

Manager Bob Stokoe had announced his intention to retire from the game at the end of the season and, with this in mind, he handed over to his assistant Bryan Robson at the end of August, Mr Stokoe remaining as number two.

But, a couple of months later, with the club anchored to the foot of the table, Mr Robson felt unable to continue so Mr Stokoe resumed control until the end of the season.

At that point, Carlisle had won only once in 15 League games, were five points behind the next club and nine behind the safety line. Even Mr Stokoe had to admit: ''To be quite honest, we need a miracle.''

The club's financial restrictions meant there was no cash for investing in experienced players. With attendances dipping to as low as two thousand at times, it was as much as the Cumbrians could do to make ends meet.

Victory over Middlesbrough on Boxing Day still left them eight points behind their nearest rivals. Defeats in the following two games removed just about the last hopes anyone at Brunton Park could have had about 2nd Division survival.

But a run of five games without defeat gave rise to a faint spark of hope and, by mid-March, they scored their first away victory of the season at Barnsley. It lifted them out of bottom place, above Fulham.

They ended March with four successive victories, success at Middlesbrough leaving them one point behind fourth-from-bottom Sunderland. And the Cumbrians had a game in hand.

Was Mr Stokoe's miracle about to occur?

Until well into April it seemed it might. The situation remained much the same with Sunderland still holding a point advantage. And Carlisle still had a game in hand.

Sadly for Carlisle, Sunderland managed to match them win for win during those critical closing games and in the end it was a battle between Carlisle and Blackburn to avoid the third relegation place.

When the Cumbrians lost their final home game to Charlton, the two clubs were level on points with one game each to play. Blackburn had a better goal-difference.

Carlisle fought well at Oldham, leading at the interval. But they eventually lost 1-2. Blackburn won their final game so Carlisle were back in Division 3.

Upon the retirement of Mr Stokoe, Harry Gregg — the former N. Ireland and Manchester United goalkeeper — was appointed as his successor.

Back Row L to R: Paul Haigh, Mick Halsall, Mick McCartney, Geoff Lomax, John Cooke. **Centre:** Ken Oliver, Paul Gorman, Paul Baker, Kevin Carr, Scott Endersby, Andy Hill, Wes Saunders, Scott McGarvey. **Front Row:** Ian Bishop, Garry Worrall, Harry Gregg (Team Manager), John Halpin, Rob Wakenshaw.

CARLISLE UNITED

DIVISION TWO: 20th   **FA CUP:** 4th ROUND   **MILK CUP:** 1st ROUND

MATCH	DATE		COMPE-TITION	VENUE	OPPONENTS	RESULT		HALF TIME	L'GUE POS'N	GOALSCORERS/GOAL TIMES	ATTEN-DANCE
1	A	17	CL	H	Bradford City	L	1-2	0-0		Entwhistle 83	5,086
2		20	MC1/1	A	Crewe Alexandra	D	3-3	2-2		Mayes 8, 17, Gavin 51	(1,732)
3		24	CL	A	Portsmouth	L	0-4	0-3	21		(12,595)
4		27	CL	H	Crystal Palace	D	2-2	1-1	21	Entwhistle 44, Halpin 86	3,080
5		31	CL	A	Blackburn Rovers	L	0-2	0-0	21		(5,956)
6	S	3	MC1/2	H	Crewe Alexandra	L	3-4	2-1		Halpin 27, 29, Bishop 54	2,520
7		7	CL	H	Barnsley	D	1-1	0-0	21	Bishop 60	2,418
8		13	CL	A	Grimsby Town	L	0-1	0-0	21		(4,099)
9		17	CL	H	Oldham Athletic	W	3-1	1-0	21	Hill 24, 58, Gavin 64	3,303
10		21	CL	A	Hull City	L	0-4	0-0	21		(6,117)
11		28	CL	H	Shrewsbury Town	L	0-2	0-1	22		2,559
12	O	5	CL	A	Brighton & H. A.	L	1-6	0-2	22	Wakenshaw 49	(8,608)
13		8	FMC	A	Middlesbrough	L	0-2	0-1			(2,177)
14		12	CL	H	Norwich City	L	0-4	0-1	22		2,907
15		19	CL	H	Sunderland	L	1-2	0-1	22	Halpin 76	9,249
16		22	CL	A	Millwall	L	1-3	0-1	22	Walker (og) 82	(4,522)
17		26	CL	A	Huddersfield Town	D	3-3	0-0	22	Wakenshaw 48, McCartney 69, Halsall 84	(5,012)
18	N	3	CL	A	Wimbledon	L	1-4	1-0	22	Hill 15	(3,882)
19		9	CL	H	Stoke City	W	3-0	2-0	22	Halsall 32, Mayes 38, 67	2,813
20		23	CL	H	Leeds United	L	1-2	0-0	22	Baker 59	3,504
21		30	CL	A	Charlton Athletic	L	0-3	0-1	22		(3,059)
22	D	7	CL	H	Millwall	W	1-0	0-0	22	Bishop 83	2,497
23		13	CL	A	Bradford City	L	0-1	0-0	22		(5,212)
24		22	CL	H	Portsmouth	L	0-1	0-0	22		4,225
25		26	CL	H	Middlesbrough	W	1-0	0-0	22	Halpin 89	4,238
26	J	1	CL	A	Sheffield Utd	L	0-1	0-0	22		(10,561)
27		11	CL	H	Grimsby Town	L	1-2	0-2	22	Hill 50	2,483
28		13	FAC3	H	Q.P.R.	W	1-0	1-0		Cooke 6	5,080
29		18	CL	H	Blackburn Rovers	W	2-1	1-0	22	Halpin 20, Hill 54	3,801
30		25	FAC4	A	Peterborough United	L	0-1	0-1			(8,311)
31	F	1	CL	A	Crystal Palace	D	1-1	0-1	22	McCartney 68	(3,744)
32		8	CL	A	Sunderland	D	2-2	0-0	22	McGarvey 58, Bishop 73	(12,689)
33	M	1	CL	A	Shrewsbury Town	D	0-0	0-0	22		(2,364)
34		11	CL	H	Hull City	W	2-1	1-0	22	Baker 4, Halsall 78	3,248
35		15	CL	A	Norwich City	L	1-2	0-1	22	McGarvey 66	(13,852)
36		18	CL	H	Huddersfield Town	W	2-0	0-0	22	Halsall 70, Hill 84	3,334
37		22	CL	A	Barnsley	W	2-1	0-1	21	Hill 49, Halpin 88	(4,400)
38		29	CL	H	Sheffield United	W	1-0	1-0	21	Bishop 30	4,575
39		31	CL	A	Middlesbrough	W	3-1	1-1	21	Cooke 39, 47, Nattrass (og) 87	(7,603)
40	A	6	CL	H	Wimbledon	L	2-3	1-1	21	Cooke 42, McGarvey (pen) 80	5,593
41		8	CL	A	Fulham	W	1-0	1-0	21	Hill 41	(2,134)
42		12	CL	A	Stoke City	D	0-0	0-0	21		(7,159)
43		19	CL	H	Fulham	W	2-1	2-1	21	Bishop 33, Saunders 42	3,817
44		26	CL	A	Leeds United	L	0-2	0-1	21		(13,868)
45		29	CL	H	Brighton & H.A.	W	2-0	1-0	21	Tolmie (pen) 14, Cooke 56	4,854
46	M	3	CL	H	Charlton Athletic	L	2-3	2-1	20	Saunders 6, 23	6,526
47		5	CL	A	Oldham Athletic	L	1-2	1-0	20	Bishop 7	(4,491)

Best Home League Attendance: 9,249 v Sunderland 19/10   **Smallest:** 2,418 v Barnsley 7/9   **Av Home Att:** 4,011

Goal Scorers: Compared with 84-85: −70

League (47):	Hill 8, Bishop 6, Halpin 5, Cooke 4, Halsall 4, McGarvey 3, Saunders 3, Baker 2, Entwhistle 2, Mayes 2, McCartney 2, Wakenshaw 2, Galvin 1, Tolmie 1 (pen), Opponents 2
Milk Cup (6):	Halpin 2, Mayes 2, Bishop 1, Gavin 1
FA CUP (1):	Cooke 1
FM Cup (Nil):	

Carr	Haigh	McCartney	Ashurst	Baker	Halsall	Gorman	Bishop	Entwhistle	Hill	Gavin	Robson	Halpin	Mayes	Saunders	Wakenshaw	Cooke	Endersby (L)	Lomax	McGarvey (L)	Tolmie (L)	Referee	#
1	2	3	4	5	6	7*	8	9	10	11	12										A Saunders	1
1	2	3		5		4	6	9	10	11		7	8								**R Banks**	2
1	2	3	4	5		12	6	9	10	7		11	8*								R Gifford	3
1	2	3	4	5		8	6	9		11		7									T Fitzharris	4
1	4	3		5		10	2	6	9			11	8								L Robinson	5
1	2	3		5	10	8	6	9		11		7		4							**D Allison**	6
1	2	3	4†		6	8	10	9		11		7	12	5*							N Glover	7
1	2	3	4	5	6	8		9	10	11		7									D Phillips	8
1	2	3	4		6	8		9		11		7		5	10						D Hutchinson	9
1	2	3		4	6	8*		9		11		7	12	5	10						J Ashworth	10
1	2	3		4	6	8		9*		11	12	7		5	10						L Dilkes	11
1	2	3		4	6	8				11		7		5	9	10					A Ward	12
1	2	3		12	6	8		12		11	4*	7		5	9*	10					**J Worrall**	13
1	2	3	4		6	8		12		11		7		5	9	10					G Courtney	14
1	2	3	4	12	6	10			9	7*		11		5		8					A Robinson	15
1†	2	3	4	12	6	7*	10		9			11		5		8					J Deakin	16
1	2*	3	4		6		10		9			11		5		8					C Napthine	17
1		3	4	2	6		10		9			11		5	7	8					J Ball	18
		3	4	9	6	2	10					11	7	5		8	1				K Walmsley	19
		3	4	9*	6	2	10	12				11	7	5		8	1				N Wilson	20
		3	4	9	6	2	10	12				11	7*	5		8	1				A Seville	21
		3	4	9	6		10					11	7	5		8	1	2			R Guy	22
		3	4	9	6	7	10†					11		5	12	8*	1	2			R Bridges	23
		3	4	9	6		10	12				11	7*	5		8	1	2			K Redfern	24
		3	4	9	6		10		7			11		5		8	1	2			T Jones	25
		3	4	9*	6	12	10		7			11		5		8	1	2			P Tyldesley	26
		3	4	9*	6		10		7	12		11		5		8	1	2			R Nixon	27
		3	4	9	6		10		7			11		5		8	1	2			**D Scott**	28
		3	4	9	6		10		7			11		5	12	8	1	2			P Willis	29
		3	4		6	12	10		7			11		5	9*	8	1	2			**I Borrett**	30
		3	4		6		10		7			11		5		8	1	2	9		R Hill	31
12		3	4	5	6		10		7			11				8	1	2	9		T Simpson	32
3				5	6	4	10		7			11				8	1	2	9		F Roberts	33
		3	4	7	6		10					11		5		8	1	2	9		N Wilson	34
12		3	4		6		10		7			11		5		8	1	2*	9		H Taylor	35
	2	3	4		6		10		7			11		5		8	1		9		K Lupton	36
	2	3	4	7*	6		10	12				11		5		8	1		9		G Napthine	37
	2	3	4		6	12	10					11	7*	5		8	1		9		T Fitzharris	38
	2	3	4		6	12	10		7			11*		5		8	1		9		A Saunders	39
	2	3	4		6		10		7					5		8	1		9	11	J Key	40
	2	3	4	9	6		10		7					5		8	1			11	L Shapter	41
	2	3	4	9	6	12	10		7					5		8	1			11*	T Mills	42
	2	3	4	9	6	12	10		7					5		8	1			11*	N Midgeley	43
	2	3	4	9	6		10		7					5		8	1			11	T Fitzharris	44
	2	3	4	9	6	12	10		7					5		8	1			11	P Tyldesley	45
	2	3	4	9	6	12	10		7					5		8	1			11*	K Breen	46
	2		4	9*	6	11	10		7					5		8	1	3		12	J Lloyd	47
15	27	40	35	33	41	17	36	8	26	12		33	8	35	6	33	27	13	10	7	League Appearances	
2			2			7		1	4	1	2		2		2					1	Substitute Appearances	
2	2	2		2	1	2	2	2	1			2	1			1					Milk Cup Appearances	
		2	2	1	2	0-1	2		2			2	1	2		2	2				FA Cup Appearances	
1	1	1		0-1	1	1		0-1		1		1	1	1		1	1				FM Cup Appearances	

Players on Loan: Endersby (Swindon Town), McGarvey (Portsmouth), Tolmie (Man City)
Departures: Robson (Gateshead), Entwhistle (Bolton W), Gavin, (Bolton W), Ashurst (Leeds Utd)

'CUMBRIANS'

Formed: 1904
Turned Professional: **Ltd Co:** 1921

Previous Managers: W Clark   Ivor Broadis   Bill Shankly   Fred Emery   Andy Beattie   Ivor Powell   Alan Ashman   Tim Ward   Bob Stokoe   Ian MacFarlane   Alan Ashman   Dick Young   Bobby Moncur   Martin Harvey   B S Robson   Bob Stokoe
Honours: Champions Div 3, 1964-5
League Career: Elected to Div 3 (N) 1928   Transferred to Div 4 1958
Promoted to Div 3 1961-2   Relegated to Div 4 1962-3   Promoted to Div 3 1963-4
Promoted to Div 2 1964-5   Promoted to Div 1 1973-4   Relegated to Div 2 1974-5
Relegated to Div 3 1976-7   Promoted to Div 2 1981-2   Relegated to Div 3 1985-6
Colours: Blue shirts with white pinstripe, white collar with red and blue trim, blue shorts and blue stockings
Change Colours: All red
Reserves League: Carlisle District League

CLUB RECORDS

Most Appearances for Club: Alan Ross: 466, 1963-79
Most Capped Player: Eric Welsh, 4, Northern Ireland   **For England:** None
Record Goalscorer in a Match: Jim Whitehouse, 5 v Scunthorpe United, 8-0, Div 3 (N) 25.12.52
Record League Goalscorer in a Season: Jimmy McConnell, 42, Div 3 (N), 1928-9
Record League Goalscorer in a Career: Jimmy McConnell, 126, 1928-32
Record Transfer Fee Received: £275,000 from Vancouver Whitecaps for Peter Beardsley
Record Transfer Fee Paid: £120,000 to York City for Gordon Staniforth, Oct 1979
Best Performances: League: 22nd Div 1 1974-5   **FA Cup:** 6th Round 1974-5   **League/Milk Cup:** Semi-Final 1969-70
Most League Points: 80, Div 3, 1981-2   **Most League Goals:** 113, Div 4, 1963-4
Record League Victory: 8-0 v Hartlepool, Div 3 (N), 1 Sept 1928   v Scunthorpe United, Div 3 (N), 25 Dec 1952 (Carlisle also won against Nelson, Div 3, 14 Mar 1931)
Most Goals Scored in a First Class Match: 9-1 v Windermere, 2nd Qualifying Round FA Cup, 19 Oct 1907
Most Goals Scored in a Cup Tie: 6-1 v Billingham Synthonia, 1st Round FA Cup, 17 Nov 1976
Record League Defeat: 1-11 v Hull City, Div 3 (N), 14 Jan 1939
Oldest Player in League Match: Bryan 'Pop' Robson, 40 yrs
Youngest Player in League Match:
Most Consecutive Undefeated League Matches: 15 1950-51, 1983-84
Longest Run of Undefeated Home League Matches: 22 1950-51
Longest Run Without Home League Win: 8 1954
Most Consecutive League Wins: 6 1937, 1981-82
Most Consecutive League Defeats: 8 1935

League Matches Without a Win: 14 1935
Away League Matches: 12 1950-51
Away League Win: 20 1970-71
Home League Wins: 7 1930-36
Away League Wins: 4 1965-65

Club Statistician for the Directory: B Rodger

CARLISLE UNITED

PLAYERS NAME Ht Wt Birthdate	Honours	Birthplace Transfers	Clubs	League	Milk Cup	FA Cup	Other Comps	League	Milk Cup	FA Cup	Other Comps
GOALKEEPERS											
Kevin Carr 6.2 13.6 6.11.58		Ashington F F	Burnley (A) Newcastle United Carlisle United	173 15	9 2	11	1				
Scott Endersby 5.10 12.6 20.2.62	EY	Lewisham	Kettering Town Ipswich Town (A) Tranmere Rovers Swindon Town Carlisle United	79 85 27	6 4	2 6 7 2	5				
DEFENDERS											
Paul Baker 6.1 12.10 5.1.63		Newcastle £4,000 F	Bishop Auckland Southampton Carlisle United	33+2	2	1	0+1	2			
Paul Haigh 5.11 12.6 4.5.58	EU21 (1)	Scarborough £100,000	Hull City (A) Carlisle United	179+1 185+5	13 11	7 16+1	1	8 3	2 1	1	
Geoff Lomax 5.9 11.8 6.7.64		Droylsden	Manchester City Carlisle United	23+2 13+1	1	2 2		1			
Mike McCartney 5.7 10.12 28.9.54	SS	Edinburgh F £80,000 £50,000 Player exch.	WBA (A) Carlisle United Southampton Plymouth Argyle Carlisle United	148+8 22 49 108+1	11 2 4 4	7 6 4	1	17 1 5 7		1	
Wes Saunders 6.0 11.11 23.2.63		Sunderland F	Newcastle United Bradford City (L) Carlisle United	79 1+3 35	8 1	5 2	1	3			
MIDFIELD											
Ian Bishop 5.9½ 10.12 29.5.65		Liverpool £10,000+£5,000	Everton (A) Crewe Alexandra (L) Carlisle United	0+1 4 66+1	2	3		8	1		
Paul Gorman 5.10 12.0 6.8.63	EIU21, Y	Dublin F £5,000	Arsenal (A) Birmingham City Carlisle United	5+1 6 23+18	2	0+1	1	1			
John Halpin† 5.10 11.5 15.11.61		Broxburn (Scot) £10,000	Celtic Carlisle United	3+4 50+2	1+4 2	1+1 2+1	1	6	1 2		
Mike Halsall 5.10 11.6 21.7.61		Bootle F £5,000	Liverpool (A) Birmingham City Carlisle United	5+1 35+1 69	8+1 1	3 4	1	3 9			
FORWARDS											
John Cooke 5.8 11.0 25.4.62	EY	Salford F F F	Sunderland (A) Carlisle United Sheffield Wednesday Carlisle United	42+13 5+1 33	2 1	3+1 2	1	4 2 5	1	1	
Andy Hill 6.1 12.0 10.11.60		Ilkeston £16,000	Kimberley Derby County Carlisle United	18+3 73+8	3 3	3 4		2 15	1 1	1	
Alan Mayes 5.7 10.12 11.12.53	Div. 4, 78	London £80,000 £200,000 F	QPR (A) Watford Northampton Town (L) Swindon Town Chelsea Swindon Town Carlisle United Newport County (L)	110+23 10 89 61+5 52+10 8+2 3	11+1 15 1 3 1	5+3 8 9 3+1	3	31 38 18 27 2 1	4 9 1 2	1 4 5 1	
Scott McGarvey 6.0 12.7 22.4.63		Glasgow £100,000	Manchester United (A) Wolverhampton W. (L) Portsmouth Carlisle	13+12 13 17+6 10	3+2	1+1		3 2 6			
Rob Wakenshaw 5.10 12.0 22.12.65		Ashington £20,000	Everton (A) Carlisle United Doncaster Rovers (L)	8+1 6+3 8		7+1 1 1	1	1 2 3			
Garry Worral 5.9 11.5 4.11.61		Salford	Manchester United (A) Peterborough Carlisle United	93+2	2	1	2+1	16		1	

ADDITIONAL CONTRACT PROFESSIONALS

APPRENTICES

NON-CONTRACT PLAYERS

Record Attendance: 27,500 v Birmingham City, FA Cup Round 3, 5 Jan 1957 and v Middlesbrough, FA Cup Round 5, 7 Feb 1970

Smallest Home Attendance for a First Class Match: 1,855 v Darlington, Div 3, 30 Jan 1960

Record Receipts: £37,130 v Newcastle United, Div 2, 27 Dec 1982

Season Tickets: Stands: £70.00, £77.00, £80.00 (£36 juveniles). Ground: £47.50 (£25.50 juveniles)

Cost of Stand Tickets: £4.00, £4.50, £5.00 (£2 00 juveniles); **Terraces:** £2.50 (£1.30 juveniles)

Match and Ticket Information: Bookable 1 to 3 weeks before matches by postal or personal applications

Car Parking: Car park for 1,500 vehicles next to ground. Entrance in St Aidan's Road. 50p cars, £2.00 coaches. Limited street parking permitted

Nearest Railway Station: Carlisle Citadel (0228 4471)

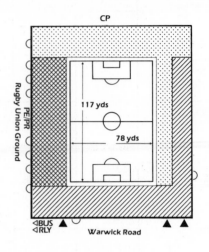

How to get to the ground

From North, East, South: Use Motorway M6 until junction 43. Leave motorway and follow signs Carlisle A69 into Warwick Road for Carlisle United FC
From West: Follow signs into Carlisle then forward A69 along Warwick Road for Carlisle United FC

Price of 1986-7 Programme: 50p
Number of Pages: 20
Subscriptions: Prices on request from CUFC

Local Newspaper: Cumbrian Newspapers

Local Radio Station: BBC Radio Cumbria

President
J B Sunley

Chairman
J A E Fryer

Directors
Richard D Collins
James W T Hill
Michael John Norris
Derek Ufton
William P Strong

Secretary
G I S Hortop (01-771 6321)

Commercial Department
(01-653 0871)

Manager
R M 'Lennie' Lawrence

Physiotherapist
C A Hall

Reserve Team Coach
B Eastick

Chief Scout
Arnie Warren

Groundsman
Len Chatterton

Quietly and efficiently Charlton Athletic worked their way into a safe promotion position. There were much more fancied clubs who faded, there was the traumatic move from the club's traditional home at the Valley and there was the leadership of a manager who had hardly made any impact as a player himself; but Charlton always looked to be 'on course'.

The move, although sad was financially sensible. The more fancied clubs created there own pressures and problems and not surprisingly their consistency suffered and in 'Lennie' Lawrence, Charlton Athletic had a 'gem' of a manager who based his footballing beliefs on common sense and putting his trust in players with character.

Ten players made at least 30 League appearances last season with Mark Reid and John Pearson 'ever presents' and only 20 players were used in the first team. Goals were shared out amongst the team with Pearson proving a superb buy from Sheffield Wednesday and finishing as top scorer with 15 goals. Mike Flanagan took his League total to over 100 for the team and the introduction of Alan Curbishley after ten games and Jim Melrose for the last 11 were shrewd additions to a very well balanced side.

Despite a disastrous cup season (that finally made concentration on League matters easier) Charlton only failed to score on four occasions in the League and on three of those the results were goalless draws. The club were never out of the top six and they only lost on three occasions in the New Year. Leadership was noticeable from the manager's office, while the captain Mark Aizlewood also won the Player of the Year award; and having steered the club through an horrendous period Mr Fryer, the Chairman, had the comforting support of Jimmy Hill, a man who has only been associated with successful club sides and Derek Ufton a very popular and experienced ex-Charlton and England player, as Directors.

Whether their lack of identity at Selhurst Park will hinder progress from now on, only time will tell but one thing is certain and that is with a leader like Lennie Lawrence in charge, the club will live sensibly within its means and will continue to produce excellent 'team' performances which should give Charlton time to consolidate.

Back Row L to R: George Shipley, Robert Lee, John Humphrey, Mark Stuart, Mark Reid, Jim Melrose. **Middle Row:** Charlie Hall (Physio), John Pender, Nicky Johns, John Pearson, Bob Bolder, Peter Shirtliff, Bill Gallagher (Assistant Physio). **Front Row:** Steve Gritt, Mark Aizlewood, Lennie Lawrence (Manager), Brian Eastick (Coach), Steve Thompson, Alan Curbishley.

CHARLTON ATHLETIC

DIVISION TWO: RUNNERS-UP **FA CUP:** 3rd ROUND **MILK CUP:** 1st ROUND

MATCH	DATE		COMPE-TITION	VENUE	OPPONENTS	RESULT		HALF TIME	L'GUE POS'N	GOALSCORERS/GOAL TIMES	ATTEN-DANCE
1	A	17	CL	H	Barnsley	W	2-1	1-0		Flanagan 5, Pearson 62	4,178
2		20	MC1/1	H	Crystal Palace	L	1-2	0-2		Stuart 69	4,930
3		24	CL	A	Grimsby Town	D	2-2	0-1	6	Gritt 54, Pearson 85	(4,261)
4		27	CL	H	Middlesbrough	W	2-0	0-0	5	Flanagan 46, Gritt 87	4,045
5		31	CL	A	Leeds United	W	2-1	1-1	4	Flanagan 27, Lee 69	(10,862)
6	S	3	MC1/2	A	Crystal Palace	D	1-1	0-0		Flanagan 51	(6,051)
7		7	CL	H	Crystal Palace	W	3-1	0-1	3	Reid (pen) 57 (pen) 69, Pearson 64	6,637
8		13	CL	A	Oldham Athletic	L	1-2	0-0	6	Reid (pen) 90	(4,700)
9		17	FMC	A	Portsmouth	L	1-4	0-0		Pender 63	(3,074)
10		21	CL	H	Stoke City	W	2-0	0-0	6	Stuart 78, Lee 83	8,858
11		28	CL	A	Wimbledon	L	1-3	1-2	6	Humphrey 19	(4,527)
12	O	1	CL	A	Sheffield Utd	D	1-1	1-0	6	Stuart 11	(9,047)
13		5	CL	H	Sunderland	W	2-1	1-0	5	Reid (pen) 30, Stuart 82	5,552
14		12	CL	A	Portsmouth	L	0-1	0-1	6		(15,549)
15		15	CL	H	Bradford City	D	1-1	1-0	6	Curbishley 5	3,247
16		19	CL	A	Brighton & H. A.	W	5-3	1-1	3	Curbishley 26, 90, Shipley 53, Lee 69, Flanagan 87	(11,546)
17		23	FMC	H	Chelsea	L	1-3	0-0		Pearson 80	3,714
18	N	2	CL	H	Shrewsbury Town	W	4-1	2-1	2	Griffin (og) 16, Stuart 31, 80, Pearson 68	3,233
19		9	CL	A	Huddersfield Town	W	2-0	1-0	2	Flanagan 18, Curbishley 87	(5,205)
20		16	CL	H	Hull City	L	1-2	1-1	4	Flanagan 43	4,140
21		23	CL	A	Blackburn Rovers	D	0-0	0-0	4		(5,321)
22		30	CL	H	Carlisle United	W	3-0	1-0	3	Pearson 38, Shipley 76, Humphrey 80	3,059
23	D	7	CL	H	Sheffield Utd	W	2-0	0-0	2	Flanagan 75, Thompson (og) 88	7,121
24		14	CL	A	Barnsley	L	1-2	0-2	3	Stuart 87	(6,231)
25		21	CL	H	Grimsby Town	W	2-0	0-0	3	Pearson 48, Reid (pen) 82	3,525
26		26	CL	A	Norwich City	L	1-3	0-0	3	Flanagan 65	(17,984)
27	J	5	FAC3	H	West Ham United	L	0-1	0-0			13,037
28		11	CL	A	Crystal Palace	L	1-2	0-2	4	Reid (pen) 59	(11,521)
29		18	CL	H	Leeds United	W	4-0	3-0	4	Reid pen 28, Lee 29, 56, Pearson 40	4,333
30	F	1	CL	A	Middlesbrough	W	3-1	0-0	3	Flanagan 46, Mowbray (og) 57, Stuart 83	(4,463)
31		4	CL	H	Brighton & H.A.	D	2-2	0-1	3	Lee 59, Aizlewood 70	5,932
32		22	CL	A	Stoke City	D	0-0	0-0	3		(9,297)
33	M	8	CL	A	Sunderland	W	2-0	0-0	3	Lee 62, 78	(11,885)
34		15	CL	H	Portsmouth	L	1-2	1-2	4	Pearson 19	10,132
35		19	CL	A	Bradford City	W	2-1	1-1	3	Pearson 15, Flanagan 75	(5,645)
36		22	CL	H	Oldham Athletic	D	1-1	1-1	4	Aizlewood 30	3,767
37		29	CL	H	Millwall	D	2-2	2-1	4	Melrose 42, Shipley 44	(7,846)
38		31	CL	H	Norwich City	W	1-0	0-0	3	Pearson 49	8,458
39	A	5	CL	A	Shrewsbury Town	L	1-2	0-2	3	Shipley 52	(3,380)
40		12	CL	H	Huddersfield Town	W	3-0	2-0	4	Melrose 19, 44, Pearson 54	4,143
41		14	CL	H	Millwall	D	3-3	2-3	4	Stuart 24, 44, Melrose 65	7,861
42		19	CL	A	Hull City	D	1-1	0-1	4	Flanagan 84	(7,139)
43		22	CL	A	Fulham	W	3-0	1-0	3	Pearson 28, Stuart 60, 65	(5,587)
44		26	CL	H	Blackburn Rovers	W	3-0	2-0	2	Melrose 8, Reid (pen) 38, Pearson 64	5,766
45		29	CL	H	Fulham	W	2-0	0-0	2	Pearson 70, Marshall (og) 87	9,393
46	M	3	CL	A	Carlisle United	W	3-2	1-2	2	Tomie (og) 40, Stuart 70, Aizlewood 80	(6,526)
47		6	CL	H	Wimbledon	D	0-0	0-0	2		13,214

Best Home League Attendance: 13,214 v Wimbledon 6/5 **Smallest: 3,059 v Carlisle United 30/11** **Av Home Att: 6,023**

Goal Scorers: **Compared with 84-85: +984**

League (78): Pearson 14, Stuart 12, Flanagan 11, Lee 8, Reid 8 (8 pen), Melrose 5, Curbishley 4, Shipley 4, Aizlewood 3, Gritt 2, Humphrey 2, Opponents 5

Milk Cup (2): Flanagan 1, Stuart 1

FA Cup (Nil):

FM Cup (2): Pearson 1, Pender 1

Johns	Friar	Reid	Aizlewood	Thompson	Berry	Gritt	Lee	Pearson	Shipley	Flanagan	Stuart	Pender	Humphrey	Loveridge	Towner	Curbishley	Lange	Melrose	Davies (L)	Referee	
1	2	3	4	5	6	7	8	9	10	11										R Milford	1
1	2	3	8	5	6	4*	7	9	10	11	12									**K Hackett**	2
1	2	3	4	5		7	12	9	10	11	8*	6								D Hutchinson	3
1	2	3	8	5		4		9	10	11	7	6								M Bodenham	4
1		3	8	5		4*	12	9	10	11	7	6	2							I Hendrick	5
1		3	8*	5			12	9	10	11	7	6†	2	4						**A Gunn**	6
1		3	8	5				9	10	11	7	6	2	4						D Hedges	7
1		3	8	5			12	9	10*	11†	7	6	2	4						T Mills	8
1		3	6			8	12	9	10		11*	5	2	4	7					**J Deakin**	9
1		3	8*	5	6		12	9	10	11	7		2	4						M James	10
1		3		5	6	4*	8	9	7	11			2		12	10				L Shapter	11
1		3		5			8	9	7	11		6	2			10				M Robinson	12
1		3		5			8	9	7	11	12	6	2			10				J Bray	13
1	11*	3		5		4	8	9	7		12	6	2			10				B Stevens	14
1		3		5		4	8*	9	7	11		6	2		12	10				J Ashworth	15
1		3		5		4	8	9	7	11		6	2			10				Alan Robinson	16
	12	3			4	7		10	8	11	9	5	2*		6			1		**M Cotton**	17
1		3	10	5			8	9	7	11	12	6*	2			4				J Martin	18
1		3	10	5			8	9	7	11		6	2			4				N Wilson	19
1		3	10	5			8	9	7*	11	12	6	2			4				G Napthine	20
1		3	10	5			8	9	7	11	12	6	2			4				D Phillips	21
1		3	10	5			8	9	7	11		6	2			4				A Seville	22
1		3	10	5			8	9	7	11		6	2			4				R Hamer	23
1		3	10	5			8	9	7*	11	12	6	2			4				J Worrall	24
1		3	10	5			8	9	7*	11	12	6	2			4				K Baker	25
1		3	10	5		7		9		11	8	6	2			4				J Ball	26
1		3	10	5		7	8	9		11		6	2			4				**B Hill**	27
1		3	10	5		7*	8	9		11	12	6	2			4				E Scales	28
1		3	10	5			8	9		11	7	6	2			4				G Ashby	29
1		3	10		5		8	9		11	7	6	2			4				A Robinson	30
1		3	10		5		8	9		11	7	6	2			4				R Lewis	31
1		3	10	5			8	9	7	11		6	2			4				K Hackett	32
1		3	10	5			8	9	7	11		6	2			4				P Tyldesley	33
1		3	10	5			8	9	7	11	12	6	2			4*				M Bodenham	34
1		3	10	5			8	9	7	11		6	2			4				D Scott	35
1		3	10	5			8	9	7	11	12	6*	2			4				R Milford	36
1		3	10	5*				9	7	11	12	6	2			4		8		J Moules	37
		3	10	5				9	7	11*	12	6	2			4	1	8		D Axcell	38
		3	10	5			12	9	7	11		6	2			4	1	8	6*	J Bray	39
		3	10*		5		12	9	7		11	6	2			4	1	8		R Groves	40
		3	10		5		12	9	7		11	6	2			4	1	8		D Reeves	41
1		3	10	5				9	7	12	11	6	2			4*		8		M Heath	42
1		3	10	5			12	9	7	4	11	6	2					8*		H Taylor	43
1		3	10	5			12	9	7	4	11	6	2					8*		I Borrett	44
1		3	10	5			12	9	7	4	11	6	2					8*		K Barratt	45
1		3	10	5			4	9	7		11	6	2					8		K Breen	46
1		3	10	5			4	9	7	12	11	6	2					8*		M James	47
38	4	42	35	38	7	11	26	42	37	33	21	38	39	5		30	4	11	1	League Appearances	
							8	9			4	9		1	1					Substitute Appearances	
2	1	2	2	2	1	1	1·1	2	2	2	1·1	1	1	1		1				Milk Cup Appearances	
1		1	1	1		1		1	1	1			1			1				FA Cup Appearances	
1	0·1	2	1		1	2	0·1	2	2	1	2	2	1	2		1				FM Cup Appearances	

Players on Loan: Davies (Newcastle)
Departures: Towner (F), Loveridge (F), Hodson (F), Berry (Brighton), Anderson, Lange (Aldershot), Flanagan (F)

HADDICKS or ROBINS

Formed: 1905
Turned Professional: 1920   **Ltd Co:** 1919

Previous Managers: 1920-5 Walter Rayner   1925-8 Alex MacFarlane   1928 Albert Lindon
1928-32 Alex MacFarlane   1932-3 Albert Lindon   1933-56 Jimmy Seed   1956-61 Jimmy Trotter
1961-5 Frank Hill   1965-7 Bob Stokoe   1967-70 Eddie Firmani   1970-4 Theo Foley
1974-80 Andy Nelson   1980-1 Mike Bailey   1981-2 Alan Mullery   1982-2 Ken Craggs
Honours: Div Three (South) Champions 1928-9, 1934-5   FA Cup Winners 1947
League Career: Elected to Div 3 (S) 1921   Promoted to Div 2 1928-9
Relegated to Div 3 (S) 1932-3   Promoted to Div 2 1934-5   Promoted to Div 1 1935-6
Relegated to Div 2 1956-7   Relegated to Div 3 1971-2   Promoted to Div 2 1974-5
Relegated to Div 3 1979-80   Promoted to Div 2 1980-1   Promoted to Div 1 1986
Colours: Red shirts, white shorts, red stockings
Change Colours: Yellow and blue
Reserves League: Football Combination   **Youth Team:** S E Counties Southern

---

CLUB RECORDS

Most Appearances for Club: Sam Bartram: Football League 582 + FA Cup 44 **Total 626**
Most Capped Player: John Hewie (Scotland) 19   **For England:** Don Welsh 3
Record Goalscorer in a Match: W Lennox, 5 v Exeter City (a) 5-2, Div 3 (S), 02.02.29
Eddie Firmani, 5 v Aston Villa (h) 6-1, Div 1 05.02.55   J Summers, 5 v Huddersfield Town (h) 6-6, Div 2
Record League Goalscorer in a Season: Ralph Allen, 32, Div 3 (S), 1934-5   **In All Competitions:** Ralph Allen, 33 (League 32 + FA Cup 1)
Record League Goalscorer in a Career: Stuart Leary, 153, 1953-62   **In All Competitions:** Stuart Leary, 163 (League 153 + FA Cup 8 + League Cup 2)
Record Transfer Fee Received: £650,000 from Crystal Palace for Mike Flanagan, Aug 1979
Record Transfer Fee Paid: £324,000 to Barcelona for Allan Simonson, Nov 1982
Best Performances: League: 2nd Div 1 1936-7   **FA Cup:** Winners 1947   **League/Milk Cup:** 4th Round 1962-3, 1964-5, 1978-9
Most League Points: 77, Div 2, 1985-6   **Most League Goals:** 107, Div 2, 1957-8
Record League Victory: 8-1 v Middlesbrough, Div 1, 12 Sept 1953
Record League Defeat: 1-11 v Aston Villa, Div 2, 14 Nov 1959
Oldest Player in League Match: Sam Bartram 42 yrs 38 days, 10.03.1956
Youngest Player in League Match: Mark Penfold 16 yrs 258 days, 25.08.1973
Most Consecutive Undefeated League Matches: 15 1980   **League Matches Without a Win:** 16 1955
Longest Run of Undefeated Home League Matches: 28 1935-36   **Away League Matches:** 7 1980
Longest Run Without Home League Win: 9 1955   **Away League Win:** 33 1969-70
Most Consecutive League Wins: 7 1980   **Home League Wins:** 11 1937-8
Most Consecutive League Defeats: 9 1957   **Away League Wins:** 5 1935

Club Statistician for the Directory: Colin Cameron

CHARLTON ATHLETIC

PLAYERS NAME Ht Wt Birthdate	Honours	Birthplace Transfers	Clubs	APPEARANCES				GOALS			
				League	Milk Cup	FA Cup	Other Comps	League	Milk Cup	FA Cup	Other Comps
GOALKEEPERS											
Nicky Johns 6.3½ 11.8 8.6.57		Bristol	Minehead								
		£6,000	Millwall	50	6	5					
		£150,000	Tampa Bay Rowdies								
			Sheffield United (L)	1	1						
		£135,000	Charlton Athletic	267	14	14	1				
Bob Bolder 6.1 14.8 2.10.58		Dover	Sheffield Wednesday								
		£125,000	Liverpool								
			Sunderland	22	2	3	2				
			Charlton Athletic								
DEFENDERS											
John Humphrey 5.10½ 10.13 31.1.61		Paddington	Wolverhampton W. (A)	149	8	4		3			
		£60,000	Charlton Athletic	39	1	1	2	2			
John Pender 6.0½ 12.3 19.11.53	EU21 (1), Y	Luton	Wolverhampton W. (A)	115+2	8	4		3		1	
		£35,000	Charlton Athletic	38	1	1	2				
Mark Reid 5.8½ 11.5 15.9.61	SU21 (2), Y, SP Div. (2), SLgC (1)	Kilwinning	Celtic	120+4	21+2	17	10	5	6	1	
		£40,000	Charlton Athletic	42	2	1	2	8			
Peter Shirtliff 6.2 12.10 6.4.61		Chapeltown	Sheffield Wed. (A)	188	17+2	16+1		4		2	
			Charlton Athletic								
Mark Stuart 5.10½ 10.12 15.12.66		Chiswick	Charlton Athletic	25+1	1+1		2	13	1		
Steve Thompson 5.10 12.0 28.7.55		Sheffield	Boston United								
		£15,000	Lincoln City	153+1	16	9	3	8		1	1
		£225,000	Charlton Athletic	38	2	1					
MIDFIELD											
Mark Aizlewood*+ 6.0 12.8 1.10.59	W (3), U21 (2), Div. 2, 82	Newport	Newport County (A)	35+3		2		1			
		£50,000	Luton Town	90+8	7	5		3		1	
		£50,000	Charlton Athletic	126	6	5	1	8		1	
Alan Curbishley 5.10½ 11.6 8.11.57	EU21 (1), Y	Forest Gate	West Ham United (A)	78+7	3	5	1+1	5			
		£25,000	Birmingham City	128+2	12	10		11	3	1	
		£100,000	Aston Villa	34+2	5	2	2	1			
		£40,000	Charlton Athletic	53		3		6			
Steve Gritt 5.9 10.10 31.10.57		Bournemouth	Bournemouth	4+2	4			3			
		F	Charlton Athletic	262+22	17+1	15	2	21			
George Shipley 5.7 10.3 7.3.59		Newcastle	Southampton (A)	2+1							
			Reading (L)	11+1							
		£45,000	Lincoln City	199	21	8	4	43	8		
		£15,000	Charlton Athletic	37	2		2	4			
Steve Jacobs 5.8 11.0 5.7.61		West Ham	Coventry City (A)	94+7	5+3	2+2		3			
		F	Brighton	47+1	5	5+1	2	3			
		F	Charlton Athletic								
Robert Lee 5.10 11.6 1.2.66	EU21 (1)	Plaistow	Charlton Athletic	72+13	3+1	3	0+1	22			
Jim Melrose 5.9 10.10 7.10.58	SU21 (8), SLG (1), S	Glasgow	Partick Thistle	103+19				31			
		£250,000	Leicester City	57+15	6	2+6		21	1	4	
		Player exch.	Coventry City	21+3	3	0+1		8	2		
		£100,000	Celtic	20+9	6+1	2+1		7	3	1	
			Wolverhampton W. (L)	6+1	2			2	2		
		£40,000	Manchester City	27+7	2+1	1	2+2	8	2		1
		£45,000	Charlton Athletic	11				5			
John Pearson 6.2 13.2 1.9.63	EY	Sheffield	Sheffield Wed. (A)	63+41	6+3	11+2		24	1	2	
		£100,000	Charlton Athletic	42	2	1	2	14			1
Roy Parkin .20.4.68		London	Charlton Athletic (A)								

ADDITIONAL CONTRACT PROFESSIONALS

APPRENTICES
Nathan Amato, Mike Bennett, Lee Featherstone, Carl Leaburn, Paul Murray, Geoff Thomas

NON-CONTRACT PLAYERS

SELHURST PARK

Selhurst Park, London SE25 6PU   Capacity: 38,500 (18,000 covered)

Record Attendance: 13,214 v Wimbledon, Div 2, 06.05.1986

Smallest Home Attendance for a First Class Match: 3,059 v Carlisle, Div 2, 30.11.1985

Record Receipts: £52,000 v West Ham, 3rd Round FA Cup, 05.01.1986

Season Tickets: Stand: Adult £96.90, Juv/OAP £56.50 before 31.5.86
Ground: Adult £64.60, Juv/OAP £32.50 before 31.5.86, Adult £43.70, Juv/OAP £24.20 before 31.5.86

Executive Box Season Tickets:

Cost of Stand Tickets:
Terraces:

Car Parking: By prior arrangement only through the Secretary. Street parking is available. Supporters may use Club Car Park (for 600 cars) **for £1 per day.** Season Tickets £50

Nearest Railway Station: Norwood Junction

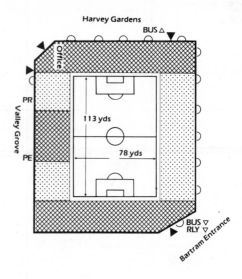

How to get to the ground

From North: From Motorway M1 or A1, use A406 North Circular Road to Chiswick. Follow signs South Circular Road A205 to Wandsworth.

Then use A3 to A214 and follow signs to Streatham. Join A23. In 1m turn left B273. At end turn left into High Street then forward into the Whitehorse Lane for Crystal Palace FC
From East: Use A232 (S.P. Croydon) to Shirley then join A215 (S.P. Norwood). In 2.2m turn left B266 into Whitehorse Lane
From South: Use A23 (S.P. London) then follow signs Crystal Palace B266 via Thornton Heath into Whitehorse Lane
From West: Use Motorway M4 to Chiswick then route from North or A232 (S.P. Croydon) to Beddington, then follow signs London A23. After follow signs Crystal Palace B266 via Thornton Heath into Whitehorse Lane

Price of 1986-7 Programme: 60p
Number of Pages: 20

Local Newspapers: Kentish Independent, Kentish Times, South East London Mercury South London Press & Croydon Advertiser

Chelsea by any standards had a satisfactory season, which was ultimately spoiled by a very poor ending to the League programme, when five of the last six matches were lost, although a victory at West Ham meant that the latter could not become Champions. The Stamford Bridge side eventually had to settle for sixth place.

In the major cup competitions there were some satisfactory results, but just when it seemed that something might be won there were disasters and the club missed out on the two trophies. In the Milk Cup there was an excellent run which took them past Mansfield Town (4-2 on aggregate), Fulham (1-0 in a replay at Craven Cottage) and Everton (in a 2-1 replay win at Goodison Park). Wembley beckoned until QPR came to the Bridge for a 5th Round replay and scored twice without reply. By then the FA Cup campaign had also ended with home defeat in a televised match against Liverpool (1-2); in appalling conditions Shrewsbury had been despatched by a single goal at the Gay Meadow in the only other match played.

Does that all sound sad? Well, it should not because there was a Wembley day of glory as Manchester City were faced in the Full Members Cup Final played on a Sunday and the day after an away victory in the League at Southampton. No-one wanted the competition — so they said! — but 68,000 watched that game and it was one of the best 'finals' ever seen at the old stadium with Chelsea leading by five goals to one near the finish (Speedie scoring a fine hat-trick and Lee the other two), but then City fought back and nearly drew level. A great game!

So, it was a good season after all and it must be said that the team was usually attractive and interesting to watch with Pat Nevin the entertainer-in-chief ably supported by McAllister, the injury-hit Kerry Dixon (when available) and Lee with various defenders doing fine work notably McLaughlin, Pates (the captain), young Wood, Rougvie and Dublin. Niedzwiecki was consistently good until badly injured and his place in goal will probably be filled in the immediate future by Tony Godden. With useful close season recruits for John Hollins in Durie (from Hibs) and McNaught (from Hamilton) team building work continues and the new season should see more entertaining shows.

A year ago we severely criticised Chelsea's following — or some of it — so it is only fair to report that on the two occasions this writer saw the team (both away from the Bridge) the behaviour was exemplary. This is the kind of reward Ken Bates, who has done so much for the club, deserves, so keep up the fine improvement everyone!
WLM

Back Row L to R: Terry Howard, Roy Wegerle, John McNaught, Colin Lee, Joe McLaughlin, Kerry Dixon, Robert Isaac, Keith Dublin. **Standing:** John Hollins, Colin West, Keith Jones, Doug Rougvie, Steve Wicks, Steve Francis, Eddie Niedzwiecki, Tony Godden, Colin Pates, Nigel Spackman, Micky Bodley, Jerry Murphy, Ernie Walley. **Seated:** Kevin McAllister, Darren Wood, Gordon Durie, Phil Priest, John Bumstead, Mick Hazard, Pat Nevin, David Speedie, John Millar, Paddy McCarthy.

CHELSEA

DIVISION ONE: 6th   **FA CUP:** 4th ROUND   **MILK CUP:** 5th ROUND   **FM CUP:** WINNERS

MATCH	DATE		COMPE-TITION	VENUE	OPPONENTS	RESULT		HALF TIME	L'GUE POS'N	GOALSCORERS/GOAL TIMES	ATTEN-DANCE
1	A	17	CL	A	Sheffield Wednesday	D	1-1	1-1		Speedie 34	(26,164)
2		20	CL	H	Coventry City	W	1-0	0-0		Speedie 76	15,679
3		24	CL	H	Birmingham City	W	2-0	1-0	3	Rougvie 17, Jones 72	16,534
4		28	CL	A	Leicester City	D	0-0	0-0	3		(11,248)
5		31	CL	H	W.B.A.	W	3-0	2-0	3	Speedie 9, 44, Spackman (pen) 69	15,376
6	S	4	CL	A	Tottenham Hotspur	L	1-4	0-3	5	Dixon 66	(23,692)
7		7	CL	A	Luton Town	D	1-1	0-1	6	Dixon 47	(10,720)
8		14	CL	H	Southampton	W	2-0	1-0	5	Dixon 34, Canoville 80	15,711
9		21	CL	H	Arsenal	W	2-1	0-0	3	Nevin 76, Spackman (pen) 86	33,241
10		25	MC2	A	**Mansfield Town**	D	2-2	0-2		**Speedie 76, Nevin 83**	**(6,018)**
11		28	CL	A	Watford	L	1-3	0-1	3	Rougvie 65	(16,035)
12	O	2	FMC	H	**Portsmouth**	W	3-0	2-0		**Bumstead 2, Hazard 5, Dixon 85**	**6,833**
13		5	CL	A	Manchester City	W	1-0	0-0	3	Dixon 10	(20,104)
14		9	MC2	H	**Mansfield Town**	W	2-0	0-0		**Dixon 47, 55**	**11,664**
15		12	CL	H	Everton	W	2-1	2-1	3	Dixon 3, Speedie 42	27,634
16		19	CL	A	Oxford United	L	1-2	0-2	3	Dixon 77	(12,072)
17		23	FMC	A	**Charlton Athletic**	W	3-1	0-0		**Nevin 78, 90, Speedie 89**	**(3,714)**
18		26	CL	H	Manchester United	L	1-2	0-1	5	McLaughlin 75	42,485
19		29	MC3	H	**Fulham**	D	1-1	0-0		**Hazard 88**	**19,669**
20	N	2	CL	A	Ipswich Town	W	2-0	2-0	4	Dixon 2, Speedie 10	(15,324)
21		6	MC3R	A	**Fulham**	W	1-0	1-0		**Dixon 18**	**(20,190)**
22		9	CL	H	Nottingham Forest	W	4-2	3-1	4	Speedie 1, Dixon 24, 61, Hazard (pen) 35	17,743
23		13	FMC	A	**W.B.A.**	D	2-2†	1-2		**Speedie 26, McAllister 70**	**(4,917)**
24		16	CL	A	Newcastle United	W	3-1	1-1	3	Speedie 43, Spackman 78, Dixon 81	(22,355)
25		23	CL	H	Aston Villa	W	2-1	1-1	3	Dixon 31, Speedie 83	17,509
26		26	MC4	H	**Everton**	D	2-2	2-2		**Dixon 1, Nevin 39**	**27,544**
27		30	CL	A	Liverpool	D	1-1	0-0	4	Nevin 89	(38,482)
28	D	4	FMCAF	A	**Oxford United**	W	4-1	1-1		**Slatter (og) 34, Dixon 3 49, 82, 87**	**(6,018)**
29		7	CL	A	Coventry City	D	1-1	1-1	4	Murphy 36	(8,721)
30		10	MC4R	A	**Everton**	W	2-1	1-0		**Dixon 1, McLauglin 74**	**(26,376)**
31		14	CL	H	Sheffield Wednesday	W	2-1	1-0	4	Speedie 27, Spackman 46	19,658
32		17	FMCAF	H	**Oxford United**	L	0-1	0-1			**8,528**
33		21	CL	A	Birmingham	W	2-1	1-0	4	Hagan (og) 35, Nevin 88	(10,594)
34		28	CL	H	Tottenham Hotspur	W	2-0	1-0	2	Dixon 18, Spackman (pen) 63	37,115
35	J	4	FAC3	A	**Shrewsbury**	W	1-0	0-0		**Speedie 81**	**(8,100)**
36		11	CL	H	Luton	W	1-0	0-0	3	Speedie 55	21,201
37		18	CL	H	W.B.A.	W	3-0	1-0	4	Speedie 19, Murphy 53, Nevin 85	(10,300)
38		22	MC5	H	**QPR**	D	1-1	1-1		**Nevin 25**	**(27,000)**
39		26	FAC4	H	**Liverpool**	L	1-2	0-1		**Speedie 63**	**33,625**
40		29	MC5R	H	**QPR**	L	0-2	0-0			**(27,937)**
41	F	1	CL	H	Leicester	D	2-2	1-1	3	Shearer 27, Jones 60	12,372
42		8	CL	H	Oxford United	L	1-4	0-2	4	Bunstead 66	16,181
43	M	8	CL	H	Manchester City	W	1-0	0-0	4	Reid (og) 80	17,573
44		16	CL	A	Everton	D	1-1	1-0	4	Murphy 12	(30,145)
45		19	CL	H	QPR	D	1-1	1-0	4	Nevin 28	17,871
46		22	CL	A	Southampton	W	1-0	0-0	4	Pates 61	(15,009)
47		23	FMC F	N	**Manchester City**	W	5-4	2-1		**Speedie 3 23, 51, 58, Lee 36, 79**	**68,000**
48		29	CL	H	West Ham United	L	0-4	0-0	4		29,955
49		31	CL	A	QPR	L	0-6	0-3	4		(18,584)
50	A	5	CL	H	Ipswich Town	D	1-1	1-1	4	Speedie 4	13,072
51		9	CL	A	Manchester United	W	2-1	0-0	4	Dixon 48, 89	(45,355)
52		12	CL	A	Nottingham Forest	D	0-0	0-0	4		(18,055)
53		15	CL	A	West Ham United	W	2-1	0-0	4	Spackman 55, Nevin 78	(29,361)
54		19	CL	A	Newcastle United	D	1-1	1-1	4	Nevin 31	18,970
55		26	CL	A	Aston Villa	L	1-3	0-1	5	Spackman (pen) 72	(17,770)
56		29	CL	A	Arsenal	L	0-2	0-0	5		(24,025)
57	M	3	CL	H	Liverpool	L	0-1	0-0	6		43,900
58		5	CL	H	Watford	L	1-5	0-2	6	Speedie 79	12,017

Best Home League Attendance: 43,900 v Liverpool 3/5   **Smallest:** 12,017 v Watford 5/5   **Av Home Att:** 21,992

Goal Scorers: Compared with 84-85: −1.070

League (57):	Dixon 14, Speedie 14, Nevin 7, Spackman 7 (4 pen), Murphy 3, Jones 2, Opponents 2, Rougvie 2, Bumstead 1, Canoville 1, Hazard 1, McLaughlin 1, Pates 1, Shearer 1
Milk Cup (11):	Dixon 5, Nevin 3, Hazard 1, McLaughlin 1, Speedie 1
FA Cup (2):	Speedie 2
FM Cup (17)	Speedie 5, Dixon 4, Lee 2, Nevin 2, Bumstead 1, Hazard 1, McAllister 1, Opponents 1 †Chelsea won 5-4 on penalties

1985-86

Niedzwieki	Lee	Rougvie	Pates	Dublin	Bumstead	Nevin	Spackman	Dixon	Speedie	Murphy	Jones	McLaughlin	Wood	McAllister	Davies	Canoville	Isaac	Hazard	Jasper	Shearer	Millar	Francis	Godden (L)	Howard	Fridge	Referee	
1	2	3	4		6*	7	8	9	10	11	12	5														K Baker	1
1	2	3	4		6	7		9	10	11	8	5														Alan Robinson	2
1	2	3	4		6	7		9	10	11	8	5														D Hedges	3
1	2	3	4		6	7	8	9	10	11		5														J Hough	4
1	2	3	4		6	7	8	9	10	11		5														D Axcell	5
1	2	3	4†		6	7	8	9	10	11*		5		12												B Stevens	6
1	2	3	4		6	7	8	9	10	11		5														K Barratt	7
1		3	4		6*	7	8	9				5	2	12	10	11										M James	8
1		3			6	7	12	9				5	2	10		11	4	8*								J Bray	9
1		3	4		6	7	12	9	10			5	2			11*		8								A Robinson	10
1		3	4		6	7*	11	9	10			5	2			12		8								J Moules	11
1		3	4		6	7	11	9	10			5	2			12		8*								G Napthine	12
1		3	4		6	7	11	9	10			5	2			12		8*								M Peck	13
1		3	4			7	11	9	10		6	5	2			11*		8								M Bodenham	14
1		3	4		6	7	11	9	10			5	2					8								V Callow	15
1		3*	4		6	7		9	10		11	5	2			12		8								J Ashworth	16
1			4	3	6*	7	11*	9	10		13	5	2	12				8								M Cotton	17
1		3	4		6*	7	8	9	10		12	5		11			2									J Martin	18
1			4	3	6	7	8	9	10			5		11*			2	12								L Shapter	19
1			4	3	6	7	8	9	10			5		11			2									B Hill	20
1			4	3		7	8	9	10		6	5	2	11*		12	5									A Seville	21
1			4	3		7	8	9	10		6	5	2			11										R Milford	22
1	13		4	3		7	8		10		6*		2	9		5		11*	12							A Banks	23
1			4	3	6	7	8	9	10			5	2			11										N Midgley	24
1			4	3	6	7	8	9	10			5	2	12		11*										A Gunn	25
1			4*	3	6	7	8	9	10			5	2	12					11							D Hedges	26
1		4		3		7	8	9		11	6	5	2	10*		12										N Ashley	27
1		4		3		7	8	9		11	6†	5	2	10												G Napthine	28
1			4	3		7	8	9	10	11*	6	5	2	12												T Jones	29
1		3	4			7	8	9	10	11	6	5	2†													K Hackett	30
1		3	4			7*	8	9	10		6	5	2	11		12										L Robinson	31
1		3	4	13	11*	7	8	9	10*		6	5	2	12												R Milford	32
1		3	4		6*	7	8	9		11†		5	2	10		12										D Scott	33
1		2	4	3		7	8	9	10		6	5		11*		12										J Deakin	34
1		2	4	3		7	8	9	10		6	5		12				11*								N Midgley	35
1	2	4		3	6	7	8	9	10			5						11								J Martin	36
1	2		4	3	6	7	8	9	10*	11		5						12								K Cooper	37
1	2	5	4	3	6	7*	8	9	10	11								12								L Shapter	38
1	2	5	4	3	6	7	8	9*	10	11								12								Alan Robinson	39
1		5	4	3*	6	7	8		10	11			2	9				12								A Gunn	40
1		5	4	3	6	7	8				12		2	10*		11				9						R Hamer	41
1		5	4		6	7	8				10		2			11				9	3					I Hemley	42
1	8*	3	4		6		12	9	10	11		5	2	7												A Seville	43
1		3	4		6	7	8	9	10	11		5	2													D Hutchinson	44
1*	12	3	4		6	7	8	9	10	11		5	2													H Taylor	45
1		3	4		6	7	8	9	10			5	2	11								1				K Cooper	46
1	9	3	4		6	7	8		10			5	2	11								1				A Saunders	47
1	9	3	4		6*	7	8		10			5	2	11		12						1				R Lewis	48
1		2	3	4		7	8	9	10†			5		11		12	6					1				M Bodenham	49
1			4	3	6	7	8	9	10	11		5										1	2			J Martin	50
		3	4			7	8	9	10	11		5	2			6						1				G Courtney	51
			4			7	8	9	10	11		5	2			6					3	1				D Shaw	52
			4		6*	7	8	9	10	11		5	2	12				10			3	1				M Bodenham	53
		3*			6	7	8	9				5	2	12				10		11	3	1				J Deakin	54
			4		6	12	8	9	10	11		5	2	7				7*			3	1				R Nixon	55
		3	6*	4		7	8	9	10	11	12	5	2									1				Alan Robinson	56
		4				7	8	9	10		6	5	2	12		11					3	1			1	L Shapter	57
		4					8		10		6	5	2	7		11					3				1	B Hill	58
30	12	34	35	11	32	39	37	38	34	21	10	40	28	13	1	4	3	17	2	7	3	8	1	1		League Appearances	
	1				1	2							4	7		9		1								Substitute Appearances	
8	1	5	8	5	5	8	7·1	7	8	3		5	6	3·1		2	2	1·2	2		2·2	1				Milk Cup Appearances	
2	1	2	2	2	1	2	2	2	2	1	1	1						0·2		1						FA Cup Appearances	
5	1·1	4	5	3·1	4	6	6	4	5	1		3·1	6	3·2		0·1	1	3	0·1			1				FM Cup Appearances	

Also Played: Position(Game): Durie 9(58)

Departures: Thomas (Newcastle), Davies (Man City), Shearer (Huddersfield), Cannoville (Brentford), Jasper (Brighton)

'THE BLUES'

Formed: 1905
Turned Professional: 1905   **Ltd Co:** 1905

Previous Managers: 1905-6 John Tait Robertson   1907-33 David Calderhead   1933-9 Leslie Knighton   1939-52 Billy Birrell   1952-62 Ted Drake   1962-7 Tommy Docherty   1967-74 Dave Sexton   1974-5 Ron Suart   1975-7 Eddie McCreadie   1977-8 Ken Shellito   1978-9 Danny Blanchflower   1979-81 Geoff Hurst   1981-84 John Neal

Honours: Champions Div 1   FA Cup Winners 1970   European Cup Winners Cup Winners   Football League Cup Winners

League Career: Elected to Div 2 1905   Promoted to Div 1 1906-7   Relegated to Div 2 1909-10   Promoted to Div 1 1911-12   Relegated to Div 2 1923-4   Promoted to Div 1 1929-30   Relegated to Div 2 1961-2   Promoted to Div 1 1962-3   Relegated to Div 2 1974-5   Promoted to Div 1 1976-7   Relegated to Div 2 1978-9   Promoted to Div 1 1983-4

Colours: Royal blue with striped trim, blue shorts with white stripe, white stockings
Change Colours: All yellow
Reserves League: Football Combination   **Youth Team:** S E Counties

---

CLUB RECORDS

Most Appearances for Club: Ron Harris: Football League 646 + 9   + FA Cup 63   + League Cup 46 + 2   + Charity Shield 1   + European Cup Winners Cup 13   + Fairs Cup 14   + Anglo-Scottish 7 + 1 **Total 790   + 12 subs**
Most Capped Player: Ray Wilkins, 24, England
Record Goalscorer in a Match: George Hilsdon, 6 v Worksop, FA Cup 1907-8
Record League Goalscorer in a Season: Jimmy Greaves, 41, 1960-1   **In All Competitions:** Jimmy Greaves, 43 (League 41 + FA Cup 2)
Record League Goalscorer in a Career: Bobby Tambling, 164   **In All Competitions:** Bobby Tambling, 202 (League 164 + FA Cup 25 + League Cup 10 + Fairs Cup 3)
Record Transfer Fee Received: £825,000 from Manchester United for Ray Wilkins, Aug 1979
Record Transfer Fee Paid: £225,000 to Celtic for David Hay
Best Performances: League: Champions (1)   **FA Cup:** Winners (1)   **League/Milk Cup:** Winners (1)   **European Cup Winners Cup:** Winners (1)   **European Fairs Cup:** Semi-Final
Most League Points: (3pts for win) 88, Div 2, 1983-4   (2pts for win) 57, Div 2, 1906-7   **Most League Goals:** 98, Div 1, 1960-61
Record League Victory: 7-0 v Lincoln City, Div 2, 29 Oct 1910
Most Goals Scored in a First Class Match: 13-0 v Jellnesse Hartcharge-Luxembourg (h) European Cup Winners' Cup First Round Second Leg, 29 Sept 1971
Most Goals Scored in a League Match: 9-2 v Glossop North End (h), Div 2, 1 Sept 1906
Record League Defeat: 1-8 v Wolverhampton Wanderers, Div 1, 26.9.53
European Competitions Entered: European Cup Winners Cup 1970-1, 1971-2   European Fairs Cup: 1958-60, 1965-6, 1968-9
Oldest Player in League Match:
Youngest Player in League Match:

Most Consecutive Undefeated League Matches: 19 1984	**League Matches Without a Win:** 14 1951
Longest Run of Undefeated Home League Matches: 34 1910-12	**Away League Matches:** 11 1966
Longest Run Without Home League Win: 9 1974	**Away League Win:** 22 1914-15, 1952-53
Most Consecutive League Wins: 8 1927	**Home League Wins:** 13 1910-11
Most Consecutive League Defeats: 7 1952	**Away League Wins:** 6 1962

Chelsea Statistics Club: c/o Neil Jenson, 90 Boyle Road, Stanford-le-Hope, Essex (0375 675507)
Club Statistician for the Directory: D Fletcher

CHELSEA

PLAYERS NAME Ht Wt Birthdate	Honours	Birthplace Transfers	Clubs	APPEARANCES				GOALS			
				League	Milk Cup	FA Cup	Other Comps	League	Milk Cup	FA Cup	Other Comps
GOALKEEPERS											
Steve Francis 5.11 11.5 29.5.64	EY	Billericay	Chelsea (A)	71	6	10					
Eddie Niedzwiecki+ 6.0 11.0 3.5.59	W (1), S, Div.3, 78, Div. 2, 84	Bangor £55,000	Wrexham Chelsea	111 112	10 22	7 6					
Tony Godden 6.0½ 13.0 2.8.55		Gillingham	Ashford WBA Luton Town (L) Walsall (L) Chelsea	 267 12 19 8	 27	1 21	 12				
		F									
DEFENDERS											
Keith Dublin 5.7 10.0 29.1.66	EY	Brent	Chelsea (A)	22+1	5	2					
Terry Howard 6.1 11.7 26.2.66		Stepney	Chelsea (A) Crystal Palace (L)	5 4							
Bob Isaac 5.11 12.7 30.11.65	EY	Hackney	Chelsea (A)	4	2						
Colin Lee 6.1 11.9 12.6.56	Div. 2, 84	Torquay £8,000 £60,000 £80,000	Bristol City (A) Hereford United (L) Torquay United Tottenham Hotspur Chelsea	 7+2 35 57+5 166+16	 0+1 3 2 20+2	 2 6+1 12		 14 18 36	 1 1	 3 2	
Joe McLaughlin 6.1 11.4 2.6.60	SU21 (10) Div. 2, 84	Greenock	Morton Chelsea	134 117	17 19	5 5		3 2	 1		
John McNaught 6.0 12.0 19.6.64			Hamilton Accs Chelsea	87+19 0+1	7	5		19		1	
John Millar 5.9 11.0 8.12.66		Coatbridge	Chelsea	7							
Colin Pates* 6.0 11.0 10.8.61	EY Div. 2, 84	Carshalton	Chelsea (A)	221	27	17		6			
Doug Rougvie 6.2 12.10 24.5.56	S (1), SPD (2), SC (3), ECWC 83	Fife	Aberdeen Chelsea	161+8 61	38+5 13	26 4	26+2	20 3	2		
Steve Wicks 6.2¾ 13.2 3.10.65		Reading £275,000 £300,000 £250,000 £250,000 £450,000	Chelsea (A) Derby County QPR Crystal Palalce QPR Chelsea	117+1 24 73 14 116	3 1 5+1 17	5 3 5 2	 4	5 1 6		2	
Darren Wood 5.10 11.8 9.6.64	ES	Scarborough P/E.+£50,000	Middlesbrough (A) Chelsea	101 45+2	6 6	5 3		6 1			
MIDFIELD											
John Bumstead 5.7 10.0 27.11.58	Div. 2, 84	Rotherhithe	Chelsea (A)	212+10	22+2	11+1					
Mike Hazard 5.7 10.5 5.2.60	FAC 82, UEFAC 84	Sunderland	Tottenham Hotspur (A) Chelsea	73+18 17+1	11+3 2+2	7+3 1	22+1	12 1	5 1	2	3
Keith Jones 5.9 10.11 14.10.65	EYS	Dulwich	Chelsea	27+8	7+1	1		2	2		
Jerry Murphy 5.9 11.0 23.9.59	EI (4), Div. 2, 79, FAYC 77, 78	Stepney F	Crystal Palace (A) Chelsea	214+15 21	22 3	15+1 1		20 3	5		
Nigel Spackman 6.1 12.4 2.12.60	Div. 4, 84	Romsey	Andover Bournemouth Chelsea	 118+1 119+2	 5 22+1	 7 6	 6	 10 11		 1	
FORWARDS											
Kerry Dixon 6.0 13.0 24.7.61	E (3), U21 (1), Div. 2, 84	Luton £20,000 £175,000	Dunstable Town Reading Chelsea	 116 121	 6+1 22	 2+1 5		 51 66	 19	 4	
Gordon Durie 6.0 11.6 6.12.65		East Fife Hibernian Chelsea	 57+15 23+1 1	 6 6	 5+1 4		 19 6	 8	 1	
Kevin McAllister 5.6 10.0 8.11.62		Falkirk £34,000	Falkirk Chelsea	 13+7	 3+1						
Pat Nevin 5.6 11.9 6.9.63	S (2), U21 (5), Y, SD2 (1), Div. 2, 84,	Glasgow £95,000	Clyde Chelsea	60+13 118+1	5+3 20+1	9 6		17 24	 5	3 1	
David Speedie 5.7 10.4 20.2.60	S (5), U21 (1), Div. 2, 84	Glen Rothes F £65,000	Barnsley Darlington Chelsea	10+13 88 133+7	 4 22+1	 3 9		 21 44	 7	 1 4	
Roy Wegerle 5.11½ 11.8 19.3.64		South Africa £100,000	Tampa Bay Rowdies Chelsea								

ADDITIONAL CONTRACT PROFESSIONALS

Les Fridge (G, 1Lge), John Hollins, Philip Priest, Colin West, Gareth Hall, Mike Bodley, Pat McCarthy

APPRENTICES

Tom Byrne, Billy Dodds

NON-CONTRACT PLAYERS

STAMFORD BRIDGE London SW6

Capacity: 43,900

Record Attendance: 82,905 v Arsenal, Div 1, 12 Oct 1935

Smallest Home Attendance for a First Class Match: 5,630 v Workington, 2nd Round League Cup, 24 Oct 1960

Record Receipts: £161,218 v Manchester United, Div 1, 29 Dec 1984

Season Tickets: Stand: £159, £183, £207, £255 **Terrace:** £87 (adults), £49 (juveniles/OAPs)

Cost of Stand Tickets: £6, £7, £9, £11 **Terraces:** £4 (£2 juveniles and OAPs—Club Members only)

Match and Ticket Information: Personal or postal bookings are accepted in advance. No telephone bookings

Car Parking: Street parking only available

Nearest Railway Station: Fulham Broadway (District Line)

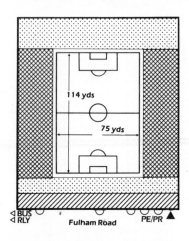

How to get to the ground

From North: From Motorway M1 and A1. Follow signs Central London to Hyde Park Corner, then follow signs Guildford (A3) into Knightsbridge A4. In 1m turn left A308 into Fulham Road for Chelsea FC
From East: Via Hyde Park Corner as above or via Embankment and Cheyne Walk A3212. Follow signs Chelsea A322C then at crossroads turn left A308 into Fulham Road for Chelsea FC
From South: Use A13 or A24 then A219 to cross Putney Bridge. Follow signs West End A304, then join A308 into Fulham Road for Chelsea FC
From West: From Motorway M4. Follow signs Central London, then Westminster A3220. In 0.8m at crossroads turn right A308 into Fulham Road for Chelsea FC

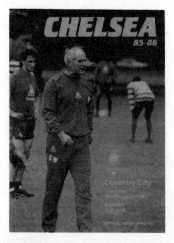

Price of 1986-7 Programme: 60p
Number of Pages: 28
Subscriptions: £17.50 (UK postage) for members per season, £19.00 (UK postage) for non-members per season

Local Newspapers: Fulham Chronicle, West London Observer

Local Radio Stations: LBC (away games only), (261 medium wave)

CHESTER CITY

Division 3

President
R Rowlands

Chairman
A E Barnes, JP

Directors
C Thompson, (Vice-Chairman)
R H Crofts
L Lloyd
F Summers

Secretary
J A Eckersley (0244 371376)

Assistant Secretary
I Ireland

Manager
Harry McNally

Reserve & Youth Manager
Cliff Sear

Commercial Manager
(0244 378162)

Club Captain
A Holden

Groundsman
G Kent

Club Doctors
Dr M Swallow
Dr J Kane

Back Row L to R: Mick Clarke (Trainer), Martin Lane, Gary Bennett, Ricky Greenough, Billy Stewart, Andy Holden, John Butcher, Barry Butler, Graham Abel, Peter Houghton, Cliff Sear (Youth Team Coach), **Front Row:** Brian Croft, Ian Richardson, Dave Glenn, Stuart Rimmer, Harry McNally (Manager), Graham Barrow, Milton Graham, Jon Kelly, Mark Sconce.

Promotion!! After all the troubles of the previous season Chester fans approached the 1985-86 season with guarded optimism. New manager Harry McNally had brought in several new players and the team had a well balanced look about it as the season commenced.

The features of the early months of the season was the goalscoring exploits of Stuart Rimmer. He just couldn't stop scoring and towards the end of November, Chester were top of the Fourth Division and Rimmer was by far the leading goalscorer in the Football League. Then whilst scoring against Orient he collided with their goalkeeper and was carried off with damaged knee ligaments that kept him out for the rest of the season. At about the same time Chester had cancelled the contract of their giant centre-back Wakeley Gage due to personal problems and also were without the services of Welsh International Andy Holden.

Chester fans were worried as these injuries could have proved so damaging to their promotion prospects. However Harry McNally acted quickly, snapping up Ian Richardson from Watford to replace the injured Rimmer and bringing in players on loan and from non-league to bolster the squad. More problems arose when player coach Micky Speight departed to Norway and injury-plagued club captain Andy Holden made a brief comeback over the holiday period at Christmas and New Year only to suffer more ankle problems which then kept him out for the rest of the season. The team kept winning though, and Richardson along with Gary Bennett and Peter Houghton kept popping the goals in whilst the energetic Kelly and the stylish Graham ticked over in midfield. At the heart of the defence the ever dependable Bobby Coy held things together aided by two sound full-backs in Glenn and Lane.

The bad weather came in February and City started to lose their way. Their form stuttered badly and with the likes of Hartlepool and Stockport charging up the table to join Chester along with Swindon, Mansfield and Port Vale doubts were beginning to set in. Injuries continued to hit Chester hard but the manager kept calm and made two loan signings which together with the improved form of goalkeeper John Butcher and utility player Ricky Greenough were to prove crucial on the promotion run in.

Earl Barrett from Manchester City and Steve Johnson from Bristol City were the two loan signings concerned. Barrett with his slinky skills and youthful exhuberance and Johnson with his physical aggression and goalscoring potential. These two gave Chester that vital impetus and a 0-0 draw at Orient proved to be the point that took Chester City back to the 3rd Division.

All the media attention was focused on Lou Macari and Swindon in the 4th Division but to my mind when you look at the crippling injuries Chester had to contend with I think that for them to finish as runners-up was a far greater achievement. Manager Harry McNally and his backroom staff and players deserve all the credit from every Chester fan for the marvellous season they gave us.

Derrick Orme

CHESTER CITY

DIVISION FOUR: RUNNERS-UP   **FA CUP:** 1st ROUND   **MILK CUP:** 2nd ROUND

MATCH	DATE	COMPE-TITION	VENUE	OPPONENTS	RESULT		HALF TIME	L'GUE POS'N	GOALSCORERS/GOAL TIMES	ATTEN-DANCE
1	A 17	CL	H	Halifax Town	D	1-1	1-0		Rimmer 34	1,750
2	24	CL	A	Perterborough United	L	0-3	0-0	20		(2,667)
3	26	CL	H	Hartlepool United	D	1-1	0-1	18	Rimmer (pen) 79	1,429
4	28	MC1/1	A	Tranmere Rovers	W	3-1	2-1		Rimmer 3 22 (pen) 27, 82	(2,207)
5	31	CL	A	Tranmere Rovers	W	3-0	1-0	13	Holden 6, Burgess (og), 62, Rimmer 67	(1,703)
6	S 4	MC1/2	H	Tranmere Rovers	D	0-0	0-0			2,384
7	7	CL	H	Hereford United	W	1-0	1-0	9	Houghton 37	1,720
8	14	CL	A	Torquay United	W	3-0	1-0	7	Houghton 7, Rimmer 78, 88	(1,111)
9	21	CL	A	Crewe Alexandra	W	4-0	1-0	5	Rimmer pen 35, Gage 84, Bennett 87, 89	2,369
10	25	MC2/1	H	Coventry City	L	1-2	0-0		Rimmer (pen) 57	4,863
11	28	CL	A	Stockport County	D	2-2	1-1	7	Bennett 15, 79	(1,801)
12	O 2	CL	H	Mansfield Town	W	1-0	1-0	4	Rimmer (pen) 42	2,127
13	5	CL	H	Burnley	W	4-0	2-0	3	Rimmer 15, Graham 20, Kelly 59, Bennett 87	3,005
14	9	MC2/2	A	Coventry City	L	2-7	?-4		Murray 20, Rimmer (pen) 35	(5,504)
15	12	CL	A	Preston North End	W	6-3	4-1	3	Rimmer 4 16, 44, 45, 85, Kelly 40, Greenhough 66	(4,073)
16	19	CL	H	Swindon Town	L	0-1	0-1	5		3,109
17	22	CL	A	Northampton	D	2-2	1-1	6	Graham 16, Murray 58	(2,323)
18	26	CL	A	Wrexham	D	1-1	1-0	6	Coy 37	(3,500)
19	N 2	CL	H	Aldershot	W	1-0	0-0	4	Rimmer (pen) 49	2,180
20	6	CL	H	Colchester United	W	4-0	0-0	1	Greenhough 16, Rimmer 58, 70, Abel 75	2,809
21	9	CL	A	Exeter City	W	3-1	2-1	1	Greenhough 21, Houghton 28, 71	(1,888)
22	16	FAC1	A	Bury	L	0-2	0-0			(3,424)
23	23	CL	H	Orient	W	3-0	1-0	1	Kelly 35, 78, Rimmer 62	2,653
24	29	CL	A	Southend United	D	1-1	1-0	1	Houghton 72	(3,525)
25	D 7	CL	A	Aldershot	D	1-1	0-1	1	Richardson (pen) 60	(1,528)
26	14	CL	H	Scunthorpe United	D	1-1	1-1	1	Kelly 12	2,657
27	21	CL	H	Peterborough United	W	2-1	1-0	1	Holden 9, Bennett 79	2,331
28	26	CL	A	Cambridge United	L	2-3	1-2	1	Richardson 10, Bennett 51	(2,395)
29	J 1	CL	H	Port Vale	W	4-1	2-1	2	Houghton 9, 77, Richardson (pen) 29, Bennett 87	5,010
30	7	CL	A	Hartlepool United	D	1-1	1-0	2	Abel 2	(3,891)
31	11	CL	H	Tranmere Rovers	W	1-0	0-0	1	Graham 69	3,700
32	17	CL	A	Halifax Town	W	2-1	0-0	2	Houghton 42, 48	(1,473)
33	20	FRT	A	Rochdale	L	0-1	0-0			(1,164)
34	22	FRT	H	Wigan	L	0-2	0-2			1,375
35	25	CL	H	Torquay	W	3-1	2-1	1	Richardson 16, 58, Bennett 21	2,808
36	F 1	CL	H	Hereford United	W	2-0	1-0	1	Bennett (pen) 35, 81	(3,255)
37	5	CL	H	Northampton Town	L	2-3	2-1	2	Richardson (pen) 3, Chard (og) 16	3,304
38	15	CL	H	Rochdale	D	1-1	1-0	1	Richardson (pen) 11	3,232
39	22	CL	A	Crewe Alexandra	D	2-2	2-1	2	Kelly 20, Richardson (pen) 26	(3,271)
40	M 1	CL	A	Stockport County	L	1-2	1-2	2	Richardson 17	2,919
41	4	CL	H	Mansfield Town	D	0-0	0-0	2		(3,957)
42	8	CL	A	Burnley	L	0-1	0-0	2		(3,690)
43	15	CL	H	Preston North End	W	2-0	1-0	2	Wright 12, Kelly 54	3,062
44	22	CL	H	Wrexham	W	2-1	1-1	2	Richardson 42, Bennett 82	4,791
45	29	CL	A	Port Vale	D	1-1	0-1	2	Greenhough 50	(4,490)
46	31	CL	H	Cambridge United	D	1-1	0-0	2	Houghton 47	2,893
47	A 4	CL	A	Colchester United	W	3-2	2-0	2	Johnson 3, Glenn 30, Greenhough 82	(2,281)
48	8	CL	A	Swindon Town	L	2-4	2-1	2	Johnson 3, (pen) 45	(12,630)
49	12	CL	H	Exeter City	W	2-1	1-1	2	Lane 45, Johnson (pen) 75	2,899
50	19	CL	A	Orient	D	0-0	0-0	2		(2,617)
51	26	CL	H	Southend United	W	2-0	1-0	2	Bennett 4, Johnson (pen) 79	4,453
52	29	CL	A	Rochdale	W	2-1	1-0	2	Kelly 30, Johnson 89	(1,963)
53	M 3	CL	A	Scunthorpe United	L	0-2	0-1	2		(2,256)

Best Home League Attendance: 5,010 v Port Vale 1/1   **Smallest:** 1,429 v Hartlepool 26/8   **Av Home Att:** 2,922

Goal Scorers: **Compared with 84-85:** +1,043

League (83):   Rimmer 16 (4 pen), Bennett 13 (1 pen), Houghton 10, Richardson 10 (5 pen), Kelly 8, Johnson 6 (3 pen), Greenhough 5, Graham 3, Abel 2, Holden 2, Opponents 2, Coy 1, Gage 1, Glenn 1, Lane 1, Murray 1, Wright 1

Milk Cup (6):   Rimmer 5 (3 pen), Murray 1

FA Cup (-):

FRT (-):

1985-86

Butcher	Glenn	Lane	Holden	Gage	Coy	Speight	Graham	Rimmer	Sconce	Brett	Wright	Kaye	Bennett	Houghton	Croft	Kelly	Greenhough	Murray	Barrett	Cashley	Abel	Johnson	Bramhall (L)	Richardson	Butler	Referee	
1	2	3	4	5	6	7	8*	9		11																T Holbrook	1
	2	3	4	5	7	6	8			11		1	9	10*	12											M James	2
	2	3	4	5	6	7		9				1	11	10		8										G Ashby	3
	2	3	4	5	6		9					1	10	11		7	8									**A Robinson**	4
	2	3	4	5	6		9					1	11	10		7	8									M Scott	5
1	2	3	4	5	6		9	8					10	11		7										**J McAulay**	6
1	2	3		5	6		8	9					11	10		7	4									A Banks	7
1	2	3		5	4	6	8	9		12			11*	10		7										B Stevens	8
1	2	3		5	6		8	9					11	10		7	4									K Walmsley	9
1	2	3	4	5	6		8	9					11	10		7										**T Mills**	10
1	2	3	4	5	6		8	9		10*			11			7	12									J Key	11
1	2	3		5	6		8	9		12			11	10*		7	4									M Heath	12
1	2	3		5	6		8	9		10			11			7	4									H King	13
1	2	3			6	4	8	9		11						7	5	10								**R Lewis**	14
1	2	3		5	6		8	9		11				10		7	12	4*								M Peck	15
	2	3	4	5	6	10	8*	9		11						7		12		1						M Reed	16
	2	3		5	6	4	8	9					10			7	12	11*		1						K Miller	17
	2	3		5	6	4	8	9					11	12		7	10*			1						N Midgley	18
		3		5	6	4	8	9					11	10		7	12			1	2*					I Hendrick	19
		3		5	6		8	9					11	10		7	4			1	2					D Allinson	20
		3		5	6		8	9					11	10		7	4			1	2					H Taylor	21
1	12	3		5	6	2	8*	9					11	10		7	4									**G Aplin**	22
1	2	3			6	4		9*					11	10		7	12			8	5					V Callow	23
1	2	3			6								11	10		7	4			8	5			9		A Robinson	24
1	2	3			6								11	10		7	4			8	5			9		M Robinson	25
1	2	3			6		4						11	10		7				8	5			9		K Barratt	26
1	2	3	4		6		8						11	10		7					5			9		T Simpson	27
1	2	3	4		6		8*						11	10		7	12				5			9		A Ward	28
1	2	3	4		6		8†						11	10		7					5			9		B Hill	29
1	2	3	4		6		8†						11	10		7					5			9		D Scott	30
1	2	3			6		12						11	10		7	4				5			9*	8	G Napthine	31
1	2	3			6								11	10		7	4				5			9	8	H Taylor	32
1*					6				2	12			9		11	4	10				5				8	**R Guy**	33
	6								2	7			11		10	4			1		5				8	**M Heath**	34
	2	3			6		8						11	10		4			1		5			9	7	A Robinson	35
	2*	3			6		8						11	10		7	4		1		5			9	12	N Butler	36
		3			6		8						11*	10		7	4	12	1		5			9	2	T Fitzharris	37
1		3			6		8				4		11	10		7	2				5			9		G Peck	38
1		3			6		8				4		11	10		7	2				5			9		G Ashby	39
1		3			6		8		2		4		11*	10		7					5			9	12	K Breen	40
1		3			6*		8				4		11	10		7	2				5			9	12	J McAulay	41
1		3					8		12		4		11	10		7	2				5			9	6*	C Seel	42
1		3					8				4		12			7	10	11*	2		5			9	6	D Phillips	43
1		3			6		8						12	10*		7	4		2		5	11		9		I Hendrick	44
1		3			6		8						11	10		7	4		2		5			9		B Hill	45
1		3			6		8						11	10*		7	4		2		5			9	12	B Stevens	46
1	2				6		8						11*	12		7	4		3			10		9	5	D Reeves	47
1	2				6		8						11	10		7	4		3			9			5	D Axcell	48
1	2	3			6		8						12	11*		7	4		5			10		9		T Simpson	49
1	2	3			6		8							11		7	4		5			10		9		R Gifford	50
1	2	3			6		8						11			7	4		5			10		9	8	R Hamer	51
1	2	3			6		8						11			7	5		4			10		9		P Willis	52
1	2*	3			6		8						11	12		7	4					10		9	5	I Borrett	53
34	33	44	10	17	44	9	37	18	1	6	6	3	40	34		43	28	3	12	9	23	10	4	27	10	League Appearances	
							1		1	2			3	3	1		5	3							4	Substitute Appearances	
3	4	4	3	3	4	1	3	4		1		1	3	3		4	2	1								Milk Cup Appearances	
1	0-1	1		1	1	1	1	1				1	1	1		1	1									FA Cup Appearances	
1	1				1				2	1+1			2		2	2	1		1	2					2	FR Trophy Appearances	

Also Played: Position(Game): Fox 10(1), Harley (NC) 12(1), Bailey (NC) 12(33), 9(34), Woodthorpe (NC) 3(33, 34), Palmer (NC) 7*(33)

Players on Loan: Bramhall (Bury), Wright (Birmingham), Barrett (Man City), Johnson (Bristol City)

Departures: Gage (CXL), Brett (F), Kaye (F)

'THE BLUES'

Formed: 1884
Turned Professional: 1902   **Ltd Co:** 1909

Previous Names: Chester until 1983
Previous Managers: 1930-36 Charles Hewitt   1936-38 Alex Raisbeck   1938-53 Frank Brown
1953-56 Louis Page   1956-59 John Harris   1959-61 Stan Pearson   1961-63 Bill Lambton
1963-68 Peter Hauser   1968-76 Ken Roberts   1976-82 Alan Oakes   1982-82 Cliff Sear*
1982-83 John Sainty*   John McGrath
* Includes period as caretaker manager
Honours: Welsh Cup Winners (3)   Debenhams Cup Winners, 1977
League Career: Elected to Div 3 (N) 1931   Div 4 1957-58   Promoted to Div 3 1974-75
Relegated to Div 4 1981-82   Promoted to Div 3 1985-86
Colours: Royal blue shirts with white pin stripe, white shorts and blue stockings
Change Colours: Gold shirts, black shorts, gold socks
Reserves League: Lancashire League

CLUB RECORDS

Most Appearances for Club: Trevor Storton: Football League 396, 23 FA Cup, 28 League Cup, 3 Football League Trophy, 3 Group Cup, **Total 453**
Most Capped Player: Bill Lewis, 7 for Wales.   **For England:** None
Record Goalscorer in a Match: Barry Jepson, 5 v York City in Div 4 08.02.58
Record League Goalscorer in a Season: Dick Yates, 36, Div 3 (N), 1946-47   **All Competitions:** Dick Yates, 44 (36 League, 8 in other first team fixtures) 1946-47
Record League Goalscorer in a Career: Gary Talbot, 83, 1963-66   **All Competitions:** Gary Talbot, 100 (83 League and 17 Cup goals), 1963-66
Record Transfer Fee Received: £300,000 from Liverpool for Ian Rush, May 1980
Record Transfer Fee Paid: £45,000 to Carlisle United for Steve Ludlam, May 1980
Best Performances: League: 5th Div 3 1977-78   **FA Cup:** 5th Round Replay, 1976-77, 1979-80   **League/Milk Cup:** Semi-Final 1974-75   **Welsh Cup:** Winners (3)
Most League Goals: 119, Div 4, 1964-65
Most League Points: 84 Div 4, 1985-86
Record League Victory and Most Goals in a First Class Match: 12-0 v York City, Div 3 (N), 1 Feb 1936
Most Goals Scored in a Cup Tie: 6-1 v Darlington, FA Cup 1st round, 1933-34
Record League Defeat: 2-11 v̇ Oldham Athletic, Div 3 (N), 19 Jan 1952
Oldest Player in League Match: Alan Oakes 35 yrs
Youngest Player in League Match: David Evans 16 yrs

Most Consecutive Undefeated League Matches: 18 1934-35	**League Matches Without a Win:** 26 1961-62
Longest Run of Undefeated Home League Matches: 27 1973-75	**Away League Matches:** 12 1939-46
Longest Run Without Home League Win: 13 1961-62	**Away League Win:** 29 1971-72, 1977-78
Most Consecutive League Wins: 8 1934, 1936, 1978	**Home League Wins:** 10 1932, 1963-64
Most Consecutive League Defeats: 7 1955, 1956, 1982	**Away League Wins:** 4 1934, 1936

Club Statistician for the Directory: Derrick Orme

CHESTER CITY

				APPEARANCES				GOALS			
PLAYERS NAME Ht Wt Birthdate	Honours	Birthplace Transfers	Clubs	League	Milk Cup	FA Cup	Other Comps	League	Milk Cup	FA Cup	Other Comps
GOALKEEPERS											
John Butcher 6.2 12.3 27.5.66		Newcastle	Blackburn Rovers	104	9	5					
			Oxford United	16	1	4	1				
			Bury (L)	5							
			Chester City	67	5	2	1				
Billy Stewart 5.11 11.7 1.1.65		Liverpool F F	Liverpool (A) Wigan Athletic Chester City	14							
DEFENDERS											
Graham Abel 6.2½ 13.0 17.9.60		Runcorn	Northwich Victoria								
			Chester	23			2	2			
Bobby Coy 5.11 11.12 30.11.61		Birmingham	Wolverhampton W. (A)	40+13	4						
			Chester City	93	6	1	3	2			
Brian Croft 27.9.67		Chester	Chester City	0+1			2				
David Glenn 5.10 10.10 30.11.62		Wigan	Wigan Athletic (A)	68+4	7	0+1		4			
			Blackburn Rovers	23+1		3					
			Chester City	33	4	0+1		1			
Martin Lane 5.9 11.4 12.4.61		Altrincham	Manchester United								
			Chester City	154	12	5	5	3			
MIDFIELD											
Graham Barrow 6.2 13.7 13.6.54	FRT 85	Chorley £10,000	Altrincham				8				
			Wigan Athletic	173+6	11	13	14	33	3		5
			Chester City								
Barry Butler 6.2 13.0 4.6.62		Farnworth	Atherton Town								
			Chester City	10+4			2				
Milton Graham 5.11 12.6 2.11.62	AMC 84	Hackney	Bournemouth	51+15	2+1	3+3	7	12	1	1	2
			Chester City	37+1	3	1		3			
Andy Holden* 6.1 13.2 14.9.62	W (1), U21 (1)	Flint	Rhyl								
			Chester City	92	8	2	4	14	2		2
John Kelly 5.10 10.10 7.10.62		Bebbington	Cammell Laird								
			Tranmere Rovers	55+9	7	1		9	1		
			Preston North End	85+8	11	4	3	20	1	1	
			Chester City	43	4	1		8			
FORWARDS											
Gary Bennett 6.1 12.6 20.9.63		Liverpool F	Wigan Athletic								
			Chester City	40+3	3	1	2	13			
Ricky Greenough 6.1 13.4 30.5.61		Mexborough	Boston								
			Alfreton Town								
			Chester City	51+6	2	1	2	7	4		
Peter Houghton 5.11 12.7 30.11.54		Liverpool	South Liverpool								
			Wigan Athletic	169+16	18	14		62	3	3	
			Preston North End	30+2	2+2		2+1	10	2		
			Wrexham (L)	5				2			
			Chester City	34+3	3	1		10			
David Murray 6.1 12.6 30.9.67		Chorley	Chorley								
			Wigan Athletic								
			Chester City	3+3	1		1	1	1		
Ian Richardson 5.8½ 10.6 5.5.64	FAYC 82	Ely	Watford (A)	5+3	1+1			2			
			Blackpool (L)	5				2			
			Rotherham United (L)	5				2			
			Chester City	27				10			
Stuart Rimmer 5.7 9.2 12.10.64	EY	Southport	Everton (A)	3							
			Chester	18	4	1		16	5		
Mark Sconce 5.9 10.6 18.2.68		Wrexham	Chester	1+1			2				

Player of the Year: Bobby Coy

ADDITIONAL CONTRACT PROFESSIONALS

APPRENTICES

NON-CONTRACT PLAYERS

Brian Croft (D) (0+1Lge, 2FRT), Ian Bailey (1+1FRT), Alec Cashley (G) (9Lge+1FRT), Mike Bates

THE STADIUM   Sealand Road, Chester CH1 4LW

Capacity: 20,000, seats

Record Attendance: 20,500 v Chelsea, FA Cup Round 3 Replay, 16 Jan 1952

Smallest Home Attendance for a First Class Match: 880 v Swindon Town, Div 4, 8 Feb 1984

Record Receipts: £15,854 v Aston Villa, League Cup Semi-Final 1st Leg, 15 Jan 1975

Size of Playing Area: 114yds × 76yds

Season Tickets: Stand: £62.00

Executive Box Season Tickets: £120.00 exclusive lounge, car park and seats

Cost of Stand Tickets: £3.50, **Terraces:** £2.50

Match and Ticket Information: No advance booking

Car Parking: Extensive at ground

Nearest Railway Station: Chester General (0244 40170)

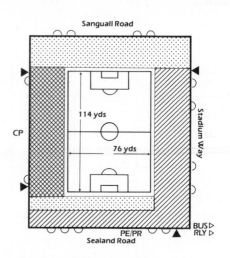

How to get to the ground

From North: Use Motorway M56, A41 or A56 S.P. Chester into town centre, then follow signs Queensferry A548 into Sealand Road for Chester FC

From East: Use A54 or A51 S.P. Chester into town centre, then follow signs Queensferry A548 into Sealand for Chester FC

From South: Use A41 or A483 S.P. Chester into town centre then follow signs Queensferry A548 into Sealand for Chester FC

From West: Use A55, A494 or A548 S.P. Chester, then follow signs to Queensferry. Follow signs Birkenhead A494 then in 1.2m branch left to join A548 S.P. Chester into Sealand Road for Chester FC

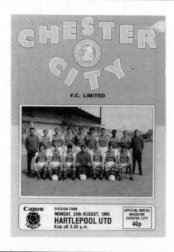

Price of 1986-7 Programme: 40p
Number of Pages: 16

Local Newspaper: Chester Chronicle

Local Radio Stations: Radio Merseyside, Marcher Sound Radio

144

President
His Grace The Duke of Devonshire
MC, DL, JP

Chairman
G M E Watterson

Directors
D P Kelly
A E Weinrich
P Taylor
K R Unwin
R A C Woodhead

Secretary
Bob Pepper (0246 209765)

Manager
John Duncan

Assistant Manager
Kevin Randall

Youth Team Coach
Derek Cluley

Commercial Manager
Jim Brown (0246 31535)

About the only thing which will please followers of Chesterfield is the fact that they will still be in the 3rd Division this coming season, but there has not been much else to provide satisfaction. After winning their first three League games the team went into steady decline and the final goals tally (61 for and 64 against) showed that a modest attack was not supported by a sound defence. A late struggle for survival was hastened by poor form in March when of seven matches at one stage only one produced even a draw, the rest being losses.

It was here that a win against the doomed visitors Wolverhampton Wanderers meant a slight rally so that there was no relegation, but it had been an unhappy time with only one instance of the team scoring even four goals in a game — against Swansea on April 5th.

The cups? Here again there was no respite from disappointment with an unlucky exit by penalties in the 1st round of the Milk Cup against Bradford City (five goals had been shared in the two legs). In the FA Cup the hard work was done when the side came away from Tranmere having shared four goals, but a second-half score by the visitors ended hopes in that competition. The Freight Rover Trophy began and ended at the Preliminary stage.

So where does Manager John Duncan look for comfort? His own previous good track record will not help, but he must hope for better work by his strikers, of whom Moss is the most consistent. Other sound performers last season were Scrimgeour, Baines, Spooner and Henderson, but it is significant that neither goalkeeper — Marples or Brown — ever inspired confidence.

This coming season could be another struggle for 3rd Division survival unless there is a dramatic improvement.   WLM

Back Row L to R: Brian Ferguson, Andy Kowalski, Gary Bellamy, Ernie Moss, Jim Brown, Brian Scrimgeour, Dave Caldwell, Jamie Hewitt, Andy Taylor, **Middle Row:** Phil Brown, Tony Reid, Ollie Bernadoux, Kevin Randall (Assistant Manager), Mick Henderson, John Duncan (Manager), Tony Coyle, Lee Coombes, Charlie Williamson, **Front Row:** Darren Wood, Keith Jones, Richard Marriott, Robert Elliott, Simon Harrison, Stephen Stoppard, Simon Grisedale, Jason MacDonald.

CHESTERFIELD

DIVISION THREE: 17th **FA CUP: 1st ROUND** **MILK CUP: 1st ROUND**

MATCH	DATE	COMPE-TITION	VENUE	OPPONENTS	RESULT		HALF TIME	L'GUE POS'N	GOALSCORERS/GOAL TIMES	ATTEN-DANCE
1	A 17	CL	H	Bury	W	4-3	2-1		Hunter 10, Spooner 41, Valentine (og) 56, Brown P. 67	3,835
2	21	MC1/1	A	**Bradford City**	D	2-2	1-2		**Brown P. (pen) 39, Moss 77**	**(2,980)**
3	24	CL	A	Cardiff City	W	2-0	1-0	1	Brown P. 22, Moss 89	(3,601)
4	27	CL	H	Rotherham United	W	2-0	0-0	1	Moss 52, Brown P. 60	5,434
5	31	CL	A	Walsall	L	0-3	0-0	5		(4,528)
6	S 3	MC1/2	H	**Bradford City**	L†	3-4	1-0		Moss 9, 84, Henderson 76	4,326
7	7	CL	H	A.F.C. Bournemouth	L	0-1	0-0	7		3,207
8	14	CL	A	Gillingham	D	1-1	1-0	8	Caldwell 16	(3,101)
9	17	CL	H	Darlington	W	1-0	0-0	5	Moss 56	3,161
10	21	CL	A	Derby County	D	0-0	0-0	5		(13,259)
11	28	CL	H	Wigan Athletic	D	1-1	0-0	6	Scrimgeour 84	3,518
12	O 2	CL	A	Reading	L	2-4	0-1	11	Moss 60, Williamson 77	(5,946)
13	5	CL	A	Bristol City	D	0-0	0-0	13		(6,416)
14	12	CL	H	York City	W	1-0	1-0	9	Moss 9	3,723
15	19	CL	A	Notts County	L	1-2	1-1	10	Moss 19	(5,776)
16	22	CL	H	Blackpool	L	1-2	0-0	13	Moss 90	3,720
17	26	CL	H	Doncaster Rovers	D	0-0	0-0	13		3,746
18	N 2	CL	A	Plymouth	D	0-0	0-0	13		(7,522)
19	5	CL	A	Swansea City	D	1-1	0-1	13	Walker 65	(3,424)
20	9	CL	H	Newport County	W	3-1	1-1	12	Scrimgeour 24, Hunter 82, Walker 84	2,420
21	16	FAC1	A	**Tranmere Rovers**	D	2-2	1-0		**Batty 38, Henderson 61**	**(2,252)**
22	19	FAC1R	H	**Tranmere Rovers**	L	0-1	0-0			**2,950**
23	23	CL	A	Brentford	L	0-1	0-1	12		(3,502)
24	D 14	CL	A	Bolton Wanderers	L	1-2	0-0	15	Walker 50	(3,621)
25	20	CL	H	Cardiff City	L	3-4	2-2	17	Spooner 4, Hunter 6, Henderson 60	1,773
26	26	CL	H	Lincoln City	D	2-2	2-1	17	Hunter 13, Scrimgeour 22	2,631
27	28	CL	A	Rotherham United	W	2-1	1-0	13	Henderson 32, Spooner 53	(4,816)
28	J 1	CL	A	Wolverhampton W.	L	0-1	0-1	14		(3,229)
29	14	FRT N	A	**Darlington**	L	0-2	0-1			**(1,057)**
30	18	CL	A	Bury	D	1-1	0-0	15	Scrimgeour 66	(2,614)
31	20	FRT N	H	**Burnley**	L	1-2	1-1		**Brown 9**	**1,053**
32	25	CL	H	Gillingham	D	1-1	1-1	15	Walker 22	2,521
33	31	CL	A	Bournemouth	L	2-3	0-1	17	Scrimgeour (pen) 75, Baines 85	(2,347)
34	F 4	CL	A	Blackpool	W	1-0	1-0	16	Baines 21	(2,988)
35	8	CL	H	Notts County	D	2-2	2-1	16	Scrimgeour (pen) 27, Moss 43	3,623
36	22	CL	H	Derby County	W	1-0	0-0	15	Baines 90	9,394
37	M 1	CL	A	Wigan Athletic	L	0-2	0-1	15		(3,209)
38	4	CL	H	Reading	L	3-4	2-1	16	Henderson 19, Moss 24, 84	2,428
39	8	CL	H	Bristol City	D	0-0	0-0	15		2,547
40	15	CL	A	York City	L	0-2	0-1	16		(3,580)
41	18	CL	H	Plymouth Argyle	L	1-2	1-2	17	Henderson 2	1,828
42	21	CL	A	Doncaster Rovers	L	0-2	0-1	17		(1,989)
43	25	CL	H	Walsall	L	2-3	1-2	18	Spooner 25, Caldwell 78	2,177
44	29	CL	H	Wolverhampton W.	W	3-0	2-0	17	Henderson 39, Moss 41, Reid 67	2,500
45	31	CL	A	Lincoln City	L	1-2	0-1	18	Caldwell 74	(2,461)
46	A 5	CL	H	Swansea City	W	4-1	1-1	17	Spooner 44, Scrimgeour (pen) 50, Moss 77, 80	2,148
47	12	CL	A	Newport County	D	3-3	2-2	18	Jones (og) 32, Reid 36, Scrimgeour 87	(1,940)
48	15	CL	H	Bristol Rovers	W	2-0	0-0	17	Reid 55, Walker 66	1,911
49	19	CL	H	Brentford	L	1-3	0-1	18	Armstrong 10	2,344
50	22	CL	A	Darlington	L	1-2	1-1	18	Bellamy 28	(2,597)
51	26	CL	A	Bristol Rovers	D	1-1	0-1	18	Scrimgeour (pen) 55	(3,576)
52	M 3	CL	H	Bolton Wanderers	W	3-0	0-0	17	Bellamy 49, Moss 54, Reid 61	3,183

Best Home League Attendance: 9,394 v Derby County 22/2 **Smallest: 1,773 v Cardiff City 20/12** **Av Home Att: 3,207**

Goal Scorers: **Compared with 84-85: −864**

League (61): Moss 14, Scrimgeour 9 (4 pen), Henderson 5, Spooner 5, Walker 5, Hunter 4, Reid 4, Baines 3, Brown 3, Caldwell 3, Bellamy 2, Opponents 2, Armstrong 1, Williamson 1

Milk Cup (5): Moss 3, Brown P 1 (pen), Henderson 1

FA Cup (2): Batty 1, Henderson 1

FRT (1): Brown P 1

†After extra time

Brown J. (NC)	Scrimgeour	O'Neill	Batty	Baines	Hunter	Spooner	Moss	Brown P.	Henderson	Kendal	Walker	Caldwell	Marples	Williamson	Reid	Hewitt	Perry (NC)	Bloomer (NC)	MacDonald (NC)	Wood (NC)	Taylor (NC)	Armstrong (NC)	Bellamy	Referee	
1	2	3	4	5	6	7	8	9	10	11														M Heath	1
1	2	3	4	5	6	7	8	9	10	11														**R Guy**	2
1	2	3	4	5	6	7	8	9	10	11														R Groves	3
1	2	3	4	5	6	7	8	9	10	11														P Vanes	4
1	2	3	4	5	6	7	8	9	10	11*	12													D Vickers	5
1	2	3	4	5	6	7*	8	9	10	11		12												**L Robinson**	6
	2	3	4*	5	6	7	8	9	10	11		12	1											K Breen	7
	2	3	4	5	6			7				9	8	1	10	11								D Axcell	8
	2	3	4	5	6		8	9	10			7		1	12	11*								K Barratt	9
	2	3	4	5	6		8	7	10	11	9		1											R Bridges	10
	2	3	4	5	6		8	9	10	11		7*		1		12								J McAulay	11
	2	3	4*	5	6		8	9	10	11				1	12	7								K Baker	12
	2	5	6	3	4		10	8				11		1	9	7								M James	13
	2	3	4	5	6	7	8		10			9		1		11								R Nixon	14
	2	3	4	5	6	7	8		10			9	12	1		11*								I Hemley	15
	2	3	4*	5	6	7	8	11	10			9		1		12								N Ashley	16
	2	3		5	6	11			10			9	8	1	7	4								C Trussell	17
	2	3		5	6	11*	8		10			9		1	4	7	12							R Lewis	18
	2	3		5	6		8	11	10			9		1	4	7								G Ashby	19
	2	3	12	5	6		8	11	10			9		1	7	4*								T Holbrook	20
	2	3	4	5	6		8	7	10			9		1	11									**A Ball**	21
	2	3	4	5	6	12	8	7	10			9		1	11*									**P Tyldesley**	22
	2	3	4*	5	6	7		12	10			9	8	1	11									B Stevens	23
	2	3	4	5		11		7*	10			9	8	1	12			6						J Lovatt	24
	2	3	4	5	6	11		7	10			9	8*	1				12						J Worrall	25
	2	3	4	5	6	11	8	7	10					1		9								M Reed	26
	2	3	4	5	6†	11	8	7	10					1		9								G Tyson	27
	2	3	4	5	6	11*		7	10			8		1	12	9								H Taylor	28
	2	3	4*	5			8	7	10			9*		1	6	11	13	12						**D Allison**	29
	2	5		3	4		10	6	7			11		1	9	8†								M Peck	30
11		5					7							8	1	3	4*	2	6*	10	12	13	9	**J Ashworth**	31
	2	3		5	6		8	7	10			9		1	4							11		K Lupton	32
	2	3		5	6	12	8	7*	10					1	4			9				11		A Gunn	33
	2	3		5	6	7	8		10					1	4			9				11		G Aplin	34
	2*	3		5	6	9	8	7	10					1	12	4						11		D Hedges	35
		3	6	5*			8	7	10	12				1	9	2	4					11		A Seville	36
	6	3		5		11*	8	7	10					1	9	2	12					4		J Ball	37
11		3		5				7	10		12	7*		1	9	2								R Guy	38
11		3		5	6	4*	8	7	10		12			1	9	2								I Hemley	39
11		3		5	6		8	7	10			9		1	4	2								N Glover	40
9		3	11	5			8	7	10		12			1	4*	2							6	G Napthine	41
	2	3		5			8		10			9*		1	12	2					7	4	6	P Vanes	42
1	9	3		5		11	8	12	10			7			4*	2							6	F Roberts	43
1	9	3		5	11		8		10			7†	3		4	2						9	5	D Scott	44
1	6				11		8		10			7	3		4	2						9	5	T Mills	45
1	6				11		8		10			7	3		4	2						9	5	T Fitzharris	46
1	6	3	10		11	7	8								4	2						9	5	B Stevens	47
1	6	3			11		8		10			9			4	2						7	5	J Bray	48
1	6	3	12		11		8		10			9			4	2						7*	5	I Hendrick	49
1	6	4	9	12	11		8		10			7	3			2*							5	D Hutchinson	50
1	6	3	9		11		8		10			7			2	4							5	J Moules	51
1	6	9			11		8		10			7	3		4	2							5	J Lloyd	52
14	45	43	24	37	32	31	39	29	43	8	18	18	32	22	24	16	1	6				12	12	League Appearances	
		2	1		1		2			1	2	4		5	4	1	1							Substitute Appearances	
2	2	2	2	2	2	2	2	2	2			0+1												Milk Cup Appearances	
	2	2	2	2	2	0+1	2	2						2	2									FA Cup Appearances	
2	1	1	2		1	2	1		1			1	2	2	1	1+1	1+1	0+1	0+1	1				FR Trophy Appearances	

Players on Loan:

Departures: Hunter (Scunthorpe), Ferguson (F), Kendal (F), Walker (F), Batty (Exeter City)

'THE SPIREITES'

Formed: 1866
Turned Professional: 1891　**Ltd Co:** 1871

Previous Managers: Bob Brocklebank　Bob Marshall　1952-8 Ted Davison
1958-62 Dugald Livingstone　1962-7 Tony McShane　1967-73 Jimmy McGuigan
1973-76 Joe Shaw　1976-80 Arthur Cox　1980-3 Frank Barlow
Honours: Champions Div 3 (N) 1930-31　Champions Div 4, 1969-70, 1984-85　Anglo Scottish Cup Winners 1980-81
League Career: Elected to Div 2 1899　Failed re-election 1908-09　Re-elected to Div 3 (N) 1921-22
Promoted to Div 2 1930-31　Relegated to Div 3 (N) 1932-33　Promoted to Div 2 1935-6
Relegated to Div 3 (N) 1950-1　Transferred to Div 3 1958　Relegated to Div 4 1960-61
Promoted to Div 3 1969-70　Relegated to Div 4 1982-83　Promoted to Div 3 1984-85
Colours: Royal blue shirts with white pin stripe, white shorts with blue stripe at sides, white stockings
Change Colours: Red shirt with white pin stripe, black shorts and stockings
Reserves League: Midland Intermediate

CLUB RECORDS

Most Appearances for Club: Dave Blakey: Football League 613 + FA Cup 32 + League Cup 6 **Total 651**
Most Capped Player: Walter McMillan, 4　**For England:** None
Record Goalscorer in a Match: No player has ever scored more than 4 goals in a match and this feat has been achieved on 19 occasions
Record League Goalscorer in a Season: Jimmy Cookson, 44, Div 3 (N), 1925-6　**In All Competitions:** Jimmy Cookson, 46 (League 44 + FA Cup 2), 1925-6
Record League Goalscorer in a Career: Ernie Moss, 128, 1968-76, 1979-81　**In All Competitions:** Ernie Moss, 158 (League 128 + FA Cup 11 + League/Milk Cup 12 + Anglo-Scottish Cup 3) 1968-76, 1979-81
Record Transfer Fee Received: £200,000 from Wolverhampton Wanderers for Alan Birch, Aug 1981
Record Transfer Fee Paid: £150,000 to Carlisle United for Phil Bonnyman, Mar 1980
Best Performances: League: 4th Div 2 1946-7　**FA Cup:** 5th Round　**League/Milk Cup:** 4th Round 1964-5
Most League Points: 64, Div 4, 1969-70, Div 3, 1981-82　**Most League Goals:** 102, Div 3 (N), 1930-1
Record League Victory: 10-0 v Glossop, Div 2, 13 Jan 1903
Record League Defeat: 1-9 v Port Vale, Div 2, 24 Sept 1932
Oldest Player in League Match:
Youngest Player in League Match:
Most Consecutive Undefeated League Matches: 13 1984

League Matches Without a Win: 16 1960-61, 1983

Longest Run of Undefeated Home League Matches: 27 1925-26
Longest Run Without Home League Win: 9 1963
Most Consecutive League Wins: 10 1933
Most Consecutive League Defeats: 9 1960

Away League Matches: 10 1935, 1969-70
Away League Win: 26 1907-08
Home League Wins: 17 1929-30
Away League Wins: 6 1933

Club Statistician for the Directory: R West

CHESTERFIELD

PLAYERS NAME Ht Wt Birthdate	Honours	Birthplace Transfers	Clubs	League	Milk Cup	FA Cup	Other Comps	League	Milk Cup	FA Cup	Other Comps
GOALKEEPERS											
Chris Marples 5.11 12.0 3.8.64	Div. 4, 85	Chesterfield	Chesterfield	70		2	2				
DEFENDERS											
Steve Baines* 6.0 12.12 23.6.54	Div. 4, 85	Newark	Nottingham Forest (A)	2							
			Huddersfield Town	113+1	11	7		10	1	1	
		£15,000	Bradford City	98+1	8	4		17	1	2	
		£50,000	Walsall	47+1	2	1		5			
			Bury (L)	7							
		£5,000	Scunthorpe United	37+1							
		F	Chesterfield	128+1	8	7	6	8	1		
Gary Bellamy 6.2 11.5 4.7.62	Div. 4, 85	Worksop	Chesterfield	139+3	10	6	1	5			
Shaun O'Neill 5.9 12.0 24.2.52	Div. 4, 85	Belfast	Leeds United (A)								
			Chesterfield	442	4	4	4	6			
Brian Scrimgeour† 6.0 12.13 11.8.59	Div. 4, 85	Dundee	Dundee	24+10	3+3	1					
			Chesterfield	98+3	7+1	6	6	12	1		
Jamie Hewitt 5.10 10.8 17.5.68		Chesterfield	Chesterfield								
MIDFIELD											
Mike Henderson 5.10 11.6 31.5.56	Div. 4, 85	Gosforth	Sunderland (A)	81+3	2	6		2			
		£140,000	Watford	50+1	8+1	4					
			Cardiff City	11							
			Sheffield United	65+2	6	11	2				
			Chesterfield	61	2	2	2	5			
Tony Reid 5.9 10.10 9.5.63		Nottingham	Derby County (A)	27+3	2	1+1		1			
			Scunthorpe United (L)	6							
			Newport County	74+2	3	6	7	12			
			Chesterfield	24+4			2	4			
Steve Spooner 5.11 12.0 25.1.61		London	Derby County (A)	7+1							
		F	Halifax Town	71+1	6	4		13			
		F	Chesterfield	89+4	3+1	0+2	3	14			1
Charlie Williamson 5.8 11.5 16.3.62		Glasgow	Sheffield Wednesday	61+1	1	1					
			Lincoln City (L)	5		1					
			Southend United (L)	10							
			Chesterfield	24+4			2				
FORWARDS											
Phil Brown 5.6 9.7 16.1.66	Div. 4, 85	Sheffield	Chesterfield (A)	72+4							
Tony Coyle 5.10 11.2 17.1.60		Glasgow	Albion Rovers	46		5					
		F	Stockport County	216+4	7+1	5		30	1		
		F	Chesterfield								
David Caldwell 5.10 11.6 31.7.60		Aberdeen	Inverness Caley								
			Mansfield Town	146+12	13	12	0+1	57	2	4	
			Carlisle United (L)								
			Swindon Town (L)								
		£15,000	Chesterfield	18+4	0+1		1	3			
Ernie Moss 6.1½ 13.2 19.10.49	Div. 4, 70, Div. 4, 85	Chesterfield	Chesterfield	271	14+1	14		94	6	8	
		£16,000	Peterborough United	34+1	5	2		9	2	1	
		£20,000	Mansfield Town	56+1	2			21			
		£16,000	Chesterfield	105+2	9	5		33	6		
		£15,000	Port Vale	74	4	5		23	3	2	
		F	Lincoln City	10+1				2			
		F	Doncaster Rovers	41+3	4	1	3	15	2		
		F	Chesterfield	71+1	4	3	2	26	3		
Andy Taylor 6.0 12.8 30.12.67		Chesterfield	Chesterfield								
Andy Kowalski 5.10 11.0 26.2.53		Mansfield	Worksop Town								
			Chesterfield	354+11	23+2	18+1		30	5		
			Doncaster Rovers	45+7	5	2	0+1	1			
			Peterborough United	35	2	7		4		1	
			Chesterfield								

ADDITIONAL CONTRACT PROFESSIONALS
Lee Coombes (monthly), Oliver Bernardeav

APPRENTICES
Kevin Randall, Andy Skelton, Mark Wing, Darren Wood (0+1FRT)

NON-CONTRACT PLAYERS
Robert Bloomer (GLge1+1FRT), Jim Brown (G62apps, 1gl), Mark Hedley, Jason MacDonald (0+1FRT), Paul Mainwaring, David Perry (1+1Lge, 1+1FRT)

RECREATION GROUND

Chesterfield S40 4SX   **Capacity:** 18,750 (12,000 cov'd)

Record Attendance: 30,968 v Newcastle United, Div 2, 7 Apr 1939

Record Receipts: £26,640 v Barnsley, Div 3, 26 Dec 1980

Season Tickets: Stand: £75 (£50 juveniles/OAP), Ground £50 (£30 juveniles/OAP)

Executive Box Season Tickets: £100

Cost of Stand Tickets: £4.00 (adults), £3.00 (juveniles/OAP) **Terraces:** £2.50 (adults), £1.50 (juveniles/OAP)

Match and Ticket Information: Centre and Wing stands bookable in advance

Car Parking: Street parking near ground allowed. Car parks ½ mile from ground in Saltergate

Nearest Railway Station: Chesterfield (0246 74371)

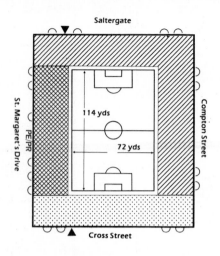

Saltergate

St. Margaret's Drive

PE/PR

114 yds

72 yds

Compton Street

Cross Street

How to get to the ground

From North: Use Motorway M1 until junction 30, then follow signs Chesterfield A619. In town centre follow signs Old Brampton into Saltergate for Chesterfield FC

From East and South: Follow signs Chesterfield A617 into town centre then follow signs Old Brampton into Saltergate for Chesterfield FC

From West: Follow signs Chesterfield 619 then at roundabout take 1st exit into Foljambe Road at end turn right into Saltergate for Chesterfield FC

Price of 1986-7 Programme: 50p
Number of Pages: 20
Subscriptions: £12.50 + £2.50 p&p

Local Newspapers: Derbyshire Times, Sheffield Star, Chesterfield Star

Local Radio Stations: Radio Hallam, Radio BBC Sheffield

COLCHESTER UNITED Division 4

Chairman	M J Cadman
Vice-Chairman	H R Piper
Directors	J T Crisp G H Parker J H Schultz
Secretary	Martin R Bennet (0206-574042)
Lottery Manager	C Harvey
Manager	Mike Walker
Youth Team Manager	Roy Massey
Physiotherapist	Charlie Simpson

Colchester United promise each season to rise from the depths of Division 4 and each time the fates conspire to cheat them of it. Some seasons failure is caused by a simple lack of consistency and if that is ever achieved the club might just one day startle fans everywhere. But this most recent season again produced the good and bad form with a late burst of nine matches without defeat bringing a final position of sixth — well away from a promotion place in terms of points.

The campaign started badly with three of the first six matches lost, but then six matches in succession were won followed by only two victories before the New Year, when another loss brought a descent to 13th place. There was another bad run in March and farewell was paid to promotion for another year. But the team did score 88 League goals and several players became consistent scorers so that another season could go well if the defence could be tightened — 63 goals were let in.

The cups provided no cheer with immediate exits from both major competitions being the team's fate. The Milk Cup brought two matches against Millwall — and defeat by a combined score of 3-7. A visit to Gola League relegation candidates Wycombe Wanderers brought humiliation (0-2). In the Freight Rover Trophy no rivers were ignited, so the late League splash was timely and welcome. Now fans wait to see whether it can be done again for a complete season.

Former goalkeeping stalwart Mike Walker holds the reins now at Layer Road and he has enough talent to produce results. The two Englishs have played well up front and Groves can also stick them away. Chamberlain did well in goal and there were good defensive efforts from Hedman, Phillips, Houston and Baker. One of these days there will be a successful promotion challenge. **WLM**

Back Row L to R: Alec Chamberlain, Andy Farrell, Simon Burman, Tony English, Keith Day, Rudi Hedman, Kirk Game, Terry Baker, Sean Norman, John Reeves.
Front Row: Charlie Simpson (Physio), Robin Turner, Perry Groves, Tom English, Ian Phillips, Mike Walker (Manager), Mike Ferguson, Tony Adcock, Keith Bowen, Steve Allen (Physio).

COLCHESTER UNITED

DIVISION FOUR: 6th   **FA CUP:** 1st ROUND   **MILK CUP:** 1st ROUND

MATCH	DATE		COMPE-TITION	VENUE	OPPONENTS	RESULT		HALF TIME	L'GUE POS'N	GOALSCORERS/GOAL TIMES	ATTEN-DANCE
1	A	17	CL	H	Stockport County	W	3-1	1-0		Osborne 36, Day 71, Adcock 74	1,719
2		21	MC1/1	H	Millwall	L	2-3	1-3		Bowen 12, 89	1,430
3		24	CL	A	Wrexham	L	1-2	1-0	11	Reeves 30	(2,298)
4		27	CL	H	Aldershot	W	4-0	1-0		English 36, Adcock 68, Groves 70, Hedman 72	1,928
5		31	CL	A	Torquay United	L	1-2	1-1	8	Adcock 27	(1,023)
6	S	3	MC1/2	A	Millwall	L	1-4	0-2		Bowen (pen) 78	(3,330)
7		6	CL	H	Halifax Town	W	3-1	2-0	6	Adcock 1, 29, Bowen 56	2,023
8		14	CL	A	Tranmere Rovers	W	4-3	3-2	4	English 23, Groves 38, Parkinson 40, Day 47	(1,362)
9		17	CL	H	Cambridge United	W	4-1	2-0		Adcock 3 2, 30, 57, Groves 85	2,574
10		21	CL	A	Orient	W	2-1	0-1	2	Parkinson 55, Bowen 88	(2,577)
11		27	CL	H	Port Vale	W	1-0	1-0	1	Bowen 33	3,110
12	O	1	CL	A	Burnley	W	2-0	0-0	1	Adcock 46, Bowen 61	(3,375)
13		4	CL	H	Exeter City	D	1-1	1-0	1	Day 29	3,927
14		12	CL	A	Mansfield Town	L	1-2	0-0	1	English 50	(3,364)
15		18	CL	H	Scunthorpe United	D	1-1	0-0	1	Reeves 78	3,462
16		22	CL	A	Southend United	W	4-2	1-0	1	Bowen 16, Groves 3 49, 66, 85	(8,120)
17		26	CL	H	Northampton Town	L	0-2	0-1	2		2,872
18	N	2	CL	A	Hereford	L	0-2	0-2	5		(3,081)
19		6	CL	A	Chester City	L	0-4	0-1	6		(2,809)
20		8	CL	A	Rochdale	L	0-1	0-0	8		2,624
21		16	FAC1	A	Wycombe	L	0-2	0-2			(3,018)
22		23	CL	A	Preston North End	L	2-3	0-2	9	Parkinson (pen) 70, Adcock 82	(2,783)
23	D	14	CL	A	Hartlepool United	L	1-4	1-2	12	Hedman 36	(2,507)
24		20	CL	H	Wrexham	W	5-2	2-0	11	Comstive (og) 9, Adcock 15, 84, Groves 77, Hedman 79	1,683
25		28	CL	A	Aldershot	D	1-1	1-1	11	Day 4	(1,757)
26	J	1	CL	A	Swindon Town	L	1-2	0-2	13	Parkinson 54	(8,802)
27		3	CL	H	Hereford	W	4-1	1-0	11	Parkinson 43, 83, English 77, Phillips 80	2,216
28		11	CL	H	Torquay United	D	0-0	0-0			2,063
29		14	FRT S	H	Southend United	W	4-1	4-0		Groves 3 12, 29, 39, Adcock 29	1,364
30		17	CL	A	Stockport County	D	1-1	1-1	10	Groves 29	(2,336)
31		21	FRTS	A	Northampton Town	L	1-2	1-1		Baker 36	(1,958)
32		24	CL	H	Tranmere Rovers	L	1-2	0-2	12	Parkinson	2,013
33		31	CL	A	Halifax Town	D	2-2	1-0	12	Baker 36, Adcock 61	(800)
34	F	4	CL	H	Southend United	W	2-0	2-0	10	Adcock 4, Clark (og) 22	1,915
35	M	1	CL	A	Port Vale	D	1-1	0-0	9	Groves 68	(2,726)
36		8	CL	A	Exeter City	D	2-2	1-0	12	Adcock 42, Burman 85	(1,520)
37		14	CL	H	Mansfield Town	D	0-0	0-0	13		1,920
38		22	CL	A	Northampton Town	L	0-1	0-1	15		(2,035)
39		24	CL	H	Crewe Alexandra	L	1-2	0-2	15	English Tony 62	1,356
40		28	CL	H	Swindon Town	D	1-1	0-0	14	English Tony 54	2,997
41		31	CL	A	Peterborough United	W	2-1	1-1	13	English Tom 6, Baker 84	(2,316)
42	A	4	CL	H	Chester City	L	2-3	0-2	14	English Tom (pen) 57, 62	2,281
43		8	CL	H	Orient	W	4-0	2-0	12	Ferguson 17, Day 33, Phillips 66, English Tony 78	1,771
44		12	CL	A	Rochdale	D	3-3	1-1	12	Ferguson 20, Farrell 76, English Tom 83	(1,182)
45		15	CL	A	Scunthorpe United	D	1-1	1-1	14	Ferguson 6	(1,067)
46		18	CL	H	Preston North End	W	4-0	1-0	12	English Tom pen 30, 75, pen 83, Ferguson 78	2,046
47		22	CL	H	Peterborough United	W	5-0	1-0	9	Reeves 26, English Tom 64, English Tom 3 66, 80, 88	1,863
48		26	CL	A	Crewe Alexandra	W	2-0	2-0	8	Groves 25, 40	(1,555)
49		29	CL	A	Cambridge United	W	3-1	3-0	7	Reeves 7, Ferguson 14, 35	(3,115)
50	M	2	CL	H	Hartlepool United	W	3-1	1-1	6	Ferguson 25, English Tom 89, English Tony 90	2,410
51		6	CL	H	Burnley	D	2-2	1-0	6	Groves 45, English Tom 80	2,726

Best Home League Attendance: 3,927 v Exeter City 4/10   **Smallest:** 1,356 v Crewe Alexandra 24/3   **Av Home Att:** 2,326

Goal Scorers: **Compared with 84-85:** +251

League (88): Adcock 15, Groves 12, English Tom 11 (3 pen), English Tony 10, Ferguson 7, Parkinson 7 (1 pen), Bowen 5, Day 5, Reeves 4, Hedman 3, Baker 2, Phillips 2, Opponents 2, Burman 1, Farrell 1, Osborne 1

Milk Cup (3): Bowen 3 (1 pen)

FA Cup (Nil):

FRT (5): Groves 3, Adcock 1, Baker 1

1985-86

Chamberlain	Hedman	Phillips	Reeves	Day	Houston	Groves	Osborne	Bowen	Adcock	English, Tony	Irving	Parkinson	Farrell	Hull	Game	Turner	English, Tom	Whymark (NC)	Burman	Baker	Ferguson	Referee	
1	2	3	4	5	6	7*	8	9	10	11	12											E Scales	1
1	2	3	8	5	6	7	4*	9	10	11		12										**I Borrett**	2
1	2	3	4*	5	6	7		9	10	11	12	8										M Reid	3
1	2	3	4	5	6	7	12	9	10	11*		8										J Baker	4
1	2	3	4	5	6	7	12	9	10	11*		8										A Robinson	5
1	2	3	4	5	6		12	9	10	11	7*	8										**J Bray**	6
1	6	3	4	5		7		9	10	11		8	2									M Cotton	7
1	2	3	4	5	6	7		9	10	11		8										D Shaw	8
1	2	3	4*	5	6	7	12	9	10	11		8										N Butler	9
1	2	3	4	5	6	7		9	10	11		8										G Napthine	10
1	2	3	4	5	6	7*		9	10	11	12	8										A Gunn	11
1	2	3	4	5*	6			9	10	11	12	8	7									A Saunders	12
1	2	3	4	5	6	7		9	10	11		8										D Reeves	13
1	2	3	4*	5	6	7	12	9	10	11		8										K Breen	14
1	2	3	4	5	6	7	12	9	10	11		8*										B Hill	15
1	2		4	5*	6	7		9	10	11		8	3	12								D Vickers	16
1	5		4		6	7	12	9	10	2		8	3	11*								M James	17
1	5		4		6	7	9		10	2	12	8	3*	11								R Groves	18
1	5		4		6	7			10	2	9	8	3	11								D Allinson	19
1	2		4		6	7			10	11		8	3		5	9						I Hemley	20
1	2		4		6	7			10	11		8	3		5	9						**E Scales**	21
1	2		5	6	7				10	11*		8	3		12	4	9					F Roberts	22
1	2		4*	5	6	7			10	11		8	3			9	12					K Walmsley	23
1	2			5	6	7	4		10	11		8	3				12	9*				A Robinson	24
1	2	3		5	6	7*	4		10	11		8					12	9				K Cooper	25
1	2	3	5*	6			4		10	11	12	8				9	7					R Lewis	26
1	2	3	5*	6			4		10	11	12	8				9	7					T Ward	27
1	2	3		6	12		4		10	11		8				7*	9		5			D Hedges	28
1	2	3		6	9*		4		10	11		8				7	12		5			**J Moules**	29
1	2	3		6	9		4		10	11		8				7			5			T Mills	30
1	2	3		5	10		6	9	11			8*			12	7			4			**G Ashby**	31
1	2	3		6*	9		4		10	11		8				7	12		5			C Downey	32
1	2						9	4	10	3	11	8			6			7	5			G Aplin	33
1	2	3		6	9		4		10	11		8					12	7	5			E Scales	34
1	2	3		6	9		4		10	11		8					12	7*	5			P Willis	35
1	2	3		6	9		4		10			8	11				12	7	5*			K Cooper	36
1	5	3		6	9		4		10	11		8	2				12	7*				L Shapter	37
1		3		6	9		4		10*	11		8	2				12	7	5			P Tyldesley	38
1	2	3		6	9		4			11		8	7				10		5			I Hemley	39
1	2	3		6	9		4			11		8	7				10		5			A Gunn	40
1	2	3		6	9		4			11		8*	7				10			5	12	M Reed	41
1		3	2	6	9		4			11			7				10			5	8	D Reeves	42
1		3	2	6	7		4			11		8					10			5	9	T Holbrook	43
1	2	3		6	7		4			11			9				10			5	8	J Bray	44
1	2	3		6	9		4*			11			7			12	10			5	8	G Tyson	45
1	2	3		6	9		4			11			7				10			5	8	T Ward	46
1	12	3	11	6	9		4			2			7*		8		10			5		M Bodenham	47
1		3	11†	6	9		4			2			7				10†			5	8	N Glover	48
1		3	11	6	9		4			2			7				10			5	8	G Napthine	49
1		3	11	6	9		4			2			7				10			5	8	H Taylor	50
1		3	11*	6	9		4			2			7			12	10			5	8	M Cotton	51
46	38	37	24	30	36	42	28	15	33	45	2	35	24	4	3	6	16	2	10	21	9	League Appearances	
	1					1	6					7	1	1	3	7	1			1		Substitute Appearances	
2	2	2	2	2	1	1+1	2	2	2	1		1+1										Milk Cup Appearances	
1	1	1		1	1					1		1	1	1	1							FA Cup Appearances	
2	2	2				2	2			2		2			0-1	2	0-1			2		FR Trophy Appearances	

Players on Loan:

Departures: Hull (F), Osborne (F), Parkinson (F), Irving (F), Houston (Plymouth as Coach)

'THE U's'

Formed: 1937
Turned Professional: 1937 **Ltd Co:** 1937

Previous Managers: Since joining the Football League:
Ted Fenton   Jimmy Allen   Jack Butler   Benny Fenton   Neil Franklin   Dick Graham   Jim Smith
Bobby Roberts   Allan Hunter   Cyril Lea
Honours: None
League Career: Elected to Div 3 (S) 1950   Transferred to Div 3 1958
Relegated to Div 4 1960-1   Promoted to Div 3 1961-2   Relegated to Div 4 1964-5
Promoted to Div 3 1965-6   Relegated to Div 4 1967-8   Promoted to Div 3 1973-4
Relegated to Div 4 1975-6   Promoted to Div 3 1976-7   Relegated to Div 4 1980-1
Colours: Blue with white pin-striped shirts, white shorts, white stockings
Change Colours: Red shirts, black shorts and stockings
Reserves League: Building Scene Eastern   **Youth Team** S.E. Counties Div 2

CLUB RECORDS

Most Appearances for Club: Micky Cook: Football League 609 + 4 subs + FA Cup 46 + League/Milk Cup 36 **Total 691 + 4**
Most Capped Player: None
Record Goalscorer in a Match: No one has scored more than four
Record League Goalscorer in a Season: Bobby Hunt, 37, Div 4, 1961-2   **In All Competitions:** Bobby Hunt, 38, (League 37, FA Cup 1)
Record League Goalscorer in a Career: Martyn King, 131, 1959-65
Record Transfer Fee Received: £90,000 from Gillingham for Trevor Lee, Jan 1981
Record Transfer Fee Paid: £25,000 to Ipswich Town for Roger Osborne, Feb 1981
Best Performances: League: 3rd Div 3 (S) 1956-7   **FA Cup:** 6th Round (shared record for Div 4) 1970-1   **League/Milk Cup:** 5th Round 1974-5
Most League Goals: 104, Div 4, 1961-2
Most League Points: 81 in Div 4, 1982-3
Record League Victory and Most Goals in a First Class Match: 9-1 v Bradford City, Div 4, 30 Dec 1961
Most Goals Scored in a Cup Tie: 7 v Yeovil, 2nd Round Replay FA Cup, 1958
Record League Defeat: 0-7 v Leyton Orient, Div 3 (S), 5 Jan 1953   0-7 v Reading, Div 3 (S), 18 Sept 1957
Oldest Player in League Match: Benny Fenton 39 yrs 6 months
Youngest Player in League Match: Peter Barlow 16 yrs 10 months

Most Consecutive Undefeated League Matches: 20 1956-57
Longest Run of Undefeated Home League Matches: 27 1956-57
Longest Run Without Home League Win: 11 1968
Most Consecutive League Wins: 7 1968-69
Most Consecutive League Defeats: 8 1954

League Matches Without a Win: 20 1968
Away League Matches: 9 1956-57
Away League Win: 19 1950-51, 1959-60
Home League Wins: 13 1976-77
Away League Wins: 5 1981

Club Statistician for the Directory: Mick Middleton

COLCHESTER UNITED

PLAYERS NAME Ht Wt Birthdate	Honours	Birthplace Transfers	Clubs	APPEARANCES League	Milk Cup	FA Cup	Other Comps	GOALS League	Milk Cup	FA Cup	Other Comps
GOALKEEPERS											
Alec Chamberlain 6.2 11.11 20.6.64		Ely	Ramsey Town								
			Ipswich Town								
			Colchester United	142	8	7	8				
DEFENDERS											
Terry Baker 5.11 12.4 3.11.65		Rochford	West Ham United (A)								
			Billericay Town								
			Colchester United	21			2				
Keith Day 6.1 11.0 29.11.62		Grays	Aveley								
			Colchester united	75	4	3	2	9			
Kirk Game 6.2 12.0 22.10.66		Rochford	Southend United (A)								
			Colchester United	3+1		1	0+1				
Rudi Hedman 6.3 12.1 16.11.64		London	Colchester United	70+4	2	2+2	5	5			
Sean Norman 5.6 10.8 27.11.66		Lowestoft	Colchester United (A)								
Ian Phillips* 5.8 12.2 23.4.59		Edinburgh	Ipswich Town								
		F	Mansfield Town	18+5		1+1		5			
		F	Peterborough United	97	7	7		3			
		F	Northampton Town	42	4			1			
		£3,000	Colchester United	117	4	6	7	8			
MIDFIELD											
Simon Burman 5.10 11.0 26.4.55		Ipswich	Colchester United (A)	18+2				1			
Tony English 5.11 11.2 19.10.66		Luton	Coventry City (A)	1							
			Colchester United	45	2	1	2				
Andy Farell 5.11 11.0 7.10.65		Colchester	Colchester United (A)	74+3	6	5	3	1			
John Reeves 5.7 9.10 8.7.63		London	Fulham (A)	10+4	1	2					
			Colchester United	24	2	1		4			
Robin Turner 5.9 10.8 10.9.55	EY FAYC 73	Carlisle	Ipswich Town (A)	22+26	1+2	5+1	1+3	1	2	2	1
			Swansea City	20		3	5				
			Colchester United	6+3		1	2				
FORWARDS											
Tony Adcock 5.10 11.0 1.10.57		Bethnal Green	Colchester United (A)	159+16	13+1	9+2	6	87	5	1	6
Keith Bowen 6.1 11.2 26.2.58	WU21 (1)	Northampton	Northampton T (NC)	61+4	8+1	2		25	1		
			Brentford	42+9	0+1	3+2		9		3	
			Colchester United	115+1	7	3+1	4	37	5	5	
Tom English 5.9 11.6 18.10.61		Cirencester	Coventry City (A)	62+4	7	3		17	4	1	
			Leicester City	29+15	2+1	0+1		3	1		
			Rochdale	3				1			
			Plymouth Argyle	0+4	1			1			
			Colchester United	36+9			0+1	14			
Mike Ferguson 6.1 12.8 3.10.54		Newcastle	Coventry City (A)	121+6	10+2	3		51	3		
		£280,000	Everton	7+1	3+1			4	2		
		£60,000	Birmingham City	22	2		9				
			Coventry City (L)	7							
		Player exch.	Brighton	17	3	1	1	7	1		
			Colchester United	9+1				7			
Perry Groves 5.11 11.2 19.4.65		London	Colchester United (A)	141+14	8	6	6	27	1	1	4

ADDITIONAL CONTRACT PROFESSIONALS

Player of the Year: Roger Osborne

APPRENTICES

Scott Daniels, Lee Hunter, Michael Jewell

NON-CONTRACT PLAYERS

Andrew Springett, Steven Turney, Scott Young

Record Attendance: 13,031 v Manchester United, Milk Cup Round 3, 8 Nov 1983

Record Receipts: £22,754 v Manchester United, Milk Cup Round 3, 8 Nov 1983

Season Tickets: B Block: £100 (£65 juveniles/OAP), includes Ass. Membership of V.I.P. club, C Block: £95 (£60 juveniles/OAP), A & D: £80 (£50 juveniles/OAP), Bench Seats: £60 (£50 juveniles/OAP), Ground Season tickets: £50 (juveniles/OAP £20). Early Bird prices are available on all prices until 4 June 1986

Executive Box Season Tickets: All taken

Cost of Stand Tickets: B & C: £5.00, A & D £4.00, Bench £3.00. **Terraces:** £2.50 (adults), £1.00 (juveniles/OAP)

Match and Ticket Information: 0206 572202 or 574042 (Bookable two weeks in advance and retained if paid for until 48 hours before kick-off)

Car Parking: Available in Butts Road and Layer Road (150 yards from ground South side of Colchester, Also in Army Barracks (150 yards from ground)

Nearest Railway Station: Colchester North (0206 64777)

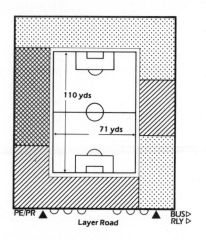

PE/PR △ ○○○ ○○○ △ BUS▷
Layer Road RLY ▷

110 yds
71 yds

How to get to the ground

From North: Follow signs in Colchester on A133/B1508 or A12, then follow signs Layer B1026 into Layer Road for Colchester United FC
From East: Follow signs into Colchester on A604 or A133 then follow signs Layer B1026 into Layer Road for Colchester United FC
From South and West: Follow signs into Colchester on A604 or A12 then follow signs Layer B1026 into Layer Road for Colchester United FC

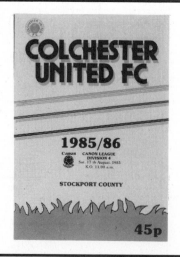

Price of 1986-7 Programme: 50p
Number of Pages:
Subscriptions: Rates available from club

Local Newspapers: Evening Gazette (Mon-Fri Evenings), East Anglian Daily Times (Mon-Sat Morning), Essex County Standard (Weekly-Fridays)

Local Radio Stations: Radio Orwell (Ipswich), Essex Radio (Southend & Chelmsford) (257 medium wave)

COVENTRY CITY

Life President
Derrick H Robins

Chairman
J Poynton

Directors
M F French FCA
G W Curtis (Managing)
J F W Reason
D W Richardson
E J Stocker

Secretary
G P Hover (0203 57171)

Managing Director
G W Curtis

Club Coach
John Sillett

Physiotherapist
George Dalton

A final victory against QPR kept the Sky Blues in the top flight for their twentieth successive season of First Division football. This escape must set them up as the "greatest Houdinis" of all time as for the third season in succession they had to win their final match of the campaign to stay up. Again the woodwork saved them late in the game and we had the usual post match pitch invasion, followed by the players accepting the cheers of their fans from the director's box. Heady stuff! But on reflection it had been another poor season with early exits from both cup competitions, and crowds down to an all-time low of 7,000 in January.

The usual flurry of bargain basement close season signings had given the squad a more balanced look and although they had a promising spell before Christmas their usual fall from grace after the FA Cup exit bracketed them in the relegation zone earlier than usual.

Morale was at rock bottom when they sold their only saleable asset Terry Gibson, leading scorer for the last three seasons, to Manchester United in a deal worth £650,000. In came Jim McInally, Alan Brazil and Nick Pickering, and for a time it looked as if they might finish in a respectable position but another terrible slump left them again teetering on the brink of relegation.

With only three matches remaining Manager Don Mackay resigned (his assistant Frank Upton had already been dismissed two weeks previously) and it was left to that old warhorse George Curtis with assistance from Youth Team coach John Sillett to raise team spirit sufficiently to obtain the six points required to keep them up.

To everybody's surprise this duo along with another 'Old Boy' Mick Coop have been given the opportunity to manage the club's affairs from now on. Enthusiasm and committment they certainly have but whether the right blend of experience is there, is another matter.

The board of the club has been totally reconstituted and with the bulk of the members being 'Coventry Kids' made good the ambition at last seems to be there. Brazil, McInally and Bowman have already gone, to be replaced by Phillips, Houchen and Painter, more signings are promised and with another new strip (very similar to Argentina!) the future certainly looks brighter than for some time.

The fans though have grown sceptical over the years and it will take a fair measure of success to get them coming through the turnstiles in any numbers again.

Back Row L to R: Paul Culpin, Cyrille Regis, Andy Williams, Graham Rodger, Keith Houchen, Brian Kilcline, Trevor Peake. **Middle Row:** Michael Gynn, Ian Painter, David Phillips, Steve Ogrizovic, Jake Findlay, Lloyd McGrath, Gareth Evans, Micky Adams. **Front Row:** Brian Borrows, Greg Downs, George Dalton (Physio), John Sillett (Chief Coach), George Curtis (Managing Director), Wayne Turner, Dave Bennett, Nick Pickering.

COVENTRY CITY

DIVISION ONE: 17th | **FA CUP:** 3rd ROUND | **MILK CUP:** 3rd ROUND

MATCH	DATE		COMPE-TITION	VENUE	OPPONENTS	RESULT		HALF TIME	L'GUE POS'N	GOALSCORERS/GOAL TIMES	ATTEN-DANCE
1	A	17	CL	H	Manchester City	D	1-1	1-1		McNab (og) 22	14,550
2		20	CL	A	Chelsea	L	0-1	0-0			(15,679)
3		24	CL	A	Everton	D	1-1	1-0	18	Gibson 43	(27,691)
4		26	CL	H	Newcastle United	L	1-2	0-0	20	Gibson 81	12,047
5		31	CL	A	Watford	L	0-3	0-2	21		(13,835)
6	S	3	CL	H	Oxford United	W	5-2	2-2	17	Bennett 19, Hibbitt 22, Briggs (og) 60, Gynn 65, Kilcline (pen) 74	10,266
7		7	CL	H	Arsenal	L	0-2	0-1	20		12,189
8		14	CL	A	Aston Villa	D	1-1	1-1	20	Culpin 6	(12,198)
9		21	CL	A	Southampton	D	1-1	0-0	18	Gibson 60	(12,674)
10		25	MC2/1	A	Chester	W	2-1	0-1		Gibson 52, Bowman 86	(4,863)
11		28	CL	H	W.B.A	W	3-0	1-0	14	Adams (pen) 17, Gibson 47, Peake 57	10,295
12	O	6	CL	H	Leicester City	W	3-0	1-0	15	Bowman 18, Gibson 47, Regis 50	10,959
13		9	MC2/2	H	Chester	W	7-2	4-2		Regis 5 3, 18, 30, 43, 88, Gibson 52, Kilcline 76	5,504
14		12	CL	A	Sheffield Wednesday	D	2-2	0-2	15	Adams 51, Gibson 77	(19,132)
15		15	FMC	H	Millwall	D	1-1	1-0		Gibson 42	1,086
16		20	CL	H	Tottenham	L	2-3	2-1	16	Bennett 17, Kilcline (pen) 24	13,545
17		26	CL	A	Birmingham City	W	1-0	1-0	14	Gibson 16	(9,267)
18		29	MC3	H	W.B.A.	D	0-0	0-0			9,804
19	N	2	CL	A	Manchester United	L	0-2	0-2	14		(46,748)
20		6	MC3R	A	W.B.A	L	3-4	2-3		Evans 2, Bennett 21, 47	(8,919)
21		9	CL	H	Liverpool	L	0-3	0-1	16		16,497
22		16	CL	A	Luton	W	1-0	1-0	15	Bowman 35	(9,607)
23		23	CL	H	West Ham United	L	0-1	0-0	15		11,042
24		30	CL	A	Queens Park Rangers	W	2-0	0-0	14	Gibson 77, Byrne (og) 88	(11,101)
25	D	7	CL	H	Chelsea	D	1-1	1-1	14	Gibson 7	8,721
26		14	CL	A	Manchester City	L	1-5	0-2	15	Gibson 72	(20,075)
27		21	CL	H	Everton	L	1-3	0-0	15	Gibson 60	11,059
28		26	CL	H	Ipswich	L	0-1	0-0	17		9,356
29	J	1	CL	A	Nottingham Forest	L	2-5	2-1	17	Gibson 19, Adams 20	(13,860)
30		4	FAC3	H	Watford	L	1-3	0-0		Kilcline 58	10,498
31		11	CL	H	Aston Villa	D	3-3	3-1	16	Regis 22, Kilcline 41, (pen) 44	10,328
32		18	CL	H	Watford	L	0-2	0-1	17		7,499
33		25	CL	A	Oxford United	W	1-0	0-0	16	Turner 64	(9,383)
34	F	1	CL	A	Newcastle United	L	2-3	1-2	16	Regis 43, Brazil 63	(16,637)
35		8	CL	A	Tottenham Hotspur	W	1-0	0-0	16	Regis 80	(13,135)
36		16	CL	H	Birmingham City	D	4-4	2-2	14	Bennett 51, 73, Kilcline (pen) 56, (pen) 88	14,271
37		22	CL	H	Southampton	W	3-2	0-2	14	Brazil 55, Pickering 58, Bennett 79	10,881
38	M	8	CL	A	Leicester City	L	1-2	1-0	15	Pickering 27	(10,774)
39		15	CL	H	Sheffield Wednesday	L	0-1	0-0	16		10,168
40		19	CL	A	WBA	D	0-0	0-0	16		(8,831)
41		22	CL	A	Arsenal	L	0-3	0-1	16		(17,189)
42		29	CL	H	Nottingham Forest	D	0-0	0-0	16		9,500
43		31	CL	A	Ipswich Town	L	0-1	0-0	16		(13,485)
44	A	5	CL	H	Manchester United	L	1-3	0-2	17	Pickering 52	17,160
45		12	CL	A	Liverpool	L	0-5	0-2	19		(42,729)
46		19	CL	H	Luton Town	W	1-0	0-0	17	Pickering 47	10,146
47		26	CL	A	West Ham United	L	0-1	0-0	18		(27,251)
48	M	3	CL	H	Queens Park Rangers	W	2-1	2-1	17	Kilcline 37, Bennett 44	14,086

Best Home League Attendance: 17,160 v Man Utd 5/4   **Smallest:** 7,499 v Watford 18/1   **Av Home Att:** 11,646

Goal Scorers: **Compared with 84-85:** −1,145

League (48): Gibson 12, Kilcline 7 (5 pens), Bennett 6, Pickering 4, Regis 4, Adams 3 (1 pen), Opponents 3, Bowman 2, Brazil 2, Culpin 1, Glynn 1, Hibbitt 1, Peake 1, Turner 1

Milk Cup (12): Regis 5, Gibson 2, Bennett 2, Bowman 1, Evans 1, Kilcline 1

FA Cup (1): Kilcline 1

FM Cup (1): Gibson 1

Ogrizovic	Borrows	Downs	Bowman	Kilcline	Peake	Bennett	Gynn	Regis	Gibson	Adams	Hibbitt	Turner	Culpin	McGrath	Stephens	Evans	Rodger	Williams	Pickering	Brazil	McNally	Referee	
1	2	3	4	5	6	7	8*	9	10	11	12											A Buksh	1
1	2	3	4	5	6	7	12	9	10	11	8*											A Robinson	2
1	2	3	4	5	6	7	12	9	10	11	8*											F Roberts	3
1	2	3	4*	5	6	7	12	9	10	11	8											R Dilkes	4
1	2	3	4	5	6	7	12	9	10	11	8*											I Borrett	5
1	2	3		5	6	7	11	9	10*		8	4	12									A Ward	6
1	2	3		5	6		·11	9*	10	7	8	4	12									I Hendrick	7
1	2	3	4	5	6	12	11*		10	7			9	8								R Nixon	8
1	2	3	4	5	6	12	11		10	7			9*	8								N Glover	9
1	2	3	4	5*	6	9	11		10	7	12			8								T Mills	10
1	2	3	4		6		11	9	10	7*	12			8		5						M Dimblebee	11
1	2	3	4	5	6	11		9*	10	7				8		12						K Cooper	12
1	2	3	4	5	6	11		9	10	7				8*		12						R Lewis	13
1	2	3	4	5	6	11		9	10	7				8								A Robinson	14
1	2		4	5	6	7	8		10*	3	11			9		12						P Tyldesley	15
1	2	3	4*	5	6	11		9	10	7				8								M Heath	16
1	2	3	4	5	6	11		9	10	7				8								K Hackett	17
1	2	3	4*	5	6	11	12	9	10	7				8								C Downey	18
1	2	3	4	5	6	11	12		7					8		9						J McAulay	19
1	2	3	4	5*	6	11						10	7	8		9	12					D Scott	20
1	2	3*	4		6	11			7					8		9	5	12				D Vickers	21
1	2	12	4		6	11	3*		7					8		9	5					J Moules	22
1	2	3	4		6	11			7			12		8		9*	5					J Worrall	23
1	2	3	4			11		9	10	7				8			5					B Stevens	24
1	2	3	4			11		9	10	7				8		6	5					T Jones	25
1	2	3	4			11		9	10	7		12		8		6*	5					D Hutchinson	26
1	2	3	4	5		11		9	10	7				8		6	5					M Scott	27
1	2	3	4	5		12		9	10	7	11			8*		6						N Midgley	28
1	2	3	4	5		11		9	10	7				8		6						M Cotton	29
1	2		12	5	6	11		9	10	7		4		8				3*				J Martin	30
1	2	3	12	5*	6	11		9	10			4		8		7						D Shaw	31
1	2	3			6	11		9		7		4		8		10*	5	12				K Hackett	32
1	2	3			6		9		7*	8	10	4		12		5	11					E Scales	33
1	2	3	4		6	12		9						8		5			11*	7	10	R Dilkes	34
1	2	3	4	5	6	7		9						8					11	10		I Borrett	35
1	2	3	4	5	6	7		9						8					11	10		K Lupton	36
1	2	3	4	5	6	7		9						8					11	10		C Trussell	37
1	2	3	4	5	6	7		9						8					11	10		G Courtney	38
1	2	3		5	6	7*		9		4				8					12	11	10	A Gunn	39
1	2	3		5	6			9		11				4				12	10	8	7*	A Ward	40
1	2			5	6	7			4*				9	8					12	10	3	L Shapter	41
1	2	3		5	6	7				9	12			4					11	10	8*	C Downey	42
1	2	3		5	6	12		9			11			4					10	8	7*	J Key	43
1		3*	4	5	6	7		9		12				8					11	10	2	R Groves	44
1	2	3	4*	5	6	7		9		12				8					11	10		D Hutchinson	45
1	2	3		5	6	7		9		4				8					11	10		D Phillips	46
1	2	3		5	6	7		9		11				4					10	8		I Hemley	47
1	2	3		5	6	7		9		4				8					11	10		N Wilson	48

42	41	40	29	32	37	33	7	34	24	29	11	14	4	32	1	5	10	2	15	15	5	League Appearances	
	1	1			5	6			2	3	1	3			1	1			5				Substitute Appearances	
4	4	4	4	4	4	4	1·1	2	3	3	0·1	1	1	4	0·1	1	0·1		1			Milk Cup Appearances	
1	1		0·1	1	1	1	1		1	1		1	1	1		1			1			FA Cup Appearances	
1	1	1	1	1	1	1		1	1	1	1		1	1			0·1		1			FM Cup Appearances	

Players on Loan:

Departures: Gibson (Man Utd), Stephens (Retired Injured), Hibbitt (Bristol R), McNally, Suckling (Man City), Bowman (Dundee Utd), Brazil (QPR)

'SKY BLUES'

Formed: 1883
Turned Professional: 1893   **Ltd Co:** 1907

Previous Managers: Until 1914 the secretary and committee undertook all managerial duties
1914-5 F Scott-Walford   1917-9 W Clayton   1919-20 H Pollitt   1920-4 A J Evans   1924-8 J Kerr
1928-31 J McIntyre   1931-45 H Storer   1945-7 R Bayliss   1947-8 W Frith   1948-53 H Storer
1954 J Fairbrother   1954-5 C Elliott   1955-6 J Carver, B Raynor (Caretaker)   1956-7 H Warren
1957-61 W Frith   1961-7 J W T Hill   1967-72 N Cantwell   1972 R Dennison   1972-81 G Milne
1981-3 D Sexton   1983-4 R Gould   1984-86 D S Mackay
Honours: Champions Div 2, 1966-7   Champions Div 3, 1963-4   Champions Div 3 (S) 1935-6
League Career: Elected to Div 2 1925-6   Relegated to Div 3 (N) 1924-5
Transferred to Div 3 (S) 1926   Promoted to Div 2 1935-6   Relegated to Div 3 (S) 1951-2
Relegated to Div 4 1957-8   Promoted to Div 3 1958-9   Promoted to Div 2 1963-4
Promoted to Div 1 1966-7
Colours: Sky blue and white vertical striped shirts, white shorts, sky blue stockings
Change Colours: All yellow
Reserves League: Central League   **Youth Team:** Midland Intermediate

---

CLUB RECORDS

Most Appearances for Club: George Curtis: Football League 486 + FA Cup 29 + League Cup 20 **Total 535**
Most Capped Player: Dave Clements, 21, N Ireland   **For England:** Reg Matthews, 5
Record Goalscorer in a Match: C Bourton, 5 v Bournemouth, 6-1 (h), Div 3 (S), 17.10.31
A Bacon, 5 v Bradford City, 7-3 (a), Div 3 (S), 30.12.34
Record League Goalscorer in a Season: Clarrie Bourton, 49   **In All Competitions:** Clarrie Bourton, 50 (League 49 + FA Cup 1), 1931-2
Record League Goalscorer in a Career: Clarrie Bourton, 171   **In All Competitions:** Clarrie Bourton, 180 (League 171 + FA Cup 9)
Record Transfer Fee Received: £1,250,000 from Nottingham Forest for Ian Wallace, July 1980
Record Transfer Fee Paid: £325,000 to Bristol City for Gary Collier, July 1979
Best Performances: League: 6th Div 1 1969-70   **FA Cup:** 6th Round 1962-3   **League/Milk Cup:** Semi-Final 1970-1   **European Fairs Cup:** 2nd Round
Most League Points: 60, Div 4, 1958-9   60 Div 3, 1963-4
Most League Goals: 108, Div 3 (S)
Record League Victory and Most Goals Scored in a League Match: 9-0 v Bristol City, Div 3 (S), 28.4.34
Most Goals Scored in a Cup Tie: 7-0 v Scunthorpe United, (h) 1st Round FA Cup, 24.11.34
Record League Defeat: 2-10 v Norwich City, Div 3 (S), 15.3.30
European Competitions Entered: European Fairs Cup 1970-1
Oldest Player in League Match:
Youngest Player in League Match:
Most Consecutive Undefeated League Matches: 25 1966-67   **League Matches Without a Win:** 19 1919
Longest Run of Undefeated Home League Matches: 19 1925-26   **Away League Matches:** 12 1966-67
Longest Run Without Home League Win: 10 1919, 1928   **Away League Win:** 28 1924-25
Most Consecutive League Wins: 6 1964   **Home League Wins:** 11 1952-53
Most Consecutive League Defeats: 9 1919   **Away League Wins:** 4 1963

COVENTRY CITY

PLAYERS NAME Ht Wt Birthdate	Honours	Birthplace Transfers	Clubs	APPEARANCES League	Milk Cup	FA Cup	Other Comps	GOALS League	Milk Cup	FA Cup	Other Comps
GOALKEEPERS											
Jake Findlay 6.1 14.1 13.7.54		Blairgowie	Aston Villa (A)	14							
			Luton Town	155							
			Barnsley (L)	6							
			Derby County (L)	1							
			Luton Town	3							
			Swindon Town	4							
			Coventry City								
Steve Ogrizovik 6.3 14.7 12.9.57		Mansfield	Chesterfield	16	2						
		£70,000	Liverpool	4							
		Player exch.	Shrewsbury Town	84	5	5					
		£72,500	Coventry City	84	6	3	1				
DEFENDERS											
Brian Borrows 5.10 10.12 20.12.60		Liverpool	Everton	27	2						
		£10,000	Bolton Wanderers	113	7	4	4				
		£80,000	Coventry City	41	4	1	1				
Greg Downs 5.9½ 10.7 13.12.58		Carlton	Norwich City (A)	162+7	15	20		7			
			Torquay United (L)	1							
		£40,000	Coventry City	40+1	4						
Brian Kilcline*	EU21 (2)	Nottingham	Notts County (A)	156+2	16	10		9	1	1	
6.2 12.0 7.5.62		£60,000	Coventry City	58	5+1	3	1	8	1	1	
Lloyd McGrath 5.8 10.6 24.2.65	EY	Birmingham	Coventry City (A)	54+1	4	3					
Trevor Peake† 6.0 12.9 10.2.57	ES-P (2)	Nuneaton	Nuneaton Borough		5						
		£27,750	Lincoln City	171	16	7		7		2	
		£100,000	Coventry City	104+1	9	6	1	5			
Graham Rodger 6.2 11.13 1.4.67		Glasgow F	Wolverhampton W. (A)	1							
			Coventry City	10	0+1	1					
MIDFIELD											
Mike Adams 5.6 10.4 8.11.61	EY	Sheffield	Gillingham (A)	85+7	5	10		4			
		£75,000	Coventry City	69+4	5	2	1	6			
Micky Gynn 5.5 10.6 19.8.61		Peterborough	Peterborough U (A)	152+4	12	13		31	1	3	
		£60,000	Coventry City	58+15	3+1	2	1	5			
David Phillips 5.10 11.2 29.7.63	W (13), U21 (4), Y	Welbourg, W.G.	Plymouth Argyle	65+8	2+1	9+1		15			
		£65,000	Manchester City	42	5	1		12			
		£150,000	Coventry City								
Ian Painter 5.7 10.2 28.12.64	EY	Wombourne	Stoke City (A)	105+8	3	4+1		20	1	2	
		£80,000	Coventry City								
Nick Pickering 6.1 11.11 4.8.63	E (1), U21 (11), Y	Newcastle	Sunderland (A)	177+2	18	9	2	18			
		£120,000	Coventry City	15				4			
Wayne Turner 5.9 12.4 9.3.61	Div. 2, 82	Luton	Luton Town (A)	80+3	4	5		2		1	
			Lincoln City (L)	16	1						
		£75,000	Coventry City	14+1	1	1		1			
Andy Williams 6.0 11.10½ 29.7.62		Birmingham	Solihull Borough								
		£20,000	Coventry City	2+5							
FORWARDS											
David Bennett 6.0 11.2 11.7.59		Manchester	Manchester City	43+9	7	5+1		9	5	1	
		£120,000	Cardiff City	75+2	4	4		18	1		
		£100,000	Coventry City								
Paul Culpin 5.10 10.8 8.2.62		Kirby Muxloe	Leicester City								
			Nuneaton Borough			3					
		£50,000	Coventry City	4+3	1		1	1			
Gareth Evans 5.8 10.8 14.1.67		Coventry	Coventry City (A)	5+1	1		0+1				
Keith Houchen 6.2 11.4 25.7.60		Middlesbrough	Chesterfield								
			Hartlepool United	160+10	8	4+1		65	1		
		£25,000	Orient	74+2	3	3		20	2		
		£15,000	York City	56+11	6	9+2	4+1	18	4	2	1
			Scunthorpe United	9				2			
		£60,000	Coventry City								
Cyrille Regis 6.0 13.4 9.2.58	E (4), B (3), U21 (6)	French Guyana	Hayes								
		£5,000	WBA	233+4	27+1	25	10	82	16	10	3
		£300,000	Coventry City	64+1	2	2		9	5		1

ADDITIONAL CONTRACT PROFESSIONALS
Steve Sedgley (A), Tony Dobson, Terry Merriman, Steve Livingstone, David Smith, Shaun McGrory, John Hathaway (M), Tony Mahan (M), John Findlay (M)

APPRENTICES
Howard Clark

NON-CONTRACT PLAYERS
Mike Cook, Kerry Dewis, John Gowens, Gary Marshall, Mark Pollard

HIGHFIELD ROAD King Richard Street, Cov. CV2 4FW Capacity: 22,500 (20,500 seats)

Record Attendance: 51,455 v Wolverhampton W., Div 2, 29 April 1967

Smallest Home Attendance for a First Class Match: 3,936 v Newport County, Div 3 (S), 4th April 1955

Record Receipts: £68,029.70 v West Ham United, League Cup Semi-Final 1st Leg, 27 Jan 1981

Season Tickets: £70, £79, £99, £112 (half-price juveniles/OAP): Terraces £60 (half-price juveniles/OAP)

Executive Box Season Tickets: £5,000 per annum (for ten), £2,250 per annum (for ten) (ground level)

Cost of Stand Tickets: £4.50, £5.50 and £6.50

Match and Ticket Information: Postal applications for stand tickets accepted (with SAE) 21 days before each match by the Ticket Office manager at the Stadium, Highfield Road, Coventry

Car Parking: Street parking around ground permitted. Special park—cars & coaches is situated at Gosford Green on Walsgrave Road (A46) 200 yards from stadium.

Nearest Railway Station: Coventry (0203 555211)

How to get to the ground

From North: Use Motorway M6 until junction 3. Leave Motorway and follow signs Coventry

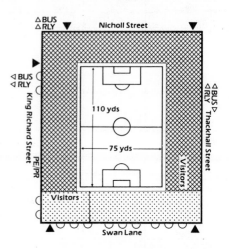

A444. In 3.5m turn left into Eagle Street B4110, then forward over all crossroads into Swan Lane for Coventry City FC
From East: Use Motorway M45 then A45 to Ryton on Dunsmore. In 1.5m at roundabout take 3rd exit A423. In 1.2m turn right B4110. Over crossroads and at T road turn left then shortly right into Swan Lane for Coventry City FC
From South: Use Motorway M1 then M45 and route from East or A46 (S.P. Coventry) into City Centre, then follow signs Market Harborough A427 into Binley Road and on nearside of railway bridge turn left into Swan Lane for Coventry City FC
From West: Use Motorway M6 and route from North or A45 (S.P. Coventry) into City Centre, then follow signs Market Harborough, A427 into Binley Road and on nearside of railway bridge turn left into Swan Lane for Coventry City FC

Price of 1986-7 Programme: 40p
Number of Pages: 24
Subscriptions: Subscriptions on request to club

Local Newspaper: Coventry Evening Telegraph

Local Radio Station: Mercia Sound

President
D Godfrey

Chairman
N Rowlinson

Directors
J McHugh
K Potts
D Rowlinson
R Clayton
J McMillan
N Hassall
J Bowler
H Smith (Vice-Chairman)

Managing Director/Manager
Dario Gradi

Assistant Manager
P Slack

Secretary
Mrs Gill Palin (0270 213014)

Sales Marketing Manager
C Wrigglesworth (0270 256557)

Physiotherapist
J Dyer

The final League position of 12th was just two places lower than in the previous campaign and the number of points obtained just three less. The season was one in which injuries to key players which kept them out for long spells, had a significant effect on the final outcome. Club captain Nigel Hart missing 24 games, Geoff Thomas 9 and Tony Cliss missing the whole season.

Cup competitions met with mixed fortunes, in the Milk Cup, having beaten Carlisle United in the two legged first round tie they were drawn against 1st Division Watford and although beaten over the two games, they provided the fans with two excellent ties. Once again in the FA Cup they were drawn away from home, this time to League opponents, Derby County. A controversial penalty decision just before the interval setting Derby County on the way to victory. In the Freight Rover competition, after convincingly beating Stockport County at Gresty Road they lost 1-0 to Bolton Wanderers who then progressed to the Final of the competition.

In mid-season the club went through a very difficult spell, failing to win a game between October 19th and January 11th. This was very quickly followed by a remarkable run of ten victories out of 11 fixtures and this included five consecutive away victories, a new club record.

Dave Waller was once again the club's leading scorer with a total of 18 goals (League 13, Milk Cup 3 and Freight Rover 2). Close behind was Gary Blissett with 11 League, 1 Milk Cup and 2 in the Freight Rover Trophy. In the final four League games of the season, regular custodian Brian Parkin was out with a damaged shoulder and Rob Powner an 18-year-old non-contract player was thrust into League action. His performance in the final games showed that here was a youngster with distinct promise for the future. He has already been rewarded with a contract. Keeper Brian Parkin was the unanimous choice of the Junior Supporters, the Sandbach Branch of the Supporters Association and the Crewe Branch of the Supporters Association as their Player of the Year, the first time this has been achieved.   H Finch

Back Row L to R: Geoff Parker, Geoff Thomas, John Pemberton, Brian Parkin, Chris Cutler, Gary Blissett, Steve Wright. **Front Row:** Norman Dougherty, Tony Cliss, Dave Pullar, Steve Davis, Ian Macowat, David Platt, Terry Milligan.

CREWE ALEXANDRA

DIVISION FOUR: 12th   **FA CUP:** 1st ROUND   **MILK CUP:** 2nd ROUND   **FRT:** 2nd Round

MATCH	DATE		COMPE-TITION	VENUE	OPPONENTS	RESULT		HALF TIME	L'GUE POS'N	GOALSCORERS/GOAL TIMES	ATTEN-DANCE
1	A	17	CL	H	Southend United	D	1-1	0-0		Waller 74	1,431
2		20	MC1/1	H	Carlisle United	D	3-3	2-2		Saunders 28, Hart 39, Waller 74	1,732
3		24	CL	A	Hartlepool United	L	1-4	0-2	19	Platt 88	(2,165)
4		27	CL	H	Hereford United	W	2-0	0-0		Allatt 67, Waller 83	1,914
5		31	CL	A	Wrexham	L	1-2	0-0	17	Waller 69	(3,081)
6	S	3	MC1/2	A	Carlisle United	W	4-3	1-2		Platt 10, (pen) 81, Waller 57, Blissett 71	(2,520)
7		6	CL	H	Stockport County	L	0-1	0-1	21		2,148
8		14	CL	A	Northampton	W	1-0	0-0	16	Blissett 60	(2,654)
9		17	CL	H	Swindon Town	W	2-0	0-0		Thomas 68, Platt 71	1,699
10		21	CL	A	Chester City	L	0-4	0-1	16		(2,369)
11		24	MC2/1	H	Watford	L	1-3	1-0		Waller 7	4,252
12		28	CL	H	Torquay United	W	1-0	1-0	11	Saunders 11	1,437
13	O	1	CL	A	Scunthorpe United	L	1-3	0-1	14	Waller 82	(1,443)
14		5	CL	H	Preston North End	D	3-3	2-2	13	Waller 6, Platt 29, Thomas 71	2,454
15		8	MC2/2	A	Watford	L	2-3	0-1		Cutler 67, Pemberton 86	(11,583)
16		12	CL	A	Rochdale	L	0-1	0-0	15		(1,776)
17		19	CL	H	Burnley	W	3-1	2-0	13	Power 20, 32, Waller 63	1,998
18		23	CL	A	Peterborough United	D	0-0	0-0	14		(2,760)
19		26	CL	A	Aldershot	L	2-3	0-0	17	Davis 49, Platt 56	(1,457)
20	N	2	CL	H	Halifax Town	D	2-2	2-1	15	Waller 8, Platt 23	1,493
21		5	CL	H	Orient	L	1-3	1-0	18	Waller 43	1,232
22		9	CL	A	Mansfield Town	D	2-2	1-0	18	Blissett 1, Thomas 58	(3,243)
23		16	FAC1	A	Derby County	L	1-5	0-1		Micklewhite (og) 58	(11,047)
24		23	CL	H	Cambridge	L	0-1	0-1	18		1,312
25	D	13	CL	H	Exeter	L	0-1	0-0	19		1,108
26		20	CL	H	Hartlepool United	D	0-0	0-0	20		1,070
27		26	CL	A	Port Vale	L	0-3	0-1	21		(5,976)
28		28	CL	A	Hereford United	L	1-4	1-1	21	Waller 39	(2,873)
29	J	4	CL	A	Halifax Town	L	0-1	0-0	23		(1,031)
30		11	CL	H	Wrexham	W	3-2	0-0	22	Platt 3, Keay (og) 65, Blissett (pen) 72	1,675
31		13	FRT N	H	Stockport County	W	4-1	3-0		Blissett 17, 37, Waller 40, 75	994
32		18	CL	A	Southend United	W	1-0	0-0	21	Platt 55	(1,848)
33		25	CL	H	Northamton Town	L	0-1	0-0	21		1,856
34		28	FRT N	A	Bolton Wanderers	L	0-1	0-0			(2,428)
35		31	CL	A	Stockport County	L	0-3	0-0	22		(2,564)
36	F	4	CL	H	Peterborough United	D	1-1	1-1	22	Cutler 19	1,009
37		22	CL	H	Chester City	D	2-2	1-2	22	Platt 42, Thomas 71	3,271
38	M	1	CL	A	Torquay United	D	0-0	0-0	22		(1,011)
39		3	CL	A	Scunthorpe United	W	4-0	1-0	21	Cutler 9, Blissett (pen) 54, 76, Waller 72	1,072
40		8	CL	A	Preston North End	W	2-1	2-0	20	Waller 22, Blissett 35	(2,922)
41		15	CL	H	Rochdale	W	4-2	1-1	18	Blissett (pen) 3, Cutler 64, Thomas 69, Johnson (og) 84	1,683
42		18	CL	H	Tranmere Rovers	W	2-1	1-1	16	Blissett (pen) 35, Platt 56	1,647
43		22	CL	H	Aldershot	W	2-0	0-0	16	Cutler 50, Blissett (pen) 78	1,701
44		25	CL	A	Colchester United	W	2-1	2-0	12	Cutler 20, Phillips (og) 31	(1,356)
45		29	CL	A	Tranmere Rovers	W	1-0	0-0	9	Thomas 51	(1,587)
46		31	CL	H	Port Vale	L	0-1	0-1	12		4,986
47	A	5	CL	A	Orient	W	1-0	1-0	9	Blissett 30	(1,975)
48		11	CL	H	Mansfield Town	W	2-1	0-0	9	Farrell 46, Waller 75	2,099
49		15	CL	A	Burnley	W	1-0	0-0	9	Waller 71	(1,961)
50		19	CL	A	Cambridge United	L	0-1	0-0	9		(2,225)
51		26	CL	H	Colchester United	L	0-2	0-2	11		1,555
52	M	3	CL	A	Exeter City	W	2-1	1-1	11	Blissett (pen) 42, Cutler 73	(1,777)
53		5	CL	A	Swindon Town	L	0-1	0-0	12		(10,976)

Best Home League Attendance: 4,986 v Port Vale 31/3   **Smallest:** 1,009 v Peterborough Utd 4/2   **Av Home Att:** 1,821

Goal Scorers: **Compared with 84-85:** −1,421

League (54): Waller 12, Blissett 11 (6 pens), Platt 9, Cutler 6, Thomas 6, Opponent 4, Power 2, Allatt 1, Davis 1, Farrell 1, Saunders 1
Milk Cup (10): Waller 3, Platt 2 (1 pen), Blissett 1, Cutler 1, Hart 1, Pemberton 1, Saunders 1
FA Cup (1): Opponent 1
FRT (4): Blissett 2, Waller 2

Longley	Booth	Pullar	Thomas	Davis	Hart	Platt	Crabbe	Waller	Bissett	Saunders	Handford (L)	Cutler	Parkin	Pemberton	Allatt	McGarrick (NC)	Edwards (NC)	Holland (M)	Johnson (NC)	Power	Anderson (L)	Farrell	Callaghan (L)	Powner (NC)	McClure (NC)	Referee	
1	2	3	4	5	6	7	8	9	10	11																G Ashby	1
1	2	3	4	5	6	7	8	9	10*	11																R Banks	2
1	2	3	4	5	6	7	8	9	10	11*		12														D Phillips	3
		3	4	5	6	7	8	9		11																F Roberts	4
	3*		4	5	6	7		9		11	12		8	1	2	10										N Glover	5
5	3	4				7	8	9		11		6*		1	2	10										D Allison	6
6	3	4				7	8*	9		11				1	2	10	12									M Scott	7
3	12	6	5			7		9		11*				1	2†	10	8	4								N Butler	8
6	12	4	5			7		9		11*				1	2	10	8	3								K Breen	9
6	11	4	5			7		9						1	2	10	8	3								K Walmsley	10
5	11	4	6			7		9						1	2	10	8	3								M Robinson	11
5		4	6			7		9	12	11				1	2	10*	8	3								N Wilson	12
6	10	4	5			7		9	12†	11				1	2*		8	3								T Simpson	13
6	10	4	5			7		9	12	11*			8	1	2			3								J McAulay	14
6*	10	4	5			7		9		11			8	1	2	12		3								A Robinson	15
6		4	5			7		9	10	11*			8	1	2	12		3								J Key	16
	10	4	5	6		7		9					8	1	2			3	11							J Ball	17
	10	4	5	6*		7		9					8	1	2	12		3	11							E Scales	18
	10	4	5			7		9					8*	1	2	12		3	11		6					I Hemley	19
	10	4	5			7		9	12					1	2		8	3*	11		6					G Napthine	20
		3	4	5		7		9		11					2	10*	12		8		6					C Trussell	21
1		3	4	5		7		9		11*	12				2		8				6	10				K Baker	22
1		3	4	5		7		9		11	12				2		8*				6	10				L Robinson	23
	2*	3	4	5		7		9		11	12			1			8				6	10				T Fitzharris	24
		3	4*	5		7		9		11			8	1	2		12				6	10				A Robinson	25
	2		5	6	7			9		11			8*	1			12	3				10	4			L Dilkes	26
	2		5	6	7			9		11			8*	1			12	3				10	4			J Bray	27
	2		5	6	7			9		11			8	1				4	3							R Hamer	28
3	2		5	6	7			9		11	12			1				4				10				C Seel	29
	2*		5	6	7			9		11	8			1			12	3				10	4			J Ashworth	30
12			5	6	7			9		11	8			1	2		3*					10	4			K Breen	31
12			5	6	7			9		11	8			1				3				10	4			B Hill	32
			5	6	7			9		11*	8			1	2		12	3				10	4			F Roberts	33
			5	6	7			9		11	8			1	2	12	12					10*	4		3	R Bridges	34
			5	6				9		11	8	7		1	2		12					10	4		3	K Barratt	35
			5	6				9			8	7*	11	1	2		12					10	4		3	J Shaw rd J McAulay	36
	12		4	5	6	7		9		11			8	1	2			3				10			3	G Ashby	37
	12		4	5	6*	7		9		11			8	1	2			3				10				R Gifford	38
6	1		4	5		7		9		11			8	1	2			3				10				T Fitzharris	39
6	12		4	5		7		9		11			8	1	2			3*				10				G Aplin	40
6	3		4	5		7		9		11	12		8	1	2							10				R Guy	41
6	3		4	5		7		9		11			8	1	2	10										C Seel	42
12	3*		4	5	6	7		9		11			8	1	2							10				D Allison	43
	3		4	5	6	7		9		11			8	1	2	12						10				I Hemley	44
	3		4	5	6	7		9		11	12		8	1	2							10*				T Phillips	45
	3		4	5	6	7		9		11			8	1	2		12					10*				K Walmsley	46
			4	5	6			9		11			8	1	2			3		7		10				M James	47
			4	5	6	7		9		11			8	1	2			3				10				I Hendrick	48
6	12		4	5		7		9		11*			8	1	2			3				10				T Holbrook	49
2	11		4	5		7		9	12				8					3				10			1	K Baker	50
6	2		4	5		7		9	11†				8				12	3				10*			1	N Glover	51
10	2		4	5		7		9	11				8					3				12			1	M Reed	52
			10	4	5	7		9	11				8		2			3							1	A Gunn	53
3	23	29	37	45	23	43	4	44	34	15	9	25	39	37	8	10	10	7	8	7	5	19	8	4	3	League Appearances	
	4	4							4	7		3		4	1	1	3		4			1				Substitute Appearances	
1	4	4	4	3	1	4	2	4	1	3			1	3	3	2	1·2	2				4			1	Milk Cup Appearances	
1	1	1	1	1	1			1		0·1			1	1								1	1			FA Cup Appearances	
0·1			2	2	2	2		2	2	2			2				1·1		0·1		2	2			1	FR Trophy Appearances	

Also Played: Position(Game): Scott 12(6), 5(7), Taylor 10(28), 8(29), 2(32), Woodhead (M) 12(2), Watkiss 6(50, 52, 53)

Players on Loan: Anderson (Charlton), Callaghan (Stoke), Taylor (Hartlepool)

'RAILWAYMEN'

Formed: 1877
Turned Professional: 1893   **Ltd Co:** 1892

Previous Managers: Since 1946
George Lillycrop   Frank Hill   Arthur Turner   Harry Catterick   Ralph Ward   Maurice Lindley
Harry Ware   Jimmy McGuigan   Ernie Tagg   Dennis Viollet   Jimmy Melia   Ernie Tagg   Harry Gregg
Warwick Rimmer   Tony Waddington   Arfon Griffiths   Peter Morris
Honours: Welsh Cup Winners 1936, 1937
League Career: Original members of Div 2 1892   Failed to gain re-election 1896
Re-joined the League in Div 3 (N) 1921   Transferred to Div 4 1958
Promoted to Div 3 1962-3   Relegated to Div 4 1963-4   Promoted to Div 3 1967-8
Relegated to Div 4 1968-9
Colours: Red shirts, white shorts, red stockings
Change Colours: All white shirts and red shorts
'A' & 'B' Team: Lancashire Divs 1 & 2

CLUB RECORDS

Most Appearances for Club: Tommy Lowry, 1966-78: Football League 436 + FA Cup 20 + League Cup 18 + Watney Cup 1 **Total 475**
Most Capped Player: Bill Lewis, 12, Wales   **For England:** J H Pearson 1
Record Goalscorer in a Match: No one has scored more than four goals
Record League Goalscorer in a Season: Terry Harkin, 35, Div 4, 1964-5   **In All Competitions:** Terry Harkin, 35
Record League Goalscorer in a Career: Bert Swindells, 126, 1928-37   **In All Competitions:** Bert Swindells, 134 (League 126 + FA Cup 7)
Record Transfer Fee Received: £40,000 from Port Vale for Paul Bowles, Sept 1979
Record Transfer Fee Paid: £10,000 to Derby County for Colin Chesters, Sept 1979   £10,000 to Sheffield United for Mike Guy, Sept 1979
Best Performances: League: 10th Div 2 1892-3   **FA Cup:** Semi-Final 1888   **League/Milk Cup:** 3rd Round 1974-5, 1975-6, 1978-9   **Welsh Cup:** Winners (2)
Most League Points: (3pts for win) 65, Div 4, 1984-5   (2pts for win) 59, Div 4, 1962-3
Record League Victory: 8-0 v Rotherham United, Div 3 (N), 1 Oct 1932
Record League Defeat: 1-11 v Lincoln City, Div 3 (N), 29 Sept 1951
Oldest Player in League Match: Frank Broome, 39 yrs 176 days
Youngest Player in League Match: David Jones, 16 yrs 131 days
Most Consecutive Undefeated League Matches: 12 1949, 1975
Longest Run of Undefeated Home League Matches: 28 1967-68
Longest Run Without Home League Win: 15 1979
Most Consecutive League Wins: 7 1928-29, 1986
Most Consecutive League Defeats: 10 1923, 1957-58, 1979

League Matches Without a Win: 30 1956-57
Away League Matches: 7 1966-67
Away League Win: 56 1955-57
Home League Wins: 16 1938
Away League Wins: 5 1986

Club Statistician for the Directory: H Finch

CREWE ALEXANDRA

PLAYERS NAME Ht Wt Birthdate	Honours	Birthplace Transfers	Clubs	League	Milk Cup	FA Cup	Other Comps	League	Milk Cup	FA Cup	Other Comps
GOALKEEPERS											
Brian Parkin† 6.1 12.0 12.10.65		Birkenhead F	Oldham Athletic Crewe Alexandra	6 51	2 3	2	2				
DEFENDERS											
Steve Davis* 6.0 12.7 26.7.65	EY	Birmingham F	Stoke City (A) Crewe Alexandra	107+2	8	3	5+1	1	1		
Nigel Hart 6.3 12.13 1.10.58		Golborne F F F	Wigan Athletic Leicester City Blackpool Crewe Alexandra	1 36+1 131+1	 4+1 5	 3 2		 7	 10		
John Pemberton 5.11 11.9 18.11.64		Oldham F F	Chadderton Rochdale Crewe Alexandra	 1 43+4					 1		
David Pullar 5.11 11.8 13.2.59		London £12,000 F	Portsmouth (A) Exeter City Crewe Alexandra	84+9 124+6 99+7	3 12+1 8	9 7 2	 2	 22 6	 2	 3	
Ian Macuwat 5.7 10.7 19.11.65		Liverpool F F	Everton (A) Gillingham Crewe Alexandra	 4+1	 0+1						
David Sutton 6.1 12.8 21.1.57	Div. 4, 80	Tarleton £10,000	Plymouth Argyle (A) Reading (L) Huddersfield Town Bolton Wanderers Crewe Alexandra	60+1 9 242 32	2+1 23 1	3 19	 6	 11	 1	 3	
MIDFIELD											
David Platt 5.11 11.7 10.6.66		Oldham F	Manchester United (A) Crewe Alexandra	 65	 4	 1	 3	 14	 2		
Philip Power 5.9 11.0 25.7.66		Salford	Northwich Victoria Witton Albion Crewe Alexandra	 7+4			 0+1	 2			
Geoff Thomas 6.1 12.0 5.8.64		Manchester	Rochdale Crewe Alexandra	10+1 80+4	 9	 3	 3+2	 11	 1		
Terry Milligan 5.10 9.5 10.1.66	NIY	Manchester	Manchester City (A) New Zealand Crewe Alexandra								
Steve Wright 6.0 11.0 6.8.59		Clapton Finland	Colchester United Wrexham Torquay United Crewe Alexandra	112+5 76	8 3	13+1 2	 2	2			
FORWARDS											
Gary Blisset 6.0 12.7 29.6.64		Manchester	Crewe Alexandra	79+10	7	3	5+1				
Chris Cutler 5.11 11.0 7.4.64		Manchester F	Bury Crewe Alexandra	8+5 25+3	 1	0+1	2	3 6	 1		
Tony Cliss 5.9 11.0 22.9.59		March F	Peterborough United Crewe Alexandra	65+20 107+1	4+1 5	1+2 1	 5	11 12			

ADDITIONAL CONTRACT PROFESSIONALS

Terry Mulligan (M), Mark Wroe (M)

APPRENTICES

NON-CONTRACT PLAYERS

Tony Gore, Matt McNair, Neil Morton, Bob Powner (G-4Lge)

Record Attendance: 20,000 v Tottenham
Hotspur, FA Cup Round 4, 30 Jan 1960

Record Receipts: £8,131 v Port Vale, Div 4, 22
Mar 1985

Season Tickets: Ground: £40 (£22
juveniles/OAPs); Paddock: £45 (£28); Stand A &
D: £55 (£40); Stand C: £64, B £69.50

Executive Box Season Tickets: None

Cost of Stand Tickets: £3.30 (A, D) (£2.40
juveniles/OAP), C £3.50, B £3.90 **Terraces:**
£2.40 (£1.40 juveniles/OAP); Paddock: £2.80
(£1.90 juveniles/OAP)

Match and Ticket Information: Advance
bookings for important cup matches only

Car Parking: Parking at the ground for 200 cars

Nearest Railway Station: Crewe (5 mins)
(0270 255245)

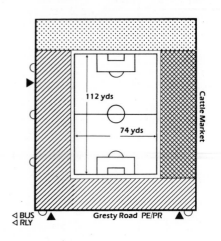

How to get to the ground

From North: Use Motorway M6 until junction
17 and follow signs Crewe A534. At Crewe
roundabout follow signs Chester into Nantwich
Road. Then take next turning on left into Gresty
Road for Crewe Alexandra FC
From East and South: Use A52 then A5020
(S.P. Crewe) then at Crewe roundabout follow
signs Chester into Nantwich Road. Then take
next turning on left into Gresty Road for Crewe
Alexandra FC
From West: Use A534 (S.P. Crewe) and
immediately before Crewe Railway Station turn
right int Gresty Road for Crewe Alexandra FC

Price of 1986-7 Programme: 50p
Number of Pages: 24
Subscriptions: Subscription rates on request
from club

Local Newspapers: Crewe Chronicle, The
World — Evening Sentinel — Hanley

Local Radio Stations: Radio Stoke (200
medium wave), Signal Radio

CRYSTAL PALACE   Division 2

Palace enjoyed a reasonable season but their fifth place in the 2nd Division does not actually indicate a really strong promotion challenge, since ten points separated them and Wimbledon, who earned the third promotion place. Another ascending team by an irony was Charlton Athletic, who early in the season started an arrangement whereby they would share the Selhurst Park ground, so it was not very neighbourly for them to leave for higher climbs!

It was a slow start which made ultimate ascent unlikely and poor form during September (only one victory) followed by four defeats and one draw over the festive period left the team with far too much to do. The subsequent form was much better and there were some excellent efforts such as a victory at Barnsley in the penultimate match (4-2), which suggested that even the limited promotion opportunities this coming season may not be too strigent for them.

Three cup competitions were entered and none provided any excitement apart from the Milk Cup 1st Round against Charlton Athletic, which was won on penalties after the teams had shared six goals over the two legs. Manchester United then won both legs of the 2nd Round tie — each by a single goal. The FA Cup brought Luton Town to Selhurst Park and out went Palace (2-1). The Full Members Cup in October read — played two, lost two; that was another brief run.

Palace have in Steve Coppell a manager who is not only competent but also one of the game's more popular people, so any successes he achieves with his team will be roundly applauded. But is his side good enough?

After being the butt of jokes around London George Wood has done well in goal at Selhurst Park; Jim Cannon continues as a model and consistent professional. Others to do well have been Brush, Nebbeling, Ketteridge, Irvine, Wright and Taylor. There is potential.

The club must now strive for an early resumption of 'Derby' matches with Charlton Athletic — in Division 1.   WLM

Back Row L to R: Andy Higginbotham, Gary Stebbing, Andy Gray, George Wood, Mark Hone, Tony Finnigan. **Middle Row:** Ian Wright, Jim Cannon (Captain), Trevor Aylott, Micky Droy, Ken O'Doherty, Gavin Nebbling, Paul Brush, David West (Physio). **Seated:** Brian Sparrow, Anton Otulakowski, Kevin Taylor, Ian Evans, Steve Coppell (Manager), Alan Irvine, Steve Ketteridge, Phil Barber.

CRYSTAL PALACE

DIVISION TWO: 5th   **FA CUP:** 3rd ROUND   **MILK CUP:** 2nd ROUND

MATCH	DATE		COMPE-TITION	VENUE	OPPONENTS	RESULT		HALF TIME	L'GUE POS'N	GOALSCORERS/GOAL TIMES	ATTEN-DANCE
1	A	18	CL	A	Shrewsbury	W	2-0	2-0		Barber 21, Gray 44	(4,295)
2		20	MC1/1	A	Charlton Athletic	W	2-1	2-0		Barber 22, 42	(4,930)
3		24	CL	H	Sunderland	W	1-0	0-0	4	Droy 70	7,040
4		27	CL	A	Carlisle United	D	2-2	1-1	6	Aylott 8, Barber 88	(3,080)
5		31	CL	H	Huddersfield Town	L	2-3	2-1	11	Barber 16, 26	6,026
6	S	3	MC1/2	H	Charlton Athletic	D	1-1	0-1		Gray 75	6,051
7		7	CL	A	Charlton Athletic	L	1-3	1-0	13	Gray 31	(6,637)
8		14	CL	H	Fulham	D	0-0	0-0	14		6,381
9		18	CL	A	Norwich	L	3-4	2-2	16	Gray 21, (pen) 26, Droy 90	(13,475)
10		21	CL	H	Millwall	W	2-1	0-1	12	Barber 66, Gray 85	8,713
11		23	MC2/1	A	Manchester United	L	0-1	0-0			21,506
12		28	CL	A	Stoke City	D	0-0	0-0	12		(7,130)
13	O	1	CL	H	Hull City	L	0-2	0-0	14		5,003
14		5	CL	A	Middlesbrough	W	2-0	2-0	10	Barber 13, Ketteridge 29	(4,991)
15		9	MC2/2	H	Manchester United	L	0-1	0-1			(26,118)
16		12	CL	H	Oldham Athletic	W	3-2	1-2	8	Irvine 37, Taylor 86, Wright 89	5,243
17		16	FMC	H	Brighton & H. A.	L	1-3	0-2		Aylott 57	2,207
18		19	CL	A	Portsmouth	L	0-1	0-1	9		(16,539)
19		23	FMC	A	W.B.A.	L	1-2	1-1		Cannon 44	(3,764)
20		26	CL	H	Blackburn Rovers	W	2-0	0-0	9	Barber 46, Wright 87	5,408
21	N	2	CL	A	Bradford City	L	0-1	0-1	10		(5,604)
22		9	CL	H	Grimsby Town	W	2-1	0-1	9	Droy 57, Taylor 82	4,620
23		16	CL	A	Leeds United	W	3-1	2-0	7	Cannon 19, Finnigan 37, 89	(10,378)
24		23	CL	H	Barnsley	W	1-0	0-0	6	Taylor 58	5,625
25		30	CL	A	Sheffield United	D	0-0	0-0	6		(13,765)
26	D	7	CL	A	Hull City	W	2-1	1-0	5	Aylott 17, 81	(6,058)
27		15	CL	H	Shrewsbury Town	L	0-1	0-0	6		8,253
28		22	CL	A	Sunderland	D	1-1	1-0	7	Barber 18	(16,710)
29		26	CL	H	Wimbledon	L	1-3	0-2	6	Droy 64	7,929
30	J	1	CL	A	Brighton & H. A.	L	0-2	0-1	9		(15,469)
31		6	FAC3	H	Luton Town	L	1-2	0-1		Taylor 86	9,886
32		11	CL	A	Charlton Athletic	W	2-1	2-0	8	Finnigan 14, Taylor 28	7,521
33		18	CL	A	Huddersfield Town	D	0-0	0-0	8		(5,729)
34		25	CL	H	Norwich City	L	1-2	0-2	8	Barber 46	8,369
35	F	1	CL	H	Carlisle United	D	1-1	1-0	6	Gray 23	3,774
36		15	CL	A	Blackburn Rovers	W	2-1	1-0	6	Gray 24, Wright 84	(4,825)
37	M	8	CL	H	Middlesbrough	W	2-1	1-1	6	Taylor 42, Wright 81	4,863
38		15	CL	A	Oldham Athletic	L	0-2	0-1	8		(3,726)
39		18	CL	H	Stoke City	L	0-1	0-1	9		4,501
40		22	CL	A	Fulham	W	3-2	0-1	8	Taylor (pen) 58, Ketteridge 64, Wright 74	(4,951)
41		29	CL	H	Brighton & H.A.	W	1-0	1-0	7	Brush 8	9,124
42	A	1	CL	A	Wimbledon	D	1-1	0-1	6	Wright 62	(8,429)
43		5	CL	H	Bradford City	W	2-1	0-0	6	Gray 80, Brush 85	5,079
44		8	CL	H	Portsmouth	W	2-1	2-0	6	Gray 18, 44	11,731
45		12	CL	A	Grimsby Town	L	0-3	0-2	5		(4,222)
46		19	CL	H	Leeds United	W	3-0	1-0	5	Wright 40, Irvine 65, 78	6,285
47		22	CL	A	Millwall	L	2-3	0-2	5	Higginbotham 58, Ketteridge 82	(5,618)
48		26	CL	A	Barnsley	W	4-2	2-1	5	Wright 10, 44, Aylott 66, Ketteridge 89	(3,862)
49	M	3	CL	H	Sheffield United	D	1-1	0-0	5	Higginbotham 49	6,375

Best Home League Attendance: 11,731 v Portsmouth 8/4   **Smallest:** 3,744 v Carlisle United 1/2   **Av Home Att:** 6,689

Goal Scorers: **Compared with 84-85:** +249

League (57): Gray 10, Barber 9, Wright 9, Taylor 6 (1 pen), Droy 4, Ketteridge 4, Aylott 4, Finnigan 3, Irvine 3, Brush 2, Higginbotham 2, Cannon 1

Milk Cup (3): Barber 2, Gray 1

FA Cup (1): Taylor 1

FM Cup (2): Aylott 1, Cannon 1

Wood	Hughton	Lindsay	Ketteridge	Droy	Cannon	Irvine	Stebbing	Barber	Gray	Sparrow	Finnigan	Aylott	Wright	Galloway	Higginbottom	Locke	Taylor	Brush	Nebbeling	Hughes	O'Doherty	Howard (L)	Hardwick (L)	Referee	
1	2	3	4	5	6	7	8	9	10	11														A Seville	1
1	2	3	8	5	6	7		9	10	11	4													K Hackett	2
1	2	3	8	5	6	7		11	10		4	9												J Deakin	3
1	2	3	8	5	6	7		11	10		4	9·												T Fitzharris	4
1	2	3*	8	5	6	7		11	10		4	9	12											H King	5
1	2	3*	8	5	6	7		11	10		4		9	12										A Gunn	6
1	2	3	8	5	6	7*		11	10		4			9	12									D Hedges	7
1		3*	8	5	6	7		9	10		4		12		11	2								M Bodenham	8
1			8	5	6	7		9	10	3	4		12		11	2								J Ball	9
1			8	5+	6	7		9	10	3	4					2	11							J Martin	10
1			8	5	6	7	11	9	10	3	4					2								G Napthine	11
1			8	5	6	7	11	9	10	3	4		12			2								J Worrall	12
1			8	5	6	7	11	9	10	4*	12					2		3						K Barratt	13
1			8		6	7		9	10	11*	12					2	4	3	5					N Midgley	14
1	3		8		6	7		9	10*			11	12			2	4		5					V Callow	15
1				5	6	7		9			8	10*	12		11	2	4	3						R Hamer	16
	8*			5		7	12	9				10	13		11*	2	4	3	6	1				I Borrett	17
1				5	6	7		11			8	9	10			2	4	3						R Groves	18
1		12		5	6	7		10*				8	9	13	11		4	3*			2			H Taylor	19
1		3			6	7		9				8	10	12	11	5*	4				2			R Gifford	20
1		3		5	6	7		10				8	9	12	11*		4				2			J Lovatt	21
1			11	5	6	7		10	12			8	9*				4	3			2			B Stevens	22
1			11	5	6	7		10				8	9				4	3			2			M Heath	23
1			11	5	6	7		10*				8	9	12			4	3			2			J Moules	24
1			11	5	6	7		10				8	9				4	3			2			K Breen	25
1			11	5	6	7		10*				8	9	12			4	3			2			K Lupton	26
1			11	5	6	7		10				8*	9	12			4	3			2			D Axcell	27
1			11	5	6	7		10					9	8			4	3			2			J Key	28
1	12		11	5	6	7		10					9	8			4	3*			2			M James	29
1	3		11	5	6	7		10				8*	9	12		2	4							A Robinson	30
1	3		11	5	6	7		10*	9			8			12	2	4							B Stevens	31
1	3			5	6	7		10	9		11	8					4				2			E Scales	32
1	3			5	6	7*		10	9		11	8	12				4				2			C Trussell	33
1	3				6			10	9	11	7	8					4				2			R Milford	34
1					6	7		10	9	3	8	12			11*		4				2			R Hill	35
1				5	6	7		10	9		11	8*				12	4	3			2			G Aplin	36
			8	5	6	7		10	9	11*			12				4	3			2	1		D Hedges	37
		8	4	3	6		11	10	9				12			7	5				2*	1		J Bray	38
	2*		8		6	7		10	9	11						12	4	3	5			1		R Hamer	39
1			8		6	7		10	9		2				11		4	3	5					M Dimblebee	40
1			8		6	7		10*	9		2				11	12	4	3	5					J Ball	41
1			8		6	7		10*	9		2				11		4	3	5					A Gunn	42
1			8		6	7		10*	9		2				11	12	4	3	5					J Ashworth	43
1			8		6	7			9		2				11	10	4	3	5					V Callow	44
1		12	8		6	7			9		2				11*	10	4+	3	5					L Dilkes	45
1			8		6	7·			9		2				11	10	4	3	5					M Reed	46
1			8		6	7*	12		9		2				11	10	4	3	5					B Stevens	47
1			8		6	7		4	9*		2		12		11	10		3	5					K Redfern	48
1			8		6	7		4	9		2*		12		11	10		3	5					R Milford	49
39	10	8	33	27	**42**	41	3	38	29	12	34	16	16	1	12	10	31	26	14		13	4	3	League Appearances	
	1	1					1	1			2	2	16		4									Substitute Appearances	
4	3	2	4	3	4	4	1	4	4	2	0-1	1	0-1				2	1			1			Milk Cup Appearances	
1	1		1	1	1	1		1	1							0-1	1	1						FA Cup Appearances	
1	1	0-1	2	1	2	0-1		2	1	2	0-2				2	1	2	2			1	1	1	FM Cup Appearances	

Players on Loan: Howard (Chelsea), Hardwick (Oxford Utd)
Departures: Locke (F), Aylott (Bournemouth), Galloway (Maidstone Utd)

'THE EAGLES'

Formed: 1905
Turned Professional: 1905   **Ltd Co:** 1905

Previous Managers: 1905-7 John Robson   1907-25 Eddie Goodman   1925-7 Alec Maley
1927-30 Fred Maven   1930-5 Jack Tresarden   1935-6 Tom Bromilow   1936 R S Moyse
1937-9 Tom Bromilow   1939-47 George Irwin   1947-9 Jack Butler   1949-50 Ronnie Rooke
1950-1 Fred Dawes & Charlie Slade   1951-4 Laurie Scott   1954-8 Cyril Spiers   1958-60 George Smith
1960-3 Arthur Rowe   1963-6 Dick Graham   1966 Arthur Rowe   1966-72 Bert Head
1972-6 Malcolm Allison   1976-80 Terry Venables   1980-1 Malcolm Allison   1981 Dario Gradi
1981-2 Steve Kember   1982-4 Alan Mullery   May 1984 Dave Bassett
Honours: Div 2: Champions 1978-9   Div 3 (S): Champions 1920-1
League Career: Original Members of Div 3 1920
Promoted to Div 2 1920-1   Relegated to Div 3 (S) 1924-5   Relegated to Div 4 1957-8
Promoted to Div 3 1960-1   Promoted to Div 2 1963-4   Promoted to Div 1 1968-9
Relegated to Div 2 1972-3   Relegated to Div 3 1973-4   Promoted to Div 2 1976-7
Promoted to Div 1 1978-9   Relegated to Div 2 1980-1
Colours: White shirts with 4" diagonal band red over blue from left shoulder, white shorts and stockings
Change Colours: All Red
Reserves League: Football Combination   **Youth Team:** S.E. Counties

---

CLUB RECORDS

Most Appearances for Club: Jim Cannon: Football League 447 + FA Cup 38 + League/Milk Cup 35 **Total 463 + 9 subs**
Most Capped Player: Peter Nicholas, 16 Wales, **For England:** Kenny Sansom 9
Record Goalscorer in a Match: Peter Simpson, 6 v Exeter C (h) 7-2, Div 3 (S) 04.10.30
Record League Goalscorer in a Season: Peter Simpson, 46, Div 3 (S), 1930-1   **All Competitions:** Peter Simpson, 54, (League 46, FA Cup 8) 1930-31
Record League Goalscorer in a Career: Peter Simpson, 154 **All Competitions:** Peter Simpson 164 (League 154, FA Cup 12) 1930-36
Record Transfer Fee Received: £800,000 (Nett) from Arsenal for Kenny Sansom, August 1980
Record Transfer Fee Paid: £800,000 to Arsenal for Clive Allen, August 1980
Best Performances: League: 13th Div 1 1979-80   **FA Cup:** Semi-Final 1975-6   **League/Milk Cup:** 5th Round 1968-9, 1970-1
Most League Points: 64 in Div 4, 1960-1
Most League Goals: 110, Div 4, 1960-1
Record League Victory: 9-0 v Barrow, Div 4, 10 Oct 1959
Record League Defeat: 0-8 v Coventry City, Div 3 (S), 6 Feb 1932   2-10 v Reading, Div 3 (S), 4 Sept 1946

Most Consecutive Undefeated League Matches: 18 1969	**League Matches Without a Win:** 20 1962
Longest Run of Undefeated Home League Matches: 32 1931-32	**Away League Matches:** 10 1928-29, 1968-69, 1975, 1978-79
Longest Run Without Home League Win: 11 1973	**Away League Win:** 31 1980-81
Most Consecutive League Wins: 8 1921	**Home League Wins:** 12 1925-26
Most Consecutive League Defeats: 8 1925	**Away League Wins:** 4 1932, 1975

Club Statistician for the Directory: Mike Purkiss

CRYSTAL PALACE

PLAYERS NAME Ht Wt Birthdate	Honours	Birthplace Transfers	Clubs	League	Milk Cup	FA Cup	Other Comps	League	Milk Cup	FA Cup	Other Comps
GOALKEEPERS											
George Wood+ 6.3 14.0 26.9.53	S (4)	Douglas	East Stirling	44	4	1		1			
			Blackpool	117	8	4					
			Everton	103	13	4	2				
		£150,000	Arsenal	60	4	1					
		F	Crystal Palace	123	10	6					
DEFENDERS											
Paul Brush 5.11 12.2 22.2.58	FAC 80, Div. 2, 81	London	West Ham United	144+7	12+1	17	1+3	1			
			Crystal Palace	26			2				
Jim Cannon* 6.0 13.0 2.10.53	Div. 2, 79	Glasgow	Crystal Palace (A)	486+3	37	39		25	3	1	
Micky Droy 6.4¼ 15.5 7.5.51		Highbury	Slough Town								
			Chelsea	262+8	17+2	21		13	2	4	
			Luton Town (L)	2	1						
		F	Crystal Palace	37	3	1		6			
Tony Finnigan 6.0 12.0 17.10.62		Fulham	Crystal Palace	44+3	4			4			
Mark Hone 6.1 12.0 31.3.68		London	Crystal Palace								
Gavin Nebbeling 6.0 12.4 15.5.63		South Africa	Arcadia Shepherds								
			Crystal Palace	70+5	4+1	3		1			
Ken O'Doherty 6.0 12.0 30.3.63	EIU21 (1)	Dublin	University of Dublin								
			Crystal Palace	13							
Brian Sparrow 5.7 10.2 24.6.66		London	Arsenal (A)	19							
			Wimbledon (L)	17							
			Millwall (L)	5							
			Gillingham (L)	5							
		F	Crystal Palace	45	6	2		2			
MIDFIELD											
Andy Higginbottom 5.10 11.0 22.10.64		Chesterfield	Chesterfield (A)	3							
			Everton								
		F	Cambridge United	1							
		F	Crystal Palace	12+4		0+1		2			
Steve Ketteridge 5.9 10.7 7.11.59	Div. 4, 83	Stevenage	Derby County (A)								
			Wimbledon	229+8	19	10	1	32	2	1	
			Crystal Palace	33	4	1		4			
Anton Otulakowski 5.9 10.13 29.1.56	Div. 4, 81	Dewsbury	Ossett Trinity								
			Barnsley	42		1		2			
		£60,000	West Ham United	10+7							
		£50,000	Southend United	161+2	12	9		8			
		£30,000	Millwall	114	6	5	3	16	1		
			Crystal Palace								
David Lindsay 5.7½ 10.7 17.5.66		Havering	Crystal Palace (A)	18+3	2	1					
Gary Stebbing 5.8 11.0 11.8.56		Croydon	Crystal Palace	55+3	4	3		3			
Kevin Taylor 5.8 11.11 22.1.61		Wakefield	Sheffield Wed. (A)	118+7	11	7		22	5	1	
		£25,000	Derby County	22	4		1	2			1
		£10,000	Crystal Palace	42+2	1	1		6		1	
FORWARDS											
Phil Barber 5.11 12.6 10.6.65		Tring	Aylesbury United								
		£7,500	Crystal Palace	68+13	4	3		15	2		
Andy Gray 5.10 10.2 22.2.64		London	Dulwich Hamlet								
			Crystal Palace	48+3	4	1					
Alan Irvine 5.8 11.4 17.7.58	S. Div. 2, 81	Glasgow	Queens Park	83+5	4+1	3		9	1		
			Everton	51+9	10+1	8		4		2	
			Crystal Palace	75+1	8	3		8			
Ian Wright 5.10 11.0 3.11.63		Woolwich	Greenwich Borough	16+16	1	1		9			
			Crystal Palace								

ADDITIONAL CONTRACT PROFESSIONALS
Richard Riches (D), Richard Shaw (D), Paul Roberts (D), Steve Forrest

APPRENTICES
John Salako

NON-CONTRACT PLAYERS

SELHURST PARK London SE25 6PU

Capacity: 38,500 (18,000 covered)

Record Attendance: 51,482 v Burnley, Div 2, 11 May 1979

Record Receipts: £103,173 v West Ham U, FA Cup, Round 4, 28 Jan 1984

Season Tickets: Membership £95 (adults) £57 (juniors/OAP), Arthur Wait Stand £114, Arthur Wait Enclosure £72 (adults) £45.50 (junior/OAP's), Palace Club Membership £2 adults £1 OAP's and Junior 'Eagles'

Executive Boxes: Negotiable; Associate Directors: Negotiable; Vice Presidents Club: £400 + £20 car park; Executive/Tudor Lounges: £200 + £20 car park; Vice Presidents: £15 per match; Exec/Tudor: £12 per match, £228 per season

Match prices: Memberships £5 (adults) £3 juniors/OAP's, Arthur Wait Stand £6, Arthur Wait Enclosure £3.80 (adults) £2.50 (junior/OAP), Holmesdale Terrace £3.20 (adults) £2 (juniors/OAP's), Members Terrace £2.70 (adults) £1.50 (junior/OAP's)

Match and Ticket Information: Seats bookable in advance, one month by post (with sae) and two weeks for personal applications. Cheques should be made payable to Crystal Palace F.C. and should record the name and address of applicant on back. Separate applications for each match.

Wheelchairs: Contact club re. special enclosure

Car Parking: By prior arrangement only through the Secretary. Street parking is available. Supporters may use Club Car Park (for 600 cars) **for £1 per day.** Season Tickets £50

Nearest Railway Station: Thornton Heath/Norwood Junction/Selhurst

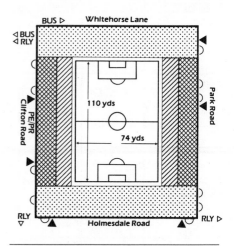

How to get to the ground

From North: From Motorway M1 or A1, use A406 North Circular Road to Chiswick. Follow signs South Circular Road A205 to Wandsworth. Then use A3 to A214 and follow signs to Streatham. Join A23. In 1m turn left B273. At end turn left into High Street then forward into Whitehorse Lane for Crystal Palace FC
From East: Use A232 (S.P. Croydon) to Shirley then join A215 (S.P. Norwood). In 2.2m turn left B266 into Whitehorse Lane
From South: Use A23 (S.P. London) then follow signs Crystal Palace B266 via Thornton Heath into Whitehorse Lane
From West: Use Motorway M4 to Chiswick then route from North or A232 (S.P. Croydon) to Beddington, then follow signs London A23. After follow signs Crystal Palace B266 via Thornton Heath into Whitehorse Lane

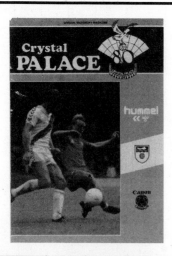

Price of 1986-7 Programme: 50p
Number of Pages: 24
Subscriptions: £18.00 from Programme Department CPFC

Local Newspapers: Croydon Advertiser, South London Press

DARLINGTON

Division 3

President
J L Moore

Chairman
A Heaton

Directors
J B Hadley
A Brown
W Mason
C H Parias
A Heaton
P Boddy
A Moore
J G Cheadle

Secretary
Brian Anderson

Manager
Cyril Knowles

Reserve Team Coach
Brian Swift

Commercial Manager
Val Armstrong (0325 465097)

Physiotherapist
Bob Farrelly

Groundsman
Colin Gray

In 1985 our colleague Tony Pullein forecast that Darlington would be promoted to the 3rd Division and they duly succeeded, but many experts would have foretold a swift descent to former places and for much of the campaign they were almost right as life was one long struggle for the team, which reached a perilous 22nd place on New Year's Day.

Only one other League game was played in January owing to bad weather, but then a wonderful revival took place and defeat was not tasted again in League or the Freight Rover matches until a visit to Newport, where the Gwent team won (3-0). In between 15 matches were played (two in the Freight Rover Trophy) and six only (one in the FRT) were drawn so that 15th place was reached. There was a slight slump then, but a win at home on 12th May against Derby County meant a most respectable 13th place in the final table and at least one more season of 3rd Division football — or even better things if the form during that long run can be repeated.

The main cup matches were contested when form was none too good and this meant that the Milk Cup run lasted only until the second round; a close tussle with Scunthorpe (3-2 and 0-0) was followed by a tie with Ipswich Town and aggregate defeat (2-7). The FA Cup was an even shorter affair with defeat in the first round at Rochdale (2-1), but the Freight Rover Trophy brought some success with Chesterfield, Burnley and Mansfield all removed before a visit from Bolton Wanderers proved disastrous (0-3).

In the League 61 goals were scored with another dozen coming in the cups. MacDonald scored 18 of the total amount with Airey contributing 16 and McLean (the penalty ace) 11. They can all only improve and others who have been sound are Barber (who will need to be replaced in goal), Morgan, Tupling and Roberts. Cyril Knowles has done a fine job as Manager so far and the fans will hope for some real success for 'The Quakers' this coming season. After all, if one campaign can be survived it becomes less difficult to improve from then onwards. WLM

Back Row L to R: Phil Lloyd, David Currie, Mike Astbury, John Huntley, Peter Robinson. **Middle Row:** Lew Clayton (Physio), Gary Hyde, Gary Graham, David Woodcock, Paul Ward, Gary Haire, Mark Hine, Mark Davis, Craig Puckering, Kenneth Hughes. **Front Row:** Garry MacDonald, Steve Tupling, Chris Evans, Cyril Knowles (Manager), John Craggs (Coach), John Green, Gary Morgan, Alan Roberts.

DARLINGTON

DIVISION THREE: 13th   FA CUP: 1st ROUND   **MILK CUP:** 2nd ROUND   **FRT:** AREA QUARTER FINAL

MATCH	DATE		COMPE-TITION	VENUE	OPPONENTS	RESULT		HALF TIME	L'GUE POS'N	GOALSCORERS/GOAL TIMES	ATTEN-DANCE
1	A	18	CL	H	Bristol Rovers	D	3-3	3-1		Poskett 6, MacDonald 17, Cook (pen) 37	4,196
2		20	MC1/1	H	Scunthorpe United	W	3-2	0-1		McLean 65, (pen) 75, Forster 73	2,159
3		24	CL	A	Gillingham	D	1-1	1-1	15	MacDonald 21	(2,929)
4		26	CL	H	Blackpool	W	2-1	1-0	12	Tupling 38, Poskett 83	3,548
5		31	CL	A	Doncaster Rovers	L	0-2	0-1	16		(2,671)
6	S	10	MC1/2	A	Scunthorpe United	D	0-0	0-0			(1,504)
7		14	CL	A	Wigan Athletic	L	1-5	1-2	19	Tupling 14	(3,694)
8		17	CL	A	Chesterfield	L	0-1	0-0	21		(3,161)
9		22	CL	H	Notts County	L	2-3	0-1	23	Airey 76, 84	3,786
10		24	MC2/2	A	Ipswich Town	L	1-3	1-1		Poskett 4	(7,667)
11		28	CL	A	A.F.C. Bournemouth	L	2-4	0-3	23	Robinson 74, Roberts 77	(2,775)
12	O	1	CL	H	Brentford	L	3-5	0-3	24	Millen (og) 49, Airey 80, McLean (pen) 90	2,477
13		5	CL	A	York City	L	0-7	0-2	24		(5,059)
14		8	MC2/2	H	Ipswich Town	L	1-4	1-2		MacDonald 6	3,321
15		19	CL	A	Bristol City	L	0-1	0-0	24		(5,878)
16		22	CL	H	Cardiff City	W	4-1	0-0	23	McLean (pen) 52, 55, Airey 70, 87	2,446
17		27	CL	H	Walsall	L	0-3	0-1	24		3,879
18		30	CL	H	Bury	D	1-1	1-1	24	Poskett 13	2,334
19	N	2	CL	A	Wolverhampton W.	L	1-2	0-0	24	MacDonald 56	(3,811)
20		5	CL	A	Bolton Wanderers	W	3-0	0-0	23	MacDonald 66, 85, Green 72	(2,902)
21		9	CL	H	Swansea City	W	6-0	4-0	21	McLean (pen) 28, (pen) 45, Poskett 33, Roberts 37 Macdonald 46, Tupling 87	2,600
22		16	FAC1	A	Rochdale	L	1-2	0-0		Hicks (og) 63	(2,153)
23		23	CL	A	Reading	W	2-0	1-0	20	Senior (og) 44, Hicks (og) 54	(5,239)
24	D	8	CL	H	Doncaster Rovers	L	0-2	0-1	20		3,370
25		14	CL	A	Plymouth Argyle	L	2-4	0-2	20	MacDonald 76, Airey 89	(6,036)
26		20	CL	H	Gillingham	W	3-2	2-2	20	Airey 16, McDonald 43, Morgan 47	2,072
27		26	CL	H	Rotherham United	D	2-2	0-0	20	MacDonald 81, Airey 87	3,727
28		28	CL	A	Blackpool	D	0-0	0-0	20		(5,595)
29	J	1	CL	A	Lincoln City	D	1-1	0-0	22	Airey 80	(2,304)
30		14	FRT	H	Chesterfield	W	2-0	1-0		Airey 38, 84	1,057
31		18	CL	A	Bristol Rovers	L	1-3	0-2	22	Airey 47	(3,395)
32	F	1	CL	A	Bury	W	1-0	0-0	21	MacDonald 54	(2,613)
33		4	CL	A	Cardiff City	W	1-0	0-0	19	MacDonald 89	(2,222)
34	M	1	CL	H	Bournemouth	D	0-0	0-0	21		2,576
35		9	CL	H	York City	W	1-0	1-0	22	Tupling 45	4,255
36		13	FRT	A	Burnley	D	1-1	1-1		Robinson 18	(1,138)
37		15	CL	A	Derby County	D	1-1	1-1	19	Ward 59	(11,824)
38		18	CL	H	Newport County	W	3-2	3-1	17	MacDonald 28, Airey 33, Ward 38	2,538
39		22	CL	A	Walsall	D	0-0	0-0	18		(4,618)
40		27	FRT QF N	H	Mansfield Town	W	3-0	1-0		MacDonald 43, Airey 48, 77	1,425
41		29	CL	H	Lincoln City	W	1-0	1-0	18	MacDonald 34	3,102
42		31	CL	A	Rotherham United	W	2-1	1-0	16	MacDonald 39, Roberts 62	(3,041)
43	A	2	CL	H	Wolverhampton W.	W	2-1	0-0	15	MacDonald 83, Roberts 85	3,887
44		12	CL	A	Swansea City	D	2-2	0-1	17	McLean (pen) 48, (pen) 75	(3,357)
45		18	CL	H	Reading	D	0-0	0-0	17		3,838
46		22	CL	H	Chesterfield	W	2-1	1-1	14	MacDonald 29, McLean (pen) 69	2,597
47		24	CL	H	Bolton Wanderers	L	0-1	0-0	15		1,870
48		26	CL	A	Newport County	L	0-3	0-1	15		(2,848)
49		29	CL	H	Wigan Athletic	D	1-1	1-0	15	Woodcock 31	2,013
50	M	1	FRT SF N	H	Bolton Wanderers	L	0-3	0-2			3,771
51		3	CL	H	Plymouth Argyle	L	0-2	0-0	15		3,306
52		5	CL	A	Brentford	L	1-2	1-1	15	Woodcock (pen) 38	(2,824)
53		6	CL	A	Notts County	L	0-5	0-2	15		(2,345)
54		12	CL	H	Derby County	W	2-1	2-1	14	Airey 3, McLean 38	3,585
55		15	CL	H	Bristol City	D	1-1	1-0	13	Roberts 43	1,615

Best Home League Attendance: 4,255 v York City 9/3   **Smallest:** 1,615 v Bristol City 15/5   **Av Home Att: 3,027**

Goal Scorers: **Compared with 84-85:** −745

League (61): MacDonald 16, Airey 12, McLean 9 (7 pen), Roberts 5, Poskett 4, Tupling 4, Opponents 3, Ward 2, Woodcock 2 (1 pen), Cook 1 pen, Green 1, Morgan 1, Robinson 1
Milk Cup (5): McLean 2 (1 pen), Forster 1, MacDonald 1, Poskett 1
FA CUP (1): Opponents 1
FRT (6): Airey 4, MacDonald 1, Robinson 1

1985-86

Barber	Aldred	Morgan	Tupling	Robinson	Carney	Haire	Poskett	MacDonald	Cook	McLean	Forster	Airey	Sbragia (L)	Woodcock	Nattress (N.C)	Ward	Roberts	Astbury	Huntley (N.C)	Evans	Green	Pallister (L)	Lloyd	Douglas (NC)	Shute (NC)	Referee	
1	2	3	4	5	6	7	8	9	10	11																D Scott	1
1	2	3	4	5	6	12		10	7*	11	8	9														**T Jones**	2
1		3	4	5	2	7	8			11	10*	9	6	12												K Miller	3
1		3	4		2	6*	12	8	7	10	11	9	5													J Key	4
1	2	3	4	5		12	8	10		11		9		6	7*											K Walmsley	5
1	2	3	4	5	6	7	8	10		11		9														**J Ball**	6
1		3	4	5	6			10		11		9	8			2	7									J Bray	7
1		3	4	2*	6		8	10		11		9	5	12			7									K Barratt	8
1		3	4		6		8	10		11		9	5			2	7									M Peck	9
1	2	3	4		6	7*	8	10		11		9		5												**D Reeves**	10
1	12	3*	4	5	6		8	10		11		9				2	7									G Ashby	11
1	2		4	5	6		8	10		11		9				3	7									D Phillips	12
1	2		4		6	12	8	10		11		9				3†	7		5*							R Banks	13
1	2		4		6	12	8	10		11*		9		7	3				5							**N Wilson**	14
1	8	5	7				11*	10		9		12					6			2	3	4				M Cotton	15
1		3	4				12	10		11		9				8	7*			2	5	6				T Simpson	16
1		3	4				7	10*		11		9		12		8				2	5	6				T Fitzharris	17
1	12	3	4				7	10		11		9				8*				2	5	6				D Hutchinson	18
1	9	3	4				7*	10		11		12				8				2	5	6				J Deakin	19
1		3	4				9	10		11		12				8	7			2	5	6				H Taylor	20
1		3	4				9	10*		11		12				8	7			2	5	6				A Robinson	21
1		3	4					10		11		9				8	7			2	5		6			**N Ashley**	22
1		3	4					10		11		9				8	7			2	5		6			A Robinson	23
1		3	4	12				10		11		9				8	7*			2	5		6			I Hendrick	24
1		3	4*					10	12	11		9				8	7			2	5		6			R Gifford	25
1		3	4					10		11		9				8	7			2	5		6			N Midgley	26
1		3		12				10		11		9	4			8*	7			2	5		6			C Seel	27
1		3	4					10		11		9				8	7			2	5		6			J McAulay	28
1		3	12					10†		11		9	4				7	8*		2	5		6			J Ashworth	29
1		3	4	12				10*		11		9	8*				7		12	2	5		6			**D Allison**	30
1		3	4	12				10		11		9					7		8*	2	5		6			R Bridges	31
1		3	4	8				10		11		9					7			2	5		6			M Robinson	32
1		3	4	8				10		11		9					7			2	5		6			R Groves	33
1		3	4	8				10				9				11	7			2	5		6			R Nixon	34
1		3	4	8				10				9				11	7			2	5		6			T Fitzharris	35
1		3	4	8				10				9		11		7*	12			2	5		6			**C Trussell**	36
1		3	4†	11				10				9		12		8	7			2	5*		6			C Trussell	37
1		3	4	11				10				9		12		8	7			2*	5		6			T Mills	38
1		3	4	11				10				9				8	7			2	5		6			B Hill	39
		3	12	11				10		4		9				8	7*			2	5		6	13		**K Redfern**	40
		3		11				10		4		9*		12		8	7	1		2	5		6			G Napthine	41
		3		11				10		12		4				8	7	1		2	5		6	9		M Heath	42
		3	12	11				10		9		4*				8	7	1		2	5		6			G Aplin	43
		3	4	11				10		9		12				8	7	1		2*	5		6			C Downey	44
		3	4	11				10		9*		12				8	7	1		2	5		6			K Breen	45
		3	4	11				10*		9		12				8	7	1		2	5		6			D Hutchinson	46
	12	3	4	11				10*				9				8	7	1	5	2			6			A Saunders	47
	5	3	4	11				12		9						8	7	1	3*	2			6		10*	P Tyldesley	48
	12	3	4	11				10				9				8	7	1		2			6	5		T Simpson	49
	12	3	4	11						10*		9				8	7			2	5*		6		12	**V Callow**	50
	12	3	4	11				10		9						8	7	1		2			6		5*	J McAulay	51
	5	3	12	11				10*		9		4				2	7	1	12				6		10*	J Ashworth	52
	5	3		11						9		8				2	7	1	12				6		10*	D Reeves	53
	2		4	11				10		9		8				3	7	1			5		6			K Hackett	54
	2		4	11				10		9		8				3	7	1			5		6			M Peck	55
32	11	41	38	29	10	3	18	35	3	37	1	31	6	13	1	35	38	14	5	33	30	7	29	3	2	League Appearances	
5		2		2	3	3	1		1			3							1							Substitute Appearances	
4	4	3	4	2	4	2·2	3	4	1	4	1	4				2	1		1							Milk Cup Appearances	
1			1		1		1			1		1					1	1					1			FA Cup Appearances	
1	0·1	3	2·1	3			2	2		3		1		3		2·1	0·1	3	3				3	0·1	0·1	FR Trophy Appearances	

Also Played: Position(Game): Sherry (NC) 1(39, 49)FRT, Sanderson (NC) 4(52), Wright (NC) 12(10)
Players on Loan: Sbragia (York), Pallister (Middlesbrough)
Departures: Cook (Middlesbrough), Poskett (Stockport), Carney (F), Barber (Everton), Forster (F)

'THE QUAKERS'

Formed: 1883
Turned Professional: 1908 **Ltd Co:** 1891

Previous Managers: Since 1946
Bill Forrest   George Irwin   Bob Gurney   Dick Duckworth   Eddie Carr   Lol Morgan
Jimmy Greenhalgh   Ray Yeoman   Len Richley   Frank Brennan   Allan Jones   Ralph Brand
Dick Conner   Billy Horner   Peter Madden   Len Walker   Billy Elliot
Honours: Div 3 (N) Champions 1924-5
League Career: Original member of Div 3 (N) 1921   Promoted to Div 2 1924-5
Relegated to Div 3 (N) 1926-7   Transferred to Div 4 1958   Promoted to Div 3 1965-6
Relegated to Div 4 1966-7   Promoted to Div 3 1984-5
Colours: White shirts with black trim, black shorts and black stockings with white hoop at top
Change Colours: All blue or all red
Reserves League: Drysbroughs Northern

CLUB RECORDS

Most Appearances for Club: Ron Greener, 442, 1955-68
Most Capped Player: None
Record Goalscorer in a Match: Tom Ruddy, 5 v South Shields, Div 2, 23.04.27, Maurice Wellock, 5 v Rotherham United, Div 3 (N), 15.02.30
Record League Goalscorer in a Season: David Brown, 39, Div 3 (N), 1924-5   **In All Competitions:** David Brown 1924-5
Record League Goalscorer in a Career: Alan Walsh, 90, 1978-84   **In all competitions:** Alan Walsh 100 (87 League + 6 FA Cup + 7 Milk Cup) 1978-84
Record Transfer Fee Received: £65,000 from Chelsea for David Speedie, May 1982
Record Transfer Fee Paid: £17,000 to Notts County for Eric Probert, Oct 1978
Best Performances: League: 15th Div 2 1925-6   **FA Cup:** 3rd Round 1910-1, 5th Round 1957-8 (both last 16)   **League/Milk Cup:** 5th Round 1967-8
Most League Points: 85 in Div 4, 1984-5
Record League Victory: 9-2 v Lincoln City, Div 3 (N), 7 Jan 1928
Record League Defeat: 0-10 v Doncaster Rovers, Div 4, 25 Jan 1964
Oldest Player in League Match: Clive Nattrass
Youngest Player in League Match: John Huntley 17
Most Consecutive Undefeated League Matches: 17 1968
Longest Run of Undefeated Home League Matches: 36 1923-25
Longest Run Without Home League Win: 10 1972-73
Most Consecutive League Wins: 5 1922, 1924, 1928, 1975, 1985

Most Consecutive League Defeats: 8 1985

League Matches Without a Win: 18 1949-50
Away League Matches: 14 1968-69
Away League Win: 36 1952-54
Home League Wins: 8 1923-24, 1924, 1935-36
Away League Wins: 4 1948

Club Statistician for the Directory: F Tweddle

DARLINGTON

				APPEARANCES				GOALS			
PLAYERS NAME Ht Wt Birthdate	Honours	Birthplace Transfers	Clubs	League	Milk Cup	FA Cup	Other Comps	League	Milk Cup	FA Cup	Other Comps
GOALKEEPERS											
Mike Astbury		Leeds	York City (A)	48	5	5	1				
5.11 13.0 22.1.64			Peterborough (L)	4							
			Darlington	14							
DEFENDERS											
Chris Evans	Div. 4, 84	Rhondda	Arsenal (A)								
5.10 11.2 13.10.62		F	Stoke City								
		F	York City	93+3	8	5+1	2+1				
			Darlington	33		1	3				
John Green		Rotherham	Rotherham United (A)	247+1	21	17		8	2	2	
5.10 12.1 7.8.58			Scunthorpe United	100	6	9	5	4			
			Darlington	30		1	3	1			
Phil Lloyd		Hemsworth	Middlesbrough (A)								
6.0 11.13 26.12.64			Barnsley								
			Darlington	84	2	10	3	2		2	
Gary Morgan		Consett	Berwick Rangers	67				4			
5.8 11.4 1.4.61			Darlington	41	3	1	3	1			
Peter Robinson	ES-P	New Biggin	Blyth Spartans								
6.1 12.4 4.9.57			Rochdale (NC)	9+3							
			Darlington	29	2		3	1			1
MIDFIELD											
Mark Hine		Middlesbrough	Grimsby Town	20+2	1	1		1			
5.8 9.11 18.5.84		F	Darlington								
David McLean*	ES	Newcastle	Newcastle United (A)	7+2	1						
5.8 11.0 24.11.57		£10,000	Carlisle United	9+6							
		F	Darlington	287+5	16	18	6+1	46	5	2	2
Steve Tupling		Wensleydale	Middlesbrough (A)								
6.0 11.3 11.7.64			Carlisle United (NC)	1							
			Darlington	76+3	4	3	6+1	8			
Paul Ward		Sedgefield	Chelsea (A)								
5.11 12.5 15.9.63			Middlesbrough	69+7	5	6+1		1			
			Darlington	35		1	3	2			
Dave Woodcock		Darlington	Sunderland (A)								
5.11 12.0 13.10.66			Darlington	13+10	2		1	2			
FORWARDS											
David Currie		Stockton	Middlesbrough	92+19	6	5+1	2	30	1		
6.0 11.13 27.11.62											
Gary Haire		Sedgefield	Oxford United (A)								
5.7 10.8 24.7.63			Whitley Bay								
			Bradford City	44+6	2+1	3+1	1	13		1	
			Darlington	16+8	2+2			2			
Gary MacDonald+		Middlesbrough	Middlesbrough	40+12	26+5	4+1		5		1	
6.0 12.1 26.3.62		F	Carlisle United	7+2	0+1						
		F	Darlington	67+2	4	6	6	20	1	2	1
Alan Roberts		Newcastle	Middlesbrough (A)	28+10	2+1	0+1		2			
5.8½ 9.12½ 8.12.64			Darlington	38		1	2+1	5			

ADDITIONAL CONTRACT PROFESSIONALS

APPRENTICES

NON-CONTRACT PLAYERS
John Craggs, John Huntley, David Mills

FEETHAMS Darlington

Record Attendance: 21,023 v Bolton Wanderers, League Cup Round 3, 14 Nov 1960

Record Receipts: £14,237 v Middlesbrough, FA Cup 3 Round Replay, 8 Jan 1985

Cost of Stand Tickets: £2.60 (adults), £1.80 (juveniles/OAP), Terraces: £2.00 (adults), £1.20 (juveniles/OAP)

Match and Ticket Information: Postal and telephone one month in advance (Secretary, 0325 465097)

Car Parking: Adequate in adjacent side streets.

Nearest Railway Station: Darlington (0325 55111)

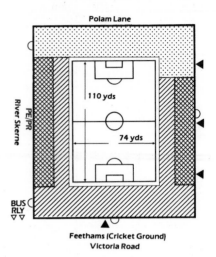

Feethams (Cricket Ground)
Victoria Road

How to get to the ground

From North: Use Motorway A1M then A167 S.P. Darlington into town centre then follow signs Northallerton into Victoria Road for Darlington F.C.

From East: Use A67 S.P. Darlington into town centre, then follow signs Northallerton into Victoria Road for Darlington F.C.

From South: Use Motorway A1M and A66M then A66 S.P. Darlington and at roundabout take 4th exit into Victoria Road for Darlington F.C.

From West: Use A67 (S.P. Darlington) into town centre and at roundabout take 3rd exit into Victoria Road for Darlington F.C.

Local Newspaper: Northern Echo, Evening Despatch

Local Radio Stations: BBC Radio Cleveland, Radio Tees

After two seasons in the comparative obscurity of the 3rd Division Derby County finally carried out a long standing threat by gaining promotion and this coming campaign will be in the 2nd Division. But it was a far from easy campaign and the last promotion spot was not achieved until the penultimate match of the season with a victory at home over Rotherham after a visit to relegated Swansea had brought them a three-clear-goal success. Still, third place was sufficient to bring the ascent and it was well deserved after some very hard work.

As so often happens the season did not start well and after the first ten matches the team was in the lower half of the table; five wins in six matches (with one draw) did produce a change and the improved form continued so that by the New Year second place had been reached. The bad weather and postponements plus a few silly points dropped here and there meant that the finish would mean some biting of nails — and ultimate rejoicing. The runaway form of Reading and Plymouth's consistency had made life hard.

The cup runs were fair with Hartlepool starting the campaigns by losing a cliff-hanger on aggregate (3-2); the next tie brought on Leicester City and the 1st Division team were also despatched on aggregate (3-1). That brought Forest to the Baseball Ground and an exciting match went to the visitors (1-2). The first two rounds of the FA Cup produced resounding successes at home against 4th Division Crewe Alexandra (5-1) and Gola League club Telford United (6-1), but Gillingham in the 3rd Round were tough opponents only being beaten in a Baseball Ground replay after extra-time (1-1 and 3-1). That brought a visit to Sheffield United and a shock 'Rams' success by a goal from Hindmarch so that Sheffield Wednesday were next faced — at the Baseball Ground. This tie needed two matches before Wednesday advanced at Hillsborough (2-0 after 1-1). That was all good stuff, but the Freight Rover Trophy provided a short campaign and early elimination.

So now Arthur Cox will have taken stock and he will know that on the whole his team has shown the kind of form which should bring survival at least in the higher division. The experienced Mark Wallington was his usual consistent self in goal until injury meant that Steele took over. Buckley, Hindmarch and MacLaren were sound at the back and others to show good form were Micklewhite, Christie, Davison, Chandler and Williams. The basis for a good showing in better company — confirmed by good cup performances — is all there.

The very loyal supporters will look forward to the coming season with optimism — and why not?   WLM

Back Row L to R: Roy McFarland (Assistant Manager), Ross MacLaren, Charlie Palmer, Michael Forsyth, John Gregory, Richard Pratley, Martin Taylor, Mark Wallington, Eric Steele, Rob Hindmarch, Andy Garner, David Linigham, Mark Lillis, Paul Blades, Gordon Guthrie (Physio). **Front Row:** Geriant Williams, David Penney, Jeff Chandler, Mel Sage, Steve Cross, Phil Gee, Arthur Cox (Manager), Bobby Davison, Gary Micklewhite, Micky Lewis, Graham Harbey, Steve McLaren, Steve Buckley (now with Lincoln).

DERBY COUNTY

DIVISION THREE: 3rd   **FA CUP:** 5th ROUND   **MILK CUP:** 3rd ROUND

MATCH	DATE		COMPE-TITION	VENUE	OPPONENTS	RESULT	HALF TIME	L'GUE POS'N	GOALSCORERS/GOAL TIMES	ATTEN-DANCE
1	A	17	CL	H	A.F.C. Bournemouth	W	3-0	1-0		Christie 31, Chandler 53, 70	11,324
2		21	MC1/1	H	Hartlepool United	W	3-0	2-0		Davison 14, 75, McLaren 44	8,415
3		24	CL	A	Wigan Athletic	L	1-2	0-1	9	Chandler 67	(4,707)
4		26	CL	H	Wolverhampton W.	W	4-2	2-1	6	Lewis 10, Christie 24, 57, Davison 87	13,154
5		31	CL	A	Bristol Rovers	D	0-0	0-0	7		(4,961)
6	S	4	MC1/2	A	Hartlepool United	L	0-2	0-1			(1,611)
7		7	CL	H	Blackpool	L	1-2	0-0	10	Davison 63	10,702
8		14	CL	A	Bury	D	1-1	0-0	12	Hindmarch 54	(3,684)
9		17	CL	A	Bristol City	D	1-1	0-1	12	Davison 57	(7,750)
10		21	CL	H	Chesterfield	D	0-0	0-0	13		13,259
11		25	MC2/1	H	Leicester City	W	2-0	2-0		MacLaren (pen) 10, Chandler 27	12,504
12		28	CL	A	Cardiff City	W	2-0	1-0	8	MacLaren (pen) 28, Christie 49	(3,435)
13	O	2	CL	H	Swansea City	W	5-1	4-0	6	Price (og) 2, Christie 20, Davison 27, Micklewhite 42, Chandler 62	9,169
14		5	CL	H	Notts County	W	2-0	1-0	5	Chandler (pen) 13, Davison 68	14,406
15		9	MC2/2	A	Leicester City	D	1-1	1-1		Davison 31	(10,373)
16		19	CL	H	York City	W	2-1	1-0	4	Garner 42, 51	11,157
17		22	CL	A	Gillingham	W	2-1	1-0	3	Garner 7, Chandler 54	(4,613)
18		26	CL	H	Plymouth Argyle	L	1-2	1-2	4	Davison 45	11,433
19		30	MC3	H	Nottingham Forest	L	1-2	1-1		Chandler (pen) 9	25,000
20	N	2	CL	A	Rotherham United	D	1-1	0-1	7	Williams 90	(6,030)
21		6	CL	A	Brentford	D	3-3	1-1	7	Hindmarch 16, 51, Davison 75	(4,707)
22		9	CL	H	Lincoln City	W	7-0	2-0	4	Chandler 13, Davison 43, Micklewhite 50, 73, Hindmarch 51, 63, Garner 86	10,560
23		16	FAC1	H	Crewe Alexandra	W	5-1	1-0		Chandler pen 43, Davison 56, 87, Christie 61, 68	11,047
24		23	CL	A	Bolton Wanderers	W	1-0	1-0	4	Micklewhite 17	(5,887)
25		30	CL	H	Reading	D	1-1	0-1	7	Davison 67	16,140
26	D	9	FAC2	H	Telford	W	6-1	1-1		Gregory 32, Chandler 3 50,63,84, M/white 73,82	12,267
27		15	CL	A	Doncaster Rovers	W	3-0	1-0	8	Davison 10, 80, Micklewhite 55	(4,617)
28		22	CL	A	Wigan Athletic	W	1-0	1-0	2	Christie 1	14,047
29		28	CL	A	Wolverhampton W.	W	4-0	1-0	2	Williams 27, Christie 52, Davison 64, Gregory 71	(9,166)
30	J	4	FAC3	A	Gillingham	D	1-1	1-0		Garner 19	(8,983)
31		13	FAC3R	H	Gillingham	W	3-1*	0-0		Micklewhite 52, Garner 103, Christie 120	10,959
32		18	CL	A	A.F.C. Bournemouth	D	1-1	1-1	5	Micklewhite 7	(4,223)
33		15	FRT S	A	Brentford	D	0-0	0-0			(2,531)
34		22	FRT S	H	Gillingham	L	0-2	0-1			3,721
35		25	FAC4	A	Sheffield United	W	1-0	1-0		Hindmarch 34	(22,658)
36	F	12	CL	A	Blackpool	W	1-0	1-0	3	Garner 31	(6,732)
37		8	CL	A	York City	W	3-1	3-0	4	Micklewhite 9, 32, Christie 27	(5,994)
38		22	CL	A	Chesterfield	L	0-1	0-0	4		(9,394)
39		26	FAC5	H	Sheffield Wednesday	D	1-1	1-1		Davison 23	22,781
40	M	1	CL	H	Cardiff City	W	2-1	0-0	4	Gregory 70, MacLaren 89	11,014
41		5	FAC 5R	A	Sheffield Wednesday	L	0-2	0-1			(29,077)
42		8	CL	H	Notts County	W	3-0	0-0	4	Micklewhite 49, Davison 67, 88	(13,086)
43		12	CL	H	Walsall	W	3-1	0-1	3	Chandler 69, Williams 81, Hart og 88	13,434
44		15	CL	H	Darlington	D	1-1	1-0	3	Christie 25	11,824
45		19	CL	A	Bristol City	W	2-0	2-0	2	Gregory 26, Christie 45	11,113
46		22	CL	H	Plymouth Argyle	L	1-4	0-0	2	Christie 12	(11,769)
47		29	CL	A	Newport County	D	1-1	1-0	4	Gregory 23	11,256
48		31	CL	A	Walsall	D	1-1	0-0	4	MacLaren 86	(8,294)
49	A	5	CL	H	Brentford	D	1-1	0-0	5	Micklewhite 52	11,026
50		7	CL	A	Gillingham	W	2-0	1-0	4	Davison 19, Micklewhite 27	11,351
51		9	CL	H	Bristol Rovers	L	0-2	0-0	4		11,033
52		12	CL	A	Lincoln City	W	1-0	1-0	3	Davison 26	(6,237)
53		19	CL	H	Bolton Wanderers	W	2-1	1-0	2	Buckley 21, Williams 64	12,232
54		21	CL	A	Newport County	D	1-1	1-1	3	Christie 27	(3,049)
55		26	CL	A	Reading	L	0-1	0-0	4		(12,266)
56		30	CL	H	Bury	D	1-1	0-1	4	MacLaren (pen) 29	11,790
57	M	3	CL	H	Doncaster Rovers	D	1-1	0-1	5	Hindmarch 90	12,030
58		6	CL	A	Swansea City	W	3-0	1-0	4	Christie 20, (pen) 80, Chandler 75	(3,974)
59		9	CL	H	Rotherham United	W	2-1	0-0	4	Gee 73, Christie 85	21,036
60		12	CL	A	Darlington	L	1-2	1-2	3	Gee 22	(3,585)

Best Home League Attendance: 16,140 v Reading 30/11   Smallest: 9,169 v Swansea City 2/10   Av Home Att: 12,369

Goal Scorers: Compared with 84-85: +1,537

League (80):	Davison 16, Christie 15 (1 pen), Micklewhite 11, Chandler 9, Hindmarch 6, Garner 5, Gregory 4, MacLaren 4 (2 pen), Williams 4, Gee 2, Opponents 2, Buckley 1, Lewis 1
Milk Cup (7):	Davison 3, Chandler 2 (1 pen), MacLaren 1 (pen), McLaren 1
FA CUP (17):	Chandler 4 (1 pen), Christie 3, Davison 3, Micklewhite 3, Garner 2, Gregory 1, Hindmarch 1

Wallington	Streete	Buckley	Lewis	Hindmarch	MacLaren	Micklewhite	Christie	Davison	McClaren	Chandler	Blades	Palmer	Williams	Garner	Harbey	Gregory	Gee	Pratley	Steele	Thomas (L)	Penney	Biggins	Referee	
1	2	3	4	5	6	7	8	9	10	11													L Dilkes	1
1	2	3	4	5	6	7	8	9	10	11													J Key	2
1	2	3	4*	5	6	7	8	9	10	11	12												N Ashley	3
1	2	3	4	5	6	7	8	9	10*	11	12												T Mills	4
1	2	3	4	5	6	7	8	9	10	11*	12												N Butler	5
1	2	3	4	5	6	7	8	9	10	11*	12												T Simpson	6
1	2	3	4	5	6	7	8	9	10	11													J Ashworth	7
1		5		4	3	6	10	11	8*	9	12	2	7										K Lupton	8
1		5		3	4	6	10	11	8	9		2	7										D Hedges	9
1		3		5	6	7	8	9	10	11		2	4										R Bridges	10
1		3*		5	6	7	8	9	10	11		2	4	12									T Jones	11
1		3		5	6	7	8	9	10*	11	12	2	4										D Reeves	12
1		3		5	6	7	8	9	10	11		2	4										D Scott	13
1		3		5	6	7	8	9	10*	11		2	4	12									A Robinson	14
1		3		5	6	7	8	9	10	11*	12	2	4										A Buksh	15
1		3		5	6	7	8*	9	10	11		2	4	12									P Tyldesley	16
1		3		5	6	7		9	10	11		2	4	8									J Moules	17
1		3		5	6	7	8	9	10*	11		2	4	12									K Breen	18
1		3		5	6	7	8	9	10	11		2	4*	12									D Shaw	19
1		3		5	6	7	8	9	10	11	12	2*	4										F Roberts	20
1		3		5	6	7	8	9		11		2	4	10									A Gunn	21
1		3		5	6	7	8	9*		11		2	4	10	12								J Lovatt	22
1		3		5	6	7	8	9		11		2	4			10							L Robinson	23
1		3		5	6	7	8	9		11*		2	4	12		10							A Saunders	24
1		3		5	6	7	8	9*		11		2	4	12		10							T Borrett	25
1		3		5	6	7	8	9		11		2	4	12		10*							R Nixon	26
1		3		5	6	7	8	9		11		2	4			10							G Tyson	27
1		3		5	6	7	8	9		11*		2	4	12		10							E Scales	28
1		3		5	6	7	8	9		11		2	4			10							J Worrall	29
1		3		5	6	7	8			11*		2	4	9	12	10							J Bray	30
1		3		5	6	7	8			11*		2	4	9	12	10							J Ashworth	31
1		3		5	6	7	8			11		2	4	9		10							M Bodenham	32
			4		10*					12	6	2		11*	3	13	8	5	1		7	9	D Hedges	33
1		3		5	6	7	8*			11		2	4*	9	12	10	13						L Dilkes	34
1		3		5	6	7	8			11		2	4	9		10							T Fitzharris	35
1		3			6	7	8			11		2	4	9		10		5					R Guy	36
1		3			6	7	8			11		2	4	9		10		5					K Breen	37
1		3		5	6	7	8			11		2	4	9		10							A Seville	38
1		3		5	6	7	8	9		11		2	4			10							N Midgley	39
1		3		5	6	7	8			11		2	4			10							D Phillips	40
1		3		5	6	7	8	9*		11		2	4	12		10							N Midgley	41
1		3		5	6	7	8	9		11		2	4			10							J Key	42
1		3		5	6	7	8	9		11		2	4			10	9						J Bray	43
		3		5	6	7	8	9		11		2	4			10			1				C Trussell	44
		3			6	7	8	9		11		2	4			10		5	1				M Reed	45
		3			6	7	8	9		11		2	4			10		5	1				G Ashby	46
		3		5*	6	7	8	9				2	4	12		10			1	11			I Hendrick	47
		3			6	7	8	9	12			2	4			10*		5	1	11			Alan Robinson	48
		3		5	6	7	8	9	10			2	4						1	11			J Deakin	49
		3			6	7	8	9	10			2	4					5	1	11			K Barratt	50
		3			6	7	8	9	10			2	4	12				5	1	11*			K Walmsley	51
		3		5	6	7	8	9	10			2*	4	12					1	11			J Lloyd	52
		3		5	6	7	8	9	10			2	4						1	11			J Key	53
		3		5	6	7	8	9				2	4						1	11			R Milford	54
		3		5	6	7	8	9				2	4	12		10			1	11*			L Robinson	55
		3		5	6	7	8	9		11		2	4			10			1				R Lewis	56
1		3		5	6	7	8	9*		11		2	4			10							M Cotton	57
1		3		5	6	7	8	9		11		2	4			10							R Groves	58
1		3		5	6	7	8	9		11		2	4*			10							T Fitzharris	59
1		3*		5	6	7	8	9		12	4	2				10				11			K Hackett	60
33	6	46	5	39	46	46	45	41	22	36	24	17	39	8		22	2	7	13	9			League Appearances	
									1	1	6	1		8	3	2							Substitute Appearances	
5	2	5	2	5	5	5	5	5	5	5	0·2	3	3	0·2									Milk Cup Appearances	
7		7		7	7	7	7	4	7	7			7	3·2		7							FA Cup Appearances	
1	1	1	1	2	1	1	1·1		2	1·1	2	1	1	2	1·1	1·1	1·1	1		1	1	1	FR Trophy Appearances	

Players on Loan: Thomas (WBA)   Departures: Christie (Man City)

'THE RAMS'

Formed: 1884
Turned Professional: 1884   **Ltd Co:** 1896

Previous Managers: Since 1946:
Stuart McMillan   Jack Barker   Harry Storer   Tim Ward   Brian Clough   Dave Mackay   Colin Murphy   Tommy Docherty   Colin Addison   John Newman

Honours: Champions Div 1, 1971-2, 1974-4   Champions Div 2, 1911-2, 1914-5, 1968-9   Champions Div 3 (N) 1956-7   FA Cup Winners 1945-6   Charity Shield Winners 1975   Texaco Cup Winners 1971-2

League Career: Founder Members of Football League 1888   Relegated to Div 2 1906-7   Promoted to Div 1 1911-2   Relegated to Div 2 1913-4   Promoted to Div 1 1914-5   Relegated to Div 2 1920-1   Promoted to Div 1 1925-6   Relegated to Div 2 1952-3   Relegated to Div 3 (N) 1954-5   Promoted to Div 2 1956-7   Promoted to Div 1 1968-9   Relegated to Div 2 1979-80   Relegated to Div 3 1983-4   Promoted to Div 2 1985-6

Colours: White shirts, blue shorts and stockings with white band on top

Change Colours: Royal blue and sky blue striped shirts, sky blue shorts and stockings

Reserves League: Central League   **Youth Team:** Midland Intermediate

---

CLUB RECORDS

Most Appearances for Club: Kevin Hector: Football League 486, 1966-78, 1980-2

Most Capped Player: Roy MacFarland, 28, England

Record Goalscorer in a Match: Steve Bloomer, 6 v Sheffield Wednesday, Div 1, 02.01.1899

Record League Goalscorer in a Season: Jack Bowers, 37, Div 1, 1930-1   Ray Straw, 37, Div 3 (N), 1956-7

Record League Goalscorer in a Career: Steve Bloomer, 291, 1892-1906, 1910-4

Record Transfer Fee Received: £400,000 from Southampton for Charlie George, Dec 1978

Record Transfer Fee Paid: £410,000 to Crystal Palace for David Swindlehurst, April 1980

Best Performances: League: Champions (2)   **FA Cup:** Winners (1)   **League/Milk Cup:** Semi-Final 1967-8   **European Cup:** Semi-Final   **UEFA Cup:** 3rd Round   **Texaco Cup:** Winners

Most League Points: 63, Div 2, 1968-9, Div 3 (N) 1958-9, Div 3 (N) 1956-7

Record League Victory: 9-0 v Wolverhampton Wanderers, Div 1, 10 Jan 1891; 9-0 v Sheffield Wednesday, Div 1, 2 Jan 1899

European Competitions Entered: European Cup 1972-3, 1975-6   UEFA Cup 1974-5, 1976-7

Oldest Player in League Match:

Youngest Player in League Match: Steve Powell

Most Consecutive Undefeated League Matches: 22 1969

Longest Run of Undefeated Home League Matches: 23 1929-30

Longest Run Without Home League Win: 7 1892, 1954, 1955, 1965

Most Consecutive League Wins: 9 1969

Most Consecutive League Defeats: 8 1965

League Matches Without a Win: 14 1955

Away League Matches: 13 1969, 1985-6

Away League Win: 33 1919-21

Home League Wins: 12 1971-72

Away League Wins: 6 1969

Club Statistician for the Directory: S McGhee

DERBY COUNTY

PLAYERS NAME Ht Wt Birthdate	Honours	Birthplace Transfers	Clubs	Appearances League	Milk Cup	FA Cup	Other Comps	Goals League	Milk Cup	FA Cup	Other Comps
GOALKEEPERS											
Eric Steele 6.0 12.8 14.5.54	Div. 4, 74	Newcastle	Newcastle United								
			Peterborough United	124	11	13					
			Brighton & H.A.	87	9	2					
			Watford	51	7	4					
			Cardiff City (L)	7	1						
			Derby County	39	2	1	3				
Mark Wallington 6.1 14.2½ 17.9.52	EU23 (2), Y, Div. 2, 80	Sleaford £35,000 £10,000	Walsall	11		1					
			Leicester City	412	23	25					
			Derby County	33	5	7	1				
DEFENDERS											
Paul Blades 6.0 11.0 5.1.65	EY	Peterborough	Derby County (A)	55+7	1+2	7	3+1				
Michael Forsyth 5.11 11.2 20.3.66	EY	Liverpool	WBA (A)	28+1	1	2					
			Derby County								
Rob Hindmarch* 6.1½ 13.4 27.4.61	EY	Stannington	Sunderland (A)	114+1	6+2	5		2	1		
			Portsmouth (L)	2							
			Derby County	61	7	7	1	1			
David Linighan 6.2 12.6 9.1.65		Hartlepool	Hartlepool United	84+7	3+1	6		1	3	1	
			Leeds United								
			Derby County								
Ross McLaren† 5.10 12.12 14.4.62		Edinburgh	Glasgow Rangers								
			Shrewsbury Town	158+3	9	7		18	3	1	
			Derby County	46	5	7	2				
Charlie Palmer 5.11 11.9 10.7.63		Aylesbury F	Watford (A)	10	2		4				
			Derby County	50	7	1	2	2			
Richard Pratley 6.1 12.6 12.1.63		Banbury	Banbury United								
			Derby County	20+2		0+1	3				
			Scunthorpe United (L)	10+1			2	1			
Mel Sage 5.8 10.4 24.3.64		Gillingham	Gillingham (A)	126+6	10	12	5	3		1	
			Derby County								
MIDFIELD											
Steve Cross 5.11 10.4 22.12.59	Div. 3, 79	Wolverhampton	Shrewsbury Town (A)	240+22	14	14	2	32	3	3	
			Derby County								
John Gregory 6.1 11.5 11.5.54	E (6), Div. 2, 83	Scunthorpe £40,000 £250,000 £300,000	Northampton Town (A)	187	8	7		8	1	1	
			Aston Villa	59+6	5	2	3+1	10	1		
			Brighton	72	6	3		7			
			QPR	162+2	16	9	4	36	4		1
			Derby County	22		7	1+1				
Mickey Lewis 5.6 10.6 25.2.65	EY	Birmingham £25,000	WBA (A)	22+2	4+1	4					
			Derby County	27	2		3				
Steve McClaren 5.7½ 9.4 3.5.61		Fulford	Hull City (A)	171+7							
			Derby County	22+1	5						
Gary Micklewhite 5.8 9.10 21.3.61	Div. 2, 83	London F £50,000	Manchester United (A)								
			QPR	97+9	12+1	6+2		11	4	1	
			Derby County	65	5	7	1	4			
David Penney 5.8 10.7 17.8.64		Wakefield	Pontefract								
			Derby County				1				
FORWARDS											
Jeff Chandler 5.7 10.1 19.6.59	EI (2)	Hammersmith	Blackpool (A)	31+6	2+1	0+1		7			
			Leeds United	21+5	1	1		2			
			Bolton Wanderers	152+5	10	7		36	4	3	
			Derby County	36+1	5	7	1+1				
Bobby Davison 5.10 11.5 17.7.59		South Shields £1,000 £20,000 £90,000	Seaham C.W.								
			Huddersfield Town	1+1							
			Halifax Town	63	5	3		29	3		
			Derby County	148+3	11	10	2	46		4	2
Andy Garner 5.11 11.9 8.3.66		Chesterfield	Derby County (A)	32+11	0+2	5+2	2	8			
Phillip Gee 5.9 10.4 19.12.64		Pelsall	Gresley Rovers								
			Derby County	2+2			1+1				
Mark Lillis 6.0 12.12 17.1.60		Manchester P/E+£100,000	Huddersfield Town	199+7	16	19+1		55	1	6	
			Manchester City	29	3	4	5	11	1		3
			Derby County								

ADDITIONAL CONTRACT PROFESSIONALS
Martin Taylor

APPRENTICES
Kevin Cresswell, Brian McCord

NON-CONTRACT PLAYERS
Karl Austin, Paul Fogerty, Ian Grostate, Roy McFarland, Stuart Stokes, Gordon Tucker

BASEBALL GROUND
Shaftesbury Crescent, Derby DE3 8NB   **Capacity:** 26,500

Record Attendance: 41,826 v Tottenham Hotspur, Div 1, 20 Sept 1969

Record Receipts: £108,000 v Manchester United, FA Cup Round 5, 19 Feb 1983

Season Tickets: Stand: From £60.00, £120.00; **Terraces:** £70 (adults), £40 (juveniles); OAP any stand £60

Cost of Stand Tickets: Home supporters £5.00, £5.50, £6.00; Visitors £5.00 (Co-op Stand juveniles/OAP £3.00); **Terraces:** Home £3.50, Visitors £4.00

Match and Ticket Information: Available 14 days prior to match

Car Parking: Eight parks within ½ mile of ground run by club in co-operation with local corporation. Street parking within same distance

Nearest Railway Station: Derby Midland (0332 32051)

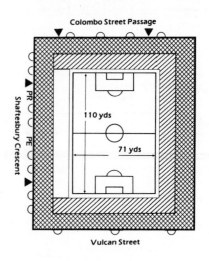

Colombo Street Passage

Shaftesbury Crescent

110 yds

71 yds

Vulcan Street

How to get to the ground

From North: Follow signs Derby A38 into Town Centre, then follow signs Melbourne A514. Then on nearside of Railway Bridge turn right into Shaftesbury Street for Derby County FC
From East, South and West: Use Derby Ring Road from East and South (S.P. Burton) and from West (S.P. Nottingham) as far as junction with A514, then follow signs town centre into Osmaston Road. In 1.3m turn left into Shaftesbury Street for Derby County FC

Price of 1986-7 Programme: 70p
Number of Pages: 28
Subscriptions: 70p plus postage per match

Local Newspaper: Derby Evening Telegraph

Local Radio Station: BBC Radio Derby

DONCASTER ROVERS   Division 3

Doncaster ended the 1985-86 season in a very respectable 11th position in the 3rd Division table and this would have been better if there had not been a bad spell at the end of the season when of the last 13 matches only three were won, which meant that a promotion situation was changed into something less spectacular. In fact, of the last seven matches none were won and only three were drawn — three points out of a possible 21! That was the vital moment in the season. Also, it was one of the periods when the strike force failed to function properly and without goals matches are not won.

Perhaps, that lack of scoring ability was the main factor in preventing Rovers from doing better, since the team never scored more than three goals in any competitive game, although there is some promising material at the club's disposal.

The cups did not provide any relief with the Milk Cup campaign being over early in September as the result of an aggregate draw with Notts County (2-2) but defeat on penalties. The FA Cup also ended abruptly with a thrashing at Wigan (1-4) and the team also failed to advance further than the opening stages of the Freight Rover Trophy.

So Dave Cusack must not look at ways and means of making the side score more goals, which is never anything but a very difficult task. Douglas was the best striker, but there is potential supply of goals to be expected from Buckley, Woods and Wakinshaw, who came through near the end of the season. In goal Rhodes took over from Peacock and did well, Rushbury, Humphries (until injured)), Cusack himself, Flynn and Stead played their parts well enough.

As with many other teams consistency is needed and if Rovers find that a return to the 2nd Division cannot be ruled out.   WLM

Back Row L to R: Colin Russell, Neil Redfern, Andy Rhodes, Micky Nesbitt, John Deakin. **Middle Row:** Micky Stead, Glen Humphries, Neil Woods, Brian Deane, Paul Holmes, Gary Clayton, Dave Rushbury, Phil Boersma. **Front Row:** Jim Dobbin, Tony Brown, Dave Cusack, John Philliben, Sean Joyce.

DONCASTER ROVERS

DIVISION THREE: 11th **FA CUP:** 1st ROUND **MILK CUP:** 1st ROUND

MATCH	DATE		COMPE-TITION	VENUE	OPPONENTS	RESULT		HALF TIME	L'GUE POS'N	GOALSCORERS/GOAL TIMES	ATTEN-DANCE
1	A	17	CL	A	Newport County	D	2-2	2-1		Nesbitt 4, Woods 29	(2,375)
2		20	MC1/1	A	Notts County	L	0-1	0-0			(2,425)
3		24	CL	H	Bolton Wanderers	D	1-1	0-0	16	Douglas 88	3,414
4		26	CL	A	Notts County	D	1-1	1-0	18	Buckley 43	(3,922)
5		31	CL	H	Darlington	W	2-0	1-0	13	Woods 9, Douglas 75	2,671
6	S	3	MC1/2	H	Notts County	W	2-1†	0-1		Dobbin 66, Douglas 89	2,679
7		8	CL	A	Lincoln City	D	3-3	2-2	13	Caswell 36, Woods 38, Dobbin 87	(3,205)
8		13	CL	H	Brentford	W	1-0	0-0	6	Douglas 90	2,831
9		17	CL	H	Plymouth Argyle	W	1-0	1-0	4	Woods 37	2,904
10		21	CL	A	Rotherham United	L	1-2	0-2	6		(5,189)
11		28	CL	H	Reading	L	0-1	0-0	9		4,012
12	O	1	CL	A	Blackpool	L	0-4	0-3	15		(4,121)
13		5	CL	H	Walsall	W	1-0	0-0	14	Harle (pen) 53	2,901
14		12	CL	A	Wolverhampton W.	W	2-1	0-1	10	Douglas 53, 56	(4,324)
15		19	CL	H	Bristol Rovers	L	0-2	0-2	11		3,032
16		22	CL	A	Swansea City	W	2-0	1-0	10	Douglas 3, Dobbin 59	(3,827)
17		26	CL	A	Chesterfield	D	0-0	0-0	11		(3,746)
18	N	2	CL	H	Bristol City	D	1-1	0-1	11	Brown, T 60	2,871
19		5	CL	H	Wigan Athletic	D	2-2	1-2	13	Dobbin 38, 85	2,069
20		8	CL	A	Cardiff City	W	1-0	0-0	11	Caswell 78	(2,015)
21		16	FAC1	A	Wigan Athletic	L	1-4	1-2		Douglas 5	(3,315)
22		23	CL	H	A.F.C. Bournemouth	D	1-1	1-1	11	Harle 27	2,390
23		30	CL	A	Gillingham	L	0-4	0-2	11		(3,159)
24	D	8	CL	A	Darlington	W	2-0	1-0	11	Woods 31, 82	(3,370)
25		15	CL	H	Derby County	L	0-3	0-1	11		4,617
26		21	CL	A	Bolton Wanderers	L	0-2	0-1	11		(4,546)
27		26	CL	A	York City	W	1-0	1-0	10	Buckley (pen) 21	(5,320)
28		28	CL	H	Notts County	W	2-1	1-1	7	Cusack 2, Buckley (pen) 47	3,673
29	J	1	CL	H	Bury	W	1-0	0-0	4	Douglas 67	3,283
30		7	CL	A	Bristol City	L	1-4	0-1	7	Douglas 65	5,385
31		16	FRT N	A	Notts County	L	0-1	0-1			(1,642)
32		18	CL	H	Newport County	D	1-1	1-0	9	Buckley 45	2,336
33		21	FRTN	H	Mansfield Town	W	1-0	1-0		Flynn 3	(1,584)
34		24	CL	A	Brentford	W	3-1	1-0	5	Dobbin 45, Joyce 60, Cusack 87	(3,678)
35	F	1	CL	H	Lincoln City	D	1-1	0-0	8	Douglas 80	2,723
36		4	CL	H	Swansea City	D	0-0	0-0	6		2,029
37		8	CL	A	Bristol Rovers	L	0-1	0-1	7		(3,894)
38		15	CL	A	Plymouth Argyle	W	1-0	0-0	6	Douglas 81	(4,827)
39	M	4	CL	H	Blackpool	D	0-0	0-0	6		2,316
40		8	CL	A	Walsall	L	0-1	0-1	7	Stead (og) 17	(4,810)
41		15	CL	H	Wolves	L	0-1	0-0	10		2,656
42		17	FRT N	A	Mansfield Town	L	2-4	0-1		Cusack 59, Woods 88	(2,895)
43		21	CL	H	Chesterfield	W	2-0	1-0	8	Wakenshaw 14, 67	1,989
44		29	CL	A	Bury	W	2-1	1-0	8	Woods 5, Wakenshaw 83	(2,294)
45		31	CL	H	York City	D	1-1	0-1	7	Holmes 57	3,319
46	A	5	CL	A	Wigan Athletic	W	1-0	1-0	7	Buckley (pen) 25	(4,143)
47		12	CL	H	Cardiff City	L	0-2	0-2	7		2,051
48		15	CL	H	Rotherham United	D	0-0	0-0	10		3,159
49		19	CL	A	AFC Bournemouth	D	1-1	0-0	9	Douglas 78	(2,796)
50		25	CL	H	Gillingham	L	2-3	0-3	10	Douglas 60, Dobbin 89	1,659
51	M	3	CL	A	Derby County	D	1-1	1-0	10	Douglas 31	(12,030)
52		5	CL	A	Reading	L	0-2	0-0	11		(8,168)

Best Home League Attendance: 4,617 v Derby Co 15/12   **Smallest:** 1,659 v Gillingham 25/4   **Av Home Att:** 2,822

Goal Scorers: Compared with 84-85: −1,324

League (45):	Douglas 13, Woods 7, Dobbing 6, Buckley 5 (3 pen), Wakenshaw 3, Caswell 2, Cusack 2, Harle 2, Brown T 1, Holmes 1, Joyce 1, Nesbitt 1, Opponents 1
Milk Cup (2):	Dobbin 1, Douglas 1
FA Cup (1):	Douglas 1
FRT (3):	Cusack 1, Flynn 1, Woods 1

1985-86

Peacock	Caswell	Rushbury	Dobbin	Brown, T.	Humphries	Buckley	Nesbitt	Douglas	Woods	Deakin	Deans	Butterworth	Travis (NC)	Philliben	Cusack	Harle	Joyce	Wakenshaw (L)	Wadsworth (NC)	Rhodes	Holmes (A)	Flynn	Stead	Walker	Peattie (L)	Referee	
1	2	3	4	5	6	7	8	9	10	11																M Cotton	1
1	2	3	4	5	6	7		9	10			8*	12	11												J Hough	2
1		3	4	5	11	7		9	10			8*		2	6	12										K Redfearn	3
1	2	3	8	5	4	7		9	10						6	11										V Callow	4
1	2	3	8	5	4	7		9	10						6	11										K Walmsley	5
1	2	3	8	5	4	7		9	10*					12	6	11										N Midgley	6
	2*	3	8	5	4	7	12	9	10			11			6											N Ashley	7
	2	3	8	5	4	7		9	10			11			6											G Napthine	8
1	2	3	8	5	4	7		9	10*			11			6	12										R Banks	9
1	2	3	10	5	4*	7	12	9				11			6	8										H Taylor	10
	2	3	8	5	4	7		9			10*	12			6	11										K Lupton	11
	2	3†	12	5	4	7		9	8			11*			6	10										J Lovatt	12
	2	3	8		4	7		9	10*			12		5	6	11										L Dilkes	13
	2	3			4	7		9	8*			12		5	6	10										R Bridges	14
	2†	3	12	4		7		9	8					5	6	10										T Fitzharris	15
	2	3	11	5		7		8				9		4	6	10				1						L Shapter	16
	2	3	11	5		7		8				12	9*	4	6	10				1						C Trussell	17
		3	11	5	4	7		8				2*	9	12	6	10				1						A Robinson	18
		3	11	5	4*	7	12	8				9			6	10				1	2					A Saunders	19
	2	3	11	5*	4	7	8					9	12		6	10				1						K Barratt	20
	2	3*	11		4	7	8					12		5	6	10				1		9				J Bray	21
		3	11		4	7	8	9*				12			6	10				1	2	5				D Allinson	22
		3	11		4	7	8	9*							6	10				1		5	2	12		D Hedges	23
		3	11*		4	7	8		10		12				6					1		5	2	9		I Hendrick	24
		3			4	7*	8		10	11				9	6					1		5	2	12		G Tyson	25
		3			4	7	8		10	11*			12		6					1		5	2			M Heath	26
		3	11		4	7	8*		10					12	6					1		5	2			N Wilson	27
		3	11		4	7			10						6					1		5	2	8		D Scott	28
		3	11		4	7	12		10						6					1		5	2	8*		J Ball	29
		12	11		4	7	8		10						6					1	3*	5	2			G Ashby	30
		3		11	4	7	13	12	12	10					6		9			1		5	2		8	T Holbrook	31
		3	12	11	4	7				10					6		9			1		5	2		8	A Seville	32
		3		11		7*		9*	13			12			6	10				1		5	2		8	T Fitzharris	33
		3	7	11	4			9							6	10				1		5	2		8	K Cooper	34
1		3	4	11		7		8				12			6	10		1				5	2		9*	R Nixon	35
1		3	12	11		7		8						4	6	10				1		5	2			P Willis	36
1		3	8		4	7		8				11*			6	10				1		5	2		12	M James	37
		3	9	11	4	7									6	10				1		5	2			I Hemley	38
		3		11	4*	7		9	8			12			6	10				1		5	2			K Baker	39
		3		11		7	8							4	6		10	9		1		5	2			K Miller	40
		3		11		7	8							4	6		10*	9	12	1		5	2			J Lovatt	41
		3		11		7	8	12	13						6†		10	9	4*	1		5	2*			H Taylor	42
		3		11		7		8	10	4				2	6					1		5				P Vanes	43
		3		11		7		8	10	4				2	6			9		1		5				K Barratt	44
		3		11		7			10*	4				2	6			9		1	8	5				K Lupton	45
		3		11		7		8	12	4				2	6		10*	9		1		5				G Napthine	46
		3	10	11		7		8	12	4*				2	6					1		5				D Allison	47
		3		11		7		8	10	4				2	6					1		5				B Hill	48
		3*		11		7		8	10	4				2	6			9		1		5	12			R Milford	49
		3	12	11		7*		8	10	4				2	6			9		1		5				J Lloyd	50
		3	9	11		7		8	10	4				12	6					1		5*	2			M Cotton	51
		3	9	11		7		8	10	5	12				6*	4				1			2			L Shapter	52
9	15	45	25	38	29	45	2	41	28	13	4	12		20	43	15	15	8	1	30	5	27	19	3	3	League Appearances	
		6					3	1	2	1	1	1	9	2	2		2			1			1	2	1	Substitute Appearances	
2	2	2	2	2	2		2	2				0-1	1	0-1	1	1										Milk Cup Appearances	
1	1	1	1	1			1	1		0-1			1		1	1						1	1			FA Cup Appearances	
		3		3	1	2	1+1	1	1-2	0-3	1	0-1			3		3	1	1	3		3	3		2	FR Trophy Appearances	

Also Played: Position(Game): Swinburne (L) 1(11, 12, 13, 14), Deane 9(36, 48), 12(45), Allen (NC) 1(7, 8, 15), Brown 11(14, 15), Rodgers (NC) 4(42)

Players on Loan: Swinburne (Leeds), Wakenshaw (Carlisle Utd), Peattie (Sheffield Utd)

Departures: Harle, Caswell, Russell (Scunthorpe), Buckley (Leeds), Saddington (Sunderland), Douglas (Rotherham U), Peacock, Deans (Retired Injured)

Doncaster Rovers Football Club Ltd.
(Founded 1879)

'ROVERS'

Formed: 1879
Turned Professional: 1885   **Ltd Co:** 1905 & 1920

Previous Managers: Since 1946: Bill Marsden   Jackie Bestall   Peter Doherty   Jack Hodgson   Syd Bycroft   Jack Crayston   Jack Bestall   Norman Curtis   Danny Malloy   Oscar Hold   Bill Leivers   Keith Kettleborough   George Raynor   Lawrie McMenemy   Maurice Setters   Stan Anderson   Billy Bremner

Honours: Champions Div 3 (N), 1934-5, 1946-7, 1949-50   Champions Div 4, 1965-6, 1968-9

League Career: Elected to Div 2 1901   Failed to gain re-election 1903
Re-elected to Div 2 1904   Failed to gain re-election 1905   Re-elected to Div 3 (N) 1923
Promoted to Div 2 1934-5   Relegated to Div 3 (N) 1936-7   Promoted to Div 2 1946-7
Relegated to Div 3 (N) 1947-8   Promoted to Div 2 1949-50   Relegated to Div 3 1957-8
Relegated to Div 4 1958-9   Promoted to Div 3 1965-6   Relegated to Div 4 1966-7
Promoted to Div 3 1968-9   Relegated to Div 4 1970-1   Promoted to Div 3 1980-1
Relegated to Div 4 1982-3   Promoted to Div 3 1983-4

Colours: Red shirts with white sleeves with red and green trim, white shorts, red stockings with white and green tops

Change Colours: Green shirts with white sleeves and red trim, green shorts with white and red stripe on sides, red stockings with green and white tops

---

CLUB RECORDS

Most Appearances for Club: Fred Emery: Football League 422 + FA Cup 19, 1924-36 **Total 441**

Most Capped Player: Len Graham, 14, N Ireland   **For England:** I Snodin 4 (under 21)

Record Goalscorer in a Match: Tom Keetley, 6 v Ashington (a), 7-4, Div 3 (N), 16.02.1929

Record League Goalscorer in a Season: Clarrie Jordan, 42, Div 3 (N), 1946-7   **In All Competitions:** Clarrie Jordan, 44 (League 42 + FA Cup 2), 1946-7

Record League Goalscorer in a Career: Tom Keetley, 175, 1923-9   **In All Competitions:** Tom Keetley, 180 (League 175 + FA Cup 5)

Record Transfer Fee Received: £200,000 from Leeds United for Ian Snodin, May 1985

Record Transfer Fee Paid: £60,000 to Stirling Albion for John Philliben, March 1984

Best Performances: League: 7th Div 2 1901-2   **FA Cup:** 5th Round 1951-2, 1953-4, 1954-5, 1955-6   **League/Milk Cup:** 5th Round 1975-6

Most League Points: (3pts for win) 85, Div 4, 1983-4   (2pts for win) 72, Div 3 (N), 1946-7 (League record)

Most League Goals: 123, Div 3 (N), 1946-7

Record League Victory: 10-0 v Darlington, Div 4, 25 Jan 1964

Record League Defeat: 0-12 v Small Heath, Div 2, 11 April 1903

Oldest Player in League Match:

Youngest Player in League Match:

Most Consecutive Undefeated League Matches: 21 1968-69	**League Matches Without a Win:** 15 1904
Longest Run of Undefeated Home League Matches: 33 1931-33	**Away League Matches:** 17 1939 & '46
Longest Run Without Home League Win: 8 1954	**Away League Win:** 44 1902-03, 1904-05, 1923-24
Most Consecutive League Wins: 10 1947	**Home League Wins:** 11 1934-35
Most Consecutive League Defeats: 9 1905	**Away League Wins:** 9 1939 & '46

Footnote: In between those seasons in the away matches without a win column, Doncaster were either an ex or non-League club

Club Statistician for the Directory: K Harrison

DONCASTER ROVERS

PLAYERS NAME Ht Wt Birthdate	Honours	Birthplace Transfers	Clubs	League	Milk Cup	FA Cup	Other Comps	League	Milk Cup	FA Cup	Other Comps
GOALKEEPERS											
Andy Rhodes 6.1 12.9 23.8.64		Doncaster F	Barnsley (A) Doncaster Rovers	36	2	1					
Mark Samways 6.0 11.12		Doncaster	Doncaster Rovers								
DEFENDERS											
Tony Brown† 6.2 12.7 17.9.58		Thacklex F F	Thacklex Leeds United Doncaster Rovers	24 49	2		3	1 1			
David Cusack 6.1½ 13.12 6.6.56		Rotherham £50,000 £30,000 £40,000	Sheffield Wednesday Southend United Millwall Doncaster Rovers	92+3 186 98 43	7 13 8 1	7 7 2 1	3	1 17 9 2		1	1
Paul Holmes 5.10 11.0 18.2.68		Wortley	Doncaster Rovers (A)	5		1		1			
Glen Humphries 6.0 12.0 11.8.44	EY	Hull	Doncaster Rovers (A)	150+5	10+1						
John Philliben 5.11 12.0 14.3.64	SY	Stirling £70,000	Stirling Albion Doncaster Rovers Cambridge United (L)	109 65+5 6	11 2+1	2 2	3	1 1	1		
Dave Rushbury 5.10 11.0 20.2.56		Wolverhampton £60,000 £60,000 £50,000 £15,000 £10,000	WBA (A) Sheffield Wednesday Swansea City Carlisle United Gillingham Doncaster Rovers	28 111+1 51+1 120+9 12 45	8 6 7 2	3 13 6 8 1	3	7 1			
Mike Stead 5.8 11.7 28.2.57	Div. 4, 81	West Ham F F	Tottenham Hotspur (A) Swansea City (L) Southend United Doncaster Rovers	14+1 5 296	19	6	5	5			
MIDFIELD											
John Deakin 5.7 10.2 29.9.66		Wortley F	Barnsley (A) Doncaster Rovers	13+1		0+1	0+3				
Jim Dobbin 5.9½ 10.7 17.9.63	SY	Dunfermline £25,000	Celtic Motherwell Doncaster Rovers	2 2 51+8	1 3	2	2	9	1		
Brian Flynn 5.4 12.3 12.10.55	W (66), U23 (2)	Port Talbot £175,000 £60,000	Burnley (A) Leeds United Burnley Cardiff City Doncaster Rovers	115+5 152+2 76+4 32	11+1 12 7+1 2	5 6+1 12 1	4 4	8 11 10	2 2 2	1 1	
FORWARDS											
Brian Deane 6.3 12.7 7.2.68		Leeds	Doncaster Rovers	2+1							
Mike Nesbitt 5.10 11.7 8.1.69	EY	Doncaster	Doncaster Rovers (A)	2+3		1+1		1			
Colin Russell 5.7 10.7 21.1.61		Liverpool F	Liverpool (A) Huddersfield Town Stoke City (L) Bournemouth Doncaster Rovers	0+1 64+2 11 65+3	10 6	4+1 9	4	23 2 14	1 2	1 2	3
Neil Woods 6.0 11.11 30.7.66		York	Doncaster Rovers	38+10	2	2	4+3	10			2

ADDITIONAL CONTRACT PROFESSIONALS

APPRENTICES

NON-CONTRACT PLAYERS
Sean Joyce

BELLE VUE GROUND Doncaster

Record Attendance: 37,149 v Hull City, Div 3 (N), 2 Oct 1948

Record Receipts: £22,000 v QPR, FA Cup Round 3, 5 Jan 1985

Season Tickets: Stand: £65; Terrace £48; Ground £42

Executive Box Season Tickets: None

Cost of Stand Tickets: £4.50 (£2.00 Juniors if accompanied by an adult); **Terraces:** £3.00 (£1.50 Junior/OAP); **Ground:** £2.50 (£1.50 Junior/OAP)

Match and Ticket Information: No advance bookings except for Cup matches

Car Parking: Very large car and coach park adjacent to ground; entrance direct from Great North Road

Nearest Railway Station: Doncaster (0302 20191)

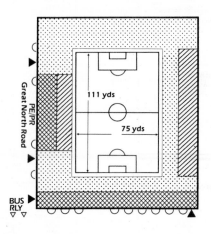

How to get to the ground

From North: Use Motorway A1 (N) then A638 S.P. Doncaster into Town Centre, then follow signs Bawtry (A638) and in 1.2m at roundabout take 3rd exit into Bawtry Road for Doncaster FC
From East: Use Motorway M18 then A630 S.P. Doncaster. In 2.7m at roundabout take 1st exit A18. In 2.5m at roundabout take 1st exit into Bawtry Road A638 for Doncaster FC
From South: Use motorway M1 then M18, take junction 3 S.P. Doncaster A6182 in 2m at roundabout take 3rd exit S.P. Racecourse and Scunthorpe A18. In 1¼m at roundabout take 3rd exit A638 into Bawtry Road for Doncaster FC
From West: Use A635 in Doncaster Town Centre then follow signs Bawtry A638 and in 1.2m at roundabout take 3rd exit into Bawtry Road for Doncaster FC

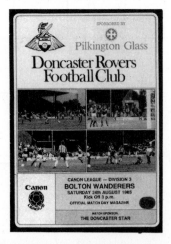

Price of 1986-7 Programme: 50p
Number of Pages: 32
Subscriptions: Apply to club for details

Local Newspapers: Doncaster Star, Yorkshire Post

Local Radio Stations: Radio Hallam, Radio Sheffield

EVERTON

Division 1

In spite of the disappointment in being pipped so narrowly to the League and FA Cup double, this was another splendid season for Everton who ultimately took runners-up place in both competitions.

Following their League Championship and European Cup Winners Cup successes of the previous season, the Toffees had been hoping to land further trophies this time. With new striker Gary Lineker, signed from Leicester for £800,000, soon finding his best form, optimism was high during the early weeks — in spite of the fact that Manchester United's fine start left Everton some way behind in the First Division.

Early season injuries to centre-back Derek Mountfield and midfield grafter Peter Reid led to re-arrangements in the side. Pat Van den Hauwe switched from left to centre defence, with Neil Pointon being signed from Scunthorpe to take the number three shirt.

Manager Howard Kendall had a different sort of problem in attack. Adrian Heath and Graeme Sharp both challenged for the right to partner Lineker up front but, with Sharp winning the verdict, Heath moved into midfield and was often nominated as substitute.

With 65 goals between them, Lineker and Sharp formed the most successful striking partnership in the First Division.

When the side became settled, Everton began to make up ground in the League and by the end of January they had closed the gap on United to just two points.

Peter Reid was welcomed back into the side in February but no sooner had he settled than Kevin Sheedy was sidelined.

A serious injury to goalkeeper Neville Southall looked likely to kill the club's championship chances but Bobby Mimms deputised so superbly that the side was in no way weakened.

The title chase really hotted up in the closing weeks. Liverpool became Everton's chief challengers but West Ham, Chelsea and Manchester United were all deeply involved. The Toffees' hopes finally ended with their defeat by a late goal at Oxford at the end of April.

That set-back was partially offset by the fact that the Toffees had reached the FA Cup final for the third time in succession, this time facing Liverpool in the first all-Merseyside confrontation at Wembley in this competition.

When Gary Lineker gave Everton a first-half lead, it looked as if the trophy would return to Goodison but an inspired second-half performance by their deadly local rivals eventually gave Liverpool a 3-1 victory.

A useful run in the Milk Cup eventually ended, rather surprisingly, with a 1-2 home defeat in a fourth round replay against Chelsea after the Toffees had drawn 2-2 at Stamford Bridge.

The European ban on all English clubs denied Everton the chance of winning the European Champions Cup. There was some small consolation in reaching the final of the Screen Sport Super Cup — a tournament hurriedly arranged for the six clubs that should have been in Europe — and their opponents in that will, once again, be Liverpool.

Back Row L to R: Paul Wilkinson, Derek Mountfield, Fred Barber, Neville Southall, Mick Stowell, Bobby Mimms, Kevin Langley, Ian Marshall. **Second Row:** John Clinkard (Physio), Jason Danskin, Robert Coyle, Pat Van Der Hauwe, Paul Bracewell, Peter Reid, Neil Pointon, Neil Adams, Graeme Sharpe, Alan Harper, Paul Power, Colin Harvey (Coach), Mick Heaton (Coach). **Sitting:** Warren Aspinall, Adrian Heath, Gary Stevens, Kevin Sheedy, Howard Kendall (Manager), Kevin Ratcliffe, Trevor Steven, Kevin Richardson, Peter Billinge, Derek Walsh. **Front Row:** Apprentices (names not available at time of going to press).

EVERTON

DIVISION ONE: 2nd   **FA CUP:** RUNNERS-UP   **MILK CUP:** 4th ROUND   **SUPER CUP:** FINALISTS

MATCH	DATE		COMPE-TITION	VENUE	OPPONENTS	RESULT		HALF TIME	L'GUE POS'N	GOALSCORERS/GOAL TIMES	ATTEN-DANCE
1	A	17	CL	A	Leicester City	L	1-3	1-1		Mountfield 24	(16,932)
2		20	CL	H	W.B.A.	W	2-0	0-0		Heath 64, 81	26,788
3		24	CL	H	Coventry City	D	1-1	0-1	11	Sharp 85	27,691
4		26	CL	A	Tottenham Hotspur	W	1-0	0-0	7	Lineker 75	(29,720)
5		31	CL	H	Birmingham City	W	4-1	2-1	5	Lineker 3 11, 22, 85, Steven (pen) 79	28,066
6	S	3	CL	A	Sheffield Wednesday	W	5-1	1-1	3	Mountfield 37, Steven 58, Lineker 62, 72, Heath 84	(30,065)
7		7	CL	A	Queens Park Rangers	L	0-3	0-2	4		(16,544)
8		14	CL	H	Luton Town	W	2-0	1-0	2	Sheedy 44, Sharp 86	26,419
9		21	CL	H	Liverpool	L	2-3	0-3	6	Sharp 51, Lineker 82	51,509
10		28	CL	A	Aston Villa	D	0-0	0-0	5		(22,048)
11		5	CL	H	Oxford United	W	2-0	1-0	4	Sharp 43, Bracewell 89	24,553
12		12	CL	A	Chelsea	L	1-2	1-2	6	Sheedy 43	(27,634)
13		19	CL	H	Watford	W	4-1	1-0	6	Heath 45, Sharp 60, 81, Bracewell 67	26,425
14		26	CL	A	Manchester City	D	1-1	0-1	6	Heath 35	(28,807)
15	N	2	CL	A	West Ham United	L	1-2	0-0	7	Steven 60	(23,844)
16		9	CL	H	Arsenal	W	6-1	2-0	6	Lineker 19, 38, Heath 50, 80, Steven 62, Sharp 84	28,620
17		16	CL	A	Ipswich Town	W	4-3	1-2	6	Heath 34, Sharp 47, Sheedy 58, Steven 78	(13,910)
18		23	CL	H	Nottingham Forest	D	1-1	0-0	6	Bracewell 76	27,860
19		30	CL	A	Southampton	W	3-2	1-1	6	Lineker 29, Heath 75, Steven 83	(16,917)
20	D	7	CL	A	W.B.A.	W	3-0	2-0	6	Sheedy 3, Van den Hauwe 15, Lineker 52	(13,600)
21		14	CL	H	Leicester City	L	1-2	1-0	6	Richardson 26	23,347
22		21	CL	A	Coventry City	W	3-1	0-0	6	Lineker 50, 86, Sharp 62	(11,059)
23		26	CL	H	Manchester United	W	3-1	2-1	5	Sharp 18, 47, Lineker 41	42,551
24		28	CL	H	Sheffield Wednesday	W	3-1	2-0	3	Stevens 19, Lineker 24, 85	41,536
25	J	1	CL	A	Newcastle United	D	2-2	1-0	2	Steven 26, Sharp (pen) 82	(27,820)
26		11	CL	H	Queens Park Rangers	W	4-3	1-2	2	Sharp (pen) 44, 67, Lineker 55, Wilkinson 56	26,015
27		18	CL	A	Birmingham City	W	2-0	1-0	2	Lineker 36, 46	(10,502)
28	F	1	CL	H	Tottenham Hotspur	W	1-0	0-0	1	Reid 82	33,178
29		11	CL	H	Manchester City	W	4-0	1-0	1	Lineker 3, 5, 46, 56, Sharp 76	30,006
30		22	CL	A	Liverpool	W	2-0	0-0	1	Ratcliffe 74, Lineker 76	(45,445)
31	:	1	CL	H	Aston Villa	W	2-0	0-0	1	Sharp 76, Lineker 82	32,133
32		16	CL	H	Chelsea	D	1-1	0-1	1	Sheedy 86	30,145
33		22	CL	A	Luton Town	L	1-2	0-0	1	Foster (og) 46	(10,949)
34		29	CL	H	Newcastle United	W	1-0	1-0	1	Richardson 29	4,116
35		31	CL	A	Manchester United	D	0-0	0-0	2		(51,189)
36	A	12	CL	A	Arsenal	W	1-0	0-0	2	Heath 80	(28,251)
37		15	CL	A	Watford	W	2-0	1-0	2	Lineker 45, Sharp 89	(18,960)
38		19	CL	H	Ipswich Town	W	1-0	0-0	2	Sharp 64	39,055
39		26	CL	A	Nottingham Forest	D	0-0	0-0	2		(30,171)
40		30	CL	A	Oxford United	L	0-1	0-0	3		(13,939)
41		3	CL	H	Southampton	W	6-1	4-0	3	Mountfield 9, Steven 28, Lineker 3 29, 34, 63, Sharp 51	33,057
42		5	CL	H	West Ham United	W	3-1	1-0	2	Lineker 42, 47, Steven (pen) 72	40,073

Best Home League Attendance: 51,509 v Liverpool 21/9   **Smallest:** 23,347 v Leicester City 14/12   **Av Home Att: 32,388**

Goal Scorers: **Compared with 84-85: +263**

League (87): Lineker 30, Sharp 19, Heath 10, Steven 9 (1 pen), Sheedy 5, Bracewell 3, Mountfield 3, Richardson 2, Ratcliffe 1, Reid 1, Stevens 1, Van den Hauwe 1

1985-86

Southall	Stevens	Van den Hauwe	Ratcliffe	Mountfield	Reid	Steven	Lineker	Sharp	Bracewell	Sheedy	Heath	Harper	Marshall	Atkins	Bailey	Richardson	Wilkinson	Mimms	Pointon	Billinge	Aspinall	Referee	
1	2	3	4	5	6	7	8	9	10	11*	12											B Stevens	1
1	2	3				7	8	9	10	11*	6	4	5	12								F Roberts	2
1	2	3	4			7	8		10	11	9	6	5									G Aplin	3
1	3	2	6			11	10	12	8	7	9*	4	5									J Bray	4
1	2	3	4	5	6	7	8		10	11	9											J McAulay	5
1	2	3	4	5	6*	7	8	9	10	11	12											G Courtney	6
1	2	3	4	5	6	7	8	9	10		11											A Gunn	7
1	2	3	4	5		7	8	12	10	11	9*	6										P Tyldesley	8
1	2	3	4			7	8	9	10	11	12	6	5*									D Shaw	9
1	2	3	4			7	8	9	10	11		6	5									R Groves	10
1	2	3	4			7	8	9	10	11		6	5									G Tyson	11
1	2	5	4			7	8	9	10	11	12				3	6*						V Callow	12
1	2	3	4			7	8	9	10	11	6	12	5*									K Hackett	13
	2	5	4			7	8	9	10	11*	6	3				12		1				K Redfern	14
1	2	5	4			7	8	9	10	11	6	3										A Seville	15
1	5		4			7	8	9	10	11	6	2							3			L Robinson	16
1	5	3	4			7	8	9	10	11	6	2										D Axcell	17
1	5	3	4			7	8	9	10	11	6	2										J Lovatt	18
1	5	3	4			7	8		10	11	6	2					9					M Cotton	19
1	5	3	4			7	8		10*	11	6	2					9		12			R Gifford	20
1	2		4			7	8	9	10		6		5			11			3			N Ashley	21
1	2	5	4			7	8	9	10	11	6								3			M Scott	22
1	2	5	4			7	8	9	10	11	6								3			D Allison	23
1	2	5	4			7	8	9	10	11	6*	12							3			M Peck	24
1	2	5	4			7	8	9	10*	11	6	12							3			C Seel	25
1	2	5	4				8	9		11*	6	7				10	12		3			T Holbrook	26
1	2	5	4			7	8	9			11	6				10			3			J Deakin	27
1	2	5	4		6	7	8	9	10							11			3			M Reed	28
1	2	5	4		6	7	8	9	10	11*						12			3			D Phillips	29
1	2	5	4		6	7	8	9	10*			12				11			3			J Worrall	30
1	2	5	4		6	7	8	9		10						11			3			G Aplin	31
1	2	4		5		7	8	9	10	11	12					6*			3			D Hutchinson	32
1		4		5		7	8	9	10	11*		2	12			6			3			R Lewis	33
	2	3*	4	5	6	7	8	9	10		12					11		1				M Heath	34
	2	3	4	5	6	7	8*	9	10		12					11		1				K Hackett	35
	2	3	4	5	6	7	8*	9	10		12					11		1				G Napthine	36
	2	3	4	5	6	7		9	10		12					11		1				K Barratt	37
	2	3	4	5	6	7		9	10	8						11		1				A Saunders	38
	2	3	4	5	6	7	8	9	10	11*	12							1				B Hill	39
	2	3	4	5		7	8	9	10	11	12					6*		1				D Shaw	40
	2	3	4	5	6	7	8	9	10*	11	12							1				P Willis	41
	2	3	4			7	8*			11	10					6	9	1		5	12	G Courtney	42
32	41	40	39	15	15	41	41	35	38	31	24	17	8		1	16	3	10	14	1		League Appearances	
								2			12	4	1	1		2	1	1			1	Substitute Appearances	

Also Played:
Players on Loan:
Departures: Bailey (Newcastle Utd), Lineker (Barcelona), Wakenshaw (Carlisle Utd)

'TOFFEEMEN'

Formed: 1878
Turned Professional: 1885 **Ltd Co:** 1892

Previous Managers: Since 1946: Theo Kelly Cliff Britton Ian Buchan John Carey Harry Catterick Billy Bingham Gordon Lee
Honours: Champions Div 1, 1890-1, 1914-5, 1927-8, 1931-2, 1938-9, 1962-3, 1969-70, 1984-5 Champions Div 2, 1930-1 FA Cup Winners 1906, 1933, 1966, 1984
League Career: Founder Members of Football League 1888 Relegated to Div 2 1929-30 Promoted to Div 1 1930-1 Relegated to Div 2 1950-1 Promoted to Div 1 1953-4
Colours: Blue shirts with white neckband, white shorts, blue stocking with white tops
Change Colours: All yellow
Reserves League: Central **'A' Team:** Lancashire

CLUB RECORDS

Most Appearances for Club: Ted Sagar: 465, 1929-53
Most Capped Player: Alan Ball, 39 for England
Record Goalscorer in a Match: Jack Southworth, 6 v WBA, Div 1, 30.12.1893
Record League Goalscorer in a Season: Bill 'Dixie' Dean, 60, Div 1, 1927-28 **In All Competitions:** Bill 'Dixie' Dean, 63 (League 60 + FA Cup 3)
Record League Goalscorer in a Career: Bill 'Dixie' Dean, 377 (League 349 + FA Cup 28)
Record Transfer Fee Received: £2.5 million from Barcelona for Gary Lineker, June 1986
Record Transfer Fee Paid: £800,000 to Leicester City for Gary Lineker, June 1985
Best Performances: League: Champions (8) **FA Cup:** Winners (4) **League/Milk Cup:** Finalists 1976-77, 1983-4 **European Cup:** Quarter Final **European Cup Winners Cup:** Winners **Fairs Cup/UEFA CUP:** 3rd Round
Most League Points: 66, Div 1, 1969-70 (3pts for win) 90 Div 1 1985 **Most League Goals:** 121, Div 2, 1930-1
Record League Victory: 9-1 v Manchester C, Div 1, 03.09.1906 9-1 v Plymouth Argyle, Div 2 1930
Record League Defeat: 4-10 v Tottenham Hotspur, Div 1, 11 Oct 1958
European Competitions Entered: European Cup 1963-4, 1970-1 European Cup Winners Cup 1966-7, 1984-5 European Fairs Cup: 1962-3, 1964-5, 1965-6 UEFA Cup 1978-9, 1979-80
Oldest Player in League Match: Ted Sagar 42
Youngest Player in League Match: Joe Royle, 16
Most Consecutive Undefeated League Matches: 20 1978

Longest Run of Undefeated Home League Matches: 39 1961-63
Longest Run Without Home League Win: 12 1957-58
Most Consecutive League Wins: 12 1894
Most Consecutive League Defeats: 6 1929-30, 1958, 1972

League Matches Without a Win: 14 1937
Away League Matches: 11 1908-09
Away League Win: 35 1970-72
Home League Wins: 15 1930-31
Away League Wins: 6 1908, 1915-19

Club Statistician for the Directory: G Smailes

EVERTON HONOURS ARE SHOWN ON PAGE 565

EVERTON

PLAYERS NAME Ht Wt Birthdate	Honours	Birthplace Transfers	Clubs	APPEARANCES				GOALS			
				League	Milk Cup	FA Cup	Other Comps	League	Milk Cup	FA Cup	Other Comps
GOALKEEPERS											
Frederick Barber 6.0 11.0 26.8.63		Ferryhill	Darlington (A) Everton	103	5	10	5				
Bobby Mimms 6.2½ 12.10 12.10.63	CS 86, EU21 (3)	York £15,000	Halifax Town (A) Rotherham United Everton Notts County (L)	83 10 2	7	3 2	1 1				
Neville Southall 6.1 12.2 16.9.58	W (27), Div. 1, 85, FAC84, CS84, 85, ECWC 85	Llandudno	Winsford United Bury Everton Port Vale (L)	39 152 9	22	5 22	9				
DEFENDERS											
Alan Harper 5.8 9.7 1.11.60	EY, FAC 84, CS 84, 86, ECWC 85, Div. 1, 85	Liverpool	Liverpool (A) Everton	53+10	11+1	5+3	3+1	1		1	
Ian Marshall 6.1 12.12 20.3.66	CS 86	Liverpool	Everton (A)	8+1	1+1					1	
Derek Mountfield 6.1 12.7 2.11.62	E B (1), EU21 (1), Div. 1, 85, FAC 84, ECWC 85, CS, 84, 85	Liverpool £30,000	Tranmere Rovers (A) Everton	26 84	1 12	1 18	9	1 16	2	2	
Neil Pointon 5.10 12.10 28.11.64		Churchwarsop	Scunthorpe United (A) Everton	159 14+1	9	13 5	4	2	1		
Paul Power 5.10 11.6 30.10.53	E B (1), CS 86	Manchester	Manchester City Everton	358+7	37+1	28		26	2	6	
Kevin Ratcliffe* 5.11 10.2 4.12.62	W (36), U21 (2), YS, FAC 84, CS 84, 85, 86, Div. 1, 85, ECWC 85	Newcastle	Everton (A)	193+1	26	23	9	2			
Gary Stevens 5.11 10.12 27.3.63	E (14), E B (1), U21 (1), Div. 1, 85, FAC 84, ECWC 85, CS 84, 85	Barrow	Everton (A)	151+1	23	28	9	6		3	
Pat Van Der Hauwe 5.10 10.6 16.12.60	W (3), Div. 1, 85, ECWC 85, CS 85	Dew Dermonde £100,000	Birmingham City Everton	119+4 71	12 8	5 14	5	1 1		1	
Dave Watson 5.11½ 11.12 20.11.61	E (6), U21 (7), MC 85, Div. 2, 86	Liverpool £100,000 £1,200,000	Liverpool Norwich City Everton	212	19	18		11	2	1	
MIDFIELD											
Paul Bracewell 5.8 10.9 19.7.62	E (3), U21 (13), Div. 1, 85, ECWC 85, CS 84, 85	Stoke £250,000 £425,000	Stoke City (A) Sunderland Everton	123+6 38 75	6 4 9	6 2 14	8	5 4 5	2		1
Kevin Langley 6.1 11.0 24.5.64	FRT 85, CS 86	St. Helens £100,000	Wigan Athletic (A) Everton	156+4	10	14	13	6	1	1	
Peter Reid 5.8 10.8 20.6.56	E (9), U21 (6), Div. 1, 85, FAC 84, ECWC 85, CS 85	Huyton £60,000	Bolton Wanderers (A) Everton	223+3 92+1	18+1 13+1	17 24	9	23 5	1 1	1	1
Kevin Richardson 5.7 10.2 4.12.62	FAC 84, Div. 1, 85 ECWC 85, CS 84, 86	Newcastle	Everton	94+14	10+3	14	3+1	15	3	1	
Kevin Sheedy 5.7 10.11 21.10.59	EI (8), U21 (1), Y, Div. 1, 85, CS 84, 85, 86, ECWC 85	Builth Wells	Hereford United (A) Liverpool Everton	47+4 1+2 128	2+1 2 19	2 21	4	4 30	6	8	2
Trevor Steven 5.10 11.7 29.9.63	E (13), U21 (2), Div. 1, 85, FAC 84, ECWC 85, Div. 3, 82, CS 84, 85, 86	Berwick	Burnley (A) Everton	74+2 104+4	10 12	13 16	9	11 22	1 1	4 2	2
FORWARDS											
Neil Adams 5.8 10.1 23.11.66	CS 86	Stoke £150,000	Stoke City Everton	31+1	3	1		4			
Warren Aspinall		£150,000	Wigan Athletic (A) Everton Wigan Athletic (L)	22+11 0+1 18	1	2+3 2	1+4	10 12		2	2 2
Adrian Heath 5.6 10.1 11.1.61	EU21 (8), Div. 1, 85, FAC 84, CS 84, 85, 86	Stoke £700,000	Stoke City (A) Everton	94+1 136+13	9 21	4 15+4	4	16 49	6	1 5	1
Graeme Sharp 6.1 11.8 16.10.60	S (7), U21 (1), Div. 1, 85, FAC 84, ECWC 85, CS 85, 86	Glasgow £125,000	Dumbarton Everton	37+3 167+10	2 25	3 25+2	8	17 76	7	2 4	4
Paul Wilkinson 5.11½ 11.0 30.10.64	EU21 (4), CS 86	Louth £250,000	Grimsby Town Everton	69+2 7+1	10	4+2 1		27 3	5	1	

ADDITIONAL CONTRACT PROFESSIONALS

Peter Billinge (D), Robert Coyle (D), Jason Danskin (M), Michael Stowell (G), Derek Walsh (M)   **Player of the Year:** Gary Lineker (now Barcelona)

APPRENTICES

Andrew Rooney

NON-CONTRACT PLAYERS

Chris Birtwhistle, James Carberry, John Ebbrall, Lee Elliott, Philip Farrelly, Phil Jones, Sam Jones, Tony Ward, Ed Youds

GOODISON PARK Liverpool L4 4EL

Record Attendance: 78,299 v Liverpool, Div 1, 18 Sept 1948

Record Receipts: £274,555 v Liverpool v Manchester United, FA Cup Semi-Final, 13 Apr 1985

Season Tickets: Stand: £93, £84, £75 Ground: £46

Executive Box Season Tickets: £7,000 pa — Box for 10 persons with restaurant and waiter service in boxes

Cost of Stand Tickets: £5.20, £4.70, £4.20
Terraces: £2.60

Match and Ticket Information: Box office open each weekday 0900 to 1700. Except matches v Liverpool reserved stand seats can be purchased for all home fixtures any time during season by post (with remittance and SAE) or personally from the box office at the Goodison Road side of the ground. Postal applications to the Box Office Manager

Car Parking: Extensive parking is available on site at the corner of Prior and Utting Avenue

Nearest Railway Station: Liverpool (Lime Street) 051-709 9696

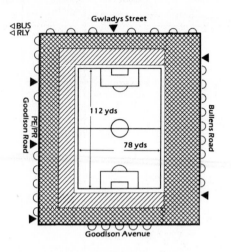

Gwladys Street

◁ BUS
◁ RLY

Goodison Road

PE/PR

112 yds

78 yds

Bullens Road

Goodison Avenue

How to get to the ground

From North: Use Motorway M6 until junction 28 then follow signs Liverpool on A58 then A580 and forward into Walton Hall Avenue for Everton FC
From East, South: Use Motorway M6 then M62 until end of Motorway then turn right A5058 into Queens Drive. In 3.7m turn left A580 into Walton Hall Avenue for Everton FC
From West: Use Mersey Tunnel into Liverpool City Centre, then follow signs Preston A580 into Walton Hall Avenue for Everton FC

Price of 1986-7 Programme: 50p
Number of Pages: 32
Subscriptions: £21.90 (postage paid UK), £29.70 (Scandinavia), £29.70 (surface USA, Canada, Saudi Arabia, Australia), £52.80 (airmail USA, Canada), £55.80 (airmail Australia), £45.90 (airmail Saudi Arabia)

Local Newspapers: Liverpool Daily Post. Liverpool Echo

Local Radio Stations: Radio Merseyside, Radio City

EXETER CITY   Division 4

With Exeter City having to apply for re-election it would be easy to despair, but a closer study of the season shows signs that the club is coming to the end of a bleak few years.

The cheery welcome that is received when a visit to St James's Park is made, proves that the appointment of Mike Cosway as General Manager was a step in the right direction. Mike Radford's work with the Youth policy is producing several very promising first team possibles.

After a short spell as Chairman, Byron Snell departed, the majority shareholding reverting to the previous Chairman, now Club President Clifford Hill, who after considering a takeover bid from the man who had been sacked from the board, millionaire, Dan McCauley, he decided to transfer the shares to Exeter businessman Ivor Doble. No doubt the supporters would be delighted if the board ended the long takeover saga, by inviting Dan McCauley back to the fold.

Colin Appleton with very little money at his disposal, juggled with various combinations to produce a side that conceded very few goals. Apart from the top four only Scunthorpe in Division 4 let in less goals. Sadly the goalscoring was the opposite, with only the bottom club Torquay managing to net fewer goals, a fact that led to the application for re-election, which could have been avoided with just two more goals.

A run of 13 games with only one defeat raised hopes of ending in a comfortable mid table position, but only one point from the last five games sealed the club's fate.

The Milk Cup saw local rivals Plymouth Argyle disposed of before a visit to Aston Villa and exit. In the FA Cup after defeating Cardiff City and Bristol City. City travelled to Goodison, and a memorable game with eventual finalists Everton, in which all that attended had to admit that Everton were lucky to have avoided a visit to St James's Park with the solitary late goal.

With just a little more bite up front City must surely turn the corner, and see better results next term.   Jim Blackstone

Back Row L to R: Chris Small, Richard Hancox, Clive Nelson, Warren Hadley, Richard Smeath, Richard Massey, Jamie Harris, Scott Hiley, Mark Robson. **Second Row:** Mike Radford (Youth Development Officer), Steve Pugh, Mel Gwinnett, Sean Priddle, Nicky Marker, Andrew Watson, Keith Viney, Aiden MaCaffery, John Shaw, Darren Gale, Colin Appleton (Team Manager). **Third Row:** Paul Batty, Steve Harrower, Brendon O'Connell, Tony Kellow, Dean Roberts, Danny Keough, Gary Jackson.

EXETER CITY

DIVISION FOUR: 21st   **FA CUP:** 3rd ROUND   **MILK CUP:** 2nd ROUND

MATCH	DATE		COMPE-TITION	VENUE	OPPONENTS	RESULT		HALF TIME	L'GUE POS'N	GOALSCORERS/GOAL TIMES	ATTEN-DANCE
1	A	17	CL	H	Port Vale	W	1-0	1-0		Ling 26	2,868
2		20	MC1/2	A	**Plymouth Argyle**	L	1-2	0-1		Pratt (pen) 71	(4,754)
3		24	CL	A	Aldershot	L	0-4	0-2	17		(1,411)
4		26	CL	H	Northampton Town	L	1-2	1-0	21	Kellow 30	2,392
5	S	4	MC1/2	H	**Plymouth Argyle**	W	2-0	2-0		Kimble 19, Marker 44	3,362
6		7	CL	H	Southend United	L	0-2	0-1	23		2,213
7		14	CL	A	Wrexham	D	1-1	0-0	22	Harrower 71	(2,417)
8		18	CL	H	Scunthorpe United	W	2-0	1-0	17	Kellow (pen) 14, Harrower 47	1,723
9		20	CL	A	Cambridge United	D	1-1	0-1	18	Gale 86	(1,479)
10		25	MC2/1	H	**Aston Villa**	L	1-4	0-2		Kellow 54	5,325
11		28	CL	H	Tranmere Rovers	W	1-0	0-0	16	Gale 83	1,881
12	O	1	CL	A	Swindon Town	L	1-2	0-1	18	Ling 70	(3,118)
13		4	CL	A	Colchester United	D	1-1	0-1	17	Gale 47	(3,927)
14		9	MC2/2	A	**Aston Villa**	L	1-8	0-6		Crawford 49	(7,678)
15		12	CL	H	Orient	D	1-1	0-0	16	Pratt 85	2,057
16		19	CL	A	Mansfield Town	L	1-2	1-1	18	Viney 16	(3,289)
17		23	CL	H	Halifax Town	W	1-0	0-0	15	Kellow (pen) 48	1,719
18		26	CL	H	Hartlepool United	L	1-2	0-1	18	Kellow (pen) 63	1,934
19	N	2	CL	A	Peterborough United	D	1-1	0-1	18	Kellow (pen) 89	(2,200)
20		5	CL	A	Rochdale	D	1-1	0-0	19	Harrower 58	(1,243)
21		9	CL	H	Chester City	L	1-3	1-2	19	Ling 2	1,888
22		16	FAC1	H	**Cardiff City**	W	2-1	1-0		Gale 29, 55	2,772
23		23	CL	A	Burnley	L	1-3	0-1	19	Ling 79	(2,874)
24		30	CL	H	Preston North End	W	3-0	1-0	18	Gale 9, 52, Pratt 53	1,896
25	D	7	FAC2	A	**Bristol City**	W	2-1	1-1		Kellow 26, Crawford 57	(8,052)
26		13	CL	A	Crewe Alexandra	W	1-0	0-0	18	Ling 62	(1,108)
27		21	CL	H	Aldershot	W	2-0	1-0	17	Crawford 3, McNichol 80	1,954
28	J	1	CL	A	Hereford United	L	1-4	0-0	17	Harrower 75	(3,157)
29		5	FAC3	A	**Everton**	L	0-1	0-0			(22,726)
30		11	CL	H	Stockport County	W	1-0	1-0	15	Harrower 41	2,161
31		14	FRT S	H	**Wolverhampton W.**	D	1-1	0-1		McNichol 69	1,278
32		17	CL	A	Port Vale	D	0-0	0-0	16		(3,382)
33		25	CL	H	Wrexham	L	0-1	0-1	16		2,397
34	J	29	FRT S	A	**Torquay Utd**	L	0-1	0-0			1,046
35		31	CL	A	Southend United	L	0-2	0-2	17	,	(1,653)
36	F	4	CL	A	Halifax Town	L	0-1	0-0	18		(1,004)
37		8	CL	H	Mansfield Town	L	0-1	0-1	19		1,798
38		21	CL	H	Cambridge United	D	0-0	0-0	19		1,369
39	F	24	CL	A	Stockport County	D	1-1	1-1	18	Ward 19	(2,048)
40		28	CL	A	Tranmere Rovers	W	1-0	0-0	17	McNichol 60	(1,031)
41	M	4	CL	H	Swindon Town	L	0-3	0-2	17		2,291
42		8	CL	H	Colchester United	D	2-2	0-1	16	Ward 50, Crawford 67	1,520
43		15	CL	A	Orient	D	2-2	2-2	19	Crawford 34, Cornwell (og) 43	(2,220)
44		19	CL	H	Peterborough United	W	1-0	0-0	17	McNichol 54	1,460
45		22	CL	A	Hartlepool United	D	0-0	0-0	18		(2,480)
46		26	CL	H	Torquay United	D	2-2	2-2	19	Ward 3 22, 56, 65, Harrower 4	2,420
47		29	CL	H	Hereford United	W	3-2	1-1	17	McNichol 34, Viney 54, Kellow (pen) 75	1,989
48	A	1	CL	A	Torquay United	W	2-1	0-0	16	Kellow 55, Ling 77	(2,555)
49		4	CL	H	Rochdale	W	2-0	2-0	11	Kellow (pen) 17, Jackson 27	1,713
50		8	CL	A	Northampton Town	D	2-2	1-2	11	Ling 30, Friar (og) 77	(2,213)
51		12	C!	A	Chester City	L	1-2	0-1	13	Kellow 72	(2,899)
52		19	CL	H	Burnley	L	0-2	0-1	14		2,019
53		22	CL	A	Scunthorpe United	L	0-1	0-0	16		(1,343)
54		26	CL	A	Preston North End	D	2-2	1-1	16	Ling 15, McNichol 80	(3,132)
55	M	3	CL	H	Crewe Alexandra	L	1-2	1-1	21	Jackson 32	1,777

Best Home League Attendance: 2,868 v Port Vale 17/8   **Smallest:** 1,369 v Cambridge Utd 21/2   **Av Home Att:** 1,975

Goal Scorers: **Compared with 84-85:** −373

League (47):	Kellow 9 (6 pens), Ling 8, Harrower 6, Gale 5, McNichol 5, Crawford 3, Ward 3, Jackson 2, Pratt 2, Opponents 2, Viney 2
Milk Cup (5):	Crawford 1, Kellow 1, Kimble G 1, Pratt 1 (pen), Marker 1
FA Cup (4):	Gale 2, Crawford 1, Kellow 1
FRT (1):	McNichol 1

Shaw	Kirkup (NC)	King	McNichol	McCaffery	Marker	Ling	Kellow (NC)	Morgan	Pratt	Crawford	Viney	Walsh (NC)	Impey	Kimble A. (L)	Kimble G. (L)	Williams (NC)	Jackson	Harrower	Gale	Gwinnett	Webber (NC)	Keough	Johnson (NC)	Massey (NC)	Referee	
1	2	3	4	5	6	7	8	9	10	11															R Hamer	1
1	2	3*	4	5	6	7	8	9	10	11	12														J Deakin	2
1	2	3	4	5	6*	7		9	10	11		8	12												B Hill	3
1	2		4	5	6	7	8	9	10	11	3														R Gifford	4
1	2		4		6	7		9			11	3		5	8	10									J Martin	5
1	2		4		6	7		9			11	3		5	8	10*	12								H King	6
1		2	4		6	7		9	12		3			5		10*	8	11							T Jones	7
1		2	4		6	7		9			3			5			10	11	8						K Cooper	8
1	2		4		6	7		9	12		3			5			8	11*	10						M Bodenham	9
1	2		4		6	7*		9	12	11	3			5			8		10†						M Cotton	10
1	2		4		6			9	7	11	3			5			8		10						R Milford	11
1	2		4		6	7		9		11	3			5			8		10						P Vanes	12
	2		4		6	7		9		11	3			5			8		10	1					D Reeves	13
1	2		4		6	7		9	10	11	3			5			8*	12							P Tyldesley	14
1		12	4		6	7		9*	10	11	3			5			8	2							R Groves	15
1			4	12	6	7				11	3			5			8	2	10			9*			T Mills	16
1			4		6	7		9		11	3			5			8	2	10						B Stevens	17
1			4		6	7		9		11*	3			5			8	2	10			12			C Downey	18
1		2	4	12				9	10	11	3		5				8*	7				6			L Robinson	19
1			4	2	6	7		9*	12	11	3		5				8		10						R Nixon	20
1		8*	4		6	7		9	12	11	3		5					2	10						H Taylor	21
1			4	5	6	7				11	3						8	2	9			10			R Hamer	22
1			4		6	7	12			11	3		5				8	2*	9			10			J Lloyd	23
			4		6	7	2*		12	11	3		5				8	9		1		10			J Ball	24
1		7	4	3	6	10			12	11			5				2	8*				9			H King	25
1			4		6	7	9*		12	11	3		5				8	2	10						A Robinson	26
1			4		6	7	12	9*		11	3		5				8	2	10						A Seville	27
1			4	5	6	7*	12			11	3						8	2	9			10			E Scales	28
1			4	5	6	7	12			11	3						8	2*	9			10			R Milford	29
1			4	5	6	7				11	3						8	2	9			10			B Stevens	30
1			4	5	6	7				11*	3					12	8	2	9			10			R Groves	31
1			4		6	7				11	3		5				8	2	9			10			R Guy	32
1			4		6	7	12			11*	3		5				8	2	9			10			G Ashby	33
1			4		6	7			12	11	3		5				8*	2	9			10			R Hamer	34
1	11		4			7	12		10		3		5					2	9*			8			A Ward	35
1	11*		4		6				10		3		5				12	2	9			8			N Ashley	36
1			4		6	7	9		10*		3		5				8	2	12			11			J Deakin	37
1			4	5	6	7					3						8	2	11			10	9		V Callow	38
1			4	5	6	7	12			11	3						8	2				10	9*		K Lupton	39
1			4	5	6	7				11	3						8	2				10	9		K Baker	40
1			4	5	6	7				11	3						8	2				10	9		R Gifford	41
1			4	5	6	7	12		8*	11	3							2				10	9		K Cooper	42
1			4	5	6	7	8			11	3							2				10	9		B Hill	43
1			4	5	6	7				11	3							2				10	9	8	J Martin	44
1			4	5	6	7				11	3							2				10	9	8	C Trussell	45
1			4	5	6	7	12			11	3							2				10	9	8*	G Ashby	46
1			4	5		7				11	3						8	2				10	9	6	R Hamer	47
1			4	5	6	7				11	3						8	2				10	9		M James	48
1			4	5	6	7				11	3						8	2				10	9		D Hedges	49
1			4	5	6	7				11	3						8*	12				10	9	2	I Borrett	50
1				5	6	7				11	3	4						12				10	9	8	T Simpson	51
1		12	4	5		7	9			11*	3						8	2				10			M Dimblebee	52
1		10	4	5		7	12			9	3		6				8*	2				11			M Heath	53
1		9	4	5	6	7	12			11	3						8	2				10*			T Mills	54
1		10	4	5		7	9			11	3		6				8	2							M Reed	55
44	8	9	45	31	40	45	25	4	10	32	45		26	1	1	1	31	36	17	2	1	31	14	5	League Appearances	
	2		2		8		8					1				1	1	2	1			1			Substitute Appearances	
4	4	1	4	1	4	4	3	2	2+1	4	3+1		3	1	1		2	0+1	1						Milk Cup Appearances	
3		3	3	3	3	1	0-2			3	3						3	3	2			3			FA Cup Appearances	
2		2	2	2	2	2	0-1				2		1+1				1	2				2	2		FR Trophy Appearances	

Players on Loan: Kimble A., Kimble G., (Charlton), Ward (Lincoln)

Departures: Morgan (Bristol Rovers), Pratt (Chard T), Impey, McNichol (Torquay Utd), Ling (Swindon Town)

'THE GRECIANS'

Formed: 1904
Turned Professional: 1908 **Ltd Co:** 1908

Previous Managers: 1908-23 Arthur Chadwick   1923-7 Fred Mavin   1927-30 David Wilson   1930-6 Billy McDevitt   1936-9 Jack English   1945-52 George Roughton   1952-3 Norman Kirkman   1953 Tim Ward   1953-7 Norman Dodgin   1957-8 Bill Thompson   1958-60 Frank Broome   1960-2 Glen Wilson   1962-3 Cyril Spiers   1963-5 Jack Edwards   1965-6 Ellis Stuttard   1966-7 Jock Basford   1967-9 Frank Broome   1969-76 John Newman   1977-9 Bobby Saxton   1979-83 Brian Godfrey   1983-4 Gerry Francis   1984-85 Jim Iley

Honours: None

League Career: Elected to Div 3 1920   Transferred to Div 3 (S) 1921   Relegated to Div 3 1957-8   Promoted to Div 3 1963-4   Relegated to Div 4 1965-6   Promoted to Div 3 1976-7   Relegated to Div 4 1983-4

Colours: Red and white striped shirts, black shorts, black stockings with red and white tops
Change Colours: Yellow shirts, green shorts and yellow stockings
Reserves League: South West Counties   **'A' Team:** Devon & Exeter Premier

---

CLUB RECORDS

Most Appearances for Club: Arnold Mitchell (1952-66): League 494 + FA Cup 17 + League Cup 4 **Total 515**
Most Capped Player: Dermot Curtis, 1 (Eire)   **For England:** None
Record Goalscorer in a Match: James Bell, 6 v Weymouth, 1st Prelim Round FA Cup 1908   Fred Whitlow v Crystal Palace, Div 3 (S) Cup 1934
Record League Goalscorer in a Season: Fred Whitlow, 34, Div 3 (S), 1932-3, 1963-6, 1967-73   **In All Competitions:** Rod Williams 36 (League 32, FA Cup 4)
Record League Goalscorer in a Career: Tony Kellow, 110   **In All Competitions:** Tony Kellow, 131 (League 110, FA Cup 11, League Cup 10)
Record Transfer Fee Received: £105,000 from Blackpool for Tony Kellow, Nov 1978
Record Transfer Fee Paid: £65,000 to Blackpool for Tony Kellow, Mar 1980
Best Performances: League: 8th Div 3 1979-80   **FA Cup:** 6th Round Replay 1930-1   **League/Milk Cup:** Never beyond 4th Round
Most League Points: 62 in Div 4, 1976-7   **Most League Goals:** 88, Div 3 (S), 1932-3
Record League Victory: 8-1 v Coventry, Div 3 (S), 4 Dec 1926   8-1 v Aldershot, Div 3 (S), 4 May 1935
Record League Defeat: 0-9 v Notts County, Div 3 (S), 16 Oct 1948   0-9 v Northampton Town, Div 3 (S), 12 Apr 1958
Most Consecutive Undefeated League Matches: 12 1947-48, 1964, 1977

Longest Run of Undefeated Home League Matches: 21 1932-33
Longest Run Without Home League Win: 9 1984
Most Consecutive League Wins: 7 1977
Most Consecutive League Defeats: 7 1936 1984

League Matches Without a Win: 18 1984
Away League Matches: 8 1964
Away League Win: 26 1936-37
Home League Wins: 13 1932-33
Away League Wins: 6 1977

Club Statistician for the Directory: Jim Blackstone

EXETER CITY

PLAYERS NAME Ht Wt Birthdate	Honours	Birthplace Transfers	Clubs	APPEARANCES				GOALS			
				League	Milk Cup	FA Cup	Other Comps	League	Milk Cup	FA Cup	Other Comps
GOALKEEPERS											
Mel Gwinnett		Stourbridge	Peterborough H.								
6.1½ 11.8 14.5.63			Hereford United	1							
			Bradford City								
			Exeter City	2							
John Shaw		Stirling	Leeds United (A)								
6.1 13.7 4.2.54			Bristol City	295	13	14	4				
			Exeter City	44	4	3	6				
DEFENDERS											
Aidan McCaffery	EY	Newcastle	Newcastle United (A)	57+2	3+1	5		4		1	
5.11 12.0 30.8.57		£25,000	Derby County	31+6	4			4			
		£110,000	Bristol Rovers	183+1	18	12	4	11	1		
			Bristol City (L)	6							
			Torquay United (L)	3							
			Exeter City	31+2	1	3	2				
Nick Marker		Budleigh Salterton	Exeter City	142+6	7	6	6	2			1
6.0 12.11 3.6.65											
Steve Pugh		Wolverhampton	Wolverhampton W. (A)								
5.10 11.3 1.2.65		F	Torquay United	50+4	3	2+1	1	1			
		F	Exeter City								
Keith Viney*		Portsmouth	Portsmouth (A)	160+6	14	13		3			
5.11 11.9 26.10.57		F	Exeter City	176	9+1	8	7	7	1		
Andy Watson		Barnsley	Huddersfield Town	17							
5.11 12.0 30.3.67		F	Exeter City								
MIDFIELD											
Paul Batty		Edington	Swindon Town (A)	102+6	2	12	3+1	7		2	
5.7 10.7 9.1.64			Chesterfield	24+2	2	2	1			1	
		F	Exeter City								
Steve Harrower†		Exeter	Dawlish								
5.8 11.1 9.10.61			Exeter City	71+11	0+1	5	6	8			
Gary Jackson		Swinton	Manchester City (A)	8							
5.6 10.6 30.9.64		F	Exeter City	31+1	2	3	1	2			
Danny Keough		Rawtenstall	Manchester United (A)								
5.8 9.11 31.1.63			Exeter City	31+1		3	2				
FORWARDS											
Darren Gale	WU21 (1)	Port Talbot	Swansea City (A)	28+11	2	2	0+2	6	1	1	
5.10½ 12.13 25.10.63			Exeter City	17+1	1	2	2	5		2	
Tony Kellow (NC)		Falmouth	Exeter City	107	12	7		40	4	4	
5.10 12.7 1.5.52		£105,000	Blackpool	57	4	3		23		1	
		£60,000	Exeter City	140+3	10	10	2	61	5	6	1
			Plymouth Argyle (NC)	8+2	3			2			
			Swansea City (NC)	0+1							
			Newport County (NC)	18+3			2+1	8			1
			Exeter City (NC)	25+8	3	1	2	9	1	1	
Brendan O'Connell		London	Portsmouth								
5.10 10.9 12.11.66		F	Exeter City								
Sean Priddle			Wimbledon								
			Exeter City								
Dean Roberts		Mexborough	Bolton Wanderers (A)			1					
5.11 10.10 12.1.67		F	Exeter City								

ADDITIONAL CONTRACT PROFESSIONALS
Symon Burgher, Jamie Harris, Scott Hiley, Richard Massey.

APPRENTICES
Mark Robson, Chris Small, Richard Smeath

NON-CONTRACT PLAYERS
Warren Hadley, Richard Hancox, Clive Nelson

ST. JAMES PARK Exeter EX4 6PX

Record Attendance: 20,984 v Sunderland, FA Cup 6th Round replay, 4 March 1931

Record Receipts: £32,007 v Newcastle United, FA Cup 5th Round replay, 18 Feb 1981

Season Tickets: Stand seat: £84, Ground £50

Executive Box Season Tickets: None

Cost of Stand Tickets: £4, **Terraces:** £2.40

Match and Ticket Information: Tickets usually bookable up to two weeks prior to each match. Clubhouse 'Center Spot' behind goal at opposite end to St James Road, refreshments in grandstand and 'Cowshed'

Car Parking: Limited street parking

Nearest Railway Station: Exeter St Davids (0392 33551)

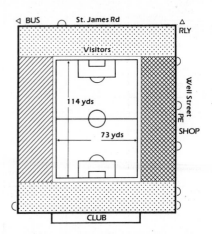

How to get to the ground

From North: Use Motorway M5 until junction 30. Leave Motorway and follow signs City Centre along Sidmouth Road for Heavitree Road, then at roundabout take 4th exit into Western Way and at roundabout take 2nd exit into Old Tiverton Road, then take next turning left into St. James Road for Exeter FC

From East: Use A30 (S.P. Exeter) into Heavitree Road, then at roundabout take 4th exit into Western Way and at Roundabout take 2nd exit into Old Tiverton Road, then take next turning left into St James Road for Exeter FC

From South and West: Use A38 and follow signs City Centre into Western Way and at roundabout take 3rd exit passing Coach Station, then at next roundabout take 2nd exit into Old Tiverton Road, and turn left into St. James Road for Exeter City

Price of 1986-7 Programme: 50p
Number of Pages: 24

Local Newspaper: Express & Echo, Western Morning News, Sunday Independent

Local Radio Stations: BBC Radio Devon, Devon Air

FULHAM

Division 3

Chairman
David W Bulstrode

Directors
Robert Noonan

Secretary
Mrs Y Haines (01-736 6561)

Commercial Manager
Miss J Baldwin (01-736 4634)

General Administrator
D Barnard

Player Manager
Ray Lewington

Coach
Jack Burkett

Youth Team Coach
Brian Nicholls

Physiotherapist
David Galley MSRG, SRRG

Fulham got entangled in the relegation net in December and, after that, never really looked capable of getting away from it. The policy of selling off most of their best players — forced upon them by economic necessity — caught up on them and now they are back in the 3rd Division.

Manager Ray Harford, who had produced so many outstanding players who were destined to bring success to rival clubs, could no longer wave his magic wand. And it was no surprise when the relegation axe finally fell.

In less than two years, Fulham had sold a complete midfield of Ray Lewington (to Sheffield United), Robert Wilson (Millwall) and Ray Houghton (Oxford) plus a complete attack of Gordon Davies (now with Manchester City following a spell with Chelsea), Leroy Rosenoir (QPR) and Tony Sealy (Leicester).

Further problems arose for Mr Harford when Welsh international defender Jeff Hopkins and England under-21 centre-back Paul Parker, plus midfielder Peter Scott, were sidelined by injuries.

Though the Cottagers started brightly with a couple of home wins, away results were poor. They failed to score in any of their opening six away matches.

A crushing 0-3 home defeat by Middlesbrough, who had not previously won away, put the Cottagers into the bottom three danger zone in mid-December. They never escaped.

From the start of February, Fulham suffered a run of 13 winless games that produced but three solitary points from drawn matches. By then they were 12 points behind the safety mark with only six games to play.

An astonishing 3-2 win at Brighton, one of the promotion-chasing clubs, raised faint hopes but defeat in their next two games cut off all the escape routes.

In the end they finished bottom, nine points behind the nearest club.

The highlight of a bitterly disappointing season came when they were drawn against neighbouring Chelsea in the 3rd Round of the Milk Cup. The tie at Stamford Bridge came to a dramatic end when Mike Hazard gave Chelsea the lead with only two minutes to go. But Fulham were awarded a penalty moments later and Cliff Carr converted it to earn a replay.

Craven Cottage's best crowd of 20,190 turned up for the replay but Fulham lost 0-1.

Manager Ray Harford left at the end of the season when the club appointed Ray Lewington as player-manager.

Back Row L to R: John Marshall, Jeff Hopkins, Tim Houghton, Shaun Gore, Jim Hicks, Dean Coney, David Harlow. **Middle Row:** David Galley (Physio), Gary Barnett, Peter Scott, Roderick Braithwaite, Brian Cottington, Laurence Batty, Chris Pike, Glen Thomas, Leo Donnellan, Kenneth Achampong, Jack Burkett (1st Team Coach). **Front Row:** Gary Elkins, Paul Parker, Wayne Kerrins, David Bulstrode (Chairman), Ray Lewington (Player/Manager), Clifford Carr, Kevin Hoddy.

FULHAM

DIVISION TWO: 22nd   **FA CUP:** 3rd ROUND   **MILK CUP:** 3rd ROUND

MATCH	DATE		COMPE-TITION	VENUE	OPPONENTS	RESULT		HALF TIME	L'GUE POS'N	GOALSCORERS/GOAL TIMES	ATTEN-DANCE
1	A	17	CL	H	Leeds United	W	3-1	0-1		Scott 78, 79, Coney 87	5,772
2		24	CL	A	Middlesbrough	L	0-1	0-0	12		(5,366)
3		26	CL	H	Grimsby Town	W	2-1	1-1	8	Sealy 37, 71	4,873
4		31	CL	A	Barnsley	L	0-2	0-1	12		(5,197)
5	S	7	CL	H	Portsmouth	L	0-1	0-0	16		9,331
6		14	CL	A	Crystal Palace	D	0-0	0-0	16		(6,381)
7		17	CL	H	Sheffield United	L	2-3	1-0	17	Coney 16, Sealy 79	4,259
8		21	CL	A	Blackburn Rovers	L	0-1	0-0	18		(5,241)
9		23	MC2/1	H	Notts County	D	1-1	0-1		Barnett 73	2,324
10		28	CL	H	Brighton & H. A.	W	1-0	0-0	15	Carr (pen) 66	5,861
11	O	5	CL	H	Shrewsbury Town	W	2-1	0-0	13	Marshall 48, Pike 52	3,412
12		8	MC2/2	A	Notts County	W†	4-2	0-2		Barnett 50, Marshall 71, Pike 96, Coney 110	(3,054)
13		12	CL	A	Wimbledon	L			14		(5,953)
14		15	FMC	A	Shrewsbury Town	D	0-0	0-0			(1,340)
15		19	CL	H	Stoke City	W	1-0	1-0	14	Pike 38	4,007
16		22	FMC	H	Oxford United	L	0-2	0-1			2,022
17		29	MC3	A	Chelsea	D	1-1	0-0		Carr (pen) 89	(19,669)
18	N	2	CL	H	Sunderland	L	1-2	1-0	18	Coney 34	5,795
19		6	MC3R	H	Chelsea	L	0-1	0-1			20,190
20		9	CL	A	Hull City	L	0-5	0-3	19		(6,122)
21		23	CL	A	Huddersfield Town	W	3-1	1-1	17	Barnett (pen) 25, 79, Carr 55	(4,650)
22		30	CL	H	Oldham Athletic	D	2-2	0-1	17	Coney 63, 86	3,544
23	D	7	CL	H	Bradford City	W	4-1	1-0	16	Barnett (pen) 24, Marshall 64, Achampong 81, Carr 89	3,724
24		14	CL	A	Leeds United	L	0-1	0-0	18		(9,998)
25		21	CL	H	Middlesbrough	L	0-3	0-2	20		3,512
26		28	CL	A	Sheffield United	L	1-2	0-1	21	Barnett 47	(10,421)
27	J	1	CL	H	Norwich City	L	0-1	0-0	21		7,463
28		11	CL	A	Portsmouth	D	1-1	1-0	21	Coney 20	(13,666)
29		13	FAC3	A	Sheffield United	L	0-2	0-0			(7,004)
30		18	CL	H	Barnsley	W	2-0	0-0	21	Carr 55, Scott 90	3,580
31	F	1	CL	A	Grimsby Town	L	0-1	0-0	21		(3,572)
32		18	CL	A	Stoke City	L	0-1	0-1	21		(6,449)
33	M	8	CL	A	Shrewsbury Town	L	1-2	0-2	21	Barnett 88	(2,563)
34		11	CL	H	Blackburn Rovers	D	3-3	1-0	21	Barnett 32, Marshall 60, Coney 69	2,555
35		15	CL	H	Wimbledon	L	0-2	0-2	22		(6,209)
36		18	CL	A	Millwall	D	1-1	0-0	21	Achampong 47	(5,645)
37		22	CL	H	Crystal Palace	L	2-3	1-0	22	Coney 11, 66	4,951
38		29	CL	A	Norwich City	L	1-2	1-2	22	Coney 29	(17,320)
39		31	CL	H	Millwall	L	1-2	0-1	22	Pike 79	4,581
40	A	2	CL	A	Bradford City	L	1-3	1-1	22	Burvill 18	(5,564)
41		5	CL	A	Sunderland	L	2-4	0-3	22	Coney 60, Burvill 71	(11,338)
42		8	CL	H	Carlisle United	L	0-1	0-1	22		2,134
43		12	CL	H	Hull City	D	1-1	0-0	22	Achampong 65	2,795
44		16	CL	A	Brighton & H.A.	W	3-2	1-1	22	Braithwaite 2, Dreyer 56, Pike 78	(6,255)
45		19	CL	A	Carlisle United	L	1-2	1-2	22	Dreyer (pen) 36	(3,818)
46		22	CL	H	Charlton Athletic	L	0-3	0-1	22		5,587
47		26	CL	H	Huddersfield Town	W	2-1	1-1	22	Scott 25, Doyle (og) 67	2,877
48		29	CL	A	Charlton Athletic	L	0-2	0-0	22		(9,393)
49	M	3	CL	A	Oldham Athletic	L	1-2	0-0	22	Coney 53	(2,510)

Best Home League Attendance: 9,331 v Portsmouth 7/9   **Smallest:** 2,134 v Carlisle Utd 8/4   **Av Home Att:** 4,611

Goal Scorers: **Compared with 84-85:** −1,567

League (45): Coney 12, Barnett 6 (2 pen), Carr 4 (1 pen), Scott 4, Pike 4, Achampong 3, Marshall 3, Sealy 3, Dreyer 2 (1 pen), Borvill 2, Braithwaite 1, Opponent 1

Milk Cup (6): Barnett 2, Carr 1 (pen), Coney 1, Marshall 1, Pike 1

FA Cup (-):

FM Cup (-):

1985-86

Peyton	Cottington	Carr	Scott	Hopkins	Parker	Marshall	Donnellan	Sealy	Coney	Houghton	Achampong	Hicks	Batty	Elkins	Grew (L)	Barnett	Pike	Kerrins	Thomas	Fishenden (L)	Gore (NC)	Dreyer (L)	Burvill (L)	Braithwaite	Smith (A)	Referee	
1	2	3	4	5	6	7	8	9	10	11																V Callow	1
1	2	3	4*		6	7	8	9	10	11	12	5														K Hackett	2
	2	3	4		6	7	8	9	10	11		5	1													R Groves	3
	2	3	4	5	6	7		9	10	11	12		1	8												D Scott	4
	2*	3	4	5	6	7	12	9	10	11		8			1											I Borrett	5
	2	3	4†	5		7		9	10			8		6	1	11										M Bodenham	6
	2	3	4	5		7		9	10			8		6	1	11*	12									D Axcell	7
	2	3	4	5		7			10			8		6	1	11	12	9								D Hutchinson	8
1	2	3	4	5		7			10			8		6		11	12	9*								**D Hedges**	9
1	2	3		5		7			9			8	6	12		4*	10	11								J Bray	10
1	2	3		5	4	7			9*			8	6			11	10	12								A Robinson	11
1	2	3	4	5	6	7			9			8				11	10									**D Shaw**	12
1	2	3	4	5	6	7			9			12	8*			11	10									J Moules	13
1	2	3	4	5		7						8	6			11	10	9*	12							**I Hendrick**	14
1	2	3	4	5	6	7			9			8				11	10									H King	15
1	2*	3	4	5	6	7			9		12	8				11	10									**J Martin**	16
1	2	3	4	5	6	7			9			8				11	10									**L Shapter**	17
1	2	3	4	5	6	7			9			8				11	10									M Scott	18
1	2	3	4	5	6	7			9			8				11	10									**A Seville**	19
1	2			5	6	7						8	4	3		11	10	9								L Dilkes	20
1	2	10	4	5	6	7			9			8		3		11										K Lupton	21
1	2	10	4	5	6	7			9			8		3				11								J Ashworth	22
1	2	10	4	5	6	7			9			8		3		11										J Deakin	23
1	2*	10	4	5	6	7			9			8		3		11		12								A Saunders	24
1	2	10	4	5	6	7			9			8		3		11										A Gunn	25
1	2	10	4	5	6	7						8	9	3		11										R Bridges	26
1	2	10	4	5	6	7	11					8		3*		12		9								M James	27
1	2	10	4	5	6	7	3	9				8				11										R Hamer	28
1	2	10	4	5	6	7	3*	9				8		12		11										**T Jones**	29
1	2	10	4	5	6	7	3	9				8				11										D Axcell	30
1	2	3		5	6	7	10	9				8				11		4								I Borrett	31
1	2	3		5	6	7	10	9				8*				11	12	4								J Bray	32
1	2	3	4		6	7	8	9						5*		11	10	12								G Napthine	33
1	2	3	4		6	7	10	9				12		5*		11	8									I Hemley	34
1	2	3	4		6	7	8	9				12				11	10					5*				K Barratt	35
1	2	3	4	6*	5		8	9	7							11	10	12								K Baker	36
1	2	3	4	6	5		8*	9	7							11	10	12								M Dimblebee	37
1	2	3	4	6*	5	7		9				8				11	12						10			T Holbrook	38
1	2	3	4*	5					9			8	6			11	12						10	7		D Vickers	39
1	2			5			8*	9								11	10	3				6	7	4	12	I Hendrick	40
1	2	3		5			12	9	8							11	10					6*	4	7		M Peck	41
1	2	3			6	4*		9	7							11	12					5	10	8		L Shapter	42
1	2	3		5		4			7							11	9	10				6	8			K Cooper	43
1	2	3*			6	4			7							11	9	10				5	8	12		J Moules	44
1	2	7			3	5	4*			11						12	9	10					6	8		N Midgeley	45
1	2		4		7	3		9								11	10	8				5	6			H Taylor	46
1	2		4		3	5		9	7							11	10						6	8		H Taylor	47
1	2		4	3	5	8		9								7	10	11					6			K Barratt	48
1	2		4		5			9	8*							7	10	11				6	3		12	C Seel	49
36	42	35	32	23	30	42	21	7	37	5	30	10	2	12	4	34	20	11		3	5	12	9			League Appearances	
							2		5					1		2	6	5						2	1	Substitute Appearances	
4	4	4	4	4	3	4			4		4			1		4	3+1	1								Milk Cup Appearances	
1	1	1	1	1	1	1			1		1				0+1	1										FA Cup Appearances	
2	2	2	2	2	1	2	1		1		2	1+1				2	2	1	0+1							FM Cup Appearances	

Players on Loan: Fishenden (Wimbledon), Burvill (Reading), Dreyer (Oxford), Grew (Ipswich)

Departures: Houghton (Oxford Utd), Rosenoir (QPR), Sealy (Leicester City), Peyton (Bournemouth)

FULHAM F.C.

'THE COTTAGERS'

Formed: 1879
Turned Professional: 1898 **Ltd Co:** 1903

Previous Managers: Jack Peart   Frank Osborne   Doug Livingstone   Bill Dodgin (Snr)   Bedford Jezzard
Vic Buckingham   Bobby Robson   Johnny Haynes   Bill Dodgin (jnr)   Alec Stock   Bobby Campbell
Malcolm Macdonald   Ray Harford   Ray Lewington
Honours: Champions Div 2, 1948-9   Champions Div 3 (S) 1931-2
League Career: Elected to Div 2 1907   Relegated to Div 3 (S) 1927-8
Promoted to Div 2 1931-2   Promoted to Div 1 1948-9   Relegated to Div 2 1951-2
Promoted to Div 1 1958-9   Relegated to Div 2 1967-8   Relegated to Div 3 1968-9
Promoted to Div 2 1970-1   Relegated to Div 3 1979-80   Promoted to Div 2 1981-2
Relegated to Div 3 1985-6
Colours: White shirts with black trim, black shorts and white stockings with black trim
Change Colours: Red shirts, red shorts and red stockings with three red hoops on tops
Reserves League: Football Combination   **Youth League:** S E Counties

CLUB RECORDS

Most Appearances for Club: Johnny Haynes: 594, 1952-70
Most Capped Player: Johnny Haynes, 56, England
Record Goalscorer in a Match: Fred Harrison, 5 v Stockport County, Div 2, 05.09.1908   Bedford Jezzard, 5 v Hull City,
Div 2, 08.10.1955   Jimmy Hill 5 v Doncaster Rovers (a), Div 2 15.03.1958   Steve Earl 5 v Halifax Town, Div 3
16.09.1969
Record League Goalscorer in a Season: Frank Newton, 41, Div 3 (S), 1931-2
Record League Goalscorer in a Career: Bedford Jezzard, 154, 1948-56
Record Transfer Fee Received: £333,333 from Liverpool for Richard Money, May 1980
Record Transfer Fee Paid: £150,000 to Orient for Peter Kitchen, Feb 1979   £150,000 to Brighton for Teddy Maybank,
Dec 1979
Best Performances: League: 10th Div 1 1959-60   **FA Cup:** Finalists 1974-5   **League/Milk Cup:** 5th Round 1967-8,
1970-1
Most League Points: 78, Div 3, 1981-2   **Most League Goals:** 111, Div 3 (S), 1931-2
Record League Victory and Most Goals Scored in a League Match: 10-1 v Ipswich Town, Div 1, 26 Sept 1963
(Fulham also beat Torquay 10-2, Div 3, 10 Sept 1931)
Most Goals Scored in a Cup Tie: 8-3 v Luton Town (a), 1st Round FA Cup, 1907-8
Record League Defeat: 0-9 v Wolverhampton Wanderers, Div 1, 16 Sept 1959
Oldest Player in League Match: Jimmy Sharpe 40, April 1920 (Played in an emergency and scored his only goal for the club
many years after officially retiring!)
Youngest Player in League Match: Tony Mahoney, 16 yrs, 1976
Most Consecutive Undefeated League Matches: 15 1957, 1970
Longest Run of Undefeated Home League Matches: 28 1921-22
Longest Run Without Home League Win: 8 1950, 1951-52,
1961-62, 1980
Most Consecutive League Wins: 8 1963
Most Consecutive League Defeats: 11 1961-62

League Matches Without a Win: 15 1950
Away League Matches: 9 1958, 1970

Away League Win: 31 1964-66
Home League Wins: 12 1959
Away League Wins: 5 1966, 1981

Club Statistician for the Directory: Dennis Turner

FULHAM

PLAYERS NAME Ht Wt Birthdate	Honours	Birthplace Transfers	Clubs	APPEARANCES League	Milk Cup	FA Cup	Other Comps	GOALS League	Milk Cup	FA Cup	Other Comps
GOALKEEPERS											
Lawrence Batty 6.0½ 13.7 15.2.64		London	Fulham	2							
John Vaughan 5.10 13.1 26.6.64		Isleworth	West Ham United (A)								
			Charlton Athletic (L)	6							
			Bristol Rovers (L)	6							
			Wrexham (L)	4							
			Bristol City (L)	2							
		£20,000	Fulham								
DEFENDERS											
Cliff Carr* 5.4 10.4 19.6.64	EU21 (1)	London	Fulham (A)	115+5	13	4	2	13	1	1	
David Harlow 5.10 9.6 2.11.67		Epsom	Fulham (A)								
Jim Hicks 6.1 12.0 16.9.60		Ipswich	Exeter City	3							
		F	Oxford United								
		F	Fulham	10			1+1				
Jeff Hopkins 6.0 11.9 14.4.64	W (14), U21 (5), Y	Swansea	Fulham (A)	167+6	23	9	2	3	1	1	
John Marshall 5.9 11.4 18.8.64		Surrey	Fulham (A)	92+7	9	3	2	4	1		
Paul Parker 5.7 10.8 4.4.64	EU21 (8), Y	Essex	Fulham (A)	109+13	12	7	1				
Glen Thomas 6.0½ 11.6 6.10.67		Hackney	Fulham (A)								
MIDFIELD											
Rod Braithwaite 5.9½ 10.10 19.12.65		Middlesex	Fulham (A)	0+2				1			
Brian Cottington 5.8 10.4 14.2.65		London	Fulham (A)	46+4	4	1	2				
Leo Donellan 5.10 11.5 19.1.65	EY	Brent	Chelsea (A)								
		F	Orient (L)	6		2	2				
		F	Fulham	21+2		1					
Gary Elkins 5.8½ 11.0 4.5.66	EY	Wallingford	Fulham (M)	33+1	2	0+1					
Kevin Hoddy 5.10¼ 11.1 6.1.68		Essex	Fulham (A)								
Peter Scott 5.8 11.0 1.10.63		London	Fulham	81+3	7	4	2	9	1		
Ray Lewington 5.6 10.5 7.9.56		Lambeth	Chelsea (A)	80+5	3	4		4			
			Vancouver W.								
			Wimbledon (L)	23	2	5					
		£50,000	Fulham	134+2	17	9+1		15	2	1	
		£40,000	Sheffield United	36	3	2					
		£20,000	Fulham								
FORWARDS											
Kenny Achampong 5.8 10.4 26.6.66		London	Fulham (A)	40+5	4	1	2	6			
Gary Barnett 5.5 9.4 11.3.63		Stratford	Coventry City (A)								
			Oxford United	37+6	6+2	3	1	9			
			Wimbledon (L)	5							
			Fulham	35+6	4	1	2	7	2		
Dean Coney 6.0 12.6 18.9.63	EU21 (3)	Dagenham	Fulham (A)	173+3	20	7	1	46	6	6	
Wayne Kerrins 5.7 11.1 5.8.65		Essex	Fulham	11+7	1			1			
			Port Vale (L)	6+2							
Chris Pike 6.2 12.7 19.10.61		Cardiff	Barry Town								
			Fulham	20+6	3+1		2	4	2		

ADDITIONAL CONTRACT PROFESSIONALS

APPRENTICES

Tim Houghton, Justin Skinner, Gary Smith (0+1Lge)

NON-CONTRACT PLAYERS

Dennis Bailey, Shaun Gore (5Lge)

CRAVEN COTTAGE Stevenage Road, Fulham, London SW6   Capacity: 25,680

Record Attendance: 49,335 v Millwall, Div 2, 8 Oct 1938

Smallest Home Attendance for a First Class Match: 1,800 v Lincoln City, Div 2, March 1915

Record Receipts: £80,247 v Chelsea, Div 2, 8 Oct 1983

Season Tickets: Stand: £94.50 to £126.00; Ground: £63.00

Executive Club Season Tickets: Riversiders' Club £168.00

Cost of Stand Tickets: £4.50, £5.00, £5.50, £6.00; **Terraces:** £3.00 (enclosure £3.20) (half price for children and OAPs on terrace and in enclosure)

Match and Ticket Information: Computerised. Bookable daily during season 9.30-4.30

Car Parking: Ample in adjacent streets

Nearest Railway Station: Putney

Nearest Tube Station: Putney Bridge

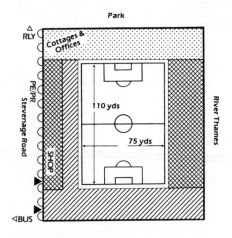

How to get to the ground

From North: Use Motorway M1 S.P. London then take North Circular Road A406 S.P. West to Neasden follow signs Harlesden A404, then Hammersmith A219 and at Broadway follow sign Fulham and in 1m turn right into Harbord Street and at end turn left for Fulham FC
From East & South: Use South Circular Road A205 and take sign Putney Bridge A219. Cross bridge and follow sign Hammersmith and in 0.5m turn left into Bishops Park Road and at end turn right for Fulham FC
From West: Use Motorway M4 then A4 and in 2m branch left S.P. other routes into Hammersmith Broadway, follow sign Fulham A219 and in 1m turn right into Harbord Street and at end turn left for Fulham FC

Price of 1986-7 Programme: 60p
Number of Pages: 28

Local Newspaper: Fulham Chroncicle

Local Radio Stations: LBC, Capital Radio

GILLINGHAM

Division 3

For the second consecutive season, Gillingham just missed out on their aim to bring Second Division football to Priestfield Stadium for the first time in their history.

Like last term, the club were always up with the leaders from the very start but in the final analysis, the month of March put paid to their ambitions. Despite gaining maximum points over the Easter period, only four points were gained out of a possible 18. All this after Manager Keith Peacock has won the Divisional 'Manager of the Month' award for February!

Peacock made just two pre-season signings, Karl Elsey from Cardiff City and David Byrne from Vauxhall Opel League side Kingstonian. Elsey went on to be ever present for the season, as did the evergreen Ron Hillyard in goal and Elsey's full-back partner Mel Sage who was just about everybody's choice as 'Player of the Year'.

Like the previous season, Gillingham had no problems scoring goals with Eire International Tony Cascarino leading the way with 21 goals and that after missing the final 11 games through injury. The rest of the goals were shared near enough by Martin Robinson, Dave Shearer, Derek Hales, Mark Weatherly, Terry Cochrane, Dave Mehmet and Karl Elsey.

Although defensively Gillingham were sound, it was in midfield where the team came unstuck on a few occasions. Hopefully this summer Keith Peacock would have solved the problem by signing a midfield player who can dominate the proceedings.

In the Cup competitions, Second Division highflyers Portsmouth put paid to the club's quest for glory in the Milk Cup whilst in the FA Cup, the club reached the third round for the the fourth time in five years. Convincing victories over Northampton Town and non-League side Bognor Regis Town brought Third Division promotions rivals Derby County to Priestfield. The match ended in a 1-1 draw and in the replay the 'Rams' needed extra-time to reach the 4th Round. Gillingham did gain revenge over Derby by defeating them in Group 8 (Southern Section) of the Freight Rover Trophy and after a 1-1 draw with Brentford met Cambridge United in the Quarter-Finals. A 2-0 home win over them gave the club a visit to Bristol City and it was only a controversial penalty decision at Ashton Gate that ended their chance of glory last season.

Like Portsmouth in the Second Division, can Gillingham do it this season at the third time of asking?   Roger Triggs

Back Row L to R: Karl Elsey, Howard Pritchard, Tony Cascarino, Mel Eves, Paul Collins. **Middle Row:** Mark Weatherly, Keith Oakes, Mark Beeney, Paul Taylor (Assistant Manager), Ron Hillyard, Joe Hinnigan, Martin Robinson. **Front Row:** Bill Collins (First Team Trainer), Russell Musker, Graham Westley, Paul Haylock, Keith Peacock (Manager), Graham Pearce, David Shearer, Trevor Quow, John Gorman (Youth Team Coach).

GILLINGHAM

DIVISION THREE: 5th   **FA CUP:** 3rd ROUND   **MILK CUP:** 2nd ROUND   **FRT:** AREA SEMI-FINAL

MATCH	DATE	COMPE-TITION	VENUE	OPPONENTS	RESULT	HALF TIME	L'GUE POS'N	GOALSCORERS/GOAL TIMES	ATTEN-DANCE
1	A 17	CL	A	Lincoln City	L	0-1	0-1			(2,099)
2	20	MC1/1	A	Southend United	D	1-1	0-0		Shearer 51	(2,008)
3	24	CL	H	Darlington	D	1-1	1-1	19	Sage 27	2,929
4	26	CL	A	Bristol City	W	2-1	0-1	13	Cascarino 49, 87	(6,052)
5	31	CL	H	Bolton Wanderers	W	2-1	0-1	9	Hinnigan 65, Cascarino 77	2,773
6	S 3	MC1/2	H	Southend United	W	2-0	1-0		Cascarino 3, 87	3,106
7	7	CL	A	Notts County	D	1-1	0-1	8	Byrne 89	(3,624)
8	14	CL	H	Chesterfield	D	1-1	0-1	10	Cascarino 54	3,101
9	17	CL	H	Wigan Athletic	W	2-0	1-0	7	Mehmet (pen) 30, Elsey 86	3,401
10	21	CL	A	Bury	W	2-1	1-1	4	Mehmet 9, Cochrane 46	(2,802)
11	24	MC2/1	H	Portsmouth	L	1-3	0-2		Cascarino 48	4,617
12	28	CL	H	York City	L	1-2	1-1	5	Collins 3	3,509
13	O 1	CL	A	Plymouth Argyle	L	0-3	0-1	9		(4,135)
14	5	CL	A	Blackpool	D	2-2	2-1	12	Elsey 35, Cascarino 42	(4,571)
15	8	MC2/2	A	Portsmouth	L	1-2	0-0		Dillon (og) 54	(7,629)
16	12	CL	H	Cardiff City	W	2-0	2-0	8	Oakes 23, Weatherly 29	3,367
17	19	CL	A	A.F.C. Bournemouth	W	3-2	1-1	5	Cascarino 29, 81, Shearer 47	(3,561)
18	22	CL	H	Derby County	L	1-2	0-1	8	Mehmet 68	4,613
19	26	CL	H	Swansea City	W	5-1	3-1	6	Shearer 3 6, 14, 62, Hales 30, (pen) 88	3,082
20	N 2	CL	A	Newport County	D	1-1	0-0	8	Byrne 63	(1,970)
21	6	CL	A	Rotherham United	D	1-1	0-1	9	Weatherly 84	(2,361)
22	9	CL	H	Walsall	W	5-2	2-1	7	Hales 7, 22, Cascarino 50, Shearer 60, Robinson 88	3,339
23	16	FAC1	H	Northampton Town	W	3-0	2-0		Mundee og 34, Mehmet 42, Cascarino 57	3,991
24	23	CL	A	Wolverhampton W.	W	3-1	0-0	5	Cochrane 53, Shearer 81, 89	(3,543)
25	30	CL	H	Doncaster Rovers	W	4-0	2-0	4	Robinson 2, Mehmet (pen) 6, Cascarino 48, Shearer 87	3,159
26	D 7	FAC2	H	Bognor	W	6-1	3-0		Cascarino 2, 13, Robinson 40, Shearer 50, Cochrane 65, Hales 80	4,228
27	14	CL	A	Bristol Rovers	L	0-1	0-0	4		(4,224)
28	20	CL	A	Darlington	L	2-3	2-2	5	Shearer 28 secs, Cascarino 40	(2,072)
29	28	CL	A	Bristol City	D	1-1	0-0	8	Cascarino 88	4,672
30	J 1	CL	A	Reading	W	2-1	1-1	7	Byrne 2, Elsey 79	(10,665)
31	4	FAC3	H	Derby County	D	1-1	0-1		Robinson 67	8,983
32	11	CL	A	Bolton Wanderers	W	1-0	0-0	3	Cochrane 61	(5,232)
33	13	FAC3R	A	Derby County	L	1-3	0-0		Robinson 88	(10,959)
34	18	CL	H	Lincoln	W	2-0	1-0	2	Cochrane 42, Weatherly 50	4,397
35	22	FRT	A	Derby County	W	2-0	1-0		Robinson 10, Cascarino 89	(3,721)
36	24	CL	A	Chesterfield	D	1-1	1-1	2	Hinnigan 7	(2,521)
37	29	FRT	H	Brentford	D	1-1	0-1		Hales 73	1,464
38	F 1	CL	A	Notts County	W	4-0	2-0	2	Robinson 8, 24, Oakes 61, Musker 77	4,368
39	8	CL	H	AFC Bournemouth	W	2-0	1-0	2	Cascarino 18, Heffernan (og) 69	3,895
40	15	CL	A	Wigan Athletic	D	3-3	2-2	2	Elsey 10, Weatherly 31, Mehmet 84	(5,017)
41	22	CL	H	Bury	W	1-0	0-0	2	Weatherly 60	4,212
42	24	FRT S QF	H	Cambridge United	W	2-0	1-0		Collins 30, Hinnigan 53	1,812
43	M 1	CL	A	York City	L	0-2	0-0	3		(4,351)
44	4	CL	H	Plymouth Argyle	D	1-1	0-0	2	Cascarino 59	3,490
45	8	CL	H	Blackpool	D	2-2	1-1	2	Cascarino 15, Robinson 76	4,537
46	15	CL	A	Cardiff City	D	1-1	1-1	4	Cascarino 24	(2,505)
47	18	CL	H	Brentford	L	1-2	0-0	4	Robinson 69	3,582
48	22	CL	A	Swansea City	D	2-2	0-2	5	Sage 75, Weatherly 83	(3,364)
49	29	CL	H	Reading	W	3-0	1-0	5	Tempest 25, 67, Horrix (og) 57	5,710
50	31	CL	H	Brentford	W	2-1	1-1	3	Robinson 43, Elsey 53	(4,702)
51	A 4	CL	H	Rotherham United	W	3-0	3-0	2	Hales 1, Weatherly 25, Robinson 38	4,525
52	7	CL	A	Derby County	L	0-2	0-2	4		(11,351)
53	12	CL	A	Walsall	L	1-4	1-2	5	Tempest 8	(3,889)
54	16	FRT S SF	A	Bristol City	L	0-3	0-0			(5,707)
55	19	CL	A	Wolverhampton W.	W	2-0	0-0	5	Hales 47, Mehmet (pen) 59	3,681
56	25	CL	A	Doncaster Rovers	W	3-2	3-0	5	Robinson 8, Tempest 13, Hales 44	(1,659)
57	29	CL	H	Newport County	L	0-1	0-0	4		2,566
58	M 3	CL	H	Bristol Rovers	W	2-0	2-0	5	Robinson 9, Mehmet (pen) 22	2,050

Best Home League Attendance: 5,710 v Reading 29/3   **Smallest:** 2,050 v Bristol Rovers 3/5 Av Home Att: 3,694

Goal Scorers: Compared with 84-85: −1,032

League (81): Cascarino 14, Robinson 10, Shearer 9, Hales 7 (1 pen), Mehmet 7 (3 pen), Weatherley 7, Cochrane 5, Elsey 4, Tempest 4, Byrne 3, Hinnigan 2, Oakes 2, Opponents 2, Sage 2, Collins 1, Musker 1

Milk Cup (5): Cascarino 3, Opponents 1, Shearer 1,

FA Cup (10): Cascarino 3, Robinson 2, Cochrane 1, Hales 1, Mehmet 1, Opponents 1, Shearer 1

FRT (5): Cascarino 1, Collins 1, Hales 1, Hinnigan 1, Robinson 1

Hillyard	Sage	Hinnigan	Oakes	Musker	Shaw	Cochrane	Shearer	Elsey	Cascarino	Mehmet	Weatherly	Collins	Byrne	Hales	Macowat	Robinson	Tong	Tempest (L)	Westley	Referee	
1	2	3	4	5	6	7†	8	9*	10	11	12									R Banks	1
1	2		4	8*	5	9	10	3	11	7	6	12								A Buksh	2
1	2		4		6†	7	8	3	11	10*	5	9	12							K Miller	3
1	2	3	9	5	7	8	6	11		4*	10	12								L Robinson	4
1	2	3	4		6		9	11		5	10	7	8							M Bodenham	5
1	2	3	4		6	8		9	11	12	5	10	7*							N Butler	6
1	2	3	4	6		8		9	11	10	5		7							T Simpson	7
1	2	3	4	6*		8		9	11		5	12	7	10						D Axcell	8
1	2	3	4		6	8		9	11	10		5	7							R Lewis	9
1	2	5	3		4	9		8	11	10	12	7	6*							J Lloyd	10
1	2	3	4		6	7		9*	11	10	8	5		12						D Vickers	11
1	8	2*	4		6	7		9	11	10		5		12	3					I Hemley	12
1	8	2	4		6	7		9*	11	10		5		12	3					A Seville	13
1	2	3*	4		6	8		9	11		5	10	7	12						G Courtney	14
1	2		4		6	7	3	11†		5	10	8	9							E Scales	15
1	2		4		6	7	3	11		5	10	8	9*			12				A Gunn	16
1	2	5	4		6	7	8	3	11	12	10					9*				J Martin	17
1	2	3	4		6	7	8*	5		10		9		12		11				J Moules	18
1	2	5	4			7	8	3		10*		6	11	9		12				I Borrett	19
1	2	5	4			7	8	3	11	10		6	9*			12				B Stevens	20
1	2	5	4				8	3	11	10	6		7*	12		9				P Tyldesley	21
1	2		4				8	3	11	10	5		6	9		7				C Downey	22
1	2		4			7	8	3	11*	10	5		12	9		6				N Butler	23
1	2	12	4			7	8	3	11	10	5			9*		6				R Nixon	24
1	2		4			7	8	3	11	10	5			9		6				D Hedges	25
1	2		4			7	8	3	11		5	10		9		6				D Axcell	26
1	2	12	4			7†	8	3	11	10	5			9		6*				M Cotton	27
1	2	4		10		7	8	3	11		5		12	9*		6				N Midgeley	28
1	2	6	4	12			8	3	11	10	5		7	9*						D Reeves	29
1	2	6	4				8	3	11	10	5		7	9						J Bray	30
1	2	6	4			7	8	3	11	10*	5		12	9						J Ashworth	31
1	2	6		5	4	7	8	3	11	10				9						N Ashley	32
1	2	6		5*	4	7	8	3	11	10			12	9						J Ashworth	33
1	2	6		10	4	7	8*	3	11		5		12	9						M James	34
1	2	6			4	7		3	11	5	10		8	9						L Dilkes	35
1	2	6			4	7		3	11	5	10		8	9						K Lupton	36
1	2	6	4	13		7		3	11	10*	12	8*		9						D Axcell	37
1	2	6	4	12		7		3	11	5	10		8*	9						J Moules	38
1	2	6	4			7	9	3	11	12	5	10	9*	8						T Ward	39
1	2	6	4			7	9	3	11	12	5	10	8*							J Lovatt	40
1	2	6	4			7		3	11		5	10	8	9						K Baker	41
1	2	6	4			7	12	3	11	13	5	10*	8*	9						A Gunn	42
1	2	6	4			7	12	3	11	10	5		8*	9						H Taylor	43
1	2	6	4			7	10	3	11		5		8	9						M Bodenham	44
1	2	6	4*		12	7	8	3	11		5		10	9						J Ashworth	45
1	2	6			4	7	8	3	11	10	5		12	9*						G Ashby	46
1	2	6			4	7		3	11*	10	5	8	12	9						M Scott	47
1	2	6	12		4	7	9*	3		10	5	8				11				T Holbrook	48
1	2		4		6	7		3		10*	5	12				11	8	9		V Callow	49
1	2	3	4		6	7		10			5			12		11*	8	9		I Borrett	50
1	2	6	4			7		3			5		10			11	8	9		I Hemley	51
1	2	6	4	10	7			3			5		12			11	8	9*		K Barratt	52
1	2	6	4			7		3		10	5	12				11	8*	9		D Phillips	53
1	2	6	4			12		3		10	5	8*	7			11		8		J Martin	54
1	2	6	4			7*		3		10	5		11	8		12		9		G Napthine	55
1	2	6	4					3		10	5		7	8		11		9		J Lloyd	56
1	2	6	4			12		3		10	5		7*	8		11		9		E Scales	57
1	2		4		6			3		10	5		7		12	11		9	8*	D Vickers	58
46	**46**	37	39	7	22	39	22	**46**	34	28	36	20	19	21	2	29	5	9	1	League Appearances	
	2	1	2	1	1	1			3	2	3	5	8	1		4				Substitute Appearances	
4	4	2	4	1	4	4	1	4	4	2-1	4	3-1	2	1		0-1				Milk Cup Appearances	
4	4	2	3	1	1	4	4	3	3	1	0-3	2				4				FA Cup Appearances	
4	4	4	3	0-1	1	3-1	0-1	4	3	1-1	4		4			4		1		FR Trophy Appearances	

Players on Loan: Tempest (Huddersfield)
Departures:

'THE GILLS'

Formed: 1893
Turned Professional: 1894   **Ltd Co:** 1893

Previous Name: New Brompton 1893-1913
Managers since 1920: John McMillan 1920-23   Harry Curtis 1923-26   Albert Hoskins 1926-30
Dick Hendrie 1930-32   Fred Maven 1932-37   Alan Ure 1937-38   Bill Harvey 1938-39
Archie Clark 1939-58   Harry Barratt 1958-62   Freddie Cox 1962-66   Basil Hayward 1966-71
Andy Nelson 1971-74   Len Ashurst 1974-75   Gerry Summers 1975-81   Keith Peacock 1981-
Honours: Champions Div 4 1963-4
League Career: Original Members of Div 3 1920   Transferred to Div 3 (S) 1921
Failed to gain re-election 1938   Southern League 1938-44   Kent League 1944-6
Southern League 1946-50   Re-elected to Div 3 (S) 1949   Transferred to Division 4 1958
Promoted to Div 3 1963-4   Relegated to Div 4 1970-1   Promoted to Div 3 1973-4
Colours: Royal blue shirts, white shorts and stockings.
Change Colours: Red shirts, black shorts, red stockings.
Reserves League: Capital   **Youth League:** S E Counties

CLUB RECORDS

Most Appearances for Club: John Simpson: Football League 571 + FA Cup 27 + League Cup 19 **Total 617**
Most Capped Player: Tony Cascarino, 3, Eire
Record Goalscorer in a Match: Fred Cheesmuir, 6 v Merthyr Tydfil (h), 6-0, Div 3 (S), 26.04.30
Record League Goalscorer in a Season: Ernie Morgan, 31, Div 3 (S), 1954-5   Brian Yeo, 31, Div 4, 1973-4   **In All Competitions:** Ernie Morgan, 33 (League 31 + FA Cup 2), 1929-30
Record League Goalscorer in a Career: Brian Yeo, 136, 1963-75   **In All Competitions:** Brian Yeo, 149 (League 136 + FA Cup 9 + League Cup 4) 1963-75
Record Transfer Fee Received: £135,000 from Norwich City for Steve Bruce, July 1984
Record Transfer Fee Paid: £90,000 to Colchester United for Trevor Lee, Jan 1981
Best Performances: League: 4th Div 3 1978-9, 1984-5   **FA Cup:** 5th Round 1969-70   **League/Milk Cup:** 4th Round 1964
Most League Points: (3pts for a win) 83, Div 3, 1984-5   (2pts for a win) 62, Div 4, 1973-4
Record League Victory: 6-0 v Brentford, Div 3 (S), 19 March 1924   v Merthyr Tydfil, Div 3 (S), 26 April 1930
Most Goals Scored in a League Match: 9-4 v Exeter City (H), Div 3 (S), 7 Jan 1951
Most Goals Scored in a Cup Tie: 10 v Gorleston (H) FA Cup 1st Round, 16 Nov 1957
Record League Defeat: 2-9 v Nottingham Forest, Div 3 (S), 18 Nov 1950
Oldest Player in League Match: John Simpson 39 years 137 days
Youngest Player in League Match: Billy Hughes, 15 years 275 days
Most Consecutive Undefeated League Matches: 20 1973-74
Longest Run of Undefeated Home League Matches: 48 1963-65
Longest Run Without Home League Win: 9 1961
Most Consecutive League Wins: 7 1954-55
Most Consecutive League Defeats: 9 1951-52
League Matches Without a Win: 15 1972
Away League Matches: 10 1973-74
Away League Win: 26 1937-38-50
Home League Wins: 10 1963
Away League Wins: 4 1953, 1981
Missing seasons in aways without a win between 1938-50 was when they were a non-league club

Club Statistician for the Directory: Roger Triggs

GILLINGHAM

PLAYERS NAME Ht Wt Birthdate	Honours	Birthplace Transfers	Clubs	APPEARANCES				GOALS			
				League	Milk Cup	FA Cup	Other Comps	League	Milk Cup	FA Cup	Other Comps
GOALKEEPERS											
Ron Hillyard		Rotherham	York City	61	2	9					
5.11 11.4 31.3.52			Hartlepool United (L)	23							
			Gillingham	453	36	31	5				
DEFENDERS											
Joe Hinnigan		Liverpool	South Liverpool								
6.0½ 12.7 3.12.55		£1,000	Wigan Athletic	66	4	7		10			
		£80,000	Sunderland	63	1	1					
		£15,000	Preston North End	51+1	3	1	1	8	2		
		F	Gillingham	73+3	5	6	5	7			1
Keith Oakes		Bedworth	Peterborough U (A)	48+13	7+2	4+1		2			
5.10 12.2 3.7.56			Newport County	232	14	13+1	1	27	1	1	
			Gillingham	84+1	8	7	4	7			
Graham Pearce		London	Barnet			7					
5.9 11.0 8.7.59		£10,000	Brighton	87+1	7	12	2	2			
Mark Weatherley*		Ramsgate	Gillingham (A)	342+37	29+3	26+4	5+1				
6.0 11.12 18.1.58											
Paul Haycock		Lowestoft	Norwich City (A)	154+1	22	13+1	1	3			
5.8 11.0 24.3.63			Sheffield United								
			Gillingham								
MIDFIELD											
Terry Cochrane	NI (26)	Killyleagh	Coleraine								
5.7½ 10.8 23.1.53			Burnley	62+5	7	4+1		13	4		
		£238,000	Middlesbrough	96+15	5	12		7	1		
		F	Gillingham	105+2	7	13	3+1	17		2	
Paul Collins		West Ham	Gillingham (A)	25+4	3+1	1	7	2			1
5.10 11.11 11.8.66											
Karl Elsey		Swansea	Pembroke Borough								
5.10 11.6 20.11.58			QPR	0+1							
			Newport County	114+9	8+3	8	6	15	1		
		Player exch.	Cardiff City	59	4	1		4			
		F	Gillingham	46	4	4	4	5			
Graham Westley		London	QPR (A)								
5.8 11.0 4.3.68			Gillingham	1							
FORWARDS											
David Byrne		London	Kingstonian								
5.8 11.0 5.3.61			Gillingham	18+5	2	0+3	1+1	3			
Tony Cascarino	EI (3)	St. Paul's Cray	Crockenhill								
6.2 11.10 1.9.62			Gillingham	166+10	14	12+1	5	60	8	7	3
Howard Pritchard	W (1), Y	Cardiff	Bristol City (A)	31+7	1	5+1		2			
5.10 12.7 18.10.58		F	Swindon Town	59+6	2+1	8		11		8	
		F	Bristol City	117+2	7	10	7+3	22		3	1
			Gillingham								
Martin Robinson	FAYC 74	Ilford	Charlton Athletic	218+10	16+3	8+1		58	6	2	
5.8½ 11.5 17.7.57			Reading (L)	2							
			Gillingham	62+4		8	4	20		4	1
David Shearer		Inverness	Inverness Caley								
5.10 12.10 16.10.58			Middlesbrough	88+9				23			
			Wigan Athletic (L)	11				9			
			Grimsby Town	1+3							
			Gillingham	41+5	2	6	0+1	21	2	4	
Trevor Quow	EY	Peterborough	Peterborough U (A)	119+12	14+1	9+1	3	17	1	2	2
5.6 10.4 28.9.60		£6,000	Gillingham								
Mel Eves	EB (3)	Wednesbury	Wolverhampton W.	169+11	12+1	19		44	3	5	
5.10½ 11.0 10.9.56			Huddersfield Town (L)	7				4			
		F	Sheffield United	25+1		1+1		10			
		F	Gillingham								

ADDITIONAL CONTRACT PROFESSIONALS
Mark Beeney (monthly)

Player of the Year: Mel Sage (now Derby County)

APPRENTICES

NON-CONTRACT PLAYERS
Ian Docker, John Gorman (Youth Team Coach), Jason Willis, Paul Taylor

Record Attendance: 23,002 v Queens Park Rangers, FA Cup Round 3, 10 Jan 1948

Smallest Home Attendance for a First Class Match: 963 v Colchester United, Freight Rover Trophy, 23 Jan 1985

Record Receipts: £35,070 v Everton, FA Cup Round 4, 6 Feb 1984

Season Tickets: Stand: £95.00 and £85.00; Ground: £65.00

Executive Box Season Tickets: Match sponsors lounge £500 (25 seats)

Cost of Stand Tickets: £5.00 and £4.50 **Terraces:** £3.00

Match and Ticket Information: Can reserve by postal application with payment and SAE

Car Parking: No car park available, but plenty of parking spaces in nearby roads

Nearest Railway Station: Gillingham

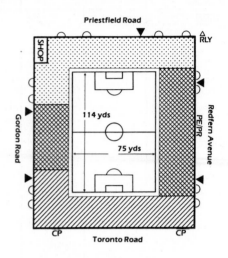

How to get to the ground

Use Motorway M2 until junction 4, leave Motorway and follow signs Gillingham A27, then A2. In 2 miles turn right A231 into Nelson Road. Pass Bus Station on right and turn right into Gillingham Road, then turn right into Gordon Road for Gillingham FC on your left

Price of 1986-7 Programme: 50p
Number of Pages: 20
Subscriptions: Rates obtainable from club

Local Newspapers: Kent Evening Post, Chatham News and Standard

Local Radio Stations: BBC Radio Kent, Invicta Radio

GRIMSBY TOWN

Once again the club has experienced a season during which more headlines have been made off the field than on it. The boardroom power struggle continued, and the half-way mark in the season had seen changes of chairman, vice-chairman, manager, assistant manager, commercial manager and youth coach.

Of the team's performance over the season all that can be said is that they survived to spend a seventh successive season in the Second Division. Of the players brought in by Dave Booth in the close season the most outstanding has been Gordon Hobson. Costing only £35,000 from Lincoln City, Hobson established himself as one of the division's best strikers, and his tally of 19 goals in league and cup matches, despite having no regular partner, speaks for itself. Having spent eight seasons un-noticed at Sincil Bank he has at the age of 28 realised his full potential, whether his ambition to prove himself at First Division level means he has said goodbye to Blundell Park remains to be seen. Of the others only Kevin Peake has established himself. A series of injuries did not give Jimmy Gilligan a chance to prove himself and Dave Felgate never regained his place after Batch's return to fitness. Tony Barratt a young full-back from non-league football impressed many supporters but found himself out of favour after the arrival of Mike Lyons as player manager, and was not retained.

The arrival of Lyons and Darracott appears to mark the disbanding of the side built by Dave Booth and Peter Grotier. By March, ten of the first team squad were made available for transfer, although only three departed on loan. With the club reported to be upwards of £500,000 in 'the red', Lyons' options for team building appear to be strictly limited. Bargains like Hobson occur very rarely. If the club can make a serious attempt for a top place in what appears to be a fairly ordinary Second Division Lyons and Darracott will have gone a long way towards establishing themselves as a managerial team.

Back Row L to R: Dean Crombie, Andy Moore, Nigel Batch, David Felgate, Neil Horwood, Neil Matthews. **Middle Row:** Don O'Riordin (Assistant Manager), Phil Bonnyman (Coach), Ian Straw, Gary Henshaw, Neil Robinson, Paul Agnew, Andy Dixon, David Burgess, Gordon Simmonite (Youth Team Coach), John Fraser (Physiotherapist). **Front Row:** Phil Turner, Andy Peake, Ian Walsh, Michael Lyons (Manager), Kevin Moore, Gordon Hobson, Bob Cummings.

GRIMSBY TOWN

DIVISION TWO: 15th   **FA CUP:** 3rd ROUND   **MILK CUP:** 3rd ROUND   **FM CUP:** 1st ROUND

MATCH	DATE		COMPE-TITION	VENUE	OPPONENTS	RESULT		HALF TIME	L'GUE POS'N	GOALSCORERS/GOAL TIMES	ATTEN-DANCE
1	A	17	CL	A	Brighton & H. A.	D	2-2	1-0		Lund 33, Hobson 90	(9,787)
2		20	CL	H	Huddersfield Town	D	1-1	1-0		Lund 30	6,180
3		24	CL	H	Charlton Athletic	D	2-2	1-0	13	Lund 9, Hobson 74	4,261
4		26	CL	A	Fulham	L	1-2	1-1	15	Lund 28	(4,873)
5		31	CL	H	Wimbledon	L	0-1	0-0	16		3,476
6	S	4	CL	A	Stoke City	D	1-1	1-0	16	Lund 1	(7,362)
7		7	CL	A	Sunderland	D	3-3	2-1	17	Ford 37, Gilligan 40, Lund 53	(14,985)
8		13	CL	H	Carlisle United	W	1-0	0-0	15	Peake 85	4,099
9		17	FMC	H	Sunderland	W	3-2	0-0		Bonnyman 57, Hobson 82, 88	2,435
10		21	CL	A	Barnsley	L	0-1	0-1	16		(5,365)
11		24	MC2/1	H	York City	D	1-1	1-1		Gilligan 36	2,908
12		28	CL	H	Bradford City	W	2-0	1-0	13	Peake 39, Emson 55	5,158
13	O	1	FMC	A	Sunderland	L†	1-2	1-1		Lund 6	(11,571)
14		5	CL	A	Oldham Athletic	L	1-2	0-1	15	Gilligan 54	(5,301)
15		8	MC2/2	A	York City	W	3-2	2-1		Hobson 14, 78, Gilligan 30	(5,030)
16		12	CL	H	Sheffield United	L	0-1	0-1	17		5,935
17		19	CL	A	Leeds United	D	1-1	0-0	16	Hobson 48	(11,244)
18		26	CL	H	Middlesbrough	W	3-2	1-1	15	Gilligan 28, 73, Hobson 55	4,454
19		29	MC3	H	Ipswich Town	L	0-2	0-2			6,700
20	N	2	CL	H	Millwall	W	5-1	2-0	12	Bonnyman 37, Hobson 3, 40, 65, 69, Moore, A. 60	3,685
21		9	CL	A	Crystal Palace	L	1-2	1-0	14	Emson 20	(4,620)
22		16	CL	H	Portsmouth	W	1-0	0-0	13	Bonnyman (pen) 61	6,380
23		23	CL	A	Norwich	L	2-3	0-1	14	Culverhouse (og) 69, Emson 85	(12,108)
24		30	CL	H	Blackburn Rovers	W	5-2	3-0	13	Ford 2, Hine 23, Moore, K. 45, Hobson 63, 76	5,016
25	D	7	CL	A	Huddersfield Town	D	2-2	2-2	13	Lyons 8, Hobson 23	(4,811)
26		14	CL	H	Brighton & H. A.	L	0-2	0-2	14		5,320
27		21	CL	A	Charlton Athletic	L	0-2	0-0	17		(3,525)
28		26	CL	A	Hull City	L	0-2	0-1	17		(12,824)
29	J	1	CL	H	Shrewsbury Town	W	3-1	1-1	16	Lyons 31, 87, Lund 71	4,750
30		4	FAC3	H	Arsenal	L	3-4	1-2		Lund 9, Lyons 53, Peake (pen) 73	12,829
31		11	CL	A	Carlisle United	W	2-1	2-0	16	Hobson 16, Emson 43	(2,483)
32		18	CL	A	Wimbledon	L	0-3	0-0	16		(2,770)
33		24	CL	H	Stoke City	D	3-3	2-3	14	Emson 19, Bonnyman 26, Ford 66	4,523
34	F	1	CL	H	Fulham	W	1-0	0-0	12	Peake 55	3,572
35		8	CL	H	Leeds United	W	1-0	0-0	10	Hobson 55	6,338
36	M	1	CL	A	Bradford City	W	1-0	0-0	10	Cumming 89	(5,185)
37		4	CL	A	Middlesbrough	L	1-3	0-0	11	Crombie 19	(4,496)
38		8	CL	H	Oldham Athletic	L	1-4	1-3	.12	Hobson 5	4,174
39		14	CL	A	Sheffield United	D	1-1	1-0	11	Henshaw 30	(9,165)
40		22	CL	H	Sunderland	D	1-1	1-0	12	Lund 31	5,339
41		29	CL	A	Shrewsbury Town	W	2-0	0-0	12	Lyons 65, Henshaw 72	(3,097)
42	A	1	CL	H	Hull City	L	0-1	0-1	12		9,121
43		5	CL	A	Millwall	L	0-1	0-1	14		(3,612)
44		12	CL	H	Crystal Palace	W	3-0	2-0	13	Cannon (og) 21, Peake 75, Henshaw 89	4,222
45		19	CL	A	Portsmouth	L	1-3	0-0	15	Cumming 61	(12,967)
46		22	CL	H	Barnsley	L	1-2	1-1	15	Hobson 6	4,009
47		26	CL	H	Norwich City	W	1-0	0-0	15	Hobson 55	8,090
48	M	5	CL	A	Blackburn Rovers	L	1-3	1-2	15	Moore 5	(7,600)

Best Home League Attendance: 9,121 v Hull City 1/4   **Smallest:** 3,476 v Wimbledon 31/8   **Av Home Att:** 5,148

Goal Scorers: Compared with 84-85: −1,492

League (58):	Hobson 16, Lund 8, Emson 5, Lyons 4, Peake 4, Bonnyman 3 (1 pen), Ford 3, Gilligan 3, Henshaw 3, Cumming 2, Moore K 2, Opponent 2, Crombie 1, Ford 1, Hine 1, Moore A 1
Milk Cup (4):	Gilligan 2, Hobson 2
FA Cup (3):	Lund 1, Lyons 1, Peake 1 (pen)
FM Cup (4):	Hobson 2, Bonnyman 1, Lund 1

†Sunderland win 3-2 on penalties

Felgate	Robinson	Agnew	Peake	Moore A.	Crombie	Ford	Lund	Gilligan	Bonnyman	Emson	Hobson	Hine	Barratt	Moore K.	Batch	Cumming	Lyons	Henshaw	Matthews	Grocock (S)	Referee	
1	2	3	4	5	6	7	8	9	10	11*	12										K Miller	1
1	2	3	4	5	6	7	8*	9	10	11	12										D Shaw	2
1	2	3	4	5		7	8	9	10	11	6										D Hutchinson	3
1	2	3	4	5	6	7	8	9	10		11	12									R Groves	4
1			4	5	3	7	8	9		11			2	6							T Jones	5
1	2		4	5	3	7	8	9	10		11			6							R Bridges	6
1	2		4	5	3	7	8	9	10	12	11*			6							C Seel	7
1	2*		4	5	3	7	8	9	10	12	11			6							D Phillips	8
		5		3	4	6	10	11*	7		12	9	8	2	1						**T Simpson**	9
1		3	4	5		7	8	12	10	11*	9		2	6							D Allison	10
1		3	4	5		7		8	10	11	9		2	6							**M Scott**	11
1		3	4	5		7		8		11	9	10	2	6							G Napthine	12
		3	4	5		7		8	9		11	10	2	6	1						**N Wilson**	13
1		3	4	5		7	12	8		11*	9	10	2	6							N Ashley	14
1			4	5	3	7	12	9			8	10	2	6		11*					**L Dilkes**	15
			4	5	3	7*	12	8		11	9	10	2	6	1						J Bray	16
			4	5	3*	7	12	8	10		9		2	6	1	11					N Midgley	17
			4	5	3	7		8	10	11	9		2	6	1						H Taylor	18
			7	4	3	6	12	10*	8	9	11		2	5	1						**J Key**	19
			4	5	3	7	9		10	11	8		2	6	1	12					N Glover	20
			4	5	3	7	8*		10	11	9		2	6	1	12					B Stevens	21
			4		3	7		9	10	11	8		2	6	1		5				P Tyldesley	22
		3	4	12		7	9*			10	11	8	2	6	1		5				C Downey	23
			4			7		8	10		9	11	2	6	1	3	5				G Tyson	24
		12		4			7		8*	10		9	11†	2	6	1	3	5			K Walmsley	25
				4	12	7		8*	10		9	11	2	6	1	3	5				T Mills	26
				4	3	7		12	10†	11*	9†		2	6	1	8	5				K Baker	27
				4	3	7	12		10		9	8	2	6	1	11	5*				I Hendrick	28
				3		7		8	10		9	4	2	6	1	11	5				K Hackett	29
		3	4		6	7	8	12		11*	9	10	2		.1		5				**J Bray**	30
1		3	4		6	7	8	12		11	9	10*	2				5				R Nixon	31
		3	4		6	7*	8	12	10	11	9		2		1		5				Alan Robinson	32
	2		4		6	7	8		10	11	9				1	3	5				J Ashworth	33
	2		5		6	7	8	12	10	11	9*				1	3	4				I Borrett	34
	2		4		6	7	8*	12	10	11	9				1	3	5				G Napthine	35
	2		4	5	6	7			10	11	9				1	8					M Reed	36
	2	3	4	5	6	7			10	11	9				1	8					I Hendrick	37
	2	3	4		6	7			10*	11	9		12		1	8	5				K Breen	38
10		4	2	3	12		8				9			6	1	11*	5	7			J Ball	39
10		4	2	3	12	8					9			6	1	11	5	7*			T Fitzharris	40
10		3	4	2		8				7*	9	12		6	1		5	11			J McAulay	41
		4	2	3		8				9	10	12		6	1	11	5	7*			J Key	42
	2		4	12	3	8				10	7			6	1	11	5	9*			R Gifford	43
10		4	2	3		8					9			6	1	11*	5	7	12		L Dilkes	44
10	12	4	2	3		8*					9			6	1	11	5	7			J Moules	45
8		7	2	5		11					10		4		1	9	3	6	12		P Willis	46
10		4	2	3		12					9			6	1	11	5	7	8*		N Midgeley	47
10		4		3				2			9			6	1	11*	5	7	8	12	J Lovatt	48
12	22	14	36	31	33	32	24	19	29	21	39	12	20	30	30	22	24	10	2		League Appearances	
	2		2	1	2	5	6		2	2	1	2	1		2			2	1		Substitute Appearances	
2		1	3	3	2	3	0-2	3	2	2	3	1		3	3	1	1				Milk Cup Appearances	
1	1		1	1	1	0-1	1	1	1	1		1			1		1				FA Cup Appearances	
2	1	2	2	2	2	1	1-1	1	2	2	1	2									FM Cup Appearances	

Players on Loan:
Departures: Barratt (Free), Hine (Free), Emson (Wrexham), Ford (Stoke City)

'THE MARINERS'

Formed: 1878
Turned Professional: 1890 **Ltd Co:** 1890

Previous Names: Grimsby Pelham
Previous Managers: 1920-1 Haydn Price 1921-5 George Fraser 1925-32 Wilf Gillow 1932-6 Frank Womack 1937-51 Charlie Spencer 1951-4 Bill Shankly 1954-5 Billy Walsh 1955-9 Allenby Chilton 1960-2 Tim Ward 1962-4 Tom Johnston 1964-7 Jimmy McGuigan 1967-8 Don McEvoy 1968-9 Bill Harvey 1969-71 Bobby Kennedy 1971-3 Lawrie McMenemy 1973-5 Ron Ashman 1975-6 Tom Casey 1976-9 John Newman 1979-82 George Kerr
Honours: Champions Div 2, 1900-1, 1933-4 Champions Div 3 (N) 1925-6, 1955-6 Champions Div 3 1979-80 Champions Div 4 1971-2
League Career: Original Members of Div 2 1892 Promoted to Div 1 1900-1 Relegated to Div 2 1902-3 Failed re-election 1910 Re-elected to Div 2 1911 Relegated to Div 3 1919-20 Transferred to Div 3 (N) 1921 Promoted to Div 2 1925-6 Promoted to Div 1 1928-9 Relegated to Div 2 1931-2 Promoted to Div 1 1933-4 Relegated to Div 2 1947-8 Relegated to Div 3 (N) 1950-1 Promoted to Div 2 1955-6 Relegated to Div 3 1958-9 Promoted to Div 2 1961-2 Relegated to Div 3 1963-4 Relegated to Div 4 1967-8 Promoted to Div 3 1971-2 Relegated to Div 4 1976-7 Promoted to Div 3 1978-9 Promoted to Div 2 1979-80
Colours: Black and white striped shirts, black shorts and white stockings
Change Colours: All red
Reserves League: Central League **Youth Team:** Northern Intermediate **Colts:** Grimsby League Div 1

CLUB RECORDS

Most Appearances for Club: Keith Jobling: Football League 450 + FA Cup 23 + League Cup 19 **Total 492**
Most Capped Player: Pat Glover, 4, Wales **For England:** H Betmead, J Bestall, G Tweedy (1 each)
Record Goalscorer in a Match: Tommy McCairns, 6 v Leicester Fosse (H), 7-1, Div 2, 11 Apr 1896
Record League Goalscorer in a Season: Pat Glover, 42, Div 2, 1933-4 **In All Competitions:** Pat Glover, 43 (League 42 + FA Cup 1), 1933-4
Record League Goalscorer in a Career: Pat Glover, 180, 1930-9 **In All Competitions:** Pat Glover, 197 (League 180 + FA Cup 17)
Record Transfer Fee Received: £300,000 from Everton for Paul Wilkinson, March 1985
Record Transfer Fee Paid: £100,000 to Lincoln City for Jimmy Gilligan
Best Performances: League: 5th Div 1 1934-5 **FA Cup:** Semi-Final 1936, 1939 **League/Milk Cup:** 5th Round 1979-80, 1984-5
Most League Points: 70, Div 2, 1983-4 **Most League Goals:** 103, Div 2, 1933-4
Record League Victory and Most Goals Scored in a League Match: 9-2 v Darwen, Div 2, 15 Apr 1899
Most Goals Scored in a First Class Match: 10-1 v Boston United, 2nd Round FA Cup, 24 Oct 1891
Record League Defeat: 1-9 v Arsenal, Div 1, 28 Jan 1931
Oldest Player in League Match: George Tweedy
Youngest Player in League Match: Tony Ford
Most Consecutive Undefeated League Matches: 19 1980   **League Matches Without a Win:** 18 1981-82
Longest Run of Undefeated Home League Matches: 33 1974-76   **Away League Matches:** 9 1980, 1983-84
Longest Run Without Home League Win: 12 1947-48   **Away League Win:** 23 1982-83
Most Consecutive League Wins: 11 1952   **Home League Wins:** 17 1895-96
Most Consecutive League Defeats: 9 1907-08   **Away League Wins:** 5 1952

Club Statistician for the Directory: Les Triggs

GRIMSBY TOWN

PLAYERS NAME Ht Wt Birthdate	Honours	Birthplace Transfers	Clubs	APPEARANCES				GOALS			
				League	Milk Cup	FA Cup	Other Comps	League	Milk Cup	FA Cup	Other Comps
GOALKEEPERS											
Nigel Batch 5.10 12.5 9.11.57	Div. 3, 80	Huddersfield	Derby County (A)								
			Grimsby Town	327	29	20					
David Felgate 6.1 13.3 4.3.60	W (1), S	Blaenau Festiniog	Bolton Wanderers								
			Rochdale (L)	35							
			Crewe Alexandra (L)	14							
			Rochdale (L)	12							
		£25,000	Lincoln City	177	13	7	1				
			Cardiff City	4							
		£27,000	Grimsby Town	24	2						
			Bolton Wanderers	15			4				
			Grimsby Town								
DEFENDERS											
Paul Agnew 5.10 12.7 15.8.65	NI Y, S	Lisburn	Grimsby Town (A)	27+2	3	4					
David Burgess 5.10 11.2 20.1.60		Liverpool	Tranmere Rovers	217+1	16	15	11	1			
			Grimsby Town								
Dean Crombie 6.0 11.12 9.8.54	Div. 3, 80	Lincoln	Ruston Bucyrus								
			Lincoln City	33	1+1						
		F	Grimsby Town	297+4	25	17		3			
Bob Cumming 5.8 10.5 7.12.55	Div. 3, 80	Airdrie	Baillieston								
			Grimsby Town	318+24	23+2	18+1		56	5	2	
Mike Lyons 6.1 13.2 8.12.51	EU23 (5), B (1)	Liverpool	Everton (A)	364+26	37	34		48	5	6	
		£100,000	Sheffield Wednesday	129	20	15		11	2	1	
			Grimsby Town	24		1		4		1	
Andrew Moore+ 6.0 12.0 14.11.65		Cleethorpes	Grimsby Town (A)	52+3	3			1			
Kevin Moore 5.11 11.7 29.5.58	ES, Div. 3, 80	Grimsby	Grimsby Town	372+3	38	23		18	2	2	
Neil Robinson 5.8 10.6 20.4.57		Liverpool	Everton (A)	13+3	3	1		1			
			Swansea City	114+9	6	6	2	7			
			Grimsby Town	39							
MIDFIELD											
Phil Bonnyman 6.0 12.0 6.2.54		Glasgow	Hamilton Ac.	71	17	3		7	2		
		£20,000	Carlisle United	149+3	10	14		26	2	5	
		£150,000	Chesterfield	98+1	6	8		25	1	2	
		£80,000	Grimsby Town	133+2	13	6		15	2		
			Stoke City (L)	7							
Gary Hanshaw 5.9½ 9.10 18.2.65		Leeds	Grimsby Town	19+2				4			
Andy Peake 5.9½ 11.2 1.11.61	EU21 (1), Y, Div. 2, 80	Market H'borough	Leicester City (A)	141+6	5+1	9		13			
			Grimsby Town	36	3	1		4		1	
Phil Turner 5.8 10.7 12.2.62		Sheffield Player exch.	Lincoln City	203+2	18	11	5	19		1	
			Grimsby Town								
FORWARDS											
Gordon Hobson+ 5.8 10.5 27.11.57		Sheffield	Lincoln City	260+1	20	8+1	6	72	3		3
		£35,000	Grimsby Town	39+2	3	1		16	2		
Neil Matthews 5.11 12.0 19.9.66		Humberston	Grimsby Town	6+2				1			
			Scunthorpe United (L)	1							
Gary Lund 5.11 11.0 13.9.64	EU21 (1), Y	Grimsby	Grimsby Town	47+13	6+2	4	2	24	1	5	

ADDITIONAL CONTRACT PROFESSIONALS
Andrew Dixon

APPRENTICES
Christopher Grocock (0+1)

NON-CONTRACT PLAYERS

Record Attendance: 31,657 v Wolverhampton Wanderers, League Cup Round 5, 4 Dec 1979

Smallest Home Attendance for a First Class Match: 1,833 v Brentford, Div 4, 3 May 1969

Record Receipts: £44,137 v Norwich City, Milk Cup 5th Round, 16 Jan 1985

Season Tickets: Findus Stand: £79.50 adults, £59.50 juniors/OAPs; Main Stand: £65.00 adults, £50.00 juniors/OAPs; Osmond Stand: £65.00 adults, £50.00 juniors/OAPs; Standing: £42.50 adults, £29.50 juniors/OAPs

Executive Box Season Tickets: Consult Commercial Manager

Cost of Stand Tickets: Findus Stand: £4.50 adults, £3.50 juniors/OAPs; Main Stand: £3.80 adults, £2.80 juniors/OAPs; Osmond Stand: £3.80 adults, £2.80 juniors/OAPs; Standing: £2.50 adults, £1.50 juniors/OAPs

Match and Ticket Information: Seats bookable two weeks in advance of each match

Car Parking: Street parking available

Nearest Railway Station: Cleethorpes, Grimsby (0472 53556)

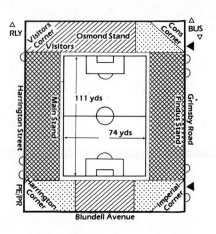

How to get to the ground

From North and West: Use Motorway M180 then A180 (S.P. Grimsby) then follow signs to Cleethorpes A1098

From South: Use A1 then A16 and follow signs to Cleethorpes and at roundabout take 1st exit into Grimsby Road A1098 for Grimsby Town FC

Price of 1986-7 Programme: 50p
Number of Pages: 24
Subscriptions: £16.50 per season (home matches postage included)

Local Newspapers: Grimsby Evening Telegraph, Grimsby Gazette, Grimsby Target

.ocal Radio Stations: Radio Humberside, Viking Radio

Chairman
J Madeley

Vice-Chairman
Roger Newby

Directors
Frank Hinchliffe
Tony McLean
Derek Wilkinson
Jack Turner
Tom Dawson BEM
John Robinson

Secretary
Mrs Carol Bell (0422 53423)

Assistant Secretary
Mrs Ann Pettifor (0422 53423)

Manager
Mick Jones

Assistant Manager
Billy Ayre

Commercial Manager
Tony Thwaites (0422 66593)

Physiotherapist
Alan Sutton

A win at home over Port Vale in their 44th Fourth Division match of the season gave Halifax just enough points to avoid another supplicatory visit to the League's AGM to ask for clemency. Five goals were conceded in the remaining two matches with two scored and in ordinary circumstances those results at home would have made sure of a further humiliation, but when the sums were done Halifax had scored more goals than Exeter City and had a goals difference which was a sole counter better than that of the team from Devon. Things could hardly have been 'hairier'.

This, of course, is standard practice for the club from the Shay, which still manages to keep its League place, but a new headache now appears as the club must in future avoid bottom place; the alternative is to face a spell in the Gola League. With a win over Wrexham by five goals to two as their best performance they could not be said to have provided any reasons for optimism, but who can tell?

After dismally mediocre seasons it is customary to look at the cups and show how things were not too bad after all, but here swift exits were the order of the day, Hull City (by 4-1 aggregate) leading the way for Halifax in the Milk Cup. A visit from Scunthorpe United immediately ended FA Cup interest in round one (the score 3-1), whilst the Freight Rover Trophy later rounds did not include the Town, who went out again at the first hurdle. In fact, the players earned no overtime with the team playing the least possible number of matches designated for any season.

One bright spot was the striking form of Billy Kellock with 18 League goals and Longhurst with 13 also earned an honourable mention. Others to do consistently well were Roche (in goal), Brown, Ward, Lowe, Shaw, Nicholson and Knill.

No-one will envy the task of Mick Jones, who holds the 'hot-seat' of Manager now. If the team can improve we may be referring to him again next year.

Back Row L to R: Mick Galloway, Jimmy Willis, Paul Sanderson, Dave Robinson, Phil Whitehead, Alan Knill, Paddy Roche, Phil Brown, Adrian Shaw, Dean Martin, Nigel Foster. **Front Row:** Paul Fleming, Gary Nicholson, Russel Black, Billy Ayre (Assistant Manager), Mick Jones (Manager), Dave Longhurst, Steve Thornber, Barry Diamond.

HALIFAX TOWN

DIVISION FOUR: 20th   **FA CUP:** 1st ROUND   **MILK CUP:** 1st ROUND

MATCH	DATE	COMPE-TITION	VENUE	OPPONENTS	RESULT		HALF TIME	L'GUE POS'N	GOALSCORERS/GOAL TIMES	ATTEN-DANCE
1	A 17	CL	A	Chester City	D	1-1	0-1		Ward 72	(1,750)
2	20	MC1/1	H	Hull City	D	1-1	1-1		Shaw 6	820
3	23	CL	H	Scunthorpe United	W	2-1	0-1	6	Graham (og) 48, Lowe 85	1,094
4	27	CL	A	Mansfield Town	L	0-2	0-1	10		(3,299)
5	30	CL	H	Preston North End	W	2-1	0-0	6	Longhurst 63, 76	2,011
6	S 3	MC1/2	A	Hull City	L	0-3	0-3			(3,299)
7	6	CL	A	Colchester United	L	1-3	0-2	11	Gallagher 60	(2,023)
8	13	CL	H	Orient	W	2-1	0-0	10	Nicholson 72, Longhurst 85	1,243
9	17	CL	H	Southend United	L	2-3	0-2	12	Longhurst 53, Kendall 62	1,514
10	21	CL	A	Port Vale	L	2-3	1-2	15	Kellock 25, 82	(2,754)
11	27	CL	H	Cambridge United	D	1-1	0-1	15	Kellock 67	1,409
12	O 1	CL	A	Torquay United	L	0-2	0-0	19		(1,131)
13	5	CL	H	Aldershot	D	1-1	1-1	18	Kellock (pen) 35	1,066
14	12	CL	A	Wrexham	L	1-2	1-2	18	Gallagher 16	(1,609)
15	18	CL	H	Tranmere Rovers	L	1-2	0-1	20	Gallagher 50	1,412
16	23	CL	A	Exeter City	L	0-1	0-0	23		(1,719)
17	26	CL	H	Burnley	D	2-2	0-1	23	Kellock 54, Lowe 55	2,334
18	N 2	CL	A	Crewe Alexandra	D	2-2	1-2	23	Longhurst 16, 84	(1,493)
19	4	CL	A	Stockport County	L	1-2	1-1	23	Gallagher 4	(1,673)
20	9	CL	H	Peterborough United	D	1-1	1-1	21	Gallagher (pen) 21	1,007
21	16	FAC1	H	Scunthorpe United	L	1-3	1-1		Kendall 3	1,501
22	23	CL	A	Northampton Town	L	0-4	0-2	23		(1,514)
23	D 3	CL	H	Hereford United	W	1-0	0-0	20	Lowe 56	(1,015)
24	14	CL	A	Swindon Town	L	2-3	1-1	22	Coleman (og) 42, Kellock 73	(4,516)
25	22	CL	A	Scunthorpe United	D	3-3	3-1	22	Brown 8, 36, Kellock 21	(2,285)
26	26	CL	H	Rochdale	D	1-1	0-0	22	Kellock 85	2,253
27	J 1	CL	A	Hartlepool United	L	0-3	0-2	22		(3,392)
28	4	CL	H	Crewe Alexandra	W	1-0	0-0	21	Lowe 52	1,031
29	11	CL	A	Preston North End	W	1-0	1-0	20	Kellock 42	(3,184)
30	17	CL	H	Chester City	L	1-2	0-0	22	Kellock (pen) 75	1,473
31	21	FRT N	A	Scunthorpe United	L	2-3	1-2		Longhurst 34, Gallagher 79	(1,244)
32	31	CL	H	Colchester United	D	2-2	0-1	22	Sanderson 70, Kellock 73	800
33	F 4	CL	H	Exeter City	W	1-0	0-0	19	Longhurst 62	1,004
34	7	CL	A	Tranmere Rovers	W	3-0	3-0	16	Diamond 5, 39, Nicholson 42	(1,357)
35	11	FRT N	H	Lincoln City	D	1-1	1-1		Shaw 8	150
36	M 5	CL	A	Southend United	L	1-2	1-1	21	Diamond 20	(1,006)
37	8	CL	A	Aldershot	W	2-1	0-1	19	Kellock 65, Longhurst 70	(1,314)
38	14	CL	H	Wrexham	W	5-2	3-2	17	Kellock 3 (pen) 30, 76, 79, Knill 36, Sanderson 42	1,268
39	22	CL	A	Burnley	W	3-1	2-1	17	Nicholson 19, Lowe 28, Longhurst 80	(3,321)
40	28	CL	H	Hartlepool United	W	3-2	2-1	18	Longhurst 2, Kellock (pen) 11, Lowe 75	2,064
41	31	CL	A	Rochdale	L	0-1	0-0	18		(1,931)
42	A 4	CL	H	Stockport County	D	0-0	0-0	18		1,836
43	8	CL	A	Cambridge United	L	0-4	0-2	19		(1,909)
44	12	CL	A	Peterborough United	D	1-1	1-1	19	Knill 20	(2,260)
45	14	CL	H	Torquay United	D	0-0	0-0	19		1,062
46	15	CL	H	Northampton Town	W	2-0	2-0	18	Longhurst 20, 40	1,105
47	22	CL	A	Orient	L	0-1	0-1	20		(1,443)
48	26	CL	A	Hereford United	L	1-2	0-0	21	Kellock 84	(2,212)
49	29	CL	H	Port Vale	W	2-0	0-0	18	Longhurst 50, Kellock (pen) 84	1,389
50	M 2	CL	H	Swindon Town	L	1-3	0-1	19	Lowe 73	1,626
51	5	CL	H	Mansfield Town	L	1-2	0-0	20	Longhurst 89	1,414

Best Home League Attendance: 2,334 v Burnley 26/10   **Smallest:** 800 v Colchester Utd 31/1   **Av Home Att:** 1,410

Goal Scorers: Compared with 84-85: +29

League (60): Kellock 17 (5 pen), Longhurst 13, Lowe 7, Gallagher 5 (1 pen), Diamond 3, Nicholson 3, Brown 2, Knill 2, Kendall 2, Opponents 2, Sanderson 2, Ward 1

Milk Cup (1): Shaw 1
FA Cup (1): Kendall 1
FRT (3): Gallagher 1, Longhurst, Shaw 1

1985-86

Roche	Brown	Ward	Shaw	Kendall	Ayre	Gallagher	Kellock	Lowe	Longhurst	Nicholson	Podd	Knill	Sanderson	Thornber	Hotte (NC)	Robinson (L)	Fleming	Galloway	Diamond (NC)	Martin	Sharpe	Referee	
1	2	3	4	5	6	7	8	9	10*	11	12											T Holbrook	1
1	2	3	4	5	6	7	8	9	10	11												**M Peck**	2
1	2	3	4	5	6	7	8	9	10	11*	12											K Breen	3
1	2	11	4	5	6	7	8	9	10		3											I Hemley	4
1	2	3	4	5	6	7	8	9	10	11*	12											J Lloyd	5
1	2	3	4	5		7	8	9	10	11	12	6*										**G Tyson**	6
1	2	3	4	5	6	7	8	9	10*	11	12											M Cotton	7
1	2	3	4	5	6	7	8	9	10	11												R Guy	8
1	2	3	4	5	6	7*	8	9	10	11	12											K Redfern	9
1	2	3	4	5			8	9*	10	11		6	7	12								M Reed	10
1	2	3	4	5	6		8		10	11			9	7								C Trussell	11
1	2	3	4	5	6		8		10	11			7	9								V Callow	12
1	2	3	4	5	6	7*	8		10	11					12							T Fitzharris	13
1	6	3	4*	5		7	8	9	10	11	2		12									G Ashby	14
1	6	3	4	5		7	8	9	10	11*	2			12								K Lupton	15
1	6	3	4				8	9	10	11	2	5	7									B Stevens	16
1	6	3	4				8	9	10	11	2	5	7									J Worrall	17
1	6	3	4			12	8*	9		11	2	5	7									G Napthine	18
1	6	3	4				8	9	10	11	2	5	7									F Roberts	19
1	6*	3	4			12		9	10	11	2	5	7	8								M Heath	20
1	2	3	4		6	9	12		10*	11		5	7	8			12					**G Courtney**	21
1			4	12	6		8	9	10	11	2	5	7*	3								R Lewis	22
1	2	3	4		6	7	8	9	10	11		5										I Hendrick	23
1	2	3			6	7	8	9	10	11		5		4								T Ward	24
1	2	3			7	6	8	9	10	11		5		4								J-Bray	25
1	2	3			6	7	8	9	10	11		5		4	12							A Saunders	26
1	2	9			6	7	8		10	11*	3†	5		4		12						M Scott	27
1	2	3				7	8	9	10	11		5		4		6						C Seel	28
1	2	3				7	8	9	10	11		5		4		6						P Vanes	29
1	2	3				7	8	9	10	11		5		4		6						H Taylor	30
1	2	3			6	7	8	9*	10	11		5		4	12							**V Callow**	31
1	2	3					8	9	10	11		5	7	4				6				G Aplin	32
1	2	3					8*	12	10	11		5	7	4				6	9			N Ashley	33
1	2		4						10	11		5	7	8			3	6	9			D Allison	34
	3		4*					9	12	10	2	5	11				7*	6	12	1	8	**K Lupton**	35
1	2		4					12	8*	11		5	7	10			3	6	9			J Ball	36
1	2		4					12		11		5	7	8*			3	6	9†			D Axcell	37
1	2	12	4				8		10	11*		5	7				3	6	9			K Redfern	38
1	2		4				8	9	10	11		5	7				3	6				M Peck	39
1	2	12	4				8	9	10	11		5	7				3*	6				M Robinson	40
1	2	12	4				8		10	11		5	7				3*	6	9			R Bridges	41
1	2		4				8		10	11		5	7				3	6	9			I Hendrick	42
1	2	12	4				8	10		11		5	7				3	6	9*			C Downey	43
1	2		4				8		10	11		5	7				3	6	9			N Wilson	44
1	2	3	4				8	12	10	11		5	7					6	9*			F Roberts	45
1	2	3					8	9	10	11		5	7	4				6				R Nixon	46
1	2	3				7*	8	12	10	11		5		4				6	9			D Hedges	47
1	2	3	4			12	8	9	10	11		5	7*					6				E Scales	48
1	2*	12	4				8	9	10	11		5	7				3	6				T Fitzharris	49
1	2*	12	4				8	9	10	11		5	7				3	6				J Worrall	50
1	2						8	9	10	11		5	7	4			3	6				R Glover	51

Roche	Brown	Ward	Shaw	Kendall	Ayre	Gallagher	Kellock	Lowe	Longhurst	Nicholson	Podd	Knill	Sanderson	Thornber	Hotte (NC)	Robinson (L)	Fleming	Galloway	Diamond (NC)	Martin	Sharpe		
46	45	32	34	18	10	23	41	32	44	44	11	33	27	17	2	3	13	19	12			League Appearances	
	6		2			2	2	3		5		1	1	2	2							Substitute Appearances	
2	2	2	2	1		2	2	2	2	0-1	1											Milk Cup Appearances	
1	1	1	1	1		1	0-1	1	1			1	1	1								FA Cup Appearances	
1	2	1	1		1	1	2	1-1	1		2	1	1				1-1	1	0-1	1	1	FR Trophy Appearances	

Players on Loan: Robinson (Darlington)

Departures: Lowe (Hartlepool), Podd, Kendall, Gallagher (Scarborough), Kellock (Kettering T), Hotte (Frickley)

'THE SHAYMEN'

Formed: 1911
Turned Professional: 1911   **Ltd Co:** 1911

Previous Managers: Since 1946
Jack Breedon   W Wooton   Jimmy Thompson   Gerald Henry   Bobby Browne   Willie Watson
Billy Burnicle   Harry Hooper   Willie Watson   Vic Metcalfe   Alan Ball (Snr)   George Kirby
Ray Henderson   George Mulhall   John Quinn   Alan Ball (Snr)   Jimmy Lawson   George Kirby
Mickey Bullock   Mick Jones

Honours: None

League Career: Original Members of Div 3 (N) 1920   Transferred to Div 3 1958
Relegated to Div 4 1962-3   Promoted to Div 3 1968-9   Relegated to Div 4 1975-6

Colours: Royal blue shirts with white trim, white shorts with blue trim, blue stockings with white tops

Change Colours: Yellow shirts with blue trim, blue shorts, yellow stockings with blue tops

---

CLUB RECORDS

Most Appearances for Club: John Pickering: 367, 1965-74

Most Capped Player: None

Record Goalscorer in a Match: William Chambers, 5 v Hartlepool United, Div 3 (N), 07.04.1934   Albert Valentine, 5 v New Brighton, Div 3 (N), 09.03.1935

Record League Goalscorer in a Season: Albert Valentine, 34, Div 3 (N), 1934-5

Record League Goalscorer in a Career: Ernest Dixon, 129, 1922-30

Record Transfer Fee Received: £98,000 from Huddersfield Town for Bobby Davison, Nov 1982

Record Transfer Fee Paid: £25,000 to Huddersfield Town for Kevin Johnson, Aug 1978

Best Performances: League: 3rd Div 3 1970-1   **FA Cup:** 5th Round 1932-3, 1952-3   **League/Milk Cup:** 4th Round. 1964

Most League Points: 60, Div 4, 1982-3

Record League Victory: 6-0 v Bradford (P.A), Div 3 (N), 3 Dec 1955

Most Goals Scored in a League Match: 6 on 9 occasions

Most Goals Scored in a Cup Tie: 7-0 (h) v Bishop Auckland, FA Cup 2nd Round Replay, 1966

Record League Defeat: 0-13 v Stockport County, Div 3 (N), 6 Jan 1934

Oldest Player in League Match: Bob Souter, 52 yrs

Youngest Player in League Match:

Most Consecutive Undefeated League Matches: 17 1969	**League Matches Without a Win:** 22 1978-79
Longest Run of Undefeated Home League Matches: 19 1974-75	**Away League Matches:** 11 1970-71
Longest Run Without Home League Win: 11 1972-73	**Away League Win:** 40 1950-52
Most Consecutive League Wins: 7 1964	**Home League Wins:** 8 1935
Most Consecutive League Defeats: 8 1946-47	**Away League Wins:** 4 1927

Club Statistician for the Directory: M Belshaw

HALIFAX TOWN

PLAYERS NAME Ht Wt Birthdate	Honours	Birthplace Transfers	Clubs	APPEARANCES				GOALS			
				League	Milk Cup	FA Cup	Other Comps	League	Milk Cup	FA Cup	Other Comps
GOALKEEPERS											
Paddy Roache 6.1 11.9 4.1.51	EI (7)	Dublin £15,000 F	Shelbourne Manchester United Brentford Halifax Town	 46 71 89	 5 7 6	 6 3	 1				
DEFENDERS											
Billy Ayre 5.11 12.10 7.5.52		Crookhill £15,000	Scarborough Hartlepool United Halifax Town Mansfield Town Halifax Town	 141 63 67 32	 6 2 2 4	 8 1 3 2	 1 1	 27 5 7 2			
Phil Brown* 5.11 11.6 30.5.57		Hartlepool F	Hartlepool United Halifax Town	211+6 45	12 2	11 1	3	8 2			1
Paul Fleming 5.7 10.0 6.9.67		Halifax	Halifax Town	13+1							
Alan Knill 6.2½ 10.9 8.10.64		Slough	Southampton Halifax Town	 77	 4	 3	 1	 3			
David Robinson 6.0 12.3 14.1.65		Cleveland	Hartlepool United Halifax Town	64+1	4	5	3	1			
MIDFIELD											
Mike Galloway 5.11 11.7 30.5.65		Oswestry	Mansfield Town Halifax Town	39+15 19	1+1	1	1	3			
Dean Martin 5.10 10.2 9.9.67		Halifax	Halifax Town								
Adrian Shaw 5.9½ 11.6 30.4.66			Nottingham Forest Halifax Town	 55	 2	 1+1	 1	 1	 1		 2
Steve Thornber 5.9¾ 11.2 11.10.65			Halifax Town	43+6	2	2+1	1	2			
FORWARDS											
Russell Black 5.9½ 11.6 29.7.60		Dumfries F	Gretna Green Sheffield United Dundee (L) Halifax Town	 10+4 1		 				 1	
Barry Diamond (NC) 5.7 11.5 20.2.60		Dunbarton 	Barrow Rochdale Stockport County (L) Halifax Town	 50+2 6 12	 3+1	 2 0+1	 2	 16 3			
Dave Longhurst† 5.8 10.12 15.1.65		Northampton	Nottingham Forest (A) Halifax Town	 44	 2			 13			 1
Paul Sanderson 6.1 12.0 16.2.66		Leeds F F	Manchester City (A) Chester Halifax Town	 24 46+5	 2	 1	 2	 3			
Gary Nicholson 5.7½ 9.11 4.11.60		Newcastle £10,000 F F	Newcastle United (A) Mansfield Town York City Halifax Town	7+5 74+3 23+1 44	3 5 4 2	 3+1 1	 1 3	 4 3			

ADDITIONAL CONTRACT PROFESSIONALS

Jimmy Willis

APPRENTICES

NON-CONTRACT PLAYERS

THE SHAY   Halifax HX1 2YS

Record Attendance: 36,885 v Tottenham Hotspur, FA Cup Round 5, 14 Feb 1953

Smallest Home Attendance for a First Class Match: 856 v Colchester United, Div 3, 26 April 1976

Record Receipts: £14,000 v Manchester City, FA Cup Round 3, 5 Jan 1980

Season Tickets: Main Stand: £60.00 (£30.00 OAP/juveniles); Patrons & 160 Stand £70.00 (£35.00 juveniles/OAP); Ground: £50.00 (£25.00 juveniles/OAP)

Executive Box Season Tickets: 50 Club £120, Vice-Presidents £100

Cost of Stand Tickets: £5.50 (50 Club & Vice-Presidents), £3.00; Main Stand (£1.50 juveniles/OAP); £3.50 (Patrons & 160 Stand), £1.75 (juveniles/OAP); **Terraces:** £2.50 (£1.25 juveniles/OAP)

Match and Ticket Information: Applications in advance may be sent to secretary

Car Parking: Car park available with entrance in Shaw Hill

Nearest Railway Station: Halifax

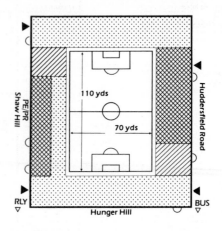

How to get to the ground

From North: Use A629 into Halifax Town centre, then at roundabout take 2nd exit into Broad Street and follow signs Huddersfield A629 into Skircoat Road for Halifax Town FC
From East, South and West: Use Motorway M62 until junction 24, leave Motorway and follow signs Halifax A629, then follow signs to town centre into Skircoat Road for Halifax Town FC

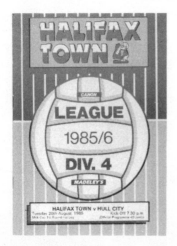

Price of 1986-7 Programme: 40p
Number of Pages: 24
Subscriptions: Apply to club for details with an S.A.E.

Local Newspapers: Halifax Courier, Yorkshire Post, Telegraph Argus

Local Radio Stations: Radio Pennine, Radio Leeds

HARTLEPOOL UNITED — Division 4

President
E Leadbitter, MP

Executive Vice-Presidents
R Boyes, MP
J C Thomas
E Ord

Chairman
J W Smart

Vice-Chairman
D Jukes

Directors
A Bamford ARICS
M Brown
M H Lancaster FCA
G Lormor
J McCardle
M Gough
P Montgomery

Secretary
Mr M Kirby (0429 725841)

Manager
W Horner

Commercial Manager
Alan Stevenson (0429 222077)

Assistant Manager
J Bird

Physiotherapist
T Johnson

The club certainly enjoyed one of Hartlepool's better seasons, and yet in the end there was still some disappointment for the club's supporters. Finishing 7th was their second best season since the Fourth Division was formed in 1958, but this came as an anti-climax after promotion had looked likely. The good season was achieved mainly through a much improved home record, and for once the Victoria Ground was not a place for easy pickings for the away club. Also with 13 penalties being scored in League games 'Pool cannot complain they were hard done by.

The season started with some mixed results, but then there was a steady improvement and in mid-October Hartlepool had reached third place. No doubt many thought this a flash in the pan, but in the event 'Pool were able to maintain a strong promotion challenge well in to the new year. A three-week winter lay-off proved to be disastrous with Hartlepool playing nine matches without a win. This all but ended the promotion chances although there was a short revival. Finally after looking to have secured fifth place, a bad finish saw 'Pool slip down to seventh — their lowest position since October.

In Cup football Hartlepool also had disappointments. They had started the season by defeating Darlington in the Durham Senior Professional Cup Final, but good wins against Derby County (Milk Cup) and York City (FR Trophy) proved meaningless as 'Pool went out on aggregate scores. A shock 1-0 home defeat to Frickley Athletic in the FA Cup is now best forgotten.

As for the players, record signing Bob Newton had a disastrous return ruined by a knee injury. His replacement John Borthwick came on well, but it was veteran Alan Shoulder who took on the major goalscoring responsibilities. Brian Honour continued to prove Darlington were wrong to release him and quite rightly was voted Hartlepool Player of The Year. He was an ever-present in League games as were goalkeeper Eddie Blackburn and captain Tony Smith. David Linighan had his best season so far, while Roy Hogan took his chance while Alan Little was out with a broken leg. Nigel Walker had a good first season with Hartlepool and Keith Nobbs made a successful return to League football.

Overall, a satisfactory season for manager Billy Horner and his assistant John Bird. For once the club's playing fortunes over-shadowed any problems off the field. Chairman John Smart looks to have got Hartlepool United running on the right lines, and it has to be said that he and Commercial Manager Alan Stevenson have done much to improve the club's image locally. Of course there is still a lot to be done — the Victoria Ground's 3,300 capacity will need to be increased if 'Pool are to make any money at the gate.   Gordon Small

Back Row L to R: Nigel Walker, Simon Lowe, John Gollogly, Tommy Sword, Bob Newton. **Middle Row:** John Bird (Assistant Manager), Alan Little (Coach), Kevin Dixon, Rob McKinnon, Eddie Blackburn, John Borthwick, Dean Gibb, Keith Nobbs, Tommy Johnson (Physio). **Front Row:** Alan Shoulder, Tony Smith, Billy Horner (Manager), Roy Hogan, Brian Honour.

HARTLEPOOL UNITED

DIVISION FOUR: 7th **FA CUP:** 2nd ROUND **MILK CUP:** 1st ROUND

MATCH	DATE	COMPE-TITION	VENUE	OPPONENTS	RESULT	HALF TIME	L'GUE POS'N	GOALSCORERS/GOAL TIMES	ATTEN-DANCE
1	A 17	CL	A	Cambridge United	L 2-4	1-0		Shoulder 11, Newton (pen) 69	(1,821)
2	21	MC1/1	A	Derby County	L 0-3	0-2			(8,415)
3	24	CL	H	Crewe Alexandra	W 4-1	2-0	10	Davis (og) 9, Dixon 25, Newton 68, Shoulder 70	2,165
4	26	CL	A	Chester City	D 1-1	1-0		Smith 22	(1,429)
5	31	CL	H	Orient	L 1-2	0-1	16	Shoulder 49	2,876
6	S 4	MC1/2	H	Derby County	W 2-0	1-0		Linighan 15, Hogan 74	1,611
7	7	CL	A	Burnley	L 0-2	0-1	20		(3,154)
8	13	CL	H	Rochdale	W 2-0	1-0	15	Dixon 35, Borthwick 84	1,942
9	18	CL	H	Northampton Town	W 2-1	2-0		Honour 3, Walker 14	1,892
10	21	CL	A	Torquay United	W 3-1	2-1	7	Borthwick 8, Honour 13, 49	(1,094)
11	28	CL	H	Swindon Town	W 1-0	0-0	6	Dobson 74	2,727
12	30	CL	A	Port Vale	L 0-4	0-2			(3,015)
13	O 5	CL	H	Peterborough	W 2-1	1-1	5	Borthwick 38, Hogan (pen) 88	2,584
14	11	CL	A	Stockport County	W 3-1	1-0	4	Gollogly 36, Honour 47, Shoulder 84	(1,827)
15	19	CL	H	Hereford United	W 2-1	1-0	3	Smith 42, Shoulder 65	3,490
16	22	CL	A	Preston North End	L 1-2	0-1		Hogan (pen) 47	(3,538)
17	26	CL	A	Exeter City	W 2-1	1-0	5	Hogan 44, Shoulder 57	(1,934)
18	N 2	CL	H	Mansfield Town	D 1-1	0-0	6	Hogan (pen) 51	4,220
19	6	CL	H	Aldershot	W 2-1	1-0		Nobbs 10, Dobson 72	3,329
20	9	CL	A	Southend United	L 2-3	2-1	6	Walker 42, Borthwick 44	(2,755)
21	16	FAC1	A	Macclesfield	W 2-1	1-0		Shoulder 40, 47	(3,000)
22	N 23	CL	A	Tranmere Rovers	W 1-0	1-0	3	Walker 23	3,107
23	D 7	FAC2	H	Frickley	L 0-1	0-0			4,100
24	14	CL	H	Colchester United	W 4-1	2-1	3	Shoulder 2, (pen) 43, Dixon 74, Robinson 78	2,507
25	20	CL	A	Crewe Alexandra	D 0-0	0-0	3		(1,070)
26	26	CL	A	Scunthorpe United	L 0-1	0-1	6		(2,495)
27	J 1	CL	H	Halifax Town	W 3-0	2-0	4	Shoulder 25, 37, Dixon 70	3,392
28	8	CL	H	Chester City	D 1-1	0-1	4	Holden (og) 78	3,891
29	11	CL	A	Orient	D 1-1	0-1	4	Honour 80	(3,667)
30	18	CL	H	Cambridge United	W 2-1	1-0	4	Honour 37, 65	3,300
31	21	FRT N	A	Rotherham United	L 0-3	0-1			(1,309)
32	25	CL	A	Rochdale	W 2-0	0-0	4	Borthwick 56, Shoulder (pen) 87	(2,301)
33	28	FRT N	H	York City	W 3-2	2-0		Lester 12, Honour 31, 81	1,080
34	F 1	CL	H	Burnley	W 3-1	0-0	4	Shoulder (pen) 62, pen 74, Linighan 69	3,336
35	5	CL	H	Preston North End	W 1-0	1-0	4	Shoulder 29	3,102
36	25	CL	A	Wrexham	L 0-1	0-0	4		(957)
37	M 5	CL	H	Port Vale	D 1-1	1-1	5	Sproson (og) 20	2,562
38	8	CL	A	Peterborough United	L 1-3	0-1	6	Borthwick 70	(2,300)
39	11	CL	A	Northampton Town	L 0-3	0-2	6		(1,815)
40	14	CL	H	Stockport County	D 1-1	1-1	6	Lester 4	2,662
41	22	CL	H	Exeter City	D 0-0	0-0	5		2,480
42	25	CL	A	Swindon Town	L 1-3	1-2	6	Smith 7	(6,172)
43	28	CL	A	Halifax Town	L 2-3	1-2	6	Shoulder 17, pen 66	(2,064)
44	A 1	CL	H	Scunthorpe United	L 0-1	0-0	6		2,781
45	5	CL	A	Aldershot	W 1-0	1-0	7	Walker 18	(1,277)
46	8	CL	H	Hereford United	D 2-2	1-1	6	Hogan (pen) 41, Honour 72	(2,023)
47	11	CL	H	Southend United	W 3-2	0-1	5	Little 46, Honour 49, Walker 60	2,235
48	15	CL	H	Torquay United	W 1-0	1-0	5	Compton (og) 19	2,080
49	18	CL	A	Tranmere Rovers	L 2-4	0-1	5	Hogan 53, Shoulder (pen) 63	(1,161)
50	22	CL	A	Mansfield Town	L 0-4	0-2	5		(5,523)
51	26	CL	H	Wrexham	D 3-3	1-0	5	Borthwick 35, Dixon 71, Hogan (pen) 72	1,520
52	M 2	CL	A	Colchester United	L 1-3	1-1	7	Hogan (pen) 8	(2,410)

Best Home League Attendance: 4,220 v Mansfield Town 2/10 **Smallest:** 1,520 v Wrexham 26/4 **Av Home Att:** 2,790

Compared with 84-85: +450

Goal Scorers:

League (68): Shoulder 17 (7 pens), Honour 9, Hogan 8, Borthwick 7, Dixon 5, Walker 5, Opponents 4, Smith 3, Dobson 2, Newton 2, Gollogly 1, Lester 1, Linighan 1, Little 1, Nobbs 1, Robinson 1

Milk Cup (2): Hogan 1, Linighan 1

FA Cup (2): Shoulder 2

FRT (3): Honour 2, Lester 1

Blackburn	Nobbs	Kelly	Little	Smith	Linighan	Shoulder	Honour	Newton	Walker	Dixon	Gollogly (NC)	Hogan	Borthwick	Dobson	Robinson	Taylor	Chilton (NC)	Chambers	Proudlock	Lester (L)	Wilson (NC)	Hewitt (NC)	Carney	Poskett	Referee	
1	2	3	4	5	6	7	8	9	10	11*	12														J Ball	1
1	2	3	4	5	6	7	8	9	10	11															J Key	2
1	2	3	4	5	6	7	8	9	10	11															D Phillips	3
1	2	3	4	5	6	7	8	9	10	11		12													G Ashby	4
1	2	3	4*	5	6	8	7	9†	10	11			12												A Robinson	5
1	2	3		6	5		8	9	10	11			4			7									T Simpson	6
1	2	3		5	6*		8	9	10	11		12	4			7									R Bridges	7
1	2	3		5	6		7		10	11		8	4		9										G Aplin	8
1		3		5	6		7		10	11	12	8	4	2	9*										N Glover	9
1	2	3		5	6		7		10	11		8	4		9										J Deakin	10
1	2	3		5	6		7		10	11	12	8	4		9*										T Mills	11
1	2	3*		5	6		7		10	11		8	4		9			12							R Nixon	12
1	2	3		5	6	11*	7		10		12	8	4		9										K Hackett	13
1	2	3		5	6	11	7		10			8	4		9										G Napthine	14
1	2	3*		5	6	11	7		10		12	8	4		9										J McAulay	15
1	2			5	6	11	7		10		12	8*	4		9			3							T Jones	16
1	11			5	6	8	7		10			12	4		9*		2	3							C Downey	17
1	11			5	6	8	7		10			12	4		9*		2	3							D Allison	18
1	11			5	6	8	7		10			12	4		9*		2	3							N Wilson	19
1	2			5	6	8	7		10	11		12	4		9*			3							E Scales	20
1	2			5	6	11	7		10				4		9			3	8						K Walmsley	21
1	2			5	6	8	7		10	11		12	4		9*			3							M Peck	22
1	2			5	6	8	7		10	11		12	4		9*			3							D Scott	23
1	2			5	6	8	7		10	9	11		4					3							K Walmsley	24
1	2			5	6	8	7	9	10	11	12		4*					3							L Dilkes	25
1	2			5	6	8	7	9	10				4					3		11					P Tyldesley	26
1	2			5	6	8	7	9	10				4					3		11					M Scott	27
1	2		4*	5	6*	8	7	12	10	9			4					3		11					D Scott	28
1	2			5			7	12	10*	9	11		4	8	6			3							K Cooper	29
1	2			5			8	7	9	10			4		6			3		11					C Seel	30
1	2			5			7	9*	10				4	12	8	6		3		11					H Taylor	31
1	2			5	6	8	7		10				4	12	9			3		11					J McAulay	32
	2	3		5	6	8*	7						4		9	10*			12	11	1	13			M Peck	33
1	2			5	6	8	7		10				4		9			3		11					D Phillips	34
1	2			5	6	8	7		10				4		9			3		11					T Mills	35
1	2			3	4	8	7		10				6		9			5		11					N Midgley	36
1	2			5	6	8	7		10				4	12	9*			3		11					N Glover	37
1	2			5	6	8	7		10				4		9			3		11					E Scales	38
1	2			5	6	8	7						4	12	9*	10		3		11					J Moules	39
1	2	4*		5	6	8	7		12	10			9					3		11					J Key	40
1	2	4		5	6	8	7	9	10*				12					3		11					C Trussell	41
1				5	6	8	7	9	12				4		10*	2		3		11					J Borrett	42
1	2			5	6	8	7		10				4		9			3				11			M Robinson	43
1	2			5	6	11	7		10				4		9	12		3						8*	C Seel	44
1		11*		5	12	8	7		10				4		2			3					6	9	K Barratt	45
1		9		5	11†		7		10				4	12	2			3					6	8*	R Gifford	46
1		11		5		8	7		10				4	12	2			3					6	9*	K Walmsley	47
1		11		5		8	7		10				4	9	2			3					6		T Simpson	48
1	2			11*	5	8	7		10				4	9				3					6	12	F Roberts	49
1	12	3		5	6		7		10*				4	8	9					11			2		R Guy	50
1	2			5	6		7		10	8			4	9		11*		3				12			M Peck	51
1		12	11	5			7		10	8			4	9*		6	2	3							H Taylor	52
46	**38**	**14**	**12**	**46**	**38**	**36**	**46**	**8**	**44**	**21**	**11**	**36**	**29**	**4**	**20**	**2**	**3**	**29**	**1**	**11**			**7**	**4**	League Appearances	
2	2	2	1		1					3	1	1	2	2	4							1	1		Substitute Appearances	
2	2	2		2	2	2		2				1	2	0-1	1						2	1			Milk Cup Appearances	
1	2	1		2	1	1	2	1	1			2	1+1	1	1	1		1		0-1	2	1	0-1		FA Cup Appearances	
																									FR Trophy Appearances	

Players on Loan: Lester (Scunthorpe)

Departures: Linighan (Leeds Utd), Robinson (F), Proudlock (F), Taylor (F), Dobson (F), Kelly (F)

'THE POOL'

Formed: 1908
Turned Professional: 1908   **Ltd Co:** 1908

Previous Names: Until 1968 Hartlepools United; 1968-77 Hartlepool
Previous Managers: 1908-15 Fred Priest   1919-20 Jack Manners   1920-22 Cecil Potter
1922-24 David Gordon   1924-27 Jack Manners   1927-31 Bill Norman   1932-35 Jackie Carr
1935-39 Jimmy Hamilton   1943-57 Fred Westgarth   1957-59 Ray Middleton   1959-62 Bill Robinson
1962-63 Allenby Chilton   1963-64 Bob Gurney   1964-65 Alvan Williams   1965 Geoff Twentyman
1965-67 Brian Clough   1967-70 Angus McLean   1970-71 John Simpson   1971-74 Len Ashurst
1974-76 Ken Hale   1976-83 Billy Horner   1983 John Duncan   1983 Mick Docherty   1984 W Horner
Honours: None
League Career: Original Members of Div 3 (N) 1921   Transferred to Div 4 1958
Promoted to Div 3 1967-8   Relegated to Div 4 1968-9
Colours: Blue and white striped shirts, blue shorts, blue stockings
Change Colours: All red with thin white stripes on shirt, red shorts, black stockings
Reserves League: Drybrough Northern   **Youth Team:** Northern Intermediate

---

CLUB RECORDS

Most Appearances for Club: Wattie Moore: Football League 448 + FA Cup 25 **Total 473**, 1948-64
Most Capped Player: Ambrose Fogarty, 1, Eire   **For England:** None
Record Goalscorer in a Match: Harry Simmons, 5 v Wigan Borough, (6-1), Div 3 (N), 1 Jan 1931   Bobby Folland,
5 v Oldham Athletic (5-1), Div 3 (N), 15 Apr 1961
Record League Goalscorer in a Season: Billy Robinson, 28, Div 3 (N), 1927-8   **In All Competitions:** Billy Robinson, 28
Record League Goalscorer in a Career: Ken Johnson, 98, 1949-60   **In All Competitions:** Ken Johnson, 106 (League
98 + FA Cup 6 + League Cup 2)
Record Transfer Fee Received: £60,000 from Brighton for Malcolm Poskett, Feb 1978
Record Transfer Fee Paid: £17,500 to Chesterfield for R Newton, Aug 1985
Best Performances: League: 22nd Div 3 1968-9   **FA Cup:** 4th Round 1954-5, 1977-8   **League/Milk Cup:** 4th Round
1974-5
Most League Points: 70, Div 4, 1985-6   **Most League Goals:** 90, Div 3 (N), 1956-7
Record League Victory and Most Goals Scored in a League Match: 10-1 v Barrow, Div 4, 4 Apr 1959
Most Goals Scored in a Cup Tie: 10 v St Peters Albion, 17 Nov 1923
Record League Defeat: 1-10 v Wrexham, 3 Mar 1962
Oldest Player in League Match: Terry Turnbull 34
Youngest Player in League Match: Craig Farnaby, 17
Most Consecutive Undefeated League Matches: 17 1968
Longest Run of Undefeated Home League Matches: 27 1967-68
Longest Run Without Home League Win: 8 1977, 1984
Most Consecutive League Wins: 7 1956, 1968
Most Consecutive League Defeats: 8 1950

League Matches Without a Win: 18 1962-63
Away League Matches: 7 1968
Away League Win: 31 1937-38
Home League Wins: 12 1933, 1951
Away League Wins: 4 1921-22, 1979

Club Statistician for the Directory: Gordon Small

HARTLEPOOL UNITED

PLAYERS NAME Ht Wt Birthdate	Honours	Birthplace Transfers	Clubs	APPEARANCES				GOALS			
				League	Milk Cup	FA Cup	Other Comps	League	Milk Cup	FA Cup	Other Comps
GOALKEEPERS											
Eddie Blackburn		H'ton-le-Spring	Hull City (A)	68	2	5					
5.9 10.5 18.4.57		£6,000	York City	76	6	5					
		F	Hartlepool	116	4	2	3				
DEFENDERS											
Rob McKinnon		Glasgow	Newcastle United								
5.11 11.1 31.7.66		F	Hartlepool United	1							
Roy Hogan		Hartlepool	Hartlepool United	224+12	9+1	9+1	5	8	1		
5.8 10.6 24.9.60											
Keith Nobbs		Bishop Auckland	Middlesbrough (A)	1							
5.10 11.10 18.9.61			Halifax Town	46	2	1	1				
			Hartlepool United	38+1	2	2	2				
Tony Smith	ES	Sunderland	Newcastle United	1+1							
5.10 11.11 20.2.57		£10,000	Peterborough United	68	3	4		5			
		F	Halifax Town	44	4	1		2			
		F	Hartlepool United	90	4	4	4	5			
Tommy Sword		Bishop Auckland	Bishop Auckland								
6.2 14.0 12.11.57		£6,000	Stockport County	236+2	15	6	3	51			
		F	Hartlepool United								
MIDFIELD											
Brian Honour		Hordern	Hartlepool United	63	2	2	2	9			2
5.7 12.5 16.2.64											
Nigel Walker		Gateshead	Whickham								
5.10 11.11 7.4.59			Newcastle United	65+5	1	3					
		San Diego	Sunderland								
			Crewe Alexandra (NC)	20		5					
			Sunderland	0+1							
			Blackpool (L)	8+2							
			Chester	41	2	1	2	9			
			Hartlepool United	44+1	2	2	1	5			
FORWARDS											
John Borthwick		Hartlepool	Hartlepool United	29+7				7			
6.0 10.12 24.3.64											
Kevin Dixon		Consett	Carlisle United	5+4							
5.11 11.0 27.7.60			Hartlepool United	65+1	4	2	2	18		1	
Bob Newton		Chesterfield	Huddersfield Town (A)	37+5	3+1	3		7	3	2	
5.11 12.6 23.11.56			Hartlepool United	150	5	12		48	2	10	
			Port Vale	48	2	1		22	2		
			Chesterfield	78	2	5	2	29	2	4	
			Hartlepool United	8+3	2		1	2			
Alan Shoulder		Bishop Auckland	Blyth Spartans								
5.5 10.5 4.2.53		£20,000	Newcastle United	99+8	4+2	6+1		35	2	1	
		F	Carlisle United	110+2	5	5		32		2	
		F	Hartlepool United	36	1	2	1	17		2	
Simon Lowe		London	Barnsley								
5.11 12.11 26.12.62		F	Halifax Town	74+3	5	2+1		19	2		
			Hartlepool United								

ADDITIONAL CONTRACT PROFESSIONALS

APPRENTICES

NON-CONTRACT PLAYERS

Ken Dodds, John Gollogly (18+2Lg+1FAC app/2Lge gls), Martin Hewitt (0+1Lg, 0+1FRT), Peter Judson, Alan Stevenson, Stuart Wilson (1FRT), Richard Edwards

Record Attendance: 17,426 v Manchester United, FA Cup Round 3, 18 Jan 1957

Smallest Home Attendance for a First Class Match: 655 v Bradford City, Football League Trophy, 18 Aug 1982　790 v Stockport County, Div 4, 5 May 1984

Record Receipts: £17,000 v Leeds United, FA Cup Round 3, 18 Jan 1979

Season Tickets: Seats: £68 (Stand) £39 (juveniles/OAP), Standing: £52.50 (Stand) £29.50 (juveniles/OAP)

Executive Box Season Tickets: None

Cost of Stand Tickets: £3.50 (£2.00 juveniles/OAP), Ground £2.70 (£1.50 juveniles/OAP)

Match and Ticket Information: No pre-booking of tickets

Car Parking: Side street parking is ample

Nearest Railway Station: Hartlepool Church Street (0429) 74039

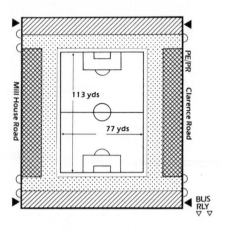

How to get to the ground

From North: Use A1, A19 then A179 S.P. Hartlepool to Hart. In 2.5m at traffic signals forward, then at crossroads turn right into Clarence Road for Hartlepool United FC
From South and West: Use A1, A19 and A689 into Hartlepool town centre, then bear right into Clarence Road for Hartlepool United FC

Price of 1986-7 Programme: 45p
Number of Pages: 16
Subscriptions: Please apply to club

Local Newspapers: Hartlepool Mail, Northern Echo

Local Radio Stations: Radio Tees, Radio Cleveland

HEREFORD UNITED — Division 4

Chairman
P S Hill, FRICS

Directors
M B Roberts (Vice-Chairman)
D Vaughan
J Jackson
A J Phillips
G R E Rivers
G C E Hales

Secretary
D H Vaughan (0432 276666)

Assistant Secretary
Mrs J Fennessey

Manager
John Newman

Assistant Manager
Alan Ashman

Commercial Manager
K Butler (0432 273155)

Physiotherapist
Peter Isaac

Back Row L to R: Wayne Cegielski, Kevin Rose, Michael Cartor. **Third Row:** Mel Pejic, Steve Devine, Ian Rogerson, Paul Butler, Ian Dalziel, Jimmy Harvey, Steve Spooner, John Delve, Danny Corner. **Second Row:** Ian Benbow, Stewart Phillips, Ollie Kearns, John Newman (Manager), Ian Wells, Bruce Halliday, Sean Edwards. **Front Row:** Jason Lee, David Thomas, Paul Mallender.

Hereford United lost at Mansfield on the first day of the season by four clear goals and followed this by beating Bristol City at home in the Milk Cup by five goals to one at home. The team finally finished ninth in Division 4 after being one of the pre-season favourites for promotion. Those two bare facts in the opening sentence give the cause for their failure; home form (only two defeats) was offset by very poor work away from home where only three games were won — at Northampton, Wrexham and Tranmere Rovers (the latter right at the end of the season).

The poor form on their travels meant that the players never placed the team in even a challenging position, although at the same time a re-election spot never seemed to be threatening. Victories in five of the last eight matches brought a final position which was better than it might have been, but it was still very disappointing.

The cups did bring some consolation. Bristol City only managed two goals in the second leg of that Milk Cup tie, which brought another confrontation with Arsenal, who at Hereford managed a goal-less draw; but in the return 'The Gunners' only went through by the odd goal of three in extra-time. The FA Cup saw Yeovil Town beaten at home (4-2), before a Second Round visit to Reading brought defeat by two unanswered goals. In the Freight Rover Trophy great things were done with Bristol Rovers, Swindon Town, Orient (2-1 away after extra-time) and Swansea City (0-0 at home and 5-4 on penalties) all despatched before Bristol City were encountered in the Southern Final over two legs. All went well at home (2-0), but the poor away form continued and a blank first-half was followed by disaster as City overtook the first leg advantage and they went on to victory at Wembley. So near! So far!

So wither Hereford? They obviously can do better and can at least claim consistency since only 18 players were used last season in competitive matches with Rose in goal an 'ever present'. Price, Dalziel, Pejic and Harvey were others to appear in most matches and Kearns with occasional injury problems did well to score 16 goals in the major competitions, but a total League scoreline of 74 fell short of promotion requirements with just two less conceded suggesting that the defence needed tightening.

Manager John Newman will have thought over these things and must now try again to put together a real promotion challenge. Like good wine the team will need to travel well.
WLM

HEREFORD UNITED

DIVISION FOUR: 9th   **FA CUP:** 2nd ROUND   **MILK CUP:** 2nd ROUND   **FRT:** SOUTHERN AREA-FINAL

MATCH	DATE	COMPE-TITION	VENUE	OPPONENTS	RESULT	HALF TIME	L'GUE POS'N	GOALSCORERS/GOAL TIMES	ATTEN-DANCE
1	A 17	CL	A	Mansfield Town	L 0-4	0-1			(2,405)
2	21	MC1/1	H	Bristol City	W 5-1	3-0		Kearns 1, Price 14, Harvey (pen) 43, Phillips 59, 77	2,449
3	24	CL	H	Swindon Town	W 4-1	1-0	13	Delve 14, 90, Dalziel 73, Phillips 89	4,049
4	27	CL	A	Crewe Alexandra	L 0-2	0-0	16		(1,914)
5	31	CL	A	Cambridge United	W 1-0	1-0	11	Phillips 29	2,924
6	S 3	MC1/2	A	Bristol City	L 0-2	0-1			(2,373)
7	7	CL	A	Chester City	L 0-1	0-1	15		(1,720)
8	14	CL	H	Burnley	D 2-2	0-1	17	Wells 57, Carter 87	3,411
9	16	CL	A	Stockport County	D 1-1	1-1	17	Wells 32	(2,255)
10	21	CL	H	Peterborough United	W 2-1	2-0	14	Phillips 17, Harvey (pen) 19	3,261
11	25	MC2/1	H	Arsenal	D 0-0	0-0			6,049
12	28	CL	A	Preston North End	L 0-2	0-1	17		(3,387)
13	O 2	CL	H	Aldershot	W 4-1	2-0	12	Kearns 20, Dalziel 29, Halliday 48, Price 78	2,256
14	5	CL	A	Northampton Town	W 3-1	3-1	9	Wells 3, Kearns 20, Carter 24	(1,998)
15	8	MC2/2	A	Arsenal †	L 1-2	1-1		Wells 24	(15,789)
16	12	CL	H	Torquay United	W 4-1	4-1	8	Dalziel 3, Maddy 18, Kearns 31, 36	3,053
17	19	CL	A	Hartlepool	L 1-2	0-1	9	Kearns 90	(3,490)
18	23	CL	A	Rochdale	D 2-2	2-0	9	Price 20, Pejic 36	2,761
19	25	CL	H	Scunthorpe United	L 1-2	0-0	10	Phillips 53	(1,564)
20	N 2	CL	H	Colchester United	W 2-0	2-0	9	Phillips 7, 37	3,081
21	6	CL	H	Port Vale	D 1-1	0-0	10	Harvey (pen) 80	3,305
22	9	CL	A	Wrexham	W 1-0	0-0	9	Wells 53	(2,190)
23	16	FAC1	A	Yeovil	W 4-2	2-1		Carter 3 13, 86, 89, Kearns 45	(4,533)
24	D 3	CL	A	Halifax Town	L 0-1	0-0	12		(1,015)
25	7	FAC2	A	Reading	L 0-2	0-1			(6,096)
26	14	CL	H	Tranmere Rovers	L 1-4	1-1	14	Delve 23	2,731
27	22	CL	A	Swindon Town	L 0-1	0-0	14		(7,364)
28	26	CL	A	Orient	D 2-2	0-1	14	Delve 47, Carter 63	(2,700)
29	28	CL	H	Crewe Alexandra	W 4-1	1-1	12	Wells 33, Devine 70, Pemberton (og) 74, Kearns 88	2,873
30	J 1	CL	H	Exeter City	W 4-1	0-0	10	Wells 56, 88, Kearns 58, Delve 73	3,157
31	3	CL	A	Colchester United	L 1-4	0-1	12	Delve 84	(2,216)
32	11	CL	A	Cambridge United	L 0-4	0-2	12		(2,149)
33	15	FRT S	H	Bristol Rovers	W 2-0	1-0		Wells 29, 51	1,770
34	18	CL	H	Mansfield Town	W 4-2	1-0	13	Kearns 13, 51, Wells 60, Harvey 63	2,883
35	25	CL	A	Burnley	L 2-3	2-1	13	Rodgerson 27, Carter 33	(3,920)
36	F 1	CL	H	Chester City	L 0-2	0-1	14		3,255
37	4	CL	A	Rochdale	D 1-1	1-1	14	Rodgerson 25	(1,081)
38	M 1	CL	A	Preston North End	D 1-1	1-0	14	Harvey (pen) 24	1,857
39	8	CL	H	Northampton Town	W 3-0	1-0	13	Maddy 13, 60, Carter 80	2,478
40	11	FRT S	A	Swindon Town	D 1-1	0-0		Maddy 48	(3,692)
41	15	CL	A	Torquay Utd	L 1-2	0-0	14	Harvey 47	(1,438)
42	19	CL	H	Southend United	W 2-1	0-0	10	Maddy 52, 85	2,002
43	22	CL	H	Scunthorpe United	D 1-1	0-1	10	Price 74	2,367
44	24	FRT S	A	Orient	W 2-1†	1-1		Carter 27, Harvey (pen) 111	(1,113)
45	26	CL	A	Peterborough United	D 0-0	0-0	11		(1,560)
46	29	CL	H	Exeter City	L 2-3	1-1	13	Maddy 8, Harvey 58	(1,989)
47	31	CL	H	Orient	W 3-2	2-1	10	Price 9, Carter 28, Harvey 68	(2,854)
48	A 2	FRT S SF	H	Swansea City	D 0-0	0-0		(won 5-4 on pens)	3,725
49	5	CL	A	Port Vale	L 0-1	0-1	12		(3,344)
50	9	CL	H	Hartlepool	D 2-2	1-1	12	Kearns 2, Cegielski 90	2,033
51	12	CL	H	Wrexham	W 3-1	2-1	10	Harvey 8, Carter 45, Cegielski 65	(2,588)
52	16	CL	H	Stockport County	W 3-2	1-1	9	Beacock 21, Kearns 58, 84	2,003
53	18	CL	A	Southend United	L 1-3	0-3	10	Harvey 84	(1,554)
54	26	CL	H	Halifax Town	W 2-1	0-0	9	Maddy 79, Carter 83	2,212
55	29	CL	H	Aldershot	L 0-2	0-1	10		(1,164)
56	M 2	CL	A	Tranmere Rovers	W 2-1	1-0	9	Kearns 27, Carter 67	(1,346)
57	6	FRTS F1	H	Bristol City	W 2-0	2-0		Phillips 32, Kearns 44	7,608
58		FRTS F2	A	Bristol City	L 0-3	0-0		(Bristol City win 3-2 on aggregate)	(11,558)

Best Home League Attendance: 4,049 v Swindon Town 24/8   **Smallest:** 1,857 v Preston N E 1/3   **Av Home Att:** 2,557

Goal Scorers: Compared with 84-85: −1,324

League (74): Kearns 13, Carter 9, Harvey 9 (3 pen), Wells 8, Maddy 7, Delve 6, Phillips 6, Price 4, Dalziel 3, Rodgerson 2, Cegielski 2, Beacock 1, Devine 1, Halliday 1, Pejic 1, Opponent 1
Milk Cup (6): Phillips 2, Harvey 1 (pen), Kearns 1, Price 1, Wells 1
FA Cup (4): Cater 3, Kearns 1
FRT (7): Wells 2, Carter 1, Harvey 1 (pen), Kearns 1, Maddy 1, Phillips 1   †After extra time

Rose	Price	Dalziel	Halliday	Cegielski	Pejic	Harvey	Delve	Phillips	Kearns	Butler	Rodgerson	Maddy	Carter	Wells	Davies	Beacock	Devine	Referee	
1	2	3	4	5	6	7	8	9	10	11								C Trussell	1
1	**2**	**3**	**4**	**5**	**6**	**7**	**8**	**9**	**10**	**11**								**K Barratt**	**2**
1	2	3	4	5	6	7	8	9	10	11								J Bray	3
1	2	3	4	5	6	7	8*	9	10	11		12						F Roberts	4
1	2	3	4	5	6	7		9	10	11		8						M Reed	5
1	**2**	**6**	**3**	**4**	**5**	**7**		**9**	**10**	**11**		**8**						**R Gifford**	**6**
1	2†	3	4	5		7	8	9	10	11	6*	12						A Banks	7
1	2	3	4	5		7	8	9				6	11	10				D Hedges	8
1	2	3	4	5		7	8	9				6	11	10*	12			R Guy	9
1		3	4	5		7	8	9			2	6	11	10				C Downey	10
1		**3**	**4**	**5**		**7**	**8**	**9**		**12**	**2**	**6**	**11**	**10***				**H Taylor**	**11**
1	2	3	4	12	5	7	8	9*	10	11		6						A Saunders	12
1	2	3	4	5		7	8		10			6	11	9				J Deakin	13
1	2	3	4	5		7	8		10			6	11	9				M Scott	14
1	**2**	**3**	**4**	**5**		**7**	**8**		**10**	**12**		**6**	**11***	**9**				**I Borrett**	**15**
1	2	3	4	5		7	8		10	11		6		9				M Heath	16
1	2	3	4	5		7	8		10	11		6		9				J McAulay	17
1	2	3	4	5		7	8	9	10	11	12	6*						V Callow	18
1	2	3	4	5		7	8	9		11		6		10				J Ashworth	19
1	2	3	4	5		7	6	9		11		8		10				R Groves	20
1	2	3*	4	12	5	7	6		10	11		8		9				J Ball	21
1	2		4	5	3	7	8		10			6	11	9				D Scott	22
1	**2**		**4**	**5**	**3**	**7**	**8**		**10**			**6**	**11**	**9**				**J Deakin**	**23**
1	2		4*	5	3		8		10	7		6	11	9	12			I Hendrick	24
1	**2**		**5**	**4**			**8**		**10**	**7**	**6**	**11**	**9**			**3**		**B Stevens**	**25**
1	2		5	4		8	9*	10	11	7	12	6				3		K Cooper	26
1	2	3†	5	4		7	8		10			6	11	9		6		M Dimblebee	27
1	2	3	5	4		7	8		10			6	11	9				M Cotton	28
1	2	3	5	4		7	8		10			6	11*	9	12			R Hamer	29
1	2	3		5	4	7	8		10	11	6*			9		12		E Scales	30
1	2	3		5	4	7	8		10	11*		12		9		6		T Ward	31
1	2	3		5	4	7	8		10*			6	11		9	12		D Axcell	32
1	**2***	**3**		**5**	**4**	**7**	**8**		**10**			**12**	**6**	**11**	**9**			**K Vanes**	**33**
1		3		5	4	7	8		10		2	6	11	9				J Lovatt	34
1	2	5		4	3	8*		10			12	6	11†	9				J Key	35
1	2	3	5		4	7		10			8	6	11	9	10			N Butler	36
1	2	3	4		5	7		10	11	8	6		9					C Seel	37
1	2	3	6	5	4	7				12	8	11	9	10*				T Jones	38
1	**2**	**3**	**4**	**6**	**5**	**7**			**10**			**8**	**11**	**9**				**G Napthine**	**40**
1	2	3	4	6	5	7			10			8	11	9*	12			T Holbrook	41
1	2	3	4	6	5	7			10			8	11	9				L Shapter	42
1	2	3			5	7	6	12				8	11	9	10*	4		K Miller	43
1	**2**	**3**	**4**	**6**	**5**	**7**		**9**				**8**	**11**	**10**				**I Hemley**	**44**
1	2			4	7	6	5	9		11		8		10		3		R Lewis	45
1	2	3		4	5	7	6	9*				8	11	12	10			R Hamer	46
1	2	3		4	5	7	6	9				8	11	10				R Nixon	47
1	**2**	**3**		**4**	**5**	**7**	**6**	**9**	**12**			**8**	**11**	**10***				**T Mills**	**48**
1		3		4		7	6	9	10	12	2	8	11*			5		R Tyldesley	49
1	2*	3	4	6	5		7		10			8	11	9	12			R Gifford	50
1	2		4	5	3	7	6	9	10			8	11					M Dimblebee	51
1	2		4	5	3	7	6		10			8	11	9				C Downey	52
1		3		4	5	7	6			11	2	8		10	9			P Vanes	53
1	2	9*	4	5	3	7	6		10			8	11		12			E Scales	54
1	2	3	4*		5			10	11	7	8			12	9	6		D Hedges	55
1		3		4	5	7	6	12	10			2		11	9*		8	T Simpson	56
1	**2**	**3**		**5**	**4**	**7**	**6**	**9**	**10**			**8**	**11**					**G Napthine**	**57**
1	**2**	**3**		**5**	**4**	**7**	**6**		**10**			**8**	**11**	**9***	**12**			**R Lewis**	**58**
46	41	40	30	29	45	42	38	18	32	19	14	32	31	31		9	9	League Appearances	
			2				2	1			4	1	1	3	1	4	3	Substitute Appearances	
4	3	4	4	2	4	4	3	3	3	2-2	1	3	2	2				Milk Cup Appearances	
2	2	1	2	1	2	2	2	2	2	1								FA Cup Appearances	
6	6	6	2	6	6	6	4	3	4-1	0-1	6	6	6	5	0-1			FR Trophy Appearances	

Players on Loan:

Departures: Maddy (Brentford), Price (Blackburn)

'UNITED'

Formed: 1924
Turned Professional: 1924   **Ltd Co:** 1939

Previous Managers: Since joining the Football League
Colin Addison   John Sillett   Tony Ford   Mike Bailey   Frank Lord
Honours: Div 3, 1975-6
League Career: Elected to Div 4 1972   Promoted to Div 3 1972-3
Promoted to Div 2 1976-7   Relegated to Div 3 1976-7   Relegated to Div 4 1977-8
Colours: White shirts with red and black trim, black shorts, white stockings with red and black tops
Change Colours: All red
Reserves League: Macbar League

CLUB RECORDS

Most Appearances for Club: Tommy Hughes: Football League 240, 1973-82, Chris Price, 289, 1976-
Most Capped Player: Brian Evans, 1, Wales   **For England:** None
Record Goalscorer in a Match: No player has scored more than four goals
Record League Goalscorer in a Season: 'Dixie' McNeil, 35, Div 3, 1975-6   **In All Competitions:**
Record League Goalscorer in a Career: 'Dixie' McNeil, 85, 1974-7   **In All Competitions:**
Record Transfer Fee Received: £100,000 from Derby Countyy for Steve Emery, Sept 1979
Record Transfer Fee Paid: £25,000 to Aston Villa for David Cunningham, Aug 1979
Best Performances: League: 22nd Div 2 1976-7   **FA Cup:** 4th Round 1971-2, 1976-7, 1981-2   **League/Milk Cup:** 3rd Round 1974-5   **Welsh Cup:** Finalists (3)
Most League Points: 77, Div 4, 1984-5   **Most League Goals:** 86, Div 3, 1975-6
Record League Victory: 5-0 v Chesterfield, Div 3, 28 Sept 1974   5-0 v Chester, Div 3, 10 Aug 1975   6-1 v Crewe Alexandra, Div 4, 16 Sept 1978   5-0 v Hartlepool, Div 4, 7 March 1984
Record League Defeat: 0-5 v Wrexham, Div 3, 22 Dec 1973   1-6 v Tranmere Rovers, Div 3, 29 Nov 1974
1-6 v Wolverhampton Wanderers, Div 2, 2 Oct 1976
Oldest Player in League Match: John Jackson 40 yrs 6 days
Youngest Player in League Match: Stuart Phillips 16 yrs 112 days
Most Consecutive Undefeated League Matches: 14 1972-73, 1984

Longest Run of Undefeated Home League Matches: 21 1972-73
Longest Run Without Home League Win: 11 1981-82
Most Consecutive League Wins: 5 1984
Most Consecutive League Defeats: 7 1976

League Matches Without a Win: 13 1977-78, 1978
Away League Matches: 6 1972-73, 1984
Away League Win: 28 1977-78
Home League Wins: 12 1973
Away League Wins: 3 1975, 1976, 1984

Club Statistician for the Directory: L Appleby

HEREFORD UNITED

PLAYERS NAME Ht Wt Birthdate	Honours	Birthplace Transfers	Clubs	APPEARANCES				GOALS			
				League	Milk Cup	FA Cup	Other Comps	League	Milk Cup	FA Cup	Other Comps
GOALKEEPERS											
Kevin Rose 5.11 12.12 23.11.60		Evesham	Ledbury Town								
			Lincoln City								
		F	Hereford United	153	8	8	9				
DEFENDERS											
Wayne Cebielski 6.0 12.3 11.1.56		Bedwelty	Blackpool	5+1							
			Hereford United	29+3	2	2	6	2			
Ian Dalziel 5.8 11.10 24.10.62		Sunderland	Derby County (A)	22	5+1	2+1		4			
			Hereford United	89+8	7	4	7	7			
Bruce Halliday 5.11 11.2 3.1.61		Sunderland	Newcastle United (A)	32							
			Darlington (L)	4							
			Bury	29							
			Bristol City	52+1	4	7	0+1	1		1	
			Hereford United	30	4	1	2	1			
Mel Pejic 5.7½ 10.6 27.4.59		Newcastle-u-Lyme	Stoke City	1							
			Hereford United	220	11+1	8	9	3	2	1	
MIDFIELD											
John Delve* 5.7 11.0 27.9.53		London	QPR (A)	9+6	0+1	1					
		£25,000	Plymouth Argyle	127+5	8	8					
		£15,000	Exeter City	215	17	13		20	3		
		F	Hereford United	93+1	7	4	4	9	1		
Jim Harvey 5.9½ 11.4 2.5.58	NI U23 (1)	Lurgan	Glenavon								
		£20,000	Arsenal	2+1							
		£35,000	Northampton Town								
		F	Hereford United	242+2	14	13+1	8	33	4	1	1
Ian Rogerson 5.8 10.7 9.4.66		Hereford	Pegasus Juniors								
			Hereford United	14+4	1	1	0+1	2			
FORWARDS											
Paul Butler 5.7 10.4 9.6.64		Stockton	Wolverhampton W. (A)	18+10	3+2			1			
			Hereford United	93+4	2+2			4			
Mike Carter 5.9 10.7 18.4.60		Warrington	Bolton Wanderers (A)	37+12	3+1	3		8			
			Mansfield Town (L)	18							
			Swindon Town (L)	4+1							
		F	Plymouth Argyle	6+6	0+1			1			
		F	Hereford United	65+4	3	4	7+1	9		3	1
Ollie Kearns 6.2 12.9 12.6.56	Div. 4, 79	Banbury	Banbury United								
			Reading	75+11	4+2	6+1		40	1	2	
			Oxford United	9+9	0+2	0+1		4			
			Walsall	31+7	2	2		11		1	
			Hereford United	127+2	5	7	7+1	41	1	5	1
Stewart Phillips 6.0½ 11.7 30.12.61		Halifax	Hereford United	216+8	10+1	11	5	71	6	4	1
Ian Wells 6.0 13.0 27.10.64		Wolverhampton	Harrisons								
			Hereford United	32+3	2	2	5	8	1		2
Steve Devine 5.9 10.7 11.12.64	NI Y	Strabane	Wolverhampton W. (A)								
		F	Derby County	10+1							
		F	Stockport County (NC)	2							
		F	Hereford United	8+3		1		1			

ADDITIONAL CONTRACT PROFESSIONALS

Player of the Year: Chris Price (now Blackburn Rovers)

APPRENTICES

NON-CONTRACT PLAYERS

Kevin Davies (0+1Lge)

EDGAR STREET Hereford

Record Attendance: 18,114 v Sheffield Wednesday, FA Cup Round 3, 4 Jan 1958

Record Receipts: £51,234 v Arsenal, FA Cup Round 3, 5 Jan 1975

Season Tickets: Merton Stand: £00.00 (£00.00 juveniles/OAPs); Len Weston Stand: £00.00 (£00.00 juveniles/OAPs); Ground: £00.00 (£00.00 juveniles/OAPs)

Executive Box Season Tickets:

Cost of Stand Tickets: £3.00 **Terraces:** £2.00 (£1.30 juveniles/OAPs)

Match and Ticket Information: Bookable in advance

Car Parking: Available near ground for 1,000 cars (approx)

Nearest Railway Station: Hereford (0432 266534)

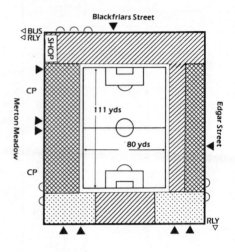

How to get to the ground

From North: Use A49 (S.P. Hereford) into Edgar Street for Hereford United FC
From East: Use A465 or A438 (S.P. Hereford) into town centre, then follow signs Leominster A49 into Edgar Street for Hereford United FC
From South: Use A49 or A465 (S.P. Hereford) into town centre, then follow signs Leominster A49 into Edgar Street for Hereford United FC
From West: Use A438 (S.P. Hereford) into town centre, then follow signs Leominster A49 into Edgar Street for Hereford United FC

Price of 1986-7 Programme: 40p
Number of Pages: 12
Subscriptions: Contact Ron Parrott c/o Club

Local Newspapers: Herefordshire Times, Evening News

Local Radio Station: Radio Wyvern

HUDDERSFIELD TOWN — Division 2

Chairman
K Longbottom

Directors
J Christie (Vice-Chairman)
E Lodge
C Senior
F L Thewlis
B Buckley
D G Headey
R B Fielding

Secretary
G S Binns (0484 20335/6)

Assistant Secretary
Mrs M Baldwin

Commercial Manager
Maurice Porter (0484 34867)

Promotions Manager
Steve Kindon

Manager
Mick Buxton

Assistant Manager/Physiotherapist
John Haselden

Reserve Team Coach
Jimmy Robson

Youth Team Coach
Steve Smith

Chief Scout
Steve Smith

Groundsman
Raymond Chappell

A disappointing season ended with The Terriers battling to avoid relegation to the 3rd Division. They eventually missed by six points.

Manager Mick Buxton made an important signing shortly before the start of the season, securing the transfer of Wales' international defender Joey Jones from Chelsea. In March Jones smashed Ivor Allchurch's caps record for Wales when he played his 69th international against the Republic of Ireland.

Huddersfield opened the season well by coming from 0-2 down to beat Millwall 4-3 at Leeds Road, a hat-trick from Dale Tempest doing the trick. With only one defeat in their opening nine League games, Huddersfield seemed to be lining up for a promotion challenge. But after they had lost at Sunderland, form became erratic and run of ten games without a win sent them plummeting into second-from-bottom place by mid-December.

Though they produced several good results, relegation remained a threat almost to the end of the season. When Tempest's goals supply dried up, he was allowed to join Gillingham on loan and Mr Buxton secured the transfer of Duncan Shearer from Chelsea.

The new man made a dramatic early impact, scoring a hat-trick in his first full game, at Barnsley on Easter Monday. Two more goals in his next game produced more much-needed points and Shearer finished with seven goals in only eight games, one of those as substitute.

Shearer scored the goal which beat Brighton in their 40th match and that virtually saved the club from the drop. Though Huddersfield lost their final two games, clubs below them also dropped points.

There was little to cheer in either of the Cups. The situation looked promising when the came away from Shrewsbury with a 3-2 lead in the first-leg of the Milk Cup's second round. But Huddersfield were beaten 0-2 at home in the return game.

Drawn at home to the 3rd Division's runaway leaders Reading in the 3rd round of the FA Cup, Huddersfield were held to a draw and then went out in extra-time at Elm Park in the replay.

Back Row L to R: Steve Smith (Chief Scout), Simon Trevitt, David Cork, Graham Mitchell, Joey Jones, Brian Cox, Simon Webster, Malcolm Brown, Julian Winter, Duncan Shearer, Jimmy Robson (Coach). **Front Row:** Andrew Thackeray, Phil Wilson, David Cowling, David Burke, Steve Doyle, M J Buxton (Manager), Ian Bray, Graham Cooper, Paul Raynor, Paul Wilson, Gary Worthington.

HUDDERSFIELD TOWN

DIVISION TWO: 16th   **FA CUP:** 3rd ROUND   **MILK CUP:** 2nd ROUND

MATCH	DATE		COMPE-TITION	VENUE	OPPONENTS	RESULT		HALF TIME	L'GUE POS'N	GOALSCORERS/GOAL TIMES	ATTEN-DANCE
1	A	17	CL	H	Millwall	W	4-3	0-2		Tempest 48, (pen) 51, 89, Webster 72	6,603
2		20	CL	A	Grimsby Town	D	1-1	0-1		Curran 59	(6,180)
3		24	CL	A	Oldham Athletic	D	1-1	1-1	5	Cork 32	(6,024)
4		26	CL	H	Portsmouth	L	1-2	0-1	11	Tempest 67	9,248
5		31	CL	A	Crystal Palace	W	3-2	1-2	8	Cork 5, Tempest 55, Webster 80	(6,026)
6	S	3	CL	H	Blackburn Rovers	D	0-0	0-0	7		9,060
7		7	CL	H	Bradford City	W	2-0	1-0	4	Cowling 8, Cork 85	11,667
8		14	CL	A	Sheffield United	D	1-1	0-0	7	Cork 53	(13,854)
9		21	CL	H	Norwich City	D	0-0	0-0	7		7,225
10		24	MC2/1	A	**Shrewsbury Town**	W	3-2	2-2		Jones, J 3, Curran 43, Tempest 62	(2,251)
11		28	CL	A	Sunderland	L	0-1	0-0	9		(18,980)
12	O	5	CL	H	Leeds United	W	3-1	2-1	7	Tempest 24, Stanton 37, Curran 63	9,983
13		8	MC2/2	H	**Shrewsbury Town**	L	0-2	0-1			4,966
14		12	CL	A	Shrewsbury Town	L	0-3	0-3	9		(3,986)
15		19	CL	A	Hull City	L	1-3	1-2	11	Wilson 12	(8,128)
16		26	CL	H	Carlisle United	D	3-3	0-0	11	Tempest 49, Raynor 79, Cork 85	5,012
17	N	2	CL	A	Stoke City	L	0-3	0-2	14		(7,291)
18		9	CL	H	Charlton Athletic	L	0-2	0-1	16		5,205
19		16	CL	A	Brighton & H. A.	L	3-4	1-2	16	Tempest 3, Cowling 52, 77	(7,952)
20		23	CL	H	Fulham	L	1-3	1-1	19	Tempest 44	4,650
21		30	CL	A	Wimbledon	D	2-2	2-0	18	Cork 26, Raynor 42	(2,805)
22	D	7	CL	H	Grimsby Town	D	2-2	2-2	20	Cowling 26, 39	4,881
23		14	CL	A	Millwall	L	1-2	0-2	21	Tempest 83	(3,645)
24		21	CL	H	Oldham Athletic	W	2-0	1-0	21	Cowling 38, Bray 68	5,094
25		26	CL	H	Barnsley	D	1-1	1-1	18	Raynor 2	10,575
26	J	1	CL	A	Middlesbrough	W	1-0	1-0	20	Jones 44	(9,320)
27		4	FAC3	H	**Reading**	D	0-0	0-0			9,875
28		11	CL	H	Sheffield United	W	3-1	1-1	18	Raynor 6, 60, Tempest 64	9,268
29		13	FAC3R	A	**Reading**	L	1-2†	1-1		**Cowling 5**	(8,726)
30		18	CL	H	Crystal Palace	D	0-0	0-0	17		5,729
31	F	1	CL	A	Portsmouth	L	1-4	0-1	19	Tempest 83	(10,937)
32		25	CL	H	Hull City	W	2-1	1-0	16	Cork 43, Curran 87	4,518
33	M	1	CL	H	Sunderland	W	2-0	2-0	14	Curran 18, 25	7,150
34		8	CL	A	Leeds United	L	0-2	0-1	18		(14,667)
35		12	CL	A	Norwich City	L	1-4	1-1	18	Curran 35	(12,772)
36		15	CL	H	Shrewsbury Town	W	1-0	0-0	16	Curran 56	4,511
37		18	CL	A	Carlisle United	L	0-2	0-0	18		(3,334)
38		22	CL	A	Bradford City	L	0-3	0-1	18		(9,058)
39		29	CL	H	Middlesbrough	L	0-3	0-1	18		5,585
40		31	CL	A	Barnsley	W	3-1	1-1	15	Shearer 44, 79, 85	(5,746)
41	A	5	CL	H	Stoke City	W	2-0	0-0	15	Shearer 68, 70	5,750
42		12	CL	A	Charlton Athletic	L	0-3	0-2	17		(4,143)
43		15	CL	A	Blackburn Rovers	W	1-0	1-0	14	Cork 38	(5,183)
44		19	CL	H	Brighton & H.A.	W	1-0	0-0	12	Shearer 68	5,469
45		26	CL	A	Fulham	L	1-2	1-1	16	Shearer 42	(2,877)
46	M	3	CL	H	Wimbledon	L	0-1	0-0	16		6,083

Best Home League Attendance: 11,667 v Bradford City 7/9   **Smallest:** 4,511 v Shrewsbury Town 15/3   **Av Home Att:** 6,819

Goal Scorers: **Compared with 84-85:** −419

League (51):   Tempest 12 (1 pen), Cork 8, Cowling 7, Shearer 7, Curran 6, Raynor 5, Webster 2, Bray 1, Jones J 1, Stanton 1, Wilson, Phil 1

Milk Cup (3):   Curran 1, Jones J 1, Tempest 1

FA CUP (1):   Cowling 1   †After extra time

Cox	Brown	Bray	Doyle	Webster	Jones P.	Curran	Cork	Tempest	Wilson, Phil	Cowling	Raynor	Jones J.	Stanton	Robinson	Winter	Mason	Wilson, Paul (NC)	Shearer	Butler	Referee	
1	2	3	4	5		7	8	9	10	11		6								G Tyson	1
1	2	3	4	5		7	8	9	10	11		6								D Shaw	2
1	2	3	4	5		7	8	9*	10	11	12	6								P Vanes	3
1	2	3	4	5		7	8	9	10	11		6								R Guy	4
1	2	3	4	5		7*	8	9	10	11	12	6								H King	5
1	2*	3	4	5		7	8	9	10	11	12	6								N Ashley	6
1		3	4	5	6	7	8	9	10	11		2								K Redfern	7
1		3	4	5	6	7	8	9	10	11		2								A Saunders	8
1		3	4	5	6	7	8	9	10	11*	12	2								J Worrall	9
1		**3**	**4**	**5**	**6**	**7**	**8**	**9**	**10**	**11**		**2**								**K Baker**	**10**
1		3	4	5	6	7	8	9	10*	11		2	12							D Allison	11
1		3	4	5	6	7	8	9	10		12	2*	11							J Hough	12
1		**3**	**4***	**5**	**6**	**7**	**8**	**9**	**10**	**11**		**2**	**12**							**G Courtney**	**13**
1	2	3	4		6	7	8	9	10	11		5								K Cooper	14
1	2		4*	5	6	7	8	9	10	11	12	3								J Bray	15
1	2		4	5	6	7	8	9	10*	11	12	3								C Napthine	16
1	2		4	5	6	7	8	9*		11	10	3	12							K Barratt	17
1	12	3	4	5	6*	7	8	9		11		2	10							N Wilson	18
1	2	3	4	5		7	8	9*		11		6†	10	12						R Groves	19
1	2	3	4	5		7	8	9		11*	10	6	12							K Lupton	20
1	2	3	4	5	6		8	9*	7	11	10				12					I Hemley	21
1	2	3	4	5	6		8	9	7	11	10									K Walmsley	22
1	2	3	4	5	6		8	9	7	11*	10		12							A Seville	23
1	2	3	4	5	6		8*	9	10	11	7		12							F Roberts	24
1	2	3	4	5		10*	8		9	7	11	6	12							M Scott	25
1	2	3	4	5				9	7	11	10	6	8							D Allinson	26
1	**2**	**3**	**4**	**5**			**12**	**9***	**7**	**11**	**10**	**6**	**8**							**R Dilkes**	**27**
1	2	3	4	5				9	7	11	10	6	8							H Taylor	28
1	**2**	**3**	**4**	**5**				**9**	**7**	**11**	**10**	**6**	**8**							**J Moules**	**29**
1	2	3	4	5			12	9*	7	11	10	6	8							C Trussell	30
1	2	3	4	5			12	11	9	7	10	6	8*							D Axcell	31
1	2	3	4	5		7	8	9	10	11		6								C Seel	32
1	2	3	4	5		7*	8	9	10	11	12	6								L Robinson	33
1	2	3	4	5		7	8	9	10	11*	12	6								J Lloyd	34
	2	3	4	5		7	8			11	9	6			10	1				D Hedges	35
	2	3	4	5		7	8			11	9	6			10	1				N Wilson	36
	2	3	4	5		7	8			11	9	6			10	1				K Lupton	37
	2	3	4	5		7*	8†	12	10	11	9	6				1				J Key	38
	2		4	5		7	8		10	11*	9	6				1	3	12		M Scott	39
1	2		4	5		7*	8		10	11	12	6					3	9		D Hutchinson	40
1	2		4	5		7			10	11	8	6					3	9		G Aplin	41
1	2		4	5		7			10	11	8	6					3	9		R Groves	42
1	2		4	5		7	8		10	11		6					3	9		R Nixon	43
1	2		4	5		7	8		10	11		6					3	9		K Walmsley	44
1	2*		4	5			8		10	11	7	6					3	9	12	H Taylor	45
1	2	3	4	5		7†	8		10	11†		6						9		G Courtney	46

Cox	Brown	Bray	Doyle	Webster	Jones P.	Curran	Cork	Tempest	Wilson, Phil	Cowling	Raynor	Jones J.	Stanton	Robinson	Winter	Mason	Wilson, Paul (NC)	Shearer	Butler		
37	36	32	42	41	14	33	37	29	35	39	20	38	7		3	5	7	7		League Appearances	
	1					1	1	1			10		6	1	1			1	1	Substitute Appearances	
2		2	2	2	2	2	2	2	2			2	0-1							Milk Cup Appearances	
2	2	2	2	2		0-1	2	2	2	2	2	2	2							FA Cup Appearances	

Also Played:

Players on Loan:

Departures: Jones P. (Oldham), Curran (F), Stanton (F)

'THE TERRIERS'

Formed: 1908
Turned Professional: 1908   **Ltd Co:** 1908

Previous Managers: F Walker R Puden J Howie A Fairclough A Langlry 1921 H Chapman 1925 C B Potter C Stephenson D Steele G Stephenson A Beattie E Boot T Johnston I Greaves R Collins T Johnston (reappointed)

Honours: Div 1 Champions 1923-4, 1924-5, 1925-6 (first of only three clubs to win the Championship three years in succession), Div 2 Champions 1969-70, Div 4 Champions 1979-80, FA Cup Winners 1922

League Career: Elected to Div 1 1910   Promoted to Div 1 1919-20
Relegated to Div 2 1951-2   Promoted to Div 1 1952-3   Relegated to Div 2 1955-6
Promoted to Div 1 1969-70   Relegated to Div 2 1971-2   Relegated to Div 3 1972-3
Relegated to Div 4 1974-5   Promoted to Div 3 1979-80   Promoted to Div 2 1982-3

Colours: Blue and white striped shirts, white shorts and white stockings

Change Colours: All yellow

Reserves League: Central   **Youth Team:** Northern Intermediate

---

CLUB RECORDS

Most Appearances for Club: W H Smith: Football League 519 + FA Cup 53 **Total 572**

Most Capped Player: Jimmy Nicholson, 31, Northern Ireland   **For England:** Ray Wilson 30

Record Goalscorer in a Match: D Mangall, 5 v Derby County (h) 6-0 Div 1, 21.11.31   A P Lythgoe, 5 v Blackburn Rovers (h) 6-0 Div 1, 13.04.35

Record League Goalscorer in a Season: Sam Taylor, 35, Div 2, 1919-20   **In All Competitions:** Dave Mangall, 42 (League 33, FA Cup 9) 1931-2

Record League Goalscorer in a Career: Jimmy Glazzard, 142, 1946-56   George Brown, 142, 1921-29   **In All Competitions:** George Brown, 161 (League 142, FA Cup 19)

Record Transfer Fee Received: £100,000 from Leeds United for Trevor Cherry, June 1972

Record Transfer Fee Paid: £110,000 to Mansfield for Terry Austin, Dec 1980

Best Performances: League: Champions (3)   **FA Cup:** Winners (1)   **League/Milk Cup:** Semi-Final 1967-8

Most League Points: 82 in Div 3, 1982-3

Record League Victory and Most Goals Scored in a League Match: 10-1 v Blackpool, Div 1, 13 Dec 1930

Most Goals Scored in a Cup Tie: 11-0 v Heckmondwike (H) FA Cup, 1910-11

Record League Defeat: 0-8 v Middlesbrough, Div 1, 30 Sept 1950

Oldest Player in League Match:

Youngest Player in League Match: Dennis Law 15 yrs 10 months

Most Consecutive Undefeated League Matches: 27 1925

Longest Run of Undefeated Home League Matches: 28 1982-83

Longest Run Without Home League Win: 11 1971-72

Most Consecutive League Wins: 11 1920

Most Consecutive League Defeats: 7 1913-14, 1955

League Matches Without a Win: 22 1971-72
Away League Matches: 18 1925
Away League Win: 31 1936-38
Home League Wins: 11 1925-26
Away League Wins: 5 1925

Club Statistician for the Directory: J D Loughrey

HUDDERSFIELD TOWN

PLAYERS NAME Ht Wt Birthdate	Honours	Birthplace Transfers	Clubs	APPEARANCES				GOALS			
				League	Milk Cup	FA Cup	Other Comps	League	Milk Cup	FA Cup	Other Comps
GOALKEEPERS											
Brian Cox		Sheffield	Sheffield Wed. (A)	22	4						
6.0 13.3 7.5.61		F	Huddersfield Town	156	16	9					
Keith Mason		Leicester	Huddersfield Town	30		2					
6.0 12.7 19.7.58											
DEFENDERS											
Ian Bray		Neath	Hereford United	105+3	2	7	3	4			
5.9 11.2 6.12.62			Huddersfield Town	32	2	2		1			
Malcolm Brown	Div. 4, 80	Salford	Bury (A)	10+1							
6.2 13.0 13.12.56		F	Huddersfield Town	256	22	18		16	2	2	
David Burke	EY	Liverpool	Bolton Wanderers (A)	65+4	5	1+1		1			
5.10 10.7 6.8.60		F	Huddersfield Town	158	17	11		3			
Joey Jones†	W (70), EC 77,	Llandudno	Wrexham	98	3	8		2			
5.10 11.7 4.3.55	Div. 1, 76, 77,	£110,000	Liverpool	72		9	15	3			
	Div. 2, 84, ESC 77	£210,000	Wrexham	145+1	15	14		6	1	2	
		£34,000	Chelsea	76+2	8	5		2			
		£30,000	Huddersfield Town	38	2	2		1	1		
Paul Wilson		Bradford	Huddersfield Town	7							
2.8.68											
MIDFIELD											
David Cork		Doncaster	Arsenal	5+2		1		1			
5.9 11.8 28.10.62			Huddersfield Town	37+1	2	0+1		8			
Stephen Doyle	WU21 (2)	Neath	Preston North End (A)	178+19	16+1	17+1		14			
5.9½ 11.1 2.6.58		F	Huddersfield Town	153+3	13	5		4			
Simon Webster		Hinckley	Tottenham Hotspur (A)	2+1							
6.0 11.0 20.1.64			Exeter City (L)	26			3				
			Huddersfield Town	57	2	2		3			
Phil Wilson		Hemsworth	Bolton Wanderers (A)	35+4	1	2		4			
5.6 10.4 16.10.60		F	Huddersfield Town	192+3	20	12		15	1		
Julian Winter		Huddersfield	Huddersfield Town (A)	18+2	1	0+1					
5.10 11.10 6.9.65											
FORWARDS											
Graham Cooper		Huddersfield	Huddersfield Town	3				1			
5.10 11.0 22.5.62											
David Cowling	Div. 4, 80	Doncaster	Mansfield Town (A)								
5.7 10.6 27.11.58		F	Huddersfield Town	292+8							
Paul Raynor		Nottingham	Nottingham Forest	3	1						
5.8 11.12 29.4.66			Huddersfield Town	20+10		2		5			
Duncan Shearer		Fort William	Chelsea	2				1			
5.10 10.10 28.8.62			Huddersfield Town	7+1				7			
Gary Worthington	EY	Cleethorpes	Manchester United (A)								
5.10 10.5 10.11.66			Huddersfield Town								

ADDITIONAL CONTRACT PROFESSIONALS

Graham Mitchell (A), Simon Trevitt (A), Andy Thackeray (M), Graham Cooper (M)

APPRENTICES

Junior Bent, Michael France, Carl Madrick, Lee Martin, Richard Shelton

NON-CONTRACT PLAYERS

Richard Gledhill

Record Attendance: 67,037 v Arsenal, FA Cup Round 6, 27 Feb 1932

Record Receipts: £52,607 v Newcastle United Division 2, 7 Mar 1984

Size of Playing Area: 115yds × 76yds

Season Tickets: Centre Stand: £80 (£40 Juniors/OAP), £70 Outer Centre Stand (£35 Juniors/OAP), £60 Wing Stand (£20 Juniors/OAP), £48 Ground (£24 Juniors/OAP).

Executive Box Season Tickets: Consult Secretary

Cost of Stand Tickets: £5.00, £2.50 Junior/OAP; **Terraces:** £3.00 (£1.50 Juniors/OAP)

Match and Ticket Information: Advance reservations only for special matches, otherwise admission to ground and stands on days of matches

Car Parking: Ample parking on all sides of the ground for 6,000 cars approx. All within 200 yards of ground

Nearest Railway Station: Huddersfield (0484 31226)

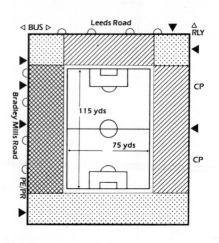

How to get to the ground

From East and M1 (Junction 38): Use A642 (S.P. Huddersfield) into town centre, then follow signs Leeds A62 into Leeds Road for Huddersfield Town FC
From South: Use A616 (S.P. Huddersfield) into town centre, then follow signs Leeds A62 into Leeds Road for Huddersfield Town FC
From West: Use Motorway M62 until junction 23 then A640 or A62 into town centre, then follow signs Leeds A62 into Leeds Road for Huddersfield Town FC

Price of 1986-7 Programme: 50p
Number of Pages: 32
Subscriptions: Apply to club

Local Newspaper: Huddersfield Examiner

Local Radio Stations: Radio Leeds, Pennine Radio, Radio Aire

 # HULL CITY

Chairman
D Robinson

Vice-Chairman
T C Waite, FIM, MIRTE

Directors
J Johnson MP
G H C Needler BA, FCA
C M Thorpe
H Bermitz
R Chetham

General Manager/Secretary
R M Linney (0482 51119)

Commercial Department
P Roper (0482 51119)

Player-Manager
Brian Horton

Assistant Manager/Coach
Chris Chilton

Reserve Team Player Manager
Dennis Booth

Physiotherapist
Jeff Radcliffe

The Tigers ended their first season back in the Second Division in a highly creditable sixth position—a placing they have bettered only six times before, and a mere twice since 1919. And yet there was an inescapable impression that it could have been an even more successful finish.

An all-winning January lifted the side into a position to mount a challenge for promotion, but when a string of good results was imperative, points were trifled away against some of the division's lowlier outfits and the chance was gone. It would be easy, although doubtless oversimplification, to point to Brian Horton's absence from the final third of the season as the decisive factor. The City boss stepped down for his new signing, the classy Garry Parker, but the former Evertonian, like most newcomers, needed time to settle in.

This was true also of Horton's earlier midfield acquisition, Bobby Doyle, who came into the side at a time when the Tigers were realising the difference in Third and Second Division standards. A difficult opening programme did not ease the transition, against teams who seemed able to exploit every error to the full. Here too it was the presence of Horton which helped put the side back on an upward path. Switching to a sweeper system brought, paradoxically, a glut of seven goals in his first two games, as the old campaigner led his men from behind.

However, as Frankie Bunn and Billy Whitehurst began to get the measure of Second Division defences, and spearheaded a bold bid for Wembley in the Full Members' Cup, Newcastle United stepped in with an offer of £230,000 for Whitehurst. With the bustling striker's contract finishing at the end of the season, it had to make sense to accept the offer, despite the criticism from the terraces, but a few months later the inevitable question was being asked: would the Tigers have been in the First Division if Billy had stayed? Bunn certainly missed the big target man's presence in the penalty box, although Andy Flounders was regularly amongst the goals in the second half of the campaign.

Defensively, special praise is due to Tony Norman, whose fine performances were rewarded with inclusion in the Welsh national side. In front of him, Skipper, McEwan and Jobson were highly competent performers, although the latter's attacking flair might have found freer expression in midfield.

Much depends on Brian Horton's ability to blend that middle line into an efficient, creative unit, and upon the front-runners to make the most of their opportunities. Then we could reach greater heights in 1987 than in its predecessor. Chris Elton

Back Row L to R: Steve Corkain, Andy Flounders, Paul Olssen, Nicky Brown, Lawrie Pearson, Gary Parker, Gary Swann, Steve Brentano. **Middle Row:** Andy Saville, Stan McEwan, Peter Skipper, John Davies, Richard Jobson, Tony Norman, Frankie Bunn, Bobby Doyle, Tom Wilson (Youth Team Coach). **Front Row:** Dennis Booth (Assistant Manager), Andy Payton, Pat Heard, Garreth Roberts, Brian Horton (Manager), Billy Askew, Neil Williams, Ray Daniel, Jeff Radcliffe (Physio).

HULL CITY

DIVISION TWO: 6th   **FA CUP:** 4th ROUND   **MILK CUP:** 2nd ROUND   **FM Cup:** NORTHERN AREA FINAL

MATCH	DATE	COMPE-TITION	VENUE	OPPONENTS	RESULT	HALF TIME	L'GUE POS'N	GOALSCORERS/GOAL TIMES	ATTEN-DANCE
1	A 17	CL	H	Portsmouth	D 2-2	1-1		Bunn 10, Whitehurst 76	8,221
2	20	MC1/1	A	Halifax Town	D 1-1	1-1		Flounders 41	(820)
3	24	CL	A	Leeds United	D 1-1	0-0	17	Jobson 69	(16,689)
4	26	CL	H	Blackburn Rovers	D 2-2	2-0	15	Rathbone (og) 26, Bunn 30	7,288
5	31	CL	A	Oldham Athletic	L 1-3	0-1	17	Whitehurst 60	(4,500)
6	S 3	MC1/2	H	Halifax Town	W 3-0	3-0		Bunn 22, 42, Whitehurst (pen) 33	3,299
7	7	CL	H	Middlesbrough	D 0-0	0-0	18		7,710
8	14	CL	A	Bradford City	L 2-4	0-1	19	McEwan (pen) 70, Swann 89	(4,930)
9	17	CL	H	Millwall	W 3-0	1-0	15	Bunn 7, 83, McEwan (pen) 90	6,021
10	21	CL	H	Carlisle United	W 4-0	0-0	13	Doyle 57, Swann 63, Whitehurst 81, Roberts 89	6,117
11	24	MC2/1	A	Queens Park Rangers	L 0-3	0-1			(7,201)
12	28	CL	A	Norwich City	L 0-2	0-1	14		(12,639)
13	O 1	CL	A	Crystal Palace	W 2-0	0-0	9	McEwan 70, Bunn 90	(5,003)
14	5	CL	H	Stoke City	L 0-2	0-1	12		6,890
15	8	MC2/2	H	Queens Park Rangers	L 1-5	1-1		Whitehurst 3	4,287
16	12	CL	A	Sunderland	D 1-1	1-1	13	Whitehurst 39	(16,613)
17	19	CL	H	Huddersfield Town	W 3-1	2-1	10	Whitehurst 2, 82, Williams 26	8,128
18	23	FMC	H	Bradford City	W 4-1	1-1		Whitehurst 41, McEwan 66, Bunn 68, 78	2,177
19	26	CL	A	Shrewsbury Town	D 0-0	0-0	10		(3,587)
20	N 2	CL	A	Sheffield United	L 1-3	1-1	13	Skipper 42	(13,272)
21	5	FMC NSF	H	Middlesbrough	W† 3-1	0-0		Bunn 49, Whitehurst 104, 115	3,637
22	9	CL	H	Fulham	W 5-0	3-0	11	Whitehurst 5, Roberts 40, McEwan 44 (pen) 85, Bunn 54	6,122
23	16	CL	A	Charlton Athletic	W 2-1	1-1	11	Bunn 15, 71	(4,140)
24	23	CL	A	Wimbledon	D 1-1	0-1	10	McEwan (pen) 59	6,576
25	26	FMC NF1	H	Manchester City	W 2-1	0-0		Bunn 48, McEwan 82	5,213
26	30	CL	A	Brighton & H. A.	L 1-3	1-2	11	Saville 23	(8,487)
27	D 7	CL	H	Crystal Palace	L 1-2	0-1	14	Bunn 64	6,058
28	11	FMC NF2	A	Manchester City	L 0-2	0-1			(10,180)
29	14	CL	A	Portsmouth	D 1-1	0-0	13	McEwan 81	(13,596)
30	22	CL	H	Leeds United	W 2-1	2-1	11	Jobson 29, Bunn 41	11,852
31	26	CL	H	Grimsby Town	W 2-0	1-0	10	Jobson 3, Askew 67	12,824
32	28	CL	A	Millwall	L 0-5	0-1	10		(3,783)
33	J 1	CL	A	Barnsley	W 4-1	1-1	8	Jobson 12, McEwan (pen) 57, Doyle 72, Ring 78	(8,363)
34	3	FAC3	H	Plymouth Argyle	D 2-2	1-2		Flounders 20, 56	6,776
35	7	FAC3R	A	Plymouth Argyle	W 1-0	1-0		Roberts 6	(13,940)
36	11	CL	H	Bradford City	W 1-0	0-0	7	Jobson 53	9,333
37	18	CL	H	Oldham Athletic	W 4-2	3-1	6	Flounders 30, 34, Jobson 37, 47	6,909
38	25	FAC4	H	Brighton & H.A.	L 2-3	1-2		Roberts 35 McEwan (pen) 58	12,228
39	F 1	CL	A	Blackburn Rovers	D 2-2	1-0	7	Bunn 45, McEwan 77	(5,414)
40	25	CL	A	Huddersfield	L 1-2	0-1	9	Roberts 59	(4,518)
41	M 4	CL	H	Shrewsbury Town	W 4-3	2-1	7	Flounders 3 10, 43, 87, Bunn 55	6,253
42	8	CL	A	Stoke City	W 1-0	1-0	5	McEwan 30	(9,112)
43	11	CL	A	Carlisle United	L 1-2	0-1	5	Flounders 76	(3,248)
44	15	CL	H	Sunderland	D 1-1	1-0	5	Roberts 1	9,295
45	22	CL	A	Middlesbrough	W 2-1	0-0	6	Bunn 51, Flounders 70	(6,233)
46	29	CL	H	Barnsley	L 0-1	0-1	6		7,903
47	A 1	CL	A	Grimsby Town	W 1-0	1-0	5	Flounders 21	(9,121)
48	5	CL	H	Sheffield United	D 0-0	0-0	5		9,645
49	12	CL	A	Fulham	D 1-1	1-0	6	Bunn 88	(2,795)
50	19	CL	H	Charlton Athletic	D 1-1	1-0	6	Askew 6	7,139
51	26	CL	A	Wimbledon	L 1-3	1-2	7	Flounders 34	(5,155)
52	29	CL	H	Norwich City	W 1-0	0-0	6	Williams 80	6,146
53	M 2	CL	H	Brighton & H.A.	W 2-0	0-0	6	Flounders 52, Williams 72	5,459

Best Home League Attendance: 12,824 v Grimsby T 26/12   **Smallest:** 5,459 v Brighton & H.A. 2/5   **Av Home Att:** 7,709

Goal Scorers: Compared with 84-85: −301

League (65): Bunn 14, Flounders 10, McEwan 10 (5 pen), Jobson 7, Whitehurst 7, Roberts 4, Williams 3, Askew 2, Doyle 2, Swann 2, Ring 1, Saville 1, Skipper 1, Opponent 1

Milk Cup (5): Bunn 2, Whitehurst 2 (1 pen), Flounders 1

FA Cup (5): Flounders 2, Roberts 2, McEwan 1 (pen)

FM Cup (9): Bunn 4, Whitehurst 3, McEwan 2

†After extra time

Norman	Jobson	Pearson	Swann	Skipper	McEwan	Williams	Bunn	Whitehurst	Askew	Roberts	Flounders	Doyle	Ring	Horton	Brentano	Saville	Parker	Heard	Brown	Referee	No
1	2	3	4	5	6	7	8	9	10	11										T Simpson	1
1	2	3	4	5	6	7	8		10	11	9									**M Peck**	2
1	2	3	4	5	6	7	8	9	10	11										G Courtney	3
1	2	3	4	5	6	7	8	9	10	11										H Taylor	4
1	2	3	7	5	6		8	9	10*	11	12	4								R Bridges	5
1	2	3	7	5	6		8	9	10	11		4	12							**G Tyson**	6
1	2	3	7*	5	6		8	9	10	11		4	12							J Ball	7
1	2	3	12	5	6		8	9	10*	11		4	7							N Wilson	8
1	2	3	7	5	6		8	9		11		4		10						A Robinson	9
1	2	3	7	5	6		8	9		11		4		10						J Ashworth	10
1	2	3	7	5	6		8*	9		11	12	4		10						**J Martin**	11
1	2	3	7*	5	6		8	9		11		4		10	12					M Cotton	12
1	2	3	7	5	6		8	9		11		4		10						K Barratt	13
1	2	3*	7	5	6		8	9		11	12	4		10						K Redfern	14
1	2	3		5	6	7	8	9	10	11		4								**D Scott**	15
1	2	3			6	7	8*	9	10	11		4		5		12				J Worrall	16
1	5	3			6	7	8	9	10	11		4			2					J Bray	17
1	5	3	12		6	7	13	9	10	11	8*	4*			2					**M Scott**	18
1	5	3	12		6	7	8	9	10	11*		4			2					H King	19
1	2	3		5	6	7	8	9	10*	11	12	4								V Callow	20
1	2	3		5	6	7	8*	9	10*	11	13	4				12				**D Hutchinson**	21
1	2	3		5	6	7	8	9	10	11*		4				12				L Dilkes	22
1	2	3		5	6	7	8	9	10			4			11					G Napthine	23
1		3		5	6	7	8	9	10	11		4			2					R Banks	24
1	2	12	3*	5	6	7	8	9	10			4			11	13				**G Courtney**	25
1	2			5	6	7	8		10	11*		4	12	3	9					E Scales	26
1	2			5	6	7*	8		10	11		4	12	3	9					K Lupton	27
1	2	3		5	6	7	8		10	11		4				9				**K Baker**	28
1	2	3		5	6	7*	8		10	11	12	4				9				K Miller	29
1	2	3		5	6	7	8		10	11		4	12			9*				B Eland rpd N Glover	30
1	2	3		5	6	7	8		10	11		4		9						I Hendrick	31
1	2	3		5	6	7*	8		10		12	4		9	11					I Hemley	32
1	2	3		5	6		8		10		9	4		7	11					T Fitzharris	33
1	2	3		5	6		8		10	11	9	4			7					**J Worrall**	34
1	2	3		5	6		8		10	11	9	4			7					**J Deakin**	35
1	2	3		5	6		8		10	11	9	4			7					A Saunders	36
1	2	3		5	6		8		10	11	9	4			7					K Redfern	37
1	2	3		5	6		8		10	11	9	4			7					**P Tyldesley**	38
1	2*	3		5	6		8		10	11	9	4	12		7					T Holbrook	39
1		2	3	5	6		8		10	11	9	4					7			C Seel	40
1	3	2		5	6		8		10	11	9	4				12	7*			K Walmsley	41
1	3	2		5	6		8		10	11	9	4					7			K Barratt	42
1	3	2		5	6		8		10	11	9	4					7			N Wilson	43
1	2	3		5	6		8		10	11	9	4					7			P Vanes	44
1	2*	3	12	5	6		8		10	11	9	4					7			T Mills	45
1	3*	2		5	6		8		10	11	9	4					7	12		A Seville	46
1	2	3		5	6		8		10	11	9	4					7	10		J Key	47
1	2	3		5	6		8			11	9	4					7*	10		A Robinson	48
1	2	3		5	6		8			11	9*	4					7	10	12	K Cooper	49
1	2	3		5	6		8			11		9	4				7	10		M Heath	50
1	2	3		5	6		8			12	11*	9	4				7	10		G Napthine	51
1	2	11	3	5	6		8				9*	4				12		10		D Allison	52
1	2	11	3*	5	6	7	8				9	4				12		10		N Glover	53
42	**36**	**20**	**37**	**39**	**42**	**18**	**42**	**18**	**32**	**33**	**20**	**39**	**4**	**10**	**7**	**4**	**12**	**7**		League Appearances	
	2	1		1			1				5		5			5		1	1	Substitute Appearances	
4	4	3	4	4	4	2	4	3	3	4	3	4	0-1	1						Milk Cup Appearances	
3	3		3	3	3		3		3	3	3	3		1	2					FA Cup Appearances	
4	4	0-1	4	3-1	4	4	3-1	3	4	3		1-1	4			2	1-2			FM Cup Appearances	

Players on Loan:

Departures: Whitehurst (Newcastle Utd), Ring (Aldershot)

'THE TIGERS'

Formed: 1904
Turned Professional: 1904   **Ltd Co:** 1904

Previous Managers: 1905-13 Ambrose Langley   1913-4 Harry Chapman   1914-6 F G Stringer
1916-21 David Menzies (1)   1921-3 Harry Lewis   1923-31 Bill McCracken   1931-4 Haydn Green
1934-6 Jack Hill   1936 David Menzies (2)   1936-46 Ernie Blackburn   1946-8 Frank Buckley
1948-51 Raich Carter   1952-5 Bob Jackson   1955-61 Bob Brocklebank   1961-70 Cliff Britton
1970-4 Terry Neill   1974-7 John Kaye   1977-8 Bobby Collins   1978-9 Ken Houghton
1980-2 Mike Smith   1982-4 Colin Appleton
Honours: Champions Div 3 (N) 1932-3, 1948-9   Champions Div 3, 1965-6
League Career: Elected to Div 2 1905   Relegated to Div 3 (N) 1929-30
Promoted to Div 2 1932-3   Relegated to Div 3 (N) 1935-6   Promoted to Div 2 1948-9
Relegated to Div 3 (N) 1955-6   Division 3 1958   Promoted to Div 2 1958-9
Relegated to Div 3 1959-60   Promoted to Div 2 1965-6   Relegated to Div 3 1977-8
Relegated to Div 4 1980-1   Promoted to Div 3 1982-3   Promoted to Div 2 1984-5
Colours: Amber shirts with red pin stripe and black trim, black shorts with amber and red stripe, black
stockings with red and amber tops
Change Colours: All white
Reserves League: Central Div 1   **Youth League:** Northern Intermediate

CLUB RECORDS

Most Appearances for Club: Andy Davidson: Football League 520 + FA Cup 43 + League Cup 16 **Total 579**
Most Capped Player: Terry Neill, 15, Northern Ireland   **For England:** The following all went on Dominions tours—Stan
Alexander (Canada, 1931) Chris Chilton (Australia, 1971) David Mercer (South Africa, 1920) Ken Wagstaff (Australia,
1971). Gordon Wright won 20 caps at Amateur level—including one for the 1912 Olympic Games. He also won a full England
cap on 19th March 1906 against Wales, which was just three weeks before his first appearance for Hull City. Most lists of
international appearances show Portsmouth as his club, but the City management had been negotiating with Wright since the
turn of the year. It may be that he was already a Hull City player when he won that full cap.
Record Goalscorer in a Match: Ken McDonald, 5 v Bristol City (5-1), Div 2, 17.11.28
Sim Raleigh, 5 v Halifax Town (10-0), Div 3 (N) 26.12.30
Record League Goalscorer in a Season: Bill McNaughton, 41, Div 3 (N), 1932-33   **In All Competitions:** Bill
McNaughton, 42 (League 41, FA Cup 1) 1932-33
Record League Goalscorer in a Career: Chris Chilton, 194, 1960-71   **In All Competitions:** Chris Chilton, 220 (League
194 + FA Cup 16 + League Cup 10)
Record Transfer Fee Received: £200,000 from Manchester United for Stuart Pearson, May 1974
Record Transfer Fee Paid: £150,000 to Carlisle for Mick Tait, Sept 1979
Best Performances: League: 3rd Div 2 1909-10   **FA Cup:** Semi-Final 1930   **League/Milk Cup:** 4th Round, 1973-4,
1975-6, 1977-8
Most League Points: (2pts for a win) 69, Div 3, 1965-6   (3pts for a win) 90, Div 4 1982-3
Most League Goals: 109, Div 3, 1965-6
Record League Victory and Most Goals in a First Class Match: 11-1 v Carlisle United, Div 3 (N), 14 Jan 1939
Most Goals Scored in a Cup Tie: 8-1 v Grimethorpe United 1st Qualifying Round FA Cup (H), 7 Oct 1905   8-2 v
Stalybridge Celtic 1st Round FA Cup (A), 26 Nov 1932
Record League Defeat: 0-8 v Wolverhampton Wanderers, Div 2, 4 Nov 1911 (At the time this game was played, Hull City
were top of Div 2)
Oldest Player in League Match: Eddie Burbanks 40 yrs 3 months
Youngest Player in League Match: Andy Flounders 16 yrs 269 days
Most Consecutive Undefeated League Matches: 15 1964-65   **League Matches Without a Win:** 16 1936
Longest Run of Undefeated Home League Matches: 25 1932-33,
1965-66   **Away League Matches:** 13 1948-9
Longest Run Without Home League Win: 12 1935-36   **Away League Win:** 35 1979-81
Most Consecutive League Wins: 10 1948, 1966   **Home League Wins:** 19 1965-66
Most Consecutive League Defeats: 8 1934   **Away League Wins:** 5 1905-06, 1909-10,
1913-14, 1964-65, 1966

Club Statistician for the Directory: Chris Elton

HULL CITY

PLAYERS NAME Ht Wt Birthdate	Honours	Birthplace Transfers	Clubs	APPEARANCES League	Milk Cup	FA Cup	Other Comps	GOALS League	Milk Cup	FA Cup	Other Comps
GOALKEEPERS											
John Davies 6.3 13.2 18.11.59	.	Llandysull £12,000	Cardiff City (A) Hull City Notts County (L)	7 24 10	1	2					
Tony Norman+ 6.1½ 12.8 24.2.58	WY	Mancot £30,000	Burnley Hull City	265	17	20	7				
DEFENDERS											
Dennis Booth 5.7½ 11.3 9.4.49		Stanley £7,000 £7,000 £9,000 £10,000 £40,000	Charlton Athletic (A) Blackpool Southend United Lincoln City Watford Hull City	67+10 12 77+1 162 97+3 121+1	1 3 3 10+1 11 7	4 3 13 6 12	0+1	5 1 9 2 2	1		
Steve Brentano 5.8½ 10.12 9.11.62		Hull	Hull City	9							
Laurie Pearson 6.0 11.2 2.7.65		Wallsend	Manchester United Hull City	51+1	7	3	1				
Peter Skipper* 5.11 12.6 16.4.58		Hull F £10,000	Hull City Scunthorpe United (L) Darlington Hull City	22+1 0+1 91 177+1	4 12	1 3 10	7	4 11	1		
Gary Swann 5.8½ 10.10 11.4.62		York	Hull City (A)	167+10	7+1	11					
MIDFIELD											
Billy Askew 5.6½ 10.2 2.10.59		Lumley F F	Middlesbrough (A) Gateshead Hull City	10+2 143	9	9	5+2	15			1
Frank Bunn 5.11 10.6 6.11.62		Birmingham	Luton Town (A) Hull City	52+7 42	6+1 4	2 3	1	8 14	3 2		
Robert Doyle 6.0 11.2 27.12.53	Div. 3, 83	Dumbarton £20,000 £120,000 £90,000	Dumbarton Barnsley Peterborough United Blackpool Portsmouth Hull City	148+1 130 47+2 169+4	5 18 6 13	6 8 5 4		16 10 2 16	2 1		
Pat Heard 5.10 11.0 17.3.60	EY	Hull	Everton (A) Aston Villa Sheffield Wednesday Newcastle United Middlesbrough Hull City	10+1 20+4 22+3 34 25 7+1	0+1 1	6 2 1		2 3 2 2			
Brian Horton 5.9 11.4 4.2.49	Div. 2, 80, 82	Hednesford £30,000 £100,000 F	Hednesford Town Port Vale Brighton & H.A. Luton Town Hull City	232+4 217+1 118 32	6 24 8 3	16 10 6 4	1	33 33 8	3 6 2	2 2	
Richard Jobson 6.1 12.2 9.5.63		Hull £22,000 £40,000	Burton Albion Watford Hull City	26+2 42+2	2 4	3		4 7			
Stan McEwan 5.11 12.8 8.6.57		Cambuskenneth	Blackpool (A) Exeter City Hull City	204+10 65 95	16 4 8	13 3 6	5	24 15 22	6 1 2	2 1	1
Garry Parker 5.8 11.0 7.9.65	EY	Oxford	Luton Town (A) Hull City	18+4 12	1+3	1+1		1	1		
Garreth Roberts 5.4 10.2 15.11.60		Hull	Hull City (A)	253+3	17	20	5+1	36	3	4	4
Neil Williams 5.10 11.0 23.10.64	EY FAYC 82	Waltham Abbey F	Watford (A) Hull City	30+6	2	1	1	16			
FORWARDS											
Andy Flounders 5.7½ 10.0 13.12.63		Hull	Hull City (A)	108+23	3+2	8+2	3+2	51	13	14	
Paul Olsson 5.10 10.7 24.12.65		Hull	Hull City (A)								
Andy Saville 6.0 12.0 12.12.64		Hull	Hull City	7+6				1			

ADDITIONAL CONTRACT PROFESSIONALS

APPRENTICES

NON-CONTRACT PLAYERS

David Anderson, Michael Barrett, Neal Buckley, Anthony Dobson, David England, Leigh Jenkinson, Gavin Kelly, Mark Richardson, Michael Smith, Dean Windass

BOOTHFERRY PARK Hull HU4 6EU

Record Attendance: 55,019 v Manchester United, FA Cup Round 6, 26 Feb 1949

Smallest Home Attendance for a First Class Match: 1,621 v Hartlepools (Group Cup), 22 Aug 1981

Record Receipts: £37,778 v Southampton, Milk Cup, 2nd Round 2nd Leg, 9 Oct 1984

Season Tickets: Stand: £90.00 (Main Stand), £60.00 (South), £42.00, £32.00 respectively juveniles/OAP; Ground: £48.00 (£26 juveniles/OAP)

Executive Box Season Tickets: None available

Cost of Stand Tickets: £6.00, £4.00 (£3.50, £2.50 respectively juveniles/OAP); **Terraces:** £3.00 (£1.50 juveniles/OAP)

Match and Ticket Information:

Car Parking: Limited parking in front of ground

Nearest Railway Station: Hull Paragon (0482 26033) or Boothferry Halt by the ground

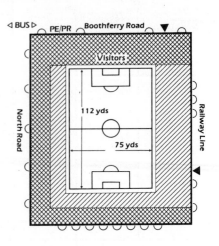

How to get to the ground

From North: Use A1 or A19 then A1079 S.P. Hull into town centre then follow signs Leeds A63 into Anlaby Road, then at roundabout take 1st exit into Boothferry Road for Hull City FC
From West: Use Motorway M62 then A63 S.P. Hull into Boothferry Road for Hull City FC
From South: Use Motorway M1, M18 then M62 and A63 S.P. Hull into Boothferry Road for Hull City FC

Price of 1986-7 Programme: 50p
Number of Pages: 24
Subscriptions: £20.00 (postage paid UK) for season

Local Newspaper: Hull Daily Mail

Local Radio Stations: BBC Radio Humberside (202 medium wave), Viking Radio

President
Lady Blanche Cobbold

Chairman
Patrick Cobbold

Directors
Kenneth Brightwell
John Kerr
John Kerridge
Murray Sangster
Harold Smith

Secretary
David Rose (0473-219211)

Ticket Office Manager
Roger Serjeant

Sales and Marketing Manager
Brian Scott

Manager
Bobby Ferguson

Reserve Team Coach
Brian Owen

Coach
Charlie Woods

Youth Team Coach
Peter Trevivian

Physiotherapist
John Chandler

Chief Scout
Ron Gray

Groundsman
Winston Chapman

A disappointing campaign ended with Ipswich's 18-year run as a 1st Division club coming to an end.

Ipswich sorely missed the steadying influence of injured England defender Terry Butcher for the first three months and, by the time he returned, they were in serious trouble close to the bottom of the table.

They won only two of their opening 14 1st Division games and, after investing £100,000 in Everton midfield man Ian Atkins, manager Bobby Ferguson had no more cash for the purchase of experienced players.

But, it's an ill wind as they say. And Mr Ferguson made a rare find in Nigel Gleghorn who, at the start of the season, had only been a fireman in Newcastle. He took over in midfield half-way through the season and held his place for much of the remainder of the campaign.

After Butcher's return in November, Ipswich began to achieve better results, yet they tended to throw away points they could scarcely afford. They ran up a 2-0 lead at home to Champions Everton, only to let it slip and lose 3-4. A week later they led 3-0 at Oxford but, again went down 3-4.

That latter defeat was particularly costly as a point gained from that one would ultimately have saved them from relegation.

In mid-season they scored useful away victories over relegation rivals Coventry and Birmingham but their best performance was at Portman Road in February when they recovered from conceding an early goal at home to Liverpool to beat the eventual champions 2-1.

At that point confidence was rising and they appeared to be pulling clear of danger but it was a disastrous run of five games without a win in April that plunged them into serious trouble again.

They ended the month on a high note, though, coming from behind to score a 3-2 home win over Oxford. They then led Oxford, who were third from bottom but had a game in hand, by five points.

Their fate was effectively decided in a mid-week match at West Ham. Kevin Wilson gave them a shock lead after an hour at Upton Park but, after the Hammers had equalised, they were awarded a hotly disputed penalty four minutes from the end. It went in and Ipswich were denied a precious point.

Defeat at Sheffield Wednesday left them fourth from bottom but Oxford, just below them, had one game still to play. They needed to win to save themselves and put Ipswich down. Oxford beat Arsenal 3-0 and that meant Ipswich's proud long run at the top was over.

The directors, as expected, immediately gave Mr Ferguson a vote of confidence and the time to rebuild for a return to the 1st Division in the not-too-distant future.

Back Row L to R: Mick Stockwell, Tommy Parkin, Mark Brennan, Ian Cranson, Mich D'Avray, Frank Yallop. **Middle Row:** Charlie Woods (First Team Coach), Romeo Zondervan, Nigel Gleghorn, Jon Hallworth, Paul Cooper, Michael Cole, Jason Dozzell, Bobby Ferguson (Manager). **Front Row:** Steve McCall, Kevin Wilson, Ian Atkins, John Deehan, Irvin Gernon.

IPSWICH TOWN

DIVISION ONE: 20th   **FA CUP:** 4th ROUND   **MILK CUP:** 5th ROUND

MATCH	DATE		COMPE-TITION	VENUE	OPPONENTS	RESULT	HALF TIME	L'GUE POS'N	GOALSCORERS/GOAL TIMES	ATTEN-DANCE
1	A	17	CL	A	Queens Park Rangers	L	0-1	0-0		(12,755)
2		20	CL	H	Manchester United	L	0-1	0-0		18,777
3		24	CL	H	Tottenham	W	1-0	0-0	15	Zondervan 64	17,758
4		26	CL	A	Liverpool	L	0-5	0-3	20		(29,383)
5		31	CL	H	Southampton	D	1-1	1-0	19	Cranson 17	11,588
6	S	7	CL	A	W.B.A.	W	2-1	2-0	16	Putney 19, Sunderland 30	(7,733)
7		14	CL	H	Birmingham City	L	0-1	0-0	18		11,616
8		21	CL	H	Aston Villa	L	0-3	0-2	19		11,598
9		24	MC2/1	H	Darlington	W	3-1	1-1		Wilson 45, 88, Yallop 75	7,667
10		28	CL	A	Leicester City	L	0-1	0-1	21		(7,290)
11	O	1	CL	A	Luton Town	L	0-1	0-1	21		(8,553)
12		5	CL	A	Nottingham Forest	L	1-3	0-3	21	Atkins 48	(12,120)
13		8	MC2/2	H	Darlington	W	4-1	2-1		Wilson 3, 21, 43, 50, Dozzell 65	(3,321)
14		12	CL	H	Newcastle United	D	2-2	2-1	21	Cole 29, Zondervan 38	12,537
15		19	CL	A	Arsenal	L	0-1	0-1	21		(19,522)
16		26	CL	H	West Ham United	L	0-1	0-1	21		16,849
17		29	MC3	A	Grimsby Town	W	2-0	2-0		Cole 1, Wilson 24	(6,700)
18	N	2	CL	H	Chelsea	L	0-2	0-2	21		15,324
19		9	CL	A	Manchester City	D	1-1	1-1	21	Gleghorn 15	(20,853)
20		16	CL	H	Everton	L	3-4	2-1	21	D'Avray 5, Wilson 31, Butcher 72	13,910
21		23	CL	A	Oxford United	L	3-4	2-0	21	Wilson 24, Brennan (pen) 43, Dozzell 53	(9,387)
22		26	MC4	H	Swindon Town	W	6-1	2-0		Brennan 8, Wilson 36, Butcher 68, 75, Cole 78, 82	12,083
23		30	CL	H	Sheffield Wednesday	W	2-1	1-1	21	D'Avray 21, 75	12,918
24	D	7	CL	A	Manchester United	L	0-1	0-1	21		(37,981)
25		14	CL	H	Queens Park Rangers	W	1-0	1-0	21	Wilson 3	12,032
26		21	CL	A	Tottenham Hotspur	L	0-2	0-1	21		(18,845)
27		26	CL	A	Coventry City	W	1-0	0-0	20	D'Avray 88	(9,356)
28		28	CL	H	Luton Town	D	1-1	1-0	20	Gleghorn 10	16,155
29	J	1	CL	H	Watford	D	0-0	0-0	20		15,922
30		4	FAC3	H	Bradford City	D	4-4	3-3		Evans (og) 12, Wilson 18, Brennan 29, D'Avray 73	13,003
31		11	CL	A	Birmingham City	W	1-0	1-0	20	Wilson 34	(6,856)
32		13	FAC3R	A	Bradford City	W	1-0†	0-0		Brennan 101	(10,108)
33		18	CL	A	Southampton	L	0-1	0-1	19		(13,164)
34		21	MC5	A	Liverpool	L	0-3	0-2			(19,762)
35		25	FAC4	A	West Ham United	D	0-0	0-0			(25,035)
36	F	1	CL	A	Liverpool	W	2-1	0-1	19	D'Avray 53, Wilson 79	20,551
37		4	FAC4R	H	West Ham United	D	1-1†	0-0		Dozzell 93	25,384
38		6	FAC4R	H	West Ham United	L	0-1	0-0			14,515
39	M	8	CL	H	Nottingham Forest	W	1-0	0-0	19	Butcher 52	12,658
40		11	CL	H	Arsenal	L	1-2	1-1	19	Dozzell 40	13,967
41		15	CL	A	Newcastle United	W	3-1	1-0	19	Wilson 10	(18,851)
42		22	CL	H	W.B.A.	W	1-0	0-0	18	Butcher 67	12,100
43		29	CL	A	Watford	D	0-0	0-0	19		(14,988)
44		31	CL	H	Coventry City	W	1-0	0-0	17	Brennan 78	13,485
45	A	5	CL	A	Chelsea	D	1-1	1-1	16	Brennan 37	(13,072)
46		8	CL	H	Leicester City	L	0-2	0-2	17		11,718
47		12	CL	H	Manchester City	D	0-0	0-0	18		13,586
48		16	CL	A	Aston Villa	L	0-1	0-0	19		(13,611)
49		19	CL	A	Everton	L	0-1	0-0	19		(39,055)
50		26	CL	H	Oxford United	W	3-2	0-1	17	Dozzell 53, Butcher 55, Atkins 90	17,827
51		30	CL	A	West Ham United	L	1-2	0-0	19	Wilson 63	(31,121)
52	M	3	CL	A	Sheffield Wednesday	L	0-1	0-0	10		(22,369)

Best Home League Attendance: 20,551 v Liverpool 1/2   **Smallest:** 11,588 v Southampton 31/8   **Av Home Att: 14,413**

Goal Scorers: Compared with 84-85: −2,637

League (32):	Wilson 7, D'Avray 5, Butcher 4, Brennan 3 (1 pen), Dozzell 3, Atkins 2, Gleghorn 2, Zondervan 2, Cole 1, Cranson 1, Putney 1, Sunderland 1
Milk Cup (15):	Wilson 7, Cole 3, Butcher 2, Brennan 1, Dozzell 1, Yallop 1
FA Cup (6):	Brennan 2, D'Avray 1, Dozzell 1, Wilson 1, Opponent 1

†After extra time

Cooper	Yallop	Cranson	Gernon	Putney	Sunderland	Brennan	McCall	Zondervan	Wilson	D'Avray	Dozzell	Burley	Parkin	Cole	Butcher	Steggles	Rimmer	Atkins	Gleghorn	Halworth	Stockwell	Referee	
1	2	3	4	5	6	7	8	9	10	11	12											H King	1
1	2	5	6	12	11	8	3*	4	10	9		7										D Vickers	2
1	3	5	6	7	10	8		4		9	11	2										H Taylor	3
1	3	5	6		10	8		4		9	11	2	7	12								T Holbrook	4
1	3	5	6	7	10	8		4		9	11	2										J Moules	5
1	3	5		7	10	8		4	12	9*	11	2			6							D Allison	6
1	3	5	6	7	10*	8		4	12	9	11	2										E Scales	7
1	3	5	6*	7	10	8		4		9	11	2		12								K Miller	8
1	2	5	3	7	10	8		4		9	11				6			7				D Reeves	9
1	2	5	3		10	8		4	9*		11				6	7		12				R Gifford	10
1	2	6	3	8	11	9		4	10		12					5*		7				M Cotton	11
1		6	3	8	11*	9	2	4	10		5					12		7				T Jones	12
1	3	5	6	7		8	10*		9	11				12	2			4				N Wilson	13
1	2	5	3*	12		9		4	10	11				8	6			7				N Butler	14
1	2	5				8	3	4	10		11			9	6*			7	12			J Milford	15
1	2	5				8	3	4	9	12	11			10	6			7*				M Scott	16
1	2	5				8	3	4	10		11			9	6			7				J Key	17
1	2	5	7*			8	3	4	10	11	9			12	6							B Hill	18
1	2	5				8	3	9	7	12	10				6*	4		11				K Hackett	19
1	2	5	4			8	3		10	9	11				6			7				D Axcell	20
	2	5	4			8	3		10	9*	11				6			7	12	1		M Dimblebee	21
1	2	5				8	3*		10	11			4	9	6			7	12			C Downey	22
1	2	5				8	3		10	9	11		4		6			7*	12			T Ward	23
	2	5	12			8	3		10	9*	11		4		6			7		1		P Vanes	24
1	2	5	9			8	3	4*	10		11				6			7				J Ball	25
1	2	5				8	3	4	10	9			7		6			11*	12			R Groves	26
1	2	5	12			8	3		10	9	11				6	4			7*			N Midgeley	27
1	2	5*	12			8	3		10	9	11				6	4			7			A Gunn	28
1	2	5				8	3		10	9	11				6	4			7			A Seville	29
1	2	5				8	3	4	10	9	11				6				7			R Lewis	30
1	2	5	12			8	3	4*	10	9	11				6				7			J Worrall	31
1	2	5	4*			8	3		10	9	11				6				7		12	N Wilson	32
1	2	5	4			8	3		10	9	11				6				7*		12	D Reeves	33
1	2	5	4			8	3		10	9	11				6	7*					12	J Deakin	34
1	2	5	7			8	3	12	10	9	11				6			4*				J Martin	35
1	2*	5	7			8	3	4	10	9	11			12	6							V Callow	36
1	2	5	7*			8	3	4	10	9	11			12	6							J Martin	37
1	2	5	7*			8	3	4	10	9	11				6						12	K Baker	38
1	2	5	7			8	3	4	10		11			9	6							D Reeves	39
1	2*	5	7			8	3	4	10	9	11			12	6							D Axcell	40
1	2	5	7†				3	4	10	9	11		8		6						12	K Walmsley	41
1	2*	5	7				3	4	10	9	11		8		6							M James	42
		5				8	3		10	11		2		9	6	4*		7		1	12	J Lovatt	43
		5				8	3		10	12	11*	2		9	6	4		7		1		J Key	44
		5	12			8	3	2	10	11				9	6	4*		7		1		J Martin	45
		5	11*			8	3	4	10			2		9	6			7		1	12	R Lewis	46
1		5				8	3	4	10	9	11	2			6			7				I Hemley	47
1		5				8	3	4	10	9	11	2			6			7*			12	K Breen	48
1		5				8	2	4*	10	9	11				6	3		7			12	A Saunders	49
1	3	5				8	11		10		9	4*		12	6	2		7				T Holbrook	50
1	12	5				8	3		10		9	4		11	6	2*		7				G Ashby	51
1		5				8	3		10		9	4		11	6	2		7				D Allison	52

Cooper	Yallop	Cranson	Gernon	Putney	Sunderland	Brennan	McCall	Zondervan	Wilson	D'Avray	Dozzell	Burley	Parkin	Cole	Butcher	Steggles	Rimmer	Atkins	Gleghorn	Halworth	Stockwell		
36	32	42	11	18	13	40	33	27	37	24	38	6	13	12	28	5	1	20	17	6	3	League Appearances	
	1		3	4					2	2	3		1	6		1	1	2	4		5	Substitute Appearances	
5	5	5	2	3	1	5	4	2	5	2	5		1	2+1	2	2		4	0+1		0+1	Milk Cup Appearances	
5	5	5	4			5	5	3+1	5	5	5			0+1	5			2			1+2	FA Cup Appearances	

Also Played:

Players on Loan:

Departures: Burley (Sunderland), Butcher (Glasgow Rangers)

'BLUES' or 'TOWN'

Formed: 1887
Turned Professional: 1936   **Ltd Co:** 1936

Previous Managers: Since the club turned professional:
1936-7 M T O'Brien   1937-55 A Scott-Duncan   1955-63 Sir A E Ramsey   1963-4 J E T Milburn
1964-8 W H McGarry   1969-82 R W Robson
Honours: Div 1 Champions 1961-2   Div 2 Champions 1960-61, 1967-8
Div 3 (S) Champions 1953-4, 1956-7   UEFA Cup Winners 1980-1   FA Cup Winners 1977-8
League Career: Elected to Div 3 (S) 1954-5   Promoted to Div 2 1953-4
Relegated to Div 3 (S) 1954-5   Promoted to Div 2 1956-7   Promoted to Div 1 1960-1
Relegated to Div 2 1963-4   Promoted to Div 1 1967-8
Colours: Royal blue Shirts, white shorts, blue stockings with three white hoops
Change Colours: White shirts, black shorts and white stockings
Reserves League: Football Combination   **Youth Team:** S.E. Counties

---

CLUB RECORDS

Most Appearances for Club: Mick Mills **Total 737 + 4 subs**
Most Capped Player: Allan Hunter, 47, N. Ireland. For England: Mick Mills, 40 + 2 subs
Record Goalscorer in a Match: Ray Crawford, 5 v Floriana (10-1), European Cup, 25.9.62
Record League Goalscorer in a Season: Ted Phillips, 41, Div 3 (S), 1956-7   **In All Competitions:** Ted Phillips, 46,
(League 41, FA Cup 5), 1956-7
Record League Goalscorer in a Career: Ray Crawford, 203   **All Competitions:** Ray Crawford, 244, 1958-63, 1966-9
Record Transfer Fee Received: £500,000 from Tottenham Hotspur for Alan Brazil, March 1983
Record Transfer Fee Paid: £250,000 to Millwall for Kevin O'Callaghan, Jan 1980
Best Performances: League: Champions (2)   **FA Cup:** Winners   **League/Milk Cup:** Semi-Final 1981-2, 1984-5
Most League Points: 64 in Div 3 (S), 1954-5
Most League Goals: 106, Div 3 (S), 1955-6
Record League Victory: 7-0 v Portsmouth, Div 2, 7 Nov 1964   7-0 v Southampton, Div 1, 2 Feb 1974   7-0 v W.B.A., Div
1, 6 Nov 1976
Record League Defeat: 1-10 v Fulham, Div 1, 16.12.63
European Competitions Entered: European Cup: 1962-3   **European Cup Winners Cup:** 1978-9   **UEFA Cup:** 1973-4,
1974-5, 1975-6, 1977-8, 1979-80, 1980-1, 1981-2, 1982-3
Oldest Player in League Match: John Jackson 39 yrs
Youngest Player in League Match: Jason Dozzell 16 yrs

Most Consecutive Undefeated League Matches: 23 1979-80	**League Matches Without a Win:** 21 1963
Longest Run of Undefeated Home League Matches: 33 1979-81	**Away League Matches:** 11 1979-80
Longest Run Without Home League Win: 9 1963	**Away League Win:** 27 1963-64
Most Consecutive League Wins: 8 1953	**Home League Wins:** 14 1956-57
Most Consecutive League Defeats: 10 1954	**Away League Wins:** 5 1976

Club Statistician for the Directory: P Voller

IPSWICH TOWN

PLAYERS NAME Ht Wt Birthdate	Honours	Birthplace Transfers	Clubs	APPEARANCES				GOALS			
				League	Milk Cup	FA Cup	Other Comps	League	Milk Cup	FA Cup	Other Comps
GOALKEEPERS											
Paul Cooper 5.11 12.7 21.12.53	FAC 78, UEFAC 81	Brierley Hill £27,000	Birmingham City (A) Ipswich Town	17 411	1 40	4 44	34				
John Hallworth 5.10 11.3 26.10.65		Bilston	Ipswich Town (A) Bristol Rovers (L)	6 2		1					
DEFENDERS											
Ian Atkins 5.10 11.0 16.1.57	Div. 3, 79	Birmingham Player exch. £70,000	Shrewsbury Town (A) Sunderland Everton Ipswich Town	273+5 76+1 6+1 20+2	13 7 4	23 4 0+1		58 6 1 2			
Andy Crane 5.9 11.1 3.1.67		Ipswich	Ipswich Town	0+1							
Ian Cranson 5.11½ 12.4 2.7.64	EU21 (3)	Easington	Ipswich Town (A)	69+1	12	10		2			
Irvin Gernon 6.0 11.13 30.12.62	EU21 (1), Y	Birmingham	Ipswich Town (A)	73	6	4					
Steve McCall 5.11 11.3 15.10.60	EU21 (6), B (1), Y, UEFAC 81	Carlisle	Ipswich Town (A)	223+8	28	12+1		7		1	2
Kevin Steggles 6.0 11.1 19.3.61		Ditchingham	Ipswich Town (A) Southend United (L)	49+1 3	6	3	2	1	1		
Frank Yallop 5.10½ 10.3 4.4.64	EY	Watford	Ipswich Town (A)	45+5	5	7		1			
MIDFIELD											
Mark Brennan 5.9 11.1 4.10.65	EY	Bicester	Ipswich Town (A)	94+1	14+1	10		6	1	3	
Nigel Gleghorn 6.0 12.13 12.8.62		Seaham	Seaham Red Star Ipswich Town	17+4	0+1	2		2			
Tommy Parkin 5.7 10.4 1.2.56	EY, FAYC 73	Gateshead	Ipswich Town (A) Grimsby Town (L) Peterborough United (L)	51+16 12+4 3	3 1 2	2	1+1				
Mike Stockwell 5.7 10.10 14.2.65		Chelmsford	Ipswich Town (A)	3+5	0+1	1+2					
Romeo Zondervan 5.9½ 11.2 4.3.59	Hol (6)	Surinam (W.I)	F.C. Twente WBA Ipswich Town	82+2 77	6 11	5 8+1		5 5	2	2	
FORWARDS											
Mike Cole 6.0 11.9 3.9.66		Stepney	Ipswich Town (A)	12+8	2+1	0+1		1			
Mich D'Avray 6.1 13.0 19.2.62	EU21 (2)	South Africa	Ipswich Town (A)	98+21	3	8+2	1+2	16	8	2	
John Deehan 6.0 11.3 6.8.57	EU21 (7), Y, LgC 77, MC 85	Birmingham £400,000 £175,000 F	Aston Villa (A) WBA Norwich City Ipswich Town	107+3 44+3 158+3	13 18	7+1 2 17		42 5 62	2 1	3 2	
Jason Dozzell 6.1 11.6 9.12.67		Ipswich	Ipswich Town (A)	47+8	7	7		5	1	3	
Alan Sunderland 5.9 11.7 1.7.53	E (1), B (7), U23 (1) U21 (1), LgC 74	Mexborough	Wolverhampton W. (A) Arsenal Ipswich Town	139+9 204+2 51+7	13+1 26 6+1	16 34 2+1	13	29 55 11	4 13 1	15 1	7
Kevin Wilson 5.7 10.7 18.4.61		Banbury £20,000 £100,000	Banbury United Derby County Ipswich Town	105+16 52+4	8+3 5	8 9		30 14	8 7	3 3	

ADDITIONAL CONTRACT PROFESSIONALS

Dalian Atkinson (F), Keith Gorman (F), Craig Ferries (G), Tony Humes (D), Chris O'Donnell (D), Neil Rimmer (M) (1+1Lge), George Watson

APPRENTICES

Andrew Dickinson, Neil Emmerson, Paul Homewood, Lee Howey, Steven McGavin, Chris Nunn, Paul Tynan

NON-CONTRACT PLAYERS

PORTMAN ROAD Ipswich, Suffolk IP1 2DA

Record Attendance: 38,010 v Leeds United, FA Cup Round 6, 8 Mar 1975

Record Receipts: £105,950 v AZ Alkmaar, UEFA Cup Final 1st Leg, 6 May 1981

Size of Playing Area: 112yds × 72yds

Season Tickets: Stand: £85.00 (lowest), £230 (highest); Ground £53 (adults) £26 (OAP/juveniles); Family Seating £75.00 (adult), £30.00 (children)

Executive Boxes: Box rental £5,500-£5,700 per year

Cost of Stand Tickets: £5.50, £6.00, £7.00. Family Seating £3.80 (adults) £1.50 children   **Terraces:** £3.00 (adults) £1.50 (OAP/juveniles)

Match and Ticket Information: On sale 12 days prior to each match. Postal, Access/Visa bookings accepted

Car Parking: Large parks in Portman Road & Portman's Walk

Nearest Railway Station: Ipswich (0473 57373)

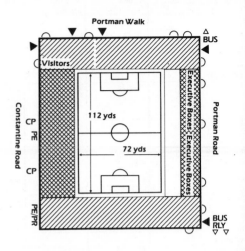

How to get to the ground

From North and West: Use A45 (S.P. Ipswich) into Town Centre then follow signs Manningtree A137 then at roundabout take 3rd exit into Princes Street. In 0.2m turn right into Portman Road for Ipswich Town FC

From South: Use A12 S.P. Ipswich into town centre and follow signs Manningtree A137 then at roundabout take 3rd exit into Princes Street. In 0.2m turn right into Portman Road for Ipswich Town FC

Local Newspaper: East Anglian Daily Times, Evening Star

Local Radio Stations: Radio Orwell, Saxon Radio

LEEDS UNITED

President
Rt Hon Earl of Harewood

Chairman
L Silver OBE

Directors
M Cussins (Vice-Chairman)
R Barker MCIT, MBIM
W J Fotherby
P J Gilman
G M Holmes B Sc (Econ)
J W G Marjason
M J Bedford
E Carlile
A Hudson
R Feldman

Company Secretary
D J Dowse

Commercial Manager
M Price (0532 706560)

Manager
Billy Bremner

Assistant Manager
Dave Bentley

Reserve Team Coach
P Gunby

Chief Scout
Dave Blakey

Physiotherapist
G Ladley

Groundsman
J Reynolds

Having set out confidently as one of the favourites in Division 2 it must have been a nasty shock for Eddie Gray and his established squad when it took six games before their first victory was recorded.

Indeed their defeat at Fulham on the first day of the season was probably the major blow to their confidence and when Stoke City scored six past them nine days later perhaps the defence's solidarity came under question. In fact if you compare the defence on the first day and last day of the season one can see how the team has changed.

Regulars last season were Mervyn Day who certainly seemed to get a new lease of football life from his move to Elland Road, Neil Aspin who changed position but only missed four League games and new signing from Doncaster Rovers, Ian Snodin. In attack the partnership of Ian Baird and Andy Ritchie managed 23 of the 56 League goals and if Tommy Wright can find the form he showed in the previous season then United could again be challenging for promotion.

When Billy Bremner returned to Elland Road the scene was set for one of Leeds favourite sons to lift the club back to previous glories. However, it's not as easy as that and steadily a new formation was moulded together. Unfortunately Andy Linighan didn't hold down the centre-back position but by the end of the season the new formation of David Rennie and Brendan Ormsby from Aston Villa were settling down in the middle of the defence. However ten goals were conceded in the last four games so this department may need further strengthening.

The final League position was just under half-way and sadly the cups gave no compensation as Aston Villa won 3-0 at Elland Road in the 3rd Round of the Milk Cup and Peterborough United did morale no good at all by winning 1-0 in the 3rd Round of the FA Cup. Neither did the Full Members Cup do anything for confidence as Manchester City progressed after an impressive 6-1 victory.

Sadly the very promising side that finished the 1984-5 season with such high hopes had just disappeared. Leeds fans can only hope that Billy Bremner with time to prepare a 'new Leeds' for the coming season, can enjoy that very necessary little bit of luck at the beginning of the campaign.

Back Row L to R: Andy Ritchie, Neil Aspin, Ronnie Robinson, Mervyn Day, Ron Sinclair, Peter Swan, Peter Maddock, David Rennie. **Middle Row:** Geoff Lodley (now left the club), David Bentley (Assistant Manager), Jack Ashurst, Bob Taylor, Brian Caswell, Brendan Ormsby, Ian Baird, Peter Gunby (Coach), Billy Bremner (Manager). **Front Row:** Nigel Thompson, John Stles, John Sheridan, Ian Snodin, Tommy Wright, Russell Doig, John Buckley .

LEEDS UNITED

DIVISION TWO: 14th   **FA CUP:** 3rd ROUND   **MILK CUP:** 3rd ROUND

MATCH	DATE		COMPE-TITION	VENUE	OPPONENTS	RESULT		HALF TIME	L'GUE POS'N	GOALSCORERS/GOAL TIMES	ATTEN-DANCE
1	A	17	CL	A	Fulham	L	1-3	1-0		Lorimer 1	(5,772)
2		21	CL	H	Wimbledon	D	0-0	0-0			12,426
3		24	CL	H	Hull City	D	1-1	0-0	18	Baird 83	16,689
4		26	CL	A	Stoke City	L	2-6	0-1		Aspin 61, Snodin 70	(7,047)
5		31	CL	H	Charlton Athletic	L	1-2	0-1	20	Lorimer (pen) 45	10,862
6	S	4	CL	A	Brighton & H.A.	W	1-0	0-0		McCluskey 50	(9,798)
7		7	CL	A	Shrewsbury Town	W	3-1	1-0	11	Wright 32, McCluskey 60, Baird 79	(4,168)
8		14	CL	H	Sunderland	D	1-1	0-1	11	Sheridan 81	19,693
9		21	CL	A	Bradford City	W	2-1	0-0	11	Lorimer 46, Sellars 84	21,104
10		25	MC2/1	H	**Walsall**	D	0-0	0-0			8,869
11		28	CL	H	Sheffield United	D	1-1	0-1	11	Baird 64	15,622
12	O	5	CL	A	Huddersfield Town	L	1-3	1-2	14	Baird 15	(9,983)
13		8	MC2/2	A	**Walsall**	W	3-0	2-0		**Linighan 10, Snodin 40, 81**	(7,085)
14		12	CL	H	Middlesbrough	W	1-0	0-0	12	Lorimer (pen) 19	14,117
15		14	FMC	A	**Manchester City**	L	1-6	0-3		**Lorimer (pen) 62**	(4,029)
16		16	FMC	H	**Sheffield United**	D	1-1	0-0		**Sellars 71**	2,274
17		19	CL	H	Grimsby Town	D	1-1	0-0	12	Baird 66	11,244
18		27	CL	A	Barnsley	L	0-3	0-1	13		(8,302)
19		30	MC3	H	**Aston Villa**	L	0-3	0-1			15,444
20	N	2	CL	H	Portsmouth	W	2-1	0-1	11	Simmonds 64, (pen) 71	15,672
21		9	CL	A	Millwall	L	1-3	0-1	13	Ritchie 85	(9,158)
22		16	CL	H	Crystal Palace	L	1-3	0-2	14	McCluskey 55	10,378
23		23	CL	A	Carlisle United	W	2-1	0-0	13	Linighan 50, Ritchie 77	(3,504)
24		30	CL	H	Norwich City	L	0-2	0-1	15		11,480
25	D	7	CL	A	Wimbledon	W	3-0	0-2	12	Snodin 38, Baird 41, Dickenson 48	(3,492)
26		14	CL	H	Fulham	W	1-0	0-0	11	Sheridan 67	9,998
27		22	CL	A	Hull City	L	1-2	1-2	12	Sheridan 17	(11,852)
28		26	CL	A	Blackburn Rovers	L	0-2	0-2	14		(8,666)
29		28	CL	H	Brighton & H.A.	L	2-3	0-1	14	Baird 52, Snodin 86	13,110
30	J	1	CL	H	Oldham Athletic	W	3-1	1-0	12	Baird 16, 76, Ritchie 73	10,830
31		4	FAC3	A	**Peterborough United**	L	0-1	0-0			(10,137)
32		11	CL	A	Sunderland	L	2-4	0-1	14	Baird 47, Sheridan 71	(15,139)
33		18	CL	A	Charlton Athletic	L	0-4	0-3	15		(4,333)
34	F	1	CL	H	Stoke City	W	4-0	1-0	14	Stiles 33, Baird 52, Swan 59, 85	10,425
35		8	CL	A	Grimsby Town	L	0-1	0-0	15		(6,338)
36		15	CL	H	Barnsley	L	0-2	0-0	15		11,765
37	M	8	CL	H	Huddersfield Town	W	2-0	1-0	16	Ormsby 12, Snodin 86	14,667
38		15	CL	A	Middlesbrough	D	2-2	1-1	18	Simmonds 38, Rennie 88	(6,899)
39		22	CL	H	Shrewsbury Town	D	1-1	0-0	17	Rennie 65	9,641
40		28	CL	A	Oldham Athletic	L	1-3	0-1	17	Ritchie 78	(4,937)
41		31	CL	H	Blackburn Rovers	D	1-1	0-0	18	Ritchie 74	9,919
42	A	5	CL	A	Portsmouth	W	3-2	0-1	17	Ritchie 55, 83, Baird 65	(14,430)
43		9	CL	A	Bradford City	W	1-0	1-0	15	Aspin 14	(10,751)
44		12	CL	H	Millwall	W	3-1	2-1	12	Sellars 9, Swan 14, Ritchie 63	15,067
45		19	CL	A	Crystal Palace	L	0-3	0-1	14		(6,285)
46		22	CL	A	Sheffield United	L	2-3	1-1	16	Ritchie 18, Snodin 55	(9,158)
47		26	CL	H	Carlisle United	W	2-0	1-0	14	Ritchie 10, 63	13,868
48	M	3	CL	A	Norwich City	L	0-4	0-1	14		(17,942)

Best Home League Attendance: 21,104 v Bradford City 21/9   **Smallest:** 9,641 v Shrewsbury Town 22/3   **Av Home Att:** 13,265

Goal Scorers: **Compared with 84-85:** −1,396

League (56): Baird 12, Ritchie 11, Snodin 5, Lorimer 4 (2 pen), Sheridan 4, McClusky 3, Simmonds 3 (1 pen), Swann 3, Aspin 2, Rennie 2, Sellars 2, Dickenson 1, Linighan 1, Ormsby 1, Stiles 1, Wright 1

Milk Cup (3): Snodin 2, Linighan 1

FA Cup (Nil):

FM Cup (2): Lorimer 1 (pen), Sellars 1

Day	Irwin	Hamson	Snodin	Linighan	Aspin	McCluskey	Sheridan	Baird	Lorimer (M)	Sellars	Wright	Dickenson	Phelan	Ritchie	Swann	Stiles	Simmonds	Thompson	Swinburne	McGregor (L)	Caswell	Robinson	Harle	Rennie	Ormsby	Referee	
1	2	3	4	5	6	7	8	9	10	11																V Callow	1
1	2	3	4	5	6	7	8	9	10	11																K Walmsley	2
1	2	3	4	5	6	7	8	9	10*	11	12															G Courtney	3
1	2	3	4	5	6	7*	8	9	10	11	12															P Tyldesley	4
1	2	3	4	5	6	12	8	9*	10	11	7															I Hendrick	5
1	2	3	4	5	6	9	8		10		7	11														J Moules	6
1	2		4	5	6	9	8	12	10		7	11*	3													J Deakin	7
1	2		4	5	6	11	8	9	10	12	7*		3													T Fitzharris	8
1	2		4	5*	6	7	8	9	10	11	12		3													R Nixon	9
1	2		4	5		7*	8	9	10	11	12	6	3													J Worrall	10
1	2		4	5			8	9	10	11	7	6	3													D Scott	11
1	2		4	5		12	8†	9	10	11	7	6*	3													J Hough	12
1	2	11	4	5		12	8	9	10			6*	3	7												N Ashley	13
1	2	4		5	6	7	8	9	10		12		3	11*												M Scott	14
1	2	4		5*	6	7*	8	9	10	11			3		12	13										J Bray	15
1	2*			5	6*		8	9	10	4			3		12	13	7	11								M Peck	16
	2	4		5	6	7		9	10			8	3	11*				1								N Midgley	17
1		8	4	5	6	7		9	10			2	3	11												R Bridges	18
1		11	4	5	6	10	8	9				2	3	7												K Redfern	19
1	2	10		5	6		8	9				3		7		11					4					T Jones	20
1		11		5	6	10	8	9				2	3	7							4					M Bodenham	21
1		10	4	5*	6	9	8					12	3	7		11					2					M Heath	22
1		10	4	5		9	8					11		7							6	2	3			N Wilson	23
		10	4	6		9	8					11		7	12					1	5	2	3*			C Trussell	24
1		10	4	6	5			9†				11		7			8					2	3			J Ashworth	25
1		10	4	6	5	9	8					11		7								3				A Saunders	26
1		10	4	5	6	9*	8					11	12	7							2	3				N Glover/B Eland	27
1		10	4	6*	5	9	8					12	11	7	3						2					J Lovatt	28
1		10	4		5		8	9				12	11	7								3				D Allison	29
1	2	10	4		5			9				3	11	7	6									8		K Lupton	30
1	2	10	4	6	5		12	9				3†	11	7	8*											P Tyldesley	31
1	2	10	4		6		10	9				5		7								3		8		N Midgley	32
1	2	11	4		6		10	9				5		7								3		8		G Ashby	33
1		10	4	5				9				12		7	8	11					2	3		6		K Breen	34
1		10	4	5				9				12		7	8	11					2*	3		6		G Napthine	35
1		10	4	5				9				12		7	8	2						3	11*	6		L Dilkes	36
1		4	2				8	9						10	11	7						3		6	5	J Lloyd	37
1		4	2				8	9					12	10	11	7						3*		6	5	V Callow	38
1		3	4	2			8	9						10	11	7								6	5	A Seville	39
1		3†	4	2			8	9						10	11	7								6	5	G Aplin	40
1		3	4	2			8	9						10	11									6	5	K Redfern	41
1		4		2		7	8	9						10	11							3		6	5	J Ball	42
1		4		2		7*	8	9						10	11	12						3		6	5	K Barratt	43
1		4		2				9		7*				10	8	12						3		6	5	T Holbrook	44
1		4		2			8†	9				12		11	10							3		6	5	M Reed	45
1		4		2			8	9						11	10	7						3		6	5	C Seel	46
1		3	4*	2			12	9			8			7	10	11								6	5	T Fitzharris	47
1		3	2				8	9						7	10	11						4		6	5	K Miller	48
40	19	30	37	24	38	20	31	34	14	13	6	17	12	28	16	11	6	1	2	5	8	16	3	16	12	League Appearances	
					2	1	1		4	4	2	2	1		1		2									Substitute Appearances	
3	2	2	3	3	1	2-1	3	3	2	1		0-1	3	3	2											Milk Cup Appearances	
1	1	1	1	1	1	0-1	1	1		1		1		1	1											FA Cup Appearances	
2	2	1	2	2	1	2	2	2	2				2				0-2	0-1	1-1	1						FM Cup Appearances	

Also Played: Position(Game): Eli 6(29), Taylor 11(44), 7(45)

Players on Loan: McGregor (Liverpool)

Departures: Linighan (Oldham), Eli (Wolves), Dickinson (W.B.A.), Harle (Bristol City), Hamson (Bristol City), McCluskey (Hibs), Sellars (Blackburn), Phelan (Swansea), Irwin (Oldham), Swinburne (Lincoln), Lorimer (Whitby Town)

'THE WHITES'

Formed: 1919 as Leeds United
Turned Professional: 1919   **Ltd Co:** 1920

Previous Names: Leeds City 1904-19 (disbanded on order by FA)
Previous Managers: 1920-7 Arthur Fairclough   1927-35 Dick Ray   1935-47 Billy Hampson
1947-48 Willis Edwards   1948-53 Major Frank Buckley   1953-8 Raich Carter   1958-9 Bill Lambton
1959-61 Jack Taylor   1961-74 Don Revie, OBE   1974 Brian Clough   1974-8 Jimmy Armfield
1978 Jock Stein   1978-80 Jimmy Adamson   1980-2 Allan Clarke   1982-85 Eddie Gray
Honours: Div 1 Champions 1968-9, 1973-4   Div 2 Champions 1923-4, 1963-4   FA Cup Winners
1972   Football League Cup Winners 1967-8   European Fairs Cup Winners 1967-8, 1970-1
League Career: Elected to Div 2 1920   Promoted to Div 1 1923-4
Relegated to Div 2 1926-7   Promoted to Div 1 1927-8   Relegated to Div 2 1930-1
Promoted to Div 1 1931-2   Relegated to Div 2 1946-7   Promoted to Div 1 1955-6
Relegated to Div 2 1959-60   Promoted to Div 1 1963-4   Relegated to Div 2 1981-2
Colours: All white with blue and yellow trim
Change Colours: All yellow with blue shorts
Reserves League: Central Div 1   **Youth League:** Northern Intermediate

---

CLUB RECORDS

Most Appearances for Club: Jack Charlton, 1953-73 (League 629, FA Cup 52, League Cup 35, European Cups 56, Charity Shield 1) **Total 773**
Most Capped Player: Billy Bremner 54, Scotland   **For England:** Jack Charlton, 35
Record Goalscorer in a Match: Gordon Hodgson, 5 v Leicester City (H), Div 1 (8-2), 1 Oct 1938
Record League Goalscorer in a Season: John Charles, 42, Div 2, 1953-4   **In All Competitions:** John Charles, 43, (League 42 + FA Cup 1) 1953-54
Record League Goalscorer in a Career: Peter Lorimer, 165, 1962-79, 1983-85   **In All Competitions:** Peter Lorimer, 234 (165 League + 20 FA Cup + 19 League Cup + 30 European Cups)
Record Transfer Fee Received: £500,000 from Nottingham Forest for Frank Gray, July 1979
Record Transfer Fee Paid: £930,000 (gross fee) to Manchester City for Peter Barnes, Aug 1981
Best Performances: League: Champions (2)   **FA Cup:** Winners (1)   **League/Milk Cup:** Winners (1)   **European Cup:** Finalists   **European Cup Winners Cup:** Finalists   **Fairs/U.E.FA Cup:** Winners (2)
Most League Points: 67 in Div 1, 1968-9   **Most League Goals:** 98, Div 2, 1927-8
Record League Victory and Most Goals in a League Match: 8-0 v Leicester City, Div 1, 7 April 1934
Most Goals Scored in a Cup Tie: 10-0 v Lynoslo, European Cup, 1st Rnd/1st Leg, 17 Sept 1969
Record League Defeat: 1-8 v Stoke City, Div 1, 27 Aug 1934
European Competitions Entered: European Cup: 1969-70, 1974-5   European Cup Winners Cup: 1972-3   European Fairs Cup: 1965-6, 1966-7, 1967-8, 1968-9, 1970-1   U.E.F.A Cup: 1971-2, 1973-4, 1979-80

Most Consecutive Undefeated League Matches: 35 1968-69	**League Matches Without a Win:** 17 1947
Longest Run of Undefeated Home League Matches: 39 1968-70	**Away League Matches:** 17 1968-69
Longest Run Without Home League Win: 10 1982	**Away League Win:** 26 1939-46-47
Most Consecutive League Wins: 9 1931	**Home League Wins:** 13 1968-69
Most Consecutive League Defeats: 6 1947	**Away League Wins:** 8 1963

Club Statistician for the Directory: Julian Barker

LEEDS UNITED

PLAYERS NAME Ht Wt Birthdate	Honours	Birthplace Transfers	Clubs	League	Milk Cup	FA Cup	Other Comps	League	Milk Cup	FA Cup	Other Comps
GOALKEEPERS											
Mervyn Day 6.2 15.1 26.6.55	EU 23 (5), Y	Chelmsford £100,000 £15,000 £30,000	West Ham United Orient Aston Villa Leeds United	194 170 30 58	14 10 3 3	14 8 1	9				
Ronnie Sinclair 5.9 11.12½ 19.11.64		Stirling	Nottingham Forest (A) Wrexham (L)	11		1					
DEFENDERS											
Jack Ashurst 6.0 12.4 12.10.64	Div. 2, 76	Coatbridge £110,000 £40,000 £35,000	Sunderland Blackpool Carlisle United Leeds United	129+11 53 194	7 2 10	8 4 12	4 2	3 1			
Neil Aspin 6.0 12.6 12.4.65		Gateshead	Leeds United (A)	106+1	3	9	4				
Brian Caswell 5.10 10.7 14.2.56		Wednesbury £40,000	Walsall (A) Leeds United	388+12	29	23	4	7		1	
Peter Haddock 5.11 11.5 22.9.57		Newcastle £40,000	Newcastle United (A) Leeds United	53+4	5	6					
David Linighan 6.2 11.0 9.1.65		Hartlepool £20,000	Hartlepool United Leeds United	84+7	3+1	6	1	5	1		
Brendan Ormsby 5.11 11.3 1.10.60	EY, S	Birmingham £65,000	Aston Villa (A) Leeds United	115+2 12	11+1	3+1	7	4 1	2		1
David Rennie 6.0 12.0 29.8.64	SY	Edinburgh £50,000	Leicester City Leeds United	21 16	2			2			
Ronald Robinson 5.11 11.5 22.10.66		Sunderland	Ipswich Town (A) Leeds United	16							
Nigel Thompson 5.7 10.7 1.3.67		Leeds	Leeds United	2							
MIDFIELD											
John Sheridan 5.9 10.8 1.10.64	EU21 (1), Y	Stretford	Leeds United (A)	111+1	6	3+1		12	1		
Ian Snodin+ 5.7 8.12 15.8.63	EU21 (4), Y	Rotherham	Doncaster Rovers (A) Leeds United	181+7 37	9 3	11+1 1	3	23 5			
John Stiles 5.10½ 11.3 6.5.64		Manchester F	Shamrock Rovers Vancouver Whitecaps Leeds United	12+1							
Peter Swan 6.0 12.0 28.9.66		Leeds	Leeds United (A)	16		1					
FORWARDS											
Ian Baird 6.0 12.9 1.4.64		Rotherham £75,000	Southampton (A) Cardiff City (L) Newcastle United (L) Leeds United	21+4 12 4+1	1+1		1				
John Buckley 5.9 10.7 18.5.62		East Kilbride £35,000	Partick Thistle Doncaster Rovers Leeds United	42+3 79+4 44+1	1 3 3	1 5 1	3	11 18			
Russell Doig 5.8 10.9 17.1.64		Millport	St Mirren East Stirling Leeds United	93+16				9			
Keith Edwards 5.10 10.3 16.7.57	Div. 4, 82	Stockton £60,000 £95,000 £125,000	Sheffield United Hull City Sheffield United Leeds United	64+6 130+2 183+8	2 9 12+3	3 10 16	3	29 57 114	1 10	5 10	2
Andy Ritchie 5.9½ 11.11 28.11.60	EU21 (1), YS	Manchester £500,000 Player exch.	Manchester United (A) Brighton & H.A. Leeds United	26+7 82+7 98+7	3+1 9	3 9 4	3	13 23 33	1 3	2 1	
Lyndon Simmonds 5.4½ 9.12 11.11.64	WY	Pontypool	Leeds United (A)	6+3				3			
Bob Taylor 5.10 11.9 3.2.67		Horden	Horden CW Leeds United	2							
Tommy Wright 5.7 9.9 10.1.66		Dunfermline	Leeds United (A)	73+8	3+2	4		24	1	3	

ADDITIONAL CONTRACT PROFESSIONALS

APPRENTICES
Richard Annan, Andrew Armitage, David Batty, David Bentley, Mark Fella, David Mills, Peter Mumby, Dean Walling, Lee Warren

NON-CONTRACT PLAYERS
Vince Brookie, Nigel Smith

ELLAND ROAD Leeds LS11 0ES

Record Attendance: 57,892 v Sunderland, FA Cup Round 5 Replay, 15 Mar 1967

Smallest Home Attendance for a First Class Match: 4,500 v Brentford League Cup, 1st Round, 13 Sept 1961

Record Receipts: £146,483, FA Cup Semi-Final Replay, Everton v West Ham United, 16 Apr 1980

Season Tickets: Stands: From £90 to £110 (juveniles & OAP £45), Standing £45

Executive Box Season Tickets: £5,000 per annum (box of 8)

Executive Suite Membership £275 per annum

Cost of Stand Tickets: £5.50, £6.50 (£4.00 unreserved), half-price before 12 noon; **Terraces:** £3.00; Half-price for Junior Club Members and OAPs only

Match and Ticket Information: Computerised for sale match by match. 24-hr answer phone: 0532 702621

Car Parking: Leeds Greyhound Association has park for 1,000 cars (approx), one minute walk from ground

Nearest Railway Station: Leeds City (0532 448133)

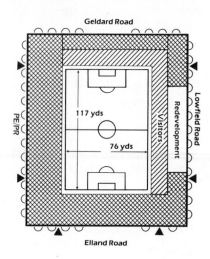

Geldard Road

117 yds

76 yds

PE/PR

Visitors

Redevelopment

Lowfield Road

Elland Road

How to get to the ground

From North: Use A58 or A61 into Leeds City Centre, then follow signs Motorway M621 to join Motorway. In 1.6m leave motorway and at roundabout join A643 into Elland Road for Leeds United FC

From East: Use A63 or A64 into Leeds City Centre, then follow signs Motorway M621 to join motorway. In 1.6m leave motorway and at roundabout join A643 into Elland Road for Leeds United FC

From South: Use Motorway M1 then M621 until junction with A643, leave motorway and at roundabout join A643 into Elland Road for Leeds United FC

From West: Use Motorway M62 then M621 until junction with A643. Leave motorway and at roundabout join A643 into Elland Road for Leeds United FC

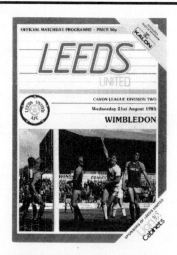

Price of 1986-7 Programme: 50p
Number of Pages: 32
Subscriptions: £15.70 (UK postage included), £16.70 overseas. £25 airmail (overseas), £36.00 airmail (elsewhere)

Local Newspaper: Yorkshire Post, Yorkshire Evening Post, Bradford Telegraph & News

Local Radio Stations: BBC Radio Leeds, Radio Aire (Leeds), Pennine Radio (Bradford)

LEICESTER CITY

Chairman
T W Shipman

Vice-Chairman
T E Bloor

Directors
W G Page
D E Sharp
W K Shooter FCA
T Smeaton
J M Elson FCA
M F George

General Secretary
A K Bennett (0533 555000)

PRO
Alan Birchenall

Club Manager
Gordon Milne

Team Manager
Brian Hamilton

Youth Team Coach
Dave Richardson

Physiotherapist
John McVey

Commercial Manager
P Hill (0533 555000)

The 1985-86 campaign was huge disappointment for Leicester City. The club managed to stave off relegation at the eleventh hour, but only due to the failure of Ipswich to gain some reward from their final fixture. The reaction of the supporters on that final day was not one of euphoria at the result, but one of concern for the future — a sad reflection of the direction in which the team had gradually slid throughout the season.

Over the previous 18 months the club had generated income in excess of £1.3m from transfer deals. However, less than £0.5m had been reinvested in new players and the effects of that policy, whilst keeping the club on a sound financial base, have shown up dramatically on the field.

Of the newcomers, Russell Osman started the season as though he was likely to regain his England place, suffered a gashed leg in September, and never looked the same player again. Meanwhile, Gary McAllister and Ally Mauchlen, both from Motherwell, met with varying success. McAllister showed great potential but was prone to display the inconsistency which affected most of his colleagues, whilst Mauchlen took longer to adapt to English conditions, but, during the latter stages of the season, looked the team's most accomplished player. The departure of Gary Lineker, however, was like losing the crown jewels and it left a gap which could not be adequately filled.

Over the years Leicester have always tended to produce shock results against the top clubs, but slip up against the lesser lights. In 1985-86 City seemed to take this to extremes, completing the double over reigning champions Everton yet struggling to scramble two draws with a West Brom team detached at the foot of the table. More significantly, these results came as no surprise whatsoever to the fans. Motivation against the top clubs was never a problem, but the approach to the more mundane fixtures caused great concern. This attitude was summed up most forcibly in the two cup competitions, where the performances on the grounds of Third Division opponents, Derby and Bristol Rovers, were nothing short of disgraceful. How these contrasted to the afternoon in November when runaway League leaders Manchester United were thrashed 3-0 at Filbert Street!

This question of approach has to be remedied for 1986-87 if any significant improvement is to come about. It can only be hoped that the change in management structure at the club has the desired effect, or four figure attendances will become the rule rather than the exception.   Dave Smith

Back Row L to R: Paul Reid, Andy Feeley, Ian Banks, Ian Andrews, Jeremy Roberts, John O'Neill, Robert Kelly, Kevin Jobling. **Middle Row:** Dave Richardson (Youth Team Manager), Paul Ramsey, Simon Morgan, Mark Venus, Phil Horner, Alan Smith, Steve Walsh, Gary McAllister, Mark Bright, Russell Osman, John McVey (Physio). **Front Row:** Ali Mauchlen, Steve Lynex, Paul Bunce, Gordon Milne (Manager), Bryan Hamilton (Team Manager), Ian Wilson, Bobby Smith, Tony Sealy.

LEICESTER CITY

DIVISION ONE: 18   **FA CUP:** 3rd ROUND   **MILK CUP:** 2nd ROUND   **FRT:**

MATCH	DATE	COMPE-TITION	VENUE	OPPONENTS	RESULT		HALF TIME	L'GUE POS'N	GOALSCORERS/GOAL TIMES	ATTEN-DANCE
1	A 17	CL	H	Everton	W	3-1	1-1		Smith R 44, Bright 61, 77	16,932
2	21	CL	A	Manchester City	D	1-1	1-1		Wilson 44	(25,528)
3	24	CL	A	Oxford United	L	0-5	0-2	13		(9,626)
4	28	CL	H	Chelsea	D	0-0	0-0	15		11,248
5	31	CL	A	Arsenal	L	0-1	0-1	15		(18,207)
6	S 4	CL	H	Watford	D	2-2	0-1	16	Ramsey 51, Bright 64	(9,672)
7	8	CL	H	Nottingham Forest	L	0-3	0-1	19		14,272
8	14	CL	A	West Ham United	L	0-3	0-1	21		(12,125)
9	21	CL	A	Birmingham City	L	1-2	1-0	21	Sealy 12	(9,834)
10	25	MC2/1	A	Derby County	L	0-2	0-2			(12,504)
11	28	CL	H	Ipswich Town	W	1-0	0-0	19	Smith 70	7,290
12	O 2	CL	H	Oxford United	W	4-2	2-2	16	Smith 24, Wilson 27, McAllister 74, Lynex (pen) 83	7,711
13	6	CL	A	Coventry City	L	0-3	0-1	19		(10,959)
14	9	MC2/2	H	Derby County	D	1-1	1-1		Wilson 21	10,373
15	12	CL	H	W.B.A.	D	2-2	1-2	19	Smith A 43, Lynex (pen) 65	7,237
16	19	CL	H	Sheffield Wednesday	L	2-3	0-1	19	Lynex 50, Smith A. 67	10,259
17	26	CL	A	Tottenham Hotspur	W	3-1	3-1	19	Smith A 6, Lynex (pen) 25, Bright 37	(17,944)
18	N 2	CL	A	Liverpool	L	0-1	0-0	19		(37,718)
19	9	CL	H	Southampton	D	2-2	1-1	19	Smith A. 2, Lynex (pen) 65	8,080
20	16	CL	A	Q.P.R.	L	0-2	0-0	20		(11,085)
21	23	CL	H	Manchester United	W	3-0	3-0	19	McAllister 7, Smith A. 15, 30	22,008
22	30	CL	A	Newcastle United	L	1-2	0-2	19	Smith A. 59	(17,304)
23	D 7	CL	A	Manchester City	D	1-1	1-0	18	Smith A. 2	10,289
24	14	CL	A	Everton	W	2-1	0-1	18	McAllister (pen) 59, Smith A. 77	(23,347)
25	26	CL	H	Aston Villa	W	3-1	2-1	16	Smith A. 15, 40, Bright 84	13,752
26	28	CL	A	Watford	L	1-2	1-0	16	Smith A. 15	(14,709)
27	J 1	CL	A	Luton Town	L	1-3	0-1	16	Bright 70	(10,917)
28	4	FAC3	A	Bristol Rovers	L	1-3	0-0		McAllister (pen) 79	(9,392)
29	11	CL	H	West Ham United	L	0-1	0-0	17		11,359
30	18	CL	H	Arsenal	D	2-2	0-1	17	Banks 46, Sealy 86	11,246
31	F 1	CL	A	Chelsea	D	2-2	1-1	17	Mauchlen 30, Lynex (pen) 71	(12,372)
32	M 8	CL	H	Coventry City	W	2-1	0-1	17	McAllister 81, Smith A. 87	10,774
33	12	CL	H	Birmingham City	W	4-2	3-2	17	McAllister 6, Sealy 16, Smith A. 27, Lynex (pen) 81	8,458
34	15	CL	A	W.B.A.	D	2-2	1-1	17	Sealy 31, 63	(8,300)
35	18	CL	A	Sheffield Wednesday	L	0-1	0-1	17		(18,874)
36	22	CL	A	Nottingham Forest	L	3-4	1-1	17	Smith A. 5, 68, Sealy 48	(14,484)
37	29	CL	H	Luton Town	D	0-0	0-0	17		9,912
38	31	CL	A	Aston Villa	L	0-1	0-0	18		(12,200)
39	A 5	CL	H	Tottenham Hotspur	L	1-4	1-1	18	Lynex (pen) 44	9,572
40	8	CL	A	Ipswich Town	W	2-0	2-0	16	McAllister 12, Smith A. 15	(11,718)
41	12	CL	A	Southampton	D	0-0	0-0	16		(13,403)
42	14	CL	H	Q.P.R.	L	1-4	0-2	17	McAllister (pen) 61	7,724
43	26	CL	A	Manchester United	L	0-4	0-1	19		(38,840)
44	30	CL	H	Liverpool	L	0-2	0-2	20		25,797
45	M 3	CL	H	Newcastle United	W	2-0	0-0	18	Mauchlen 58, Banks (pen) 70	13,170

Best Home League Attendance: 25,797 v Liverpool   Smallest: 7,237 v W.B.A.   Av Home Att: **11,750**

Goal Scorers: Compared with 84-85: **−58,368**

League (54):   Smith A. 19, Lynex 8 (7 pen), McAllister 7 (2 pen), Bright 6, Sealy 6, Banks 2, Mauchlen 2, Wilson 2, Ramsey 1, Smith R. 1

Milk Cup (1):   Wilson 1
FA CUP (1):   McAllister 1 (pen)

1985-86

Andrews	Ramsey	Smith R	Kelly	Osman	O'Neil	Lynex	Bright	Smith A	Wilson	Banks	Mauchlen	Williams	Jones	Feeley	Sealy	Venus	Rennie	McAllister	Morgan	Roberts	Christensen (NC)	Cunningham (NC)		Referee	
1	2	3	4	5	6	7	8	9	10	11														B Stevens	1
1	2	3	4	5	6	7	8	9	10	11														T Mills	2
1	2	3	4	5	6	7	8	9*	10	11	12													D Vickers	3
1	4	3		5	6	7	8	9	10†	11		2												J Hough	4
1	4		11	5	6	7	8	9*	10	12	3	2												J Martin	5
1	4			5	6	7	8	9*	3	12	10	2	11											P Tyldesley	6
1	4			5	6	7	8	12	3	11	10	2	9*											T Holbrook	7
1	4*	3	7	5	6		8	9		11	10	2	12											I Borrett	8
1	4		11	5*	6			9			12	10		2	3	7	8							M Heath	9
1	4					7	9		3	11	10	5		2	8		6							**T Jones**	**10**
1	2				6	7	9	12	11		10	5			8*		3	4						R Gifford	11
1	2				6	7	8	9	11		10	5			12			4	3					K Miller	12
1	10				6	7	8	9	11					2	5			4	3					K Cooper	13
1	10*			5	6	7	8	9	11					2	12			4	3					**A Buksh**	**14**
				5	6	7	8	9	11					2	10			4	3	1				E Scales	15
1				5	6	7	8	9	11		12			2	10*			4	3					D Reeves	16
1				5	6	7	8	9	11		10			2				4	3					D Hedges	17
1				5	6	7	8	9	11		10			2				4	3					K Redfern	18
1				5	6	7	8*	9	11		10			2				4	3			12		R Banks	19
1				5	6		8	9	11	12	10			2				4	3		7*			L Shapter	20
1				5	6			9	11	7	10			2				4	3			8		N Butler	21
1				5	6			9	11	7	10			2				4	3			8		J McAuley	22
1				5	6			9	11	7	10			2				4	3			8		C Downey	23
1				5	6	12		9	11	7	10			2				4	3			8*		N Ashley	24
1				5	6	12		9	11	7	10			2				4	3			8*		L Dilkes	25
1				5	6		8	9	11	7	10			2				4	3					M Cotton	26
1	11			5	6	12	8		9	7	10			2				4*	3					I Borrett	27
1	11			5	6		8	9		7	10			2				4	3					**A Gunn**	**28**
1	12			5	6	7	8*	9	11		10			2				4	3					A Robinson	29
1	8			5	6	7		9	11		10*			2	12			4	3					T Fitzharris	30
1				5	6	7		9	11		10	4		2	8				3					R Hamer	31
1				5	6	7		9		11*	10			2	8			4	3			12		G Courtney	32
1				5	6	7		9			10			2	8			4	3			11		F Roberts	33
1				5	6	7		9			10			2	8			4	3			11		J Worrall	34
				5	6	7		9	11		10			2	8			4	3	1				I Hendrick	35
1				5	6	7*		9	12		10			2	8			4	3			11		D Scott	36
1				5	6	7		9		12	10			2	8			4	3			11*		K Walmsley	37
1			12	5	6		3	9		7	10			2	8			4				11*		N Midgley	38
1				5	6	7		9	11		10			2	8			4	3					T Mills	39
1	2			5	6	7		9	11		10				8			4	3					R Lewis	40
1	2			5	6	7		9	11		10				8			4	3					K Miller	41
		3		5	6	7†	9			11	10				8			4	2*	1		12		M Reed	42
1	7*	3		5	6	12				11	10				8			4	2			9		N Ashley	43
1		3	11	5	6			9		12	10				8			4*	2			7	8	R Milford	44
1		3	4	5	6			9	11	12	10				8*				2			7		G Ashby	45
39	13	13	8	40	41	28	22	38	24	24	35	8	2	26	19	1	3	31	30	3	1	13		League Appearances	
	1	1			2	2	2	1	7	2			1		2						1	2	1	Substitute Appearances	
2	2			1	1	2	2	1	2	1	1	1		2	1+1	1	1	1						Milk Cup Appearances	
		1	1			1			1		1		1					1	1			1		FA Cup Appearances	

Also Played:
Players on Loan:
Departures: Peake (Grimsby) Rennie (Leeds United)

THE FILBERTS

Formed: 1884
Turned Professional: 1894   **Ltd Co:** 1894

Previous Names: Leicester Fosse 1884-1919
Previous Managers: From 1884-1919 the club secretary took charge of all team matters. The first full time manager was appointed in 1919. The full list is:
1919-26 Peter Hodge   1926-32 Willie Orr   1932-4 Peter Hodge   1934-6 Arthur Lockhead
1936-9 Frank Womack   1939-45 Tom Bromilow   1945-6 Tom Mather   1946-9 John Duncan
1949-55 Norman Bullock   1955-8 David Halliday   1959-68 Matt Gillies   1968-71 Frank O'Farrell
1971-7 Jimmy Bloomfield   1977-8 Frank McLintock   1978-82 Jock Wallace
Honours: Div 3 Champions 1924-5, 1936-7, 1953-4, 1956-7, 1970-1, 1979-80
Football League Cup Winners 1964
League Career: Elected to Div 2 1894   Promoted to Div 1 1907-8
Relegated to Div 2 1908-9   Promoted to Div 1 1924-5   Relegated to Div 2 1934-5
Promoted to Div 1 1936-7   Relegated to Div 2 1938-9   Promoted to Div 1 1953-4
Relegated to Div 2 1954-5   Promoted to Div 1 1956-7   Relegated to Div 2 1968-9
Promoted to Div 1 1970-1   Relegated to Div 2 1977-8   Promoted to Div 1 1979-80
Relegated to Div 2 1980-1   Promoted to Div 1 1982-3
Colours: Royal blue shirts with white pin stripe and trim, white shorts with blue side stripe, white stockings with blue stripes at top
Change Colours: Red shirts, black shorts, black stockings with yellow rings at top
Reserves League: Central Div 1   **'A' Team:** Midland Intermediate

---

CLUB RECORDS

Most Appearances for Club: Graham Cross: Football League 495 + 3 + FA Cup 59 + League Cup 40 + European Cup Winners Cup 2 **Total 596** + 3 subs
Most Capped Player: Gordon Banks, 37, England
Record Goalscorer in a Match: John Duncan, 6 v Port Vale (7-0) (h), Div 2, 25.12.24
Arthur Chandler, 6 v Portsmouth (10-0) (h), Div 1, 20.10.28
Record League Goalscorer in a Season: Arthur Rowley, 44 (5 pens), Div 2, 1956-7   **In All Competitions:** Arthur Rowley, 44 (all League)
Record League Goalscorer in a Career: Arthur Chandler, 259, 1923-35   **In All Competitions:** Arthur Chandler, 273 (League 259, FA Cup 14)
Record Transfer Fee Received: £800,000 from Everton for Gary Lineker, July 1985
Record Transfer Fee Paid: £250,000 to FC Bruges for Roger Davies, Dec 1977
£250,000 to Oldham Athletic for Alan Young, July 1979
£250,000 to Partick Thistle for Jim Melrose, July 1980
£250,000 to Ipswich Town for Russell Osman, July 1985
Best Performances: League: Runners up Div 1 1928-9   **FA Cup:** Finalists 1949, 1961, 1963, 1969   **League/Milk Cup:** Winners   **European Cup Winners Cup:** 2nd Round
Most League Points: (3pts for win) 70, Div 2, 1982-3   (2pts for win) 61, Div 2, 1956-7
Most League Goals: 109, Div 2, 1956-7
Record League Victory and Most Goals in a First Class Match: 10-0 v Portsmouth, Div 1, 20 Oct 1928
Most Goals Scored in a Cup Tie: 13-0 v Notts Olympic (away but switched to home match) FA Cup 1st Qual Rnd, 13 Oct 1894
Record League Defeat: 0-12 v Nottingham Forest, Div 1, 21 Apr 1909 (as Leicester Fosse)
European Competitions Entered: European Cup Winners Cup 1961-2 (Tottenham Hotspur, the winners of the FA Cup, were competing in the European Cup as League Champions)
Oldest Player in League Match:
Youngest Player in League Match: Peter Shilton 16 yrs 228 days 04.05.1966
Most Consecutive Undefeated League Matches: 19 1971   **League Matches Without a Win:** 18 1975
Longest Run of Undefeated Home League Matches: 40 1898-1900
Away League Matches: 10 1971
Longest Run Without Home League Win: 8 1932, 1975   **Away League Win:** 22 1977-78
Most Consecutive League Wins: 7 1908, 1925, 1962-63   **Home League Wins:** 13 1906
Most Consecutive League Defeats: 7 1931-32   **Away League Wins:** 4 1971

Club Statistician for the Directory: Dave Smith

LEICESTER CITY

PLAYERS NAME Ht Wt Birthdate	Honours	Birthplace Transfers	Clubs	APPEARANCES				GOALS			
				League	Milk Cup	FA Cup	Other Comps	League	Milk Cup	FA Cup	Other Comps
GOALKEEPERS											
Ian Andrews 6.2 12.12 1.12.64	EY	Nottingham	Leicester City (A)	72	3	5					
			Swindon Town (L)	1							
Jeremy Roberts 6.0 13.0 24.11.66		Middlesbrough	Leicester City	3							
DEFENDERS											
Andy Feeley 5.9 10.10 30.9.61		Hereford F £10,000	Hereford United (A)	50+1				3			
			Trowbridge Town								
			Leicester City	63+1	4	5					
Simon Morgan 5.10½ 11.7 5.9.66		Birmingham	Leicester City (YTS)	30	1	1					
John O'Neill 6.0 13.3 11.3.58	NI (39), U21 (1), Div. 2, 80	Lanark	Denny AFC								
			Leicester City	284	13	19					
Russell Osman 6.0 11.10 14.2.59	E (11), B (1), U21 (7), UEFAC 81, FAYC 75	Ilkeston £200,000	Ipswich Town (A)	294	28	30+2	29+1	14	3	1	
			Leicester City	40	1	1					
Bobby Smith 5.7 11.8 21.12.53	Div. 2, 80	Dalkeith £85,000	Hibernian	146+6	13+2	8+1	11	19	2	2	
			Leicester City	175+6	8+1	10		20		1	
			Peterborough United (L)	5							
			Hibernian (L)	5							
Steve Walsh 6.2 11.10 7.10.62	FRT 85	Preston £100,000	Wigan Athletic	123+3	6	6	10+2	4			
			Leicester City								
Ian Wilson 5.7 10.11 27.3.58	Div. 2, 80	Aberdeen £20,000	Elgin City								
			Leicester City	232+8	15	14		14	1	1	
MIDFIELD											
Ian Banks 5.10½ 12.2 9.1.61		Mexborough	Barnsley (A)	158+6	20	11		37	3		
			Leicester City	76+14	3+2	6		14	1		
Robert Kelly 5.9 10.13 25.11.65		Birmingham	Leicester City (A)	9+1				2			
			Tranmere Rovers (L)	5				2			
Gary McAllister 6.1 11.5 25.12.64		Motherwell	Motherwell	51+6	3+1	6		6		2	
			Leicester City	31	1	1		7	1		
Alister Mauchley 5.7½ 11.5 29.6.60		West Kilbride	Kilmarnoch	82+6	27	5		9			2
			Motherwell	75+1	6	8		4	1		
			Leicester City	35+2	1	1		2			
Paul Ramsey 5.10 12.0 3.9.62	NI (9)	Londonderry	Leicester City (A)	135+3	10	5		3	1	1	
FORWARDS											
Mark Bright 6.0 11.0 6.6.62		Stoke F £33,333	Leek Town								
			Port Vale	18+11	1+1	0+1	2	10		1	
			Leicester City	25+16	3+1	1		6			
Phil Horner 6.1 12.1 10.11.66		Lincoln	Leicester City (A)								
			Rotherham United (L)	3+1							
Steve Lynex 5.9 11.5 23.1.58	FAYC 76	West Bromwich	WBA (A)								
			Shamrock Rovers								
			Birmingham City	28+18	3	1+3		9	1		
			Leicester City	193+10	13	11		59	2	1	
Tony Sealy 5.8½ 10.11 7.5.59	Div. 2, 83	London £50,000	Southampton (A)	2+5	0+1						
			Crystal Palace	16+8	0+2	1		5			
			Port Vale (L)	17				6			
			Fulham (L)	5				1			
			Port Vale (L)	6				4			
		£75,000	QPR	57+6	3+1			18			
			Fulham	17+3	0+1			7			
			Leicester City	19+2	1+1			6			
Alan Smith 6.2¾ 12.0 2.11.62	ESP (1)	Bromsgrove	Alvechurch								
			Leicester City	158+10	5+1	7		59	2	3	
Mark Venus 6.0 11.8 6.4.67		Hartlepool	Leicester City	1							

ADDITIONAL CONTRACT PROFESSIONALS
Paul Bunce (A)

APPRENTICES
Tony Brian, Jason Garwood, Sean Kimberley, Andy Ling, Carl Muggleton, Steve Prondiville, Steve Wilkinson, Darren Williams

NON-CONTRACT PLAYERS
Robert Alleyne, Ian Millne

Record Attendance: 47,298 v Tottenham Hotspur, FA Cup Round 5, 18 Feb 1928

Smallest Home Attendance for a First Class Match: 6,155 v Shrewsbury Town, Div 2, 22 Feb 1983

Record Receipts: £86,782 v Liverpool, Div 1, 30 Apr 1986

Season Tickets: Stand: £115.00, £105.00, £98.00, £95.00, £85.00; reductions for juveniles. Family Enclosures: (£35.00 OAP)

Executive Box Season Tickets: £5,000 per annum (19 people each) (3 year contracts), 20 boxes have been constructed

Cost of Stand Tickets (Standard Matches): £6.50, £6.00, £5.50, £5.00, Family Club £4.00 Juveniles £2.50, £2.00. **Terraces:** £3.50, Family Club £3.00, Juveniles £2.00

Match and Ticket Information: Applications with SAE are accepted two months prior to each match

Car Parking: Parking adjacent to stadium for season ticket holders only. Street parking is available and there is also a public car park five minutes walk from the ground

Nearest Railway Station: Leicester (0533 29811)

How to get to the ground

From North: Use Motorway M1 until junction 22 or A46/A607 into Leicester City Centre.

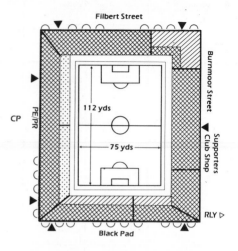

Follow signs Rugby into Almond Road, then at end turn right into Aylestone Road. Shortly turn left into Walnut Street, then turn left into Filbert Street for Leicester City FC

From East: Use A47 into Leicester City Centre. Follow signs Rugby into Almond Road, then at end turn right into Aylestone Road. Shortly turn left into Walnut Street, then turn left into Filbert Street for Leicester City FC

From South: Use Motorway M1 or M69 until junction 21 then A46 (S.P. Leicester). Under railway bridge and in 0.2m turn right into Upperton Road, then turn right into Filbert Street for Leicester City FC

From West: Use Motorway M69 or A50 into Leicester City centre and follow signs Rugby into Almond Road, then at end turn into Aylestone Road. Shortly turn left into Walnut Street, then turn left into Filbert Street for Leicester City FC

Price of 1986-7 Programme: 60p
Number of Pages: 20

Local Newspapers: Leicester Mercury, Leicester Trader

Local Radio Stations: Leicester Sound, Radio Leicester

LINCOLN CITY

Chairman
K J Reames

Directors
M B Pryor (Vice-Chairman)
G R Davey
G D Overton

Chief Executive
C J N Rodman MSC (0522 22224)

Manager
George Kerr

Assistant Manager/Physiotherapist
B Loxley

Administration
Miss Lisa Shammon

Lotteries Manager
B Baldwin

Club Doctor
M Locher

Life Vice-Presidents
V C Withers
D W L Bocock

Twelve months ago we recorded that survival in the 3rd Division was about the only good thing to come out of the 1984-85 season for Lincoln City. Now with genuine sadness — but with no feelings of surprise — we have to talk about their descent to the 4th Division in a season of unending humiliation. The team in fact played the minimum number of matches available to any club of their status in the process.

At the very best the season could be said to have started moderately well with sixth place being achieved on October 2nd, but form soon fell away and from October 5th until January 11th, when Bury were beaten at Sincil Bank in the League, not a match was won and defeat was avoided on only five occasions; the penultimate place was the price paid plus elimination from the FA Cup (0-1 at home to Blackpool).

There was a slight improvement, but it was not good enough, and with a final shameful home defeat against already-relegated Wolves came the coup-de-grace. Down go Lincoln, but the warning signs had been there for each season after the club almost gained promotion in 1982. Now it is back to the drawing board!

One cup result has already been mentioned and the other competitions are best dismissed briefly. The Milk Cup saw first round aggregate elimination at the hands of York City, who won both legs by the same score (2-1). The Freight Rover Trophy saw immediate loss of interest against Scunthorpe and Halifax.

Only four players in the recent season could be described as first team regulars — Redfearn, West, Turner and Strodder. Two goalkeepers were used (Naylor and Swinburne) and the new season starts with a change of manager, George Kerr having replaced Pickering. Kerr has done well as a manager in the past, but he has a frightening job on his hands now and must virtually build a new team from scratch. We wish him well.   WLM

Back Row L to R: Ian McInnes, Phil Turner (now at Grismby), Willie Gamble, Gary West, Trevor Swinburne, Lee Butler, Gary Strodder, John McGinley, Kevin Kilmore, Bobby Mitchell. **Middle Row:** Mark Cook (Apprentice), Richard Cooper, Neil Redfearn (now at Doncaster), Bert Loxley (Asst. Manager/Physio), Peter Daniel, Simeon Hodson, Neil Franklin (Apprentice). **Front Row:** Richard Ranshaw, Alex Buck, Gary Hare, David Parkin, Shane Nicholson (Apprentices).

LINCOLN CITY

DIVISION THREE:			**FA CUP:** 1st ROUND				**MILK CUP:** 1st ROUND			**FRT:**

MATCH	DATE	COMPE-TITION	VENUE	OPPONENTS	RESULT	HALF TIME	L'GUE POS'N	GOALSCORERS/GOAL TIMES	ATTEN-DANCE
1	A 17	CL	H	Gillingham	W 1-0	1-0		Redfern 43	2,099
2	20	MC1/1	A	York City	L 1-2	1-1		Burke 43	(3,630)
3	24	CL	A	Rotherham United	L 0-1	0-0	13		(3,356)
4	26	CL	H	Walsall	W 3-2	1-0		McGinley 4, 66, Toman 47	2,282
5	31	CL	A	Bury	L 0-4	0-1	15		(2,888)
6	S 4	MC1/2	H	York City	L 1-2	1-1		Richards, S. 1	2,257
7	8	CL	H	Doncaster Rovers	D 3-3	2-2	14	Redfern (pen) 11, McGinley 15, Ward 46	3,205
8	14	CL	A	Bristol Rovers	D 0-0	0-0	13		(3,077)
9	17	CL	A	Bolton Wanderers	D 1-1	1-1	12	Ward 9	(3,928)
10	21	CL	H	Brentford	W 3-0	1-0	9	Turner 43, 70, Toman 87	1,856
11	28	CL	A	Wolverhampton W.	D 1-1	0-1	10	Toman 80	(3,351)
12	O 2	CL	H	Bournemouth	W 3-2	0-0	6	Ward 53, McGinley 70, Redfearn 81	1,962
13	5	CL	H	Newport County	D 1-1	0-0	6	McGinley 57	1,989
14	11	CL	A	Swansea City	L 1-3	1-0	13	Redfearn 36	(3,600)
15	19	CL	H	Reading	L 0-1	0-1	13		4,007
16	22	CL	A	Plymouth Argyle	L 1-2	0-0	15	Ward 65	(6,552)
17	27	CL	A	Notts County	L 2-3	2-2	17	Latchford 7, Toman 12	(6,143)
18	N 2	CL	H	Blackpool	L 0-3	0-0	20		2,373
19	6	CL	H	Bristol City	D 1-1	1-1	20	Redfearn 18	1,379
20	9	CL	A	Derby County	L 0-7	0-2	21		(10,580)
21	N 16	FAC1	H	Blackpool	L 0-1	0-0			2,596
22	24	CL	H	York City	L 3-4	2-1	21	McGinley 26, Redfearn (pen) 38, Turner 72	2,295
23	30	CL	A	Wigan Athletic	L 2-3	1-3	21	Latchford 10, Mair 54	(3,014)
24	D 14	CL	H	Cardiff City	L 0-4	0-0	21		2,127
25	22	CL	H	Rotherham United	D 0-0	0-0	21		3,007
26	26	CL	A	Chesterfield	D 2-2	1-2	22	White 39, Ward 83	(2,631)
27	28	CL	A	Walsall	L 1-2	1-1	22	Daniel 41	(4,493)
28	J 1	CL	H	Darlington	D 1-1	0-0	22	McGinley 49	2,304
29	11	CL	H	Bury	W 2-0	1-0	23	McInnes 36, 77	2,226
30	15	FRT	H	Scunthorpe	L 1-3	0-1		Daniel 52	1,235
31	18	CL	A	Gillingham	L 0-1	0-1	23		(4,397)
32	F 1	CL	A	Doncaster Rovers	D 1-1	0-0	23	Daniel (pen) 64	(2,723)
33	11	FRT	A	Halifax Town	D 1-1	1-1		McInnes 18	(150)
34	25	CL	A	Blackpool	L 0-2	0-1	23		(1,995)
35	M 4	CL	A	Bournemouth	D 2-2	0-2	23	West 78, Gamble 83	(1,873)
36	8	CL	A	Newport County	W 2-1	0-0	23	Mair 78, Kilmore 88	(1,540)
37	12	CL	A	Reading	W 2-0	0-0	23	Redfearn 63, Gamble 90	(4,792)
38	16	CL	H	Swansea City	W 4-1	1-0	23	Turner 18, Gamble 51, 75, Mair 81	(2,846)
39	22	CL	H	Notts County	L 0-2	0-0	21		3,468
40	25	CL	H	Bolton Wanderers	D 1-1	1-1	21	Kilmore 32	2,329
41	29	CL	A	Darlington	L 0-1	0-1	21		(3,102)
42	31	CL	H	Chesterfield	W 2-1	1-0	20	Kilmore 9, White 84	2,461
43	A 5	CL	A	Bristol City	D 1-1	1-0	19	White 16	(5,395)
44	12	CL	H	Derby County	L 0-1	0-1	21		6,237
45	16	CL	H	Plymouth Argyle	D 1-1	1-0	21	West 3	2,297
46	19	CL	A	York City	L 1-2	0-2	23	Strodder 74	(3,874)
47	22	CL	A	Brentford	W 1-0	0-2	22	Ward 27	(3,011)
48	26	CL	H	Wigan Athletic	D 0-0	0-0	21		3,074
49	30	CL	H	Bristol Rovers	D 2-2	1-2	21	Ward 45, Redfearn 47	2,233
50	M 3	CL	A	Cardiff City	L 1-2	1-2	21	Kilmore 45	(1,904)
51	5	CL	H	Wolverhampton W.	L 2-3	1-2	21	Gamble 29, Ward (pen) 71	2,174

Best Home League Attendance: 6,237 v Derby County	Smallest: 1,379 v Bristol City	Av Home Att: 2,618
Goal Scorers:		Compared with 84-85: +68

League (55): Redfearn 8 (2 pen), Ward 8 (1 pen), McGinley 7, Gamble 5, Kilmore 4, Toman 4, Turner 4, Mair 3, White 3, Latchford 2, Daniel 2 (1 pen), McGinnes 2, West 2, Strodder 1

Milk Cup (2): Burke 1, Richards S. 1

FA CUP (-):

FRT (2): Daniel 1, McInnes 1

1985-86

Naylor	McCarrick	Collins	Redfearn	West	Richards S.	Toman	Turner	Latchford	White	McGinley	Strodder	Ward	Burke	Mair	Cooper	Greygoose	Gamble	Measham (L)	McNeil (NC)	Mitchell	Richards G.	Daniel	Swinburne	Hodson	McInnes	Referee	
1	2	3	4	5	6	7	8	9	10*	11	12															R Banks	1
1	2	3	4	5	6	7	8			11		9	10													**K Redfern**	2
1	2*	3	4	5	6	7	8			9	12	10	11													R Guy	3
1		3	2	5	6	7	8			9		10	11	4												M Scott	4
1		5	2	3	4	6*	7		12	10				11	9	8										A Saunders	5
1	2	3	8	5	6	7				9	12	10		11	4*											**M Heath**	6
1		3†	8	5	6	7			12	9	2	10*		11	4											N Ashley	7
1	4	3	8	5	6	7				9	2	10		11												G Ashby	8
1	4	3	8	5	6	7				9	2	10*	12	11												G Tyson	9
		3	4	5	6	7	8			9	2	10		11		1										T Fitzharris	10
		3	4	5	6	7	8			9	2	10		11*		1	12									I Hendrick	11
1		3	4	5	6	7	8			9	2	10		11												J McCauley	12
1	12	3	4	5	6	7	8			9	2	10*		11												D Hutchinson	13
1		3	4	5	6	7	8	9		10	2			11												P Vanes	14
		3	4	5	6*	7	8	9		10	2	12				1	11									D Phillips	15
		3	4	5		7	8	9		11	6	12				1	2									R Hamer	16
		3	4			7	8	9		10	6*	12		11		1	5	2								M Dimblebee	17
		3	4			7	8	9		10	5	12		11		1	6	2*								K Hackett	18
		3	4			7	8	9		10	5	11					6*	2			12					L Dilkes	19
		3*	4				8	9		11	5	10		12			7	2			6					J Lovatt	20
1	3	7	4	5	6		8	9		10	2			11												**J Ashworth**	21
1	3*		4	5	6	7	8	9		10	2			11							12					K Barratt	22
1	3		2		6	7*	8	9		10	5			11								4				T Jones	23
1			2	5		7	8	9		10	6						11			3†		4				H Taylor	24
1			3	5	6		8	9	7	11	2				10							4				N Wilson	25
1			3	5	6		8*	9	7	11	2	12			10							4				M Reed	26
1			3	5	6		8	9	7	11	2				10							4				C Trussell	27
1			3	5	6		8	12	7*	9	2			11	10							4				J Ashworth	28
1			3	5			8			9	11	6										4		2	7	B Hill	29
1	3	10*		5	13					9*	11	6	8		12							4		2	7	**M Scott**	30
1			3	5			8			9*	11	6			12							4		2	7	M James	31
1			12	5			8			9*	11	6								3		4		2	7	R Nixon	32
1			3	5			4*			11*		12	8		9					13	6			2	7	**K Lupton**	33
			12	5			8			9	11*	6								3		4	1	2	7	T Holbrook	34
			4	5			8				6			11	9					3			1	2	7	C Downey	35
			4	5			8				6			11	12		9			3*			1	2	7	R Groves	36
			4	5			8				6			11	9	3*					12		1	2*	7	A Gunn	37
			4	5			8*				6			11*	9					3	12		1	2	7	T Jones	38
			4	5			8				6			11*	9					3	12		1	2	7	T Simpson	39
			4	5			8				6			11	9					3*	12		1	2	7	K Miller	40
			4	5			8				6			11	9					3*	12		1	2	7	G Napthine	41
			3	5*			8				6	12		11	9								1	2	7	T Mills	42
			3	5*	12		8		4		6			11	9								1	2	7	R Bridges	43
			3			12	8		4	5	6	10			9*								1	2	7	J Lloyd	44
			3	5			8		9		6			11								4	1	2	7	P Tyldesley	45
			3	5			8		9		6	12		11								4	1	2	7	J Ball	46
			4	5			8		9*		6	10		11	12					3			1	2	7	L Robinson	47
			4	5			8		9*		6	10		11	12					3			1	2	7	F Roberts	48
			4	5			8		9*		6	10		11	12					3			1		7	I Hemley	49
			4	5			8				6	9*		11	2		12			3			1		7	D Reeves	50
				5	4		8	12			6	10		11*	2		9			3			1		7	J McAulay	51
20	13	11	43	38	21	21	43	14	17	29	41	15	4	26	16	6	12	6	4	14	2	16	18	15	21	League Appearances	
	1		2			3		1	5		2	5	1		4	4					5					Substitute Appearances	
2	2	2	2	2	2	1				2	0·1	1	2	1	1											Milk Cup Appearances	
1	1	1	1	1	1			1	1			1	1	1												FA Cup Appearances	
2	1	2		1	1	0·1	1		1	2	1	1		0·2	1		1			0·1	1	1		2	2	FR Trophy Appearances	

Also Played: Position(Game): Harrison 12(23), Judge 1(19, 20)
Players on Loan: Burke (QPR), Greygoose (Cambridge), Measham (Huddersfield), Judge (Oxford)
Departures: Naylor (WBA), Collins (Peterborough), Richards G, Richards S (Cambridge Utd), Redfearn (Doncaster)

'THE RED IMPS'

Formed: 1883
Turned Professional: 1892   **Ltd Co:** 1892

Previous Managers: Bill Anderson   Bob Chapman   Ron Gray   Bert Loxley   David Herd   Graham Taylor   George Kerr   Willie Bell
Honours: Champions Div 3 (N), 1931-2, 1947-8, 1951-2   Champions Div 4, 1975-6
League Career: Original Members of Div 2 1892   Not re-elected to Div 2 1908
Re-elected to Div 2 1909   Not re-elected to Div 2 1911   Re-elected to Div 2 1912
Not re-elected 1920   Elected to Div 3 1921   Promoted to Div 2 1931-2
Relegated to Div 3 (N) 1933-4   Promoted to Div 2 1947-8   Relegated to Div 3 (N) 1948-9
Promoted to Div 2 1951-2   Relegated to Div 3 1960-1   Relegated to Div 4 1961-2
Promoted to Div 3 1975-6   Relegated to Div 4 1978-9   Promoted to Div 3 1980-1
Colours: Broad red and white striped shirts, black shorts and red stockings
Change Colours: Royal blue with white pinstipe, black shorts and royal blue stockings
Reserves League: **'A' Team:**

CLUB RECORDS

Most Appearances for Club: Tony Emery: 402, 1946-59
Most Capped Player: David Pugh, 3, Wales   George Moulson, 3, Eire
Record Goalscorer in a Match: Andy Graver, 6 v Crewe Alexandra (h), 11-1, Div 3 (N), 29.09.1951   Frank Keetley, 6 v Halifax Town (h), 9-1, Div 3 (N), 16.01.1932
Record League Goalscorer in a Season: Allan Hall, 42, Div 3 (N), 1931-2
Record League Goalscorer in a Career: Andy Graver, 144, 1950-1 & 1958-61
Record Transfer Fee Received: £180,000 from Newcastle United for Mick Harford, Dec 1980
Record Transfer Fee Paid: £45,000 to Southampton for George Shipley, Jan 1980
Best Performances: League: 5th Div 2 1901-2   **FA Cup:** Equivalent of 5th Round 1886-7, 1889-90, 1901-2   **League/Milk Cup:** 4th Round 1967-8
Most League Points: (3pts for win) 77, Div 3, 1981-2   (2pts for win) Div 4, 1975-6
Record League Victory and Most Goals Scored in a League Match: 11-1 v Crewe Alexandra, Div 3 (N), 29 Sept 1951
Most Goals Scored in a Cup Tie: 13-0 v Peterborough (a), FA Cup 1st Qualifying Round, 12 Oct 1895
Record League Defeat: 3-11 v Manchester City, Div 2, 23 March 1895
Oldest Player in League Match:
Youngest Player in League Match:
Most Consecutive Undefeated League Matches: 18 1980
Longest Run of Undefeated Home League Matches: 35 1975-6
Longest Run Without Home League Win: 11 1978-79
Most Consecutive League Wins: 10 1930
Most Consecutive League Defeats: 12 1896-97

League Matches Without a Win: 19 1978
Away League Matches: 12 1980
Away League Win: 35 1896-98
Home League Wins: 14 1982
Away League Wins: 5 1968, 1975

Club Statistician for the Directory: Paul Harbridge

LINCOLN CITY

PLAYERS NAME Ht Wt Birthdate	Honours	Birthplace Transfers	Clubs	APPEARANCES League	Milk Cup	FA Cup	Other Comps	GOALS League	Milk Cup	FA Cup	Other Comps
GOALKEEPERS											
Trevor Swinburne	FAYC 69	East Rainton	Sunderland (A)	10		1					
6.0 12.12 20.6.53		F	Carlisle United	248	16	9					
		Player exch.	Brentford	45	8	5	2				
			Leeds United	2							
			Doncaster Rovers (L)	4							
			Lincoln City								
DEFENDERS											
Steve Buckley		Brinsley	Burton Albion								
5.11 12.4 16.10.53		£2,000	Luton Town	123	7	5		9			
		£165,000	Derby County	323	21	17	3	8			
			Lincoln City								
Simeon Hodson		Lincoln	Notts County	27	3						
5.10 11.2 5.2.66		F	Charlton Athletic	5							
			Lincoln City	15			2				
Robert Mitchell		Grimsby	Sunderland (A)	1+2							
5.10 11.6 4.1.55			Blackburn Rovers	17+12		2		6			
			Grimsby Town	142	16	8		6		1	
			Carlisle United	2							
			Rotherham United	86+9	11	6	2	2		1	
		Malta	Lincoln City	14			0+1				
Gary Strodder+		Spenborough	Lincoln City	67+6	3+1	1+1	4+1	4			
6.1 11.3½ 1.4.65											
Gary West	EY	Scunthorpe	Sheffield United (A)	75	3	7	2		1		
6.1 12.2 25.8.64		£35,000	Lincoln City	38	2	1	1	2			
MIDFIELD											
Richard Cooper		London	Sheffield United	2+4		1					
5.8½ 10.10½ 7.5.65		F	Lincoln City	16+4	1		1				
Peter Daniel	EU23 (3), U21 (7),	Hull	Hull City (A)	113	2	8		9			
5.8½ 11.3 12.12.55	LgC 80	£150,000	Wolverhampton W.	157	17	19		13	2	1	
			Sunderland	33+1	10	1	1				
			Lincoln City	16			1	2			1
FORWARDS											
Simon Gamble		Cottam	Lincoln City (A)	12+4			1	5			
5.9 11.7½ 5.3.68											
Kevin Kilmore	EY, Div. 3, 80	Scunthorpe	Scunthorpe United	93+9	6+2	3		28	1		
5.10½ 11.11 11.11.59		£60,000	Grimsby Town	70+32	4	4+1		27			
		F	Rotherham United	82+2	10+1	6	2	20	5	3	
		Malta	Lincoln City	18			1	4	1		
John McGinley		Highfield	Sunderland								
6.2 13.6¼ 11.6.59		Tyne & Wear	Lincoln City								
		Charleroi, Belgium	Lincoln City	29	2	3	6	11			
Ian McInnes		Hamilton	Rotherham United	5+2							
5.8 9,11 23.3.67			Lincoln City	21			2	2			1

ADDITIONAL CONTRACT PROFESSIONALS
Lee Butler, Steve Richards

APPRENTICES

NON-CONTRACT PLAYERS
Alan Crombie

Record Receipts: £34,843.30 v Tottenham Hotspur, Milk Cup, 26 Oct 1983

Season Tickets: £70.00, £55.00* (South Park); Ground: £45.00 (concession £20).
*Concession
Family: £103.50 (one adult one child), £132.25 (one adult two children)

Cost of Stand Tickets: £3.50 (concessions £3.00 or £3.20) **Terraces:** £2.30 (concessions £1.10)

Match and Ticket Information: Contact Club

Car Parking: Street parking available

Nearest Railway Station: Lincoln Central (0522 39502)

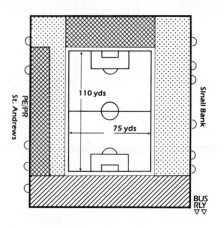

How to get to the ground

From North, East and West: Use A15, A57, A46 or A158 into Lincoln city centre then follow Newark (A46) into High Street. Under railway bridge then take next turning left into Queen Street for Lincoln City FC
From South: Use A1 then A46 (S.P. Lincoln) then following signs city centre into High Street and on nearside of railway bridge turn right into Queen Street for Lincoln City FC

Price of 1986-7 Programme: 50p
Number of Pages: 24
Subscriptions: £20.00

Local Newspapers:

Local Radio Stations:

LIVERPOOL

Chairman
J W Smith CBE, JP, DL

Directors
S C Reakes JP
J T Cross
W D Corkish
Coun S T Moss JP
R Paisley OBE
G A Ensor
N White

Chief Executive/General Secretary
P B Robinson (051-263 2361)

Assistant Secretary
R E Jones

Team Manager
Kenny Dalglish

Chief Coach
Ronnie Moran

First Team Assistant Coach
Roy Evans

Reserve Team Coach
Phil Thompson

Youth Team Coaches
M Cook
J Bennison

Chief Scout
Geoff Twentyman

Commercial Manager
K Addison (051-263 6391)

Stadium Foreman
K Myers

Groundsman
R Summers

In May of last year the good name of Liverpool was in ruins thanks to the violent behaviour of a small number of supporters in Brussels. EUFA banned the club from their competitions for a minimum of three years and there were other problems. For a great club like Liverpool there was the sad prospect of a bleak future, but the men of Anfield have courage and character and instead of gloom and despondency with heads down they hit back and gave the public a glimpse of astonishing achievement which is to their eternal credit. They did the League and Cup double and became only the fifth side to do so. And in the League they came from behind to win through.

In fact, early form in the League was at best modest and later (in December) five matches went by without a victory, whilst the team failed to win any game of three played in February. But then the charge happened and of the final 12 matches only a drawn game away to Sheffield Wednesday provided any hint of a set-back so that they overtook the front-runners and were 'home and dry' with one match remaining after a success away to their erstwhile bogey-team, Leicester City.

The cups were almost equally rewarding. The Milk Cup could also have reached Anfield, since Oldham Athletic, Brighton, Manchester United and Ipswich Town all fell to their power. But then a potentially easy semi-final over two legs against QPR was thrown away by courtesy of two own goals. No such mistakes were made in the FA Cup, where Norwich City (5-0 at home), Chelsea (2-1 away), York City (after a replay and extra-time) and Watford (also after a replay — away — and more extra-time at Watford) were eliminated. The semi-final also required an extra half hour before Southampton were despatched (2-0) and at Wembley an Everton lead at half-time was only overtaken in the last half-hour of the match thanks to the opportunism (as usual) of Ian Rush, who plays the coming season on loan from Juventus. The team also reached the Final of the domestic Super Cup and if that is won early this coming season . . . well!

What more can be said about this paragon of a club? They show incredible consistency and the apparent gamble of making Kenny Dalglish player-manager seems to have worked a miracle. In the Cup Final at Wembley the only Englishman in the party was McMahon the substitute, who did not play, and the season's main stars in a team of no stars (?) were Whelan, Hansen, Dalglish himself, Nicol, Molby, Beglin, Johnston, Gillespie and (who else) that man Rush. Even if they might have been a League of Nations team at Wembley it must be emphasised that Liverpool are once again a credit to English Football and it is hoped that the lifting of EUFA's ban will include the club when it does happen — we hope for next season.   WLM

Back Row L to R: Mark Lawrenson, Jan Molby, Mike Hooper, Gary Gillespie, Bruce Grobbelaar, Kevin Macdonald. **Middle Row:** Roy Evans (Trainer), Steve Nicol, Steve McMahon, Jim Beglin, Ian Rush, Barry Venison, Paul Walsh, Ronnie Moran (Coach). **Front Row:** Ronnie Whelan, John Wark, Bob Paisley (Team Consultant), Kenny Dalglish (Player/Manager), Alan Hansen (Captain), Craig Johnston, Sammy Lee (now with QPR).

LIVERPOOL

DIVISION ONE: 1st   **FA CUP:** WINNERS   **MILK CUP:** SEMI-FINAL   **SUPER CUP:**

MATCH	DATE	COMPE-TITION	VENUE	OPPONENTS	RESULT	HALF TIME	L'GUE POS'N	GOALSCORERS/GOAL TIMES	ATTEN-DANCE
1	A 17	CL	H	Arsenal	W 2-0	1-0		Whelan 37, Nicol 66	38,261
2	21	CL	A	Aston Villa	D 2-2	1-1		Rush 38, Molby 84	(20,197)
3	24	CL	A	Newcastle United	L 0-1	0-0	10		(29,670)
4	26	CL	H	Ipswich Town	W 5-0	3-0		Nicol 16, Molby 27, Rush 33, 67, Johnston 89	29,383
5	31	CL	A	West Ham United	D 2-2	0-1	8	Johnston 52, Whelan 83	(19,762)
6	S 3	CL	H	Nottingham Forest	W 2-0	0-0		Whelan 55, 70	27,135
7	7	CL	H	Watford	W 3-1	1-1	2	Neal 28, Johnston 66, Rush 71	31,395
8	14	CL	A	Oxford United	D 2-2	0-1	4	Rush 62, Johnston 75	(11,474)
9	21	CL	A	Everton	W 3-2	3-0	2	Dalglish 1, Rush 16, McMahon 43	(51,509)
10	28	CL	H	Tottenham Hotspur	W 4-1	1-0	2	Lawrenson 45, Rush 56, Molby (pen) 61, (pen) 66	41,521
11	O 5	CL	A	Q.P.R.	L 1-2	1-1	2	Walsh 7	(24,621)
12	12	CL	H	Southampton	W 1-0	0-0	2	McMahon 59	31,070
13	19	CL	A	Manchester United	D 1-1	0-0	2	Johnston 46	(54,492)
14	26	CL	H	Luton Town	W 3-2	2-0	2	Walsh 29, 33, Molby 76	31,488
15	N 2	CL	H	Leicester City	W 1-0	0-0	2	Rush 83	31,718
16	9	CL	A	Coventry City	W 3-0	1-0	2	Beglin 5, Walsh 48, Rush 62	(16,497)
17	16	CL	H	W.B.A.	W 4-1	1-1	2	Nicol 45, Molby 63, Lawrenson 74, Walsh 87	28,407
18	23	CL	A	Birmingham City	W 2-0	2-0	2	Rush 9, Walsh 26	(15,062)
19	30	CL	H	Chelsea	D 1-1	0-0	2	Molby (pen) 85	38,482
20	D 7	CL	H	Aston Villa	W 3-0	1-0	2	Molby 2, Walsh 67, Johnston 81	29,418
21	14	CL	A	Arsenal	L 0-2	0-2	2		(35,048)
22	21	CL	H	Newcastle United	D 1-1	1-1	2	Nicol 34	30,746
23	26	CL	A	Manchester City	L 0-1	0-0	2		(35,484)
24	28	CL	A	Nottingham Forest	D 1-1	0-1	4	MacDonald 55	(27,141)
25	J 1	CL	H	Sheffield Wednesday	D 2-2	0-1	3	Rush 49, Walsh 75	38,964
26	12	CL	A	Watford	W 3-2	1-1	3	Walsh 44, 85, Rush 75	(16,692)
27	18	CL	H	West Ham United	W 3-1	0-0	3	Molby (pen) 58, Rush 67, Walsh 70	41,056
28	F 1	CL	A	Ipswich Town	L 1-2	1-0	4	Whelan 36	(20,551)
29	9	CL	H	Manchester United	D 1-1	1-1	3	Wark 40	35,084
30	22	CL	H	Everton	L 0-2	0-0	3		45,454
31	M 2	CL	A	Tottenham Hotspur	W 2-1	0-1	3	Molby 65, Rush 90	(16,463)
32	8	CL	H	Q.P.R.	W 4-1	3-1	2	McMahon 19, 74, Rush 29, Wark 43	26,219
33	15	CL	A	Southampton	W 2-1	0-0	2	Wark 53, Rush 59	(19,784)
34	22	CL	H	Oxford United	W 6-0	3-0	2	Rush 3 (1, 70, 89) Lawrenson 18, Whelan 38, Molby (pen) 50	37,861
35	29	CL	A	Sheffield Wednesday	D 0-0	0-0	2		(37,946)
36	31	CL	H	Manchester City	W 2-0	1-0	1	McMahon 32, 58	43,316
37	A 12	CL	H	Coventry City	W 5-0	2-0	1	Whelan 3 (19, 26, 82) Molby 46, Rush 75	42,729
38	16	CL	A	Luton Town	W 1-0	1-0	1	Johnston 16	(15,390)
39	19	CL	A	W.B.A.	W 2-1	1-1	1	Dalglish 23, Rush 66	(20,200)
40	26	CL	H	Birmingham City	W 5-0	1-0	1	Rush 27, Gillespie 3 (47, 59, (pen) 63) Molby (pen) 49	42,021
41	30	CL	A	Leicester City	W 2-0	2-0	1	Rush 19, Whelan 25	(25,797)
42	M 3	CL	A	Chelsea	W 1-0	1-0	1	Dalglish 23	(43,900)

Best Home League Attendance: 45,445 v Everton   **Smallest:** 26,219 v Q.P.R.   **Av Home Att:** 35,320

Goal Scorers: **Compared with 84-85:** −534

League (89): Rush 23, Molby 14 (6 pen), Walsh 11, Whelan 10, Johnston 7, McMahon 5, Nicol 4, Dalglish 3, Gillespie 3, Lawrenson 3, Wark 3, Beglin 1, MacDonald 1, Neal 1

Milk Cup (?):
FA CUP (?):

Grobbelar	Neal	Kennedy	Lawrenson	Whelan	Hansen	Dalglish	Nicol	Rush	Molby	Beglin	Walsh	Johnston	Lee	McMahon	MacDonald	Wark	Gillespie	Referee	
1	2	3	4	5	6	7	8	9	10	11								D Hutchinson	1
1	2	3	4	5	6		8	9	10	11	7*	12						K Cooper	2
1	2	3	4	5	6	7*	8	9	10	11		12						J Key	3
1	2*	3	4	5	6		8	9	10		12	7	11					T Holbrook	4
1	2	3	4	6	5		8	9	10			7	11					B Hill	5
1	2	3	4	5	6		8	9	10			7	11					T Mills	6
1	2	3	4	5	6		8	9	10			7	11					M Peck	7
1	2	3	4	5*	6		8	9	10		12	7		11				J Moules	8
1	12		4	5	6	7	2*	9	10	3		8		11				D Shaw	9
1	2		4	5	6	7		9	10	3		8		11*	12			C Seel	10
1	2		4	5	6			9	10	3	7	8		11				G Napthine	11
1	2		4	5		7		9	10	3		8		11	12	6*		J Lovatt	12
1	2		4	5	6			9	10	3		7		11	12	8*		A Saunders	13
1			4	5	6	7	2		10	3	9	8		11				L Robinson	14
1			4	5	6	12	2	9	10	3	7	8*		11				K Redfern	15
1	12		4	5	6		2	9	10	3	7	8		11*				D Vickers	16
1			4	5*	6	12	2	9	10	3	7	8		11				T Simpson	17
1			4	5	6		2	9	10	3	7	8		11				H King	18
1			4	5	6		2	9	10	3	7	8		11				N Ashley	19
1			4		6		2	9	10	3	7	8	5	11				G Courtney	20
1			4		6		2	9	10	3	7	8	5*	11	12			D Hedges	21
1			4		6	12	2	9		3	7	8	5	11		10*		K Hackett	22
1			4		6	12	2	9		3	7*	8		11	10			A Seville	23
1			4	5	6	7	2	9	10	3		8*	12	11				K Baker	24
1			4	5	6	7*	2	9	10		12	8		11	3			R Bridges	25
1			4	5	6		2	9	10		7	8		11	3			M Bodenham	26
1			4	5	6		2	9	10		7	8			11	3		G Tyson	27
1			4	5	6		2		10	3	7	8*	9		12	11		V Callow	28
1			4	5	6			9	10	3	7*	8	2		12	11		N Ashley	29
1			4	5	6			9	10*	3		8	2	11	12		7	J Worrall	30
1			4	5	6			9	10	3		8	2	11			7	Alan Robinson	31
1			4	5	6	7		9	10	3		12	2	11	8*			B Hill	32
1			4	5	6			9	10	3		7	2	11		8		A Ward	33
1			4*	5	6	7	12	9	10	3		8		11			2	G Courtney	34
1				5	6	4		9	10	3	7*	8		11	12		2	P Willis	35
1				5	6	7	4	9	10	3		8		11			2	D Hough	36
1				5	6	7	4	9*	10	3		8			12	11	2	D Hutchinson	37
1				5	6	7	4	9	10	3		8	12	11			2*	P Vanes	38
1		2		5	6	7	4	9	10	3		8		11				R Lewis	39
1				5	6	7	4	9	10	3		8		11			2	G Tyson	40
1		12		5	6	7	4	9*	10	3		8		11			2	R Milford	41
1		10		5	6	7	4	9		3		8		11			2	L Shapter	42
42	11	8	36	39	41	17	33	40	39	34	17	38	13	23	10	7	14	League Appearances	
	2		1			4	1					3	3	2	7	2		Substitute Appearances	

Also Played:
Players on Loan:
Departures: Neal (Bolton), Kennedy (Sunderland), Bolder (Sunderland)

'THE REDS or POOL'

Formed: 1892
Turned Professional: 1892   **Ltd Co:** 1892

Sponsored by
Crown Paint

Previous Managers: 1892-6 John McKenna   1896-1920 Tom Watson   1920-3 David Ashworth   1923-8 Matthew McQueen   1928-35 George Patterson   1935-51 George Kay   1951-6 Don Welsh   1956-9 Phil Taylor   1959-74 Bill Shankly   1974-84 Bob Paisley   1984-5 Joe Fagan

Honours: Champions Div 1, 1900-1, 1905-6, 1921-2, 1922-3, 1946-7, 1963-4, 1965-6, 1972-3, 1975-6, 1976-7, 1978-9, 1979-80, 1981-2, 1982-3, 1983-4 (Third club to win the Championship in three consecutive years) 1985-6   Champions Div 2, 1893-4, 1895-6, 1904-5, 1961-2   FA Cup Winners 1965-6, 1974, 1986   Football League/Milk Cup Winners 1981, 1982, 1983, 1984   European Cup Winners 1976-7, 1977-8, 1980-1, 1983-4   UEFA Cup Winners 1972-3, 1975-6   European Super Cup Winners 1977

League Career: Elected to Div 2 1893   Promoted to Div 1 1893-4   Relegated to Div 2 1894-5   Promoted to Div 1 1895-6   Relegated to Div 2 1903-4   Promoted to Div 1 1904-5   Relegated to Div 2 1953-4   Promoted to Div 1 1961-2

Colours: All red with white and yellow trim

Change Colours: White with red and yellow trim

CLUB RECORDS

Most Appearances for Club: Ian Callaghan: Football League 640 + FA Cup 77 + League Cup 42 + European Cups 87 **Total 846**

Most Capped Player: Emlyn Hughes, 59, England

Record Goalscorer in a Match: Andy McGuigan, 5 v Stoke City, 7-0 (h), Div 1, 04.01.1902   John Evans, 5 v Bristol Rovers, 5-3 (h), Div 2, 15.09.1954

Record League Goalscorer in a Season: Roger Hunt, 41, Div 2, 1961-2   **In All Competitions:** Ian Rush, 47 (League 32 + FA Cup 2 + Milk Cup 8 + European Cup 5), 1983-4

Record League Goalscorer in a Career: Roger Hunt, 245, 1959-69   **In All Competitions:** Roger Hunt, 285 (League 245 + FA Cup 18 + League Cup 5 + European Cups 17)

Record Transfer Fee Received: £650,000 from Sampdoria for Graeme Souness, June 1984

Record Transfer Fee Paid: £900,000 to Brighton for Mark Lawrenson, Aug 1981

Best Performances: As in honours

Most League Points: (3pts for win) 87, Div 1, 1982-3 (record)   (2pts for win) 68, Div 1, 1978-9

Most League Goals: 106, Div 2, 1895-6 (30 games)

Record League Victory and Most Goals Scored in a League Match: 10-1 v Rotherham United, Div 2, 18 Feb 1896

Most Goals Scored in a Cup Tie: 11-0 v Stromsgodset, 1st Round European Cup Winners Cup, 17 Sept 1974

Record League Defeat: 1-9 v Birmingham City, Div 2, 11 Dec 1954

European Competitions Entered: European Cup: 1964-5, 1966-7, 1973-4, 1976-7, 1977-8, 1978-9, 1979-80, 1980-1, 1981-2, 1982-3, 1983-4, 1984-5   European Cup Winners Cup: 1965-6, 1971-2, 1974-5   European Fairs Cup: 1967-8, 1968-9, 1969-70, 1970-1   UEFA Cup: 1972-3, 1975-6   European Super Cup: 1977, 1978   World Club Championship: 1981, 1983

Oldest Player in League Match:

Youngest Player in League Match:

Most Consecutive Undefeated League Matches: 30 1893-94

Longest Run of Undefeated Home League Matches: 63 1978-81

Longest Run Without Home League Win: 10 1951-52

Most Consecutive League Wins: 11 1982

Most Consecutive League Defeats: 9 1899

League Matches Without a Win: 14 1953-54

Away League Matches: 16 1893-94

Away League Win: 24 1953-54

Home League Wins: 21 1972

Away League Wins: 6 1904, 1982

Club Statistician for the Directory: Brian Pead

LIVERPOOL

PLAYERS NAME Ht Wt Birthdate	Honours	Birthplace Transfers	Clubs	APPEARANCES				GOALS			
				League	Milk Cup	FA Cup	Other Comps	League	Milk Cup	FA Cup	Other Comps
GOALKEEPERS											
Bruce Grobbelaar	·	Zimbabwe	Vancouver W.								
6.1 12.0 6.10.57			Crewe Alexandra	24			1				
			Vancouver W.								
		£250,000	Liverpool	210	28	24	32				
Mike Hooper		Bristol	Bristol City	1							
6.3 13.0 10.2.64		F	Wrexham	33	4		1				
			Liverpool								
DEFENDERS											
Gary Ablett		Liverpool	Liverpool (A)								
6.0 11.4 19.11.65			Derby County (L)	3+3			2				
Jim Beglin		Waterford	Shamrock Rovers								
5.11 11.0 29.7.63			Liverpool	44	7	10	3	2			
Gary Gillespie		Stirling	Falkirk	22	2	1					
6.2 12.1 5.7.60		£75,000	Coventry City	171+1	15	1		6			
		£325,000	Liverpool	24+2	5	9+1	3+2	4			
Alan Hansen	·	Alloa	Partick Thistle	82+4	14	4		6			
6.1 13.0 13.6.55		£100,000	Liverpool	329	41	38+1	44+1	7	1	2	
John McGregor		Airdrie	Queens Park	103	9	5		19	2	1	
5.11 12.0 5.1.63			Liverpool								
			St Mirren (L)	5							
			Leeds United (L)								
Mark Lawrenson		Preston	Preston North End	73	2	5		2			
6.0 11.7 2.6.57		£100,000	Brighton & H.A.	152	15	7		5	1	1	
		£900,000	Liverpool	188+3	27	19	27+1	11	2	2	1
Steve Nicol		Irvine	Ayr United	57+2	9	3		5			
5.10 11.0 11.12.61		£300,000	Liverpool	82+9	5	12	10+2	14			2
Barry Venison		Consett	Sunderland (A)	169+4	21	7+1	3				1
5.10½ 11.12 16.8.64		£200,000	Liverpool								
MIDFIELD											
Wayne Harrison			Oldham Athletic (A)		5+1		1				
5.8 10.7 15.11.67		£250,000	Liverpool								
			Oldham Athletic (L)	1		0+1					
Craig Johnston		Johannesburg	Middlesbrough (A)	61+3	4+2	5+2		16			
5.9 11.2 8.12.60		£575,000	Liverpool	120+12	14+2	10+4	14+2	22	3	3	2
Kevin MacDonald		Inverness	Inverness Caley								
6.0¼ 11.11 27.12.60		£40,000	Leicester	133+5	10	4		8			
		£400,000	Liverpool	23+7	0+2	9	4	1	1	1	
Steve McMahon		Liverpool	Everton (A)	99+1	11	9		11		3	
5.9 12.1½ 20.8.61		£175,000	Aston Villa	74+1	9	3	4	7			
			Liverpool	23	5	4		5	3	1	
Jan Molby	·	Kolding, Jutland	Ajax								
6.1 13.8 4.7.83		£575,000	Liverpool	58+3	5+1	8	1	15	2	3	
John Wark		Glasgow	Ipswich Town (A)	295+1	24+1	36+1	25	94	12	10	18
5.10½ 11.12 4.8.57		£450,000	Liverpool	56+3	4+2	10+2	11	23	1	6	5
Ronnie Whelan		Dublin	Home Farm								
5.9 10.13 25.9.61			Liverpool	152+8	21+3	19	23+2	34	9	5	6
FORWARDS											
Kenny Dalglish		Glasgow	Celtic	200+4	59+3	28	22	112	34	11	7
5.8 11.13 4.3.51		£440,000	Liverpool	330+4	45	37	48+1	112	23	13	10
Ian Rush		St. Asaph	Chester City (A)	33+1		5		14		3	
6.0½ 12.6 25.10.61		£300,000	Liverpool	182	26	23	26+1	110	13	18	15
		£3,500,000	Juventus								
			Liverpool (L)								
Paul Walsh		Plumstead	Charlton Athletic (A)	85+2	9	4		24	6	1	
5.8 10.4 1.10.62		£400,000	Luton Town	80	5	4		24	1	2	
		£700,000	Liverpool	39+7	6	3+3	6	19	4	3	3
Mark Seagraves		Bootle	Liverpool		1	1					
6.0 11.10 22.10.66											

LIVERPOOL HONOURS ARE SHOWN ON PAGE 565

ADDITIONAL CONTRACT PROFESSIONALS

Ian Toale (A), Alex Watson (A), Ian Fairborther, Ken de Mange, Brian Mooney, Sean Curry, Phil Thompson although coaching has also signed playing contract

APPRENTICES

John Jeffers, Terry McPhillips, Paul Reddington, Chris Rogers

NON-CONTRACT PLAYERS

Andy Doyle, Curtis Eaton, Karl Edmunds, Ian McNab, William Mercer

Record Attendance: 61,905 v Wolverhampton Wanderers, FA Cup Round 4, 2 Feb 1952

Smallest Home Attendance for a First Class Match: 1,000 v Loughborough Trinity, Div 2, 7 Dec 1895

Record Receipts: £164,000 v Panathinaikos, Semi-final European Cup, 10 Apr 1985

Season Tickets: Stand: £82.00, £95.00: Ground: £47.50 (adult)

Cost of Stand Tickets: £5.20 Main Stand/Kemlyn Road/Paddock; £4.50 Anfield Road, £6.35 combined Adult/Juvenile: **Terraces:** £2.60 adults, £1.80 OAP/juveniles

Match and Ticket Information: Postal applications 19 days before match. Phone numbers: 051-263 2361; 24-hr service 051-260 9999 or normal office hours 051-260 8680

Car Parking: Limited street parking. Mainly privately-owned car park in Priory Road (5 minutes walk from ground)

Nearest Railway Station: Kirkdale or Lime Street (051-709 9696)

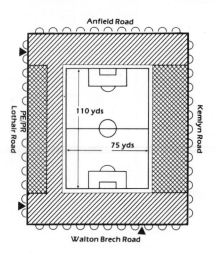

How to get to the ground

From North: Use Motorway M6 until junction 28 then follow signs Liverpool on A58 and forward into Walton Hall Avenue pass Stanley Park and turn left into Anfield Road for Liverpool FC

From East and South: Use Motorway M6 then M62 until end of Motorway then turn right A5058 into Queens Drive. In 3m turn left into Utting Avenue. In 1m turn right into Anfield Road for Liverpool FC

From West: Use Mersey tunnel into Liverpool City Centre then follow signs Preston A580 into Walton Hall Avenue, then on nearside of Stanley Park turn right into Anfield Road for Liverpool FC

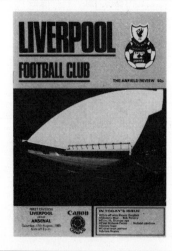

Price of 1986-7 Programme: 50p
Number of Pages: 24

Local Newspapers: Liverpool Daily Post, Liverpool Echo

Local Radio Stations: Radio Merseyside, Radio City

LUTON TOWN

President
Tom Hodgson

Chairman
D J Evans

Directors
R J Smith
E S Pearson, LLM, BSc
R L Banks
J R Smith
M Alleyan

Executive Director
J R Smith

Company Secretary
G H Mackrell, FCCA

Manager
John Moore

Physiotherapist
D Kirby

Commercial Director
W J Tomlins (0582 411622)

Back Row L to R: Marcus Tuite, David Preece, Mark Stein, Emeka Nwajiobi, Mark North, Ricky McEvoy, Rob Johnson. **Middle Row:** Jim Ryan (Coach), Tim Breacker, Les Sealey, Mick Harford, Stacey North, Andy Dibble, Mike Newell, John Faulkner (Coach). **Front Row:** Ray Harford (Coach), Ricky Hill, Mal Donaghy, Steve Foster, John Moore (Manager), Peter Nicholas, Brian Stein, Ashley Grimes, Dave Kirby (Physio).

I t would be easy to be disappointed with a side that was up with the leaders for most of the second half of the season but yet only finished ninth. However, considering the traumas that have surrounded Luton Town both on and off the field since their return to Division 1, ninth position was a magnificent achievement which further amplified the belief in manager David Pleat, his astute dealing in the transfer market and further fruition of his youth policy.

The defence, for so long regarded as weak by Division 1 standards conceded only 44 goals which was bettered by only four other sides whilst the team in general retained the free-flowing style of previous seasons.

Skipper and central defender Steve Foster had probably his best ever season and was mentioned to Bobby Robson on more than one occasion with regard to possible additions to his England cap collection, whilst Mick Harford could feel himself extremely unlucky to be excluded from the original World Cup Squad. A consensus of opinion gleaned from his fellow professionals would doubtless have seen him included.

There is little doubt that the artificial surface suited Luton's close passing style of play but until they got used to it, early season form was decidedly patchy. This changed after a fighting 1-1 draw with Manchester United, which ruined the Old Trafford side's opening sequence, quickly followed by the 7-0 demolition of Southampton.

David Pleat's locally christened "A" team was hampered by a long term injury sustained by Emeka Nwajiobi in November followed by a long lay-off for Brian Stein, back to his very best form, starting in February. These injuries undoubtedly affected the pattern of the team despite the introduction of Mike Newell the free scoring forward from Wigan and would account for the gradual tail off toward the end of the season.

In the Milk Cup Sheffield United were comfortably seen off in the 2nd Round but a shock 2-0 defeat by Norwich at Kenilworth Road at the next stage was a disappointment. Everton, for the second season running knocked the Hatters out of the FA Cup in the latter stages. Crystal Palace and Bristol Rovers were accounted for in the early rounds before a three-match epic against Arsenal stirred the imagination in Round 5. Luton were unfortunate to meet an Everton side at the top of their form in the Quarter-Finals but it took a replay at Goodison to "lower the flag" for another season.

All in all therefore an immensely satisfying year with the hope of an even better showing in 1986/7 as youngsters such as Tim Breacker, Mitchell Thomas, Rob Johnson, David Preece and Newall continue to mature alongside seasoned professionals Les Sealey, Mal Donaghy, Peter Nicholas, Ricky Hill, Stein, Nwajiobi, Harford and Foster.   Roger Wash

LUTON TOWN

DIVISION ONE: 9th   **FA CUP:** 6th ROUND   **MILK CUP:** 3rd ROUND

MATCH	DATE	COMPE-TITION	VENUE	OPPONENTS	RESULT	HALF TIME	L'GUE POS'N	GOALSCORERS/GOAL TIMES	ATTEN-DANCE
1	A 17	CL	H	Nottingham Forest	D 1-1	1-0		Stein B. 20	11,318
2	21	CL	A	Newcastle United	D 2-2	1-0		Nwajiobi 33, Harford 48	(21,304)
3	24	CL	A	West Ham United	W 1-0	0-0	7	Harford (pen) 48	(14,104)
4	27	CL	H	Arsenal	D 2-2	1-0		Nwajiobi 2, Stein B. 68	10,012
5	31	CL	A	Aston Villa	L 1-3	0-3	11	Stein B. 53	(10,524)
6	S 7	CL	H	Chelsea	D 1-1	1-0	15	Harford 35	10,720
7	14	CL	A	Everton	L 0-2	0-1	16		(26,419)
8	21	CL	H	Q.P.R.	W 2-0	2-0	14	Harford 21, Foster 28	9,508
9	24	MC2/1	A	Sheffield United	W 2-1	0-1		Stein B. 79, Nwajiobi 89	(8,948)
10	28	CL	A	Sheffield Wednesday	L 2-3	1-2	15	Harford 45, 63	(17,887)
11	O 1	CL	H	Ipswich Town	W 1-0	0-0		Nwajiobi 59	8,553
12	5	CL	H	Manchester United	D 1-1	0-0	14	Stein B. 68	17,454
13	8	MC2/2	H	Sheffield United	W 3-0	2-0		Preece 13, North 42, Hill 64	5,560
14	12	CL	A	Oxford United	D 1-1	1-0	14	Stein B. 24	(10,626)
15	19	CL	H	Southampton	W 7-0	3-0	12	Nwajiobi 5, Stein B. 32, 54, (pen) 90, Hill 35, Preece 59, Daniel 88	8,876
16	26	CL	A	Liverpool	L 2-3	0-2	13	Foster 46, Harford 65	(21,488)
17	29	MC3	H	Norwich City	L 0-2	0-2			8,202
18	N 2	CL	H	Birmingham City	W 2-0	0-0	10	Stein B. 46, Harford 70	8,550
19	9	CL	A	Tottenham Hotspur	W 3-1	1-0	10	Harford 20, Stein B. 61, Hill 90	(19,163)
20	16	CL	H	Coventry City	L 0-1	0-1	11		9,607
21	23	CL	A	Watford	W 2-1	1-0	8	Thomas 28, Terry (og) 87	(16,107)
22	30	CL	H	Manchester City	W 2-1	1-0	8	Stein B. 2, 64	10,096
23	D 7	CL	H	Newcastle United	W 2-0	1-0	7	Harford 6, North M. 75	10,319
24	14	CL	A	Nottingham Forest	L 0-2	0-1	8		(12,087)
25	21	CL	H	West Ham United	D 0-0	0-0	8		14,599
26	26	CL	A	W.B.A.	W 2-1	2-1	8	North M. 4, Harford 45	(12,508)
27	28	CL	A	Ipswich Town	D 1-1	0-1	8	North M. 82	(16,155)
28	J 1	CL	H	Leicester City	W 3-1	1-0	8	Harford 27, 65, 75	10,917
29	J 6	FAC3	A	Crystal Palace	W 2-1	1-0		Stein B. 9, Preece 87	(9,886)
30	11	CL	A	Chelsea	L 0-1	0-0	8		(21,201)
31	18	CL	H	Aston Villa	W 2-0	1-0	7	Newell 16, Stein B. 77	10,271
32	25	FAC4	H	Bristol Rovers	W 4-0	2-0		Harford 22, Hill 29, North M. 63, Parkin og 87	12,463
33	F 1	CL	A	Arsenal	L 1-2	1-1	9	Harford 30	(22,473)
34	8	CL	A	Southampton	W 2-1	1-0	6	Newell 28, Stein B. 86	(13,740)
35	15	FAC5	H	Arsenal	D 2-2	2-2		Hill 9, Harford 40	15,799
36	22	CL	A	Q.P.R.	D 1-1	0-1	6	Newell 62	(16,252)
37	M 1	CL	H	Sheffield Wednesday	W 1-0	1-0	6	Harford 16	10,206
38	3	FAC5R	A	Arsenal	D 0-0	0-0			(26,547)
39	5	FAC5R2	H	Arsenal	W 3-0	1-0		Foster 23, O'Leary (og) 52, Stein M. 79	13,251
40	8	FAC6	H	Everton	D 2-2	1-0		Harford 22, Stein M. 63	15,529
41	12	FAC6R	A	Everton	L 0-1	0-1			(44,264)
42	14	CL	H	Oxford United	L 1-2	1-0	8	Preece 15	10,633
43	19	CL	A	Manchester United	L 0-2	0-1	9		(33,668)
44	22	CL	H	Everton	W 2-1	0-0	8	Foster 81, 85	10,949
45	29	CL	A	Leicester City	D 0-0	0-0	8		(9,912)
46	A 1	CL	H	W.B.A.	W 3-0	2-0	8	Newell 14, Harford (pen) 15, Hill 50	9,226
47	6	CL	A	Birmingham City	W 2-0	0-0	6	Harford 49, 89	(8,836)
48	12	CL	H	Tottenham Hotspur	D 1-1	0-1	6	Newell 88	13,141
49	16	CL	A	Liverpool	L 0-1	0-1	7		15,390
50	19	CL	A	Coventry City	L 0-1	0-0	8		(10,146)
51	26	CL	H	Watford	W 3-2	2-0	7	Harford 10, 13, 74	11,810
52	M 3	CL	A	Manchester City	: 1-1	0-1	9	Nwajiobi 50	(20,361)

Best Home League Attendance: 17,454 v Man Utd   **Smallest: 8,550 v Birmingham City**   **Av Home Att:**

Goal Scorers: **Compared with 84-85:**

League (61):   Harford 22 (2 pen), Stein B. 14 (1 pen), Newell 5, Nwajiobi 5, Foster 4, Hill 4, North M. 3, Preece 2, Daniel 1, Thomas 1, Opponent 1

Milk Cup (5):   Stein 1, Nwajiobi 1, Preece 1, North 1, Hill 1

FA CUP (13):   Harford 3, Hill 2, Stein M. 2, Foster 1, North M. 1, Preece 1, Stein B. 1, Opponents 2

1985-86

Dibble	Breacker	Thomas	Nicholas	Foster	Donachie	Hill	Stein B.	Harford	Nwajiobi	Preece	Parker	Grimes	Elliott	Johnson	Sealey	Stein M.	North M.	Daniel	King	North S.	Newell	Referee	No.
1	2	3	4	5	6	7*	8	9	10	11	12											J Martin	1
1		2	4		6		8	9	10	11	7	3	5									I Hendrick	2
1		3	4		6		8	9	10	11	7		5	2								T Holbrook	3
1	2	3	4		6	7	8	9	10	11	5											A Seville	4
1	2	3	4		6	7	8	9	10	11	12				5*							D Shaw	5
1		3	4	5	6	7	8	9	10	11*			12	2								K Barratt	6
1	2	3	4	5	6	7*	8	9†	10	11	12											P Tyldesley	7
	2	3	4	5	6	7	8	9	12	11					1	10*						V Callow	8
	2	3	4	5	6	7	8	9	10	11					1							J Lovatt	9
	2	3	4	5	6	7	8	9	10	11				12	1							R Banks	10
	2	3	4	5	6	7	8	9	10	11					1							M Cotton	11
	2	3	4	5	6	7	8		10	11				12	1	9*						K Baker	12
	2	3	4	5	6	7	8		10	11					1	9						B Stevens	13
	2	3†	4	5	6	7	8	9	10	11					1							R Lewis	14
	2	3	4	5	6	7	8	9	10	11					1		12					C Downey	15
	2			5	6	7	8	9	10	11*			12	3	1			4				L Robinson	16
	2			5	6	7	8	9	10			4	12	3*	1			11				B Hill	17
	2	3	4	5	6	7	8	9	10	11					1							K Miller	18
	2	3	4	5	6	7	8	9	10	11					1							L Shapter	19
	2*	3	4	5	6	7	8	9	10	11	12				1							J Moules	20
	2	3	4	5	6	7	8	9	10	11					1							G Napthine	21
	2	3	4		6	7	8	9	10*	11					1				12			D Axcell	22
	2	3	4	5	6	7	8	9		11					1		10*		12			D Vickers	23
	2	3	4	5	6		8	9		11	7				1		10*		12			J Bray	24
	2	3	4	5	6		8	9		11					1		10					D Hedges	25
	2	3	4	5	6	7	8	9		11					1		10					A Robinson	26
	2	3	4		6	7	8	9		11					1		10			5		A Gunn	27
	2	3	4	5	6	7	8	9		11					1		10					I Borrett	28
	2	3	4	5	6	7	8	9		11					1		10					B Stevens	29
	2	3	4	5	6	7	8		11						1		10*	12		9		J Martin	30
	2	3	4	5	6	7	8			11					1		10			9		R Lewis	31
	2	3	4	5	6	7	8	9		11					1		10					J Moules	32
	2	3	4	5	6	7	8	9*		11					1			12			10	H Taylor	33
	2	3	4	5*	6	7	8	9		11					1						10	L Shapter	34
		3	4	5	6	7	8*	9		11		12		2	1		10					A Gunn	35
		3	4	5	6	7		9		11				2	1		10				8	J Ashworth	36
		3	4	5	6	7		9		11				2	1		10				8	D Axcell	37
		3	4	5	6	7		9		11				2	1		10				8	A Gunn	38
		3	4	5	6	7		9		11				2	1		10				8	D Scott	39
		3	4	5	6	7		9		11				2	1			12	10*		8	K Hackett	40
		3	4	5	6	7		9		11			10*	2	1			12			8	K Hackett	41
	2	3	4	5	6	7		9		11					1		8*	12			10	C Downey	42
	10	3	4	5	6	7		9		11				2	1		8		11*	5	9	G Napthine	43
	10	3	4		6	7		9		11				2	1						8	R Lewis	44
	10	3	4	5	6			9		11				2	1		12		7*		8	K Walmsley	45
1		3	4	5	6	7		9		11*				2			12				8	A Ward	46
	10	3	4	5	6	7		9		11				2	1						8	K Breen	47
		3	4	5	6	7	8	9		11				2	1						10	R Hamer	48
	12	3	4	5	6	7	8*	9		11				2	1						10	P Vanes	49
8		3	4	5	6	7		9		11				2*	1		12				10	D Phillips	50
	2	3	4	5	6	7	8	9	10	11					1							D Hedges	51
	12	3	4	5	6	7	8		10	11*				2	1						9	A Saunders	52
7	34	41	41	35	42	38	33	37	20	40	4	2	3	15	35	3	9	2	3	2	16	League Appearances	
2									1	1	4	1	3			3	4	3				Substitute Appearances	
	3	2	2	3	3	3	3	2	3	2				1	0-1	1	3	1	1			Milk Cup Appearances	
2	7	7	7	7	7	3	7	0-1	1	7				5	7	3	4-1	0-1	3			FA Cup Appearances	

Also Played:

Players on Loan:

Departures: Elliot (Aston Villa), Parker (Hull), Thomas (Tottenham)

'THE HATTERS'

Formed: 1885
Turned Professional: 1890 **Ltd Co:** 1897

Previous Managers: 1925 George Thomson 1927-9 John McCartney 1929-31 George Kay 1931-5 Harold Wightman 1936-8 Edward Liddell 1938-9 Neil McBain 1939-47 George Martin 1947-58 'Dally' Duncan 1959-60 Syd Owen 1960-2 Sam Bartram 1962 Jack Crompton 1962-4 Bill Harvey 1965-6 George Martin 1966-8 Allan Brown 1968-72 Alec Stock 1972-8 Harry Haslam 1978-86 David Pleat

Honours: Champions Div 2, 1981-2 Champions Div 4, 1967-8 Champions Div 3 (S) 1936-7

League Career: Elected to Div 2 1897 Failed to gain re-election 1900 Re-elected to Div 3 1920 Transferred to Div 3 (S) 1921 Promoted to Div 2 1936-7 Promoted to Div 1 1954-5 Relegated to Div 2 1959-60 Relegated to Div 3 1962-3 Relegated to Div 4 1964-5 Promoted to Div 3 1967-8 Promoted to Div 2 1969-70 Promoted to Div 1 1973-4 Relegated to Div 2 1974-5 Promoted to Div 1 1981-2

Colours: White shirts with navy and orange trims, navy blue shorts, white stockings with orange and navy tops

Change Colours: Orange shirts with navy blue sleeves and shoulders with white and navy stripes across shoulders and sleeves, navy shorts with orange trim, orange stockings with white and navy trim

---

CLUB RECORDS

Most Appearances for Club: Bob Morton: Football League 494 + FA Cup 48 + League Cup 7 **Total 549**

Most Capped Player: Mal Donaghy, 31 **For England:** Bob Hawkes, 5

Record Goalscorer in a Match: Joe Payne, 10 v Bristol Rovers (12-0) (H), Div 3 (S) 13 Apr 1936

Record League Goalscorer in a Season: Joe Payne, 55, Div 3 (S), 1936-7 **In All Competitions:** Joe Payne, 58 (League 55 + FA Cup 3)

Record League Goalscorer in a Career: Gordon Turner, 243 **In All Competitions:** Gordon Turner, 265 (League 243 + FA Cup 18 + League Cup 44) 1949-64

Record Transfer Fee Received: £750,000 from Liverpool for Paul Walsh, May 1984

Record Transfer Fee Paid: £270,000 to Birmingham City for Mick Harford, Dec 1984

Best Performances: League: 8th Div 1 1957-8 **FA Cup:** Finalists 1959 **League/Milk Cup:** 5th Round 1978-9

Most League Points: (3pts for win) 88, Div 2, 1981-2 (record) (2pts for Win) 66, Div 4 1967-8

Most League Goals: 103, Div 3 (S), 1936-7

Record League Victory and Most Goals Scored in a League Match: 12-0 v Bristol Rovers, Div 3 (S), 13 April 1936

Most Goals Scored in a Cup Tie: 15-0 v Gt Yarmouth, 4th Qual Round FA Cup, 21 Nov 1914

Record League Defeat: 0-9 v Small Heath, Div 2, 12 Nov 1898

Oldest Player in League Match:

Youngest Player in League Match:

Most Consecutive Undefeated League Matches: 19 1968, 1969   **League Matches Without a Win:** 15 1924-25

Longest Run of Undefeated Home League Matches: 39 1925-27   **Away League Matches:** 10 1981

Longest Run Without Home League Win: 10 1964, 1972-73   **Away League Win:** 32 1898-1900 4'20

Most Consecutive League Wins: 9 1977   **Home League Wins:** 15 1967

Most Consecutive League Defeats: 8 1899-1900   **Away League Wins:** 5 1981

Between 1900-22 they were a non-league club. In the undefeated matches column they went 19 matches undeated twice

Club Statistician for the Directory: R Wash

LUTON TOWN

PLAYERS NAME Ht Wt Birthdate	Honours	Birthplace Transfers	Clubs	League	Milk Cup	FA Cup	Other Comps	League	Milk Cup	FA Cup	Other Comps
GOALKEEPERS											
Andy Dibble 6.2½ 13.7 8.5.65	WU21 (3), YS	Cwmbran	Cardiff City (A)	62	8	1					
			Luton Town	20							
			Sunderland (L)	12							
Les Sealey 6.0 11.6 29.9.57		Bethnal Green	Coventry City (A)	158	11	9					
			Luton Town	103	5	9					
			Plymouth Argyle (L)	6							
DEFENDERS											
Tim Breacker 6.0 12.6 2.7.65		Bicester	Luton Town (A)	70+3	5	2					
Mal Donaghy 5.10 12.7 13.9.57	NI (45), U21 (1), Div. 2, 82	Belfast £20,000	Larne Luton Town	330	24	17		15	2	3	
Steve Foster 6.0 14.0 24.9.57	E (3), U21 (1)	Portsmouth £150,000 £200,000	Portsmouth (A)	101+8	10	8		6		2	
			Brighton	171+1	13	15		6	2		
			Aston Villa	15	2			3			
			Luton Town	60	3	7		5		2	
Mark North 5.11 11.0 29.5.66		Ware	Luton Town	9+4	1	4+1		3	1	1	
			Lincoln City (L)	3							
Stacey North 6.2 12.6 25.11.64		Luton	Luton Town (A)	10	1						
			Wolverhampton W. (L)	3							
MIDFIELD											
Ashley Grimes 5.11½ 11.7 2.8.57	EI (16), U21 (2), FAC 83	Dublin £200,000	Bohemians	62+28	8	5		10		1	
			Coventry City	29+3	3			1	1		
		Player exch.	Luton Town	11+1	2+1	1					
Ricky Hill 5.10 11.10 5.3.59	E (3), Y, Div. 2, 82	London	Luton Town (A)	350+6	27	19		47	2	6	
Bob Johnson 5.7 10.6 22.2.62		Bedford Norway	Luton Town (A)	17	1	5					
			Lincoln City (L)	4							
Peter Nicholas 5.8½ 11.8 10.11.59	W (43), U21 (3)	Newport £100,000 £150,000 £165,000	Crystal Palace (A)	127	10	7		7			
			Arsenal	57+3	8	8		1	1	1	
			Crystal Palace	69	4	4		7	1		
			Luton Town	60	2	7					
David Preece 5.6 10.0 28.5.63		Bridgend Part exch.	Walsall (A)	107+4	18	5	1	7	5	1	
			Luton Town	61+1	2	7		2	1	1	
Marcus Tuite 5.9 9.0 11.5.68	EY	Dublin	Luton Town (A)								
Robert Wilson 5.10 11.2 5.6.61	E1, U21 (1)	Kensington £57,500 £40,000	Fulham	168+7	16+1	7+1		46	3		
			Millwall	28	3	5					
			Luton Town								
FORWARDS											
Mick Harford 6.1 12.4 12.2.59		Sunderland £180,000 £160,000 £100,000 £250,000	Lincoln City	109+6	8	3		41	5		
			Newcastle United	18+1				4			
			Bristol City	30	5	5		11	6	2	
			Birmingham City	92	9	7		26	1	7	
			Luton Town	59	2	7		37		4	
Mike Newell 6.0 11.0 27.1.65	FRT 85	Liverpool F	Crewe Alexandra	3							
			Wigan Athletic	64+8	6	8	5+1	25	1	6	3
			Luton Town	16				5			
Brian Stein 5.10 11.8 19.10.57	E (1), U21 (3), Div. 2, 82	South Africa	Edgware Town Luton Town	312+10	25	12		107	9	4	
Mark Stein 5.6 10.0 29.1.66	EY	South Africa	Luton Town (A)	4+4		3				2	
			Aldershot (L)	2							
Chuck Nwajiobi 5.7 12.2 25.5.59		Nigeria	Dulwich Hamlet Luton Town	43+11	4			14	1	1	

ADDITIONAL CONTRACT PROFESSIONALS

Richard McEvoy, David Oldfield, Gary Cobb, Kingley Black, Aaron Tigue

APPRENTICES

Sean Farrell, Richard Harvey, Marvin Johnson, John Kennedy, Paul Lewis, Ian Scott

NON-CONTRACT PLAYERS

KENILWORTH ROAD Luton

Record Attendance: 30,069 v Blackpool, FA Cup Round 6 replay, 4 Mar 1959

Smallest Home Attendance for a First Class Match: 2,272 v Bristol Rovers, Div 3 (S), 13 Mar 1933

Record Receipts: £55,906 v Manchester United, FA Cup Round 4, 29 Jan 1983

Season Tickets: £100 (£40 OAPs), £100, £65 (£40 juveniles/OAPs), £35 for Junior Hatters Club Enclosure

Executive Members Clubs: 'Club 82' £1,100 (for two seats, meal and bar); 'Century Club' £300 (includes buffet); 'Vice-President's Suite' **Executive Boxes:** North Stand match day hire, 12 and 14 seater boxes. Unique choice of viewing. Personal open balcony, 12 feet from the action. Prices contact Commercial Director.

Cost of Stand Tickets: £6.00, £4.00 (£2.00 juveniles). **Terraces:** £4.00 (visitors), £3.00 (£2.00 juveniles)

Match and Ticket Information: Entry by membership only

Car Parking: Street parking near ground only available

Nearest Railway Station: Luton Midland Road (0582 27612)

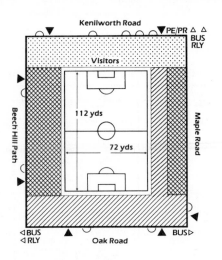

How to get to the ground

From North and West: Use Motorway M1 until junction 11 then follow signs Luton A505 into Dunstable Road. Forward through one-way system and then turn right into Kenilworth Road for Luton Town FC

From South and East: Use Motorway M1 until junction 10 or A6/A612 into Luton town centre, then follow signs Dunstable into Dunstable Road A505. Under railway bridge then turn left into Kenilworth Road for Luton Town FC

Price of 1986-7 Programme: £1.00
Number of Pages: 32 16 full colour, 16 two colour

Local Newspapers: Luton News, The Herald

Local Radio Stations: Chiltern Radio, BBC Radio Bedfordshire

MANCHESTER CITY

Division 1

Chairman
P J Swales

Vice-Chairman
F Pye

Directors
I L G Niven MBE
C B Muir
M T Horwich
W C Adams
A Thomas
G Doyle
W A Miles
B Turnbull
J Greibach
J K White

Honorary Presidents
J F Smith
S Rose
E Alexander

Secretary
J B Halford (061-226 1191/2/3)

Commercial Manager
P Critchley (061-226 3143)

Manager
W McNeil MBE

Assistant Manager
J Frizzell

Youth & Reserve Team Coaches
T Book & G Pardoe

Chief Scout
K Barnes

Physiotherapist
R Bailey

Groundsman
S Gibson

Administration Assistant
I S Niven

Here we have another 'sleeping giant' who must be wondering whether to be pleased with staying away from the danger zone most of the season or whether to be disappointed that they really couldn't force their way into the upper strata of the 1st division.

To be generous, as it was only City's second season back in Division 1 perhaps consolidation was the aim. If so, is the team ready for progress next season? For consistency David Phillips, Paul Power and Mick McCarthy led the way but promising goalkeeper Alex Williams missed practically the whole season and midfield formations varied. Nicky Reid came in to play consistently after a great 6-1 victory over Leeds United in the Full Members Cup and indeed it was this competition that brought the highlight to City's season.

Having eliminated Leeds, Sheffield United, Sunderland and Hull City they played the most amazing final at Wembley a day after a 1st Division fixture and lost despite scoring three goals in the last 15 minutes and a total of four. It was some game and certainly did both sides great credit.

In the other Cup competitions Arsenal stopped 'The Blues' Milk Cup run in the 3rd Round and Watford knocked them out of the FA Cup 4th Round at the third attempt.

It's difficult to forecast what City can achieve next season, youngsters Paul Simpson and Clive Wilson could mature dramatically, Neil McNab had a good season so should be confident, but up front their must be some questions to answer. In mid-season City were regular scorers but in the last 14 League games they failed to score in eight and in the last seven matches only three goals were recorded, all by Gordon Davies, a very valuable signing from Chelsea.

David Lillis proved his worth by finishing overall top scorer but he certainly faded at the end of the season. It was his first in the 1st Division however and perhaps he can form an exciting partnership with Davies.

Manager Billy McNeil has also had time to get used to the English 1st Division and I wouldn't be surprised to see City 'showing their claws' a little this season and if they do, thousands of City fans will be roaring out a challenge to the other team across the City.

Back Row L to R: Ian Brightwell, Trevor Christie, Mick McCarthy, Steve Redmond, Andy May. **Middle Row:** Jimmy Frizzell (Assistant Manager), Nigel Johnson, Eric Nixon, Billy McNeill (now with Aston Villa), Perry Suckling, Kenny Clements (Captain), Roy Bailey (Physio). **Front Row:** Graham Baker, Steve Kinsey, Clive Wilson, Neil McNab, Gordon Davies, Paul Simpson.

MANCHESTER CITY

DIVISION ONE: 15th   **FA CUP:** 4th ROUND   **MILK CUP:** 3rd ROUND   **FM Cup:** FINALIST

MATCH	DATE		COMPE-TITION	VENUE	OPPONENTS	RESULT		HALF TIME	L'GUE POS'N	GOALSCORERS/GOAL TIMES	ATTEN-DANCE
1	A	17	CL	A	Coventry City	D	1-1	1-1		McIlroy 10	(14,550)
2		21	CL	H	Leicester City	D	1-1	1-1		Lillis (pen) 42	25,528
3		24	CL	H	Sheffield Wednesday	L	1-3	0-1	19	Simpson 50	26,934
4		26	CL	A	W.B.A.	W	3-2	2-1		Lillis 29, Simpson 44, Wilson 78	(12,122)
5		31	CL	H	Tottenham Hotspur	W	2-1	1-0	9	Simpson 37, Miller (og) 83	27,789
6	S	3	CL	A	Birmingham City	L	0-1	0-0			(11,706)
7		7	CL	A	Southampton	L	0-3	0-1	13		(14,308)
8		14	CL	H	Manchester United	L	0-3	0-2	14		48,773
9		21	CL	H	West Ham United	D	2-2	1-2	16	Lillis 10, Melrose 49	22,001
10		25	MC2/1	A	Bury	W	2-0	2-0		Melrose 6, Wilson 29	(11,377)
11		28	CL	A	Oxford United	L	0-1	0-1	18		(9,796)
12	O	5	CL	H	Chelsea	L	0-1	0-1	20		20,104
13		8	MC2/2	H	Bury	W	2-1	1-0		Melrose 29, Lillis 87	9,799
14		12	CL	A	Watford	L	2-3	0-2	20	Lillis 65, McNab 72	(15,418)
15		14	FMC	H	Leeds United	W	6-1	3-0		Davies 3 (15, 26, 32) Baker 49, Lillis 65 Power 89	4,029
16		19	CL	A	Q.P.R.	D	0-0	0-0	20		(13,471)
17		22	FMC	A	Sheffield United	W	2-0	0-0		Phillips 60, Baker 89	(3,420)
18		26	CL	H	Everton	D	1-1	0-1	20	Simpson 47	28,807
19		30	MC3	H	Arsenal	L	1-2	1-0		Davies 16	18,279
20	N	2	CL	A	Arsenal	L	0-1	0-0	20		(22,264)
21		4	FMC	H	Sunderland	D	0-0†	0-0		(Won 4-3 on pens)	6,642
22		9	CL	A	Ipswich Town	L	1-1	1-1	20	Lillis (pen) 44	20,853
23		16	CL	A	Nottingham Forest	W	2-0	1-0	18	Wilson 28, Simpson 55	(15,140)
24		23	CL	H	Newcastle United	W	1-0	1-0	17	Lillis 31	25,179
25		26	FMC N F1	A	Hull City	L	1-2	0-0		Phillips 60	(5,213)
26		30	CL	A	Luton Town	L	1-2	0-1	17	Lillis (pen) 83	(10,096)
27	D	7	CL	A	Leicester City	D	1-1	0-1	17	Davies 75	(10,289)
28		11	FMC N F2	H	Hull City	W	2-0	1-0		Phillips 24, Melrose 89	10,180
29		14	CL	H	Coventry City	W	5-1	2-0	16	Davies 18, 56, Simpson 44, 85, Lillis 74	20,075
30		21	CL	A	Sheffield Wednesday	L	2-3	1-3	16	Lillis 13, McNab 66	(23,117)
31		26	CL	H	Liverpool	W	1-0	0-0	15	Wilson 61	35,384
32		28	CL	H	Birmingham City	D	1-1	0-1	15	McNab 89	24,955
33	J	1	CL	A	Aston Villa	W	1-0	0-0	15	Lillis 53	(14,215)
34		4	FAC3	A	Walsall	W	3-1	1-1		Davies 45, Simpson 65, 89	(10,779)
35		11	CL	H	Southampton	W	1-0	0-0	13	Phillips 84	21,675
36		18	CL	A	Tottenham Hotspur	W	2-0	1-0	13	Davies 27, Lillis 86	(17,009)
37		25	FAC4	H	Watford	D	1-1	0-0		Davies 53	31,632
38	F.	1	CL	A	W.B.A.	W	2-1	1-0	12	Power 15, Davies 89	20,540
39		3	FAC4R	A	Watford	D	0-0†	0-0			(19,347)
40		6	FAC4R	H	Watford	L	1-3	0-0		Kinsey 81	27,260
41		8	CL	H	Q.P.R.	W	2-0	2-0	11	Simpson 9, Davies 43	20,414
42		11	CL	A	Everton	L	0-4	0-1	11		(30,006)
43	M	1	CL	H	Oxford United	L	0-3	0-2	11		20,099
44		8	CL	A	Chelsea	L	0-1	0-0	12		(17,573)
45		15	CL	H	Watford	L	0-1	0-0	13		18,899
46		22	CL	A	Manchester United	D	2-2	0-1	13	Wilson 71, Albiston (og) 78	(52,174)
47		23	FMC Final	N	Chelsea	L	4-5	1-2		Kinsey 9, Lillis 85 pen 89, Rougvie (og) 88	(68,000)
48		29	CL	H	Aston Villa	D	2-2	0-1	13	McNab 62, Wilson 74	20,935
49		31	CL	A	Liverpool	L	0-2	0-1	14		(43,316)
50	A	5	CL	H	Arsenal	L	0-1	0-0	14		19,590
51		12	CL	A	Ipswich Town	D	0-0	0-0	14		(13,586)
52		19	CL	H	Nottingham Forest	L	1-2	0-0	15	Davies 85	19,715
53		26	CL	A	Newcastle United	L	1-3	1-0	15	Davies 18	(22,689)
54		28	CL	A	West Ham United	L	0-1	0-1	15		(27,153)
55	M	3	CL	H	Luton Town	D	1-1	1-0	15	Davies 22	20,361

Best Home League Attendance: 48,773 v Manchester United   **Smallest:** 18,899 v Watford   **Av Home Att:** 24,229

Goal Scorers: **Compared with 84-85:** +23

League (43): Lillis 11 (3 pen), Davies 9, Simpson 8, Wilson 5, McNab 4, Opponents 2, McIlroy 1, Melrose 1, Phillips 1, Power 1
Milk Cup (5): Melrose 2, Wilson 1, Lillis 1, Davies 1
FA Cup (5): Davies 2, Simpson 2, Kinsey 1
FM Cup (15): Lillis 3 (1 pen), Baker 2, Davies 3, Phillips 3, Melrose 1, Kinsey 1, Opponents 1

†After Extra Time

1985-86

Williams	Phillips	Power	Clements	Johnson	Wilson	Lillis	McNab	Kinsey	McIlroy	Simpson	McCarthy	May	Tolmie	Beckford	Smith	Melrose	Nixon	Baker	Davies	Reid	Moulden	Redmond	Siddall (L)	Barrett	Referee	No.
1	2	3	4	5	6	7	8	9	10	11															N Buksh	1
1	2	3	4		6	7	8	9	10	11	5														T Mills	2
1	6*	3	4			7	8	9	10	11	5	2	12												A Saunders	3
1	6		4	3		7	8	9	10	11	5	2													R Milford	4
1	6		4	3		7	8	9	10	11	5	2													G Courtney	5
1	6		4	3			8	9	10	11	5	2	7*	12											H Taylor	6
1	6		4	3		7	8	9	10*	11	5	2				12									D Reeves	7
1	6	8	4	3		7		9*	10	11	5	2				12									G Tyson	8
	6	8	4	3		7	10			11	5	2				9	1								M Robinson	9
	6	3	4		8	7	10			11	5	2				9	1								**K Barrett**	10
	6	3	4		8	7		12	10*		5	2	11			9	1								P Vanes	11
	6	3	4		8	7	10			11	5	2	12			9*	1								M Peck	12
	6	3	4			7	10			11	5	2				9	1	8							**J McAuley**	13
	6	3	4			7	10			11	5	2					1	8	9						J Ball	14
		3	4	5		7	10			11*	6			13		12	1	8	9*	2					**J Bray**	15
	6		4		11	7	10				5	3					1	8	9	2					R Gifford	16
	6	3	5			7	10			11*	12	2					1	8	9	4					**T Holbrook**	17
	6	3	4			7	10			11	5						1	8	9	2					K Redfern	18
	6	3	4			7	10			11	5					12	1	8*	9	2					**R Bridges**	19
	6	8	4			7	10*			11	5	3				12	1		9	2					J Ashworth	20
	6	10	4	5		7				11	3					12	1	8*	9*	2	13				**C Seel**	21
	6	8	4			7	10			11	5	3					1		9	2					K Hackett	22
	6	3	4		11	7	10			12	5	8					1		9*	2					V Callow	23
	6	3	4		11	7	10			12	5	8					1		9*	2					M Heath	24
	6	3	4		11		10			12	5	8				7*	1		9	2					**G Courtney**	25
	6	3	4	11*		7	10				5	8					1	12	9	2					D Axcell	26
	6	3	4			7	10			11	5	8*				12	1		9	2					C Downey	27
	6	3	4			7	10			11*	5	8				12	1		9	2					**K Baker**	28
	6	3	4			7	10			11	5*	8				12	1		9	2					D Hutchinson	29
	6	3	4	8		7*	10			11	5					12	1		9	2					G Aplin	30
	6	3	4		11		10				5	8				7	1		9	2					A Seville	31
	6	3	4	11*		7	10			12	5	8					1		9	2					F Roberts	32
	6	3	4			7	10			11	5	8					1			2	9				N Ashley	33
	6	3	4			7	10			11	5	8					1		9*	2	12				**D Hedges**	34
	6	3	4			7	10			11	5	8					1		9	2					J Key	35
	6	3	4			7	10			11	5	8					1		9	2					G Napthine	36
	6	3	4			7	10			11	5	8					1		9	2					**M Heath**	37
	6	3	4			7	10			11	5	8					1		9	2					M Scott	38
	6	3	4			7	10	12		11*	5	8					1		9	2					**M Heath**	39
	6	3	4			7	10	12		11	5	8*					1		9	2					**V Callow**	40
	6	3				7				11	5	8					1	10	9	2		4			A Saunders	41
	6	3				7	10			11	5	12					1	8*	9	2		4			D Phillips	42
	6	3	4	5		7	10			11							1	8	9	2		4			D Hutchinson	43
	6	3	4			7	10			11	5	8					1		9	2		12			A Seville	44
	6	3	4			7	10			11	5	8					1		9*	2		12			K Baker	45
	6	3	4*		11	7	10	9		12		8					1			2		5			D Shaw	46
	6*	3			11	7	10	9		12	5	8					1		13	2*		4			**A Saunders**	47
	6*	3			11	7	10	9		12	5	8					1			2		4			J Lloyd	48
	6	3				7	10	9		11	5	8								2		4	1		D Hough	49
	6	3				7	10	9		11	5	8								2		4	1		K Lupton	50
		3			11	7	10				5	8						6		2		4	1		I Hemley	51
		3			12	7	10				5	8						6	9*	2		4	1		J Lovatt	52
		3*			11	7	10				5	8						6	9	2		4	1		J McAuley	53
2					6	7	10	8		11*	5	3	12						9	4			1		R Gifford	54
	6*				11	7	10	8		12	5	3					1		9	4				2	A Saunders	55
8	39	36	30	4	24	39	37	12	12	30	38	36	1	2	0	4	28	9	26	30	1	9	6	1	League Appearances	
				1				1	7		1	2	1	1	6		1				1				Substitute Appearances	
	3	3	3		1	3	2				3	3				2·1			4	1					Milk Cup Appearances	
	4	4	4		4	4	4				4	0·2					4		4	4		0·1			FA Cup Appearances	
5	6	4	3	2	5	4	1	2	3·2	3	6		0·1		0·1	2·2	6		2·1	5	6	0·1	1		FM Cup Appearances	

Players on Loan: Siddall (Stoke City)

Departures: Melrose (Charlton Athletic), Smith (Oldham Athletic), Power (Everton), Lomax (Carlisle), Lillis (Derby Co)

'CITY' or 'BLUES'

Formed: 1887
Turned Professional: 1887   **Ltd Co:** 1894

Previous Names: Ardwick 1887 until reformed as Manchester City in 1894
Previous Managers: 1892-3 L W Furniss   1893-5 W J Parlby   1895-1902 S Ormrod   1902-6 T E Maley
1906-12 H W Newbould   1912-26 J E Magnell   1926-32 P Hodge   1932-46 W Wild
1946-7 S Cowan   1947-50 J R Thompson   1950-63 L McDowell   1963-5 G Poysor   1965-71 J Mercer
1971-3 M Allison   1973 Mar-Nov J Hart   1973-4 R Saunders   1974-9 T Book   1979-80 M Allison
1980-3 J Bond   1983 Feb-Jun J Benson   1983 to date B McNeill
Honours: Champions Div 1, 1936-7, 1967-8   Champions Div 2, 1898-9, 1902-3   FA Cup Winners
1904, 1934, 1956, 1969   Football League Cup Winners 1970, 1976   European Cup Winners Cup
Winners 1969-70   FA Youth Cup Winners 1986   Full Members Cup Finalists 1986
League Career: Elected as Ardwick as founder members of Div 2 1892
Manchester City elected to Div 2 1894
Promoted to Div 1 1898-9   Relegated to Div 2 1901-2   Promoted to Div 1 1902-3
Relegated to Div 2 1908-9   Promoted to Div 1 1909-10   Relegated to Div 2 1925-6
Promoted to Div 1 1927-8   Relegated to Div 2 1938-9   Promoted to Div 1 1946-7
Relegated to Div 2 1949-50   Promoted to Div 1 1950-1   Relegated to Div 2 1962-3
Promoted to Div 1 1965-6   Relegated to Div 2 1982-3   Promoted to Div 1 1984-5
Colours: Sky blue with white shorts and sky blue stockings
Change Colours: White shirts with red/black diagonal stripes across chest, black shorts and stockings
Reserves League: Central Div 1   **'A' Team:** Lancashire League Div 1

CLUB RECORDS

Most Appearances for Club: Alan Oakes: Football League 564 + FA Cup 41 + League Cup 46 + European Cup
2 + European Cup Winners Cup 13 + UEFA Cup 2 + Charity Shield 3 + Texaco Cup 3 + Anglo-Scottish Cup 2 + Anglo-Italian 2 **Total 679**
Most Capped Player: Colin Bell, 48, England
Record Goalscorer in a Match: Denis Law, 6 v Luton Town, 4th Round FA Cup 28.01.1961 (match abandoned)
Tommy Johnson, 5 v Everton, (h) 5-1, Div 1, 15.09.1928   George Smith 5 v Newport County (h) 5-1, Div 2, 14.06.1947
Record League Goalscorer in a Season: Tommy Johnson, 38, Div 2, 1928-9   **In All Competitions:** Tommy Johnson, 38
(all League)
Record League Goalscorer in a Career: Eric Brook, 159, 1927-39 (including one goal in season 1939-40)   **In All
Competitions:** Eric Brook, 178 (League 159 + FA Cup 19)
Record Transfer Fee Received: £800,000 from Sampdoria for Trevor Francis, July 1982
Record Transfer Fee Paid: £1,150,000 to Wolverhampton Wanderers for Steve Daley, Sept 1979
Best Performances: League: Champions (2)   **FA Cup:** Winners (4)   **League/Milk Cup:** Winners (2)   **European Cup
Winners Cup:** Winners   **European Cup:** 1st Round   **UEFA Cup:** Quarter-Final
Most League Points: 70, Div 2, 1983-4   **Most League Goals:** 108, Div 2, 1926-7
Record League Victory and Most Goals Scored in a League Match: 11-3 v Lincoln City, Div 2, 23 March 1895
Record League Defeat: 1-9 v Everton, Div 1, 3 Sept 1906
European Competitions Entered: European Cup 1968-9   European Cup Winners Cup 1969-70, 1970-1   UEFA Cup
1972-3, 1976-7, 1977-8, 1978-9
Oldest Player in League Match: Billy Meredith, 49 yrs 245 days
Youngest Player in League Match: Glyn Pardoe, 15 yrs 314 days
Most Consecutive Undefeated League Matches: 22 1936-37, 1946-47

Longest Run of Undefeated Home League Matches: 41 1919-21
Longest Run Without Home League Win: 9 1979-80
Most Consecutive League Wins: 9 1912
Most Consecutive League Defeats: 6 1910, 1960

League Matches Without a Win: 17 1979-80
Away League Matches: 12 1946-47
Away League Win: 27 1900-02
Home League Wins: 16 1920-21
Away League Wins: 6 1903

Club Statistician for the Directory: Ray Goble

MANCHESTER CITY

PLAYERS NAME Ht Wt Birthdate	Honours	Birthplace Transfers	Clubs	APPEARANCES League	Milk Cup	FA Cup	Other Comps	GOALS League	Milk Cup	FA Cup	Other Comps
GOALKEEPERS											
Eric Nixon 6.2 14.3 4.10.62		Manchester	Curzon Ashton Manchester City	28	3	4	6				
Alex Williams 6.2½ 13.4 13.11.61	EY	Moss Side	Manchester City	114	9	2					
Perry Suckling 6.1½ 11.2 12.10.65		Leyton	Coventry City Manchester City								
DEFENDERS											
Kenny Clements* + 6.1 12.6 9.4.55		Manchester £200,000	Manchester City (A) Oldham Athletic Manchester City	116+3 204+2 41+1	18 11 3	7 9 4	4				
Nigel Johnson 6.3 12.3 17.1.60		Rotherham £75,000	Rotherham United Manchester City	85 4	11	5 3		3	1		
Mick McCarthy 6.1½ 13.3 7.2.59	EI (12)	Barnsley £200,000	Barnsley (A) Manchester City	272 101	27 7	16 6	3	7 1	3		
Andy May 5.8 11.1 26.2.64		Bury	Manchester City (A)	124+9	9	5	6	8			
Steve Redmond 5.10½ 11.2 2.11.67		Liverpool	Manchester City	9		1	1	1			
Nicky Reid 5.10 11.10 30.10.60	EU21 (6)	Urmston	Manchester City (A)	205+5	20	17	6	2			
MIDFIELD											
Graham Baker 5.9 10.12 3.12.58	EU21 (2)	Southampton £200,000	Southampton (A) Manchester City	111+2 101+1	6+1 12	3 2	2+1	22 16	2	1	2
Earl Barrett 5.10 11.2 28.4.67		Rochdale	Manchester City (A)	1							
Paul Simpson 5.6 10.5 26.7.66	EY	Carlisle	Manchester City (A)	40+10	6	5	3+2	13	3	2	
Neil McNab 5.7 10.10 6.6.57	SU21 (1), S, FAYC 74	Greenock £75,000 £250,000 £220,000 £30,000	Morton Tottenham Hotspur Bolton Wanderers Brighton & H.A. Leeds United (L) Manchester City	11+3 63+9 33+2 100+3 5 85+3	4+1 5 2 3 6	1 2 2 5 5	5	1 3 4 4 5			
Sammy McIlroy 5.10 11.8 2.8.54	NI (87), U23 (1), FAC 77, CS 78, Div. 2, 75	Belfast	Manchester United Stoke City Manchester City	320+22 132+1	25+3 5	35+3 6	10	57 14	6	6	2
FORWARDS											
Darren Beckford 6.1 11.1 12.5.67		Manchester	Manchester City (A) Bury (L)	3+4 12	0+1						
Gordon Davies 5.7 10.6 3.8.55	W (16)	Merthyr Tydfil £5,000 £90,000	Merthyr Tydfil Fulham Chelsea Manchester City	244+3 10+2 26	24 1	18 2 4	5	113 6 9	9 1	4 2	2
Steve Kinsey 5.7 10.2 2.1.63	U21 (1)	Gorton	Manchester City Chester (L) Chesterfield (L)	87+14 3 3	6+1 1	4+2	1	15 1 7		1	1
Paul Mouldon 5.10 11.0 6.9.67	EY	Bolton	Manchester City	1+1		0+1	0+1				
Clive Wilson 5.7 9.10 13.11.61		Greenleys	Manchester City Chester City (L)	65+2 21	7	1	2	9	2 2		
Trevor Christie 6.2 12.0 28.2.59		Newcastle £60,000 £175,000 £100,000 Part exch.	Leicester City (A) Notts County Nottingham Forest Derby County Manchester City	28+3 158+29 14 20	1 19+1 2	8+2 2 1		8 64 5 7	5 1	3 1	1

ADDITIONAL CONTRACT PROFESSIONALS
Ian Brightwell (A), John Clarke (A), Steve Crompton (YTS), Ian Scott (A), David White, Carl Lewis

APPRENTICES
Andy Hinchcliffe, Paul Lake, Steve McCauley, Steve Mills

NON-CONTRACT PLAYERS

Record Attendance: 84,569 v Stoke City, FA Cup Round 6, 3 Mar 1934 (record in Britain for match outside London or Glasgow)

Smallest Home Attendance for a First Class Match: 8,015 v Swindon Town, Div 2, 1964

Record Receipts: £274,281
Liverpool v Manchester United, 17 April 1985, FA Cup Semi-Final Replay, Mar 1984

Season Tickets: Stands: £73.00 (£50.00 Juv/OAP), £82.00, £110.00; Ground £42.00 (£35 Juv/OAP) £52.00 (£37.00 Juv/OAP)

Cost of Stand Tickets: £4.50. £6.00 (Reserved); £3.50 (Unreserved); Ground: £2.50 (£2.00 Juv/OAP) £3.50 (£2.50 Juv/OAP)

Match and Ticket Information: Advance booking 14 days prior to matches

Car Parking: Kippax Street car park holds 400 vehicles (approx). Some street parking is permitted

Nearest Railway Station: Manchester Piccadilly (061-832 8353)

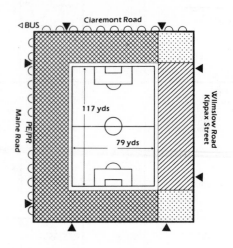

How to get to the ground

From North: Use Motorway M61 then M63 until Junction 9. Leave Motorway and follow signs Manchester A5103. In 2.8m at crossroads turn right into Claremont Road. In 0.4m turn right into Maine Road for Manchester City FC

From East: Use Motorway M62 until junction 17 then A56 into Manchester. Follow signs Manchester Airport then turn left to join Motorway A57(M). Follow signs Birmingham to join A5103. Then in 1.3m turn left into Claremont Road. In 0.4m turn right into Maine Road for Manchester City FC

From South: Use Motorway M6 until junction 19 then A556 and M56 until junction 3. Keep forward A5103 S.P. Manchester. In 2.8m at crossroads turn right into Claremont Road. In 0.4m turn right into Maine Road for Manchester City FC

From West: Use Motorway M62 then M63 and route as from north. Or use M56 and route as from south.

Price of 1986-7 Programme: 50p
Number of Pages: 24
Subscriptions: £19.00 (postage); (£3 extra abroad & Eire)

Local Newspapers: Manchester Evening News, Sunday Pink

Local Radio Stations: BBC Radio Manchester, Piccadilly Radio

MANCHESTER UNITED Division 1

President
Sir Matt Busby CBE

Chairman
C M Edwards

Directors
J M Edelson
R Charlton CBE
E M Watkins

Secretary
R L Olive (061-872 1661/2)

Assistant Secretary
K R Merrett

Commercial Manager
D A McGregor (061-872 1661/2/3)

Ticket Officer
K Ramsden

Manager
R Atkinson

Assistant Manager
M Brown

Reserve Team Coach
Brian Whitehouse

Youth Team Coach
E Harrison

Chief Scout
T Collins

Physiotherapist
J McGregor

Groundsman
P Solski

History has a sad habit of repeating itself at Old Trafford and the recently ended season followed an all-too-familiar pattern—top place in the 1st Division for the best part of the season followed by a slump in form and a failure to realise potential. The latest 'fade-out' left the team in a final position of fourth and nothing of any importance was won; with UEFA competitions out of bounds it must have left the average fan in a state of frustration. There was a poor start to the season at Wembley with the FA Charity Shield match against Everton being won by the Merseysiders (2-0) in a very mediocre match, but the first ten League games were won and defeat (0-1 at Sheffield Wednesday) was not tasted until 9th November—in the 16th match. Of course, top place had been gained, but now the process of undoing all the good work began and points— plus matches—were thrown away with prodigal purposelessness, which was also transferred to cup matches. When will United be consistent for a complete season?

As Cup holders United desperately needed to repeat the success as League form fell away, but the desperation produced sub-standard performances with a struggle to beat Rochadale at home (2-0) followed by a goalless match against Sunderland (when Bryan Robson was despatched to an early bath), redeemed by a convincing replay performance at home (3-0). But 'the writing was on the wall' and the next venture saw a draw at home (1-1) followed by elimination at West Ham (0-2). The Milk Cup pursued a similar pattern with survival not being extended beyond two ties—against Crystal Palace (two single goal wins) and West Ham United (another lone goal success at Old Trafford). Then a visit to Anfield found United on the wrong end of sharing three goals against Liverpool. The Super Cup began and ended with a visit by Everton in September (2-4).

On paper United have the talent to win competitions—as they occasionally do—but their ability to dissipate good situations is sad. Their leading striker, Mark Hughes, is now about to 'earn his crust' with Barcelona and the club hopes that Blackmore can fill that gap. The remaining talent reads like a star international array—Olsen, Robson, Stapleton, Strachan, Whiteside, McGrath, Albiston, Duxbury, Davenport, etc . . . Mogg is a very promising central defender and Turner looked the part when he replaced Bailey in goal during the season.

Consistency is needed and Ron Atkinson will be required to provide the necessary motivation so that it can be achieved. He will also hope that Bryan Robson can play a full season free of injury to provide the inspiration on the field. United fans will never tolerate second best or a bare sideboard.   WLM

Back Row L to R: Frank Stapleton, John Sivebaek, Mark Higgins, Paul McGrath, Graeme Hogg, Norman Whiteside, Billy Garton. **Middle Row:** Mick Brown (Assistant Manager), Peter Davenport, Gary Bailey, Bryan Robson, John Gidman, Chris Turner, Kevin Moran, Jim McGregor (Physio). **Front Row:** Gordon Strachan, Clayton Blackmore, Colin Gibson, Mike Duxbury, Ron Atkinson (Manager), Peter Barnes, Arthur Albiston, Jesper Olsen, Terry Gibson.

MANCHESTER UNITED

DIVISION ONE: 4th   **FA CUP:** 5th ROUND   **MILK CUP:** 4th ROUND

MATCH	DATE	COMPE-TITION	VENUE	OPPONENTS	RESULT		HALF TIME	L'GUE POS'N	GOALSCORERS/GOAL TIMES	ATTEN-DANCE
1	A 17	CL	A	Aston Villa	W	4-0	0-0		Whiteside 47, Hughes 48, 74, Olsen 82	49,743
2	20	CL	A	Ipswich Town	W	1-0	0-0		Robson 63	(18,777)
3	24	CL	A	Arsenal	W	2-1	1-0	1	Hughes 19, McGrath 64	(37,145)
4	26	CL	H	West Ham United	W	2-0	0-0	1	Hughes 55, Strachan 75	50,773
5	31	CL	A	Nottingham Forest	W	3-1	3-0	1	Hughes 2, Barnes 5, Stapleton 40	(26,274)
6	S 4	CL	H	Newcastle United	W	3-0	2-0	1	Stapleton 5, 11, Hughes 61	51,102
7	7	CL	H	Oxford United	W	3-0	2-0	1	Whiteside 28, Robson 44, Barnes 74	51,820
8	14	CL	A	Manchester City	W	3-0	2-0	1	Robson (pen) 8, Albiston 18, Duxbury 73	(48,773)
9	18	SC	H	Everton	L	2-4	1-2		Robson (pen) 45, Stapleton 61	33,859
10	21	CL	A	W.B.A.	W	5-1	2-0	1	Brazil 6, 78, Strachan 22, Blackmore 68, Stapleton 72	(25,068)
11	24	MC2/1	A	Crystal Palace	W	1-0	0-0		Barnes 60	(21,506)
12	28	CL	H	Southampton	W	1-0	0-0	1	Hughes 75	52,449
13	O 5	CL	A	Luton Town	D	1-1	0-0	1	Hughes 60	17,454
14	9	MC2/2	H	Crystal Palace	W	1-0	1-0		Whiteside 1	26,118
15	12	CL	H	Q.P.R.	W	2-0	1-0	1	Hughes 31, Olsen 52	48,845
16	19	CL	H	Liverpool	D	1-1	0-0	1	McGrath 65	54,492
17	26	CL	A	Chelsea	W	2-1	1-0	1	Olsen 42, Hughes 77	(42,485)
18	29	MC3	H	West Ham United	W	1-0	0-0		Whiteside 77	32,057
19	N 2	CL	H	Coventry City	W	2-0	2-0	1	Olsen 18, 40	46,748
20	6	SC	H	Norwich City	D	1-1	0-1		Whiteside (pen) 54	20,130
21	9	CL	A	Sheffield Wednesday	L	0-1	0-0	1		(48,105)
22	16	CL	H	Tottenham Hotspur	D	0-0	0-0	1		54,575
23	23	CL	A	Leicester City	L	0-3	0-3	1		(22,008)
24	26	MC4	A	Liverpool	L	1-2	1-0		McGrath 7	(41,291)
25	30	CL	H	Watford	D	1-1	1-1	1	Brazil 67	42,181
26	D 7	CL	H	Ipswich Town	W	1-0	1-0	1	Stapleton 33	37,981
27	11	SC	A	Norwich City	D	1-1	0-1		Gibson C. 71	(15,449)
28	14	CL	A	Aston Villa	W	3-1	1-1	1	Blackmore 19, Strachan 67, Hughes 71	(27,626)
29	21	CL	H	Arsenal	L	0-1	0-0	·1		44,386
30	26	CL	A	Everton	L	1-3	1-2	1	Stapleton 14	(42,551)
31	J 1	CL	H	Birmingham City	W	1-0	0-0	1	Gibson C. 47	43,095
32	9	FAC3	H	Rochdale	W	2-0	1-0		Stapleton 15, Hughes 75	38,500
33	11	CL	A	Oxford United	W	3-1	1-0	1	Whiteside 11, Hughes 74, Gibson C. 83	(13,280)
34	18	CL	H	Nottingham Forest	L	2-3	0-1	1	Olsen (pen) 46, 67	46,717
35	25	FAC4	A	Sunderland	D	0-0	0-0			(35,484)
36	29	FAC4R	H	Sunderland	W	3-0	2-0		Whiteside 28, Olsen 38 (pen), 53	43,402
37	F 2	CL	A	West Ham United	L	1-2	1-0	2	Robson 25	(22,642)
38	9	CL	A	Liverpool	D	1-1	1-1	2	Gibson C. 15	(35,084)
39	22	CL	H	W.B.A.	W	3-0	2-0	2	Olsen 3 (pen) 26, (pen) 43, 70	45,193
40	M 1	CL	A	Southampton	L	0-1	0-0	2		(19,012)
41	5	FAC5	A	West Ham United	D	1-1	0-1		Stapleton 73	(26,441)
42	9	FAC5R	H	West Ham United	L	0-2	0-1			30,441
43	15	CL	A	Q.P.R.	L	0-1	0-0	3		(23,407)
44	19	CL	H	Luton Town	W	2-0	1-0	3	Hughes 37, McGrath 76	33,668
45	22	CL	H	Manchester City	D	2-2	1-0	3	Gibson C. 2, Strachan (pen) 56	51,274
46	29	CL	A	Birmingham City	D	1-1	0-0	3	Robson 85	(22,551)
47	31	CL	H	Everton	D	0-0	0-0	3		51,189
48	A 5	CL	A	Coventry City	W	3-1	2-0	3	Gibson C. 13, Robson 28, Strachan 83	(17,160)
49	9	CL	H	Chelsea	L	1-2	0-0	3	Olsen (pen) 68	45,355
50	13	CL	H	Sheffield Wednesday	L	0-2	0-0	3		32,331
51	16	CL	A	Newcastle United	W	4-2	3-1	3	Robson (pen) 2, Hughes 13, 45, Whiteside 50	(31,840)
52	19	CL	A	Tottenham Hotspur	D	0-0	0-0	3		(32,357)
53	26	CL	H	Leicester City	W	4-0	1-0	3	Stapleton 17, Hughes 83, Blackmore 84, Davenport (pen) 86	38,840
54	M 3	CL	A	Watford	D	1-1	1-0	4	Hughes 23	(18,414)

Best Home League Attendance: 54,575 v Tottenham Hotspur   **Smallest:** 32,331 v Sheffield Wed   **Av Home Att:** 43,880

Goal Scorers: Compared with 84-85: −1,194

League (70): Hughes 17, Olsen 11 (4 pen), Robson 7 (2 pen), Stapleton 7, Gibson C. 5, Strachan 5 (1 pen), Whiteside 4, Blackmore 3, Brazil 3, McGrath 3, Barnes 2, Albiston 1, Davenport 1, Duxbury 1

Milk Cup (4): Whiteside 2, Barnes 1, McGrath 1

FA Cup (6): Olsen 2 (1 pen), Stapleton 2, Hughes 1, Whiteside 1

Super Cup (4): Gibson C. 1, Whiteside 1 (1 pen), Robson 1 (1 pen), Stapleton 1

1985-86

Bailey	Gidman	Albiston	Whiteside	McGrath	Hogg	Robson	Moses	Hughes	Stapleton	Olsen	Duxbury	Strachan	Brazil	Moran	Blackmore	Garton	Turner	Gibson C.	Dempsey	Davenport	Higgins	Barnes	Gibson T.	Sivebaek	Referee	
1	2	3	4	5	6	7	8*	9	10	11	12														C Seel	1
1	2*	3	4	5	6	7		9	10	11	12	8													D Vickers	3
1		3	4	5	6	7		9	10	11	2	8													B Stevens	3
1		3	4	5	6	7		9	10	11	2	8													R Bridges	4
1		3	4	5	6	7		9	10		2	8*	12									11			K Hackett	5
1		3	4	5	6	7		9	10*		2	8	12									11			D Hutchinson	6
1		3	4	5	6	7		9	10*		2	8	12									11			G Aplin	7
1		3	4	5	6	7		9	10*		2	8	12									11			G Tyson	8
1		3	4	5		7		9	10		2	8		6								11			J Key	9
1		3	4	5	6	7		9			2	8*	10	12								11			M Scott	10
1		3	4	5		7			10		2		9	6	8							11			G Napthine	11
1		3	4*	5		7	8	9	10		2		12	6								11			K Redfern	12
1		3	4	5		7	8	9	10		2			6								11			K Baker	13
1		3	4	5		7		9*	10	8	2		12	6								11			V Callow	14
1		3	4	5		7		9	10	8	2			6								11			A Seville	15
1		3	4	7	6		8*	9	10	11	2			5								12			A Saunders	16
1		3	4	7	6†			9	10	8	2			5								11			J Martin	17
1		3	4	7	6			9	10	8	2*		12	5								11			F Roberts	18
1		3	4	7	6			9	10	8				5		2						11			J McAuley	19
	2	3	4	5	6			9	8				12	10		7	1					11*			T Mills	20
1	2	3	4	5		7*		9	10	8			12	6								11			J Bray	21
1	2	3	4	5				9	10	8		7		6								11			M Peck	22
1	2	3*	4	7	6			9	10	11		8	12	5											N Butler	23
1	2		4	7	6			9	11			8	10	5	3										D Shaw	24
1	2		4	7	6			9	10			8		5*				3							G Courtney	25
1	2		4	5	6			9*	10	11		8	12					3		7					P Vanes	26
1	2		4	5		7		9	10	11		8		6				3							D Vickers	27
	2		4	5		7		9	10*	11		8	12	6			1	3							D Reeves	28
1	2		4	5		7		9	10	11		8		6				3							T Holbrook	29
1	2		4	5	6	7		9	10	11*		8						3							D Allinson	30
	2	3	4	5*		7		9	10			8	12	6			1	11							D Hutchinson	31
		3	4					9*	10	12	2	8		6	7		1	11					5		V Callow	32
1	2	3	4					9	10			8		5	7	6		11							A Gunn	33
1	2	3	4					9	10	7		8		5		6		11							J Key	34
1	2	3	4	5		7		9	11			8		6				10							C Seel	35
1	2	3	4	5		7		9	11			8*		6	12			10							C Seel	36
1	2	3	4	5		7*		9	10			8		6				11				12			J Ball	37
	2	3	4	5				9	12	11*		8		6			1	10					8	7	N Ashley	38
	2*	3		5				9	10	11		7		6	4		1	8				12			G Tyson	39
		3		5		7		9	10	11*	2	8		6			1	4				12			R Milford	40
		3	4	5		7*		9	10	12	2	8		6			1	11							B Stevens	41
		3	4	5				9	10	7	2	8			12		1	11			6*				B Stevens	42
		3		5				9		7	2	8		6	4*		1	11		10			12		J Deakin	43
		3	4	5				9	12	11	2	8		6*			1	7		10					G Napthine	44
		3	4	5				9	12		2	8					1	7		10	6	11*			D Shaw	45
	2	3	4	5		7		9	12			8					1	11*		10	6				A Ward	46
	2	3	4	5		7		9	12			8					1	11		10*	6				K Hackett	47
	2	3		5		7		9	12			8					1	11*		10	6				R Groves	48
	2	3		5		7		9	12	11	4	8*					1			10	6				G Courtney	49
	2	3		5		7		9		11	4						1			10*	6		12	8	V Callow	50
	2	3	4	5		7		9	10					6	11		1			8*			8*	12	T Mills	51
	2	3	4	5				9	10	12		7		6	11		1								J Martin	52
	2	3	4*	5				9	10	12		7		6	11		1			8					N Ashley	53
		3	4	5	6			9	10	12		7			11	2	1			8*					A Gunn	54
25	24	37	37	40	17	21	4	40	34	25	21	27	1	18	12	10	17	18	1	11	6	12	2	2	League Appearances	
									7	3	2	1	10	1								1	5	1	Substitute Appearances	
4	1	3	4	4	2	2		2	4	3	3	1		2·2	4	2						3			Milk Cup Appearances	
2	2	5	5	4		3		3	5	5	3	3		4				2							FA Cup Appearances	
2	2	2	3	3	1	1		2	2	1	1	2·1		2	1	1	1	1				2			Super Cup Appearances	

Also Played: Position (Game): Wood 12(30)
Departures: Brazil (Coventry), Hughes (Barcelona)

'RED DEVILS'

Formed: 1878
Turned Professional: 1885   **Ltd Co:** 1907

Previous Name: Newton Heath 1880-1902

Previous Managers: Since 1946: Matt Busby 1945-70   Wilf McGuiness 1970   Sir Matt Busby 1970-71   Frank O'Farrell 1971-2   Tommy Docherty 1972-77   Dave Sexton 1977-81

Honours: Champions Div 1, 1907-8, 1910-11, 1951-2, 1955-6, 1956-7, 1964-5, 1966-7   Champions Div 2, 1935-6, 1974-5,   FA Cup Winners 1909, 1948, 1963, 1977, 1983, 1985   European Cup Winners 1967-8

League Career: Elected to Div 1 1892   Relegated to Div 2 1893-4   Promoted to Div 1 1905-6   Relegated to Div 2 1921-2   Promoted to Div 1 1924-5   Relegated to Div 2 1930-1   Promoted to Div 1 1935-6   Relegated to Div 2 1936-7   Promoted to Div 1 1937-8   Relegated to Div 2 1973-4   Promoted to Div 1 1974-5

Colours: Red shirts with white and black trim, white shorts, black stockings with white top with three red hoops

Change Colours: White shirts with black and red trim, black shorts with white trim, white stockings with three black hoops on tops

Reserves League: Central   **'A' Team:** Lancs Div 1   **'B' Team:** Lancs Div 2   **Youth Team:** Cup Ties only

CLUB RECORDS

Most Appearances for Club: Bobby Charlton 1956-73: Football League 604 + 2 subs + FA Cup 78 + League Cup 24 + European Cups 45 + FA Charity Shield 3 **Total 754 + 2 subs**

Most Capped Player: Bobby Charlton, 106, England

Record Goalscorer in a Match: R Smith, 6 for Newton Heath v Walsall Town Swifts, Div 2, 9 March 1895 (match replayed)   Harold Halse, 6 v Swindon Town, Charity Shield, (8-4), 1911   George Best 6 v Northampton Town, FA Cup 5th Round (8-2), 7 Feb 1970

Record League Goalscorer in a Season: Dennis Viollet, 32, Div 1, 1959-60   **In All Competitions:** Dennis Law, 46 (League 30 + FA Cup 10 + European Cup Winners Cup 6), 1963-4

Record League Goalscorer in a Career: Bobby Charlton   **In All Competitions:** Bobby Charlton, 248 (League 198 + FA Cup 19 + League Cup 7 + European Competitions 22 + Charity Shield 2)

Record Transfer Fee Received: £1,500,000 from A C Milan for Ray Wilkins, June 1984

Record Transfer Fee Paid: £1,500,000 to WBA for Bryan Robson, Oct 1981

Best Performances: League: Champions Div 1 (7)   **FA Cup:** Winners (6)   **League/Milk Cup:** Finalists   **European Cup:** Winners   **European Cup Winners Cup:** Semi-Finalists   **European Fairs Cup/UEFA CUP:** Semi-Finalists

Most League Points: (3pts for win) 78, Div 1, 1981-2 (2pts for win) 64 Div 1 1956-7

Most League Goals: 103, Div 1, 1956-7 & 1958-9

Record League Victory: 10-1 v Wolverhampton Wanderers, Div 2, 15 Oct 1892 (as Newton Heath)

Most Goals Scored in a First Class Match: as in record victory and 10-0 v Anderlecht (h), European Cup, 26 Sept 1956

Record League Defeat: 0-7 v Wolverhampton Wanderers, Div 2, 26 Dec 1931   0-7 v Blackburn Rovers, Div 1, 10 April 1926   0-7 v Aston Villa, Div 1, 27 Dec 1931

European Competitions Entered: European Cup: 1956-7, 1957-8, 1965-6, 1967-8, 1968-9   European Cup Winners Cup: 1963-4, 1977-8, 1983-4   European Fairs/UEFA Cup: 1964-5, 1976-7, 1980-1, 1982-3, 1984-5

Oldest Player in League Match:

Youngest Player in League Match:

Most Consecutive Undefeated League Matches: 26 1956

Longest Run of Undefeated Home League Matches: 37 1966-68

Longest Run Without Home League Win: 7 1920. 1930, 1933-34, 1958, 1978

Most Consecutive League Wins: 14 1904-05

Most Consecutive League Defeats: 14 1930

Club Statistician for the Directory: John Hewitt

League Matches Without a Win: 16 1930

Away League Matches: 14 1956

Away League Win: 26 1930-31

Home League Wins: 18 1904-05

Away League Wins: 6 1904-05

United recorded the worst ever start to a League season, losing their first 12 games in the 1930-31 season

MANCHESTER UNITED

				APPEARANCES				GOALS			
PLAYERS NAME Ht Wt Birthdate	Honours	Birthplace Transfers	Clubs	League	Milk Cup	FA Cup	Other Comps	League	Milk Cup	FA Cup	Other Comps
GOALKEEPERS											
Gary Bailey 6.1½ 12.10 9.8.58	E (2), B (2), U21 (14), FAC 83, 85	Ipswich	Manchester United	289	28	29	18				
Chris Turner 5.10½ 11.11 15.9.58	EY	Sheffield	Sheffield Wed. (A)	91	11	13					
			Lincoln City (L)	5		1					
		£80,000	Sunderland	195	21	7					
		£275,000	Manchester United	17		3					
DEFENDERS											
Arthur Albiston 5.7½ 10.13 14.7.57	S (11), U21 (5), FAC 77, 83, 85	Edinburgh	Manchester United	340+6	36+2	36	21+1	6	1		
Mark Dempsey 5.8 10.4 14.1.64		Manchester	Manchester United (A)	1							
			Swindon Town (L)	5		1					
Mike Duxbury 5.9 10.12 1.9.59	E (10), U21 (7), FAC 83, 85	Blackburn	Manchester United (A)	174+16	20+1	6+3	15+1	5		1	
Colin Gibson 5.8 10.10 6.4.60	E B (1), U21 (1), ESC 82, Div. 1, 81, EC 82	Bridport	Aston Villa (A)	181+5	26	12	13+1	10	4	1	2
			Manchester United	18		4		5			
John Gidman 5.11 12.2 10.1.54	E (1), B (2), Y, U23 (4), LgC 77, FAC 85, FAYC 72	Liverpool	Liverpool (NC)								
			Aston Villa	196+1	21	12		9			
		£650,000	Everton	64	6	11		2	1		
		£450,000	Manchester United	95+1	5	9	7	5			
Mark Higgins 6.1 13.4 29.9.58	EY	Buxton	Everton (A)	150+2	20	7		6			
			Manchester United	6							
Graeme Hogg 6.1 12.12 19.6.64	SU21 (4)	Aberdeen	Manchester United (A)	62	5	6	10	1			
Paul McGrath† 6.0 13.2 4.12.52	EI (10, FAC 83, 85,	Ealing £30,000	St Patrick's Athletic								
			Manchester United	86	5	11	4	7	1	2	
Kevin Moran 5.10½ 12.8 29.4.56	EI (21), FAC 83, 85	Dublin	Manchester United	176+1	20	15	12+1	21	2	1	2
Bill Garton 5.11 11.8 15.3.65		Salford	Manchester United	12	1		0+1				
MIDFIELD											
Remi Moses 5.6 10.7 14.11.60	EU21 (8)	Manchester £650,000	WBA	63	7	2	1	5	1		
			Manchester United	110+5	17+1	10	11	7	2		
Jesper Olsen 5.6 10.0 20.3.61	FAC 85	Fakse	Ajax								
			Manchester United	61+3	5	11	6+1	16	1	2	
Bryan Robson* 5.10½ 11.9 11.1.57	E (53), U21 (7), B (2), Y, S, FAC 83, 85	Chester-le-Street £1,500,000	WBA (A)	193+4	17+1	10+2		39	2	2	
			Manchester United	151+1	19	15	25	43	2	5	6
John Sivebaek 5.11 12.0 25.10.61		Vejle	Manchester United	3							
Gordon Strachan 5.6 10.8 9.2.57	S (37), U21 (1), Y, SPD 80, 84, SC 82, 83, 84, ECWC 83, FAC 85	Edinburgh	Dundee	56+13	10+1	7		13	1	1	
			Aberdeen	175+9	43+2	29+1	30+4	55	20	7	8
		£500,000	Manchester United	68+1	3	12	7	20		2	2
Norman Whiteside 6.0 12.3 8.5.65	NI (29), Y, S, FAC 83, 85	Belfast	Manchester United (A)	130+12	18+2	19	10+2	31	6	8	1
FORWARDS											
Peter Barnes 5.10 11.0 10.6.57	E (22), B (1), U21 (9), Y, S, LgC 76, Flg XI	Manchester £748,000	Manchester City (A)	108+7	15+2	6	9	15	11	2	
		£930,000	WBA	76+1	9+1	4	1	23	1	1	
		£115,000	Leeds United	30	2						
		F	Real Betis								
		£65,000	Leeds United	25+2	3	1		41			
		£50,000	Coventry City	18	1			2			
			Manchester United	12+1	3			2	1		
Clayton Blackmore 5.9 11.3 23.9.64	W (6), U23 (3) YS	Neath	Manchester United (A)	14	3	4		3			
Peter Davenport 5.10 11.12 24.3.61	E (1), B (1)	Birkenhead	Cammell Lairds								
			Nottingham Forest	114+11	10	7+1	10+1	54	1	1	2
			Manchester United	11				1			
Terry Gibson 5.5 10.0 23.10.62	EY	Walthamstow	Tottenham Hotspur (A)	16+2	1	5		4	1	1	
			Coventry City	73+1	4	5		32	1	5	
			Manchester United	2+5							
Frank Stapleton 5.11 13.0 10.7.56	EI (148), Y, FAC 79, 83, 85	Dublin £900,000	Arsenal (A)	223+2	26	32	15	75	14	15	4
			Manchester Utd	179+10	22+1	19	12+1	54	4	7	5

ADDITIONAL CONTRACT PROFESSIONALS

Nick Wood (EY, 0+1Lge), Martin Russell, Simon Ratcliffe, Gary Walsh (A), Aiden Murphy, Denis Cronin (A), Tony Gill (A), Jo Hanrahan, Andy McBride (A), Lee Martin, Mark Todd, Steve Gardiner (A).

APPRENTICES

Russell Beardsmore, Paul Harvey, Tony Hopley, Ian Scott, Phil Steer, David Wilson

NON-CONTRACT PLAYERS

James O'Donnell, Andy Comyw

Record Attendance: 76,962 Wolverhampton W v Grimsby Town, FA Cup Semi-Final, 25 March 1939

Smallest Home Attendance for a First Class Match: 7,800 v Stoke City (played at Maine Road) 5 Feb 1947

Record Receipts: £221,899.60 v Juventus, 11 Apr 1984

Season Tickets: Stand: £73.00, £86.00, £93.00, £104.00; Ground: £44.00, £47.50 (half price for children)

Executive Box Season Tickets: Executive Seat: £605; Boxes: £3,250, £3,575, £11,250

Cost of Stand Tickets: £4.30 (£2.20 for children in Family Stand) £5.20 **Terraces:** £2.60, £2.80 (half-price for children)

Match and Ticket Information: For up-to-date information, phone 061-872 0199, 24-hour service. Seats can be reserved one calendar month before a match, by post only

Car Parking: Several large parks: 1. Lancashire County Cricket Ground, Talbot Road and Great Stone Road (1200), 2. White City Stadium, Chester Road (900)

Manchester United FC Museum: The only one of its type in the World. Situated at the Warwick Road End of Old Trafford. Open everyday except Saturday. Admission £1.50, £1.00 for Children & OAPs

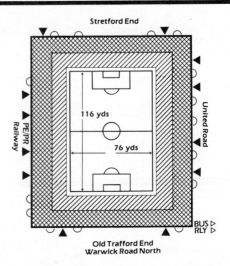

Stretford End

116 yds

76 yds

Railway PE/PR

United Road

BUS ▷
RLY ▷

Old Trafford End
Warwick Road North

How to get to the ground

From North: Use Motorway M61 then M63 until junction 4. Leave Motorway and follow signs Manchester A5081. In 2.5m turn right into Warwick Road, then turn right into United Road for Manchester United FC

From East: Use Motorway M62 until junction 17 then A56 into Manchester. Follow signs South then Chester into Chester Road. In 2m turn right into Warwick Road, then turn left into United Road for Manchester United FC

From South: Use Motorway M6 until junction 19 then follow signs Stockport A556 then Altrincham A56. From Altrincham follow signs Manchester. In 6m turn left into Warwick Road, then turn left into United Road for Manchester United FC

From West: Use Motorway M62 then M63 and route from north or as route from south

Price of 1986-7 Programme: 40p
Number of Pages: 24
Subscriptions: £15 (UK) and £19 (overseas)

Local Newspapers: Manchester Evening News, Sunday Pink

Local Radio Stations: BBC Radio Manchester, Piccadilly Radio

Chairman
J W Pratt

Vice-Chairman
J B Almond JP

Directors
G Hall
Ian Greaves

Secretary
J D Eaton (0623 23567)

Manager
Ian Greaves

Assistant Manager
John Jarman

Commercial Manager
S J Burgan (0623 25877)

Groundsman
D May

Chief Coach
W Dearden

Promotion to the 3rd Division, after six campaigns in Division 4, was achieved last season and undoubtedly the major contributory factor was the increase in the amount of goals scored compared to the previous season. With the sound defensive record being maintained the 'Stags' finished in 3rd place and but for a disappointing lapse towards the end of the season, only three victories in the last 12 matches, the championship itself may well have been within reach.

The dream of promotion seemed far away during the 1985 close season when leading players Colin Calderwood and David Caldwell both departed from the club. The loss of Calderwood being particularly upsetting as he appears to have an outstanding future in the game. New arrivals at the club were Mike Graham, Keith Cassells, Neville Chamberlain and Kevin Kent.

The highlight of the various knock-out cup campaigns was the meeting with Chelsea in the second round of the Milk Cup. The first leg, played at Field Mill, lived up to all expectations with Mansfield at one stage leading 2-0 only for the 1st Division team to draw level in the final 15 minutes. At Stamford Bridge the team were far from disgraced despite losing 2-0. A unique situation occurred in the group matches of the Freight Rover Trophy when all three clubs, Mansfield, Notts County and Doncaster Rovers finished with identical playing records. All matches therefore had to be replayed at a time when the fixture list was proving to be very demanding. The 'Stags' were eventually eliminated from the competition at the Quarter-Final stage after playing 11 matches in a period of 27 days. Although all-round teamwork and performance was a notable feature the major successes on the field were undoubtedly, player of the year, team captain and inspirational central defender George Foster and keeper Kevin Hitchcock. Football League debuts were given to two players, both strikers, Roddy Collins, a £10,000 buy from Dundalk and youngster Ian Stringfellow, nephew of a former 'Stags' favourite Mike Stringfellow. Of much importance to the club and supporters alike was manager Ian Greaves decision to remain at Mansfield instead of accepting an offer to take charge of West Bromwich Albion.

Predictions for the 1986/87 season are that the club will more than hold their own in the higher grade and that a lengthy cup run may well occur!

P Stevenson

Back Row L to R: Gareth Price, Ian Stringfellow, Stephen Williams, David Hodge, Glen Russell, Mark Place, Stephen Beeston, John Blair, Nicholas Anderson. **Middle Row:** Mike Graham, Leslie Robinson, Neil Whatmore, Mark Koarney, Kevin Hitchcock, Gary Pollard, Craig McKernon, David Logan, Simon Coleman. **Front Row:** W. Deardon (Trainer/Coach), Neville Chamberlain, Keith Cassells, Tony Lowery, Kevin Kent, Ian Greaves (Manager), George Foster, Paul Garner, Roddy Collins, John Jarman (Asst. Manager).

MANSFIELD TOWN

DIVISION FOUR: 3rd   **FA CUP: 1st ROUND**   **MILK CUP: 2nd ROUND**   **FRT: AREA QUARTER FINAL**

MATCH	DATE		COMPE-TITION	VENUE	OPPONENTS	RESULT		HALF TIME	L'GUE POS'N	GOALSCORERS/GOAL TIMES	ATTEN-DANCE
1	A	17	CL	H	Hereford United	W	4-1	1-0		Cassells 3 43, 52, 83, Chamberlain 58	2,405
2		21	MC1/1	H	Middlesbrough	W	2-0	2-0		Chamberlain 5, Vinter 26	3,179
3		24	CL	A	Port Vale	D	0-0	0-0	5		(2,930)
4		27	CL	H	Halifax Town	W	2-0	1-0		Vinter 12, Chamberlain 61	3,299
5		31	CL	A	Northampton Town	L	0-1	0-1	5		(2,739)
6	S	3	MC1/2	A	Middlesbrough	D	4-4	3-2		Kearney 21, Graham 24, Chamberlain 27, Vinter 88	(4,051)
7		7	CL	H	Wrexham	D	1-1	0-0	8	Whatmore 46	3,063
8		14	CL	A	Aldershot	W	2-1	1-0	6	Cassells 38, Kearney 84	(1,307)
9		18	CL	H	Orient	D	1-1	1-1		Chamberlain 45	4,185
10		21	CL	A	Scunthorpe United	W	3-0	2-0	4	Pollard 17, Whatmore 28, Vinter 76	(1,780)
11		25	MC2/1	H	Chelsea	D	2-2	2-0		Pollard 3, Cassells 16	6,018
12		28	CL	H	Southend United	W	3-0	0-0	3	Kearney pen 54, Vinter 88, Westley og 90	3,701
13	O	2	CL	A	Chester City	L	0-1	0-1			(2,127)
14		5	CL	A	Cambridge United	L	2-4	0-1	7	Kearney (pen) 46, Chamberlain 55	(1,957)
15		9	MC2/2	A	Chelsea	L	0-2	0-0			(11,664)
16		12	CL	H	Colchester United	W	2-1	0-0	6	Luke 56, Chamberlain 62	3,364
17		19	CL	H	Exeter City	W	2-1	1-1	6	Kearney 44, Lowery 56	3,289
18		22	CL	A	Tranmere Rovers	W	2-1	1-0	3	Kearney 23, Chamberlain 84	(1,540)
19		26	CL	H	Torquay United	W	4-0	2-0	1	Whatmore 25, 28, Chamberlain 67, Lowery 84	3,506
20	N	2	CL	A	Hartlepool United	D	1-1	0-0	2	Chamberlain 50	(4,220)
21		5	CL	A	Burnley	L	1-2	0-1		Kearney 46	(2,200)
22		9	CL	H	Crewe Alexandra	D	2-2	0-1	4	Chamberlain 51, Kent 68	3,243
23		16	FAC1	H	Port Vale	D	1-1	0-0		Chamberlain 51	5,207
24		18	FAC1R	A	Port Vale	L	0-1	0-0			(6,749)
25		23	CL	A	Swindon Town	L	1-2	0-1	6	Ramsey (og) 53	(4,784)
26		30	CL	H	Rochdale	W	3-2	2-0	3	Whatmore 12, 47, Luke 41	2,586
27	D	14	CL	A	Peterborough United	L	2-4	1-2	5	Garner 31, Kent 66	(3,128)
28		22	CL	H	Port Vale	W	2-1	1-0	4	Garner 6, Kent 53	3,722
29		26	CL	H	Stockport County	W	4-2	2-1	3	Lowery 3, 71, Garner S 5, Chamberlain 62	4,206
30	J	1	CL	A	Preston North End	W	2-0	1-0	3	Cassells 6, Chamberlain 77	(3,705)
31		11	CL	H	Northampton Town	W	1-0	1-0	3	Kearney (pen) 13	3,829
32		18	CL	A	Hereford United	L	2-4	0-1	3	Logan 48, Kent 64	(2,883)
33		21	FRT	A	Doncaster Rovers	L	0-1	0-1			(1,584)
34		25	CL	H	Aldershot	W	2-0	2-0	3	Whatmore 26, 37	3,097
35	F	1	CL	A	Wrexham	W	2-1	2-0	3	Cassells 37, Vinter 44	(1,363)
36		8	CL	A	Exeter City	W	1-0	1-0	3	Kent 24	(1,798)
37		15	CL	A	Orient	W	1-0	0-0	3	Kent 85	(3,713)
38	M	4	CL	H	Chester City	D	0-0	0-0	3		3,957
39		8	CL	H	Cambridge United	W	2-0	0-0	3	Chamberlain 82, Cassells 89	3,373
40		11	FRT	H	Notts County	W	1-0	1-0		Lowery 37	3,447
41		14	CL	A	Colchester United	D	0-0	0-0	3		(1,920)
42		17	FRT	H	Doncaster Rovers	W	4-2	1-0		Cassells (pen) 32, Chamberlain 57, Collins 66, 87	2,895
43		20	FRT	A	Notts County	W	1-0	0-0		Luke 60	(2,409)
44		22	CL	A	Torquay United	W	2-1	1-0	3	Cassells 41, Luke 90	(1,880)
45		25	CL	H	Scunthorpe United	D	1-1	1-0	3	Garner 17	3,919
46		27	FRT QF	A	Darlington	L	0-3	0-1			(1,425)
47		29	CL	H	Preston North End	L	2-3	2-1	3	Cassells 27, Chamberlain 39	3,737
48		31	CL	A	Stockport County	W	2-0	1-0	3	Chamberlain 28, Cassells 89	(4,635)
49	A	5	CL	H	Burnley	D	0-0	0-0	3		3,671
50		11	CL	A	Crewe Alexandra	L	1-2	0-0	4	Kent 52	(2,099)
51		15	CL	A	Southend United	L	1-3	1-1	4	Lowery 38	(1,140)
52		19	CL	H	Swindon Town	D	1-1	1-1	4	Chamberlain 33	8,416
53		22	CL	H	Hartlepool United	W	4-0	2-0	3	Cassells 18,68, Kelly (og) 29, Chamberlain 81	5,523
54		26	CL	A	Rochdale	D	1-1	0-1	3	Cassells 70	(1,936)
55		29	CL	H	Tranmere Rovers	D	0-0	0-0	3		3,470
56	M	3	CL	H	Peterborough United	L	0-1	0-1	4		3,008
57		5	CL	A	Halifax Town	W	2-1	0-0	3	Kent 56, Whatmore 85	(1,414)

Best Home League Attendance: 8,416 v Swindon Town   **Smallest: 2,405 v Hereford United**   **Av Home Att: 3,764**

Goal Scorers: **Compared with 84-85: +1448**

League (74): Chamberlain 16, Cassells 13, Whatmore 9, Kent 8, Kearney 7 (3 pen), Lowery 5, Garner 4, Vinter 4, Luke 3, Opponents 3, Logan 1, Pollard 1

Milk Cup (8): Chamberlain 2, Vinter 2, Kearney 1, Graham 1, Pollard 1, Cassells 1

FA CUP (1): Chamberlain 1

FRT (6): Collins 2, Cassells 1 (pen), Chamberlain 1, Lowery, Luke 1

1985-86

Hitchcock	Graham	Garner	Lowery	Foster	Pollard	Chamberlain	Whatmore	Cassells	Vinter	Kearney	Logan	Luke	Gallaway	Kent	McKernon	Robinson	Collins	Kenworthy (L)	Beasley	Anderson	Cunningham	Coleman	Gunn (L)	Stringfellow	Referee	
1	2	3	4	5	6	7	8	9	10	11															C Trussell	1
1	2	3	4	5	6	7	8	9	10	11															**J Lovatt**	2
1	2		4	5	6	7	8	9	10*	11	3	12													N Wilson	3
1			4	5	6	7	8	9	10	11	3	12	2*												I Hemley	4
1	2		4	5	6	7	8*	9	10	11	3	12													A Ward	5
1	2		4	5	6	7	8	9	10	11	3														**T Fitzharris**	6
1	2		4	5	6	7	8	9	10	11	3	12													R Dilkes	7
1	2		4	5	6	7	8	9	10	11	3														M Dimblebee	8
1	2		4	5	6	7	8*	9	10	11	3			12											N Ashley	9
1	2		4	5	6	7	8*	9	10	11	3		12												J McAulay	10
1	2		4	5	6	7		9	10	11*	3	12		8											**A Robinson**	11
1	2			5	6	7	8	9	10	11	3			4											N Midgley	12
1	2		4	5		7*	8	9	10	11	3	12		6											M Heath	13
1	2		4	5		7	8		10	11	3	6		9											C Downey	14
1	2		4	5	6	7	8		10		3	11		9											**M Bodenham**	15
1	2		4	5	6	7	8	9*			3	11		10	12										K Breen	16
1	2		4	5	6	7	8	9	10*	11	3			12											T Mills	17
1	2		4	5	6	7	8			11	3	9		10											K Walmsley	18
1	2		4	5	6	7	8			11	3			10	9										P Tyldesley	19
1	2		4	5	6	7	8			11	3	9*	12	10											D Allison	20
1	2		4	5	6	7	8			11	3	12	9*	10											T Jones	21
1	2		4	5	6	7	8	9		11	3			10											K Baker	22
1	2		4	5	6	7	8*	9	12	11	3			10											**T Fitzharris**	23
1	2		4	5	6	7*	12	9	10	11	3			8											**T Fitzharris**	24
1	2	8	4	5	6			9	10	11	3			7											K Cooper	25
1	2	11	5*				8	9	10					4	7	3	12								G Ashby	26
1	2	11	4*	5	6	7		9			3			8	10	12									N Butler	27
1	2	8	4	5	6	7		9		11	3			10											D Phillips	28
1	2	8	4	5	6	7		9		11	3			10											J Ashworth	29
1	2	8	4	5	6	7		9		11	3			10											R Nixon	30
1	2	8	4	5	6*	7		9		11	3			10			12								T Simpson	31
1	2	8	4	5		7		9		11	6	3		10			12								J Lovatt	32
1	2	8*	4	5		7	13	9		11	6	3		12			10*								**T Fitzharris**	33
1	2	3	4	5	6	7*	8	9	10	11				12											J Worrall	34
1	2	3	4	5	6		8	9*	10	11				7			12								T Jones	35
1	2	3	4	5	6		8	9	10	11				7											J Deakin	36
1	2	3	4	5	6	9	8			11				7		10									J Martin	37
1	2	3	4	5	6	12	8	9	10	11*				7											J McAulay	38
1	2	3	4	5	6	11	8*	9						7	12	10									M Heath	39
1	2	3	4		6	11		8					12	7		10	9*	5							**J Ball**	40
1	2	3	4	5	6	11		9						8*	7		12	10							L Shapter	41
	2	3	12	5		11	10*	8						7		4	9	6	1						**H Taylor**	42
	2	3	4	5		11	9	8						7			10*	6	1	12					D Phillips	43
1	2	3	4	5	6	11		10						7			9	8							M Cotton	44
1	2	3	4	5	6	11		10	8					7			9								J Lloyd	45
1	2	3*		5	6	11		9						7	4		10			12	13	8*			**K Redfern**	46
1	2	3	4*	5		7	12		10	11							9	6				8			I Hemley	47
1	2	3		5		7			10	11					4		9	8				6			D Allison	48
1	2	3	4	5		7			10	11					12		9*	8				6			I Borrett	49
1	2	3	4	5		7		9	10	11							8					6			I Hendrick	50
1	2	3	4	5				9	10					8			7	11				6			D Hedges	51
1	2	3	4	5	6	11		10						7			9*	12				8			G Ashby	52
1	2	3	4	5	6	11		10						7			9	8							R Guy	53
1	2			5	6			9	10	11				7	4	8	3								A Seville	54
1	2	3		5				8	10	11				7	4		9*					6	12		T Holbrook	55
1	2	3	4*	5		7	8		10	11							9					6	12		J Bray	56
1	2	3		5			8		10	11				9	7	4	6*						12		R Glover	57
46	45	28	40	46	35	39	30	40	21	31	24	8	4	31	7	6	7	13					5	0	League Appearances	
							1	1						6	2	3	4	1	5					3	Substitute Appearances	
4	4	1	4	4	4	3	3	4	3	3	1·1			2											Milk Cup Appearances	
2	2		2	2	2	1·1	2	2	1·1	2				2											FA Cup Appearances	
3	5	5	3·1	5	1	4	2·1	2	5	1	1	3·1		1·1	3	1	4	3	2	0·2	0·1	1			FR Trophy Appearances	

Players on Loan: Gunn (Nottm Forest, Kenworthy (Sheff Utd)
Departures: Galloway (Halifax Town), Luke (F), Vintner (Newport County)

303

'THE STAGS'

Formed: 1905
Turned Professional: 1905   **Ltd Co:** 1905

Previous Managers: 1931-3 J Hickling   1933-5 H Martin   1935 C Bell   1936 H Whiteman
1936-8 H Parkes   1938-9 J Poole   1939-45 C Barke   1945-9 R Goodall   1949-51 F Steele
1952-3 G Jobey   1953-5 S Mercer   1956-8 C Mitten   1958-60 S Weaver   1960-3 R Carter
1963-7 T Cummings   1967-70 T Eggleston   1970-1 J Basford   1971-4 D Williams   1974-6 D Smith
1976-8 P Morris   1978-9 B Bingham   1979-81 M Jones   1981-3 S Boam
Honours: Champions Div 3, 1976-7   Champions Div 4, 1974-5
League Career: Elected to Div 3 (S) 1931   Transferred to Div 3 (N) 1932
Transferred to Div 3 (S) 1936   Transferred to Div 3 (N) 1947   Transferred to Div 3 1958
Relegated to Div 4 1959-60   Promoted to Div 3 1962-3   Relegated to Div 4 1971-2
Promoted to Div 3 1974-5   Promoted to Div 2 1976-7   Relegated to Div 3 1977-8
Relegated to Div 4 1979-80   Promoted to Div 3 1985-6
Colours: Amber shirts with dark blue trim, blue shorts and stockings
Change Colours: Red and white
Reserves League: Midland Intermediate **'A' Team:** North Football Combination Premier Division

---

CLUB RECORDS

Most Appearances for Club: Rod Arnold: Football League 440 + FA Cup 29 + League/Milk Cup 24 **Total 493**
Most Capped Player: John McClelland, 6, N Ireland   **For England:** None
Record Goalscorer in a Match: Ted Harston, 7
Record League Goalscorer in a Season: Ted Harston, 58
Record League Goalscorer in a Career: Harold Johnson, 104
Record Transfer Fee Received: £200,000 from Luton Town for Mike Saxby, July 1979
Record Transfer Fee Paid: £75,000 to Luton Town for Steve Taylor, July 1979
Best Performances: League: 21st Div 2 1977-8   **FA Cup:** 6th Round, 1968-9   **League/Milk Cup:** 5th Round 1975-6
Most League Points: 68, Div 4, 1974-5   **Most League Goals:** 108, Div 4, 1962-3
Record League Victory and Most Goals Scored in a League Match: 9-2 v Rotherham United, Div 3 (N), 27 Dec 1932
Most Goals Scored in a Cup Tie: 9-2 v Hounslow, FA Cup 1st Replay, 1962
Record League Defeat: 1-8 v Walsall, Div 3 (N), 19 Jan 1934
Oldest Player in League Match:
Youngest Player in League Match:
Most Consecutive Undefeated League Matches: 20 1976

League Matches Without a Win: 12 1959, 1974, 1979-80

Longest Run of Undefeated Home League Matches: 38 1976-77
Away League Matches: 8 1976
Longest Run Without Home League Win: 11 1959
Away League Win: 37 1931-33
Most Consecutive League Wins: 7 1962
Home League Wins: 10 1949
Most Consecutive League Defeats: 7 1947
Away League Wins: 7 1976

Club Statistician for the Directory: Pete Stevenson

MANSFIELD TOWN

PLAYERS NAME Ht Wt Birthdate	Honours	Birthplace Transfers	Clubs	League	Milk Cup	FA Cup	Other Comps	League	Milk Cup	FA Cup	Other Comps
GOALKEEPERS											
Andy Beasley 6.2 12.2 5.2.64	F	Wolverhampton	Luton Town (A)								
			Mansfield Town	5							
Kevin Hitchcock 6.1 12.2 5.10.62		Custom House	Nottingham Forest								
			Mansfield Town	89	6	4	3				
DEFENDERS											
George Foster† 5.10 11.2 26.9.56		Plymouth	Plymouth Argyle (A)	201+11	19	10		6			
			Torquay United (L)	6							
			Exeter City (L)	28							
			Derby County	30	7	5					
			Mansfield Town	132	8	6	6				
Mike Graham 5.9½ 11.7 24.2.59		Lancaster F F	Bolton Wanderers (A)	43+3	3	2					
			Swindon Town	105	6	9	2				
			Mansfield Town	45	4	2	5		1		
Mark Kearney 5.10 11.0 12.6.62		Ormskirk £23,000 F	Marine								
			Everton								
			Mansfield Town	96+1	7	3+2	1	11	1		
David Logan 5.9 10.11 5.12.63		Whitley	Mansfield Town	41	3	2	1	1			
Gary Pollard 6.1 11.10 30.12.59		Staveley	Chesterfield	83+4	4+1	9					
			Port Vale	17+1	3	2	1+1				
			Mansfield Town	52+1	4	2	1	1	1		
MIDFIELD											
Simon Coleman 6.0 10.8 13.6.68		Worksop	Mansfield Town				1				
Paul Garner 5.9 10.10 1.12.55	EY, Div. 4, 82	Doncaster £60,000	Huddersfield Town (A)	96	8	2		2			
			Sheffield United	248+3	8+1	14	3	7			2
			Mansfield Town	66+1	1	1	5	6			
Tony Lowery 5.9½ 10.6 6.7.61		Wallsend	Ashington								
			WBA	1							
			Walsall	4+2				1			
			Mansfield Town	131	7	6	4+1	14		1	1
Craig McKernon 5.8 10.2 23.2.68		Gloucester	Mansfield Town (A)	8+5			3				
FORWARDS											
Keith Cassells 5.10 11.12 10.2.57		London £500	Wembley								
			Watford	6+6	2	1+1					
			Peterborough (L)	8							
		£51,000	Oxford United	43+2	5	8		13			
		£115,000	Southampton	13+6	5	1		4			
		£25,000	Brentford	80+6	4	5	5+2	28			
		£17,000	Mansfield Town	40	3	2	2	13	1	1	
Roderick Collins 5.10 12.10 7.8.62		Dundalk	Dundalk								
			Mansfield Town	7+5			4	2			
Neville Chamberlain 5.7½ 11.5 22.1.60		Stoke	Port Vale (A)	133+8	7	10		33	3	6	
			Stoke City	6							
			Newport County (L)	6							
			Plymouth Argyle (L)	7+4							
		F	Newport County	39+2	1	2	5	13	1		1
			Mansfield Town	39+1	4	2	4	16	2	1	1
Kevin Kent 5.8 11.0 19.3.65		Birmingham F F	WBA (A)	1							
			Newport County	23+9	2	2+1	3+1	1			
			Mansfield Town	31+3	2	2	1+1	8			
Les Robinson 5.8 11.1 1.3.67		Mansfield	Mansfield Town	10+3			1				
Neil Whatmore 5.9½ 11.8 17.5.55		Ellesmere Port £340,000	Bolton Wanderers (A)	262+15	22+1	20		102	7	6	
			Birmingham City	24+2							
			Bolton Wanderers (L)	10							
		£25,000	Oxford United	33+3	3+1	2+2	1	15	1		
			Bolton Wanderers (L)	7							
		Player exch.	Burnley	15	1			1			
			Mansfield Town	56	3	1+1	2+1	16			
Ian Stringfellow 5.9½ 10.4 8.5.69		Retford	Mansfield Town	0+3							

ADDITIONAL CONTRACT PROFESSIONALS

APPRENTICES

NON-CONTRACT PLAYERS
Nicholas Anderson (0+2FRT), Russell Black, Nick Anderson

FIELD MILL GROUND   Quarry Lane, Mansfield   Capacity: 8,500

Record Attendance: 24,467 v Nottingham
Forest, FA Cup Round 3, 10 Jan 1963

**Smallest Home Attendance for a First Class
Match:** 1,086 v Darlington, Associate Members
Cup, 1983-4

Record Receipts: £19,227 v Sheffield
Wednesday, Div 3, 15 Mar 1980

Season Tickets: £76 (£55 juniors/OAP), £57
(£33 juniors/OAP); Ground: £51 (£25.50
juniors/OAP)

Executive Box Season Tickets: Vice-
Presidents £190 single, Vice-Presidents £300
double

Cost of Stand Tickets: £5.00; Ground £3.00
(£1.50 ground)

Match and Ticket Information: Advance
booking for five days prior to match

Car Parking: Space for 500 cars at the ground
and for another 3,000 within 500 yards

Nearest Railway Station: Mansfield Alfreton
Parkway

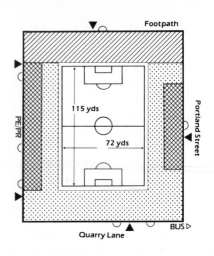

How to get to the ground

From North: Use Motorway M1 until junction
29. Leave Motorway and follow signs Mansfield
A617. In 6.3m turn right into Rosemary Street
B6030. In 1m turn right into Quarry Lane for
Mansfield Town FC
From East: Use A617 to Rainworth. In 3m at
crossroads turn left B6030 into Windsor Road.
At end turn right into Nottingham Road. Shortly
turn left into Portland Street, then turn left into
Quarry Lane for Mansfield Town FC
From South and West: Use Motorway M1 until
junction 28 then follow signs Mansfield A38. In
6.4m at crossroads turn right into Belvedere
Street B6030. In 0.4m turn right into Quarry
Lane for Mansfield Town FC

Price of 1986-7 Programme: 50p
Number of Pages: 16

Local Newspapers: Chronicle Advertiser,
Nottingham Evening Post

Local Radio Stations: Radio Trent, Radio
Nottingham

MIDDLESBROUGH

Division 3

Chairman
Colin Henderson

Directors
Steve Gibson
Henry Muskovitch
Graham Fordy

Secretary
David Thorne (0642 819659/815996)

Manager
Bruce Rioch

Club Coach
Colin Todd

Commercial Manager
Colin Busfield

Unfortunately Middlesborough hadn't had a new team photo taken at the time of going to print, so we apologise that last year's group photo cannot obviously include all of this season's squad.

Back Row L to R: Don O'Riordan, Gary Hamilton, Tony McAndrew, Stephen Pears, Archie Stephens, David Cume, Andrew Strong.
Middle Row: Steve Smelt (Physio), Paul Ward, Tony Mowbray, Alan Kernaghan, Garry Gill, Garry Pallister, John Coddington (Coach).
Front Row: Alan Roberts, David Mills, Brian Laws, Alf Duffield (Chairman), Willie Maddren (Manager), Peter Beagrie, Irving Nattrass, Gary Rowell.

This was, without doubt, the worst season in the club's 88-year history. Devastated by off-field financial problems, the Borough struggled to find any sort of cohesion on the pitch and ended up being relegated to the 3rd Division.

After that the club was wound up in the High Court, all non-playing staff were sacked and there were grave doubts about the club being able to carry on in League football.

Middlesbrough's luck really was out from the start. Young Steve Corden had the misfortune to break a leg on his League debut on the opening day of the season as the Borough crashed 0-3 away to Wimbledon.

They managed only one goal in their opening five matches — that against a Fulham side that was to suffere equally as wretched a season.

With only two wins from 15 games, Middlesbrough were settling down among the bottom three at the beginning of November. By then Carlisle already looked booked for the drop but Middlesbrough had hope as many other clubs around them were also struggling.

One consolation was that home form was good and, largely because of this, they began to pull clear of the danger zone for a while. But a disastrous run at the start of January plunged them back into trouble.

Following a home defeat by Charlton at the start of February — which once again gave rise to serious relegation fears — manager Willie Maddren left the club by mutual consent. Former Scotland international Bruce Rioch took over but, though the team won its first match under his charge, the situation remained grim.

But, with Sunderland, Blackburn and Huddersfield, also in difficulties, there was still hope that Middlesbrough could save their 2nd Division status. A 1-0 victory over second-placed Portsmouth in mid-April, gave rise to real hope of survival but then came two away games that both ended in defeat.

A 3-0 home win over Millwall in Borough's penultimate match actually lifted them out of the bottom three. But Sunderland, one point behind, had two games to play.

Sunderland, in fact, won those closing two games so Middlesbrough's 1-2 reverse at Shrewsbury put them down into Division 3.

There was little to cheer in any of the Cups, either. They lost 2-6 on aggregate to Mansfield in the 1st Round of the Milk Cup and then lost 1-3 at home to Southampton in the 3rd Round of the FA Cup.

Though they defeated Carlisle in the new Full Members Cup, they were beaten at Hull in the Northern semi-final.

MIDDLESBROUGH

DIVISION TWO: 21st   **FA CUP:** 3rd ROUND   **MILK CUP:** 1st ROUND   **FM CUP:** AREA SEMI-FINAL

MATCH	DATE		COMPE-TITION	VENUE	OPPONENTS	RESULT		HALF TIME	L'GUE POS'N	GOALSCORERS/GOAL TIMES	ATTEN-DANCE
1	A	17	CL	A	Wimbledon	L	0-3	0-2			(2,844)
2		21	MC1/1	A	Mansfield Town	L	0-2	0-2			(3,179)
3		24	CL	H	Fulham	W	1-0	0-0	16	Stephens 76	5,366
4		27	CL	A	Charlton Athletic	L	0-2	0-0			(4,045)
5		31	CL	H	Brighton & H.A.	L	0-1	0-1	19		5,543
6	S	3	MC1/2	H	Mansfield Town	D	4-4	2-3		Pollard og 13, Currie 19, Rowell 60 pen 81	4,051
7		7	CL	A	Hull City	D	0-0	0-0	20		(7,710)
8		10	CL	H	Stoke City	D	1-1	0-0	19	Rowell 51	4,255
9		14	CL	H	Norwich City	D	1-1	1-0	18	Rowell (pen) 4	5,475
10		21	CL	A	Sheffield United	W	1-0	0-0	15	Rowell 89	(10,535)
11		28	CL	H	Barnsley	D	0-0	0-0	16		5,589
12	O	5	CL	H	Crystal Palace	L	0-2	0-2	18		4,991
13		8	FMC	H	Carlisle United	W	2-0	1-0		Saunders (og) 22, O'Riordan	2,177
14		12	CL	A	Leeds United	L	0-1	0-1	20		(14,117)
15		19	CL	H	Bradford City	D	1-1	1-0	20	Slaven 17	6,130
16		22	CL	A	Sunderland	L	0-1	0-1	20		(20,541)
17		26	CL	A	Grimsby Town	L	2-3	1-1	21	Stephens 35 secs, Laws 72	(4,454)
18	N	2	CL	H	Blackburn Rovers	D	0-0	0-0	20		5,126
19		5	FMC	A	Hull City	L	1-3†	0-0		Slaven 66	(3,637)
20		16	CL	H	Oldham Athletic	W	3-2	2-0	20	Currie 4, Heard 39, Rowell 89	4,249
21		23	CL	A	Millwall	L	0-3	0-2	21		(3,188)
22		30	CL	H	Shrewsbury Town	W	3-1	2-1	20	Rowell 6, Heard 32, McAndrew 55	4,506
23	D	7	CL	A	Stoke City	L	2-3	1-2	21	Stephens 6, O'Riordan 56	(7,646)
24		14	CL	H	Wimbledon	W	1-0	0-0	19	Mowbray 72	4,693
25		21	CL	A	Fulham	W	3-0	2-0	18	Slaven 6, Rowell 40, 52	(3,512)
26		26	CL	A	Carlisle United	L	0-1	0-0	19		(4,238)
27		28	CL	H	Sunderland	W	2-0	1-0	17	Mowbray 3, McAndrew 89	19,774
28	J	1	CL	H	Huddersfield Town	L	0-1	0-1	19		9,320
29		11	CL	A	Norwich City	L	0-2	0-1	20		(13,730)
30		13	FAC3	H	Southampton	L	1-3	1-2		O'Riordan 31	12,735
31		18	CL	A	Brighton & H.A.	D	3-3	2-1	20	Rowell 40, 90, Slaven 44	(10,106)
32		25	CL	A	Portsmouth	L	0-1	0-0	20		(10,611)
33	F	1	CL	H	Charlton Athletic	L	1-3	0-0	20	Rowell (pen) 59	4,463
34	M	4	CL	H	Grimsby Town	W	3-1	0-0	20	Slaven 48, 79, Mowbray 56	4,496
35		8	CL	H	Crystal Palace	L	1-2	1-1	20	Slaven 33	(4,863)
36		15	CL	A	Leeds United	D	2-2	1-1	20	Currie 44, 53	6,899
37		18	CL	H	Sheffield United	L	1-2	1-1	20	O'Riordan 30	5,678
38		22	CL	H	Hull City	L	1-2	0-0	20	Currie 89	6,233
39		25	CL	A	Barnsley	D	0-0	0-0	20		(3,827)
40		29	CL	A	Huddersfield Town	W	3-0	1-0	20	Hamilton 16, 89, Slaven 74	(5,585)
41		31	CL	H	Carlisle United	L	1-3	1-1	20	Hamilton 29	7,603
42	A	5	CL	A	Blackburn Rovers	W	1-0	0-0	20	Hamilton 46	(4,049)
43		12	CL	H	Portsmouth	W	1-0	0-0	19	Mowbray 63	7,160
44		19	CL	A	Oldham Athletic	L	0-1	0-0	21		(4,192)
45		23	CL	A	Bradford City	L	1-2	0-2	21	Oliver (og) 77	(3,426)
46		26	CL	H	Millwall	W	3-0	1-0	19	Beagrie 35, Slaven (pen) 47, Laws 79	5,494
47	M	3	CL	A	Shrewsbury Town	L	1-2	0-1	21	Stephens 48	(6,695)

Best Home League Attendance: 19,774 v Sunderland	**Smallest: 4,249 v Oldham Athletic**		**Av Home Att: 6,335**
Goal Scorers:			**Compared with 84-85: +1,208**

League (44):	Rowell 10 (2 pen), Slaven 8 (1 pen), Currie 4, Hamilton 4, Mowbray 4, Stephens 4, Laws 2, Heard 2, McAndrew 2, O'Riordan 2, Beagrie 1, Opponent 1
Milk Cup (4):	Rowell 2 (1 pen), Currie 1, Opponent 1
FA Cup (1):	O'Riordan 1
FM Cup (3):	O'Riordan 1, Slaven 1, Opponent 1

†After extra time

Appearance grid (shirt numbers per match; * = substituted, † / · as printed). Player columns left→right: Pears, Laws, Corden, Pallister, Mowbray, Nattrass, Roberts, O'Riordan, Stephens, McAndrew, Rowell, Currie, Ward, Kernaghan, Beagrie, Hamilton, Heard, Gill, Cook, Slaven, Cooper, Turnbull, McManus (L), Ripley, Kite (L).

Pears	Laws	Corden	Pallister	Mowbray	Nattrass	Roberts	O'Riordan	Stephens	McAndrew	Rowell	Currie	Ward	Kernaghan	Beagrie	Hamilton	Heard	Gill	Cook	Slaven	Cooper	Turnbull	McManus (L)	Ripley	Kite (L)	Referee	
1	2	3*	4	5	6	7	8	9	10	11	12														K Barratt	1
1	2	6	5			7*	8	9	4	10	11	3	12												J Lovatt	2
1	2		5				8	9	4	10	11*	3	12	6	7										K Hackett	3
1	2		6				8	9	4	10	12	3	11*	5	7										M Bodenham	4
1	2		5				8	9	4	10		3*	12	11	7	6									A Banks	5
1	2		5				8	12	4	10	11	3	9	6	7*										T Fitzharris	6
1	2		5				8	9	4	10	11*		12	6		3	7								J Ball	7
1	2		5				8	9	4	10	11			6		3	7								T Mills	8
1	2		5	6			8	9	4	10			11			3	7*	12							J McAuley	9
1	2		5	6			8	9	4	10			11		7	3									A Robinson	10
1	2		5	6			8	9	4	10			11*	7		3	12								K Walmsley	11
1	2		5*	6			8		4	10		9	11	7		3	12								N Midgeley	12
1	2		5	6			8		4	10*	9		11	7		3	12								J Worrall	13
1	2		5	6			8	10	4		12		11*	7		3			9						M Scott	14
1	2			6			5		4	10			11	7		3	8	9							G Alpin	15
1	2			6			5	10†	4		11		12	7		3	8*	9							L Dilkes	16
1	2			6			5	10	4		11		12	7		3	8*	9							H Taylor	17
1	2			6			5	10	4		11		8	7		3		9							M Peck	18
1	2						5	4*		8		10	13	6		3	11	9	12	7*					D Hutchinson	19
1	2	6					5	4	10	11			7	8	3		9								J Key	20
1	2	6					5	12	4	10	11		7*	8	3		9								M Robinson	21
1	2	6	4				5	10	3	11				7	8		9								C Seel	22
1	2	6	4				5	10	3	11*	12			7	8		9								C Trussell	23
1	2	6	4				5	10	3	11				7	8		9								D Phillips	24
1	2	6	4				5	10	3	11				7	8		9								A Gunn	25
1	2	6	4				5	10	3	11				7	8		9								T Jones	26
1	2	6	4				5	10	3	11				7	8		9								I Hendrick	27
1	2	6	4				5	10	3	11				7	8		9								D Allinson	28
1	2	6	4				5	10	3	11				7	8		9								I Hemley	29
1	2	6		4			5	10*	3	11	12			7	8		9								N Ashley	30
	2	6		4			5	10	3	11				7	8		9			1					M Dimblebee	31
	2	6	5				5	10	3*	11			12	7	8		9			1					R Groves	32
1	2	6*	4				5	10	3	11			12	7	8		9								A Robinson	33
1	2	6	4	3			5			10	9		11			8	7								I Hendrick	34
1	2	6	4	3			5*			10	9		11			8	7	12							D Hedges	35
1	2	6	4	3			5			10	9		11			8	7								V Callow	36
1	2	6	4	3			5			10	9		11			8*	7	12							R Nixon	37
1	2	6	4	3			5				9		11			8	7	10*		12					T Mills	38
	2	6	4	3			5				9			11			7	10		8					P Vanes	39
	2	6	4	3			5				9			10			7	8		11					M Scott	40
1	2	6	4	3			5				9		12	10			7*	8		11					A Saunders	41
1	2	6	4				5		3		9			11			7	10		8					N Ashley	42
1	2	6	4				5		3		10			11			9	8		7					K Hackett	43
	2	6	4				5*		3		10			11			9	8		7	11*	1			M Peck	44
	2	6	4						3		10		9			5	7	8		11*	1				R Guy	45
1	2	6	4				5	9	3				11	10			7	8*	12						N Wilson	46
1	2	6†	4				5	9	3		12		11	10			7		8*						N Butler	47

38	42	1	28	35	19	1	41	26	34	27	21	3	2	21	33	25	9	3	32	9	1	2	7	2	League Appearances	
								2			5		4	5					3		2	1	1		Substitute Appearances	
2	2		1	2		1	2	1·1	2	2	2	2		1·1	1	1									Milk Cup Appearances	
1	1		1		1		1	1	1	1	1	0·1			1	1			1						FA Cup Appearances	
2	2		1	1			2	1	2		1		1·1	2	2		1·1	1	0·1	1					FM Cup Appearances	

Players on Loan: McManus (Bradford), Kite (Southampton)
Departures: Ward, Bell, Roberts (Darlington), Heard (Hull), O'Hanlon (Rotherham), Beagrie (Sunderland)

'THE BORO'

Formed: 1892
Turned Professional: 1889 (amateur 1992-99)   **Ltd Co:** 1892

Previous Managers: Since 1946
David Jack   Walter Rowley   Bob Dennison   Raich Carter   Stan Anderson   Jack Charlton OBE
John Neal   Bobby Murdoch   Willie Maddren
Honours: Champions Div 2, 1926-7, 1928-9, 1973-4   Anglo Scottish Cup Winners 1975-6   FA
Amateur Cup Winners 1895, 1898
League Career: Elected to Div 2 1899   Promoted to Div 1 1901-2
Relegated to Div 2 1923-4   Promoted to Div 1 1926-7   Relegated to Div 2 1953-4
Relegated to Div 3 1965-6   Promoted to Div 2 1966-7   Promoted to Div 1 1973-4
Relegated to Div 2 1981-2   Relegated to Div 3 1985-6
Colours: Red shirts with three narrow stripes down sleeves, red shorts with 'hummel' style white trim
and stockings
Change Colours: All blue with same style white trim

CLUB RECORDS

Most Appearances for Club: Tim Williamson, 563, 1902-23
Most Capped Player: Wilf Manion, 26, England
Record Goalscorer in a Match: Andy Wilson, 5 v Nottingham Forest, Div 1, (h) 5-2 06.10.1953
George Camsell, 5 v Manchester City, Div 2, (a) 5-3, 25.12.1926   George Camsell, 5 v Aston Villa, Div 1, (a) 7-2, 09.09.1935
Brian Clough, 5 v Brighton, Div 2, (h) 9-0, 23.08.1958
Record League Goalscorer in a Season: George Camsell, 59, Div 2, 1926-7 (a record for the division)
Record League Goalscorer in a Career: George Camsell, 326, 1925-39
Record Transfer Fee Received: £600,000 from Southampton for David Armstrong, Aug 1981
Record Transfer Fee Paid: £475,000 to Newcastle for Irving Nattrass, Aug 1979
Best Performances: League: 3rd Div 1 1913-14   **FA Cup:** 6th Round 1935-6, 1946-7, 1969-70, 1976-7, 1977-8, last
eight 1900-1, 1903-4   **League/Milk Cup:** Semi-Final 1975-5
Most League Points: 65, Div 2, 1973-4   **Most League Goals:** 122, Div 2, 1926-7
Record League Victory: 9-0 v Brighton, Div 2, 23 Aug 1958
Record League Defeat: 0-9 v Blackburn Rovers, Div 2, 6 Nov 1954
Oldest Player in League Match:
Youngest Player in League Match:
Most Consecutive Undefeated League Matches: 24 1973-74   **League Matches Without a Win:** 19 1981-82
Longest Run of Undefeated Home League Matches: 27 1936-37   **Away League Matches:** 14 1973-74
Longest Run Without Home League Win: 10 1984-85   **Away League Win:** 33 1903-05
Most Consecutive League Wins: 9 1974   **Home League Wins:** 11 1913-14, 1927
Most Consecutive League Defeats: 8 1954   **Away League Wins:** 5 1974

Club Statistician for the Directory: I Tewson

MIDDLESBROUGH

PLAYERS NAME Ht Wt Birthdate	Honours	Birthplace Transfers	Clubs	League	Milk Cup	FA Cup	Other Comps	League	Milk Cup	FA Cup	Other Comps
GOALKEEPERS											
Steve Pears		Brandon	Manchester United (A)								
6.0 12.0 22.1.62			Middlesbrough	54	2	2	2				
DEFENDERS											
Brian Laws	Div. 3, 82	Wallsend	Burnley	125	14	15		12	2	1	
5.8 11.0 14.10.61		£10,000	Huddersfield Town	56	7	3		1			
		£30,000	Middlesbrough	53	2	1	2	3			
Tony Mowbray		Saltburn	Middlesbrough (A)	133+3	6+2	8	1	8			
6.1 12.2 22.11.63											
Donal O'Riordan	EIU21 (1)	Dublin	Derby County (A)	2+4	0+1		1				
5.11 12.0 14.5.57		£30,000	Doncaster Rovers (L)	2							
		Tulsa Roughnecks	Preston North End	153+5	10		8				
		£30,000	Carlisle United	84	4	2	18				
		£55,000	Middlesbrough	41	2	1	2	2		1	1
Gary Pallister		Ramsgate	Middlesbrough	28	1	1					
6.4 13.0 30.6.65			Darlington (L)	7							
MIDFIELD											
Mitchell Cook			Scarborough								
5.7 10.10 15.10.61			Darlington	3.	1	3	3	4			
			Middlesbrough	3+3			1+1				
Steve Corden		Middlesbrough	Middlesbrough	1							
5.8 10.7 9.1.67											
Gary Gill		Middlesbrough	Middlesbrough (A)	27+2	0+1						
5.10 10.9 28.11.64			Hull City (L)	0+1							
Gary Hamilton		Glasgow	Middlesbrough (A)	101+8	3	6	2	9			
5.9 11.2 27.12.65											
Heine Otto		Holland	F.C. Twente								
6.0 12.0 24.8.54		£125,000	Middlesbrough	163+3	9	12		24	2	1	
Stuart Ripley	EY	Middlesbrough	Middlesbrough (A)	7+2							
5.11½ 12.6 20.11.67											
Gary Rowell	EU21 (1)	Seaham	Sunderland	229+25	19+2	15		88	7	4	
5.10 10.13 6.6.57		F	Norwich City	2+4				1			
		£25,000	Middlesbrough	27	2	1	1	10	2		
FORWARDS											
Colin Cooper		Trimdon	Middlesbrough (A)	9+2			0+1				
5.8 9.3½ 28.2.67											
Alan Kernaghan		York	Middlesbrough (A)	10+4	1+1		1	1			
6.1 12.12½ 25.4.67											
Bernard Slavey			Morton	22				1			
5.10 10.10 13.11.60			Airdrie	2							
			Queen of the South	3							
			Albion Rovers	42				27			
			Middlesbrough	32		1	1	8			1
Archie Stephens		Liverpool	Melksham Town								
5.11 12.7 19.5.54			Bristol Rovers	100+27	9+4	8+1	2+1	40	3	2	1
			Middlesbrough	35+2	1+1	1		6			

ADDITIONAL CONTRACT PROFESSIONALS
Lee Turnbull (1+1Lge/1FRT), Gary Parkinson

APPRENTICES
Kevin Barrow, Peter Duffield, Geoffrey Thompson

NON-CONTRACT PLAYERS
Peter Flear

AYRESOME PARK
Middlesbrough, Cleveland TS1 4PB

Capacity: 42,000

Record Attendance: 53,596 v Newcastle United, Div 1, 27 Dec 1949

Record Receipts: £57,710 v Barnsley, FA Cup Round 5, 14 Feb 1981

Season Tickets: Stands £90 (£40 Juniors/OAP), £75 (£35 Juniors/OAP), South Terrace £55 (£25 Juniors/OAP)

100 Club Tickets: £190 (£100 OAPs & children)

Cost of Stand Tickets: £4.50, £3.00 (adults), £1.70 & £1.50 (OAPs & children

Match and Ticket Information: Postal or personal applications two weeks prior to any match

Car Parking: Off-street near the ground; on-street around the ground

Nearest Railway Station: Middlesbrough (0624 243208)

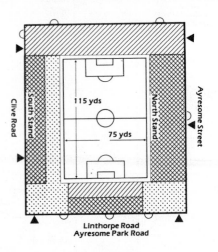

How to get to the ground

From North: Use A19 (S.P. Middlesbrough) cross Tees Bridge and in 0.2m join A66, in 1,5m at roundabout take 3rd exit into Heywood Street, at end turn left in Ayresome Street for Middlesbrough FC

From South: Use A1, and A19 to junction with A1130. In 1m join A66, 1m further at roundabout take 4th exit into Heywood Street, at end turn left into Ayresome Street to Middlesbrough FC

From West: Use A66 (S.P. Middlesbrough) 1.6m after Teeside Park Race Course at roundabout take 4th exit in Heywood Street, at end turn left into Ayresome Street for Middlesbrough FC

Price of 1986-7 Programme: 20p
Number of Pages: 24
Subscriptions: On request from club (£14.00 per season approximately subject to confirmation)

Local Newspapers: Journal, Chronicle, Sunday Sun, Northern Star

Local Radio Stations: Radio Tees, Metro Radio

MILLWALL

Division 2

President
R J Mellish

Chairman
R I Burr

Directors
B E Mitchell
J D Burnige

Chief Executive
Tony Shaw

Secretary
Sylvia Shaw (01-639 3143/4)

Manager
John Docherty

Coach
R Cross

Reserve & Youth Coach
Roger Cross

Chief Scout
Bob Pearson

Commercial Manager
Billy Neill (01-639 4590)

Physiotherapist
Joe Miller

Groundsman
Ernie Godden

In a season when consolidation in the Second Division was probably the best the 'Lions' supporters could have wished for, George Graham's club achieved a respectable ninth position and certainly had some fun in the cup competitions. Sixteen goals in the first six games of the season certainly raised hopes at the Den but this spell was followed by six matches in which only one more goal was scored and that by a defender!

This inconsistency probably prevented Millwall from ever challenging the leaders and indeed it wasn't until the last games of the season that the club lifted itself above a mid-table position.

Cup football was a different matter however and it was Southampton and Peter Shilton in particular who were to play an important part in Millwall's season. Two goalless draws in the Milk Cup when Southampton hardly deserved to survive, finally saw the south coast club win on penalties and then having captured the impressive scalp of Aston Villa in the FA Cup Fourth Round, having eliminated Wimbledon in Round Three, it was 'The Saints' again who just pipped Millwall 1-0 in a replay at the Den after yet another 0-0 draw in Southampton.

Stirring stuff but goals were hard to come by and although Steve Lovell who scored 15 and John Fashanu, before his departure to Wimbledon, teamed up well, another striker will be needed for the coming season. Robert Wilson had an excellent first season in midfield and scored a valuable 12 goals while the consistent Alan McLeary won the supporters 'Player of the Year' award.

The excellent job done by George Graham has earned him the Arsenal manager's position and although the club came through the difficulties thrust on it by a misguided section of their supporters and certainly last season's form was solid enough, it may take another season of hard work and rebuilding under the new leadership to enable 'The Lions' to prepare for a top of the table challenge in the seasons ahead.

Back Row L to R: Dave Mehmet, Alan McLeary, Paul Hinshelwood, Keith Stevens, Alan Walker, Micky Nutton, Michael Marks, Danis Salman. **Middle Row:** Roger Cross (Coach), Nick Chatterton, Nicky Coleman, Paul Sansome, Brian Horne, Teddy Sheringham, Steve Lovell, Joe Miller (Physio). **Front Row:** Darren Morgan, Robert Wilson, David Byrne, John Docherty (Manager), John Leslie, Steve Lowndes, Les Briley. John Leslie and Steve Lowndes are no longer with Millwall F.C.

313

MILLWALL

DIVISION TWO: 9th   **FA CUP:** 5th ROUND   **MILK CUP:** 2nd ROUND

MATCH	DATE	COMPE-TITION	VENUE	OPPONENTS	RESULT	HALF TIME	L'GUE POS'N	GOALSCORERS/GOAL TIMES	ATTEN-DANCE
1	A 17	CL	A	Huddersfield Town	L 3-4	2-0		Fashanu 35, Lovell 37, Lowndes 87	(6,603)
2	21	MC1/1	A	Colchester United	W 3-2	3-1		Lovell (pen) 7, (pen) 10, Fashanu 14	(1,430)
3	24	CL	H	Norwich City	W 4-2	1-1		Kinsella 5, Lovell (pen) 47, Wilson 68, Hinshelwood 77	7,100
4	27	CL	A	Shrewsbury Town	D 1-1	0-0		Roffey 76	(3,008)
5	31	CL	H	Sunderland	W 1-0	1-0	10	Fashanu 30	7,910
6	S 3	MC1/2	H	Colchester United	W 4-1	2-0		Lovell 8, Lowndes 35, Fashanu 72, Leslie 89	(7,187)
7	7	CL	A	Stoke City	D 0-0	0-0	9		8,013
8	14	CL	H	Brighton & H.A.	L 0-1	0-0	12		(6,021)
9	17	CL	A	Hull City	L 0-3	0-1	15		(8,713)
10	21	CL	A	Crystal Palace	L 1-2	1-0	17	Nutton 32	7,958
11	25	MC2/1	H	Southampton	D 0-0	0-0			5,700
12	28	CL	H	Oldham Athletic	L 0-1	0-1	18		1,741
13	O 2	FMC	H	Stoke City	D 2-2	1-0		Fashanu 28, Lovell 54	(9,159)
14	5	CL	A	Sheffield United	W 3-1	2-0	16	Lovell 4, Fashanu 20, 67	(9,480)
15	8	MC2/2	A	Southampton	D 0-0†	0-0		(Southampton win 5-4 on pens)	6,050
16	12	CL	H	Blackburn Rovers	L 0-1	0-1	18		(1,088)
17	15	FMC	A	Coventry City	D 1-1	0-1		Chatterton 85	(4,644)
18	19	CL	A	Wimbledon	D 1-1	1-1	17	Lovell 21	4,522
19	22	CL	H	Carlisle United	W 3-1	1-0	16	Lovell 5, Chatterton (pen) 53, (pen) 89	6,810
20	26	CL	H	Portsmouth	L 0-4	0-2	19		(3,685)
21	N 2	CL	A	Grimsby Town	L 1-5	0-2	19	Chatterton 84	9,158
22	9	CL	H	Leeds United	W 3-1	1-0	17	Lovell (pen) 41, Lowndes 54, Baird (og) 65	3,188
23	25	CL	H	Middlesbrough	W 3-0	2-0	15	Chatterton 17, Briley 21, Lovell 72	(4,340)
24	30	CL	A	Barnsley	L 1-2	0-1	16	Leslie 89	(2,497)
25	D 7	CL	A	Carlisle United	L 0-1	0-0	17		3,645
26	14	CL	H	Huddersfield Town	W 2-1	2-0	16	Lovell (pen) 9, 29	(12,349)
27	21	CL	A	Norwich City	L 1-6	0-4	19	Sherringham 83	
28	28	CL	H	Hull City	W 5-0	1-0	18	Lowndes 15, Walker 49, Wilson 79, 83, Fashanu 89	3,783
29	J 4	FAC3	H	Wimbledon	W 3-1	2-0		Lovell 11, Fashanu 35, Walker 77	5,840
30	11	CL	H	Stoke City	L 2-3	1-2	19	Wilson 31, Lovell 55	4,611
31	18	CL	A	Sunderland	W 2-1	0-0	19	Agboola (og) 55, Fashanu 88	(14,294)
32	25	FAC4	A	Aston Villa	D 1-1	1-1		McLeary 7	(12,205)
33	29	FAC4R	H	Aston Villa	W 1-0	0-0		Fashanu 56	10,273
34	F 1	CL	H	Shrewsbury Town	W 2-0	0-0	17	Wilson (pen) 55, Walker 65	4,487
35	15	FAC5	A	Southampton	D 0-0	0-0			(16,356)
36	M 1	CL	H	Oldham Athletic	D 0-0	0-0	17		(3,482)
37	5	FAC5R	H	Southampton	L 0-1	0-0			10,625
38	8	CL	H	Sheffield United	W 3-0	1-0	17	Hinshelwood 43, Lowndes 73, Walker 77	4,270
39	11	CL	H	Wimbledon	L 0-1	0-0	17		4,634
40	15	CL	A	Blackburn Rovers	W 2-1	1-0	13	Fashanu 11, Lovell 89	(4,336)
41	18	CL	H	Fulham	D 1-1	0-0	13	Fashanu 79	5,645
42	22	CL	A	Brighton & H.A.	L 0-1	0-0	14		(9,370)
43	25	CL	A	Portsmouth	L 1-2	1-2	14	Lovell 25	(9,570)
44	29	CL	H	Charlton Athletic	D 2-2	1-2	13	Lowndes 2, Wilson (pen) 50	7,846
45	31	CL	A	Fulham	W 2-1	1-0	12	Stevens 15, Lovell 85	(4,581)
46	A 5	CL	H	Grimsby Town	W 1-0	1-0	12	Wilson (pen) 40	3,612
47	12	CL	A	Leeds United	L 1-3	1-2	14	Wilson 12	(15,067)
48	15	CL	A	Charlton Athletic	D 3-3	3-2	13	McLeary 3, Wilson 9, 18	(7,861)
49	19	CL	H	Bradford City	W 2-1	1-0	10	Sherringham 24, 73	3,763
50	22	CL	H	Crystal Palace	W 3-2	2-0	10	Lowndes 17, Sherringham 34, Lovell 71	5,618
51	26	CL	A	Middlesbrough	L 0-3	0-1	10		(5,494)
52	30	CL	A	Bradford City	W 2-0	1-0	8	Wilson 38, 73	(3,826)
53	M 3	CL	H	Barnsley	D 2-2	0-1	9	McLeary 49, 54	(4,230)

Best Home League Attendance: 9,158 v Leeds Utd 9/11   **Smallest:** 3,188 v Middlesbrough 25/11   **Av Home Att:** 5,457

Compared with 84-85: −985

Goal Scorers:

League (64): Lovell 14 (3 pen), Wilson 12 (3 pen), Fashanu 8, Lowndes 6, Chatterton 4 (2 pen), McLeary 3, Sherringham 4, Opponents 2, Hinshelwood 2, Walker 3, Briley 1, Leslie 1, Nutton 1, Roffey 1, Stevens 1, Kinsella 1

Milk Cup (7): Lovell 3 (2 pens), Fashanu 2, Lowndes 1, Leslie 1

FA Cup (5): Fashanu 2, Lovell 1, McLeary 1, Walker 1

FM Cup (3): Chatterton 1, Fashanu 1, Lovell 1

†After extra-time

Sansome	Hinshelwood	Roffey	Briley	Smith	Nutton	Lowndes	Wilson	Fashanu	Lovell	Kinsella	McLeary	Leslie	Chatterton	Stevens	Walker	Granville (NC)	Sherringham	Otulakowski	Coleman	Referee	
1	2	3	4	5*	6	7	8	9	10	11	12									G Tyson	1
1	2	3	4		6	7	8	9	10	11	5									I Borrett	2
1	2	3	4		6	7	8	9	10	11	5									Alan Robinson	3
1	2	3	4		6	7	8	9	10	11	5									J Ball	4
1	2	3	4		6	7	8	9	10	11	5									V Callow	5
1	2	3	4		6	7	8	9	10*	11	5	12								J Bray	6
1	2	3	4		6	7	8	9	10	11	5									J Key	7
1	2	3	4		6	7	8	9	10	11*	5	12								R Milford	8
1	2†	3	4		6	7	8	9	10	11*	5		12							A Robinson	9
1	3		4		6	7	8	9	10		5	11*	12	2						J Martin	10
1	3		4	5	6	7	8	9	10	12		11*		2						D Axcell	11
1	3		4	5	6	7	8	9	10*	12		11		2						B Stevens	12
1		3	4	5	6	7		9	10	11			8	2						D Hedges	13
1		3	4	5	6	7		9	10	11			8	2						I Hendrick	14
1		3	4		6	7		9†	10*	11	5	12	8	2						R Gifford	15
1	12	3	4		6	7*		9	10	11	5		8	2						B Hill	16
1	3		4		6	7*		9		11	12	10	8	2	5					P Tyldesley	17
1	3		4		6	7			10	11	12		8*	2	5					A Gunn	18
1	3		4		6	7			10	11	9		8	2	5					J Deakin	19
1	3		4		6	7			10	11	9		8	2	5					P Vanes	20
1	3		4		6			9†	10	11	12	7	8	2	5					N Glover	21
	3		4	5	6*	7			10	11			8	2		1				M Bodenham	22
	3	12	4		6*	7			10		7	9	8	2	5	1		12		M Robinson	23
	3		4	5*	6	7			10	11		9	8	2	5	1				J Lloyd	24
	3		4	5*	6	7			10	11		9	8	2		1		12		R Guy	25
	3		4		6				10		7	12	8*	2	5	1	9	11		A Seville	26
	3		4		6				10		7	12	8*	2	5	1	9	11		V Callow	27
1	3		4		6	7	8	9	10					2	5			11		I Hemley	28
1	3		4		6	7	8	9	10				12	2	5			11*		H King	29
1	2	3	4		6	7	8	9	10						5			11		J Ball	30
1	3	2*	4		6	7	8	9	10				12		5			11		D Phillips	31
1	3				6	7	8	9	10		4			2	5			11		K Hackett	32
1	3				6	7	8	9	10		4			2	5			11		K Hackett	33
1	3		4			7	8	9*	10		6	12		2	5			11		L Shapter	34
1	3		4			7	8	9	10		6			2	5			11		B Hill	35
1	3					7	8	9	10		6		4	2	5			11		A Saunders	36
1	3					7	8	9	10		6		4	2	5			11		B Hill	37
1	3		4			7	8	9	10		6			2	5		12	11*		H Taylor	38
1	3		4			7	8	9	10		6			2	5			11		E Scales	39
1	3		4*			7	8	9	10		6			2	5		12	11		R Bridges	40
1	3*		4			7	8	9	10		6			2	5		12	11		K Baker	41
1	3		4			7*		9	10		6		8	2	5		12	11		R Groves	42
1	3		4				8	9	10		6	7*		2	5		12	11		G Napthine	43
1	3		4			7	8	9	10		6			2	5			11		J Moules	44
1	3		4			7	8	9*	10		6			2	5		12	11		D Vickers	45
1	3		4				8		10		6	9*		2	5		12	11		R Gifford	46
1			4			7	8		10		6			2	5		9	11	3	T Holbrook	47
1	3		4			7	8		10		6	12		2	5		9	11*		D Reeves	48
1			4	5		7	8		10		6			2			9	11	3	M James	49
1			4	5		7	8		10		6			2			9	11	3	B Stevens	50
1			4	5		7	8		10		6			2			9	11	3	N Wilson	51
1				5		7	8		10		6			2	4		9	11	3	T Jones	52
1	12			5*		7	8		10		4			2	6		9	11	3	T Holbrook	53
36	34	11	39	14	22	39	28	25	42	13	32	9	15	33	26	6	9	23	6	League Appearances	
	2									1	3	6	2				9			Substitute Appearances	
4	3	3	4	1	4	4	3	4	4	3·1	3	1·2	1	2						Milk Cup Appearances	
5	5		2		3	5	5	5	5		4		2	5	5		5			FA Cup Appearances	
2	1	1	2	1	2	2		2	1	2	0·1	1	2	2	1					FM Cup Appearances	

Departures: Neal (Southend), Fashanu (Wimbledon), Roffey (Retired), Kinsella (Enfield), Ruddock (Tottenham Hotspur), Otulakowski (Crystal Palace), Smith (Cambridge United)

'THE LIONS'

Formed: 1885
Turned Professional: 1893   **Ltd Co:** 1894

Previous Names: 1885 Millwall Rovers   1889 Millwall Athletic
Previous Managers: The managers before 1909 were directors who were known as 'Honorary Team Managers' and were F B Kidd (1907-8), and G A Sauders (1908-9).   H B Lipsham (signed as player c1909)-1921   1921-33 R Hunter
1933-6 W McCracken   1936-40 C Hewitt   1940-4 W Voisey   1944-8 J Cock   1948-56 C Hewitt
1957-8 R Gray   1958-9 J Seed   1959-61 J R Smith   1961-3 R Gray   1963-6 W Gray
1966-74 B Fenton   1974-7 G Jago   1978-80 G Petchey   1980 B Kitchener (Caretaker)
1980-2 P Anderson   1982 B Kitchener (Caretaker)   1982-86 G Graham
Honours: Champions Div 3 (S), 1927-8   Champions Div 4, 1961-2
League Career: Original Members of Division 3 1920   Transferred to Division 3 (S) 1921
Promoted to Div 2 1927-8   Relegated to Div 3 (S) 1933-4   Promoted to Div 2 1937-8
Relegated to Div 3 (S) 1947-8   Relegated to Div 4 1957-8   Promoted to Div 3 1961-2
Relegated to Div 4 1963-4   Promoted to Div 3 1964-5   Promoted to Div 2 1965-6
Relegated to Div 3 1974-5   Promoted to Div 2 1975-6   Relegated to Div 3 1978-9
Promoted to Div 2 1984-5
Colours: Royal blue shirts, white shorts, blue stockings
Change Colours: All red with white trim
Reserves League: Football Combination **'A' Team:** South East Counties

---

CLUB RECORDS

Most Appearances for Club: Barry Kitchener: Football League 518 + 5 + FA Cup 29 + 2 + League Cup 42 **Total 589 + 7 subs**
Most Capped Player: Eamonn Dunphy, 22, Eire   **For England:** J R Smith and L Graham 2
Record Goalscorer in a Match: Richard Parker, 5 v Norwich City (h), 6-1, Div 3 (S), 28.08.1926
Record League Goalscorer in a Season: Richard Parker, 37, Div 3 (S), 1926-7   **In All Competitions:** Peter Burridge, 39, 1960-1 (League 36 + FA Cup 2 + League Cup 1)
Record League Goalscorer in a Career: Derek Possee, 79, 1967-73   **In All Competitions:** Derek Possee, 87 (League 79 + FA Cup 4 + League Cup 4)
Record Transfer Fee Received: £250,000 from Ipswich Town for Kevin O'Callaghan, Jan 1980
Record Transfer Fee Paid: £150,000 to Barnsley for Trevor Aylott, August 1982
Best Performances: League: 3rd Div 2 1971-2   **FA Cup:** Semi-Final (3) including 1937 when Millwall was the first 3rd Div Club to reach this stage   **League/Milk Cup:** 5th Round 1973-4, 1976-7
Most League Points: (3pts for win) 90, Div 3, 1984-5   (2pts for win) 65, Div 3 (S) 1927-8, 65, Div 3 1965-6
Most League Goals: 127, Div 3 (S), 1927-8
Record League Victory: 9-1 v Torquay United, Div 3 (S), 29 Aug 1927   9-1 v Coventry City, Div 3 (S), 19 Nov 1927
Record League Defeat: 1-8 v Plymouth Argyle
Oldest Player in League Match:
Youngest Player in League Match:
Most Consecutive Undefeated League Matches: 19 1959   **League Matches Without a Win:** 17 1929
Longest Run of Undefeated Home League Matches: 59 1964-66   **Away League Matches:** 10 1921
Longest Run Without Home League Win: 8 1929, 1933, 1967   **Away League Win:** 26 1979-80
Most Consecutive League Wins: 10 1928   **Home League Wins:** 13 1923-24
Most Consecutive League Defeats: 11 1929   **Away League Wins:** 5 1928

Club Statistician for the Directory: R Lindsay

MILLWALL

<table>
<thead>
<tr><th colspan="4"></th><th colspan="4">APPEARANCES</th><th colspan="4">GOALS</th></tr>
<tr>
<th>PLAYERS NAME
Ht Wt Birthdate</th><th>Honours</th><th>Birthplace
Transfers</th><th>Clubs</th>
<th>League</th><th>Milk Cup</th><th>FA Cup</th><th>Other Comps</th>
<th>League</th><th>Milk Cup</th><th>FA Cup</th><th>Other Comps</th>
</tr>
</thead>
<tbody>
<tr><td colspan="12">GOALKEEPERS</td></tr>
<tr><td>John Granville
6.2 12.0</td><td>Trinidad</td><td>Tobago
F</td><td>QPR (NC)
Millwall</td><td>
6</td><td></td><td></td><td></td><td></td><td></td><td></td><td></td></tr>
<tr><td>Paul Sansome
5.11 11.10 6.10.61</td><td></td><td>New Addington
F</td><td>Crystal Palace (A)
Millwall</td><td>
145</td><td>
10</td><td>
13</td><td>
8</td><td></td><td></td><td></td><td></td></tr>
<tr><td colspan="12">DEFENDERS</td></tr>
<tr><td>Nick Coleman
5.9 11.2 6.5.61</td><td></td><td>Crayford</td><td>Millwall (A)</td><td>6+1</td><td></td><td></td><td>4</td><td></td><td></td><td></td><td></td></tr>
<tr><td>Mickey Nutton
5.11 10.12 3.10.59</td><td></td><td>St Johns Wood

£65,000</td><td>Chelsea (A)
Reading (L)
Millwall</td><td>77+2
6
81+1</td><td>1

10</td><td>3

5</td><td>

9</td><td>

4</td><td></td><td></td><td>

2</td></tr>
<tr><td>Paul Hinshelwood
6.0 12.6 14.5.56</td><td>EU21 (12)
Div. 2, 79, Div.
3, 84, FAYC 72</td><td>Bristol
F
F</td><td>Crystal Palace (A)
Oxford United
Millwall</td><td>271+5
45
55+2</td><td>18
11
3</td><td>24
7
8</td><td>
1
2</td><td>23

2</td><td>2
1</td><td>1</td><td></td></tr>
<tr><td>Danis Salman
5.10 11.8 12.3.60</td><td>EY</td><td>Famagusta</td><td>Brentford (A)
Millwall</td><td>316+9</td><td>16+1</td><td>16+1</td><td>10</td><td>8</td><td></td><td></td><td></td></tr>
<tr><td>Keith Stevens
6.0 12.5 21.6.64</td><td></td><td>Merton</td><td>Millwall (A)</td><td>124+1</td><td>7</td><td>12</td><td>8</td><td>1</td><td></td><td></td><td></td></tr>
<tr><td>Alan Walker
6.1 12.2 17.12.59</td><td>FAT 83</td><td>Ashton-u-Lyme

£32,500</td><td>Stockport Co.
Telford United
Lincoln City
Millwall</td><td>

32+1
26</td><td>

2</td><td>
4
4
5</td><td>

4
1</td><td>

4
3</td><td></td><td>
1
1
1</td><td></td></tr>
<tr><td>Alan McLeary+
5.10 10.9 6.10.64</td><td>EY</td><td>London</td><td>Millwall (A)</td><td>75+14</td><td>4+1</td><td>10+1</td><td>9+1</td><td>4</td><td></td><td>2</td><td>2</td></tr>
<tr><td colspan="12">MIDFIELD</td></tr>
<tr><td>Les Briley*
5.6 9.11 2.10.56</td><td></td><td>Lambeth
F
£18,000
£43,000
Player exch.</td><td>Chelsea (A)
Hereford United
Wimbledon
Aldershot
Millwall</td><td>
60+1
59+2
157
72</td><td>
3+1
4+1
11
7</td><td>
2
8+1
6
7</td><td>

1
2</td><td>
2
2
3
1</td><td></td><td></td><td></td></tr>
<tr><td>Nicky Chatterton
5.9 11.0 18.5.54</td><td>Div. 2, 79</td><td>Norwood
£100,000</td><td>Crystal Palace
Millwall</td><td>142+9
258+6</td><td>15
18</td><td>15
19+2</td><td>
6</td><td>31
56</td><td>3
4</td><td>2
5</td><td>
1</td></tr>
<tr><td>Dave Mehmet
5.9 11.9 2.12.60</td><td>FAYC 79</td><td>London
£120,000
£80,000
F
F</td><td>Millwall (A)
Tampa Bay Rowdies
Charlton
Gillingham
Millwall</td><td>97+17

29
128+4</td><td>6+1

1
8+1</td><td>9+1

11</td><td>

2+1</td><td>15

2
39</td><td></td><td>

3</td><td></td></tr>
<tr><td colspan="12">FORWARDS</td></tr>
<tr><td>Dave Byrne
5.8 11.10 5.3.61</td><td></td><td>London

F</td><td>Kingstonian
Gillingham
Millwall</td><td>
18+7</td><td></td><td></td><td></td><td>

3</td><td></td><td></td><td></td></tr>
<tr><td>John Leslie
5.8 11.2 25.10.55</td><td></td><td>London

£10,000
£5,000</td><td>Dulwich Hamlet
Wimbledon
Gillingham
Millwall</td><td>
242+11
60+5
9+6</td><td>
20+1
6
1+2</td><td>
14+2
8</td><td>

2
1</td><td>
86
12
1</td><td>
10
1
1</td><td>
5
4</td><td></td></tr>
<tr><td>Steve Lovell
5.9 11.13 16.7.60</td><td>W (4)</td><td>Swansea

F</td><td>Crystal Palalce (A)
Stockport Co. (L)
Millwall</td><td>68+4
12
143+3</td><td>10+1

12</td><td>1+1

14</td><td>

6</td><td>3

43</td><td>1

5</td><td>

6</td><td>

3</td></tr>
<tr><td>Steve Lowndes
5.7 10.7 17.6.60</td><td>W (6), U21 (4)</td><td>Cwmbran
£55,000</td><td>Newport County
Millwall</td><td>200+8
95+1</td><td>10+1
9</td><td>12
12</td><td>
3</td><td>29
16</td><td>2
2</td><td></td><td></td></tr>
<tr><td>Ed Sherringham
5.10½ 12.4 2.4.66</td><td>EY</td><td>London</td><td>Millwall (A)
Aldershot (L)</td><td>13+12
4+1</td><td>0+1</td><td>
</td><td>1+2
1</td><td>5</td><td></td><td></td><td>1</td></tr>
</tbody>
</table>

ADDITIONAL CONTRACT PROFESSIONALS

APPRENTICES

Brian Horne (G), David Thompson, Paul Malcolm (F) 0+1 FRT, Darren Morgan (D) 1 FRT, Mike Marks (F), Steve Middleton (MF)

NON-CONTRACT PLAYERS

Sean Sparham, Steve Anthrobus, Paul Malcolm

Record Attendance: 48,672 v Derby County, FA Cup Round 5, 20 Feb 1937

Record Receipts: £52,637 v Leicester City, FA Cup Round 5, 19 Feb 1985

Season Tickets: £95 to £114 (adults stand), £67 to £80 (OAP/juveniles stand); £66 (adult ground) £47 (juvenile/OAP ground); £262 (wing forecourt, 2 adults, 2 children); £178 (wing forecourt, 1 adult, 2 children)

Executive Box Season Tickets: Executive Club £260 per annum (usual VP facilities and car park)

Cost of Stand Tickets: £5.00, £6.00; **Terraces:** £3.50 (£2.50 juveniles/OAP on production of Pensions/Bus Pass)

Match and Ticket Information: Bookable 10-14 days in advance from club office

Car Parking: Good street parking. Also car park near the ground

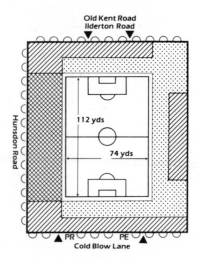

How to get to the ground

From North: From Motorway M1 and A1 follow signs London A1 then City, then follow signs Shoreditch, Whitechapel. Then follow signs Ring Road, Dover to Cross Tower Bridge. In 1m at roundabout take 1st exit A2. In 1.8m turn left into Avonley Road then take 3rd turning right into Edric Road, at end turn right then turn left into Cold Blow Lane for Millwall FC

From East: Use A2 S.P. London. At New Cross follow signs City, Westminster, into Kender Street and at end keep forward into Avonley Road. Take 3rd turning right into Edric Road. At end turn right then left into Cold Blow Lane for Millwall FC

From South: Use A20 and A21 S.P. London. At New Cross follow signs City, Westminster, into Kender Street, and at end keep forward into Avonley Road then take 3rd turning right into Edric Road. At end turn right then left into Cold Blow Lane for Millwall FC

From West: From Motorway M4 and M3 take South Circular Road A205. Then follow signs Clapham, City A3 then signs Camberwell, New Cross and later Rochester A202 and in 0.8m turn left into Kender Street and at end forward into Avonley Road. Take 3rd turning right into Edric Road, at end turn right then left into Cold Blow Lane for Millwall FC

Price of 1986-7 Programme: 60p
Number of Pages: 24
Subscriptions: £16.50 per season

Local Newspapers: South London Press, South East London Mercury

Local Radio Station: LBC

NEWCASTLE UNITED · Division 1

The dramatic pre-season resignation of manager Jack Charlton caused a stir at St James Park but the situation was resolved by appointing his right-hand man, Willie McFaul, as caretaker-manager. After the team's successful start, Mr McFaul was given the job on a permanent basis.

Following the departure of Chris Waddle to Spurs, cash was available for team-building and some of this was used in the acquisition of two international players—Alan Davies (Wales), from Manchester United, and Ian Stewart (N Ireland), from QPR.

With Peter Beardsley producing some sparkling displays, and the new players settling quickly, the team got off to a fine start. A morale-boosting home win over Liverpool started a run of three successive victories, a sequence that took the club into fourth place in the First Division.

It was unfortunate for the Magpies that Manchester United had made such a breath-taking start, otherwise they might have gone right to the top.

The first defeat was, in fact, sustained at Old Trafford and, when they were beaten 1-5 at Tottenham, it seemed the team had lost its confidence. But this was soon restored with good home wins over WBA (4-1) and Oxford (3-0).

Mr McFaul was not happy with his defence, though, so he signed left-back John Bailey from Everton.

The manager was also anxious to give Beardsley more support up front and in December he signed the big Billy Whitehurst from Hull City. To make way for him, George Reilly moved on to WBA.

As expected, Whitehurst took a little while to settle into First Division football but, towards the end of the season, he began to score at almost the same rate as he had done for Hull.

Beardsley remained the club's chief goalscorer and it was no surprise when England manager Bobby Robson eventually felt he could be an asset to our World Cup campaign. Peter really played his way into Mr Robson's heart with a fine display against the USSR in Tbilisi and he later proved one of England's biggest successes in Mexico.

February marked the start of a new surge of success. A run of five successive victories sent the club into the top half of the table and there they remained for the rest of the season.

One of the most remarkable games took place at West Ham towards the end of the season. The Hammers were challenging strongly for the Championship so the Magpies expected no sympathy when injuries caused them to use three players in goal as West Ham ran up an 8-1 victory.

Sadly, Newcastle enjoyed little success in Cup competitions. They defeated Barnsley on the away-goals-double rule in the second round of the Milk Cup but then went out to the eventual winners at Oxford (1-3). In the FA Cup they were beaten at home by Brighton in round three.

Back Row L to R: Colin Suggett (Coach), Ken Wharton, Brian Tinnion, Martin Thomas, Jeff Clarke, Billy Whitehurst, Tony Cunningham, Neil McDonald, Joe Allon, Gary Kelly, Paul Stephenson, John Anderson, Derek Wright (Physio). **Front Row:** Paul Gascoigne, John Bailey, Paul Ferris, Peter Beardsley, Willie McFaul (Manager), Glenn Roeder (Captain), David McCreery, Ian Stewart, Alan Davies.

NEWCASTLE UNITED

DIVISION ONE: 11th   **FA CUP:** 3rd ROUND   **MILK CUP:** 3rd ROUND

MATCH	DATE		COMPE-TITION	VENUE	OPPONENTS	RESULT		HALF TIME	L'GUE POS'N	GOALSCORERS/GOAL TIMES	ATTEN-DANCE
1	A	17	CL	A	Southampton	D	1-1	0-1		Beardsley (pen) 49	(16,401)
2		21	CL	H	Luton Town	D	2-2	0-1		Beardsley 72, Roeder 76	21,304
3		24	CL	H	Liverpool	W	1-0	0-0	8	Reilly 68	29,670
4		26	CL	A	Coventry City	W	2-1	0-0	6	Reilly 87, Stewart 89	(12,047)
5		31	CL	H	Q.P.R.	W	3-1	1-0	4	McDonald 21, Reilly 64, Beardsley 65	(25,026)
6	S	4	CL	A	Manchester United	L	0-3	0-2	6		(51,102)
7		7	CL	A	Tottenham Hotspur	L	1-5	1-2	8	Davies 5	(23,883)
8		14	CL	H	W.B.A.	**W**	**4-1**	2-0	6	McDonald 14, Clarke 25, Reilly 52, 66	21,885
9		21	CL	H	Oxford United	W	3-0	0-0	4	Beardsley 60, McDonald 70, Gascoigne 90	23,596
10		25	MC2/1	H	Barnsley	D	0-0	0-0			18,544
11		28	CL	A	Arsenal	D	0-0	0-0	4		(24,104)
12	O	5	CL	H	West Ham United	L	1-2	0-2	7	Reilly 84	26,709
13		8	MC2/2	A	Barnsley	D	1-1†	1-0		Cunningham 1, New'le win on away goals	(10,084)
14		12	CL	A	Ipswich Town	D	2-2	1-2	8	Beardsley 43, McDonald 54	(12,537)
15		19	CL	H	Nottingham Forest	L	0-3	0-1	10		23,151
16		26	CL	A	Aston Villa	W	2-1	1-1	9	Gascoigne 4, Beardsley 77	(12,033)
17		30	MC3	A	Oxford United	L	1-3	1-1		Cunningham 37	(8,096)
18	N	2	CL	H	Watford	D	1-1	0-1	8	Gascoigne 87	20,649
19		9	CL	A	Birmingham City	W	1-0	1-0	8	Reilly 12	(8,162)
20		16	CL	H	Chelsea	L	1-3	1-1	8	Roeder 1	22,355
21		23	CL	A	Manchester City	L	0-1	0-1	11		25,179
22		30	CL	H	Leicester City	W	2-1	2-0	9	Clarke 1, Beardsley 15	17,304
23	D	7	CL	A	Luton Town	L	0-2	0-1	9		(10,319)
24		14	CL	H	Southampton	W	2-1	1-0	9	Roeder 27, Beardsley 79	19,229
25		21	CL	A	Liverpool	D	1-1	1-1	9	Beardsley 22	(30,746)
26		26	CL	A	Sheffield Wednesday	D	2-2	0-1	10	Roeder 53, Beardsley 73	(30,269)
27	J	1	CL	H	Everton	D	2-2	0-2	11	Gasgoigne 59, Beardsley 73	27,820
28		3	FAC3	H	Brighton & H.A.	L	0-2	0-1			24,643
29		11	CL	A	W.B.A.	D	1-1	1-0	10	Wharton 35	(9,100)
30		18	CL	H	Q.P.R.	L	1-3	0-2	11	Gascoigne 73	(14,159)
31	F	1	CL	H	Coventry City	W	3-2	2-1	11	Beardsley 13, Allon 36, Wharton 78	16,637
32		8	CL	A	Nottingham Forest	W	2-1	0-0	10	Beardsley 66, 73	(15,388)
33	M	1	CL	H	Arsenal	W	1-0	0-0	10	Roeder 81	21,860
34		15	CL	H	Ipswich Town	W	3-1	0-1	10	Beardsley 69, Whitehurst 83, Gasgoigne 88	18,851
35		19	CL	A	Oxford United	W	2-1	1-0		Gascoigne 31, Beardsley 62	(10,052)
36		22	CL	H	Tottenham Hotspur	D	2-2	1-1	9	Whitehurst 17, Anderson 66	30,615
37		29	CL	A	Everton	L	0-1	0-1	9		(41,116)
38		31	CL	H	Sheffield Wednesday	W	4-1	3-0	9	Stephenson 9, Gasgoigne 34, Beardsley 36, Whitehurst 46	25,614
39	A	5	CL	A	Watford	L	1-4	0-2	10	McClelland (og) 81	(14,706)
40		9	CL	H	Aston Villa	D	2-2	1-1	10	Whitehurst 18, Gascoigne 79	20,107
41		12	CL	H	Birmingham City	W	4-1	1-0	9	Beardsley 14, 64, Anderson 79, Whitehurst 88	19,981
42		16	CL	H	Manchester United	L	2-4	1-3	10	Stewart 20, Cunningham 72	15,390
43		19	CL	A	Chelsea	D	1-1	1-1	10	Anderson 44	(18,970)
44		21	CL	A	West Ham United	L	1-8	0-4	11	Whitehurst 76	(24,735)
45		26	CL	H	Manchester City	W	3-1	0-1	10	Clarke 78, Roeder 80, Whitehurst 89	22,689
46	M	3	CL	A	Leicester City	L	0-2	0-0	11		(13,170)

Best Home League Attendance: 30,615 v Tottenham H.   **Smallest:** 15,390 v Manchester Utd   **Av Home Att:** 22,402

Goal Scorers: **Compared with 84-85:** −3,644

League (67):	Beardsley 19 (1 pen), Gascoigne 9, Reilly 7, Whitehurst 7, Roeder 6, McDonald 4, Anderson 3, Clarke 3, Stewart 2, Wharton 2, Allon 1, Cunningham 1, Stephenson 1, Opponent 1, Davies 1
Milk Cup (2):	Cunningham 2
FA Cup (-):	

†After extra time

1985-86

Thomas	Anderson	Wharton	Davies	Clarke	Roeder	McDonald	Megson	Reilly	Beardsley	Gascoigne	McCreery	Stewart	McKinnon	Hedworth	Haddock	Cunningham	Bailey	Allon	Whitehurst	Stephenson	McKellar (L)	Referee	
1	2	3	4	5	6	7	8	9	10	11*	12											D Hedges	1
1	2	3		5	6	7	8*	9	10	4	12	11										I Hendrick	2
1	2	3		5	6	7		9	10	4	8	11										J Key	3
1	2	3		5	6	7		9	10	4	8	11										R Dilkes	4
1	2	3		5	6	7	12	9	10	4	8	11*										T Fitzharris	5
1	2	3		5	6	7		9	10	4	8	11										D Hutchinson	6
1	2		4	5	3	7		9	10	12	8	11	6*									Alan Robinson	7
1	3		4	5	6	7		9	10	12	8*	11		2								K Walmsley	8
1	3		4	5	6	7		9	10	12	8	11		2*								T Simpson	9
1	**12**		**4**	**5**	**6**	**7**		**9***	**10**	**8**	**3**	**11**			**2**							**C Seel**	**10**
1	3		4	5	6	7			10		8	11			2	9						K Barratt	11
1	3		4	5	6	7		9	10		8	11			2							D Scott	12
1	**3**		**4**	**5**	**6**	**7**		**9**			**8**	**11**			**2**	**10**						**M Dimblebee**	**13**
1	3		4	5	6	7		9	10		8	11			2							N Butler	14
1	3		4	5	6	7		9	10		8	11			2*	12						N Wilson	15
1	2		4	5	7		12	9*	8	11	6	10					3					N Glover	16
1	**3**	**12**	**5**	**6**	**7**	**2**		**10**	**8***	**4**	**11**					**9**						**J Bray**	**17**
1	2			5	6	7*		9	10	11	4	12					3					T Mills	18
1	3	2		5	6	12		9	10	7	4	11*						8				R Bridges	19
1	2	11		5	6			9	10	7	4*	12					3	8				N Midgley	20
1	2	11	8	5	6	12		9	10	7*	4						3					M Heath	21
1	4	8	2	5	6	7			10			11				9	3					J McAuley	22
1	7	8	2	5	6				10		4	11					3		9			D Vickers	23
1	2	11	8	5	6				10		4						3		9	7		D Allinson	24
1	2			5	6				10	8	4	11					3		9	7		K Hacken	25
1	2			5	6				10	8	4	11					3		9	7		G Napthine	26
1	2			5	6				10	8	4	11					3		9	7		C Seel	27
1	**2**			**5**	**6**				**10**	**8**	**4**	**11**					**3**		**9**	**7**		**J Key**	**28**
1	2	11		5	6				10	8	4						3		9	7		P Tyldesley	29
1	2	11		5	6	12			10	8	4						3		9	7*		K Miller	30
1	2	11		5	6	12			10	8*	4						3		9			R Dilkes	31
1	2	11		5	6				10	8	4					9	3			7		J Lloyd	32
1	2	11		5	6				10*	8	4					12	3		9	7		N Midgley	33
	2			5	6	11*			10	8	4					12	3		9	7	1	K Walmsley	34
	2			5	6				10	8	4					11	3		9	7	1	M Cotton	35
	2			5	6				10	8	4					11	3		9	7	1	K Breen	36
	2			5	6				10	8	4	11					3		9	7	1	M Heath	37
	2			5	6				10	8	4	11*				12	3		9	7	1	M Peck	38
	2			5	6				10	8	4	11*				12	3		9	7	1	M Reed	39
				5	6				10	8	4	11*		2		12	3		9	7	1	D Scott	40
1	2			5	6	11			10	8†	4						3		9	7		N Glover	41
1				5	6	2			10	8*	4	11				12	3		9	7		T Mills	42
	8			5	6	2			10		4					11	3		9	7	1	J Deakin	43
1*				5	6	2			10		4	12	8			11	3		9	7		T Hamer	44
				5	6	2			10		4				8	11	3		9	7	1	J McAuley	45
				5	6	2			10		4	11			8		3		9	7	1	G Ashby	46
32	38	15	14	41	**42**	23	2	17	**42**	28	39	25	1	4	6	9	28	3	21	22	10	League Appearances	
						4	2			3	2	3				7						Substitute Appearances	
3	2·1		2·1	3	3	3	1	2	2	2	3	3			2	2						Milk Cup Appearances	
1	1			1	1				1	1	1	1					1		1	1		FA Cup Appearances	

Also Played:

Players on Loan: McKellar (Hibernian)

Departures: Reilly (W.B.A.), Megson (Sheff W), Haddock (Leeds U), Hedworth (Barnsley), Saunders (Carlisle U), Heard (Middlesbrough)

'THE MAGPIES'

Formed: 1882
Turned Professional: 1889 **Ltd Co:** 1890

Previous Names: Until 1892 Newcastle East End
Previous Managers: Since 1946
George Martin   Duggie Livingstone   Charlie Mitten   Norman Smith 1961-62   Joe Harvey
Gordon Lee   Richard Dinnis   Bill McGarry   Arthur Cox
Honours: Champions Div 1, 1904-5, 1906-7, 1908-9, 1926-7   Champions Div 2, 1964-5
FA Cup Winners 1910, 1924, 1932, 1951, 1952, 1955   European Fairs Cup Winners 1968-9   Anglo Italian Cup Winners 1973   Texaco Cup Winners 1973-4, 1974-5
League Career: Elected to Div 2 1893   Promoted to Div 1 1897-8   Relegated to Div 2 1933-4
Promoted to Div 1 1947-8   Relegated to Division 2 1960-1   Promoted to Div 1 1964-5
Relegated to Div 2 1977-8   Promoted to Div 1 1983-4
Colours: Black and white striped shirts, black shorts and black stockings with two white hoops on tops
Change Colours: All silver/grey
Reserves League: Central   **Youth Team:** Northern Intermediate

---

CLUB RECORDS

Most Appearances for Club: Jim Lawrence: **Total 432**, 1904-22
Most Capped Player: Alf McMichael, 40, N Ireland   **For England:** Malcolm Macdonald 14
Record Goalscorer in a Match: Len Shackleton, 6 v Newport County, Div 2, 05.10.46 (his debut)
Record League Goalscorer in a Season: Hughie Gallacher 36 Div 1, 1926-7
Record League Goalscorer in a Career: Jackie Milburn, 177, 1946-57
Record Transfer Fee Received: £590,000 from Tottenham Hotspur for Chris Waddle, July 1985
Record Transfer Fee Paid: £250,000 to West Bromwich Albion for John Trewick, Dec 1980
Best Performances: League: Champions (4)   **FA Cup:** Winners (6)   **League/Milk Cup:** Finalists 1975-6
Most League Points: (3 points for win) 80, Div 2, 1983-4   (2 points for win) 57, Div 2, 1964-5
Record League Victory: 13-0 v Newport County, Div 2, 5 Oct 1946
Record League Defeat: 0-9 v Burton Wanderers, Div 2, 15 Apr 1895
European Competitions Entered: European Fairs Cup 1968-9, 1969-70, 1970-1   UEFA Cup 1977-8   Anglo-Italian Cup Winners 1973
Oldest Player in League Match: William Hampson 41 yrs 2 months
Youngest Player in League Match: Neil McDonald, 16 yrs 326 days

Most Consecutive Undefeated League Matches: 14 1950	**League Matches Without a Win:** 21 1978
Longest Run of Undefeated Home League Matches: 31 1905-07	**Away League Matches:** 10 1907-08
Longest Run Without Home League Win: 12 1977-78	**Away League Win:** 17 1967-68
Most Consecutive League Wins: 7 1904, 1909, 1964-65	**Home League Wins:** 20 1906-07
Most Consecutive League Defeats: 10 1977	**Away League Wins:** 5 1909

Club Statistician for the Directory: F Evans

NEWCASTLE UNITED

PLAYERS NAME Ht Wt Birthdate	Honours	Birthplace Transfers	Clubs	APPEARANCES League	Milk Cup	FA Cup	Other Comps	GOALS League	Milk Cup	FA Cup	Other Comps
GOALKEEPERS											
Martin Thomas 6.1 13.0 28.11.59	WU21 (2)	Senghenydd	Bristol Rovers (A)	162	12	9					
			Cardiff City (L)	15	4						
			Southend United (L)	6							
			Newcastle United	76	5	2					
			Middlesbrough (L)	4							
Gary Kelly 5.11 12.3	FAYC 85	Preston	Newcastle United (A)								
DEFENDERS											
John Anderson 5.11 11.6 7.11.59	EI (8), U21 (3), Y	Dublin £40,000 F	WBA (A)								
			Preston North End	47+4	2	1					
			Newcastle United	141+6	10+1	6		6			
John Bailey 5.8 11.3 1.4.57	FAC 84, Div. 1, 85, CS 84, 85, ECWC 85	Liverpool £300,000	Blackburn Rovers (A)	115+5	8	8					
			Everton	173	20	23	4	3			
			Newcastle United	28		1					
Jeff Clarke 5.10½ 13.8 18.1.54	Div 2 76	Pontefract £100,000 F	Manchester City	13	2						
			Sunderland	178+3	14	15		6			
			Newcastle United	117	5	3		4			
			Brighton (L)	4	1	2					
Glenn Roeder* 6.2½ 12.8 13.12.58	EB (6)	Woodford £250,000 £125,000	Orient (A)	107+8	8	13		4			
			QPR	157	13	11		17		1	
			Notts County (L)	4							
			Newcastle United	101	6	1		6			
Ken Wharton 5.8 9.0 28.11.60		Newcastle	Newcastle United	190+16	10+1	12		23	1		
MIDFIELD											
Alan Davies 5.8 10.8 5.12.61	W (8), U21 (6), FAC 83	Manchester	Manchester United	6			2	1			
			Newcastle United	14	2+1						
Paul Gascoigne 5.10 11.7 27.5.67	FAYC 85	Gateshead	Newcastle United (A)					9			
David McCreery 5.6½ 10.7 16.9.57	NI (56), U21 (1), YS	Belfast £200,000 £125,000 £80,000	Manchester United (A)	48+39	4	1		7	1		
			QPR					4	1		
			Tulsa Roughnecks								
			Newcastle United	136+6	11	2+1		1			
Neil McDonald 5.11 11.4 2.11.65	EY, S	Wallsend	Newcastle United (A)	84+15	7	2+1		13	2		
FORWARDS											
Joe Allon 5.11 11.2 12.11.66	EY, FAYC 85	Gateshead	Newcastle United (YTS)	4				1			
Peter Beardsley+ 5.8 11.7 18.1.61	E (9)	Newcastle £275,000 £150,000	Carlisle United	93+4	6+1	15		22		7	
			Vancouver Whitecaps								
			Manchester United (L)								
			Newcastle United	114+1	7	2+1		13	2		
Tony Cunningham 6.1 13.2 12.11.57		Jamaica £20,000 £85,000	Stourbridge								
			Lincoln City	111+12	13	5+1		32	7		
			Barnsley	40+2	4	5+1		11			
			Sheffield Wednesday	26+2							
			Manchester City	16+2	5	0+1		2	3		
			Newcastle United	22+7	2			2	2		
Ian Stewart 5.6½ 11.9 10.9.61	NI (29), Y, S, Div. 2, 83	Belfast	QPR	55+11	3+3	2+1		2			
			Millwall (L)	10+1	3		2+1	3			
			Newcastle United	25+3	3	1		2			
Billy Whitehurst 6.0 13.0 10.6.59		Thurnscoe £1,500	Mexborough								
			Hull City	176+17	13+1	10	7	47	5	3	1
			Newcastle United	21		1		7			

ADDITIONAL CONTRACT PROFESSIONALS
Paul Ferris (M), Kevin Scott, Brian Tinnion, Tony Nesbit, Ian Bogie, Peter Harback, Paul Stephenson, Paul Rutherford, Neil Wilson.

APPRENTICES
Stuart Dickenson, Jeff Wrightson

NON-CONTRACT PLAYERS
Kevin Caizley, Philip Coxall, Chris Hutchinson, Michael Robinson, Paul Thompson, Paul Watson

ST. JAMES' PARK   Newcastle-upon-Tyne NE1 4ST   **Capacity:** 36,581

Record Attendance: 68,386 v Chelsea, Div 1, 3 Sept 1930

Record Receipts: £83,000 v Liverpool (Kevin Keegan Farewell Match), 17 May 1984

Season Tickets: £130 (£80 juvenile), £110 (£75 juvenile), £63.50 (£40 juvenile); West Stand: £130 (£80 juvenile) £115 (£75 juvenile), £85 (£65 juvenile); East Stand: £50 (£25 juvenile) family enclosure

Executive Box Season Tickets: All Sold

Cost of Stand Tickets: £3.50, £5.75, £6.75, (£4.25, £4.75 OAP/juveniles); West Stand: £4.75, £6.00, £6.75 (£3.75, £4.25, £4.75 OAP/juveniles) East Stand: **Terraces:** £3.00 (£1.50 OAP/juveniles); **Paddocks:** £3.00 (£1.50 OAP/juveniles)

Match and Ticket Information: Postal applications 14 days before each match, personal ten days before each

Car Parking: Parking on the north side of the ground. Also street parking is permitted

Nearest Railway Station: Central Station (091-232 6262)

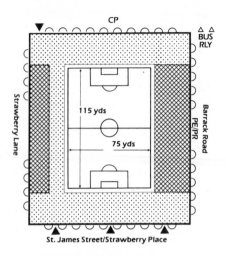

St. James Street/Strawberry Place

How to get to the ground

From North: Use A1 into Newcastle then follow sign Hexham into Percy Street, then turn right into Leaze Park Road (or turn left then right into St James' Street) for Newcastle United FC

From South: Use A1, A68 and then A6127, cross River Tyne and at roundabout take 1st exit into Mosley Street. One-way keep to left hand lane into Neville Street. At end turn right into Clayton Street for Newgate Street. Then turn left into Leaze Park Road (one-way) turn left then right into St. James' Street for Newcastle United FC

From West: Use A69 (S.P. Newcastle) enter city centre then turn left into Clayton Street for Newgate Street. Then turn into Leaze Park Road (one-way) turn left then right into St. James' Street for Newcastle United FC

Price of 1986-7 Programme:
Number of Pages:
Subscriptions:

Local Newspapers: Newcastle Chronicle, Newcastle Journal, Sunday Sun, Northern Echo, South Shields Gazette

Local Radio Stations: Metro Radio, Radio Newcastle, Radio Tees

NEWPORT COUNTY Division 3

Chairman
A O Menzies

Directors
G P Prosser
J Turner

Secretary
K Saunders (0633 277543/277271/
277472)

General Manager
R A Ford

Player/Manager
Jimmy Mullen

Player Coach
Leighton James

Physiotherapist
D Williams

**Youth Development Officer/
Chief Scout**
R Skyrme

Commercial Manager
P Jones (0633 277472)

N ot for the first time Newport County flattered to deceive and the 1985-86 season provided another example of this. A sound enough start in the 3rd Division, with second place beingh achieved early in September, was followed by a period when not a single match was won out of fifteen played in the League—nine were drawn! Wolves were then beaten, but more draws in the Old Year left a dangerous position of 20th, which was still the situation with six games left.

At this stage three wins and three draws brought relief and a rise to the final position of 19th, but it was far too close for comfort and the traumas were not relieved by cup successes. Particularly galling was the Welsh Cup elimination at the hands of Kidderminster Harriers. The Milk Cup 1st Round produced defeat on aggregate against Bristol Rovers (1-2), but in the FA Cup things were better with an early win at Southend by a single Mardenborough goal, which brought Torquay to Somerton Park and a tie which ended in extra-time at Plainmoor with James scoring the seventh goal of the epic to take County through to face Sunderland at Roker Park. There the run ended (0-2).

Being a Newport County fan is none too rewarding these days and fans will hope that the club with no worthwhile funds can find the right blend of players to avoid joining the rest of the Welsh clubs in Division 4. At least they can claim the dubious distinction of being the senior Welsh club in terms of League situation, but that is hardly a 'big deal'.

Jimmy Mullen manages a club, whose most consistent players were all in defence or midfield; the strike force only managed 52 League goals. Kendall played well in goal and the evergreen John Relish as usual gave of his best. Boyle, Carter, Mardenborough and Staniforth were really the only others to show any signs of being first-team reliables, so without some kind of injection of new talent the future must remain bleak.

Back Row L to R: Mick Vinter, Steve Berry, Steve Mardenborough, Mark Kendall, Roger Freestone, Roy Carter, Roger Gibbins, Lyndon Jones. **Front Row:** Tony Bolton, Darren Peacock, John Lewis, Jimmy Mullen (Player Manager), Peter Jones, Sean Mills, Gordon Staniforth.

NEWPORT COUNTY

DIVISION THREE: 19th **FA CUP:** 3rd ROUND **MILK CUP:** 1st ROUND

MATCH	DATE	COMPE-TITION	VENUE	OPPONENTS	RESULT	HALF TIME	L'GUE POS'N	GOALSCORERS/GOAL TIMES	ATTEN-DANCE
1	A 17	CL	H	Doncaster Rovers	D 2-2	1-2		Boyle 20, Carter (pen) 63	2,375
2	20	MC1/1	A	Bristol Rovers	L 0-2	0-1			(2,777)
3	24	CL	A	Wolverhampton W.	W 2-1	1-0	6	Miles 15, 80	(6,073)
4	26	CL	H	Cardiff City	L 1-2	0-1		Carter 46	(5,027)
5	31	CL	A	Bournemouth	W 1-0	0-0	8	Carter 59	(3,381)
6	S 3	MC1/2	H	Bristol Rovers	W 1-0	1-0		Reck 23	2,012
7	7	CL	H	Bristol Rovers	W 3-0	1-0	2	James 45, Staniforth 65, Dowman 77	2,775
8	14	CL	A	Plymouth Argyle	L 0-2	0-1	7		(3,686)
9	17	CL	A	Swansea City	D 1-1	0-1		Boyle 75	(5,534)
10	21	CL	H	Bolton Wanderers	L 0-1	0-0	12		2,212
11	28	CL	A	Walsall	L 0-2	0-0	14		(4,586)
12	O 1	CL	H	Bristol City	D 1-1	0-0	15	Boyle 89	3,776
13	5	CL	A	Lincoln City	D 1-1	0-0	16	Staniforth (pen) 73	(1,989)
14	12	CL	H	Reading	L 0-2	0-1	18		6,449
15	19	CL	A	Brentford	D 0-0	0-0	19		(3,646)
16	22	CL	H	Rotherham United	D 0-0	0-0	18		1,817
17	26	CL	A	Wigan Athletic	D 0-0	0-0	18		(3,719)
18	N 2	CL	H	Gillingham	D 1-1	0-0	18	Jones P. 66	(1,970)
19	6	CL	H	York City	D 1-1	1-0	18	Senior (og) 27	1,529
20	9	CL	A	Chesterfield	L 1-3	1-1	18	Gill 22	(2,420)
21	16	FAC1	A	Southend United	W 1-0	0-0		Mardenborough 83	(3,343)
22	23	CL	H	Notts County	L 1-2	1-1	19	Carter 35	1,946
23	D 7	FAC2	H	Torquay United	D 1-1	0-1		Berry 67	2,386
24	10	FAC2R	A	Torquay United	W 3-2†	0-1		Boyle 48, Jones P. 79, James 114	(1,937)
25	14	CL	H	Blackpool	D 1-1	1-0	19	Berry 32	1,991
26	21	CL	H	Wolverhampton W.	W 3-1	0-1	19	Mardenborough 64, 82, Boyle 74	2,222
27	26	CL	A	Bury	D 1-1	0-1	19	Mardenborough 68	(3,013)
28	28	CL	A	Cardiff City	D 1-1	0-0	20	Staniforth 52	(7,450)
29	J 4	FAC3	A	Sunderland	L 0-2	0-2			(12,352)
30	11	CL	H	Bournemouth	W 2-1	0-0	18	Boyle 76, Staniforth 79	2,333
31	18	CL	A	Doncaster Rovers	D 1-1	0-1	18	Relish 61	(2,336)
32	20	FRT	A	Swansea City	D 1-1	1-1		Berry 45	(2,863)
33	21	FRT	H	Cardiff City	W 1-0	0-0		Mardenborough	1,863
34	25	CL	H	Plymouth Argyle	W 3-1	2-1	14	Staniforth 29, Berry 37, Hodges (og) 50	3,007
35	F 1	CL	A	Bristol Rovers	L 0-2	0-0	18		(3,284)
36	4	CL	A	Rotherham United	D 0-0	0-0	17		(2,975)
37	16	CL	H	Swansea City	W 2-0	1-0	17	Relish 18, Mayes 47	2,805
38	22	CL	A	Bolton Wanderers	L 0-4	0-3	17		(4,063)
39	28	CL	H	Walsall	L 1-5	0-1	17	Boyle 51	1,530
40	M 4	CL	A	Bristol City	L 1-3	0-1	18	Mardenborough 53	(4,395)
41	8	CL	H	Lincoln City	L 1-2	0-0	18	James 85	1,540
42	11	CL	H	Brentford	L 1-2	1-1	18	Berry 38	1,508
43	15	CL	A	Reading	L 0-2	0-0	20		4,783
44	18	CL	A	Darlington	L 2-3	1-3	20	Carter 20, Latchford 49	(2,538)
45	22	CL	H	Wigan Athletic	L 3-4	2-1	20	Mardenborough 3, Latchford 10, 74	1,700
46	29	CL	A	Derby County	D 1-1	0-1	20	Carter 82	(11,256)
47	31	CL	H	Bury	W 1-0	0-0	19	Staniforth (pen) 87	1,983
48	A 5	CL	A	York City	L 1-3	0-1	20	Lewis 73	(3,038)
49	12	CL	H	Chesterfield	D 3-3	2-2	20	Carter 9, Latchford 15, Staniforth 52	1,940
50	19	CL	A	Notts County	W 2-1	2-0	20	Staniforth (pen) 34, Mardenborough 37	(3,279)
51	22	CL	H	Derby County	D 1-1	1-1	20	Boyle 39	3,049
52	26	CL	H	Darlington	W 3-0	1-0	20	Mardenborough 21, Staniforth 54, Latchford 68	2,848
53	29	CL	A	Gillingham	W 1-0	0-0	19	Jones L. 89	(2,566)
54	M 3	CL	A	Blackpool	D 0-0	0-0	19		(3,407)

Best Home League Attendance: 6,449 v Reading 12/10 **Smallest:** 1,508 v Brentford **Av Home Att:** 2,536

Goal Scorers: **Compared with 84-85:** +105

League (52): Staniforth 9 (3 pen), Boyle 7, Carter 7 (1 pen), Mardenborough 7, Latchford 5, Berry 3, James 2, Miles 2, Opponents 2, Relish 2, Dowman 1, Gill 1, Jones L. 1, Jones P. 1, Lewis 1, Mayers 1
Milk Cup (1): Reck 1
FA Cup (5): Mardenborough 1, Berry 1, Boyle 1, Jones P. 1, James 1
FRT (2): Berry 1, Mardenborough 1

†After extra-time

Kendall	Rogers	Jones L	Pulis	Dowman	Boyle	Carter	James	Mardenborough	Staniforth	Lewis	Miles	Relish	Giles	Jones P	Reck (L)	McManus (L)	Peacock	Tyler (NC)	Gill (NC)	Berry	Moore (L)	Latchford (L)	Mayes (L)	Hamer	Referee	
1	2		4	5	6	7	8	9	10	11	12			3*											M Cotton	1
1	2			5	6	4	8	9	10	11	12		3	7*											K Baker	2
1	12	2		5	6	4	8	7*	10	11	9			3											D Allinson	3
1		2	4	5	6	7	8	12	9	11	10*			3											J Martin	4
1		2		5	6	7	8	12	10	11	9*			3	4										M James	5
1		2		5	6	7	8	12	10	11	9*		3		4										V Callow	6
1		2		5	6	7	8		10	11				3	4	9									C Downey	7
1		2		5	6	7	8		10	11				3	4	9*	12								Alan Robinson	8
1		2		5	6	7		8	10	11				3	4	9									L Robinson	9
1		2		5	6	7	8	12	10	11				3	4	9*									A Seville	10
1		8	5*		6			9	7	10	11			3	4		12	2							K Breen	11
1		2			6		8	9	7*	10				3	4		5	12	11						H Taylor	12
1		2			6	8	9		10	11				3	4		5		7						D Hutchinson	13
1		2			6	8	9	12	10	11				3*	4		5		7						L Shapter	14
1		2			6	8	9*	12	10	11				3	4		5		7						K Barratt	15
1		2			6	8	9	10*	11	12				3	4		5		7						D Reeves	16
1	8	2			6	5	9*		12	10	11			3	4				7						K Lupton	17
1	8	2			6	5		9	10	11				3	4				7						B Stevens	18
1	8	2			6	5	12	9*	10	11				3	4				7						R Groves	19
1	8	2			6	5	12	9*	10	11				3			4		7						T Holbrook	20
1	8	2			6	5	7	9	10	11				3	4										F Ward	21
1	8	2*			6	5	7	9	10	11				3	4				12						D Vickers	22
1	2	8			6	5	12	7*	10	11				3					4	9					V Callow	23
1	2	8			6	5	11	12	10	7				3					4	9*					V Callow	24
1	2	8			6	5	11		12	10	7			3					4	9*					G Ashby	25
1	2	8			6	5	11	12	10	7				3					4	9*					N Butler	26
1	2	8			6	5	11		10	7				3					12	4*					J Key	27
1	2	8*			6	5	11	9	10	7				3					12	4					G Napthine	28
1	2			6	5*	11	9	10	7				12	3			4		8						M Heath	29
1	2			5		8	9	11	7					3			4		6		10				J Bray	30
1	2		6	5	8*		10	11	7					3			12		4	9					A Seville	31
1	2		6	12	8	13	10*	11						3			5*		7	4		9			K Cooper	32
1	2		6	5	12	10*	11	8						3			12	13	7	4		9*			E Scales	33
1	2		6	5	12	10*	11	8						3					7	4		9			M Reed	34
1	2	12	6	5*		10	11	8						3			12		4			9			J Martin	35
1	2	11	6	5	7*	10	8							3			12		4			9			J Lovatt	36
1	2		6	5	12	10	11	8						3					4	9		7*			L Shapter	37
1	2*	12	6	5	7	10	11	8						3					4	9*					G Courtney	38
1		2	6	2	7	10	11	8*						3			5		12	4		9*			I Hemley	39
1		2	6	5	12	7	10	11					8*	3			12		9	4					J Moules	40
1	2		6	5	12	7	10	11						3			8		4			9*			R Groves	41
1	2	8	6	9	12	7	11							3			5		4		10*				T Jones	42
1	2	8	6	7	12	10	11							3			5		4	9*					R Nixon	43
1	2	8	6	5	7	10	11*							3			12		4	9					T Mills	44
1	2	7	5	4	9	11	8							3*			12		6	10					D Axcell	45
1	2	8	6	11	12	7	10	3						3			5*		4	9					I Hendricks	46
1	2	8	6	5	7	10	11							3*					4	9					D Reeves	47
1	2*	8	6	5	11	7	10						3						4	9				12	J Lloyd	48
1	2	8	6	11	7	10	3							3			5		4	9					B Stevens	49
1	5	2	8	6	11	7	10	3						3					4	9					M Cotton	50
1	5	2	8	6	11	7	10	3											4	9					R Milford	51
1	5	2	8	6	11	7	10	3											4	9					P Tyldesley	52
1	5	2	8	6	11	12	7	10	3										4*	9					E Scales	53
1	5	2	8	6	11		10	3									7		4	9					K Lupton	54
46	6	31	38	9	46	42	21	30	45	44	3		12	36	15	4	14	0	13	26	2	20	3	0	League Appearances	
	1		2				7	9			1		2			1	4	2	6					1	Substitute Appearances	
2		1	1	2	2	2	2	1·1	2	2	1·1	2	1			1									Milk Cup Appearances	
4		4	3		4	4	4	3·1	4	4			0·1	4	1	1		3	2						FA Cup Appearances	
2		2			2	1·1		1·1	1	2			1		2		1·1	0·1	2	2		2			FR Trophy Appearances	

Players on Loan: McManus (Southampton), Reck (Oxford United), Moore (Sunderland), Mayes (Carlisle), Latchford (Lincoln Cty)

Departures: Boyle (Cardiff), Dowman (Cambridge), Matthewson (Stockport Co.), Giles (Cardiff), Pulis (Bournemouth), Chamberlain (Mansfield)

'THE IRONSIDES'

Formed: 1912
Turned Professional: 1912   **Ltd Co:** 1912

Previous Managers: Since 1946: Billy McCandless   Tom Bromilow   Fred Stansfield   Bill Lucas
Bobby Evans   Bill Lucas   Trevor Morris   Les Graham   Bob Ferguson   Bill Lucas   Brian Harris
Dave Elliot   Jimmy Scoular   Colin Addison   Len Ashurst   Colin Addison   Bob Smith   John Relish
Honours: Champions Div 3 (S) 1938-9
League Career: Original Members of Div 3 1920   Reverted to Div 3 (S) 1921
Dropped out of the Football League 1931   Re-elected to Div 3 (S) 1932
Promoted to Div 2 1938-9   Relegated to Div 3 (S) 1946-7
Transferred to Div 3 1958   Relegated to Div 4 1961-2
Promoted to Div 3 1979-80
Colours: Amber shirts, black shorts, amber stockings
Change Colours: White shirts, black shorts white stockings
Reserves League: Welsh Premier   **'A' Team:** Newport & District Premier   **Youth League:** Macbar League

---

CLUB RECORDS

Most Appearances for Club: Len Weare: Football League 526 + FA Cup 35 + League Cup 13 **Total 574**
Most Capped Player: Nigel Vaughan, 3, Wales   **For England:** None
Record Goalscorer in a Match: Tudor Martin, 5 v Merthyr Tydfil (h), 10-0, Div 3 (S), 10 Apr 1930
Tony Buck, 5 v Bradford (P.A.) (a), 21 Sept 1968
Record League Goalscorer in a Season: Tudor Martin, 34, Div 3 (S), 1929-30   **In All Competitions:** Tudor Martin, 36
(League 34 + FA Cup 2), 1929-30
Record League Goalscorer in a Career: Reg Parker, 99, 1948-54   **In All Competitions:** Reg Parker 109 (League
99 + FA Cup 10) 1948-54
Record Transfer Fee Received: £70,000 from Oxford United for Mark Aizlewood, Mar 1978
Record Transfer Fee Paid: £80,000 to Swansea City for Alan Waddle, Jan 1981
Best Performances: League: 4th Div 3 1982-3   **FA Cup:** 5th Round 1948-9   **League/Milk Cup:** Never past 3rd
Round   **Welsh Cup:** Winners 1979-80   **European Cup Winners Cup:** Quarter Final
Most League Points: 78 in Div 3, 1982-3   **Most League Goals:** 85, Div 4, 1964-5
Record League Victory and Most Goals in a First Class Match: 10-0 v Merthyr Tydfil, Div 3 South, 10 Apr 1930
Record League Defeat: 0-13 v Newcastle United, (a), Div 2, 5 Oct 1946
European Competitions Entered: European Cup Winners Cup 1980-1
Oldest Player in League Match: Billy Lucas (over 40)
Youngest Player in League Match: Darren Peacock, Kevin Hamer, 17
Most Consecutive Undefeated League Matches: 12 1938   **League Matches Without a Win:** 25 1970-71
Longest Run of Undefeated Home League Matches: 20 1923-24   **Away League Matches:** 7 1972
Longest Run Without Home League Win: 12 1970-71   **Away League Win:** 35 1968-70
Most Consecutive League Wins: 10 1980   **Home League Wins:** 9 1959, 1977-78
Most Consecutive League Defeats: 10 1970   **Away League Wins:** 5 1980

Club Statistician for the Directory: Tony Ambrosen

NEWPORT COUNTY

PLAYERS NAME Ht Wt Birthdate	Honours	Birthplace Transfers	Clubs	League	Milk Cup	FA Cup	Other Comps	League	Milk Cup	FA Cup	Other Comps
GOALKEEPERS											
Roger Freestone 6.2 13.3		Newport	Newport County								
Mark Kendall 6.0 13.9 20.9.58	W.U21 (1) S	Blackwood	Tottenham H (A)	29	1	6					
			Chesterfield (L)	9							
		£45,000	Newport County	25	13	18	7				
DEFENDERS											
Linden Jones 5.6 10.8 5.3.61	W.U21 (3)	Tredegar	Cardiff City (A)	143+2	10	4		2		1	
		Player Exchange	Newport County	107	2	6	6	1			2
Peter Jones 5.5 10.5 22.9.57		Caerphilly	Merthyr T								
			Newport County	36		1	4	1		1	
John Lewis 5.10 11.3 15.10.55		Tredegar	Pontllanfraith								
			Cardiff City	135+5	10	10	1	9	1	1	
		Player Exchange	Newport County	102	4	6	3	3			1
James Mullen 5.10 12.12 8.11.52		Jarrow	Sheffield Wed (A)	222+7	23	9+1		10			
		£25,000	Rotherham Utd	49	3	2		1			
			P.N.E. (L)	1							
		£10,000	Cardiff City	128+5	8+1	5	2	8			
			Newport County								
Darren Peacock 6.2 12.6 3.2.68		Bristol	Newport County	14+4		1					
MIDFIELD											
Stephen Berry 5.8 10.6 4.4.63		Gosport	Portsmouth (A)	26+2	2+1		2	2	1		
		F	Sunderland	31+3	10	1	2				
			Newport County	26		3		3		1	1
Roy Carter 6.0 11.7 19.2.54	Div 3 1976	Torpoint	Falmouth Town								
			Hereford Utd	64+7	9	4+1		9	3	1	
		£22,000	Swindon Town	193+7	22+1	11		34	2	2	
			Torquay Utd (L)	6							
			Bristol Rovers (L)	4							
		F	Torquay Utd	21							
		£10,000	Newport County	71	2	4	3	11			
FORWARDS											
Tony Bolton 5.7 11.4 15.1.68		Newport	Charlton Athletic (A)								
			Newport County								
Roger Gibbins 5.10½ 11.9 6.9.55	E.S. FAYC 74	Enfield	Tottenham H (A)								
		F	Oxford Utd	16+3				2			
		F	Norwich City	47+1	1	2		12		1	
		£60,000	New England Teamen								
		F	Cambridge U	97+3	7	2+1		12	3		
		F	Cardiff City	135+5	12	5		17	5	1	
		F	Swansea City	35		2	4	6			
		F	Newport County								
Steve Mardenborough 5.7 11.9 11.9.64		Birmingham	Coventry City								
		F	Wolverhampton W	17		0+1		2			
		F	Swansea City	62+13	3+1	5+1	3+1	14		1	1
			Newport County								
Gordon Staniforth 5.6 9.12 23.5.57		Hull	Hull City (A)	7+5				2			
		£10,000	York City	128	7	6		33	2	4	
		£120,000	Carlisle United	118+8	7	17		33	2	3	
			Plymouth Argyle	87+4	8	0+1	4	19	3	1	
			Newport County	45	2	4		9			
Mark Vinter 5.9 11.0 23.5.54	Div.3 '84	Boston	Boston United								
			Notts County	135+81	8+2	7+1		53	2	5	
		£150,000	Wrexham	90+12	9	10+1		25	5	7	
		£25,000	Oxford United	67+2	12+1	11		21	3	4	
		£15,000	Mansfield Town	53+2	6	2	5	7	3		
		F	Newport County								
Ken Gill 6.0 11.8 5.11.55		Bath	Forest Green Rovers								
			Newport County								

ADDITIONAL CONTRACT PROFESSIONALS
Sean Mills

APPRENTICES
David Abruzzese, Richard Jones, Normal Parselle

NON-CONTRACT PLAYERS
Kenneth Gill (13 + 6 Lge, 1gl), Kevin Hamer, Andrew Roberts, Graham Rogers, Stuart Spencer, Simon Tyler

SOMERTON PARK Newport, Gwent

Capacity: 18,000 (1,200 seats)

Record Attendance: 24,268 v Cardiff C, Div 3 (S), 16 Oct 1937

Record Receipts: £28,050 v Carl Zeiss Jena, European Cup Winners Cup Quarter Final 2nd Leg, 18 Mar 1981

Season Tickets: Stand (Main Upper): £90.00; Lower: £60.00; Ground: £50.00, (juveniles/OAPs £60.00, £45.00, £30,00 respectively)

Executive Box Season Tickets: Vice-Presidents Club £120 (£5 per match)

Cost of Stand Tickets: £4.50 (Main Upper); £3.00 (Main Lower), (OAP/Juveniles £3.00 & £2.25 respectively); **Ground:** £2.50, (OAP/Juveniles £1.50)

Match and Ticket Information: Seats can be purchased from Club Secretary

Car Parking: Street parking under police control

Nearest Railway Station: Newport (0633) 842222

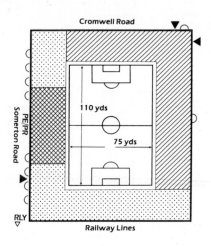

How to get to the ground

From North and East: Use Motorway M4 until junction 24. Leave Motorway and follow signs Newport A48. In 1.8m turn left into Somerton Road B4237. In 0.4m turn right into Cromwell Road for Newport County FC
From West: Use Motorway M4 until junction 28. Leave Motorway and follow signs Newport A48. In 2.3m turn right A467. Cross Railway Bridge then turn right into A455 into Corporation Road. In 0.4m turn left into Cromwell Road for Newport County FC

Price of 1986-7 Programme: 40p
Number of Pages: 20
Subscriptions: Apply to club for rates

Local Newspapers: Western Mail, South Wales Argus

Local Radio Stations: Red Dragon Radio, BBC Radio Wales

NORTHAMPTON TOWN — Division 4

Chairman
D Banks

Vice-Chairman
S Wilson

Directors
E P Northover
B Stonehill
M Pell
M Deane
G Wilson
D Underwood
R Church
M Conroy

Secretary/Director
David Gifford (0604 721103)

Manager
Graham Carr

Assistant Manager
Clive Walker

Back Row L to R: Glen Donegal, Mark Bushell, Bob Coy, Mark Schiavi, Richard Hill. **Middle Row:** Clive Walker (Coach), Ian Benjamin, Graham Reid, Peter Gleasure, Russell Wilcox, Keith McPherson, Dennis Casey (Physio). **Front Row:** Paul Curtis, David Gilbert, Trevor Morley, Graham Carr (Manager), Phil Chard, Warren Donald, Adi Mann.

S upporters of Northampton Town awaited the start of the 1985-86 season with anticipation. New manager Graham Carr had been busy in the transfer market during the close season and only six of last season's side remained. However, the opening game was a disapointment, Northampton were trailing by 3-0 at Burnley at half-time, although they did pull two back by the end of the game.

As the side began to settle so the results became more favourable, a 6-0 thrashing of Preston was followed by a 5-0 win against local rivals, Peterborough at London Road.

Slowly manager Graham Carr added to his squad, Phil Chard from Peterborough, Warren Donald from West Ham. Gavin Nebbelling the giant South African came on loan from Crystal Palace with a view to staying but after his loan period the club felt that Palace's asking price was too high and instead Northampton signed West Ham's Keith McPherson, first on loan and then on a contract.

By mid March, Northampton were on the fringe of the promotion race but unfortunately had their worst spell in the following matches, this was highlighted by the fact that teams around them also began to stutter, and a good run during this period could have clinched promotion.

The cups brought little cheer and by falling to Gillingham in the first round of the FA Cup the side made a first round exit for the first time since 1980. Victory over Peterborough in the Milk Cup turned sour when First Division Oxford won both legs in the second round, despite 'The Cobblers' scoring first at Oxford, and missing a penalty. The Freight Rover Trophy saw Northampton win both their 'section' matches, but lose to Bristol City in a close game in the knock out competition.

In all a great season, as despite all the problems with the ground, the directors made every effort to make sure there was seating for the fans. Northampton were the first side to score 50 goals, but the remainder of the season consisted of breaking other club's records rather than creating more of their own: The first side to score against Mansfield, the first to beat Peterborough and Colchester on their own ground and unfortunately the first club to draw under 1,000 to the Roots Hall in the Freight Rover Cup match v Southend.   Frank Grande

NORTHAMPTON TOWN

DIVISION FOUR: 8th   **FA CUP:** 1st ROUND   **MILK CUP:** 2nd ROUND   **FRT:** AREA QUARTER-FINAL

MATCH	DATE		COMPE-TITION	VENUE	OPPONENTS	RESULT		HALF TIME	L'GUE POS'N	GOALSCORERS/GOAL TIMES	ATTEN-DANCE
1	A	17	CL	A	Burnley	L	2-3	0-3		Morley 49, Reed 86	(4,214)
2		21	MC1/1	A	Peterborough United	D	0-0	0-0			(3,117)
3		26	CL	A	Exeter City	W	2-1	0-1		Morley 66, Benjamin 81	(2,392)
4		31	CL	H	Mansfield Town	W	1-0	1-0	10	Cavener (pen) 12	2,739
5	S	3	MC1/2	H	Peterborough United	W	2-0	0-0		Cavener (pen) 55, Chard 81	2,464
6		6	CL	A	Swindon Town	L	2-3	0-2	13	Hill 54, Cavener (pen) 89	(3,879)
7		10	CL	H	Preston North End	W	6-0	3-0	9	Benjamin 1, 11, Morley 41, Hill 3 52, 77,88	2,171
8		14	CL	H	Crewe Alexandra	L	0-1	0-0	11		2,654
9		18	CL	A	Hartlepool United	L	1-2	0-2	13	Benjamin 84	(1,892)
10		21	CL	H	Stockport County	W	3-1	2-1	10	Benjamin 16, Hill 17, Morley 46	1,954
11		25	MC2/1	A	Oxford United	L	1-2	1-1		Benjamin 21	(5,644)
12		28	CL	A	Rochdale	L	2-3	1-2	12	Hill 10, Benjamin 66	(1,954)
13	O	1	CL	H	Wrexham	L	1-2	0-1	14	Hill 82	2,234
14		5	CL	H	Hereford United	L	1-3	1-3	16	Chard 1	1,998
15		8	MC2/2	H	Oxford United	L	0-2	0-0			5,076
16		12	CL	A	Peterborough United	W	5-0	2-0	13	Chard 2, Mann 9, 72, Cavener 75, Benjamin 85	(3,872)
17		19	CL	A	Torquay United	D	1-1	0-1	14	Chard 75	(1,282)
18		22	CL	H	Chester City	D	2-2	1-1	14	Morley 4, Benjamin 71	2,323
19		26	CL	A	Colchester United	W	2-0	1-0	12	Chard 2, Mann 63	(2,872)
20	N	2	CL	H	Scunthorpe United	D	2-2	1-1	13	Benjamin 22, Cavener (pen) 60	2,343
21		5	CL	H	Tranmere Rovers	D	2-2	2-0	13	Donald 27, Benjamin 34	2,005
22		9	CL	A	Aldershot	L	0-1	0-0	15		(1,556)
23		16	FAC1	A	Gillingham	L	0-3	0-2			(3,991)
24		23	CL	H	Halifax Town	W	4-0	2-0	14	Chard (pen) 1, Benjamin 14, Morley 49, Schiavi 73	1,514
25		30	CL	A	Cambridge United	W	5-2	2-1	11	Benjamin 3 8, 18 (pen) 74, Schiavi 64, Morley 76	(2,235)
26	D	6	CL	A	Southend United	W	4-0	1-0	9	Schiavi 5, Curtis 48, Benjamin 60, 63	(2,527)
27		14	CL	H	Port Vale	D	2-2	0-1	9	Morley 69, Chard 86	3,030
28		21	CL	A	Preston North End	D	1-1	1-0	10	Hill 10	(2,570)
29	J	11	CL	A	Mansfield Town	L	0-1	0-1	14		(3,829)
30		18	CL	H	Burnley	W	2-0	1-0	13	Morley 35, Hill 88	3,095
31		21	FRT	H	Colchester United	W	2-1	1-1		Schiavi 4, Benjamin 82	1,958
32		25	CL	A	Crewe Alexandra	W	1-0	0-0	10	Morley 60	(1,856)
33	F	1	CL	H	Swindon Town	L	0-1	0-0	11		4,449
34		5	CL	A	Chester City	W	3-2	1-2	9	Hill 38, Schiavi 72, Morley 73	(3,304)
35		21	CL	A	Stockport County	L	0-1	0-0	9		(2,011)
36	M	1	CL	H	Rochdale	W	1-0	0-0	8	Benjamin 56	2,146
37		4	CL	A	Wrexham	L	0-1	0-1	9		(1,433)
38		8	CL	A	Hereford United	L	0-3	0-1	10		(2,478)
39		11	CL	H	Hartlepool United	W	3-0	2-0	8	Benjamin 30, 81, Hill 34	1,815
40		13	FRT	A	Southend United	W	3-1	1-0		Hill 12, Benjamin 49, 80	(683)
41		15	CL	H	Peterborough United	D	2-2	2-0	9	Morley 17, Hill 40	3,332
42		18	CL	A	Scunthorpe United	L	0-1	0-0	9		(1,355)
43		22	CL	H	Colchester United	W	1-0	1-0	8	Donald 13	2,035
44		27	FRT QF	A	Bristol City	L	2-3	1-1		Hamil 9, Hill 75	(3,038)
45		29	CL	A	Orient	W	1-0	0-0	8	Benjamin 84	(2,920)
46		31	CL	H	Southend United	D	0-0	0-0	7		3,527
47	A	4	CL	A	Tranmere Rovers	W	3-1	1-0	6	Hamil 1, Benjamin 60, Sugrue 80	(1,103)
48		8	CL	H	Exeter City	D	2-2	2-1	6	Donald 5, Hill 8	2,213
49		12	CL	H	Aldershot	L	2-3	1-0	7	Sugrue 19, Chard (pen) 73	2,049
50		15	CL	H	Orient	L	2-3	1-1	7	Morley 19, Hill 52	1,731
51		18	CL	A	Halifax Town	L	0-2	0-2	8		(1,105)
52		26	CL	A	Cambridge United	L	0-2	0-0	10		2,100
53		29	CL	H	Torquay United	W	5-1	1-0	8	Hill 3 23, 46, (pen) 53, Schiavi 66, Compton (og) 74	3,470
54	M	3	CL	A	Port Vale	D	0-0	0-0	8		(3,873)

Best Home League Attendance: 4,449 v Swindon Town   **Smallest:** 1,514 v Halifax Town   **Av Home Att:** 2,418

Goal Scorers: **Compared with 84-85:** +577

League (79):	Benjamin 21 (1 pen), Hill 17 (1 pen), Morley 13, Chard 6 (1 pen), Cavener 5 (4 pen), Schiavi 5, Donald 3, Mann 3, Sugrue 2, Curtis 1, Hamil 1, Opponent 1, Reed 1
Milk Cup (3):	Cavener 1 (pen 1), Chard 1, Benjamin 1
FA CUP (-):	
FRT (7):	Benjamin 3, Hill 2, Hamil 1, Schiavi 1

1985-86

Gleasure	Curtis	Mundee	Dawes	Lewis	Hill	Mann	Benjamin	Reed	Morley	Cavener	Chard	Schiavi	Donald	Nebbelling (L)	McPherson	Friar	Sugrue	Hamil (NC)	Garner	Referee	
1	2	3	4	5	6	7	8	9	10	11										J Lloyd	1
1	2	3		5	6	7	8	9	10	11	4									**J Moules**	2
1	2	3		5	6	7	8	9	10	11	4									R Gifford	3
1	2	3	12	5	6	7	8	9*	10	11	4									A Ward	4
1	2	3	4	5	6	8*	9		10	11	7	12								**M Cotton**	5
1	2	3		5	6	7	8	9	10	11	4									R Milford	6
1	2	3			6	7	8*	9	4	10	11	5	12							J Martin	7
1	2	3		5		7	8*	9	4	10	11	6	12							N Butler	8
1	2	3		5	6*	12	8	9	10	11	4	7								N Glover	9
1	2	3		5	6*	12	8	9	10	11	4	7								A Buksh	10
1	2	3		5	6		8	9	10	11	4	7								**T Holbrook**	11
1	2	3		5	6	12	8	9	10	11	4	7*								G Courtney	12
1	2	3		5	6	12	8	9	10	11	4	7*								E Scales	13
1	2	3	12	5	6†	7	8	9	10		4	11*								M Scott	14
1	2	3		5	6	11*	8	9	10	12	4		7							**A Seville**	15
1	2	3		5	6	11	8	9	10	12	4*		7							D Axcell	16
1	2	3	6	5		11	8		10	9	4		7							R Hamer	17
1	2*	3	6	5		11	8		10	9	4	12	7							K Miller	18
1		3		5	9	11	8	2	10		4		7		6					M James	19
1		3		5	7	9*	11	2	10	12	6		8	4						M Reed	20
1		3		5	9		8	2	10	7	4		11		6					R Vickers	21
1		3		5	9	11	8	2	10*	12	4		7		6					A Gunn	22
1	2	3		5	9		8	6	10	11	4		7							**N Butler**	23
1		3		5	9		8	2	10		4	11	7		6					R Lewis	24
1		3		5	9	12	8	2	10		4*	11	7		6					D Reeves	25
1	2	3		5	9	4	8		10			11	7		6					C Downey	26
1	2	3		5	9		8		10		4	11	7		6					B Stevens rd Millidge	27
1		3		5	11		8	2	10		4	9	7		6					P Tyldesley	28
1		3		5	11†		8	2	10		4	9	7		6					T Simpson	29
1		3		5	11		8	2	10		4	9	7		6					V Callow	30
1		3	4		8*	12	9	2	10		6	11	7	5						**G Ashby**	31
1		3		5		11	8	2	10		4	9	7		6					F Roberts	32
1		3		5	11		8	2	10		4	9	7		6					D Reeves	33
1		3		5	11	7	8	2	10		4	9			6					T Fitzharris	34
1		3		5	11	7	8	2*	10	12	4	9			6					R Guy	35
1	2	3		5	11	9	8		10		4		7		6					R Groves	36
1	2	3		5		11	8		10		4	9	7		6					N Wilson	37
1	2			5		11	8		10		4	9	7		6	3				N Ashley	38
1				5	11	7	8		10		2	9	4		6	3				J Moules	39
1				5	11	7	8	12	10		2*	9	4		6	3				**I Borrett**	40
1			4	11	7*	8	12		10		2	9	6		5	3				I Hemley	41
1	2*			5	11		8		10		9†	7	4		6	3	12			D Phillips	42
1				5	11		8	2	10		9	7*	4		6	3	12			P Tyldesley	43
1				5	11		8	2	10		6	9	4			3	12	7*		**T Ward**	44
1				5	11		8	2	10		9	7	4		6	3				L Shapter	45
1				5*	11	12	8	2	10		9	7	4		6	3				G Ashby	46
1	2				11		8	5	10		9	4*	6			3	12	7		K Hackett	47
1	2				11		9	4	10		8*	6	5			3	12	7		I Borrett	48
1	2				11	12	8	5	10		3	9			6	4	7*			N Midgley	49
1				5	11		8	2	10*		9	7	4		6	3	12			M Scott	50
1	2			5	11		8		10		9	7	4		6	3*	12			R Nixon	51
1	2			5	11	7	8	12		10		4			6	3	9*			D Axcell	52
	2			5	11	7	8	9				10	4		6	3			1	J McAulay	53
	2			5	11	7	8	9			6	10	4			3			1	G Aplin	54
44	27	31	3	43	41	25	46	34	43	13	41	31	32	11	20	14	2	3	2	League Appearances	
			2			7		2		4			3				6			Substitute Appearances	
4	4	4		4	4	3	4	3	4	3+1	4	1+1	1							Milk Cup Appearances	
1	1	1		1	1		1	1	1	1	1		1							FA Cup Appearances	
3		1		3	3	1+1	3	2+1	3		3	3	3	1	1	2	0+1	1		FR Trophy Appearances	

Players on Loan: Nebbelling (Crystal Palace)
Departures: Lewis (Kettering)

'THE COBBLERS'

Formed: 1897
Turned Professional: 1901 **Ltd Co:** 1901

Previous Managers: 1903-12 Herbert Chapman 1912-14 no manager 1920-5 Bob Hewison
1925-31 Jack Tresadern 1931-6 Jack English Snr 1936-7 Sid Puddefoot 1937-War Warney Cresswell
War-1949 Tom Smith 1949-55 Bob Dennison 1955-9 Dave Smith 1959-63 Dave Bowen
1963 Jack Jennings (caretaker) 1963-7 Dave Bowen 1967-8 Tony Marchi 1968-9 Ron Flowers
1969-72 Dave Bowen 1972-3 Bill Baxter 1973-6 Bill Dodgin 1976-7 Pat Crerand 1977 Committee*
1977-8 John Petts 1978-9 Mike Keen 1979-80 Clive Walker 1980-1 Bill Dodgin
1981-4 Clive Walker
*Committee: 1 director, 1 coach, 2 senior players
Honours: Champions Div 3 1962-3
League Career: Original Members of Div 3 1920 Transferred to Div 3 (S) 1921
Relegated to Div 4 1957-8 Promoted to Div 3 1960-1 Promoted to Div 2 1962-3
Promoted to Div 1 1964-5 Relegated to Div 2 1965-6 Relegated to Div 3 1966-7
Relegated to Div 4 1967-8 Promoted to Div 3 1975-6 Relegated to Div 4 1976-7
Colours: White shirts with claret sleeves, maroon shorts, white stockings with claret top
Change Colours: Yellow shirts with claret trim, yellow shorts and stockings
Youth Team: South East Counties League

CLUB RECORDS

Most Appearances for Club: Tommy Fowler: Football League 521 + FA Cup 31 + League Cup 31 **Total 583**
Most Capped Player: E Lloyd, 12, Wales **For England:** None
Record Goalscorer in a Match: R Hoten, 5 v Crystal Palace (h), 8-1, Div 3 (S), 27.10.1928 A Dawes, 5 v Lloyds Bank (h), 8-1, FA Cup 1st Round, 26.11.1932
Record League Goalscorer in a Season: Cliff Holton, 36, Div 3, 1961-2 **In All Competitions:** Cliff Holton, 39 (League 36 + FA Cup 3), 1961-2
Record League Goalscorer in a Career: Jack English, 135, 1948-60 **In All Competitions:** Jack English, 143 (League 135 + FA Cup 8)
Record Transfer Fee Received: £140,000 from Cambridge United for George Reilly, Nov 1979
Record Transfer Fee Paid: £40,000 to Brentford for Steve Phillips
Best Performances: League: 21st Div 1 1965-6 **FA Cup:** 5th Round 1933-4, 1949-50, 1969-70 **League/Milk Cup:** 5th Round 1964-5, 1966-7
Most League Points: 68, Div 4, 1975-6 **Most League Goals:** 109, Div 3, 1962-3, Div 3 (S) 1952-3
Record League Victory: 10-0 v Walsall, Div 4 (S), 5 Nov 1927
Most Goals Scored in a Cup Tie: 10 v Sutton, FA Cup
Record League Defeat: 0-10 v Bournemouth, Div 3 (S), 2 Sept 1939
Oldest Player in League Match:
Youngest Player in League Match:
Most Consecutive Undefeated League Matches: 17 1964
Longest Run of Undefeated Home League Matches: 29 1932-33, 1975-76
Longest Run Without Home League Win: 9 1984
Most Consecutive League Wins: 8 1960
Most Consecutive League Defeats: 8 1935

League Matches Without a Win: 18 1969
Away League Matches: 8 1964
Away League Win: 33 1921-22
Home League Wins: 12 1927
Away League Wins: 5 1978

Club Statistician for the Directory: Frank Grande

NORTHAMPTON TOWN

PLAYERS NAME Ht Wt Birthdate	Honours	Birthplace Transfers	Clubs	APPEARANCES League	Milk Cup	FA Cup	Other Comps	GOALS League	Milk Cup	FA Cup	Other Comps
GOALKEEPERS											
Peter Gleasure	FAYC 79	Luton	Millwall (A)	55	7	4					
5.11 12.13 8.10.60			Northampton Town	144	8	10	6				
Alan Harris	Nuneaton		Nuneaton Borough			1					
5.10 11.0 13.4.69		£7,500	Northampton Town								
DEFENDERS											
Mark Bushell		Northampton	Northampton Town	1							
5.7½ 10.12 5.6.68											
Philip Chard		Corby	Notts Forest (N-C)								
5.8 11.12 16.10.60			Peterborough Utd	153+19	15+2	9	1	18	2	1	
			Northampton Town	41	4	1	3	6	1		
Paul Curtis		London	Charlton Ath. (A)	69+3	3+1	4		5			
5.10 11.2 1.7.63		F	Northampton Town	27	4	1		1			
Keith McPherson		Greenwich	West Ham Utd (A)	1							
5.11 10.11 11.9.63			Northampton Town	20			1				
MIDFIELD											
Warren Donald		Hillingdon	West Ham Utd (A)	2+1							
5.7 10.3 7.10.64			Northampton Town	43	1	1	3	5			
David Gilbert			Boston United								
			Northampton Town								
Richard Hill		Hinckley	Leicester City								
6.0 12.1 20.9.63		Finland	Nuneaton Borough		3				1		
			Northampton Town	41	4	1	3	17			2
Adrian Mann		Northampton	Northampton Town	61+8	3	4	2+1	5			
5.5 9.0 12.7.67											
Mark Schiavi	EY	London	West Ham Utd (A)								
5.7½ 10.6 1.5.64		F	Bournemouth	24+3		0+3					
		F	Northampton Town	31+3	1+1		3	5			1
FORWARDS											
Ian Benjamin	EY	Nottingham	Sheffield Utd (A)	4+1	1+1			3			
5.11 12.0 11.12.61		F	West Bromwich A.	43+3		1		18		1	
		F	Peterborough Utd	77+3	7+1	5		14	1		1
		F	Northampton Town	88+2	6	5	5	39	1		3
Eddie McGoldrick		Corby	Nuneaton Borough			1					
5.11 11.0 30.4.65	£7,500	Northampton T									
Graham Reed		Doncaster	Barnsley (A)								
5.11½ 12.7 24.6.61			Doncaster								
			Frickley Athletic		3				1		
		£23,000	Northampton Town	34+2	3	1	2+1	1			
Paul Sugrue		Coventry	Nuneaton Borough		2						
5.7 9.10 6.11.60		£30,000	Manchester City	5+1							
		F	Cardiff City	2+3							
		Kansas	Middlesbrough	66+3	5	10		6	1	5	
			Portsmouth	4	1						
			Northampton Town	2+6			0+1	2			
Trevor Morley*	ESP (5)	Nottingham	Derby County								
5.11 12.1 20.3.61		£7,700	Corby Town								
			Nuneaton Borough		4						
			Northampton Town	43	4	1	3	13			

ADDITIONAL CONTRACT PROFESSIONALS
Russell Willcox   **Player of the Year:** Russell Lewis (now Kettering Town)

APPRENTICES
David Beazeley, Paul Dempsey, Gavin Eyles, Stephen Kenchington, Tyrone Kene, Peter Larkin, Darren Moore, Nicholas Petrisor, Karl Richardson, Bradley Sandeman, Gerald Sylvester, Mark Wood

NON-CONTRACT PLAYERS
Glenville Donegal, John Flowerden, Timothy Garner, Shane Geary, Daniel Wells

THE COUNTY GROUND   Northampton NN1 4PS   Capacity: 13,250 (1,450 seats)

Record Attendance: 24,523 v Fulham, Div 1, 23 April 1966

Smallest Home Attendance for a First Class Match: 942 v Chester, 9 March 1985

Record Receipts: £25,000 v Aston Villa, FA Cup Round 3

Season Tickets:

Executive Box Season Tickets: None on sale

Cost of Stand Tickets: £4.00 **Terraces:** £2.50/£3.00

Match and Ticket Information: No pre-match bookings

Car Parking: Ample street parking

Nearest Railway Station: Northampton Castle (0788 60116)

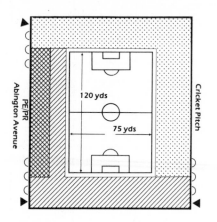

How to get to the ground

From North and West: Use A45 into Northampton. Follow signs Kettering A43 into Kettering Road. In 0.9m turn right into Abington Avenue for Northampton Town FC

From East: Use A45 S.P. Northampton to Wilby. In 5.2m at roundabout forward. In 2.5m turn right then over crossroads into Abington Avenue for Northampton Town FC

From South: Use Motorway M1 until junction 15. Leave Motorway and follow signs Northampton A508. Follow signs Kettering A43 into Kettering Road. In 0.9m turn right into Abington Avenue for Northampton Town FC

Price of 1986-7 Programme: 50p
Number of Pages: 24
Subscriptions: Please contact club

Local Newspapers: Chronicle and Echo, Evening Telegraph, Northants Post

Local Radio Stations: Homeward Radio, Radio Northampton

NORWICH CITY Division 1

President
G C Watling

Chairman
R T Chase, JP

Directors
E J Abbs
R J Munby
B W Lockwood
J A Jones
G A Paterson

Secretary
Nigel Pleasants (0603 612131)

Assistant Secretary
Jon Pollard

Marketing & Promotions Manager
Ray Cossey

Manager
Ken Brown

Chief Coach
Mel Machin

Coaches
Dave Stringer
Keith Webb

Physiotherapist
Tim Sheppard

Groundsman
Russ Allison

City put behind them the triumph followed by disaster of 1984-85 and after a few early problems regained their Top Division status with something in hand after taking top spot on December 14th and staying there. Five consecutive wins from 23rd November made this happen and with generally good form in the New Year the return to glamour games was not really in doubt at any time. Only when promotion had been achieved did form slump slightly with late defeats at Grimsby and Hull, but it had been a good campaign.

The cups were less happy events than the previous season — but there were no tears thanks to that first place in the 2nd Division. As Milk Cup holders they made a spirited defence of the trophy beating Preston North End (only 3-2 on aggregate) and Luton Town away (2-0) before a visit to Oxford (whose name was fated to replace theirs in any case) saw and honourable exit (1-3). The FA Cup campaign ended in Round 3 at Anfield, where Liverpool were at the top of their form (5-0), but in the new domestic Super Cup the team did some great things by despatching Everton and Manchester United both by penalties before Liverpool followed a draw at Carrow Road (1-1) with success at Anfield (3-1).

Now Ken Brown must decide whether the squad he has at his disposal is good enough for the 1st Division, which is due to be reduced in size. Woods has left for Glasgow Rangers and Graham Benstead will be given his chance to take over in goal. Van Wyk, Bruce, Phelan and Watson have all been models of consistency and Drinkell did well in a strike force which scored 84 League goals and another 14 in the cups. With Biggins and Barham also capable of finding the back of the net on a regular basis the goals tally should be good enough in higher company, but it will less easy than against 2nd Division defences.

Norwich enjoy excellent support and given a good start City should be able to give them good reasons for singing 'On the ball, City!' with gusto and frequency.
WLM

Back Row L to R: Ian Crook, Kevin Drinkell, Dennis Van Wyk, Robert Rosario, Graham Benstead, Dave Watson, Steve Bruce, Michael Phelan, Wayne Biggins.
Front Row: David Hodgson, Trevor Putney, Mark Barham, Dale Gordon, Garry Brooke, Peter Mendham, David Williams, Ian Culverhouse.

NORWICH CITY

DIVISION TWO: 1st   **FA CUP: 3rd ROUND**   **MILK CUP: 4th ROUND**   **SUPER CUP: SEMI-FINAL**

MATCH	DATE		COMPE-TITION	VENUE	OPPONENTS	RESULT		HALF TIME	L'GUE POS'N	GOALSCORERS/GOAL TIMES	ATTEN-DANCE
1	A	17	CL	H	Oldham Athletic	W	1-0	1-0		Mendham 26	12,508
2		20	CL	A	Blackburn Rovers	L	1-2	1-0		Bruce 40	(6,567)
3		24	CL	A	Millwall	L	2-4	1-1	15	Brooke 22, Deehan (pen) 89	(7,100)
4		26	CL	H	Barnsley	D	1-1	0-0		Bruce 90	13,510
5		31	CL	A	Portsmouth	L	0-2	0-1	14		(15,504)
6	S	7	CL	H	Sheffield United	W	4-0	1-0		Bruce 40, Drinkell 61, 78, Haylock 89	12,899
7		14	CL	A	Middlesbrough	D	1-1	0-1	13	Drinkell 60	(5,475)
8		18	CL	H	Crystal Palace	W	4-3	2-2		Watson 23, Drinkell 44, Phelan 55, Barham 78	13,475
9		21	CL	A	Huddersfield Town	D	0-0	0-0	10		(7,225)
10		28	CL	H	Hull City	W	2-0	1-0	8	Rosario 9, Mendham 62	12,639
11		30	MC2/1	A	Preston North End	D	1-1	1-1		Bruce 44	(4,330)
12	O	2	SC	A	Everton	L	0-1	0-0			(10,329)
13		5	CL	H	Wimbledon	L	1-2	1-2	9	Drinkell 5	12,707
14		9	MC2/2	H	Preston North End	W	2-1	0-1		Brooke 63, Rosario 87	11,537
15		12	CL	A	Carlisle United	W	4-0	1-0	7	Rosario 20, Phelan 54, Drinkell 89, Brooke 90	(2,907)
16		19	CL	H	Shrewsbury Town	W	3-1	2-1	6	Mendham 29, Drinkell 35, Barham 83	11,732
17		23	SC	H	Everton	W	1-0	0-0		Mendham 61	12,196
18		26	CL	A	Sunderland	W	2-0	0-0	5	Williams 61, Mendham 87	(17,908)
19		29	MC3	A	Luton Town	W	2-0	2-0		Mendham 28, Bruce 32	(8,202)
20	N	2	CL	A	Brighton & H.A.	D	1-1	0-0	6	Biggins 63	(10,423)
21		6	SC	A	Manchester United	D	1-1	1-0		Biggins 6	(20,130)
22		9	CL	H	Bradford City	D	0-0	0-0	6		13,939
23		16	CL	A	Stoke City	D	1-1	0-0	5	Drinkell 70	(6,469)
24		20	MC4	A	Oxford United	L	1-3	1-1		Drinkell 14	(7,851)
25		23	CL	H	Grimsby Town	W	3-2	1-0	5	Watson 43, Biggins 51, Lyons (og) 54	12,108
26		30	CL	A	Leeds United	W	2-0	1-0	4	Drinkell 38, Bruce 57	(11,480)
27	D	7	CL	A	Blackburn Rovers	W	3-0	2-0	3	Bruce 22, Van Wyk 29, Barham 54	12,820
28		11	SC	H	Manchester United	D	1-1	1-0		Williams 9	15,449
29		14	CL	A	Oldham Athletic	W	3-1	0-0	1	Drinkell 51, Barlow (og) 69, Watson 84	(3,949)
30		21	CL	H	Millwall	W	6-1	4-0	1	Mendham 4, Williams 8, 33, Barham 30, Drinkell 58, Phelan 76	12,349
31		26	CL	H	Charlton Athletic	W	3-1	0-0	1	Drinkell 67, 84, Deehan 88	17,984
32	J	1	CL	A	Fulham	W	1-0	0-0	1	Drinkell 89	(7,463)
33		4	FAC3	A	Liverpool	L	0-5	0-2			(29,082)
34		11	CL	H	Middlesbrough	W	2-0	1-0	1	Williams (pen) 44, Bruce 84	13,730
35		18	CL	H	Portsmouth	W	2-0	0-0	1	Barham 77, Drinkell 85	20,129
36		25	CL	A	Crystal Palace	W	2-1	2-0	1	Mendham 16, Biggins 36	(8,369)
37	F	1	CL	A	Barnsley	D	2-2	2-1	1	Deehan 39, Mendham 43	(5,608)
38		5	SC S/F	H	Liverpool	D	1-1	0-0		Drinkell 49	15,313
39		8	CL	H	Shrewsbury Town	W	3-0	2-0	1	Drinkell 4, 64, Barham 20	(5,157)
40	M	8	CL	A	Wimbledon	L	1-2	1-0	1	Barham 22	(5,827)
41		12	CL	H	Huddersfield Town	W	4-1	1-1	1	Drinkell 4, Biggins 59, 85, Bruce 72	12,772
42		15	CL	H	Carlisle United	W	2-1	1-0	1	Williams (pen) 32, 55	13,852
43		22	CL	A	Sheffield United	W	5-2	2-1	1	Smith P. (og) 6, Drinkell 42, Mendham 65, Barham 88, Biggins 89	(11,894)
44		29	CL	H	Fulham	W	2-1	2-1	1	Barham 21, Deehan 40	17,320
45		31	CL	A	Charlton Athletic	L	0-1	0-0	1		(8,458)
46	A	5	CL	H	Brighton & H.A.	W	3-0	0-0	1	Connor og 51, Drinkell 71, Williams pen 81	15,155
47		9	CL	A	Sunderland	D	0-0	0-0	1		17,752
48		12	CL	A	Bradford City	W	2-0	1-0	1	Drinkell 1, Biggins 46	(7,190)
49		19	CL	H	Stoke City	D	1-1	0-0	1	Gordon 75	17,757
50		26	CL	A	Grimsby Town	L	0-1	0-0	1		(8,090)
51		29	CL	A	Hull City	L	0-1	0-0	1		(6,146)
52	M	3	CL	H	Leeds United	W	4-0	1-0	1	Ormsby (og) 33, Drinkell 59, Bruce 66, Williams 79	17,942
53		6	SC S/F2	A	Liverpool	L	1-3	1-0		Brooke 2	(26,696)

Best Home League Attendance: 20,129 v Portsmouth	Smallest: 11,732 v Shrewsbury Town	Av Home Att 14,528
Goal Scorers:		Compared with 84-85: −1,530

League (84): Drinkell 22, Barham 9, Mendham 8, Williams 8 (3 pen), Biggins 7, Bruce 7, Opponents 5, Deehan 4, Brooke 3, Phelan 3, Watson 3 Rosario 2, Gordon 1, Haylock 1, Van Wyk 1

Milk Cup (4): Bruce 2, Brooke 1, Rosario 1

FA CUP (-):

Super Cup (5): Biggins 1, Brooke 1, Drinkell 1, Mendham 1, Williams 1

Woods	Haylock	Van Wyk	Bruce	Phelan	Watson	Mendham	Drinkell	Deehan	Brooke	Williams	Donawa	Barham	Spearing	Rosario	Culverhouse	Biggins	Gordon	Clayton	Referee	
1	2	3	4	5	6	7	8	9	10	11									J Bray	1
1	2	3	4	5	6	7	8	9	10	11									M Scott	2
1	2	3	4	5	6	7	8	9	10	11*	12								Alan Robinson	3
1	2	3*	4	5	6	10	8	9		11	12	7							E Scales	4
1	2*		4	5	6	10	8	9		11	12	7	3						D Reeves	5
1	2		4	5	6	10	8	9		11		7	3						R Lewis	6
1	2	12	4	5	6	10	8			11		7	3	9*					J McAuley	7
1	2		4	5	6	10	8			11		7	3	9					J Ball	8
1	2		4	5	6	10	8			11		7	3	9					J Worrall	9
1	2		4	5	6	10	8			11		7	3	9					M Cotton	10
1	2	6	4	5		10	8			11		7	3	9					**G Tyson**	**11**
1	2	6	4	5		10	8			11		7*	3	9					**J Hough**	**12**
1	2	11	4	5		10	8		12			7	3*	9					H Taylor	13
1		3	4	5	6	10	8			11		7		9	2				**G Napthine**	**14**
1		3	4	5	6	10	8			11		7		9	2				G Courtney	15
1		3	4	5	6	10	8			11	12	7		9*	2				N Butler	16
1		3	4	5	6	10*	8		12	11		7			2	9			**T Ward**	**17**
1		3	4	5	6	10	8			11		7			2	9			R Banks	18
1		3	4	5	6	10	8			11		7		9	2				**B Hill**	**19**
1		3	4	5	6	10				11		7	8		2	9			D Axcell	20
1		3	4	5	6	10	8			11		7			2	9			**T Mills**	**21**
1		3	4	5	6	10	8		12	11*		7			2	9			K Miller	22
1		3	4	5	6	10	8			11*		7			2	9	12		G Ashby	23
1		3	4	5	6	10	8		12	11*		7		9	2				**Alan Robinson**	**24**
1		3	4	5	6	10	8			11		7			2	9			C Downey	25
1		3	4	5	6	10	8		12	11		7*			2	9			C Trussell	26
1		3	4	5	6	10	8			11		7			2	9*	12		M Dimblebee	27
1		3	4	5	6	10	8			11		7			2	9			**D Vickers**	**28**
1		3	4	5	6	10	8		12	11		7			2	9*			R Nixon	29
1		3	4	5	6*	10	8		12	11		7			2	9			V Callow	30
1		3	4	5	6	10	8		12	11*		7			2	9			J Ball	31
1		3	4	5	6	10	8		12	11		7			2	9*			M James	32
1		3	4	5	6	10	8		12	11*		7			2	9			**D Hutchinson**	**33**
1		3	4	5	6	10	8			11		7			2	9			I Hemley	34
1		3	4	5	6	10	8			11		7			2	9			N Butler	35
1			4	5	6	10	8	3		11		7			2	9			R Milford	36
1			4	5	6	10	8	3		11		7			2	9			I Hendrick	37
1			4	5	6	10	8	3*		11		7			2	9	12		**J Moules**	**38**
1			4	5	6	10	8	3		11		7			2	9			J Worrall	39
1			4	5	6	10	8	3		11		7			2	9			G Ashby	40
1			4	5	6	10	8	3		11		7			2	9			D Hedges	41
1			4	5	6	10	8	3		11		7			2	9			H Taylor	42
1			4	5	6	10	8	3		11		7			2	9			K Redfearn	43
1			4	5	6	10	8	3		11		7			2	9			T Holbrook	44
1	12		4	5	6	10	8	3		11		7			2*	9			D Axcell	45
1		3	4	5	6		8	10		11		7*			2	9	12		K Baker	46
1		3	4	5	6		8	10				7			2	9	11		B Hill	47
1		3	4	5	6		8	10		11		7			2	9			T Fitzharris	48
1		3	4	5	6		8	10	12	11					2	9*	7		M Scott	49
1		3	4	5	6		8	10	12	11					2	9	7*		N Midgley	50
1	2	3	4	5	6		8	10		11	12	7				9*			D Allison	51
1		3	4	5	6		8	9		11		7			2		10		K Miller	52
1		3	4	5	6		8	9		11*		7			2		12	10	**A Seville**	**53**
42	12	27	**42**	**42**	**42**	35	41	22	8	37		35	7	8	30	28	3	1	League Appearances	
	2							4	4	2	2	1					3		Substitute Appearances	
4	1	4	4	4	3	4	4			1+1	3	4	1		4	3			Milk Cup Appearances	
1		1	1	1	1	1	1			1		1			1	1			FA Cup Appearances	
6	1	5	6	6	5	5	6	2	1·2	6		5	1	1	5	4	0·2	1	Super Cup Appearances	

Players on Loan:
Departures: Devine (Stoke), Rigby (Aldershot), Wood (Glasgow Rangers), Watson (Everton), Deehan (Ipswich), Haylock (Sheff Utd)

NORWICH CITY FC

'THE CANARIES'

Formed: 1905
Turned Professional: 1905   **Ltd Co:** 1905

Previous Managers: 1905-6 J W Bowman   1907-8 J McEwen   1908-10 A Turner
1910-5 J B Stansfield   1919-20 F C Buckley   1920-1 C O'Hagan   1921-6 A A Gosnell
1926-7 J B Stansfield   1927-8 C B Potter   1929-33 J Kerr   1933-7 T Parker   1937-8 R T Young
1938-9 R T Young & A J Jewell   1946-7 C H Spiers   1947-8 C H Spiers & D Lochhead
1948-50 D Lochhead   1950-5 N H Low   1955-7 T R Parker   1957-62 A Macaulay   1962 B Reid
1962-3 G Swindin   1963-6 R Ashman   1966-9 L Morgan   1969-73 R Saunders   1973-80 J Bond
Honours: Div 2 Champions 1971-2, 1985-6   Div 3 (S) Champions 1933-4
Football League Cup Winners 1962   Milk Cup Winners 1985
League Career: Original member of Div 3 1920   Transferred to Div 3 (S) 1921
Promoted to Div 2 1933-4   Relegated to Div 3 1938-9   Promoted to Div 2 1959-60
Promoted to Div 1 1971-2   Relegated to Div 2 1973-4   Promoted to Div 1 1974-5
Relegated to Div 2 1980-1   Promoted to Div 1 1981-2   Relegated to Div 2 1984-5
Promoted to Div 1 1985-6
Colours: Yellow shirts with green trim, green shorts with yellow trim, yellow stockings
Change Colours: White shirts with green trim, white shorts, green stockings
Reserves League: Football Combination   **Youth League:** S E Counties

---

CLUB RECORDS

Most Appearances for Club: Kevin Keelan, 1963-79: League 571 + Cup ties 110 **Total 681**
Most Capped Player: Martin O'Neill, 19, Northern Ireland   **For England:** Dave Watson
Record Goalscorer in a Match: Roy Hollis, 5 v Walsall (H) 8-0 Div 3 (S), 29.12.51
Record League Goalscorer in a Season: Ralph Hunt, 31, Div 3 (S), 1955-6   **In All Competitions:** Terry Alcock, 37, 1962-3
Record League Goalscorer in a Career: Johnny Gavin, 122   **In All Competitions:** Johnny Gavin 132 (League 122 + Cup 10) 1945-54, 1955-8
Record Transfer Fee Received: £1,000,000 from Manchester City for Kevin Reeves, Mar 1980   £1,000,000 from Nottingham Forest for Justin Fashanu, Aug 1981
Record Transfer Fee Paid: £300,000 to Hadjuk Split for Drazen Muzinic, Sept 1980
Best Performances: League: 10th Div 1 1975-6   **FA Cup:** Semi-Final 1959   **League/Milk Cup:** Winners 1962, 1985
Most League Points: (3pts for win) 84 in Div 2, 1985-6; (2 pts for win) 64 in Div 3(S), 1950-2   **Most League Goals:** 99, Div 3 (S) 1952-3
Record League Victory: 10-2 v Coventry City, Div 3 (S), 15 Mar 1930
Record League Defeat: 0-7 v Walsall (a), Div 3 (S), 13 Sept 1930
Oldest Player in League Match: Albert Sturgess 42 yrs
Youngest Player in League Match: Justin Fashanu 16 yrs

Most Consecutive Undefeated League Matches: 20 1950
Longest Run of Undefeated Home League Matches: 31 1971-72
Longest Run Without Home League Win: 12 1956-57
Most Consecutive League Wins: 10 1985-86
Most Consecutive League Defeats: 7 1935, 1957

League Matches Without a Win: 25 1956-57
Away League Matches: 12 1985-86
Away League Win: 41 1977-79
Home League Wins: 12 1952
Away League Wins: 4 1934, 1952, 1953, 1985-86

Club Statistician for the Directory: Dave Pease

NORWICH CITY

PLAYERS NAME Ht Wt Birthdate	Honours	Birthplace Transfers	Clubs	APPEARANCES League	Milk Cup	FA Cup	Other Comps	GOALS League	Milk Cup	FA Cup	Other Comps
GOALKEEPERS											
Graham Benstead 6.1 12.11 20.8.63	EY	Aldershot	QPR (A) Norwich City	1		1					
Harvey Lim 6.0 13.7 30.8.67		Halesowen	Norwich City Plymouth Argyle (L)								
DEFENDERS											
Kenneth Brown 5.8 11.6 11.7.67		Barking	Norwich City (A)								
Steve Bruce 6.0½ 12.6 31.12.60	EY	Corbridge £125,000	Gillingham Norwich City	205+3 81	15 13	8 6	23 6	23 8	6 2	1	
Phil Chapple 6.2 12.6 26.11.66		Norwich	Norwich City								
Ian Culverhouse 5.10 11.2 22.9.64	EY	Bishops Stortford	Tottenham H (A) Norwich City	1+1 30	3	1	5				
Shaun Elliott 6.0 11.6¼ 26.1.58	E 'B' (3)	Hebden Bridge	Sunderland Norwich City	316+5	28	14	2	10			
Paul Folkes 5.8 10.6 9.8.67		Great Yarmouth	Norwich City								
Mike Phelan 5.10½ 11.2 24.9.62		Nelson	Burnley (A) Norwich City	166+2 42	16 4	16 1	8 6	9 3	2		1
Tony Spearing 5.9½ 10.12 7.10.64	EY FAYC '83	Romford	Norwich City Stoke City (L) Oxford United (L)	11+1 9 5	1	1	1				
Dennis van Wijk 5.9½ 11.2 16.2.62	MC '85	Oostzaan, Holland	Ajax Norwich City	109+9	16+1	15	5	3		1	
MIDFIELD											
Mark Barham 5.7 11.0 12.7.62	E (2) Y MC '85	Folkestone	Norwich City (A)	158+6	22+1	9	5	21		1	
Garry Brooke 5.6 10.5 24.11.60	FAC '81, '82	Bethnal Green	Tottenham H (A) Norwich City	49+24 8+4	4+1 1+1	4+8	6+3 1+2	15 3	1 1	1	1 1
Ian Crook 5.8 10.6 18.1.63		Romford	Tottenham H (A)	10+11	1	0+2	1+2	1			
Ruel Fox 5.6 10.0 14.1.68		Ipswich	Norwich City (A)								
Dale Gordon 5.10 11.8 9.1.67	EY,S	Gt. Yarmouth	Norwich City (A)	24+5	4	0+2		4			
Jeremy Goss 5.9 10.9 11.5.65	FAYC '83	Cyprus	Norwich City (A)	1+5		1					
Peter Mendham 5.10 11.6 9.4.60	MC '85	King's Lynn	Norwich City (A)	192+11	23+1	23	5	23		1	1
Steve Pritchard 5.11 13.0 5.12.67		Acton	Norwich City (A)								
Trevor Putney 5.7 10.11 11.2.61		Harold Hill	Brentwood & Warley Ipswich Town Norwich City	94+9	14	9		8	1		
David Williams 5.10 11.8 11.3.55	W.U23 (1) U21 (1)	Cardiff	Bristol Rovers Norwich City	342+10 37+2	12 3	17+1 1	6 6	66	6	7 1	
FORWARDS											
Wayne Biggins 5.11 11.0 20.11.61		Sheffield £7,500	Lincoln City Burnley Norwich City	8 78 28	6	3 1	7 4	1 29 7	1	1	5 1
Paul Clayton 5.11 11.3 4.1.65	FAYC '83	Dunstable	Norwich City (A)	8+5	1		1	1			
Lou Donowa 5.9 11.0 24.9.64	E. U21 (3) FAYC '83, MC '85	Ipswich	Norwich City (A) Stoke City (L)	56+6 4	13+1	1+1 0+1		11 1			
Kevin Drinkell† 5.10½ 12.6 18.6.60	Div.3 '80	Grimsby £105,000	Grimsby Town (A) Norwich City	242+28 41	20+4 4	12+3 1	6	89 22	8	5	1
David Hodgson 5.10 12.2 1.11.60	E.U21 (7) Div 1 '83	Gateshead £450,000 £125,000 F	Middlesbrough Liverpool Sunderland Norwich City	116+9 21+7 42+8	6 4+1 8+1	9 3 1	3+4 1+1	16 4 4	2 1	4 1	2 1
Jamie Hoyland 6.0 12.8½ 23.1.66	EY	Sheffield	Manchester City Norwich City	2	1			1			
Robert Rosario 6.3 12.1 4.3.66		Hammersmith	Norwich City Wolverhampton W (L)	18+2 2	4		1	5 1	1		

ADDITIONAL CONTRACT PROFESSIONALS
Richard Garwood, Mark Metcalf

APPRENTICES
Christopher Davy, Andrew Fensome, Jonathan Sheffield

NON-CONTRACT PLAYERS

CARROW ROAD Norwich NR1 1JE

Capacity: 26,000

Record Attendance: 43,984 v Leicester City, FA Cup Round 6, 30 Mar 1963

Record Receipts: £71,948 v Tottenham Hotspur, FA Cup Round 4 Replay, 1 Feb 1984

Season Tickets: Stands: £75.00 to £140.00; Ground: £45.00

Executive Box Season Tickets: Variable according to match

Cost of Stand Tickets: £4.50 to £5.50 **Terraces:** £3.00

Match and Ticket Information: Applications to Box Office 14 days before match with payment and SAE (0603 612591)

Car Parking: Numerous private parks nearby. Multi-storey parks in Malt House Road and St. Andrews Street. Street parking nearby in Rose Lane, Carrow Hill and side streets off King Street. Coaches must park at Lower Clarence Road Car Park

Nearest Railway Station: Norwich (0603 632055)

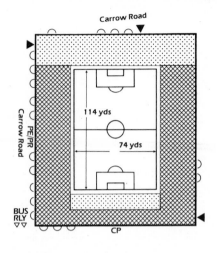

How to get to the ground

From North: Use A140 to junction with Ring Road, then follow signs Yarmouth A47. In 3.5m at T road turn right. In 0.5m turn left into Carrow Road for Norwich City FC
From East: Use A47 S.P. Norwich on entering city, keep left into Ring Road for Carrow Road for Norwich City FC
From South and West: Use A11, A140 into Norwich and follow signs Yarmouth A47 into Ring Road, Carrow Road for Norwich City FC

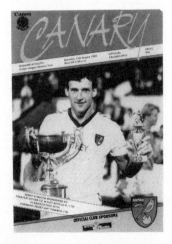

Price of 1986-7 Programme: 50p
Number of Pages: 20

Local Newspaper: Eastern Counties Newspapers

Local Radio Stations: Radio Norfolk, Radio Broadland

NOTTINGHAM FOREST — Division 1

Forest quickly settled after a poor opening but, though they finished well up the table, they were never really serious contenders for the Championship.

Manager Brian Clough made three major close-season signings — England under-21 midfield man Neil Webb, from Portsmouth, and defenders Ian Butterworth and Stuart Pearce, from Coventry. Butterworth is also an England under-21 cap.

Butterworth took over from Paul Hart, who had moved on to Sheffield Wednesday, but his intended centre-back partner Chris Fairclough was to miss the whole season through injury. Des Walker took over here.

The season was an exciting one for former apprentice David Campbell who earned his place in the N. Ireland squad with only a handful of first-team games behind him and then went to Mexico for the World Cup finals.

Nigel Clough finally played himself into the senior side, ending the season top scorer with 18 goals, a performance that earned him his first England under-21 cap.

Clough junior enjoyed such an impressive season that his father felt able to agree to the sale of England striker Peter Davenport to Manchester United towards the end of the season. That deal netted Forest a much-needed cash injection of £525,000.

Johnny Metgod once again proved an inspiration, whether he played in midfield or as a sweeper, and it was hoped that he would be renewing his contract with the club before the start of 1986/87.

Forest lost four of their opening six games and, at that point, were second from bottom. But they made a quick recovery and, at the end of five successive victories in November, they had joined the fringe of the Championship chase.

But they lacked consistency. In January they won successive away games at Tottenham and Manchester United but then lost at home to Newcastle and were held at home by Aston Villa.

Towards the end of the season, the manager introduced two young full-backs in Gary Fleming and Brett Williams and, with the rest of the side showing more confidence, Forest finished very well indeed, unbeaten in their closing 12 League matches.

Their Milk Cup run ended on Queen's Park Rangers' plastic pitch in the 4th Round so Forest fans were looking to the FA Cup to give them their last chance of honours. But they were surprisingly held at home by struggling 2nd Division Blackburn Rovers in the 3rd Round and, worse, went out in the replay at Ewood Park.

Back Row L to R: Colin Walsh, Garry Birtles, Steven Sutton (Goalkeeper), Ian Butterworth, Hans Segers (Goalkeeper), Brian Rice, Ian Bowyer (Team Captain). **Middle Row:** Ron Fenton (Coach), David Campbell, Stuart Pearce, Gary Mills, Johnny Metgod, Neil Webb, Mark Smalley, Liam O'Kane (Coach). **Front Row:** Des Walker, Nigel Clough, Gary Fleming, Franz Carr, Brett Williams.

NOTTINGHAM FOREST

DIVISION ONE: 8th   **FA CUP:** 3rd ROUND   **MILK CUP:** 4th ROUND

MATCH	DATE		COMPE-TITION	VENUE	OPPONENTS	RESULT		HALF TIME	L'GUE POS'N	GOALSCORERS/GOAL TIMES	ATTEN-DANCE
1	A	17	CL	A	Luton Town	D	1-1	0-1		Webb 52	(11,318)
2		21	CL	H	Sheffield Wednesday	L	0-1	0-1			18,361
3		24	CL	H	Southampton	W	2-1	2-0	12	Metgod 22, Wright (og) 44	12,643
4		27	CL	A	Q.P.R.	L	1-2	1-2	15	Webb 17	(10,748)
5		31	CL	H	Manchester United	L	1-3	0-3	18	Davenport 46	26,274
6	S	3	CL	A	Liverpool	L	0-2	0-0	21		(27,135)
7		8	CL	A	Leicester City	W	3-0	1-0	14	Webb 35, Davenport 78, Rice 89	(14,272)
8		14	CL	H	Tottenhan Hotspur	L	0-1	0-0	17		17,554
9		21	CL	H	Watford	W	3-2	1-1	15	Clough 28, Campbell 54, Davenport 71	12,921
10		25	MC2/1	H	Bolton Wanderers	W	4-0	0-0		Campbell 66, 74, Rice 70, Clough 79	10,530
11		28	CL	A	West Ham United	L	2-4	0-3	16	Metgod 61, Clough 70	(15,540)
12	O	5	CL	H	Ipswich Town	W	3-1	3-0	15	Pearce 8, Bowyer 11, 27	12,120
13		7	MC2/2	A	Bolton Wanderers	W	3-0	0-0		Rice 62, Davenport 74, Clough 84	(4,010)
14		12	CL	A	Aston Villa	W	2-1	0-0	12	Ormsby (og) 60, Clough 72	(15,315)
15		19	CL	A	Newcastle United	W	3-0	1-0	9	Rice 28, Davenport 78, 87	(23,151)
16		25	CL	H	Arsenal	W	3-2	1-0	8	Davenport 3 (pen) 29, 65, 72	17,756
17		30	MC3	A	Derby County	W	2-1	1-1		Metgod 12, Carr 68	(25,000)
18	N	3	CL	H	W.B.A.	W	2-1	1-0	8	Webb 38, Davenport 75	19,610
19		9	CL	A	Chelsea	L	2-4	1-3	9	Clough 10, 55	(17,743)
20		16	CL	H	Manchester City	L	0-2	0-1	10		15,140
21		23	CL	A	Everton	D	1-1	0-0	10	Clough 70	(27,860)
22		26	MC4	A	Q.P.R.	L	1-2	0-1		Clough 80	(13,052)
23	D	1	CL	H	Oxford United	D	1-1	0-1	10	Davenport (pen) 59	15,315
24		7	CL	A	Sheffield Wednesday	L	1-2	0-0	11	Webb 54	(22,495)
25		14	CL	H	Luton Town	W	2-0	1-0	10	Clough 30, Webb 78	12,087
26		20	CL	A	Southampton	L	1-3	1-2	11	Carr 43	(12,500)
27		26	CL	A	Birmingham City	W	1-0	1-0	10	Webb 17	(10,376)
28		28	CL	H	Liverpool	D	1-1	1-0	10	Webb 11	27,141
29	J	1	CL	H	Coventry City	W	5-2	1-2	9	Webb 3 40, 52, 76, Metgod 80, Davenport 84	13,860
30		4	FAC3	H	Blackburn Rovers	D	1-1	0-1		Birtles 55	15,772
31		11	CL	A	Tottenham Hotspur	W	3-0	0-0	9	Davenport 47, 69, Walsh 51	(19,043)
32		13	FAC3R	A	Blackburn Rovers	L	2-3	1-3		Walsh 24, Birtles 88	(11,710)
33		18	CL	A	Manchester United	W	3-2	1-0	8	Walsh 43, 80, Clough 88	(46,717)
34	F	1	CL	H	Q.P.R.	W	4-0	2-0	6	Walsh 20, 84, Carr 27, Webb 59	11,538
35		8	CL	H	Newcastle United	L	1-2	0-0	7	Walsh 80	15,388
36	M	8	CL	A	Ipswich Town	L	0-1	0-0	9		(12,658)
37		15	CL	H	Aston Villa	D	1-1	0-0	10	Clough (pen) 62	12,933
38		22	CL	H	Leicester City	W	4-3	2-1	10	Bowyer 7, Carr 38, Clough 65, 89	14,484
39		29	CL	A	Coventry City	D	0-0	0-0	10		(9,500)
40		31	CL	H	Birmingham City	W	3-0	1-0	10	Clough (pen) 28, Metgod 48, Webb 88	12,134
41	A	2	CL	H	West Ham United	W	2-1	1-0	8	Metgod 39, Rice 88	17,498
42		5	CL	A	W.B.A.	D	1-1	1-0	8	Metgod 21	(7,901)
43		8	CL	A	Arsenal	D	1-1	0-1	8	Campbell 65	(15,098)
44		12	CL	H	Chelsea	D	0-0	0-0	8		18,055
45		19	CL	A	Manchester City	W	2-1	0-0	7	Webb 71, Campbell 82	(19,715)
46		21	CL	A	Watford	D	1-1	1-1	7	Clough 22	(11,510)
47		26	CL	H	Everton	D	0-0	0-0	8		30,171
48	M	3	CL	A	Oxford United	W	2-1	1-1	8	Clough 16, 81	(11,845)

Best Home League Attendance: 30,171 v Everton   **Smallest:** 11,538 v Q.P.R.   **Av Home Att:** 16,809

Goal Scorers: Compared with 84-85: +2,279

League (69):	Clough 15 (2 pen), Webb 14, Davenport 13 (2 pen), Metgod 6, Walsh 6, Bowyer 3, Campbell 3, Carr 3, Rice 3, Opponents 2, Pearce 1
Milk Cup (10):	Clough 3, Campbell 2, Rice 2, Davenport 1, Metgod 1, Carr 1
FA Cup (3):	Birtles 2, Walsh 1

Segars	McInally	Pearce	Butterworth	Walker	Hodge	Mills	Webb	Birtles	Davenport	Robertson	Wigley	Metgod	Clough	Bowyer	Rice	Campbell	Carr	Walsh	Sutton	Williams	Flemming	Referee	
1	2	3	4	5	6		7	8	9	10	11											J Martin	1
1	2	3	4	5	6		8	9	10	11	7											D Scott	2
1	2	3	4	5			6	9	10	11	7	8										A Robinson	3
1	2	3	4	5		12	6		10	11*	7	8	9									J Deakin	4
1	2*	3	4	5			6		10	11	7	8	9	12								K Hackett	5
1		3	2	4			8	9*	10		7	5	12	6	11							T Mills	6
1		3	2	4			8	9*	10		7	5	12	6	11							T Holbrook	7
1		3	4	2			8		10		7	5	9	6	11							P Willis	8
1		3	4	2			8		10		7	5	9	6*	11	12						R Guy	9
1		3	4	2*			8		10		7	5	9		11	6	12					P Vanes	10
1*		3	4	2		7	11		10			5	9	6		8		12				D Axcell	11
	2	3	4	5			12		10	11		7	9	6		8*			1			T Jones	12
		3	4		2	6	5		10		7	8*	9		11			12	1			D Hutchinson	13
		3	4		2	6	5		10			8	9		11		7		1			A Buksh	14
		3	4		2	6	5		10			8	9		11		7		1			N Wilson	15
		3	4	12	2	6	5		10			8*	9		11		7		1			J McAuley	16
		3	4		2	6	5		10			8	9		11		7		1			D Shaw	17
		3	4		2	6	5		10			8	9		11		7		1			N Midgley	18
		3	4		2	6	5		10			8	9		11		7		1			R Milford	19
		3	4	12	2	6	5*		10			8	9		11		7		1			V Callow	20
	2	3	4	5		7	6		10			8	9				11		1			J Lovatt	21
	2	3	4			7	6	5	10†			8	9				11		1			M James	22
	2	3	4			7	6	5	10			8	9				11		1			P Tyldesley	23
	2	3	4				8	5	10				9	6			7	11	1			T Holbrook	24
	2	3	5	4					10	11		8*	9	6			7	12	1			J Bray	25
	2		5	4					10	3*	11	12	9	6			7	8	1			H King	26
	2*		4				8	5	10	11		7	9	6				12	1	3		K Walmsley	27
			4		2		8	5	10	11		7	9	6					1	3		K Baker	28
			4		2		8	5	10	11		7	9	6					1	3		M Cotton	29
			4		2		8	5	10	11		7	9	6*				12	1	3		G Courtney	30
		2	4				9	5	10	12		7	8*	6				11	1	3		R Milford	31
		2	4				8	5	10			7	9	6				11	1	3		G Courtney	32
			4				8		10			5	9	6			7	11	1	3	2	J Key	33
			4				8		10			5	9	6		12	7*	11	1	3	2	T Fitzharris	34
			4				8		10			5	9	6		12	7*	11	1	3	2	J Lloyd	35
			4				8		10			5	9	6	11*	12	7		1	3	2	D Reeves	36
1			4			7	10	5				12	9	6		8		11*		3	2	J Moules	37
			4				10					5	9	6	11	8	7		1	3	2	D Scott	38
			4				10					5	9	6	11	8	7		1	3	2	C Downey	39
		3	4				8		10*			5	9	6	11		7	12	1		2	J Worrall	40
		3	4				8					5	9	6	11	10	7		1		2	L Dilkes	41
		3	5	4			10						9		11	8	7	6	1		2	C Trussell	42
		3	4				10					5	9	6		8	7	11	1		2	L Robinson	43
		3	4				8					5	9	6		10	7	11	1		2	D Shaw	44
		3	12	4			8					5	9	6*		10	7	11	1		2	J Lovatt	45
		3	4				8					5	9		6	10	7	11	1		2	A Gunn	46
		3	4				8					5	9		11	10	7	6	1		2	B Hill	47
		3	4				8					5	9		11	10	7	6	1		2	R Hamer	48
11	12	30	24	34	2	13	38	24	27	10	8	37	37	25	19	13	24	16	31	11	16	League Appearances	
	1	2						1		1		2	2	1		4		4				Substitute Appearances	
1	1	4	4	1		3	4	3	4		2	4	4		3	1	1+1	1+1	3			Milk Cup Appearances	
		1	2		1	2	2	2	1			2	2	2			1+1		2	2		FA Cup Appearances	

Also Played:

Players on Loan:

Departures: Sinclair (Leeds Utd), McInally (Coventry C), Davenport (Man Utd), Wigley (Sheff Utd)

'FOREST'

Formed: 1865
Turned Professional: 1889   **Ltd Co:** 1982

Previous Managers: Until 1936, a secretary fulfilled the role of manager:
1889-97 Harry Radford   1897-1909 Harry Hallam   1909-12 F W Earp   1912-25 Bob Marsters
1925-9 Jack Baynes   1930-1 Stan Hardy   1931-6 Noel Watson   1936-9 Harold Wightman
1939-60 Billy Walker   1960-3 Andy Beattie   1963-8 Johnny Carey   1969-72 Matt Gillies
1972-3 Dave Mackay   1973-5 Allan Brown
Honours: Champions Div 1, 1977-8   Champions Div 2, 1906-7, 1921-2,   Champions Div 3 (S)
1950-1   FA Cup Winners 1898, 1959   Football League Cup Winners 1977-8, 1978-9   Anglo Scottish
Cup Winners 1976-7   European Cup Winners 1978-9, 1979-80   European Super Cup Winners
1979-80
League Career: Elected to Div 1 1892   Relegated to Div 2 1905-6
Promoted to Div 1 1906-7   Relegated to Div 2 1910-11   Promoted to Div 1 1921-2
Relegated to Div 2 1924-5   Relegated to Div 3 (S) 1948-9   Promoted to Div 2 1950-1
Promoted to Div 1 1956-7   Relegated to Div 2 1971-2   Promoted to Div 1 1976-7
Colours: Red shirts, white shorts, red stockings
Change Colours: All white

CLUB RECORDS

Most Appearances for Club: Bobby McKinlay: Football League 614 + FA Cup 54 + League Cup 11 + Inter Cities Fairs
Cup 6 **Total 685**
Most Capped Player: Martin O'Neill, 36, N Ireland   **For England:** Peter Shilton, 19
Record Goalscorer in a Match: A Higgins, 5 v Clapton, 14-0 (a), FA Cup 1st Round, 1890
Record League Goalscorer in a Season: Wally Ardron, 36   **In All Competitions:** Wally Ardron, 36 (all League), 1950-1
Record League Goalscorer in a Career: Grenville Morris, 199   **In All Competitions:** Grenville Morris, 217 (League
199 + FA Cup 18)
Record Transfer Fee Received: £1,250,000 from Manchester United for Gary Birtles, Oct 1980
Record Transfer Fee Paid: £1,250,000 to Coventry City for Ian Wallace, July 1980
Best Performances: League: As in Honours
Most League Points: (3pts for win) 74, Div 1, 1983-4   (2pts for win) 70, Div 3 (S), 1950-1
Record League Victory: 12-0 v Leicester City, Div 1, 21 April 1909
Record League Defeat: 1-9 v Blackburn Rovers, Div 2, 10.4.1937
European Competitions Entered: European Cup 1978-9, 1979-80, 1980-1   Fairs Cup 1961-2, 1967-8   UEFA Cup
1983-4, 1984-5   Super Competition 1979-80, 1980-1   World Club Championship 1980-1
Oldest Player in League Match: F H Scott 39 yrs 345 days v Rotherham United 15.9.56
Youngest Player in League Match: S J Burke, 16 yrs 22 days v Ayr United, Anglo Scottish Cup, 20.10.76
Most Consecutive Undefeated League Matches: 42 1977-78
(record)

Longest Run of Undefeated Home League Matches: 51 1977-79	**League Matches Without a Win:** 16 1913
Longest Run Without Home League Win: 10 1909-10, 1982	**Away League Matches:** 21 1977-78 (record)
Most Consecutive League Wins: 7 1892, 1906, 1921, 1979	**Away League Win:** 37 1913-15
Most Consecutive League Defeats: 14 1913	**Home League Wins:** 12 1980
	Away League Wins: 5 1907, 1983

NOTTINGHAM FOREST

PLAYERS NAME Ht Wt Birthdate	Honours	Birthplace Transfers	Clubs	APPEARANCES League	Milk Cup	FA Cup	Other Comps	GOALS League	Milk Cup	FA Cup	Other Comps
GOALKEEPERS											
Paul Chrichton 6.0 12.1		Pontefract	Notts Forest								
Darren Heyes 5.11 12.9 11.1.67	EY, S	Swansea	Notts Forest								
Hans Segers 5.11 12.7½ 30.10.61		Eindhoven, Holl. £50,000	PSV Eindhoven Notts Forest	39	1	4					
Steve Sutton 6.0 13.1½ 16.4.61		Hartington	Notts Forest (A) Mansfield Town (L) Derby County (L)	70 8 14	9 1	4 2					
DEFENDERS											
Gary Andrews 5.11 11.13½ 12.5.68		Nottingham	Notts Forest (A)								
Ian Butterworth 6.1 12.6 25.1.65	E. U21 (2)	Crewe	Coventry City (A) Notts Forest	80+10 24+1	5 4	5+1 1					
Chris Fairclough 5.11 11.12½ 12.4.64	E. U21 (3)	Nottingham	Notts Forest (A)	78+3	7	5	9+2				
Gary Fleming 5.9½ 11.1 17.2.67		Londonderry	Notts Forest (A)	18							
Stuart Pearce 5.10 11.2 24.4.62		London £25,000	Wealdstone Coventry City Notts Forest	51 30	4	2		1			
Mark Smalley 5.11 11.6 2.1.65		Newark	Notts Forest (A) Birmingham C (L)	1+2 7							
Desmond Walker 5.11 11.3 26.11.65	E. U21 (1)	Hackney	Notts Forest (A)	40+3	1	2					
Brett Williams 5.10 11.11 19.3.68		Dudley	Notts Forest (A)	11		2					
MIDFIELD											
Ian Bowyer 5.10 11.11 6.6.51	Div 1 '78 Lg.C 70,78,79 E.Cup 79, 80	Ellesmere Port £25,000 £40,000 £50,000 £50,000	Manchester C (A) Orient Notts Forest Sunderland Notts Forest	42+8 75+3 222+17 15 168+3	6+8 31+1 1 10	4 25 8	5+3 15 12	13 49 1 16	2 12 1	5 2	5 1
David Campbell 5.9 10.9 2.6.65	NI (2)	Londonderry	Notts Forest (A)	13+5	1						
Johnny Metgod 6.4 13.6 27.2.58	Holland	Amsterdam, Holland £300,000	(DWS, Haarlem, AZ67) Real Madrid Notts Forest	77+2	8	6	2	12	1		
Gary Mills 5.8 11.1 11.11.61	E. U21 (2), Y, S E. Cup '80	Northampton Seattle Sounders Seattle Sounders	Notts Forest (A) Derby County Notts Forest	50+8 18 26+10	7+3 2 6	3 3 1	4+2 3+1	8 4	2		
Colin Murphy 5.7 10.5 1.5.68		Birmingham	Notts Forest (A)								
Steve Murray 5.7½ 10.13 1.12.67		Kilmarnock	Notts Forest (A)								
Leigh Palin 5.9½ 10.3 12.9.65	EY	Worcester	Aston Villa Shrewsbury Town (L) Notts Forest	2							
Brian Rice 6.0 11.10 11.10.63	S.U21 (1) Y	Glasgow	Hibernian Notts Forest	53+9 19	7+2 3	2		9 3	1 2		
Colin Walsh 5.9 11.0 22.7.62	S.U21 (5) Y	Hamilton	Notts Forest (A)	115+24	9+4	8+2	11	32		2	3
Neil Webb 6.1 11.12 30.7.63	E.U21 (1) Y Div.3 '83	Reading £83.000 £250,000	Reading Portsmouth Notts Forest	65+7 123 38	2 13 4	2 8 2		22 34 14	5		
Terry Wilson 6.0 10.10		Broxburn	Notts Forest (A)								
FORWARDS											
Garry Birtles 6.0 12.0 27.7.56	E (3) U.21 (2) B (1) LgC '79 E.Cup '79, '80 ESC '79	Nottingham £3,000 £1,250,000 £275,000	Long Eaton United Notts Forest Manchester Utd Notts Forest	87 57+1 94+2	18 2 8	5 4 4	20 7+2	32 11 24	10	1 6	8
Franz Carr 5.6 10.8½ 24.9.66	EY		Blackburn Rovers (A) Notts Forest	24	1+1			3	1		
Nigel Clough† 5.9 11.4 19.3.66	E.U21	Sunderland	Notts Forest (A)	45+3	4	2		16	3		
David Riley 5.7 10.10 8.12.60		Northampton	Keyworth United Notts Forest	7+4	1			2			

ADDITIONAL CONTRACT PROFESSIONALS

APPRENTICES
Antony Abrahams, Raymond Campbell, David Carlin, Gary Charles, Stephen Chettle, Steven McLoughlin

NON-CONTRACT PLAYERS
Paul Chalmers, Mark Crossley, Graham Forbes, Philip Spall, Philip Starbuck, Darren Wassall

CITY ROAD   Nottingham NG2 5FJ

Capacity: 35,000 (14,561 seats)

Record Attendance: 44,945 v Manchester United, Div 1, 28 Oct 1967

Record Receipts: £132,000 v Ajax, European Cup Semi-Final 1st Leg, 9 Apr 1980

Season Tickets: £70.00, £90.00, £98.00 (stands); £135.00 & £108.00 (Tandems of 1 adult and 1 juvenile); £46.00 (ground); £25.00 (juveniles/OAP)

Executive Box Season Tickets: Phone Commercial Office for details (820444)

Cost of Stand Tickets: £6.00, £5.50, £5.00 (Tandems £9.00 and £8.00); **Terraces:** £3.00 (adults), £1.50 (OAP/juveniles)
For pre-season games an extra 50p is charged

Match and Ticket Information: 14 days in advance (personal); 12 days (postal)

Car Parking: Space for 300 cars in East Stand car park plus street parking off Loughborough and Radcliffe Roads

Nearest Railway Station: Nottingham Midland (0602 46151)

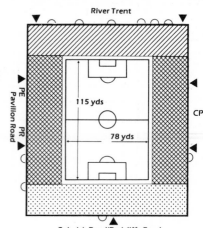

River Trent

115 yds

78 yds

PE Pavilion Road

PR

CP

Colwick Road/Radcliffe Road

How to get to the ground

From North: Use Motorway M1 until junction 26, leave Motorway and follow signs into Nottingham A610. Follow signs Melton Mowbray, Trent Bridge A606. Cross river and turn left into Radcliffe Road, then turn left into Colwick Road for Nottingham Forest FC

From East: Use A52 S.P. Nottingham into West Bridgeford, then turn right into Colwick Road for Nottingham Forest FC

From South: Use Motorway M1 until junction 24, leave Motorway and follow signs Nottingham (South) to Trent Bridge, turn right into Radcliffe Road, then turn left into Colwick Road for Nottingham Forest FC

From West: Use A52 into Nottingham, then follow signs Melton Mowbray, Trent Bridge A606, cross river and turn left into Radcliffe Road, then turn left into Colwick Road for Nottingham Forest FC

Price of 1986-7 Programme: 50p
Number of Pages: 24
Subscriptions: Apply to club

Local Newspapers: Nottingham Evening Post, Derby Telegraph

Local Radio Stations: Radio Nottingham, Radio Trent

Chairman
J J Dunnett, MA, LLB (Cantab), MP

Managing Director
N Hook

Directors
R Sweet
J Mounteney
J Sirrel

Company Secretary
Neal Hook, M Inst M (0602 861155)

Manager
Jimmy Sirrel

Reserve Team Coach
Michael Walker

Physiotherapist
Wayne Jones

Commercial Manager
Elaine Howes

Chief Coach
Dick Bate

After the glamour of the 1st Division the drudgery of the 3rd was something that gave no pleasure to County fans, who cannot be happy about the team's failure to return at least to the 2nd Division immediately, but this might have been premature for a side which must be rebuilt and the ultimate evidence appears to suggest that Jimmy Sirrel, back as team manager, has gone some way to achieving that. County did not start the League campaign well and three defeats in six matches during March made it certain that another season in the 3rd Division would be necessary: only one of those games was won. A final position of eighth was disappointing particularly as a promotion place seemed possible early in the New Year.

The cups provided some encouragement with the Milk Cup starting well; Doncaster were despatched on aggregate in the first round (2-2 and penalties) before Fulham in extra-time at Meadow Lane delivered a knock-out blow (5-3 on aggregate). The FA Cup went much better with an easy 1st Round victory over Scarborough (6-1 at home) followed by a win in a replay at Wrexham (3-0) after a draw (2-2) at Meadow Lane. Then a visit to the Victoria Ground brought success over Stoke City by two clear goals, which brought a draw at home against Tottenham Hotspur, who needed a replay at White Hart Lane before advancing (5-0). In the Freight Rover Trophy neighbours Mansfield Town made a successful visit to Meadow Lane (1-0) and that was that!

Fans of the League's oldest club will want nothing less than promotion this coming season and Jimmy Sirrel must use a blend of consistent experienced men and younger players to achieve it. Last season Clarke, Benjamin, Sims, Yates, McParland and Goodwin all showed the right kind of form, so a few adjustments here and there could 'do the trick' for the club.   WLM

Back Row L to R: Darren Davis, Tristan Benjamin, Mick Leonard, David Hunt, Paul Barnes. **Middle Row:** Wayne Jones (Physio), Steve Sims (Capt), Mick Waitt, Dean Yates, Dick Bate (Chief Coach). **Front Row:** Paul Smalley, David Clarke, Declan Edge, Jimmy Sirrel (Manager), David Kevan, Mark Harbottle, Ian McParland.

NOTTS COUNTY

DIVISION THREE: 8th   **FA CUP:** 4th ROUND   **MILK CUP:** 2nd ROUND   **FRT:** PRELIMINARY ROUND

MATCH	DATE	COMPE-TITION	VENUE	OPPONENTS	RESULT	HALF TIME	L'GUE POS'N	GOALSCORERS/GOAL TIMES	ATTEN-DANCE
1	A 17	CL	H	Cardiff City	L	1-4	0-3		Young 47	5,436
2	20	MC1/1	H	Doncaster Rovers	W	1-0	0-0		Clarke 84	2,425
3	24	CL	A	Blackpool	W	3-1	3-1	14	Clarke 21, Young 30, Harkouk 38	(4,011)
4	26	CL	H	Doncaster Rovers	D	1-1	0-1		McParland 61	3,922
5	31	CL	A	Plymouth Argyle	W	1-0	1-0	11	Harkouk 13	(5,105)
6	S 3	MC1/2	A	Doncaster Rovers	L	1-2†	1-0		Goodwin 26	(2,679)
7	7	CL	H	Gillingham	D	1-1	1-0	9	Young 14	3,624
8	14	CL	A	Bournemouth	D	0-0	0-0	11		(4,235)
9	17	CL	H	York City	W	3-1	3-0	7	Goodwin 3, Young 27, McParland 39	3,708
10	22	CL	A	Darlington	W	3-2	1-0	4	Harbottle 45, McParland 72, Waitt 86	(3,786)
11	24	MC2/1	A	Fulham	D	1-1	1-0		Goodwin 24	(2,324)
12	28	CL	H	Bury	D	2-2	1-0	4	Young 34, Waitt 89	4,622
13	O 1	CL	A	Bristol Rovers	D	1-1	1-0	5	McParland 14	(3,549)
14	5	CL	A	Derby County	L	0-2	0-1	7		(14,406)
15	8	MC2/2	H	Fulham	L	2-4†	2-0	·	Young 15, McParland 44	3,054
16	12	CL	H	Bristol City	W	4-0	2-0	5	Hunt 3 21, 28, 60, McParland 70	4,332
17	19	CL	H	Chesterfield	W	2-1	1-1	3	Waitt 6, Goodwin (pen) 62	5,776
18	22	CL	A	Wigan Athletic	L	1-5	1-2	7	Robinson 3	(3,555)
19	27	CL	H	Lincoln City	W	3-2	2-2	5	Harkouk 6, 59, McParland 21	6,143
20	N 2	CL	A	Walsall	D	0-0	0-0	5		(4,967)
21	6	CL	H	Reading	L	1-3	0-2	9	Harkouk (pen) 74	(6,766)
22	9	CL	H	Bolton Wanderers	W	1-0	0-0	8	Yates 78, McParland 75	4,497
23	17	FAC1	H	Scarborough	W	6-1	3-0		Hunt 20, Harkouk 3 28, 29, 78, Young 68,	5,621
24	23	CL	A	Newport County	W	2-1	1-1	6	McParland 20, Goodwin 81	(1,946)
25	30	CL	H	Swansea City	W	3-0	2-0	4	Hunt 19, Goodwin (pen) 41, McParland 89	3,912
26	D 7	FAC2	H	Wrexham	D	2-2	0-0		Waitt 57, 89	4,569
27	10	FAC2R	A	Wrexham	W	3-0	1-0		Clarke 7, Waitt 60, McParland 79	(2,645)
28	14	CL	A	Rotherham United	L	0-1	0-0	5		(3,820)
29	22	CL	H	Blackpool	L	1-2	0-1	8	Hunt 49	5,926
30	26	CL	H	Wolverhampton W.	W	4-0	1-0	4	Harkouk 6, McParland 48, Waitt 75, Goodwin 89	5,264
31	28	CL	A	Doncaster Rovers	L	1-2	1-1	9	Edge 25, Goodwin 89	(3,673)
32	J 11	CL	H	Plymouth Argyle	W	2-0	1-0	5	Hunt 26, McParland 73	4,953
33	13	FAC3	A	Stoke City	W	2-0	1-0		Waitt 40, McParland 64	(12,219)
34	16	FRT	H	Doncaster Rovers	W	1-0	1-0		McParland 35	1,642
35	18	CL	A	Cardiff City	W	3-1	1-1	4	Waitt 22, Mullen (og) 70, McParland 87	(2,410)
36	20	CL	A	Brentford	D	1-1	1-0	3	Hunt 36	(4,002)
37	25	FAC4	H	Tottenham Hotspur	D	1-1	1-1		McParland 21	17,546
38	29	FAC4R	A	Tottenham Hotspur	L	0-5	0-3			(17,393)
39	F 1	CL	A	Gillingham	L	0-4	0-2	6		(4,368)
40	4	CL	H	Wigan Athletic	D	1-1	0-1	6	Yates 61	3,369
41	8	CL	A	Chesterfield	D	2-2	1-2	6	Edge 12, Waitt 90	(3,623)
42	M 1	CL	A	Bury	W	4-2	2-2	6	Waitt 25, Hunt 35, Harkouk 46, Barnes 68	(2,379)
43	4	CL	H	Bristol Rovers	D	0-0	0-0	6		3,183
44	8	CL	H	Derby County	L	0-3	0-0	6		13,086
45	11	FRT	A	Mansfield Town	L	0-1	0-1			(3,447)
46	15	CL	A	Bristol City	L	0-3	0-1	9		(5,701)
47	20	FRT	H	Mansfield Town	L	0-1	0-0			2,409
48	22	CL	A	Lincoln City	W	2-0	0-0	7	Waitt 65, 84	(3,468)
49	29	CL	H	Brentford	L	0-4	0-3	11		3,857
50	31	CL	A	Wolverhampton W.	D	2-2	2-2	12	Waitt 4, Goodwin 26	(3,774)
51	A 5	CL	H	Reading	D	0-0	0-0	11		3,711
52	8	CL	H	Walsall	W	3-1	2-0	9	Waitt 6, 47, Barnes 19	2,490
53	12	CL	A	Bolton Wanderers	L	0-1	0-0	9		(4,688)
54	15	CL	H	Bournemouth	W	3-1	2-0	8	Davis 2, McParland 8, Waitt 53	2,423
55	19	CL	H	Newport County	L	1-2	0-2	8	Waitt 46	3,279
56	22	CL	A	York City	D	2-2	1-2	8	Barnes 20, McParland (pen) 57	(3,211)
57	26	CL	A	Swansea City	D	0-0	0-0	8		(3,869)
58	M 3	CL	H	Rotherham United	W	1-0	0-0	8	McParland 50	3,213
59	6	CL	H	Darlington	W	5-0	2-0	8	Yates 4, 40, Barnes 53, Clarke 74, McParland 82	2,345

Best Home League Attendance: 13,086 v Derby County   **Smallest:** 2,345 v Darlington   **Av Home Att: 4,481**

Goal Scorers: Compared with 84-85: +709

League (71): McParland 15 (1 pen), Waitt 14, Hunt 8, Harkouk 7 (1 pen), Goodwin 6 (2 pen), Young 5, Barnes 4, Yates 4, Clarke 2, Edge 2, Davis 1, Harbottle 1, Opponent 1, Robinson 1

Milk Cup (5): Goodwin 2, Clarke 1, Young 1, McParland 1

FA Cup (14): McParland 4, Waitt 4, Harkouk 3, Clarke 1, Hunt 1, Young 1

FRT (1): McParland 1   †After Extra Time

1985-86

Leonard	Richards	Clarke	Benjamin	Sims	Yates	McParland	Goodwin	Young	Harkouk	Downing	Davis	Smalley	Hunt	Waitt	Harbottle (A)	Fairclough (A)	Robinson	Daws	Hesford (L)	Edge	Kevan (A)	Barnes	Mimms	Davies	Dalton	Referee	
1	2	3	4	5	6	7	8	9	10	11																P Tyldesley	1
1	2	11	4	5	6	7	8*	9	10		3	12														J Hough	2
1	2	3	4	5	6	7	8*	9	10			12	11													T Jones	3
1	2	3	4	5	6	7		9	10	11*		12	8													V Callow	4
1	2	3	4	5	6	7		9	10				11													R Groves	5
1	2	3	4	5	6	7	8	9	10*				11	12												N Midgley	6
1	2	3	4	5	6	7	8	9					11	10												T Simpson	7
1	2	3	4	5	6	7	8	9					11	10												R Gifford	8
1	2	3	4	5	6	7	8	9*					11	10	12											C Downey	9
1		3	4	5	6	7	8						11	9	10*	2	12									M Peck	10
1	2	3	4	5	6	7	8						11	9		12	10*									D Hedges	11
1	2	3	4	5	6	7	8	9*					11	10			12									E Scales	12
1	2	3	4	5	6	7	8	9					11	10												R Lewis	13
1	2	3	4	5	6	7	8*	9					11	10			12									A Robinson	14
1	2	11	4	5	6	7		9			3*		8	10			12									D Shaw	15
1	2	3	4	5	6	7*	8	9					11	10			12									C Trussell	16
1	2	3	4	5	6	7	8	9					11	10*			12									I Hemley	17
1	2	3	4	5	6	7	8*	9					11		12		10									G Aplin	18
1	2	3	4	5	6	7	8	9	10*				11				12									M Dimblebee	19
1	2	3	4	5	6	7	8	9	10				11													R Nixon	20
1	2	3	4	5	6	7	8*	9	10				11				12									M Bodenham	21
1	2	3	4	5	6	7	8	9					11				10									D Reeves	22
1	2	3	4	5	6	7	8	9	10				11													R Banks	23
1		3	4	5	6	7	8		10*			2	11	9			12									D Vickers	24
		3	4	5	6	7	8					2	11	9			10			1						J Lovatt	25
1		3	4	5	6	7	8	9				2	11	10												N Midgley	26
1		3	4	5	6	7	8	9				2	11	10												N Midgley	27
		3	4	5	6†	7	8	9*				2	11	10			12			1						K Breen	28
		3	4		6	7	8	9*	12		5	2	11	10						1						I Borrett	29
		3	4	5	6	7	8	10				2*	11	9					1	12						T Fitzharris	30
		3	4	5	6	7	8				6	2*	11	9	12				1†	10						D Scott	31
1		3	4	5*		7	8				6		11	9	2		12			10						R Dilkes	32
1		3	4	5	2	7	8				6		11	9			12			10*						G Napthine	33
		3*	4	5	2	7*	8				6	12	11	9			13		1	10						T Holbrook	34
			4	5	6	7	8				3	2	11	9					1	10						L Shapter	35
			4		6	7	8		3		5	2	11	9					1	10						K Miller	36
1			4	6	7	8			12		3	5	11	9	2					10*						R Lewis	37
1			4	5	6	7			8		3	2	11	9						10						R Lewis	38
		3	4		6	7			10		5	8*	11	9	2				1		12					J Moules	39
		3	4		6				7		5	8	11	9	2				1	10*		12				R Hamer	40
		3		5	6		8		7			4	11	9	2				1	10						D Hedges	41
1	6		4	2	9	7			11*		5	3	8	10								12				G Ashby	42
1	3*		5	2	7	8					6	4	11	9						10		12				V Callow	43
1	3	4	5	2	7*	8			10		6		11	9						12						J Key	44
1		4	5	2	7	8			10		3	6	11	9												J Ball	45
	3	4	5	6	12	8			10*			2	11	9								7	1			R Gifford	46
		4	5	6	7	8			10		3	2*	11	9						12			1			D Phillips	47
		4	5	6	7	8			10		3	2	11*	12								9	1			T Simpson	48
		12	4	5	6	7	8		10		3	2*		9								11		1		N Glover	49
		11	4	5	6	7	8		10*		3	2		9						12				1		F Roberts	50
		11	4	5	6	7	8		10		3	2		9								10		1		N Midgley	51
		11	4	5	6	7	8				3	2		9								10		1		J McAuley	52
5		11	4		6	7	8				3	2		9								10		1		G Tyson	53
		11	4	5	6	7	8				3	2		9								10		1		N Wilson	54
		11	4	5	6	7	8				3	2		9								10		1		M Cotton	55
		11	4	5	6	7	8				3	2		9								10			1	K Redfern	56
12		11	4	5	6	7	8				3*	2		9								10		1		R Guy	57
		11	2	5	6	7	8				3			9						4		10		1		R Bridges	58
		11	2	5*	6	7	8				3			9						4		10		1		D Reeves	59
23	19	41	43	41	44	43	43	19	19	3	22	24	34	36	1	5	3		10	7	2	11	2	10	1	League Appearances	
1	1		1		1			1			2		1	3			9	1	3	1		3				Substitute Appearances	
4	4	4	4	4	4	3	3	2			2	0-1	3	2-1		0-2	1									Milk Cup Appearances	
6	1	4	6	5	6	6	5	3	3		3	4	6	5	1	1	3									FA Cup Appearances	
3	3	3	3	3	3	2	2-1	3		2-1-1	3	0-1	1	1-1	1				0-1	1	1-1		1			FR Trophy Appearances	

Players on Loan: Hesford (Sheffield Wednesday), Davies (Hull)
Also Played: Position (Game): Jackson 12(59)

'THE MAGPIES'

Formed: 1862 (oldest League club)
Turned Professional: 1885   **Ltd Co:** 1890

Previous Managers: (Before 1913 the team was chosen by directors)
1913-27 Albert Fisher   1927-34 Horace Henshall   1934 Charlie Jones   1935 David Pratt
1935-36 Percy Smith   1936-37 Jimmy McMullan   1938-39 Harry Parkes   1939-42 Tony Towers
1942-43 Frank Womack   1944-46 Maj. Frank Buckley   1946-49 Arthur Stollery
1949-53 Eric Houghton   1953-57 George Poyser   1957-58 Tommy Lawton   1958-61 Frank Hill
1961-63 Tim Coleman   1963-65 Eddie Lowe (player-manager)   1965-66 Tim Coleman
1966-67 Jack Burkitt   1967 Andy Beattie   1967-68 Billy Gray   1968-69 Jack Wheeler
(caretaker manager for 14 months)   1969-75 Jimmy Sirrel   1975-77 Ronnie Fenton
1977-82 Jimmy Sirrel   1982-83 Howard Wilkinson   1983-84 Larry Lloyd   1984-85 Ritchie Barker
Honours: Div 2 Champions 1896-7, 1913-4, 1922-3   Div 3 (S) Champions 1930-1, 1949-50   Div 4
Champions 1970-1 FA Cup Winners 1893-4
League Career: Founder member of Football League 1888   Relegated to Div 2 1892-3
Promoted to Div 1 1896-7   Relegated to Div 2 1912-3   Promoted to Div 1 1913-4
Relegated to Div 2 1919-20   Promoted to Div 1 1922-3   Relegated to Div 2 1925-6
Relegated to Div 3 (S) 1929-30   Promoted to Div 2 1930-1   Relegated to Div 3 (S) 1934-5
Promoted to Div 2 1949-50   Relegated to Div 3 1957-8   Relegated to Div 4 1958-9
Promoted to Div 3 1959-60   Relegated to Div 4 1963-4   Promoted to Div 3 1970-1
Promoted to Div 2 1972-3   Promoted to Div 1 1980-1   Relegated to Div 2 1983-4
Relegated to Div 3 1984-5
Colours: White with thin black striped shirts, black shorts with white stripe, white stockings with black
hoops on tops
Change Colours: All yellow with green trim   **Reserves League:** Central   **'A' Team:** Midland Intermediate

CLUB RECORDS

Most Appearances for Club: Albert Iremonger, 564, 1904-26   **All Competitions:** Albert Iremonger 601 (564 League, 35
Cup)
Most Capped Player: Aki Lahtinen, 10, Finland   **For England:** Harry Cursham 8
Record Goalscorer in a Match: Bob Jardine, 5 v Burnley, Div 1, 27 Oct 1888   Dan Bruce, 5 v Burslem Port Vale, Div 2, 26
Feb 1985   Paddy Mills, 5 v Barnsley, Div 2, 19 Nov 1927
Record League Goalscorer in a Season: Tom Keetley 39, Div 3 (S), 1930-1   **In All Competitions:** Tom Keetley, 41,
1930-31 (League 39 + 2 FA Cup)
Record League Goalscorer in a Career: Les Bradd, 125, 1967-8   **All competitions:** Les Bradd, 138
Record Transfer Fee Received: £350,000 from Tottenham Hotspur for John Chiedozie, Aug 1984
Record Transfer Fee Paid: £350,000 to Orient for John Chiedozie, Aug 1981
Best Performances: League: 3rd Div 1 1890-1, 1900-1   **FA Cup:** Winners   **League/Milk Cup:** 5th Round 1963-4,
1972-3, 1975-6
Most League Points: 71 in Div 3, 1985-6   **Most League Goals:** 107, Div 4, 1959-60
Record League Victory and Most Goals in a First Class Match: 11-1 v Newport Co (H), Div 3 (S), 15 Jan 1949
Most Goals Scored in a Cup Tie: 15-0 v Rotherham Town (H), 1st Round FA Cup, 24 Oct 1885
Record League Defeat: 1-9 v Blackburn Rovers, Div 1, 16 Nov 1889   1-9 v Aston Villa, Div 1, 29 Sept 1930   1-9 v
Portsmouth, Div 2, 9 Apr 1927
Oldest Player in League Match: Albert Iremonger 41 yrs 320 days, May 1926
Youngest Player in League Match: Tony Bircumshaw 16 yrs 54 days, April 61

Most Consecutive Undefeated League Matches: 19 1930	**League Matches Without a Win:** 18 1904-05
Longest Run of Undefeated Home League Matches: 25 1970-71	**Away League Matches:** 10 1971
Longest Run Without Home League Win: 13 1904-05. 1979-80	**Away League Win:** 24 1933-35
Most Consecutive League Wins: 8 1914	**Home League Wins:** 14 1959-60
Most Consecutive League Defeats: 7 1888-89, 1912, 1933, 1983	**Away League Wins:** 5 1896

Club Statistician for the Directory: K Warsop

NOTTS COUNTY

PLAYERS NAME Ht Wt Birthdate	Honours	Birthplace Transfers	Clubs	APPEARANCES				GOALS			
				League	Milk Cup	FA Cup	Other Comps	League	Milk Cup	FA Cup	Other Comps
GOALKEEPERS											
Mick Leonard 5.11 11.0 9.5.59		Carshalton £30,000	Epsom & Ewell Halifax Town Notts County	 69 91	 6 10	 1 9	 1				
DEFENDERS											
Tristan Benjamin† 6.0 11.1 1.4.57	EY	St. Kitts W.I.	Notts County (A)	271+5	27+1	14	3	4			
David Clarke 5.10 11.0 3.12.64	EY	Nottingham	Notts County	92+8	7+2	10	1	2	2	1	
Darren Davis 6.0 11.0 5.2.67		Nottingham	Notts County (A)	27	2	3	3	1			
Keith Downing 5.8 11.0 23.7.65		Birmingham	Mile Oak Rovers Notts County	15							
Wayne Fairclough 5.10½ 9.12 27.4.64		Nottingham	Notts County	5	0+2	1					
Steve Sims 6.1 13.9 2.7.57	E. B (1) U.21 (10) Y	Lincoln £175,000 £50,000	Leicester City (A) Watford Notts County	78+1 150+2	5 14	3 14	 4+1	3 4	 3		
Paul Smalley 5.11 11.0 17.11.66			Notts County (A)	24+2	0+1	4	2+1				
Dean Yates 6.1 11.0 26.10.67		Leicester	Notts County (A)	52	4	6	3	4			
MIDFIELD											
Mark Goodwin 5.10 10.9 23.2.60	Div.2 '80	Sheffield £60,000	Leicester City (A) Notts County	69+22 181+11	3 16+1	4+1 12+1	 3	8 20	 3		
Mark Harbottle 5.10 10.4 26.9.68	EY	Nottingham	Notts County (A)	1+3				1			
David Hunt 5.11 11.0 17.4.59		Leicester £30,000	Derby County (A) Notts County	5 39+5	 25+1	 20+1	 3	 26	 3	 2	
David Kevan 5.8 9.10 31.8.68		Wigtown	Notts County (A)	2+1							
Craig Jackson 5.10½ 10.9 17.1.69		Rennishaw	Notts County (YTS)	1							
FORWARDS											
Paul Barnes 5.10 10.6 16.11.67		Leicester	Notts County (A)	10+3				4			
Dellan Edge 5.10 10.1 18.9.65	New Zealand	Malacca, Malaya	Shrewsbury Town (A) Gisbourne N.Z. Notts County	 7+3		 3	 1+1	 2			
Ian McParland 5.8 10.8 4.10.61		Edinburgh	Ormiston Primrose Notts County	 85+25	 6+2	 8+2	 3	 18	 1	 6	 1
Mick Waitt 6.4 13.7 25.6.60		Newcastle	Keyworth United Arnold Kingswell Notts County	 43+7	 2+1	 7	 3	 15		 4	
Alan Young 6.0 12.7 26.10.55	S.Sch Div.2 '80	Kirkcaldy £250,000 £160,000 £140,000 £55,000	Oldham Athletic Leicester City Sheffield United Brighton Notts County	107+15 102+2 23+2 25+1 39+4	3 5 4 2 6	6 10 2 1 5		30 26 7 12 12	1 1 3 2	4 2 3 1	

ADDITIONAL CONTRACT PROFESSIONALS

Richard Young   Departures: Dalton, Beavon, Richards (Boston United)

APPRENTICES

Luke Betteridge, Tony Wood

NON-CONTRACT PLAYERS

Eddie Snook

Record Attendance: 47,310 v York City, FA Cup Round 6, 10 Mar 1955

Smallest Attendance for a First Class Match: 1,927 v Chesterfield, Div 4, 2 Apr 1966

Record Receipts: £63,505 v Everton, FA Cup Round 6, 10 Mar 1984

Season Tickets: £60 to £95 (Stands), £40 (£25 OAPs/Juniors) (Ground)

Executive Box Season Tickets: Consult Commercial Manager

Cost of Stand Tickets: £4.50, £5.50 (£3 adult £2 OAP/juveniles)

Match and Ticket Information: Applications by post (with remittance and SAE) or in person 14 days before each match

Car Parking: No street parking near ground but ample space in the City of Nottingham Corporation car park on the Cattle Market, Meadow Lane, 400 yards from the main entrances

Nearest Railway Station: Nottingham Midland (0602 46151)

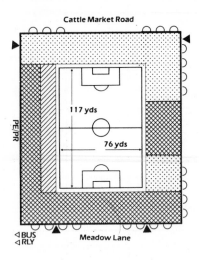

How to get to the ground

From North: Use Motorway M1 until junction 26, leave motorway and follow signs into Nottingham A610. Follow signs Melton Mowbray, Trent Bridge A606. On nearside of River Trent turn left into Meadow Lane for Notts County FC

From East: Use A52 S.P. Nottingham to Trent Bridge, cross River and then turn right into Meadow Lane for Notts County FC

From South: Use Motorway M1 until junction 24, leave motorway and follow signs Nottingham (South) to Trent Bridge, cross river and then turn right into Meadow Lane for Notts County FC

From West: Use A52 into Nottingham, then follow signs Melton Mowbray, Trent Bridge A606 on nearside of River Trent turn left into Meadow Lane for Notts County FC

Price of 1986-7 Programme: 50p
Number of Pages: 32

Local Newspaper: Nottingham Evening Post

Local Radio Stations: Radio Nottingham, Radio Trent

OLDHAM ATHLETIC   Division 2

President
R Schofield

Chairman
I H Stott

Directors
D A Brierley (Vice-Chairman)
R Adams
G T Butterworth
P Chadwick
J C Slevin
D R Taylor

Secretary
T M Finn (061-624 4972)

Commercial Manager
A Hardy (061-652 0966)

Manager
Joe Royle

Coach
W Urmson

Player/Coach
Willie Donachie

Chief Scout
J Cassell

Youth Development Officer
G Hollinshead

Physiotherapist
I Liversedge

Groundsman
H Wood

Club Statistician
Mark Blackbourne

After losing at Norwich on the opening day of the season, the Latics quickly struck form and, after beating Charlton in mid-September, moved into second place in the table. For several weeks it seemed they would make a serious bid to make their long-awaited return to the 1st Division.

With Ron Futcher, Roger Palmer and Mike Quinn all scoring consistently, Oldham's attack was a match for most rivals.

At the end of October, after crushing promotion rivals Brighton 4-0 at Boundary Park, Oldham were still in second place but then, for no logical reason, the defence disintegrated.

Sheffield United hit five past them at Boundary Park, Stoke scored four times there. In ten games, the Latics collected only one point and conceded 26 goals.

That effectively ended any hopes of promotion and, for a week or two, they were more concerned with relegation.

Manager Joe Royle went into the market for four new players. Centre-back Paul Jones was signed from Huddersfield, right-back Gary Williams came from Bristol City. Gordon Smith, a midfield player was signed from Manchester City following a successful loan spell and Andy Linighan, another centre-back, was bought from Leeds.

Mr Royle also gave Bob Colville a run in the senior side up front.

After that, results started to improve and the relegation threat was quickly dispelled. A good run at the end saw the Latics rise into eighth place in the table.

Quinn, who scored 11 times, moved on to Portsmouth shortly before the transfer deadline.

Latic's fans had precious little Cup excitement. Their Milk Cup venture was catastrophic. Drawn against Mersey giants Liverpool, they went down 0-3 at Anfield and 2-5 at Boundary Park. Rather surprisingly, Liverpool's visit drew only 7,719 spectators.

In the third round of the FA Cup, Oldham received the bitter blow of being beaten at home by 4th Division Orient.

At least, improved form towards the end of the season gave rise to optimism for 1986/87. It they can find more consistency, the Latics could be ready for a promotion bid in the new season.

Back Row L to R: Dennis Irwin, Paul Jones, Andy Goram, Andy Gorton, Andy Linighar, Roger Palmer. **Middle Row:** Mike Flynn, Willie Donachie (Player Coach), Andy Barlow, Ron Futcher, Darron McDonough, Ian Liversedge (Physiotherapist), John Ryan, Tony Henry, Mick McGuire, Billy Urmson (Coach), Bob Monaghan. **Front Row:** Dave Williams, Gary Williams, Bob Colville, Paul Atkinson, Joe Royle (Team Manager), Mike Cecere, Mike Milligan, Gary Hoolickin, Andrew Arrol. **Sitting:** Andrew Sleney, Ashley Hughes, Brian Adams, Chris Joughin, Neil Edmonds, Chris Blundel, Nick Henry, Dean Hanley, Paul Ogden.

OLDHAM ATHLETIC

DIVISION TWO: 8th   FA CUP: 3rd ROUND   MILK CUP: 2nd ROUND

MATCH	DATE		COMPE-TITION	VENUE	OPPONENTS	RESULT		HALF TIME	L'GUE POS'N	GOALSCORERS/GOAL TIMES	ATTEN-DANCE
1	A	17	CL	A	Norwich City	L	0-1	0-1			(12,508)
2		20	CL	H	Shrewsbury Town	W	4-3	2-1		Futcher 4, 45, Palmer 73, Henry 85	3,092
3		24	CL	H	Huddersfield Town	D	1-1	1-1	8	Atkinson 44	6,024
4		26	CL	A	Sunderland	W	3-0	2-0		Quinn 10, McGuire 36, Palmer 89	(16,414)
5		31	CL	H	Hull City	W	3-1	1-0	3	Futcher 44, Quinn 69, Palmer 86	4,500
6	S	7	CL	A	Wimbledon	D	0-0	0-0	6		(2,749)
7		13	CL	H	Charlton Athletic	W	2-1	0-0	3	Palmer 81, Quinn 89	4,700
8		17	CL	A	Carlisle United	L	1-3	0-1	6	Futcher 66	(3,138)
9		21	CL	A	Portsmouth	W	2-0	0-0	3	Palmer 48, Futcher 59	5,815
10		24	MC2/1	A	**Liverpool**	L	0-3	0-2			(16,150)
11		28	CL	A	Millwall	W	1-0	1-0	2	Futcher 10	(5,700)
12	O	5	CL	H	Grimsby Town	W	2-1	1-0	2	Quinn 44, 63	5,301
13		9	MC2/2	H	**Liverpool**	L	2-5	0-2		**Fairclough 46, 60**	7,719
14		12	CL	A	Crystal Palace	L	2-3	2-1	3	Palmer 14, Fairclough 45	(5,243)
15		19	CL	A	Blackburn Rovers	D	0-0	0-0	4		(9,666)
16		26	CL	H	Brighton & H.A.	W	4-0	1-0	2	Futcher 6, Quinn 63 (pen) 83, Palmer 85	4,970
17	N	2	CL	A	Barnsley	L	0-1	0-0	3		(7,118)
18		9	CL	H	Sheffield United	L	1-5	1-4	5	Palmer 2	8,193
19		16	CL	A	Middlesbrough	L	2-3	0-2	6	Futcher 48, Quinn 70	(4,249)
20		23	CL	H	Stoke City	L	2-4	0-2	8	Quinn (pen) 67, 70	4,817
21		30	CL	A	Fulham	D	2-2	1-0	9	Palmer 19, Futcher 88	(3,544)
22	D	7	CL	A	Shrewsbury Town	L	0-2	0-1	9		(2,702)
23		14	CL	H	Norwich City	L	1-3	0-0	12	Phelan (og) 75	3,949
24		21	CL	A	Huddersfield Town	L	0-2	0-1	13		(5,094)
25		26	CL	H	Bradford City	L	0-1	0-0	16		6,680
26	J	1	CL	A	Leeds United	L	1-3	1-1	17	Palmer 21	(10,830)
27		6	FAC3	H	**Orient**	L	1-2	0-1		**Palmer 87**	3,604
28		11	CL	A	Wimbledon	W	2-1	1-0	17	Futcher 9, Palmer 81	3,035
29		18	CL	A	Hull City	L	2-4	1-3	18	Futcher (pen) 13, 52	(6,909)
30	F	1	CL	H	Sunderland	D	2-2	2-1	18	Palmer 30, Quinn 41	3,827
31		8	CL	H	Blackburn Rovers	W	3-1	3-0	13	Futcher 14, Henry 36, Palmer 42	5,314
32		22	CL	A	Portsmouth	W	2-1	1-0	12	Colville 10, Henry 77	(10,891)
33	M	1	CL	H	Millwall	D	0-0	0-0	12		3,483
34		4	CL	A	Bradford City	L	0-0	0-0	13		(3,964)
35		8	CL	A	Grimsby Town	W	4-1	3-1	11	Futcher 8, Colville 25, Henry 40, 84	(4,174)
36		15	CL	H	Crystal Palace	W	2-0	1-0	9	Henry 22, Williams 79	3,726
37		22	CL	A	Charlton Athletic	D	1-1	1-1	9	Palmer 10	(3,767)
38		28	CL	H	Leeds United	W	3-1	1-0	9	Linighan 32, Futcher 47, Jones P. 56	4,937
39	A	2	CL	A	Brighton & H.A.	D	1-1	0-0	9	Pearce (og) 90	(8,200)
40		6	CL	H	Barnsley	D	1-1	0-1	9	Palmer 49	3,971
41		12	CL	A	Sheffield United	L	0-2	0-1	10		(7,782)
42		19	CL	H	Middlesbrough	W	1-0	0-0	8	McGuire 52	4,192
43		26	CL	A	Stoke City	L	0-2	0-1	12		(8,585)
44	M	3	CL	H	Fulham	W	2-1	0-0	9	Henry 60, Futcher 66	2,510
45		5	CL	H	Carlisle United	W	2-1	0-1	8	Milligan 65, Futcher (pen) 71	4,434

Best Home League Attendance: 8,193 v Sheffield Utd   **Smallest:** 2,510 v Fulham   **Av Home Att: 4,641**

Goal Scorers: **Compared with 84-85: −100**

League (62):	Futcher 17 (2 pen), Palmer 15, Quinn 11 (2 pen), Henry 7, Colville 2, McGuire 2, Opponents 2, Atkinson 1, Fairclough 1, Linighan 1, Jones P. 1, Milligan 1, Williams 1
Milk Cup (2):	Fairclough 2
FA Cup (1):	Palmer 1

Goram	Donachie	Barlow	McDonough	O'Callaghan	McGuire	Palmer	Henry	Quinn	Futcher	Atkinson	Fairclough	Bullock	Hoolickin	Ryan	Milligan	Williams (NC)	Jones P.	Colville	Smith	Linighan	Gorton	Referee	
1	2	3	4	5*	6	7	8	9	10	11	12											J Bray	1
1	2	3	4		6	7	8	9	10	11		5										P Willis	2
1	2	3	4		6*	7	8	9	10	11	12		5									P Vanes	3
1	2		4		6	7	8	9	10	11			5	3								M Peck	4
1	2		4		6	7	8	9	10	11			5	3								R Bridges	5
1	2		4		6	7	8	9	10	11			5	3								M Dimblebee	6
1	2		4*		6	7	8	9	10	11	12		5	3								T Mills	7
1	2				6	7	8	9	10	11*	12	4	5	3								D Hutchinson	8
1	2		4		6	7	8	9	10	11			5	3								J Lovatt	9
1	**2**		**4**		**6**	**7**	**8**	**9**	**10***	**11**	**12**		**5**	**3**								**K Walmsley**	**10**
1	2		4		6	7	8	9	10	11*	12		5	3								B Stevens	11
1	2		4		6	7	8	9		11	10		5	3								N Ashley	12
1			**4**		**6**	**7**	**8**	**9***		**11**	**10**	**2**	**5**	**3**	**12**							**D Allison**	**13**
1	2		4		6	7	8	9		11	10		5	3								R Hamer	14
1	2		4		6	7	8	9	10	11			5	3								C Seel	15
1	2		4		6	7	8	9	10*	11	12		5	3								T Holbrook	16
1	2		4		6	7	8	9*	10	11	12		5	3								G Courtney	17
1	2		4		6	7	8	9	10	11	12		5	3*								K Redfearn	18
1	2	3	4		6	7	8*	9	10	11	12		5									J Key	19
1	2		4		6*	7	8	9	10	11	12		5	3								G Alpin	20
1	2		4		6	7	8	9*	10	11	12		5	3								J Ashworth	21
1	2				6	7	8	12	10	11	9*	4	5	3†								M Reed	22
1	2*	3	4		6	7	8	9	10	11		12	5									R Nixon	23
1		3	4*		6	7	8		10	11	9	12	5				2					F Roberts	24
1	2	3			6	7	8		10*	11	9		4				5	12				M Heath	25
1	2	3				7	8		10	11	9		4		6		5					K Lupton	26
1	**2**	**3**			**8**	**7**			**10**	**11**	**9**		**4**		**6***		**5**	**12**				**R Bridges**	**27**
1	2*	3			8	7			10	11			4			12	5	9	6			G Courtney	28
1		3			8*	7			10	11			2			12	4	9	6	5		K Redfern	29
1		3			8	7			11	9*	10		2				4	12	6	5		G Napthine	30
1		3			8	7			11	9*	10		2				4	12	6	5		K Hackett	31
1		3			8				11	12	10		2		7		4	9*	6	5		K Cooper	32
1		3			8	7			11	9	10		2				4	12	6	5		A Saunders	33
1		3			8	7			11	9	10*		2				4	12	6	5		G Tyson	34
1	2	3			8	7			11	10			5			12	4	9	6*			K Breen	35
1	2	3			6	7			11	10			5			12	4	9	8*			J Bray	36
1		3			6	7			11	10			2*			12	4	9	8	5		R Milford	37
1		3			6*	7			11	10						12	4	9	8	5		G Alpin	38
1	2	3				7			11	10*			12		6		4	9	8	5		I Hemley	39
1	2	3			8	7			11	10	12				6		4*	9		5		J Lovatt	40
1	2†	3			8	7			11	10					6		4	9		5		K Baker	41
1	2	3			8	7			11	10	12		2		4			9	6*	5		M Peck	42
1		3			8	7			11	10			2		6		4	9*	12	5		C Downey	43
	2	3			8	7			11	10			12		6		4	9*	5		1	C Seel	44
1	2	3			8*	7			11	10			12		6		4	9	5			J Lloyd	45
41	33	26	20	1	40	41	40	24	40	26	6	4	32	19	5	3	18	13	14	15	1	League Appearances	
								2			11	4	3				6	4	1			Substitute Appearances	
2	1		2		2	2	2	2	1	2	1·1	1	2	2			0·1					Milk Cup Appearances	
1	1				1	1			1	1	1			1	1		1⁻	0·1				FA Cup Appearances	

Also Played:

Players on Loan:

Departures: O'Callaghan (F), Quinn (Portsmouth) A Jones (P.N.E), Parker (Burnley), Fairclough (F), Hudson (Sweden), Bowden (Port Vale)

'THE LATICS'

Formed: 1894
Turned Professional: 1899   **Ltd Co:** 1906

Previous Names: Pine Villa 1894-1899
Previous Managers: Since 1946
Bob Mellor   Frank Womack   Billy Wooton   George Hardwick   Ted Goodier   Peter McKennan
Norman Dodgin   Jack Rowley   Les McDowell   Gordon Hurst   Jimmy McIlroy   Jack Rowley
Jimmy Frizell
Honours: Champions Div 3 (N), 1952-3   Champions Div 3, 1973-4
League Career: Elected to Div 2 1907   Promoted to Div 1 1909-10
Relegated to Div 2 1922-3   Relegated to Div 3 (N) 1934-5   Promoted to Div 2 1952-3
Relegated to Div 3 1953-4   Relegated to Div 4 1957-8   Promoted to Div 3 1962-3
Relegated to Div 4 1968-9   Promoted to Div 3 1970-1   Promoted to Div 2 1973-4
Colours: Royal blue shirts with red and white trim, white shorts and stockings with red and white trim
Change Colours: All green
Reserves League: Central League Div 1   **'A' Team:** Lancashire League Div 2

CLUB RECORDS

Most Appearances for Club: Ian Wood, 525, 1966-80
Most Capped Player: Albert Gray, 9, Wales
Record Goalscorer in a Match: Eric Gemmell, 7 v Chester, 11-2, 19 Jan 1953   Bert Lister, 7 v Southport, 11-0, 20 Dec 1962
Record League Goalscorer in a Season: Tom Davis, 33, Div 3 (N), 1936-7
Record League Goalscorer in a Career: Eric Gemmell, 110, 1947-54
Record Transfer Fee Received: £275,000 from Queens Park Rangers for Simon Stainrod, Nov 1980
Record Transfer Fee Paid: £200,000 to Manchester City for Kenny Clements, Sept 1979
Best Performances: League: 2nd Div 1 1914-15   **FA Cup:** Semi-Final 1913   **League/Milk Cup:** Never past 3rd Round
Most League Points: 62, Div 3, 1973-4   **Most League Goals:** 95, Div 4, 1962-3
Record League Victory: 11-0 v Southport, Div 4, 26 Dec 1962
Record League Defeat: 4-13 v Tranmere Rovers, Div 3 (N), 26 Dec 1935
Oldest Player in League Match:
Youngest Player in League Match: Wayne Harrison, 15 yrs 11 months
Most Consecutive Undefeated League Matches: 15 1937-38,
1952   **League Matches Without a Win:** 17 1920
Longest Run of Undefeated Home League Matches: 28 1923-24   **Away League Matches:** 11 1973
Longest Run Without Home League Win: 9 1920   **Away League Win:** 31 1974-75
Most Consecutive League Wins: 10 1974   **Home League Wins:** 12 1908-09
Most Consecutive League Defeats: 8 1932-33, 1934-35   **Away League Wins:** 5 1974

Club Statistician for the Directory: D Williams

OLDHAM ATHLETIC

PLAYERS NAME Ht Wt Birthdate	Honours	Birthplace Transfers	Clubs	APPEARANCES League	Milk Cup	FA Cup	Other Comps	GOALS League	Milk Cup	FA Cup	Other Comps
GOALKEEPERS											
Andy Goram 5.10 11.6 13.4.44	S (3) U.21	Bury	W.B.A. (A)								
			Oldham Athletic	145	6	5					
Andy Gorton 6.0 12.0 23.9.66		Salford	Oldham Athletic	1							
DEFENDERS											
Andy Barlow 5.8 9.10 24.11.65		Oldham	Oldham Athletic	57+2	2	3					
Steve Bullock 5.8 11.1 5.10.66		Stockport	Oldham Athletic	10+7	1						
Willie Donachie 5.9 11.5 5.10.51	S (35) U.23 (2) Lg.C '76	Glasgow £200,000 £200,000 £200,000 F	Manchester City Portland Timbers Norwich City Portland Timbers Burnley Oldham Athletic	347+4 11 60 72	40 4 3	21 12 2	4	2 3			
Gary Hoolickin 5.11 11.1 29.10.57		Middleton	Oldham Athletic	191+2	20	6+1		2			
Mike Milligan 5.8 11.0 20.2.67		Manchester	Oldham Athletic	5	0+1			1			
Paul Jones 6.1 12.9 13.5.53	Div.3 '73 Div.2 '78	Ellesmere Port	Bolton Wanderers (A) Huddersfield Town Oldham Athletic	440+4 73 18	30 10	31 1		38 8 1	4 1	1 2	
Andy Linighan 6.3½ 12.6 18.6.62		Hartlepool £200,000	Hartlepool United Leeds United Oldham Athletic	110 42	7+1 3	8 1	1	4 2	1		1
John Ryan 5.10 11.7 18.2.62	E.U21 (1)	Oldham	Oldham Athletic (A) Newcastle United Sheffield Weds. Oldham Athletic	77 28 5+3	6 2 1+1	2 1		8 1 1			
Gary Williams 5.8 10.11 8.6.63		Bristol	Bristol City Portsmouth Swansea City Bristol Rovers Oldham Athletic	98+2 6 3+6	6	11	1	1 1			
MIDFIELD											
Paul Atkinson 5.10 11.5 1.4.61	EY	Pudsey £175,000 £30,000	Oldham Athletic (A) Watford Oldham Athletic	139+4 26	9+1 2	5 1		11 1			
Tony Henry 5.11 12.0 26.11.57		Newcastle £125,000 £21,000	Manchester City (A) Bolton Wanderers Oldham Athletic	68+11 80 130+3	7 3 6	3+1 3 3		6 22 15	6 2 1		
Darren McDonough 5.11 11.0 7.11.62		Antwerp	Oldham Athletic	174+5	12	5		14	1		
Ron Futcher 6.0 12.10 25.9.56		Chester U.S.A. £30,000 £15,000	Chester C. (A) Luton Town Manchester City Barnsley Oldham Athletic	4 116+4 10+7 18+1 40	5 2 1	8 1 4 1		40 7 5 17	2	1 2	
Mick Maguire 5.7 10.5 4.9.52	EY	Blackpool £50,000 £30,000 F	Coventry City Norwich City Barnsley Oldham Athletic	60+12 172+10 63 40	3 11 2 2	5 7+1 1 2		1 11 7 2	1		
FORWARDS											
Michele Cecere 6.0 11.4 4.1.68		Chester	Oldham Athletic (A)								
Bob Coalville 5.11 11.12 27.4.63		Nuneaton	Oldham Athletic	19+7		0+1		4			
Roger Palmer† 5.10 10.10 30.1.59		Manchester £70,000	Manchester City (A) Oldham Athletic	22+9 216+3	3+3 14	7		9 65	1	1	

ADDITIONAL CONTRACT PROFESSIONALS

APPRENTICES
Mike Flynn

NON-CONTRACT PLAYERS
Brian Adams, Neil Edmonds, Nick Henry, Ashley Hughes, Paul Moreton, Bob Pullar, David Williams, Godfrey Williams, David Wilson

BOUNDARY PARK Oldham, Greater Manchester

Record Attendance: 47,671 v Sheffield Wednesday, FA Cup Round 4, 25 Jan 1930

Record Receipts: £44,998.30 v Manchester City, Div 2, 20 Apr 1984

Season Tickets: £76.00 (stand), £47.50 (enclosure—adult; £28.50 juvenile/OAP), £43.50 (ground—adult, £28.50 juvenile/OAP)

Executive Box Season Tickets: V P Box £207, V P Stand £154

Cost of Stand Tickets: Centre £5.00, Wing £4.00, Juvenile/OAP £2.50; **Terraces:** Enclosures £2.50 (adult), £1.50 (juvenile/OAP), £2.50 (adult), £1.50 (child/OAP) Chadderton End

Match and Ticket Information: 12 days in advance postal or personal

Car Parking: Parking for 800 cars on site adjacent to ground

Nearest Railway Station: Werneth

Junior Supporters: Secretary: Mrs B Pascall, Junior Lattice, Boundary Park, Oldham

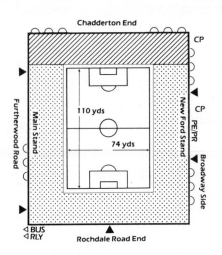

How to get to the ground

From North, East, South and West: Use Motorway M62 until junction 20, then A627 to junction with A664. Leave Motorway and at roundabout take 2nd exit into Burnley Lane. In 0.3m turn left into Boundary Park Road for Oldham Athletic FC

Price of 1986-7 Programme: 50p
Number of Pages: 24
Subscriptions: No subscriptions

Local Newspapers: Oldham Chronicle, Manchester Evening News (Sat Pink), Oldham Advertiser

Local Radio Stations: Radio Piccadilly, Radio Manchester, Radio Cavell (Hospital)

ORIENT

Division 4

Chairman
N Ovenden

Directors
A Pincus
D L Weinrabe
A Harding
M Ovenden

Secretary
Miss Carol Stokes (01-539 2223/4)

Assistant Secretary
Mrs Sue Tilling

Manager
Frank Clark

Physiotherapist
Bill Songhurst

Commercial Manager
F Woolf (01-539 4483)

Perhaps, Orient were not quite ready for a return to the 3rd Division, in which case their failure by one place to ascend might have been a blessing in disguise. They can at least approach the new season confident in the knowledge that they have the proven ability to go up and a good start should make that happen. If one were to look at a narrow failure in that light then it was not a bad season for the team from London's East End.

In fact, there were many good things for the club. The cup form was most encouraging and it suggested that a maturing team could live in better company. The Milk Cup run did only last two rounds, but aggregate victory over Aldershot (5-3) was followed by a really brave effort against Tottenham, who lost the first leg at Brisbane Road (0-2) and were still in deficit at half-time in the return before they rallied in the second half and ran in enough goals to survive (4-2 on aggregate). That was good going for the 'O's' and the FA Cup also was full of interest. First, V S Rugby provided stiff opposition before bowing out in a replay (4-1 at Brisbane Road) and then another non-League club, Slough Town, produced a severe headache by drawing in Leyton after leading at half-time (2-0) before the Londoners pulled back that lead. At Slough in the replay a thriller was won by the League club (3-2), which meant a visit to 2nd Division Oldham Athletic and a shock win (2-1). The romance was ruthlessly ended at Hillsborough where Sheffield Wednesday took no chances and won by five clear goals. In the Freight Rover Trophy there was a win at home against Bournemouth (3-1) and at all-conquering Reading (3-0), but an extra-time goal at Hereford saw the ending of that campaign. Even so, it was good stuff.

In the League there was just not quite enough consistency and four consecutive defeats from March 29th made it certain that there would be no promotion, but a team which scores 106 goals in a season must have some potential and Shinners, Jones and Juryeff certainly have plenty of that quality. Elsewhere, Manager Frank Clark has consistent men in Wells (the goalkeeper), Dickenson, Sussex, Sitton, Cornwell and Brooks. It should be the turn of Orient this coming season.   WLM

Back Row L to R: Chris Jones, Steve Castle, Alan Comfort, Stephen John, Ian Juryeff. **Middle Row:** Pat Holland (Youth Manager), Colin Foster, John Cornwell, Robert Quinnell, Peter Wells, Dean Greygoose, Peter Mountford, Kevin Godfrey, Andy Sussex, Bill Songhurst (Physio). **Front Row:** Tommy Cunningham, Shaun Brooks, John Sitton, Frank Clark (Manager), Lee Harvey, Paul Shinners, Kevin Hales, Kevin Dickenson.

ORIENT

DIVISION FOUR: 5th   **FA CUP:** 4th ROUND   **MILK CUP:** 2nd ROUND   **FRT:** QUARTER-FINAL

MATCH	DATE		COMPE-TITION	VENUE	OPPONENTS	RESULT		HALF TIME	L'GUE POS'N	GOALSCORERS/GOAL TIMES	ATTEN-DANCE
1	A	17	CL	H	Tranmere Rovers	W	3-1	0-1		Godfrey 58, Brooks 74, Cornwell 84	2,857
2		20	MC1/1	A	Aldershot	W	3-1	2-1		Godfrey 8, Jones 44, Sussex 69	(1,423)
3		23	CL	A	Southend United	L	1-5	0-2	16	Jones 89	(3,643)
4		27	CL	H	Peterborough	D	2-2	2-1		Mountford 15, Hales 27	2,577
5		31	CL	A	Hartlepool	W	2-1	1-0	7	Cornwell 2, 86	(2,876)
6	S	3	MC1/2	H	Aldershot	D	2-2	1-0		Shinners 8, Brooks 60	1,761
7		7	CL	H	Port Vale	W	1-0	1-0	5	Cornwell 26	2,455
8		13	CL	A	Halifax Town	L	1-2	0-0	9	Shinners 70	(1,243)
9		18	CL	A	Mansfield Town	D	1-1	1-1		Shinners 2	(4,185)
10		21	CL	H	Colchester United	L	1-2	1-0	13	Godfrey	2,577
11		23	MC2/1	H	Tottenham Hotspur	W	2-0	0-0		Godfrey 63, 76	13,828
12		28	CL	A	Wrexham	W	3-1	1-1	9	Shinners 14, 63, Godfrey 88	(1,842)
13	O	1	CL	H	Rochdale	W	5-0	4-0		Juryeff 9, Jones 10, 64, Brooks pen 30, Shinners 33	2,650
14		5	CL	H	Scunthorpe United	W	3-0	1-0	4	Shinners 21, 55, Brooks 68	2,847
15		12	CL	A	Exeter City	D	1-1	0-0	7	Godfrey 75	(2,057)
16		19	CL	A	Cambridge United	W	2-1	1-0	7	Jones 32, Dowman (og) 87	(2,743)
17		22	CL	H	Aldershot	D	1-1	1-0		Shinners 37	2,833
18		26	CL	H	Stockport County	L	0-1	0-1	7		3,021
19		30	MC2/2	A	Tottenham Hotspur	L	0-4	0-1			(21,046)
20	N	2	CL	A	Torquay United	D	2-2	0-1	7	Brooks 76, Sussex 89	(1,282)
21		5	CL	A	Crewe Alexandra	W	3-1	0-1	6	Juryeff 58, Sussex 74, Brooks 90	(1,232)
22		9	CL	H	Preston North End	W	2-0	1-0	6	Cornwell 21, Juryeff 75	2,805
23		16	FAC1	A	V S Rugby	D	2-2	1-1		Brooks 9 (pen) 79	(2,500)
24		19	FAC1R	H	V S Rugby	W	4-1	3-0		Jones 17, Castle 32, Juryeff 38, Brooks 46	2,311
25		23	CL	A	Chester City	L	0-3	0-1	7		(2,653)
26		30	CL	H	Swindon Town	W	1-0	1-0	4	Cornwell 32	3,100
27	D	7	FAC2	H	Slough	D	2-2	0-2		Cornwell 55, Juryeff 64	3,450
28		10	FAC2R	A	Slough	W	3-2	1-1		Juryeff 19, Godfrey 63, Shinners 71	(3,200)
29		14	CL	A	Burnley	L	0-1	0-1	6		(3,007)
30		21	CL	H	Southend United	W	3-0	1-0	5	Brooks 44, Shinners 52, Juryeff 60	3,545
31		26	CL	A	Hereford United	D	2-2	1-0	5	Juryeff 41, Hales 90	2,700
32		28	CL	A	Peterborough United	D	2-2	0-0	5	Cunningham 75, Sussex 80	(3,283)
33	J	6	FAC3	A	Oldham Athletic	W	2-1	1-0		Shinners 45, Foster 74	(3,604)
34		11	CL	H	Hartlepool United	D	1-1	1-0	6	Brooks 21	3,667
35		14	FRT	H	Bournemouth	W	3-1	2-0		Juryeff 6, Shinners 41, 78	947
36		17	CL	A	Tranmere Rovers	W	3-0	0-0	6	Shinners 49, Juryeff 67, Cornwell 86	(1,677)
37		25	FAC4	A	Sheffield Wednesday	L	0-5	0-3			(19,087)
38	F	1	CL	A	Port Vale	L	0-2	0-1	7		(3,074)
39		4	CL	A	Aldershot	D	1-1	1-1	8	Shinners 44	(1,248)
40		8	CL	H	Cambridge United	W	3-1	1-0	6	Juryeff 15, Shinners 68, Jones 84	2,727
41		15	CL	H	Mansfield Town	L	0-1	0-0	6		3,713
42	M	1	CL	H	Wrexham	L	1-3	0-0	7	Juryeff 55	2,160
43		6	FRT	A	Reading	W	3-0	2-0		Juryeff 3, Cunningham 13, Jones 50	(1,403)
44		8	CL	A	Scunthorpe United	D	2-2	0-0	7	Shinners 51, Jones 53	(1,478)
45		15	CL	H	Exeter City	D	2-2	2-2	7	Cunningham 8, Sussex 18	2,220
46		18	CL	H	Torquay United	W	4-2	2-1	7	Cornwell 1, Jones 4, Wright og 63, Shinners 78	1,828
47		21	CL	A	Stockport County	W	3-2	2-1	7	Shinners 9, Jones 36, Comfort 77	(3,119)
48		24	FRT QF	H	Hereford United	L	1-2†	1-1		Cornwell 12	1,113
49		29	CL	H	Northampton Town	L	0-1	0-0	7		2,920
50		31	CL	A	Hereford United	L	2-3	1-2	8	Dickenson 17, Foster 89	(2,854)
51	A	5	CL	H	Crewe Alexandra	L	0-1	0-0	8		1,975
52		8	CL	A	Colchester United	L	0-4	0-2	8		(1,771)
53		12	CL	A	Preston North End	W	3-1	2-0	8	Juryeff 11, 14, Comfort 46	(4,750)
54		15	CL	H	Northampton Town	W	3-2	1-1	6	Jones 20, Comfort 54, Foster 84	(1,731)
55		19	CL	H	Chester City	D	0-0	0-0	6		2,617
56		22	CL	H	Halifax Town	W	1-0	1-0	6	Godfrey 7	1,443
57		27	CL	A	Swindon Town	L	1-4	0-1	6	Comfort 69	(8,081)
58	M	3	CL	H	Burnley	W	3-0	1-0	7	Harvey 41, 46, Comfort 53	1,995
59		5	CL	A	Rochdale	W	4-1	1-0	5	Castle 4 25, 54, 80, 83	(1,299)

Best Home League Attendance: 3,713 v Mansfield Town   **Smallest:** 1,443 v Halifax Town   **Av Home Att:** 2,661

Goal Scorers: Compared with 84-85: +85

League (79):	Shinners 15, Jones C, 9, Juryeff 9, Cornwell 8, Brooks 7, Comfort 5, Godfrey 5, Castle 4, Sussex 4, Cunningham 2, Foster 2, Hales 2, Harvey 2, Opponents 2, Dickenson 1, Mountford 1
Milk Cup (7):	Godfrey 3, Jones 1, Sussex 1, Shinners 1, Brooks 1
FA CUP (13):	Brooks 3 (1 pen), Juryeff 3, Shinners 2, Jones 1, Castle 1, Cornwell 1, Godfrey 1, Foster 1
FRT (7):	Juryeff 2, Shinners 2, Cunningham 1, Cornwell 1, Jones 1

†After extra time

Wells	Hales	Dickenson	Sussex	Sitton	Cornwell	Godfrey	Brooks	Jones C	Castle	Mountford	Shinners	Corbett	Cunningham	Foster	Juryeff	John	Harvey	Greygoose	Comfort		Referee	
1	2	3	4	5	6	7	8	9*	10	11	12										I Borrett	1
1	2	3	4	5	6	7	8	9*		11	12	10									**M Bodenham**	2
1	2	3	4	5	6	7	8	9	10*	11	12										A Gunn	3
1	2	3	4	5	6		8	9		11	7	10									K Barratt	4
1	2	3	4	5	6		8		10		9	11†	7†								A Robinson	5
1	2	3	4	5	6		8		11		9	10	7								**J Ashworth**	6
1	2	3	4*	5	6		8	12		11	9	10	7								M James	7
1	2	3	4	5	6		8	11			9	10	7								R Guy	8
1	2	3	4	5	6		8*	11	10		9			7	12						N Ashley	9
1	2	3	4	5	6*	10	8			11	9			7	12						G Napthine	10
1	2	3	4	5		10	8	11			9	6		7							**H King**	11
1	2	3	4	5	12	10*	8	11			9	6		7							K Baker	12
1	2	3	4	5†			8	11			9	6		7	10						J Martin	13
1	2	3*	4	5	12		8	11			9	6		7	10						R Hamer	14
1	2	3	4	5*	8	10		11	12		9	6		7							R Groves	15
1	2	3	4		6	10	8	11			9		5	7							T Holbrook	16
1	2	3	4	5	6	10*	8	11	12		9			7							D Axcell	17
1	2	3	4	5	6		8	11	12		9*			7	10						B Hill	18
1	2	3	4	5	6	9	7	8						10	11						**K Hackett**	19
1	2	3	4	5†	6		8	11	9					7	10						R Milford	20
1	2	3	4	5	6		8	9	10					7	11						C Trussell	21
1	2	3	4	5	6		8	9	10	12				7*	11						Alan Robinson	22
1	2	3	4*		6		8	9	12	7		10		5	11						**D Reeves**	23
1	2	3			6	7*	8	9	10	5					11	4	12				**D Reeves**	24
1	2	3	4	7	6	10	8	9						5	11						V Callow	25
1	2	3	4	5	6	10*	8	9	12					11	7						M Bodenham	26
1	2	3	4	5	6	10	8	9						7	11						**D Hedges**	27
1	2	3	4	5	6	10	8	12			9			7	11*						**D Hedges**	28
1	2	3	4	7†	6	10	8	9*	12					5	11						K Lupton	29
1	2	3	4	7	6		8		10		9			5	11						H Taylor	30
1	2	3	4	7	6	12	8*		10		9			5	11						M Cotton	31
1	2	3	4		6		8		10		9	7		5	11						J Ball	32
1	2	3	4		6		8		10		9	7		5	11						**R Bridges**	33
1	2	3	4		6		8		10	12	9	7*		5	11						K Cooper	34
		3			6	7*	8		13	10	9	2		5	11*	4	12	1			**K Barratt**	35
1	2	3	4		6		8		10		9	7		5	11						T Jones	36
1	2*	34	4		6	11	8		10	12	9	7		5							**K Redfern**	37
1		3	4		6		8		10	7	2	9		5	11						M Peck	38
		3	2		6		8		10	7	4	9		5	11		1				G Ashby	39
1		3	2				8		10	7	4	9	6	5	11						R Milford	40
1		3	2		12		8	10*		7	4	9	6	5	11						J Martin	41
1	2	3	10		6	7	8*				4	9		5	11	12					J Bray	42
1		3	10		6	12	13	4			9	2	7	11*	5	8*					**M Cotton**	43
1	2	3	10			7	4	9			6			5	8					11	T Simpson	44
1	2*	3	10			7	12	4	9		6			5	8					11	B Hill	45
1		3*	10	2		7	12	4	9		6			5	8					11	P Vanes	46
1		3	10	2		7		4	9		6			5	8					11	J McAuly/R Jones	47
1		3	10*	2		7	13	4	9		6*			5	11	12	8				**I Hemley**	48
1	6	3	10	2		7		4	9					5	8					11	L Shapter	49
1		3	10		6	7	4	2	9					5	8					11	R Nixon	50
1		3	10		6	7	4	2	9					5	8					11	M James	51
1	2	3	10		6	7	12	9						5	4		8*			11	T Holbrook	52
1		3	12		6	7	4		10	5	9	2			8					11*	P Willis	53
1		3			6	7	8	4	10	5	9	2								11	M Scott	54
1		3			6	7	12	8	4	10*	5	9	2							11	R Gifford	55
1		3			6	7	8	4	10	5	9	2								11	D Hedges	56
1		3			6	7	12	8	4*	10	5	9	2							11	K Miller	57
1		3			6	7	4	12	10	9*	5	2			8					11	J Deakin	58
1		3			6	7	5	87	4	10	2	9								11	J Key	59
45	31	46	35	39	41	13	35	40	19	11	31	10	13	36	25	8	11	1	1	15	League Appearances	
			1		3	3	3	1	4	4	2				2	1					Substitute Appearances	
4	4	4	4	4	3	3	4	3	1	1	2-1	3	1	2	1						Milk Cup Appearances	
6	6	6	5	2	6	4	6	4	1-1	2-2	5			3	4	4	5	1	0-1		FA Cup Appearances	
2		3	2	1	3	1	1-2	0-1	0-1	3	3	2	2	3	2-1	2-1	1				FR Trophy Appearances	

Players on Loan:

Departures:

'THE O's'

Formed: 1881
Turned Professional: 1903 **Ltd Co:** 1906

Previous Names: 1881-86 Glyn Cricket and Football Club   1886-88 Eagle Football Club   1888-98 Orient Football Club   1898-1946 Clapton Orient   1946-67 Leyton Orient
Previous Managers: 1905-7 S Ormerod   1907-22 W Holmes   1923-8 P Proudfoot
1929-30 A Grimsdell   1930-1 P Proudfoot   1931-3 J Seed   1933-5 D Pratt   1935-9 P Proudfoot
1939-40 T Halsey   1940-5 W Wright   1945 W Hall   1945-6 W Wright   1946-8 C Hewitt
1948-9 N McBain   1949-56 A Stock   1956 L Gore (Caretaker)   1956-7 A Stock
1957-8 L Gore (Caretaker)   1958-9 A Stock   1961-3 J Carey   1963 L Gore (Caretaker)
1963-4 B Fenton   1964-5 L Gore (Caretaker)   1965 D Sexton   1965-6 L Gore (Caretaker)
1966-8 R Graham   1968-71 J Bloomfield   1971 G Petchey   12/8/77-27/8/77 J Bloomfield
23/9/81-12/10/81 P Went (20 days)   13/10/81-24/5/83 K Knighton
Honours: Div 3 Champions 1969-70, Div 3 (S) Champions 1955-56
League Career: Elected to Div 2 1905   Relegated to Div 3 (S) 1928-9
Promoted to Div 2 1955-6   Promoted to Div 1 1961-2   Relegated to Div 2 1962-3
Relegated to Div 3 1965-6   Promoted to Div 2 1969-70   Relegated to Div 3 1981-2
Colours: All red
Change Colours: All blue
Reserves League: Capital League   **Youth Team:** S E Counties

---

CLUB RECORDS

Most Appearances for Club: Peter Allen: Football League 431 + FA Cup 25 + League Cup 24 **Total 480**
Most Capped Player: Tony Grealish, 8, Eire   **For England:** J Townrow, 2
Record Goalscorer in a Match: Ron Heckman, 5 v Lovells Athletic (H) 7-1 1st Rnd FA Cup, 19.08.55
Record League Goalscorer in a Season: Tom Johnston, 35, Div 2, 1957-8   **In All Competitions:** Tom Johnston, 36, Football League 35 + FA Cup 1 **Total 36**
Record League Goalscorer in a Career: Tom Johnston, 126   **In All competitions:** Tom Johnston, 128, Football League 126 + 2 FA Cup, 1956-8, 1959-61
Record Transfer Fee Received: £600,000 from Notts County for John Chiedozie, Aug 1981
Record Transfer Fee Paid: £150,000 to Tottenham Hotspur for Peter Taylor, Nov 1980
Best Performances: League: 22nd Div 1 1962-3   **FA Cup:** Semi-Final 1977-8   **League/Milk Cup:** 5th Round 1963
Most League Points: 66 in Div 3, 1955-6   **Most League Goals:** 106, Div 3, (S) 1955-6
Record League Victory: 8-0 v Crystal Palace, Div 3, 12 Nov 1955
Most Goals in a First Class Match: 9-2 v Aldershot, Div 3 (South) 10 Feb 1934, 9-2 v Chester, 3rd Round League Cup, 15 Oct 1962
Record League Defeat: 1-7 v Torquay United (A), Div 3 (S), 16 April 1949   v Stoke City (A), Div 2, 7 Sept 1956

Most Consecutive Undefeated League Matches: 14 1954-55	**League Matches Without a Win:** 23 1962-3
Longest Run of Undefeated Home League Matches: 25 1913-14	**Away League Matches:** 9 1954-55
Longest Run Without Home League Win: 14 1962-63	**Away League Win:** 34 1938-47
Most Consecutive League Wins: 10 1956	**Home League Wins:** 12 1954
Most Consecutive League Defeats: 8 1927-28	**Away League Wins:** 6 1956

Club Statistician for the Directory: T Higgins

ORIENT

PLAYERS NAME Ht Wt Birthdate	Honours	Birthplace Transfers	Clubs	APPEARANCES				GOALS			
				League	Milk Cup	FA Cup	Other Comps	League	Milk Cup	FA Cup	Other Comps
GOALKEEPERS											
Peter Wells 6.1 13.4 13.8.56		Nottingham £16,000 F	Notts Forest (A) Southampton Millwall Orient	27 141 78	3 6	2 12 8	5				
Dean Greygoose 5.11 11.5 18.12.54	EY	Thetford	Cambridge United (A) Lincoln City (L) Orient	26 6 1	1						
DEFENDERS											
Tommy Cunningham* 6.0 11.3 7.12.55		London F £45,000 £60,000	Chelsea (A) Q.P.R. Wimbledon Orient	27+3 99 131	1+1 1 3	3 6 12	4	2 12 13	1		1
Kevin Dickenson† 5.6 10.6 24.11.61		London F F	Tottenham Hotspur (A) Charlton Athletic Orient	72+3 46	5 4	2 6	3	1 1		1	
Colin Foster 6.4 13.10 16.7.64		Chislehurst	Orient (A)	152+1	8	6	3	8	3	2	1
Kevin Hales 5.7 10.4 13.1.61		Dartford F	Chelsea (A) Orient	18+2 106+1	10	11	4	4			
Lee Harvey 27.12.66		Harlow	Orient (A)	13+7		0+2	5+1	2			1
John Sitton 5.11 12.4 21.10.59 Orient		Hackney £10,000 £10,000	Chelsea (A) Millwall Gillingham	11+2 43+2 141+5	2 9	2 13+1	4	5			
MIDFIELD											
Shaun Brooks 5.7 11.0 9.10.62	EY.S	London	Crystal Palace Orient	47+7 95+9	6 8	4+2 8	5+3	4 22	1	3	1
Steve Castle 5.11 12.5 17.5.66		Ilford	Orient (A)	39+5	1	4+1	5+1	5		1	
John Cornwell 6.0 12.0 13.10.64		Bethnal Green	Orient (A)	148+8	7+1	10	5	28	2	2	2
Peter Mountford 5.10 10.6 30.9.60		Stoke	Stoke City Norwich City (A) Charlton Ath (A) Orient	1+3 10+1 25+6	0+1 1	2+2	5	1 2			
Paul Shinners 6.2 13.3 8.1.59		London	Gillingham Colchester (L) Orient	1+3 6 31+2	2+1	2 5	2 3	15	1	2 2	2
FORWARDS											
Kevin Godfrey 5.10 11.2 24.2.60		Kennington	Orient (A) Plymouth Argyle (L)	193+22 7	12+1	23	2	46 1	4	4	
Chris Jones 5.11 10.7 18.4.56	E.U21 (1)	Jersey F F F F	Tottenham H (A) Manchester City Crystal Palace Charlton Athletic Orient	149+15 3 18 17+6 76+1	7+1 4 2 4	10+2 1 8	4+1	37 3 2 13	1 1 1	4 2	2
Ian Juryeff 5.11 12.0 24.11.67		Gosport £5,000	Southampton Mansfield Town (L) Reading (L) Orient	0+2 12 7 44+2	1	3 5	6	5 2 16	3	2 4	
Andy Sussex 6.0 11.6 23.11.64		Islington	Orient (A)	106+9	7+1	8	3+3	15	2		1

ADDITIONAL CONTRACT PROFESSIONALS
Robert Quinnell (Monthly)

APPRENTICES
Steve Davis, Paul Hammond

NON-CONTRACT PLAYERS
Warren Barton, David Dobson, Kevin Nugent, Chris Snell, Tony St. Pier

Record Attendance: 34,345 v West Ham U, FA Cup Round 4, 25 Jan 1964

Smallest Home Attendance for a First Class Match: 1,668 v Preston North End, Div 3, 17 Dec 1982

Record Receipts: £54,891.50 v Southampton FA Cup Round 4, 26 Jan 1985

Size of Playing Area: 110yds × 75yds

Season Tickets: Stand (Main): £100, £80 (OAP/children) (Centre), £80 (£70 children/OAP) (wing); Unreserved seats of Ground £60 (£40 OAP, £30 children)

Executive Box Season Tickets: Double O Directors Box, Seats £200

Cost of Stand Tickets: £6.00, £4.00 **Ground:** £3.00 (£1.80 OAP/Juveniles)

Match and Ticket Information: Bookable at least two weeks in advance

Car Parking: Street parking around the ground. NCP five minutes from Brisbane Road (off Oliver Road)

Nearest Railway Station: Leyton Central

Nearest Tube Station: Leyton (Central Line)

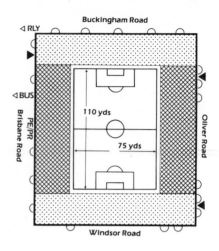

How to get to the ground

From North and West: Use A406 North Circular Road (S.P. Chelmsford) to Edmonton, then in 2.6m at roundabout take 3rd exit A112 (S.P. Leyton). Pass Leyton Midland Road Station and in 0.5m turn right into Windsor Road, then turn left into Brisbane Road for Orient FC

From East: Use A12 (S.P. London then City) to Leytonstone and follow signs Hackney into Grove Road. At Leyton cross main road and forward into Ruckholt Road, then turn right then left into Leyton High Road and in 0.2m turn left into Buckingham Road then right into Brisbane Road for Orient FC

From South: Use A102M through Blackwall Tunnel and follow signs Newmarket A102 to join A11 to Stratford. Follow signs Stratford Station into Leyton Road A112, to Leyton Station then keep forward. In 0.4m keep left then turn right then left into Leyton High Road and proceed as from East.

Price of 1986-7 Programme: 50p
Number of Pages: 20
Subscriptions: Rates obtainable from shop manager

Local Newspapers: Waltham Forest Guardian, Ilford Recorder, Hackney Gazette, East London Advertiser, Stratford Express

Local Radio Stations: Radio Goodmayes, Whipps Cross Hospital Radio

OXFORD UNITED

Division 1

Back Row L to R: Jeremy Charles, Andy Thomas, Alan Judge, Gary Briggs, Steve Hardwick, David Langan, Bobby McDonald, John Dreyer. **Middle Row:** Ken Fish (Trainer), David Fogg (Reserve Team Coach), Kevin Brock, David Leworthy, Neil Slatter, Peter Rhoades-Brown, Robbie Mustoe, Trevor Hebberd, Sean Reck, Paul Swannack, Tony Obi, Mark Jones, Ray Graydon (Assistant Manager), David Coates (Chief Scout). **Front Row:** Ray Houghton, Les Phillips, Malcolm Shotton, Maurice Evans (Manager), Steve Perryman, John Aldridge, John Trewick.

T his was the greatest season in Oxford's history. They were playing in the 1st Division for the the first time and they battled their way to Wembley to produce a classic performance and crush QPR in the Milk Cup final.

When Jim Smith, who had plotted the club's rise from the 3rd Division to the 1st Division, moved on to QPR during the summer of 1985, his assistant Maurice Evans very reluctantly took charge of the team, stressing that he far preferred his role as coach.

But he took to the task well, even though he received the shattering blow of losing N Ireland international striker Billy Hamilton early in the season through injury. Initially, midfield man Andy Thomas switched successfully to attack, later Mr Evans paid a club record £175,000 fee to sign Dave Leworthy from Spurs but in the end it was the versatile Jeremy Charles who set up a new partnership with top scorer John Aldridge.

Welsh international right-back Neil Slatter, signed from Bristol Rovers during the close-season, spent most of the season out of position on the left side of the back four.

To give his midfield more authority, Mr Evans paid what was then a club record fee of £125,000 to Fulham for Ray Houghton. As the season progressed his stylish displays on the right, coupled with the terrier-like qualities of Les Phillips and the guile of Trevor Hebberd gave the club an excellent balance in the middle of the field.

There was competition for the fourth midfield place between Kevin Brock and Peter Rhoades-Brown.

One of the strong features of the Oxford side was the centre-back partnership of Malcolm Shotton and Gary Briggs. With David Langan at right-back for much of the season and Steve Hardwick performing well in goal until his injury, Oxford quickly found that they were not being over-run by their more famous 1st Division opponents.

But it was to be expected that they would have to battle to retain their newly-won place at thet top. And so it proved. And it wasn't until they produced another outstanding performance, to clout Arsenal 3-0 in their final match, that they were guaranteed survival.

Oxford, in fact, always seemed to come good when it most mattered. They defeated Newcastle, Nowich (the holders), Portsmouth and Aston Villa on the way to the Milk Cup final at Wembley. But they were still the underdogs as they prepared to meet QPR — ironically, the side managed by their former boss Jim Smith — at Wembley.

But they rose to the occasion splendidly. After quickly gaining control of the game, Oxford produced on of the best club performances ever seen at this famous stadium. Goals from Trevor Hebberd, Ray Houghton and Jeremy Charles in no way exaggerated their superiority — a fact readily acknowledged by Mr Smith.

There was no time for too many celebrations. Oxford had to buckle down to their 1st Division survival programme and in the end they missed the drop by just one point.

OXFORD UNITED

DIVISION ONE: 19th   **FA CUP:** 3rd ROUND   **MILK CUP:** WINNERS   **FM CUP:** AREA FINAL

MATCH	DATE	COMPE-TITION	VENUE	OPPONENTS	RESULT		HALF TIME	L'GUE POS'N	GOALSCORERS/GOAL TIMES	ATTEN-DANCE
1	A 17	CL	A	W.B.A.	D	1-1	0-0		McDonald 78	(14,626)
2	21	CL	H	Tottenham Hotspur	D	1-1	0-1		Charles 87	10,634
3	24	CL	H	Leicester City	W	5-0	2-0	6	Hebberd 25, Hamilton 40, 81, Charles 60, Trewick (pen) 69	9,626
4	26	CL	A	Birmingham City	L	1-3	1-2		Aldridge 13	(10,568)
5	31	CL	H	Sheffield Wednesday	L	0-1	0-1	13		9,934
6	S 3	CL	A	Coventry City	L	2-5	2-2	17	McDonald 2, 36	(10,266)
7	7	CL	A	Manchester United	L	0-3	0-2	19		(51,820)
8	14	CL	H	Liverpool	D	2-2	1-0	19	Aldridge 15, Kennedy (og) 87	11,474
9	18	FMC	H	Shrewsbury Town	W	3-0	2-0		Briggs 1, Charles 3, Houghton 48	1,898
10	21	CL	A	Newcastle United	L	0-3	0-0	20		(23,596)
11	25	MC2/1	H	Northampton Town	W	2-1	1-1		Rhoades-Brown 40, Houghton 73	5,644
12	28	CL	H	Manchester City	W	1-0	1-0	17	Trewick (pen) 31	9,796
13	O 2	CL	A	Leicester City	D	4-4	2-2	16	Thomas 3, Trewick pen 41, Aldridge 51, 80	(7,711)
14	5	CL	A	Everton	L	0-2	0-1	18		(24,553)
15	8	MC2/2	A	Northampton Town	W	2-0	0-0		Aldridge 61, 63	(5,076)
16	12	CL	H	Luton Town	D	1-1	0-1	18	Hebberd 88	(10,626)
17	19	CL	H	Chelsea	W	2-1	2-0	17	Aldridge 32, Rhoades-Brown 42	12,072
18	22	FMC	A	Fulham	W	2-0	1-0		Thomas 3, 51	(2,022)
19	26	CL	A	Watford	D	2-2	0-1	16	Rhoades-Brown 71, Houghton 78	(16,126)
20	30	MC3	H	Newcastle United	W	3-1	1-1		Thomas 19, 50, Hebberd 77	8,096
21	N 2	CL	A	Aston Villa	L	0-2	0-1	18		(12,922)
22	6	FMCS S/F	A	Stoke City	W	1-0	0-0		Aldridge 86	(5,820)
23	9	CL	H	West Ham United	L	1-2	1-1	18	Aldridge 21	13,140
24	16	CL	A	Arsenal	L	1-2	0-2	19	Charles 50	(19,632)
25	20	MC4	H	Norwich City	W	3-1	1-1		Aldridge 19, Thomas 51, Phillips 63	7,851
26	23	CL	H	Ipswich Town	W	4-3	0-2	18	Aldridge 3, 54 55, 63, Slatter 80	9,387
27	D 1	CL	A	Nottingham Forest	D	1-1	1-0	18	Thomas 19	(15,315)
28	4	FMCS F1	H	Chelsea	L	1-4	0-1		Aldridge (pen) 80	6,018
29	7	CL	A	Tottenham Hotspur	L	1-5	1-4	19	Aldridge 43	(17,698)
30	14	CL	H	W.B.A.	D	2-2	1-0	18	Aldridge (pen) 42, Charles 61	9,020
31	17	FMCS F2	A	Chelsea	W	1-0	1-0		Hebberd 45	(8,528)
32	26	CL	H	Southampton	W	3-0	2-0	18	Leworthy 23, 30, Aldridge 61	11,266
33	J 1	CL	A	Q.P.R.	L	1-3	0-2	19	Leworthy 67	(16,348)
34	4	FAC3	H	Tottenham Hotspur	D	1-1	1-0		Slatter 10	10,638
35	8	FAC3R	A	Tottenham Hotspur	L	1-2†	1-0		Aldridge 31	(19,136)
36	11	CL	H	Manchester United	L	1-3	0-1	19	Leworthy 53	13,280
37	18	CL	A	Sheffield Wednesday	L	1-2	0-1	19	Slatter 53	(18,565)
38	22	MC5	H	Portsmouth	W	3-1	2-0		Briggs 2, Phillips 44, Slatter 67	10,334
39	25	CL	H	Coventry City	L	0-1	0-0	19		9,383
40	F 1	CL	H	Birmingham City	L	0-1	0-0	20		9,086
41	8	CL	A	Chelsea	W	4-1	2-0	18	Rhoades-Brown 11, Charles 40, Hebberd 76, Aldridge 78	(16,181)
42	M 1	CL	A	Manchester City	W	3-0	2-0	17	Aldridge 3, 61, Charles 39	(20,099)
43	4	MC S/F1	A	Aston Villa	D	2-2	1-1		Aldridge 8 (pen) 56	(23,098)
44	12	MC S/F2	H	Aston Villa	W	2-1	0-0		Phillips 57, Charles 73	13,989
45	15	CL	A	Luton Town	L	2-1	0-1	18	Aldridge (pen) 49, Charles 60	(10,633)
46	19	CL	H	Newcastle United	L	1-2	0-1	18	Aldridge 82	10,052
47	22	CL	A	Liverpool	L	0-6	0-3	18		(37,861)
48	29	CL	H	Q.P.R.	D	3-3	2-3	18	Houghton 21, Aldridge (pen) 37, (pen) 82	11,910
49	A 1	CL	A	Southampton	D	1-1	1-1	19	Aldridge 34	(15,350)
50	5	CL	H	Aston Villa	D	1-1	0-0	19	Charles 49	11,406
51	9	CL	H	Watford	D	1-1	0-1	19	Aldridge 51	10,680
52	12	CL	A	West Ham United	L	1-3	1-0	20	Houghton 13	(23,956)
53	20	MC Final	N	Q.P.R.	W	3-0	1-0		Hebberd 40, Houghton 52, Charles 86	(90,390)
54	26	CL	A	Ipswich Town	L	2-3	1-0	20	Aldridge 30, Phillips 61	(17,827)
55	30	CL	H	Everton	W	1-0	0-0	20	Phillips 88	13,939
56	M 3	CL	H	Nottingham Forest	L	1-2	1-1	20	Charles 27	11,845
57	5	CL	H	Arsenal	W	3-0	1-0	19	Houghton 3, Aldridge pen 71, Hamilton 82	13,651

Best Home League Attendance: 13,939 v Everton   **Smallest:** 9,020 v W.B.A.   **Av Home Att:** 11,057

Goal Scorers: Compared with 84-85: +544

League (62):	Aldridge 23 (5 pen), Charles 9, Houghton 4, Leworthy 4, Hamilton 3, Hebberd 3, McDonald 3, Rhoades-Brown 3, Trewick 3 (3 pen), Phillips 2, Slatter 2, Thomas 2, Opponent 1
Milk Cup (20):	Aldridge 5 (1 pen), Phillips 3, Thomas 3, Hebberd 2, Houghton 2, Charles 2, Briggs 1, Rhoades-Brown 1, Slatter 1
FA Cup (2):	Slatter 1, Leworthy 1
FM Cup (8):	Aldridge 2 (1 pen), Thomas 2, Briggs 1, Charles 1, Hebberd 1, Houghton 1 †After Extra Time

Hardwick	Langan	McDonald	Trewick	Briggs	Shotton	Jones	Aldridge	Hamilton	Hebberd	Brock	Charles	Thomas	McDermott	Barnett	Houghton	Rhoades-Brown	Phillips	Slatter	Judge	Leworthy	Perryman	Referee	
1	2	3	4	5	6	7	8	9*	10	11	12											N Ashley	1
1	2	3	4	5	6	7*		9	10	11	12	8										V Callow	2
1	2	3	4	5	6			9	10	11*	7	8	12									D Vickers	3
1	2	3	4	5	6		8		10	11	9	7*	12									J Lovatt	4
1	2	3	4	5	6		8	9	10	11	7*	12										C Downey	5
1	2	3	4	5	6		8*		10	11	9		7	12								A Ward	6
1	2	3	4*	5	6		8		10	11	9		7	12								G Aplin	7
1	2	3	4	5	6		8		10	11*	9				7	12						J Moules	8
1	2	3	4	5	6		8		10	11	9*				7	12						G Napthine	9
1	2	3	4	5	6		8		10	11	9*				7	12						T Simpson	10
1	2	3	4	5*	6		8		10		9				7	11	12					T Holbrook	11
1	2		4	5	6		8		10	11	9				7			3				P Vanes	12
1	2		4*	5	6		8		10	11	12	9			7			3				K Miller	13
1	2			5	6		8		10	11*	9	12			7		4	3				G Tyson	14
1	2			5	6		8		10	11	9				7		4	3				A Seville	15
1	2			5	6		8†		10	12	9*				7	11	4	3				R Lewis	16
1	2			5	6		8		10		9				7	11	4	3				J Ashworth	17
1	2	12			6		8		10	5	9				7	11	4*	3				J Martin	18
1	2			5	6				10	8	9				7	11	4	3				D Axcell	19
1	2	12		5	6				10		9	8			7	11	4*	3				J Bray	20
1	2			5	6		8		10		9				7	11	4	3				R Guy	21
1	2	13		5	6		8		10	12	9*				7	11*	4	3				L Robinson	22
1	2		4	5	6		8		10	12	9				7	11*						J Ball	23
1	2		4	5	6		8		10		9				7	12	11*	3				M Bodenham	24
1	2*		4		6	12	8			5	7				9	11	10	3				Alan Robinson	25
1	2		4		6		8			5	9				7	11	10	3				M Dimblebee	26
1	2	3	4		6		8			11	9				7		10	5				P Tyldesley	27
1	2	13		5	6	12	8		10		9				7	11	4*	2*				G Napthine	28
1	6	9	3	5					10		4	11*			7	12	8	2				M James	29
1	2	3		5	6		8		10	11	9				7		4					R Groves	30
	2			5	6	12	8		10	11	9*				7		4	3	1			R Milford	31
	2	3		5	6		8		10	11					7		4		1	9		B Stevens	32
	2*	3	12	5	6		8			11					7		4	10	1	9		J Martin	33
	2			5	6		8		10	11					7		4	3	1	9		L Shapter	34
	2			5	6	11	8		10						7	12	4*	3	1	9		L Shapter	35
	2				6	7*	8		10	5	11				12		4	3	1	9		A Gunn	36
	2				6	12	8		10	11	5*				7		4	3	1	9		A Saunders	37
	2			5	6	12	8		10	11	9*				7		4	3	1			N Ashley	38
	2			5	6	12	8		10	11*					7		4	3	1	9		E Scales	39
	2			5	6		8		10	11		12			7		4*	3	1	9		M Heath	40
	2			5	6		8		10		9				7	11	4	3	1			I Hemley	41
	12	3*		5	6		8		10		9				7	11	4	2	1			D Hutchinson	42
	2			5	6		8		10		9				7	11	4	3	1			J Worrall	43
	2			5	6		8		10		9				7	11	4	3	1			Alan Robinson	44
	2			5	6		8		10		9*	12			7	11	4	3	1			C Downey	45
	12	2*		5	6		8		10						7	11	4	3	1	9		M Cotton	46
1	2	3		5*	6		8		10		9	12			7	11	4					G Courtney	47
	2	3		5	6		8		10	12	9				7	11*	4		1			N Midgley	48
	2	3		5	6		8		10		9				7		4	3	1		11	J Moules	49
	2	3		5	6		8		10	12	9*				7		4		1		11	T Jones	50
	2	3		5	6		8	9	10						7		4		1		11	T Simpson	51
	2	3		5	6		8	9*	10			12			7		4		1		11	K Butler	52
	2	3		5	6		8		10	11	9				7		4		1			K Hackett	53
	2	3		5	6		8		10	12	9*				7		4		1		11	T Holbrook	54
	2	3		5	6		8	9	10						7		4		1		11	D Shaw	55
	2	3		5*	6		8	9	10	12	9				7		4		1		11	R Hamer	56
	2	3		5	6	4	8	9	10						7				1		11	D Axcell	57
League Appearances																							
23	32	14	34	38	42	4	39	8	41	18	23	12	2	0	35	12	28	22	19	7	9	League Appearances	
	2	1			2					5	5	5	2	2	5							Substitute Appearances	
4	5	1	6-1	7	8	0-2	7		8	4	5	4			7	5	7-1	6	4			Milk Cup Appearances	
								2	2	2	1	2	2	1	2	0-1	2	2	2	2		FA Cup Appearances	
4	3	2-1	2-2	4	5	0-2	5		5	2	3-1	3			5	3-1	4	4	1			FM Cup Appearances	

Players on Loan:

Departures: Barnett (Fulham), Hicks (Fulham)

OXFORD UNITED F.C.

'THE U's'

Formed: 1896
Turned Professional: 1949   **Ltd Co:** 1949

Previous Names: Headington United (until 1960)
Previous Managers: Since 1962:
Arthur Turner   Ron Saunders   Gerry Summers   Mike Brown   Bill Asprey   Ian Greaves   Jim Smith
Honours: Champions Div 3, 1967-8, 1983-4   Champions Div 2, 1984-5   Milk Cup 1985-6
League Career: Elected to Div 4 1962   Promoted to Div 3 1965   Promoted to Div 2 1968
Relegated to Div 3 1976   Promoted to Div 2 1984   Promoted to Div 1 1985
Colours: Yellow shirts, navy blue shorts and stockings
Change Colours: All white
Reserves League: Football Combination   **Youth Team:** S E Counties

CLUB RECORDS

Most Appearances for Club: John Shuker 480, 1962-77
Most Capped Player: Dave Roberts, 6(17), Wales   **For England:** None
Record Goalscorer in a Match: No one more than four
Record League Goalscorer in a Season: John Aldridge, 30, Div 2, 1984-5   **In All Competitions:** John Aldridge, 34
(League 30 + FA Cup 1 + Milk Cup 3)
Record League Goalscorer in a Career: Graham Atkinson, 73, 1962-73   **In All Competitions:** Peter Foley, 87 (League
70 + FA Cup 9 + League/Milk Cup 8) 1974-83
Record Transfer Fee Received: £100,000 from Watford for Les Taylor, Nov 1980
Record Transfer Fee Paid: £175,000 to Tottenham Hotspur for David Leeworthy, Dec 1985
Best Performances: League: Champions Div 2 1984-5   **FA Cup:** 6th Round 1963-4 (best by Div 4 club)   **League/Milk
Cup:** Winners 1985-6
Most League Points: 95 in Div 3, 1983-4   **Most League Goals:** 91, Div 3, 1983-4
Record League Victory: 7-0 v Barrow, Div 4, 19 Dec 1964
Record League Defeat: 0-5 v Cardiff City, Div 2, 8 Feb 1969   v Cardiff City, Div 2, 12 Sept 1973
Oldest Player in League Match: Colin Todd 35 yrs 4 months
Youngest Player in League Match: Jason Seacole 16 yrs 5½ months

Most Consecutive Undefeated League Matches: 20 1984	**League Matches Without a Win:** 11 1975-76
Longest Run of Undefeated Home League Matches: 20 1964-65	**Away League Matches:** 12 1984
Longest Run Without Home League Win: 12 1980	**Away League Win:** 24 1974-5
Most Consecutive League Wins: 6 1968, 1982-83, 1985	**Home League Wins:** 10 1984
Most Consecutive League Defeats: 6 1968-69, 1975	**Away League Wins:** 4 1982-83, 1984

Club Statistician for the Directory: Mick Brown

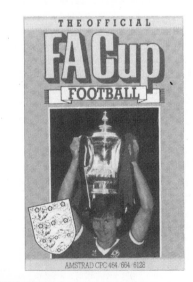

PLAYERS NAME t Wt Birthdate	Honours	Birthplace Transfers	Clubs	League	Milk Cup	FA Cup	Other Comps	League	Milk Cup	FA Cup	Other Comps
				APPEARANCES				GOALS			
GOALKEEPERS											
Steve Hardwick .11 13.0 6.9.56	EY Div.3 '84 Div.2 '85	Mansfield £80,000 £20,000	Chesterfield	38	2	4					
			Newcastle United	92	3	4					
			Oxford United	129	21	9	4				
			Crystal Palace (L)	3							
Ian Judge .11 11.5 21.6.59	Lg.C '86	Kingsbury F £10,000	Luton Town (A)	11	1						
			Reading	77	4	3	1				
			Oxford United	19	4	2	1				
			Lincoln City (L)	2							
DEFENDERS											
Gary Briggs .3 12.10 21.6.59	Div.3 '84 Div.2 '85, Lg.C '86	Leeds £12,500	Middlesbrough (A)								
			Oxford United	345+2	41	22	5	13	1		1
David Fogg .10½ 11.8 28.5.51		Liverpool	Wrexham	159+2	4	13+1					
			Oxford United	289+4	23+1	16		16	2	2	
David Langan .10 11.2 15.2.57	EI. (20) Div.2 '85 Lg.C '86	Dublin £350,000	Derby County (A)	143	6	6					
			Birmingham City	92	6	4					
			Oxford United	71+2	11	2	3	1	1		
Bobby McDonald .10 12.1 13.4.55	FAYC '72, Lg.C '75 Div.3 '84 Div.2 '85	Aberdeen £40,000 £270,000	Aston Villa (A)	33+6	4	3		3			
			Coventry City	161	11+1	7		14			
			Manchester City	96	5	10+1		11	1	4	
			Oxford United	87	16	9	4+1	14	3	4	
Steve Perryman .8 10.0 21.12.51	E (1) U.23 (17) Y FAC'80,'81,LgC (2) UEFA '72	Ealing F	Tottenham Hotspur (A)	653+2	66	69	68+1	31	3	2	3
			Oxford United	9							
Malcolm Shotton* .3 13.12 16.2.57	Div.3 '84 Div.2 '85 Lg.C '86	Newcastle F £15,000	Leicester City (A)								
			Nuneaton Borough			1					
			Oxford United	251	39	21	6	12	2	1	
Neil Slatter .11 10.10 30.5.64	W (12) U.21 (6) Y	Cardiff £70,000	Bristol Rovers (A)	147+1	14	8	3	4	1	1	
			Oxford United	22	6	2	4	2	1	1	
MIDFIELD											
Kevin Brock .9 10.12 9.9.62	E.U21 (3) S Div.3'84, Div.2'85 Lg.C '86	Middleton Stoney	Oxford United	198+17	28+1	15+1	2	25	5	1	
Trevor Hebberd .11½ 11.4 19.6.58	Div.3 '84 Div.2 '85 Lg.C '86	Winchester	Southampton (A)	69+28	9+1	4+3		7	3		
			Bolton W (A)	6							
			Leicester City (L)	4							
			Oxford United	183	28	14	6	32	3	1	1
Ray Houghton .7 10.10 9.1.62	EI. (4) Lg.C '86	Glasgow F	West Ham United	0+1							
			Fulham	129	12	4		16	3	2	
			Oxford United	35	7	2	5	4	2	1	
Mark Jones .8 9.12 26.9.61	Div.2 '85	Berinsfield	Oxford United (A)	101+28	10+4	6+2	0+2	7			
Les Phillips† .8 10.6 7.1.63	Lg.C '86	Lambeth £5,000	Birmingham City (A)	36+6	7+1	1		3	1		
			Oxford United	39+5	7+2	2	4	2	3		
Sean Reck .10 12.7 5.5.67		Oxford	Oxford United (A)								
			Newport County (A)	15	1	1		1			
			Reading (L)	3+2							
Andy Thomas .0 10.10 16.12.62	Div.3 '84 Lg.C '86	Oxford	Oxford United (A)	89+27	17+2	9	3	32	7	3	2
			Fulham (L)	3+1				2			
			Derby County (L)	0+1							
John Trewick .10 10.13 3.6.57	EY, S Div.2 '85, Lg.C '86	Bedlington £250,000	W.B.A. (A)	84+12	10+2	2		11			
			Newcastle United	76+2	2	7		8			
			Oxford United	78+2	12+1	4	2+2	3			
FORWARDS											
John Aldridge .11 10.4 18.9.58	Ei (4), Div.2 '85 Lg.C '86	Liverpool £3,500 £78,000	South Liverpool								
			Newport County	159+11	11	12+1		69	5	7	
			Oxford United	86+3	13	4	5	57	8	1	2
Jeremy Charles .1¾ 13.8 26.5.59	W (18), U.21 (2) WC '81, '83 Lg.C '86	Swansea £100,000	Swansea City (A)	224+23	19	11	8	53	7	3	5
			Q.P.R.	10+2	0+1	1	1+1	5			1
			Oxford United	34+5	5		3+1	13	2		1
Billy Hamilton .1 12.0 9.5.57	NI (41), U.23 (1) Div.3 '84 Div.2 '85	Belfast £25,000 £38,000 £80,000+PE	Linfield					2			
			Q.P.R.	9+3		1		58	5	7	
			Burnley	200	16	22	3	13	8		
			Oxford United	31	6	2		2			
Dave Leworthy .8½ 11.11 22.10.62		Portsmouth £150,000	Portsmouth	1							
			Fareham Town								
			Tottenham Hotspur	8+3	0+1		0+1	3	1		1
			Portsmouth (L)	8+3	0+1		0+1	3	1		1
			Oxford United	7				4		1	
Brian McDermott .9 11.7 8.4.61	EY, Div.2 '85	Slough £40,000	Arsenal	38+23	3+1	0+1	0+1	12			
			Fulham (L)	0+3							
			Oxford United	54+14	9	2+1	4+1	11	2		1
Peter Rhoades-Brown .9 11.4 2.1.62	Div.3 '84 Div.2 '85	Hampton	Chelsea	80+10	4	7+2		2		1	
			Oxford United (A)	54+14	9	2+1	4+1	11	2		1

ADDITIONAL CONTRACT PROFESSIONALS John Dreyer, Robbie Mustoe, Anthony Obi, Paul Swannack. **APPRENTICES** Edward Denton **NON-CONT. PLAYERS** Paul Whittington

Record Attendance: 22,730 v Preston North End, FA Cup Round 6, 29 Feb 1964

Record Receipts: £68,091 v Arsenal, Milk Cup Round, 3 Oct 1984

Season Tickets: Stand: £150.00 adult, £90.00 juvenile/OAP; Ground £65.00 adult, £32.50 juvenile/OAP

Executive Box Season Tickets: None available

Cost of Stand Tickets: £5.00 (adults), £3.00 (juvenile/OAP); **Terraces:** £3.00 (adults), £1.50 (juveniles/OAP)

Match and Ticket Information: It is expected that matches will be all-ticket. Admission by season ticket only for home supporters. Away fans should apply to their clubs for scarce terrace tickets as there will be no cash admission on the day of the match

Car Parking: Street parking near ground

Nearest Railway Station: Oxford (0865 722333)

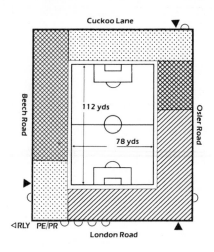

How to get to the ground

From North: Follow signs Ring Road, London A40, then at roundabout take 4th exit A420 S.P. Headington. In 0.8m turn right into Sandfield Road, then turn right into Beech Road to Oxford United FC

From East: Use Motorway M40 then A40 and at roundabout take 2nd exit A420 S.P. Headington. In 0.8m turn right into Sandfield Road, then turn right into Beech Road for Oxford United FC

From South: Use A34 then follow signs bypass, London A4142, then at roundabout take 1st exit A420 S.P. Headington. In 0.8m turn right into Sandfield Road then turn right into Beech Road for Oxford United FC

From West: Use A420 into Oxford, then follow signs London along Headington Road. In 2m turn left into Sandfield Road then turn right into Beech Road for Oxford United FC

Price of 1986-7 Programme: 50p
Number of Pages: 32
Subscriptions: £16.50 per season (UK postage paid): £25.00 (overseas)

Local Newspapers: Oxford Mail, Oxford Times

Local Radio Stations: Radio Oxford

PETERBOROUGH UNITED   Division 4

President
G H Woodcock

Chairman
S E Kendrick

Vice-Chairman
W O'N Wylde

Directors
S E Nicholas
A H Hand
G H Woodcock
D E Ringham Chief Executive
J C Duddington
M J Lewin

General Manager/Secretary
A V Blades

Manager
John Wile

Club Coach/Pysiotherapist
Bill Harvey

Commercial Manager
Ellis Stafford (0733 69760)

Back Row L to R: Bill Harvey (Physio), Paul Price, Noel Luke, John Turner, Andy Beasley, Les Lawrence, Jeff Doyle, Mark Nightingale, Lil Fuccillo (1st Team Coach).

Front Row: David Gregory, Steve Collins, Alan Paris, John Wile (Manager), Wakeley Gage (Captain), Greig Shepherd, Jackie Gallagher, Derrick Christie. Bryn Gunn, missing from picture.

The season started off brightly enough after the gloom that had descended on the club at the end of the 84/85 season. After only four League games a visit to Rochdale brought the top two teams together, how things were to change!! By this time local rivals Northampton had ruined Posh's Milk Cup hopes.

October seemed to take a dislike to 'Posh' as six games brought only two points, but worse than that, two unwanted records were set up. Record League defeat 0-7 at Tranmere, after the first game had been abandoned with 'Posh' a goal up. Also record home defeat 0-5 against county-rivals Northampton. A game which saw goalkeeper John Turner sent off after only five minutes, and all the more annoying was the fact that for 70 minutes 'Posh' were the better team, but once the third goal went in it could have been a cricket score as Peterborough ran out of steam.

After that the League could be forgotten and the quicker the better!!

As time passes the 85/86 season will be remembered for the FA Cup, which saw 'Posh' progress to the 5th Round.

The 1st round saw the club travel to non-league Bishop Stortford and although 'Posh' were twice in the lead a replay was needed. Two goals in the last five minutes did the trick but for 20 minutes in the second-half the only victors seemed to be Bishop Stortford.

A very poor 2nd Round game at home to Bath saw progress into the 3rd Round and a home game with Leeds. The game, although not the most skillful had everything possible and summed up the perfect David v Goliath match. The game was played on a frozen pitch and local hero 'Kelly' was injured early on and had to be replaced by substitute Sheperd. The second-half was played in a worsening snow storm. Substitute Sheperd scored for 'Posh' and within minutes Posh were down to ten men after goalkeeper Turner suffered a broken leg. Full-back Pike went in goal and the team fought out the rest of the game with their backs to the wall. Leeds did find the net in the last minute only to have it disallowed for off-side which saw Sellars sent off for protesting and Peterborough held on for a famous victory. They don't write them like that any more!!

The 4th Round saw Carlisle visit London Road and in a poor game another Sheperd goal brought a visit from Brighton in the 5th Round.

The game was played on a blanket of snow and was goalless until the 70th minute when up popped Sheperd again tp put Posh a goal up. Within two minutes Brighton were level. Kelly with the help of a snow divit, set the home fans dreaming of a 6th Round tie, but it was not to be as a late equaliser took the tie back to Brighton when a 79th minute goal finished off the Poshs' cup run and for some people that was the end of the season!!

PETERBOROUGH UNITED

DIVISION FOUR: 17th **FA CUP:** 5th ROUND **MILK CUP:** 1st ROUND **FRT:** 1st ROUND

MATCH	DATE		COMPE-TITION	VENUE	OPPONENTS	RESULT	HALF TIME	L'GUE POS'N	GOALSCORERS/GOAL TIMES	ATTEN-DANCE
1	A	17	CL	A	Preston North End	W 4-2	2-1		Gallagher 1, 79, Worrall 44, 72	(3,177)
2		21	MC1/1	H	Northampton Town	D 0-0	0-0			3,117
3		24	CL	H	Chester City	W 3-0	0-0	1	Pike 47, 57, Kowalski 56	2,667
4		27	CL	A	Orient	D 2-2	1-2		Worrall 24, Holmes 73	(2,577)
5		31	CL	A	Scunthorpe United	W 1-0	1-0	1	Fuccillo 9	2,928
6	S	3	MC1/2	A	Northampton Town	L 0-2	0-0			(2,464)
7		7	CL	A	Rochdale	L 1-2	0-2	4	Kowalski 57	(2,600)
8		14	CL	H	Swindon Town	W 3-0	2-0	2	Gallagher 2, 85, Holmes (pen) 17	2,946
9		18	CL	H	Torquay United	W 2-0	1-0		Kowalski 44, Quow 66	3,432
10		21	CL	A	Hereford United	L 1-2	0-2	3	Holmes (pen) 63	(3,261)
11		28	CL	H	Burnley	D 0-0	0-0	4		3,700
12	O	5	CL	A	Hartlepool United	L 1-2	1-1	8	Gallagher 36	(2,584)
13		12	CL	H	Northampton Town	L 0-5	0-2	11		3,872
14		18	CL	A	Stockport County	D 2-2	1-0	12	Shepherd 44, Gallagher 53	(1,634)
15		23	CL	H	Crewe Alexandra	D 0-0	0-0			2,760
16		26	CL	A	Cambridge United	L 1-3	0-0	13	Holmes (pen) 87	(3,234)
17		29	CL	A	Tranmere Rovers	L 0-7	0-1			(1,318)
18	N	2	CL	H	Exeter City	D 1-1	1-0	14	Rees 1	2,200
19		6	CL	H	Wrexham	D 1-1	1-0		Rees 18	1,948
20		9	CL	A	Halifax Town	D 1-1	1-1	16	Worrall 4	(1,007)
21		16	FAC1	A	Bishops Stortford	D 2-2	2-1		Hull (og) 17, Worrall 35	(2,000)
22		19	FAC1R	H	Bishop Stortford	W 3-1	1-0		Cassidy 24, Gallagher 85, Kowalski 87	2,778
23		23	CL	H	Port Vale	W 1-0	1-0	16	Worrall 6	2,852
24		30	CL	A	Aldershot	L 0-1	0-1	16		(1,375)
25	D	7	FAC2	H	Bath	W 1-0	0-0		Gallagher 53	3,388
26		14	CL	H	Mansfield Town	W 4-2	2-1	16	Cassidy 25, 67, Slack 40, Kelly 56	3,128
27		21	CL	A	Chester City	L 1-2	0-1	16	Gallagher 83	(2,231)
28		28	CL	H	Orient	D 2-2	0-0	16	Kelly 70, Gallagher 89	3,283
29	J	1	CL	H	Southend United	D 1-1	0-0	15	Kelly 55	3,104
30		4	FAC3	H	Leeds United	W 1-0	0-0		Shepherd 67	10,137
31		11	CL	A	Scunthorpe United	L 0-2	0-2	16		(1,832)
32		18	CL	H	Port Vale	D 1-1	0-1	17	Shepherd 60	2,711
33		21	FRT	A	Cambridge United	L 1-4	1-0		Gallagher 1	(2,253)
34		25	FAC4	H	Carlisle United	W 1-0	1-0		Shepherd 5	8,311
35	F	4	CL	A	Crewe Alexandra	D 1-1	1-1	18	Shepherd 24	(1,009)
36		15	FAC5	H	Brighton H.A.	D 2-2	0-0		Shepherd 73, Kelly 77	15,812
37	M	1	CL	A	Burnley	D 1-1	0-0	19	Slack 52	(2,686)
38		3	FAC5R	A	Brighton H.A.	L 0-1	0-0			(19,010)
39		5	CL	H	Tranmere Rovers	L 0-1	0-1	19		1,512
40		8	CL	H	Hartlepool United	W 3-1	1-0	17	Slack 37, Shepherd 47, Gallagher 89	2,300
41		11	CL	A	Torquay United	L 0-2	0-1	21		(1,243)
42		14	CL	A	Northampton Town	D 2-2	0-2	20	Slack 73, Kelly 78	(3,332)
43		19	CL	A	Exeter City	L 0-1	0-0	21		(1,460)
44		22	CL	H	Cambridge United	D 0-0	0-0	21		2,894
45		26	CL	H	Hereford United	D 0-0	0-0	20		1,560
46		29	CL	H	Southend United	W 1-0	0-0	19	Gallagher 87	(1,687)
47		31	CL	H	Colchester United	L 1-2	1-1	19	Fuccillo 29	2,316
48	A	5	CL	A	Wrexham	W 1-0	1-0	19	Shepherd 5	(1,138)
49		8	CL	H	Stockport County	W 2-0	2-0	18	Kowalski 14, Shepherd 18	1,610
50		12	CL	A	Halifax Town	D 1-1	1-1	18	Slack 30	2,260
51		15	CL	A	Swindon Town	L 0-3	0-1	20		(6,426)
52		19	CL	A	Port Vale	L 0-2	0-1	21		(3,765)
53		22	CL	A	Colchester United	L 0-5	0-1	21		(1,863)
54		26	CL	H	Aldershot	W 3-0	2-0	19	Fuccillo 42, Gallagher 44, Shrubb (og) 75	1,942
55	M	3	CL	A	Mansfield Town	W 1-0	1-0	17	Quow 14	(3,008)
56		7	CL	H	Rochdale	D 1-1	1-0	17	Quow 32	1,592

Best Home League Attendance: 3,872 v Northampton **Smallest:** 1,512 v Tranmere Rovers **Av Home Att:** 2,588

Goal Scorers: Compared with 84-85: −546

League (52): Gallagher 11, Shepherd 6, Slack 5, Worrall 5, Holmes 4 (3 pen), Kelly 4, Kowalski 4, Fuccillo 3, Quow 3, Cassidy 2, Pike 2, Rees 2, Opponent 1

Milk Cup (-):
FA CUP (10): Shepherd 3, Gallagher 2, Cassidy 1, Kelly 1, Kowalski 1, Worrall 1, Opponent 1
FRT (1): Gallagher 1

1985-86

Turner	Paris	Pike	Quow	Wile (NC)	Holmes	Kowalski	Fuccillo (NC)	Gallagher	Kelly	Worrall	Cassidy	Slack	Whymark (NC)	Johnson	Shepherd	Corder (L)	McClure (NC)	Rees (L)	Gage	Astbury (L)	Collins	O'Keeffe (NC)	Nuttell (NC)	McManus (L)	Cavener (NC)	Referee	
1	2*	3	4	5	6	7	8	9		10	11	12														K Lupton	1
1	2	3	4	5	6	7	8	9		11	10															J Moules	2
1	2	3	4	5	6	7	8	9*		11		12	10													M James	3
1	2	3	4	5	6	7	8	9		11			10													K Barratt	4
1	2	3	4	5	6	7	8	9		11			10													M Dimblebee	5
1	2	3	4	5	6	7	8	9	12	11			10*													M Cotton	6
1	2	3	4	5	6	7	8	9		10	11															J Lovatt	7
1	2	3	4	5	6	7	8	9		10	11															K Miller	8
1	2	3	4		6	7	8	9		10	11	5														A Ward	9
1	2	3	4		6	7	8*	9		10	11	5		12												C Downey	10
1	2	3	4		6*	7	8	9		11		5		12	10											R Lewis	11
1	2	3	4	5		7	8	9	12	11*		6			10											K Hackett	12
1†	2	3	4		6	7	8	9		10	11	5*			12											D Axcell	13
1	2	3	4	5		7	8	9		11		6			10											J Lloyd	14
1	2	3	4	5			8	9	12	11		6					7	10*								E Scales	15
	2	3	4	5			8*	9		11		6			12	1	7	10								A Vickers	16
	2	3	4	5	6		8	9							11	1	7	10								T Holbrook	17
1	2	5	6		3		8	9	12	11	4*						7	10								L Robinson	18
1	2	3	4		6		8	9		11	7	5						10								D Hedges	19
1	2	3	4		6		8	9		11	7	5			10											M Heath	20
1	2	3	4		6	7	8	9		11		5			10											K Barratt	21
1	2	3			6	7	8	9	12	11	4	5			10*											K Barratt	22
1	2	3				7	8	9	10	11	4	5							6							D Reeves	23
1	2	3				7	8	9	10	11	4	5							6							R Groves	24
1	2	3	5			7	8	9	10	11	4	6														A Ward	25
1	2	3				7	8	9	10	11	4	5							6							N Butler	26
1	2	3				7	8	9	10	11	4	5							6							T Simpson	27
1	2	3				7	8	9	10	11	4	5							6							J Ball	28
1	2	3				7	8	9	10	11	4	5							6							M Dimblebee	29
1	2	3	5			7	8	9		10*	4				12				6							P Tyldesley	30
	2	3				7	8	9	12		4*	5			10				6	1	11					N Glover	31
	2	3				7	8*	9		11	4	5			10				6	1	12					K Barratt	32
	2	3					8*	9		11	12	6			10				5	1	7	4				J Hemley	33
	2	3	5			7	8		10		4	6			9					1						I Borrett	34
	2	3	12			7	8			11	10	5			9				6*	1	4					J McAulay/J Shaw	35
	2	3	5			7	8			11	4	6			10					1	4					J Worrall	36
	2	3				7	8			11	10	5			9				6	1	4					J Lovatt	37
	2	3	5			7	8	12	10	11	4*	6			9					1	4					C Downey	38
	2	3				7	8	12	10*		11	5			9				6		4			1		M Heath	39
	2	3				7	8		10		11	5			9				6		4			1		E Scales	40
	2	3				7	8		10	11*	12	5			9				6		4			1		R Groves	41
	2	3	7				8		10	12	11*	5			9				6		4			1		I Hemley	42
	2	3	12			7	8		10	11*		5			9				6		4			1		J Martin	43
	2	3	11			7*	8		10		12	5			9				6		4			1		A Robinson	44
	2	3	11				8		10		7	5			9				6		4			1		R Lewis	45
	2	3	11				8		10			5			9				6		4			1	7	A Buksh	46
	2	3				7	8		10	11		5			9				6		4			1		M Reed	47
	2	3	10			7	8					5			9				5		4			1	11	L Robinson	48
	2	3	10*			7	8					5			9				6		4			1	11	K Baker	49
	2	3	10			7	8*	12				5			9				6		4			1	11*	N Wilson	50
	2	3	10			7	8	12				5			9				6		4			1	11*	L Shapter	51
	2	3	10*			7	8	11				5			9				6		4			1	12	G Tyson	52
	2	3				7	8		10			5		12					6		4		9*	1	11	M Bodenham	53
	2	3	10			7	8	9				5			8				6*		4			1	11	D Vickers	54
	2	3	10			7	8	9				5							6*		4			1	11	J Bray	55
	2	3	10			7	8	9				5	6						4*					1	11	T Mills	56

22	46	46	29	13	15	35	45	40	15	29	13	39	3	2	23	2	4	5	27	4	21		1	18	9	League Appearances	
	1	1						2	6	1	2	1		3	2						1		2		1	Substitute Appearances	
2	2	2	2	2	2	2	2	0-1	2	1				1												Milk Cup Appearances	
4	7	7	1	5	2	7	7	4-1	5-1	7	6	7			5-1				3							FA Cup Appearances	
1	1	1	1		1	1	0-1	1				1			1		1				1		1	1	1	FR Trophy Appearances	

Players on Loan: Corder (Tottenham), Rees (Birmingham), Astbury (York), McManus (Bradford)

Departures: Whymark, McClure, Chard (Northampton), Pike (Sheff Wed), Worrall (Carlisle), Quow (Peterborough), Kowalski (Chesterfield)

'THE POSH'

Formed: 1934
Turned Professional: 1934   **Ltd Co:** 1934

Previous Managers: 1934-6 Jock Porter   1936-7 Fred Taylor   1937-8 V Poulter   1938-48 Sam Maden   1948-50 Jack Blood   1950-2 Bob Gurney   1952-4 Jack Fairbrother   1954-8 George Swindin   1958-62 Jimmy Hagan   1962-4 Jack Fairbrother   1964-7 Gordon Clark   1967-9 Norman Rigby   1969-72 Jim Iley   1972-7 Noel Cantwell   1977-8 John Barnwell   1978-9 Billy Hails   1979-82 Peter Morris   1982-3 Martin Wilkinson   1983- John Wile

Honours: Champions Div 4, 1960-1

League Career: Elected to Div 4 1960   Promoted to Div 3 1960-1
Demoted to Div 4 for financial irregularities 1968   Promoted to Div 3 1973-4
Relegated to Div 4 1978-9

Colours: All blue

Change Colours: All yellow with blue trim

Reserves League: Midland Intermediate

CLUB RECORDS

Most Appearances for Club: Tommy Robson: Football League 440 + 42 + FA Cup 43 + 2 + League Cup 31 + 1 **Total 514 + 45 subs**

Most Capped Player: Tony Millington, 8, Wales   **For England:** None

Record Goalscorer in a Match: Laxton, 6 v Rushden, FA Cup 3rd Qual. Round, 6 Oct 1945

Record League Goalscorer in a Season: Terry Bly, 52, Div 4, 1960-1   **In All Competitions:** Terry Bly, 54 (League 52 + FA Cup 2), 1960-1

Record League Goalscorer in a Career: Jim Hall, 122, 1967-75   **In All Competitions:** Jim Hall, 137 (League 122 + FA Cup 11 + League Cup 4)

Record Transfer Fee Received: £110,000 from Blackpool for Bobby Doyle, July 1979

Record Transfer Fee Paid: £60,000 to West Ham United for Bill Green, July 1978

Best Performances: League: 4th Div 3 1977-8   **FA Cup:** 6th Round, 1965   **League/Milk Cup:** Semi-Final 1966

Most League Points: 82, Div 4, 1981-2   **Most League Goals:** 134, Div 4, 1960-1

Record League Victory: 8-1 v Oldham Athletic, Div 4, 26 Nov 1969   7-0 v Barrow, Div 4, 9 Oct 1971

Most Goals Scored in a Cup Tie: 9-1 v Rushden (A), 6 Oct 1945

Record League Defeat: 0-7 v Tranmere Rovers, Div 4, 29 Oct 1985

Oldest Player in League Match:

Youngest Player in League Match:

Most Consecutive Undefeated League Matches: 17 1960-61   **League Matches Without a Win:** 17 1978

Longest Run of Undefeated Home League Matches: 32 1973-74   **Away League Matches:** 8 1969

Longest Run Without Home League Win: 9 1985   **Away League Win:** 26 1976-77

Most Consecutive League Wins: 7 1960-61, 1973   **Home League Wins:** 15 1960-61

Most Consecutive League Defeats: 4 1967-68, 1971, 1972,
1977, 1978, 1982, 1985   **Away League Wins:** 4 1969

The last time that Peterborough United lost their first League game of the season was in 1976

Club Statistician for the Directory: Mick Robinson

PETERBOROUGH UNITED

PLAYERS NAME Ht Wt Birthdate	Honours	Birthplace Transfers	Clubs	APPEARANCES League	Milk Cup	FA Cup	Other Comps	GOALS League	Milk Cup	FA Cup	Other Comps
GOALKEEPERS											
Andrew Beasley .2 12.2 5.2.64		Sedgley Temp. Transfer	Luton Town (A) Mansfield Town Peterborough United	5							
DEFENDERS											
Steve Collins .8 12.4 21.3.62		Stamford F F F	Peterborough Utd (A) Southend United Lincoln City Peterborough Utd	92+2 51 23	9 2	8 2 1	1 5	1			
Wakeley Gage .4 13.7 5.5.58		Northampton £5,000	Desborough Town Northampton Town Chester City Peterborough Utd	173+2 17 27	10 3	14 1	1	17 1		2	
Mark Nightingale .10 10.7 1.2.57	EY AMC '84	Salisbury F F Bulova HR F	Bournemouth (A) Crystal Palace Norwich City Bournemouth Peterborough Utd	44+5 28+7 144+5	2 8	8 10	12	4 4			
Paul Price .11 12.0 23.3.54	W (25) U.21 (7)	St. Albans £200,000 Minnesota S. Saltash	Luton Town Tottenham H. Swansea City Peterborough Utd	206+1 35+4 62	13 6 4	9 6 1	8	8 1			
Trevor Slack .2 12.2 26.9.61	EY	Peterborough	Peterborough Utd (A)	201+1	13	13	2	14	1	1	1
MIDFIELD											
Alan Paris .11 10.12 15.8.64		Slough	Slough Town Watford Peterborough United	46	2	7	1				
Jol Fuccillo (N/C) .11 11.4 2.5.56	Div. 2 '82	Bedford Tulsa Roughnecks	Luton Town Southend United Peterborough Utd (N/C)	153+7 40+5 45	2	2 7	1+1 1	24 5 3			
FORWARDS											
Derek Christie .8 11.0 15.3.57		Bletchley F F F F	Northampton Town (A) Cambridge United Reading Cardiff City Peterborough United	116+22 132+6 8+6 18+1	11+1 11+1 1	4+2 3+1 1	2 1	18 19 1 2	2 2	1	
Jackie Gallagher .10½ 12.9 6.4.58		Wisbech Wisbech Town Hong Kong F F	March Town Utd Lincoln City Peterborough United Torquay United Peterborough United	1 11+2 38+4 40+2	2 2	5 4+1	27 1	11	2	1 2	1
David Gregory .9 11.6 6.10.51		Peterborough £55,000 £30,000 £30,000 F	Chatteris Town Peterborough United Stoke City Blackburn Rovers (L) Bury Portsmouth Wrexham Peterborough Utd	125+17 22+1 5 50+2 64+10 143+7	10+1 1 1 2 7 5	13+1 1 4 4 3+1	3	32 3 3 13 18 30	2 1 1 1 2 4	6 6 1 2	1
es Lawrence .3 11.0 18.5.57	22+9	Wolverhampton Telford United Weymouth F £15,000 Burnley	Stourbridge Shrewsbury Town Torquay United Port Vale Aldershot Rochdale Peterborough United	10+4 170+9 5+3 39 15 2+2	11+4 0+1 4 2 8	9+1 2 1	1	45 23 4 1	4 2 1	4	
Noel Luke 5.11 10.11 28.12.61		Birmingham F	W.B.A. (A) Mansfield Town Peterborough United	8+1 41+7	3 1+1	4+2 3+1	7	3	1		1
Greg Shepherd 5.1 12.0 29.9.60		Edinburgh F £8,000	Musselburgh Norwich City Southend United Peterborough United	13+3 47+6 50+2	2 2	4	2 1	2 11 12	3	1 3	1

ADDITIONAL CONTRACT PROFESSIONALS

APPRENTICES
Mark Amps, Nicholas Brooker, Stephen George, Graham Harford, Lee Philpott, Matthew Sanderson

NON-CONTRACT PLAYERS
Jeremy Moulds

Record Attendance: 30,096 v Swansea Town, FA Cup Round 5, 20 Feb 1965

Smallest Home Attendance for a First Class Match: 1,464 v Exeter City, Div 4, 4 May 1985

Record Receipts: £51,315 v Brighton, FA Cup 5th Round, 15 Feb 1986

Season Tickets: Stands: £100.00 (centre); £80.00 (wing stand); £65.00 (enclosure); £55.00 (ground). Senior Citizens ½ price. All season ticket prices include match programme

Executive Box Season Tickets: Four Boxes, £250 in the new executive suite for Vice-Presidents (single)

Cost of Stand Tickets: Ground £2.50; Enclosure £3.00; Wing Stand £4.00; Centre Stand £5.00

Match and Ticket Information: Tickets bookable 14 days in advance

Car Parking: Ample parking available at ground

Nearest Railway Station: Peterborough (0733 68181)

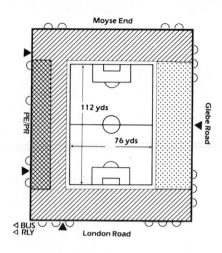

How to get to the ground

From North and West: Use A1 then A47 S.P. Peterborough into town centre. Follow signs Whittlesey and cross river bridge into London Road for Peterborough United FC
From East: Use A47 into Peterborough town centre and follow signs Whittlesey and cross river bridge into London Road for Peterborough United FC
From South: Use A1 then A15 S.P. Peterborough into London Road for Peterborough United FC

Price of 1986-7 Programme: 50p
Number of Pages: 20
Subscriptions: Please apply to club

Local Newspapers: Peterborough Standard, Evening Telegraph

Local Radio Stations: Cambridgeshire Radio, Hereward Radio

P LYMOUTH ARGYLE Division 2

Whew! What a season. A poor start saw only four points obtained from a possible 15 which did not promise well.

An early exit from the Milk Cup to our Devon rivals Exeter City did nothing to boost confidence. Results slightly improved in the next three months with the signing of John Clayton from Tranmere Rovers to play alongside Steve Cooper. A good result at Boothferry Park in the 3rd round fo the FA Cup against Hull City 2-2 was welcome, but were narrowly defeated 1-0 in the replay at Home Park. Previous to this game a large following of supporters went to Reading to see Argyle take a 3-1 lead at half-time only to be finally defeated 4-3. With more points being regularly dropped thoughts of promotion for this season seemed to fade.

However, on March 4th in an away game to Gillingham manager Dave Smith intoduced a loan signing from Orient, a lad called Kevin Godfrey, a 1-1 draw resulted. For the next six games in which Kevin Godfrey played Argyle remained undefeated and were back in the promotion hunt. Kevin Godfrey's loan period was now up and he returned to Orient and I think a word of thanks should be extended to Kevin for the part he played during this period.

Manager Dave Smith immediately pulled off a master stroke of business by getting Tommy Tynan, Argyle's top scorer the previous season, back on loan from Rotherham United. During the next six games Argyle moved up and down the top four in the table but on Tuesday 29th April, before 20,000 spectators, they clinched promotion with a power display of football against Bristol City winning 4-0 much to the delight of all their fans, who now look forward to a good season in Division 2.

A word of praise is due to manager Dave Smith and his assistant Martin Harvey for the way they have orchestrated this success with the co-operation of all the players.

So supporters, let's keep the support forthcoming in Division 2.   F J Lee

Back Row L to R: Dave Smith (Team Manager), John Matthews, John Uzzell, Harvey Lim, Gordon Nisbet, Geoff Crudgington, Kevin Summerfield, Clive Goodyear, Malcolm Musgrove (Physio). **Front Row:** Darren Rowbotham, Leigh Cooper, John Clayton, Gerry McElhinney, Steve Cooper, Garry Nelson, Kevin Hodges, Russell Coughlin, Adrian Burrows.

PLYMOUTH ARGYLE

DIVISION THREE: 2nd   **FA CUP:** 3rd ROUND   **MILK CUP:** 1st ROUND

MATCH	DATE		COMPE-TITION	VENUE	OPPONENTS	RESULT		HALF TIME	L'GUE POS'N	GOALSCORERS/GOAL TIMES	ATTEN-DANCE
1	A	17	CL	A	York City	L	1-3	0-2		McElhinney (pen) 55	(4,246)
2		20	MC1/1	H	Exeter City	W	2-1	1-0		Summerfield 15, McElhinney (pen) 63	4,754
3		24	CL	H	Reading	L	0-1	0-1	22		4,261
4		26	CL	A	Swansea City	W	2-0	0-0		McElhinney (pen) 55, Cooper S 80	(3,903)
5		31	CL	H	Notts County	L	0-1	0-1	19		5,105
6	S	4	MC1/2	A	Exeter City	L	0-2	0-2			(3,362)
7		7	CL	A	Brentford	D	1-1	0-1	20	Cooper S (pen) 90	(3,927)
8		14	CL	H	Newport County	W	2-0	1-0	15	Burrows 31, Nelson 79	3,686
9		17	CL	A	Doncaster Rovers	L	0-1	0-1			(2,904)
10		21	CL	H	Wolverhampton W.	W	3-1	1-0	14	Cooper S (pen) 44, Nelson 50, 62	5,241
11		28	CL	A	Bolton Wanderers	L	1-3	0-3	18	Clayton 65	(4,270)
12	O	1	CL	H	Gillingham	W	3-0	1-0	14	Hodges 43, Nelson 53, Cooper S (pen) 84	4,135
13		5	CL	H	Bristol Rovers	W	4-2	3-0	11	Clayton 14, Coughlin 19, Hodges 37, Parkin (og) 72	5,662
14		12	CL	A	Walsall	D	2-2	0-1	12	Nelson 85, 90	(4,253)
15		19	CL	A	Rotherham United	D	1-1	0-0	12	Hodges 48	(2,942)
16		22	CL	H	Lincoln City	W	2-1	0-0	9	Hodges 47, Nelson 87	6,552
17		26	CL	A	Derby County	W	2-1	2-1	7	Hodges 7, Goodyear 30	(11,433)
18	N	2	CL	H	Chesterfield	D	0-0	0-0	10		7,522
19		4	CL	H	Bournemouth	W	2-1	1-1	5	Hodges 42, Cooper S. 56	6,186
20		9	CL	A	Bury	W	1-0	1-0	3	Clayton 39	(2,975)
21		16	FAC1	H	Aldershot	W	1-0	1-0		Coughlin 20	7,209
22		23	CL	H	Wigan Athletic	W	2-1	0-0	2	Summerfield 68, Coughlin (pen) 83	6,714
23		30	CL	A	Blackpool	D	1-1	0-1	5	Nelson 82	(6,184)
24	D	7	FAC2	H	Maidstone	W	3-0	2-0		Cooper S. 12, Nelson 29, Summerfield 84	7,597
25		14	CL	H	Darlington	W	4-2	2-0	2	Hodges 37,64, Cooper 45, Summerfield 58	6,036
26		21	CL	A	Reading	L	3-4	2-0	4	Hodges 10, Cooper S (pen) 44, Clayton 49	(8,512)
27		26	CL	A	Bristol City	L	0-2	0-2	5		(8,298)
28		28	CL	H	Swansea City	W	2-0	1-0	3	Clayton 21, 50	8,622
29	J	1	CL	H	Cardiff City	D	4-4	2-2	3	Nelson 33, Summerfield 40, Clayton 83, Hodges 86	8,920
30		4	FAC3	A	Hull City	D	2-2	2-1		Clayton 28, Cooper S. 34	(6,776)
31		7	FAC3R	H	Hull City	L	0-1	0-1			13,940
32		11	CL	A	Notts County	L	0-2	0-1	6		(4,953)
33		14	FRT	A	Bristol City	D	0-0	0-0			(2,402)
34		18	CL	H	York City	D	2-2	1-1	7	Brimacomb 6, Coughlin (pen) 68	5,942
35		21	FRT	H	Walsall	L	0-1	0-1			3,198
36		25	CL	A	Newport County	L	1-2	1-2	8	Clayton 7	(3,007)
37	F	1	CL	H	Brentford	W	2-0	1-0	8	Nelson 30, 55	4,873
38		15	CL	H	Doncaster Rovers	L	0-1	0-0	8		4,827
39	M	4	CL	A	Gillingham	D	1-1	0-0	8	Summerfield 87	(3,490)
40		8	CL	A	Bristol Rovers	W	2-1	1-0	8	Coughlin (pen) 18, Godfrey 80	(4,667)
41		11	CL	A	Wolverhampton W.	W	3-0	2-0	7	Coughlin (pen) 21, Summerfield 23, Clayton 81	(2,367)
42		15	CL	H	Walsall	W	2-0	1-0	6	Cooper L. 34, Coughlin 59	6,079
43		18	CL	A	Chesterfield	W	2-1	2-1	5	Summerfield 42, Goodyear 44	(1,828)
44		22	CL	H	Derby County	W	4-1	0-1	4	Clayton 47,57, Rowbotham 79, Hodges 83	11,769
45		28	CL	A	Cardiff City	W	2-1	2-0	3	Hodges 15, Matthews 32	(3,834)
46	A	5	CL	A	Bournemouth	W	3-1	2-0	4	Cooper S 12, Coughlin pen 45, Hodges 84	(5,351)
47		8	CL	H	Rotherham United	W	4-0	2-0	3	Pickering (og) 17, Tynan 33, 59, Summerfield 90	13,034
48		12	CL	H	Bury	W	3-0	2-0	2	Hodges 12, Tynan 30, 59	13,626
49		16	CL	A	Lincoln City	D	1-1	0-1	3	Tynan 54	(2,297)
50		19	CL	A	Wigan Athletic	L	0-3	0-1	4		(9,485)
51		22	CL	H	Bolton Wanderers	W	4-1	0-1	3	Hodges 72, Coughlin (pen) 82, Tynan 84, Burrows 88	12,183
52		26	CL	H	Blackpool	W	3-1	0-1	2	Nelson 50, Coughlin (pen) 78, Clayton 87	14,975
53		29	CL	H	Bristol City	W	4-0	1-0	2	Tynan 32, 64, Nelson 54, Coughlin 60	19,900
54	M	3	CL	A	Darlington	W	2-0	0-0	2	Hodges 66, Tynan 84	(3,306)

Best Home League Attendance: 19,900 v Bristol City   Smallest: 3,686 v Newport County   Av Home Att: 8,080

Goal Scorers: Compared with 84-85: +2,947

League (88): Hodges 16, Nelson 13, Clayton 12, Coughlin 10 (7 pen), Tynan 9, Cooper S. 8 (4 pen), Summerfield 7, Burrows 2, Goodyear 2, McElhinney 2, Opponents 2, Brimacomb 1, Cooper L 1, Godfrey 1, Matthews 1, Rowbotham 1

Milk Cup (2): Summerfield 1, McElhinney 1 (pen)

FA Cup (6): Coughlin 1, Cooper L. 1, Nelson 1, Summerfield 1, Clayton 1, Cooper S. 1

FRT (-):

1985-86

Croughton	Nisbet	Goodyear	Uzzell	McElhinney	Matthews	Coughlin	Cooper S	Rowbotham	Nelson	Hodges	Summerfield	Cooper L	Burrows	Clayton	Philip (NC)	Brimacomb (NC)	Godfrey (L)	Tynan (L)	Referee	No.
1	2	3	4	5	6	8	9	10	11	7									J Worrall	1
1	2	4		5	6	8	9		11	7	10	3							**J Deakin**	2
1	2	4	3	5	6	8	9		11	7		10							R Milford	3
1	2	4	3	5	6	8	9		11	7		10							B Stevens	4
1	2			5	6	8	9		11	7		3	4	10					R Groves	5
1	2	12		5	6	8	9		11	7		3*	4	10					**J Martin**	6
1	2	3		5		8	9	6	11	7			4	10					K Baker	7
1	2	3		5	6	8	9		11	7			4	10					Alan Robinson	8
1	2	3*		5	6	8	9	12	11	7			4	10					R Banks	9
1	2	3		5	6	8*	9	12	11	7			4	10					K Cooper	10
1	2	3		5	6	8	9		11	7			4	10					G Aplin	11
1	2	3		5	6	8	9		11	7	4			10					A Seville	12
1	2	4		5	6	8	9		11	7		3		10					L Robinson	13
1	2	3		5	6*	8	9		11	7	12		4	10					I Hemley	14
1	2	4		5	6	8	9		11	7		3		10					I Hendrick	15
1	2	4		5	6	8	9		11	7		3		10					R Hamer	16
1	2	4		5	6	8	9		11	7		3		10					K Breen	17
1	2	4		5		8	9	12	11*	7	6	3		10					R Lewis	18
1	2	4		5	6	8	9		11	7		3		10					P Vanes	19
1	2	3		4*	7	8	10		9	6	12	5		11					D Phillips	20
1	2	4		5		8	9	12	11	7*	6	3		10					**B Stevens**	21
1	2	4		5	12	8	9*		11	7	6	3		10					D Hedges	22
1	2	4		5		8	9		11	7	6	3		10					J Key	23
1	2	4		5		8	9		11	7	6	3		10					**R Milford**	24
1	2	4		5		8	9	12	11	7	6	3*		10					R Gifford	25
1	2†	4		5		8	9		11	7	6	3		10					D Axcell	26
1	2	4		5		8	9	12	11	7*	6	3		10					D Vickers rpd J Carter	27
1	2	4		5		8	9		11	7	6	3		10					C Downey	28
1*	2	4		5	12	8	9		11	7	6	3		10					R Hamer	29
		4		5		8	9		11	7	6	3	2	10	1				**J Worrall**	30
		4	12	5	6		9		11	7	8*	3	2	10	1				**J Deakin**	31
1	2	4		5	6	12	9*		11	7	8	3		10					R Dilkes	32
1	2	4*	3	5	6	8			11	7	9	12		10					**J Bray**	33
1	2	3*		5	6	8			11	7	9	12		10		4			R Milford	34
1	2	4		5	6	8	12		11	7	9*	3		10					**B Stevens**	35
1	2	4		5	6	8	9		11	7		3		10					M Reed	36
1	2	4		5	6	8	9		11	7		3		10					R Groves	37
1	2	4		5	6	8	9		11	7		3		10					I Hemley	38
1	2	4		5		8			11	7	6	3		10			9		M Bodenham	39
1	2	4		5		8*		12	11	7	6	3		10			9		M Scott	40
1	2	4		5		8		12	11*	7	6	3		10			9		D Hutchinson	41
1	2	4		5		8			11	7	6	3		10			9		R Hamer	42
1	2	4		5		8		12	11	7	6	3		10			9*		G Napthine	43
1	2	4		5		8*		12	11	7	6	3		10			9		G Ashby	44
1	2	4		5		8		12	11	7	6	3		10			9*		M Dimblebee	45
1	2	4		5		8	6	10	11*	7	12	3						9	J Moules	46
1	2	4		5	6	8	10		11*	7	12	3						9	K Cooper	47
	2	4		5	6	8	10		11*	7		3						9	R Gifford	48
1	2	4		5	6	8	10		11*	7	12	3						9	P Tyldesley	49
1	2	4		5	6*	8	10		11	7	12	3						9	G Alpin	50
1	2	4				8			11	7	6	3	5	10				9	Alan Robinson	51
1	2	4		5		8			11	7	6	3		10				9	J Martin	52
1	2	4		5	6	8			11	7	10	3						9	J Deakin	53
1	2	4		5*	6	8			11	7	10	3						9	J McAulay	54
46	46	41	8	44	29	44	34	7	41	46	21	39	7	36	1		7	9	League Appearances	
					2	1		4	7	1	5	1							Substitute Appearances	
2	2	1·1		2	2	2	2		2	2	1	2	1	1					Milk Cup Appearances	
2	2	4	0·1	4	2	4	0·1		4	4	4	2	4	2					FA Cup Appearances	
2	2	2	1	2	2	2	0·1		2	2	2	1	0·1	2					FR Trophy Appearances	

Players on Loan: Godfrey (Orient), Tynan (Rotherham)
Departures: Rogers (Reading), Staniforth (Newport), Harrison (F), Philip (F)

'THE PILGRIMS'

Formed: 1886
Turned Professional: 1903 **Ltd Co:** 1903

Previous Names: 1886-1903 Argyle Athletic Club
Previous Managers: 1903-5 Frank Brettell 1905-6 Bob Jack 1906-7 William Fullerton
1910-38 Bob Jack 1938-48 Jack Tresardern 1948-55 Jimmy Rae 1955-60 Jack Rowley
1960-1 George Taylor/Neil Dougall 1961-3 Ellis Stuttard 1963 Vic Buckingham
1963-4 Andy Beattie 1964-5 Malcolm Allison 1965-8 Derek Ufton 1968-70 Billy Bingham
1970-2 Ellis Stuttard 1972-77 Tony Waiters 1977-8 Mike Kelly 1978 Lenny Lawrence
1978-9 Malcolm Allison 1978-81 Bobby Saxton 1981-3 Bobby Moncur 1983-4 John Hore
Vic Buckingham was only with the club for six weeks during the summer of 1963 and never fielded an
'Argyle' team.
Lennie Lawrence was acting manager only for 5 games early in 1978. George Taylor and Neil Dougall
worked together in 1960-1
Honours: Champions Div 3 (S) 1929-30, 1951-2, Champions Div 3 1958-9
League Career: Original Member of Div 3 1920 Reverted to Div 3 (S) 1921
Promoted to Div 2 1929-30 Relegated to Div 3 (S) 1949-50 Promoted to Div 2 1951-2
Relegated to Div 3 (S) 1955-6 Transferred to Div 3 1958 Promoted to Div 2 1958-9
Relegated to Div 3 1967-8 Promoted to Div 2 1974-5 Relegated to Div 3 1976-7
Colours: Green shirts with black trim, black shorts, green stockings with black and white tops
Change Colours: All yellow
Reserves League: Macbar S W Counties League **'A' Team:** Great Mills Western League **Youth Team:**
Plymouth & District League

CLUB RECORDS

Most Appearances for Club: Sammy Black: Football League 470 + FA Cup 22 **Total 492**
Most Capped Player: Moses Russell, 20, Wales **For England:** None
Record Goalscorer in a Match: Wilf Carter, 5 v Charlton Athletic, Div 2, 27.12.1960
Record League Goalscorer in a Season: Jack Cock, 32, 1926-7 **In All Competitions:** Wilf Carter, 32 (League 26 + FA
Cup 6), 1957-8 and Jack Cock (all League) 1926-7
Record League Goalscorer in a Career: Sammy Black, 180 **In All Competitions:** Sammy Black, 184 (League 176 + FA
Cup 8) 1924-38
Record Transfer Fee Received: £250,000 from Everton for Gary Megson, Feb 1980
Record Transfer Fee Paid: £75,000 to Carlisle United for David Kemp, Sept 1979
Best Performances: League: 4th Div 2 1931-2, 1952-3 **FA Cup:** Semi-Final (as Third Div Club) **League/Milk Cup:**
Semi-Final, 1965, 1974
Most League Points: 68, Div 3 (S), 1929-30 **Most League Goals:** 107, Div 3 (S), 1925-6, 1951-2
Record League Victory: 8-1 v Millwall, Div 2, 16 Jan 1932. Plymouth also scored an 8-3 victory v Mansfield Town, Div 3,
7 Mar 1959
Record League Defeat: 0-9 v Stoke City, Div 2, 17 Dec 1980
Oldest Player in League Match: John Oakes 41 yrs
Youngest Player in League Match: Alec Govan, 16 yrs
Most Consecutive Undefeated League Matches: 22 1929
Longest Run of Undefeated Home League Matches: 47 1921-23
Longest Run Without Home League Win: 7 1947, 1949-50,
1977-78
Most Consecutive League Wins: 9 1930, 1986
Most Consecutive League Defeats: 9 1947

League Matches Without a Win: 13 1963
Away League Matches: 9 1929

Away League Win: 27 1975-76
Home League Wins: 17 1921-22
Away League Wins: 6 1929

Club Statistician for the Directory: F Lee

LYMOUTH ARGYLE

PLAYERS NAME / t Wt Birthdate	Honours	Birthplace / Transfers	Clubs	League	Milk Cup	FA Cup	Other Comps	League	Milk Cup	FA Cup	Other Comps
OALKEEPERS											
eoff Crudgington / 0 13.5 14.2.52	ES	Wolverhampton	Wolves (N/C)								
			Aston Villa	4							
			Bradford City (L)	1							
			Crewe Alexandra	250	15	14					
		£20,000	Swansea City	52	9	4					
		£40,000	Plymouth Argyle	298	16	26	7				
EFENDERS											
drian Burrows / 11 11.12 16.1.59		Sutton	Mansfield Town	77+1	6	1+2		6			
		£10,000	Plymouth Argyle	45	5	0+1	2				
		F	Northampton Town	173+2	10	14	1	13		2	
eigh Cooper / 8 11.0 7.5.61		Reading	Plymouth Argyle (A)	230+1	12	26	8	15		1	1
live Goodyear / 0 11.4 15.1.61	Div. 2 '82	Lincoln	Luton Town	85+5	5	4		4	1		
			Plymouth Argyle	74	5+1	5	3	4			
erry McElhinney* / 2 13.0 19.9.56	N.I. (5)	Londonderry	Distillery								
			Bolton Wanderers	107+2	5	8	1	2			
			Rochdale (L)	20							
		£30,000	Plymouth Argyle	64+1	2	4	2	1			
ordon Nisbet / 10 12.4 31.2.59	E. U23 (1)	Wallsend	W.B.A.	136	8	13					
		£30,000	Hull City	190+3	11	10		1			
		£30,000	Plymouth Argyle	246	16	21	8	9	2		
		15+1	6	5		1					
ohn Uzzell / 10 11.13 31.3.59		Plymouth	Plymouth Argyle	236+2	10+1	15+1	6	5		1	
IDFIELD											
ussell Coughlin / 8 11.8 15.2.60		Swansea	Manchester City (A)								
		£40,000	Blackburn Rovers	22+2	1+1						
		£20,000	Carlisle United	114+16	5	12		13	1		
		£20,000	Plymouth Argyle	81+1	6	5	3	13		1	
evin Hodges† / 8 10.0 12.6.60		Bridport	Plymouth Argyle (A)	315+8	23+1	26	6+1	62		1	2
ohn Matthews / 0 12.6 1.11.55		London	Arsenal (A)	38+7	6	4		2	2	1	
		£90,000	Sheffield United	98+5	5	5		14			
			Mansfield Town	70+2	3	5	1	6			
			Chesterfield	38	2	1	2+1	1			1
			Plymouth Argyle	29+2	2	2	2	1			
arren Rowbotham / 10 11.5 22.10.67		Cardiff	Plymouth Argyle	10+10		0+1	0+1	1			
ORWARDS											
ohn Clayton / 11 11.7 20.8.61		Elgin	Derby County (A)	11				1			
		Hong Kong	Chesterfield								
			Tranmere Rovers	72+8	5+1	6	3	40	2	2	1
			Plymouth Argyle	36	1	4	2	12		1	
teve Cooper / 1 11.10 22.6.64		Birmingham	Newport County	38		2	5	11			
			Plymouth Argule	34+4	2	4	0+1	8		1	
ary Nelson / 10 11.10 16.1.61		Braintree	Southend United	106+23	3+1	6+2		17	1		
		£10,000	Swindon Town	78+1	4	5	5	7			
		£15,000	Plymouth Argyle	41+1	2	4	2	13		1	
evin Summerfield / 0 10.7 7.1.59	FAYC '76, EY	Walsall	WBA (A)	5+4	2	1+1		4		1	
		F	Birmingham City	2+3	1			1			
		F	Walsall	42+12	5+2	1		17	2		
			Cardiff City	10	2			1			
		F	Plymouth Argyle	36+7	1	4	5	9	1	1	
mmy Tynan / 10 13.0 17.11.55		Liverpool	Liverpool (A)								
		£10,000	Sheffield Wednesday	89+2	12	4		31	5	1	
		£33,000	Lincoln City	9				9			
		£25,000	Newport County	168+15	11+1	7+1		66	5	4	
		£55,000	Plymouth Argyle	80	8	13	3+1	43	1	3	4
			Rotherham United	20	2	4	3	13		4	
			Plymouth Argyle (L)	9				9			

DDITIONAL CONTRACT PROFESSIONALS

PPRENTICES

ON-CONTRACT PLAYERS
hn Brimacombe, Tony Kenealy, Steve Nute

Record Attendance: 43,596 v Aston Villa, Div 2, 10 Oct 1936

Record Receipts: £118,000 v Derby County, FA Cup Round 6, 3 Mar 1984

Season Tickets: Stands (Centre): £95 (Adults), £62.50 (Juveniles/OAP), £165 (Married Couples). Stands (Wing): £80 (Adults), £135 (Married Couples). Ground (North): £40 (Adults), £17.50 (Juveniles), £27.50 (OAP). Ground (South): £48 (Adults), £25.00 (Juveniles), £35.00 (OAP) (16/OAP), £55 (Wing), £40 (under 16/OAP); Ground: £30, £20 (under 16/OAP)

Executive Box Season Tickets: None free

Cost of Stand Tickets (Match Days): Grandstand: Centre £6.00 (No reduction for Juveniles). Wing: £5.00 (Juveniles under 16 £4.00). OAPs Centre: £5.00. Wing: £4.00. Mayflower Stand: £5.00 (OAP £4.00). Ground Northside (Lyndhurst Road & Devonport End): £3.00 (Adults), £1.50 (Juveniles under 16), £2.00 (OAP). Ground Southside (Mayflower Enclosure): £3.50 (Adults), £2.00 (Juveniles under 16), £2.50 (OAP). Mayflower (Family Enclosure) 1 Adult standing with 2 children under 12 yrs (max) £5.00. Junior Pilgrims same price

Match and Ticket Information: Grandstand and Mayflower stand tickets are available 2 to 3 weeks before each first-team game

Free Car Parking: Car park (2,000 vehicles) adjoins ground

Nearest Railway Station: Plymouth (0752 21300)

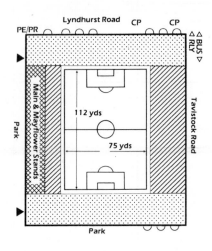

How to get to the ground

From All Directions: Use A38 Plymouth bypass as far as the Tavistock Road A386, then branch left and follow signs Plymouth A386. In 0.7m turn right then left A3041 into Outland Road for Plymouth Argyle FC

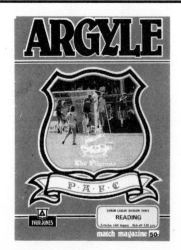

Price of 1986-7 Programme: 50p
Number of Pages: 32

Local Newspapers:

Local Radio Stations:

PORTSMOUTH

Chairman
B J Deacon CBE

Directors
J R Parkhouse
G G Gauntlett
D K Deacon
S W Sloan
Mrs J Deacon

Company Secretary
W B J Davis (0705 731204)

Commercial Manager
L Allen (0705 827111)

Manager
Alan Ball

Back Row L to R: Kevin Russell, Nicky Morgan, Mick Tait, Lee Sandford, Darren Angell, Noel Blake, Billy Gilbert, Malcolm Waldron, Scott McGarvey (Now with Carlisle United), Mick Quinn. **Middle Row:** Graham Paddon (Coach), Peter Osgood (Youth Team Coach), Kevin O'Callaghan, Marcus Winter, Martin Roderick, Alan Knight, Tony Oliver, Andrew Gosney, Kevin Dillon, Paul Wood, Kevin Ball, Eammon Collins, Mr J Dickens (Physio), Mr G Neave (Trainer). **Front Row:** Vince Hilaire, Mick Kennedy, Kenny Swain, Mr J R Parkhouse (Vice-Chairman), Mr D K Deacon (Director), Mrs J Deacon (Director), Mr B J Deacon CBE (Chairman), Mr G G Gauntlett (Director), Mr S W Sloan (Director), Mr W J B Davis (Company Secretary), Mr A Ball (Team Manager), Paul Hardyman, Robbie Taylor.

P ompey suffered the mortiying fate of being narrowly pipped to promotion for the second season in succession. Goal difference had robbed them of their 1st Division dream a year earlier. This time, due to some sensational late failures, they missed by three points.

Manager Alan Ball signed the veteran former England striker Mick Channon to lend his experience as the team attempted to make sure this time. A fine start saw Pompey go to the top of the 2nd Division table.

After poor home performances had cost so dearly a year earlier, it was heartening to see Portsmouth win their first seven home League matches without conceding a goal. The 100 per cent record went when Sheffield United won 3-0 at Fratton Park and that was the signal for another run of disappointing home results.

A home defeat by Brighton on Boxing Day enabled Norwich City to jump over Pompey to take over the leadership of the division. Mr Ball demanded a very special effort to halt the slide and the players responded well. Norwich took full advantage to establish themselves in top place but, in early February, Portsmouth looked well on course for promotion.

They held second place with a lead of nine points over third-placed Charlton. In spite of another run of adverse results, Pompey scored an important 2-1 victory over Charlton at Selhurst Park in mid-March and still held second place.

Because of deteriorating results, Mr Ball went into the transfer market to sign striker Mike Quinn from Oldham for £150,000 and he made his debut in that clash with Charlton. He scored his first goal in the next match, securing a 2-1 home win over Millwall, and by the end of March there seemed no reason why Pompey should not go on to clinch promotion.

A run of three consecutive defeats at the start of April altered the complexion of things, though. Though Portsmouth were clinging to second place still, Wimbledon, and particularly Charlton, below them had games in hand.

A 3-1 home win over Grimsby restored confidence to a point but, by now, the club's fate was in the hands of others. Wimbledon and Charlton were both producing excellent results, and had those precious games in hand.

A 0-2 defeat at Stoke worsened the situation but the real mortal blow was suffered at Sheffield United where they drew 0-0. With one game remaining, Portsmouth had slipped to third place with Wimbledon only two points behind and with four matches to play.

Pompey finished with a 4-0 home win over Bradford City. But, by then, it was too late. Wimbledon and Charlton both moved above them and that 1st Division dream was snatched from them once again on the final day of the season.

One of the highlights of the season was a 1-0 victory over Tottenham in a second replay of a 4th Round Milk Cup tie. Sadly, they went out at the next stage away to Oxford, the eventual winners.   T P

PORTSMOUTH

DIVISION TWO: 4th   **FA CUP:** 3rd ROUND   **MILK CUP:** QUARTER-FINAL

MATCH	DATE		COMPE-TITION	VENUE	OPPONENTS	RESULT		HALF TIME	L'GUE POS'N	GOALSCORERS/GOAL TIMES	ATTEN-DANCE
1	A	17	CL	A	Hull City	D	2-2	1-1		Morgan 25, Hilaire 60	(8,221)
2		20	CL	H	Sunderland	W	3-0	0-0		Hilaire 59, Dillon 67, Morgan 79	14,681
3		24	CL	H	Carlisle United	W	4-0	3-0	1	Hilaire 4, Morgan 28, 41, Hardyman 53	12,595
4		26	CL	A	Huddersfield Town	W	2-1	1-0	1	Jones (og) 16, Morgan 84	(9,248)
5		31	CL	H	Norwich City	W	2-0	1-0	1	Morgan 25, 83	15,504
6	S	3	CL	A	Shrewsbury Town	D	1-1	1-1	1	O'Callaghan 21	(3,719)
7		7	CL	A	Fulham	W	1-0	0-0	1	O'Callaghan 62	(9,331)
8		14	CL	H	Stoke City	W	3-0	0-0	1	Morgan 53, Dillon (pen) 64, Wood 77	13,720
9		17	FMC	H	Charlton Athletic	W	4-1	0-0		Wood 61, 74, Blake 66, Morgan 85	3,074
10		21	CL	H	Oldham Athletic	L	0-2	0-0	1		(5,815)
11		24	MC2/1	A	Gillingham	W	3-1	2-0		O'Callaghan 24, Tait 28, Wood 52	(4,617)
12		28	CL	H	Blackburn Rovers	W	3-0	1-0	1	Channon 7, Hilaire 75, O'Callaghan 85	16,870
13	O	2	FMC	A	Chelsea	L	0-3	0-2			(6,833)
14		5	CL	A	Barnsley	W	1-0	1-0	1	Blake 14	(7,064)
15		8	MC2/2	H	Gillingham	W	2-1	0-0		Sandford 56, Morgan 77	7,629
16		12	CL	H	Charlton Athletic	W	1-0	1-0	1	Dillon (pen) 44	15,549
17		19	CL	H	Crystal Palace	W	1-0	1-0	1	Morgan 37	16,539
18		26	CL	A	Millwall	W	4-0	2-0	1	O'Callaghan 10, 22, Morgan 49, 87	(6,810)
19		29	MC3	H	Stoke City	W	2-0	0-0		Dillon (pen) 46, (pen) 64	13,319
20	N	2	CL	A	Leeds United	L	1-2	1-0	1	Morgan 6	(15,672)
21		16	CL	A	Grimsby Town	L	0-1	0-0	1		(6,380)
22		20	MC4	A	Tottenham Hotspur	D	0-0	0-0			(28,619)
23		23	CL	H	Sheffield United	L	0-3	0-2	1		17,558
24		27	MC4R	H	Tottenham Hotspur	D	0-0†	0-0			28,100
25	D	3	CL	A	Bradford City	L	1-2	1-1	1	Kennedy 39	(4,701)
26		7	CL	A	Sunderland	W	3-1	2-0	1	Christensen 26, O'Callaghan 44, Wood 66	(17,229)
27		10	MC4/2R	H	Tottenham Hotspur	W	1-0	1-0		Blake 44	26,306
28		14	CL	H	Hull City	D	1-1	0-0	2	Christensen 55	13,596
29		22	CL	A	Carlisle United	W	1-0	0-0	2	Channon 75	(4,225)
30		26	CL	H	Brighton & H.A.	L	1-2	1-1	2	O'Callaghan 33	15,265
31		28	CL	A	Shrewsbury Town	W	4-0	1-0	2	Kennedy 33, Wood 84, 88, Channon 86	12,302
32	J	1	CL	A	Wimbledon	W	3-1	2-0	2	Channon 29, 49, Hilaire 34	(9,025)
33		4	FAC3	H	Aston Villa	D	2-2	0-1		Blake 56, Dillon (pen) 70	17,732
34		11	CL	A	Fulham	D	1-1	1-1	2	Tait 86	13,666
35		13	FAC3R	A	Aston Villa	L	2-3†	0-1		Stanley 83, (pen) 106	(14,958)
36		18	CL	A	Norwich City	L	0-2	0-0	2		(20,129)
37		22	MC.QF	A	Oxford United	L	1-3	0-2		Stanley 89	(10,334)
38		25	CL	H	Middlesbrough	W	1-0	0-0	2	Morgan 75	10,611
39	F	1	CL	H	Huddersfield	W	4-1	1-0	2	Tait 33, Dillon (pen) 63, Morgan 77, O'Callaghan 81	10,937
40		22	CL	H	Oldham Athletic	L	1-2	0-1	2	Hilaire 66	10,891
41	M	1	CL	A	Blackburn Rovers	L	0-1	0-0	2		(4,980)
42		8	CL	H	Barnsley	D	1-1	1-1	2	O'Callaghan 35	10,426
43		15	CL	A	Charlton Athetic	W	2-1	2-1	2	Channon 8, O'Callaghan 26	(10,132)
44		25	CL	H	Millwall	W	2-1	2-1	2	O'Callaghan 37, Quinn 45	9,570
45		29	CL	H	Wimbledon	D	1-1	0-0	2	Blake 53	18,859
46		31	CL	A	Brighton & H.A.	W	3-2	3-0	2	Quinn 13, (pen) 45, Hilaire 42	(16,640)
47	A	5	CL	H	Leeds United	L	2-3	1-0	2	Blake 11, 85	14,430
48		8	CL	A	Crystal Palace	L	1-2	0-2	2	Gray (og) 68	(11,731)
49		12	CL	A	Middlesbrough	L	0-1	0-0	2		(7,160)
50		19	CL	H	Grimsby Town	W	3-1	0-0	2	Quinn 59, Hilaire 77, McGarvie 83	12,967
51		22	CL	A	Stoke City	L	0-2	0-2	2		(8,529)
52		26	CL	A	Sheffield United	D	0-0	0-0	3		(12,234)
53	M	3	CL	H	Bradford City	W	4-0	1-0	4	Quinn 19, 70, Dillon (pen) 78, Wood 84	9,568

Best Home League Attendance: 17,558 v Sheffield United 23/11   **Smallest:** 9,568 v Bradford City 3/5   **Av Home Att:** 13,624

Goal Scorers: **Compared with 84-85:** −1,568

League (69):	Morgan 14, O'Callaghan 11, Hilaire 8, Channon 6, Quinn 6 (1 pen), Dillon 5 (4 pen), Wood 5, Blake 4, Christensen 2, Kennedy 2, Tait 2, Hardyman 1, McGarvie 1, Opponents 2
Milk Cup (9):	Dillon 2 (2 pens), Blake 1, Morgan 1, O'Callaghan 1, Sandford 1, Stanley 1, Tait 1, Wood 1
FA Cup (4):	Stanley 2 (1 pen), Blake 1, Dillon 1 (pen)
FM Cup (4):	Wood 2, Blake 1, Morgan 1

† A.E.T.

Knight	Tait	Swain	Blake	Doyle	Gilbert	Kennedy	Hilaire	O'Callaghan	Channon	Morgan	Hardyman	Dillon	Wood	Ball	Money	Sandford	Russell	Stanley	Lambert	McGarvie	Christensen (NC)	Sugrue	Gosney	Quinn	Referee	
1	2	3	4	5	6	7	8	9	10	11															T Simpson	1
1		2	5		6	8	11	7	10*	9	3	4	12												C Downey	2
1		2	5		6	8	11	7	10	9	3	4													R Gifford	3
1		2	5		6	8	11	7	10*	9	3	4	12												R Guy	4
1		2	5			8	11	7	10*	9	3	4	12	6											D Reeves	5
1			5			8	11	7	9*	10	3	4	12	6	2										D Scott	6
1	12	2	5			8	11	7	10*	9	3	4		6											I Borrett	7
1	2	3	5		6	8	11	7	10*	9		4	12												T Ward	8
1	2	3*	5			8*	11			9		4	10	6		12	7	12							J Deakin	9
1	2	3	5		6		11	7	10*	9		4					8	12							J Lovatt	10
1	8	2	5		6		11	7		9	3	4	10												D Vickers	11
1		2	5		6	8	11	7	10*	9	3	4	12												K Cooper	12
1	12	2	5			8	11*	7		9	3	4	10	6											G Napthine	13
1	12	2	5		6	8	11	7	10	9	3*	4													M Heath	14
1	2		5		6	8	11	7		9		4	10†			3									E Scales	15
1	2	3	5		6	8†	11	7	10	9		4													B Stevens	16
1	2	3	5		6	8	11	7	10*	9		4	12												R Groves	17
1	8	3*	5		6		11	7		9		4						2	12						P Vanes	18
1	8		5		6		11	7	10*	9		4				3		2		12					A Buksh	19
1	2	3	5		6	8	11	7	10*	9		4						12							T Jones	20
1		2	5		6	8	11	7	10	9		4				3									P Tyldesley	21
1	3		5		6	8	11	7*	10	9		4	12					2							D Axcel	22
1	3		5		6	8	11		10*	9		4	7					2		12					M James	23
1	12	2	5		6	8	11	7	10*	9	3	4													A Gunn	24
1	12	2	5		6	8	11*	7		9	3	4										10			J Worrall	25
1	4	2	5		6	8	11	7					9			3						10			K Hackett	26
1	4	2	5		6	8	11	7			12		9*			3						10			B Stevens	27
1	4	2	5		6	8	11	7	9							3						10	12		K Miller	28
1	4	2	5		6	8	11	7	10	9						3									K Redfern	29
1	2	3	5		6	8	11	7	10*	9		4											12		L Shapter	30
1	2	3	5		6	8	11	7		9		4	10												J Moules	31
1	2	3	5		6	8	11	7		9		4	10												M Reed	32
1	2	3	5		6†	8	11	7*		9		4	10					12							C Downey	33
1	8	3	5		6		11			9	12		10	4				2				7*			R Hamer	34
1	8	2	5		6		11		9*	12			10			3		4	7						A Ward	35
	6	2	5			8	11	7		9		4	10			3							1		N Butler	36
	6	2	5			8	11	7	9			4	10			3*		12					1		N Ashley	37
	2	3	5		6	8	11	7		9		4	10										1		R Groves	38
	2	3	5		6	8	11	7		9		4	10										1		D Axcell	39
	6	2	5			8	11	7		9	3	4	10										1		K Cooper	40
1	6		5			8	11	7	10*	9	3	4	12			2									K Barratt	41
1		2	5		6	8	11	7	10*	9	3	4	12												C Downey	42
1	4	2	5		6	8	11	7	10*		3		12											9	M Bodenham	43
1	4	2	5		6	8	11	7	10		3		12											9	G Napthine	44
1	4*	2	5		6	8	11	7	10		3	12												9	R Groves	45
1		2	5		6	8	11	7*		10	3		12	4										9	E Scales/P Alcock	46
1		2	5		6	8	11	7	10*	12	3			4										9	J Ball	47
1		2	5		6	8	11	7*	10		12	4				3								9	V Callow	48
1		3	5		6	8	11	7		10*		12		2†					4					9	K Hackett	49
1		2	5		6	8	11	7	10*		3	4								12				9	J Moules	50
1		2	5		6	8	11	7	10*		3	4								12				9	J Worrall	51
1		2	5		6	8	11*	7	10		3	4	12											9	T Jones	52
1		2	5		6	8			10*		3	4	7				12			11				9	B Stevens	53
38	23	39	42	1	36	39	41	39	34	28	21	30	10	9	1	6		4		2	3	1	4	11	League Appearances	
3											2	1	15					1	2	1	3	2			Substitute Appearances	
6	5-1	5	7		6	5	7	7	4	5	2	6-1	4-1			4	2-1	0-1	1	1					Milk Cup Appearances	
2	1-1	2	2		2	1	2	1	0-1		1	2				1	1-1	1							FA Cup Appearances	
2	1-1	2	2			2	2	1			2	1	2	2		2				0-1	1	0-1			FM Cup Appearances	

Players on Loan:

Departures: Money (Scunthorpe Utd), Doyle (Hull C), McGarvie (Carlisle Utd), Channon (Retired)

'POMPEY'

Formed: 1898
Turned Professional: 1898   **Ltd Co:** 1898

Previous Managers: 1898-1901 Frank Brettell   1901-4 Robert Blyth   1904-8 Richard Bonney
1909-20 Robert Brown   1920-7 John McCartney   1927-47 John W Tinn   1947-52 J R (Bob) Jackson
1952-8 Eddie Lever   1958-61 Freddie Cox   1961 William Thompson   1961-70 George Smith
1970-3 Ron Tindall   1973-4 John Mortimore   1974 Ron Tindall   1974-7 Ian St John
1977-9 Jimmy Dickinson   1979-82 Frank Burrows   1982-4 Bobby Campbell
Honours: Div 1 Champions 1948-9, 1949-50   Div 3 (S) Champions 1923-4
Div 3 Champions 1961-2, 1982-3   FA Cup Winners 1939
League Career: Original members of Div 3 1920   Transferred to Div 3 (S) 1921
Promoted to Div 2 1923-4   Promoted to Div 1 1926-7
Relegated to Div 2 1958-9   Relegated to Div 3 1960-1
Promoted to Div 2 1961-2   Relegated to Div 3 1975-6
Relegated to Div 4 1977-8   Promoted to Div 3 1979-80
Promoted to Div 2 1982-3
Colours: Royal blue shirts with white collars and cuffs, white shorts, red stockings
Change Colours: Red shirts with white collar and cuffs, red shorts and white stockings
Reserves League: Football Combination   **Youth League:** S E Counties

---

CLUB RECORDS

Most Appearances for Club: Jimmy Dickinson (1946-65): Football League 764 + FA Cup 64 **Total 828** (Also 26 League and 5 Cup appearances during the war)
Most Capped Player: Jimmy Dickinson, 48, England
Record Goalscorer in a Match: Alf Strange, 5 v Gillingham (H) 6-1 Div 3, 27.01.23
Peter Harris, 5 v Aston Villa (H) 5-2 Div 1, 03.09.58
Record League Goalscorer in a Season: Billy Haines, 40, Div 2, 1926-7   **In All Competitions:** Billy Haines, 43 (League 40, FA Cup 3) 1926-7
Record League Goalscorer in a Career: Peter Harris, 194   **In All Competitions:** Peter Harris, 209 (League 194 + FA Cup 15) 1946-60
Record Transfer Fee Received: £1,000,000 from Inter Milan for Mark Hateley, June 1984
Record Transfer Fee Paid: £180,000 to Coventry City for Mark Hateley, June 1983
Best Performances: League: Champions (2)   **FA Cup:** Winners   **League/Milk Cup:** 5th Round 1967
Most League Points: 91 in Div 3, 1982-3   **Most League Goals:** 91, Div 4, 1979-80
Record League Victory and Most Goals in a First Class Match: 9-1 v Notts County, Div 2, 9 Apr 1927
Most Goals Scored in a Cup Tie: 10-0 v Ryde, Qual Rnd FA Cup, 30 Sept 1899
Record League Defeat: 0-10 v Leicester City, Div 1, 20 Oct 1928
Oldest Player in League Match: Jimmy Dickinson MBE 40 yrs
Youngest Player in League Match:
Most Consecutive Undefeated League Matches: 15 1924
Longest Run of Undefeated Home League Matches: 32 1948-49
Longest Run Without Home League Win: 16 1958-59
Most Consecutive League Wins: 7 1980, 1983
Most Consecutive League Defeats: 9 1959, (2) 1963, 1975

League Matches Without a Win: 25 1958-59
Away League Matches: 14 1924
Away League Win: 24 1938-9
Home League Wins: 11 1931-2, 1938
Away League Wins: 6 1980

Club Statistician for the Directory: Doug Robinson

PORTSMOUTH

PLAYERS NAME / Ht Wt Birthdate	Honours	Birthplace / Transfers	Clubs	APP League	Milk Cup	FA Cup	Other Comps	GOALS League	Milk Cup	FA Cup	Other Comps
GOALKEEPERS											
Andrew Gosney 5.4 13.5 8.11.63	EY	Southampton	Portsmouth (A)	5	2						
Alan Knight 6.1 13.1 3.7.61	E.U21 (2) Y Div.3, '83	Balham	Portsmouth (A)	223	19	13	2				
DEFENDERS											
Kevin Ball 5.9 11.6 12.11.64		Hastings	Portsmouth (A)	10	1		2				
Joel Blake† 6.0 13.5 12.1.62		Jamaica / F / £55,000 / £150,000	Aston Villa / Shrewsbury (L) / Birmingham City / Portsmouth	4 / 6 / 76 / 84	/ / 12 / 11	/ / 8 / 4	/ / / 2	/ / 5 / 7	/ / / 1	/ / / 1	/ / / 1
Billy Gilbert 5.11 12.0 10.11.59	E.U21 (11) Y, S FAYC 78, Div.2 78	Lewisham / £100,000	Crystal Palace (A) / Portsmouth	235+2 / 71	19 / 10	15 / 3				
Paul Hardyman 5.8½ 11.4 15.9.65	E.U21 (2)	Manchester	Fareham Town / Portsmouth	2+1 / 38+1	/ 2	/ 2	/ 1	/ 1		
Kenny Swain 5.11 11.7 28.1.52	E.Cup '82 Div.1 '81	Birkenhead / £100,000	Wycombe W. / Chelsea / Aston Villa / Nottingham Forest / Portsmouth	/ 114+5 / 148 / 73 / 39	/ 6 / 12 / 6 / 5	/ 7 / 10 / 2 / 2.	/ / 8 / 10 / 2	/ 26 / 2 / 2 / 2	/ 1 / 1 / /	/ 2 / / /
Gary Stanley 5.9 12.6 4.3.54		Burton / £300,000 / £150,000 / F	Chelsea (A) / Everton / Swansea City / Portsmouth	105+4 / 52 / 60+12 / 43+4	5 / 7 / 4 / 6+1	4+1 / 2 / 1 / 1+1	/ / 2 / 0+1	15 / 1 / 3 / 1	/ / / 1	/ / / 2
Mick Tait 5.11 12.5 30.9.56	Div.2 '83	Wallsend / £65,000 / £150,000 / £100,000	Oxford U (A) / Carlisle United / Hull City / Portsmouth	61+3 / 101+5 / 29+4 / 203+9	2+1 / 7 / / 22+3	7 / 7 / 1 / 11	/ / / 1+1	23 / 20 / 3 / 30	1 / / / 1	/ 2 / 1 / 1	
Malcolm Waldron 6.0 12.4 6.9.56	E.'B' (1)	Emsworth / £60,000	Southampton (A) / Burnley / Portsmouth	177+1 / 16 / 23	19	15	4	10		
MIDFIELD											
Eamonn Collins 5.6½ 8.13 22.10.65	Ei. Y	Dublin / F	Blackpool (N/C) / Southampton (A) / Portsmouth	1+2	1+1					
Kevin Dillon 6.0 11.0 18.12.59	E.U21 (1), Y Div.3 '83	Sunderland / £200,000	Birmingham City (A) / Portsmouth	181+5 / 114+1	14 / 14+1	9 / 5	/ 2	15 / 28	3 / 5	/ 1	
Mick Kennedy 5.10 10.6 9.4.61	Ei. (2), U.21	Salford / £50,000 / £100,000 / £100,000	Halifax Town (A) / Huddersfield Town / Middlesbrough / Portsmouth	74+2 / 80+1 / 68 / 76	2 / 4+2 / 4 / 8	6 / 8 / 7 / 3	/ / / 2	4 / 9 / 5 / 2		
Lee Sandford 6.1 12.2 22.4.68	E.Y	Basingstoke	Portsmouth	6	4	1				
FORWARDS											
Vince Hilaire 5.6 10.3 10.10.59	E.U21 (9) B (1) Y Div.2 '79 FAYC '77, '78	Forest Gate / Player Exchange	Crystal Palace (A) / Luton Town / Portsmouth	239+16 / 5+1 / 67	20 / 2+1 / 7	16+1 / / 4	/ / 2	29 / / 8	4	3	
Paul Mariner 6.0 12.2 22.5.53	E (35), B (7) UEFA '81, FAC '78	Bolton / £22,500 / £200,000 + P/E / £150,000 / F	Chorley / Plymouth Argyle / Ipswich Town / Arsenal / Portsmouth	/ 134+1 / 260 / 52+8	/ 12 / 20 / 3+1	/ 11 / 28 / 5+1	/ / 27	/ 56 / 97 / 14	/ 2 / 8 / 1	/ 3 / 19 / 2	/ / 12
Nicky Morgan 5.10½ 13.5 30.10.59		East Ham / £50,000	West Ham United (A) / Portsmouth	14+7 / 75+16	1 / 8+1	/ 2+2	/ 2	2 / 33	/ 1	/ 1	/ 1
Kevin O'Callaghan 5.8½ 10.9 29.10.61	Ei (19) U.21 (1) Y, FAYC '79	London / £220,000 / £90,000	Millwall (A) / Ipswich Town / Portsmouth	15+5 / 71+43 / 54	2 / 8+3 / 7	3+1 / 5+6 / 1	/ 1+7 / 1	3 / 3 / 13	2 / 1 / 1	1	
Mike Quinn 5.9½ 10.0 2.5.62		Liverpool / F / F / £52,000	Derby County (A) / Wigan Athletic / Stockport County / Oldham Athletic / Portsmouth	56+13 / 62+1 / 78+2 / 11	5 / 5 / 4	3 / 2 / 2		19 / 39 / 34 / 6	/ 2 / 2	/ / 1	
Kevin Russell 5.8 10.10 6.12.66	EY	Brighton / F	Brighton (A) / Portsmouth							
Paul Wood 5.9 10.1 1.11.64		Middlesbrough	Portsmouth (A)	21+18	4+2	2	2	6	1		2

ADDITIONAL CONTRACT PROFESSIONALS
Darren Angell (D), Martin Roderick, Robert Taylor, Philip Carroll, Lee Darby, Shaun Gale, Lee Gosling, Mark Kelly, Robert Moore, David Motecine, David Newton, Lee Russell

APPRENTICES
Brett Angell, John Cox, Leam Daish, Jason Millar, Paul Mulvaney, Paul Musselwhite, Nick O'Brien, Tony Oliver, Julian Ake, Simon Stapleton

NON-CONTRACT PLAYERS
John Oliver, Martin Roderick, Bob Taylor

FRATTON PARK Portmouth PO4 8RA

Record Attendance: 51,385 v Derby County, FA Cup Round 6, 26 Feb 1949

Smallest Home Attendance for a First Class Match: 4,688 v Middlesbrough, Div 2, 16 Dec 1972

Record Receipts: £122,000 v Southampton, FA Cup Round 4, 28 Jan 1984

Size of Playing Area: 116yds × 73yds

Season Tickets: Stand: £122; Ground £65

Executive Box Season Tickets: None

Cost of Stand Tickets: £6.50 **Terraces:** £3.20

Match and Ticket Information: South Stand (central section) bookable ten days in advance

Car Parking: Side-street parking only

Nearest Railway Station: Fratton (by Fratton Park), Portsmouth (0705 825711)

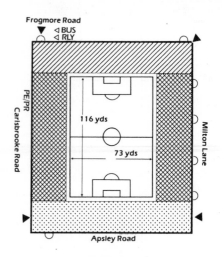

How to get to the ground

From North and West: Use Motorway M27 and M275 and at end at roundabout take 2nd exit and in 0.2m at T road turn right A2047 into London Road. In 1.3m over railway bridge and turn left into Goldsmith Avenue. In 0.6m turn left into Frogmore Road for Portsmouth FC

From East: Use A27 then follow signs Southsea A2030. In 3m at roundabout turn left A288. Then turn right into Priory Crescent then take next turning right into Carisbrooke Road for Portsmouth FC

Price of 1986-7 Programme: 50p
Number of Pages: 24
Subscriptions: Available from club

Local Newspaper: Portsmouth Evening News

Local Radio Stations: Radio Victory, Radio Solent

PORT VALE

Division 3

President
J Burgess

Chairman
J D Lloyd

Directors
D P McGrath (Vice-Chairman)
A McPherson
W T Bell

Secretary
R J Fairfax (0782 814134)

Assistant Secretary
Mrs S Everton

Manager
J Rudge

Youth Team Coach
G Barnett

Chief Scout
R Williams

Groundsman
R Fairbanks

Back Row L to R: Chris Banks, Russel Bromage, Phil Spronson, Eric Mountford, John Williams, John Bowden, Andy Jones, Robbie Earle. **Middle Row:** John Rudge (Manager), Martain Copeland, Alan Webb, Mark Grew, Ray Walker, Mike Pejic, Alan Oakes. **Front Row:** Paul Smith, Geoff Hunter, Wayne Ebanks, Richard O'Kelly, Paul Maguire.

Port Vale returned to Division Three after an absence of only two years thanks largely to the best defensive record in the division and an unbeaten run of 18 games, just one short of a club record. An unspectacular start of only one win in five games suddenly exploded as 22 goals flew into the opposing net in the next six homes games. Hartlepool, Wrexham and Southend, three teams chasing promotion all perished 4-0 in successive games and then the icing on the cake came with a 3-0 win over champions-elect Swindon Town, although the euphoria over the latter was tempered somewhat by an injury to central defender John Williams who was forced to miss ten weeks of the season.

The club's first win at Preston in over 50 years took them to the top of the league giving cause for optimism for the championship but a run of four games without a win, allied to four tough FA Cup games (v Mansfield and Walsall) kept everyone's feet on the ground.

The New Year got off to a bad start with a 4-1 defeat at promotion rivals Chester, Vale's biggest defeat of the season and this was followed by their only home defeat, 0-1 against struggling Preston on a snowbound pitch in which they also missed a penalty. This result sparked off a renewed effort for the task in hand and after recovering from a 2-0 deficit to earn a 3-3 draw at Rochdale the team remained undefeated until promotion had been clinched.

At one stage it looked as though too many draws would prove detrimental, even with a 0-0 scoreline at Swindon which halted their run of 14 successive home wins but important victories at Crewe and Stockport turned their fate into their own hands. Promotion was mathematically secured at Torquay when backed by 1000 travelling supporters a Robbie Earle goal was enough to clinch a 1-0 victory.

Robbie scored 17 goals altogether sharing the honours with Andy Jones who notched 18 in his first season of league football, whilst at the back Webb, Sproson, John Williams and Bromage all had excellent seasons backed by the evergreen Jim Arnold in goal who was a deserving winner of the club's player of the year award.

In the cup competitions Third Division Wigan were beaten in the Milk Cup and West Brom were given a close shave whilst in the FA Cup their run ended in Round 2 against deadly rivals Walsall. Wigan gained their revenge in the Freight Rover Trophy by winning the Northern Area Semi-Final 2-1 at Vale Park.

Hopefully with a couple of new signings in the right places the Vale should consolidate their new found status in Division Three.   Phil Sherwin

PORT VALE

DIVISION FOUR: 4th **FA CUP:** 2nd ROUND **MILK CUP:** 2nd ROUND **FRT:** AREA-FINAL

MATCH	DATE		COMPE-TITION	VENUE	OPPONENTS	RESULT		HALF TIME	L'GUE POS'N	GOALSCORERS/GOAL TIMES	ATTEN-DANCE
1	A	17	CL	A	Exeter City	L	0-1	0-1			(2,868)
2		20	MC1/1	A	Wigan Athletic	L	1-2	0-0		Sproson 65	(2,260)
3		24	CL	H	Mansfield Town	D	0-0	0-0	18		2,930
4		26	CL	A	Burnley	W	2-1	1-1	12	Sproson 25, Griffiths 50	(3,940)
5		31	CL	A	Rochdale	D	1-1	0-1	12	Jones 65	3,043
6	S	2	MC1/2	H	Wigan Athletic	W	2-0	1-0		Jones 8, Earle 48	2,772
7		7	CL	A	Orient	L	0-1	0-1	17		(2,455)
8		14	CL	H	Cambridge United	W	4-1	1-1	14	Earle 4, Brown 46, Maguire (pen) 64, 70	2,674
9		17	CL	A	Aldershot	D	0-0	0-0	14		(1,027)
10		21	CL	H	Halifax Town	W	3-2	2-1	11	Hunter 7, 63, Maguire 42	2,754
11		24	MC2/1	A	W.B.A.	L	0-1	0-1			(6,268)
12		27	CL	A	Colchester United	L	0-1	0-1	13		(3,110)
13		30	CL	H	Hartlepool United	W	4-0	2-0	10	Williams O. 10, Williams J. 23, Jones 49, Maguire 85	3,015
14	O	5	CL	H	Wrexham	W	4-0	1-0	6	Maguire 20 secs, pen 89, Johnson 52, Hooper (og) 75	3,351
15		7	MC2/2	H	W.B.A.	D	2-2	0-2		Jones 68, Maguire 87	7,895
16		12	CL	A	Tranmere Rovers	W	2-1	1-0	5	Earle 25, Maguire 64	(2,328)
17		19	CL	H	Southend United	W	4-0	3-0	4	Jones 10, 46, Webb 34, Earle 36	4,736
18		22	CL	A	Scunthorpe United	D	0-0	0-0	4		(1,888)
19		26	CL	H	Swindon Town	W	3-0	1-0	3	Williams O. 33, Earle 46, Brown 82	5,073
20	N	2	CL	A	Preston North End	W	1-0	0-0	1	Maguire (pen) 78	(4,531)
21		6	CL	A	Hereford United	D	1-1	0-0	3	Sproson 88	(3,305)
22		9	CL	H	Stockport County	D	1-1	1-1	3	Bowden 9	5,248
23		16	FAC1	A	Mansfield Town	D	1-1	0-0		Earle 69	(5,207)
24		18	FAC1R	H	Mansfield Town	W	1-0	0-0		Maguire (pen) 89	6,749
25		23	CL	A	Peterborough United	L	0-1	0-1	7		(2,852)
26	D	8	FAC2	H	Walsall	D	0-0	0-0			11,736
27		10	FAC2R	A	Walsall	L	1-2	0-0		Brown 74	(5,671)
28		14	CL	A	Northampton Town	D	2-2	1-0	8	Sproson 45, Earle 78	(3,030)
29		17	CL	H	Torquay United	W	1-0	1-0		Hunter 7	3,421
30		22	CL	H	Mansfield Town	L	1-2	0-1	6	Williams O 90	(3,722)
31		26	CL	H	Crewe Alexandra	W	3-0	1-0	4	Maguire 27, Brown 66, Earle 89	5,976
32	J	1	CL	A	Chester City	L	1-4	1-2	5	Earle 35	(5,010)
33		4	CL	H	Preston North End	L	0-1	0-1	5		3,592
34		11	CL	A	Rochdale	D	3-3	0-2	5	Jones 50, 83, Brown 75	(2,445)
35		17	CL	H	Exeter City	D	0-0	0-0	6		3,382
36		21	FRT	A	Wrexham	D	1-1	0-1		Jones 49	(992)
37		25	CL	A	Cambridge United	W	3-1	1-0	5	Williams J. 32, Hunter 75, Earle 79	(2,437)
38	F	1	CL	H	Orient	W	2-0	1-0	5	Earle 8, 66	3,074
39		3	CL	H	Scunthorpe United	W	3-1	2-0	5	Williams J 33, Jones pen 37, Bromage 83	2,977
40		10	FRT	H	Blackpool	W	3-1	0-1		Maguire 57, Hunter 72, Jones 80	1,569
41		24	CL	H	Burnley	D	1-1	1-0	5	Banks 15	3,030
42	M	1	CL	A	Colchester United	D	1-1	0-0	6	Jones 77	2,726
43		5	CL	A	Hartlepool United	D	1-1	1-1	6	Bowden 42	(2,562)
44		8	CL	A	Wrexham	W	3-1	1-1	5	Shankland 41, Earle 84, Jones 88	(2,614)
45		10	FRT QF N	A	Scunthorpe United	D	1-1†	0-0		Jones 85	(1,415)
46		15	CL	H	Tranmere Rovers	D	0-0	0-0	5		3,427
47		18	CL	A	Aldershot	W	3-1	2-0		Bowden 4, Hunter 19, Earle 86	2,461
48		23	CL	A	Swindon Town	D	0-0	0-0	4		(10,122)
49		26	FRT SF N	H	Wigan Athletic	L	1-2	1-2		Jones (pen) 11	4,832
50		29	CL	H	Chester City	D	1-1	1-0	4	Sproson 17	4,490
51		31	CL	A	Crewe Alexandra	W	1-0	1-0	4	Earle 36	(4,986)
52	A	5	CL	H	Hereford United	W	1-0	1-0	4	Jones (pen) 22	3,344
53		11	CL	A	Stockport County	W	2-1	2-1	3	Maguire 27, Brown 42	(4,690)
54		19	CL	A	Peterborough United	W	2-0	1-0	3	Jones (pen) 43, 66	3,765
55		26	CL	A	Torquay United	W	1-0	0-0	4	Earle 1	(1,794)
56		29	CL	H	Halifax Town	L	0-2	0-0	4		(1,389)
57	M	3	CL	H	Northampton Town	D	0-0	0-0	4		3,873
58		5	CL	A	Southend United	L	1-2	0-1	4	Earle 89	(1,687)

Best Home League Attendance: 5,976 v Crewe Alex. 26/12 **Smallest:** 2,461 v Aldershot 18/3 **Av Home Att:** 3,581

Goal Scorers: Compared with 84-85: +339

League (67):	Earle 15, Jones 12 (3 pen), Maguire 10 (4 pen), Brown 5, Hunter 5, Sproson 4, Bowden 3, Williams J 3, Williams O 3, Banks 1, Bromage 1, Griffiths 1, Johnson 1, Shankland 1, Webb 1, Opponents 1
Milk Cup (5):	Jones 2, Earle 1, Maguire 1, Sproson 1
FA Cup (3):	Brown 1, Earle 1, Maguire 1 (pen)
FRT (6):	Jones 4 (1 pen), Hunter 1, Maguire 1

†A.E.T. Port Vale won on penalties

Arnold	Webb	Bromage	Hunter	Sproson	Williams J	Griffiths	Earle	Brown	Johnson	Maguire	Jones	Williams O	Bowden	Banks	Ewood	Ebanks	Pearce	Cammack (L)	Perry (NC)	Shankland	Biggins (L)	Referee	
1	2	3	4	5	6	7*	8	9	10	11	12											R Hamer	1
1	2	3	4	5	6	7	8	9*	10	11	12											F Roberts	2
1	2	3	4	5	6		8	9	10	11	7											N Wilson	3
1	2	3	4	5	6	12	8		10	11*	9	7										C Trussel	4
1	2	3	4	5	6		8		10	11	9	7										K Cooper	5
1	2	3	4	5	6		8		10	11	9	7										M Scott	6
1	2	3	4	5	6	12	8		10	11	9*	7										M James	7
1	2	3	4	5	6		8	9		11	12	7	10*									I Hendrick	8
1	2	3	4	5	6		8	9	10	11		7										K Miller	9
1		3	4		6		8	9	10	11	5	7		2								M Reed	10
1	2	3	4		6		8	9	10	11	5	7										J Ashworth	11
1	2	3	4	5	6		8	9*		11	10	7	12									A Gunn	12
1	2	3	4*	5	6		8		10	11	9	7	12									R Nixon	13
1	2	3		5	6		8		10	11	9	7	4*	12								T Simpson	14
1	2	3	12	5	6		8		10*	11	9	7	4									R Bridges	15
1	2	3	4	5	6		8			11	9	7	10									D Allison	16
1	2	3	4*	5	6		8	12		11	9	7	10									K Breen	17
1	2	3	4	5	6		8			11	9	7	10									K Redfern	18
1	2	3	4	5	6*		8	12		11	9	7	10									D Scott	19
1	2	3	4	5			8	6		11	9	7	10									G Aplin	20
1	2	3	4	5			8	6		11	9*	7	10			12						J Ball	21
	2	3	4	5			8	6		11	9*	7	10			12	1					A Seville	22
1	2	3	4	5			8	6		11	9	7	10									T Fitzharris	23
1	2	3	4	5			8	6		11	9	7	10									T Fitzharris	24
1	2	3	4	5			8	6		11	9*	7	10			12						D Reeves	25
1	6	3	4	5			8	9		11		7	10			2						G Napthine	26
1	6	3	4	5			8	9		11	12	7*	10			2						G Napthine	27
1	6	3	4	5	12		8	9*		11		7	10			2						B Stevens/M Millidge	28
		3	4	5			8	9		11		7	10	6		2						L Dilkes	29
1	6	3	4*	5			8			11	12	7	10			2		9				D Phillips	30
	6	3	4	5			8	9		11		7	10			2	1					J Bray	31
	6	3	4	5			8	9		11		7	10			2*	1	12				B Hill	32
	6	3	4	5			8	9		11		7*	10			2	1	12				H Taylor	33
		3	4	5	6		8	9		11		7	10			2	1					K Redfearn	34
1		3	4	5	6		8	9		11*		7	12	10		2						R Guy	35
1	2	3	4*	5	6	7	8			11	9		10					12				P Tyldesley	36
1	2	3	4	5	6		8			11	9	7	10									D Hedges	37
1	2*	3	4	5	6		8	12		11	9	7	10									M Peck	38
1		3	4	5	6		8			11	9	7	10	2								N Midgley	39
1	2	3	4	5	6		8			11	9	7		10								J Key	40
1	2	3	4	5	6		8			11	9	7		10								G Ashby	41
1	2	3	4	5	6	7*	8	12		11	9		10									P Willis	42
1	2	3	4	5*	6		8	12		11	9		10	7								N Glover	43
1	2	3	4		6		8			11	9		10	5						7		T Mills	44
1			4*		6	12	8		7	11	9		10	5		2				3		A Seville	45
1	2	3	4	5	6		8			11	9	12	10							7*		J Lloyd	46
1	2	3	4	5	6		8	9		11		7	10									A Robinson	47
1	2	3	4	5	6		8			11	9	7	10									J Ashworth	48
	2	3*	4	5*	6	12	8		7	11	9		10	12			1					T Jones	49
1	2		4	5	6		8	9*		11		7	10	3							12	B Hill	50
1	2		4	5	6		8	9†		11		7	10	3								K Walmsley	51
1	2		4	5	6		8	9*		11		7	10	3							12	P Tyldesley	52
1			4	5	6		8	9		11		7	10	3		2						M Scott	53
1	2		4	5	6		8			11	9	7	10	3								G Tyson	54
1	2		4	5	6		8			11	9	7	10	3								P Vanes	55
1	2	12	4	5	6		8			11	9		10	3						7*		T Fitzharris	56
1	2*	3	4	5	6		8			11	9	7	10	12								G Aplin	57
1		3	4	5	6		8			11	9	7*	10	2							12	N Butler	58
41	39	39	45	44	36	2	46	22	10	45	38	31	35	15		9	5	1		2	1	League Appearances	
	1				3			5		3	1	1	4	1		2		2			3	Substitute Appearances	
4	4	4	3·1	3	4	1	4	2	4	4	3·1	3	1									Milk Cup Appearances	
4	4	4	4	4		4	4	4		4		2·1	4	4		2						FA Cup Appearances	
3	3	3	4	3	4	1·2	4		2	4	4	1	3	2·1		1	1		0·1	1		FR Trophy Appearances	

Players on Loan: Cammack (Scunthorpe United), Biggins (Derby County)
Departures: Griffiths (F), Johnson (F), Brown (F)

PORT VALE F.C.

'THE VALIANTS'

Formed: 1876
Turned Professional: 1885   **Ltd Co:** 1911

1876

Previous Names: Burslem Port Vale (until 1913)
Previous Managers: Since 1946: Billy Smith   Gordon Hodgson   Ivor Powell   Freddie Steele   Norman Low   Freddie Steele   Jackie Mudie   Sir Stanley Matthews   Gordon Lee   Roy Sproson   Colin Harper   Bob Smith   Dennis Butler   Alan Bloor   John McGrath
Honours: Div 3 (N) Champions, 1929-30, 1953-4   Div 4 Champions 1958-9
League Career: Original Member Div 2 1892   Not re-elected to Div 2 1896
Re-elected to Div 2 1898   Resigned from Div 2 1907   Returned to Div 2** 1919
Relegated to Div 3 (N) 1929   Promoted to Div 2 1930   Relegated to Div 3 (N) 1936
Transferred to Div 3 (S) 1938   Transferred to Div 3 (S) 1952   Promoted to Div 2 1954
Relegated to Div 3 (S) 1957   Original members of Div 4 1958   Promoted to Div 3 1959
Relegated to Div 4 1965   Promoted to Div 3 1970   Relegated to Div 4 1978
Promoted to Div 3 1983   Relegated to Div 4 1984
**Port Vale took over the fixtures of Leeds City — expelled from the League for irregularities — in October 1919
Colours: White shirts with black trim, white shorts, black stockings
Change Colours: Yellow shirts, green shorts, yellow stockings
Reserves League: Central Div 2   **'A' Team:** Midland Intermediate

---

CLUB RECORDS

Most Appearances for Club: Roy Sproson, 1950-72: Football League 761 + 5 subs + FA Cup 65 + League Cup 21
Total 831 + 5 subs
Most Capped Player: Sammy Morgan, 7 (18), Northern Ireland   **For England:** None
Record Goalscorer in a Match: Stewart Littlewood, 6 v Chesterfield, Div 2, 24.09.32
Record League Goalscorer in a Season: Wilf Kirkham, 38, Div 2, 1926-7   **In All Competitions:** Wilf Kirkham, 41 (League 38 + FA Cup 3)
Record League Goalscorer in a Career: Wilf Kirkham, 154, 1923-9 & 1931-3   **In All Competitions:** Wilf Kirkham, 165 (League 154 + FA Cup 11)
Record Transfer Fee Received: £135,000 from Stoke City for Mark Chamberlain, 1982
Record Transfer Fee Paid: £40,000 to Bury for Peter Farrell, Nov 1978   £40,000 to Wolverhampton Wanderers for Ken Todd, Aug 1978   £40,000 to Crewe Alexandra for Paul Bowles, Sept 1979
Best Performances: League: 5th Div 2 1930-1   **FA Cup:** Semi-Finalists 1953-4   **League/Milk Cup:** Never past 2nd Round
Most League Points: 88, Div 4, 1982-3   **Most League Goals:** 110, Div 4, 1958-9
Record League Victory and Most Goals Scored in a League Match: 9-1 v Chesterfield, Div 2, 24 Sept 1932
Most Goals Scored in a Cup Tie: 8-2 v Alfreton (A), FA Cup 6th Qualifying Round, 13 Dec 1924
Record League Defeat: 0-10 v Sheffield United (H), Div 2, 10 Dec 1892   0-10 v Notts County, Div 2, 26 Feb 1895
Oldest Player in League Match: Roy Sproson 41 yrs 228 days
Youngest Player in League Match: Ronnie Allen 16 yrs 306 days
Most Consecutive Undefeated League Matches: 20 1969   **League Matches Without a Win:** 15 1894-95, 1983

Longest Run of Undefeated Home League Matches: 42 1952-54   **Away League Matches:** 10 1969
Longest Run Without Home League Win: 12 1978   **Away League Win:** 29 1903-04
Most Consecutive League Wins: 8 1893   **Home League Wins:** 12 1952
Most Consecutive League Defeats: 9 1957   **Away League Wins:** 4 1930

Club Statistician for the Directory: Steve Askey

PORT VALE

PLAYERS NAME Ht Wt Birthdate	Honours	Birthplace Transfers	Clubs	League	Milk Cup	FA Cup	Other Comps	League	Milk Cup	FA Cup	Other Comps
GOALKEEPERS											
Mark Green 5.10 11.3 15.2.58	FAYC '76	Bilston	W.B.A.	33	8	5	0+1				
			Wigan Athletic (L)	4							
		£25,000	Leicester City	5							
			Oldham Athletic (L)	5							
		£60,000	Ipswich Town	6							
			Fulham (L)	4							
			W.B.A. (L)	1							
			Port Vale								
DEFENDERS											
Chris Banks 5.8 10.8 12.11.65		Stone	Port Vale	20+6			3+3	1			
Wayne Ebanks 5.10 11.5 2.10.64		Birmingham	W.B.A.								
			Stoke City (L)	10	2						
		F	Port Vale	20+7		2	1				
Phil Sproson 6.0 12.0 13.10.59		Trent Vale	Port Vale	314+1	20	18+1	8	25	3		
Ray Walker 5.10 11.9 28.9.63		North Shields	Aston Villa (A)	15+8	2+1	2					
			Port Vale	15				1			
Alan Webb 5.9½ 12.0 1.1.63		Wrockwardine	W.B.A. (A)	23+1		0+1					
			Lincoln City (L)	11							
		F	Port Vale	76	8	7	5	1			
John Williams 6.2 13.6 3.10.60		Liverpool	Tranmere Rovers	167+6	13	9	2	16			
			Port Vale	36	4	4	4				
MIDFIELD											
John Bowden 6.0 11.7 21.1.63		Stockport	Oldham Athletic	73+9	5	4		5		1	
			Port Vale	35+1	1	4	3	3			
Russell Bromage 5.11 11.5 9.11.59		Stoke	Port Vale (A)	222+7	17	14	1	10	1	1	
			Oldham Athletic (L)	78+1	4	4	3	2			
Geoff Hunter 5.9 10.5 27.10.59		Hull	Manchester United								
			Crewe Alexandra	86+1	4	2		8	1		
		£10,500	Port Vale	214+2	15+1	14	9	15	1	1	
Richard O'Kelly 5.10 11.0 8.1.57		West Bromwich	Alvechurch								
		£8,000	Walsall	189+15	15+1	9+2	7	55	4	2	1
			Port Vale								
FORWARDS											
Steve Cammack 5.10 11.9 20.3.54	EY	Sheffield	Sheffield United (A)	21+15	1+1			5			
			Chesterfield	95+18	7+1	4		21	3		
		£12,500	Scunthorpe United	84	2	4		27		1	
		£29,000 + P/E	Lincoln City	18	4+1	2+1		6		1	
		£3,000 + P/E	Scunthorpe United	155+2	6	14	4	82	1	6	2
			Port Vale								
Robbie Earle 5.9 10.0 27.1.65		Stoke	Stoke City (N/C)								
		F	Port Vale	104+8	9+1	7	7+1	31	2	2	2
Andy Jones 5.10 12.7 9.1.63			Rhyl								
		£3,000	Port Vale	36+2	3+1	2+1	4	12	2	4	
Osher Williams 5.9½ 11.7 21.4.58		Stockton	Middlesbrough (A)								
			Manchester United								
			Chesterfield								
			Southampton	4+2							
			Exeter City (L)	2+1							
		£10,000	Stockport County	191+1	17	6		26	2	3	
		F	Port Vale	49+2	3	7	3	6			
Paul Maguire 5.8 11.3 21.8.56		Glasgow	Kilbernie								
			Shrewsbury T.	143+8	8	18		35	1	12	
			Stoke City	93+14	8+1	4		24	1		
		U.S.A.	Port Vale	45	4	4	4	10	1	1	

ADDITIONAL CONTRACT PROFESSIONALS
Paul Smith, Eric Mountford (M), Andrew Shankland (M)

Player of the Year: Jim Arnold

APPRENTICES

NON-CONTRACT PLAYERS
Mike Barnes, Mike Bates, Steve Harper, Kelvin Johnson, Andy Porter, Wayne Simpson, Kevin Finney

VALE PARK
Burslem, Stoke-on-Trent

Capacity: 16,500

Record Attendance: 50,000 v Aston Villa, FA Cup Round 5, 20 Feb 1960

Smallest Home Attendance for a First Class Match: 1,924 v York City, 1 May 1982

Record Receipts: £45,873 v Manchester United, Milk Cup Round 2, 3 Oct 1983

Season Tickets: Stand: £72, (£45 OAP/agents/juveniles): Ground £50 (£35 OAP/agents/juveniles)

Vice-Presidents Box Season Tickets: £175

Cost of Stand Tickets: £3.50 (£1.80 Juveniles/OAP); **Terraces:** £2.20, (£1.20 Juveniles/OAPs)

Match and Ticket Information: No advance bookings

Car Parking: Parking (ample) behind the Railway Stand on Hamil Road and on Lorne Street sides of ground

Nearest Railway Station: Longport, Stoke-on-Trent (0782 411411)

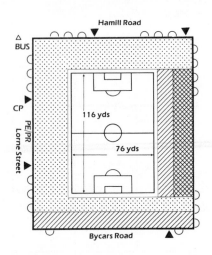

How to get to the ground

From North: Use Motorway M6 until junction 16 then join A500 S.P. Stoke. In 5.9m branch left and at roundabout take 1st exit A50. In 0.4m turn right B5051 into Newcastle Street and at end over crossroads into Moorland Road. Shortly turn left into Hamil Road for Port Vale FC

From East: Use A50 or A52 into Stoke-on-Trent then follow signs Burslem A50 into Waterloo Road. At Burslem crossroads turn right into Moorland Road. Shortly turn left into Hamil Road for Port Vale FC

From South and West: Use Motorway M6 until junction 15 then A5006 and A500. In 6.3m branch left and at roundabout take 3rd exit A50. In 0.4m turn right B5051 into Newcastle Street and at end over crossroads into Moorland Road. Shortly turn left into Hamil Road for Port Vale FC

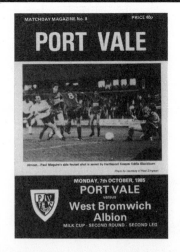

Price of 1986-7 Programme: 50p
Number of Pages: 20
Subscriptions: No fixed rate

Local Newspapers: Staffordshire Evening Sentinel

Local Radio Stations: Radio Stoke, Signal Radio

PRESTON NORTH END   Division 4

Chairman
Keith W Leeming

Directors
J T Garratt (Joint Vice-Chairman)
M J Woodhouse (Joint Vice-Chairman)
B J Campbell (Managing Director)
J Francis
E Griffiths BVsc, MRCVS
J E Wignall
J W Wilding
J T Worden

Company Secretary
Edward Griffiths BCsc MRCVS

Club Secretary
Derek J Allan (0772 795919)

Manager
John McGrath

Assistant Manager
Les Chapman

Commercial Manager
David Bradshaw
(0772 795465, 795156)

Youth Development Officer
Walter Joyce

I described the 1984-85 season as a disaster, last season was even worse, nothing seemed to go right. The club's first season in Division 4 was a disappointing dreary affair, culminating in the inevitable disgrace in having to seek re-election. The season started with the supporters fairly confident of a quick promotion back to Division 3, but their hopes were soon dashed by a home defeat in the first game, followed soon after by a 6-0 loss at Northampton. Plagued with injuries, especially to Jonathan Clark who missed most of the season, it showed that the team was again going to struggle, and it rarely moved out of the bottom four all season. The Milk Cup saw two good wins over Blackpool and two fighting displays against Norwich before losing to two late goals in the second leg.

Further poor results including a 3-6 home defeat by Chester and a dreadful 3-7 at Walsall in the FA Cup, led to manager Tommy Booth resigning on December 5th. Assistant manager Brian Kidd was appointed manager on January 24th after a spell as caretaker manager. He was very popular, worked hard, but only managed one win in the 17 games in charge. He also resigned rather suddenly before the home game against Southend on March 22nd. This was after demonstrations calling for the board and chairman to resign at the games at Chester and at home to Cambridge (when the new floodlights were switched on, the old lights were condemned in October and last used against Hartlepool). Injured captain Jonathan Clark took over as temporary manager for the rest of the season, winning his first five games in charge (the best run since 1963-64), but only two draws in the last five games left the team in the final position of 23rd. The team was well supported, both home and away, with the home gates I believe the second highest average in Division 4. A midweek afternoon game on November 5th against Scunthorpe saw a record low of 2,007, although only 751 saw a Freight Rover Trophy game v Bury on January 29th. New signings at the start of the season were—John Platt and Wayne Foster (both Bolton), John Thomas (Lincoln), Nigel Keen (Barrow). Later signings were Brian Chippendale (Burnley, released after a month), Vernon Allatt (Crewe), Mick Martin (Rotherham), Bobby McNeil (ex-Hull). Shaun Reid (Rochdale), Phil Harrington (Blackpool) and Robert Cooper (Leicester) came on loan. Scottish trialist Mark Rodgers started the game against Scunthorpe, but was replaced at half-time by local amateur Mel Tottoh. 17 year old goalkeeper Alan Kelly (son of more famous father Alan, ex PNE goalkeeper and manager) made his debut in March, and looks a fine prospect. Two more juniors (Danny Ibbotson and Andy Pilling) made their debuts in the final game (another junior was sub, Nigel Jemson).

Things will be different next season, when a plastic pitch is laid down. John Thomas was the Player of the Season, Alan Kelly won the Young Player of the Year Award, with Simon Gibson winning the local press PNE 'Starman' of the year prize.   Lawrence Bland

Back Row L to R: Osher Williams, Andy McAteer, Bob Atkins, Paul Welsh, Alex Jones, David Brown, Sam Allardyce, Vernon Allatt, Sean Allen, George Shepherd, Steven Saunders.
Front Row: Shayne Beeby, Bob McNeil, Barry Brazil, Jonathan Clark, Les Chapman, John Thomas, Peter Bulmer, Ronnie Hildersley.

PRESTON NORTH END

DIVISION FOUR: 23rd   **FA CUP:** 1st ROUND   **MILK CUP:** 2nd ROUND

MATCH	DATE		COMPE-TITION	VENUE	OPPONENTS	RESULT	HALF TIME	L'GUE POS'N	GOALSCORERS/GOAL TIMES	ATTEN-DANCE
1	A	17	CL	H	Peterborough United	L 2-4	1-2		Brazil 15, Thomas 53	3,177
2		20	MC1/1	H	Blackpool	W 2-1	1-0		Keen 17, Foster 46	4,704
3		26	CL	H	Tranmere Rovers	D 2-2	2-0	18	Brazil 3, Thomas 31	(4,206)
4		30	CL	A	Halifax Town	L 1-2	0-0	24	Greenwood 89	(2,011)
5	S	3	MC1/2	A	Blackpool	W 3-1	0-1		Rudge 46, Twentyman 52, Brazil 81	(5,043)
6		7	CL	H	Torquay United	W 4-0	2-0	18	Brazil 12, 32, Greenwood 64, 73	3,403
7		10	CL	A	Northampton Town	L 0-6	0-3	20		(2,171)
8		13	CL	H	Stockport County	L 1-2	0-1	21	Thomas 49	3,436
9		17	CL	H	Burnley	W 1-0	1-0	19	Thomas 3	5,585
10		28	CL	H	Hereford United	W 2-0	1-0	19	Greenwood 37, Brazil 83	3,387
11		30	MC2/1	H	Norwich City	D 1-1	1-1		Brazil (pen) 20	4,330
12	O	2	CL	A	Cambridge United	L 0-2	0-1	20		(1,543)
13		5	CL	A	Crewe Alexandra	D 3-3	2-2	20	Brazil 12, Gibson 45, Greenwood 83	(2,454)
14		9	MC2/2	A	Norwich City	L 1-2	1-0		Brazil 5	(11,537)
15		12	CL	H	Chester City	L 3-6	1-4	21	Foster 40, Welsh 77, Brazil 80	4,073
16		19	CL	A	Rochdale	D 1-1	0-0	21	Brazil 49	(2,527)
17		22	CL	H	Hartlepool United	W 2-1	1-1	19	Greenwood 38, Foster 53	3,538
18		25	CL	A	Southend United	L 1-2	1-2	20	Greenwood 10	(2,789)
19	N	2	CL	H	Port Vale	L 0-1	0-0	20		4,531
20		5	CL	H	Scunthorpe United	L 0-1	0-1	21		2,007
21		9	CL	A	Orient	L 0-2	0-1	22		(2,805)
22		16	FAC1	A	Walsall	L 3-7	1-4		Thomas 26, Brazil 62, Martin 66	(4,035)
23		23	CL	H	Colchester United	W 3-2	2-0	20	Thomas 17, Gray 40, Stevens 47	2,783
24		30	CL	A	Exeter City	L 0-3	0-1	21		(1,896)
25	D	7	CL	A	Swindon Town	L 1-4	1-2	22	Allatt (pen) 34	(2,945)
26		14	CL	H	Aldershot	L 1-3	1-1	23	Thomas 45	2,774
27		21	CL	H	Northampton Town	D 1-1	0-1	23	Thomas 57	2,570
28		26	CL	A	Wrexham	D 1-1	0-1	23	Atkins 70	(2,217)
29	J	1	CL	H	Mansfield Town	L 0-2	0-1	23		3,705
30		4	CL	A	Port Vale	W 1-0	1-0	22	Jones 21	(3,592)
31		11	CL	H	Halifax Town	L 0-1	0-1	23		3,184
32		18	CL	A	Peterborough United	D 1-1	1-0	23	Allatt 33	(2,711)
33		20	FRT	A	Tranmere Rovers	L 0-2	0-1			(1,047)
34		24	CL	A	Stockport County	L 1-2	0-1	23	Thomas 49	(3,035)
35		29	FRT	H	Bury	W 2-0	0-0		Greenwood 46, Allatt (pen) 82	751
36	F	1	CL	A	Torquay United	L 0-1	0-1	23		(1,215)
37		5	CL	A	Hartlepool United	L 0-1	0-1	23		(3,102)
38		8	CL	H	Rochdale	D 1-1	1-1	23	Greenwood 23	3,266
39		22	CL	H	Swindon Town	L 0-3	0-1	23		3,361
40	M	1	CL	A	Hereford United	D 1-1	0-1	23	Brazil 89	(1,857)
41		8	CL	H	Crewe Alexandra	L 1-2	0-2	23	Thomas 84	2,922
42		15	CL	A	Chester City	L 0-2	0-1	24		(3,062)
43		18	CL	H	Cambridge United	L 1-2	1-1	24	Brazil 42	2,840
44		22	CL	H	Southend United	W 3-2	2-0	24	Brazil (pen) 28, Thomas 36, 65	2,600
45		25	CL	A	Tranmere Rovers	W 3-2	2-2	23	Brazil 6, Thomas 42, 47	(1,574)
46		29	CL	H	Mansfield Town	W 3-2	1-2	23	Foster 24, Atkins 62, Allatt 69	(3,737)
47		31	CL	H	Wrexham	W 1-0	0-0	23	Thomas 54	5,163
48	A	4	CL	A	Scunthorpe United	W 3-1	2-1	22	Thomas 2, 38, Greenwood 67	(2,261)
49		12	CL	H	Orient	L 1-3	0-2	23	Brazil (pen) 61	4,750
50		18	CL	A	Colchester United	L 0-4	0-1	23		(2,046)
51		22	CL	A	Burnley	D 1-1	0-0	23	Brazil (pen) 83	(3,783)
52		26	CL	H	Exeter City	D 2-2	1-1	23	Thomas 32, Gibson 68	3,132
53	M	3	CL	A	Aldershot	L 0-4	0-0	23		(1,866)

Best Home League Attendance: 5,585 v Burnley 17/9   **Smallest:** 2,007 v Scunthorpe United 5/11   **Av Home Att:** 3,495

Goal Scorers: Compared with 84-85: −253

League (54): Thomas 17, Brazil 14 (3 pens), Greenwood 9, Allatt 3 (1 pen), Foster 3, Atkins 2, Gibson 2, Gray 1, Jones 1, Stevens 1, Welsh 1
Milk Cup (7): Brazil 3 (1 pen), Foster 1, Keen 1, Rudge 1, Twentyman 1
FA Cup (3): Brazil 1, Martin 1, Thomas 1
FRT (2): Allatt 1 (pen), Greenwood 1

Platt	Jones	McAteer	Atkins	Twentyman	Gray	Keen	Foster	Thomas	Rudge	Brazil	Greenwood	Clark	Gibson	Welsh	Martin	Chippendale M	Stevens	Tottoh N.C	Allatt	McNeil	Reid L	Cooper L	Houston	Kelly	Harrington (L)	Referee	
1	2	3	4	5	6*	7	8	9	10	11	12															K Lupton	1
1	**2**	**3**	**4**	**5**		7	8*	9	10	11	12	6														**P Tyldesley**	**2**
1	2	3	4	5		7	8	9	10	11		6														T Simpson	3
1	2	3*	4	5		7	8	9	10	11	12	6														J Lloyd	4
1	**2**	**3**	**4**	**5**			8	9	10	11	12	6		7												**R Nixon**	**5**
1	2	3	4	5		7	8	9*	10	11	12	6														K Hackett	6
1	2	3	4*	5		7	8		10	11	9	6		12												J Martin	7
1	2		4	3		7		9	10	11	8	6	5													G Courtney	8
1	2		4	3		7	8	9		11	10	6*	5	12												C Seel	9
1	3	4	2	10	7		9		11	8			5		6											A Saunders	10
1	**3**	**4**	**2**	**10**	**7**		**9**		**11**	**8**			**5**		**6**											**G Tyson**	**11**
1	3	4	2	10	7		9			11*	8		5	12	6											A Gunn	12
1	3†	4	2	10	7		9			11	8		5		6											J Mcaulay	13
1	**3**	**4**	**2**	**10***	**7**		**8**	**9**		**11**	**12**		**5**		**6**											**G Napthine**	**14**
1	3	4	2		7		8*	9		11			5	12	6					10						M Peck	15
1		2		10*	7		8†	3		11	9		5	4	6					12						R Bridges	16
1	3		2			7	8	10		11	9		5	4	6											T Jones	17
1	3		5	2			8	10		11	9			4	6	7										R Lewis	18
1	3	4	2					10		11	9		5	4	6	7*	12									G Aplin	19
1	3	4	2					10*		11	9		5			7	6	12								N Ashley	20
1	3	4	2					12	10	11	9*		5				7	6	8							Allan Robinson	21
1	**3**	**4**	**2**				**8***	**9**	**7**	**11**	**12**		**5**		**6**					**10**						**J Lovatt**	**22**
1	3	4	5	8				9	2	11					6		7			10						F Roberts	23
1	3		5	8	12			9	2	11*				4	6		7			10						J Ball	24
1	3†		5	8*	4			9	2	11	12				6		7			10						K Miller	25
1	8*	3		5				9		11	12				6		7			10	2	4				K Redfearn	26
1	8		4	5				9	8	11					6					10	2		11			P Tyldesley	27
1	3		4	5				9	8	11					6					10	2	7*	12			V Callow	28
1	3		4	5				9		11					6					10	2	7	8			R Nixon	29
1	3	7	4	5	8			9		11					6					10	2					H Taylor	30
1	3*	7	4	5	8			9		11					6					10	2		12			P Vanes	31
1	3	7	4		5		12	9		11					6*					10	2	8				K Barratt	32
1			**4**				**2**	**12**	**9***	**7**			**6**	**5**		**8**				**10**	**3**		**11**			**D Phillips**	**33**
1	8	3	4			7	12	9		11			5		6					10*	2					R Bridges	34
1	**2**	**3**	**6**		**8**		**10***		**11**		**9**		**4**	**5**						**12**			**7**			**J Lovatt**	**35**
1	8	3	4			7	12	9		11			5		6					10*	2					R Milford	36
1	8		4		7	2	10	9*		11	12		5		6					3						T Mills	37
1	4	3		8	7	10	12			11*	9		5		6					2						C Trussell	38
	4	3		8	7	10	12			11	9		5		6*					2				1		A Saunders	39
	4	3		8	7	10	12			11	9		5	6						2				1*		T Jones	40
	4	3	6	8	7*	10	12			11	9		5			1				2						G Aplin	41
	4	3		8	7	10	5			11	9			6		1				2						D Phillips	42
	4	3		8	7*	10	12			11	9		5	6		1				2						G Courtney	43
	4	3	7	8		12	9			11*			5	6		1				10	2*					K Baker	44
	2	4	7	8		9	3			11*			5	6		1				10						L Robinson	45
	2			8	7	9	3			11			5	4	6	1				10						I Hemley	46
	4	2		8	7	9	3			11			5*	12	6	1				10						T Simpson	47
	4	2		8	7	9	3			11	10			5	6	1				12						J McAulay	48
	2	4	7	8		9	3			11	10*			5	6	1										P Willis	49
	3	4	2†	8		7	9			11			5†		6	1										T Ward	50
	2	4	3	8		7	10			11	9		5		6	1										K Breen	51
	4	2		8		7	9			11	10*		5		6	1				12	3					T Mills	52
	3			8		7	9			10			5		6*	1				2						M Scott	53
31	37	29	34	26	27	24	25	34	23	43	25	6	25	11	35	5	6	13		17	19	3	3		2	League Appearances	
						6	6				5				6					1	1		2		2	Substitute Appearances	
4	4	2	4	4	2	3	4	2	4	1·3	2	3	2							1	2				2	Milk Cup Appearances	
1	1		1	1		1	1	1	1	0·1	1		1		1					1						FA Cup Appearances	
2	1	1	2		1	1	1·1	1	1	1				2	2					1·1	1				2	FR Trophy Appearances	

Also Played: Position (Game): Rodgers (NC) 8(20), Pilling 4(53), Jemson 12(53), Ibbotson (NC) 11(53)

Players on Loan: Cooper (Leicester) Reid (Rochdale), Harrington (Blackpool)   Departures: Keen (Enfield), Campbell (F)

'THE LILLYWHITES'

Formed: 1881
Turned Professional: 1885   **Ltd Co:** 1893

Previous Managers: 1919 V Hayes   1924 T Lawrence   1925 F Richards   1927 A Gibson
1931-32 L Hyde   1932-36 No Manager   1936-7 T Muirhead   1937-49 No Manager   1949-53 W Scott
1953-4 Scot Symon   1954-6 F Hill   1956-61 C Britton   1961-8 J Milne   1968-70 R Seith
1970-3 A Ball Snr   1973 F Lord (Caretaker)   1973-5 R Charlton   1975-7 H Catterick
1977-81 N Stiles   1981 T Docherty   1981-3 G Lee   1983-5 A Kelly   1985 T Booth, 1986 B Kidd
1986 (Caretaker) J Clark
Honours: Champions Div 1, *1888-89 (first winners), 1889-90   Champions Div 2, 1903-4, 1912-13,
1950-51   Champions Div 3 1970-1   FA Cup Winners *1889, 1938
*League and FA Cup 'Double'
League Career: Original Members of Football League 1888   Relegated to Div 2 1900-1
Promoted to Div 1 1903-4   Relegated to Div 2 1911-2   Promoted to Div 2 1912-3
Relegated to Div 1 1913-4   Promoted to Div 1 1914-5   Relegated to Div 2 1924-5
Promoted to Div 1 1933-4   Relegated to Div 2 1948-9   Promoted to Div 1 1950-1
Relegated to Div 2 1960-1   Relegated to Div 3 1969-70   Promoted to Div 2 1970-1
Relegated to Div 3 1973-4   Promoted to Div 2 1977-8   Relegated to Div 3 1980-1
Relegated to Div 4 1984-5
Colours: White shirts with navy blue trim, navy blue shorts, white stockings with navy blue rings
Change Colours: All yellow
Reserves League: Central League **Youth Team:** Lancashire League Div 2

CLUB RECORDS

Most Appearances for Club: Alan Kelly: Football League 447 + Cup games 65 **Total 512**
Most Capped Player: Tom Finney, 76, England
Record Goalscorer in a Match: Jimmy Ross, 8 v Hyde (h), 26-0, 1st Round FA Cup, 15.10.1887
Record League Goalscorer in a Season: Ted Harper, 37, Div 2, 1932-3   **In All Competitions:** Ted Harper, 37 (League 37) 1932-3
Record League Goalscorer in a Career: Tom Finney, 187   **In All Competitions:** Tom Finney, 210 (League 187 + FA Cup 23) 1946-60
Record Transfer Fee Received: £765,000 from Manchester City for Michael Robinson, June 1979
Record Transfer Fee Paid: £95,000 to Nottingham Forest for Steve Elliott, March 1979
Best Performances: League: Champions Div 1 (2)   **FA Cup:** Winners (2)   **League/Milk Cup:** 4th Round 1963, 1966, 1972, 1981
Most League Points: 61, Div 3, 1970-1, 1981-2   **Most League Goals:** 100, Div 2, 1927-28; 100 Div 1, 1957-8
Record League Victory: 10-0 v Stoke City, (h), Div 1, 14 Sept 1889
Most Goals Scored in a Cup Tie: 26-0 v Hyde, FA Cup, 1887
Record League Defeat: 0-7 v Blackpool, (h), Div 1, 1 May 1948, 0-7 v Nottingham Forest (a) Div 2, 9 April 1927
Oldest Player in League Match:
Youngest Player in League Match: Nigel Jameson, 16 yrs 8 months

Most Consecutive Undefeated League Matches: 23 1888-89
Longest Run of Undefeated Home League Matches: 31 1903-04
Longest Run Without Home League Win: 9 1965-66
Most Consecutive League Wins: 14 1950-51
Most Consecutive League Defeats: 8 1983

League Matches Without a Win: 15 1923
Away League Matches: 11 1888-89
Away League Win: 33 1897-99
Home League Wins: 20 1891-92
Away League Wins: 8 1950-51

Club Statistician for the Directory: L Bland

PRESTON NORTH END

PLAYERS NAME Ht Wt Birthdate	Honours	Birthplace Transfers	Clubs	League	Milk Cup	FA Cup	Other Comps	League	Milk Cup	FA Cup	Other Comps
GOALKEEPERS											
David Brown 6.1 12.8 28.1.57		Hartlepool	Horden C.W.								
			Middlesbrough	10							
			Plymouth Argyle (L)	5							
		£40,000	Oxford United	21	2						
		£5,000	Bury	146	7	7	3				
		F	Preston N.E.								
Alan Kelly 6.2 12.5 11.8.68	Ei.Y	Preston	Preston N.E.	13							
DEFENDERS											
Shaun Allen 5.11 12.5		Preston	Preston N.E.								
Bob Atkins 6.1 12.2 16.10.62		Leicester	Sheffield United	21+3	6+1		2+1	3			
			Preston N.E.	39+1	4	2	2	2			
Simon Gibson 6.2 13.2 10.12.64	Sc.Y.S.	Nottingham	Chelsea (A)								
		F	Swindon Town	29+2	1	6	4	5			
		F	Preston N.E.	25	3	1	2				
Alex Jones 6.0 11.6 27.11.64		Blackburn	Oldham Athletic	8+1	0+1						
			Stockport County (L)	3							
			Preston N.E.								
Andy McAteer 5.10 11.10 24.4.61		Preston	Preston N.E. (A)	187+2	16	8	2	5		1	
Bobby McNeil 5.8½ 10.9 1.11.62		Bellshill	Hull City (A)	135+3	5	17	5	3			
		F	Lincoln City	4							
		F	Preston N.E.	19		1					
Paul Welsh 6.2 12.4 10.5.66		Liverpool	Formby								
			Preston N.E.	10+6	2		2	1			
Ronnie Hildersley 5.4 9.2 6.4.65		Kirkcaldy	Manchester City (A)			1					
		F	Chester	18							
		F	Rochdale	12+2							
		F	Preston N.E.								
MIDFIELD											
Shayne Beeby 5.8 10.7 27.2.67		Leeds	Bradford City (A)								
			Preston N.E.								
Gary Brazil 5.8½ 10.2 19.9.62		Tunbridge Wells	Crystal Palace (A)								
		F	Sheffield United	39+23	4+1	4+5	1+1	9		1	
			Port Vale (L)	6				3			
		£5,000	Preston N.E.	43	4	1	2	14	3	1	
Les Chapman 5.7 10.0 27.9.48		Oldham	Oldham Athletic	75+1	5	1		9		1	
		£20,000	Huddersfield Town	120+13	8	11		8		2	
		£10,000	Oldham Athletic	186+1	9	11		11		1	
		F	Stockport County	32	4	1		1			
		£10,000	Bradford City	137+2	14+1	6		3		1	
		F	Rochdale	87+1	4	3	4				
		F	Stockport County	38	2	1	1	3			
			Preston N.E.								
Jon Clarke 5.10 11.10 12.11.58	W.U21 (2), S	Swansea	Manchester United	0+1							
		£50,000	Derby County	48+5	4	4		3			
		F	Preston N.E.	58	10	3	3	5	1		
FORWARDS											
Vernon Allatt 5.11 12.7 28.5.59		Hednesford	Hednesford Town								
		£2,000	Walsall								
		F	Halifax Town	93+5	3	9		14		1	
		F	Bolton Wanderers								
		F	Rochdale	40	2	3	1	8			
		F	Crewe Alexandra	36+3	2	0+1	2	7			
		F	Preston N.E.	17+2	1	1+1	3				
Wayne Foster 5.8½ 11.0 11.9.63	EY	Leigh	Bolton Wanderers (A)	91+13	3+2	6	2+2	13	1	3	
			Preston N.E.	25+6	3	1	1+1	3		1	
Nigel Greenwood 5.11 12.0 27.11.60		Preston	Preston N.E. (A)	25+5	2+3	0+1	1+1	9			1
John Thomas† 5.8 11.3 5.8.58		Wednesbury	Everton								
			Tranmere Rovers (L)	10+1				2			
			Halifax Town (L)	5							
		F	Bolton Wanderers	18+4	1	2		6	1		
		F	Chester City	44	2			20	1		
		£22,000	Lincoln City	31+6	2+1	1	4+1	18	3		
		F	Preston N.E.	34+6	4	1	1	17		1	

ADDITIONAL CONTRACT PROFESSIONALS

Peter Bulmer

APPRENTICES

NON-CONTRACT PLAYERS

Steven Saunders, George Shepherd, Stephen Wilkes

DEEPDALE Preston PR1 6RU

Record Attendance: 42,684 v Arsenal, Div 1, 23 April 1938

Smallest Home Attendance for a First Class Match: 2,007 v Scunthorpe, Div 4, 5 Nov 1985

Record Receipts: £28,300 v Blackburn Rovers, Div 2, 21 Apr 1981

Season Tickets: Pavilion: £60 (£44 Under 15/OAPs); West Stand: £54 (£33 Under 15/OAPs); Paddock £48 (30 Under 15/OAPs); Ground £43 (£25 Under 15/OAPs)

Executive Box Season Tickets: None available

Cost of Stand Tickets: Pavilion: £3.50 (all) (£2.50 Juvenile/OAP); West Stand: £3.00 (£2.20 Under 15/OAPs); Paddock; £2.80 (£1.90 Under 15/OAPs); Ground: £2.50 (£1.50 Under 15/OAPs)

Match and Ticket Information: Postal applications with payment and SAE 14 days before match

Car Parking: Club park on Deepdale Road (West Stand) side of ground for 500 vehicles. Limited off-street parking

Nearest Railway Station: Preston (0772 59439)

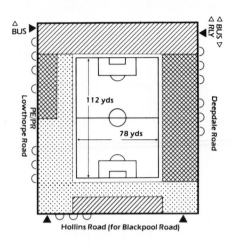

Hollins Road (for Blackpool Road)

How to get to the ground

From North: Use Motorway M6 then M55 until junction 1, leave motorway and follow signs Preston A6. In 1.9m at crossroads turn left A5085 into Blackpool Road. In 0.8m turn right A6063 into Deepdale for Preston North End FC
From East and South: Use Motorway M6 until junction 31, leave motorway and follow signs Preston A59. In 1m at roundabout take 2nd exit into Blackpool Road. In 1.3m turn left A6063 into Deepdale for Preston North End FC
From West: Use Motorway M55 until junction 1, leave motorway and follow signs Preston A6. In 1.9m at crossroads turn left A5085 into Blackpool Road. In 0.8m turn right A6063 into Deepdale for Preston North End FC

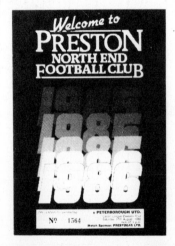

Price of 1986-7 Programme: 50p
Number of Pages: 16
Subscriptions: 50p per programme plus 21p for postage

Local Newspaper: Lancashire Evening Post

Local Radio Stations: Red Rose Radio, Radio Lancashire

QUEENS PARK RANGERS Division 1

What should have been the highlight of a successful season turned into a nightmare at Wembley. Rangers went into the Milk Cup final firm favourites to beat Oxford United but, in the words of manager Jim Smith, his team "froze" on the day and was well beaten.

Optimism had been high as Rangers had eliminated such sides as Nottingham Forest, Chelsea — in a Stamford Bridge replay — and Liverpool on the way to Wembley and, on the run-up to Wembley, they had been in superb form unbeaten in eight matches.

Mr Smith took over at The Bush during the summer of 1985 and made one or two changes in the side after a few weeks. Paul Barron took over from Peter Hucker in goal and Alan McDonald was given his head in the middle of the defence, performing so well that by the end of the season he was an established international, playing for N Ireland in the World Cup finals.

Another World Cup player was Terry Fenwick but, though he played in the middle of the defence for England, he spent much of the season in a midfield role for Rangers.

Steve Wicks was recalled to play alongside McDonald at the heart of the defence.

Martin Allen was given the chance to play himself into the side in midfield.

Though Gary Bannister and John Byrne proved a good striking partnership, scoring 33 goals between them, Mr Smith signed Leroy Rosenior, from Fulham, for £50,000 as cover.

Rangers got away to a reasonable start in the 1st Division but a disastrous run of five successive defeats in November and December gave rise for concern.

Another bad run into March placed the club in some danger of relegation. But victory over Liverpool in the semi-final of the Milk Cup, and the prospect of a trip to Wembley, revived their fortunes. During their eight-game unbeaten run, Rangers whacked Championship-chasing Chelsea by 6-0 and they got into the right frame of mind for the big event by winning 4-1 at Leicester a few days earlier.

Sadly, there were no celebrations at Wembley.

In the FA Cup, Rangers took a shock 3rd Round exit at Carlisle, who were bottom of the 2nd Division.

Back Row L to R: Warren Neill, Clive Walker, David Kerslake, Gary Chivers, Martin Allen, Gary Waddock, Wayne Fereday. **Middle Row:** David Butler (Physio), Alan Brazil, Alan McDonald, Peter Hucker, David Seaman, Michael Fillery, Robbie James, Frank Sibley (Asst. Manager). **Front Row:** Ian Dawes, Gary Bannister, Terry Fenwick, Jim Smith (Manager), Michael Robinson, Leroy Rosenior, John Byrne.

QUEENS PARK RANGERS

DIVISION ONE: 13th   **FA CUP:** 3rd ROUND   **MILK CUP:** RUNNERS-UP

MATCH	DATE	COMPE-TITION	VENUE	OPPONENTS	RESULT	HALF TIME	L'GUE POS'N	GOALSCORERS/GOAL TIMES	ATTENDANC
1	A 17	CL	H	Ipswich Town	W 1-0	0-0		Byrne 71	12,7
2	20	CL	A	West Ham United	L 1-3	0-2		Byrne 54	(15,53
3	24	CL	A	Aston Villa	W 2-1	1-0	5	Bannister 3, 89	(11,89
4	27	CL	H	Nottingham Forest	W 2-1	2-1	5	Bannister 6, Fenwick (pen) 37	10,7
5	31	CL	A	Newcastle United	L 1-3	0-1	7	Fenwick 52	(25,02
6	S 3	CL	H	Arsenal	L 0-1	0-0	9		15,9
7	7	CL	H	Everton	W 3-0	2-0	7	Bannister 29, 55, Byrne 42	16,5
8	14	CL	A	Watford	L 0-2	0-2	11		(15,7
9	21	CL	A	Luton Town	L 0-2	0-2	12		(9,5C
10	24	MC2/1	H	Hull City	W 3-0	1-0		Kerslake 13, Dawes 51, Bannister 65	7,2
11	28	CL	H	Birmingham City	W 3-1	2-1	11	Rosenoir 8, Bannister 18, Dawes 56	10,9
12	O 5	CL	H	Liverpool	W 2-1	1-1	8	Fenwick 43, Bannister 63	24,6
13		MC2/2	A	Hull City	W 5-1	1-1		Kerslake 35, 81, Rosenoir 78, 88, Fillery 59	(4,28
14	12	CL	A	Manchester United	L 0-2	0-1	9		(48,84
15	19	CL	H	Manchester City	D 0-0	0-0	11		13,4
16	26	CL	A	Southampton	L 0-3	0-1	12		(15,6
17	29	MC3	A	Watford	W 1-0	0-0		Byrne 54	(16,82
18	N 2	CL	H	Sheffield Wednesday	D 1-1	0-0	13	James 81	12,12
19	9	CL	A	W.B.A.	W 1-0	1-0	11	Robinson 4	(9,01
20	16	CL	H	Leicester City	W 2-0	0-0	9	Wicks 56, Fereday 76	11,08
21	23	CL	A	Tottenham Hotspur	D 1-1	0-1	9	Byrne 60	(20,33
22	25	MC4	J	Nottingham Forest	W 3-1	1-0		Fenwick (pen) 8, Bannister 87, Byrne 90	13,05
23	30	CL	H	Coventry City	L 0-2	0-0	10		11,10
24	D 7	CL	H	West Ham United	L 0-1	0-0	12		23,50
25	14	CL	A	Ipswich Town	L 0-1	0-0	13		(12,03
26	17	CL	H	Aston Villa	L 0-1	0-1	14		11,23
27	28	CL	A	Arsenal	L 1-3	0-1	14	Bannister 70	(25,77
28	J 1	CL	H	Oxford United	W 3-1	2-0	14	Allen 22, Fereday 36, Byrne 71	16,34
29	11	CL	A	Everton	L 3-4	1-2	15	Bannister 12, 87, Byrne 25	(26,01
30	13	FAC3	A	Carlisle United	L 0-1	0-1			(5,08
31	18	CL	H	Newcastle United	W 3-1	2-0	15	Fenwick 31 (pen) 79, Robinson 43	14,15
32	22	MCQF	H	Chelsea	D 1-1	1-1		Byrne 12	27,00
33	29	MCQFR	A	Chelsea	W 2-0†	0-0		McDonald 109, Robinson 119	(27,93
34	F 1	CL	A	Nottingham Forest	L 0-4	0-2			(11,53
35	8	CL	A	Manchester City	L 0-2	0-2	15		(20,41
36	12	MCSF 1	H	Liverpool	W 1-0	1-0		Fenwick 25	15,05
37	22	CL	H	Luton Town	D 1-1	1-0	16	Byrne 36	16,25
38	M 1	CL	A	Birmingham City	L 0-2	0-0	16		(7,09
39	5	MCSF 2	A	Liverpool	D 2-2	0-1		Whelan (og) 58, Gillespie (og) 84	(23,86
40	8	CL	A	Liverpool	L 1-4	1-3	16	Rosenoir 7	(26,21
41	11	CL	A	Southampton	L 0-2	0-2	16		14,17
42	15	CL	H	Manchester United	W 1-0	0-0	15	Byrne 81	23,40
43	19	CL	A	Chelsea	D 1-1	0-1	15	Kerslake 85	(17,87
44	22	CL	H	Watford	W 2-1	1-0	14	Fenwick (pen) 5, Robinson 59	14,06
45	29	CL	A	Oxford United	D 3-3	3-2	14	Walker 11, Allen S 22, Fenwick (pen) 44	(11,91C
46	31	CL	H	Chelsea	W 6-0	3-0	13	Bannister 3 (7, 25, 58), Byrne 43, 64 Rosenior 82	18,58
47	A 8	CL	A	Sheffield Wednesday	D 0-0	0-0	14		(13,157
48	12	CL	H	W.B.A.	W 1-0	0-0	13	Bannister 51	11,86
49	14	CL	A	Leicester City	W 4-1	2-0	12	Allen 4, Bannister 44, Robinson 47, Byrne 77	(7,724
50	20	MCF	N	Oxford United	L 0-3	0-1			(90,39C
51	26	CL	H	Tottenham Hotspur	L 2-5	0-3	13	Rosenoir 62, Bannister 80	17,76
52	M 3	CL	A	Coventry City	L 1-2	1-2	13	Byrne 28	(14,086

Best Home League Attendance: 24,621 v Liverpool 5/10   **Smallest:** 10,748 v Nottingham Forest 27/8   **Av Home Att:** 15,272

Goal Scorers:

Compared with 84-85: +908

League (53):	Bannister 16, Byrne 12, Fenwick 7 (4 pen), Robinson 4, Rosenoir 4, Allen 3, Fereday 2, Dawes 1, James 1, Kerslake 1, Walker 1, Wicks 1
Milk Cup (18):	Byrne 3, Kerslake 3, Bannister 2, Fenwick 2 (1 pen), Rosenoir 2, Dawes 1, Fillery 1, McDonald 1, Robinson 1, Opponents 2
FA Cup (Nil):	

† After extra tim

404

1985-86

Hucker	Chivers	Fenwick	McDonald	Dawes	James	Waddock	Fereday	Gregory	Robinson	Bannister	Byrne	Allen	Rosenoir	Wicks	Kerslake	Barron	Fillery	Walker	Neill	Bakholt	Referee	No.
1	2	3	4	5	6*	7	8	9	10	11	12										H King	1
1	2	6	5	3	12	4	10	11	9*	8	7										M James	2
1	2	6	5	3	8	4	12	11	9	10*	7										N Midgley	3
1	2	6	5	3	8*	4	12	11	9	10	7										J Deakin	4
1	2	6	5	3	8	4	12	11	9	10*	7										T Fitzharris	5
1	2*	6	5	3		4	8	11	9	10	7	12									K Baker	6
1	2	6	5	3		4	8	11	9	10	7										A Gunn	7
1	2	6	5	3		4*	8	11	9	10	7	12									J Ashworth	8
1	2	6	5	3		4	8	11†	9	10	7										V Callow	9
	2*	6		3		4	8	11	9		10		12	5	7	1					**J Martin**	10
		6	2	3		4	8	11	9		10			5	7	1					M Bodenham	11
		6	2	3		4	8		9		10			5	7	1	11				G Napthine	12
		6	2	3		4	9		12	8	10			5	7	1	11*				**D Scott**	13
		6	2	3		4	8		9	12	10			5	7*	1	11				A Seville	14
		6	2	3		4	8		11	9	12	10		5	7	1	8*				R Gifford	15
		6	2	3	8	4			11	9	12	10		5	7*	1	8				R Milford	16
		6*	2	3		4			11	12	9	10		5	7	1	8				**D Hedges**	17
			2	3	12	4*	11		6	9	10	7		5		1	8				I Borrett	18
		6	2	3		4	7		11	9	10*	12		5		1	8				N Glover	19
		6	2	3		4	7*		11	9	10	12		5		1	8				L Shapter	20
		6	2	3		4	7		11*	9	10	12		5		1	8				B Hill	21
		6	2	3		4	7			9	10	12		5	11*	1	8				**M James**	22
		6	2	3		4	7			9	10	11*		5	12	1	8				B Stevens	23
		6	2	3		4	11			9*	10	7	12	5		1	8				J Bray	24
	6		2	3		4	7		11	9	10			5		1	8				J Ball	25
	2	6		3		4	9		11		10			5		1	8	7			Allan Robinson	26
		6	4	3			12		7	9	10			5		1	8	11*	2		R Lewis	27
		6	2	3			11		7	9	10	8		5		1			4		J Martin	28
		6	2	3	12		11		7*	9	10	8		5		1			4		T Holbrook	29
		6	4*	3	7				11	9	10	8	12	5		1			2		**D Scott**	30
		6	2	3	8		11			7	9	10		5		1			4		K Miller	31
		6	2	3	8		11			7	9	10		5		1			4		**L Shapter**	32
			2	3	8		11			7	9	10*	12	5		1	6		4		**A Gunn**	33
			2	3	8†		11			7*	9	10	12	5		1	6		4		T Fitzharris	34
1		6	2	3	8*					11	10	5	9					7	4	12	A Saunders	35
		6	2	3			11			9	10	7		5		1			4		**G Courtney**	36
		6	2	3			11			9	10	8		5		1	7		4		J Ashworth	37
		6	2	3			11			10*	7	9		5	12	1	8		4		N Ashley	38
		6	2	3	8		12		7	9*	10			5		1	11		4		**D Hutchinson**	39
		6	2	3	8				7	10*	9			5	12	1	11		4		B Hill	40
		6	2	5	10				7	12	9*	3	8		1		11		4		A Seville	41
		6	2	3	8		12		9	10	7			5	11*	1			4		J Deakin	42
		6	2	3	8		11		9*	7				5	12	1	10		4		H Taylor	43
		6	2	3	8		10*		11	9	7			5	12	1			4		Alan Robinson	44
		6	2	3	8		11		9	12	7	5				1	10	4*			N Midgley	45
		6*	2	3	8		4		11	9	10	7	12	5		1					M Bodenham	46
		6	2	3	8		4		11	9	10	7		5		1					G Ashby	47
		6	2	3	8		4		11	9	10	7*	12	5		1					A Gunn	48
5		6	2	3			4*		11	9	12	7†	10			1		8			M Reed	49
		6	2	3	8				11	9	10	7*	12	5		1			4		**K Hackett**	50
1	5		2	3	8		4		11*	9	10	7	12		6						M Dimblebee	51
12	6*	2	3	8			11				10		9	5	7	1		4			N Wilson	52
11	13	37	**42**	**42**	25	15	30	11	25	36	30	26	12	29	9	31	17	5	16		League Appearances	
	1		3	4		1					6	5	6		5				1		Substitute Appearances	
1	8	8	9	6	3	5-1	1	5-1	9	7-1	4-2	1-2	9	4	9	5		5			Milk Cup Appearances	
	1	1	1	1	1		1		1	1	1	0-1	1				1				FA Cup Appearances	

Also Played:
Players on Loan:
Departures: Gregory (Derby County), Stewart (Newcastle)

'RANGERS' or 'R's'

Formed: 1885
Turned Professional: 1898 **Ltd Co:** 1899

Previous Names: St Jude's 1885-7
Previous Managers: 1907-13 James Cowan   1913-20 James Howie   1920-5 E (Ned) Liddell
1925-31 R (Bob) Hewison   1931 John Bowman   1931-3 Archie Mitchell   1933-5 Michael T O'Brien
1935-9 William Birrell   1939-44 E (Ted) Vizard   1944-52 Dave Mangnall   1952-9 Jack Taylor
1959-68 Alec Stock   1968 Tommy Docherty   1969-71 Les Allen   1971-4 Gordon Jago
1974-7 Dave Sexton   1977-8 Frank Sibley (acting)   1978-9 Steve Burtenshaw
1979-80 Tommy Docherty   1980-4 Terry Venables   1984 Alan Mullery   1984-5 Frank Sibley (acting)
Honours: Champions Div 2, 1982-3   Champions Div 3 (S) 1947-8   Champions Div 3 1966-7   Football
League Cup Winners 1966-7
League Career: Original Members of Div 3 1920   Transferred to Div 3 (S) 1921
Promoted to Div 2 1947-8   Relegated to Div 3 (S) 1951-2   Transferred to Div 3 1958
Promoted to Div 2 1966-7   Promoted to Div 1 1967-8   Relegated to Div 2 1968-9
Promoted to Div 1 1972-3   Relegated to Div 2 1978-9   Promoted to Div 1, 1982-3
Colours: Blue and white hooped shirts, white stockings with three blue hoops
Change Colours: Red shirts, black shorts, red stockings with four red bands on tops
Reserves League: Football Combination   **Youth Team:** S E Counties

---

CLUB RECORDS

Most Appearances for Club: Tony Ingham: Football League 514 + FA Cup 30 League Cup 4 **Total 548** (1950-63)
Most Capped Player: Don Givens, 26, Eire   **For England:** Gerry Francis 12
Record Goalscorer in a Match: Alan Wilks, 5 v Oxford United, 3rd Round League Cup, 10.10.1967
Record League Goalscorer in a Season: George Goddard, 37, Div 3 (S), 1924-30   **In All Competitions:** Rodney Marsh
44, (League 30 + FA Cup 3 + League Cup 11), 1966-7
Record League Goalscorer in a Career: George Goddard, 174   **In All Competitions:** George Goddard, 186 (League
174 + FA Cup 12) 1926-34
Record Transfer Fee Received: £1,250,000 from Arsenal for Clive Allen, June 1980
Record Transfer Fee Paid: £400,000 to Leeds United for Tony Currie, Aug 1979
Best Performances: League: Runners-Up 1975-6   **FA Cup:** Runners-Up 1982   **League/Milk Cup:** Winners
1966-7   **UEFA CUP:** Quarter-Finals
Most League Points: (2pts for win) 67, Div 3, 1966-7   (3pts for win) 85, Div 2, 1982-3
Most League Goals: 111, Div 3, 1961-2
Record League Victory and Most Goals Scored in a League Match: 9-2 v Tranmere Rovers, Div 3, 3 Dec 1960
Most Goals Scored in a Cup Tie: 8-1 v Bristol Rovers, (a), 1st Round FA Cup, 1937-8   8-2 v Sheffield Wednesday (h), 3rd
Round League Cup 1973-4   8-1 v Crewe A (a), 2nd Round, 1st Leg Milk Cup 1983-4
Record League Defeat: 1-8 v Mansfield Town, Div 3, 15 March 1965   1-8 v Manchester United, Div 1, 19 March 1969
European Competitions Entered: UEFA Cup 1977-6, 1984-5
Oldest Player in League Match: Jim Langley, 38 yrs 96 days
Youngest Player in League Match: Frank Sibley, 15 yrs 274 days
Most Consecutive Undefeated League Matches: 20 1966-67 | **League Matches Without a Win:** 20 1968-69
Longest Run of Undefeated Home League Matches: 25 1972-74 | **Away League Matches:** 17 1966-67
Longest Run Without Home League Win: 10 1968-69 | **Away League Win:** 22 1954-55. 1968-69
Most Consecutive League Wins: 8 1931 | **Home League Wins:** 11 1972-73
Most Consecutive League Defeats: 9 1969 | **Away League Wins:** 7 1927

Club Statistician for the Directory: Stewart Fell   **Club Statistician:** Derek Buxton

Queens Park Rangers

PLAYERS NAME Wt Birthdate	Honours	Birthplace Transfers	Clubs	APPEARANCES				GOALS			
				League	Milk Cup	FA Cup	Other Comps	League	Milk Cup	FA Cup	Other Comps
DALKEEPERS											
ul Barron 2 13.5 16.9.53		London	Slough Town								
			Plymouth Argyle	44	4	4					
		£60,000	Arsenal	8							
		£140,000	Crystal Palace	90	13	5					
		£60,000	W.B.A.	63							
			Stoke City (L)	1							
		£35,000	Q.P.R.	31	9	1					
ter Hucker 2 13.0 28.10.59	S.U21 (2) Div.2 '83	London	Q.P.R. (A)	160	13	11	4				
avid Seaman 2 13.0 19.9.63	E.U21 (10)	Rotherham	Leeds United (A)								
		£4,000	Peterborough United	91	10	5					
		£100,000	Birmingham City	75	4	5					
		£225,000	Q.P.R.								
EFENDERS											
ary Chivers 11 11.5 15.5.60		Stockwell	Chelsea (A)	128+5	8	7	4				
			Swansea City	10	1	8					
			Q.P.R.	35+2	3	1	1				
n Dawes 8 10.2 22.2.63	ES Div.2 '83	Croydon	Q.P.R. (A)	173	22	4	4	3	1		
rry Fenwick* 10 10.11 17.11.59	E (19) U.21 (1) Y. Div.2 '79 Div.2 '83	Durham	Crystal Palace (A)	62+8	4+1	7					
			Q.P.R.	213	25	14	4	29	6	2	
ayne Fereday 9½ 11.8 16.6.63	E.U21 (4)	London	Q.P.R. (A)	66+23	11+3	1+3	4	15	2		1
lan McDonald 2½ 12.7 12.10.63	NI (8), Y	Belfast	Q.P.R. (A)	47	8	1		1			
			Charlton Athletic (L)	24+1	4	1	1	1			
arren Neill 10½ 12.5 21.11.62	ES Div.2 '83	Acton	Q.P.R. (A)	128+1	16+1	6+1	3	3	1		1
IDFIELD											
artin Allen 10 11.0 18.8.65	EY	Reading	Q.P.R. (A)	30+6	4+3	1		3			
ke Fillery 10 11.2 17.9.60	EY,S	Mitcham	Chelsea (A)	156+5	9	11		32	6	3	
		£150,000	Q.P.R.	78+1	11+1	2	4	7	1		
bbie James 11 13.1 23.3.57	W (38) U.21 (3)	Swansea	Swansea City (A)	386+8	21	19		99	6	5	
		£160,000	Stoke City	48	7	1		6	1		
		£100,000	Q.P.R.	41+4	6	1		3			
ammy Lee 7 10.6 7.2.59	E (14) U.21 (6) Y EC '81,'84,Div.1 '82 '83 '84 '86, MC83,84,FAC '86	Liverpool	Liverpool (A)	190+7	26	21	33	13	2		4
			Q.P.R.								
ark Loram 0 12.0 13.8.67		Brixham	Torquay United								
			Q.P.R.								
ary Waddock 10 11.12 17.3.62	Ei (19), U.21 (1) Div.2 '83	Kingsbury	Q.P.R. (A)	187+12	20+1	14	1	8	1		
RWARDS											
ary Bannister 8½ 11.3 22.7.60	E.U21 (1)	Warrington	Coventry City (A)	17+5	2	2		3			
		£100,000	Sheffield Wednesday	117+1	13	12		55	2	1	
		£200,000	Q.P.R.	78	17	2	4	33	7		6
lan Brazil 0 12.4 15.6.59	S(13), U.21(8) UEFAC '81	Glasgow	Ipswich Town (A)	143+11	14+1	18+2	21	70	3	6	1
		£500,000	Tottenham Hotspur	29+2	0+1	1	3+2	9			4
		£700,000	Manchester United	18+13	4+3	0+1	2	7	3		1
			Coventry City	15				2			
		£120,000	Q.P.R.								
ohn Byrne 0 12.4 1.2.61	Ei (3), Div.4 '84	Manchester	York City (A)	167+8	8+3	10+1	1	55	5	3	
			Q.P.R.	48+8	7+1	2		15	3		
ichael Robinson 0 13.4 12.7.58	Ei (24), Div.1 '84 Lg.C '84 EC '84	Leicester	Preston N.E.	45+3	4	2		15	1		
		£750,000	Manchester City	29+1	4	1		8	1		
		£400,000	Brighton	111+2	8	12		37	3	3	
		£200,000	Liverpool	25+4	3	2	7+1	6	1	1	2
		£100,000	Q.P.R.	33+4	5+1			5	1		
roy Rosenoir 1 11.10 24.3.64	ES	London	Fulham	53+1		3		15			
			Q.P.R.	12+7	1+2	0+1		4	2		
ive Walker 8½ 11.4 26.5.57	ES	Oxford	Chelsea	168+30	9+1	14+2		60	2	3	
		£75,000	Sunderland	48+2	11	1	1+1	10	6		1
			Q.P.R.								

ODDITIONAL CONTRACT PROFESSIONALS
mmy Carter, Paul Davis, Gavin Maguire, Gavin Peacock, Tony Fowler (M), Andrew Cronin, Mark Fleming, Roberto Herrera, Stephen Lynch, John Murray, Darren Woodhurst, Bradley right

PPRENTICES
ustin Channing, Greg Costello, Brian Law, Billy McArthur, Scott Singleton, David Southwell

Player of the Year: Steve Wicks (now Chelsea)

ON-CONTRACT PLAYERS

Record Attendance: 35,353 v Leeds United, Div 1, 27 April 1974

Smallest Home Attendance for a First Class Match: 3,245 (at White City) v Coventry City, Div 3 (S), 22 May 1963

Record Receipts: £114,743 v Tottenham Hotspur, Div 1, 12 Jan 1985

Season Tickets: Stands: £105, £119, £126, £143, £147, £191; Terraces: £69 adults £25 (boys & OAPs)

Executive Box Season Tickets: Negotiable with the office

Cost of Stand Tickets: £5.00, £6.00, £7.00, £8.00; Ground: £4.00 (£1.50 juveniles/OAPs)

Match and Ticket Information: Seats bookable one month in advance of each match

Car Parking: Limited side-street parking available

Nearest Railway Station: Shepherds Bush (tube), White City (Central Line)

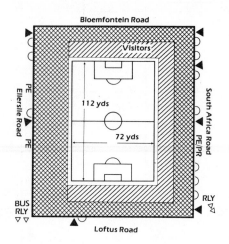

How to get to the ground

From North: Use Motorway M1 and A406 North Circular Road as for Neasden. In 0.7m turn left then join A404 S.P. Harlesden then follow signs Hammersmith and turn right into White City Road then turn left into South Africa Road for Queens Park Rangers FC

From East: Use A12, A406 then A503 then join Ring Road and follow signs Oxford to join A40 (M). In 2m branch left (S.P. The West) to join M41. At roundabout take 3rd exit A40 then join A4020 S.P. Acton. In 0.3m turn right into Loftus Road for Queens Park Rangers FC

From South: Use A206, A3 to cross Putney Bridge and follow signs to Hammersmith. Follow signs Oxford A219 to Shepherds Bush then join A4020 S.P. Acton. In 0.3m turn right into Loftus Road for Queens Park Rangers FC

From West: Use Motorway M4 to Chiswick then A315 and A402 to Shepherds Bush, then join A4020 S.P. Acton. In 0.3m turn right into Loftus Road for Queens Park Rangers FC

Price of 1986-7 Programme: 50p
Number of Pages: 20
Subscriptions: Full Season £20.00, Half-Season £11.00 (both UK postage paid). Full Season (European addresses) £25.00

Local Newspapers: Shepherds Bush Gazette, Acton Gazette

Local Radio Stations: LBC, Capital Radio

Life President
J H Brooks

Chairman
R G Smee

Directors
C M Brooks
J Campbell
M J Lewis
B Roach

Managing Director
M J Lewis

Secretary
Miss A Meek (0734 507878/9)
(0734 507880)

Manager
Ian Branfoot

Coach
Stewart Henderson

Youth Team Coach
Bobby Williams

Commercial Manager
(0734 507878)

Physiotherapist
Glenn Hunter

Groundsman
Gordon Neate

Marketing
Ms A Bassett

How can anyone adequately review the best season in the history of any club? It is not easy but we can try. The club, which only a few years ago was supposed to become part of the 'Thames Valley Royals' as it faced a season of 4th Division football, suddenly rediscovered its pride and decided not to become part of some eccentric hybrid located 'out in the sticks' and the extent of their revival was finally revealed last season, when within some 20 weeks the only question being asked in 3rd Division circles was 'Who is going to be second?'

By then a club called Reading had played 24 League games with only two draws and two defeats on their record plus a massive 20 wins and a points total of 62. The first 13 matches had been won — a League record — and defeat was only tasted for the first time in the 15th match at Bury (0-3). It was not surprising that subsequent form fell away slightly but even so well over half the games were won for a final points total of 94. The title had been earned in style with an effort notable more for consistency and perseverance in each game than for any really spectacular wins — 4-2 at home to Chesterfield being the highest score. Just to prove that champions are never perfect a visit to Walsall on February 1st provided an 'anti' scoreline of 0-6!

Amidst those 13 early victories in the League appeared two Milk cup games against Bournemouth, who won the Elm Park match (3-1) and added two more goals at home for an aggregate of five goals to one! The FA Cup run was much longer with a nasty match against Wealdstone at home (won by a lone goal) being followed by a win against Hereford at home (2-0) and a Third Round tie against Huddersfield, which was won by a Trevor Senior goal in extra-time (2-1) after the away match was drawn with no scoring. Bury brought an end to all that (as they had done to the unbeaten record earlier) by scoring three unchallenged goals at Gigg Lane after another no-scoring affair at Elm Park. The Freight Rover Trophy ended when the campaign started with a visit from Orient bringing victory to the visitors (3-0).

So how will Reading under Ian Branfoot fare in the 2nd Division? Their attack even with the free-scoring Trevor Senior (27 League goals) may find it difficult in the 2nd Division; another striker in needed. The defence has mostly been sound with Westwood good in goal and consistent defenders in Hicks (the captain), Richardson, Wood and Williams. Beavon, Horrix and Peters were also good performers, but again Mr. Branfoot might look for another player or two to strengthen the challenge.

It will be much harder, but the team must be confident — and that counts for a lot.   WLM

Back Row L to R: Gary Peters, Steve Wood, Robert Bassett, Martin Hicks, Gary Westwood, Trevor Senior, Paul Canonville. **Middle Row:** Glen Hunter (Physio), Steve Head, Andy Rogers, Colin Balie, Terry Hurlock, Brian Roberts, Jerry Williams, Dean Horrix. **Front Row:** Stuart Beavon, Mark White, Ian Banfoot, Kevin Bremner, Steve Richardson.

READING

DIVISION THREE: CHAMPIONS   FA CUP: 4th ROUND   **MILK CUP:** 1st ROUND

MATCH	DATE		COMPE-TITION	VENUE	OPPONENTS	RESULT		HALF TIME	L'GUE POS'N	GOALSCORERS/GOAL TIMES	ATTEN-DANCE
1	A	17	CL	H	Blackpool	W	1-0	0-0		Williams 83	3,190
2		21	MC1/1	H	AFC Bournemouth	L	1-3	0-0		Rogers 63	2,614
3		24	CL	A	Plymouth Argyle	W	1-0	0-0	5	Senior 23	(4,261)
4		26	CL	H	Bristol Rovers	W	3-2	1-1	1	Bater (og) 40, Hicks 60, Horrix 72	3,529
5		31	CL	A	Cardiff City	W	3-1	1-0	1	Senior 3 (6, 76, 86)	(3,539)
6	S	3	MC1/2	A	AFC Bournemouth	L	0-2	0-0			(2,590)
7		7	CL	H	Walsall	W	2-1	1-0	1	Brazier (og) 22, Senior 51	3,573
8		14	CL	A	Rotherham United	W	2-1	1-0	1	Rogers 14, White 83	(3,076)
9		17	CL	A	Brentford	W	2-1	1-1	1	Peters 41, Senior 88	(6,351)
10		21	CL	H	Swansea City	W	2-0	1-0	1	Horrix 6, Senior 78	5,126
11		28	CL	A	Doncaster Rovers	W	1-0	0-0	1	White 77	(4,012)
12	O	2	CL	H	Chesterfield	W	4-2	1-0	1	Senior 3 (39, 59, 66), Williams 83	5,946
13		5	CL	H	Bolton Wanderers	W	1-0	1-0	1	Wood 10	8,000
14		12	CL	A	Newport County	W	2-0	1-0	1	Beavon 20, Bremner 65	(6,449)
15		19	CL	A	Lincoln City	W	1-0	1-0	1	Senior 41	(4,007)
16		23	CL	H	Wolverhampton W.	D	2-2	0-1	1	Bremner 60, Senior 63	11,500
17		26	CL	A	Bury	L	1-3	0-2	1	Rogers 88	(3,967)
18	N	2	CL	H	Wigan Athletic	W	1-0	1-0	1	Williams 35	5,378
19		6	CL	H	Notts County	W	3-1	2-0	1	Bremner 28, 51, Senior 44	6,776
20		9	CL	A	York City	W	1-0	1-0	1	Bremner 18	(6,045)
21		16	FAC1	H	Wealdstone	W	1-0	0-0		Horrix (pen) 58	7,169
22		23	CL	H	Darlington	L	0-1	0-1	1		5,239
23		30	CL	A	Derby County	D	1-1	1-0	1	Gilkes 32	(16,140)
24	D	7	FAC2	H	Hereford United	W	2-0	1-0		Senior 23, Horrix 71	6,096
25		14	CL	H	Bristol City	W	1-0	0-0	1	Gilkes 86	5,565
26		21	CL	H	Plymouth Argyle	W	4-3	0-2	1	Horrix pen 65, Senior 79, 80, Bremner 83	8,512
27		26	CL	A	AFC Bournemouth	W	1-0	0-0	1	Horrix 66	(6,105)
28		28	CL	A	Bristol Rovers	W	2-0	1-0	1	Senior 15, Rogers 64	(7,555)
29	J	1	CL	H	Gillingham	L	1-2	1-1	1	Horrix 16	10,665
30		4	FAC3	A	Huddersfield Town	D	0-0	0-0			(9,875)
31		11	CL	H	Cardiff City	D	1-1	0-0	1	Bremner 80	6,784
32		13	FAC3R	H	Huddersfield Town	W	2-1†	1-1		Senior 18, 109	8,726
33		18	CL	A	Blackpool	D	0-0	0-0			(5,295)
34		21	FRT	H	AFC Bournemouth	L	0-5	0-2			(1,974)
35		25	FAC4	H	Bury	D	1-1	0-1		Senior 63	9,495
36		28	FAC4R	A	Bury	L	0-3	0-2			(5,527)
37	F	1	CL	A	Walsall	L	0-6	0-2	1		(5,113)
38		22	CL	A	Swansea City	W	3-2	1-1	1	Senior 4, Beavon 48, 50	(4,965)
39	M	4	CL	A	Chesterfield	W	4-3	1-2	1	Senior 29, 79, Peters 51, Williams 62	2,428)
40		6	FRT	H	Orient	L	0-3	0-2			1,403
41		8	CL	A	Bolton Wanderers	L	0-2	0-0	1		(4,903)
42		12	CL	H	Lincoln City	L	0-2	0-0	1		4,792
43		15	CL	H	Newport County	W	2-0	0-0	1	Wood 46, Hicks 82	4,783
44		19	CL	H	Rotherham United	W	2-1	0-1	1	Wood 76, Senior 89	4,970
45		22	CL	H	Bury	W	2-0	1-0	1	Senior 3, Horrix (pen) 66	5,347
46		29	CL	A	Gillingham	L	0-3	0-1	1		(5,710)
47		31	CL	H	Bournemouth	L	1-2	1-0	1	Senior 14	7,122
48	A	5	CL	A	Notts County	D	0-0	0-0	1		(3,711)
49		8	CL	A	Wolverhampton W.	W	3-2	0-1	1	Rogers 70, 78, White 75	(4,467)
50		12	CL	H	York City	D	0-0	0-0	1		6,133
51		16	CL	H	Brentford	W	3-1	1-0	1	Senior 36, 66, Wood 69	6,635
52		19	CL	A	Darlington	D	0-0	0-0	1		(3,838)
53		22	CL	A	Wigan Athletic	L	0-1	0-0	1		(6,056)
54		26	CL	H	Derby County	W	1-0	0-0	1	Senior 64	12,266
55	M	3	CL	A	Bristol City	L	0-3	0-3	1		(7,814)
56		5	CL	H	Doncaster Rovers	W	2-0	0-0	1	Senior 51, 82	8,168

Best Home League Attendance: 12,266 v Derby County 26/4   Smallest: 3,190 v Blackpool 17/8   Av Home Att: 6,521

Goal Scorers: Compared with 84-85: +3,056

League (67): Senior 27, Bremner 7, Horrix 6 (2 pen), Rogers 5, Williams 4, Wood 4, Beavon 3, White 3, Gilkes 2, Hicks 2, Peters 2, Opponents 2

Milk Cup (1): Rogers 1
FA Cup (6): Senior 4, Horrix 2 (1 pen)
FRT (Nil):

† A.E.T

Westwood	Bailie	Richardson	Beavon	Hicks	Wood	Williams	White	Senior	Bremner	Rogers	Horrix	Burvill	Peters	Gilkes	Williams	Foster	Roberts	Staker (N.C)	Head (N.C)	Hurlock	Platnauer (L)	Reck (L)	Stevenson (L)	Referee	
	2	3	4	5	6	7	8	9	10*	11	12													M Dimblebee	1
	2	3	4	5	6	7	8*	9		11	10	12												**E Scales**	**2**
	2	3	4	5	6	7	8	9		10	11													R Milford	3
	2	3	4	5	6	7	8*	9		11	10	12												A Gunn	4
	2	3	4	5	6	7	8	9		11	10													P Vanes	5
	2	3	4	5	6	7	8	9		11	10													**K Cooper**	**6**
	2	3	4	5	6		8	9		11	10		7											R Groves	7
	2	3	4	5	6	12	8	9		11	10		7*											A Seville	8
	2	3	4	5	6	12	8	9		11	10*		7											J Moules	9
		3	4	5	6*	7	8	9	12	11	10		2											B Hill	10
		3	4	5	6	7	8	9		11	10		2											K Lupton	11
		3	4	5	6	7	8	9	12	11	10*		2											K Baker	12
		3	4	5	6	7*	8	9	12	11	10		2											G Ashby	13
3			4	5	6	7	8	9	12	11	10*		2											L Shapter	14
		3	4	5	6	7	8	9		10	11		2											D Phillips	15
3			4	5	6	7	8	9	10*	11	12		2											M James	16
5		7	4	3	6			10	11	9		8	2											J Lovatt	17
		3	4	5	6	7	8	9		10	11		2											T Ward	18
		3	4	5	6	7*	8	9		10	11	12	2											M Bodenham	19
		3	4	5	6			9	10	8	7		2	11										K Breen	20
		3	4	5	6			9	10	8	7†		2	11										**A Gunn**	**21**
		3*	4	5	6			9	10	11	8	7	2	12										A Robinson	22
		3	4	5	6			9	10	7	8		2	11										T Borrett	23
12		3*	4	5	6			9	10	7	8		2	11										**B Stevens**	**24**
		3	4	5	6			9	10	7	8		2	11										I Hemley	25
		3	4	5	6			9	10	7	8	12	2	11*										D Axcell	26
		3	4	5	6			9	10	11	8	7	2											K Miller	27
		3	4	5	6			9	10	11	8	7	2											R Gifford	28
		3	4	5	6			9		10	8	7	2	10										J Bray	29
		3	4	5	6			9	10	11	8	7	2											**R Dilkes**	**30**
		3	4	5	6			9	10	8	7		2	11										M Reed	31
		3	4	5	6	2		9	10	8	7			11										**J Moules**	**32**
		3	4	5	6			9	10	11	8	7												M Heath	33
		3	4	5*	6						10*	8	7	11		1	2	9	12	12				**D Reeves**	**34**
12		3	4	5	6	7		9	10*	11	8		2											**K Baker**	**35**
10*		3	4	5	6	11		9		8	7		2	12										**K Baker**	**36**
		3	4	5	6			9		8	7		2	11*			12				10			N Wilson	37
		3	4	5	6			9		11*	8		2	12						7	10			N Butler	38
		3	4	5	6	12		9			8		2	11*						7	10			R Guy	39
			4	12		7		9			8*	3	5	11*		2	12	6		10				**M Cotton**	**40**
		3	4	5	6	11		9			8*		2	12						7	10			T Jones	41
		3	4	5	6		8	9			11		2							7	10			A Gunn	42
		3	4	5	6	7		9		11	8		2							10				R Nixon	43
		3		5*	6	7		9		11	8	12	2							10†		4		R Groves	44
	2	3			6	7		9		11	8		5							10		4		B Stevens	45
	2	3	4		6			9	10*		8		5	12				7						V Callow	46
		3	4		6			9	7	11	8		2							10			5	J Ashworth	47
		3	4		6	7	10	9		11	8		2										5	N Midgley	48
12		3	4		6		10	9		8*	11		2							7			5	J Key	49
	2	3	4		6	12	10	9		11	8*		5							7				D Reeves	50
	2*	3	4		6	12	10	9		11	8		5							7				T Holbrook	51
		3	4		6	2	10	9		11	8		5							7				K Breen	52
		3	4		6	2	10	9		11	8		5							7†				G Tyson	53
		3	4		6	2	10	9		11	8		5							7				L Robinson	54
		3	4		6	2	10	9		11	8		5							7				M James	55
		3	4		6	2	10	9		11	8		5							7				L Shapter	56
6	25	32	44	34	46	26	25	46	18	40	38	11	41	7						16	7	1	3	League Appearances	
1					5				4		3	5		2		1								Substitute Appearances	
2	2	2	2	2	2	2			2	2			2	0-1										Milk Cup Appearances	
3-2	4	6	6	6	3		6	5	2	6	5	5	3-1											FA Cup Appearances	
1		2	1-1	1	1		1	1	2	2	1	2	1	2	1-1	1-1	0-1				1			FR Trophy Appearances	

Players on Loan: Platnauer (Birmingham City), Reck (Oxford United), Stevenson (Swansea City)

Departures: Burvill (Aldershot), Crown (Cambridge Utd), Christie (Cardiff)

'THE ROYALS'

Formed: 1871
Turned Professional: 1895   **Ltd Co:** 1895

Previous Managers: 1923-6 Arthur Chadwick   1926-31 Angus Wylie   1931-5 Joe Smith
1935-9 Billy Butler   1939 Johnny Cochrane   1939 Joe Edelston   1947-52 Ted Drake
1952-5 Jack Smith   1955-63 Harry Johnston   1963-9 Roy Bentley   1969-72 Jack Mansell
1972-7 Charlie Hurley   1977-84 Maurice Evans
Honours: Div 3 Champions 1985-6   Div 3 (S) Champions 1925-6
Div 4 Champions 1978-9
League Career: Original Members Div 3 1920   Transferred to Div 3 (S) 1921
Promoted to Div 2 1925-6   Relegated to Div 3 (S) 1930-1   Transferred to Div 3 1958
Relegated to Div 4 1970-1   Promoted to Div 3 1975-6   Relegated to Div 4 1976-7
Promoted to Div 3 1978-9   Relegated to Div 4 1982-3   Promoted to Div 3 1983-4
Promoted to Div 2 1985-6
Colours: White shirts with blue shoulders and yellow and blue trim, blue shorts and stockings
Change Colours: All yellow
Reserves League: Football Combination   **Youth League:** S E Counties

---

CLUB RECORDS

Most Appearances for Club: Steve Death: Football League 471 + FA Cup 33 + League Cup 32 **Total 536**
Most Capped Player: Billy McConnell, 8, Northern Ireland   **For England:** Herbert Smith 4
Record Goalscorer in a Match: Arthur Bacon, 6 v Stoke City (h) 7-3 Div 2, 03.04.31
Record League Goalscorer in a Season: Ronnie Blackman, 39, Div 3 (S)   **In All Competitions:** Trevor Senior 41 (League 36, FA Cup 1, Milk Cup 4) 1983-4
Record League Goalscorer in a Career: Ronnie Blackman, 158   **In All Competitions:** Ronnie Blackman 166 (League 158 FA Cup 8) 1946-54
Record Transfer Fee Received: £170,000 from Chelsea for Kerry Dixon, July 1983
Record Transfer Fee Paid: £82,500 to Brentford for Terry Hurlock, Feb 1986
Best Performances: League: 14th Div 2 1926-7   **FA Cup:** Semi-Final 1927   **League/Milk Cup:** 4th Round 1965, 1966, 1978
Most League Points: 94 in Div 3, 1985-6   **Most League Goals:** 112, Div 3 (S), 1951-2
Record League Victory and Most Goals in a First Class Match: 10-2 v Crystal Palace, Div 3 (S), 4 Sept 1946
Most Goals Scored in a Cup Tie: 8-3 v Corinthians, 1st Round FA Cup, 1935
Record League Defeat: 1-8 v Burnley, Div 2, 13 Sept 1930
Oldest Player in League Match: J R Blandford
Youngest Player in League Match: Steve Hetzke 16 yrs 193 days
Most Consecutive Undefeated League Matches: 19 1973   **League Matches Without a Win:** 14 1927
Longest Run of Undefeated Home League Matches: 55 1933-36   **Away League Matches:** 11 1985
Longest Run Without Home League Win: 8 1954   **Away League Win:** 21 1952-53
Most Consecutive League Wins: 13 1985 (record for start of a season)   **Home League Wins:** 19 1931-32
Most Consecutive League Defeats: 6 1971   **Away League Wins:** 7 1951-52, 1985

Club Statistician for the Directory: David Downs

READING

PLAYERS NAME / Wt Birthdate	Honours	Birthplace / Transfers	Clubs	League	Milk Cup	FA Cup	Other Comps	League	Milk Cup	FA Cup	Other Comps
GOALKEEPERS											
ry Westwood 13.0 3.4.63	EY Div.3 '86	Barrow F	Ipswich Town (A) Reading	19	2	9	2				
DEFENDERS											
in Baillie 10.11 31.3.64	Div.3 '86	Belfast £22,500	Swindon Town (A) Reading	105+2 23+1	3 2	7 3+2	4 1	4			
rtin Hicks* 13.6 27.2.57	Div.4 '79 Div.3 '86	Stratford-on-Avon F £3,000	Stratford Town Reading (N/C) Charlton Athletic Reading	288+1	18	19	3+1	14			
ry Peters 11.12 3.8.54	Div.3 '86	Carshalton F F F F F	Guildford Aldershot (A) Reading Fulham Wimbledon Aldershot Reading	150+6 57+4 83 17 58+1	15 4 2 6	9+1 4 3 5	1 1 1	3 7 5 4 1 2	1		
eve Richardson 10.3 11.2.62	Div.3 '86	Slough F	Southampton (A) Reading	150+1	7	10	2	1			
rry Williams 11.10 24.3.60	Div.3 '86	Didcot	Reading (A)	234+22	11	12	4	14		1	
eve Wood† 12.7 2.2.63	Div.3 '86	Bracknell	Reading (A)	186+1	8	14	3	8			
MIDFIELD											
uart Beavon 10.6 30.11.58	Div.3 '86	Wolverhampton F	Tottenham H (A) Notts County (L) Reading	3+1 6 241+8	0+1 12+	15	5	27	1	2	1
vin Bremner 12.3 7.9.52	Div.3, '86	Banff £40,000 £25,000	Keith Colchester United Birmingham City (L) Wrexham (L) Plymouth Argyle (L) Millwall Reading	89+6 3+1 4 5 58+1	5+2 4	10 2	4	31 1 1 1 21	3	2	
rry Hurlock 13.2 22.9.58	Div.3 '86	Hackney £6,000	Leytonstone Brentford Reading	180 16	17	17	3	18	2	2	1 3
ark White 11.12 26.10.58	Div.4 '79 Div.3 '86	Sheffield F	Sheffield United (A) Reading	254+6	16+1	12+1	3	9		1	
FORWARDS											
ul Canoville 11.0 4.3.62	Div.2 '84	Hillingdon £2,000 £50,000	Hillingdon Borough Chelsea Reading	53+26	12+6	2+3		10	3	1	
chael Gilkes 10.10 20.7.65		Hackney F	Leicester City Reading	15+8		3+2	3+1	4			
an Horrix 10.8 21.11.61	Div.3 '86	Taplow Player Exchange £11,000	Millwall (A) Gillingham Reading	65+7 7+7 120+3	5+1 6	3 8	5	19 33	3	3	
ian Roberts 3.2.67		Windsor	Reading	0+5			1+1				
dy Rogers 10.0 1.12.56	Div.3 '86	Chatteris F F £50,000	Chatteris Town Peterborough United Hampton Southampton Plymouth Argyle Reading	25+4 0+5 159+1	3 9	17	5+1	1 15		3	1
evor Senior 12.8 28.11.61	Div.3 '86	Dorchester £35,000 £30,000	Dorchester Town Portsmouth Aldershot (L) Reading	11 10 122	0+2 6	11	4 3	2 7 85	5	9	

ADDITIONAL CONTRACT PROFESSIONALS

APPRENTICES

NON-CONTRACT PLAYERS
aren Bailey, Steve Head, Neville John, John Staker, Robert Bassett

Record Attendance: 33,042 v Brentford, FA Cup Round 5, 19 Feb 1978

Smallest Home Attendance for a First Class Match: 1,713 v Preston North End, Div 3, 1984/5

Record Receipts: £30,834.50 v Derby Co., Div 3, 1985/6

Season Tickets: Stand A & E: £85.00, £65.00 (juveniles/OAP), B & D £100.00 & £80.00, 'C' £110.00 & £95.00. Ground: £55.00 (adults), £42 (juveniles/OAP)

Coronettes Club: £70.00 (adults), £50 (under 14), juniors must be accompanied by an adult

Executive Box Season Tickets: None

Cost of Stand Tickets: A & E: £4.50, B & D £5.00, C £6.00; **Terraces:** £3.00 (adult) £2.00 (junior/OAP). Juveniles and OAPs can only sit in 'E' stand

Match and Ticket Information: Stand tickets bookable 14 days in advance of match

Car Parking: Space for 300 cars in Norfolk Road and Tilehurst Road

Nearest Railway Station: Reading (0734 595911) and bus or Reading West (10 minutes walk)

How to get to the ground

From North: From Oxford use A423, A4074 and A4155 and cross railway bridge into Reading, then follow signs Newbury A4 into Castle Hill, then turn right into Tilehurst Road. In

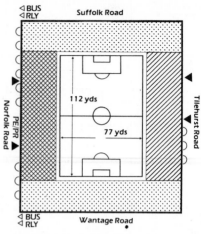

0.7m turn right into Cranbury Road, then turn left then take 2nd left into Norfolk Road for Reading FC
From East: Use Motorway M4 until junction 10, leave Motorway and use A329 and A4 into Reading. Follow signs Newbury into Bath Road. Over railway bridge then take 3rd turning on right into Liebenrood Road. At end turn left then right into Waverley Road, and turn right into Norfolk Road for Reading FC
From South: Use A33 into Reading then follow signs Newbury A4 into Bath Road. Over railway bridge then take 3rd turning on right into Liebenrood Road. At end turn left then right into Waverley Road and turn right into Norfolk Road for Reading FC
From West: Use Motorway M4 until junction 12, then leave Motorway and follow signs Reading A4. In 3.3m turn left into Liebenrood Road. At end turn left then right into Waverley Road and turn right into Norfolk Road for Reading FC

Price of 1986-7 Programme: 50p
Number of Pages: 32
Subscriptions: Rates obtainable from club

Local Newspapers: Reading Evening Post, Reading Chronicle

Local Radio Station: Radio 210

ROCHDALE

Division 4

President
Mrs L Stoney

Chairman
T Cannon

Directors
D F Kilpatrick, (Vice-Chairman)
G Morris
C D Walkden
W A C Dromsfield

Secretary
M Davies (0706 44648/9)

Assistant Secretary
T Nichol

Manager
Vic Halom

Reserve Team Manager
B Taylor

Commercial Manager
B Johnson (0706 44648)

A season which promised so much and almost ended in disaster. On September 7th Rochdale beat Peterborough at Spotland and went to the top of the 4th Division. The four wins and a draw represented the club's best ever start to a season. Eight months to the day later and Rochdale entered the last game of the season, ironically against the same Peterborough side, needing a point to avoid the bottom four. A draw, and safety, was achieved. The explanation for this turn round in fortunes was the miserly 17 points taken from 69 on offer in the second half of the season. Indeed if the season had started at Christmas Rochdale would have been anchored at the foot of the League. Responsibility for this decline was partly the distraction of the FA Cup. After exciting home wins over Darlington and Scunthorpe the 'Dale' finally fell to the mighty Manchester United in a twice-postponed 3rd Round tie at Old Trafford. To the dismay of the supporters the directors chose to spend the £40,000 from these cup ties to pay off debts (which would have had to be settled anyway) and promotion chances, still alive in the New Year, soon faded. The Milk Cup exit at the hands of Wrexham and a 6-0 thrashing at Wigan prevented any progress in the other cups. However some consolation for the faithful fans came in an undefeated home run until the end of January, first ever wins at Torquay and Colchester (indeed the only wins on their travels), and a post war club record of 31 goals from Steve Taylor. Nevertheless in the end it was very much a case of "as you were" at Spotland.   Stephen Birch

Back Row L to R: Trevor Jones (Trainer), Keith Hicks, Dave Grant, Carl Hudson, Ian Johnson, Keith Welch, Dave Redfern, Simon Gibson, Peter Shearer, John Bramhall, Alan Young, Brian Taylor (Reserve Team Coach). **Middle Row:** Shaun Reid, Neil Mills, Steve Taylor, Vic Halom (Manager), Graham Hurst, Peter Cunning, John Seasman. **Front Row:** Lee Chadwick, Carl Hallam, Mark Hunt, David Mycock, Jason Smart, Thomas McKenna.

ROCHDALE

DIVISION FOUR: 18th　　　　　**FA CUP:** 3rd ROUND　　　　　**MILK CUP:** 1st ROUND

MATCH	DATE		COMPE-TITION	VENUE	OPPONENTS	RESULT		HALF TIME	L'GUE POS'N	GOALSCORERS/GOAL TIMES	ATTEN-DANCE
1	A	17	CL	H	Aldershot	W	2-0	1-0		Taylor 25, Diamond (pen) 82	1,069
2		20	MC1/1	A	Wrexham	L	0-4	0-3			(1,751)
3		24	CL	A	Torquay United	W	2-1	1-0	2	Compton (og) 32, Moore 46	(1,247)
4		26	CL	H	Stockport County	W	4-0	3-0	2	Moore (pen) 19, Seasman 26, Taylor 33, Heaton 62	2,070
5		31	CL	A	Port Vale	D	1-1	1-0	2	Taylor 37	(3,043)
6	S	3	MC1/2	H	Wrexham	W	2-1	1-0		Cooke 30, Taylor 68	1,251
7		7	CL	H	Peterborough United	W	2-1	2-0	1	Gamble 20, 43	2,600
8		13	CL	A	Hartlepool United	L	0-2	0-1	3		(1,942)
9		21	CL	A	Burnley	L	0-1	0-1	6		(4,177)
10		28	CL	H	Northampton Town	W	3-2	2-1	5	Heaton 30, Moore 33, Grant 64	1,954
11	O	1	CL	A	Orient	L	0-5	0-4			(2,650)
12		5	CL	A	Swindon Town	L	0-4	0-3	10		(3,086)
13		12	CL	H	Crewe Alexandra	W	1-0	0-0	9	Taylor 61	1,776
14		19	CL	H	Preston North End	D	1-1	0-0	10	Taylor 68	2,527
15		23	CL	A	Hereford United	D	2-2	0-2	10	Taylor 79, 81	(2,761)
16		26	CL	A	Tranmere Rovers	L	0-2	0-1	11		(1,552)
17	N	2	CL	H	Wrexham	W	3-2	1-0	10	Taylor (pen) 17 (pen) 59, Gamble 72	1,600
18		5	CL	H	Exeter City	D	1-1	0-0		Taylor (pen) 70	1,243
19		8	CL	A	Colchester United	W	1-0	0-0	10	McMahon 70	(2,624)
20		16	FAC1	H	Darlington	W	2-1	0-0		Taylor 77, 83	2,153
21		23	CL	A	Scunthorpe United	W	1-0	0-0	8	Taylor 54	1,430
22		30	CL	A	Mansfield Town	L	2-3	0-2	8	Taylor 68, Hicks 83	(2,586)
23	D	7	FAC2	A	Scunthorpe United	D	2-2	0-1		Taylor (pen) 50, 83	(2,868)
24		10	FAC2R	H	Scunthorpe United	W	2-1	1-1		Taylor 13, Moore 75	5,066
25		21	CL	H	Torquay United	W	5-0	1-0	9	Taylor 29,60, Moore 75,89, Thompson 76	1,685
26		26	CL	A	Halifax Town	D	1-1	0-0	9	Taylor 68	(2,253)
27		28	CL	A	Stockport County	L	0-3	0-1	9		(4,005)
28	J	1	CL	H	Cambridge United	W	2-1	1-1	9	Moore 7, Cooke 58	2,046
29		9	FAC3	H	Manchester United	L	0-2	0-1			(38,500)
30		11	CL	H	Port Vale	D	3-3	2-0	9	Seasman 21, Gamble 43, Taylor (pen) 87	2,445
31		18	CL	A	Aldershot	L	1-2	0-1	9	Johnson S 59	(1,375)
32		20	FRT	H	Chester City	W	1-0	0-0		Butler (og) 63	1,164
33		25	CL	H	Hartlepool United	L	0-2	0-0	11		2,301
34		28	FRT	A	Wigan Athletic	L	0-6	0-4			(2,106)
35	F	4	CL	H	Hereford United	D	1-1	1-1	11	Moore 27	1,081
36		8	CL	A	Preston North End	D	1-1	1-1	12	Taylor 36	(3,266)
37		15	CL	A	Chester City	D	1-1	0-1	11	Taylor 47	(3,232)
38	M	1	CL	A	Northampton Town	L	0-1	0-0	12		(2,146)
39		8	CL	H	Swindon Town	L	1-2	0-0	15	Moore 55	1,989
40		11	CL	A	Wrexham	L	0-2	0-0	15		(1,378)
41		15	CL	H	Crewe Alexandra	L	2-4	1-1	15	McMahon 12, Booth (og) 59	(1,683)
42		18	CL	A	Burnley	W	1-0	0-0	13	Taylor (pen) 61	2,597
43		22	CL	H	Tranmere Rovers	D	1-1	1-1	13	McMahon (pen) 62	1,558
44		28	CL	A	Cambridge United	L	0-1	0-1	16		(1,992)
45		31	CL	H	Halifax Town	W	1-0	0-0	14	Moore 85	1,931
46	A	4	CL	A	Exeter City	L	0-2	0-2	15		(1,713)
47		12	CL	H	Colchester United	D	3-3	1-1	15	Baker (og) 32, Taylor 50, (pen) 74	1,182
48		18	CL	A	Scunthorpe United	L	1-3	1-0	20	Heaton 17	(1,406)
49		21	CL	H	Southend United	W	2-1	2-0	15	Taylor 5, Thompson 44	1,060
50		26	CL	H	Mansfield Town	D	1-1	1-0	15	Taylor 16	1,936
51		29	CL	H	Chester City	L	1-2	0-1	20	Taylor (pen) 60	1,963
52	M	2	CL	A	Southend United	L	0-5	0-3	22		(1,153)
53		5	CL	H	Orient	L	1-4	0-1	22	Taylor 77	1,299
54		7	CL	A	Peterborough United	D	1-1	1-0	18	Heaton 56	(1,592)

Best Home League Attendance: 2,600 v Peterborough Utd 7/9　　　Smallest: 1,060 v Southend Utd 2/5　　　Av Home Att: 1,797

Goal Scorers:　　　　　　　　　　　　　　　　　　　　　　　　　　Compared with 84-85: +343

League (57): Taylor 25 (7 pens), Moore 9 (1 pen), Gamble 4, Heaton 4, McMahon 3 (1 pen), Seasman 2, Thompson 2, Cooke 1, Diamond 1 (pen), Grant 1, Hicks 1, Johnson S 1, Opponents 3

Milk Cup (2): Cooke 1, Taylor 1
FA Cup (6): Taylor 5 (1 pen), Moore 1
FRT Cup (1): Opponents 1

Johnston I	Grant	Reid	Cooke	Hicks	McMahon	Taylor	Moore	Diamond	Heaton	Chambers (NC)	Seasman	Ashworth	Gamble	Hildersley (NC)	Tong (NC)	McCluskie	Haire (L)	Thompson	Towner (NC)	Johnson S (L)	Mossman	Carney (L)	Smart (NC)	Measham (L)	Referee	
2	3	4	5	6*	7	8	9	10	11	12															D Phillips	1
6		4*	5		7	8	9	10	2	3	11	12													**P Vanes**	2
6			5		4	8	9	7	2	3	10		11												K Barratt	3
2	4		6		5	8	9		3	10	7		11												G Tyson	4
2	6		5		4	8	9		7	3	10		11			12									K Cooper	5
2	6		5		4	8	9	12	7	3*	10		11												**M Peck**	6
2	6		5		4	8	9		7	3	10		11												J Lovatt	7
2	6		5		4	8	9	12	7*	3	10		11												G Aplin	8
5	6				4	8	9	7*	2	3	10		11	12											N Ashley	9
2	6		5		4	8	9		7	3	10		11*		12										G Courtney	10
2*	6		5		4	8	9†		7	3	10		11		12										J Martin	11
2	6		5		4	8	9		7	3	10		11*			12									J Deakin	12
2	3*		5	6	4	8	9		7		10		11			12									J Key	13
3		5	6	4	8						2	10	11			9*		7	12						R Bridges	14
3	6		5	4	8			9*			2	10	11					7	12						V Callow	15
3	6		5	4	8						2	10*	11					7	12						C Seel	16
3	6		5	4	8	9		12			2	10	11					7*							K Lupton	17
3		5	6	4	8	9		7			2	10	11												R Nixon	18
3		5	6	4	8	9		7			2	10	11												I Hemley	19
3		5	6	4	8	9	7				2	10	11												**N Ashley**	20
3		5	6	4	8	9	7*				2	10	11						12						T Holbrook	21
12	3	5	6	4	8	9					2	10	11*					7							G Ashby	22
	3	5	6	4	8	9					2	10	11*					12	7						**D Phillips**	23
	3	5	6	4	8	9					2	10						11	7						**D Phillips**	24
	3	5	6	4	8	9					2	10						7	11*	12					D Hutchinson	25
	3	5	6	4	8	9					2*	10						7	11	12					A Saunders	26
	3	5†	6	4	8	9					2	10						7	11*	12					K Hackett	27
12	3	5	6*	4	8	9					2	10						7	11						M Heath	28
	3	5	6	4	8	9					2	10						7	12	11*					**V Callow**	29
2	3		6		8		5		4			10	11					7	9						K Redfearn	30
4	3		6		8		5					10	12					7	9*	11					J Moules	31
3	5		6*	4	8	9					2	10*	12			12		7		11					**R Guy**	32
10	3		6		8	9					2	12						7*		11	5				J McAulay	33
10	3	8		6	4						2							7		9*	11	5			**D Allison**	34
2	3	10		6	4	8	9											7			11	5			C Seel	35
2	3	10		6		8	9	4				7						7			11	5			C Trussell	36
2	3	10		6	4	8	9					7									11	5			M Peck	37
2	3		5	6	4	8	9		10		7*		12					7			11				R Groves	38
2	3		5	6	4	8	9		10			12	7*					7			11				T Holbrook	39
2	3		5	6*	4	8	9		10			11	12					7*							M Scott	40
2	3		5	6*	4	8	9		10			11	12					7							R Guy	41
2	3		5		4	8	9		10			11						7					6		D Allison	42
2	3		5		4		9	8	10			11						7						6	G Tyson	43
2	3		5			8	9	4	10			11						7						6	N Butler	44
2	3		5			8	9	4	10			11						7						6	R Bridges	45
2	3		5			8	9	4	10†			11						7						6	D Hedges	46
2	3		5	6		8		4	10			9						7						11	J Bray	47
3			5	6		8	9	11			10							4	7					2	J Worrall	48
3			5	6		8	9	2	10				11					7						4	M Reed	49
2			5	6*		8	9	3	10				11			12		7						4	A Seville	50
2	6	12	5*			8	9	3	10				11					7						4	P Willis	51
12	3	5		6		8	9	2	10							11*		7						4	C Downey	52
12	3	10*		6		8	9	2					11			4		7						5	J Key	53
3	5	10		6		8	9	2					11					7						4	T Mills	54

Johnston I	Grant	Reid	Cooke	Hicks	McMahon	Taylor	Moore	Diamond	Heaton	Chambers (NC)	Seasman	Ashworth	Gamble	Hildersley (NC)	Tong (NC)	McCluskie	Haire (L)	Thompson	Towner (NC)	Johnson S (L)	Mossman	Carney (L)	Smart (NC)	Measham (L)		
6	35	41	7	34	31	32	45	43	7	43	9	30	22	12		10	3	24	4	3	8	4	1	12	League Appearances	
4	1		2		1						2			1		3	4	2	4		3	1	3		Substitute Appearances	
2	1	1	2		2	2	1+1	2	2	2	0+1	1													Milk Cup Appearances	
4		4	4	4	4	1	4		4		2							2+1	2+1	1					FA Cup Appearances	
2	2	1		2	2	1	1		2		1		0+1		0+1	2		1	2	1					FR Trophy Appearances	

yers on Loan: Haire (Darlington), Johnson (Bristol City), Carney (Darlington), Measham (Huddersfield)

partures: Tong (NC), Chambers (NC), Diamond (Halifax), Towner (NC), Hildersley (Preston N E)

'THE DALE'

Formed: 1907
Turned Professional: 1907   **Ltd Co:** 1910

Previous Managers: 1920-1 William Brodshaw   1921-2 No appointment made
1922-3 Thomas C Wilson   1923-30 Jack Peart   1930 C Martin (caretaker)
1930-1 William Smith Cameron   1931-2 Vacant   1932-4 Herbert Hopkinson
1934-5 William H Smith   1935-7 Ernest Nixon (caretaker)   1937-8 Sam Jennings   1938-52 Ted Good
1952 Jack Warner   1953-8 Harry Catterick   1958-60 Jack Marshall
1960-7 Tony Collins   1967-8 Bob Stokoe   1968-70 Len Richley   1970-3 Dick Connor
1973-6 Walter Joyce   1976-7 Brian Green   1977-8 Mike Ferguson   1978-9 Peter Madden (caretaker
1979 Doug Collins   1979-80 Bob Stokoe   1980-3 Peter Madden   1983-4 Jimmy Greenhoff
Honours: None
League Career: Elected to Div 3 (N) 1921   Transferred to Div 3 1958
Relegated to Div 4 1958-9   Promoted to Div 3 1968-9   Relegated to Div 4 1973-4
Colours: White shirts, blue shorts, blue stockings
Change Colours: Blue shirts, white shorts, blue stockings
Reserves League: Lancashire League

CLUB RECORDS

Most Appearances for Club: Graham Smith: Football League 316 + 1 + FA Cup 15 + League Cup 13 **Total 344 + 1 su**
Most Capped Player: No Rochdale player has won an international cap
Record Goalscorer in a Match: Tommy Tippett, 6 v Hartlepool United (a), 8-2, Div 3 (N) 21.04.1930
Record League Goalscorer in a Season: Albert Whitehurst, 44   **In All Competitions:** Albert Whitehurst, 46 (League
44 + FA Cup 2) in 43 games, 1926-7
Record League Goalscorer in a Career: Reg Jenkins, 119   **In All Competitions:** Reg Jenkins, 130 (League 119 + FA
Cup 5 + League Cup 6) 1964-73
Record Transfer Fee Received: £40,000 + player from Norwich City for David Cross, Oct 1971
Record Transfer Fee Paid: £15,000 to Aldershot for Les Lawrence, Aug 1984
Best Performances: League: 9th Div 3 1969-70, Runners-Up Div 3 (N), 1923-4, 1926-7   **FA Cup:** 1914-18 Last 32, 4th
Round Replay 1970-1   **League/Milk Cup:** Runners-Up 1962 (4th Div Record)
Most League Points: 62, Div 3 (N), 1923-4   **Most League Goals:** 105, Div 3 (N), 1926-7
Record League Victory: 8-1 v Chesterfield, Div 3 (N), 18 Dec 1926
Most Goals in a First Class Match: Record League victory (above), 8-2 v Crook Town (h) 1st Round FA Cup, 26 Nov 192
8-2 v Hartlepool United (a) Div 3 (N), 22 April 1930
Record League Defeat: 1-9 v Tranmere Rovers, Div 3 (N), 25 Dec 1931   0-8 v Wrexham (a) Div 3, 28 Sept 1929
Oldest Player in League Match:
Youngest Player in League Match:
Most Consecutive Undefeated League Matches: 20 1923-24   **League Matches Without a Win:** 28 1931-32
Longest Run of Undefeated Home League Matches: 34 1923-25   **Away League Matches:** 9 1923-24
Longest Run Without Home League Win: 16 1931-32   **Away League Win:** 37 1977-78
Most Consecutive League Wins: 8 1969   **Home League Wins:** 16 1926-27
Most Consecutive League Defeats: 17 1931-32   **Away League Wins:** 4 1923-24, 1926, 1946,
1947, 1969

Club Statistician for the Directory: S Birch

PLAYERS NAME Wt Birthdate	Honours	Birthplace Transfers	Clubs	APPEARANCES League	Milk Cup	FA Cup	Other Comps	GOALS League	Milk Cup	FA Cup	Other Comps
GOALKEEPERS											
id Redfern 13.8 8.11.62		Sheffield F	Sheffield Wednesday Rochdale	65	2	4	2				
DEFENDERS											
n Bramhall 13.6 20.11.56		Warrington £10,000	Tranmere Rovers Bury Chester (L) Rochdale	164+6 165+2 4	16 8	8 9	3	7 17	1 2	1	
Cooke* 12.7 15.2.55		Dominica W.I. £40,000 £50,000 £25,000 £10,000 F	Bradford City (A) Peterborough United Oxford United Exeter City Bradford City Rochdale	184+20 18 71+1 17 61+1 74	10+1 5 3 6 4	15 2 1 4 5	2	62 5 13 3 6 4	5 2 1	4 4	
id Grant 12.8 2.6.60		Sheffield	Sheffield Wednesday Oxford United Chesterfield (L) Cardiff City Rochdale	132+1 24 7 25 42	11 1	4+2 4	2	4 1	1		
h Hicks 13.2 9.8.54	EY Div.3 '74	Oldham F F	Oldham Athletic (A) Hereford United Rochdale	240+2 201 31	12 5	15 11 4	1 1 2	11 2 1			
Johnson 12.0 11.11.60		Oldham	Chadderton Rochdale	40+9	2						
er Shearer 11.8 4.2.67		Coventry F	Birmingham City (A) Rochdale	2+2	0+1						
ham Hurst 23.11.67		Oldham	Rochdale (YTS)	0+1							
MIDFIELD											
McMahon 12.0 7.10.64		Wells	Oldham Athletic (A) Rochdale	2 89+2	3	4	5	7			
un Reid 11.8 13.10.65		Huyton	Rochdale	44+3	2		3				
n Seasman 11.3 21.2.55		Liverpool £5,000 £10,000 £90,000 F F	Tranmere Rovers (A) Luton Town Millwall Rotherham United Cardiff City Chesterfield (L) Rochdale	15+2 7+1 157+1 93+7 10+2 8+2 38	16+1 7 4 2	11 4 4	1 1	35 25 2 1 2	5 1	1 1	
FORWARDS											
nie Moore 12.13 29.1.53	Div.3 '81	Liverpool £120,000 £100,000 £35,000 F	Tranmere Rovers Cardiff City Rotherham United Charlton Athletic Rochdale	248+1 54+2 124+1 60+2 43	18 2 9 2 2	12 2 5 4 4	1	72 6 51 13 9	4 2	1 1 1	
ve Taylor† 10.9 18.10.55	Div.2 '78 Div.3 '82	Royton £40,000 £50,000 £50,000 £35,000 F F F	Bolton Wanderers (A) Port Vale (L) Oldham Athletic Luton Town Mansfield Town Burnley Wigan Athletic Stockport County Rochdale	34+6 4 45+2 15+5 30+7 80+6 29+1 14 75	7 5 11+1 1 4 2	1 2 3 12 4 1 4	1 4	16 2 25 1 7 37 7 2 37	4 1 2 1	5 2 1 5	2
id Thompson 11.6 27.5.62		Manchester	Rochdale	148+5	6+1	9+2	6	13			

ADDITIONAL CONTRACT PROFESSIONALS
ence Conning, Carl Hudson, Neil Ashworth (M)

APPRENTICES

NON-CONTRACT PLAYERS
id Hallam, Carl Hughes, Jason Smart, Neal Tyndall, Sau Lau, David Fairclough, Gordon Raynor, Steven Watson, Michael Wood

Record Attendance: 24,231 v Notts County, FA Cup Round 2, 10 Dec 1949

Smallest Home Attendance for a First Class Match: 588 v Cambridge United, Div 3, 5 Feb 1974 (played on a Thursday afternoon during power cuts)

Record Receipts: £8,834 v Telford United, FA Cup Round 3, 7 Jan 1984

Season Tickets: Stand: £60.00 (£45 OAPs/Juv); Ground: £45.00 (£22.50 OAPs/Juv)

Executive Box Season Tickets: £100.00 Stand Seat. Car Park, Bar, Refreshments

Cost of Stand Tickets: Ground: £2.50 (£1.30 OAPs/Juv) **Terraces:**

Match and Ticket Information: Seats bookable in advance

Car Parking: At the Ground and in adjacent streets

Nearest Railway Station: Rochdale

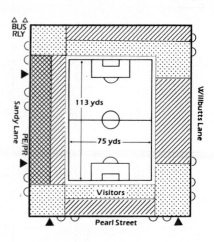

How to get to the ground

From North: Use A680 S.P. Rochdale then turn right into Willbutts Lane for Rochdale FC

From East and West: Use Motorway M62 until junction 20 then follow signs Rochdale. In 1.5m at roundabout take 2nd exit into Roch Valley Way and in 1.5m turn right into Willbutts Lane for Rochdale FC

Price of 1986-7 Programme: 40p
Number of Pages: 20
Subscriptions: Please contact club

Local Newspapers: Rochdale Observer, Manchester Evening News

Local Radio Stations: Radio Manchester, Radio Piccadilly

ROTHERHAM UNITED   Division 3

Chairman
S Wood

Vice-Chairman
G Humphries

Directors
C R Wright
J Layden

Secretary
N Darnill (0709 562434)

Manager
Norman Hunter

Assistant Manager/Physiotherapist
A B Claxton

Commercial Manager
Commercial Department (0709 562434)

The new manager worked hard in the close season to start the new campaign with a small first team squad and as might have been expected it took some time for the players to settle; it was not until November that any kind of run was put together. Then there were five successive wins including two in FA Cup games (Wolves by 6-0 and Burnley by 4-1 both at Millmoor) so that a relegation-threatened spot was cleared. An away win at Frickley United in January brought a 4th Round FA Cup place for the first time in 14 seasons.

This led to a match at Highbury where Arsenal won (5-1) before a crowd of 28,490 — the season's largest crowd. From then until the end of the season good home form with some free scoring brought a final, satisfactory position of 14th in the 3rd Division, which would have been better if away form had produced more commitment by all the players.

In the other two cup competitions there was elimination immediately from the Milk Cup in the first round against Sheffield United — the aggregate being 2-8. The Freight Rover Trophy with its final at Wembley brought more effort with elimination at the Northern Quarter-Final stage at Wigan (0-3); York City (0-0) and Hartlepool (3-0 at Millmoor) were the earlier victims.

Congratulations go to John Dungworth for being selected as Player of the Year — a well-merited award. His consistency and versatility is welcomed by the supporters, who do appreciate someone who earns his wage and is truly professional.

For the future is is heartening to note the performances of the nursery side Millers United and the Juniors, who operate in the Northern Intermediate League and Central League respectively. It is hoped that this is the way ahead — and up! — for Rotherham United.   Mike Smith

Back Row L to R: P. Chambers (Youth Team Manager), N. Pepper, J. Dungworth, K. Smith, K. O'Hanlon, T. Slack, M. Trusson, P. Crosby, B. Claxton (Assistant Manager). **Middle Row:** D. Pugh, D. Emerson, C. Douglas, N. Hunter (Manager), T. Simmons, T. Tynan (now Plymouth) M. Gooding. **Front Row:** K. Eley, M. Scott, A. Morris, R. Warburton, M. Ash.

ROTHERHAM UNITED

DIVISION THREE: 14th   **FA CUP:** 4th ROUND   **MILK CUP:** 1st ROUND   **FRT:** QUARTER-FINAL (North

MATCH	DATE		COMPE-TITION	VENUE	OPPONENTS	RESULT		HALF TIME	L'GUE POS'N	GOALSCORERS/GOAL TIMES	ATTEN-DANCE
1	A	17	CL	A	Bolton Wanderers	D	1-1	0-1		Trusson 85	(5,129)
2		20	MC1/1	H	Sheffield United	L	1-3	0-2		Emerson 80	9,087
3		24	CL	H	Lincoln City	W	1-0	0-0	7	Smith 80	3,356
4		27	CL	A	Chesterfield	L	0-2	0-0	14		(5,434)
5		31	CL	H	Bristol City	W	2-0	1-0	10	Forest 12, Tynan (pen) 56	3,134
6	S	3	MC1/2	A	Sheffield United	L	1-5	0-3		Birch 55	(7,486)
7		7	CL	A	Swansea City	L	0-1	0-0	13		(3,760)
8		14	CL	H	Reading	L	1-2	0-1	16	Simmons 86	3,076
9		17	CL	A	Walsall	L	1-3	1-2	18	Emerson 14	(4,861)
10		21	CL	H	Doncaster Rovers	W	2-1	0-0	15	Birch 19, Simmons 36	5,189
11		28	CL	A	Brentford	D	1-1	0-1	15	Gooding 87	(3,257)
12	O	1	CL	H	Cardiff City	W	3-0	2-0	12	Gooding 11, 81, Simmons 19	2,906
13		5	CL	H	Wolverhampton W.	L	1-2	1-1	15	Tynan 26	4,015
14		12	CL	A	Bristol Rovers	L	2-5	1-3	16	Tynan 26, Birch 63	(3,499)
15		19	CL	H	Plymouth Argyle	D	1-1	0-0	18	Tynan 85	2,942
16		22	CL	A	Newport County	D	0-0	0-0	18		(1,817)
17		26	CL	A	York City	L	1-2	1-1	19	Pugh 34	(4,444)
18	N	2	CL	H	Derby County	D	1-1	1-0	19	Trusson 20	6,030
19		6	CL	H	Gillingham	D	1-1	1-0	19	Birch 42	2,361
20		9	CL	A	Wigan Athletic	L	0-2	0-1	19		(3,084)
21		16	FAC1	H	Wolverhampton W.	W	6-0	2-0		Tynan 15, Simmons 44, Gooding 74, Birch 80, 82, Smith 86	3,507
22		23	CL	H	Bury	W	2-0	1-0	17	Tynan 7, Birch 89	3,335
23	D	7	FAC2	H	Burnley	W	4-1	1-0		Birch 33, Trusson 76, 83, Tynan 86	4,264
24		14	CL	H	Notts County	W	1-0	0-0	16	Birch (pen) 77	3,820
25		17	CL	A	AFC Bournemouth	W	2-1	2-0	12	Trusson 6, Tynan 12	(2,489)
26		22	CL	A	Lincoln City	D	0-0	0-0	12		(3,007)
27		26	CL	A	Darlington	D	2-2	0-0	13	Pugh 56, Gooding 65	(3,727)
28		28	CL	H	Chesterfield	L	1-2	0-1	14	Birch (pen) 67	4,816
29	J	1	CL	H	Blackpool	W	4-1	4-0	12	Gooding 15, Emerson 22, Dungworth 25, Simmons 44	4,200
30		4	FAC3	A	Frickley Athletic	W	3-1	2-0		Gooding 14, Pugh 31, Tynan 75	(5,932)
31		11	CL	A	Bristol City	L	1-3	0-2	13	Tynan 52	(6,672)
32		14	FRT	A	York City	D	0-0	0-0			(2,122)
33		18	CL	H	Bolton Wanderers	W	4-0	2-0	13	Tynan 24, 76, Trusson 32, Emerson 82	3,821
34		21	FRT	H	Hartlepool United	W	3-0	1-0		Emerson 36, Trusson 57, Pugh 89	1,309
35		25	FAC4	A	Arsenal	L	1-5	0-2		Tynan 77	(28,490)
36	F	1	CL	H	Swansea City	W	4-1	2-0	13	Tynan 3 (9, 12, 89), Gooding 78	2,932
37		4	CL	A	Newport County	D	0-0	0-0	13		2,975
38		15	CL	H	Wigan Athletic	W	3-0	1-0	11	Smith 7, Tynan 50, Birch 71	3,512
39		18	FRT QF N	A	Wigan Athletic	L	0-3	0-1			(2,597)
40	M	1	CL	H	Brentford	L	1-2	0-1	13	Gooding (pen) 85	3,268
41		8	CL	A	Wolverhampton W.	D	0-0	0-0	13		(2,838)
42		15	CL	H	Bristol Rovers	W	2-0	1-0	13	Birch 40, Emerson 70	2,734
43		19	CL	A	Reading	L	1-2	1-0	14	Birch (pen) 25	(4,970)
44		22	CL	H	York City	W	4-1	3-0	13	Smith 8, Birch 10, (pen) 13, Emerson 85	3,240
45		25	CL	A	Cardiff City	W	3-2	1-1	12	Birch 30, Simmons 75, 89	(1,863)
46		29	CL	A	Blackpool	L	1-2	0-0	13	Dungworth 77	(4,007)
47		31	CL	H	Darlington	L	1-2	0-1	13	Emerson 60	3,041
48	A	4	CL	A	Gillingham	L	0-3	0-3	13		(4,525)
49		8	CL	A	Plymouth Argyle	L	0-4	0-2	13		(13,034)
50		12	CL	H	Wigan Athletic	D	0-0	0-0	13		3,004
51		15	CL	A	Doncaster Rovers	D	0-0	0-0	13		(3,159)
52		19	CL	A	Bury	L	0-2	0-1	13		(2,166)
53		26	CL	H	Bournemouth	W	4-1	3-1	13	Trusson 25, Simmons 29, Gooding 44, Emerson 51	2,101
54	M	3	CL	A	Notts County	L	0-1	0-0	13		(3,213)
55		9	CL	A	Derby County	L	1-2	0-0	14	Trusson 79	(21,036)

Best Home League Attendance: 6,030 v Derby Co. 2/11   **Smallest:** 2,101 v Bournemouth 26/4   **Av Home Att:** 3,470

Goal Scorers: Compared with 84-85: −971

League (61):	Tynan 13 (2 pen), Birch 12 (4 pen), Gooding 8 (1 pen), Emerson 7, Simmons 7, Trusson 6, Smith 3, Dungworth 2, Pugh 2, Forest 1
Milk Cup (2):	Birch 1, Emerson 1
FA CUP (14):	Tynan 4, Birch 3, Gooding 2, Trusson 2, Pugh 1, Smith 1, Simmons 1
FRT (3):	Emerson 1, Pugh 1, Trusson 1

1985-86

O'Hanlon	Barnsley	Crosby	Trusson	Smith	Pickering	Birch	Gooding	Tynan	Dungworth	Emerson	Simmons	Forrest	Pugh	Martin (M)	Eley	Cowdrill (L)	Pepper	Horner (L)	Referee	
	2	3*	4	5	6	7	8	9	10	11	12								J Hough	1
			4	5	6	7*	8	9	3	11	10	2	12						**G Courtney**	2
			4	5	6	12	8*	9	3	11	10	2	7						R Guy	3
			4	5	6	12		9	3	11	10	2	7*	8					P Vanes	4
			4*	5	6	7	12	9	3	11	10	2		8					R Nixon	5
				5	6	7	4	9	3	11	10	2		8					**P Willis**	6
			4	5	6	7	12	9	3	11	10*	2		8					R Hamer	7
			4	5	6	7	12	9	3	11	10	2	8*						A Seville	8
			4	5	6	7	8	9	3	11	10	2							T Jones	9
			4	5	6	7	8	9	3	11	10			2					H Taylor	10
			4	5	6	7*	8	9	3	11	10	2	12						I Borrett	11
			4	5	6	7	8	9	3	11	10	2							C Trussell	12
			4	5	6	7	8*	9	3	11	10	2	12						N Wilson	13
			4	5	6	7	8*	9	3	11	10	2	12						D Vickers	14
			4	5	6	7	8*	9	3	11	10	2	12						I Hendrick	15
			4	5	6	7		9	3	11	10	2	8						D Reeves	16
			4	5	6	7	12	9*	3	11	10	2	8						A Saunders	17
			4	5	6	7	12		9	11*	10	2	8			3			F Roberts	18
			4	5	6	7		9	3	11	10	2	8						P Tyldesley	19
			4	5	6		8	9	10*	11	12	2	7			3			M Peck	20
				5	6	7	4	9	3	8	10	2	11						**A Robinson**	21
				5	6	7	4	9	3	8	10	2	11						M Scott	22
	2	10		5	6	7	4	9	3	8			11						**R Bridges**	23
	2	10		5	6	7	4	9	3	8			11						K Breen	24
	2	10		5	6	7	4	9	3	8			11						J Moules	25
	2	10		5	6	7	4	9	3	8			11						N Wilson	26
	2	10*		5	6	7	4	9	3	8		12	11						C Seel	27
	2	10		5	6	7	4*	9	3	8		12	11						G Tyson	28
	2			5	6	7	4	9	3	8	10		11*		12				V Callow	29
	2	10		5	6	7	4	9	3	8			11						**R Nixon**	30
	2			5*	6	7	4	9	3	8	10		11		12				H King/L Loosemoore	31
	2	3			6	7	4	9	5	8			11		10				**A Robinson**	32
	2	3	10		6	7*	4	9	5	8			11		12				J Bray	33
	2	10*		5	6		4	9	3	8		12	11	7					**H Taylor**	34
	2	10		5	6	7	4	9	3	8			11						**A Seville**	35
	2	10		5	6	7	4	9	3	8			11						D Scott	36
	2	10		5	6	7	4	9	3	8			11						J Lovatt	37
	2	10		5	6	7	4	9	3	8			11						J Ashworth	38
	2	10		5	6	7	4	9	3	8			11						**K Baker**	39
	2	10		5	6	7*	4	9	3	8		12	11						K Lupton	40
	2	3	10		6	7			5	8	9		11			4			Alan Robinson	41
	2	3		5	6	7		9*		8	10		11	12		4			A Saunders	42
	2	3		5	6	7		9		8	10		11†			4			R Groves	43
	2	3		5	6	7	4	9		8	10		11						R Guy	44
	2	3		5	6	7	4	9		8	10		11						R Milford/J Connock	45
	2	3		5	6	7	4	9		8	10*		11				12		N Ashley	46
	2	3		5	6	7	4	9		8		12	11					10*	M Heath	47
	2	3	9	5*	6	7	4		11	8		12						10	I Hemley	48
	2	3	9		6	7	4		5				11			8		10	K Cooper	49
	2	9		5	6	7	4		3	8	10		11						J Ashworth	50
	2	9		5	6	7	4		3	8	10		11						B Hill	51
	2	9		5	6	7	4		3	8	10*		11				12		C Trussell	52
	2	9*		5	6	7	4		3	8	10		11				12		D Allison	53
	2	3	9	5	6	7*	4		10	8			11				12		R Bridges	54
	2	9		5	6	7	4		3†	8	10		11						T Fitzharris	55
6	28	12	37	43	46	43	35	30	46	45	31	17	33	5		2	4	3	League Appearances	
				2	5							7		4	5		3	1	Substitute Appearances	
			1	2	2	2	2	2	2	2	2	2	0+1	1					Milk Cup Appearances	
	3		3	4	4	4	4	4	4	4		1	1	4					FA Cup Appearances	
	3	2	2	3	3	3	3	3	3	0+1		3		2					FR Trophy Appearances	

yers on Loan: Cowdrill (W.B.A.)

partures: Eley, Martin, Forrest (Southampton), Raynes (Wolves), Conroy, Pickering (York), McInnes (Lincoln)

THE MERRY MILLERS

Formed: 1884
Turned Professional: 1905 **Ltd Co:** 192

Previous Names: Thornhill United (1884), Rotherham County (1905) amalgamated in 1925 with Rotherham Town as Rotherham United
Previous Managers: Since 1946:
Reg Freeman   Andy Smailes   Tom Johnston   Danny Williams   Jack Mansell   Tommy Docherty   Jimmy McAnearney   Jimmy McGuigan   Ian Porterfield   Emlyn Hughes   George Kerr
Honours: Div 3 (N) Champions 1950-1   Div 3 Champions 1980-1
League Career: Rotherham Town: Elected to Div 2 1893   Not re-elected to Div 2 1896
Rotherham County: Elected to Div 2 1919   Relegated to Div 3 (N) 1923
Promoted to Div 2 1951   Relegated to Div 3 1968   Relegated to Div 4 1973
Promoted to Div 3 1975   Promoted to Div 2 1981   Relegated to Div 3 1983
Colours: Red shirts, white collar and sleeves, white shorts with red trim, red stockings
Change Colours: Yellow shirts with blue trim, blue shorts with yellow trim, yellow stockings
Reserves League: Central   **Youth Team:** Northern Intermediate

---

CLUB RECORDS

Most Appearances for Club: Danny Williams: 459, 1946-52
Most Capped Player: Harold Millership, 6, Wales   **For England:** None
Record Goalscorer in a Match: No player has scored more than four goals
Record League Goalscorer in a Season: Wally Ardron, 38, Div 3 (N), 1946-7
Record League Goalscorer in a Career: Gladstone Guest, 130, 1946-56
Record Transfer Fee Received: £100,000 from Sunderland for Dave Watson, Dec 1970
Record Transfer Fee Paid: £100,000 to Cardiff City for Ronnie Moore, Aug 1980
Best Performances: League: 3rd Div 2 1954-5   **FA Cup:** 5th Round 1952-3, 1967-8   **League/Milk Cup:** Finalists 1960-1
Most League Points: (2 pts for a win) 71 Div 3, (N), 1950-1   **Most League Goals:** 114, Div 3 (N), 1946-7
Record League Victory: 8-0 v Oldham Athletic, Div 3 (N), 26 May 1947
Record League Defeat: 1-11 v Bradford City, Div 3 (N), 25 Aug 1928**
**First match of the season. Rotherham United won their second match—at home!
Most Consecutive Undefeated League Matches: 18 1950-51

Longest Run of Undefeated Home League Matches: 27 1939'46-47
Longest Run Without Home League Win: 9 1983

Most Consecutive League Wins: 8 1982
Most Consecutive League Defeats: 8 1956

Club Statistician for the Directory: M G Smith

League Matches Without a Win: 14 1934, 1977-78

Away League Matches: 16 1950-51
Away League Win: 33 1894-96-1919 (as Non League club)
Home League Wins: 22 1939'46-47
Away League Wins: 8 1948

ROTHERHAM UNITED

PLAYERS NAME Ht Wt Birthdate	Honours	Birthplace Transfers	Clubs	League	Milk Cup	FA Cup	Other Comps	League	Milk Cup	FA Cup	Other Comps
GOALKEEPERS											
elham O'Hanlon 1 13.6 16.5.62	EiU.21	Saltburn F	Middlesbrough (A) Rotherham United								
DEFENDERS											
ail Crosby 9 10.8 9.11.62	EY	Leeds	Grimsby Town (A) Rotherham United	34+5 91	3 10	1 5	3	1			
ohn Dungworth† 0 11.0 30.3.55		Rotherham F F F £100,000 F F	Huddersfield Town (A) Barnsley (L) Oldham Athletic Rochdale (L) Aldershot Shrewsbury Town Hereford United (L) Mansfield Town Rotherham United	18+5 2+1 2+2 14 105 81+2 7 50+6 106+7	 4 2 3+1 8	 9 3 3 5	 4+2	1 3 58 17 3 16 13			
evor Slack 1 13.0 26.9.62		Peterborough	Peterborough Utd (A) Rotherham United	201+1	13	13	2	14	1	1	1
evan Smith* 3 12.0 13.12.59		Eaglescliffe F F	Stockton Darlington Rotherham United	 243+3 99+2	 10+1 8	 17 5	 6 5	 11 18	 1 4	 3	
MIDFIELD											
ean Emerson 8 10.8 27.12.62		Salford	Stockport County Rotherham United	156 45	10 2	3 4	3 3	7 7	3 1		1 1
ke Gooding 7½ 10.7 16.2.59		Newcastle	Bishop Auckland Rotherham United Chesterfield Rotherham United	 90+15 12 103+2	 9 14	 3 10	 5	 9 25	 1 3	 3	
gel Pepper 0 10.3 25.4.68		Rotherham	Rotherham United (A)	4+3							
aryl Pugh 8 10.7 5.6.61	W.U21 (2)	Sunderland Player Exchange	Doncaster Rovers (A) Huddersfield Town Rotherham United	136+18 52+33 33	12 2+1 0+1	9+1 3+2 4	 3	15 7 2	1 	1 1 1	1
ke Trusson 0 10.2 27.2.58	Div.4 '82	Northolt	Plymouth Argyle (A) Sheffield United Rotherham United	65+8 125+1 107	12 12 7	1+1 11 4	 5	15 31 15	4 2	 2	2
FORWARDS											
olin Douglas 1 11.0 9.9.62		Hurlford F	Celtic Doncaster Rovers Rotherham United	 202+10	 13+1	 11	 6	 48	 5	 13	
ny Simmons 0½ 11.3 9.2.65	EY	Sheffield	Sheffield W. (A) Q.P.R. Rotherham United	1+3 84+3	 8	 1	 2+1	 27	 2	 1	

ADDITIONAL CONTRACT PROFESSIONALS
ark Ash, Andy Martin, Martin Scott, Ray Warburton

APPRENTICES
by Bubb, Gregory Burrows, Carl Calvert, Ian Clarke, Ian Dennis, Shaun Goodwin, Giles Newcombe, David Stoker, Simon Thompson

NON-CONTRACT PLAYERS
mon Dolby

Record Attendance: 25,000 v Sheffield U, Div 2, 13 Dec 1952

Record Receipts: £34,217 v Sheffield W, Div 2, 4 May 1982

Size of Playing Area: 115yds × 76yds

Season Tickets: Main stand: £70 (£47.00 Juveniles/OAPs); Millmoor Lane Stand: £50 (£36 Juveniles/OAPs); Enclosure: £47 (£28 Juveniles/OAPs); Ground; £40 (£28 youths, £28 Juveniles/OAPs)

Cost of Stand Tickets: Main Stand: £4.00 (£2.50 Juveniles/OAPs); Millmoor Lane End Stand: £2.50 (£2.00 Juveniles/OAPs); Ground £2.20 (£1.50 Youths, £1.50 Juveniles/OAPs); Enclosure £2.50 (£1.50 Juveniles/OAPs)

Match and Ticket Information: Seats can be reserved one month before match

Car Parking: There are parks within easy distance of the ground in Kimberworth Road and Main Street

Nearest Railway Station: Rotherham (0709-563336)

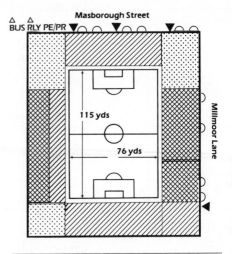

How to get to the ground

From North: Use Motorway M1 until junction 34, leave Motorway and follow signs Rotherham A6109. Cross railway bridge and then turn right into Millmoor Lane for Rotherham United FC
From East: Use A630 into Rotherham and then follow signs Sheffield into Masborough Street, then turn left into Millmoor Lane for Rotherham United FC
From South and West: Use Motorway M1 until Junction 24, leave Motorway and follow signs Rotherham A6178. At roundabout take 1st exit into Ring Road and at next roundabout take 1st exit into Masborough Street A6109. Take 1st turning left into Millmoor for Rotherham United FC

Price of 1986-7 Programme: 50p
Number of Pages: 16
Subscriptions: Apply to club

Local Newspapers: Sheffield Morning Telegraph, Sheffield Star (including Saturday special)

Local Radio Stations: Radio Hallam (194 medium wave), Radio Sheffield (290 medium wave)

SCUNTHORPE UNITED — Division 4

A 4-0 home victory on the opening day of the season seemed to confirm the bookmakers faith in making United one of the promotion favourites. A flood of goals towards the end of the previous season had led to optimism at the Old Show Ground and around the town. However a disastrous run which saw only one point gleaned from the next eight games, meant a long hard struggle to climb away from the re-election zone. The team gradually improved as the season went on, both at home and away. After Swindon triumphed 2-0 at the Show Ground in November, only two more visiting sides, were to leave with maximum points. The Iron also gained three wins and three draws in the last seven away fixtures to eventually achieve respectability in 14th position.

The Cup competitions provided little respite from League duty as Darlington and Rochdale in the Milk and FA Cups respectively, prevented the Iron from playing lucrative ties against Ipswich and Manchester United. If the club had lost out in monetary terms in these competitions they more than made up for it on the transfer market. In November Neil Pointon was signed by League Champions Everton and went on to make over 20 appearances for the Merseyside club before injury brought a premature end to his season. The move brought United a record fee of £75,000 and more was to follow with the departure of striker Keith Houchen. The tall striker joined Scunthorpe on March 27th (deadline day) for around £20,000 from York City. Shortly after the end of the campaign Coventry City paid £60,000 leaving United with an amazing profit for a player who made only nine appearances.

During the season experienced defenders Richard Money and Les Hunter returned to the club and brought stability to the back four. The big success was undoubtedly left-back Paul Longden who only got into the side following the departure of Pointon. He performed so well that the supporters club named him their player of the season. Activity on the transfer market during the summer has seen the arrival of Dave McLean (Darlington), Alan Birch (Rotherham) and Steve Johnson (Bristol City).

The team should perform much better than last time as the club starts its final season at the Old Show Ground. Planning permission has been given for the erection of a large 'superstore complex' and the sale of the ground is expected to bring in several million pounds which will pay for a new 11,000 capacity stadium for the start of the 1987-88 campaign. The future of Scunthorpe United looks assured as the club celebrates its 75th anniversary.

Front Row L to R: K Young, R Huxford, K Oulston, Jimmy Shaw, D Mountain. **Second Row:** W Russell, S Cammack, B Green, F Barlow (Manager), P McLoughlin, D McLean, D Hill. **Third Row:** A Birch, D Travis, M Atkins, R Money, P Gregory, L Hunter, A Stevenson, J Broddle, P Longden. **Fourth Row:** S Johnson, S Lister, A Whitehead, W Perry, P Nicol, J Hawley.

SCUNTHORPE UNITED

DIVISION FOUR: 15th   **FA CUP:** 2nd ROUND   **MILK CUP:** 1st ROUND   **FRT:** QUARTER-FINAL

MATCH	DATE		COMPE-TITION	VENUE	OPPONENTS	RESULT		HALF TIME	L'GUE POS'N	GOALSCORERS/GOAL TIMES	ATTEN-DANCE
1	A	17	CL	H	Torquay United	W	4-0	2-0		Graham 16, Broddle 28, Cammack 47, Green 60	1,929
2		20	MC1/1	A	Darlington	L	2-3	1-0		Lister 45, Cammack 47	(2,159)
3		23	CL	A	Halifax Town	L	1-2	1-0	7	Cammack (pen) 45	(1,094)
4		26	CL	H	Wrexham	D	1-1	1-0	9	Broddle 36	2,097
5		31	CL	A	Peterborough United	L	0-1	0-1	14		(2,928)
6	S	6	CL	H	Tranmere Rovers	L	0-1	0-1	19		2,058
7		10	MC1/2	H	Darlington	D	0-0	0-0			1,504
8		14	CL	A	Southend United	L	1-2	1-1	20	Cammack (pen) 15	(2,974)
9		18	CL	A	Exeter City	L	0-2	0-1	21		(1,723)
10		21	CL	H	Mansfield Town	L	0-3	0-2	22		1,780
11		28	CL	A	Aldershot	L	1-2	1-2	23	Graham 20	(1,056)
12	O	1	CL	H	Crewe Alexandra	W	3-1	0-0	23	Graham 14, Holland (og) 46, Hill 90	1,443
13		5	CL	A	Orient	L	0-3	0-1	24		(2,847)
14		11	CL	H	Cambridge United	D	0-0	0-0	24		1,496
15		18	CL	A	Colchester United	D	1-1	0-0	24	Broddle 63	(3,462)
16		22	CL	H	Port Vale	D	0-0	0-0	24		1,888
17		25	CL	H	Hereford United	W	2-1	0-0	22	Whitehead 47, Cammack 67	1,564
18	N	2	CL	A	Northampton Town	D	2-2	1-1	22	Brolly 26, Lister 55	(2,343)
19		5	CL	A	Preston North End	W	1-0	1-0	20	Cammack 5	(2,007)
20		9	CL	H	Swindon Town	L	0-2	0-2	20		1,920
21		16	FAC1	A	Halifax Town	W	3-1	1-1		Hill 8, Broddle 49, Lister 86	(1,501)
22		23	CL	A	Rochdale	L	0-1	0-0	22		(1,430)
23		30	CL	H	Burnley	D	1-1	0-1	20	Hawley 61	2,001
24	D	7	FAC2	A	Rochdale	D	2-2	1-0		Graham 12, Hill 63	2,868
25		10	FAC2R	H	Rochdale	L	1-2	1-1		Broddle 30	(5,066)
26		14	CL	A	Chester City	D	1-1	1-1	20	Hawley 2	(2,657)
27		22	CL	H	Halifax Town	D	3-3	1-3	21	Hawley 3 (43, (pen) 48, 78)	2,285
28		26	CL	H	Hartlepool United	W	1-0	1-0	20	Matthews 40	2,495
29	J	1	CL	A	Stockport County	D	0-0	0-0	20		(3,504)
30		11	CL	H	Peterborough United	W	2-0	2-0	20	Broddle 25, Whitehead 44	1,832
31		15	FRT	A	Lincoln City	W	3-1	1-0		Money 39, Hawley pen 60, Whitehead 78	(1,235)
32		18	CL	H	Torquay United	L	0-1	0-0	20		(1,064)
33		21	FRT	H	Halifax Town	W	3-2	2-1		Matthews 20, Hawley 27, 56	1,244
34		24	CL	H	Southend United	W	2-0	0-0	19	Hill 49, Broddle 59	1,463
35		31	CL	A	Tranmere Rovers	L	1-2	1-0	19	Hawley 7	(1,417)
36	F	3	CL	A	Port Vale	L	1-3	0-2	19	Graham 79	(2,977)
37	M	1	CL	H	Aldershot	W	1-0	0-0	18	Hawley 80	1,270
38		4	CL	A	Crewe Alexandra	L	0-4	0-1	21		(1,072)
39		8	CL	H	Orient	D	2-2	0-0	21	Whitehead 82, Cammack 84	1,478
40		10	FRT QF N	H	Port Vale	L	1-1†	0-0		Hawley 76	1,415
41		15	CL	A	Cambridge United	W	1-0	0-0	21	Cammack 14	(1,785)
42		18	CL	H	Northampton Town	W	1-0	0-0	19	Broddle 83	1,355
43		22	CL	A	Hereford United	D	1-1	1-0	19	Graham 29	(2,367)
44		25	CL	A	Mansfield Town	D	1-1	0-1	19	Travis 59	(3,919)
45		28	CL	H	Stockport County	L	2-3	0-1	20	Dixon 51, Cammack 53	2,025
46	A	1	CL	A	Hartlepool United	W	1-0	0-0	18	Cammack 57	(2,781)
47		4	CL	H	Preston North End	L	1-3	1-2	19	Cammack 12	2,261
48		12	CL	A	Swindon Town	D	1-1	1-0	20	Hunter 62	(6,783)
49		15	CL	H	Colchester United	D	1-1	1-1	20	Dixon 21	1,067
50		18	CL	H	Rochdale	W	3-1	0-1	19	Broddle 60, Houchen 64, Lister 83	1,406
51		22	CL	H	Exeter City	W	1-0	0-0	16	Cammack 50	1,343
52		26	CL	A	Burnley	W	2-1	1-1	14	Houchen 11, Overson (og) 78	(2,563)
53		29	CL	A	Wrexham	L	0-1	0-0	16		(1,042)
54	M	3	CL	H	Chester City	W	2-0	1-0	15	Brolly 29, Cammack 87	2,256

Best Home League Attendance: 2,495 v Hartlepool Utd 26/12   **Smallest:** 1,067 v Colchester Utd 15/4   **Av Home Att:** 1,770

Goal Scorers: **Compared with 84-85:** −295

League (50):	Cammack 12 (2 pens), Broddle 7, Hawley 7 (1 pen), Graham 5, Whitehead 3, Brolly 2, Dixon 2, Hill 2, Houchen 2, Lister 2, Green 1, Hunter 1, Matthews 1, Travis 1, Opponents 2
Milk Cup (2):	Cammack 1, Lister 1
FA Cup (6):	Broddle 2, Hill 2, Graham 1, Lister 1
FRT (7):	Hawley 4 (1 pen), Matthews 1, Money 1, Whitehead 1 †A.E.T. Scunthorpe Lost on Penalties

Russell	Pointon	Lister	Whitehead	Green	Brolly	Cammack	Broddle	Graham (NC)	Hill (NC)	Hawley	Lester	Matthews	Smith (NC)	Longden	Money	Ferry	Barnes (L)	Dixon (L)	Stevenson	Webster	Travis (NC)	Johnson (NC)	Hunter	Houchen	Referee	
2	3	4	5	6	7	8	9	10	11																H Taylor	1
2	3	4	5	6	7*	8	9	10	11	12															T Jones	2
2	3	4	5	6	7	8	9	10	11																K Breen	3
2	3	4	5	6	7	8	9	10	11																D Hutchinson	4
2	3	4	5	6		8	9	7	11*	12				10											M Dimblebee	5
2	3	4	5	6	7*	8	9		11	12				10											M Heath	6
2	3	4	5	6	7	8*	9		11	12				10											J Ball	7
2	3	4	5	6	7	8	9*		11	12				10											I Henley	8
2	3	4	5	6		8	12	7*	11		9			10											K Cooper	9
2	3	4	5	6	7	8			11		9			10	12										J McAulay	10
2*	3	4	5			8	9	7	11		12			10	6										A Buksh	11
	3		5	6	7	8	9	4	11					10	2										T Simpson	12
12	3	6	5		7	8	9*	4	11					10	2										R Hamer	13
	3	6	5		7	8		4	11		9			10	2										L Dilkes	14
2	3	4	5		7	8	9		11					10	6										B Hill	15
2	3	4	5		7	8	9		11					10	6										K Redfern	16
2	3	4	5		7	8	9		11					10	6										J Ashworth	17
2	3	4	5		7	8	9		11					10	6										M Reed	18
2	3	4	5		7	8	9		11					10	6	11									N Ashley	19
2		4	5		7	8	12		11	10				3	6	11*									K Lupton	20
2		4	5		7	8*	9	12	11	10				3	6										G Courtney	21
2		4	5		7	8*	9	12	11	10				3	6										T Holbrook	22
2		4	5				9	10	11		8			3	6			7							K Hackett	23
2		4	5				9	10	11		8	7		3	6										D Phillips	24
2		4	5				9	7	11		8			3	6										D Phillips	25
2			5				9	4	11	10	8			3	6			7							K Barrett	26
2	12		5				9	4	11	10	8			3	6			7							J Bray	27
2	10		5				9	4	11		8			3	6			7							P Tyldesley	28
2	10		5				9	4	11		8			3	6			7							D Scott	29
2		4	5				9	10	11		8	12		3	6			7*							N Glover	30
2		4	5				9	10	11		8			3	6			7							M Scott	31
2		4	5				9	10	11		8			3	6			7							B Stevens	32
2		4	5*				9*	10	11		8	7		3	6				12	12					V Callow	33
2		4*	5				9	10	11		8			3	6			7	12						G Napthine	34
2		4	5				9	10	11		8			3	6			7							G Ashby	35
2		4	5				9*	10	11		8			3	6			7	12						N Midgley	36
2		4	5				9	10	11		8	7		3	6										C Trussell	37
2		4	5				9	10	11		8	7		3	6										T Fitzharris	38
2		4	5				9	12	11		8			3	6			7			10*				T Simpson	39
2		4	5				9	12	11		8	7		3	6						10*				A Seville	40
2		4	5				9	12	11		8			3	6*			7			10				M Reed	41
2		4	5				9	12	11		8*			3	6			7			10				D Phillips	42
2			5			8	9	4	11					3				7			10	1	6		K Miller	43
2			5			8	9	4	11					3				7			10	1	6		J Lloyd	44
2		4*	5			8	9	12	11					3				7			10	1	6		A Saunders	45
2			5			8		4	11					3				7			10	1	6	9	C Seel	46
12			5			8		4	11					3				7			10	1	6	9	J McAulay	47
2		4	5			8			11					3				7			10	1	6	9	M Bodenham	48
2		4	5			8	12		11					3				7*			10	1	6	9	G Tyson	49
2		4				8	12	7	11					3				5			10*	1	6	9	J Worrall	50
2		4				8		7	11	10				3				5		7*		1	6	9	M Heath	51
2		4				8	12		11	10				3				5		7*		1	6	9	D Phillips	52
2		4	5			8		7	11	10				3						12		1	6	9	R Guy	53
2		4				8		7	11	10*				3				5		12		1	6	9	I Borrett	54
41	17	35	41	9	19	32	36	27	42	18	18	9		31	25	2	6	14		4	12	12	12	9	League Appearances	
1	2			1	1	5	4		3			2	1						2	1					Substitute Appearances	
2	2	2	2	2	2	2	2	1	2	0·2	1														Milk Cup Appearances	
3		3	3	1	1	3	2·1	3	2	2	1			3	3										FA Cup Appearances	
3	2	3	1	3	2·1	3	3	3	3									0·1	1·1	1					FR Trophy Appearances	

Also Played: Position (Game): Matthews (L) 9(20)

Players on Loan: Barnes (West Ham), Matthews (Grimsby)

Departures: Brolly, Graham (Scarborough), Cammack (Port Vale)

'THE IRON'

Formed: 1904
Turned Professional: 1912 **Ltd Co:** 1912

Previous Managers: Leslie Jones 1950-51   Bill Corkhill 1951-56   Ron Stuart 1956-58
Tony Macshane 1958-59   Bill Lambton 3 days 1959   Frank Soo 1959-1960
Dick Duckworth 1960-64   Freddie Goodwin 1964-67   Ron Ashman 1967-73
Ron Bradley 1973-74   Dickie Rooks 1974-76   Ron Ashman 1976-81
John Duncan 1981-83   Allan Clarke 1983-84
Honours: Div 3 (North) Champions 1957-8
League Career: Elected to Div 3 (N) 1950   Promoted to Div 2 1957-8
Relegated to Div 3 1963-4   Relegated to Div 4 1967-8   Promoted to Div 3 1971-2
Relegated to Div 4 1972-3   Promoted to Div 3 1982-3   Relegated to Div 4 1983-4
Colours: Claret and blue shirts, blue shorts and stockings with claret trim
Change Colours: Yellow with claret trim
Reserves League: Central Div 2   **Youth League:** Northern Intermediate

CLUB RECORDS

Most Appearances for Club: Jack Brownsword: Football League 600 + Cup 56 **Total 656**
Most Capped Player: No Scunthorpe player has won an international cap
Record Goalscorer in a Match: Barrie Thomas, 5 v Luton Town (h) 8-1, Div 3, 24 April 1965
Record League Goalscorer in a season: Barrie Thomas, 31, Div 2, 1961-2   **In All Competitions:** Barrie Thomas, 31 (all League)
Record League Goalscorer in a career: Steve Cammack, 109   **In All Competitions:** Steve Cammack 120 (League 109 Cups 11)
Record Transfer Fee Received: £50,000 + £25,000 from Everton for Neil Pointon, Nov 1985
Record Transfer Fee Paid: £34,000 to Brentford for Alan Whitehead, March 1984
Best Performances: League: 4th Div 2 1961-2   **FA Cup:** 5th Round 1957-8, 1969-70   **League/Milk Cup:** Never beyond 3rd Round
Most League Points: 83 in Div 4, 1982-3   **Most League Goals:** 88, Div 3 (N), 1957-8
Record League Victory and Most Goals in a League Match: 8-1 v Luton Town, Div 3, 24 April 1965
Most Goals Scored in a First Class Match: 9-0 v Boston United, 1st Round FA Cup, 21 Nov 1953
Record League Defeat: 0-8 v Carlisle United, Div 3 (N), 25 Dec 1952
Oldest Player in League Match: Wally Boyes, 37 yrs
Youngest Player in League Match:
Most Consecutive Undefeated League Matches: 15 1957-58, 1971-72

League Matches Without a Win: 14 1974, 1975

Longest Run of Undefeated Home League Matches: 21 1950-51   **Away League Matches:** 9 1982
Longest Run Without Home League Win: 7 1963, 1972-73 1974   **Away League Win:** 29 1977-78
Most Consecutive League Wins: 6 1954, 1965   **Home League Wins:** 7 1985
Most Consecutive League Defeats: 7 1973   **Away League Wins:** 5 1965

Club Statistician for the Directory: M Girdham

SCUNTHORPE UNITED

PLAYERS NAME / Wt Birthdate	Honours	Birthplace / Transfers	Clubs	League	Milk Cup	FA Cup	Other Comps	League	Milk Cup	FA Cup	Other Comps
GOALKEEPERS											
ul Gregory *0 11.7 26.7.61		Sheffield	Chesterfield (A)	23		1					
		F	Doncaster Rovers	1	1						
		F	Scunthorpe United	66	2	3	5				
DEFENDERS											
s Hunter 2 13.6 15.1.55	Div4 '85	Middlesbrough	Chesterfield (A)	156+9	15+1	13+1		8	2	1	
			Scunthorpe United	61	4	4		7			
			Chesterfield	99	4	4		5			
			Scunthorpe United								
ul Longdon† 7 10.3 28.9.62		Wakefield	Burnley (A)	5							
			Scunthorpe United	87	3	12	7	2			
chard Money* 1½ 11.5 13.10.44	E.U23 (1) Div.2 '82	Lowestoft	Lowestoft Town								
			Scunthorpe United	165+8	10	6		4			
		£30,000	Fulham	106	4	6		3		1	
		£333,000	Liverpool	12+2	1	1					
			Derby County (L)	5							
		£100,000	Luton Town	44	4	1		1			
		£50,000	Portsmouth	17	4						
			Scunthorpe United								
ly Russell 0 11.4 14.9.59	SY	Glasgow	Everton (A)								
			Celtic								
		£15,000	Doncaster Rovers	241+3	17	19	5	15			
		F	Scunthorpe United								
an Whitehead 3 12.0 20.11.56		Bury	Bury	98+1	6	10		13			
		£75,000	Brentford	101+1	13	9		4			
		£35,000	Scunthorpe United	101	6	6	5	7	1		1
MIDFIELD											
vid Hill 9 10.3 6.6.66		Nottingham	Scunthorpe United	72+1	2	4	5+1	4		2	
eve Lister 11.10 18.11.61			Doncaster Rovers (A)	227+9	14	15	2	30			
			Scunthorpe United	35+2	2	3	2	2	1	1	
vid McLean 3 11.0 24.11.57	ES	Newcastle	Newcastle United	7+2	1						
		£10,000	Carlisle United	9+6							
		F	Darlington	287+5	16	18	6+1	46	5	2	2
			Scunthorpe United								
dy Stevenson 12.3 29.9.67		Scunthorpe	Scunthorpe United	0+1			1+1				
vid Travis 0 10.7 4.7.64		Doncaster	Doncaster Rovers (N/C)	12		1		1			
		F	Scunthorpe United								
an Birch 10.5 12.8.56		West Bromwich	Walsall	158+13	9	9		23	1		
		£25,000	Chesterfield	90	8	8		35	4	1	
		£200,000	Wolverhampton W.	13+2	2	1					
		£100,000	Barnsley	43+1	4	2			11		1
			Chesterfield	30+2	4	3		5	2		
			Rotherham United	99+2	8	5	15	18	4	3	
			Scunthorpe United								
FORWARDS											
lian Broddle 9 11.3 1.11.64		Laughton	Sheffield United (A)	1							
			Scunthorpe United	87+12	6	8	3	21		3	
lie Ferry 2 12.2 21.11.66		Sunderland	Scunthorpe United	3							
hn Hawley 13.12 8.5.54		Withersea	Hull City	101+13	10+1	5		22	2	1	
		£75,000	Leeds United	30+3	6	3		16	1		
		£200,000	Sunderland	25	3	3		11			
		£50,000	Arsenal	14+6	1			3			
			Orient (L)	4				3			
			Hull City (L)	3				1			
		£15,000	Bradford City	62+6	4	3	3	28	3		1
		£15,000	Scunthorpe United	18+3	0+2	2	3	7			4
eve Johnson 12.9 22.6.55		Liverpool	Altrincham				11				
			Bury	139+15	8+1	14+1		52	5	4	
			Rochdale	17+2	2	2		7	1	2	
			Wigan Athletic	50+1	4	5	3	22	3	1	1
			Bristol City	14+7	1+1			3	2		1
			Scunthorpe United								

DDITIONAL CONTRACT PROFESSIONALS
rk Atkins, Paul Nicol

PRENTICES

N-CONTRACT PLAYERS
vin Dulston, Richard Huxford, Paul Johnson,, William Ferry, Darren Mountain, James Shaw, Kirk Young

THE OLD SHOW GROUND Scunthorpe

Record Attendance: 23,935 v Portsmouth, FA Cup Round 4, 30 Jan 1954

Smallest Home Attendance for a First Class Match: 1,106 v Bury, Div 4, 4 May 1982

Record Receipts: £28,612 v Leeds United, FA Cup Round 3 Replay, Jan 1984

Size of Playing Area: 111yds × 73yds

Season Tickets: Stand: £73 adult (£36 OAP/child); Ground: £52 adult (£26 OAP/child)

Executive Box Season Tickets: Adult £125; OAP/child £90

Cost of Stand Tickets: £3.75 adult (£1.85 OAP/child) **Terraces:** £2.65 adult (£1.35 OAP/child)

Match and Ticket Information: No telephone bookings Ground. Can reserve until day of match unless otherwise notified in press (for seats by phoning office)

Car Parking: Club park adjacent to Ground for 40/50 vehicles. Ample street parking

Nearest Railway Station: Scunthorpe

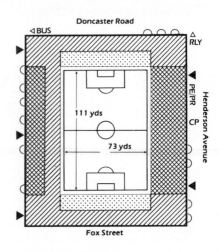

How to get to the ground

From North and West: Use Motorway M180 to end of Motorway then join A161 and A18 S.P. Scunthorpe. At Motorway Terminal roundabout take 1st exit and at next take 2nd exit into Doncaster Road for Scunthorpe United FC
From East: Use A18 S.P. Scunthorpe into town centre and at roundabout take 3rd exit into Ashby Road. In 0.8m at crossroads turn left into Doncaster Road for Scunthorpe United FC
From South: Use A1 then A1133 and A156 to Gainsborough then follow signs into Scunthorpe town centre on A159. At roundabout take 2nd exit into Ashby Road. In 0.8m at crossroads turn left into Doncaster Road for Scunthorpe United FC

Price of 1986-7 Programme: 50p
Number of Pages: 24
Subscriptions: £16.00 (Home) £32.00 (H&A)

Local Newspapers: Scunthorpe Evening Telegraph, Scunthorpe Star

Local Radio Stations: Radio Humberside, Radio Viking

Chairman
R J Brealey

Directors
A H Laver
M A Wragg
R Wragg M Inst BM
D Dooley (Managing Director)
P G Woolhouse

Secretary
G E Smith

Team Manager
W McEwan

Club Coaches
P Henson
D Bergara

Physiotherapist
I Bailey

Groundsman
Frank Holland

Marketing Executive
Andy Daykin

After a promising start, it seemed the Blades might mount a promotion challenge but, as time went on, it was seen that they lacked the consistency to remain among the leaders.

Manager Ian Porterfield's close-season transfer activities had brought England striker Peter Withe (from Aston Villa), centre-back Ken McNaught (WBA) and midfield man Ray Lewington (Fulham) to Bramall Lane.

A 3-1 away win over newly-relegated Stoke City gave the side a promising start and, in the next game, they slammed Wimbledon 4-0 at Bramall Lane. They remained unbeaten in four games, suffering the first defeat at Norwich (0-4).

Mr Porterfield signed midfield man Steve Foley, from Grimsby, and later took the decision to sell Glenn Cockerill to Southampton for £225,000, reasoning that he could probably buy two new players with the cash raised. Some of that was re-invested in the signing of Steve Wigley, from Nottingham Forest, for £90,000.

Initially, Keith Edwards had been unable to get into the team but, when goals were at a premium, he was recalled to partner Withe in attack. Edwards completed the season as top scorer for the third season in succession, netting 21 times.

In one early spell he scored nine times in four matches, form which inspired the side to a run of five wins in a row. That culminated in a remarkable 5-1 victory at Oldham which took the Blades into third place in the table.

By the end of November, the Blades had moved into second place, just one point behind leaders Portsmouth and that 1st Division goal really began to look attainable.

But, just as rapidly as they had climbed into that lofty position, so the Blades began to slip out of contention again. A five-goal hammering at Wimbledon and defeat at lowly Sunderland dented the club's pride.

Further defeats saw them slide out of the mainstream. A 2-5 home defeat by Nowich in March was a great set-back and a few days later manager Ian Porterfield left the club.

Youth team coach Billy McEwan was given the job as caretaker-manager but, before the season was over, he was confirmed as full-time manager.

The Blades finally finished in a creditable seventh place in the 2nd Division.

Back Row L to R: Tony Philliskirk, Martin Pike, Kenneth Geelan, John Burridge, Paul Tomlinson, Paul Stancliffe, Jeff Eckhardt, Peter Withe. **Middle Row:** Kevin Arnott, Brian Smith, Lee Walshaw, Phil Henson (Youth Team Coach), Andrew Barnsley, Paddy McGeeney, Chris Wilder. **Front Row:** Ian Bailey (Physio) Peter Beagrie, Steve Foley, Steve Wigley, Billy McEwan (Team Manager), Colin Morris, Mark Dempsey, David Frain, Danny Bergara (Coach).

SHEFFIELD UNITED

DIVISION TWO: 7th   **FA CUP:** 4th ROUND   **MILK CUP:** 2nd ROUND

MATCH	DATE	COMPE-TITION	VENUE	OPPONENTS	RESULT		HALF TIME	L'GUE POS'N	GOALSCORERS/GOAL TIMES	ATTEN-DANCE
1	A 17	CL	A	Stoke City	W	3-1	1-1		Cockerill 13, Morris (pen) 52, 77	(11,679)
2	20	MC1/1	A	Rotherham United	W	3-1	2-0		Cockerill 18, McNaught 34, Bolton 82	(9,087)
3	24	CL	H	Wimbledon	W	4-0	3-0	3	Gayle (og) 2, Morris (pen) 12, (pen) 51, McNaught 29	11,914
4	27	CL	A	Brighton & H.A.	D	0-0	0-0			(10,128)
5	31	CL	H	Shrewsbury Town	D	1-1	1-1	6	Withe 37	11,248
6	S 3	MC1/2	H	Rotherham United	W	5-1	3-0		Morris 23, Withe 27, 88, Bolton 35, 53	7,486
7	7	CL	A	Norwich City	L	0-4	0-1	10		(12,899)
8	14	CL	H	Huddersfield Town	D	1-1	0-1	9	Webster (og) 47	13,854
9	17	CL	A	Fulham	W	3-2	0-1		Foley 63, 83, Cockerill 77	(4,259)
10	21	CL	H	Middlesbrough	L	0-1	0-0	9		(10,535)
11	24	MC2/1	H	Luton Town	L	1-2	1-0		Foley 44	8,948
12	28	CL	A	Leeds United	D	1-1	1-0	11	Withe 36	(15,622)
13	O 1	CL	H	Charlton Athletic	D	1-1	0-1		McNaught 63	9,047
14	5	CL	H	Millwall	L	1-3	0-2		Eckhardt 82	9,159
15	8	MC2/2	A	Luton Town	L	1-3	0-2		Edwards 52	(5,560)
16	12	CL	A	Grimsby Town	W	1-0	1-0	10	Withe 30	(5,935)
17	16	FMC	A	Leeds United	D	1-1	0-0		Morris 79	(2,274)
18	19	CL	H	Barnsley	W	3-1	2-0	8	Withe 18 secs, Edwards 43, 82	11,167
19	22	FMC	H	Manchester City	L	1-2	0-0		Morris (pen) 48	3,420
20	26	CL	A	Bradford City	W	4-1	2-0	7	Withe 2, 73, Edwards 15, 86	(7,448)
21	N 2	CL	A	Hull City	W	3-1	1-1		Edwards 3 (10, 53 (pen), 75)	13,272
22	9	CL	A	Oldham Athletic	W	5-1	4-1		Morris 25, 32, Edwards 28, 44, Arnott 48	(8,193)
23	16	CL	H	Blackburn Rovers	D	3-3	2-2	3	McNaught 19, Morris 39, Wigley 48	13,610
24	23	CL	A	Portsmouth	W	3-0	2-0	2	Foley 11, 81, Withe 33	(17,558)
25	30	CL	H	Crystal Palace	D	0-0	0-0	2		13,765
26	D 7	CL	A	Charlton Athletic	L	0-2	0-0	4		(7,121)
27	14	CL	H	Stoke City	L	1-2	1-1	5	Edwards 14	12,370
28	21	CL	A	Wimbledon	L	0-5	0-3	7		(3,756)
29	26	CL	A	Sunderland	L	1-2	1-2	7	Edwards 15	(17,643)
30	28	CL	H	Fulham	W	2-1	1-0	5	Withe 18, McNaught 49	10,421
31	J 1	CL	H	Carlisle United	W	1-0	0-0	6	Edwards 52	10,561
32	11	CL	A	Huddersfield Town	L	1-3	1-1	6	Bolton 43	(9,268)
33	13	FAC3	H	Fulham	W	2-0	0-0		Morris 51, 63	7,004
34	18	CL	A	Shrewsbury Town	L	1-3	0-1	7	Morris (pen) 49	(4,261)
35	25	FAC4	H	Derby County	L	0-1	0-1			(22,658)
36	F 1	CL	H	Brighton & H.A.	W	3-0	0-0	5	Morris 54, Edwards 75, Withe 79	7,367
37	M 8	CL	A	Millwall	L	0-3	0-1	8		(4,270)
38	11	CL	H	Bradford City	W	3-1	1-1	5	Edwards 11, 86, Eves 47	8,405
39	15	CL	H	Grimsby Town	D	1-1	0-1	6	Stancliffe 82	9,165
40	18	CL	A	Middlesbrough	W	2-1	1-1	5	Withe 13, Edwards 52	(5,678)
41	22	CL	H	Norwich City	L	2-5	1-2	7	Edwards 34, 81	11,894
42	29	CL	A	Carlisle United	L	0-1	0-1	8		(4,575)
43	31	CL	H	Sunderland	W	1-0	1-0	5	Foley 18	9,839
44	A 5	CL	A	Hull City	D	0-0	0-0	7		(9,645)
45	8	CL	A	Barnsley	L	1-2	1-0	7	Arnott 12	(5,451)
46	12	CL	H	Oldham Athletic	W	2-0	1-0	7	McNaught 35, Eckhardt 82	7,782
47	19	CL	A	Blackburn Rovers	L	1-6	0-2	7	Edwards 83	(4,736)
48	22	CL	H	Leeds United	W	3-2	1-1	6	Morris (pen) 38, Frain 64, Walshaw 74	9,158
49	26	CL	H	Portsmouth	D	0-0	0-0	6		12,234
50	M 3	CL	A	Crystal Palace	D	1-1	0-0	7	Edwards 73	(6,375)

Best Home League Attendance: 13,854 v Huddersfield 14/9   **Smallest:** 7,367 v Brighton 1/2   **Av Home Att:** 10,798

Goal Scorers:

Compared with 84-85: −1,617

League (64):	Edwards 20 (1 pen), Morris 10 (5 pen), Withe 10, Foley 5, McNaught 5, Arnott 2, Cockerill 2, Eckhardt 2, Bolton 1, Eves 1, Frain 1, Stancliffe 1, Walshaw 1, Wigley 1, Opponents 2
Milk Cup (10):	Bolton 3, Withe 2, Cockerill 1, Edwards 1, Foley 1, McNaught 1, Morris 1
FA Cup (2):	Morris 2
FM Cup (2):	Morris 2 (1 pen)

Burridge	Eckhardt	Kenworthy	Thompson	Stancliffe	McNaught	Morris	Cockerill	Withe	Lewington	Bolton	Edwards	Foley	McGeeney	Smith B	Arnott	Wigley	Smith P	Eves	Frain	Black	Phillskink	Walshaw	Referee	
1	2	3	4	5	6	7	8	9	10	11													N Wilson	1
1	2	3	4*	5	6	7	8	9	10	11	12												**G Courtney**	2
1	2	3	4	5	6	7	8	9	10	11													M Heath	3
1	2	3	4	5	6	7	8	9	10	11													A Buksh	4
1	2	3	4	5	6	7	8	9	10	11													N Midgley	5
1	2	3	4	5	6	7	8	9		11		10											**P Willis**	6
1	2	3	4	5	6	7	8	9		11	12	10*											R Lewis	7
1	2	3	4	5	6	7	8	9	10	11*	12												A Saunders	8
1	2	3	4	5*	6	7	8	9	10	11	12												D Axcell	9
1	2	3	4		6	7	8	9	10	11*	12	5											A Robinson	10
1	2		4		6	7	8	9	10	3	11	5											**J Lovatt**	11
1	2			5	6	7	8	9	10†	3	11	4†											D Scott	12
1	2			5	6	7	8	9	10	3	11	4			12								M Robinson	13
1	2			5	6	7	8	9	10	3	11												I Hendrick	14
1			4	5	6	7	8	9	10	3	11		2										**B Stevens**	15
1			4	5	6	7		9		3	11		2*		10		12						J Bray	16
1	2		4	5	6	7		9	10	3	11	8											**M Peck**	17
1			4	5	6	7		9	10	3	11	8	2										N Ashley	18
1	4			5	6	7		9	10	3		8	2*	12	11								**T Holbrook**	19
1	2		4	5	6	7		9	10	3		8			11		12						D Allison	20
1	2		4	5	6	7*		9	10	3		8			11		12						V Callow	21
1	2		4	5	6	7		9	10	3		8			11								K Redfearn	22
1	2		4	5	6	7		9	10		11	8		3	11*		12						M Reed	23
1	2		4	5	6	7		9	10		11	8		3									M James	24
1	2		4	5	6	7		9	10		11	8		3*			12						K Breen	25
1	2		4	5	6	7		9	10		11	8		3*		12							R Hamer	26
1	2*		4	5	6	7		9	10	3		8			11	12							C Seel	27
1	2	3	4	5	6†			9†	10		11	8				7							M Bodenham	28
1	2*	3	4	5	6	7		9	10			8			12		11						G Aplin	29
1	2	3*	4	5	6	7		9	10			8			12		11						R Bridges	30
1	2	3	4	5	6	7		9	10		11	8											P Tyldesley	31
1	2	3	4	5		7			10		11	8			6		9						H Taylor	32
1		3	4	5		7			10		11	8			6		9	2					**T Jones**	33
1			4	5	6	7		9	10	3	11*	8	12					2					I Hendrick	34
1		3	4*	5	6	7		9	10		11	8					12	2					**T Fitzharris**	35
1				5	6	7		9	4	8	11		3					2	10				P Vanes	36
1				5	6				4	8	9		3	7			11	2	10				H Taylor	37
1				5	6	7			4	3	8	12			10		11*	2	9				P Willis	38
1	6			5		7		9	4	3	8				11			2	10				J Ball	39
1	6			5	6	7		9	4	3	8				11			2	10				R Nixon	40
1	6			5	6	7		9*	4	3	8				12			2	10				K Redfern	41
1	6			5		7			4	3	8	11	12				10	2	9*				T Fitzharris	42
1	6			5		7			4	3	8	9*					10	2	12	11			J Lovatt	43
1	6		12	5		7			4	3	8*	9					10	2		11			A Robinson	44
1	6			5		7			4	3	8	12					10	2	9	11*			C Trussell	45
1	6			5	7				4*		8	10	3					2	11	12	9		K Baker	46
1	6		4	5	7					8	11*	3					10	2	9			12	D Shaw	47
1	5	2	6*		7				3		8	4					12		11		9	10	C Seel	48
1	6			5		7			3		8	4					2		11		9	10	T Jones	49
1	6			5*		7			3		8	12	4				2		11		9	10	R Milford	50
42	33	13	26	40	34	40	12	30	36	30	32	22	5	7	17	7	13	8	7	1	4	3	League Appearances	
			1									3	6	1	1	1	3	5	1		1	1	Substitute Appearances	
4	3	2	4	3	4	4	4	4	3	4	2+1	2	1				1		2	0+1			Milk Cup Appearances	
2	2		2	2	2	2		2	2	1	2	0+1	2				1		2				FA Cup Appearances	
2	2		1	2	2			2	2	1	2	0+1	2		2								FM Cup Appearances	

Players on Loan:

Departures: Cockerill (Southampton), Kenworthy (Mansfield), Eves (Gillingham), Bolton (F), Black (F), Edwards (Leeds Utd)

'THE BLADES'

Formed: 1899
Turned Professional: 1899   **Ltd Co:** 1899

Previous Managers: Since 1946:
Ted Davison   Reg Freeman   Joe Mercer   John Harris   Arthur Rowley   John Harris   Ken Furphy
Jimmy Sirrel   Harry Haslam   Martin Peters   Ian Porterfield
Honours: Champions Div 1, 1897-8   Champions Div 2, 1952-3   Champions Div 4 1981-2   FA Cup
Winners 1898-9, 1901-2, 1914-5, 1924-5
League Career: Elected to Div 2 1892   Promoted to Div 1 1893
Relegated to Div 2 1934   Promoted to Div 1 1939   Relegated to Div 2 1949
Promoted to Div 1 1953   Relegated to Div 2 1956   Promoted to Div 1 1961
Relegated to Div 2 1968   Promoted to Div 1 1971   Relegated to Div 2 1976
Relegated to Div 3 1979   Relegated to Div 4 1981   Promoted to Div 3 1982   Promoted to Div 2 1984
Colours: Red and white striped shirts, black shorts, red and white stockings
Change Colours: Yellow shirts, shorts and stockings with red trim, yellow shorts
Reserves League: Central League   **Youth League Team:** Northern Intermediate League

---

CLUB RECORDS

Most Appearances for Club: Joe Shaw, 629, 1948-66
Most Capped Player: Billy Gillespie, 25, N Ireland
Record Goalscorer in a Match: Harry Hammond, 5 v Bootle, Div 2, 26.11.1892
Harry Johnson, 5 v West Ham United, Div 1, 26.12.1927
Record League Goalscorer in a Season: Jimmy Dunne, 41, Div 1, 1930-1
Record League Goalscorer in a Career: Harry Johnson, 205, 1919-30
Record Transfer Fee Received: £400,000 from Leeds United for Alex Sabella, May 1980
Record Transfer Fee Paid: £160,000 to River Plate for Alex Sabella, July 1978   £160,000 to Leicester City for Alan
Young, Aug 1982
Best Performances: League: Champions Div 1 (1)   **FA Cup:** Winners (4)   **League/Milk Cup:** 5th Round 1961-2,
1966-7, 1971-2
Most League Points: 96, Div 4, 1981-2   **Most League Goals:** 102, Div 1, 1925-6
Record League Victory and Most Goals Scored in a League Match: 10-0 v Port Vale, Div 2, 10 Dec 1892
(a)   10-0 v Burnley, Div 1, 19 Jan 1929
Record League Defeat: 3-10 v Middlesbrough, Div 1, 18 Nov 1937
Oldest Player in League Match:
Youngest Player in League Match:
Most Consecutive Undefeated League Matches: 22 1899-1900   League Matches Without a Win: 19 1975-76
Longest Run of Undefeated Home League Matches: 27 1936-37   Away League Matches: 11 1892-93
Longest Run Without Home League Win: 10 1949   Away League Win: 20 1975-76
Most Consecutive League Wins: 8 1893, 1903, 1958, 1960   Home League Wins: 11 1960
Most Consecutive League Defeats: 7 1975   Away League Wins: 6 1892-93

Club Statistician for the Directory: Andrew Trehearne

SHEFFIELD UNITED

PLAYERS NAME Ht Wt Birthdate	Honours	Birthplace Transfers	Clubs	APPEARANCES League	Milk Cup	FA Cup	Other Comps	GOALS League	Milk Cup	FA Cup	Other Comps
GOALKEEPERS											
John Burridge 6.10½ 12.3 3.12.51	Div.2 '79 Lg.C '77	Workington £10,000 £100,000 £65,000 £200,000 £75,000 £10,000	Workington (A) Blackpool Aston Villa Southend (L) Crystal Palace Q.P.R. Wolverhampton W. Derby County (L) Sheffield United	27 134 65 6 88 39 74 6 72	1 10 9 7 4 3 2 4	4 4 6 7 2 5 3					
Paul Tomlinson 6.2 13.6 22.2.64		Brierley Hill	Sheffield United	32	5	3					
DEFENDERS											
Andy Barnsley 6.0 11.11 9.6.62		Sheffield £25,000	Denaby United Rotherham United Sheffield United	28	3	3					
Peter Beagrie 5.8½ 9.10 28.11.65		Middlesbrough £10,000	Middlesbrough Sheffield United	24+9	1		1+1	2			
Jeff Eckhardt 6.10½ 11.10 7.10.65		Sheffield	Sheffield United	40	3			2			
Paul Haylock 5.8 11.0 24.3.63	MC '85	Lowestoft	Norwich City (A) Sheffield United	154+1	22	13+1	1	3			
Pat McGeeney 6.10½ 11.5 31.10.66		Sheffield	Sheffield United	15+1	1						
Martin Pike 5.9 10.11 21.10.64		South Shields F £20,000	W.B.A. (A) Peterborough Utd Sheffield United	119+7	8	10	4	7	2		1
Ken McNaught 5.11 11.1 11.1.55	EC '82 ESC '82 Div.1 '81	Kirkcaldy £125,000 £10,000	Everton (A) Aston Villa W.B.A. Manchester City (L) Sheffield United	64+2 207 42 34	10 17 4 4	10 13 4 1	14	3 8 1 5	1		
Paul Smith 5.9 11.0 9.11.64		Rotherham	Sheffield United (A)	29+7	2	2	1	1			
Paul Stancliffe†* 6.0 11.10 5.5.58	Div.3 '81	Sheffield	Rotherham U (A) Sheffield United	285 116	10 10	22 7	2	8 3	2	2 1	
MIDFIELD											
Kevin Arnott 5.10 11.12 28.9.58		Bensham	Sunderland (A) Blackburn Rovers (L) Sheffield United Blackburn Rovers (L) Rotherham United (L)	132+1 17 97+1 11+1 36	7 11	6 6	2+1	16 2 12 1 4	1 1	1	
Lee Walshaw 5.9 11.5 20.1.67			Sheffield United (A)	6+1				1			
FORWARDS											
Steve Foley 5.7 10.12 4.10.62		Liverpool	Liverpool (A) Fulham (L) Grimsby Town Sheffield United	3 31 22+6	2	2		2 5	1		
David Frain 5.8 10.8 11.10.62			Rowlinson YC Sheffield United (A)	7				1			
Colin Morris 5.7 10.5 22.8.53	Div.4 '82	Blyth £111,111 £100,000	Burnley (A) Southend Blackpool Sheffield United	9+1 133 87 178	11 6 15+1	12 7 14	0+1 3	25 26 55	4 3 5	1 3 5	1
Tony Philliskirk 6.1 11.2 10.2.65		Sheffield	Sheffield United	38+10	2+1	3	3	10			
Brian Smith 5.9½ 11.2 27.10.66		Sheffield	Sheffield United	13+1							
Steve Wigley 5.9 10.12 15.10.61		Ashton-u-Lyme	Curzon Ashton Notts Forest Sheffield United	69+13 7+3	8+1	5 1	10	2	1		
Peter Withe 6.2 13.0 30.8.51	E(11) Div.1 78 81 LgC 78 EC 82 ESC 82	Liverpool Arcadia S £50,000 £40,000 £225,000 £500,000 F	Southport Barrow Wolverhampton W. Birmingham City Nottingham Forest Newcastle United Aston Villa Sheffield United	3 1 12+5 35 74+1 76 182 30	3 21 3 19 4	2 14 4 9 1	21	9 28 25 73 10	12 5 2	10 2 2	9

ADDITIONAL CONTRACT PROFESSIONALS Ken Geelan

APPRENTICES
Martin Ashworth, Patrick Atkinson, Richard Aubray, Simon Copeland, Christopher Downes, Kurt Elliott, Christopher France, Paul Heald, Mark Kelly, Paul Norton, Mark Russell, Paul Wood, Simon Grayson, Chris Marsden, Clive Mendoncia

NON-CONTRACT PLAYERS Chris France, Carl Fuller, Darren Lancaster, Alan Pashley, Darren Potts

Record Attendance: 68,287 v Leeds United, FA Cup Round 5, 15 Feb 1936

Record Receipts: £65,092 v Sheffield Wednesday, Div 3, 5 Apr 1980

Season Tickets: New South Stand/Bramall Lane/John Street, Front, £92 (Adults), £46 (OAPs/Juv); John Street Rear, £74 (Adults), £37 (OAPs/Juv); Ground £46 (Adults), £23 (OAPs/Juv); Terrace £58 (Adults), £28 (OAPs/Juv); £28 (Juv East Wing only); New South Stand/Bramall Lane Stand (Special Family Seasons) Accompanied juveniles £23 with an adult paying £92—up to three juveniles/adult

Executive Box Season Tickets: Small number of seats still available

Cost of Stand Tickets: £6.00 (£3.00 Juveniles/OAPs), £7.50 Family Ticket (1 Adult, 1 Child); Ground: £3.00 (£2.20 OAPs): Terrace: £3.50 (£2.20 OAPs, £2.80 Junior Blade) & Special Rates for Families

Match and Ticket Information: Tickets bookable fourteen days prior to each match

Car Parking: The ground is five minutes away from car parks in the City Centre. Side-street parking is ample

Nearest Railway Station: Sheffield Midland (0742 26411)

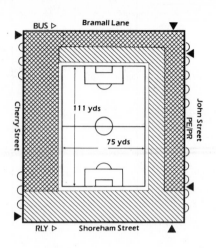

How to get to the ground

From North: Use Motorway M1 until junction 34. Leave Motorway and follow signs, Sheffield A6109. In 3.4m turn left and shortly at roundabout take 4th exit into Sheaf Street. Then at 2nd roundabout take 5th exit into St. Mary's Road (S.P. Bakewell). In 0.5m left into Bramall Lane for Sheffield United FC

From East and South: Use A57 from Motorway M1 (junction 31 or 33) then at roundabout take 3rd exit into Sheaf Street. Then at 2nd roundabout take 5th exit into St Mary's Road and proceed as above

From West: Use A57 (S.P. Sheffield) and at roundabout take 4th exit A6134 into Upper Hanover Street. Then at 2nd roundabout take 3rd exit into Bramall Lane

Price of 1986-7 Programme: 50p
Number of Pages: 24
Subscriptions: £16.50 (post paid British Isles), £24.00 (postage overseas)

Local Newspapers:

Local Radio Stations:

Chairman
H E McGee

Directors
M Sheppard JP, FCA (Vice-Chairman)
S L Speight OBE
C Woodward
K T Addy
E Barron
G K Hulley

Secretary
R H Chester (0742 343122)

Commercial Manager
D Woodhead (0742 337235)

Manager
Howard Wilkinson

Assistant Manager
Peter Eustace

Chief Scout
John Harris

Physiotherapist
Alan Smith

Groundsman
David Barber

Chief Coach
Clive Baker

Sheffield Wednesday finished fifth in the 1st Division, which was their best League placing for 25 years; in the interim period — believe it or not — they have actually experienced 3rd Division football, but the Wednesday of these days is a formidable proposition for anyone. It is just a pity that European Football is presently 'out of bounds' to English teams.

There was a good start in the League with four of the first five games being won and there was soon to be a similar run, but by now Manchester United were on a very 'hot streak' so the 'Owls' never actually took top position; a thrashing by Everton at Hillsborough (1-5) showed that the team probably did not quite have the equipment to take the title and so it proved particularly before the New Year, when silly points were thrown away. This trend continued until the closing weeks of the season when dramatically five matches out of seven were won (the other two were drawn) and these included good wins at Old Trafford and The Dell. The placing improved to fifth which was probably a fair return for the side's efforts.

The cups started with disappointment in the Milk Cup as aggregate victory over Brentford (4-2) was followed by a shock single goal failure at Swindon, but in the FA Cup there was another excellent run with a place in the semi-finals. To reach that point the team had to win an away replay at the Hawthorns against West Bromwich (3-2 after 2-2), but Orient offered few problems in the next round at Hillsborough (5-0). Derby County were a much tougher proposition with a draw at the Baseball Ground (1-1) being followed by success in the replay with two goals from the season's discovery Carl Shutt, who scored again in the 6th Round when West Ham came to Hillsborough and lost (2-1). The semi-final opposition was Everton and after a tremendous tussle in which Shutt scored yet again the Owls bowed out to two second-half goals from the Liverpool team. There was no shame in that.

Most people will rightly say that Howard Wilkinson's team can only improve and the nucleus of his good side remains, from which as an irony only two players were capped during the season — Worthington for Northern Ireland and Jonsson for Iceland. But that should not detract from the fact that many others were very consistent starting with Hodge in goal and supplemented by Sterland, Hart, Marwood, Thompson (now away), Shelton, Shutt (a returned former reject), Snodin and Morris. The only newcomer for the coming season is Ken Brannigan from Queen's Park (a central defender), but with the talent available new signings were not important.

Wednesday are a team with potential and the fans will hope for some trophies to prove that point.   WLM

Back Row L to R: Mel Sterland, Lee Chapman, Paul Hart, Martin Hodge, Kevin Pressman, Ian Knight, Mark Smith, Lawrie Madden. **Middle Row:** Peter Eustace (Assistant Manager), Brian Marwood, Gary Shelton, Mark Chamberlain, Siggi Jonsson, Gary Megson, Nigel Worthington, Alan Smith (Physio). **Front Row:** Colin Walker, Carl Shutt, David Hirst, Howard Wilkinson (Manager), Glynn Snodin, Chris Morris, Tony Gregory.

SHEFFIELD WEDNESDAY

DIVISION ONE: 5th   **FA CUP:** SEMI-FINAL   **MILK CUP:** 3rd ROUND

MATCH	DATE		COMPE-TITION	VENUE	OPPONENTS	RESULT		HALF TIME	L'GUE POS'N	GOALSCORERS/GOAL TIMES	ATTEN-DANCE
1	A	17	CL	H	Chelsea	D	1-1	1-1		Lyons 3	26,164
2		21	CL	A	Nottingham Forest	W	1-0	1-0		Stainrod 2	(18,361)
3		24	CL	A	Manchester City	W	3-1	1-0	2	Thompson 27, Marwood 68, 83	(26,934)
4		26	CL	H	Watford	W	2-1	1-0	2	Sterland 7, Chapman 64	21,962
5		31	CL	A	Oxford United	W	1-0	0-0	2	Jonsson 50	(9,934)
6	S	3	CL	H	Everton	L	1-5	1-1	2	Marwood (pen) 23	30,065
7		7	CL	H	West Ham United	D	2-2	1-1	3	Chapman 18, Thompson 58	19,287
8		14	CL	A	Arsenal	L	0-1	0-1	7		(23,108)
9		21	CL	A	Tottenham Hotspur	L	1-5	1-1	9	Chapman 20	(23,601)
10		25	MC2/1	A	Brentford	D	2-2	0-1		Chapman 66, 81	(5,352)
11		28	CL	H	Luton Town	W	3-2	2-1	7	Marwood 44, (pen) 61, Chapman 45	17,887
12	O	5	CL	A	Birmingham City	W	2-0	1-0	6	Sterland 41, Armstrong (og) 47	(11,708)
13		12	CL	H	Coventry City	D	2-2	2-0	5	Chapman 20, Shutt 44	19,132
14		15	MC2/2	H	Brentford	W	2-0	1-0		Sterland (pen) 9, Chapman 81	11,132
15		19	CL	A	Leicester City	W	3-2	1-0	5	Marwood 27, Jonsson 74, Chapman 79	(10,259)
16		26	CL	H	W.B.A.	W	1-0	1-0	3	Chapman 35	19,873
17		29	MC3	A	Swindon Town	L	0-1	0-1			(12,110)
18	N	2	CL	A	Queens Park Rangers	D	1-1	0-0	3	Snodin 77	(12,123)
19		9	CL	H	Manchester United	W	1-0	0-0	3	Chapman 83	48,105
20		16	CL	A	Aston Villa	D	1-1	1-1	5	Hart 21	(13,849)
21		23	CL	H	Southampton	W	2-1	1-0	5	Chapman 18, Marwood 71	18,955
22		30	CL	A	Ipswich Town	L	1-2	1-1	5	Yallop (og) 16	(12,918)
23	D	7	CL	H	Nottingham Forest	W	2-1	0-0	5	Marwood 57, Chamberlain 85	22,495
24		14	CL	A	Chelsea	L	1-2	0-1	5	Marwood (pen) 65	(19,658)
25		21	CL	H	Manchester City	W	3-2	3-1	5	Thompson 14, Megson 25, Sterland 42	23,177
26		26	CL	H	Newcastle United	D	2-2	1-0	6	Marwood 40, Thompson 80	30,269
27		28	CL	A	Everton	L	1-3	0-2	6	Stevens (og) 51	(41,536)
28	J	1	CL	A	Liverpool	D	2-2	1-0	6	Shutt 1, Thompson 85	(38,964)
29		13	FAC3	H	W.B.A.	D	2-2	1-1		Sterland 38, Smith 47	17,042
30		16	FAC3R	A	W.B.A.	W	3-2	2-1		Marwood (pen) 9, Chapman 41, Chamberlain 87	(11,152)
31		18	CL	H	Oxford United	W	2-1	1-1	6	Shotton (og) 17, Marwood 85	18,565
32		25	FAC4	H	Orient	W	5-0	3-0		Thompson 1, Chapman 11, Sterland 25, Blair 51, Marwood 81	19,087
33	F	1	CL	A	Watford	L	1-2	0-1	8	Megson 64	(13,144)
34		22	CL	H	Tottenham Hotspur	L	1-2	1-0	9	Thompson 20	23,232
35		26	FAC5	A	Derby County	D	1-1	1-1		Christie (og) 33	(22,781)
36	M	1	CL	A	Luton Town	L	0-1	0-1	9		(10,206)
37		5	FAC5R	H	Derby County	W	2-0	1-0		Shutt 43, 83	29,077
38		8	CL	H	Birmingham City	W	5-1	3-0	8	Shutt 3 (9, 28, 66), Chapman 41, Chamberlain 64	17,491
39		12	FAC6	H	West Ham United	W	2-1	2-0		Worthington 16, Shutt 35	35,522
40		15	CL	A	Coventry City	W	1-0	0-0	6	Sterland 63	(10,168)
41		18	CL	H	Leicester City	W	1-0	1-0	6	Sterland 30	18,874
42		22	CL	A	West Ham United	L	0-1	0-1	6		(16,604)
43		29	CL	H	Liverpool	D	0-0	0-0	7		37,946
44		31	CL	A	Newcastle United	L	1-4	0-3	7	Shutt 68	(25,614)
45	A	5	FAC SF	N	Everton	L	1-2†	0-0		Shutt 51	(47,711)
46		8	CL	H	Q.P.R.	D	0-0	0-0	9		13,157
47		13	CL	A	Manchester United	W	2-0	0-0	9	Shutt 54, Sterland (pen) 61	(32,331)
48		16	CL	A	Arsenal	W	2-0	1-0	7	Sterland (pen) 25, Shutt 67	16,344
49		19	CL	H	Aston Villa	W	2-0	1-0	6	Megson 29, Sterland 64	19,782
50		22	CL	A	W.B.A.	D	1-1	1-0	6	Marwood 10	(6,201)
51		26	CL	A	Southampton	W	3-2	1-0	6	Shutt 6, Shelton 64, Hart 89	(15,375)
52	M	3	CL	H	Ipswich Town	W	1-0	0-0	5	Marwood 82	22,369

Best Home League Attendance: 48,105 v Manchester United 9/11   **Smallest:** 13,157 v Q.P.R. 8/4   **Av Home Att:** 23,10

Goal Scorers: Compared with 84-85: − 4,66

League (63):   Marwood 13 (3 pen), Chapman 10, Shutt 9, Sterland 8 (2 pen), Thompson 6, Megson 3, Chamberlain 2, Jonsson 2, Hart 2, Lyons 1, Shelton 1, Snodin 1, Stainrod 1, Opponents 4
Milk Cup (4):   Chapman 3, Sterland 1 (pen)
FA Cup (16):   Shutt 4, Chapman 2, Marwood 2 (1 pen), Sterland 2, Blair 1, Chamberlain 1, Smith 1, Thompson 1, Opponents 1

†A.E.T.

Hodge	Sterland	Worthington	Shirtliff	Lyons	Hart	Marwood	Blair	Thompson	Chapman	Shelton	Stainrod	Jonsson	Gregory (A)	Shutt	Morris	Smith	Madden	Chamberlain	Snodin	Megson	Knight	Referee	
1	2	3	4	5	6	7	8*	9	10	11	12											K Baker	1
1	2	3	4	5	6	7		12	10*	11	9	8										D Scott	2
1	2	3	4	5	6	7		10	12		9*	8	11									A Saunders	3
1	2	3*	4	5	6	7		10	12		9	8	11									K Redfern	4
1	2	3	4	5	6	7		8*	9	11		10		12								C Downey	5
1	2	3	4	5	6*	7		8	9	11	12	10										G Courtney	6
1		3		5		7		8*	9	11	12	10			2	4	6					N Midgley	7
1		3		5		7		8	9*	11		10			2	4	6	12				A Gunn	8
1				5		7		8	9	11		10			2	4	6		3			R Milford	9
1	2			5		7*	10	8	9	11						4	6	12	3			M James	10
1	2		6	5		7	10	8*	9	11						4		12	3			R Banks	11
1	2	6		5		7	10	8	9*	11					3	4		12				R Nixon	12
1	2	6		5			8		9	11				10	3	4		7				A Robinson	13
1	2	6		5			8	10	9	11*				7	3	4		12				K Walmsley	14
1	2		5	6		7	8		9				11	10		4		3				D Reeves	15
1	2			6		7	8		9				4	10	11	5		3				N Wilson	16
1	2		5	6		7	8	12	9	11				10*		4		3				Allan Robinson	17
1	2			6		7	8	10	9	11					5	4		3				I Borrett	18
1	2			6		7*	8	10	9	11					5	4		12	3			J Bray	19
1	2			6		7	8	10	9	11					5	4			3			I Hendrick	20
1	2			6		7	8	10	9	11					5	4			3			R Betts	21
1	2			6		7	8*	10	9	11			12		5	4			3			T Ward	22
1	2			6		7	8*	10	9	11					5	4		12	3			T Holbrook	23
1	2†	10		6		7	8		9	11					5*	4		12	3			L Robinson	24
1	2			6		7	8	10	9*	11					5	4		12	3	8		G Aplin	25
1	2			6		7	8	10	9	11					5	4		12	3*	8		G Napthine	26
1		3	2			7	8	9					12		5	6*	4	11		10		M Peck	27
1	12	10*	2					9					11	8	5	3	4	7		6		R Bridges	28
1	2			5		7	10	9	12				6	8*	11	3	4					K Walmsley	29
1	2	4		5		7	10	9	8				6*		11	3		12				K Walmsley	30
1	2	4		5*		7	10	9						8	11	3		12	6			A Saunders	31
1	2	4*				7	8	9	10	12					3	5		11	6			K Redfern	32
1	2		4			7	8	9	10						3	5		11	6			R Gifford	33
1	2		4			7	8	9	10	12					3	5*		11	6			C Seel	34
1	2	5				7	8*	9	10						3	4		12	11	6		N Midgley	35
1	2	5	4			7		9		10*	12				3	6			11	8		D Axcell	36
1	2	5				7*		9		6				10	3	4		12	11	8		N Midgley	37
1	2	5				7		9		6*				10	3	4		12	11	8		D Scott	38
1	2	6	5			7*		9						10	3	4		12	11	8		J Worrall	39
1	2	6	5	4		7		9						10	3				11	8		A Gunn	40
1	2	6	5	4		7		10	9*						3			12	11	8		I Hendrick	41
1	2	6	5	4		7		10	9*						3				11	8		K Barratt	42
1	2	6*	5			7		9						10	3	4		12	11	8		P Willis	43
1	2			5		7		9		6*				10	3	4		12	11	8		M Peck	44
1	2	3	5					9	7*	6				10		4		12		11	8	B Hill	45
1	2	3	5					9	7	6*				10		4		12		11	8	G Ashby	46
1	2	3	5					9	10*	6				7		4		12		11	8	V Callow	47
1	2			5				9	10*	6				7	3	4		12		11	8	J Lovatt	48
1	2			5		7		9		6				10*	3	4		12		8	11	G Courtney	49
1	2			5		7		9		6				10	3	4		12		8*	11	T Jones	50
1	2			5		7		9		6			8	10	12	4*			3		11	R Groves	51
1	2	4		5		7		9*		6				10				12	3	8	11	D Allison	52
42	37	15	21	11	34	37	17	35	29	30	3	9	4	17	29	13	25	3	27	20	4	League Appearances	
	1						1	2	1	3	1	1	2	1					18	1		Substitute Appearances	
3	3		1	2	2	2	3	2+1	3	3					2	1	2	2	0+1	2+1		Milk Cup Appearances	
7	7	1	6		3	6	4	5	6+1	2+1			2		4	5	6	3	0-5	5	5	FA Cup Appearances	

Also Played:

Departures: Stainrod, Blair, Thompson (A Villa), Cooke (Carlisle), Oliver (Bradford), Lyons (Grimsby), Redfern (Rochdale) Hesford (Sunderland)

'THE OWLS'

Formed: 1867
Turned Professional: 1887   **Ltd Co:** 1899

Previous Managers: Since 1946: Eric Taylor (Secretary/Manager)   1959-61 Harry Catterick
1961-4 Vic Buckingham   1964-7 Alan Brown   1967-8 Jack Marshall   1969 Tom McAnearney
1969-71 Danny Williams   1971-4 Derek Dooley   1974-6 Steve Burtenshaw   1976-8 Len Ashurst
1978-83 Jack Charlton   1983- Howard Wilkinson
Honours: Champions Div 1, 1902-3, 1903-4, 1928-9, 1929-30   Champions Div 2, 1899-1900,
1925-6, 1951-2, 1955-6, 1958-9   FA Cup Winners 1896, 1907, 1935
League Career: Elected to Div 1 1892   Relegated to Div 2 1898-9
Promoted to Div 1 1899-1900   Relegated to Div 2 1919-20   Promoted to Div 1 1925-6
Relegated to Div 2 1936-7   Promoted to Div 1 1949-5   Relegated to Div 2 1950-1
Promoted to Div 1 1951-2   Relegated to Div 2 1954-5   Promoted to Div 1 1955-6
Relegated to Div 2 1957-8   Promoted to Div 1 1958-9   Relegated to Div 2 1969-70
Relegated to Div 3 1974-5   Promoted to Div 2 1979-80   Promoted to Div 1 1983-4
Colours: Blue and white striped shirts, blue shorts white stockings
Change Colours: Yellow shirts with blue trim, white shorts, yellow stockings with blue band

CLUB RECORDS

Most Appearances for Club: Andrew Wilson: Football League 502 + FA Cup 44 **Total 546**
Most Capped Player: Ron Springett, 33, England
Record Goalscorer in a Match: Douglas Hunt, 6 v Norwich City, 7-0 (h), Div 2, 19.11.38
Record League Goalscorer in a Season: Derek Dooley, 46   **In All Competitions:** Derek Dooley, 47 (League 46 + FA
Cup 1), 1951-2 (in 31 appearances)
Record League Goalscorer in a Career: Andrew Wilson, 200   **In All Competitions:** Andrew Wilson, 216 (League
200 + FA Cup 16) 1900-20
Record Transfer Fee Received: £120,000 from Newcastle United for Tommy Craig, Jan 1975
Record Transfer Fee Paid: £200,000 to Budocnost for Ante Mirocevic, 1980
Best Performances: League: Champions (4)   **FA Cup:** Winners (3)   **League/Milk Cup:** 5th Round 1982-3   **European
Fairs Cup:** Quarter Final
Most League Points: (2pts for win) 62, Div 2, 1968-94   (3pts for win) 77, Div 2, 1983-4
Most League Goals: 106, Div 2, 1958-9
Record League Victory and Most Goals Scored in a League Match: 9-1 v Birmingham City, Div 1, 13 Dec 1930
Most Goals Scored in a Cup Tie: 12-0 v Halliwell, (h), FA Cup 1st Round, 17 Jan 1891
Record League Defeat: 0-10 v Aston Villa, Div 1, 5 Oct 1912
European Competitions Entered: Fairs Cup 1961-2, 1963-4
Oldest Player in League Match: Tom Brittleton 41 yrs, 1920
Youngest Player in League Match: Peter Fose, 15 yrs 10 months

Most Consecutive Undefeated League Matches: 19 1960-61 | **League Matches Without a Win:** 20 1954-55, 1975

Longest Run of Undefeated Home League Matches: 31 1902-04 | **Away League Matches:** 11 1979-80
Longest Run Without Home League Win: 13 1974-75 | **Away League Win:** 35 1975-76
Most Consecutive League Wins: 9 1904 | **Home League Wins:** 19 1899-1900
Most Consecutive League Defeats: 7 1893 | **Away League Wins:** 5 1930, 1961

Club Statistician for the Directory: Mick Renshaw

442

SHEFFIELD WEDNESDAY

PLAYERS NAME Ht Wt Birthdate	Honours	Birthplace Transfers	Clubs	APPEARANCES				GOALS			
				League	Milk Cup	FA Cup	Other Comps	League	Milk Cup	FA Cup	Other Comps
GOALKEEPERS											
Martin Hodge† 6.2 14.2 4.2.59		Southport	Plymouth Argyle (A)	43	1	1					
			Everton	25		6					
			Preston (L)	28							
			Oldham (L)	4							
			Gillingham (L)	4							
			Preston (L)	16							
		£50,000	Sheffield Wednesday	126	16	15					
DEFENDERS											
Paul Hart 6.2 12.8 4.5.53		Manchester	Stockport County	88	7	5+1		5			
		£30,000	Blackpool	143	7	6		17	1		
		£300,000	Leeds United	191	17	11	4	16	1	1	2
		£50,000	Notts Forest	70	3	3	10	1		1	
			Sheffield Wednesday	34	2	3		2			
Lawrie Madden 5.11 13.1 28.9.53		London	Arsenal (N/C)								
			Mansfield (N/C)	9+1	2	2					
		Manchester Univ.	Charlton A.	109+4	4+2	8		7			
		£10,000	Millwall	44+3	2	1		2			
		F	Sheffield Wednesday	81+1	11	10		1	3		
Mark Smith 6.1½ 12.2 21.3.60	E.U21 (3)	Sheffield	Sheffield W. (A)	265+1	29	33		16	1	3	
Mel Sterland 5.11 13.2 1.10.61	E.U21 (7)	Sheffield	Sheffield W. (A)	181+8	20	24+1		21	4	5	
Ken Branigan 6.2 12.10 23.6.67		Glasgow	Queens Park								
			Sheffield Wednesday								
MIDFIELD											
Tony Gregory 5.8 10.10 21.3.68	E,S,Y	Doncaster	Sheffield W. (A)	4+1		2					
Siggi Johnsson 5.11 11.11 27.9.66		Akranes, Iceland	I.A. Akranes								
			Sheffield Wednesday	11+2				2			
			Barnsley (L)	5							
			Sheffield Wednesday								
Ian Knight 6.2 12.4 26.10.66		Hartlepool	Barnsley (A)								
			Sheffield Wednesday	4							
Gary Megson 5.10 11.6 2.5.59		Manchester	Plymouth Argyle (A)	78	9	5		10			
		£200,000	Everton	20+2		3		2		1	
		£130,000	Sheffield Wednesday	123	13	12		13	2	5	
		£175,000	Notts Forest								
		£130,000	Newcastle United	19+1		2		1		1	
		£60,000	Sheffield Wednesday	20		5		3			
Chris Morris 5.8 11.6 24.12.63	ES	Dronfield	Sheffield Wednesday	48+9	5+4	5+1		1	1		
Gary Shelton 5.7 11.3 21.3.58	E.U21 (1)	Nottingham	Walsall (A)	12+12	0+1	2+2				1	
			Aston Villa	23	2+1			7	1		
			Notts County (L)	8							
		£50,000	Sheffield Wednesday	158+3	17	17+1		15	3	2	
Glynn Snodin 5.6 9.5 14.2.60		Rotherham	Doncaster R. (A)	288+21	12+2	16+1	5	63	1	1	1
		£115,000	Sheffield Wednesday	27+1	2+1	5		1			
Nigel Worthington 5.10 12.6 4.11.61	NI (10) Y	Ballymena	Ballymena United								
			Notts County	67	11	4		4			
		£100,000	Sheffield Wednesday	66+1	6	4		1		1	
FORWARDS											
Mark Chamberlain 5.8½ 9.8 19.11.61	E (8) U.21 (4) S	Stoke	Port Vale (A)	90+6	4	10		17		2	
			Stoke City	110+2	9	4		17		1	
		£300,000	Sheffield Wednesday	3+18	0+1	0+5		2		1	
Lee Chapman 6.1½ 13.0 5.12.59	E.U21 (1)	Lincoln	Stoke City	95+4	5	3		34	3	1	
			Plymouth Argyle (L)	3+1							
		£500,000	Arsenal	15+8	0+2	0+1		4			
		£200,000	Sunderland	14+1		2		3		1	
		£100,000	Sheffield Wednesday	69+2	10	8+1		24	5	5	
David Hirst 5.11 12.5 7.12.67	EY	Barnsley	Barnsley	26+2	1			9			
		£250,000	Sheffield Wednesday								
Brian Marwood 5.7 9.13 5.2.60		Easington	Hull City (A)	154+4	4+1	16	5	51		1	
		£115,000	Sheffield Wednesday	78	9	9		20	4	3	
Carl Shutt 5.10½ 11.13 10.10.61		Sheffield	Spalding United								
			Sheffield Wednesday	17+2	2	4		9		4	

ADDITIONAL CONTRACT PROFESSIONALS
Desmond Hazell, Kevin Pressman, Alan Smith

APPRENTICES
C. Bradshaw, S. Chambers, C. Greenfield, W. Jacobs, G. Lee, P. Mullen, L. Oliver, J. Thackray, D. Tomlinson

NON-CONTRACT PLAYERS

HILLSBOROUGH Sheffield S6 1SW   Capacity: 50,174

Record Attendance: 72,841 v Manchester
City, FA Cup Round 5, 17 Feb 1934

**Smallest Home Attendance for a First Class
Match:** 2,500 v Everton, 5 April 1902

Record Receipts: £192,162 Tottenham
Hotspur v Wolverhampton Wanderers, FA Cup
Semi-Final, 11 Apr 1981

Season Tickets: N & S Stands (centre):
£120.00 (adults), £65.00 (juveniles/OAP); N &
S Stands (wings) £103.00 (adults), £50.00
(juveniles/OAP); Uncovered seating: £91.00
(adults), £47.00 (juveniles/OAP). For family
special offer contact club

Cost of Stand Tickets: N & S (centre): £6.50
(adult), £4.50 (juvenile/OAP); N & S (wings)
£5.50, £3.00; Uncovered £5.00, £3.00;
Terraces: £3.50 (adult), £2.00 (juveniles/OAP)

Match and Ticket Information: South and
North Stand. Applications not more than 3
weeks in advance subject to tickets being
unsold. Payment and SAE must accompany
application

Car Parking: Street parking is available

Nearest Railway Station: Sheffield Midland
(0742 26411)/Wadsley Bridge

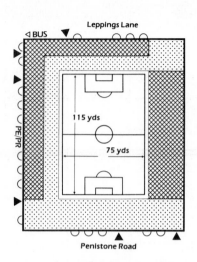

Leppings Lane
◁ BUS
PE/PR
115 yds
75 yds
Penistone Road

How to get to the ground

From North: Use Motorway M1 until junction
34, leave Motorway and follow signs Sheffield
A6109. In 1.5m at roundabout take 3rd exit
A6102. In 3.2m turn left into Herries Road South
for Sheffield Wednesday FC
From East and South: Use A57 from Motorway
M1 (junction 31 or 33) then at roundabout
junction with Ring Road take 3rd exit A610 into
Prince of Wales Road. In 5.8m turn left into
Herries Road South for Sheffield Wednesday FC
From West: Use A57 (S.P. Sheffield) then turn
left A6101. In 3.8m at T road turn left A61 into
Penistone Road for Sheffield Wednesday FC

Price of 1986-7 Programme: 50p
Number of Pages: 28
Subscriptions: £16.00 (League matches, 2nd
class postage, UK included); £17.00 (League
matches, surface mail to Europe); £20.00
(League matches, surface mail outside Europe);
£32.00 (League matches, airmail outside
Europe)

Local Newspapers: Sheffield Newspapers Ltd
(The Star, Morning Telegraph)

Local Radio Stations: BBC Radio Sheffield,
Radio Hallam

SHREWSBURY TOWN   Division 2

President
L Tudor-Owen

Chairman
H S Yates

Vice-Chairman
K R Woodhouse

Directors
L Tudor-Owen
A C Williams
F C G Fry
P W Newbrook
R Bailey

Secretary
M J Starkey (0743 60111)

Player/Manager
Chic Bates

Physiotherapist
D Mann

Chief Scout
H Maney

Commercial Manager
I Hookway (0743 56316)

Back Row L to R: Paul Johnson, Nigel Pearson, Steve Perks, Ken Hughes, Richard Green, Darren Hughes. **Middle Row:** Derek Mann (Physio), Gerry Daly, Wayne Williams, Paul Tester, Mark Kelly, Gary Leonard, Michael Brown, Neil Meredith, Chich Bates (Manager). **Front Row:** Gary Hackett, Colin Robinson, Bernard McNally, Colin Griffin, Dave Waller, Tim Steele.

It looked for a good part of Town's seventh season in Division Two that at last the miracle seemingly worked each season at Gay Meadow had failed. In true 'Roy of the Rovers' style through a first League goal for the club by substitute Darren Hughes six minutes from the end of the last game against Middlesbrough secured the necessary points and condemned Boro to division three at the same time. The necessity of running the club on such a small squad was at the root of the problem. Rarely was it possible to field the same team in consecutive games.

Ross Maclaren had left for Derby and there were long term lay offs for regulars Paul Tester, Paul Petts, Wayne Williams and Paul Johnson who broke a leg in only the 2nd game of the season. An abysmal start to the season with the first win coming only after nearly a quarter of the season, away at Carlisle, coupled with a poor away record bringing only three wins left the club to rely heavily on a reasonably consistent home record. This included seven consecutive home wins in mid season.

The squad was strengthened in October with the signing of Eire international Gerry Daly and for a loan period full-back Bryn Gunn from Notts Forest. Of great comfort to Town's followers in such a season was the gradual improvement after a lay off of over 12 months of centre-back Nigel Pearson who by May had re-established himself as arguably one of the best central defenders in the division.

The season could perhaps be best summed up in cup performances. After a 3-2 home defeat Town progressed to the third round of the Milk Cup with a fine 2-0 victory in the second leg against Huddersfield at Leeds Road. Everton were the visitors next but Town were well beaten 4-1. In the FA Cup front runners Chelsea were the visitors and left with a 1-0 victory. Rarely have the 1st division sides left Gay Meadow with a victory let alone two in a season.

Naturally it was not all gloom and despondency as there were both good results and fine performances. There were double victories over Brighton and a home win over Charlton, promoted to Division 1, at the run in. The club were lucky to be able to rely heavily on regulars Perks, Cross, Pearson, Hackett, Daly, Stevens, Robinson and McNally who whilst others were out injured provided the backbone of the team. McNally was rewarded for his hard work with a place in the Northern Ireland World Cup squad and for the first time ever Town were able to boast two internationals in their ranks.

A season then when both club and supporters were glad to hear the final whistle. Time to look forward to next season and improved fortunes in the club's centenary season.

Richard Stocken

SHREWSBURY TOWN

DIVISION TWO: 17th   **FA CUP:** 3rd ROUND   **MILK CUP:** 3rd ROUND   **FMC:** PRELIM ROUND

MATCH	DATE		COMPE-TITION	VENUE	OPPONENTS	RESULT		HALF TIME	L'GUE POS'N	GOALSCORERS/GOAL TIMES	ATTEN-DANCE
1	A	18	CL	H	Crystal Palace	L	0-2	0-2			(4,295)
2		20	CL	A	Oldham Athletic	L	3-4	1-2		McNally 20, (pen) 79, Robinson	(3,092)
3		24	CL	A	Blackburn Rovers	D	1-1	0-0	20	Nardiello 63	(6,071)
4		27	CL	H	Millwall	D	1-1	0-0		Tester	3,008
5		31	CL	A	Sheffield United	D	1-1	1-1	18	Nardiello 33	(11,246)
6	S	3	CL	H	Portsmouth	D	1-1	1-1		Robinson 43	3,719
7		7	CL	H	Leeds United	L	1-3	0-1	19	Cross 50	4,168
8		14	CL	A	Barnsley	L	0-2	0-1	20		(4,516)
9		18	FMC	A	Oxford United	L	0-3	0-2			(1,898)
10		21	CL	H	Sunderland	L	1-2	1-1	22	Robinson 10	3,919
11		24	MC2/1	H	Huddersfield Town	L	2-3	2-2		Wilson (og) 7, Stevens 38	2,251
12		28	CL	A	Carlisle United	W	2-0	1-0	21	Stevens 44, Robinson 62	(2,559)
13	O	5	CL	A	Fulham	L	1-2	0-0	21	Pearson 74	(3,412)
14		8	MC2/2	A	Huddersfield Town	W	2-0	1-0		Hackett 31, Robinson 70	(4,966)
15		12	CL	H	Huddersfield Town	W	3-0	3-0	19	Cross 18, Daly 20, Nardiello 26	3,986
16		15	FMC	H	Fulham	D	0-0	0-0			1,340
17		19	CL	A	Norwich City	L	1-3	1-2	21	Van Wyk (og) 28	(11,732)
18		26	CL	H	Hull City	D	0-0	0-0	20		3,587
19		29	MC3	H	Everton	L	1-4	0-1		Robinson 51	10,246
20	N	2	CL	A	Charlton Athletic	L	1-4	1-2	21	Stevens 9	(3,233)
21		9	CL	H	Brighton & H.A.	W	2-1	2-1	20	Robinson 24, Hutchings (og) 40	2,942
22		16	CL	A	Wimbledon	L	1-2	1-1	21	Daly 23	(2,584)
23		23	CL	H	Bradford City	W	2-0	1-0	20	Cross 31, Nardiello 81	3,148
24		30	CL	A	Middlesbrough	L	1-3	1-2	21	Cross 17	(4,506)
25	D	7	CL	H	Oldham Athletic	W	2-0	1-0	19	Hackett 33, Robinson 86	2,702
26		15	CL	A	Crystal Palace	W	1-0	0-0	20	Hackett 55	(8,253)
27		20	CL	H	Blackburn Rovers	W	2-0	0-0	15	Daly 51, Cross 78	3,174
28		26	CL	H	Stoke City	W	1-0	1-0	13	Dyson (og) 44	9,595
29		28	CL	A	Portsmouth	L	0-4	0-1	13		(12,302)
30	J	1	CL	A	Grimsby Town	L	1-3	1-1	14	Daly 35	(4,750)
31		4	FAC3	H	Chelsea	L	0-1	0-0			8,100
32		11	CL	H	Barnsley	W	3-0	2-0	13	Nardiello 15, McNally 24, 85	2,756
33		18	CL	H	Sheffield United	W	3-1	1-0	12	Hackett 21, Robinson 66, 76	4,261
34	F	1	CL	A	Millwall	L	0-2	0-0	13		(4,487)
35		8	CL	H	Norwich City	L	0-3	0-2	14		5,157
36	M	1	CL	H	Carlisle United	D	0-0	0-0	15		2,364
37		4	CL	A	Hull City	L	3-4	1-2	15	McNally 15, Leonard 58, Cross 85	(6,253)
38		8	CL	H	Fulham	W	2-1	2-0	15	Hackett 13, Stevens 27	2,563
39		15	CL	A	Huddersfield Town	L	0-1	0-0	17		(4,511)
40		22	CL	A	Leeds United	D	1-1	0-0	16	Stevens 89	(9,641)
41		29	CL	H	Grimsby Town	L	0-2	0-0	16		3,097
42		31	CL	A	Stoke City	D	2-2	1-1	17	McNally (pen) 17, Callaghan (og) 80	(8,988)
43	A	5	CL	H	Charlton Athletic	W	2-1	2-0	16	Williams 8, Hackett 10	3,380
44		12	CL	A	Brighton & H.A.	W	2-0	0-0	16	Daly 51, Robinson 89	(7,210)
45		19	CL	H	Wimbledon	D	1-1	0-1	16	Hackett 50	3,948
46		26	CL	A	Bradford City	L	1-3	0-3	17	Cross 80	(4,663)
47		29	CL	A	Sunderland	L	0-2	0-0	17		(15,507)
48	M	3	CL	H	Middlesbrough	W	2-1	1-0	17	Robinson 16, Hughes 84	6,695

Best Home League Attendance: 9,595 v Stoke City   **Smallest:** 2,364 v Carlisle United   **Av Home Att:** 3,927

Goal Scorers: **Compared with 84-85: −783**

League (52):	Robinson 10, Cross 7, Hackett 6, McNally 6 (2 pen), Daly 5, Nardiello 5, Opponents 4, Stevens 4, Hughes 1, Leonard 1, Pearson 1, Tester 1, Williams 1
Milk Cup (5):	Robinson 2, Hackett 1, Stevens 1, Opponent 1
FA Cup (-):	
FM Cup (-):	

Perks	Williams	Johnson	Cross	Pearson	Griffin	Hackett	Hughes	Stevens	Robinson	Tester	Nardiello	McNally	Kerr	Bates	Leonard	Malcolm	Daly	Brown	Gunn (L)	Steele	Rees (L)	Referee	
1	2	3	4	5	6	7	8	9*	10	11	12											A Seville	1
1	2	3*	4	5	6	8	12	9	10	11		7										P Willis	2
1	2		4	5		8		6	10	11	9	7	3									D Aplin	3
1	2		4	5		8		6	10	11	9	7	3									I Ball	4
1	2		4		5	8*		6	10	11	9	7	3	12								N Midgley	5
1	2		4		6	8		5	10	11	9	7	3									D Scott	6
1	2		4		5	8		6	10	11	9*	7	3	12								J Deakin	7
1	2		4	5	6	8	3		10*	11	9	7			12							J Hough	8
1	2		4	6	5	8*	3	9	10	12		7	11									**G Napthine**	9
1	2		4	5	6	8	3	9	10	11		7										F Roberts	10
	2		4	5	6	8	3	9	10	11*		7	12			1						**K Baker**	11
1	2		4	5	6	8	3	9	10			7					11					L Dilkes	12
1	2		4	5	6	8	3	9	10			7					11					Alan Robinson	13
1	2		4	5	6	8	3	9	10			7					11					**G Courtney**	14
1	2		4	5		8	3	6	10		9	7					12	11*				K Cooper	15
	2		4	5		13	11*	6	12		9*		3		7	1	8	10				**I Hendrick**	16
1			4	5†		8	3	6	10		9	7	2				11					N Butler	17
1	2*		4	5	6	8	3	9	10		12	7					11					H King	18
1			4	5	6	8	3	9	10			7	2				11					**H Taylor**	19
1			4		6	8		5	10		9	7	2	3	11							J Martin	20
1			4		6	8		5	10		9	7	2				11	3				T Fitzharris	21
1			4	5	6	8			10		9	7	2				11	3				I Borrett	22
1			4	5	6	8	3		10		9				7		11	2				R Hamer	23
1			4	5	6	8	3	9	10						7		11	2				C Seel	24
1			4	5		8	3	9	10		9	7					11	2				M Reed	25
1			4	5	6	8	3	9	10						7		11	2				D Axcell	26
1			4	5	6	8	3	9	10						7		11	2				G Ashby	27
1			4	5	6	8	3	9	10						7		11	2				R Guy	28
1			4	5	6	8	3	9	10		12				7*		11	2				J Moules	29
1	2		4	5	6	8	3	9	10						7		11					K Hackett	30
1	2	7	3			8	5	4	9						10	6	11					**N Midgley**	31
1	2		4	5		8	3	6	10		9	7					11					R Gifford	32
1	2		4	5		8	3	6	10		9	7					11					I Hendrick	33
1	2		4	5*		8	3	6	10		9	7			12		11					L Shapter	34
1	2		4	5		8	3	6	10		9*	7			12		11					J Worrall	35
1	2		4		6	8	3	5	10		9*	7			12		11					F Roberts	36
1	2	9*		5		8	3	6	10			7			4		11					K Walmsley	37
1	3	9*		5		8	2	6	10			7			4		11		12			G Napthine	38
1	7	3		5	6	8*	2	9	10						4		11†		12			N Wilson	39
1	2	3		5*	6	8	11	9	10		12	7			4							A Seville	40
1	2*	3		5	6	8	11	9	10		7				4						12	J McAuley	41
1	2	3		5	6	8	11	9	10		7		12								4*	V Callow	42
1	2	3		5	6	8	11	9	10		7						4					J Bray	43
1	2	3	4	5	6	8		9	10		7						11					H Taylor	44
1	2	3	4	5	6	8		9†	10		7						11					D Scott	45
1	2	3	4*	5	6	8		9	10		7				12		11					D Shaw	46
1	2	3		5	6	8	11*	9	10		12	7					4					R Bridges	47
1	2	3		5	6	8	12		10		9*	7					4	11				N Butler	48
42	30	13	35	35	32	42	29	38	42	9	19	34	9	1	15		27	9		1		League Appearances	
								2			3	1		9	4	6			2	1		Substitute Appearances	
2	2		3	3	3	3	3	3	3	1		3	1+1		1	1	1					Milk Cup Appearances	
1	1		1	1	1	1	1	1	1			1			1		1					FA Cup Appearances	
1	2		2	2	1	1+1	2	2	1+1	0+1	1	1	2		1	1	1					FM Cup Appearances	

Players on Loan: Gunn (Nottingham Forest)

Departures: Malcolm (Barnsley), Cross (Derby)

'THE TOWN'

Formed: 1886
Turned Professional: 1905 **Ltd Co:** 1936

Previous Managers: Since 1950: Sammy Crooks   Walter Rowley   Harry Potts   John Spuhler
1957-68 Arthur Rowley   1968-72 Harry Gregg   1972-4 Maurice Evans   1974-8 Alan Durban   1978
Richie Barker   1978-84 Graham Turner
Honours: Div 3 Champions   Welsh Cup Winners (5)
League Career: Elected to Div 3 (N) 1950   Reverted to Div 3 (S) 1951   Joined Div 4 1958
Promoted to Div 3 1958-9   Relegated to Div 4 1973-4   Promoted to Div 3 1974-5
Promoted to Div 2 1978-9
Colours: Blue shirts with amber trim, amber shorts and stockings
Change Colours: Red/white or all white
Reserves League: Macbar South West Counties   **'A' Team:** Midland Intermediate

---

CLUB RECORDS

Most Appearances for Club: Ken Mulhearn: Football League 370 + FA Cup 22 + League Cup 19 **Total 411**
Most Capped Player: Jimmy McLaughlin, 5, Northern Ireland   **For England:** None
Record Goalscorer in a Match: Alf Wood, 5 v Blackburn Rovers, (H) 7-1, Div 3, 7 Oct 1971
Record League Goalscorer in a Season: Arthur Rowley, 38, Div 3, 1958-9   **In All Competitions:** Alf Wood, 40 (League 35 + FA Cup 2 + League Cup 3), 1971-2
Record League Goalscorer in a Career: Arthur Rowley, 152, 1958-65
Record Transfer Fee Received: £262,000 from Stoke City for Paul Maguire, Sept 1980
Record Transfer Fee Paid: £100,000 to Aldershot for John Dungworth, Nov 1979
Best Performances: League: 8th Div 2 1983-4   **FA Cup:** 6th Round 1978-9, 1981-2   **League/Milk Cup:** Semi-Final 1961   **Welsh Cup:** Winners 1891, 1938, 1977, 1979, 1984
Most League Points: 62, Div 4, 1974-5   **Most League Goals:** 101, Div 4, 1958-9
Record League Victory: 7-0 v Swindon Town, Div 3 (S), 6 May 1955
Most Goals Scored in a League Match: 7-2 v Luton Town, (A), Div 3, 10 March 1965   7-1 v Blackburn Rovers (H), Div 3, 2 Oct 1971
Most Goals Scored in a Cup Tie: 7-1 v Banbury Spencer (H), 1st Round FA Cup, 4 Nov 1961
Record League Defeat: 1-8 v Norwich City, (H), Div 3 (S), 13 Sept 1952   v Coventry City, Div 2, 22 Oct 1963
Oldest Player in League Match:
Youngest Player in League Match:
Most Consecutive Undefeated League Matches: 12 1960
Longest Run of Undefeated Home League Matches: 31 1978-79
Longest Run Without Home League Win: 6 1977
Most Consecutive League Wins: 7 1950, 1955
Most Consecutive League Defeats: 7 1951-52

League Matches Without a Win: 11 1974, 1976
Away League Matches: 13 1974
Away League Win: 20 1981-82
Home League Wins: 8 1955, 1975
Away League Wins: 3 1955, 1974, 1976, 1980

Club Statistician for the Directory: Richard Stocken

SHREWSBURY TOWN

PLAYERS NAME / Wt Birthdate	Honours	Birthplace / Transfers	Clubs	APPEARANCES League	Milk Cup	FA Cup	Other Comps	GOALS League	Milk Cup	FA Cup	Other Comps
GOALKEEPERS											
Hughes 9.1.66		Barmouth	Crystal Palace								
ve Perks† 11.4 19.4.63		Shrewsbury	Shrewsbury Town	65	2	2	1				
DEFENDERS											
hard Green 11.8		Wolverhampton	Shrewsbury Town								
in Griffin* 11.7 8.1.56	Div.3 '79	Dudley £10,000	Derby County (A) / Shrewsbury Town	395+2	20	30	1	7			
ren Hughes 10.9 6.10.65	FAYC '84	Prescot F	Everton (A) / **Shrewsbury Town**	3 / 28+2	3	1		1			
l Johnson 11.3 25.5.59		Stoke £20,000	Stoke City (A) / Shrewsbury Town	33+1 / 140+2	6	7+1		3			
el Pearson 12.6 21.8.63		Nottingham £5,000	Heanor Town / Shrewsbury Town	100	8	4	2	2			
yne Williams 11.10 17.11.63		Telford	Shrewsbury Town (A)	138+2	9	4	2	5	2		
MIDFIELD											
ry Daly 11.2 30.4.54	Ei (37) Div.2 '75	Dublin £175,000 £310,000	Bohemians / Manchester United / Derby County / Coventry City / Leicester City (L) / Birmingham City / Shrewsbury Town	107+4 / 111+1 / 82+2 / 17 / 31+1 / 27	17 / 5 / 10+1 / / 2 / 1	9 / 5 / 6 / / 4 / 1	4 / / / / / 1	23 / 31 / 15 / / 1 / 5	4 / 1 / 1	5 / 2 / 4	
rk Kelly 10.4 7.10.66		Blackpool	Shrewsbury Town								
y Leonard 10.10 28.11.65		Newcastle	W.B.A. (A) / Shrewsbury Town	15+5	1						
nard McNally 9.11 17.2.63	NI (1)	Shrewsbury	Shrewsbury Town (A)	174+3	11	10	1	14			
l Meredith 10.9		Telford	Shrewsbury Town (A)								
l Petts 10.11 27.9.61	EY	Hackney £30,000	Bristol Rovers (A) / Shrewsbury Town	12+1 / 138+10	0+2 / 9+1	7		16			
FORWARDS											
c Bates 11.7 28.11.49		West Bromwich £5,000 £40,000 £50,000 £10,000	Stourbridge / Shrewsbury Town / Swindon Town / Bristol Rovers / Shrewsbury Town	160 / 50+13 / 26+3 / 114+20	9 / 5+1 / 5+1 / 7	14 / 4 / / 10		45 / 15 / 4 / 18	2 / 1 / 2 / 2	5 / 2 / / 3	
hael Brown 10.12 8.2.68		Birmingham	Shrewsbury Town								
y Hackett 10.13 11.10.62		Stourbridge £5,000	Bromsgrove Rovers / Shrewsbury Town	107+4	8	5	1+1	14	2	1	
in Robinson 11.0 15.5.60		Birmingham	Mile Oak Rovers / Shrewsbury Town	114+12	8	3+2		31	2	2	
Steele 11.0 1.2.67		Coventry	Shrewsbury Town (A)	0+2							
l Tester 10.10 10.3.59		Stroud £10,000	Cheltenham Town / Shrewsbury Town / Hereford United (L)	36+4 / 4	2+1	1	0+2	6			
ve Waller 10.0 20.12.63		Urmston	Crewe Alexandra / Shrewsbury Town	170+3	9	4	6	42	4		1

DITIONAL CONTRACT PROFESSIONALS

PRENTICES
an Carmichael, Duane Mellors, Peter Spargo, Stephen Davis, Ian Down,

N-CONTRACT PLAYERS
athan Narbett, John Carmichael, Tony Mann, Orville Mullings, Andrew Taylor, Barry Young

Record Attendance: 18,917 v Walsall, Div 3, 26 April 1961

Smallest Home Attendance for a First Class Match: 1,232 v Charlton Athletic, Div 3, 19 Mar 1974

Record Receipts: £36,240 v Ipswich Town, FA Cup Round 5, 13 Feb 1982

Season Tickets: Stand: £70.00 (£45 juveniles)

Executive Box Season Tickets: None

Cost of Stand Tickets: £4.00 (Centre), £3.50 (Station), £3.50 (Wakeman), £2.00 (pensioners & juniors); **Terraces:** £2.50 (£1.50 juveniles/OAPs) visitors £2.50 (All)

Car Parking: Park adjacent to ground and a free public car park five minutes away

Nearest Railway Station: Shrewsbury (0743 64041)

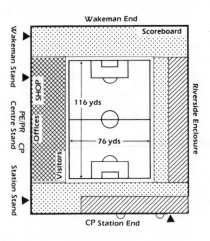

How to get to the ground

From North: Use A49 or A53 and at roundabout take 2nd exit A5112 into Telford Way. In 0.8m at roundabout take 2nd exit. Then at T road turn right into Abbey Foregate A458 for Shrewsbury Town FC

From East: Use A5 then A458 into Shrewsbury and into Abbey Foregate for Shrewsbury Town FC

From South: Use A49 and follow signs Shrewsbury town centre then at end of Coleham Head turn right into Abbey Foregate for Shrewsbury Town FC

From West: Use A458 then A5 around Shrewsbury Ring Road, Roman Road, then turn left A49 into Hereford Road, and at end of Coleham Head turn right into Abbey Foregate for Shrewsbury Town FC

Price of 1986-7 Programme: 50p
Number of Pages: 20
Subscriptions: Apply to club

Local Newspapers: Shropshire Star, Shrewsbury Chronicle

Local Radio Station: Radio Shropshire

SOUTHAMPTON

Division 1

Chairman
A A Woodford

Directors
F G L Askham FCA
E T Bates
B G W Bowyer TD, JP
J Corbett
Sir George Meyrick BMC

Secretary
Brian Truscott (0703 220505)

Assistant Secretary
Barry Fox

Marketing Executive
Bob Britten

Manager
Chris Nicholl

Assistant Manager
Tony Barton

First Team Coach
George Horsfall

Reserve Team Coach
Dennis Rofe

Physiotherapist
Don Taylor

Back Row L to R: Steve Baker, Gerry Forrest, Ian Hamilton, Phillip Parkinson, Mark Blake, Colin Clarke, Jon Gittens, Craig Maskell, Kevan Brown. **Middle Row:** Don Taylor (Physio), Dennis Rofe (Reserve Team Trainer), Joe Jordan, George Lawrence, Tim Flowers, Peter Shilton, Glenn Cockerill, Andy Townsend, George Horsfall (First Team Trainer), Dave Merrington (Youth Team Trainer), **Front Row:** Tony Barton (Assistant Manager), Steve Moran, Danny Wallace, Mark Wright, David Armstrong, Nick Holmes, Jimmy Case, Kevin Bond, Chris Nicholl (Manager).

At one point it seemed the Saints might celebrate their Centenary season by reaching the FA Cup final. But, after a fine run, they were eventually knocked out in the semi-final by all-conquering Liverpool.

Tragedy struck in the first-half of that semi-final when Mark Wright broke a leg. It was an injury that kept him out of the side for the remainder of the season and cost him his place in England's World Cup squad.

Peter Shilton did go to Mexico — as England's most-capped goalkeeper. During the season he surpassed Gordon Banks' record of 73 caps.

Winger Danny Wallace had the honour of scoring on his debut for England against Egypt and, though not included in the Mexico squad, he hopes to be challenging for a place in the 1990 finals. Another Saint to figure in international football was Alan Curtis, who won his 33rd cap for Wales against Hungary.

Chris Nicholl had a tough introduction to club management as several of his key players were injured at the start of his first season in charge at The Dell. Joe Jordan missed the opening matches whilst his striking partner Steve Moran suffered a knock in the first game which kept him out for several weeks.

Nick Holmes joined the list of cripples before the end of August so it was no surprise when the Saints failed to win any of their first half-a-dozen League games.

Injuries, in fact, were to plague the side throughout the season and it was a rare luxury for Mr Nicholl to be able to name an unchanged team.

A further injury to Jordan in October prompted Mr Nicholl to go into the transfer market, signing Sheffield United's Glenn Cockerill, who can play both in attack and midfield. A few weeks later the manager bought right-back Gerry Forrest from Rotherham.

Some good results were obtained at The Dell but away form gave great cause for concern and, by the turn of the year, the Saints had collected no more than two points from 11 away matches.

They had to wait until mid-March for their first away League victory, at QPR An earlier away victory had been gained at Middlesbrough, where a Wallace hat-trick earned a 3-1 win in the FA Cup.

That goal at Middlesbrough was the only one conceded in the Cup run, until that clash with Liverpool at White Hart Lane. In spite of the crippling loss of Wright, the Saints held out to draw 0-0 at 90 minutes and it was only during extra-time that Ian Rush nipped in to score the two goals which took Liverpool to Wembley.

So it was back to remaining League fixtures and another spate of injuries. Mr Nicholl decided to reward some of his best young players with a run in the First Division side. Keith Granger, Allen Tankard, Jon Gitten, Stuart McManus, Craig Maskell and Mark Blake all took their chances well.

Though the Saints were beaten in their final game at The Dell, by Sheffield Wednesday, other results meant they were free of relegation worries as they played their last three matches away from home.

SOUTHAMPTON

DIVISION ONE: 14th   **FA CUP:** SEMI-FINAL   **MILK CUP:** 4th ROUND

MATCH	DATE		COMPE-TITION	VENUE	OPPONENTS	RESULT		HALF TIME	L'GUE POS'N	GOALSCORERS/GOAL TIMES	ATTEN-DANCE
1	A	17	CL	H	Newcastle United	D	1-1	1-0		Puckett 42	16,40
2		20	CL	A	Arsenal	L	2-3	0-1		Armstrong 65, 81	(21,895
3		24	CL	A	Nottingham Forest	L	1-2	0-2	20	Armstrong 65	(12,643
4		27	CL	H	Aston Villa	D	0-0	0-0	20		14,22(
5		31	CL	A	Ipswich Town	D	1-1	0-1	20	Armstrong, (pen) 86	(11,588
6	S	3	CL	H	West Ham United	D	1-1	0-0	19	Curtis 52	14,47
7		7	CL	H	Manchester City	W	3-0	1-0	14	Case 10, McCarthy (og) 64, Lawrence 82	14,30
8		14	CL	A	Chelsea	L	0-2	0-1	17		(15,71
9		17	SC	A	Liverpool	L	1-2	1-2		Wallace 23	(16,189
10		21	CL	H	Coventry City	D	1-1	0-0	17	Armstrong 71	12,67
11		25	MC2/1	A	Millwall	D	0-0	0-0			(7,958
12		28	CL	A	Manchester United	L	0-1	0-0	20		52,449
13	O	2	SC	A	Tottenham Hotspur	L	1-2	0-2		Moran 48	(11,549
14		5	CL	H	Watford	W	3-1	2-0	16	Moran 3 (16, 21, 70)	14,17
15		8	MC2/2	H	Millwall	W	0-0†	0-0			9,48(
16		12	CL	A	Liverpool	L	0-1	0-0	18		(31,070
17		19	CL	A	Luton Town	L	0-7	0-3	18		8,876
18		22	SC	H	Liverpool	D	1-1	0-0		Armstrong (pen) 79	10,50
19		26	CL	H	Q.P.R.	W	3-0	0-1	18	Wallace 4, 85, Cockerill 72	15,61
20		29	MC3	H	Birmingham City	D	1-1	1-1		Puckett 14	(4,832
21	N	2	CL	H	Tottenham Hotspur	W	1-0	0-0	16	Puckett 68	17,74
22		6	MC3R	H	Birmingham City	W	3-0	2-0		Armstrong 34, (pen) 40, Wallace 58	9,08(
23		9	CL	A	Leicester City	D	2-2	1-1	15	Armstrong 29, Puckett 56	(8,08(
24		16	CL	H	Birmingham City	W	1-0	0-0	13	Wallace 67	13,16
25		19	MC4	A	Arsenal	D	0-0	0-0			(18,244
26		23	CL	A	Sheffield Wednesday	L	1-2	0-1	14	Wright 82	(18,955
27		26	MC4R	H	Arsenal	L	1-3	0-0		Armstrong (pen) 59	14,01(
28		30	CL	H	Everton	L	2-3	1-1	16	Cockerill 1, Moran 70	16,91
29	D	7	CL	H	Arsenal	W	3-1	1-0	13	Bond 29, Armstrong (pen) 64, Moran 67	15,05
30		14	CL	A	Newcastle United	L	1-2	0-1	14	Moran 69	(19,229
31		17	SC	H	Tottenham Hotspur	L	1-3	0-3		Wallace 55	4,68(
32		20	CL	H	Nottingham Forest	W	3-1	2-1	13	Moran 10, 38, Armstrong 73	12,50(
33		26	CL	A	Oxford United	L	0-3	0-2	13		(11,266
34	J	1	CL	H	W.B.A.	W	3-1	0-0	13	Cockerill 47, Wallace 58, Armstrong 83	13,154
35		11	CL	A	Manchester City	L	0-1	0-0	15		(21,674
36		13	FAC3	A	Middlesbrough	W	3-1	2-1		Wallace 3 11, 40, 89	(12,735
37		18	CL	A	Ipswich Town	W	1-0	0-0	14	Wallace 50	13,164
38		25	FAC4	H	Wigan Athletic	W	3-0	0-0		Cockerill 69, Armstrong (pen) 85, 89	14,46
39	F	1	CL	A	Aston Villa	D	0-0	0-0	14		(8,456
40		8	CL	H	Coventry City	L	1-2	0-1	14	Armstrong 63	13,74(
41		15	FAC5	H	Millwall	D	0-0	0-0			16,35
42		22	CL	A	Coventry City	L	2-3	2-0	15	Wright 17, Cockerill (pen) 38	(10,881
43	M	1	CL	H	Manchester United	W	1-0	0-0	14	Cockerill 81	19,01
44		5	FAC5R	A	Millwall	W	1-0	0-0		Wallace 15	(10,625
45		8	FAC6	A	Brighton & H.A.	W	2-0	2-0		Moran 13, Cockerill 39	(25,069
46		11	CL	A	Q.P.R.	W	2-0	2-0	14	McManus 22, Cockerill 42	(14,174
47		15	CL	H	Liverpool	L	1-2	0-0	14	Lawrence 49	19,784
48		22	CL	H	Chelsea	L	0-1	0-0	15		15,00
49		29	CL	A	W.B.A.	L	0-1	0-0	15		(7,325
50	A	1	CL	H	Oxford United	D	1-1	1-1	15	Wright 43	15,35(
51		5	FAC SF	N	Liverpool	L	0-2†	0-0			(44,605
52		8	CL	A	West Ham United	L	0-1	0-1	15		(22,459
53		12	CL	H	Leicester City	D	0-0	0-0	15		13,403
54		19	CL	A	Birmingham City	W	2-0	1-0	14	Wallace 42, Cockerill 70	(5,833
55		26	CL	H	Sheffield Wednesday	L	2-3	0-1	14	Case 55, Wallace 72	(15,375
56		29	CL	A	Watford	D	1-1	1-1	14	Townsend 12	(11,868
57	M	3	CL	A	Everton	L	1-6	0-4	14	Puckett 58	(33,057
58		5	CL	A	Tottenham Hotspur	L	3-5	2-3	14	Wallace 22, Baker 42, Maskell 65	(13,036

Best Home League Attendance: 19,784 v Liverpool   **Smallest:** 12,500 v Nottingham Forest   **Av Home Att:** 14,888

Goal Scorers: **Compared with 84-85:** −3,022

League (51):	Armstrong 10 (3 pen), Moran 8, Wallace 8, Cockerill 7 (1 pen), Puckett 4, Wright 3, Case 2, Lawrence 2, Baker 1, Bond 1, Curtis 1, Maskell 1, McManus 1, Townsend 1, Opponents 1
Milk Cup (5):	Armstrong 3 (2 pen), Puckett 1, Wallace 1
FA CUP (9):	Wallace 4, Armstrong 2 (1 pen), Cockerill 2, Moran 1
Super Cup (4):	Wallace 2, Armstrong 1 (pen), Moran 1

†A.E.T. (†Southampton won 5-4 on penalties

Shilton	Golac	Townsend	Case	Wright	Bond	Holmes	Moran	Puckett	Armstrong	Wallace	Curtis	Lawrence	Dennis	Whitlock	Jordan	Baker	Cockerill	Collins	Forrest	Kite	McManus	Gittens	Maskell	Tankard (A)	Granger (A)	Referee	
1	2	3	4	5	6	7	8*	9	10	11		12														D Hedges	1
1	2	3	4	5	6	7		9*	10	8	12	11														G Napthine	2
1	2	3	4	5	6	7*	12		10	11	9	8														A Robinson	3
1	2		4†	5	6			8	10*	9	12		3	7												A Ward	4
1	2	7	4	5	6			8	10	11	9		3													J Moules	5
1	2	7	4	5	6			10	11	8	12		3		9*											J Deakin	6
1	2	7	4	5	6			10	11	8	12		3		9*											D Reeves	7
1	2	7		5	6		4*	10	11	8	12		3		9											M James	8
1	2	7		5	6			10	11	8*	12		3	4	9											**M Scott**	9
1	2*	7		5	6	8		10	11	4	12		3		9											N Glover	10
1		3	4	5	6	8			10	11	7			9	2											**D Axcell**	11
1		7	4	5	6	8	3	11	10*		12			9	2											K Redfern	12
1		7	4	5	6	8	3	11*	10		12			9	2											**M Bodenham**	13
1		7*	4	5	6	8		10		11	12	3		9	2											R Groves	14
1			4	5	6	8	12	10	11*	7	3			9	2											**R Gifford**	15
1			4	5	6	8	10		11	7	3	12	9*	2												J Lovatt	16
1	11		4	5	6	8		10		7	3			2	9											C Downey	17
1	12		4	5		3	9	11	10	7			6*				2	8								**R Lewis**	18
1	11		4	5	6	3	9		10	7							2	8								R Milford	19
1			4	5	6	8		9	10	7	11		3				2									**T Fitzharris**	20
1			4	5	6	7		9	10	11			3				2	8								K Cooper	21
1			4	5	6	7	12	9	10	11	8*		3				2									**A Buksh**	22
1	6		4	5		7		9	10	11			3				2	8								R Banks	23
1			4	5		7*	12	9	10	11			3			6	2	8								M Dimblebee	24
1		3	4	5				9	10	11	7			6		2	8	8								**A Gunn**	25
1		3*	4	5	6		12	9	10	11	7						2	8								P Vanes	26
1		3	4	5		7	8	9	10	11				6			2									**R Gifford**	27
1			4	5	6	7		9	10	11			3				8		2							M Cotton	28
1			4	5	6	7		9	10	11			3				8		2							B Hill	29
			4	5	6	7		9	10	11			3				8		2	1						D Allinson	30
1		12	4	5	6	7	13	9	10*	11			3				8		2	1						**K Baker**	31
		3	4	5	6	7		9	10	11							8		2	1						H King	32
		3	4*		6	7		9	10	11		12		5			8		2	1						B Stevens	33
1			4	5	6	7		9	10	11			3				8		2							D Hedges	34
1			4	5	6	7		9	10	11			3				8		2							J Key	35
1			4	5	6	7		9	10	11			3			2	8									**N Ashley**	36
1			4	5	6	7		9	10	11			3				8		2							D Reeves	37
1			4	5	6	7	12	9*	10	11			3			2	8									**M Dimblebee**	38
1			4	5	6	7		9	10	11			3				8		2							R Bridges	39
1			4	5	6	7		9	10	11			3				8		2							L Shapter	40
1			4	5	6	7		9	10	11		12	3			2*	8									**B Hill**	41
1			4	5	6			9	10	11		7					8		2							C Trussell	42
1			4	5	6			9	10	11		7					8		2							R Milford	43
1		12	4	5*	6			9	10	11		7	3			2	8									**B Hill**	44
1		12	4	5	6			9	10	11*		7	3			2	8									N Midgley	45
1		12	4	5	6			9	10			7*	3				8		2		11					A Seville	46
1		12	4	5	6			9	10			7	3				8		2		11*					A Ward	47
1					6			4	11	10	12	7*	3	5	9		8		2							K Cooper	48
1		3*	4	5	6		12	10	11			7			9		8		2							L Dilkes	49
1			4	5	6	7	11		10				3		9	2	8									J Moules	50
1		12	4	5*	6		2	9	10	11		7	3				8									**A Saunders**	51
1		5	4		6	7	11*	10					3	12	9		8		2							P Vanes	52
1		7	4	5*			12		10	11			3	6	9		8		2							K Miller	53
1		7	4					9	10	11		3*		6			8		2			5	12			R Guy	54
1		7	4					9	10	11				6			8		2			5		3		R Groves	55
1		7	4						10	11	9			6			8		2			5		3		D Vickers	56
1		7	4				12		10	11	9			6			8		2			5*		3	1	P Willis	57
		10	4				9	3		11*				6		2	8		7				12		1	K Barratt	58

Shilton	Golac	Townsend	Case	Wright	Bond	Holmes	Moran	Puckett	Armstrong	Wallace	Curtis	Lawrence	Dennis	Whitlock	Jordan	Baker	Cockerill	Collins	Forrest	Kite	McManus	Gittens	Maskell	Tankard (A)	Granger (A)		
37	9	25	36	33	34	26	24	13	41	34	10	12	24	12	12	13	30		22	3	2	4	0	3	2	League Appearances	
	2						4	2				1	1	9	2							2				Substitute Appearances	
6	3	6	6	4	3	3+1	4+1	6	5	5	1		3	2	2	6		1								Milk Cup Appearances	
6	0-3	6	6	6	4	4+1	2	6	6	3+1	4		5	6												FA Cup Appearances	
3	1	2-2	3	4	3	2	3	1-1	4	4	2		0-2	2	2	2	2	2	2			1		1		Super Cup Appearances	

Also Played: Position (Game): Blake (A) 5(58)

Departures: Whitlock, Puckett (Bournemouth), Curtis (Cardiff), Collins (Portsmouth), Golac (F)

'THE SAINTS'

Formed: 1885
Turned Professional: 1894   **Ltd Co:** 1897

Previous Names: Southampton St. Mary's (until 1885)
Previous Managers: (Since 1946) Bill Dodgin (Sr)   Sid Cann   George Roughton   Ted Bates
L McMenemy
Honours: Champions Div 3 (S) 1921-22   Champions Div 3, 1959-60   FA Cup: Winners 1975-76
League Career: Original Members of Div 3 1920   Allocated to Div 3 (S) 1921
Promoted to Div 2 1922   Relegated to Div 3 (S) 1953   Original Members of New Div 3 1958
Promoted to Div 2 1960   Promoted to Div 1 1966   Relegated to Div 2 1974
Promoted to Div 1 1978
Colours: Red and white striped shirts, black shorts, white stockings
Change Colours: Light and dark blue striped shirts, dark blue shorts, light blue stockings
Reserves League: Football Combination   **Youth Team:** S E Counties

---

CLUB RECORDS

Most Appearances for Club: Terry Paine: Football League 713 + FA Cup 51 + League Cup 37 + European Fairs Cup 8 **Total 809**, 1956-74
Most Capped Player: Mike Channon 45 (46)
Record Goalscorer in a Match: Derek Reeves, 5 v Newport County 1st Round Replay, Milk Cup (5-3), 1960
Record League Goalscorer in a Season: Derek Reeves, 39, Div 3, 1959-60, in All Competitions
Record League Goalscorer in a Career: Mike Channon, 183, 1966-77, 1979-82   **In All Competitions:** Mike Channon, 226 (League 183 + FA Cup 17 + League Cup 12 + European Cup 4 + UEFA 5 + Texaco 5)
Record Transfer Fee Received: £525,000 from Arsenal for Steve Williams, Dec 1984
Record Transfer Fee Paid: £600,000 to Middlesbrough for David Armstrong, Aug 1981
Best Performances: League: 2nd Div 1 1983-4   **FA Cup:** Winners 1975-76   **League/Milk Cup:** Finalists 1978-79
Most League Points: (3 points for win) 77, Div 1, 1983-4   (2 points for win) 61, Div 3 (S) 1921-2 & Div 3 1959-60
Most League Goals: 112, Div 3 (S), 1957-58
Record League Victory: 9-3 v Wolverhampton Wanderers, Div 2, 8 Sept 1965   8-2 v Coventry City, Div 1, 28 Apr 1984
Record League Defeat: 0-8 v Tottenham Hotspur, Div 2, 28 Mar 1936   0-8 v Everton, Div 1, 20 Nov 1971
European Competitions Entered: European Fairs Cup 1969-70   UEFA Cup 1971-2, 1981-2, 1982-3, 1984-5   European Cup Winners Cup 1976-7
Oldest Player in League Match: Alan Ball 37 yrs 5 months
Youngest Player in League Match: Danny Wallace, 16 yrs 10 months

Most Consecutive Undefeated League Matches: 19 1921   **League Matches Without a Win:** 20 1969
Longest Run of Undefeated Home League Matches: 31 1921-22   **Away League Matches:** 9 1971-78
Longest Run Without Home League Win: 10 1969   **Away League Win:** 33 1933-34
Most Consecutive League Wins: 6 1964   **Home League Wins:** 11 1959-60
Most Consecutive League Defeats: 5 1927, 1957, 1967-68   **Away League Wins:** 3 1921, 1926, 1928, 1931, 1946, 1950, 1958, 1960, 1961

Club Statistician for the Directory: D Buckle

SOUTHAMPTON

PLAYERS NAME Ht Wt Birthdate	Honours	Birthplace Transfers	Clubs	APPEARANCES League	Milk Cup	FA Cup	Other Comps	GOALS League	Milk Cup	FA Cup	Other Comps
GOALKEEPERS											
Tim Flowers .2 14.0 3.2.67	EY	Kenilworth	Wolverhampton W. (A)	63							
			Southampton								
Peter Shilton† .0 14.0 18.9.49	E (86) U.23 (3) Div.2 '71, Div.1 '78 LgC'79 EC'79/80 ESC '79 FLX1	Leicester £300,000 £270,000 £325,000	Leicester City (A)	286	20	30	.	1			
			Stoke City	110	4	7					
			Notts Forest	202	26	18	24				
			Southampton	159	20	16	4				
DEFENDERS											
Stephen Baker .5 10.8 15.6.67		Newcastle	Southampton (A)	40	7	5		1			
			Burnley (L)	10+1		2					
Mark Blake .0½ 12.4 19.12.67	E(Y)	Southampton	Southampton (A)	1				.			
Kevin Bond .1½ 13.4 22.6.57	E'B' (2)	London Seattle Sounders £350,00 £75,000	Bournemouth (A)			.					
			Norwich City	137+5	12	7		12		2	
			Manchester City	108+2	8	6		11			
			Southampton	66+1	11	9		2			
Mark Dennis .9 11.2 2.5.61		Streatham	Birmingham City (A)	130	8	7	1	1			
			Southampton	75	10	14	2				
Gerry Forrest .10 10.11 21.1.57	Div.3 '81	Stockton	South Bank								
			Rotherham United	357	36	22	3	8	1		
			Southampton	22							
Nick Holmes .3 12.2 1.8.63	FAC '76 Dorchester	Southampton Oxford United	Southampton (A)	429+6	36	44	1	54	5	2	
Mark Wright			8+2								
			Southampton	140	18	16	4	6	2	1	1
MIDFIELD											
David Armstrong* .8 11.10 26.12.54		Durham	Middlesbrough (A)	357+2	27	29		59	6	8	
			Southampton	200	19						
Jimmy Case .9 12.5 18.5.54	E.U23 (1) ESC '77 LgC '81,Div1 73/77 78/9,EC 77/78/81 UEFAC '76	Liverpool £500,000 £30,000	South Liverpool								
			Liverpool	170+16	21+1	20+1	28+3	23	3	7	13
			Brighton	124+3	8	14		10	4		
			Southampton	46	6	6		3			
Glen Cockerill .0 12.4 25.8.55		Grimsby	Louth United								
			Lincoln City	65+6	2	2		10			
			Swindon Town	23+3	3			1			
			Lincoln City	114+1	16	6		25	1		
			Sheffield United	62	6	1		10	1		
			Southampton	30		6		7		2	
Andy Townsend .10½ 12.7 23.7.63		London	Weymouth			1					
			Southampton	30+2	3	'0+3		1			
FORWARDS											
Colin Clarke .11 12.10 30.10.62	NI (6)	Newry £22,500 P/E + £400,000	Ipswich Town (A)								
			Peterborough United	76+6	7	4		18	2	2	
			Gillingham (L)	8							
			Tranmere Rovers	45	2	2	4	22	1	3	3
			Bournemouth	46	4	4	2	26	3	2	4
			Southampton								
Joe Jordan .1 12.1 15.12.51	S (52) U.23 (1) Div.1 '74	Carlisle AC Milan Verona £150,000	Morton	7+3				1			
			Leeds United	139+31	9+1	16+1	18+3	35	3	4	6
			Manchester United	109	6	11+1	1	37	2	2	
			Southampton	46	9	3	2	12	2	2	
George Lawrence .10 12.10 14.9.62	Div.3 '84	London	Southampton (A)	7+3	2+1			1			
			Oxford United	78	13	10		25	1	1	
			Southampton	24+10	1	5+2		3			
Steve Moran .8 11.0 10.1.61	E.U21 (2)	Croydon	Southampton (A)	173+7	16+3	18+1	7	78	6	12	2
Danny Wallace .4½ 10.4 21.1.64	E (1) U.21 (14) Y	London	Southampton (A)	145+8	20+1	16	2+3	38	5	4	

ADDITIONAL CONTRACT PROFESSIONALS
Jon Gittens, Kevan Brown, Ian Hamilton, Philip Parkinson, Craig Maskell

APPRENTICES
Keith Granger, Allen Tankard, Francis Benali, Andrew Cook, Matthew Le Tissier, Gregory Llewellyn

NON-CONTRACT PLAYERS
Nigel Barnes, Stephen Davis, Ian Down, Peter Spargo

Record Attendance: 31,044 v Manchester United, Div 1, 8 Oct 1969

Record Receipts: £79,784 v Barnsley, FA Cup Round 5, Mar 1985

Season Tickets: Stands: £121-£131; Ground: £57; Bench Seats: £81-£88

Executive Box Season Tickets: None

Cost of Stand Tickets: £6, £6.50 **Terraces:** £3.00 (adults), £1.50 (juveniles/OAP), Bench Seats £4.50

Match and Ticket Information: Advance seat tickets 10 days before match. Terraces pay on day

Car Parking: Street parking and nearby municipal parks

Nearest Railway Station: Southampton Central (0703 29393)

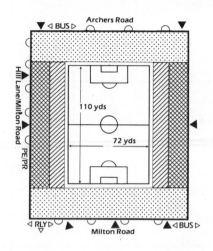

How to get to the ground

From North: Use A33 S.P. Southampton into The Avenue then turn right into Northlands Road and at end turn right into Archers Road for Southampton FC

From East: Use Motorway M27 then A334 and follow signs Southampton A3024. Then follow signs The West into Commercial Road then turn right into Hill Lane and take 1st turning right into Milton Road for Southampton FC

From West: Use A35 then A3024 S.P. Southampton City Centre. Forward into Fourposts Hill then turn left into Hill Lane and take 1st turning right into Milton Road for Southampton FC

Price of 1986-7 Programme: 50p
Number of Pages: 32
Subscriptions: Obtainable from club

Local Newspapers: Southern Evening Echo, Portsmouth News

Local Radio Stations: Radio Solent, Radio Victory

SOUTHEND UNITED   Division 4

When a club has boardroom problems with its consequent 'chopping and changing' it is usual for these events to be reflected in poor field performances, so a final League position of ninth in the 4th Division for Southend United is, if anything, quite praiseworthy. In fact, the earlier days of the campaign produced reasonable consistency and four consecutive wins in September left the team riding high at the top. A slump followed with only four League wins before the New Year and that effectively ended the promotion challenge for another season.

Worse followed with only one win before the end of February in 1986 (only one match was played in the latter month owing to bad weather), whilst in the congested March revised fixture list only two more wins were recorded. In the final 'run-in' it was only slightly improved but the last two matches were won with Rochdale going down by five clear goals in the penultimate game at Roots Hall. In the end more matches were lost than were won and it was a disappointing season, which could have been worse, and affairs will be better if players are allowed to concentrate on the game without unnecessary distractions.

As always we look to the cups for consolation but can find little to provide it. The Milk Cup 1st Round tie with Gillingham was lost on aggregate (1-3) and the FA Cup run was also ended in the 1st Round with Newport scoring the only goal at Roots Hall. It was a similar tale in the Freight Rover Trophy — exit Southend early!

Now everyone hopes that Dave Webb will bring in a brave new era. As a player he was 'Mr Courage' personified and he enjoyed plenty of success. Can he do it as a manager for Southend? He starts with one useful asset in Cadette, the scorer of 25 League goals. In goal Stannard proved that his good reputation was justified and the veteran Lampard was sound. O'Shea, Westley, Hatter, Pennyfather and Silkman all did their stuff and Clark when fit also played well. So Mr Webb has the potential at Roots Hall and he will hope that he will be able to exploit it to advantage.   WLM

Back Row L to R: David Webb (Manager), Dean Neal, David Martin, Paul Roberts, Roy McDonough, Paul Clark, Glenn Pennyfather. **Middle Row:** Barry Silkman, Derek Hall, Danny O'Shea, Mervyn Cawston, Jim Stannard, Shane Westley, Buster Footman (Physio), Kevin Lock (Youth Team Manager), **Front Row:** Richard Cadette, Micky Engwell, Steve Wiggins, John Seaden, John Gymer, Kevin Spires, Phil Cavener.

SOUTHEND UNITED

DIVISION FOUR: 9th   **FA CUP:** 1st ROUND   **MILK CUP:** 1st ROUND

MATCH	DATE		COMPE-TITION	VENUE	OPPONENTS	RESULT		HALF TIME	L'GUE POS'N	GOALSCORERS/GOAL TIMES	ATTEN-DANCE
1	A	17	CL	A	Crewe Alexandra	D	1-1	0-0		Pennyfather 89	(1,431)
2		20	MC1/1	H	Gillingham	D	1-1	0-0		Clark 77	2,008
3		23	CL	H	Orient	W	5-1	2-0	4	Cadette 4 (36, 44, 51, 88) O'Shea 47	3,643
4		27	CL	A	Cambridge United	W	2-1	1-0	2	Cadette 10, Phillips 85	(2,038)
5		30	CL	A	Swindon Town	D	0-0	0-0	4		4,037
6	S	3	MC1/2	A	Gillingham	L	0-2	0-1			(3,106)
7		7	CL	A	Exeter City	W	2-0	1-0	2	Pennyfather 35, Clark 65	(2,213)
8		14	CL	H	Scunthorpe United	W	2-1	1-1	1	Cadette 17, Phillips 69	2,974
9		17	CL	A	Halifax Town	W	3-2	2-0	1	O'Shea 21, Cadette 23, Phillips 84	(1,514)
10		20	CL	H	Wrexham	W	3-0	1-0	1	Westley 3, Silkman 64, Cadette 74	4,957
11		28	CL	A	Mansfield Town	L	0-3	0-0	2		(3,701)
12	O	1	CL	H	Stockport County	D	0-0	0-0	2		3,672
13		4	CL	H	Tranmere Rovers	D	2-2	1-0	2	Westley 9, Cadette 88	4,175
14		12	CL	A	Aldershot	W	3-1	1-0	2	Pennyfather 32, 90, Cadette 62	(1,816)
15		19	CL	A	Port Vale	L	0-4	0-3	3		(4,736)
16		22	CL	H	Colchester United	L	2-4	0-1	5	Gymer 75, McDonough 77	8,120
17		25	CL	H	Preston North End	W	2-1	2-1	4	Rogers 2, McDonough 43	2,789
18	N	2	CL	A	Burnley	W	3-1	1-0	3	Gymer 75, Cadette 78, O'Shea 90	(2,641)
19		6	CL	H	Torquay United	D	2-2	2-1	3	O'Shea 29, Pennyfather 45	(1,169)
20		9	CL	A	Hartlepool United	W	3-2	1-2	2	Cadette 43, 89, Gymer 90	2,755
21		16	FAC1	H	Newport County	L	0-1	0-0			3,343
22		29	CL	A	Chester City	D	1-1	0-0	3	Cadette 53	3,525
23	D	6	CL	A	Northampton Town	L	0-4	0-1	5		2,527
24		21	CL	A	Orient	L	0-3	0-1	6		(3,545)
25		28	CL	H	Cambridge United	W	1-0	0-0	7	McDonough 83	2,528
26	J	1	CL	A	Peterborough United	D	1-1	0-0	7	Cadette 72	(3,104)
27		3	CL	H	Burnley	L	2-3	1-0	7	Cadette 11, 67	2,619
28		12	CL	A	Swindon Town	L	1-2	1-1	8	Westley 5	(7,619)
29		14	FRT5	A	Colchester United	L	1-4	0-4		Clark 47	(1,364)
30		18	CL	H	Crewe Alexandra	L	0-1	0-0	8		1,848
31		24	CL	H	Scunthorpe United	L	0-2	0-0	9		(1,463)
32		31	CL	H	Exeter City	W	2-0	2-0	8	Neal 1, Westley 33	1,653
33	F	4	CL	A	Colchester United	L	0-2	0-2	10		(1,915)
34	M	3	CL	A	Stockport County	L	1-2	0-1	11	O'Shea 55	(2,425)
35		5	CL	H	Halifax Town	W	2-1	1-1	9	Lampard 13, O'Shea 82	1,006
36		7	CL	A	Tranmere Rovers	D	1-1	1-1	8	Neal 25	(1,184)
37		13	FRT S	H	Northampton Town	L	1-3	0-1		Lampard 85	683
38		15	CL	H	Aldershot	W	2-0	2-0	8	Neal 15, McDonough 29	1,505
39		19	CL	A	Hereford United	L	1-2	0-0	8	McDonough 69	(2,002)
40		22	CL	A	Preston North End	L	2-3	0-2	9	Cadette 60, 73	(2,600)
41		29	CL	H	Peterborough United	L	0-1	0-0	10		1,687
42		31	CL	A	Northampton Town	D	0-0	0-0	11		(3,527)
43	A	4	CL	H	Torquay United	L	1-2	0-0	13	Cadette 67	1,656
44		8	CL	A	Wrexham	D	0-0	0-0	13		(1,055)
45		12	CL	A	Hartlepool United	L	2-3	1-0	14	O'Shea 19, Hatter (pen) 77	(2,235)
46		15	CL	H	Mansfield Town	W	3-1	2-1	12	Cadette 44, 65, McDonough 34	1,140
47		18	CL	H	Hereford United	W	3-1	3-0	11	O'Shea 9, McDonough 27, Westley 36	1,554
48		20	CL	A	Rochdale	L	1-2	0-2	12	Hatter (pen) 75	(1,060)
49		26	CL	A	Chester City	L	0-2	0-1	13		(4,453)
50	M	2	CL	H	Rochdale	W	5-0	3-0	12	Cadette 3 (11, 35, 54), Pennyfather 33, Engwell 83	1,153
51		5	CL	H	Port Vale	W	2-1	1-0	9	Pennyfather 28, Sproson (og) 82	1,687

Best Home League Attendance: 8,120 v Colchester United   **Smallest:** 1,006 v Halifax Town   **Av Home Att:** 2,748

Goal Scorers: **Compared with 84-85:** +860

League (69): Cadette 25, O'Shea 8, McDonough 7, Pennyfather 7, Westbury 5, Gymer 3, Neal 3, Phillips 3, Hatter 2 (2 pen), Clark 1, Engwell 1, Lampard 1, Rogers 1, Silkman 1, Opponents 1

Milk Cup (1): Clark 1

FA CUP (-):

FRT (2): Clark 1, Lampard 1

Stannard	Stead	Lampard	O'Shea	Westley	Hatter	Pennyfather	Silkman	McDonough	Rogers	Phillips	Clark	Cadette	Gymer	Lock	May	Seaden	Stebbing (L)	Neal	Engwell	Pryer (NC)	Referee	#
1	2	3	4	5	6	7	8	9	10*	11	12										G Ashby	1
1	2	3	4	5	6		8	9*	11	10	7	12									A Buksh	2
1	2	3	4	5	6		8		11	10	7	9									A Gunn	3
1	2	3	4	5	6		8		11	10	7	9									D Hedges	4
1	2	3	4	5	6		8		11*	10	7	9									M Cotton	5
1	2	3	4	5	6		8	12	11		7	9	10*								N Butler	6
1	2	3*	4	5	6	11	8	12		10	7	9									H King	7
1	2	3	4	5	6	11	8			10	7	9									I Henley	8
1	2	3*	4	5	6	11	8	12		10	7	9									K Redfern	9
1	2		4	5	6	11	8			10	7	9		3							D Reeves	10
1	2*	3	4	5	6	11	8	12		10	7	9									N Midgley	11
1		2	4	5	6	11	8*	12		10	7	9		3							I Borrett	12
1	2	3	4	5	6	11	8	10*			7	9									M Bodenham	13
1	2	3	4	5	6	11	8	10			7	9	12								R Milford	14
1	2	3	4	5	6	11	8	10*			7	9	12								K Breen	15
1	2	3	4	5	6	7	8	10	11			9*	12								D Vickers	16
1	2	3	4	5	6	7	8	10	11			9									R Lewis	17
1	2	3	4	5	6	11	8	10				9	12	7*							G Tyson	18
1	2	3	4	5	6	11	8	10				9		7							K Cooper	19
1	2	3	4	5	6	7	8*	10	11			9	12								E Scales	20
1	2	3	4	5	6	7	8	10†	11			9*	12								F Ward	21
1		3	4	5	6	7	8	10	11			9			2						A Robinson	22
1		3	4*	5	6	7	8		11	10		9	12		2						C Downey	23
1		3			6	7	8		11	10*	5	9	12		2	4					H Taylor	24
1		3		5	6	7	8	10	11		4	9			2						M James	25
1		3		5	6	7	8	10	11		4	9			2						M Dimblebee	26
1		3		5	6	7*	8	10	11		4	9	12		2						I Hemley	27
1		3		5	6			10			7	9	11	4	2		8				K Baker	28
1		3		5	6			10	13		7	9	11*	4	2*	8	12				J Moules	29
1		3		5	6				11	10	7	9	12	4	2	8*					B Hill	30
1		3			6	2	8	10			5	9		4*	7	11	12				G Napthine	31
1		3		5		2		6	11		7	9*		4	12		8	10			A Ward	32
1			5		2	4*	6	11		7	9		3	12		8	10				E Scales	33
1		3	4		5	8	6	11		7	9				2			10			G Aplin	34
1		6	4	5	3		8	11		7	9				2			10			J Ball	35
1		6	4	5	3		8	11		7	9				2			10			I Hendrick	36
1		8	4	5	6	3*		11		7*	9				2			10	12	13	I Borrett	37
1		6	4	5	3	12	8	11		7*	9				2			10			M Robinson	38
1		6	4	5	3		8	11		7	9				2			10			L Shapter	39
1		4	5	3	6		8	11		7	9	12			2			10*			K Baker	40
1		4	5	6*	3		8	10	11	7	9	12			2						A Buksh	41
1		4	12	5	3	6	8	11		7	9				2			10*			G Ashby	42
1		4	5	6	3	12	8	11		7	9				2			10*			M Bodenham	43
1		4	5	6	3	10	8	11		7	9				2						M Heath	44
1		4	5	6	3		8	10	11	7	9				2						K Walmsley	45
1		4	5	6	3	10	8	11		7	9				2						D Hedges	46
1		4	5	6	3		8	10	11	7	9				2						P Vanes	47
1		4	5	6	3*	10	8	11		7	9				2	12					M Reed	48
1		4	5	6	3	10		11		7	9				2*		8	12			R Hamer	49
1	2		6	3	8			11		7	9			4					10	5	C Downey	50
1		4		6	3	8		10	11	7	9				2	5					N Butler	51
46	17	34	35	35	44	41	38	32	32	13	38	44	2	10	23	4	5	10	1	2	League Appearances	
		1						2	6				1		11	2	1		1	1	Substitute Appearances	
2	2	2	2	2	2		2	1·1	2	1	2	1·1	1								Milk Cup Appearances	
1	1	1	1	1	1		1		1	1	1	1		1	0·1						FA Cup Appearances	
2		2	1	2	2	1	2	0·1	2		2	2	1	1	2		1	1·1	0·1	0·1	FR Trophy Appearances	

Players on Loan:

Departures: Hatter, May (Maidstone), Stead (Doncaster R), Rogers (Cardiff C)

'THE SHRIMPERS'

Formed: 1906
Turned Professional: 1906   **Ltd Co:** 1919

Previous Managers: Since 1946:
Harry Warren   Eddie Perry   Frank Broome   Ted Fenton   Alvan Williams   Ernie Shepherd
Geoff Hudson   Arthur Rowley   David Smith   Bobby Moore
Honours: Champions Div 4, 1980-1
League Career: Original members of Div 3 1920   Allocated Div 3 (S) 1921
Original members of new Div 3 1958   Relegated to Div 4 1966   Promoted to Div 3 1972
Relegated to Div 4 1976   Promoted to Div 3 1978   Relegated to Div 4 1980
Promoted to Div 3 1981   Relegated to Div 4 1984
Colours: Blue shirts with gold chest band collar and cuff, yellow shorts, blue stockings
Change Colours: All yellow
Reserves League: **'A' Team:**

CLUB RECORDS

Most Appearances for Club: Sandy Anderson: 451, 1950-63
Most Capped Player: Georgen McKenzie, 9, Eire   **For England:** None
Record Goalscorer in a Match: Jim Shankley, 5 v Merthyr Town, Div 3 (S) 01.03.1930
Record League Goalscorer in a Season: Jim Shankley, 31, Div 3 (S), 1928-9;   Sam McCrory, 31, Div 3 (S), 1957-8
Record League Goalscorer in a Career: Roy Hollis, 122, 1953-60
Record Transfer Fee Received: £120,000 from Crystal Palace for Peter Taylor, Oct 1973
Record Transfer Fee Paid: £111,111 to Blackpool for Derek Spence, Dec 1979
Best Performances: League: 3rd Div 3 (S) 1930-1   **FA Cup:** Last sixteen 1920-1, 1925-6, 1951-2,
1975-6   **League/Milk Cup:** Never past 3rd Round
Most League Points: 69, Div 3, 1981-2   **Most League Goals:** 92, Div 3 (S), 1950-1
Record League Victory: 9-2 v Newport County, Div 3 (S), 5 Sept 1936
Record League Defeat: 1-9 v Brighton, Div 3, 27 Nov 1965
Oldest Player in League Match:
Youngest Player in League Match:
Most Consecutive Undefeated League Matches: 16 1932
Longest Run of Undefeated Home League Matches: 32 1980-81
Longest Run Without Home League Win: 8 1948-49
Most Consecutive League Wins: 6 1932, 1972, 1978, 1980
Most Consecutive League Defeats: 6 1931-32, 1955

League Matches Without a Win: 17 1984
Away League Matches: 9 1931 1950, 1972
Away League Win: 27 1920-22
Home League Wins: 18 1980-81
Away League Wins: 5 1931

Club Statistician for the Directory: P Esdaile

SOUTHEND

PLAYERS NAME Ht Wt Birthdate	Honours	Birthplace Transfers	Clubs	League	Milk Cup	FA Cup	Other Comps	League	Milk Cup	FA Cup	Other Comps
GOALKEEPERS											
Jim Stannard†		London	Fulham (A)	41	3	1					
6.0 13.1 6.10.62			Southend Utd. (L)	6							
			Charlton Athletic (L)	1						·	
			Southend United	46	2	1	2			·	
DEFENDERS											
Kevin Lock	E.U23 (4) Y	Plaistow	West Ham United (A)	122+10	13	11+1		2			
6.0 12.2 27.12.53	FAC '75		Fulham	220+1	16+1	10+1		27	2		
			Southend United	10			1	·			
Glen Pennyfather		Billericay	Southend Utd (A)	178+5	5+1	9+3	3				
5.8½ 10.10 11.2.63											
Paul Roberts	FAYC '79	London	Millwall (A)	142+4	7+1	9					
5.10 12.0 27.4.62			Brentford	61+1	4	7	2+1				1
			Swindon (N/C)	25+2	1	1	2				
			Southend Utd								
Shane Westley		Canterbury	Charlton Ath. (A)	8							
6.2½ 12.7 16.6.65			Southend Utd.	47+1	2	1	2	5			
MIDFIELD											
Paul Clark	EY	Benfleet	Southend Utd. (A)	29+4	0+1	1		1			
5.10 12.5 14.9.58		£55,000	Brighton	69+10	8+1	4+1		9			
			Reading (L)	2							
		F	Southend Utd.	115+4	5	6+1	2	3	1	1	1
Dean Neal		Edmonton	Q.P.R. (A)	20+3	2			8	1		
5.10½ 12.0 5.1.61		Tulsa Rghncks.	Millwall	101+19	8+2	4+1	7+1	42	8	1	1
			Southend	10+1			1	3			
Danny O'Shea		Kennington	Arsenal (A)	6							
6.0 12.8 26.3.63			Charlton Ath. (L)								
			Exeter City	45	2	2	2		2		
			Southend Utd.	35	2	1	2	8			
John Seaden		Southend	Southend Utd. (A)	19+1			2				
5.10½ 11.8 4.6.67											
Barry Silkman	Div.3 '76	London	Barnet								
5.8 10.13 29.6.52			Hereford Utd.	18+19	1	1		2			
			Crystal Palace	40+8	1	5					
		£53,000	Plymouth Argyle	14							
			Luton Town (L)	3							
			Manchester City	19	2			3			
			Brentford	14	2			1			
			Q.P.R.	22+1		2		2			
			Orient	133+7	7	9	6	14	1	1	
			Southend Utd.	38+2	2	1		1			
FORWARDS											
Richard Cadette		London	Wembley								
5.6 10.7 21.3.65			Orient	19+1	4	1	2	4		1	
			Southend Utd.	44	1+1	1	2	25			
Mike Engwell		Grays	Southend Utd.	8+2			1+1	3			
5.10½ 11.0 27.9.66											
John Gymer		Romford	Southend Utd.	21+16	1	0+1	2+1	9			1
5.10½ 11.8 11.11.66											
Roy McDonough		Solihull	Birmingham City (A)	2				1			
6.1 11.11 16.10.58		£15,000	Walsall	76+6	4	5		15			
		£15,000	Chelsea								
		£15,000	Colchester Utd.	89+4	9	6		24	2		
			Southend Utd.	22	2	2		4		1	
			Exeter City	19+1	2		2+1	1			
			Cambridge United	30+2		1	1	5			
			Southend Utd.	31+6	1+1	1	2	7			
Ian Rogers	Div.3 '84	Plymouth	Plymouth Argyle (A)	107+10	13	7		5			
6.10 10.7 6.7.54		£15,000	Portsmouth	154+8	13+1	9+2		15	2		
		£20,000	Southend Utd.	85+2	4	3	1+2	4			

ADDITIONAL CONTRACT PROFESSIONALS

Philip Cavener

APPRENTICES

Michael Copping, Justin Edinburgh, Neil Gray, Paul Newell, Daniel Schneider, Nicholas Thurston

NON-CONTRACT PLAYERS

Russell Short, Nicholas Smith, Stephen Wiggins, Kevin Spiers

ROOTS HALL Victoria Avenue, Southend-on-Sea

Capacity: 13,500

Record Attendance: 31,033 v Liverpool, FA Cup Round 3, 10 Jan 1979

Smallest Home Attendance for a First Class Match: 1,362 v Halifax Town, Div 4, 8 Feb 1985

Record Receipts: £36,599 v Liverpool, FA Cup Round 3, 10 Jan 1979

Season Tickets: Stand (East) (Red/Yellow/Green): £85; (Blue) £100; Paddock: £55 (£20 OAP/juveniles); North Bank & West Standing: £55 (£20 OAP/juveniles); South Bank: Visitors only

Executive Box Season Tickets: Vice-Presidents £230

Cost of Stand Tickets: £5.00; Paddock: £3.50 (£1.70 OAP/juveniles); Standing North Bank & West: £2.80 (£1.60 OAP/juveniles); South Bank Standing: £2.80 (£1.60 OAP/juveniles)

Match and Ticket Information: Seats can be bought 14 days before match

Car Parking: Two parks at the ground hold 700 vehicles (approximately). Ample street parking is available

Nearest Railway Station: Southend Central (0702 611811) Prittlewell

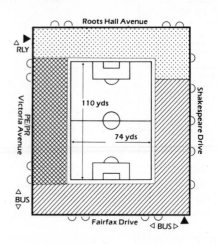

How to get to the ground

From North and East: Use A127 S.P. Southend, and then at roundabout take 3rd exit into Victoria Avenue for Southend United FC
From South: Use A13 S.P. Southend and then turn left into West Road and at end turn left into Victoria Avenue for Southend United FC

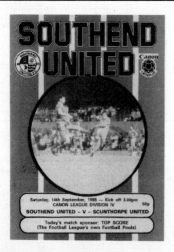

Price of 1986-7 Programme: 50p
Number of Pages: 16

Local Newspapers: Evening Echo, Southend District News, London Advertiser (Southend Edition)

Local Radio Station: Essex Radio

STOCKPORT COUNTY — Division 4

A rise of twelve places in the 4th Division was a fine achievement for Stockport County, who usually struggle to avoid re-election pleas and also have to survive under the massive shadows of their Manchester neighbours, United and City. But the sad fact is that none of the final eight matches were won and only two were drawn and this sudden slump may well have cost 'County' promotion.

The League programme initially gave few hints about the later satisfactory position. It was very much 'business as usual' at the outset and by October 11th (for nearly three weeks) a position only just above the danger zone was reached, but then came a gradual improvement, which included seven League wins in eight games from October 29th. Although form was never that good again early in March the team was in a promotion spot, which was to be succeeded by that final slump.

Cup progress was less good and it was ironical that the team played the minimum number of matches open to it during the season. All campaigns ended immediately with Bolton Wanderers (5-2 on aggregate) applying the 'coup de grace' in the Milk Cup and Telford United of the Gola League scoring the only goal of the FA Cup 1st Round tie at Edgeley Park. The Freight Rover Trophy provided an equally brief campaign — an away thrashing at Crewe (1-4) and home draw with ultimate Wembley finalists Bolton Wanderers.

The flamboyant Jimmy Melia is the man at the helm and he knows as well as anyone that a bad season could end in Stockport becoming a non-League club, which would be sad. But there does seem to be the basis for consistency in the team with Walker seeming to be a good replacement for Salmon in goal. Chapman, Sword, Hodkinson and Leonard are other men of consistency with the latter the main strike weapon. Hendrie, Evans and Matthewson are others who have shown reliability, but there must not be another late season slump if survival is to be achieved. WLM

Back Row L to R: Tom McAdam, David Mossman, Gary Walker, Trevor Mathewson, Clive Evans, **Middle Row:** David Wilkes, Jim Creaney, Bill Williams, Peter Grant, Mark Leonard, Paul Willis, Andy Cockhill, Martin Melvin, **Front Row:** Ronnie Glavin, Paul Hendrie, Jimmy Melia (Manager), Andy Hodkinson, Neil Bailey.

STOCKPORT COUNTY

DIVISION FOUR: 10th   **FA CUP:** 1st ROUND   **MILK CUP:** 1st ROUND

MATCH	DATE		COMPE-TITION	VENUE	OPPONENTS	RESULT		HALF TIME	L'GUE POS'N	GOALSCORERS/GOAL TIMES	ATTEN-DANCE
1	A	17	CL	A	Colchester United	L	1-3	0-1		Smith P. 78	(1,719)
2		20	MC1/1	A	Bolton Wanderers	L	1-4	1-0		Smith P. 28	(3,311)
3		23	CL	A	Burnley	W	1-0	0-0	14	Smith P. 77	(3,966)
4		26	CL	A	Rochdale	L	0-4	0-3	19		(2,070)
5	S	3	MC1/2	H*	Bolton Wanderers	D	1-1	1-0		Leonard 18	2,573
6		6	CL	A	Crewe Alexandra	W	1-0	1-0	16	Smith P. 33	(2,148)
7		13	CL	A	Preston North End	W	2-1	1-0	14	Smith P. 22, Hodkinson 47	(3,436)
8		16	CL	H	Hereford United	D	1-1	1-1	15	Sword (pen) 16	2,255
9		21	CL	A	Northampton Town	L	1-2	1-2	17	Sword 32	(1,954)
10		28	CL	H	Chester City	D	2-2	1-1	18	Leonard 39, Smith P. 53	1,801
11	O	1	CL	A	Southend United	D	0-0	0-0	18		(3,672)
12		5	CL	A	Torquay United	L	3-4	2-0	19	Sword 16, Leonard 30, 54	(1,274)
13		11	CL	H	Hartlepool United	L	1-3	0-1	20	Hodkinson 70	1,827
14		18	CL	H	Peterborough United	D	2-2	0-1	20	Hodkinson 47, Mossman 66	1,634
15		22	CL	A	Swindon Town	L	0-1	0-0	20		(7,172)
16		29	CL	A	Orient	W	1-0	1-0	19	Leonard 29	(3,021)
17	N	1	CL	H	Cambridge United	W	3-1	3-1	16	Mossman 7, Sword 12, Leonard 44	1,734
18		4	CL	A	Halifax Town	W	2-1	1-1	14	Chapman 24, Mossman 47	1,673
19		9	CL	A	Port Vale	D	1-1	1-1	14	Leonard 38	(5,248)
20		16	FAC1	H	Telford United	L	0-1	0-1			2,994
21		23	CL	H	Aldershot	W	3-2	2-1	13	Chapman 21, Sword pen 23, Hodkinson 85	1,354
22		29	CL	A	Tranmere Rovers	W	3-2	1-1	10	Leonard 11, 74, Mossman 78	(1,605)
23	D	6	CL	A	Cambridge United	W	2-1	2-1	8	Coyle 35, Wroe 37	(1,535)
24		13	CL	H	Wrexham	W	2-0	1-0	7	Coyle 22, Leonard 90	2,405
25		20	CL	H	Burnley	D	1-1	0-0	7	Leonard 82	3,472
26		26	CL	A	Mansfield Town	L	2-4	1-2	8	Leonard 18, 70	(4,206)
27		28	CL	H	Rochdale	W	3-0	1-0	8	Coyle 37, Sword (pen) 60, (pen) 63	4,005
28	J	1	CL	H	Scunthorpe United	D	0-0	0-0	8		3,504
29		11	CL	A	Exeter City	L	0-1	0-1	8		(2,161)
30		14	FRT N	A	Crewe Alexandra	L	1-4	0-3		Leonard (pen) 57	(994)
31		17	CL	H	Colchester United	D	1-1	1-1	7	Hodkinson 8	2,336
32		20	FRT N	H	Bolton Wanderers	D	2-2	1-0		Leonard 19, 67	1,874
33		24	CL	H	Preston North End	W	2-1	1-0	7	Coyle 3, Leonard 88	3,035
34		31	CL	H	Crewe Alexandra	W	3-0	0-0	6	Hodkinson 54, Leonard 75, 86	2,564
35	F	3	CL	H	Swindon Town	L	0-2	0-0	7		3,899
36		21	CL	H	Northampton Town	W	1-0	0-0	6	Cammack 65	2,011
37		24	CL	H	Exeter City	D	1-1	1-1	6	Wroe 45	2,048
38	M	1	CL	A	Chester City	W	2-1	2-1	5	Wroe 9, 15	(2,919)
39		3	CL	H	Southend United	W	2-1	1-0	4	Sword (pen) 37, Poskett 75	2,425
40		7	CL	H	Torquay United	D	1-1	0-0	4	Sword (pen) 61	3,010
41		14	CL	A	Hartlepool United	D	1-1	1-1	4	Leonard 23	(2,662)
42		21	CL	H	Orient	L	2-3	1-2	6	Chapman 3, Sword (pen) 52	3,119
43		28	CL	A	Scunthorpe United	W	3-2	1-1	5	Sword (pen) 8, Leonard 47, 85	(2,025)
44		31	CL	H	Mansfield Town	L	0-2	0-1	5		4,635
45	A	4	CL	A	Halifax Town	D	0-0	0-0	5		(1,836)
46		8	CL	A	Peterborough United	L	0-2	0-2	6		(1,610)
47		11	CL	H	Port Vale	L	1-2	1-2	6	Newton 2	4,690
48		16	CL	A	Hereford United	L	2-3	1-1	7	Sword 20, Hodkinson 71	(2,003)
49		19	CL	A	Aldershot	L	1-6	0-2	7	Mossman 73	(1,369)
50		24	CL	H	Tranmere Rovers	D	1-1	1-0	7	Evans 42	1,896
51	M	3	CL	A	Wrexham	L	0-3	0-1	10		(1,352)

Best Home League Attendance: 4,690 v Port Vale   **Smallest:** 1,354 v Aldershot   **Av Home Att:** 2,667

Goal Scorers: **Compared with 84-85:** +771

League (62): Leonard 18, Sword 12 (8 pen), Hodkinson 7, Mossman 5, Smith P. 5, Coyle 4, Wroe 4, Chapman 3, Cammack 1, Evans 1, Newton 1, Poskett 1

Milk Cup (2): Leonard 1, Smith P. 1

FA CUP (0):   *Played at Burnden Park

FRT (3): Leonard 3 (1 pen)

Salman	Rutter	Chapman	Lodge (NC)	Sword	Smith N.	Hodkinson	Thorpe	Leonard	Smith P. (L)	Sherlock	Coyle	Wroe	Hendrie	Yates (NC)	Devine (NC)	Williams	Evans	Matthewson	Mossman	Diamond (L)	Walker	Power	Cammack (L)	Poskett	Newton (L)	Referee	
1	2	3	4	5*	6	7	8	9	10	11	12															E Scales	1
1	2	3	4		6		5	9	10	11			7	8												**C Seel**	2
1		4			6		2	9	10	3	11		7	5	8											P Willis	3
1		4		12	6		2	9	10	3	11		7	5*	8											G Tyson	4
1		4		5	6	7	2	9	10	3	11		8													**T Holbrook**	5
1	2	4		5		11	6	9	10	3			7	8												M Scott	6
1	2	4		5		11	6	9	10	3			7	8												G Courtney	7
1	2	4		5		11	6	9		3	10		7	8												R Guy	8
1	2	4		5		11	6	9		3	10		7	8												A Buksh	9
1		4		5		11	2	9	10	3			7			6	8									J Key	10
1		4		5		7	2	9		3	10					6	8	11								I Borrett	11
1		4		5		7	2	9		3						6	8	11	10							R Gifford	12
1		4		5		7	2	9		3	10					6	8*	12	11							G Napthine	13
1		4		9		8	5			3	10	7					2	6	11							J Lloyd	14
1	3	4		9			5*			10	7	8					2	12	6	11						G Ashby	15
1	2	4		11				9		3	10	7	8			5	6									B Hill	16
1	2	4		10		7		9		3			8			5	6		11							T Simpson	17
1	2	4		10		7		9		3			8			5	12	6	11*							F Roberts	18
1	2	4		10		7		9		3			8			5		6	11							A Seville	19
1	2†	4		10		7		9		3			8			5		6	11							T Holbrook	20
1	2	4		10		7		9		3			8			5		6	11							D Hutchinson	21
1		4		5		7		9	10				8				6	2	3	11						G Aplin	22
1		4		5		7		9			10	11	8				6	2	3							M Cotton	23
1		4		5		7		9			10	11	8				6	2	3							N Wilson	24
1		4		5		7		9				11	8				6	2	3	10						L Robinson	25
1	4†	5		7				9				11	8				6	2	3	10						J Ashworth	26
1		4		5		7		9				11	8				6	2	3	10						K Hackett	27
1	4*	5		7				9			11	12	8				6	2	3	10						D Scott	28
1				7	5	9					·	11	4	8			6	2	3	10						B Stevens	29
				7	5	9					11	4	8			6	2	3			1	10				**K Breen**	30
	4	5		7		9					11		8			6	2	3		10	1					T Mills	31
3	4	5		7	6	9					11		8				2				1	10				**J Lloyd**	32
12	4	5*		7		9					11		8			6	2	3			1		10			R Bridges	33
3	4			7		9							8			6	2	5			1		11	10		K Barrat	34
3	4			7		9							8			6	2	5			1		11	10		J Bray	35
	4	5		7	6	9					11*		8				2	3			1		12	10		R Guy	36
	4	5		7	6	9						11	8				2	3			1			10		K Lupton	37
	2	5		7	6	9						11	8				4	3			1			10		K Breen	38
	2	5		7	6	9						11	8				4	3			1			10		G Aplin	39
	2	5		7	6	9						11	8				4	3			1			10		M Peck	40
	4	5		7	6	9						11	8				2	3			1			10		J Key	41
	4	5		7	6	9				12	10	11*	8				2	3			1					J McAuley/R Jones	42
		5		7	2	9				3	10	11	8				4	6			1					A Saunders	43
	4	5		7	6	9				3			8				2		11		1				10	D Allison	44
	4	5			6	9				3		7	8				2		11		1				10	I Hendrick	45
	4	5		7	6	9				3			8				2		11		1				10	K Baker	46
	4	5		7	6	9							8				2	3	11		1				10	M Scott	47
		5		4	6	9						11	8				2	3	7		1				10	C Downey	48
	8	5		4	6	9				12	10	7					2	3*	11		1		12			A Seville	49
	2			4	5	9				3	10	7				8	6	11*			1					K Walmsley	50
		4		5	7	9				3	10	7	8				2	6	11		1					J Ball	51
26	16	38	1	39	3	41	30	44	7	23	24	25	36	2	2	22	33	34	17	6	20		3	8	6	League Appearances	
	1		1								2	1	1					2	1				1	1		Substitute Appearances	
2	1	2	1		2	1	2	2	2	1	2	1	2						1		1	1				Milk Cup Appearances	
1	1	1		1		1		1		1			1			1		1	1							FA Cup Appearances	
1	1			2	2	2				2	1	2				1	2	1			2	2				FR Trophy Appearances	

Players on Loan: P. Smith (Sheff Utd), Diamond (Rochdale), Cammack (Scunthorpe), Newton (Hartlepool)

Departures: Rutter (Retired), Sherlock (Cardiff), Smith (Northwich Vic), Thorpe (F), Coyle (Chesterfield), Power (F), Sword (Hartlepool), Wroe (F)

'COUNTY'

Formed: 1883
Turned Professional: 1891   **Ltd Co:** 1908

Previous Managers: 1900-11 Fred Stewart   1911-4 Harry P Lewis   1914-9 David Ashworth   1919-24 Albert Williams   1924-6 Fred Scotchbrook   1926-31 Lincoln Hyde   1931-2 No Manager   1932-3 Andrew Wilson   1933-4 No Manager   1934-6 Fred Westgarth   1936-8 Bob Kelly   1938-9 No Manager   1939-49 Bobbie Marshall   1949-52 Andy Beattie   1952-6 Dick Duckworth   1956-60 Willie Moir   1960-3 Reg Flewin   1963-5 Trevor Porteous   1965-6 Bert Trautman   1966-6 Eddie Quigley   1966-9 Jimmy Meadows   1969-70 Walter Galbraith   1970-1 Matt Woods   1972-4 Brian Doyle   1974-5 Jimmy Meadows   1975-6 Roy Chapman   1976-7 Eddie Quigley   1977-8 Alan Thompson   1978-9 Mike Summerbee   1979-82 Jimmy McGuigan
Honours: Div 3 (N) Champions 1936-7   Div 4 Champions 1966-7
League Career: Elected to Div 2 1900   Failed Re-election 1904   Elected to Div 2 1905   Relegated to Div 3 (N) 1920-1   Promoted to Div 2 1921-2   Relegated to Div 3 (N) 1925-6   Promoted to Div 2 1936-7   Relegated to Div 3 (N) 1937-8   Transferred to Div 3 1958   Relegated to Div 4 1958-9   Promoted to Div 3 1966-7   Relegated to Div 4 1969-70
Colours: Royal blue and white striped shirts blue shorts, white stockings with three blue bands at the top
Change Colours: Yellow shirts, green shorts and stockings with yellow bands at top
Reserves League: Lancashire Div 1

CLUB RECORDS

Most Appearances for Club: Bob Murray, 1952-63: Football League 465 + FA Cup 27 + League Cup 3 **Total 495**
Most Capped Player: Harry Hardy (England) 1
Record Goalscorer in a Match: Joe Smith, 5 v Southport (h) 6-3, Div 3 (N) 07.01.28
Joe Smith, 5 v Lincoln County (h) 7-3, Div 3 (N) 15.09.28   Jack Connor, 5 v Workington (h) 6-0, Div 3 (N) 08.11.52
Jack Connor, 5 v Carlisle United (h) 8-1, Div 3 (N) 07.04.56
Record League Goalscorer in a Season: Alf Lythgoe, 46   **In All Competitions:** Alf Lythgoe, 46 League + 1 FA Cup = 47, 1933-4
Record League Goalscorer in a Career: Jack Connor, 132   **All Competitions:** Jack Connor 132, League + 8 FA Cup = 140, 1951-6
Record Transfer Fee Received: £80,000 from Manchester City for Stuart Lee, Sept 1979
Record Transfer Fee Paid: £25,000 to Albion Rovers for Tony Coyle, Dec 1979
Best Performances: League: 17th Div 2 1905-6   **FA Cup:** 5th Round 1935, 1950   **League/Milk Cup:** 4th Rd 1972-3
Most League Points: 64 in Div 4, 1966-7   **Most League Goals:** 115, Div 3 (N), 1957-8
Record League Victory and Most Goals in a First Class Match: 13-0 v Halifax Town, Div 3 (N), 6 Jan 1934
Most Goals Scored in a Cup Tie: 7-2 v Kings Lynn, 5th Qualifying Round FA Cup, 14 Dec 1912
Record League Defeat: 1-8 v Chesterfield, Div 2, 19 Apr 1902
Oldest Player in League Match: Jack Bowles 39
Youngest Player in League Match: David Herd 17
Most Consecutive Undefeated League Matches: 18 1933
Longest Run of Undefeated Home League Matches: 48 1927-29

Longest Run Without Home League Win: 8 1913, 1973
Most Consecutive League Wins: 8 1927-28
Most Consecutive League Defeats: 9 1908-09

League Matches Without a Win: 13 1947
Away League Matches: 8 1921-22, 1929, 1929-30
Away League Win: 37 1901-03
Home League Wins: 13 1928-29, 1930
Away League Wins: 7 1951

Club Statistician for the Directory: Howard Jones

STOCKPORT COUNTY

PLAYERS NAME t Wt Birthdate	Honours	Birthplace Transfers	Clubs	APPEARANCES				GOALS			
				League	Milk Cup	FA Cup	Other Comps	League	Milk Cup	FA Cup	Other Comps
GOALKEEPERS											
ary Walker .2 12.10 11.10.63		Manchester	Ashton Town								
			Stockport County	20							
DEFENDERS											
evor Mathewson .1 12.5 12.2.65		Sheffield F	Sheffield Wed. (A)	3		2					
			Newport County								
			Stockport County								
ill Williams .10 12.7 9.10.60		Littleborough	Rochdale	89+6	6	4	2	2			
			Stockport County	22		1	1				
MIDFIELD											
live Evans .10 11.5 1.5.57		Birkenhead £25,000 F F	Tranmere Rovers (A)	175+3				27			
			Wigan Athletic	29+3				2			
			Crewe Alexandra	26+2				7			
			Stockport County	106+2	4	1	4	9			
aul Hendrie* .6 10.3 27.3.55		Glasgow	Kirkintolloch Rob Roy								
			Birmingham City	19+4	3	3		1			
			Portland Timbers								
			Bristol Rovers	17+3		0+1		1			
			Halifax Town	187	8	11	1	12		1	
			Stockport County	75	4+1	2	4	4	1		
ndrew Hodginson .9 10.2 4.11.65	ES	Ashton-u-Lyme F	Bolton W. (A)								
			Oldham Athletic	4+1				1			
			Stockport County	41	1	1	2	7			
eil Bailey 5.6 11.4 26.9.58		Wigan F F F	Burnley (A)								
			Newport County	129+5	8	9		7			
			Wigan Athletic	31+10	3	4+2	1+1	2			
			Stockport County								
FORWARDS											
Mark Leonard† 5.11 11.10 27.9.62		St. Helens F F F	Witton Albion								
			Everton								
			Tranmere Rovers	6+1							
			Crewe Alexandra	51+3	4	2	3+1	15	1		
			Stockport County	67	2	1	2	22	1		3
David Mossman 5.11 12.11 27.7.64		Sheffield	Sheffield Weds.								
			Bradford City (L)	0+4				1			
			Stockport County (L)	9		1		4			
			Rochdale	9			2	1			
			Stockport County	8				1			
Malcolm Poskett 6.0 11.11 19.7.53		Middlesbrough Whitby Town £60,000 £110,000 £25,000	South Bank								
			Middlesbrough	0+1							
			Hartlepool Utd.	50+1	3	3		20	1		
			Brighton	33+12	4+1	1		16	1		
			Watford	57+6	9	5+1		17	6	6	
			Carlisle Utd.	108+7	6	8		40	2	2	
			Darlington	18+3	3	1		4	1		
			Stockport County	8				1			

ADDITIONAL CONTRACT PROFESSIONALS
Peter Grant, David Wilkes

APPRENTICES

NON-CONTRACT PLAYERS

EDGELEY PARK

Hardcastle Rd, Edgeley, Stockport, Cheshire SK3 9DD   **Capacity:** 16,500

Record Attendance: 27,833 v Liverpool, FA Cup Round 5, 11 Feb 1950

Smallest Home Attendance for a First Class Match: 1,034 v Aldershot Div 4, 25 Feb 1985

Record Receipts: £19,382 v Arsenal, League Cup Round 3, 22 Sept 1980

Season Tickets: Stand: £25 (OAP), £30 (Child), £37 (Ladies) £52 (Gentlemen)

Executive Box Season Tickets: For match sponsorship — on application to Assistant Secretary

Cost of Stand Tickets: Cheadle Stand £2.50 (Adults), £2.00 (OAP/Child); Main Stand £3.00 (All). **Terraces:** £2.00 (Adults), £1.50 (OAP/Child)

Match and Ticket Information: Seats can be reserved in the main stand by telephone or post (with remittance & SAE)

Car Parking: Ample street parking around the ground

Nearest Railway Station: Edgeley (short walk to ground)

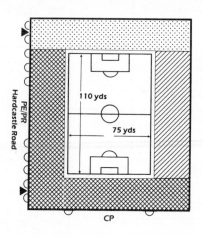

How to get to the ground

From North, South and West: Use Motorway M63 until end then join A560 S.P. Stockport. In 0.4m turn right into Edgeley Road. In 1m turn right into Caroline Street for Stockport County FC

From East: Use A6 or A560 into Stockport town centre, then turn left into Greek Street. At roundabout take 2nd exit into Castle Street then turn left into Caroline Street for Stockport County FC

Local Newspaper: Stockport Express Advertiser

Local Radio Stations: Radio Piccadilly, Radio Manchester

Stoke supporters went into the 1985-86 season with well founded apprehension. The dismal collection of records amassed in the previous season of relegation from the premier section suggested that the club faced the prospect of a hard fight ahead to avoid the ignominy of a slide down the divisions that had taken so many other traditional old industrial city clubs. The recruitment of Mick Mills as player-manager gave some hope but it was well known there was no money to spend to strengthen what looked on paper a thin squad.

The spectre of the sale of Mark Chamberlain after a couple of outstanding performances only caused more concern but with the club facing a series of injuries and illnesses to key players there emerged a number of young players who took their chance with an air of authority that augurs well for the future.

By the season's close Adams and Painter had been called into the under 21 squad whilst Heath, Shaw and Hemming were firmly established on the path to success. Keith Bertschin's goals were vital and his season's total was the highest at the club for 20 years. In many ways it was these players who stole the headlines over the season but it was the experience of Peter Fox, George Berry, John Devine and of course Mick Mills which enabled their development to blossom. A fund-raising promotion (Lifeline) gave the club a welcome boost in the arm financially with an enlarged directorate demonstrating the ambition demanded by the supporters for so long.

For the first time for many seasons the Stoke fans are anxiously awaiting a new season to savour what is hoped to be a campaign of challenging for a promotion place. The Lifeline funds are rolling in to assist viability, new players have arrived and with further progress for the young players the hopes and expectations seem better founded than for many years.   Wade Martin

Back Row L to R: Terry Williams, Carl Beeston, Tony Kelly, Philip Heath, Graham Shaw, Tony Ford, Steve Parkin, **Middle Row:** Keith Rowley (Physio), Tony Lacey (Youth Coach), Lee Dixon, Paul Reece, Carl Saunders, Peter Fox, Chris Maskery, Sammy Chung (Coach), Mick Mills (Manager), **Front Row:** Chris Hemming, Steve Bould, George Berry, Keith Bertschin, Aaron Callaghan.

STOKE CITY

DIVISION TWO: 10th   **FA CUP:** 3rd ROUND   **MILK CUP:** 3rd ROUND   **FM CUP:** SEMI-FINAL

MATCH	DATE	COMPE-TITION	VENUE	OPPONENTS	RESULT		HALF TIME	L'GUE POS'N	GOALSCORERS/GOAL TIMES	ATTEN-DANCE
1	A 17	CL	H	Sheffield United	L	1-3	1-1		Heath 43	11,679
2	24	CL	A	Barnsley	D	0-0	0-0	19		(6,598)
3	26	CL	H	Leeds United	W	6-2	1-0	10	Berry 15, Bertschin 56, 83, Chamberlain 72, 88, Maskery 74	7,047
4	S 1	CL	A	Bradford City	L	1-3	1-1	13	Painter 19	(6,999)
5	4	CL	H	Grimsby Town	D	1-1	0-1	13	Chamberlain 89	7,362
6	7	CL	H	Millwall	D	0-0	0-0	14		7,187
7	10	CL	A	Middlesbrough	D	1-1	0-0	14	Parkin 78	(4,255)
8	14	CL	A	Portsmouth	L	3-0	0-0	17		(13,720)
9	18	FMC	H	Coventry City	W	3-0	1-0		Bertschin (pen) 44, Saunders 49, Beeston 56	3,516
10	21	CL	A	Charlton Athletic	L	0-2	0-0	19		(8,858)
11	24	MC2/1	A	Wrexham	W	1-0	0-0		Bertschin 50	(5,241)
12	28	CL	H	Crystal Palace	D	0-0	0-0	19		7,130
13	O 2	FMC	A	Millwall	D	2-2	1-0		Bertschin (pen) 54, Maskery 82	(1,741)
14	5	CL	A	Hull City	W	2-0	1-0	17	Bertschin 10, Saunders 74	(6,890)
15	9	MC2/2	H	Wrexham	W	1-0	0-0		Bertschin 78	6,784
16	12	CL	H	Brighton & H.A.	D	1-1	0-1	17	Maskery 62	7,662
17	19	CL	A	Fulham	L	0-1	0-1	19		(4,007)
18	25	CL	H	Wimbledon	D	0-0	0-0	19		6,708
19	29	MC3	A	Portsmouth	L	0-2	0-0			(13,319)
20	N 2	CL	H	Huddersfield Town	W	3-0	2-0	17	Heath 12, Shaw 43, Bertschin 65	7,291
21	6	FMC (SF)	H	Oxford United	L	0-1	0-0			5,820
22	9	CL	A	Carlisle United	L	0-3	0-2	18		(2,813)
23	16	CL	H	Norwich City	D	1-1	0-0	18	Bertschin (pen) 53	6,469
24	23	CL	A	Oldham Athletic	W	4-2	2-0	16	Bertschin 35, 59, Heath 44, Maskery 48	(4,817)
25	30	CL	H	Sunderland	W	1-0'	0-0	14	Bertschin 80	9,034
26	D 7	CL	H	Middlesbrough	W	3-2	2-1	12	Berry 23, Adams 32, Bertschin 55	7,646
27	14	CL	A	Sheffield United	W	2-1	1-1	10	Adams 7, Shaw 46	(12,370)
28	21	CL	A	Barnsley	D	0-0	0-0	10		9,856
29	26	CL	A	Shrewsbury Town	L	0-1	0-1	11		(9,595)
30	J 1	CL	H	Blackburn Rovers	D	2-2	2-1	13	Bertschin (pen) 32, Adams 36	11,875
31	11	CL	A	Millwall	W	3-2	2-1	11	Donowa 15, Painter 17, Bertschin 71	(4,611)
32	13	FAC3	H	Notts County	L	0-2	0-1			12,219
33	18	CL	H	Bradford City	W	3-1	1-0	9	Shaw 41, Bertschin 49, 82	8,808
34	25	CL	A	Grimsby Town	D	3-3	3-2	9	Shaw 9, Bertschin 21, Adams 44	(4,523)
35	F 1	CL	A	Leeds United	L	0-4	0-1	9		(10,425)
36	18	CL	H	Fulham	W	1-0	1-0	9	Devine 9	6,449
37	22	CL	H	Charlton Athletic	D	0-0	0-0	9		9,297
38	M 8	CL	H	Hull City	L	0-1	0-1	10		9,112
39	15	CL	A	Brighton & H.A.	L	0-2	0-1	12		(8,783)
40	18	CL	A	Crystal Palace	W	1-0	1-0	11	Bertschin 36	(4,501)
41	29	CL	A	Blackburn Rovers	W	1-0	0-0	10	Saunders 77	(5,408)
42	31	CL	H	Shrewsbury	D	2-2	1-1	10	Bertschin (pen) 12, 62	8,988
43	A 5	CL	A	Huddersfield Town	L	0-2	0-0	10		(5,750)
44	12	CL	H	Carlisle United	D	0-0	0-0	11		7,159
45	19	CL	A	Norwich City	D	1-1	0-0	13	Bertschin 65	(17,757)
46	22	CL	H	Portsmouth	W	2-0	2-0	10	Berry 17, Heath 44	8,529
47	26	CL	A	Oldham Athletic	W	2-0	1-0	8	Shaw 39, Bertschin	8,585
48	29	CL	A	Wimbledon	L	0-1	0-0	9		(5,959)
49	M 3	CL	A	Sunderland	L	0-2	0-1	10		(20,631)

Best Home League Attendance: 11,875 v Blackburn Rovers   **Smallest:** 6,449 v Fulham   **Av Home Att:** 8,280

Goal Scorers: **Compared with 84-85:** −2,366

League (48): Bertschin 19 (3 pen), Shaw 5, Adams 4, Heath 4, Berry 3, Chamberlain 3, Maskery 3, Painter 2, Saunders 2, Devine 1, Donowa 1, Parkin 1

Milk Cup (2): Bertschin 2

FA Cup (-):

FM Cup (5): Bertschin 2 (2 pen), Beeston 1, Maskery 1, Saunders 1

1985-86

Mills	Maskery	Hudson	Dyson	Berry	Chamberlain	Beeston	Bertschin	Painter	Heath	Parkin	Bould	Saunders	Fox	Williams	Adams	Hemming	Shaw (A)	Devine	Donowa (L)	Callaghan	Curtis (L)	Bonnyman (L)	Kelly	Referee	
2	3	4	5	6	7	8	9	10	11															N Wilson	1
2	3	4	5	6	7		9	10	11	8														M Peck	2
3	8	4	5	6	7		9	10	11		2													P Tyldesley	3
3	8		5	6	7		9	10	11		2*	12												G Tyson	4
3	8	4*	5	6	7		9	10	11		2	12												R Bridges	5
3	8		5	6	7	12	9	10*	11		4	2	1											J Key	6
3	8		5	6	7		9		11		2	10	1	4										T Mills	7
3	8		5	6		4	9		11		2	10	1	7										T Ward	8
3*	8		5	6		4	9		11		2	10	1	12	7									**T Fitzharris**	9
3*	8		5	6		12	9		11	4	2	10	1	7										M James	10
3			5	6			9		11	4	2	10	1	8	7									**I Hendrick**	11
3	8	4*	5	6			9		11	12	2	10	1	7										J Worrall	12
3	8		5	6			9		11	4	2	10	1	7										**D Hedges**	13
3	8		5	6			9		11	4	2	10	1	7										K Redfern	14
3	8		5	6			9		11	4	2	10	1	7										**A Banks**	15
3	8		5	6			9		11	4	2	10	1	7										T Simpson	16
3	8		5	6			9		11	4	2	10	1	7										H King	17
3	8		5	6			9		11		2	10	1	12	7	4*								K Cooper	18
3*	8		5	6			9		11	10	2	12	1	7	4									**A Buksh**	19
3*	8		5	6			9		11	12	2		1	7	4	10								K Barratt	20
	8		5	6			9*		11	4	2	13	1	10*	7	3	12							**L Robinson**	21
	8		5	6			9		11	4	2	10	1	7	3									K Walmsley	22
3	8		5	6			9		11		2		1	4	7	10								G Ashby	23
3	8		5	6			9		11		2	12	1	7		10	4							G Aplin	24
3	8*		5	6			9		11		2	12	1	7		10	4							N Glover	25
3			5	6			9		11		2	8	1	7		10	4							C Trussell	26
3			5	6			9		11		2	8	1	12	7	10*	4							C Seel	27
			5	6			9		11		2	8	1	12	7	3	10*	4						A Robinson	28
3*			5	6			9		11		2	8	1	7	12	10	4							R Guy	29
			5	6			9		11		2	8	1	7	3	10	4							K Baker	30
			5	6			9	11			2	8	1		3	10	4	7						J Ball	31
2*			5	6			9	10				8	1	7	3	11	4	12						**G Napthine**	32
2			5	6			9					8	1	7	3	10	4	11						R Groves	33
3			5	6			9	12				8	1	7	2*	10	4	11						J Ashworth	34
3*			5	6			9	12				8	1	7	2	10	4	11						K Breen	35
			5	6			9		11		2	8	1	7	3	10*	4		12					J Bray	36
			5	6			9	10	11		2	8	1	7	3		4							K Hackett	37
3*			5				9	12	11		6	8	1	7	2		4			10				K Barratt	38
				6			9	8	11		5	2	1	7	3		4*		12	10				D Reeves	39
				6			9	10	11		5	8	1	7	3				2	4				R Hamer	40
4				6			9		11		5	8	1	7	3		2			10				R Guy	41
				6			9		11		5	8	1	7	3	10			2	4				V Callow	42
				6			12	9	10	11	5	8	1	7	3				2	4*				G Aplin	43
2				6			9	10	11		5	8	1	7	3					4				T Mills	44
2*				6			9	10	11		5	8	1	7	3	12				4				M Scott	45
2				6			9	7	11		5	8	1	7	3	10				4				J Worrall	46
				6			9	7*	11		5	2	1		12	3	10					8	4	C Downey	47
2				4			9		11		3	8	1	7	5	10		6						B Stevens	48
4				6			9	12	11		5	8	1	7	3	10		2*						D Hutchinson	49
35	31	19	6	31	41	7	2	42	15	38	10	33	33	37	3	31	23	19	15	4	6	3	7	League Appearances	
				3				4		2		4			3	1	1	1			2			Substitute Appearances	
3	2		3	3				3		3	3	3	2+1	3	1	3	1					2		Milk Cup Appearances	
1			1	1		1	1			1	1	1	1	1	1	1	0+1			0+1				FA Cup Appearances	
2	3		3	3		1	3		3	3	2	2+1	3	1+1	3	1	0+1							FM Cup Appearances	

Players on Loan: Donowa (Norwich), Curtis (Southampton), Bonnyman (Grimsby)

Departures: Dyson (WBA), Chamberlain (Sheff Wed), Painter (Coventry), Roberts (F), Siddall (F)

'THE POTTERS'

Formed: 1863
Turned Professional: 1885   **Ltd Co:** 1908

Previous Managers: 1875-82 Tom C Slaney   1882 Walter Cox   1982-90 Harry Lockett
1890-2 J Bradshaw   1892-5 A F Reeves   1895-7 J Rowley   1897-1908 A D Austerberry
1923 Jock Rutherford   1923-35 Tom Mather   1935-52 Bob McGrory   1952-60 Frank
Taylor   1960-77 Tony Waddington   1977-8 George Eastham   1978 Alan A'court (Caretaker)
1978-81 Alan Durban   1981-3 Richie Barker   1983-5 Bill Asprey
Honours: Champions Div 2, 1932-3, 1962-3   Champions Div 3 (N) 1926-7   Football League Cup
Winners 1971-2
League Career: Founder Members of Football League 1888   Failed re-election 1890
Re-elected to Football League 1891   Relegated to Div 2 1906-7   Resigned from League 1908
Re-elected to Div 2 1919   Promoted to Div 1 1921-2   Relegated to Div 2 1922-3
Relegated to Div 3 (N) 1925-6   Promoted to Div 2 1926-7   Promoted to Div 1 1932-3
Relegated to Div 2 1952-3   Promoted to Div 1 1962-3   Relegated to Div 2 1976-7
Promoted to Div 1 1978-9
Colours: Red and white striped shirts, white shorts and stockings
Change Colours: Yellow shirts, navy blue shorts, yellow stockings
Reserves League: Central League Div 2 **'A' Team:** Midland Intermediate League

---

CLUB RECORDS

Most Appearances for Club: Eric Skeels: Football League 495 + 11 + FA Cup 42 + 2 + League Cup 36 + 2 + UEFA Cup
1 + Texaco Cup 1 + 1 + Watney Cup 1 sub **Total 575 + 17 subs**
Most Capped Player: Gordon Banks, 36, England
Record Goalscorer in a Match: Neville (Tim) Coleman, 7 v Lincoln, 8-0, (h), Div 2, 23.02.1957   (Coleman played as an
orthodox outside right in this match)
Record League Goalscorer in a Season: Freddie Steele, 33   **In All Competitions:** Freddie Steele, 36 (League 33 + FA
Cup 3), 1936-7
Record League Goalscorer in a Career: Freedie Steele, 142   **In All Competitions:** Freddie Steele, 161 (League
142 + FA Cup 19)
Record Transfer Fee Received: £700,000 from Everton for Adrian Heath, Jan 1982
Record Transfer Fee Paid: £350,000 to Manchester United for Sammy McIlroy, Feb 1982
Best Performances: League: 4th Div 1 1935-6, 1946-7   **FA Cup:** Semi-Final 1899, 1971, 1972   **League/Milk Cup:**
Winners 1971-2   **UEFA Cup:** First Round (2)
Most League Points: 63, Div 3 (N), 1926-7   **Most League Goals:** 92, Div 3 (N), 1926-7
Record League Victory and Most Goals Scored in a League Match: 10-3 v West Bromwich Albion, Div 1, 4 Feb 1937
Most Goals Scored in a Cup Tie: 7-1 v Burnley (h), 2nd Round Replay FA Cup, 20 Feb 1896   0-7 v Leicester City (h), Qua
Round FA Cup, 14 Nov 1910
Record League Defeat: 0-10 v Preston North End, Div 1, 14 Sept 1889
European Competitions Entered: UEFA Cup 1972-3 1974-5
Oldest Player in League Match: Sir Stanley Matthews
Youngest Player in League Match:
Most Consecutive Undefeated League Matches: 18 1962   **League Matches Without a Win:** 17 1985
Longest Run of Undefeated Home League Matches: 23 1973-74   **Away League Matches:** 11 1978-79
Longest Run Without Home League Win: 9 1963   **Away League Win:** 30 1897-99
Most Consecutive League Wins: 7 1905, 1947   **Home League Wins:** 11 1895
Most Consecutive League Defeats: 11 1985   **Away League Wins:** 5 1922, 1947

Club Statistician for the Directory: Wade Martin

STOKE CITY

AYERS NAME / Wt Birthdate	Honours	Birthplace / Transfers	Clubs	League	Milk Cup	FA Cup	Other Comps	League	Milk Cup	FA Cup	Other Comps
				APPEARANCES				**GOALS**			
GOALKEEPERS											
er Fox 0½ 12.4 5.7.57		Scunthorpe	Sheffield Utd. (A)	49		3					
			Barnsley (L)	1							
		£15,000	Stoke City	232	16	9					
DEFENDERS											
orge Berry* ¾ 11.12 19.11.57	W (5) Lg.C '80	W. Germany	Wolverhampton W. (A)	124	14	21		4		2	
			Stoke City	138+6	5	3		3			
			Doncaster R (L)	1	1						
			Stoke City								
ephen Bould ½ 11.13 16.11.62		Stoke	Stoke City (A)	121+4	9	3		5	1		
			Torquay Utd. (L)	9							
ron Callaghan 1 11.2 8.10.66		Dublin	Stoke City (A)	8+6							
ris Hemming ¼ 11.2 13.4.66		Newcastle	Stoke City	43	1	1		1			
ris Maskery ½ 10.8 25.9.64		Stoke	Stoke City (A)	72+7	5+1	3+1		3			1
ck Mills ½ 11.0 4.1.49	E(42), U.23(5) Y FAC '78 Flg XI UEFAC '81	Godalming F	Portsmouth (A)								
			Ipswich Town	588+3	43+3	57	40	22	2	5	1
			Southampton	103	9	9	2	3			
			Stoke City	31	3	1					
ry Williams ¾ 11.0 23.10.66			Stoke City (A)	19+3	1						
MIDFIELD											
rl Beeston 10.3 30.6.67		Stoke	Stoke City (A)	3+3							1
hn Devine 0½ 12.0 11.11.58	Ei (13) MC '85 U.21 (2)	Dublin	Arsenal (A)	86+3	25	6					
			Norwich City	51+2	8	8		3			
			Stoke City	15		1		1			
e Dixon ½ 10.12 17.3.64		Manchester F F	Burnley	4	1						
			Chester City	56+11	2	1	3	1			
			Bury	45	4	8	1	6		1	
			Stoke City								
an Hudson 0½ 11.6 21.6.51	E(2) U.23(10) ECWC '71	London £240,000 £200,000 £120,000 £23,000	Chelsea (A)	144+1				10			
			Stoke City	105							
			Arsenal	36							
			Seattle Sounders								
			Chelsea								
			Stoke City	38+1							
hy Kelly 0 11.9 1.10.64	FRT '85	Prescot	Liverpool (A)								
			Wigan Athletic	98+3	4	10	12	15	2	1	4
			Stoke City	1							
eve Parkin 10.7 7.11.65	EYS	Mansfield	Stoke City (A)	21+7	4	2		2			
FORWARDS											
il Adams 10.1 23.11.65		Stoke	Stoke City	30+2	3	1		4			
ith Bertschin† 11.8 25.8.56	E.U21 (3) Y FAYC '75	Enfield £100,000 £200,000 £50,000	Barnet								
			Ipswich Town	19+13	1			8			
			Birmingham City	113+5	7+1	8+1		29	1	8	
			Norwich City	112+2	11	13		29	4	5	
			Stoke City	66	3	3		21	2		5
hy Ford 12.2 14.5.59	Div.3 '80	Grimsby £40,000	Grimsby Town	321+33	31+3	15+4		54	5	1	
			Sunderland (L)	8+1							
			Stoke City								
il Heath 11.5 24.11.64		Stoke	Stoke City (A)	75+4	3+1	2		7			
rl Saunders 10.12 28.12.64		Marston	Stoke City	50+10	4+1	1+2		4	1		1
aham Shaw 10.3 7.6.67		Stoke	Stoke City (A)	19+1		1		5			

ADDITIONAL CONTRACT PROFESSIONALS

APPRENTICES
orge Blackstock, Lee Fowler, Philip Howard, Justin Edwards, Ian Gibbons, Neil Prestridge, Jonathan Farmer, Paul Reece

NON-CONTRACT PLAYERS
dy Holmes, Brenton Degg, Sean Dobbin, Michael Mills (Manager)

Record Attendance: 51,380 v Arsenal, Div 1, 29 Mar 1937

Smallest Home Attendance for a First Class Match: 4,070 v Ipswich Town, Div 2, 30 March 1960

Record Receipts: £58,000 v Manchester United, Div 1, 20 Dec 1981

Season Tickets: Main Stands: £114 (£57 Juveniles/OAPs); Stoke-End: £95 (£47 Juveniles/OAPs); Ground: £57 (£28 Juveniles/OAPs)

Executive Box Season Tickets: Consult Secretary

Cost of Stand Tickets: £6.00 (£3.00 Juveniles/OAPs), £5.00 (advance price for Stoke-End stand, £6.00 on match day); Ground £3.00 (£1.50 Juveniles/OAPs)

Match and Ticket Information: Bookable two weeks before each match from ticket office

Car Parking: Street parking

Nearest Railway Station: Stoke (0782 411411)

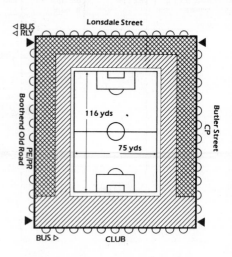

How to get to the ground

From North, West and South: Use Motorway M6 until junction 15, leave Motorway and follow signs Stoke A5006 then join A500. In 0.8m branch left and shortly at roundabout take 2nd exit into Campbell Road for Stoke City FC
From East: Use A50 into Stoke town centre and at crossroads turn left into Lonsdale Street for Campbell Road for Stoke City FC

Price of 1986-7 Programme: 60p
Number of Pages: 24

Local Newspapers: The Sentinel, Raymonds News

Local Radio Stations: Radio Stoke BBC, Signal Radio

SUNDERLAND

President
J M Ditchburn

Chairman
T Cowie, OBE

Managing Director
L McMenemy

Directors
B Batey FRICS
R S Murray FCCA
G W Hodgson FCA

General Manager/Secretary
G Davidson FCA

Assistant Manager
L Chatterley

Youth Development Officer
J Morrow

Youth Team Coach
C McMenemy

Commercial Consultant
A King

Marketing Executive
K V Douglas B.Ed, M.ILAM

Physiotherapist
J Goodfellow

ack Row L to R: Nigel Saddington, teven Jones, David Corner, Gordon rmstrong, Steve Hetzke, John ornforth, David Swindlehurst, Paul mon, **Middle Row:** David Buchanan, aul Atkinson, Iain Hesford, Gary ennett, Cameron Duncan, John oore, Dale White, **Front Row:** Mark utterside, Reuben Agboola, Alan ennedy, Shaun Elliott (now with orwich), George Burley, Eric Gates, ark Proctor, Frank Gray.

N ew manager Lawrie McMenemy found plenty of problems when he took over at Roker Park shortly after the club's relegation from the 1st Division in 1985. His main priority was to sign an experienced goalkeeper.

He eventually decided to sign Republic of Ireland international Jim McDonagh on loan from Notts County and he opened the season in Sunderland's goal.

Most of the manager's new signings were men of experience. Frank Gray, a Scottish international signed from Leeds, opened the season at left-back but also played in midfield.

Striker David Swindlehurst, from West Ham, brought a decade of scoring experience to the attack. And former England forward Eric Gates was recruited from Ipswich.

A large crowd of 21,202 turned up for the opening match of the season against Blackburn Rovers. But it was a disappointing start as Sunderland went down 0-2. In fact, they went on to lose their opening five matches, without scoring a goal, in what was the club's worst start in its history. By then they were anchored at the foot of the 2nd Division table.

More new signings were inevitable. Mr McMenemy signed two international full-backs—Alan Kennedy (England) from Liverpool and George Burley (Scotland) from Ipswich. Goalkeeper Bob Bolder was loaned from Liverpool but the full transfer was later completed.

With so many new faces in the side, it was to be expected that the team would take time to find an understanding. Relegation continued to threaten.

Home wins over promotion-chasing Wimbledon and Brighton gave the side's confidence a boost but, though there were other occasional signs of revival, inconsistency remained the big problem.

Fortunately, several of the clubs below them were experiencing similar problems so, after beating Sheffield United at Roker on Boxing Day, Sunderland were still five points clear of the danger mark.

That proved of little comfort, however, as a run of nine games without a win plunged the club into serious trouble again. By the end of the Easter programme, a solitary point was all that separated them from the third-from-bottom club.

Prior to the transfer deadline, Mr McMenemy signed centre-back Steve Hetzke from Blackpool and secured the services of goalkeeper Andy Dibble (Luton) and winger Tony Ford (Grimsby) on loan.

By mid-April, neighbouring Middlesbrough moved above Sunderland and there were real fears that the club would disappear into the 3rd Division for the first time.

That remained a possibility until they went into the final game of the season, at home to Stoke City. There was much relief when they were awarded an early penalty, which was converted by Mark Proctor. But tension remained until the 67th minute when Frank Gray scored a second goal.

When the final whistle blew, there was a dramatic wait until news filtered through that, with other results assisting them, Sunderland would remain in the 2nd Division.

SUNDERLAND

DIVISION TWO: 18th   **FA CUP:** 4th ROUND   **MILK CUP:** 2nd ROUND

MATCH	DATE		COMPE-TITION	VENUE	OPPONENTS	RESULT		HALF TIME	L'GUE POS'N	GOALSCORERS/GOAL TIMES	ATTEN-DANCE
1	A	17	CL	H	Blackburn Rovers	L	0-2	0-0			21,20
2		20	CL	A	Portsmouth	L	0-3	0-0			(14,68
3		24	CL	A	Crystal Palace	L	0-1	0-0	22		(7,04(
4		26	CL	H	Oldham Athletic	L	0-3	0-2	22		16,41
5		31	CL	A	Millwall	L	0-1	0-1	22		(7,91(
6	S	7	CL	H	Grimsby Town	D	3-3	1-2	22	Swindlehurst 34, 73, Gates (pen) 54	14,98
7		14	CL	A	Leeds United	D	1-1	1-0	22	Gray 23	(19,69:
8		17	FMC	A	Grimsby Town	L	2-3	0-0		Venison 57, Walker 75	(2,43!
9		21	CL	A	Shrewsbury Town	W	2-1	1-1	20	Pickering 44, 82	(3,91!
10		24	MC2/1	H	Swindon Town	W	3-2	1-1		Walker 28, Gates (pen) 66, Bennett 77	14,20
11		28	CL	H	Huddersfield Town	W	1-0	0-0	20	Gates 72	18,98
12	O	1	FMC	H	Grimsby Town	W	2-1	1-1		Gates (pen) 15, Hodgson 46	11,57
13		5	CL	A	Charlton Athletic	L	1-2	0-1	20	Gates 58	(5,55:
14		8	MC2/2	A	Swindon Town	L	1-3	0-0		Walker 70	(9,11
15		12	CL	H	Hull City	D	1-1	1-1	20	Gray 9	16,61
16		19	CL	A	Carlisle United	W	2-1	1-1	17	Elliott 22, Gayle 58	(9,25
17		22	CL	A	Middlesbrough	W	1-0	0-0	15	Gates 20	20,54
18		26	CL	H	Norwich City	L	0-2	0-0	17		17,90
19	N	2	CL	A	Fulham	W	2-1	1-0	15	Gates (pen) 54, Bennett 84	(5,79!
20		4	FMC S/F	A	Manchester City	L	0-0†	0-0			(6,64:
21		9	CL	H	Wimbledon	W	2-1	1-0	12	Swindlehurst 44, 74	15,51
22		16	CL	A	Barnsley	D	1-1	0-1	12	Swindlehurst 80	(9,41(
23		23	CL	H	Brighton & H.A.	W	2-1	1-0	12	Gates 6, Bennett 78	14,71
24		30	CL	A	Stoke City	L	0-1	0-0	14		(9,034
25	D	7	CL	H	Portsmouth	L	1-3	0-0	14	Gates 88	17,22
26		14	CL	A	Blackburn Rovers	L	0-2	0-1	15		(6,04!
27		22	CL	H	Crystal Palace	D	1-1	0-1	17	Armstrong 65	16,71
28		26	CL	H	Sheffield United	W	2-1	2-1	15	Gates 20, Bennett 24	17,64
29		28	CL	A	Middlesbrough	L	0-2	0-1	15		(19,774
30	J	1	CL	A	Bradford City	L	0-2	0-1	15		(8,369
31		4	FAC3	H	Newport County	W	2-0	2-0		Burley 33, Corner 44	12,35:
32		11	CL	H	Leeds United	W	4-2	1-0	13	Pickering 3 (23, 49 (pen), 85) Wallace 67	15,13!
33		18	CL	A	Millwall	L	1-2	0-0	14	Gray 89	14,294
34		25	FAC4	H	Manchester United	D	0-0	0-0			35,48
35		29	FAC4R	A	Manchester United	L	0-3	0-2			(43,402
36	F	1	CL	A	Oldham Athletic	D	2-2	1-2	17	Proctor 17, Hodgson (pen) 88	(3,827
37		8	CL	H	Carlisle	D	2-2	0-0	16	Kennedy 48, 80	12,68!
38	M	1	CL	H	Huddersfield Town	L	0-2	0-2	18		(7,150
39		8	CL	H	Charlton Athletic	L	1-2	0-0	19	Proctor 65	11,88!
40		15	CL	A	Hull City	D	1-1	0-1	19	Wallace 82	(9,295
41		22	CL	A	Grimsby Town	D	1-1	0-1	19	Armstrong 66	(5,339
42		29	CL	A	Bradford City	D	1-1	0-0	19	Ford 72	14,87(
43		31	CL	A	Sheffield United	L	0-1	0-1	19		(9,839
44	A	5	CL	H	Fulham	W	4-2	3-0	19	Elliott 2, Proctor 23, 51, Wallace 38	11,338
45		8	CL	A	Norwich City	D	0-0	0-0	19		(17,752
46		12	CL	A	Wimbledon	L	0-3	0-0	20		(6,051
47		19	CL	H	Barnsley	W	2-0	1-0	19	Futcher (og) 34, Gayle 50	12,34!
48		26	CL	A	Brighton & H.A.	L	1-3	0-1	20	Proctor 53	(9,189
49		29	CL	H	Shrewsbury Town	W	2-0	0-0	18	Gates 63, Proctor 84	15,50
50	M	3	CL	H	Stoke City	W	2-0	1-0	18	Proctor (pen) 2, Gray 68	20,63

Best Home League Attendance: 21,202 v Blackburn   **Smallest:** 11,338 v Fulham   **Av Home Att:** 16,055

Goal Scorers: Compared with 84-85: −2,303

League (47): Gates 9 (2 pen), Proctor 7 (1 pen), Pickering 5, Swindlehurst 5, Gray 4, Bennett 3, Wallace 3, Opponents 1

Milk Cup (4): Walker 2, Bennett 1, Gates 1 (pen)
FA Cup (2): Burley 1, Corner 1
FM Cup (4): Gates 1 (pen), Hodgson 1, Venison 1, Walker 1

†After Extra Time, Lost on Penaltie

McDonagh (L)	Venison	Gray	Agboola	Bennett	Elliott	Pickering	Wallace	Swindlehurst	Gates	Walker	Hodgson	Daniel	Gayle	Bolder	Kennedy	Burley	Atkinson	Corner	Proctor	Armstrong (A)	Dibble (L)	Lemon	Hetzke	Ford (L)	White	Referee	
1	2	3	4	5	6	7	8	9	10	11*	12															T Mills	1
1	2	3	4	5	6	7	8	9	10	11																C Downey	2
1	2	3	4*	5	6	7	8	9	10	11		12														J Deakin	3
1	2	3		5	6*	7	12	9	10	11	8	4														M Peck	4
1	2	3			6	7		9	10	12	8	4														V Callow	5
1	2	3		5	6	7*		9	10	11	8	4	12													C Seel	6
1	2	3		5	6	7		9	10	11	8	4														T Fitzharris	7
1	**2**	**3**		**5**		**7**		**10**	**11**	**9**	**8**		**4**													**T Simpson**	**8**
	2	3	6	5		7		9	10	11	8*		4	12	1											F Roberts	9
	2	**6**	**4**	**5**		**7***		**9**	**10**	**11**	**8**			**12**	**1**	**3**										**N Midgley**	**10**
	8	7		5	6			9	10	11			4		1	3	2									D Allison	11
	8	7		5	6			9*	10	13	12		4		1	3	2	11*								N Wilson	12
	8	7		5	6			9*	10	11	12		4		1	3	2									J Bray	13
	8	**7**		**5**	**6**				**10**	**11**	**12**		**4**		**1**	**3**	**2**									**L Shapter**	**14**
	8	7		5	6			12	10	11	9		4*		1	3	2									J Worrall	15
	8	7		5	6		4		10	9					1	3	2	11								A Robinson	16
	8	7		5	6		4	12	10	9					1	3	2	11*								L Dilkes	17
	8	7		5	6		4*	9	10	11					1	3	2	12								R Banks	18
	8	7		5	6		4	9	10	11					1	3	2									M Scott	19
	8	**7**		**5**	**6**		**4**	**9**	**10**	**11***					**1**	**3**	**2**	**12**								**C Seel**	**20**
	4	7		5	6		8	9	10	11					1	3	2									D Hutchinson	21
	4	7		5	6		8*	9	10	11					1	3	2	12								R Guy	22
	8	7		5				9	10	11					1	3	2	6								D Scott	23
	4*	7		5	6		8	9	10	12	11				1	3	2									N Glover	24
	8			5†	6		4	9	10	11		7*			1	3	2	12								K Hackett	25
	8			5	6	4	7*	9	10	12					1	3	2	11								M McAulay	26
		4		6			8	9	10	12					1	3	2	11	7	5*						J Key	27
	8			5	6		4	9	10					3	1	2			7	11						G Aplin	28
	8			5	6		4	12	10	9				3	1	2*			7	11						I Hendrick	29
	8	4		5*	6			9	10		12			3	1	2			7	11						K Breen	30
	8			**6**			**4**	**9**	**10**					**3**	**1**	**2**		**11**	**7**	**5**						**M Heath**	**31**
	8			6			4	9	10					3	1	2		11	7	5						N Midgley	32
	8	12		6			4	9	10*					3	1	2		11	7	5						D Philips	33
	8			**6**			**4**	**9***	**10**				**12**	**3**	**1**	**2**		**11**	**7**	**5**						**C Seel**	**34**
	8			**6**			**4**	**9**	**10**				**12**	**3**	**1**	**2**		**11**	**7***	**5**						**C Seel**	**35**
	8			6			4	9*	10				12	3	1	2		11	7	5						G Napthine	36
	8*	4		6				9	10		12			3	1	2		11	7	5						T Simpson	37
	8	12		6	5			9						3		2		7*	11	4	1			10		L Robinson	38
	8			6				9*	10					3		2		11	7	4	1		12	5		P Tyldesley	39
	8			6			12	10						3*		2		11	7	4	1		9	5		P Vanes	40
11	8			6			12	10						3		*2			7	4			9	5		T Fitzharris	41
8	11			6				10						3		2		4	7		1		9*	5	12	T Jones	42
11	8		6				9		12					3		2*		4		1			5	7	10	J Lovatt	43
2	10		6				9*	8						3		11		4		1		5	7	12	M Peck	44
2	4		*6	9	10		8							3		11				1	5	7		12	B Hill	45
2	10		6				9	12						3*		11		4		1	5	7		8	I Borrett	46
2	6		5	9	10		8							3		11		4	1			7			C Seel	47
2	4		5	6	9	10	8							3		11			1			7			M Scott	48
2	4		5	6	9	10	8							3		11			1			7			R Bridges	49
2	4		5	6	9	10	12	8						3*		11			1			7			D Hutchinson	50

7	36	32	12	28	32	22	14	25	38	10	9	8	20	22	32	27	10	9	19	13	12	4	8	8	2	League Appearances	
	2			2	5		1	2	6	1	3				3			1		1			1	1	2	Substitute Appearances	
2	2	1	2	1	1		1	2	1·1	1			0·1	2	2	1										Milk Cup Appearances	
3	1	3		2	3	2	1					0·2	3	3	3	3	3	3								FA Cup Appearances	
3	3		3	2	2		3	1·1	1·1	1		2	2	2	2	1·1										FM Cup Appearances	

Also Played: Position (Game): Berry 11*(5), Moore 9*(14), Duncan 1(41), Chisolm S 5(5), 6(8)

Players on Loan: McDonagh (Notts County), Dibble (Luton Town), Ford (Grimsby)

Departures: Chisholm (Hibs), Elliot (Norwich), Pickering (Coventry), Venison (Liverpool), Hodgson (Norwich)

'THE ROKERITES'

Formed: 1879
Turned Professional: 1886 **Ltd Co:** 1906

Previous Names: Sunderland & District Teachers AFC
Previous Managers: 1889-96 Tom Watson 1896-99 Robert Campbell 1899-1905 Alex Mackie
1905-28 Bob Kyle 1928-39 John Cochrane 1939-57 Billy Murray 1957-64 Alan Brown
1964-5 George Hardwick 1965-8 Ian McColl 1968-72 Alan Brown
1972-6 Bob Stokoe/Ian McFarlane (caretaker manager) 1976-8 Jim Adamson/D Merrington (Caretaker
manager) 1978-9 Billy Elliott 1979-81 Ken Knighton 1981-4 Alan Durban 1984-5 Len Ashurst
1985- L McMenemy
Honours: Champions Div 1, 1891-2, 1892-3, 1894-5, 1901-2, 1912-3, 1935-6 Champions Div 2,
1975-6 FA Cup Winners 1937, 1973
League Career: Elected to Div 1 1890 Relegated to Div 2 1957-8
Promoted to Div 1 1963-4 Relegated to Div 2 1969-70 Promoted to Div 1 1975-6
Relegated to Div 2 1976-7 Promoted to Div 1 1979-80 Relegated to Div 2 1984-5
Colours: Red and white striped shirts, black shorts red stockings with white band
Change Colours: Blue shirts with navy, blue shorts, blue stockings with navy band
Reserves League: Central League Div 1

CLUB RECORDS

Most Appearances for Club: Jim Montgomery: Football League 537 + FA Cup 39 **Total 576**
Most Capped Player: Billy Bingham, M Harvey (N Ireland), Charlie Hurley (Eire) 33 **For England:** Dave Watson 14
Record Goalscorer in a Match: C Buchan, N Sharkey, 5
Record League Goalscorer in a Season: Dave Halliday, 43 **In All Competitions:** Dave Halliday, 43 (all League), 1928-9
Record League Goalscorer in a Career: Charles Buchan, 209 **In All Competitions:** Charles Buchan, 223 (League
209 + FA Cup 14) 1911-25
Record Transfer Fee Received: £275,000 from Manchester City for Dennis Tueart, March 1974 £275,000 from Everton
for Paul Bracewell, April 1984 £275,000 from Manchester United for Chris Turner, July 1985
Record Transfer Fee Paid: £320,000 to San Lorenzo for Claudio Marangoni, Dec 1979
Best Performances: League: Champions Div 1 (6) **FA Cup:** Winners (2) **League/Milk Cup:** Runners-Up 1985
Most League Points: 61, Div 2, 1963-4 **Most League Goals:** 109, Div 1, 1935-6
Record League Victory and Most Goals Scored in a League Match: 9-1 v Newcastle United (a), Div 1, 5 Dec 1908 (1-1
half-time) — Newcastle went on to win the championship
Most Goals Scored in a Cup Tie: 11-1 v Fairfield (h), 1st Round FA Cup, 2 Feb 1895
Record League Defeat: 0-8 v West Ham United, Div 1, 19 Oct 1968 0-8 v Watford, Div 1, 25 Sept 1982
European Competitions Entered: European Cup Winners Cup 1973-4
Oldest Player in League Match: Bryan Robson 38 yrs 182 days
Youngest Player in League Match: Derek Forster 15 yrs 184 days
Most Consecutive Undefeated League Matches: 16 1922-23,
1980
Longest Run of Undefeated Home League Matches: 44 1890-93
Longest Run Without Home League Win: 12 1981-82, 1985
Most Consecutive League Wins: 13 1891-92
Most Consecutive League Defeats: 9 1976-77

League Matches Without a Win: 14 1985
Away League Matches: 14 1978-79
Away League Win: 28 1952-54
Home League Wins: 19 1890-92
Away League Wins: 5 1891-92, 1892,
1912-13, 1963

Club Statistician for the Directory: Billy Simmons

SUNDERLAND

PLAYERS NAME Ht Wt Birthdate	Honours	Birthplace Transfers	Clubs	League	Milk Cup	FA Cup	Other Comps	League	Milk Cup	FA Cup	Other Comps
GOALKEEPERS											
Ian Hesford 6.2 14.11 4.3.60	E.U21 (7)	Kenya £40,000	Blackpool (A)	202	14	13					
			Sheffield Weds.								
			Fulham (L)	3							
			Notts County (L)	10							
			Sunderland								
DEFENDERS											
Reuben Agboola 5.10 11.2 30.5.62		London £150,000	Southampton (A)	89+1	10	7	5				
			Sunderland	20	1	3					
Peter Beagrie 5.8½ 9.10 28.11.65		Middlesbrough	Middlesbrough Sunderland	24+9	1		1+1	2			
Gary Bennett* 6.1 12.1 4.12.61		Manchester	Manchester City								
			Cardiff City	85+2	4	3		11			
			Sunderland	65	2	1		6	1		
George Burley 5.9½ 11.0 3.6.56	S(11) U.23(2) YS U.21(5) FAC '78 UEFAC '81	Cumnock	Ipswich Town (A)	394	35	43	27	6		4	1
			Sunderland	27	1	3	2			1	
Frank Gray 5.10 11.10 27.10.54	S(32) U.23(5) S EC'80 ESC '79	Glasgow £500,000	Leeds United (A)	188+5	18+1	19+1	12+2	7	4		3
		£300,000	Nottm Forest	81	14	8	14	5	2	1	
		£50,000	Leeds United	141+1	12	7		10			
			Sunderland	32+2	2	1		4			
Stephen Hetzke 6.2 13.4 3.6.55	Div.4 '79	Marlborough	Hungerford Town Reading (A)	254+7	28	8+3		23	5	1	
		£30,000	Blackpool	117	10	8		14			
			Sunderland								
Alan Kennedy 5.9 10.7 31.8.54	E(2) U.23(6) 'B'7 Div1 79/80/82/83 84, LgC'81 MC'82 83/84 EC 81,84	Sunderland £300,000	Newcastle United (A)	155+3	16	20+2		9			
			Liverpool	249+2	32	22	36	14	2		
			Sunderland	32	2	3					
Nigel Saddington 6.1 12.6 9.12.65		Sunderland	Doncaster Rovers Sunderland	6							
MIDFIELD											
Paul Atkinson 5.9 10.10 19.1.66	EY	Chester le Street	Sunderland (A)	22+3	1	3		2			
David Corner 6.1¾ 12.13 15.5.66		Sunderland	Sunderland (A)	12	2	3					
			Cardiff City (L)	5							
Mark Proctor† 5.10 11.9 30.1.61	E.U21 (4) Y	Middlesbrough £115,000	Middlesbrough (A)	107+2	6	10		12	1	1	
		£115,000	Notts Forest	60+4	10	2		5	3	1	
			Sunderland	81+1	9	5		11	1		
FORWARDS											
Eric Gates 5.6 10.4 28.6.55	E(2) FAYC '73 UEFAC '81	Ferryhill £150,000	Ipswich Town (A)	267+29	28+1	23+3	46	73	5	5	7
			Sunderland	38+1	2	1		9	1		
Paul Lemon 5.10¾ 11.6½ 3.6.66		Middlesbrough	Sunderland (A)	14+2							
			Carlisle Utd. (L)	2							
John Moore 6.0 11.11 1.10.66		Sunderland	Sunderland	3+1				1			
			St. Patricks Ath (L)	2							
			Newport Co. (L)	2							
Dave Swindlehurst 6.2 11.0 9.6.67	E.U21(1) Y Div.2 '79	Edwards £41,000	Crystal Palace	221+16	17	22		73	3	4	
		£200,000	Derby County	110	8	7		29	3		
			West Ham United	52+9	5		44+1	16	1	1	
			Sunderland	25	1	2		5			
Dale White 5.10 11.4 17.3.68	ES	Sunderland	Sunderland (A)	2+2							

ADDITIONAL CONTRACT PROFESSIONALS
Cameron Duncan, John Cornforth, Mark Outterside, Gordon Armstrong, Stephen Jones

APPRENTICES
Nicholas Jimson, Paul McKenzie, Sean Mills, Gary Owers, Jarrod Suddick, Sean Wharton, Mitchell Whellans,

NON-CONTRACT PLAYERS
Gary Breeds, Gary Gilchrist, David Buchanan, John Hepple

Record Attendance: 75,118 v Derby County,
FA Cup 6th Round Replay,
8.3.1933   68,004 v Newcastle United, Div 1,
4.3.1950

**Smallest Home Attendance for a First Class
Match:** 4,832 v Portsmouth, Div 1, 29.4.1935

Record Receipts: £111,000 v Chelsea, Milk
Cup Semi-Final (1st leg), 13.2.1985

Season Tickets: Stand: £99 (£50
Juniors/OAPs); Ground: £49 (£40
Juniors/OAPs)

Executive Box Season Tickets: £4,000 (None
available)

Cost of Stand Tickets: Seats: £5.00,
Restricted view £4.25; OAP Concession
(Clockstand) £2.50; Family Enclosure: Adult
£5.00; Child £2.50; Standing: Paddock: £3.00;
Terraces: £2.50 Adult £1.50 Child

Match and Ticket Information: Bookable ten
days prior to a match

Car Parking: Parking for 1,500 cars 200 yards
from ground

Nearest Railway Station: Seaburn

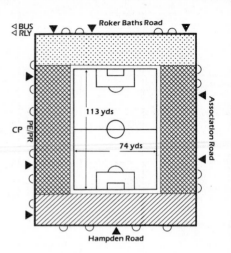

How to get to the ground

From North: Use A184 and A19 into
Sunderland and at roundabout take 1st exit into
Roker Avenue. In 0.2m turn left into Fulwell
Road then turn right one-way and then left into
Roker Baths Road for Sunderland FC
From South: Use A1 and A690 into Sunderland
then follow signs Gateshead A1018 and cross
Wearmouth Bridge. Then at roundabout take 4th
exit into Roker Avenue. In 0.2m turn left into
Fulwell Road then turn right one-way and then
left into Roker Baths Road for Sunderland FC
From West: Use A1231 into Sunderland then at
roundabout take 2nd exit shortly turn right into
Sunderland Road for Southwick Road then at
roundabout take 2nd exit into Roker Avenue. In
0.2m turn left into Fulwell Road then turn right
one-way and then left into Roker Baths Road for
Sunderland FC

Price of 1986-7 Programme: 50p
Number of Pages: 32
Subscriptions: Home, 1st class £16.50; 2nd
class £15.50; home and away, 1st class
£24.50; overseas £27.00

Local Newspapers: Journal/Chronicle/Sunday
Sun, Sunderland Echo, Northern Echo,
Sunderland and Washington Times

Local Radio Stations: Memo Radio, Radio
Tees, Radio Newcastle

Joint Presidents
P E Holden
I C Pursey MBE

Chairman
D J Sharpe

Directors
M Griffiths
D G Hammond FCA, MBM

Secretary
G M Taylor (0792 474114)

Manager
Terry Yorath

Player Coach
Tommy Hutchinson

Commercial Department
Club Shop (0792 462584)

Stadium Manager
H Woolacott

It is doubtful whether any other League club had such an eventful season as did Swansea City during 1985-6. Apart from anything else, on the blackest day in its sporting history, the club was wound up on 20th December 1985. The receiver sacked manager John Bond and the club was to be no more. Happily, two days later there was a "resurrection" and the club met the requirements of the Football League by playing Cardiff away on Boxing Day.

From that day, however, until the end of the season the club operated 'in liquidation' and several visits needed to be made to the High Court in order to allow 'The Swans' to continue. Finally, on 7th May 1986 the club's creditors accepted the rescue package of Doug Sharpe and, subject to the blessing of the High Court, Swansea City will emerge as a corporate entity again for the 1986/7 season.

Sadly the financial drama of the season, particularly the uncertainty of the club's very existence had an adverse effect on results. New manager, Tommy Hutchinson, had to operate with a team of nomads. Not surprisingly players who were signed were not prepared to move to Swansea, when it was unclear what was going to happen to the club. Then, at one stage the Players Union had to meet the club's wage bill. To add to Hutchinson's difficulties his injury list could only be described as 'crippling'. No fewer than six players of his small squad had limbs in plaster during the season, one, talented winger Colin Pascoe, was twice affected.

Nevertheless, and despite eventual relegation to Division 4, the team played some good football on occasions. Also, the many difficulties of the season forced the manager to blood several talented youngsters. Thus, in the midst of the gloom of financial difficulty and relegation there were some bright spots.

McCarthy, Burrows, French, Melville, Hughes, Hough and Williams have a great chance of joining the long list of Swansea players who have made names in the football world. Certainly, if they follow the tremendous example of 39-year-old manager Tommy Hutchinson they will do well. Nobody could have done more than the likeable Scot to help save the club on and off the field. During the season he made more than 50 League and Cup appearances plus countless reserve and friendly games. What an example for the youngsters! It should be noted too, that despite the club's results, its 'average' gate of around 4,000 was better than several in superior places in the League.   David Farmer

ck Row L to R: Ron Walton, Andrew
lville, Nigel French, Phil Williams, Mike
ghes, Chris Harrison, Sean McCarthy, Colin
scoe, David Hough, Graham Davies.
ated: Keri Andrews, Colin Randell, Dudley
wis, Tommy Hutchison, Terry Yorath
anager), Gary Emmanuel, Terry Phelan,
ul Burrows.

SWANSEA CITY

DIVISION THREE: 24th **FA CUP:** 2nd ROUND **MILK CUP:** 2nd ROUND **FRT:** Semi-Fi

MATCH	DATE		COMPE-TITION	VENUE	OPPONENTS	RESULT		HALF TIME	L'GUE POS'N	GOALSCORERS/GOAL TIMES	ATTEN-DANCE
1	A	17	CL	H	Wigan Athletic	L	0-1	0-0			4,70
2		20	MC1/1	A	Cardiff City	L	1-2	0-1		Marustik 48	(4,21
3		24	CL	A	Walsall	L	1-3	1-1	23	McHale 33	(3,77
4		26	CL	H	Plymouth Argyle	L	0-2	0-0	23		3,90
5		31	CL	A	Blackpool	L	0-2	0-0	23		(3,08
6	S	3	MC1/2	H	Cardiff City	W	3-1	1-1		Randell 45, 50, Pascoe 56	4,62
7		7	CL	H	Rotherham United	W	1-0	0-0	22	Hutchinson 60	3,68
8		14	CL	A	Wolverhampton W.	W	5-1	4-0	19	Emmanuel 16, Randell 26, Turner 40, 44, Hutchinson 56	(4,06
9		17	CL	H	Newport County	D	1-1	1-0	19	Turner 38	5,53
10		21	CL	A	Reading	L	0-2	0-1	20		(5,126
11		24	MC2/1	A	West Ham United	L	0-3	0-0			(9,28
12		28	CL	H	Bristol Rovers	L	0-1	0-0	22		4,00
13	O	2	CL	A	Derby County	L	1-5	0-4	22	Emmanuel 48	(9,16
14		5	CL	A	Brentford	L	0-1	0-1	22		(3,50
15		8	MC2/2	H	West Ham United	L	2-3	2-3		Waddle 6, Randell 23	3,58
16		11	CL	H	Lincoln City	W	3-1	0-1	19	Pascoe 61, Waddle 77, Emmanuel 89	3,60
17		19	CL	A	Bolton Wanderers	D	1-1	0-0	19	Pascoe 52	(3,55
18		22	CL	H	Doncaster Rovers	L	0-2	0-1	20		3,82
19		29	CL	A	Gillingham	L	1-5	1-3	21	French 9	(3,08
20	N	2	CL	H	Bury	W	1-0	0-0	21	Waddle 60	3,53
21		5	CL	H	Chesterfield	D	1-1	1-0	21	Pascoe (pen) 8	3,42
22		9	CL	A	Darlington	L	0-6	0-4	23		(2,60
23		16	FAC1	H	Leyton Wingate	W	2-0	1-0		Waddle 16, Williams 50	3,29
24		23	CL	H	Bristol City	L	1-2	1-2	23	Harrison 20	4,41
25		30	CL	A	Notts County	L	0-3	0-2	23		(3,91
26	D	7	FAC2	H	Bristol Rovers	L	1-2	0-2		Burrows 79	4,23
27		14	CL	H	York City	W	1-0	0-0	22	Waddle 63	2,77
28		26	CL	A	Cardiff City	L	0-1	0-0	23		(9,37
29		28	CL	A	Plymouth Argyle	L	0-2	0-1	23		(8,62
30	J	1	CL	H	Bournemouth	D	1-1	0-1	24	McCarthy 89	6,98
31		7	CL	H	Walsall	W	2-1	1-0	21	Gibbins 20, 67	4,25
32		11	CL	H	Blackpool	W	2-0	1-0	20	Gibbins 8, Harrison (pen) 72	5,70
33		18	CL	A	Wigan Athletic	L	0-5	0-1	21		(3,308
34		20	FRT	H	Newport County	D	1-1	1-1		French 3	2,86
35		25	CL	H	Wolverhampton W.	L	0-2	0-1	21		4,96
36		28	FRT	A	Cardiff City	W	2-0	1-0		McCarthy 44, 78	(1,006
37	F	1	CL	A	Rotherham United	L	1-4	0-2	23	Gibbins 77	(2,932
38		4	CL	A	Doncaster Rovers	D	0-0	0-0	22		(2,029
39		8	CL	H	Bolton Wanderers	W	3-1	2-1	22	Foley 5, 8, Hough 50	4,24
40		16	CL	A	Newport County	L	0-2	0-1	22		(2,805
41		19	FRT	H	Torquay United	W	1-0	0-0		Fowler D (og) 89	2,20
42		22	CL	H	Reading	L	2-3	1-1	22	Harrison (pen) 35, Hutchison 85	4,96
43	M	1	CL	A	Bristol Rovers	D	0-0	0-0	22		(3,098
44		8	CL	H	Brentford	W	2-0	0-0	20	McCarthy 61, Gibbins 64	3,68
45		16	CL	A	Lincoln City	L	1-4	0-1	22	McCarthy 75	(2,846
46		22	CL	H	Gillingham	D	2-2	2-0	23	Williams 11, Gibbins 27	3,364
47		25	CL	A	Bury	D	2-2	0-1	23	Williams 61, Harrison 80	(2,049
48		29	CL	H	Bournemouth	L	0-4	0-1	23		(3,328
49		31	CL	H	Cardiff City	W	2-0	0-0	21	Hough 52, Williams 63	6,64
50	A	2	FRT SF	A	Hereford	L	0-0†	0-0			(3,725
51		5	CL	A	Chesterfield	L	1-4	1-1	22	Hough 13	(2,148
52		12	CL	H	Darlington	D	2-2	1-0	23	Harrison (pen) 37, Waddle 52	3,35
53		19	CL	A	Bristol City	W	1-0	0-0	22	Price 80	(6,013
54		26	CL	H	Notts County	D	0-0	0-0	22		3,86
55	M	3	CL	A	York City	L	1-3	0-2	23	Waddle 53	(3,132
56		6	CL	H	Derby County	L	0-3	0-1	24		3,974

Best Home League Attendance: 6,989 v Bournemouth   **Smallest:** 2,779 v York City   **Av Home Att:** 4,584

Goal Scorers: **Compared with 84-85:** +187

League (43):	Gibbins 6, Harrison 5 (3 pen), Waddle 5, Emmanuel 3, Hough 3, Hutchison 3, McCarthy 3, Pascoe 3 (1 pen), Turner 3, Williams 3, Foley 2, French 2, McHale 1, Price 1, Randell 1
Milk Cup (6):	Randell 3, Marustik 1, Pascoe 1, Waddle 1
FA Cup (3):	Burrows 1, Waddle 1, Williams 1
FRT (4):	McCarthy 2, French 1, Opponents 1

† A.E.T. Lost on Penalti

Lewis	Sullivan	Price P.	Stevenson	Marustik	Hutchinson	Turner	Waddle	McHale	Pascoe	French	Andrews	Emmanuel	Randell	Burrows	Harrison	Sharpe (NC)	Hughes	Gibbins	McCarthy	Hough	Williams	Melville (NC)	Davies (NC)	Foley (NC)	Referee	
2	3	4	5	6	7	8	9	10	11*	12															N Butler	1
2	3	4	5	6	7	8*	9	10		11	12														**A Seville**	2
2	3	4	5	6	7	8	9	10		11															G Napthine	3
2	3	4	5	6	7		9			11	10														B Stevens	4
2	3	4	5	6	7		9			11		8	10												P Willis	5
2	3	4	5	6	7		9	10		11		8	10												**R Milford**	6
2	3	4	5	6	7		9*	10		11	12	8													R Hamer	7
2	3	4	5	6*	7		9	10		11		8	12												R Trussell	8
2	3	4	5	6	7		9	10		11		8													L Robinson	9
2	3	4	5	6*	7		9	10		11		8	12												B Hill	10
2	3	4	5	6	7		9			11		8	10												**A Gunn**	11
2	3	4	5		7		9	12	10	11		8			6*										T Holbrook	12
2	3	4	5*		7		9	12	11	10		8			6										D Scott	13
	3	4				7	9	5		11		10	8		6			2							D Hedges	14
	3	4	12			7	9	10*	5	11		8			6	2	1								**R Groves**	15
	3	4*				7	9	6		11	12	8			5	2		10							P Vanes	16
	3					7	10	6		11	4	8			5	2†		9							G Courtney	17
12	3	8*				7	11	10	6		4				5	2		9							L Shapter	18
12	3					7	10	6		11	4	8			5	2*		9							I Borrett	19
2	3	4*				7	10			11		8			5			9	12	6					J Bray	20
	3	2				7	10*			11	12				5			9	8	6	4				G Ashby	21
	3	4*					10			11	8	6			5			9		2	7				A Robinson	22
	3						10	6	11*			9	8		5		4	2	7		12				**M James**	23
	3						10	7				6	8		5		4	9	2	12					A Seville	24
	3	5					10	7				6					1	4	9	2	8*		11		J Lovatt	25
	4						10	7		12		6	8	3			1	5	2	9*			11		**G Ashby**	26
	4						10	7				6	8	3			1	9	2	5			11		V Callow	27
3*	4				8		10	7				6					1	9	12	2	5		11		R Lewis	28
	3	4					10	7				6	8				1	9		2			11		C Downey	29
	4				11*	7	8					6	12		5		1	9	10	2			3		B Stevens	30
	3	4			12	7	8*					6			5		1	9	10	2			11		J Martin	31
	3	4				7	8					6			5		1	9	10	2			11		K Barratt	32
	3	4				7	8					6*			5		1	9	10	2			11		D Hutchinson	33
	3	4				7	8					6			5		1	9	10	2			11		**K Cooper**	34
	3	4			12	7*	8					6			5		1	9	10	2			11		R Hamer	35
2*	4*					7	12	8				6			5		1	9	10	11			3	13	**R Gifford**	36
	4	5*				7	10	8				6			11		1	9		2			3	12	D Scott	37
2		4				7	10			12		6			5		1	9		11			3*	8	P Willis	38
2	3	4				7	10					6			5		1	9	12	11				8*	K Baker	39
2*	3	4				7	10					6			5		1	9	12	11				8	L Shapter	40
2	3	4				7	10					6			5		1	9		11				8	**L Robinson**	41
2	3	4				7	10					6			5		1	9		11				8	N Butler	42
3*	4				8	6	7								5		1	9	10	2	11		12		K Miller	43
	4					7	11	6				8			5		1	9	10	2	3				A Gunn	44
	3	4				7	8	11*				6			5		1	9	10	2	12				T Jones	45
	3	4				7						6			5		1	9	10	8	11				T Holbrook	46
2	3	4				7						6	12		5		1	9	10	8*	11				J Lloyd	47
2	3*	4				7						6	8		5		1	9	10	12	11				D Hedges	48
	3	4				7	12					6	8		5		1	9*	10	2	11				J Bray	49
	3	4					6	10		5		8			7		1	9		2	11				**T Mills**	50
	3	4				7	10			12		6*	8		5		1	9		2	11				T Fitzharris	51
	3	4				7	10			8		6			5		1	9		2	11				C Downey	52
2	3	4				7	10	9		8		6					1	5			11				D Vickers	53
2	3	4				7	10	9*		8		6			5			12			11				R Guy	54
2	3	4				7*	10	9		8		6			12		1	5			11				J Heath	55
2	3					7	10	9		8		6					1	5			11				R Groves	56
22	41	41	12	8	38	9	27	26	18	11	1	38	18	1	33	5	27	35	16	30	11	2	11	4	League Appearances	
2			3				1	2	1	3		2	1	2	2				5	1		3		1	Substitute Appearances	
3	4	4	3-1	3	4	3	3	3	3	1	0-1	3		2	1	1									Milk Cup Appearances	
	1	1					2	2		1	0-1	2	1		1	2		1	2		2	1	1-1	1	FA Cup Appearances	
2	3	4					3		1-1	1	1	2			4	1		4	3	4	2	4	1		2	1-1	FR Trophy Appearances	

Also Played: Position (Game): Budd 11(24), Hamson 4(56), Price N 12(22, 25)

Departures: Ray McHale (Scarborough), Price (Saltash), Marustik (Cardiff C)

'THE SWANS'
Formed: 1900
Turned Professional: 1912   **Ltd Co:** 1912

Previous Names: Swansea Town until Feb 1970
Previous Managers: 1912-4 Walter Whittaker   1914-5 William Bartlett   1919-26 Joe Bradshaw
1927-31 James Thompson   1934-9 Neil Harris   1939-47 Haydn Green   1947-55 Billy McCandless
1955-8 Ron Burgess   1958-65 Trevor Morris   1965-6 Glyn Davies   1967-9 Billy Lucas
1969-72 Roy Bentley   1972-5 Harry Gregg   1975-8 Harry Griffiths   1978-84 John Toshack
1984 Colin Appleton   1985-6 John Bond
In addition B Watts-Jones, Joe Sykes, Walter Robins, Doug Livermore and Les Chappel all acted in a
"caretaker" capacity for short periods. 1984 Colin Applton, Wyndham Evans (caretaker)
Honours: Champions Div 3 (S), 1924-5, 1948-9   Welsh Cup Winners (8)
League Career: Original Members of Div 3 1920   Promoted to Div 2 1924-5
Relegated to Div 3 (S) 1946-7   Promoted to Div 2 1948-9   Relegated to Div 3 1964-5
Relegated to Div 4 1966-7   Promoted to Div 3 1969-70   Relegated to Div 4 1972-3
Promoted to Div 3 1977-8   Promoted to Div 2 1978-9   Promoted to Div 1 1980-1
Relegated to Div 2 1982-3   Relegated to Div 3 1983-4
Colours: All white
Change Colours: All blue
Reserves League: Macbar

CLUB RECORDS

Most Appearances for Club: 'Wilfy' Milne: Football League 587 + FA Cup 44 + Welsh Cup 28 **Total 659**
Most Capped Player: Ivor Allchurch, 48, Wales   **For England:** None
Record Goalscorer in a Match: Jack Fowler, 5 v Charlton Athletic, 6-1, Div 3, 27.09.1924
Record League Goalscorer in a Season: Cyril Pearce, 35, 1931-2   **In All Competitions:** Cyril Pearce, 39 (League 35 + Welsh Cup 4), 1931-2   Jack Fowler, 36 (League 28 + FA Cup 8) 1924-5
Record League Goalscorer in a Career: Ivor Allchurch, 166   **In All Competitions:** Ivor Allchurch, 189 (League 166 + F Cup 9 + League Cup 4 + Welsh Cup 10)
Record Transfer Fee Received: £370,000 from Leeds United for Alan Curtis, May 1979
Record Transfer Fee Paid: £340,000 to Liverpool for Colin Irwin, Aug 1981
Best Performances: League: 6th Div 1 1981-2   **FA Cup:** Semi-Finals 1926, 1964   **League/Milk Cup:** 4th Round 1964-5, 1976-7   **European Cup Winners Cup:** 2nd Round   **Welsh Cup:** Winners (8)
Most League Points: 69, Div 1, 1981-2   **Most League Goals:** 92, Div 4, 1976-7
Record League Victory and Most Goals Scored in a League Match: 8-0 v Hartlepool United, Div 4, 1 April 1978
Most Goals Scored in a Cup Tie: 12-0 v Sliema Wanderers (Malta), 1st Round 1st Leg European Cup Winners Cup, 1982-83
Record League Defeat: 1-8 v Fulham, Div 2, 22 Jan 1938
European Competitions Entered: European Cup Winners Cup 1961-2. 1966-7, 1981-2, 1982-3
Oldest Player in League Match: 'Wilfy' Milne
Youngest Player in League Match: Nigel Darling, 15 yrs 10 months
Most Consecutive Undefeated League Matches: 19 1961, 1970-71

Longest Run of Undefeated Home League Matches: 28 1925-27
Longest Run Without Home League Win: 9 1938
Most Consecutive League Wins: 8 1961
Most Consecutive League Defeats: 6 1935, 1957

League Matches Without a Win: 12 1937-3 1963
Away League Matches: 12 1970-71
Away League Win: 46 1982-84
Home League Wins: 17 1948-49
Away League Wins: 4 1955

Club Statistician for the Directory: David Farmer

SWANSEA CITY

PLAYERS NAME Wt Birthdate	Honours	Birthplace Transfers	Clubs	League	Milk Cup	FA Cup	Other Comps	League	Milk Cup	FA Cup	Other Comps
GOALKEEPERS											
e Hughes ½ 11.3 19.8.64	WY	Swansea	Swansea City (A)								
my Rimmer 11.12 10.2.48	E (1), Div. 1, 81 EC 82	Southport £40,000 £70,000 £35,000	Manchester United (A) Swansea City (L) Arsenal Aston Villa Swansea City	34 17 124 229 66	3 10 23 7	6 12 12 3	 13 3				
DEFENDERS											
Andrews 10.1 24.4.68		Swansea	Swansea City (A)	2	0+1						
s Harrison 11.1 17.10.56		Launceston	Plymouth Argyle (A) Swansea City	315+4 35+2	22 2	26+1 2	5 4	7 5	1		
ley Lewis ¾ 10.9 17.11.62	WU21 (3)	Swansea	Swansea City (A)	65+2	4	2	6	1			
rew Melville 12.6 29.11.68		Swansea	Swansea City (A)	2+3		1+1					
y Phelan 16.3.67	EY	Manchester F	Leeds United Swansea City	12+2	3						
el Stevenson 12.0 12.11.58	W (4), U21 (2)	Swansea	Swansea City (A) Cardiff City (L) Reading (L)	235+9 14 3	14+1	10 1	6	15			1
MIDFIELD											
y Emmanuel 11.0 1.2.54	WU23	Swansea £50,000 Player exch. F F F	Birmingham City Bristol Rovers Swindon Town Newport County Bristol City Swansea City	61+10 59+6 109+2 12 2 38+2	1 4 6	5 3 12 2	 2 3 4	6 2 8 3			
d Hough† 12.0 20.2.66	WY	Crewe	Swansea City	55+3	1+1	4	6	5			
my Hutchinson 12.5 22.9.47	S (7), U23 (1)	Cardenden, Fife £45,000	Alloa Athletic Blackpool Coventry City Manchester City Burnley Swansea City	68 163+2 312+2 46 46 38	17 18 3+1 6 3	6 23 10 8 4	 4	4 10 24 4 4 3	2 2	1 4	1
n Randell 10.8 12.12.52	WU23 (1), YS	Skewen £10,000 £60,000 £40,000 F	Coventry City (A) Exeter City Plymouth Argyle Blackburn Rovers Newport County (L) Swansea City	137+12 78 110 72+1 15 18+1	10 5 12 4 3	8 5 3 5 1	 1	9 4 8 7 1	2 2 3		
p Williams 11.9 24.11.66		Morriston	Swansea City (A)	23+5	1	1	3	3		1	
FORWARDS											
Burrows 10.4 2.10.67		Swansea	Swansea City (A)	1+2		1				1	
el French 9.13 24.3.68		Swansea	Swansea City (A)	11+3	1	0+1	2	1			1
n Pascoe ½ 10.0 9.4.65	W (2), U21 (4), Y	Aberavon	Swansea City (A)	92+7	7	4	3	15	2		
n McCarthy 11.7 12.9.65		Bridgend	Bridgend Town Swansea City (A)	16+5			2	3		2	

ADDITIONAL CONTRACT PROFESSIONALS

APPRENTICES

NON-CONTRACT PLAYERS
k Wilkins

VETCH FIELD Swansea

Capacity: 26,2

Record Attendance: 32,796 v Arsenal, FA Cup Round 4, 17 Feb 1968

Smallest Home Attendance for a First Class Match: 1,311 v Brentford, Div 4, 26 April 1976

Record Receipts: £33,141 v Manchester United, Div 1, 30 Jan 1982

Season Tickets: Stands (centre) £85.50: East £85.50 (£45 OAPs): New Stand (Quadrant): £69; Terrace: £35.50 (£23 Juveniles/OAPs)

Executive Box Season Tickets: Vice-Presidents £107

Cost of Stand Tickets: £4.50; £4.00 (£5.50 Family); **Terraces:** £2.00 (£1.50 Juveniles/OAPs), £3.00 (Family — 1 Adult, 1 Child); Enclosure: £4.00 (Family — 1 Adult, 2 Children)

Match and Ticket Information: Tickets are on sale at the ticket office in the ground, Vetch Field, two weeks before each match

Car Parking: Car Park 200 yards from ground in The Kingsway. There is also ample street parking

Nearest Railway Station: Swansea High St (0792 46 7777)

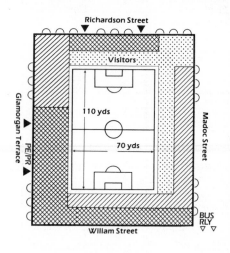

How to get to the ground

Five minutes walk from city bus station or take South Wales Transport Co Ltd from High Street General station to Lowere Oxford Street. Car parking near ground at Quadrant

Price of 1986-7 Programme: 50p
Number of Pages: 20
Subscriptions: Please contact club

Local Newspapers: Evening Mail, Western Mail

Local Radio Stations: Swansea Sound, BBC Radio Wales

SWINDON TOWN

Division 3

President
W H Castle

Chairman
B Hillier

Vice-Chairman
G Herbert

Directors
T J R Kearsey
L Smart
N Arkell
R Mattick
C Howard
D Alderton
C J Green

Admin Manager/Secretary
D G King (0793 642984)

Commercial Manager
D Buswell (0793 642984)

Player/Manager
L Macari

Finance Manager
J Humphreys

**Assistant Manager/
Youth Team Manager**
John Trollope

Physiotherapist
Kevin Morris

After a four-year absence Swindon returned to Division Three in style as runaway 4th Division Champions. The faith which the supporters had placed in Lou Macari was amply rewarded and it was perhaps appropriate that the title should have been clinched during the actual anniversay of his five-day dismissal during April 1985.

The close season had passed under the cloud of a crippling and rapidly rising debt owed to Thamesdown Council, the club's landlords, which threatened the very survival of Swindon Town. Happily, a settlement was reached and the new season was faced with growing optimism. There were a number of new signings, including David Moss and Chris Kamara, both former Swindon favourites and the first team squad looked to be the strongest for some years. However, it started badly with a home defeat and October arrived with Swindon in 23rd place having lost five of the first eight games. To make matters worse the side had suffered a crop of injuries and no less than three goalkeepers had appeared in the first team.

Milk Cup victories over Sunderland and Sheffield Wednesday lifted spirits and so began a run of 38 League games during which time the club record book was virtually re-written. Thirty of those games were won and only three lost, the last on January 4th. Because of postponement six successive League games were played away from home in the New Year, and all were won, a feat unique in League history and it virtually assured promotion. As rivals faltered Swindon proved unstoppable and were promoted with eight games to play.

Colin Calderwood was chosen Player of the Year, Lou Macari won 4th Division Manager of the Season but who could have forecast that Charlie Henry—having previously scored three goals in 138 appearances—would be leading goalscorer with 17 goals? Tony Angell

Back Row L to R: Mark Gardner, Steve White, Jimmy Gilligan, Chris Kamara, Tim Parkin, Alan Churchward, Kenny Allen, Dave Bamber, Charlie Henry, David Cole, Colin Calderwood, Chris Ramsey. **Middle Row:** Philip Bell, Nicky Hughes, Tony Berry, Peter Lango, Andy Rowland (Youth Coach), Garry Gillen, Dave Barnett, Dean Casserly, Adrian Viveash.**Front Row:** John Trollope (Assistant Manager), Alan McLoughlin, Lee Barnard, Martin Ling, Peter Coyne, Lou Macari (Manager), Mark Hughes, Jamie Reynolds, Bryan Wade, David Hackaday, Kevin Morris (Physiotherapist).

SWINDON TOWN

DIVISION FOUR: CHAMPIONS   **FA CUP:** 1st ROUND   **MILK CUP:** 4th ROUND

MATCH	DATE	COMPE-TITION	VENUE	OPPONENTS	RESULT	HALF TIME	L'GUE POS'N	GOALSCORERS/GOAL TIMES	ATTEN-DANCE
1	A 17	CL	H	Wrexham	L 0-1	0-0			4,159
2	20	MC1/1	A	Torquay United	W 2-1	1-1		Hockaday 41, Moss 55	(1,266)
3	24	CL	A	Hereford United	L 1-4	0-1	23	Calderwood 64	(4,049)
4	26	CL	H	Torquay United	W 2-1	1-1	18	Coyne 44, Henry 70	3,378
5	30	CL	A	Southend United	D 0-0	0-0	18		(4,037)
6	S 3	MC1/2	H	Torquay United	D 2-2	1-1		Coyne 17, Pugh (og) 54	2,846
7	6	CL	H	Northampton Town	W 3-2	2-0	12	Coyne 3 (18, 30, 82 all pens)	3,879
8	14	CL	A	Peterborough United	L 0-3	0-2	17		(2,946)
9	17	CL	A	Crewe Alexandra	L 0-2	0-0	20		(1,699)
10	24	MC2/1	A	Sunderland	L 2-3	1-1		Rowland 35, Coyne (pen) 74	(14,207)
11	28	CL	A	Hartlepool United	L 0-1	0-0	21		(2,727)
12	O 1	CL	H	Exeter City	W 2-1	1-1	17	Gordon 30, Calderwood 89	3,118
13	5	CL	H	Rochdale	W 4-0	3-0	14	Coyne 10, Cole 17, Wade 26, Hockaday 86	3,086
14	8	MC2/2	H	Sunderland	W 3-1	0-0		Rowland 59, Wade 90, 98	9,111
15	12	CL	A	Burnley	W 2-0	1-0	11	Gordon 12, 49	(2,979)
16	19	CL	A	Chester City	W 1-0	1-0	9	Gordon 38	(3,109)
17	22	CL	H	Stockport County	W 1-0	0-0	7	Coyne 62	7,172
18	26	CL	A	Port Vale	L 0-3	0-1	9		(5,073)
19	29	MC3	H	Sheffield Wednesday	W 1-0	1-0		Coyne 10	12,110
20	N 2	CL	H	Tranmere Rovers	W 2-1	1-0	8	Barnard 10, Wade 74	4,358
21	6	CL	H	Cambridge United	W 1-0	0-0	7	Henry 64	5,489
22	9	CL	A	Scunthorpe United	W 2-0	2-0	7	Henry 12, Wade 20	(1,920)
23	17	FAC1	H	Bristol City	D 0-0	0-0			10,468
24	20	FAC1R	A	Bristol City	L 2-4	0-1		Ramsey 47, Barnard 51	(8,979)
25	23	CL	H	Mansfield Town	W 2-1	1-0	4	Coleman (pen) 32, Wade 47	4,784
26	26	MC4	A	Ipswich Town	L 1-6	0-2		Yallop (og)	(12,083)
27	30	CL	A	Orient	L 0-1	0-1	5		(3,100)
28	D 7	CL	H	Preston North End	W 4-1	2-1	3	Henry 3 (14, 30, 79) Coleman (pen) 65	3,945
29	14	CL	H	Halifax Town	W 3-2	1-1	2	Coleman (pen) 42, (pen) 56, Henry 62	4,516
30	22	CL	A	Hereford United	W 1-0	0-0	2	Henry 87	7,364
31	28	CL	A	Torquay United	W 1-0	0-0	2	Gordon 55	(1,710)
32	J 1	CL	H	Colchester United	W 2-1	2-0	1	Cole 4, Wade 45	8,802
33	4	CL	A	Tranmere Rovers	L 1-3	0-2	1	Gordon (pen) 75	(1,795)
34	12	CL	H	Southend United	W 2-1	1-1	1	Gordon (pen) 17, Ramsey 50	7,619
35	18	CL	H	Wrexham	W 1-0	1-0	1	Gordon (pen) 2	(1,767)
36	21	FRT S	A	Bristol Rovers	L 1-2	0-2		Barnard 47	(2,335)
37	F 1	CL	A	Northampton Town	W 1-0	0-0	2	Henry 70	(4,449)
38	3	CL	A	Stockport County	W 2-0	0-0	1	Henry 80, Gordon 89	(3,899)
39	22	CL	A	Preston North End	W 3-0	1-0	1	Ramsey 10, Henry 60, Coyne 80	(3,361)
40	M 4	CL	A	Exeter City	W 3-0	2-0	1	Coyne 19, Gordon 37, Ramsey 83	(2,291)
41	8	CL	A	Rochdale	W 2-1	0-0	1	Gordon (pen) 77, Henry 79	(1,989)
42	11	FRT S	H	Hereford United	D 1-1	0-0		Hockaday 90	3,692
43	15	CL	H	Burnley	W 3-1	1-1	1	Henry 37, Bamber 58, Gordon 85	7,212
44	23	CL	H	Port Vale	D 0-0	0-0	1		10,122
43	25	CL	H	Hartlepool United	W 3-1	2-1	1	Wade 2, 71, Smith (og) 25	6,172
46	28	CL	A	Colchester United	D 1-1	0-0	1	Bamber 62	(2,997)
47	31	CL	H	Aldershot	W 4-1	3-1	1	Bamber 20, 54, Henry 25, Gordon 33	8,437
48	A 5	CL	A	Cambridge United	D 1-1	1-1	1	Gordon 43	(3,128
49	8	CL	H	Chester City	W 4-2	1-2	1	Bamber 41, 51, Wade 53, Barnard 67	12,630
50	12	CL	H	Scunthorpe United	D 1-1	1-0	1	Bamber 40	6,783
51	15	CL	H	Peterborough United	W 3-0	1-0	1	Bamber 14, Wade 79, Gordon 85	6,426
52	19	CL	A	Mansfield Town	D 1-1	1-1	1	Barnard 43	(8,416
53	22	CL	A	Aldershot	W 4-2	3-1	1	Gordon 4, 23, Henry 25, Cole 65	(3,723
54	27	CL	H	Orient	W 4-1	1-0	1	Wade 13, Bamber 53, Kamara 57, Coyne 89	8,081
55	M 2	CL	A	Halifax Town	W 3-1	1-0	1	Henry 3 (22, 49, 65)	(1,626
56	5	CL	H	Crewe Alexandra	W 1-0	0-0	1	Coyne 70	10,976

Best Home League Attendance: 12,630 v Chester City   **Smallest:** 3,086 v Rochdale   **Av Home Att:** 6,457

Goal Scorers: **Compared with 84-85:** +3,437

League (82): Henry 18, Gordon 17 (4 pen), Coyne 10 (3 pen), Wade 10, Bamber 9, Coleman 4 (4 pen), Barnard 3, Cole 3, Ramsey 3, Calderwood 2, Hockaday 1, Kamara 1, Opponents 1

Milk Cup (11): Coyne 3 (1 pen), Rowland 2, Wade 2, Hockaday 1, Moss 1, Opponents 2

FA Cup (2): Barnard 1, Ramsey 1

FRT (2): Barnard 1, Hockaday 1

1985-86

Ramsey	Barnard	Evans	Rowland	Calderwood	Hockaday	Coyne	Gordon	Hall	Moss	Macari (NC)	Henry	Cole	Endersby	Wade	Allen	Coleman (L)	Roberts (NC)	Key (NC)	Gardiner	Bamber	Kamara	Referee	
2	3	4	5	6	7	8	9	10*	11	12												I Hemley	1
2	3	4	5	6	7		9		11	10	8											R Groves	2
2	3	4	5	6	7*		9		11	12	8	10										J Bray	3
2		4	5	6		8	9		11	10	7	3										J Moules	4
2		4	5	6		8	9	11		10	7	3										M Cotton	5
2		4	7	6		8	9	11		10	3	5										H King	6
2		4	7	6		8	9	11		10	3	5	1									R Milford	7
2		4*	7	6		8	9†	11		10	3	5	1	12								K Miller	8
2		12	5	7	6		9	4*	8	10	11	3				1						K Breen	9
2		12	7	6		8	9*	11			10	5			1	3	4					N Midgley	10
2	8		5	6		7				4	10	11*		12	1		3			9		T Mills	11
2		12	7	6	11*	8	9				10	5			1	3	4					P Vanes	12
2		12		6	11	8	9	10*				5		7	1	3	4					J Deakin	13
2	4		7	6	11	8	9					5	1	10			3					L Shapter	14
2	6	7*	4				9	11			8	3		10	1	5	12					D Phillips	15
2	4		7	6	11	8*	9					5		10	1		3			12		M Reed	16
2	4			6	11	8	9					5		10	1		3			7		G Ashby	17
2	4	12		6	11	8	9					5		10	1		3			7*		D Scott	18
2	4		11	6	7	8	9					5		10	1	3						A Robinson	19
2	4	12		6	11	8	9*					5		10	1		3			7		N Butler	20
2	4	7*	9	6	11	8				12		5		10	1		3					R Gifford	21
2	4	12		6	7	8*	9			11		5		10	1		3					K Lupton	22
3	4		7	6	11		9	8*			2	5		10	1				12			K Miller	23
5	8	7*	4				9	10	12		2	3		11	1	6						K Miller	24
3	4			6	11		9				8	5		10	1	2				7		K Cooper	25
3	4		12	6*	11		9				8	5		10	1	2		1		7		C Downey	26
3	4		12	6	11*		9				8	5		10	1	2				7		M Bodenham	27
2	4		12	6	11		9*				8	5		10	1		3			7		K Miller	28
2	4			6	11		9				8	5		10	1		3			7		T Ward	29
2	4			6	11*		9				3	5		10	1	8				7	12	M Dimblebee	30
2	4			6	11		9				8	5		10	1		3			7		J Martin	31
2	4			6	11		9				3	5		10	1	8				7		R Lewis	32
2	4			6	12		9				8	5		10	1		3			7	11*	N Wilson	33
2	4			6	11		9				8	5		10	1		3			7		K Baker	34
2	4			6	11		9				8	5		10	1		3			7		D Allison	35
2	4			6	11	7					8	5		10	1		3			9		D Reed	36
2	4			6	11	7	9				8	5		10	1		3					D Reeves	37
	4			6	2	7	9				8	5		10	1		3				11	J Bray	38
2	4			6	11	7	9				8*	5			1		3		12	10		A Saunders	39
2	4			6	11	7	9				8	5			1		3			10		R Gifford	40
2	4			6	7	10					11	5			1		3			8		T Holbrook	41
2	4*	12		6	11	7*	9				8	5		10	1		3				13	G Napthine	42
2	4			6	3	10	9				8	5			1					7	11	A Robinson	43
2	4			6	12	10*	9				8	5			1		3			7	11	J Ashworth	44
2	4			6			9				8	5		10	1		3			7	11	J Borrett	45
2	4			6				11			8	5		7	1		3			9	10	A Gunn	46
2	4*			6	12		9				8	5		10	1		3			7	11	P Tyldesley	47
2	4			6			9				8	5		10	1		3			7	11	M Cotton	48
2	4			6	3	7					8	5		10	1					9	11	D Axcell	49
2	4			6	3		9				8	5		10	1					7	11	M Bodenham	50
	4			6	3	12	9*				8	5		10	1	2				7	11	L Shapter	51
	4			6	3	7					8	5		10	1	2				9	11	G Ashby	52
4		12		6	3	7*	9				8	5		10	1	2					11	C Downey	53
3	4			6	2	12	9				8*	5		10	1					7	11	K Miller	54
3	4			6	2		9		10		8	5			1					7	11	J Worrall	55
3	4			6	2		9		10		8	5			1					7	11	A Gunn	56
43	37	8	12	46	34	30	38	9	4	7	37	44	2	31	40	13	25			23	19	League Appearances	
	1	2	6		3	1	1			2	1				2		2	1			1	Substitute Appearances	
6	4	2+1	5+1	6	4	4	6	2	1		3	3	5	2	3	5	2	3	4	1	2	Milk Cup Appearances	
2	2		2	2	2		2	1+1			2	2		2	2		2		0+1	1		FA Cup Appearances	
2	2	0+1	2	2	2		1				2	2		2	2		2				1+1	FR Trophy Appearances	

Players on Loan: Coleman (Millwall)
Departures: Endersby (Carlisle Utd), Gordon (Wimbledon)

'THE ROBINS'

Formed: 1881
Turned Professional: 1894   **Ltd Co:** 1894

Previous Managers: The club did not actually have the post of manager before the 1933/4 season; the Secretary was in charge of team matters. This post was held for a great many years by Sam Allen who was appointed in 1902 and who still held the position on his death in 1946. In 1933 a team manager was appointed (Ted Vizard). He was replaced in 1939 by Neil Harris who continued until the wartime closure 1940. The full list of modern day managers since Sam Allen's death is:

1945-53 Louis Page   1953-8 Maurice Lindley   1957-65 Bert Head   1965-9 Danny Williams
1969-71 Fred Ford   1971-2 Dave Mackay   1972-4 Les Allen   1974-8 Danny Williams
1978-80 Bob Smith   1980-83 John Trollope   1983-4 Ken Beamish

Honours: Football League Cup: Winners 1968-9   Anglo-Italian Trophy 1970
Div 4 Champions 1985-6
League Career: Elected to Div 3 1920   Transferred to Div 3 (S) 1921
Transfered to Div 3 1958   Promoted to Div 2 1962-3   Relegated to Div 3 1964-5
Promoted to Div 2 1968-9   Relegated to Div 3 1973-4   Relegated to Div 4 1981-2
Promotion to Div 3 1985-6
Colours: Red shirts with white pinstripe, white shorts, red stockings
Change Colours: Yellow shirts, blue shorts, yellow stockings
Reserves League: Football Combination   **Youth League:** S E Counties Div 2

CLUB RECORDS

Most Appearances for Club: John Trollope: **Total 770**
Most Capped Player: Rod Thomas, 30, Wales   **For England:** Harold Fleming 11
Record Goalscorer in a Match: Harry Morris, 5 v QPR (H) Div 3 (S) 6-2, 18 Dec 1927
Harry Morris, 5 v Norwich (A), Div 3 (S) 5-1 26 April 1930
Keith East, 5 v Mansfield (H) Div 3 6-2, 20 Nov 1965
Record League Goalscorer in a Season: Harry Morris, 47, Div 3 (S)   **In All Competitions:** Harry Morris, 53 (League 47, FA Cup 6) 1926-7
Record League Goalscorer in a Career: Harry Morris, 216   **In All Competitions:** Harry Morris, 230 (League 216, FA Cup 14), 1926-33
Record Transfer Fee Received: £250,000 from Aston Villa for Paul Rideout, May 1983
Record Transfer Fee Paid: £150,000 to Southampton for David Peach, Mar 1980
Best Performances: League: 5th Div 2 1969-70   **FA Cup:** Semi-Finals 1910, 1912   **League/Milk Cup:** Winners (1)   **Anglo-Italian Trophy:** Winners (1)
Most League Points: (3pts for win) 68, Div 4, 1982-3   (2pts for win) 64, Div 3, 1968-9
Most League Goals: 100, Div 3 (S), 1926-7
Record League Victory and Most Goals in a First Class Match: 9-1 v Luton Town, Div 3 (S), 28 April 1921
Most Goals Scored in a Cup Tie: 10-1 v Farnham United Breweries, FA Cup Round 1, 28 Nov 1925
Record League Defeat: 0-9 v Torquay United, Div 3 (S), 8 March 1952
European Competitions Entered: Anglo-Italian Trophy
Oldest Player in League Match:
Youngest Player in League Match: Paul Rideout
Most Consecutive Undefeated League Matches: 20 1986

League Matches Without a Win: 13 1956, 1974

Longest Run of Undefeated Home League Matches: 26 1968-69
Longest Run Without Home League Win: 10 1956
Most Consecutive League Wins: 8 1926, 1986
Most Consecutive League Defeats: 6 1967, 1980

Away League Matches: 11 1986
Away League Win: 30 1972-74
Home League Wins: 14 1985-86
Away League Wins: 6 1986

Club Statistician for the Directory: Tony Angell

SWINDON TOWN

Players Name / Wt Birthdate	Honours	Birthplace / Transfers	Clubs	League	Milk Cup	FA Cup	Other Comps	League	Milk Cup	FA Cup	Other Comps
				APPEARANCES				GOALS			
GOALKEEPERS											
nny Allen 13.8 12.1.57	Div. 4, 86	Thornaby	Hartlepool United	7							
			Bath City			2					
			Bournemouth	152	9	8					
			Peterborough	11							
			Torquay United	47	3	2	3				
			Swindon Town	40		2	2				
DEFENDERS											
lin Calderwood+ 12.0 20.1.65	Div. 4, 86	Glasgow £27,500	Mansfield Town	97+3	4	6	1	3		1	
			Swindon Town	46	6	2	2	2			
vid Cole 11.10 28.9.62	Div. 4, 86	Barnsley	Swansea City	5+1		2				2	
			Swindon Town	64	5	2	2	3			
n Parkin 13.2 31.12.57		Penrith Malmo £15,000 £27,500	Blackburn Rovers (A)	13	3						
			Almondsbury G.								
			Bristol Rovers	205+3	16	13	6	12	1		
			Swindon Town								
ris Ramsey 10.12 23.4.62	Div. 4, 86	Birmingham F	Bristol City (W-C)								
			Brighton & H.A.	30	1	6					
			Swindon Town	75	6	2	4	4		1	
dy Rowland* 0½ 12.1 8.9.54	EY, Div. 4, 86	Derby	Derby County (W-C)								
			Bury	169+5	19	10		58	8	4	
			Swindon Town	280+7	26+1	3+1	5+1	80	7	8	
MIDFIELD											
igh Barnard 7½ 9.10 29.10.58	Div. 4, 86	Worsley	Portsmouth (A)	71+8	4	6		8			
			Peterborough United (L)	1+3							
			Swindon Town	149+3	8+1	14	5	14		12	1
			Exeter City (L)	6							
arlie Henry 1 12.8 13.2.62	Div. 4, 86	Acton	Swindon Town	173+3	11	12	3				
ris Kamara 12.0 25.12.57	Div. 4, 86	Middlesbrough £20,000 £50,000 Player exch.	Portsmouth (A)	56+7	1	4		7		1	
			Swindon Town	133+14	18+4	14		21	1	4	
			Portsmouth	11	3					1	
			Brentford	150+2	15	13	7	29		2	2
			Swindon Town	19+1			1+1	1			
u Macari (NC—Player M'ger) 5½ 10.13 4.6.49	S (24), U23 (2), FAC 77, Div. 2, 75, SD1 (4), SFAC (2)	Aberdeen	Celtic								
			Manchester United	311+18	23+5	31+3	9	78	2	8	
			Swindon Town	33+3	4	1	1+1	3			1
FORWARDS											
ter Coyne 10.7 13.11.58	ES, Div. 4, 86	Hartlepool F F	Manchester United (A)	2				1			
			Crewe Alexandra	134	6+1	6		47	1	1	
			Hyde United			1					
			Swindon Town	72+4	5	2	4	25	4		
ark Gardiner 1 12.3 25.12.66		Cirencester	Swindon Town (A)	4+2	1	0+3					
mes Gilligan 2 11.2 24.1.64	EY, FAYC 82	Hammersmith	Watford (A)	18+9	2+1	2	3+1	6	1	1	2
			Lincoln City (L)	0+3		3					
		£100,000	Grimsby Town	19+6	3	0+1		3	2		
			Swindon Town								
avid Hockaday 10 10.9 9.11.57	Div. 4, 86	Billingham	Blackpool	131+16	18+1	10+2		23		2	
			Swindon Town	88+17	7	8	5	5	1		1
artin Ling 7 9.12 15.7.66		West Ham £25,000	Exeter City (A)	109+8	8	4	5	14			
			Swindon Town								
mie Reynolds 7½ 10.3 27.10.67		Swindon	Swindon Town	0+1							
yan Wade 8 11.5 25.6.63	Div. 4, 86	Bolton	Trowbridge								
			Swindon Town	31+2	3	2	2	10	2		
ave Bamber 3 13.10 1.2.59		St. Helens £50,000 £20,000	Blackpool	81+5	6	7+1		29	5	2	
			Coventry City	18+1	2			3	1		
			Walsall	17+3	3			7	1		
			Plymouth	4				1			
			Swindon	23	1			9			

ADDITIONAL CONTRACT PROFESSIONALS

APPRENTICES

an Churchward, Gary Gillett, Nicholas Hughes, Peter Lango

ON-CONTRACT PLAYERS

THE COUNTY GROUND   Swindon

Capacity: 25,000 (6,500 seat

Record Attendance: 32,000 v Arsenal, FA Cup Round 3, 15 Jan 1972

Smallest Home Attendance for a First Class Match: 1,681 v Darlington, Div 4, 17 April 1984

Record Receipts: £56,024 v Tottenham H, FA Cup Round 4, 26 Jan 1980

Season Tickets: Stand (North): £70 (£43 OAP/juveniles); Stand (South); closed; Ground (covered) £52 (£32 OAP/juveniles); Ground (uncovered) £43 (£28 OAP/juveniles)

Executive Box Season Tickets: Rendezvous Box: £90 (£55 OAP/juveniles); Vice-President's Club: £200

Cost of Stand Tickets: (Main Stands) £3.50, (£2.00 OAP/juveniles); Ground (covered): £2.50 (£1.50 OAP/juveniles); Ground (uncovered): £2.00 (£1.50 OAP/juveniles); Rendezvous Box £4.50 (£2.50 OAP/juveniles)

Match and Ticket Information: Available three weeks in advance

Car Parking: Corporation car park adjacent to the west end of ground off County Road

Nearest Railway Station: Swindon (0793 36804) five minutes walk

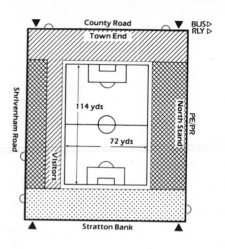

How to get to the ground

Two miles towards Town Centre from M4 (Exit 15)

Price of 1986-7 Programme: 50p
Number of Pages: 32

Local Newspapers: Wiltshire Newspapers (Evening Advertiser), Western Daily Press

Local Radio Station: Wiltshire Radio

Chairman
L W Pope

Vice-Chairman
G J Harvey

Directors
W W Rogers
J Farrell, OBE
S Latter
F M Mossley, TD
R Daniel
R Harvey
A J Boyce
R Milden

Secretary
D Turner (0803 38666)

Team Manager
Stuart Morgan

Assistant Manager
Les Chappell

Physiotherapist
A Morris

Lottery Manager
D Easton (0803 37378)

The worst side in the Canon League. For the second season running that was the sad label worn by the Plainmoor Club.

Cost-cutting and a vast improvement in United's cash situation marks David Webb as something of a miracle worker off the field, but a team is judged by its supporters on playing performances and despite an upturn in results during January, February and March it was always going to be difficult to pull clear of the danger zone.

A pay dispute which led to last season's Player of the Year, Kenny Allen joining Swindon and early season managerial changes which saw United hire and fire John Sims within one month did not help and it is to his credit that the current Manager, Stuart Morgan, has impressed everyone with his hard work and enthusiasm. Since the departure of coaches Brian Wilson and Eddie Kelly, Morgan has run the playing side virtually single-handed.

In addition to the disappointing League season United's Cup campaigns were all too quickly ended. Swindon eliminated them at the first hurdle in the Milk Cup after two very close battles. In the FA Cup United progressed to the second round where they gained a very creditable draw at Somerton Park, only to be beaten by a superb Leighton James free kick in extra-time in the Plainmoor replay. The Freight Rover Trophy saw United qualify for the Southern Quarter finals by winning a group which included Exeter and Wolves, but an own goal in the last minute at Swansea dashed United's hopes of a money-spinning trip to Wembley.

At the season's end Morgan wielded the axe to such an extent that only five senior players have been retained and even the Player of the Year, Derek Dawkins, has been released.

The promising Mark Loram has been sold to QPR and it is to be hoped that other younger players will emerge to complement the experience of Steve Phillips and the other new signings Morgan hopes to make during the summer.

Morgan knows that should United be re-elected, the bottom position must be avoided next season, otherwise the sixty-year battle to keep League Soccer alive in South Devon will be finally lost.   John Lovis

Back Row L to R: Darren Cann, Chris Myers, Trevor Webber, Dave Wreyford. **Middle Row:** Les Chappell (Assistant Manager), Mario Walsh, John Impey, Gerry Nardiello, John Smeulders, Mark Ellacott, Mark Crowe, Paul Compton, Jim McNichol, Alan Morris (Physio). **Seated:** Derek Dawkins, Steve Phillips, Gary Richards, Stuart Morgan (Manager), Paul Dobson, Steve Pyle, Tom Kelly

TORQUAY UNITED

DIVISION FOUR: 24th   **FA CUP:** 2nd ROUND   **MILK CUP:** 1st ROUND

MATCH	DATE		COMPE-TITION	VENUE	OPPONENTS	RESULT		HALF TIME	L'GUE POS'N	GOALSCORERS/GOAL TIMES	ATTEN-DANCE
1	A	17	CL	A	Scunthorpe United	L	0-4	0-2			(1,929)
2		20	MC1/1	H	Swindon Town	L	1-2	1-1		Smith 13	1,266
3		24	CL	H	Rochdale	L	1-2	0-1		Loram 89	1,247
4		26	CL	A	Swindon Town	L	1-2	1-1		Lambert 3	(3,378)
5		31	CL	H	Colchester United	W	2-1	1-1		Lambert 3, Crowe 54	1,023
6	S	3	MC1/2	A	Swindon Town	D	2-2	1-1		Pugh 22, Kelly 78	(2,846)
7		7	CL	A	Preston North End	L	0-4	0-2			(3,403)
8		14	CL	H	Chester City	L	0-3	0-1			1,111
9		18	CL	A	Peterborough United	L	0-2	1-0			(3,432)
10		21	CL	H	Hartlepool United	L	1-3	1-2		Dawkins 14	1,094
11		28	CL	A	Crewe Alexandra	L	0-1	0-1			(1,437)
12	O	1	CL	H	Halifax Town	W	2-0	0-0		Kelly 59, Pugh 90	1,131
13		5	CL	H	Stockport County	W	4-3	0-2		Smith (pen) 47, Walsh 52, West 65, Loram 81	1,274
14		12	CL	A	Hereford United	L	1-4	1-4		Dawkins 23	(3,053)
15		19	CL	H	Northampton Town	D	1-1	1-0		Dawkins 45	1,282
16		22	CL	A	Burnley	L	0-3	0-0			(2,235)
17		29	CL	A	Mansfield Town	L	0-4	0-2			(3,506)
18	N	2	CL	H	Orient	D	2-2	1-0		Pugh 16, Walsh 67	1,282
19		6	CL	H	Southend United	D	2-2	1-2		Loram 7, Crabbe 78	1,169
20		9	CL	A	Tranmere Rovers	D	2-2	0-0			(1,508)
21		16	FAC1	A	Windsor & Eton	D	1-1	1-0		Durham 2	(1,477)
22		19	FAC1R	H	Windsor & Eton	W	3-0	1-0		Walsh 38, 75, Loram 68	1,429
23		23	CL	H	Wrexham	L	1-3	0-1		Durham 67	1,158
24	D	7	FAC2	A	Newport County	D	1-1	1-0		Loram 24	(2,386)
25		10	FAC2R	H	Newport County	L	2-3	1-0		Walsh 5, 56	1,937
26		14	CL	H	Cambridge United	D	1-1	0-1		Loram 86	1,066
27		17	CL	A	Port Vale	L	0-1	0-1			(3,421)
28		21	CL	A	Rochdale	L	0-5	0-1			(1,685)
29		28	CL	H	Swindon Town	L	0-1	0-0			1,710
30	J	11	CL	A	Colchester United	D	0-0	0-0			(2,063)
31		18	CL	H	Scunthorpe United	W	1-0	0-0		Phillips 55	1,064
32		22	FRT	A	Wolverhampton W.	D	1-1	1-0		Pyle 8	(1,618)
33		25	CL	A	Chester City	L	1-3	1-2		Phillips 35	(2,808)
34		29	FRT	H	Exeter City	W	1-0	0-0		Walsh 56	1,046
35	F	1	CL	H	Preston North End	W	1-0	1-0		Compton 18	1,215
36		4	CL	H	Burnley	W	2-0	1-0		Walsh 41, Fowler D 74	1,430
37		19	FRT	A	Swansea City	L	0-1	0-0			(2,200)
38	M	1	CL	H	Crewe Alexandra	D	0-0	0-0			1,011
39		7	CL	A	Stockport County	D	1-1	0-0		West 48	(3,010)
40		11	CL	H	Peterborough United	W	2-0	1-0		Phillips 26, Pyle 54	1,243
41		15	CL	H	Hereford United	W	2-1	0-0		Phillips 53, Pugh 63	1,438
42		18	CL	A	Orient	L	2-4	1-2		Phillips 43, 66	(1,828)
43		22	CL	H	Mansfield Town	L	1-2	0-1		Crowe 68	1,880
44		26	CL	A	Exeter City	D	2-2	2-2		Walsh 12, Pyle 33	(2,420)
45		29	CL	A	Aldershot	D	1-1	0-1		Loram 57	(1,396)
46	A	1	CL	H	Exeter City	L	1-2	0-0		Phillips (pen) 50	2,555
47		4	CL	A	Southend United	W	2-1	0-0		Fowler 50, Loram 60	(1,656)
48		8	CL	H	Aldershot	L	1-2	1-1		Walsh 35	1,245
49		12	CL	H	Tranmere Rovers	L	1-2	0-0		Phillips (pen) 62	1,120
50		14	CL	A	Halifax Town	D	0-0	0-0			(1,062)
51		15	CL	A	Hartlepool United	L	0-1	0-1			(2,080)
52		19	CL	A	Wrexham	L	2-3	1-1		Walsh 15, Crabbe 90	(1,077)
53		26	CL	H	Port Vale	L	0-1	0-0			1,794
54		29	CL	A	Northampton Town	L	1-5	0-1		Walsh 49	(1,167)
55	M	3	CL	A	Cambridge United	L	0-3	0-2			(2,209)

Best Home League Attendance: 2,555 v Exeter   **Smallest: 1,011 v Crewe Alexandra**   **Av Home Att: 1,817**

Goal Scorers: **Compared with 84-85: −109**

League (43):	Phillips 8 (2 pen), Walsh 7, Loram 6, Dawkins 3, Pugh 3, Crabbe 2, Crowe 2, Fowler D 2, Lambert 2, Pyle 2, West 2, Compton 1, Durham 1, Kelly 1, Smith 1
Milk Cup (3):	Kelly 1, Pugh 1, Smith 1
FA Cup (7):	Walsh 4, Loram 2, Durham 1
FRT (2):	Pyle 1, Walsh 1

1985-86

Fowler D	Crowe	Wright	Compton	Dawkins	Pugh	Loram	Perry	Lambert	Smith	Durham	Walsh	Allen	Kelly	Wheeldon (NC)	Hirst (L)	West	Leigh (L)	Crabbe	Fry (NC)	Pyle	Dreyer (L)	Phillips	Weber (NC)	Carpenter (NC)	Referee	
2	3	4	5	6	7	8	9	10*	11	12															H Taylor	1
2	3	4	5	6	7	8*	9	10	11		12														R Groves	2
2	3	4	5	6	7	8	9*	12	11	10		1													K Barratt	3
2	3	4	5	12	7		8*		10	11	9		1	6											J Moules	4
2	3	6	5		7	8			11	9	10	1	4												A Robinson	5
2	3	6	5		8	11			9	10		1	4	7											H King	6
2	3	6	5	12	10	11*			9	8		1	4	7											K Hackett	7
	3	6	5†	12	2	8*			10	9			4	7		11									B Stevens	8
	3	6	5	8	2	10*			12	9			4	7		11									A Ward	9
	3	6	5	8	2	12			10	9			4*	7		11									J Deakin	10
2	5	6	3	9	10						12		4	7*	8	11			1						N Wilson	11
2	5	6	3	8	9						10		4			11		7							V Callow	12
2*	5	6	3	8	9				10		12		4			11		7	1						R Gifford	13
12	6	5	3	2	9	10					8		4*			11		7	1						M Heath	14
11	6	5	3	2	9*	10					8		4					7	1						R Hamer	15
11	6	5	3	2	9	10			12		8		4*					7	1						R Nixon	16
	6	4	5	3	2	9			10		12					8*		7	1						P Tyldesley	17
	6	4	5	3	2	9			10		8					11		7	1						R Milford	18
4	6	5	3	2	9	10			11		8					12		7	1						K Cooper	19
4	6	5	3	2	9	10*			12		8					11		7	1						T Mills	20
4*	6	5	3	2	9	10					8					11		7	1						J Martin	21
	6	5	3	2	9	11			10		8		4					7	1						R Groves	22
	6	5	3	2	9	11*			10		8		4			12		7	1						M Cotton	23
	6	5	3	2	9	10					8		4					7	1	11					V Callow	24
	6	5	3	2	9	10					8		4			12		7	1	11*					V Callow	25
	6	5	3	2	9	11			10		8							7	1		4				H King	26
	6	5	3	2	9	10					8					11		7	1		4				L Dilkes	27
	6	5	3	2	9	12			10		8					11		7*	1		4				D Hutchinson	28
	6	5	3	2	9	12			10		8					11*		7			4				J Martin	29
10	6	4	5	2	3*						12					8		7	1	11		9			D Hedges	30
	6	4	5	2	3						11					8		7	1	10		9			B Stevens	31
7	4	6	5	2	3	9*					12					11			1	8		10			B Hill	32
10	6	4	5	2	3						11					8		7	1			9			A Robinson	33
10	6	4	5	2	3						11					8		7	1			9			R Hamer	34
10	6	4	5	2	3						11					8		7	1			9			R Milford	35
10	6	4	5	2	3						11					8		7	1			9			K Cooper	36
10	6	4	5	2	3						11					8		7	1			9			L Robinson	37
2	6	4	5		3						11					8		7	1	10		9			R Gifford	38
2	6	4	5		3						10					8	11	7	1			9			M Peck	39
2	6	4	5		3						10					8	11	7	1			9			R Groves	40
2	6	4	5		3						10					8	11	7	1			9			T Holbrook	41
2	6	4	5		3						10					8	11*	12	1	7		9			P Vanes	42
2	6	4	5		3						10					8	11	7	1			9			M Cotton	43
2	6	4*	5	12	3						10					8	11	7	1			9			G Ashby	44
2	6	5	4	6	3						10					8	11	7	1			9			J Borrett	45
2	4	5	6		3						10					8	11	7	1			9			M James	46
2	6	4	5		3						10					8	11	7	1			9			M Bodenham	47
2	6	4	5	12	3						10					8	11*	7	1			9			R Gifford	48
11	6	4	5	2	3						10					8	12	7*				9			D Hedges	49
	6	4	5	2	3						10					8		7	1	10		9	11		F Roberts	50
12	6	4	5	2	3						10*					8		7	1	10		9	11		T Simpson	51
11	6	4	5	2	3											8		7	1			9	10		A Robinson	52
12	6	4	5	2	3											8		7	1	11*		9	10		P Vanes	53
11	6	4*	5	2	3											8	12	7				9	10		J McAuley	54
8	6		5	2	3						12							7		11*		9	10	4	K Barratt	55
31	**45**	**33**	**43**	**34**	**45**	**38**	**3**	**4**	**20**	**7**	**37**	**4**	**13**	**6**	**4**	**20**	**4**	**27**	**30**	**14**	**5**	**23**	**5**	**2**	League Appearances	
3				5			2	3	5	4			1			2		2							Substitute Appearances	
2	2	2	2	1	2	2	1	2	2	0-1	1	1	1					2	2						Milk Cup Appearances	
1	4	4	4					1	4	4			2	2				0-1	4	4		2			FA Cup Appearances	
3	3	3	3	3	3	3			2									0-1	3	3	1		3		FR Trophy Appearances	

lso Played: Position (Game): Viner 12(21)

ayers on Loan: Hirst (Bristol City), Leigh (Bournemouth), Dreyer (Oxford), Loram (QPR)

'THE GULLS'

Formed: 1898
Turned Professional: 1921   **Ltd Co:** 1921

Previous Names: Torquay Town (1910)
Previous Managers: Since 1946:
John Butler   John McNeil   Bob John   Alex Massie   Eric Webber   Frank O'Farrell   Allan Brown
Jack Edwards   Malcolm Musgrove   Frank O'Farrell   Mike Green   Frank O'Farrell   Bruce Rioch
Honours: None
League Career: Elected to Div 3 (S) 1927   Original members of Division 4 1958
Promoted to Div 3 1960   Relegated to Div 4 1962   Promoted to Div 3 1966
Relegated to Div 4 1972
Colours: All blue, white stockings
Change Colours: All white
Reserves League: Macbar League

CLUB RECORDS

Most Appearances for Club: Dennis Lewis: 1947-59 Football League 443 + FA Cup 30 **Total 473**
Most Capped Player: None
Record Goalscorer in a Match: Robin Stubbs, 5 v Newport County, Div 4, 19.10.1963
Record League Goalscorer in a Season: Sammy Collins, 40, Div 3 (S), 1955-6   **In All Competitions:** Sammy Collins, 42 (League 40 + FA Cup 2)
Record League Goalscorer in a Career: Sammy Collins, 204, 1948-58   **In All Competitions:** 219 (League 204 + FA Cup 15)
Record Transfer Fee Received: £80,000 from Tottenham Hotspur for Colin Lee, Oct 1977
Record Transfer Fee Paid: £25,000 to Exeter City for Vince O'Keefe, Mar 1980
Best Performances: League: 2nd Div 3 (S) 1956-7   **FA Cup:** 4th Round 1948-9, 1954-5, 1970-1   **League/Milk Cup:** Never past 3rd Round
Most League Points: 67, Div 4, 1983-4   **Most League Goals:** 89, Div 3 (S), 1956-7
Record League Victory and Most Goals Scored in a League Match: 9-0 v Swindon Town, Div 3 (S), 8 Mar 1952
Most Goals Scored in a Cup Tie: 7-1 v Northampton Town, (h) 1st Round FA Cup, 14 Nov 1959 (all goals scored by Torquay-born players: Graham Bond (3), Emil Pym (3) and Tommy Northcott)
Record League Defeat: 2-10 v Fulham, Div 3 (S), 7 Sept 1931   2-10 v Luton Town, Div 3 (S), 2 Sept 1933
Oldest Player in League Match:
Youngest Player in League Match:

Most Consecutive Undefeated League Matches: 15 1960	**League Matches Without a Win:** 17 1938
Longest Run of Undefeated Home League Matches: 31 1956-57	**Away League Matches:** 7 1976
Longest Run Without Home League Win: 11 1961	**Away League Win:** 25 1950-51
Most Consecutive League Wins: 6 1953	**Home League Wins:** 13 1966-67
Most Consecutive League Defeats: 8 1948 1971	**Away League Wins:** 5 1959

Club Statistician for the Directory: John Lovis

TORQUAY UNITED

PLAYERS NAME / Ht Wt Birthdate	Honours	Birthplace / Transfers	Clubs	League	Milk Cup	FA Cup	Other Comps	League	Milk Cup	FA Cup	Other Comps
				APPEARANCES				**GOALS**			
GOALKEEPERS											
John Smeulders	EY	Hackney	Orient (A)								
5.10 13.0 28.3.57			Bournemouth	14							
			Trowbridge Town								
			Bournemouth	75	4	9	5				
			Torquay United			·					
DEFENDERS											
Paul Compton		Stroud	Trowbridge Town								
5.11½ 13.1 6.6.63		£10,000	Bournemouth	64	5	2					
		F	Aldershot	13		2					
		F	Torquay United	81	4	4	4+1	2			
Mark Crowe	FAYC 83	Southend	Norwich City	0+1							
5.10 10.10 21.1.65			Torquay United	45	2	4	3	2			
Derek Dawkins		Luton	Leicester City (A)	3							
5.9 10.0 28.5.57			Mansfield Town	73							
			Bournemouth	4							
			Torquay United	94+7	3	6	6	4			
John Impey		Exeter	Cardiff City (A)	13+8		0+2				1	
6.0 11.12 11.8.54			Bournemouth	4							
			Torquay United	72	6	3	3				
			Exeter City	26	3						
			Torquay United								
Jim McNichol	SU21 (17)	Glasgow	Ipswich Town (A)								
6.0 12.10 9.6.58		F	Luton Town	13+2							
		F	Brentford	151+4	7	8		22	1		
		F	Exeter City	87	6	5	3	10			1
		F	Torquay United								
MIDFIELD											
Tom Kelly		Bellshill	Torquay United								
5.10 11.10 28.3.64											
Phil King			Exeter City (A)	22+3	1		1+1				
5.8 11.9 28.12.67			Torquay United								
Gary Richards		Swansea	Torquay United								
5.8½ 11.2 2.8.63											
Stephen Pyle		North Shields	Cambridge United (A)	58+13	15	1	2	8			
5.7 10.3 28.9.63			Torquay United								
FORWARDS											
Paul Dobson		Hartlepool	Torquay United								
5.11 10.2 17.12.62											
Gerry Nardiello	EY	Warley	Shrewsbury Town (A)	32+6	1	1+1	1	11			
5.11 11.0 5.5.66			Cardiff City (L)								
			Torquay United								
Steve Phillips		Edmonton	Birmingham City (L)	15+5	2		·	1			
5.6 10.9 4.8.54			Torquay United (L)	6							
			Northampton Town	50+1	3	1		8			
		£19,000	Brentford	156+1	5	4		65	1	3	
		£40,000	Northampton Town	75	7	4		29	3	2	
		£15,000	Southend United	157+1	5+1	9	5	67	1	3	
			Torquay United								
Mario Walsh		London	Portsmouth								
6.1 11.10 19.1.66			Torquay United	57+5	0+1	4	5	7		4	1

ADDITIONAL CONTRACT PROFESSIONALS

APPRENTICES
Martin Ellacott

NON-CONTRACT PLAYERS
Darren Cann, Chris Myers, Trevor Webber, Dave Wreyford

PLAINMOOR   Torquay, Devon TQ1 3PG   Capacity: 4,999

Record Attendance: 21,908 v Huddersfield, FA Cup Round 4, 29 Jan 1955

Smallest Home Attendance for a First Class Match: 967 v Chester, Div 4, 2 May 1984

Record Receipts: £14,300 v Sheffield Wednesday, FA Cup Round 4, 29 Jan 1983

Season Tickets: £60 (adult), £35 (juveniles/OAP)

Executive Box Season Tickets: £100 for one

Cost of Stand Tickets: £3.50 (£2.00 juveniles/OAP), £2.50 (£1.50 juveniles/OAP)

Match and Ticket Information: Seat bookings accepted two weeks before each match. Postal applications must include remittance and sae

Car Parking: Some street parking. Coaches park at Lymington Road Coach Station

Nearest Railway Station: Torquay (0803 25911)

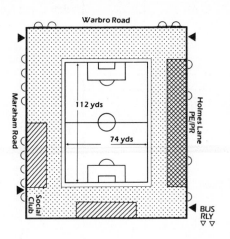

How to get to the ground

From North: Use A38 then A380 to Kings Kerswell. In 1m at roundabout take 1st exit. In 1m turn left A3022 S.P. Babbacombe. In 0.8m turn left then right into Westhill Road and Warbro Road for Torquay United FC

From West: Use A380 into Torquay town centre then follow signs Teignmouth A379 into Lymington Road, then turn right into Upton Hill then keep forward into Bronshill Road. Take 2nd turning on left into Derwent Road and at end turn right then turn right again into Marnham Road for Torquay United FC

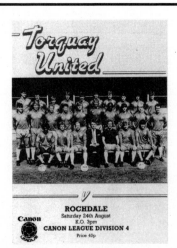

Programme Editor: David Turner
Price of 1986-7 Programme: 50p
Number of Pages: 16

Local Newspapers: Herald Express, Torbay News, Western Morning News

Local Radio Stations: BBC Radio Devon, Devon Air

TOTTENHAM HOTSPUR   Division 1

Tottenham are amongst the game's big spenders and as a public company their market price depends on results, which in recent seasons have been very disappointing, since a successful football team must win things and there have been two totally blank seasons. The club is also the domicile of a number of 'big-name' players, so the shareholders have every right to expect to see their investments 'pay off', but they have not done so thus far. A final position of tenth in the 1st Division at the end of the most recent season has meant only one thing—a change of manager with Peter Shreeves 'carrying the can' and being replaced by David Pleat from Luton Town.

After five games in the most recent campaign Spurs had only gained four points (for 16th place) and that subsequently proved too much of a burden to recover even though there were good spells. There were also periods of inconsistency and the vital matches—both Everton and Liverpool did the double over them—were all lost. Championships are lost that way and if the same form is shown in cup matches it is unlikely that those competitions will be won; after all Liverpool and Everton do enter those events and a club must be at least as good as they are to survive.

So, no cups were won to provide cheer and the Milk Cup was the first disappointment with the elimination of Orient of the 4th Division (0-2 and 4-0) and Wimbledon (2-0 at home) being followed by a four-match marathon against 2nd Division Portsmouth which ended with a single-goal defeat at Fratton Park. The FA Cup progress was similar with Oxford United losing a replay at White Hart Lane (2-1 after extra-time) and Notts County also losing a replay at Tottenham (but by 5-0 this time). The last 16 brought Everton to North London and the Toffeemen took their chances to advance (2-1). The latter and Liverpool also put paid to the Spurs Super-Cup run, so no trophies!

The Spurs 'hot-seat' is now occupied by David Pleat and few will envy him his task. It is true that he can call on numerous great men but can he blend them into something viable? How much longer can the great Ray Clemence last in goal? Hughton had a sound season but Allen did not really shine in his first season at White Hart Lane. Miller still gave 100% and Falco and Waddle did their best up front, but neither Roberts nor Hoddle realised their full potential. Mabbutt, a newcomer, suffered too many injuries. Others were 'in and out'—almost literally—and we have seen the last (in Tottenham terms) of Perryman and that great little Argentinian Ardiles. Great things are expected from new signings Richard Gough of Dundee United and Mitchell Thomas of Luton, but will they blend with the rest?

For a team of all the talents Spurs should not cause us to ask so many questions, but this is only what the supporters are doing and they will be none to happy if by this time next year the answers are still wrong.   WLM

Back Row L to R: Tony Galvin, Chris Waddle, Tony Parkes, Mitchell Thomas, Ray Clemence, Neil Ruddock, Paul Miller. **Middle Row:** Keith Blunt (Youth Team Manager), Mark Bowen, Richard Cooke, Glenn Hoddle, Ossie Ardiles, Chris Houghton, Gary Mabbutt, Mark Falco, Doug Livermore (Reserve Team Manager). **Front Row:** Trevor Hartley (First Team Coach), Clive Allen, Danny Thomas, Gary Stevens, David Pleat (Manager), Graham Roberts, John Chedozie, Paul Allen, John Sheridan (Physio).

TOTTENHAM HOTSPUR

DIVISION ONE: 10th   **FA CUP:** 5th ROUND   **MILK CUP:** 4th ROUND

MATCH	DATE	COMPE-TITION	VENUE	OPPONENTS	RESULT	HALF TIME	L'GUE POS'N	GOALSCORERS/GOAL TIMES	ATTEN-DANCE
1	A 17	CL	H	Watford	W 4-0	1-0		Waddle 23, 69, Allen 57, Falco 62	29,804
2	21	CL	A	Oxford United	D 1-1	1-0		Thomas 33	(10,634)
3	24	CL	A	Ipswich Town	L 0-1	0-0	9		(17,758)
4	26	CL	H	Everton	L 0-1	0-0	13		29,720
5	31	CL	A	Manchester City	L 1-2	0-1	16	Miller 85	(27,789)
6	S 4	CL	H	Chelsea	W 4-1	3-0	12	Roberts 15, Miller 22, Chiedozie 44, Falco 71	23,692
7	7	CL	H	Newcastle	W 5-1	2-1	9	Falco 15, Chiedozie 16, 57, Hoddle 63	23,883
8	14	CL	A	Nottingham Forest	W 1-0	0-0	7	Hughton 85 Hazard 88	(17,554)
9	21	CL	H	Sheffield Wednesday	W 5-1	1-1	5	Waddle 13, 52, Falco 48, 61, Hoddle 74	23,601
10	23	MC2/1	A	Orient	L 0-2	0-0			(13,828)
11	28	CL	A	Liverpool	L 1-4	0-1	8	Chiedozie 46	(41,521)
12	O 2	SC	H	Southampton	W 2-1	2-0		Falco 14, 38	11,549
13	5	CL	A	W.B.A.	D 1-1	1-1	9	Waddle 4	(12,040)
14	20	CL	A	Coventry City	W 3-2	2-1	8	Hoddle (pen) 3, Falco 54, Chiedozie 60	(13,545)
15	26	CL	H	Leicester City	L 1-3	1-3	10	Falco 2	17,944
16	30	MC2/2	H	Orient	W 4-0	1-0		Roberts 44, 57, Galvin 65, Waddle 72	21,046
17	N 2	CL	A	Southampton	L 0-1	0-0	12		(17,740)
18	6	MC3	H	Wimbledon	W 2-0	0-0		Mabbutt 56, Leworthy 74	16,919
19	9	CL	H	Luton Town	L 1-3	0-1	13	Cooke 80	19,163
20	16	CL	A	Manchester United	D 0-0	0-0	13		(54,575)
21	20	MC4	H	Portsmouth	D 0-0	0-0			28,619
22	23	CL	A	Q.P.R.	D 1-1	1-0	12	Mabbutt 25	20,334
23	27	MC4R	A	Portsmouth	D 0-0†	0-0			(28,100)
24	30	CL	A	Aston Villa	W 2-1	0-0	12	Mabbutt 51, Falco 70	(14,099)
25	D 3	SC	A	Liverpool	L 0-2	0-2			(14,855)
26	7	CL	A	Oxford United	W 5-1	4-1	11	Allen C 7,42, Falco 15, Hoddle 43, Waddle 89	17,698
27	10	MC4R2	A	Portsmouth	L 0-1	0-1			(26,306)
28	14	CL	A	Watford	L 0-1	0-1	12		(16,327)
29	17	SC	A	Southampton	W 3-1	2-0		Falco 9, Allen C 20, Leworthy 84	(4,680)
30	21	CL	H	Ipswich Town	W 2-0	1-0	10	Allen C 21, Hoddle 59	18,845
31	26	CL	H	West Ham United	W 1-0	0-0	9	Perryman 85	33,835
32	28	CL	A	Chelsea	L 0-2	0-1	9		(37,115)
33	J 1	CL	A	Arsenal	D 0-0	0-0	10		(45,109)
34	4	FAC3	A	Oxford United	D 1-1	0-0		Chiedozie 76	(10,638)
35	8	FAC3R	H	Oxford United	W 2-1†	0-1		Waddle 72, Allen C 112	19,136
36	11	CL	H	Nottingham Forest	L 0-3	0-0	11		19,043
37	14	SC	H	Liverpool	L 0-3	0-0			10,078
38	18	CL	A	Manchester City	L 0-2	0-1	12		17,009
39	25	FAC4	A	Notts County	D 1-1	1-1		Allen C 2	(17,546)
40	29	FAC4R	H	Notts County	W 5-0	3-0		Chiedozie 19, Allen C 29, Falco 34, Waddle 81, Hoddle 88	17,393
41	F 1	CL	A	Everton	L 0-1	0-0	13		(33,178)
42	5	SC(1)	H	Everton	D 0-0	0-0			7,548
43	8	CL	H	Coventry City	L 0-1	0-0	13		13,135
44	22	CL	A	Sheffield Wednesday	W 2-1	1-0	13	Chiedozie 60, Howells 66	(23,232)
45	M 2	CL	H	Liverpool	L 1-2	1-0	13	Waddle 2	16,436
46	4	FAC5	H	Everton	L 1-2	0-0		Falco 79	23,338
47	8	CL	A	W.B.A.	W 5-0	4-0	11	Mabbutt 3, Falco 9, 44, Galvin 21, Waddle 55	10,841
48	15	CL	A	Birmingham City	W 2-1	2-0	11	Stevens 4, Waddle 33	(9,394)
49	19	SC(2)	A	Everton	L 1-3	0-0		Falco 48	(12,008)
50	22	CL	A	Newcastle United	D 2-2	1-1	11	Hoddle 4, Waddle 47	(30,615)
51	29	CL	H	Arsenal	W 1-0	0-0	11	Stevens 33	33,427
52	31	CL	A	West Ham United	L 1-2	1-2	11	Ardiles 22	(27,497)
53	A 5	CL	A	Leicester City	W 4-1	1-1	12	Falco 3 (22, 64, 72), Bowen 54	(9,572)
54	12	CL	A	Luton Town	D 1-1	1-0	12	Allen C 18	(13,141)
55	16	CL	H	Birmingham City	W 2-0	1-0	11	Falco 20, Chiedozie 64	9,355
56	19	CL	H	Manchester United	D 0-0	0-0	11		32,357
57	26	CL	A	Q.P.R.	W 5-2	3-0	11	Allen C 19, 39, Falco 41, 53, Hoddle 50	(17,768)
58	M 3	CL	H	Aston Villa	W 4-2	1-1	11	Falco 3, 50, Allen C 61, 80	14,854
59	5	CL	H	Southampton	W 5-3	3-2	10	Waddle 8, Galvin 3 (29, 34, 55) Allen C 74	13,036

Best Home League Attendance: 33,835 v West Ham Utd   **Smallest:** 9,355 v Birmingham City   **Av Home Att:** 28,932

Goal Scorers: Compared with 84-85: − 8,074

League (74):   Falco 19, Waddle 11, Allen C 9, Chiedozie 7, Hoddle 7 (1 pen), Galvin 4, Mabbutt 3, Miller 2, Stevens 2, Allen P 1, Ardiles 1,
Bowen 1, Cooke 1, Hazard 1, Hughton 1, Howell S 1, Perryman 1, Roberts 1, Thomas 1

Milk Cup (6):   Roberts 2, Galvin 1, Leworthy 1, Mabbutt 1, Waddle 1

FA Cup (10):   Allen C 3, Chiedozie 2, Falco 2, Waddle 2, Hoddle 1

Super Cup (6):   Falco 4, Allen C 1, Leworthy 1   †After extra time

1985-86

Clemence	Thomas	Hughton	Allen P.	Miller	Perryman	Ardiles	Falco	Waddle	Hazard	Galvin	Leworthy	Roberts	Hoddle	Crook	Chiedozie	Mabbutt	Allen C.	Stevens G.	Cooke	Stevens T.	Dick	Howells	Bowen	Jennings (NC)	Referee	
	2	3	4	5	6*	7	8	9	10	11	12														A Gunn	1
	2	3	4	5	6	7	8	9	10	11															V Callow	2
	2	3	6	5		7	8	9	10	11*	12	4													H Taylor	3
	2	3	4	5	7*	8	9		11			6	10	12											J Bray	4
	2	3	6	5	7	8	9		11*			4	10		12										G Courtney	5
	2	3	6	5	10	7	11					12	4	9*	8										B Stevens	6
	2	3	6	5	7	8*	11	12				4	10	9											A Robinson	7
	2	3	6*	5	12	7	8	11				4	10	9											P Willis	8
	2	3	6	5		7*	8	11				4	10	9	12										R Milford	9
	2	3	6	5		7	8	11				4	10	9											H King	10
	2	3	5		6	7*	8	11				4	10	9	12										C Seel	11
	2	3	5		6	7*	8	11				4	10	13	12	9*									M Bodenham	12
	2	3		5	6	7	8*	11				4	10		12	9									J Worrall	13
		3		5	6	7*	8	11		9		4	10		12			2							M Heath	14
		3		5	6		8	11		9		4	10	7				2							D Hedges	15
		3			6	12	8	11		9		4	10	7*	5			2							K Hackett	16
		3			6	7	8	11		9*	10	4			12		5	2							K Cooper	17
		3		5	6		8	11			12	4	10		9		2	7*							G Napthine	18
		3			6		8	11		9	4	10	7*			5	2	12							L Shapter	19
		3	7		6		8	11		9		4	10				5	2							M Peck	20
		3	7		6		8	11		9*		4	10				5	2	12						D Axcell	21
		3	7		6		8	11		9		4	10				5	2							B Hill	22
12		3	7		6	10*	8	11		9		4					5	2							A Gunn	23
		3	7		6		8	11				4	10				5	9	2						F Roberts	24
12		3	7*		6*	13	8	11				4	10				5	9	2						G Aplin	25
2		5			12		8	11	9			4*	7		3	10	6								M James	26
6		3	12			7*	8	11				4	10				5	9	2						B Stevens	27
2		3	7		6	12	8		11			4					5	9*	10						T Holbrook	28
2		3	11		6	7*	8		12	4							5	9*	10	13					K Baker	29
		3	12		6	7	8	11				10*					5	9	2	4					R Groves	30
2		3	12		6	7*	8	11				10					5	9	4						C Downey	31
2*		3	7		6	12	8	11				10					5	9	4						J Deakin	32
		3			6	7	8	11				4	10				5	9	2						J Moules	33
		3	8		6	7		11				4	10		12	5	9*	2							L Shapter	34
		3	8		6	7*		11				4	10		9	5	12	2							L Shapter	35
		3	8		6	7		11				4	10		9	5		2							R Milford	36
		3	7	5	6			11*				4		8	10	9	2	12				1			J Martin	37
		3	9	5	6	7	11					4	12		10	8*	2								G Napthine	38
		3	7*	5	6		9	11				10	12		4	8	2								R Lewis	39
		3	12	5	6		8	11				10			7	4	9*	2							R Lewis	40
		3	12	5	6		8	11				10			7	4	9*	2							M Reed	41
	12	12	5		6		8*	11		3*		10	7		4	9	2								R Milford	42
		8		5	6			11		3*		10	12	7	4		2		9						I Borrett	43
3		2		5	6		8	11				7	4			10				9					C Seel	44
3		2		5	6		8	11				10	9	4	7										A Robinson	45
3		2	5*		6		8	11		4		10	12	7	9										J Martin	46
5		2	3				10	11	9*		8	7		4	12	6									L Shapter	47
3		2	5				8	11	9		4	10		7	6										D Allison	48
2*	3	4	5				8	11	9					10	7		6						12		G Tyson	49
3	2*	5			12		8	11	9		4	10		7			6								K Breen	50
3	2	5					8	11	9		4	10		7			6								P Vanes	51
3	2	5			10*		8	11	9		4			7	12	6									B Hill	52
	3	2	5		7*		8	11	9			12	4	10						6					T Mills	53
	3	2	5				8	11	9			7	4	10	6										R Hamer	54
	3	2	5				8*	11		10		7	4	9	6						12				I Borrett	55
2	3		5				8	11		4		10	12	7	9*	6									J Martin	56
3		2	5				8	11	6		4	10		7	9	2									M Dimblebee	57
	2	3		5			8	11	10		6	9		4	7										M Bodenham	58
2	3		5				8	11	6		4	10*		7	9	12									K Barratt	59
2	26	33	28	29	22	20	40	39	3	23	2	32	31	1	13	29	17	18	1	1	1	1			League Appearances	
		4		1	3		1		3			4	4	3	2	1	1			1					Substitute Appearances	
2+1	6	3+1	2	4	3+1	6	6	3	0+1	6	5		2	5	1	5	1+1								Milk Cup Appearances	
1	4	4+1	3	5	2	3	5	0+1	2+2	5	3+1	5													FA Cup Appearances	
3+1	5+1	5+1	3	5	2+1	5	4	2	0+1	5	2	1	3+1	5+1	5								1		Super Cup Appearances	

Departures: Perryman (Oxford Utd), Hazard (Chelsea), Leworthy (Oxford Utd), Jennings (Retired), Dick (Ajax), Culverhouse, Crook (Norwich City)

'THE SPURS'

Formed: 1882
Turned Professional: 1895   **Ltd Co:** 1898

Previous Names: Hotspur Football Club 1882-4
Previous Managers: 1895-8 Frank Brettell   John Cameron   1898-1907 Fred Kirkham
1907-08 Peter McWilliam   1927-30 Billy Minter   1930-5 Percy Smith
1935-8 Jack Tresadern   1938-45 Peter McWilliam   1945-9 Joe Hulme   1949-55 Arthur Rowe
1955-8 Jimmy Anderson   1958-74 Bill Nicholson   1974-6 Terry Neill
1976-84 Keith Burkinshaw   1984-86 Peter Shreeve
Honours: Champions Div 1, 1950-1, 1960-1   Champions Div 2, 1919-20, 1949-50   FA Cup Winners
1901 (only Non-League club to win), 1921, 1961, 1962, 1967, 1981, 1982 (no final has been
lost)   Football League Cup Winners 1970-1, 1972-3   European Cup Winners Cup Winners
1962-3   UEFA Cup Winners 1971-2, 1983-4
League Career: Elected to Div 2 1908   Promoted to Div 1 1908-9
Relegated to Div 2 1914-5   Promoted to Div 1 1919-20   Relegated to Div 2 1927-8
Promoted to Div 1 1932-3   Relegated to Div 2 1934-5   Promoted to Div 1 1949-50
Relegated to Div 2 1976-7   Promoted to Div 1 1977-8
Colours: All white   **Change Colours:** All sky blue

CLUB RECORDS

Most Appearances for Club: Steve Perryman: Football League 631 + 1 + FA Cup 64 + League Cup 62 + European Cup
63 + 1 + Anglo-Italian 2 + Texaco Cup 3 + Charity Shield 1 + 1 **Total 826 + 3 subs**
Most Capped Player: Pat Jennings, 68, N Ireland   **For England:** Jimmy Greaves 42
Record Goalscorer in a Match: Jack Rowley, 7 v Luton Town, Wartime South Regional League
In League or Cup: Ted Harper, 5 v Reading, 7-1, Div 2, 30.08.30   Alf Stokes, 5 v Birmingham City 7-1, Div 1,
18.09.57   Les Allen, 5 v Crewe Alexandra 13-2, 4th Round, FA Cup 03.02.60
Record League Goalscorer in a Season: Jimmy Greaves, 37, 1962-3   **In All Competitions:** Jimmy Greaves, 43 (League
37 + European 6), 1962-3
Record League Goalscorer in a Career: Jimmy Greaves, 220   **In All Competitions:** Jimmy Greaves, 267 (League
220 + FA Cup 32 + League Cup 5 + European Competitions 10)
Record Transfer Fee Received: £1,150,000 from Barcelona for Steve Archibald, July 1984
Record Transfer Fee Paid: £800,000 to Aberdeen for Steve Archibald, May 1980
Best Performances: League: Winners (2)   **FA Cup:** Winners (7)   **League/Milk Cup:** Winners (2)   **European Cup:** Semi
Final   **European Cup Winners Cup:** Winners   **UEFA Cup:** Winners 2
Most League Points: (2pts for win) 70, Div 2, 1919-20   (3pts for win) 77, Div 1, 1984-5
Most League Goals: 115, Div 1, 1960-1
Record League Victory: 9-0 v Bristol Rovers, Div 2, 22.10.1977
Most Goals Scored in a League Match: 10-4 v Everton, Div 1, 11 Oct 1958
Most Goals Scored in a Cup Tie: 13-2 v Crewe Alexandra, FA Cup 4th Round Replay, 3 Feb 1960
Record League Defeat: 0-7 v Liverpool (A), Div 1, 2 Sept 1978
European Competitions Entered: European Cup 1961-2   European Cup Winners Cup 1962-3, 1963-4, 1967-8, 1981-2,
1982-3   UEFA Cup 1971-2, 1972-3, 1973-4, 1983-4, 1984-5
Oldest Player in League Match: Jimmy Cantrell 40 yrs 349 days v Birmingham, Div 1, 24.4.23
Youngest Player in League Match: Ally Dick, 16 yrs 301 days v Manchester City, Div 1, 20.2.82

Most Consecutive Undefeated League Matches: 23 1949-50	**League Matches Without a Win:** 16 1934-35
Longest Run of Undefeated Home League Matches: 33 1932-33	**Away League Matches:** 16 1984-85
Longest Run Without Home League Win: 8 1935	**Away League Win:** 22 1928-29
Most Consecutive League Wins: 13 1960	**Home League Wins:** 12 1919-20
Most Consecutive League Defeats: 5 1912, 1955, 1975	**Away League Wins:** 10 1960*

(*A record, but 8 is the record in one season, shared with Cardiff City, Preston North End and Leeds United)

Club Statistician for the Directory: Andy Porter

TOTTENHAM HOTSPUR

PLAYERS NAME ᴴ Wt Birthdate	Honours	Birthplace Transfers	Clubs	Appearances League	Milk Cup	FA Cup	Other Comps	Goals League	Milk Cup	FA Cup	Other Comps
GOALKEEPERS											
ᴐngsley Banks 0½ 12.0		Hertford	Tottenham Hotspur								
ᴀy Clemence 11½ 12.9 5.8.48	E (61), U23 (4), Div. 1 (5), FAC (2), LgC, EC (3), UEFAC (2), ESC	Skegness £300,000	Notts County (NC) Scunthorpe United Liverpool Tottenham Hotspur	48 470 189	55 27	2 54 19	80 32				
ᴀny Parks 10½ 10.8 28.1.63	UEFAC 84	Hackney	Tottenham Hotspur (A)	19		3	5+1				
DEFENDERS											
ᴀark Bowen 8 11.2 7.12.63	WU21 (3), YS	Neath	Tottenham Hotspur (A)	13+1		3					
ᴀchard Gough 0 12.0 5.4.62	S (26), U21 (5), SLG 84	Stockholm, Sw. £725,000	Dundee United Tottenham Hotspur	161+8	33+3	19	30+1	24	9	2	3
ᴀris Hughton 7½ 11.5 11.12.58	EI (30), U21 (1), FAC 81, 82, UEFAC 84	Forest Gate	Tottenham Hotspur	234+2	33	29+1	34+2	12	2	1	4
ᴀul Miller 1 12.2 11.10.59	FAC 81, 82 UEFAC 84	Stepney	Tottenham Hotspur	204+2	20	30+1	26	7		1	2
ᴀaham Roberts 10 12.12 3.7.59	E (6), B (1), UEFAC 84, FAC 81, 82	Southampton £6,000 £30,000	Dorchester Weymouth Tottenham Hotspur	183+9	20+1	3 27	30+1	22	3	2	5
ᴀil Ruddock 2 12.0 9.5.68		Battersea £50,000	Millwall (A) Tottenham Hotspur			3+1					2
ᴀary Stevens 11 11.10 30.3.62	E (7), U21 (7), UEFAC 84	Hillingdon £350,000	Brighton & H.A. Tottenham Hotspur	120+13 83+4	9+1 13	15+1 12	20	2 6		1	2
ᴀanny Thomas 7 11.0 12.11.61	E (2), U21 (7), Y, S FAC 81, 82	Worksop	Coventry City (A) Tottenham Hotspur	103+5 66+3	11+1 4+1	8+1 1	11+5	5 1	1		
ᴀitchell Thomas 0 12.0 2.10.64	EY	Luton £233,000	Luton Town Tottenham Hotspur	107+1	5	10		1			
MIDFIELD											
ᴀul Allen 7 9.12 28.8.62	EU21 (3), Y (23-rec.), FAC 80, Div. 2, 81	Aveley £400,000	West Ham United (A) Tottenham Hotspur	149+3 28+4	20+4 3+1	15+3 4+1	1+1 5+1	6 1	2	3	
ᴀssie Ardiles 6 9.10 3.8.52	Arg WC, 78, FAC 81, UEFAC 84	Argentina £325,000	Huracan Tottenham Hotspur Paris St Germain Tottenham Hotspur	140 14 39+4	17 4+1	24 3	6 4+2	13 3	2	4	1 1
ᴀenn Hoddle 0 11.6 27.10.57	E (38), B (2), U21 (12), Y, FAC 81, 82	Hayes	Tottenham Hotspur (A)	336+6	36	41+1	19+4	85	6	10	1
ᴀary Mabbutt 10 10.6 23.8.61	E (9), B (1), U21 (7), UEFAC 84	Bristol £105,000	Bristol Rovers (A) Tottenham Hotspur	122+9 103+13	10 14+2	5+1 10+2	19+4	10 17	1 1	1	3
FORWARDS											
ᴀive Allen 10 12.3 20.5.61	E (3), U21 (3), Y, S, Div. 2, 83	Stepney £1,250,000 £1,250,000 £425,000+p/e £750,000	QPR (A) Arsenal Crystal Palace QPR Tottenham Hotspur	43+6 25 83+4 29+3	5 4 7 7	1 8 5+2	10+1	32 9 40 12	2 1	7 1	
ᴀhn Chiedozie 7 10.10 18.4.60	Nigeria	Owerri, E. Nigeria £450,000 £375,000	Orient (A) Notts County Tottenham Hotspur	131+14 110+1 44+7	8 10 7	7 8 5+2	10+1	20 15 12	1 1	2 2 1	
ᴀchard Cooke 7 9.7 4.9.65	EU21 (1), Y	Islington	Tottenham Hotspur (A)	9+1	1+1	1	1+2	2			
ᴀark Falco 0 12.0 22.10.60	EY UEFAC 84	Hackney	Tottenham Hotspur (A) Chelsea (L)	157+11 3	19+2	15	26+4	68	3	5	17
ᴀny Galvin 9 11.5 12.7.56	EI (14), UEFAC 84, FAC 81, 82	Huddersfield £10,000	Goole Town Tottenham Hotspur	174+3	18	4 22+1	27	19	2	2	6
ᴀris Waddle 0 11.5 14.12.60	E (20), U21 (1)	Gateshead £10,000 £590,000	Towlaw Town Newcastle United Tottenham Hotspur	169+1 39	9 6	10 5	4	46 11	2 1	4 2	

ADDITIONAL CONTRACT PROFESSIONALS
ᴀaun Close, Steve Grenfell, David Howells (1Lg), John Moncur, Paul Moran, John Pulston, Gary Poole, Vincent Samways, Mark Stimson

APPRENTICES
ᴀrren Clare, Warren Gravette, Phil Gray

NON-CONTRACT PLAYERS
ᴀt Jennings, Richard Johnston, William Manuel

Record Attendance: 75,038 v Sunderland, FA Cup Round 6, 5 Mar 1938

Smallest Home Attendance for a First Class Match: 5,000 v Sunderland, Div 1, 19 Dec 1914

Record Receipts: £245,682.10 v Anderlecht, UEFA Cup Final 2nd Leg, 23 May 1984

Season Tickets: Stand: £130, £143, £156, £182, £208, £260; Ground: £63 (£31.50 juveniles/OAPs) Family: £125, £50 (juveniles/OAPs)

Executive Box Season Tickets: Between £10,000 and £13,000

Cost of Stand Tickets: £5, £6, £7, £8, £9, £10, £11, £12: Family Section: £5 (£2 children); Ground: £3.50, £3.00 (£1.50 Members of Junior Spurs Club)

Match and Ticket Information: Seats for League matches available any time in advance. Seats are available on match days at the Park Lane ticket office. Dial a seat 01-808 3030

Car Parking: No street parking within a ¼ mile radius of the ground

Nearest Railway Station: White Hart Lane (from Liverpool Street, Central London), Northumberland Park (Liverpool St)

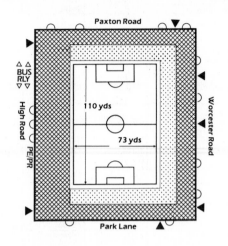

How to get to the ground

From North, East, South and West: Use A406 North Circular Road to Edmonton then at traffic signals follow signs Tottenham A1010 into Fore Street for Tottenham Hotspur FC

Price of 1986-7 Programme: 60p
Number of Pages: 32

Local Newspapers: Tottenham Herald, Waltham Forest Guardian, North London News

Local Radio Stations: LBC, Radio London, Hospital Broadcasts

TRANMERE ROVERS

President
H B Thomas

Chairman
B S Osterman USA

Directors
Ken Bracewell (Vice-Chairman)
Arthur Brew

Secretary
N Wilson (051-608 3677/4194)

Manager
Frank Worthington

Assistant Manager
George Mulhall

Commercial Manager
W Rimmer (051-608 3677/4194)

Groundsman
D Pinch

Physiotherapist
Les Helm

2nd Team Manager
Roy Lorenson

Youth Development Officer
Colin McDonald

Honorary Medical Officer
Dr Holmes-Levers

Honorary Orthopaedic Surgeon
R Johnson MCL (Ortho) FRCS

A disappointing season. At the start, with a new player-manager Frank Worthington and several new signings, there were high hopes that the club would make a strong bid for promotion, particularly after a reasonably successful season in 1984/85. Instead, the team struggled throughout the season and eventually only just managed to avoid applying for re-election.

The departure of three of the previous season's outstanding players: strikers Colin Clarke and John Clayton and defender, John Williams was a great blow and undoubtedly they were greatly missed. The main reason, however, for the club's low position was the terrible home record. No fewer than 13 of the 23 home games were lost, the club's worst home performance since entering the League in 1921. Many games were lost through giving away "silly" goals, far more than would normally be expected in a season. Defensive failings were the main reason for the poor season and the low final position. Seventy-three goals were conceded against 74 scored, compared with 84 scored and 66 conceded the previous season. Not a great difference but it certainly affected the final placing.

The various cup competitions did not offer any consolation. There were early exits from both the FA Cup and the Milk Cup and although there was slightly more progress in the Freight Rover Trophy, this ended in defeat at Bolton.

Although two high scores were recorded, 6-2 against Cambridge and 7-0 against Peterborough, at no time during the season did the team manage to put together a good run of results. Four consecutive games without defeat was the best that could be managed.

The season ended with some shocks behind the scenes. Four directors resigned just before the annual general meeting and at the meeting, according to press reports, the chairman disclosed proposals for a new stadium for the club within the next two years. This will mean the sale of the present ground. It remains to be seen whether anything will come of these plans.

Meanwhile, looking forward to next season, it is obvious that new players are required, particularly in defence and manager Frank Worthington will have a busy summer trying to strengthen the team within the club's limited resources. He has had a difficult first season as manager and all supporters will wish him success next season.

Attendances did not improve over the season and it is to be hoped that better performances next season will result in increased support.

Back Row L to R: Shaun Garnett, Andy Thorpe, Mark Hughes, Eric McManus, Darrell Grierson, Ronnie Moore, Steve Vickers, Alan Hay. **Front Row:** John Morrissey, Doug Anderson, Steve Bullock, Frank Worthington (Player/Manager), Steve Mungall, Graham Bell, Ian Muir.

TRANMERE ROVERS

DIVISION FOUR: 19th   **FA CUP:** 2nd ROUND   **MILK CUP:** 1st ROUND

MATCH	DATE	COMPE-TITION	VENUE	OPPONENTS	RESULT	HALF TIME	L'GUE POS'N	GOALSCORERS/GOAL TIMES	ATTEN-DANCE
1	A 17	CL	A	Orient	L	1-3	1-0	Worthington 22	(2,857)
2	23	CL	H	Cambridge United	W 6-3	3-2	8	Clayton 3 (6, 26, 82), Worthington 3 (7, 48, (pen) 67)	1,642
3	26	CL	A	Preston North End	D 2-2	0-2		Anderson 74, Clayton 89	(4,206)
4	28	MC1/1	H	Chester City	L	1-3	1-2	Worthington 32	2,207
5	31	CL	H	Chester City	L	2-3	0-1	15	Worthington 52, Anderson 80	1,703
6	S 4	MC1/2	A	Chester City	D 0-0	0-0			(2,384)
7	6	CL	A	Scunthorpe United	W	1-0	1-0	10	Lester (og) 11	(2,058)
8	14	CL	H	Colchester United	L	3-4	2-3	14	Sinclair 29, Muir 42, Worthington (pen) 58	1,362
9	17	CL	A	Wrexham	D	1-1	1-0		Worthington (pen) 14	(2,842)
10	21	CL	H	Aldershot	W	3-0	2-0	12	Worthington (pen) 21 (pen) 80, Muir 42	1,249
11	28	CL	A	Exeter City	L	0-1	0-0	14		(1,881)
12	O 4	CL	A	Southend United	D	2-2	0-1	15	Worthington 51, Morrissey 62	(4,175)
13	12	CL	H	Port Vale	L	1-2	0-1	17	Morrissey 81	2,328
14	18	CL	A	Halifax Town	W	2-1	1-0	15	Anderson 1, Muir 51	(1,412)
15	22	CL	H	Mansfield Town	L	1-2	0-1		Rodaway 83	(1,540)
16	26	CL	H	Rochdale	W	2-0	1-0	14	Muir 12, Rodaway 84	1,552
17	29	CL	H	Peterborough United	W 7-0	1-0		Muir 4 (36, 46, 68, 74), Worthington 50, 79, Morrissey 54	1,318
18	N 2	CL	A	Swindon Town	L	1-2	0-1	12	Miller 54	(4,358)
19	5	CL	A	Northampton Town	D	2-2	0-2		Worthington (pen) 80, Rodaway 87	(2,005)
20	9	CL	H	Torquay United	W	2-0	0-0	11	Anderson 83, Muir 90	1,508
21	16	FAC1	H	Chesterfield	D	2-2	0-1		Worthington (pen) 72, Rodaway 80	2,252
22	19	FAC1R	A	Chesterfield	W	1-0	0-0		Muir 75	(2,950)
23	23	CL	A	Hartlepool United	L	0-1	0-1	15		(3,107)
24	29	CL	H	Stockport County	L	2-3	1-1	15	Williams 21, Ashcroft 80	1,605
25	D 7	FAC2	H	Bury	D	1-1	0-1		Morrissey 54	3,398
26	10	FAC2R	A	Bury	L	1-2	0-1		Anderson 73	(3,210)
27	14	CL	A	Hereford United	W	4-1	1-1	13	Williams 37, Morrissey 69, Ashcroft 72, Anderson 89	(2,731)
28	20	CL	A	Cambridge United	L	2-3	1-2	13	Robinson 5, Worthington (pen) 84	(1,499)
29	26	CL	H	Burnley	W	2-1	0-1	13	Anderson 52, Williams 80	3,188
30	J 4	CL	H	Swindon Town	W	3-1	2-0	13	Edwards 28, Robinson 34, 80	1,795
31	11	CL	A	Chester City	L	0-1	0-0	13		(3,700)
32	17	CL	H	Orient	L	0-3	0-0	14		1,677
33	20	FRT	H	Preston North End	W	2-0	1-0		Anderson 14, Morrissey 80	1,047
34	24	CL	A	Colchester United	W	2-1	2-0	14	Hilditch 30, Mungall 41	(2,013)
35	31	CL	H	Scunthorpe United	W	2-1	0-1	10	Anderson 52, 75	1,417
36	F 7	CL	H	Halifax Town	L	0-3	0-3			1,357
37	15	CL	H	Wrexham	L	1-3	0-1	13	Muir 60	1,793
38	26	FRT	A	Bury	W	2-1	1-1		Williams 24, Miller 47	461
39	28	CL	H	Exeter City	L	0-1	0-0	13		1,031
40	M 5	CL	H	Peterborough United	W	1-0	1-0	11	Anderson 19	(1,512)
41	7	CL	H	Southend United	D	1-1	1-1	11	Pennyfather (og) 34	1,184
42	11	FRT QF	N	A	Bolton Wanderers	L	1-2	1-1		Hughes	(3,865)
43	15	CL	A	Port Vale	D	0-0	0-0	12		(3,427)
44	18	CL	A	Crewe Alexandra	L	1-2	1-1	12	Muir 40	(1,647)
45	22	CL	A	Rochdale	D	1-1	0-0	11	Rodaway 49	(1,558)
46	25	CL	H	Preston North End	L	2-3	2-2	13	Worthington 14, Muir 44	1,574
47	29	CL	H	Crewe Alexandra	L	0-1	0-0	15		1,587
48	31	CL	A	Burnley	L	1-3	1-1	16	Muir 20	(3,099)
49	A 4	CL	H	Northampton Town	L	1-3	0-1	17	Hilditch 77	1,103
50	12	CL	A	Torquay United	W	2-1	0-0	17	Worthington 48, 70	(1,120)
51	15	CL	A	Aldershot	L	1-3	0-0	18	Worthington 62	(1,067)
52	18	CL	H	Hartlepool United	W	4-2	1-0	16	Edwards 31, Anderson 52, 86, Morrissey 74	1,161
53	25	CL	A	Stockport County	D	1-1	0-1	18	Williams 61	(1,896)
54	29	CL	A	Mansfield Town	D	0-0	0-0	19		(3,470)
55	M 2	CL	H	Hereford United	L	1-2	0-1	19	Hilditch 82	1,346

Best Home League Attendance: 3,188 v Burnley 26/12   **Smallest:** 1,031 v Exeter 28/2   **Av Home Att:** 1,627

Goal Scorers: **Compared with 84-85: − 61**

League (74): Worthington 18 (8 pen), Muir 13, Anderson 11, Morrissey 5, Clayton 4, Rodaway 4, Williams 4, Hilditch 3, Robinson 3, Ashcroft 2, Edwards 2, Miller 1, Mungall 1, Sinclair 1, Opponents 2
Milk Cup (1): Worthington 1
FA CUP (5): Anderson 1, Morrissey 1, Muir 1, Rodaway 1, Worthington 1 (pen)
FRT (5): Anderson 1, Hughes 1, Miller 1, Morrissey 1, Williams 1

1985-86

Adkins	Mungall	Burgess	Edwards	Rodaway	McVicar (N.C)	Miller	Train	Worthington	Clayton	Anderson	Muir	Ashcroft	Sinclair	Hughes	Morrissey	Siddall (L)	Williams	Robinson (L)	Hilditch	Vickers	Referee	
1	2	3	4	5	6	7	8	9	10	11*	12										I Borrett	1
1	2	3	4	5	6	7	8	9*	10	11	12										N Glover	2
1	2	3*	4	5	6	7	8	9	10	11		12									T Simpson	3
1	2	3	4		6	7*	10	9		11	8	5	12								**A Robinson**	**4**
1	6	3	4	5		12	8*	9		11	7	10	2								M Scott	5
1	5	3	4		6		8	9		11	7	10	2								**J McAulay**	**6**
1	5	3	4		6	10	8	9		11	7		2								M Heath	7
1	5	3	4		6*	10	8	9		11	7	12	2								D Shaw	8
1	2	3	4	12		6	8	9		11	10	5	7								P Tyldesley	9
1	2	3	6				8	9		11	10	5	7	4							D Scott	10
1	2	3	6			12	8	9		11	10	5	7*	4							R Milford	11
1	2	3	6			5	8	9		11	10			4	7						N Bodenham	12
	2	3	6			8	5	9		11	10			4	7	1					D Allison	13
	2	3	6			8	5	9		11	10			4	7	1					K Lupton	14
	2	3	6			8	5	9		11	10			4	7	1					K Walmsley	15
	2*	3	6			8	5	9		11	10	12		4	7	1					C Seel	16
	2	3	6			8	5	9		11	10			4	7	1					T Holbrook	17
	2	3	6*			8	5	9		11	10	12		4	7	1					N Butler	18
	2	3	6			8	5	9		11	10	12		4	7*	1					R Vickers	19
	2	3	8			6		9		11	10	5		4	7	1					T Mills	20
	2	3	6			8	4	9		11	10	5			7	1					**A Ball**	**21**
	2	3	6			8	4	9		11	10	5			7	1					**P Tyldesley**	**22**
	2	3	6			8	4	9		11	10	5*		12	7	1					M Peck	23
	2	3	8				4	9		11	10	5			7	1	6				G Aplin	24
	2*	3	8			4	10	9		11		12		5	7	1	6				**M Heath**	**25**
	2	3	8			4	10	9†		11				5	7	1	6				**M Heath**	**26**
	2	3	4*			8	10	9		11		12		5†	7	1	6				K Cooper	27
	2	3	8			4		9		11				5	7	1	6	10			J Moules	28
1	2	3	9			8	4			11				5	7		6	10*			F Roberts	29
1	2	3	9			8	4			11				5	7		6	10			N Wilson	30
1	2	3	8				4	9		11				5	7		6	10			G Napthine	31
1	2	12	3			8	10	9		11		5		4	7		6*				T Jones	32
1	2	3†	6			8	10	9		11		5*		4	7		12				**D Phillips**	**33**
1	2	3	6	5		8	10			11				4	7		9				C Downey	34
1	2	3	6	5		12	8	10		11				4*	7		9				G Ashby	35
1	2	6	5			8*	12	9		11	10			4	7		3				D Allison	36
1	2	6	5			12	8*	9		11	10			4	7		3				N Ashley	37
1	2	3	6			7	4			11	10	5					8		9		**G Aplin**	**38**
1	2	3	6				4	9		11	10	5			7		8				K Baker	39
1	2	3	5			7	8			11	10			9	4		6				M Heath	40
1	2	3	5			7	8	12		11	10			9*	4		6				I Hendrick	41
1	2	3	5			7	8	12		11	10				4		6*		9		**T Simpson**	**42**
1	2	3	5			7	8	9		11	10*				4	12	6				J Lloyd	43
1	2	3	5			7	8*	9		11	10				4	12	6				C Seel	44
1	2	3	5			7	8	9		11	10				4		6				G Tyson	45
1	2	3	5			7	8	9		11	10				4*	12	6				L Robinson	46
1	2	3	4			8		9*		11	10	5			7		6		12		T Phillips	47
1	2		4			8	7	9		11	10	5		6*	12		3				J McAulay	48
1	2		8				7*			11	10	5			12		3		9	6	K Hackett	49
1	2	3	8			5	10	9		11					7		6			4	D Hedges	50
1	2	3	5		4	8*	7	10		11					12		6		9		V Callow	51
1	2	3	8			5	10	9		11				4	7		6				F Roberts	52
1	2	3	8			5	10			11	12			4	7*		6				K Walmsley	53
1	2	3	8		5	7	10	9		11							6		12	4*	T Holbrook	54
1	2	3	8			5		9		11				4	7		6		10		T Simpson	55
34	46	40	34	8	7	25	36	40	3	46	28	16	6	31	27	12	25	4	5	3	League Appearances	
			1		1			4		2				4	7	1	5		2		Substitute Appearances	
2	2	2	2		1	1	1	2		2	2	2		2	2	1+1					Milk Cup Appearances	
2	2	2	1			4	4	4		2	4	2+1		2	4	4	2				FA Cup Appearances	
3	3	3	2			2	2	3		2+1	2	2		2	1		2		2+1		FR Trophy Appearances	

Players on Loan: Hughes (Bristol City), Siddall (Stoke City), Robinson (Huddersfield)

Departures: McVicar, Clayton (Plymouth Argyle), Rodaway (Burnley), Adkins (Wigan Ath), Burgess (Grimsby Town), Hilditch (Altrincham)

'THE ROVERS'

Formed: 1883
Turned Professional: 1912 **Ltd Co:** 1920

Previous Names: None
Previous Managers: Since 1946: Ernie Blackburn   Noel Kelly   Peter Farrell   Walter Galbraith   Dave Russell   Jackie Wright   Ron Yeats   John King   Bryan Hamilton
Honours: Champions Div 3 (N) 1937-8   Welsh Cup Winners 1934-5
League Career: Original Members of Div 3 (N) 1921   Promoted to Div 2 1938
Relegated to Div 3 (N) 1939   Original members of Div 3 1958   Relegated to Div 4 1961
Promoted to Div 3 1967   Relegated to Div 4 1975   Promoted to Div 3 1976
Relegated to Div 4 1979
Colours: Royal blue shadow stripe shirts, royal blue shorts, white socks with royal blue diamond
Change Colours: All yellow
Reserves League: Lancashire League

CLUB RECORDS

Most Appearances for Club: Harold Bell: 595 (including League record of 401 consecutive appearances), 1946-64
Most Capped Player: Albert Gray, 3 (22), Wales   **For England:** None
Record Goalscorer in a Match: 'Bunny' Bell, 9 v Oldham Athletic, 26 Dec 1935
Record League Goalscorer in a Season: 'Bunny' Bell, 35, Div 3 (N), 1933-4
Record League Goalscorer in a Career: 'Bunny' Bell, 104, 1931-6
Record Transfer Fee Received: £120,000 from Cardiff City for Ronnie Moore, Feb 1979
Record Transfer Fee Paid: £20,000 to Charlton Athletic for Hugh McAuley, Aug 1978
Best Performances: League: 22nd Div 2 1938-9   **FA Cup:** 5th Round 1967-8   **League/Milk Cup:** 4th Round 1960-1, 1981-2
Most League Points: 75, Div 4, 1984-5   **Most League Goals:** 111, Div 3 (N), 1930-1
Record League Victory and Most Goals Scored in a League Match: 13-4 v Oldham Athletic, Div 3 (N), 26 Dec 1935
Most Goals Scored in a Cup Tie: 9-0 v Leamington AP, FA Cup 1st Round, 24 Nov 1979
Record Defeat: 1-9 v Tottenham Hotspur, FA Cup 3rd Round Replay, 14 Jan 1953
Oldest Player in League Match:
Youngest Player in League Match: Dixie Dean, 16 yrs, 1922-23
Most Consecutive Undefeated League Matches: 18 1970 (This
run came straight after their worst sequence, shown below)
Longest Run of Undefeated Home League Matches: 22 1964-65
Longest Run Without Home League Win: 11 1979
Most Consecutive League Wins: 8 1964
Most Consecutive League Defeats: 8 1938

League Matches Without a Win: 16 1970
Away League Matches: 10 1983-84
Away League Win: 35 1977-79
Home League Wins: 18 1964-65
Away League Wins: 4 1964, 1966

Club Statistician for the Directory: Bernard Jones

TRANMERE ROVERS

PLAYERS NAME Wt Birthdate	Honours	Birthplace Transfers	Clubs	League	Milk Cup	FA Cup	Other Comps	League	Milk Cup	FA Cup	Other Comps
GOALKEEPERS											
McManus 12.12 14.11.50	NI, Am	Limavady	Coleraine								
			Coventry City	6							
			Notts County	229	13	9					
			Stoke City	4							
			Lincoln City (L)	21							
			Bradford City	113	12	9	2				
			Middlesbrough	2							
			Tranmere Rovers								
DEFENDERS											
ve Mungall* 10.2 22.5.58		Bellshill F	Motherwell	14+6	11+2	14+1	10	6			
			Tranmere Rovers	223+9							
dy Thorpe 12.0 15.9.60		Stockport	Stockport County	312+2	22+3	7	4	3			
			Tranmere								
ve Vickers 11.7 13.10.67		Bishop Auckland	Spennymoor United								
			Tranmere Rovers	3							
ry Williams 11.7 14.5.59		Nantwich F	Tranmere Rovers	1							
			Djurgarden, Sweden								
		£40,000	Blackpool	30+1	4	2		2		1	
		£40,000	Swindon Town	37+1	2	2		3			
		F	Tranmere Rovers	82	2	4	8	9			1
		Djurgarden	Tranmere Rovers	25		2	2	4			1
MIDFIELD											
ham Bell 10.6 30.3.55	EY	Middleton	Chadderton								
			Oldham Athletic	166+4	9	6+1		9		1	
		£80,000	Preston North End	140+3	11+1	1+1		9	1		
			Huddersfield Town (L)	2							
			Carlisle United	11+3	2	1+1					
		F	Bolton Wanderers	86+6	7	2	5+1	3	2		
			Tranmere Rovers								
ve Bullock 9.9 5.10.66		Stockport	Oldham Athletic	10+7	1						
			Tranmere Rovers								
n Hay ¾ 12.0 28.11.58	Div. 4, 84	Dunfermline	Bolton Wanderers (NC)								
			Bristol City	72+2	4+2	4		1			
			York City	147+3	10	16	4+1	3			
			Tranmere Rovers								
k Hughes 12.8 3.2.62	WY	Port Talbot	Bristol Rovers (A)	64+1	9+1	3		3			
			Torquay United	9		3					
			Bristol City	21+1	1		3				
		£3,000	Tranmere Rovers	31+1		2	2				1
nie Moore 12.13 29.1.53	Div. 3, 81	Liverpool	Tranmere Rovers	248+1	18	12		72	4	1	
		£120,000	Cardiff City	54+2	2	2		6			
		£100,000	Rotherham United	124+1	9	5		51	2		
		£35,000	Charlton Athletic	60+2	2	4		13		1	
			Rochdale	43	2	4	1	9		1	
			Tranmere Rovers								
FORWARDS											
g Anderson ½ 9.8 29.8.63		Hong Kong	Port Glasgow								
			Oldham Athletic	4+5	0+1	0+1					
			Tranmere Rovers	91	3+1	7	5	13	1	2	2
n Morrissey ½ 11.4 8.3.65		Liverpool	Everton								
			Wolverhampton W.	5+5	1			1			
		£8,000	Tranmere Rovers	27+5		4	1	5		1	1
Muir ½ 11.0 5.5.63	SY	Coventry	QPR	2				2			
			Burnley (L)	1+1				1			
		F	Birmingham City	1							
		F	Brighton & H.A.	3+1							
			Swindon Town (L)	2							
			Tranmere Rovers	28+4	2	2	2	13		1	
k Worthington 11.10 23.11.48	E (8), U23 (2), FLgX (1), Div. 2, 70	Halifax	Huddersfield Town (A)	166+5	9	12		42	2	5	
		£70,000	Leicester City	209+1	10+1	18		72	2	4	
		£87,000	Bolton Wanderers	81+3	2+1	5		35	2	1	
		£150,000	Birmingham City	71+4	6	7		30	2	2	
		£100,000	Leeds United	32	5			14			
		£150,000	Sunderland	18+1				2			
		F	Southampton	34	2	6		4			
		F	Brighton & H.A.	27+4	1+1	2		7	1		
		Player Manager	Tranmere Rovers	40+2	2	4	2	18	1	1	

ADDITIONAL CONTRACT PROFESSIONALS

APPRENTICES
un Garnett, Darrell Grierson (Goal)

NON-CONTRACT PLAYERS
k Worthington

PRENTON PARK
Prenton Road West, Birkenhead   Capacity: 8,0(

Record Attendance: 24,424 v Stoke City, FA Cup Round 4, 5 Feb 1922

Record Receipts: £16,392.90 v Wolverhampton Wanderers, FA Cup Round 3, 8 Jan 1983

Season Tickets: £40 (adults), £30 (juveniles/OAPs) for Ground; £52.50 (adults), £35 (juveniles/OAPs) stands

Executive Box Season Tickets: £95.00

Cost of Stand Tickets: £3.00 (adults), £2.00 (juveniles/OAPs) **Terraces:** £2.00 (adults), £1.50 (juveniles/OAPs)

Match and Ticket Information: Not bookable in advance

Car Parking: Large park at back of stand. Also street parking

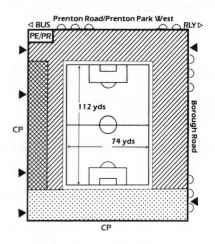

How to get to the ground

From North: Use Mersey Tunnel and Motorway M53 until junction 3. Leave motorway and at roundabout take 1st exit A552. In 1.3m at crossroads turn right B5151 then turn left into Prenton Road West for Tranmere Rovers FC
From South: Use Motorway M53 until junction 4, leave motorway and at roundabout take 4th exit B5151. In 2.5m turn right into Prenton Road West for Tranmere Rovers FC

Price of 1986-7 Programme: 50p
Number of Pages: 16

Local Newspapers: Liverpool Echo, Daily Post, Wirral News, Wirral Globe

Local Radio Stations: Radio City, Radio Merseyside

WALSALL

Division 3

Chairman
T R Ramsden

Director
R Cox

Secretary
Roy Whalley (0922 22791)

Commercial Department
(0922 22791)

Manager
Tommy Coakley

Assistant Manager/Coach
Gerry Sweeney

Physiotherapist
Fred Pedley

Groundsman
Roger Johnson

Commercial Manager
Refer to Secretary (0922 22791)

Once again Walsall's inconsistency let them down in the promotion challenge. This time, poor away results meant they missed out on a top three position.

The season started well enough, with seven of the first nine League games won; progress to the Milk Cup Second Round and a goaless draw at Leeds. However, 0-2 defeat at Wigan heralded the start of the decline, with just one win in seven games, including their only home League defeat of the season.

Walsall's problems lay in an erratic midfield. On their day they were brilliant, with home games producing seven goals once, six three times, 4 twice and 3 seven times. Added to this they scored 5 at Newport. On other occasions they were terrible, with several bad away results.

Always just off the promotion pace they were finally let down by their failure to score from the penalty spot. Penalties were missed at home against Brentford and Derby, and two away at Cardiff.

However, attendances remained steady, and matches were generally excellent with 104 goals being scored.

In cup competitions home form could not be maintained, in fact Walsall, were knocked out of all three competitions at home.

A thoroughly entertaining, but at times frustrating season had one final twist. With 14 away defeats costing them promotion the season started and ended with away wins!

Mervyn Sargeant

Back Row L to R: K. Mower, C. Brazier, P. Dolan, S. Cherry, K. Armstrong, M. Prudhoe, W. Naughton, A. Millard, P. Hawker, F. Pedley (Physio). **Middle Row:** N. Cross, G. Childs, T. Coakley (Manager), P. Hart, G. Sweeney (Coach), A. Dornan, C. Shakespeare. **Front Row:** M. Jones, M. Rees, B. Palgrave, M. Taylor, P. Jones, D. Kelly.

511

WALSALL

DIVISION THREE: 6th   **FA CUP:** 3rd ROUND   **MILK CUP:** 2nd ROUND

MATCH	DATE	COMPE-TITION	VENUE	OPPONENTS	RESULT	HALF TIME	L'GUE POS'N	GOALSCORERS/GOAL TIMES	ATTEN-DANCE
1	A 17	CL	A	Bristol City	W 3-2	1-1		Cross 27, Daley 50, O'Kelly 87 (pen)	(7,196
2	20	MC1/1	H	Wolverhampton W.	D 1-1	1-0		Cross 40	11,33◄
3	24	CL	H	Swansea City	W 3-1	1-1	2	Elliot 32, 48, Handysides 87	3,77
4	26	CL	A	Lincoln City	L 2-3	0-1	6	Elliot 73, Kelly 82	(2,282
5	31	CL	H	Chesterfield	W 3-0	0-0	3	Kelly 68, Cross 70, Handysides 88	4,52◄
6	S 3	MC1/2	A	Wolverhampton W.	W 1-0	0-0		Cross 49	(11,31C
7	7	CL	A	Reading	L 1-2	0-1	5	Hawker 48	(3,573
8	14	CL	H	Bolton Wanderers	W 2-0	1-0	2	O'Kelly (pen) 20, Cross 60	4,53
9	17	CL	H	Rotherham United	W 3-1	2-1	2	Elliot 2, 68, O'Kelly (pen) 26	4,86
10	21	CL	A	Bristol Rovers	W 1-0	1-0	2	Brazier 40	(3,787
11	25	MC2/1	A	Leeds United	D 0-0	0-0			(8,869
12	28	CL	H	Newport County	W 2-0	0-0	2	Mower 58, Kelly 82	4,58◄
13	O 1	CL	A	Wigan Athletic	L 0-2	0-1	2		(4,818
14	5	CL	A	Doncaster Rovers	L 0-1	0-0	2		(2,90'
15	8	MC2/2	H	Leeds United	L 0-3	0-2			7,08◄
16	12	CL	H	Plymouth Argyle	D 2-2	1-0	2	Rees 45, 68	4,25.
17	19	CL	A	Wolverhampton W.	D 0-0	0-0	2		(7,552
18	22	CL	H	Brentford	L 1-2	0-1	7	Elliot 47	4,31◄
19	27	CL	A	Darlington	W 3-0	1-0	4	Cross 17, Evans (og) 47, Naughton 56	(3,879
20	N 2	CL	H	Notts County	D 0-0	0-0	4		4,96
21	5	CL	H	Cardiff City	W 6-3	3-0	2	Shakespeare 21, 75, Elliot 3 (25, 84, 85), Cross 43	3,28:
22	9	CL	A	Gillingham	L 2-5	1-2		Shakespeare 28, O'Kelly 76 (pen)	(3,339
23	16	FAC1	H	Preston North End	W 7-3	4-1		Naughton 3 (6, 21, 77), Elliot 9, Childs 11, 58, O'Kelly 63	4,03
24	23	CL	H	Blackpool	D 1-1	1-1	8	O'Kelly 37	5,16
25	30	CL	A	Bury	L 1-2	0-1	10	Cross 61	(2,559
26	D 8	FAC2	A	Port Vale	D 0-0	0-0			(11,73◄
27	10	FAC2R	H	Port Vale	W 2-1	0-0		Cross 52, Hawker 81	5,67
28	14	CL	A	Bournemouth	W 4-2	1-0	9	Childs 11, Cross 55, 61, Brazier 76	4,46◄
29	28	CL	A	Lincoln City	W 2-1	1-1	10	Childs 1, Kelly 90	4,49.
30	J 1	CL	H	York City	W 3-1	2-0	6	Cross (pen) 38, 67, Elliot 43	5,64
31	4	FAC3	H	Manchester City	L 1-3	1-1		O'Kelly (pen) 23	10,83◄
32	7	CL	A	Swansea City	L 1-2	0-1	9	Kelly 61	(4,25C
33	18	CL	H	Bristol City	W 2-1	0-0	6	Cross (pen) 53, Elliot 65	4,95
34	21	FRT	A	Plymouth Argyle	W 1-0	1-0		O'Kelly 17	(3,19◄
35	24	CL	A	Bolton Wanderers	L 1-3	1-1	7	Hart 8	(4,088
36	28	FRT	H	Bristol City	L 1-2	1-2		Shakespeare 33	2,62◄
37	F 1	CL	H	Reading	W 6-0	2-0		Naughton 12, Taylor 27, O'Kelly 70, Cross 74, 85, Elliot 89	5,11
38	4	CL	A	Brentford	W 3-1	0-1	3	Cross 75, Hart 77, Shakespeare 80	(3,01◄
39	9	CL	H	Wolverhampton W.	D 1-1	1-1	5	Naughton 22	10,48◄
40	15	CL	A	Rotherham United	L 0-3	0-1	5		(3,51◄
41	28	CL	H	Newport County	W 5-1	1-0	5	Kelly 45, Jones 49, Cross (pen) 54, Childs 74, 85	(1,53C
42	M 8	CL	H	Doncaster Rovers	W 1-0	1-0	5	Stead (og) 17	4,81◄
43	12	CL	A	Derby County	L 1-3	1-0	5	Naughton 45	(13,434
44	15	CL	A	Plymouth Argyle	L 0-2	0-1	5		(6,01◄
45	18	CL	H	Bristol Rovers	W 6-0	3-0	5	Elliot 3, 80, Cross 5, Hawker 38, 84, Kelly 87	3,73◄
46	22	CL	H	Darlington	D 0-0	0-0	6 .		4,61◄
47	25	CL	A	Chesterfield	W 3-2	2-1	4	Handysides 4, Cross 42, 54	(2,177
48	29	CL	H	York City	L 0-1	0-1	6		(3,69◄
49	31	CL	H	Derby County	D 1-1	0-0	6	Cross (pen) 61	8,29
50	A 5	CL	A	Cardiff City	D 1-1	1-1	6	Brignall (og) 24	(1,77◄
51	8	CL	A	Notts County	L 1-3	0-2	6	Cross 72	(2,49C
52	12	CL	H	Gillingham	W 4-1	2-1	6	O'Kelly 23, Hawker 42, Cross 66, Elliot 70	3,88
53	15	CL	H	Wigan Athletic	D 3-3	2-0	6	Elliot 3, Palgrave 45, Kelly 89	4,29
54	19	CL	A	Blackpool	L 1-2	0-1	6	Kelly 79	(2,964
55	26	CL	H	Bury	W 3-2	2-0	6	Naughton 10, Childs 32, Kelly 85	3,45
56	M 3	CL	A	Bournemouth	W 1-0	1-0	6	Taylor 32	(3,047

Best Home League Attendance: 10,480 v Wolves 9/2   Smallest: 3,282 v Cardiff City 5/11   Av Home Att: 4,891

Goal Scorers: Compared with 84-85: +3

League (90):   Cross 21 (4 pen), Elliot 16, Kelly 10, O'Kelly 7 (4 pen), Childs 5, Naughton 5, Hawker 4, Shakespeare 4, Handysides 3, Brazier 2, Hart 2, Rees 2, Taylor 2, Daley 1, Jones 1, Mower 1, Palgrave 1, Opponents 3
Milk Cup (2):   Cross 2
FA CUP (10):   Naughton 3, Childs 2, O'Kelly 2 (1 pen), Cross 1, Elliot 1, Hawker 1
FRT (2):   O'Kelly 1, Shakespeare 1

Hart	Brazier	Hawker	Mower	Shakespeare	Handysides	Elliot	Daley	O'Kelly	Cross	Childs	Naughton	Jones	Kelly	Taylor	Rees	Gunn	Prudhoe	Palgrave	Referee	
2	5	6	3	4	7	10	11*	9	8	12									J Deakin	1
2	5	6		4	7	10	11	9*	8	3	12								N Glover	2
2	5	6	3		7	10	11		8	9		4							G Napthine	3
2	5	6	3		7	10	11*		8	9		4	12						M Scott	4
2	5	6	3		7	10	11	9	8			4*	12						D Vickers	5
2	5	6	3	4	7	10	11	9	8										K Walmsley	6
2	5	6	3	4*	7	10	11		8			12	9						R Groves	7
2	5	6*	3	4		10	11	9	8	7		12							J Ball	8
2	5	6	3	4		10	11*	9	8	7		12							T Jones	9
2	5	6	3	4		10	11		8	7	9								H King	10
	5	6	3	4		10	11		8	7	9	2							J Worral	11
	5	6	3	4		10	11		8	7*	9	2	12						K Breen	12
	5	6	3	4	12	10	11*			7	9	2	8						J Key	13
	5	6	3	4		10	11	9		7*	2	12	8†						L Dilkes	14
	5	6	3			10	11*	9	8	7	4	2	12						N Ashley	15
6		5	3*	4		10		9	8		11	2	12	7					I Hemley	16
	5		3	4		10	9	12	8*	6	11	2		7					D Hedges	17
	5		3	4		10	9	12	8	6	11	2		7*					D Shaw	18
5			3	4		10	9	12	8	6	11	2		7*					T Fitzharris	19
6		5	3	12		10		9	8	4	11	2		7*					R Nixon	20
6		5	3	4		10		9*	8	7	11	2		12					J Ashworth	21
6			3	4		10		9	8	5	11	2*	12	7					C Downey	22
6		5	3	4		10		9	8	7	11	2							J Lovatt	23
6		5	3	4	12	10*		9	8	7	11	2							R Gifford	24
6		5	3	4		10		9	8	7	11	2*		12					K Redfern	25
2	5	6	3	4		10	9		8	7	11*		12						G Napthine	26
2	5	6	3	4		10	9		8	7	11*		12						G Napthine	27
2	5	6	3	4		10	9*		8	7	11		12						I Hendrick	28
2	5	6	3	4*		10	9		8	7	11		12						C Trussell	29
2	5	6	3	4		10	9		8	7	11*		12						L Dilkes	30
2	5	6	3	4		9*	10		8	7	11		12						D Hedges	31
2	5	6	3	4		9*	10		8	7	11		12						J Martin	32
6	5		3	4		10	9*		8	7	11		12	2					D Scott	33
6		5		4		11	9		8	10	3		7	2					B Stevens	34
6	5	3		4		10			8	7*	11	9	12	2					P Willis	35
6	5		3*	4		10	9*		8	7	11		12	12	2				M Dimblebee	36
6	5		3	4		10	9		8		11	2		7					N Wilson	37
6	5		3	4		10*	9		8		11	2		7	12				M Bodenham	38
6	5		3	4		10*	9		8		11	2		7	12				M Reed	39
6	5		3	4		10			8	12	11	9		7*	2				J Ashworth	40
6		5	3				9	8	7	11	4	10		2			1		I Hemley	41
6		5	3	12			9	8	7	11*	4	10		2			1		K Miller	42
6		5	3			10	9*	8	7	11	4		12	2			1		J Bray	43
6		5	3			10		9	8	7	11	4*	2	12			1		R Hamer	44
6		5	3		7	10	9	8	4*	11		12	2				1		P Tyldesley	45
6		5	3		7	10*	9	8	4	11		12	2				1		B Hill	46
6	5		3	4		11		9	8	12	10	2		7*			1		F Roberts	47
6	5		3	4		10	9	8		11	12	2*		7			1		G Tyson	48
6	5		3			9	10	8	7	11	4	2					1		Alan Robinson	49
6	5		3			10	4*	9	8	11		2	12	7			1		R Guy	50
6	5		3			10		9	8	11	2	4		7			1	12	J McAulay	51
2	5	6	3			10		9	8	11	4		12	7*			1		D Phillips	52
2	5	6	3			10		9	8	11	4		12				1	7*	N Ashley	53
5		6	3	4		10		9	8*	7	11	12	2	7			1		R Bridges	54
5		6	3	4		10		9	8*	7	11	12	2				1		K Cooper	55
6		5	3	4		10		9	8*		11	12	2	7			1		T Ward	56
40	27	33	43	31	8	40	28	25	44	30	39	24	7	17	13	6	16	1	League Appearances	
			1	2	1		3			3		2	21	1	6			1	Substitute Appearances	
4	2	4	3	2	4	4	3	4	3	2+1	2	0+1							Milk Cup Appearances	
1	3	4	4	4	3	3	2+1	4	4	4	1	0+2							FA Cup Appearances	
2	1	2	2	1	2	1	1	1	1	1+1	1	1+1	2						FR Trophy Appearances	

...yers on Loan:

...partures: Handysides (Birmingham)

'THE SADDLERS'

Formed: 1888
Turned Professional: 1888   **Ltd Co:** 1921

Previous Names: Walsall Swifts (1877) and Walsall Town (1879) amalgamated and played as Walsall Town Swifts until 1895

Previous Managers: 1921-6 J Burchell   1926-7 D Ashworth   1927-8 J Torrance
1928-9 J Kerr   1929-30 S Scholey   1930-2 P O'Rourke   1932-4 W G Slade   1934-7 Andy Wilson
1937-44 T Lowes   1944-51 Harry Hibbs   1951-2 G McPhee   1952-3 Brough Fletcher
1953-6 Frank Buckley   1956-7 John Love   1957-64 Bill Moore   1964 Alf Wood   1964-8 Ray Shaw
1968 Dick Graham   1968-9 Ron Lewin   1969-72 Bill Moore   1972-3 John Smith
1973 Jimmy McEwan (Caretaker)   1973 Ronnie Allen   1973-7 Doug Fraser   1977-8 Dave Mackay
1978 Alan Buckley (Caretaker)   1978 Alan Ashman   1978 Frank Sibley   1979-81 Alan Buckley
1981 Alan Buckley/Neil Martin (Joint Managers)   1981-2 Neil Martin   1982-6 Alan Buckley
Honours: Champions Div 4, 1959-60
League Career: Elected to Div 2 1892   Failed to gain re-election 1895   Rejoined Div 2 1896
Failed re-election 1901   Elected as original member of Div 3 (N) 1921   Transferred to Div 3 (S) 1927
Transferred to Div 3 (N) 1931   Transferred to Div 3 (S) 1936   Joined Div 4 1958
Promoted to Div 3 1959-60   Promoted to Div 2 1960-1   Relegated to Div 3 1978-9
Relegated to Div 4 1978-9   Promoted to Div 3 1979-80
Colours: White shirts, red shorts, white stockings
Change Colours: Red shirts, white shorts, red stockings
Reserves League: **'A' Team:**

CLUB RECORDS

Most Appearances for Club: Colin Harrison: Football League 471 + Cup ties 55 **Total 526**
Most Capped Player: Mick Kearns, 15, Eire   **For England:**
Record Goalscorer in a Match: Johnny Devlin, 5 v Torquay United, 7-1, (h), Div 3 (S), 1.9.1949
Record League Goalscorer in a Season: Gilbert Alsop, 40, Div 3 (N)   **In All Competitions:** Gilbert Alsop, 44 (League 40 + FA Cup 4), 1934-5
Record League Goalscorer in a Career: Tony Richards, 184, 1954-63   **In All Competitions:** Alan Buckley, 204 (League 174 + Cups 30)
Record Transfer Fee Received: £175,000 from Birmingham City for Alan Buckley, Oct 1978
Record Transfer Fee Paid: £175,000 to Birmingham City for Alan Buckley, June 1979
Best Performances: League: 6th Div 2 1898-9   **FA Cup:** 5th Round 1939, 1975, 1978 and last sixteen 1889   **League/Milk Cup:** Semi-Final 1983-4
Most League Points: (3pts for win) 75, 1983-4   (2pts for win) 65, 1959-60   **Most League Goals:** 102, Div 4, 1959-60
Record League Victory and Most Goals Scored in a League Match: 10-0 v Darwen, Div 2, 4.3.1899
Most Goals in a First Class Match: 12-0 v Warmley (P) Qualifying Round FA Cup, 4.10.1890
Record League Defeat: 0-12 v Small Heath, Div 2, 17.12.1892   0-12 v Darwen, Div 2, 26.12.1896
Oldest Player in League Match:
Youngest Player in League Match:
Most Consecutive Undefeated League Matches: 21 1979-80

Longest Run of Undefeated Home League Matches: 26 1960-61
Longest Run Without Home League Win: 9 1952-53
Most Consecutive League Wins: 7 1933, 1959
Most Consecutive League Defeats: 9 1894-95

League Matches Without a Win: 14 1952-5 1953, 1954, 1982
Away League Matches: 13 1979-80
Away League Win: 29 1952-54
Home League Wins: 9 1972
Away League Wins: 5 1979-80

Club Statistician for the Directory:

YERS NAME Wt Birthdate	Honours	Birthplace Transfers	Clubs	League	Milk Cup	FA Cup	Other Comps	League	Milk Cup	FA Cup	Other Comps
LKEEPERS											
e Cherry 11.0 5.8.60	EY	Nottingham	Derby County	77	2	3					
			Port Vale (L)	4	2						
		£25,000	Walsall								
k Prudhoe 13.0 11.11.63		Washington	Sunderland	7							
			Hartlepool United (L)	3							
		£22,000	Birmingham City	1	4						
		£23,000	Walsall	16							
ENDERS											
Armstrong ¾ 12.1 1.8.63		Kilmarnock	Kilmarnock	82+1	8	9		3			
		£90,000	Southampton	26	2						
			Notts County (L)	10							
		£60,000	Birmingham City	58	7	4		1			
		£70,000	Walsall								
n Brazier ½ 10.13 6.6.57	LgC, 80	Birmingham	Alvechurch								
			Wolverhampton W.	69+9	1+3	1		2			
		Jacksonville M.	Birmingham City	10+1	4						
		F	Lincoln City	9							
		F	Walsall	112+1	16	5	7	4			
r Hart 12.7 14.8.57	Div. 4, 80	Mexborough	Huddersfield Town	208+2	14	5		7		1	
		£70,000	Walsall	266	25	13	8	11			
Hawker 11.6 7.12.62	EY	Solihull	Birmingham City (A)	34+1	2			1			
		F	Walsall	69	8	6	4	4	1	1	
ny Mower ¾ 12.4 1.12.60		Walsall	Walsall (A)	284+1	24	20	4+1	7		1	
FIELD											
y Childs 10.8 19.4.64	EY	Birmingham	WBA (A)	2+1							
		£15,000	Walsall	95+8	14	7	6	9	2	2	2
k Jones 10.1 4.1.68		Brownhills	Walsall (A)								
l Jones ʹ 11.3 6.9.65		Walsall	Walsall (A)	44+10	4	2	5+1	1			
g Shakespeare ʹ 12.5 26.10.63		Birmingham	Walsall (A)	142+8	19	9	7	23	3	2	1
ert Taylor 11.8 22.2.66		Birmingham	Walsall	18+5		0+1	1+1	2			
WARDS											
e Elliott ½ 11.10 15.9.58		Haltwhistle	Nottingham Forest (A)	4	2						
		£95,000	PNE	202+6	11+1	5	3	70	2	2	3
			Luton Town	12	3			2			
		Player exch.	Walsall	68+1	4	4	5	21		1	2
d Kelly 11.1 25.11.65		Birmingham	Walsall	34+32	3+1	3+2	3+3	20	2	1	2
e Naughton 12.8 20.3.62		Catrine (Ayr)	PNE	148+14	10	6	5	9	2	1	
		£43,000	Walsall	48+2	2+1	4	1	5		3	
ard O'Kelly ʹ 11.8 8.8.57		WBA	Alvechurch								
		£8,000	Walsall	189+15	15+1	9+2	7	55	4	2	1
n Palgrave 11.7 12.7.66		Walsall	Alvechurch								
			Walsall	4+2							
k Rees ½ 11.10 13.10.61	ES	Smethwick	Walsall (A)	153+36	12+2	5+3	4+1	35	5		3

)ITIONAL CONTRACT PROFESSIONALS
y Millard

RENTICES
nce Carville, Nicholas Mytton

N-CONTRACT PLAYERS
wart Franks, Michael Kearns, David Langston, Stephen Goodwin, Phillip Hill

FELLOWS PARK Walsall, West Midlands

Record Attendance: 25,433 v Newcastle United, Div 2, 29 Aug 1961

Smallest Home Attendance for a First Class Match: 500 v Bootle, Div 2, 24 Dec 1892

Record Receipts: £40,714 v Liverpool, Milk Cup Semi-Final, 2nd leg, 14 Feb 1984

Season Tickets: Stand: £60.00, Ground: £28.00

Executive Box Season Tickets: £145

Cost of Stand Tickets: £3.50; **Terraces:** £2.00

Match and Ticket Information: Seats bookable at any time by postal, telephone or personal application

Car Parking: Car park for 100 vehicles in Hillary Street, side-street parking available

Nearest Railway Station: Walsall or Bedcot

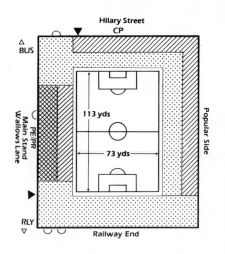

How to get to the ground

From North: Use A461 S.P. Walsall then join A4148 Broadway North around Ring Road into Broadway West for Walsall FC

From East, South and West: Use Motorway M6 until junction 9, leave motorway and follow signs Walsall A461, then turn right A4148 into Broadway West for Walsall FC

Price of 1986-7 Programme: 50p
Number of Pages: 20
Subscriptions: Apply club shop

Local Newspapers: Wolverhampton Express, Star, Birmingham Evening Mail, Birmingham Post, Mail, Walsall Observer (Wooke's)

Local Radio Stations: BBC Radio West Midlands, BRMB Radio, Beacon Radio

WATFORD

Chairman
E John

Vice-Chairman
G A Smith

Directors
J Harrowell
Bertie Mee OBE
J Reid
H M Stratford, JP
M Winwood

Chief Executive & Company Secretary
Eddie Plumley, FAAI (0923 30933)

General Manager
Graham Taylor

Marketing Manager
Caroline Gillies, M.Inst. M

Club Coaches
John Ward
Tom Walley
Steve Harrison

Physiotherapist
Billy Hails

Club Captain
Brian Talbot

Public Relations Manager
Ed Coan

Promotions Manager
Mike Sullivan

Kit Manager
Roy Clarke

This was very much a transitionory season for the Hornets. After three seasons of high drama at top level—when they were either chasing the Championship, the FA Cup or battling against relegation—Watford held a comfortable position in mid-table for much of the time and manager Graham Taylor used the situation to blood several of his younger players.

Watford did enjoy a fine run to the sixth round of the FA Cup, though. Away victories over 1st Division rivals Coventry and Manchester City took them into a fifth round confrontation with Bury from Division 3. Surprisingly, they were held to 1-1 at Vicarage Road by the Shakers and it wasn't until after the interval in the replay that the Hornets were able to force home their advantage and win 3-0.

The sixth round took them to Liverpool and, after holding the Reds to 0-0 at Anfield, there were high hopes of another trip to Wembley as the semi-final draw had placed the winners against Southampton, who were struggling in the 1st Division.

John Barnes gave Watford the lead early in the second-half and it was only a Jan Molby penalty ten minutes from time that enabled Liverpool to earn the extra half hour in which Ian Rush scored their winner.

Earlier the Hornets had been beaten at home by the eventual finalists QPR in the third round of the Milk Cup.

After a disastrous start in the League—they collapsed 0-4 at Tottenham—Watford scored eight times in their next two games and, by winning their first six home League games, assumed a position of comfort in the 1st Division.

This enabled Mr Taylor to give a few outings to players of the future, like Malcolm Allen, Paul Franklin, Gary Porter and Iwan Roberts. Allen had the remarkable experience of being called up for the Wales' national squad and he made his international debut, as substitute, against Saudi Arabia with but four League appearances behind him!

Such is the quality of player being produced at Vicarage Road that the club's future as a 1st Division side seems assured for the next few years. Nigel Gibbs, another local discovery, won himself the right-back spot this season whilst Worrell Sterling produced a serious of scintillating displays in mid-season.

When these names are added to the likes of Luther Blissett, John Barnes, Nigel Callaghan and Kenny Jackett—who have all come through from the nursery—it can be appreciated what fine work is being done by the club's youth coaches.

Some concern was shown when Watford played eight games without a win, towards the end of the season, but they finished on a high note when they defeated Chelsea—one of the chief Championship challengers until a few days earlier—by 5-1 at Stamford Bridge.

Back Row L to R: Kenny Jackett, John Barnes, Paul Franklin, John McClelland, Iwan Roberts, Steve Terry, Lee Sinnott, Paul Rumble, David Bardsley, Luther Blissett, Tim Sherwood. **2nd Row:** Billy Hails (Physiotherapist), Cliff Powell, Charlie Bishop, Nigel Callaghan, David Holdsworth, Steve Sherwood, Tony Coton, David James, Dean Holdsworth, Malcolm Allen, Worrell Sterling, Steven Thorne, Roy Clare (Kit Manager). **3rd Row:** Steve Harrison (Coach), Wilf Rostron, Neil Smillie, Les Taylor, John Ward (Assistant Manager), Brian Talbot, Graham Taylor (Manager), Chris Pullan, Nigel Gibbs, Gary Porter, Tom Walley (Youth Team Coach). **Front Row:** Neil Doherty, Greg Morris, Gary Eaton, Robert Wignall.

WATFORD

DIVISION ONE: 12th   **FA CUP:** 6th ROUND   **MILK CUP:** 3rd ROUND

MATCH	DATE		COMPE-TITION	VENUE	OPPONENTS	RESULT		HALF TIME	L'GUE POS'N	GOALSCORERS/GOAL TIMES	ATTEN-DANCE
1	A	17	CL	A	Tottenham Hotspur	L	0-4	0-1			(29,804
2		20	CL	H	Birmingham City	W	3-0	2-0		West 15, Barnes 17, 89	14,27
3		24	CL	H	W.B.A.	W	5-1	3-0	4	West 3 (7, 56, 74), Terry 35, Talbot 40	14,54
4		26	CL	A	Sheffield Wednesday	L	1-2	0-1		Blissett 54	(21,962
5		31	CL	H	Coventry City	W	3-0	2-0	6	Rostron 4, West 43, Smillie 55	13,83
6	S	4	CL	A	Leicester City	D	2-2	1-0	6	Rostron 35, 74	(9,672
7		7	CL	A	Liverpool	L	1-3	1-1	10	West 5	(31,395
8		14	CL	H	Queens Park Rangers	W	2-0	2-0	9	Blissett 7, Callaghan 9	15,77
9		21	CL	A	Nottingham Forest	L	2-3	1-1	10	Callaghan 34, Rostron 90	(12,92
10		24	MC2/1	A	**Crewe Alexandra**	W	3-1	0-1		**Rostron 56, Blissett 68, Jackett 77**	(4,252
11		28	CL	H	Chelsea	W	3-1	1-0	9	Barnes 44, Blissett 57, Terry 76	16,03
12	O	5	CL	A	Southampton	L	1-3	0-2	10	Talbot 85	(14,172
13		8	MC2/2	H	**Crewe Alexandra**	W	3-2	1-0		**Terry 24, Callaghan 70, Barnes 71**	11,58
14		12	CL	A	Manchester City	W	3-2	2-0	7	Blissett 29, Callaghan 32, Barnes 47	15,41
15		19	CL	A	Everton	L	1-4	0-1	8	Jackett (pen) 57	(26,425
16		26	CL	H	Oxford United	D	2-2	1-0	11	Rostron 4, Callaghan 60	16,12
17		29	MC3	H	**Queens Park Rangers**	L	0-1	0-0			16,82
18	N	2	CL	A	Newcastle United	D	1-1	1-0	11	West 29	(20,649
19		9	CL	H	Aston Villa	D	1-1	0-1	12	Talbot 48	14,08
20		16	CL	A	West Ham United	L	1-2	0-1	12	Sterling 66	(21,490
21		23	CL	H	Luton Town	L	1-2	0-1	13	Talbot 82	16,10
22		30	CL	A	Manchester United	D	1-1	0-0	13	West 89	(42,18
23	D	7	CL	A	Birmingham City	W	2-1	0-1	13	Blissett 49, Sterling 70	(7,043
24		14	CL	H	Tottenham Hotspur	W	1-0	1-0	11	Blissett 9	16,32
25		22	CL	A	W.B.A.	L	1-3	0-1	12	Sterling 85	(11,092
26		28	CL	H	Leicester City	W	2-1	0-1	12	West 65, 90	14,70
27	J	1	CL	A	Ipswich Town	D	0-0	0-0	12		(15,922
28		4	FAC3	A	**Coventry City**	W	3-1	0-0		**West 61, 71, Jackett 72**	(10,498
29		12	CL	H	Liverpool	L	2-3	1-1	12	Jackett 18, Sterling 86	16,69
30		18	CL	A	Coventry City	W	2-0	1-0	10	Barnes 22, 61	(7,499
31		25	FAC4	A	**Manchester City**	D	1-1	0-0		**Jackett (pen) 61**	(31,632
32	F	1	CL	H	Sheffield Wednesday	W	2-1	1-0	10	West 18, Barnes 86	13,14
33		6	FAC4R	H	**Manchester City**	W	3-1	0-0		**Smillie 46, Barnes 62, Sterling 73**	27,26
34	M	5	FAC5	H	**Bury**	D	1-1	1-0		**Barnes 13**	13,31
35		8	FAC5R	A	**Bury**	W	3-0	0-0		**Callaghan 49, West 57, Sterling 73**	(7,501
36		11	FAC6	A	**Liverpool**	D	0-0	0-0			(36,778
37		15	CL	A	Manchester City	W	1-0	0-0	12	Terry 71	(18,899
38		17	FAC6R	H	**Liverpool**	L	1-2†	0-0		**Barnes 46**	28,09
39		22	CL	H	Q.P.R.	L	1-2	0-1	12	Terry 81	(14,069
40		29	CL	H	Ipswich Town	D	0-0	0-0	12		14,98
41		31	CL	A	Arsenal	W	2-0	1-0	12	Barnes 19, Allen 68	(19,599
42	A	1	CL	A	Arsenal	W	3-0	2-0	11	Smillie 30, Jackett (pen) 35, Allen 52	18,63
43		5	CL	H	Newcastle United	W	4-1	2-0	11	Talbot 12, Porter 21, Gibbs 69, Smillie 85	14,70
44		9	CL	A	Oxford United	D	1-1	1-0	11	McClelland 6	(10,680
45		12	CL	A	Aston Villa	L	1-4	1-0	11	Sinnott 11	(12,781
46		15	CL	H	Everton	L	0-2	0-0	11		18,96
47		19	CL	H	West Ham United	L	0-2	0-0	12		16,65
48		21	CL	H	Nottingham Forest	D	1-1	1-1	12	Barnes 12	11,51
49		26	CL	A	Luton Town	L	2-3	0-2	12	Jackett (pen) 59, Sinnott 78	(11,810
50		29	CL	H	Southampton	D	1-1	1-1	12	West 43	11,86
51	M	3	CL	H	Manchester United	D	1-1	0-1	12	Blissett 72	18,41
52		5	CL	A	Chelsea	W	5-1	2-0	12	Talbot 2, 43, Bardsley 64, 77, West 85	(12,017

Best Home League Attendance: 18,960 v Everton 15/4   **Smallest:** 11,510 v Nottingham Forest 21/4   **Av Home Att:** 16,041

Goal Scorers: Compared with 84-85: – 2,334

League (69): West 13, Barnes 9, Blissett 7, Talbot 7, Rostron 5, Callaghan 4, Jackett 4 (3 pen), Sterling 4, Terry 4, Smillie 3, Allen 2, Bardsley 2, Sinnott 2, Gibbs 1, McLelland 1 Porter 1
Milk Cup (6): Barnes 1, Blissett 1, Callaghan 1, Jackett 1, Rostron 1, Terry 1
FA Cup (12): Barnes 3, West 3, Jackett 2 (1 pen), Sterling 2, Callaghan 1, Smillie 1   †A.E

Gibbs	Rostron	Talbot	Terry	McClelland	Callaghan	Blissett	West	Jackett	Barnes	Sterling	Smillie	Porter	Sherwood	Lohman	Sinnott	Taylor	Bardsley	Allen	Franklin	Roberts (NC)	Referee	#
2	3	4	5	6	7	8	9	10	11												A Gunn	1
2	3	4	5	6	7	8	9	10	11												B Hill	2
2	3	4	5	6	7	8	9	10	11												M Bodenham	3
2	3	4	5	6	12	8	9	10	11	7											K Redfern	4
2	3	4	5	6	7	8*	9	10	11			12									I Borrett	5
2	3	4	5	6	7		9	10	8		11										P Tyldesley	6
2	3	4	5	6	7	12	9	10	8		11*										M Peck	7
2	3	4	5	6	7	8	9	10	11												J Ashworth	8
2	3	4	5*	6	7	10	9	8	11			12									R Guy	9
2	3	4	5	6*	7	8	9	10	11			12									M Robinson	10
2	3	4	5		7	8	9	6	11			10	1								J Moules	11
2	3	4	5		7	8	9*	6	11			10		12							R Groves	12
2	3	4	5		7	8	9	6	11			10*		12							Allan Robinson	13
2	3	4	5		7	8	9	10	11						6						J Ball	14
2	3	4	5		7	12	9	10	11						6	8					K Hackett	15
2	3	4	5		7	8	9	10	11						6						D Axcell	16
2	3		5		7	8	12	10	9					11*	6	4					D Hedges	17
2	3	4	5		7	8	9	10	11						6						T Mills	18
2	3	4	5		7	8*	9	10	11		12				6						J Martin	19
	3	4	5					10	9	7	12	11			6		2	8			H Taylor	20
	3	4	5					10	9	7	12	11*			6		2	8			G Napthine	21
2	3	4	5				8	9	10	11	7*				6						G Courtney	22
2		4	5				8	9	10	7	11				3			6			J Lloyd	23
2	12	4	5	6			8	9	10	7*	11				3						T Holbrook	24
2	3	4	5	6			8	9	10	7	11*			12							T Fitzharris	25
2	3	4	5	6			8*	9	10	11	7						12				M Cotton	26
2	3	4	5	6		12	9	10	11	7							8*				A Seville	27
2	3	4	5	6		8	9	10	11	7											J Martin	28
2	3	4*		6		8	9	10	11	7				12				5			M Bodenham	29
2	3	4	5	6		8*	9	10	11	7				12							K Hackett	30
2	3	4	5	6		8	9	10	11	7											M Heath	31
2	3	4	5	6		8	9	10	11	7											R Gifford	32
2	3	4*	5	6			9	10	11	7	8			12							V Callow	33
2	3	4	5	6			9		11	7	8			10							R Lewis	34
2	3	4	5	6		8	9	10	11*	7							12				L Shapter	35
2	3	4	5	6			9	10	11	7					8						R Milford	36
2	3	4	5	6			9	10	11	7					8						K Baker	37
2	3	4*	5	6			9	10	11	7					8		12				R Milford	38
2	3						9*	10	11	7						4	12				Alan Robinson	39
2	3	4	5	6		8		10	11*	7							12		9		J Lovatt	40
2	3	4	5	6				10	11	7*							8	9	12		J Martin	41
2		4	5	6				10	11		7	3					8	9			K Cooper	42
2		4	5	6				10	11		7	3	1				8	9			M Reed	43
2		4	5	6					11		7	3*			10		8	9	12		T Simpson	44
2		4	5	6				10	11		7				3		8	9*	12		L Shapter	45
2		4	5	6				10	11	9	7						8	12	3*		K Barratt	46
2		4	5	6			9	10	11		7	12					8		3*		J Bray	47
2		4	5	6			9	10	11		12				3		8*				A Gunn	48
2		4	5	6	7		9*	10	11	7					3		12	8			D Hedges	49
2		4	5	6		12	9	10	11	7	8*				3						D Vickers	50
2		4	5	6		8	9	10	11	7					3						A Gunn	51
2*		4	5	6		8	9	10	11	7					3		12				B Hill	52
40	29	41	41	31	21	20	33	41	39	23	10	7	2		18	1	10	10	4	1	League Appearances	
	1			2	3				1	6	1			4			3	3		3	Substitute Appearances	
3	3	2	3	1	3	3	2+1	3	3					1+1	1+1	1	1				Milk Cup Appearances	
7	7	7	7	7	3		7	6	7	7	2			1+1	2			0-2			FA Cup Appearances	

so Played:

ayers on Loan:

partures: Jan Lohman (F), Ian Richardson (Chester), Colin West (Glasgow Rangers)

'THE HORNETS'

Formed: 1891
Turned Professional: 1897 **Ltd Co:** 1909

Previous Names: West Herts until merger with Watford St. Mary's in 1898
Previous Managers: 1903 Johnny Goodall 1910 Harry Kent 1926 Fred Pagnam 1929 Neil McBai
1938 Billy Findlay 1947 Jack Bray 1948 Eddie Hapgood 1950 Ron Gray 1951 Haydn Green
1952 Len Goulden 1955 Johnny Paton 1956 Len Goulden 1956 Neil McBain 1959 Ron Burgess
1963 Bill McGarry 1964 Ken Furphy 1971 George Kirby 1973-7 Mike Keen
Honours: Champions Div 3 1968-9 Champions Div 4 1977-8 FA Youth Cup Winners 1981-2
League Career: Original Members of Div 3 1920 Transferred to Div 3 (S) 1921
Relegated to Div 4 1958 Promoted to Div 3 1959-60 Promoted to Div 2 1968-9
Relegated to Div 3 1971-2 Relegated to Div 4 1974-5 Promoted to Div 3 1977-8
Promoted to Div 2 1978-9 Promoted to Div 1 1981-2
Colours: Yellow shirts with red and yellow trim and red/black divided band across chest, red shorts, red
stockings with black and yellow tops
Change Colours: White shirts, black shorts, black stockings with red and yellow tops
Reserves League: Football Combination **Youth League:** S E Counties Div 1

CLUB RECORDS

Most Appearances for Club: Duncan Welbourne: Football League 404 + 7 + FA Cup 28 + League Cup 17 + 1
Total 449 + 8 subs
Most Capped Player: Gerry Armstrong, 21, Northern Ireland and 21, John Barnes, England **For England:** John Barnes,
16 + 5 subs = 21
Record Goalscorer in a Match: Eddie Mummery, 5 v Newport County (8-2) (H), Div 3 (S), 05.01.24
Dennis Westcott, 5 v Q.P.R. (5-1) (A), London League, 01.11.41 (as guest player)
Record League Goalscorer in a Season: Cliff Holton, 42 **In All Competitions:** Cliff Holton, 48 (League 42, FA Cup 6)
Record League Goalscorer in a Career: Tommy Barnett, 148 **In All Competitions:** Tommy Barnett, 161 (League 145,
FA Cup 16, Div 3 (S) Cup 3)
Record Transfer Fee Received: £1,000,000 from A.C. Milan for Luther Blissett, June 1983
Record Transfer Fee Paid: £550,000 to A.C. Milan for Luther Blissett, July 1984
Best Performances: League: Runners-Up 1982-3 **FA Cup:** Runners-Up 1983-4 **League/Milk Cup:** Semi-Final
1978-9 **UEFA Cup:** 3rd Round 1983-4
Most League Points: (2pts for win) 71 in Div 4, 1959-60 (3pts for win) 80, Div 2, 1981-2
Most League Goals: 92, Div 4, 1959-60
European Competitions Entered: UEFA Cup 1983-4
Oldest Player in League Match: Joe Calvert (G) 41 yrs 25 days v Bournemouth, 28 Feb 1948
Youngest Player in League Match: Keith Mercer (F) 16 yrs 125 days v Tranmere Rovers, 16 Feb 1963
Most Consecutive Undefeated League Matches: 15 1934-35,
1978-79 | **League Matches Without a Win:** 19 1971-72
Longest Run of Undefeated Home League Matches: 27 1963-64 | **Away League Matches:** 12 1978
Longest Run Without Home League Win: 9 1971-72 | **Away League Win:** 32 1971-72
Most Consecutive League Wins: 7 1934, 1977-78 | **Home League Wins:** 8 1931, 1934-35, 1977
Most Consecutive League Defeats: 9 1972-73 | **Away League Wins:** 5 1981

Club Statistician for the Directory: Lynn Fleckney

WATFORD

AYERS NAME Wt Birthdate	Honours	Birthplace Transfers	Clubs	League	Milk Cup	FA Cup	Other Comps	League	Milk Cup	FA Cup	Other Comps
ALKEEPERS											
y Coton† 11.10 19.5.64		Tamworth	Mile Oak Rovers								
			Birmingham City	94	10	10					
		£300,000	Watford	73	6	10					
ve Sherwood 14.7 10.12.53	Div. 4, 78	Selby	Chelsea (A)	16	1						
			Millwall (L)	1							
			Brentford (L)	62	2	2					
		£4,000	Watford	200	22	23	6	1			
FENDERS											
vid Bardsley 0 10.0 11.9.64	EY	Manchester	Blackpool (A)	45	4	2		1	1		
		£150,000	Watford	52+3	3	8+1		2			
arlie Bishop 12.11 16.2.68		Nottingham	Stoke City (A)								
			Watford								
l Franklin 11.8 5.10.63	FAYC 82	Ilford	Watford (A)								
			Watford	29	1	5	4				
el Gibbs 10.2 20.11.65	EY, FAYC 82	St Albans	Watford (A)								
			Watford	53+2	3	7	4	1			
n McClelland 11.4 7.12.55	NI (38)	Portadown	Portadown								
			Cardiff City	1+3				1			
			Bangor City								
		£10,000	Mansfield Town	122+3				8			
			Glasgow Rangers								
		£225,000	Watford	60	2	12		2			
f Powell 11.5 21.2.68		Watford	Watford (A)								
f Rostron 11.1 29.9.56	E (5)	Sunderland	Arsenal (A)	12+5	1	1		2			
		£40,000	Sunderland	75+1	4	4		17			
		£150,000	Watford	227+7	20+1	28+1	6	21	2	2	3
Sinnott 11.9 12.7.65	EU21 (1), Y	Pelsall	Walsall (A)	40	3	4		2			
		£100,000	Watford	66+3	4	8		2			
ve Terry ½ 13.3 14.6.62		Clapton	Watford (A)								
			Watford	126	15	19	2+1	12	4	1	
DFIELD											
nny Jackett 0¼ 11.3 5.1.62	W (23), U21 (2), Y	Watford	Watford (A)								
			Watford	209+2	24+1	22		18	2	3	
ry Porter 9.10 6.3.66	EY FAYC 82	Sunderland	Watford (A)								
			Watford	14+5	1+1			1			
an Talbot 0 12.0 21.7.53	E (6), B (8), U21 (1), FAC 78, 99	Ipswich	Ipswich Town (A)	177	12	23	15	25	1	3	3
		£450,000	Arsenal	245+9	26	20+1	15	40	1	4	
		£150,000	Watford	41	2	7		7			
Taylor 11.7 4.12.56		North Shields	Oxford United (A)	219	16	3		15	1		
		£105,000	Watford	167+5	13	21		13	4	3	
even Thorne 0 10.6 15.9.68		Hampstead	Watford (A)								
RWARDS											
lcolm Allen ½ 10.5 21.3.67	W (1)	Deinhiolen	Watford (A)								
			Watford	10+3		0+2		2			
n Barnes 1 11.10 7.9.63	E (28), U21 (3), FAYC 82	Jamaica	Sudbury Court								
			Watford	195+1	17	23	6	55	6	8	
her Blissett 0½ 11.13 1.2.58	E (14), B (1), U21	Jamaica	Watford	222+24	26+1	17		95	13	3	
		£1,000,000	A.C. Milan								
		£550,000	Watford	58+6	7	5		28	2	6	
el Callaghan 10.9 12.9.62	E B (1), U21 (9)	Singapore	Watford (A)								
			Watford	192+10	18+2	22+1		38	4	3	
n Roberts 8 12.5 26.6.68		Bangor	Watford (A)								
l Smillie 10.7 19.7.58		Barnsley	Crystal Palace (A)	71+12	7	7					
			Brentford (L)	3							
		P/E	Brighton	61+3	2	8+11		2			
		£100,000	Watford	10+6		2		3		1	
rrell Sterling 10.8 8.6.65	FAYC 82	Bethnal Green	Watford (A)								
			Watford	45+7	2+1	11		9	1	2	

DITIONAL CONTRACT PROFESSIONALS
ris Pullan (A)

PRENTICES
l Doherty, David Holdsworth, Dean Holdsworth, Paul Rumble, Tim Sherwood, Gary Eaton, David James, Greg Morris, Robert Wignall

N-CONTRACT PLAYERS
rtin Baker

VICARAGE ROAD Watford WD1 8ER

Capacity: 28,500

Record Attendance: 34,099 v Manchester U, FA Cup Round 4, 3 Feb 1969

Record Receipts: £104,347 v Liverpool, FA Cup Round 6 Replay, 17 March 1986

Size of Playing Area: 113yds × 73yds

Season Tickets: Call Watford Ticket Office (0923 20393)

Executive Boxes: 36 Executive boxes available on three-year licence. Contact Marketing Manager (0923 30933)

Executive Clubs: Contact Marketing Department (0923 25761)

Cost of Stand Tickets: Call Watford Ticket Office (0923 20393)

Match and Ticket Information: Seats for league matches available anytime in advance

Car Parking: No public parking available at ground. There are several multi-storey parks nearby

Nearest Railway Station: Watford Junction or Watford High Street (0923 45001)

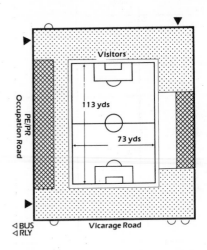

How to get to the ground

From North: Use Motorway M1 until junction 6. Leave motorway and follow signs Watford A405/A41 and A411. Follow signs Slough A412 and in 0.7m turn left into Harwoods Road. At end of T road turn left into Vicarage Road for Watford FC

From East and South: Use Motorway M1 until junction 5. Leave motorway and follow signs Watford A41 and A412. Then follow signs Slough A412 and in 0.7m turn left into Harwoods Road. At end of T road turn left into Vicarage Road for Watford FC

From West: Use A412 S.P. Watford and pass Croxley Green Station then in 0.9m turn right into Harwoods Road. At end of T road turn left into Vicarage Road for Watford FC

Price of 1986-7 Programme: 50p
Number of Pages: 24
Subscriptions: £15.00 (home programmes, £30.00 (home and away)

Local Newspapers: Watford Observer, Watford Review

Local Radio Stations: Chiltern Radio, BBC Radio Bedfordshire, LBC, Radio London, Capital Radio

President
F A Millichip

**Life Member and
Immediate Past President**
J W Gaunt

Vice-President
F T D Hall

Chairman
J S Lucas

Directors
C Edwards
A Everiss JP
D B Boundy (Vice-Chairman)
T J Summers
J G Silk

Secretary
H J Westmancoat FAAI, MBIM
(021 525 8888)

Team Manager
R Saunders

Coach
K Leonard

Youth Coach
N Stiles

Chief Scout
N Bodnell

Physiotherapist
G Wright

Marketing Manager
C A K Ross

Statistician
T Matthews

Those who have followed the fortunes of Albion in recent seasons are surprised that a very bad campaign such as the one which has just ended did not happen earlier, since the warning signs have been there. The team were in 22nd place in the 1st Division before September had arrived and they stayed there for the rest of the season, during which only four matches were won — a record which compares with Stoke's disasters of 1984-85. Inevitably, there were changes of management and Ron Saunders, who has worked miracles elsewhere, has the tough task of trying to revive a creaking machine.

There is little useful purpose to give details of the ghastly League record. The double was gained over Birmingham City, which ensured the latter's relegation, and the other two victims were Watford and Southampton at the Hawthorns when neither team had anything at stake except pride.

It was an irony that in the cup campaigns Albion did quite well with a Milk Cup effort which took them past Port Vale (3-2 on aggregate) and Coventry City (0-0 and 4-3 at the Hawthorns) before a brave draw at Villa Park (2-2) was followed by home defeat in the replay (1-2). The FA Cup effort also ended at home in a replay against the powerful Sheffield Wednesday (2-3), whilst the Full Members Cup saw wins over Brighton & Hove Albion (2-1 away) and Crystal Palace (2-1 at home) before Chelsea shared four goals at the Hawthorns and then won on penalties.

Now people will ask where Albion are going next. With the team undergoing regular changes it is not easy to forecast how they will line up for their first 2nd Division match. Consistency was so lacking last season that Statham, who played 37 times, made the largest number of appearances! Only Varadi and Mackenzie of the others played 30 times, which was quite absurd. Thirty-five goals for and 89 against in the League are figures which suggest that first-team places in every position are 'up for grabs'.

Poor Ron Saunders, when he left Birmingham earlier in the season, he must have known the difficulties, but he will need help and sympathy all the same.
WLM

Back Row L to R: David Burrows, Craig Madden, Stuart Naylor, Barry Cowdrill, Andy Thompson. **Middle Row:** Graham Doig (Physiotherapist), Martin Dickinson, George Reilly, Steve Bull, Steve Makenzie, Robbie Dennison, Carlton Palmer, Keith Leonard (Coach). **Front Row:** Stewart Evans, Clive Whitehead, Martyn Bennett, Ron Saunders (Manager), Paul Dyson, Darren Bradley, Bobby Williamson.

WEST BROMWICH ALBION

DIVISION ONE: 22nd   FA CUP: 3rd ROUND   **MILK CUP:** 3rd ROUND   FM CUP: AREA SEMI-FINAL

MATCH	DATE		COMPE-TITION	VENUE	OPPONENTS	RESULT		HALF TIME	L'GUE POS'N	GOALSCORERS/GOAL TIMES	ATTEN-DANCE
1	A	17	CL	H	Oxford United	D	1-1	0-0		Varadi 65	14,626
2		20	CL	A	Everton	L	0-2	0-0			(26,788)
3		24	CL	A	Watford	L	1-5	0-3	22	Varadi 56	(14,541)
4		26	CL	H	Manchester City	L	2-3	1-2	22	Mackenzie 8, 77	12,152
5		31	CL	A	Chelsea	L	0-3	0-2	22		(15,376)
6	S	4	CL	H	Aston Villa	L	0-3	0-2	22		17,077
7		7	CL	H	Ipswich Town	L	1-2	0-2	22	Crooks 85	7,733
8		14	CL	A	Newcastle United	L	1-4	0-2	22	Mackenzie 73	(21,855)
9		21	CL	A	Manchester United	L	1-5	0-2	22	Crooks 79	25,068
10		24	MC2/1	H	Port Vale	W	1-0	1-0		Armstrong 11	6,288
11		28	CL	A	Coventry City	L	0-3	0-1	22		(10,295)
12	O	2	FMC	A	Brighton & H. A.	W	2-1	2-1		Crooks 19, 25	(4,649)
13		5	CL	A	Tottenham Hotspur	D	1-1	1-1		Valentine 25	12,040
14		7	MC2/2	A	Port Vale	D	2-2	2-0		Varadi 16, 21	(7,895)
15		12	CL	A	Leicester City	D	2-2	2-1	22	Crooks 20, 23	(7,236)
16		19	CL	H	Birmingham City	W	2-1	2-1	22	Varadi 21, Valentine 30	14,576
17		23	FMC	H	Crystal Palace	W	2-1	1-1		Hunt 32, Nicholl 70	3,764
18		26	CL	A	Sheffield Wednesday	L	0-1	0-1	22		(19,873)
19		29	MC3	A	Coventry City	D	0-0	0-0			(9,804)
20	N	3	CL	A	Nottingham Forest	L	1-2	1-1	22	Hunt 44	(19,610)
21		6	MC3R	H	Coventry City	W	4-3	3-2		Varadi 2, 19, Crooks 9, Hunt 68	8,987
22		9	CL	H	Queens Park Rangers	L	0-1	0-1	22		9,016
23	1	13	FMC(SA)SF	H	Chelsea	L*	2-2	2-1		Valentine 13, Crooks 17	4,917
24		16	CL	A	Liverpool	L	1-4	1-1	22	Crooks 38	(28,407)
25		20	MC4	A	Aston Villa	D	2-2	1-0		Crooks 2, Bennett 51	(20,204)
26		23	CL	H	Arsenal	D	0-0	0-0	22		9,165
27		27	MC4R	H	Aston Villa	L	1-2	0-1		Hunt 69	18,868
28		30	CL	A	West Ham United	L	0-4	0-2	22		(16,325)
29	D	7	CL	H	Everton	L	0-3	0-2	22		12,206
30		14	CL	A	Oxford United	D	2-2	0-1	22	Hunt 56, Varadi 58	(9,020)
31		22	CL	H	Watford	W	3-1	1-0	22	Hunt (pen) 38, Dennison 71, Varadi 87	11,092
32		26	CL	H	Luton Town	L	1-2	1-2	22	Varadi 32	12,508
33		28	CL	A	Aston Villa	D	1-1	0-1	22	Hunt 77	(18,796)
34	J	1	CL	A	Southampton	L	1-3	0-0	22	Varadi 68	(13,154)
35		11	CL	H	Newcastle United	D	1-1	0-1	22	Varadi 53	9,106
36		13	FAC3	A	Sheffield Wednesday	D	2-2	1-1		Reilly 44, Statham 71	(17,042)
37		16	FAC3R	H	Sheffield Wednesday	L	2-3	1-2		Hunt 38, Thomas 66	11,152
38		18	CL	H	Chelsea	L	0-3	0-1	22		11,275
39	F	1	CL	A	Manchester City	L	1-2	0-1	22	Grealish 80	(20,540)
40		8	CL	H	Birmingham City	W	1-0	0-0	22	Bennett 80	(11,514)
41		22	CL	A	Manchester United	L	0-3	0-2	22		(45,193)
42	M	8	CL	A	Tottenham Hotspur	L	0-5	0-4	22		(10,841)
43		15	CL	H	Leicester City	D	2-2	1-1	22	Varadi 34, Mackenzie 59	8,337
44		19	CL	H	Coventry City	D	0-0	0-0	22		8,831
45		22	CL	A	Ipswich Town	L	0-1	0-0	22		(12,121)
46		29	CL	H	Southampton	W	1-0	0-0	22	Thompson 71	7,325
47	A	1	CL	H	Luton Town	L	0-3	0-2	22		(9,226)
48		5	CL	H	Nottingham Forest	D	1-1	0-1	22	Bennett 76	7,901
49		12	CL	A	Q.P.R.	L	0-1	0-0	22		(11,866)
50		19	CL	H	Liverpool	L	1-2	1-1	22	Madden 39	20,010
51		22	CL	H	Sheffield Wednesday	D	1-1	0-1	22	Reilly 57	6,201
52		26	CL	A	Arsenal	D	2-2	0-2	22	Reilly 81, 88	(14,843)
53	M	3	CL	H	West Ham United	L	2-3	1-2	22	Madden 30, Reilly (pen) 64	17,831

Best Home League Attendance: 25,068 v Manchester Utd 21/9   Smallest: 6,201 v Sheffield Wed 22/4   Av Home Att: 12,150

Goal Scorers: Compared with 84-85: −1,971

League (35): Varadi 9, Crooks 5, Hunt 4 (1 pen), Mackenzie 4, Reilly 4 (1 pen), Bennett 2, Madden 2, Valentine 2, Dennison 1, Grealish 1, Thompson 1

Milk Cup (10): Varadi 4, Crooks 2, Hunt 2, Armstrong 1, Bennett 1

FA CUP (4): Hunt 1, Reilly 1, Statham 1, Thomas 1

FM Cup (6): Crooks 3, Hunt 1, Nicholl 1, Valentine 1

1985-86

Nicholl	Statham	Whitehead	Bennett	Robertson	Grealish	Varadi	MacKenzie	Crooks	Valentine	Cowdrill	Hunt	Forsyth	Anderson	Robson	Armstrong	Dennison	Palmer	Thomas	Bradshaw	Reilly	Naylor	Thompson	Dyson	Bradley	Referee	
2	3	4	5	6	7	8	9	10*	11	12															N Ashley	1
2	10	7	5			8	9		11	3*	4	6	12												G Aplin	2
2	10	12	5	6*		8	9		11		3	4	7												M Bodenham	3
2	10		5			8	9		11		6	3	4	7											R Milford	4
5	10	2				8	9		11		6	3	4	7											D Axcell	5
2	3		6*	8	9	7		11				5	12	4	10										J Hough	6
2	3		10	8	9	7	11				6		12	4*	5										D Allison	7
2	3	5		9	11		6		7		4	8	10*	12											K Walmsley	8
2	3		5		9	11	10		4	6	8	7													M Scott	9
2	3		5		9*	11	10	6	4		12	8	7												J Ashworth	10
2	3	5	6	12	8	9*	11	7		4+							10								M Dimblebee	11
2	3	5	6	8	9	11	7		4									10	1						D Reeves	12
2	3*	12	5	6	8	9	11	7	4									10	1						J Worrall	13
2	3	12	5	6	4	9	11	7*		8								10	1						R Bridges	14
2	3	4	5	6	8	9	11	7										10	1						E Scales	15
	3	4	5	6	8	9	11	7									2	10	1						J Key	16
2	10		5		8	11*	7		4	6			12		9*		3								H Taylor	17
2	3	8*	5	6	9	11	7		4			12						10	1						N Wilson	18
2	3	5	6	8	9	11	7		4									10	1						C Downey	19
2	3	5	6	8	9	11	7		4									10	1						N Midgley	20
2	3	12	5	6*	8	9	11	7	4									10	1						D Scott	21
6+	3	2	5	8	9	11	7		4				12					10*	1						N Glover	22
	3	5	6	9	11	7*	4		12	8							2*					10			A Banks	23
2	3	5*	6	9	11	4	7				12						10					8			T Simpson	24
2	3	8	5	6	9	11	4		7*				12					10	1						K Hackett	25
	3*	8	5	6	9	11	4		12	7							2	10	1						J Deakin	26
	3	8	5	6	12	9	11	4		7*							2	10	1						J Worrall	27
2	8*	5	6	7	9	12	11	3	4									10	1						J Martin	28
2		5	6*	8	7			3	4		12							10		9					R Gifford	29
2	3	5	6	11	8	7			4									10		9					R Groves	30
2	3	5	6	7*	8	11	4		12									10		9					T Fitzharris	31
2	3	5	6	7*	8	11	4		12									10		9					A Robinson	32
2*	3	5	6	8	7	4			12									10		9			11		H King	33
2	3	5	6	8	7	4*			12									10		9			11		D Hedges	34
2	3	5	6	8	7*				11									10		9			12		P Tyldesley	35
2	3	5	6	8					11									10		9	7				K Walmsley	36
2	3	5*	6	8		4			11									10		9	7				K Walmsley	37
2	3				8*			11		4	6					9	5	10			7				K Cooper	38
2	3	6		7	8*	12			4								5	10		9					M Scott	39
2	3	5		7	12	10*			4		6					8				9					H Taylor	40
2	3	6		12	8	11			4		7					10*	5		1	9					G Tyson	41
2	5	6		11*	8			4		3								10		9			12		L Shapter	42
	3	2				8			10				4						1	9	7	5	11		J Worrall	43
	3	2				8			10				4						1	9	7	5	11		A Ward	44
	3	2							10		12		4						1	9	7	5	11*		M James	45
	3	2							10				4						1	9	7	5	11		L Dilkes	46
	3	2				12		9*	10				4						1		7	5	11		A Ward	47
	3	2	6						10		12		4						1	9	7*	5	11		C Trussell	48
2	10		6				9			3			4						1		7*	5	11		A Gunn	49
	3	2			7		9		11		12		4				8		1			5		6*	R Lewis	50
		2			7		9				12		4				8		1		6	5			T Jones	51
		2	6			8				3	12		4						1	9	7*	5	11		B Stevens	52
	3	2				8*					12		4	6					1	9		5	11		Alan Robinson	53
29	37	22	25	20	14	30	30	18	15	9	19	11	7	9	7	7	16	20	8	20	12	13	11	10	League Appearances	
	2			2	2	1	1		1				4	5	1	5	4			2					Substitute Appearances	
5	6	2-2	5	6	3-1	5	1	6	4	1	6		0-1	1	2	1	1-1	5	5						Milk Cup Appearances	
2	2		2	2		2				1							2	1	2	2	2		1-1		FA Cup Appearances	
2	2	1	3	2	2		2	3	3		3	1	0-1	1-1	1		2	1	1			2	1+1		FM Cup Appearances	

so Played: Position(Game): Powell 1(17) FMC, Bull 12(17, 23, 49), Owen 4(35, 36) 12(37, 38), 11 (39, 40), Robinson (A) 11(51), Dickinson 7(42, 53) 6(43, 44, 45, 46†, 47), Madden 8(45, 46, 47, 48, 49) 10(50, 51, 52, 53), Grew (L) 1(38)

ayers on Loan: Grew (Ipswich)

partures: Valentine (F), Hunt (Aston V), Forsyth (Derby), Bradshaw (F), Godden (Chelsea), Owen (F), Armstrong (Brighton), Nicholl (Glasgow Rangers)

'THROSTLES'

Formed: 1879
Turned Professional: 1885   **Ltd Co:** 1892

Previous Managers: From the time that the club turned professional, no manager was appointed until 1948. Secretary/Managers before that time were: 1885-7 Thomas Foster   1887-90 Louis Ford   1890-2 Louis Ford/W Pierre Dix   1892-4 Henry 'Swin' Jackson   1894-5 E Stephenson   1892-95 Clement Keys   1896-1902 W Frank Heaven   1902-48 Fred Everiss   1948-52 Jack Smith   1952 Jesse Carver, Manager/Coach   1953-9 Vic Buckingham   1959-61 Gordon Clark   1961-3 Archie Macaulay   1963-7 Jimmy Hagan   1967-71 Alan Ashman   1971-5 Don Howe   1975-7 Johnny Giles   1977 Ronnie Allen   1978-81 Ron Atkinson   1981-2 Ronnie Allen   1982-4 Ron Wylie   1984-5 J Giles

Honours: Champions Div 1, 1919-20   Champions Div 2, 1901-2, 1910-1   FA Cup Winners 1888, 1892, 1931, 1954, 1968   Football League Cup Winners 1966

League Career: Founder Members of Football League 1888   Relegated to Div 2 1900-1   Promoted to Div 1 1901-2   Relegated to Div 2 1903-4   Promoted to Div 1 1910-1   Relegated to Div 2 1926-7   Promoted to Div 1 1930-1   Relegated to Div 2 1937-8   Promoted to Div 1 1948-9   Relegated to Div 2 1972-3   Promoted to Div 1 1975-6   Relegated to Div 2 1985-6

Colours: Navy blue and white stripes, white shorts and stockings

Change Colours: All red

Reserves League: Central   **'A' Team:** Midland Intermediate   **Youth Team:** Sunblest Youth Cup

---

CLUB RECORDS

Most Appearances for Club: Tony Brown: Football League 561 + 13 + FA Cup 53 + 1 + League Cup 46 + 1 + European Competitions 16 + Charity Shield 1 + Other Senior Competitions 27 **Total 704 + 16 subs**

Most Capped Player: Stuart Williams, 33, Wales   **For England:** Jesse Pennington 25

Record Goalscorer in a Match: Jimmy Cookson, 6 v Blackpool, 6-3, Div 2, 17.09.1927

Record League Goalscorer in a Season: W G Richardson, 39   **In All Competitions:** W G Richardson, 40 (League 39 + FA Cup 1), 1935-6

Record League Goalscorer in a Career: Tony Brown, 218   **In All Competitions:** Tony Brown, 278 (League 218 + FA Cup 27 + League Cup 16 + European Competitions 8, Other Senior Competitions 9) 1963-79

Record Transfer Fee Received: £1,500,000 from Manchester United for Bryan Robson, Oct 1981

Record Transfer Fee Paid: £748,000 to Manchester City for Peter Barnes, July 1979

Best Performances: League: Champions Div 1 1919-20   **FA Cup:** Winners (5)   **League/Milk Cup:** Winners (1)   **EUWC:** Quarter-Final   **UEFA CUP:** Quarter-Final   **Charity Shield:** Runners-Up

Most League Points: (2pts for win) 60, Div 1, 1929-30   **Most League Goals:** 105, Div 2, 1929-30

Record League Victory and Most Goals Scored in a League Match: 12-0 v Darwen, Div 1, 4 April 1892

Most Goals Scored in a Cup Tie: 10-1 v Chatham (a), 3rd Round FA Cup, 2 March 1889

Record League Defeat: 3-10 v Stoke City, Div 1, 4 Feb 1937

European Competitions Entered: European Cup Winners Cup 1968-9   UEFA Cup 1978-9, 1979-80, 1981-2   Fairs Cup 1966-7

Oldest Player in League Match:

Youngest Player in League Match:

Most Consecutive Undefeated League Matches: 17 1901-02, 1957

Longest Run of Undefeated Home League Matches: 19 1901-02, 1908-09

Longest Run Without Home League Win: 9 1921, 1971

Most Consecutive League Wins: 11 1930

Most Consecutive League Defeats: 9 1985

League Matches Without a Win: 12 1985

Away League Matches: 11 1957, 1980

Away League Win: 27 1969-71

Home League Wins: 11 1906-07

Away League Wins: 7 1953

Club Statistician for the Directory: Tony Matthews

PLAYERS NAME Wt Birthdate	Honours	Birthplace Transfers	Clubs	League	Milk Cup	FA Cup	Other Comps	League	Milk Cup	FA Cup	Other Comps
GOALKEEPERS											
Stuart Naylor 11.13 6.12.62	EY	Leeds	Yorkshire Amateurs								
			Lincoln City	4	2	1	4				
			Peterborough United (L)	8							
			Crewe Alexandra (L)	75	5	3	5				
			Lincoln City	45	2	1	6				
			West Bromwich Albion	12							
DEFENDERS											
Colin Anderson 10.2 26.4.62		Newcastle	Burnley (A)								
			Torquay United	97+2	5	7	3	10			
			QPR (L)								
			West Bromwich Albion	7+4	0+1		0+1				
Martin Bennett* 12.12 4.8.61	ES	Birmingham	WBA	159+1	17	13	3	6	1		
Gary Cowdrill 11.4 3.1.57		Birmingham £25,000	Sutton Coldfield Town								
			West Bromwich Albion	67+3	8+1	5					
			Rotherham United (L)	2							
Paul Dyson 13.7 27.12.59	EU21 (4)	Birmingham	Coventry City	140	14	12		5			
			Stoke City	106	10	4	3	5			
			West Bromwich Albion	11		1+1					
Derek Statham ½ 11.1 24.3.59	E (3), B (2), FAYC 76, U21 (6), Y	Wolverhampton	West Bromwich Albion	291+1	35	25	2			1	
Steve Whitehead 0½ 11.4 24.11.55	EY	Birmingham £100,000	Bristol City	209+20	17+3	10		10	2	2	
			West Bromwich Albion	123+10	12+2	9	1	3	1	2	
			Wolverhampton W. (L)	2		2					
MIDFIELD											
Darren Bradley 11.2 24.11.65		Birmingham	Aston Villa (A)	16+4	3	3					
			West Bromwich Albion	10							
Martin Dickinson 11.9 14.3.63		Leeds	Leeds United	100+3	10	6		1			
			West Bromwich Albion	7							
Tony Grealish 11.7 21.9.56	EI (47), Y	Paddington	Orient (A)	169+2	6+1	17		10			
			Luton Town	78	5	3		2			
			Brighton & H.A.	95+5		7	13			6	2
			West Bromwich Albion	55+10	7+1	1	2	4			
Steve Mackenzie 11.6 23.11.61	E B (1), U21 (3), Y, FAYC 78	Romford £250,000 £650,000	Crystal Palace (A)								
			Manchester City	56+2	11	8		8		2	
			West Bromwich Albion	123+3	15+2	7	2	21	1	1	
FORWARDS											
Garth Crooks 10.3 10.3.58	EU21 (4), FAC 81, 82	Stoke £600,000 £100,000	Stoke City (A)	141+6	10+2	3+2		48	11	1	
			Tottenham Hotspur	121+4	17+1	18	14	48	9	9	9
			Manchester United (L)	6+1	2	3		2			
			West Bromwich Albion	18+1	6		3	5	2		3
Craig Madden 10.2 25.9.58		Manchester	Northern Nomads								
			Bury	278	18	19+1	2	130	10	11	1
			West Bromwich Albion	9				2			
Stewart Evans 11.5 15.11.60	Div. 4, 83	Maltby F £6,000	Rotherham United (A)								
			Gainsborough Trinity								
			Sheffield United								
			Wimbledon	165+10	13	9	1	50	13	2	
Bobby Williamson 11.0 3.8.61		Glasgow	Clydebank	66+2	14	1		26	7		
			Glasgow Rangers	36+6	5	6	1+1	12	6	4	
		Player exch.	West Bromwich Albion								
George Reilly 13.5 14.9.57		Bellshill	Corby Town								
		£140,000	Northampton Town	124+3	13	4		46	9		
		£100,000	Cambridge United	136+2	7	8		36	1	2	
		£200,000	Watford	46+2	4	8		13	1	4	
			Newcastle United	31	2			10			
			West Bromwich Albion	20		2		4		1	
Imre Varadi 11.1 8.7.59		Paddington	Letchworth GC								
		£80,000	Sheffield United	6+4				4			
		£100,000	Everton	22+4		6		6			
		£150,000	Newcastle United	81	4	5		39	1	2	
		£285,000	Sheffield Wednesday	72+4	12	7		33	1	4	
			West Bromwich Albion	44	6		3	6			1

ADDITIONAL CONTRACT PROFESSIONALS

Ian Hayward, Stephen Bull, Mark Dearlove, David Powell, Carlton Palmer, Gary Robson, Andy Thompson, Robert Dennison

THE HAWTHORNS West Bromwich B71 4LF   **Capacity:** 39,159 (12,500 seats)

Record Attendance: 64,815 v Arsenal, FA Cup Round 6, 6 Mar 1937

Smallest Home Attendance for a First Class Match: 405 v Derby County, Div 1, 29 Nov 1890. Since 1946: 6,536 v Nottingham Forest, Milk Cup 2nd Round, 2nd Leg, 27 Oct 1982

Record Receipts: £79,494.76 v Tottenham Hotspur, League Cup Semi-Final, 3 Feb 1982

Season Tickets: Stands: £65.00 to £96.00; Ground: £40.00 to £44.00 (Reductions for juveniles/OAP)

Cost of Stand Tickets: £3.70, £4.00, £4.30, £4.50, £5.00, £5.50, £6.00; **Terraces:** £2.50 & £2.70 (juveniles/OAP £1.50 & £1.60)

Match and Ticket Information: Six weeks in advance for Centre & Wing stands by post with remittance & SAE. Telephone only two days before for tickets to be collected not less than 30 minutes before kick-off. Limited availability of unreserved seats on day of match

Car Parking: Street parking in some areas within 10 minutes walk of ground

Nearest Railway Station: Rolfe St Smethwick (1¼ miles)

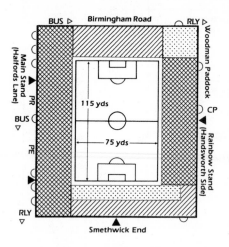

How to get to the ground

From all directions: Use Motorway M5 until junction 1. Leave motorway and follow signs Birmingham A41 into Loop Road for West Bromwich Albion FC

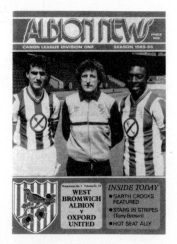

Price of 1986-7 Programme: 60p
Number of Pages: 24

Local Newspapers: Sandwell Evening Mail, Birmingham Post and Evening Mail, Express and Star Wolverhampton

Local Radio Stations: BRMB Radio, Radio WM, Beacon Radio, Mercia Sound

WEST HAM UNITED — Division 1

Chairman
L C Cearns

Directors
W F Cearns
B R Cearns, FCIS
J Petchey
M W Cearns

Secretary
K Godbee JP, BSc(Econ), FCA
as from 1/7/86
Mr Eddie Chapman retired on 30/6/86
(01-472 2740)

PRO
Jack Helliar

Manager
John Lyall

Chief Scout
E Baily

Commercial Manager
B C Blower(01-472 7352)

A marvellous season for West Ham who in finishing third gained their highest ever placing in Division One. The season started badly with only one win in the first five games. New signing Frank McAvennie however had scored twice against both QPR and Liverpool to give clear warning of his intentions. Hammers then went 18 successive league games without defeat until they lost by a single goal at Tottenham on Boxing Day. The run included a victory over the champions Everton, five successive away wins and four goals against Forest, Villa and West Bromwich. The one defeat in this period was by 1-0 to Manchester United in the Milk Cup. Gale and Martin were forming a brilliant partnership at the back, Devonshire was back to his best after nearly two years out of the game, and new signing Mark Ward added to West Ham's tougher approach with his non-stop running and tackling. Both strikers Cottee and McAvennie were scoring regularly as the Hammers approached the New Year. Live soccer returned to our screens to show West Ham gain a lucky FA Cup win over Charlton. A marathon three game meeting with Ipswich followed, where a late Cottee winner in the snow put Hammers through to the 5th round. West Ham were paired with Cup holders Manchester United and after a 1-1 draw Hammers put on a superb display at Old Trafford to win 2-0.

The euphoria soon turned to disappointment however as three days later a lethargic first half display at Hillsborough saw Hammers FA Cup hopes dashed by Sheffield Wednesday. The morale was low as within a week, League games at Arsenal and Aston Villa were lost, vital games which on reflection cost West Ham the title.

At Easter further victories over London rivals Chelsea and Spurs were gained, the 4-0 win at Stamford Bridge being particularly rewarding. The return clash with Chelsea however brought disappointment when 'The Blues' won 2-1. The Hammers of 86 are built of sterner stuff as they bounced back with a 2-0 win at Watford. With four home games in only nine days to follow the team needed determination, luck and an injury-free spell. First Newcastle were annihilated 8-1, then two narrow 1-0 wins were gained over Coventry and Manchester City as both players and fans found the tension unbearable. The final home game of the season saw 31,000 packed into Upton Park and a dramatic late penalty winner by Ray Stewart gave West Ham a 2-1 win over Ipswich. On the final Saturday of the season Hammers won 3-2 at West Bromwich, the celebrations were short lived as the news came through that Liverpool had won at Chelsea to clinch the championship.

John Lyall, his staff and all the players should be congratulated on such a fine season. The squad played entertaining football throughout and added a degree of self-belief to their game which made them hard to beat. The reserves won the Football Combination scoring 141 goals which makes the future look bright at Upton Park.

Back Row L to R: Steve Walford, Paul Milton, Tom McAlister, John Vaughan, Phil Parkes, Alvin Martin, Tony Gale. **Middle Row:** Alan Dickens, Neil Orr, Gregory Campbell, Billy Bonds, George Parris, Ray Stewart, Steve Whitton, Alan Devonshire, Paul McMenemy. **Front Row:** Mark Ward, Geoff Pike, Paul Goddard, Frank McAvennie, Tony Cottee, Kevin Keen, Steve Potts.

WEST HAM UNITED

DIVISION ONE: 3rd　　　　**FA CUP:** 6th ROUND　　　　**MILK CUP:** 3rd ROUND

MATCH	DATE	COMPE-TITION	VENUE	OPPONENTS	RESULT		HALF TIME	L'GUE POS'N	GOALSCORERS/GOAL TIMES	ATTEN-DANCE
1	A 17	CL	A	Birmingham City	L	0-1	0-0			(11,164)
2	20	CL	H	Queens Park Rangers	W	3-1	2-0		McAvennie 10, 66, Dickens 64	15,530
3	24	CL	H	Luton Town	L	0-1	0-0	14		14,104
4	26	CL	A	Manchester United	L	0-2	0-0			(50,773)
5	31	CL	H	Liverpool	D	2-2	1-0	17	McAvennie 21, 71	19,762
6	S 3	CL	A	Southampton	D	1-1	0-0		McAvennie 81	(14,477)
7	7	CL	A	Sheffield Wednesday	D	2-2	1-1	17	McAvennie 9, Cottee 88	(19,287)
8	14	CL	H	Leicester City	W	3-0	1-0	13	McAvennie 31, Devonshire 46, Cottee 70	12,125
9	21	CL	A	Manchester City	D	2-2	2-1	13	Cottee 7, McCarthy (o.g) 41	(22,001)
10	24	MC2/1	H	Swansea City	W	3-0	0-0		Cottee 48, McAvennie 56, Stewart pen 90	9,282
11	28	CL	H	Nottingham Forest	W	4-2	3-0	13	Cottee 6, McAvennie 12, 20, Dickens 59	15,540
12	O 5	CL	A	Newcastle United	W	2-1	2-0	11	McAvennie 12, Cottee 25	(26,709)
13	8	MC2/2	A	Swansea City	W	3-2	3-2		Stewart (pen) 11 (pen) 43, Cottee 13	(3,584)
14	12	CL	H	Arsenal	D	0-0	0-0	11		24,057
15	19	CL	H	Aston Villa	W	4-1	2-1	7	McAvennie 23, 79, Cottee 34, 57	15,034
16	26	CL	A	Ipswich Town	W	1-0	1-0	7	Cottee 26	(16,849)
17	29	MC3	A	Manchester United	L	0-1	0-0			(32,057)
18	N 2	CL	H	Everton	W	2-1	0-0	6	McAvennie 74, 81	23,844
19	9	CL	A	Oxford United	W	2-1	1-1	5	Cottee 38, Ward 68	(13,140)
20	16	CL	H	Watford	W	1-0	1-0	4	McAvennie 27, Ward 56	21,490
21	23	CL	A	Coventry City	W	1-0	0-0	4	McAvennie 55	(11,042)
22	30	CL	H	W.B.A.	W	4-0	2-0	3	Cottee 12, Parris 31, Devonshire 47, Orr 66	16,325
23	D 7	CL	A	Queens Park Rangers	W	1-0	0-0	3	McAvennie 73	(23,500)
24	14	CL	H	Birmingham City	W	2-0	2-0	3	McAvennie 37, Stewart (pen) 40	17,481
25	21	CL	A	Luton Town	D	0-0	0-0	3		(14,599)
26	26	CL	A	Tottenham Hotspur	L	0-1	0-0	5		(33,835)
27	J 5	FAC3	A	Charlton Athletic	W	1-0	0-0		Cottee 88	(13,037)
28	11	CL	A	Leicester City	W	1-0	0-0	4	McAvennie 54	(11,359)
29	18	CL	A	Liverpool	L	1-3	0-0	5	Dickens 82	(41,056)
30	25	FAC4	H	Ipswich Town	D	0-0	0-0			25,035
31	F 2	CL	H	Manchester United	W	2-1	0-1	5	Ward 62, Cottee 76	22,642
32	4	FAC4R	A	Ipswich Town	D	1-1†	0-0		Cottee 106	25,384
33	6	FAC4 2R	A	Ipswich Town	W	1-0†	0-0		Cottee 111	(14,515)
34	M 5	FAC5	H	Manchester United	D	1-1	1-0		McAvennie 25	26,441
35	9	FAC5R	A	Manchester United	W	2-0	1-0		Pike 18, Stewart (pen) 54	(30,441)
36	12	FAC6	A	Sheffield Wednesday	L	1-2	0-2		Cottee 48	(35,522)
37	15	CL	A	Arsenal	L	0-1	0-0	7		(31,240)
38	19	CL	A	Aston Villa	L	1-2	1-1	7	Hunt (og) 2	(11,567)
39	22	CL	H	Sheffield Wednesday	W	1-0	1-0	7	McAvennie 6	16,604
40	29	CL	A	Chelsea	W	4-0	1-0	6	Devonshire 23, Cottee 55, 64, McAvennie 68	(29,955)
41	31	CL	H	Tottenham Hotspur	W	2-1	2-1	5	Cottee 17, McAvennie 43	27,497
42	A 2	CL	A	Nottingham Forest	L	1-2	0-1	5	Cottee 69	(17,498)
43	8	CL	H	Southampton	W	1-0	1-0	5	Martin 26	22,459
44	12	CL	H	Oxford United	W	3-1	0-1	5	Trewick (og) 49, McAvennie 65, Stewart (pen) 81	23,956
45	15	CL	H	Chelsea	L	1-2	0-0	5	Cottee 51	29,361
46	19	CL	A	Watford	W	2-0	0-0	5	Cottee 59, McAvennie 89	(16,651)
47	21	CL	H	Newcastle United	W	8-1	4-0	4	Martin 3 (3,64, pen 84) Stewart 11, Orr 35 Roeder og 43, Goddard 81, McAvennie 83	24,735
48	26	CL	H	Coventry City	W	1-0	0-0	4	Cottee 61	27,251
49	28	CL	H	Manchester City	W	1-0	1-0	3	Stewart (pen) 19	27,153
50	30	CL	H	Ipswich Town	W	2-1	0-0	2	Dickens 72, Stewart (pen) 86	31,121
51	M 3	CL	A	W.B.A.	W	3-2	2-1	2	McAvennie 6, Cottee 24, Stewart (pen) 82	(17,651)
52	5	CL	A	Everton	L	1-3	0-1	3	Cottee 89	(40,073)

Best Home League Attendance: 31,121 v Ipswich T. 30/4　　**Smallest:** 12,125 v Leicester 14/9　　**Av Home Att:** 21,337

Goal Scorers:　　　　　　　　　　　　　　　　　　　　　　　　　　**Compared with 84-85:** +2,902

League (74): McAvennie 26, Cottee 20, Stewart 6 (5 pen), Dickens 4, Martin 4 (1 pen), Devonshire 3, Ward 3, Orr 2, Goddard 1, Parris 1, Opponents 4

Milk Cup (6): Stewart 3 (3 pens), Cottee 2, McAvennie 1

FA Cup (7): Cottee 4, McAvennie 1, Pike 1, Stewart 1 (pen)

†A.E.T.

Stewart	Walford	Gale	Martin	Devonshire	Ward	McAvennie	Goddard	Cottee	Orr	Dickens	Campbell	Parris	Barnes	Potts	Pike	Hilton	Referee	
2	3	4	5	6	7	8	9*	10	11	12							N Glover	1
2	3	4	5	6	7	8		10	11	9							M James	2
2	3	4	5	6	8	9		11*	7	10	12						T Holbrook	3
2	3	4	5	6	7	8		10*	11	9	12						R Bridges	4
2	3	4	5	6	7	8		10	11	9							B Hill	5
2	3	4	5	6	7	8		12	11	9	10*						J Deakin	6
2	3	4	5		7	8*		10	11	9		6	12				N Midgley	7
2	3	4	5	6	7	9		10	11	8							I Borrett	8
2	3	4	5	6	7	8		10	11	9							M Robinson	9
2	**3**	**4**	**5**	**6**	**7**	**8**		**10**	**11**	**9**							**A Gunn**	**10**
2	3	4	5	6	7	8		10	11	9							D Axcell	11
2	3	4	5	6	7	8		10	11	9							D Scott	12
2	**3**	**4**	**5**	**6**	**7**	**8***		**10**	**11**	**9**	**12**						**R Groves**	**13**
2	3	4	5	6	7	8		10	11	9*	12						Allan Robinson	14
2	3	4	5	6	7	8		10	11	9							M Bodenham	15
	3	4	5	6*	7	8		10	11	9		2	12				M Scott	16
2	**3**	**4**	**5**	**6**	**7**	**8**		**10**	**11**	**9***	**12**						**F Roberts**	**17**
2	3*	4	5	6	7	8		10	11	9	12						A Seville	18
2	3	4	5	6	7	8		10	11	9							J Ball	19
2	3	4	5	6	7	8		10	11	9							H Taylor	20
2	3	4	5	6	7	8		10	11	9							J Worrall	21
2	3	4	5	6	7			10	11	9	8						J Martin	22
2	3	4	5	6	7	8		10	11	9							J Bray	23
2	3*	4	5	6	7	8		10	11	9	12						L Shapter	24
2	3	4	5	6	7	8		10	11	9							D Hedges	25
2	3	4	5	6	7	8		10	11	9	4						C Downey	26
2	**3**	**4**	**5**	**6**	**7**	**8**		**10**		**9**	**11**						**B Hill**	**27**
2	3	4	5	6	7	8		10		9	11						A Robinson	28
2†	3	4	5	6	7	8		10		9	11						G Tyson	29
2	**3**	**4**	**5**	**6**	**7**	**8**		**10**		**9**	**11**						**J Martin**	**30**
	3	4	5	6	7	8		10		9		2		11			J Ball	31
	3*	4	5	6	7	8		10	12	9		2		11			**J Martin**	**32**
		4	5		7	8		10	6	9		2		11			**K Baker**	**33**
		4	5	6	7	8		10		9		3		11			**B Stevens**	**34**
		4	5	6	7	8		10		9		3		11			**B Stevens**	**35**
		4	5	6	7	8		10		9		3		11			**J Worrall**	**36**
		4	5†	6	7	8		10		9		3		11			J Borrett	37
	3	4	5		7	8	12	10*	6	9		2		11			K Walmsley	38
		4	5		7	8	12	10*	6	9		3		11			K Barratt	39
		4		6*	7	8		10	12	9		3		11	5		R Lewis	40
		4		6*	7	8		10	12	9		3		11	5		B Hill	41
		4	5		7	8		10	6	9		3		11			L Dilkes	42
		4	5	6	7	8		10		9		3		11			P Vanes	43
		4	5	6	7	8		10		9		3		11			N Butler	44
		4*	5	6	7	8		10	12	9		3		11			M Bodenham	45
		4	5	6	7	8		10	11	9		3					J Bray	46
		4	5	6	7	8	12	10	11	9*		3					T Hamer	47
		4	5	6	7	8		10	11	9		3					I Hemley	48
		4	5	6	7	8		10	11	9		3					R Gifford	49
		4	5	6	7	8	12	10	11*	9		3					G Ashby	50
		4	5	6	7	8		10	11	9		3					Alan Robinson	51
		4	5	6	7	8	12	10	11	9*		3					G Courtney	52
42	39	27	**42**	40	38	**42**	41	1	41	33	40	1	23		10	2	League Appearances	
							5	1	3		2	3	1	1			Substitute Appearances	
3	3	3	3	3	3	3		3	3	3	0·2						Milk Cup Appearances	
7	6	3	7	7	6	7		7	1·1	7		7		5			FA Cup Appearances	

Also Played:

Players on Loan:

Departures: McPherson, Donald (Northampton Town), Brush (Crystal Palace), Barnes (Aldershot), Whitton (Birmingham City)

'THE HAMMERS'

Formed: 1900
Turned Professional: 1900 **Ltd Co:** 1900

Previous Managers: 1900-31 Syd King   1931-50 Charlie Paynter   1950-61 Ted Fenton
1961-74 Ron Greenwood
Honours: Champions Div 2, 1957-8, 1980-1   FA Cup Winners 1964, 1975, 1980
League Career: Elected to Div 2 1919   Promoted to Div 1 1922-3
Relegated to Div 2 1931-2   Promoted to Div 1 1957-8   Relegated to Div 2 1977-8
Promoted to Div 1 1980-1
Colours: Claret shirts with sky blue and white trim and three sky blue stipes down sleeves, white shorts
and stockings
Change Colours: White shirts with three claret stripes down sleeves, blue shorts with three claret
stripes, white stockings
Reserves League: Football Combination   **Youth Team:** S E Counties

CLUB RECORDS

Most Appearances for Club: Billy Bonds: Football League 620 + 4 + FA Cup 41 + 1 + League Cup 64 + European Cup
Winners Cup 15 **Total 740 + 5 subs**
Most Capped Player: Bobby Moore, 108 for England
Record Goalscorer in a Match: Geoff Hurst, 6 v Sunderland, 8-0, Div 1, 19.10.68   Vic Watson, 6 v Leeds United, 8-2,
Div 1, 9.2.29
Record League Goalscorer in a Season: Vic Watson, 42   **In All Competitions:** Vic Watson, 50 (League 42, FA Cup 8)
1929-30
Record League Goalscorer in a Career: Vic Watson, 298   **In All Competitions:** Vic Watson, 326 (League 298 + FA Cu
28)
Record Transfer Fee Received: £400,000 from Tottenham Hotspur for Paul Allen, June 1985
Record Transfer Fee Paid: £800,000 to QPR for Paul Goddard, August 1979
Best Performances: League: 3rd Div 1 1985-86   **FA Cup:** Winners (3)   **League/Milk Cup:** Runners Up 1966,
1981   **European Cup Winners Cup:** Winners 1965
Most League Points: (2pts for win) 66, Div 2, 1980-1   **Most League Goals:** 101, Div 2, 1957-8
Record League Victory: 8-0 v Rotherham United, Div 2, 8 March 1958   8-0 v Sunderland, Div 1, 19 Oct 1968
Most Goals Scored in a Cup Tie: 10-0 v Bury, (H), Milk Cup 2nd Round 2nd Leg, 25 Oct 1984
Most Goals Conceded in a League Match: 2-8 v Blackburn Rovers (h), Div 1, 26 Dec 1963
Record League Defeat: 0-7 v Sheffield Wednesday (a), Div 1, 28 Nov 1959   0-7 v Everton (a), Div 1, 22 Oct
1927   0-7 v Barnsley (a) Div 2, 1 Sept 1919
European Competitions Entered: European Cup Winners Cup (4) 1964-5, 1965-6, 1975-6, 1980-1
Oldest Player in League Match: Billy Bonds 39 yrs 8 months
Youngest Player in League Match: Paul Allen 17 yrs 1 month
Most Consecutive Undefeated League Matches: 27 1980-81   **League Matches Without a Win:** 17 1976
Longest Run of Undefeated Home League Matches: 27 1980-81   **Away League Matches:** 13 1981
Longest Run Without Home League Win: 10 1973, 1984-85   **Away League Win:** 31 1932-33
Most Consecutive League Wins: 9 1985   **Home League Wins:** 16 1980-81
Most Consecutive League Defeats: 9 1932   **Away League Wins:** 5 1922-23, 1935-36,
1985

Club Statistician for the Directory: John Northcutt (Secretary of West Ham Statisticians Group, 7 Bells Chase, Great
Baddow, Chelmsford, Essex)

WEST HAM UNITED

ERS NAME / Wt Birthdate	Honours	Birthplace / Transfers	Clubs	APPEARANCES League	Milk Cup	FA Cup	Other Comps	GOALS League	Milk Cup	FA Cup	Other Comps
LKEEPERS											
McAllister 12.13 10.12.52		Clydebank	Sheffield United (A)	63	6	2					
		£15,000	Rotherham United	159	12	14					
		£50,000	Blackpool	16	4						
		F	Swindon Town	1							
			Bristol Rovers (L)	13							
		F	West Ham United	35	5	5					
Parkes 14.9 8.8.50	E (1), B (1), U23 (6), FAC 80, Div. 2, 73, 81	Sedgeley	Walsall	52	1	7					
		£15,000	QPR	344	27	27	8				
		£500,000	West Ham United	275	36	25	6				
ENDERS											
Bonds 13.2 17.9.46	EU23 (2), Div. 2, 81, FAC 75, 80	Woolwich	Charlton Athletic (A)	95	3	2		1			
			West Ham United	620+4	64	41+1	15	48	6	2	3
Gale 12.4 19.11.59	EU21 (1)	London	Fulham (A)	277	22	16		19	2		
		£200,000	West Ham United	78+1	6	7					
Martin 13.0 29.7.58	E (16), B (2), YFAC 80, Div. 2, 81	Bootle	West Ham United (A)								
			West Ham United	283+2	41	26	6	20	3		
Orr 12.2 13.5.59	SU21 (7), SD1 (1)	Greenock	Morton	180+6	10	14					
		£400,000	West Ham United	111+12	10+4	9+1		3	1		
rge Parris 12.7 11.9.64		Essex	West Ham United (A)	24+3	0+2	7		1			
Stewart 12.0 7.9.59	S (7), U21 (12), FAC 80, Div. 2, 81	Perth	Dundee United	44	8	1	1	4			
			West Ham United	278	40	28	6	52	13	7	1
e Walford 11.7 5.1.58	EY, FAC 79	Highgate	Tottenham Hotspur (A)	1+1							
			Arsenal	64+13	5	5		3	1		
			Norwich City	93	8	7		2			
		£165,000	West Ham United	101	12	11		2	2		
FIELD											
Devonshire 11.0 13.4.56	E (9), B (1), FAC 80, Div. 2, 81	London	Southall								
		£5,000	West Ham United	307+3	37	26	4	27	2	1	
Dickens 12.0 3.9.64	EU21 (1)	Plaistow	West Ham United (A)								
			West Ham United	83+7	4+2	12		12		2	
Hilton 11.6 8.10.59	EY	Oldham	Bury	136+12	2+3	16					
		£75,000	West Ham United	14+5		1+1		3			
ff Pike 11.3 28.9.56	FAC 80, Div. 2, 81	Clapton	West Ham United (A)								
			West Ham United	265+15	37+1	25+2	6	32	3	5	1
k Ward 10.0 10.10.62		Huyton	Everton (A)								
			Northwich Victoria			3			2		
		£10,000	Oldham Athletic	84	5	3		12			
		£250,000	West Ham United	42	3	7		3			
WARDS											
g Campbell 12.0 13.7.65		Portsmouth	West Ham United (A)	3+2							
Cottee† 11.5 11.7.65	EU21 (8), Y	West Ham	West Ham United (A)								
			West Ham United	121+9	11	17		57	9	8	
Goddard 11.8 12.10.59	E (1), U21 (8), Div. 2, 81	Harlington	QPR (A)	63+7	4+1						
		£800,000	West Ham United	156+10	25	10+1	6	53	11	3	2
k McAvennie 11.4 22.11.59	S (4), U21 (5), Y	Glasgow	St. Mirren	99+2	18	16		32	7	5	
		£340,000	West Ham United	41	3	7		26	1	1	
e Whitton 12.7 4.12.60		London	Coventry City (A)	64+10	2+2	3		21			
		£175,000	West Ham United	35+4	6	1		6	2		

DITIONAL CONTRACT PROFESSIONALS

nmon Dolan (F), Paul Ince (F), Kevin Keen (MF), Paul McMenemy (F), L. Aldershot (10Lge + 5GLS), Robert Mayes (F), Steve Potts (MF), (1+1Lge).

PRENTICES

Bracey, Simon Livett, Stuart Slater, John Strain

N-CONTRACT PLAYERS

Record Attendance: 42,322 v Tottenham Hotspur, Div 1, 17 Oct 1970

Smallest Home Attendance for a First Class Match: 4,500 v Doncaster Rovers, Div 2, 24 Feb 1958

Record Receipts: £122,268 v Manchester United, FA Cup Round 5, 5 March 1986

Season Tickets: Stand: £127, £138; Ground: £77

Executive Room Season Tickets: £400 per person

Cost of Stand Tickets: £8.00, £7.00, £6.50, (Upper Tier); £8.00, £7.00, £5.00; (Lower Tier); £8.00 (East Stand); **Ground:** East Terrace: £4.50 (Adults and Children), North & South Banks: £3.50 (Adults), £2.00 (Children & OAP's)

Match and Ticket Information: Advance bookings personally by telephone or by post are accepted one month before each League match

Car Parking: Ample side-street parking available

Nearest Railway Station: Upton Park (District Line Tube)

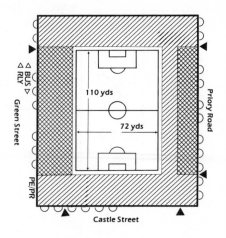

How to get to the ground

From North and West: Use A406 North Circular Road, then A104 to Leytonstone, then follow A114 to Forest Gate Station and shortly at T road turn left then shortly turn right B167 into Green Street for West Ham United FC
From East: Use A13 (S.P. London) then at crossroads turn right A117. In 0.9m at crossroads turn left A124. In 0.6m turn right into Green Street for West Ham United FC
From South: Use Blackwall Tunnel and A13 to Canning Town, then follow signs East Ham A124. In 1.7m turn left into Green Street for West Ham United FC

Price of 1986-7 Programme: 60p
Number of Pages: 24
Subscriptions:

Local Newspapers: Stratford Express, Ilford Recorder

Local Radio Stations: Essex Radio, LBC

S o near and yet so far. That is the story of Wigan Athletic in 1985/86, when much was promised and by the end of the season, nothing was won.

The season started well enough with an away win at Swansea and good home wins over Brentford (4-0) and Darlington (5-1).

However by Christmas 'Latics' were unbeaten at home, but they had only won one away match. Board room changes had seen the appointment of a new chairman, vice-chairman and three new directors, with former chairman B Heathcote leaving the board and with the new chairman announcing that the club were having serious financial problems.

Mike Newell the leading scorer, 19 goals in 28 matches, was sold to Luton Town for £85,000 to ease some of the problems.

The push for promotion increased in January with good away wins at Bolton and Brentford and a 5-0 home win over Swansea with Newell's replacement Warren Aspinall scoring five goals in three matches. It came as no surprise when Everton signed Aspinall in January in a deal that could bring the club £300,000 and Everton loaning the player back to Latics until the end of the season.

'Latics' unbeaten home record of 33 matches was ended by Bolton in April and a further home defeat by Doncaster were set backs which cost them dearly.

Midfield player Tony Kelly became discontented, and was sold to Stoke for £80,000. Good home wins over Plymouth 3-0 and Reading 1-0 were achieved but they could only draw their last two away matches at Lincoln and Darlington and so were overtaken by both Plymouth and Derby County who gained promotion along with Reading.

As holders of The Freight Rover Trophy, 'Latics' won through to the Northern Area final, but with Everton recalling leading scorer Warren Aspinall, it was going to be a hard task, and Bolton won 3-1 on aggregate. The Milk Cup was a disappointment losing 2-3 in the 1st Round to Port Vale. The FA Cup saw Wigan equal a club record by reaching the 4th Round for only the second time before losing 0-3 at Southampton.

Manager Bryan Hamilton will have to bring new faces to replace Newell, record League goalscorer in a season, Aspinall and Kelly, but cash is limited. However the future looks good, with good youngsters in Walsh, Beesley, Langley and Lowe plus the experience of Cribley, Tunks and player of the year Methven.   Geoffrey Lea

Back Row L to R: Roy Tunks (Assistant Manager), Barry Knowles, Paul Beesley, John Lowey, Nigel Adkins, Mark Schofield, Chris Thompson, Paul Cook, David Bingham (Physiotherapist). **Middle Row:** David Hamilton, Graham Houston, John Buttler, Ray Mathias (Manager), Alex Cribley, Ian Griffiths, Paul Jewell. **Front Row:** David Lowe, Jimmy Mitchell.

WIGAN ATHLETIC

DIVISION THREE: 4th   **FA CUP:** 4th ROUND   **MILK CUP:** 1st ROUND   **FRT:** AREA RUNNERS-|

MATCH	DATE		COMPE-TITION	VENUE	OPPONENTS	RESULT		HALF TIME	L'GUE POS'N	GOALSCORERS/GOAL TIMES	ATTEN-DANCE
1	A	17	CL	A	Swansea City	W	1-0	0-0		Barrow 59	(4,70
2		20	MC1/1	H	Port Vale	W	2-1	0-0		Kelly 64 (pen) 77	2,26
3		24	CL	H	Derby County	W	2-1	1-0	4	Newell 39, Lowe 82	4,70
4		26	CL	A	York City	L	1-4	0-2	7	Aspinall 78	(4,06
5		31	CL	H	Brentford	W	4-0	3-0	4	Kelly (pen) 3, Aspinall 12, Newell 25, 54	2,87
6	S	2	MC1/2	A	Port Vale	L	0-2	0-1			(2,77.
7		7	CL	A	Bristol City	L	0-1	0-0	6		(5,66:
8		14	CL	H	Darlington	W	5-1	2-1	3	Newell 3(10, 55, 88), Bailey 20, Cribley 46	3,69
9		17	CL	A	Gillingham	L	0-2	0-1	6		(3,40
10		21	CL	H	AFC Bournemouth	W	3-0	0-0	3	Aspinall (pen) 60 (pen) 89, Newell 73	3,05
11		28	CL	A	Chesterfield	D	1-1	1-0	3	Newell 32	(3,518
12	O	1	CL	H	Walsall	W	2-0	1-0	3	Kelly 26, Jewell 78	4,81
13		5	CL	A	Bury	D	0-0	0-0	4		(4,61(
14		12	CL	H	Blackpool	D	1-1	0-1	3	Cribley 46	5,99
15		19	CL	A	Cardiff City	L	1-3	0-1	6	Griffiths 47	(2,02(
16		22	CL	H	Notts County	W	3-1	2-1	4	Newell 13, 15, Kelly 65	3,55
17		26	CL	H	Newport County	D	0-0	0-0	5		3,71
18	N	2	CL	A	Reading	L	0-1	0-1	9		(5,378
19		5	CL	A	Doncaster Rovers	D	2-2	2-1	10	Newell 12, Aspinall 42	(2,069
20		9	CL	H	Rotherham United	W	2-0	1-0	9	Barrow 42, Newell 85	3,08
21		16	FAC1	H	Doncaster Rovers	W	4-1	2-1		Lowe 30, 40, Newell 53, Aspinall 60	3,31
22		23	CL	A	Plymouth Argyle	L	1-2	0-0	10	Methven 70	(6,714
23		30	CL	H	Lincoln City	W	3-2	3-1	8	Kelly 23, Newell 40, Methven 44	3,01
24	D	7	FAC2	A	Runcorn	D	1-1	0-1		Knowles 74	(4,50(
25		10	FAC2R	H	Runcorn	W	4-0	2-0		Methven 5, Newell 14, 69, Jones (o.g) 82	3,39
26		14	CL	A	Wolverhampton W	D	2-2	1-1	10	Kelly 21, Newell 60	(2,982
27		22	CL	A	Derby County	L	0-1	0-1	10		(14,047
28		26	CL	H	Bristol Rovers	W	4-0	0-0	9	Aspinall 50, Griffiths 61, Kelly pen 72, Newell 81	3,71
29	J	1	CL	A	Bolton Wanderers	W	2-1	1-1	8	Newell 19, Barrow 58	(9,252
30		4	FAC3	H	A.F.C. Bournemouth	W	3-0	0-0		Methven 50, Kelly 75, Aspinall 89	4,18
31		11	CL	A	Brentford	W	3-1	0-0	4	Aspinall 55, 61, Barrow 66	(4,048
32		18	CL	H	Swansea City	W	5-0	1-0	3	Aspinall 43, Cook 72, Methven 83, 84, Kelly 89	3,30
33		22	FRT	H	Chester City	W	2-0	2-0		Aspinall 42, 44	(1,375
34		25	FAC4	A	Southampton	L	0-3	0-0			(14,462
35		28	FRT	H	Rochdale	W	6-0	4-0		Kelly (pen) 8, Barrow 19, 39, Lowe 28, 73, Griffiths 80	2,106
36	F	1	CL	H	Bristol City	D	1-1	1-0	4	Cook 39	3,402
37		4	CL	H	Notts County	D	1-1	1-0	5	Barrow 1	(3,369
38		8	CL	H	Cardiff City	W	2-0	1-0	5	Aspinall 17, Lowe 82	3,428
39		15	CL	H	Gillingham	D	3-3	2-2	3	Kelly 18, Aspinall 23, Griffiths 80	5,01
40		18	FRT N QF	H	Rotherham United	W	3-0	1-0		Aspinall 25, Lowe 63, Barrow 82	2,597
41		22	CL	A	AFC Bournemouth	W	2-0	0-0	3	Methven 59, Jewell 72	(2,949
42	M	1	CL	A	Chesterfield	W	2-0	1-0	2	Aspinall 19, Methven 61	3,209
43		11	CL	H	Bury	W	1-0	0-0	2	Aspinall 72	3,52
44		15	CL	A	Blackpool	W	2-1	0-0	2	Langley 55, Jewell 72	(6,218
45		18	CL	H	York City	W	1-0	0-0	2	Aspinall 67	4,307
46		22	CL	A	Newport County	W	4-3	1-2	2	Kelly pen 7, Langley 50, Lowe 55, Aspinall 77	(1,700
47		26	FRT N SF	A	Port Vale	W	2-1	2-1		Barrow 4, Aspinall 20	(4,832
48		29	CL	A	Bolton Wanderers	L	1-3	0-0	2	Methven 65	8,009
49	A	1	CL	A	Bristol Rovers	D	1-1	0-0	2	Barrow 57	(3,428
50		5	CL	H	Doncaster Rovers	L	0-1	0-1	4		4,143
51		12	CL	A	Rotherham United	D	0-0	0-0	4		(3,004
52		15	CL	A	Walsall	D	3-3	0-2	4	Jewell 58, Lowe 61, Aspinall 76	(4,293
53		19	CL	H	Plymouth Argyle	W	3-0	1-0	3	Jewell 30, 67, Lowe 53	9,485
54		22	CL	A	Reading	W	1-0	0-0	3	Aspinall (pen) 85	6,056
55		26	CL	A	Lincoln City	D	0-0	0-0	3		(3,074
56		29	CL	H	Darlington	D	1-1	0-1	3	Aspinall (pen) 69	(2,013
57	M	3	CL	H	Wolverhampton W.	W	5-3	3-1	4	Aspinall 3 (pen 12, 21, pen 75), Walsh 26,	4,029
58		6	FRT N F1	H	Bolton Wanderers	L	0-1	0-0		Barrow 78	6,975
59		9	FRT N F2	A	Bolton Wanderers	L	1-2	1-0		Jewell 14	12,120

Best Home League Attendance: 9,485 v Plymouth Argyle 19/4   Smallest: 2,871 v Brentford 31/8   Av Home Att: 4,192

Goal Scorers: Compared with 84-85: +928

League (82):	Aspinall 21 (6 pen), Newell 16, Kelly 9 (3 pen), Barrow 7, Methven 7, Jewell 6, Lowe 5, Griffiths 3, Cook 2, Cribley 2, Langley 2, Bailey 1, Walsh 1
Milk Cup (2):	Kelly 2 (1 pen)
FA CUP (12):	Newell 3, Aspinall 2, Lowe 2, Methven 2, Kelly 1, Knowles 1, Opponents 1
FRT (14):	Aspinall 4, Barrow 4, Lowe 3, Griffiths 1, Jewell 1, Kelly 1 pen

1985-86

Butler	Knowles	Kelly	Cribley	Methven	Lowe	Barrow	Newell	Langley	Griffiths	Cook	Aspinall (L)	Beesley	Jewell	Stewart	Bailey	Walsh	Scholfield	Referee	
2	3	4	5	6	7	8	9	10	11									N Butler	1
2	3	4	5	6	7	8	9	10	11									F Roberts	2
2	3	4*	5	6	7	8	9	10		11	12							N Ashley	3
2	3	4		6	7		9	10	11		12	5	8*					C Seel	4
2	3	4		6	7		9	10	11		8*	5	12					J Lovatt	5
2	3	4		6	7		9	10	11		8	5*	12					M Scott	6
2	3			6	7		9	10	11	12	8	5	4*	1				M Read	7
2	3		5	6	7		9	10*		11	8		12		4			J Bray	8
2	3		5	6	7		9	10		11	8		12	4*				R Lewis	9
2*	3		5	6	7		9	10	11		6		12	4				D Phillips	10
2	3	4*	5	6	7		9	10	11	12	8							J McAulay	11
2	3	4	5	6	7		9	10	11		8*		12					J Key	12
2	3	4	5	6	7		9	10	11		8							K Walmsley	13
2	3	4	5	6	7		9	10	11		8							T Mills	14
2	3	4	5	6	7		9	10*	11		12		8					B Stevens	15
2	3	4	5	6	7		9*	10	11		12		8					G Aplin	16
2	3	4*	5	6	7		9	10	11		12		8					K Lupton	17
2	3	4	5		7	12†	9	10	11		6	8*						T Ward	18
2	3	4	5		7		9	10	11		8	6						A Saunders	19
2	3	4	5	6	7	8	9	10	11*	12								M Peck	20
2	3	4	5	6	7		9	10	11		8							J Bray	21
2	3	4	5	6	7	8	9	10	11									D Hedges	22
2	3	4	5	6	7	8	9	10	11									T Jones	23
2	3	4	5	6	7	8	9*	10	11				12					J Key	24
2	3	4	5*	6	7	8	9	10	11				12					G Aplin	25
2	3*	4	5	6	7	8	9			11			12	10				R Milford	26
2		4		6	7*	8	9			11	5	3	12	10				E Scales	27
2	3	4		6	7	8	9			11	10*	5	12					J Lloyd	28
2	3	4		6	7	8	9	12	11		10*	5						K Walmsley	29
2	3	4		6	7	8	9	10	11		12	5*						J Ball	30
2	3	4	5	6	7*	8		10		11		9	12					L Robinson	31
2	3	4	5	6	7	8		10		11		9						D Hutchinson	32
2	3	4	5	6	7	8		10		11		9*	12					M Heath	33
2	3	4	5	6	7	8		10		11		9						M Dimblebee	34
2*	3	4	5	6	7	8		10*	12	11		9				12		D Allison	35
2	3	4*	5	6	7	8		10		11	12	9						K Redfern	36
2	3		4	6	7	8		10		11		9				5		R Hamer	37
2	3	4	5	6	7	8		10	11			9						R Bridges	38
2	3	4	5	6	7	8		10	11			9						J Lovatt	39
2	3	4	5	6	7	8		10	11			9						K Baker	40
2	3	4	5	6	7	8		10	11*			9	12					M James	41
2	3	4		6	7	8		10	11*			9	12			5		J Ball	42
2	3				7	8		10	11	4*	9	6	12			5		R Dilkes	43
2	3		5	6	7	8		10	11			9*	4			12		I Hendrick	44
2	3	4	5	6	7	8		10	11			9						T Holbrook	45
2	3	4	5	6	7	8		10	11			9						D Axcell	46
2	3	4†	5	6	7*	8		10	11			9*	12			12		T Jones	47
	3	4	2	6	7	8		10*	11			9	12			5		N Wilson	48
	3	4	2	6	7	8		10	11			9	12			5*		K Barrett	49
	3	4	2	6	7	8		10	11			9*	5	12	1			G Napthine	50
	3		2	6	7		10	11	4*	9	5	8	1			12		J Ashworth	51
	3		2	6	7		10	11	4*	9	5	8	1			12		N Ashley	52
	3		2	6	7	12	10	11		9	5	8		4*				G Aplin	53
	3		2	6	7	12	10	11		9	5	8*		4				G Tyson	54
	3		2	6	7	8	10	11		9*	5	12	1	4				F Roberts	55
	3		2	6	7	12	10	11		9	5	8*	1	4				T Simpson	56
	3		2	6	7	8	10	11		9	5	12		4*				K Hackett	57
	3		2	6	7	8	10	11	12	5	9*	4						N Ashley	58
	3*		2	6	7	8	10	11		5	9	4	12					N Wilson	59
38	36	45	32	38	43	46	26	24	42	38	11	33	17	14	8	5	10	League Appearances	
							4	1		2	8		15		1	3		Substitute Appearances	
2	2	2	1	2	2			2	2		1	1	0·1					Milk Cup Appearances	
5	5	5	4	5	4	4		5	4	1		1·3	1	1				FA Cup Appearances	
4	6	4	6	6	6	6		6	4·1	2·1	3	2	3·2		*	2·2	0·1	FR Trophy Appearances	

Players on Loan: Aspinall (Everton)

Departures: Newell (Luton), Aspinall, Langley (Everton), Kelly (Stoke), Bailey (F), Stewart, Barrow (Chester), Methven (Blackpool), Walsh (Leicester)

'THE LATICS'

Formed: 1932
Turned Professional: 1932   **Ltd Co:** 1932

Previous Managers: Ted Goodier   Allan Brown   Gordon Milne   Ian McNeill   Larry Lloyd
Bobby Charlton (acting)   Harry McNally

Sponsored by
H. J. Heinz

Honours: Freight Rover Trophy 1985
League Career: Elected to Div 4 1978   Promoted to Div 3 1982
Colours: White with blue trim, blue shorts and stockings with white trim
Change Colours: All green
Reserves League: 'A' Team:

CLUB RECORDS

Most Appearances for Club: Colin Methven: Football League 295 + 1 + FA Cup 23 + League Cup 20 **Total 338 + 1 sub**
Most Capped Player: None
Record Goalscorer in a Match: No one has scored more than three goals
Record League Goalscorer in a Season: Warren Aspinal, 21, Div 3, 1985-6 **In All Competitions:** Warren Aspinal, 27 (League 21 + Cup Competitions 6)
Record League Goalscorer in a Career: Peter Houghton, 62, 1978-83 **In All Competitions:** Peter Houghton, 68 (League 62 + FA Cup 3 + League Cup 3)
Record Transfer Fee Received: £135,000 from Sunderland for Joe Hinnigan, Feb 1980
Record Transfer Fee Paid: £65,000 to Everton for Eamonn O'Keefe, Jan 1982
Best Performances: League: 4th Div 3 1985-6 **FA Cup:** 4th Round 1979-80 **League/Milk Cup:** 4th Round 1981-2
Most League Points: 91, Div 4, 1981-2 **Most League Goals:** 80, Div 4, 1981-2
Record League Victory and Most Goals Scored in a League Match: 7-2 v Scunthorpe United, Div 4, 12 March 1982
Most Goals Scored in a Cup Tie: 4-2 v Chelsea, (h), 3rd Round League Cup, 11 Nov 1981
Record League Defeat: 2-6 v Bradford City, Div 3, 27 Dec 1983   0-5 v Bristol Rovers, Div 3, 26 Feb 1983
Oldest Player in League Match:
Youngest Player in League Match:

Most Consecutive Undefeated League Matches: 21 1981-82	**League Matches Without a Win:** 12 1985
Longest Run of Undefeated Home League Matches: 25 1985-86	**Away League Matches:** 11 1986
Longest Run Without Home League Win: 5 1979, 1983, 1985	**Away League Win:** 9 1985
Most Consecutive League Wins: 6 1985	**Home League Wins:** 8 1978-79, 1985
Most Consecutive League Defeats: 5 1983	**Away League Wins:** 3 1979, 1982, 1986

Club Statistician for the Directory: G Lea

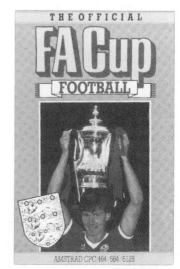

PLAYERS NAME Wt Birthdate	Honours	Birthplace Transfers	Clubs	League	Milk Cup	FA Cup	Other Comps	League	Milk Cup	FA Cup	Other Comps
GOALKEEPERS											
el Adkins 12.7 11.3.65		Birkenhead	Tranmere Rovers (A)	86	4	2	6				
			Wigan Athletic	1							
Tunks 13.11 21.1.51	FRT 85	West Germany	Rotherham United (A)	138	9	8					
			York City (L)	4							
		£7,000	Preston North End	277	20	16					
		F	Wigan Athletic	196	13	16	13				
DEFENDERS											
n Butler 11.7 7.2.62		Liverpool £100	Prescot Cables								
			Wigan Athletic	160+3	8+1	15	11	9			
Cribley* 12.9 1.4.57	FRT 85	Liverpool F	Liverpool								
			Wigan Athletic	210+3	13+1	18	10	4			
y Knowles 11.8 25.4.59	FRT 85	Barrow	Wigan Athletic	75	3	5	11	1		1	
Mitchell 11.5 13.6.67		Liverpool	Wigan Athletic (A)	2							
MIDFIELD											
n Lowey 12.7 7.8.58		Manchester £25,000 Wigan Athletic	Sheffield Wednesday	35+7		7		4		2	
			Blackburn Rovers	136+5	8	5		13	2		
l Beesley details			Wigan Athletic	19	1	1	2				
l Cook 10.10 22.2.67		Liverpool	Wigan Athletic	13+2		1	2+1	2			
Griffiths details			Wigan Athletic	38	2	4	4+1	3			1
vid Hamilton 10.0 7.11.60	EY	South Shields F	Sunderland (A)								
			Blackburn Rovers	106+2	8	1+1		7			
			Cardiff City (L)	10							
			Wigan Athletic								
FORWARDS											
ham Houston 11.4 24.2.60		Gibraltar	Preston North End	90+38	8+1	7	2+3	11		1	1
l Jewell 10.8 28.9.64	FRT 85	Liverpool	Liverpool (A)								
			Wigan Athletic	37+15	0+1	2	7+4	16	1	1	3
vid Lowe 11.0 30.8.65	EY, FRT 85	Liverpool	Wigan Athletic	134+9	4	11+1	13	24		2	7
rk Schofield details		Wigan	Wigan Athletic	1					0+1		
vis Thompson 12.2 24.1.60		Walsall	Bolton Wanderers (A)	66+7	4+1	3+1		18	1	1	
			Lincoln City (L)	5+1							
		F	Blackburn Rovers	31+4	4	9		24	1	1	
			Wigan Athletic								

ADDITIONAL CONTRACT PROFESSIONALS

Player of the Year: Colin Methven (now Blackpool)

APPRENTICES

drew Ainscow, Jason Banks, Peter Atherton, Allan Hall, Ian Rennox, Jon Crompton, Dayle Green, Barry Smith

NON-CONTRACT PLAYERS

n Coleman

Record Attendance: 27,500 v Hereford United, 2 Dec 1953

Smallest Home Attendance for a First Class Match: 2,021 v Wrexham Milk Cup Round 1 Second Leg, 4 Sept 1984

Record Receipts: £29,169 v Aston Villa, League Cup Round 4, 1 Dec 1981

Season Tickets: Stand: £80.00, Ground: £60.00

Executive Box Season Tickets: £250 + vat for seat in glass-enclosed area with buffet facilities at Half-Time and Full-Time with Licensed Bar

Cost of Stand Tickets: £4.00 **Terraces:** £3.00 (£1.50 Juveniles/OAP)

Match and Ticket Information: Stand tickets bookable 14 days in advance

Car Parking: On ground and nearby

Nearest Railway Station: Wigan Wallgate or Wigan (0942 42231)

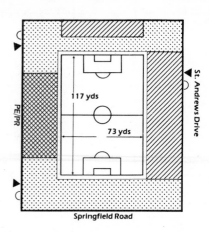

117 yds

73 yds

PE/PR

St. Andrews Drive

Springfield Road

How to get to the ground

From North: Use Motorway M6 until junction 27. Leave motorway and follow signs Wigan A5209. In 0.3m turn right B5206. In 1.1m turn left B5375. In 4.6m turn left into Springfield Road for Wigan Athletic FC

From East: Use A557 S.P. Wigan into town centre then turn left into Market Street and at end turn left into Parsons Walk B5375. In 0.7m turn right into Springfield Road for Wigan Athletic FC

From South: Use Motorway M6 until junction 25. Leave motorway and follow signs into Wigan A49. Turn left into Market Street and at end turn left into Parsons Walk B5375. In 0.7m turn right in Springfield Road for Wigan Athletic FC

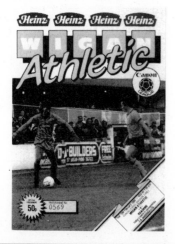

Price of 1986-7 Programme: 50p
Number of Pages: 32

Local Newspapers: Wigan Observer, Wigan Evening Post

Local Radio Stations: Radio Piccadilly, Radio Manchester, Red Rose Radio

WIMBLEDON

Division 1

Amateurs in 1964, Southern League until 1977, halting League progress until the early 'eighties'! Wimbledon have been a good club in their limited spheres and that is the kind of story the script-writers would like to invent for them. But no! What is this? Wimbledon have torn up the scripts and—Glory Be!—what have we here! A 1st Division team! Rub your eyes if you like, but it is true!

The first seven matches were very important and by the end of them second place in the 2nd Division had been achieved through four wins and two draws. There were to be occasional slumps, but the side had character and on November 3rd after the visit of Carlisle (beaten 4-1) second place was again achieved. The lowest position after that was seventh on December 14th after a visit to Middlesbrough (1-0 winners), but three victories followed in succession and from January 18th no more League matches were lost and by April 29th promotion was inevitable. This was achieved by a relatively modest attack, which scored only 58 League goals with Cork the leading scorer on only 11. Conversely the defence was a strong point with only 37 goals conceded in 2nd Division matches.

With all the 'bread and butter' successes the Dons did not really need any cup successes and early departures were the style this time. Blackburn Rovers (5-0 and 1-2) were dismissed from the Milk Cup, but a visit to White Hart Lane ended that run (0-2). In the FA Cup a short journey to the Den was enough; Millwall won comfortably (3-1).

Now even non-Wimbledon supporters will be intrigued to follow 1st Division results and their 'homespun' manager can be expected to provide his own recipe for success. Dave Bassett has some good defenders in his squad—Beasant in goal, Kay, Smith and Winterburn. His midfield is hard working—Galliers, Fairweather and Sanchez did well. But can Cork, Fishenden, Evans and Hodges produce the goals? That is the riddle.

Most followers of the game who are also romantics would like to see Wimbledon do well amongst the top teams just to prove that there are some things which plenty of money cannot buy. What else have they in store for us after making record progress to the 1st Division after only nine seasons in the League? WLM

Back Row L to R: Lawrie Sanchez, Brian Gayle, Stewart Evans, David Beasant, John Fashanu, Colin Gordon, Mark Morris. **Middle Row:** Derek French (Physiotherapist), Mick Smith, Alan Cork, Nigel Winterburn, Simon Tracey, Andrew Thorn, Carlton Fairweather, Glyn Hodges, Alan Gillett (Assistant Manager), Geoff Taylor (Youth Team Manager). **Front Row:** John Gannon, David Martin, Steve Galliers, John Kay, David Bassett (Manager), Kevin Gage, Wally Downes, Paul Fishenden, Dennis Wise.

WIMBLEDON

DIVISION TWO: 3rd   FA CUP: 3rd ROUND   **MILK CUP:** 3rd ROUND

MATCH	DATE		COMPE-TITION	VENUE	OPPONENTS	RESULT		HALF TIME	L'GUE POS'N	GOALSCORERS/GOAL TIMES	ATTEN-DANCE
1	A	17	CL	H	Middlesbrough	W	3-0	2-0		Evans 5, Gage (pen) 40, Sanchez 64	2,84
2		21	CL	A	Leeds United	D	0-0	0-0			(12,426
3		24	CL	A	Sheffield United	L	0-4	0-3	10		(11,914
4		26	CL	H	Bradford City	W	1-0	0-0		Evans 77	3,20
5		31	CL	A	Grimsby Town	W	1-0	0-0	5	Evans 85	(3,476
6	S	3	CL	H	Barnsley	W	1-0	1-0		Fishenden 15	2,35
7		7	CL	H	Oldham Athletic	D	0-0	0-0	2		2,749
8		14	CL	A	Blackburn Rovers	L	0-2	0-1	5		(5,006
9		21	CL	A	Brighton & H.A.	L	0-2	0-1	8		(9,973
10		24	MC2/1	H	**Blackburn Rovers**	W	5-0	3-0		Cork 3 (10, 24, 84), Gayle 34, Evans 51	2,07
11		28	CL	H	Charlton Athletic	W	3-1	2-1	5	Evans 2, 51, Holloway 27	4,52
12	O	5	CL	A	Norwich City	W	2-1	2-1	6	Martin (pen) 16, Cork 19	(12,707
13		8	MC2/2	A	**Blackburn Rovers**	L	1-2	1-1		Cork 24	(2,160
14		12	CL	H	Fulham	W	1-0	0-0	4	Cork 55	5,95
15		19	CL	H	Millwall	D	1-1	1-1	5	Winterburn 37	4,64
16		25	CL	A	Stoke City	D	0-0	0-0	4		(6,708
17	N	3	CL	H	Carlisle United	W	4-1	0-1	2	Smith 50, 82, Cork 54, 70	3,88
18		6	MC3	A	**Tottenham Hotspur**	L	0-2	0-0			(16,919
19		9	CL	A	Sunderland	L	1-2	0-1	4	Fairweather 82	(15,518
20		16	CL	H	Shrewsbury Town	W	2-1	1-1	2	Sanchez 31, Galliers 71	2,58
21		23	CL	A	Hull City	D	1-1	1-0	3	Sanchez 18	(6,576
22		30	CL	H	Huddersfield Town	D	2-2	0-2	5	Morris 50, Fishenden 61	2,80
23	D	7	CL	H	Leeds United	L	0-3	0-2	6		3,49
24		14	CL	A	Middlesbrough	L	0-1	0-0	7		(4,693
25		21	CL	H	Sheffield United	W	5-0	3-0	5	Kay 20, Hodges 22, 88, Sanchez 27, Stancliffe (og) 77	3,75
26		26	CL	A	Crystal Palace	W	3-1	2-0	4	Cork 3, 43, Sanchez 72	(7,929
27		28	CL	A	Barnsley	W	1-0	1-0	3	Sanchez 21	(8,949
28	J	1	CL	H	Portsmouth	L	1-3	0-2	3	Cork 50	9,02
29		4	FAC3	A	**Millwall**	L	1-3	0-2		Gage 87	(5,840
30		11	CL	A	Oldham Athletic	L	1-2	0-1	3	Holloway 51	(3,035
31		18	CL	H	Grimsby Town	W	3-0	0-0	3	Sanchez 51, Hodges 67, Cork 82	2,770
32	F	22	CL	H	Brighton & H. A.	D	0-0	0-0	4		5,79
33	M	8	CL	H	Norwich City	W	2-1	0-1	4	Evans 61, Cork 64	5,82
34		11	CL	A	Millwall	W	1-0	0-0	3	Fairweather 74	(4,643
35		15	CL	H	Fulham	W	2-0	2-0	3	Sanchez 36, Cork 42	(6,209
36		22	CL	H	Blackburn Rovers	D	1-1	1-1	3	Fairweather 29	3,26
37		29	CL	A	Portsmouth	D	1-1	0-0	3	Smith 60	·(18,859
38	A	1	CL	H	Crystal Palace	D	1-1	1-0	4	Fashanu 34	8,42
39		6	CL	A	Carlisle United	W	3-2	1-1	4	Fashanu 35, Fairweather 61, 64	(5,593
40		12	CL	H	Sunderland	W	3-0	0-0	3	Hodge 3 (63, 67, (pen) 86)	6,05
41		19	CL	A	Shrewsbury Town	D	1-1	1-0	3	Fairweather 43	(3,948
42		26	CL	H	Hull City	W	3-1	2-1	4	Fashanu 36, 60, Fairweather 37	5,15
43		29	CL	H	Stoke City	W	1-0	0-0	3	Cork 48	5,95
44	M	3	CL	A	Huddersfield Town	W	1-0	0-0	3	Sanchez 61	(6,083
45		6	CL	A	Charlton Athletic	D	0-0	0-0	3		(13,214
46		8	CL	A	Bradford City	D	1-1	1-0	3	Gannon 25	(4,316

Best Home League Attendance: 9,025 v Portsmouth 1/1   Smallest: 2,351 v Barnsley 3/9   Av Home Att: 4,817

Goal Scorers: **Compared with 84-85: +393**

League (58):	Cork 11, Sanchez 9, Fairweather 7, Evans 6, Hodges 6, Fashanu 4, Smith 3, Fishenden 2, Holloway 2, Gage 1 (pen), Galliers 1, Gannon 1, Kay 1, Martin 1 (pen), Morris 1, Winterburn 1, Opponents 1
Milk Cup (6):	Cork 4, Evans 1, Gayle 1
FA CUP (1):	Gage 1

1985-86

Kay	Gage	Galliers	Gayle	Smith	Evans	Holloway	Cork	Sanchez	Thorn	Hodges	Sayer	Morris	Winterburn	Martin	Fishenden	Downes	Fairweather	Wise	Fashanu	Gannon	Referee	
2	3	4	5	6	7	8	9	10	11	12											K Barratt	1
2	3	4	5	6	7		9*	10	11	12	8										K Walmsley	2
2	3	4	5		7†		9	10	11		8	6*	12								M Heath	3
2		4	5		7	8		10	11	12			3	6	9*						D Axcell	4
2		4	5		7	8		10	11				3	6	9						T Jones	5
2		4	5		7*		12	10	11		8		3	6	9						B Hill	6
2		4	5		7			10*	11	12	8		3	6	9						M Dimblebee	7
2		4	5		7			10	11	12	8		3	6	9*						T Holbrook	8
2*	9	4	5		7	8		10	11	12			3	6							D Hedges	9
	2	4	5		7	9*	8	10	11				3	6	12						**R Milford**	**10**
	11	4	5		7	9	8	10	2	12			3*	6							L Shapter	11
	2	4	5		7	9	8	10	12	11			3*	6							H Taylor	12
	11	4	5		7	9	8	10*	2				3	6	12						**A Saunders**	**13**
	2	4	5		7	9	8*	10	11	12			3	6							J Moules	14
	2	4	5		7	9	8	10	11				3	6							A Gunn	15
	2	4	5		7	9	8	10	11				3	6							K Cooper	16
	2	4	5		7	9	8	10	11*	12			3	6							J Ball	17
	2	4	5		7*	9	8	10	11			6	3		12						**G Napthine**	**18**
	2	4	5		7*		8†	10	11			6	3	9			12				D Hutchinson	19
	2	4	5		7		8	10	11			6	3				9				I Borrett	20
	2	4		5	7	12	8	10	11*			6	3				9				R Banks	21
	2	4		5*	7	9	8	10	11			6	3				12				I Hemley	22
	2	4*		5	7	12	8	10	11			6	3				9				J Ashworth	23
	2	4		5†	7*	9	8	10	12			6	3			11					D Phillips	24
	2	4		5		9	8	10	11			6	3				7				M Bodenham	25
	2	4		5	7	9	8	10*	11			6	3				12				M James	26
	2				7	9	8	10	11			6	3	5	4						K Breen	27
	2				7	9*	8	10	11			6	3	5	4	12					M Reed	28
	2	4		5	7	9	8	10*	11			6	3		12						**H King**	**29**
	2	4		5	7		8	10				6*	3			12	11		9		G Courtney	30
	2	4		5	7	9	8	10	11			6*	3			12					Allan Robinson	31
	2	4		6	7	9*	8	10				5	3			12	11				D Axcell	32
	2	4		6	7		8	10				5	3		9		11				G Ashby	33
	2	4		6	7		8	10				5	3		9*	12	11				E Scales	34
	2	4		6	7		8	10				5	3		9*	12	11				K Barratt	35
	2	4		6	7*		8	10				5	3		9	12	11				J Bray	36
	2	4		6	7		8	10				5	3		9*		11		12		R Groves	37
	2	4		6		12	8	10				5	3		7*		11		9		A Gunn	38
	2	4		6	7		8	10				5	3				11		9		J Key	39
	2	4		6			8	10				5	3		7		11		9		I Borrett	40
	2	4		6		12	8	10				5	3		7*		11		9		D Scott	41
	2	4		6*			8	10				5	3		7	12	11		9		G Napthine	42
	2	4		6			8	10				5	3		7*	12	11		9		B Stevens	43
	2	4		6			8	10				5	3		7	12	11*		9		G Courtney	44
	2	4*		6			8	10				5	3		7	12	11		9		M James	45
	2			6		7*	8	10				5	3			12	11		9	4	K Lupton	46
26	29	32	13	24	27	19	36	**42**	27	18	5	20	38	15	16	5	18	1	8	1	League Appearances	
			3		2		1	12	2			1		2	4	2	3	1			Substitute Appearances	
1	2	3	2	1	3	3	3	2	2	3			3	2	0-1	0-2			1		Milk Cup Appearances	
1	0-1	1		1	1	1	1	1					1	1			1				FA Cup Appearances	

Played:

Players on Loan:

Departures: Handford (Maidstone Utd), Evans (WBA)

'THE DONS'

Formed: 1889
Turned Professional: 1964   **Ltd Co:** 1964

Previous Name: Wimbledon Old Centrals 1899-1905
Previous Managers: 1977-8 Allen Batsford   1978-81 Dario Gradi
Honours: Champions, Division 4, 1982-3
League Career: Elected to Division 4 1977-8   Promoted to Division 3 1978-9
Relegated to Division 4 1979-80   Promoted to Division 3 1980-1   Relegated to Division 4 1981-2
Promoted to Division 3 1982-3   Promoted to Division 2 1983-4   Promoted to Division 1 1985-6
Colours: Royal blue shirts with yellow trim, blue shorts with yellow trim, blue and yellow stockings
Change Colours: Yellow with blue
Reserves League: Capital League   **Youth League** S.E. Counties

---

CLUB RECORDS

Most Appearances for Club: John Leslie: Football League 242 + 11 + F.A. Cup 14 + 2 + League Cup 20 + 1 **Total 276 + 14**
Most Capped Player: Glyn Hodges, 2, Wales   **For England:** None
Record Goalscorer in a Match: Alan Cork, 4 v Torquay (A), Div 4, 28 Feb 1979
Record League Goalscorer in a Season: Alan Cork, 32, Div 3, 1983-4   **In All Competitions:** Alan Cork, 32 (League 28 F.A. Cup 2, Milk Cup 2) 1983-4
Record League Goalscorer in a Career: Alan Cork, 94, 1977-84   **In All Competitions:** Alan Cork, 118 (League 106 + F.A. Cup 6 + Milk Cup 6), 1977-85
Record Transfer Fee Received: £70,000 from Crystal Palace for Steve Galliers, Oct 1981
Record Transfer Fee Paid: £45,000 to Queen's Park Rangers for Tommy Cunningham, Mar 1979
Best Performances: League: 1st Div 3 1983-4   **F.A. Cup:** 4th Round 1974-5   **League/Milk Cup:** 4th Round 1979-80 1983-4
Most League Points: 98 in Div 4, 1982-3   **Most League Goals:** 97, Div 3, 1983-4
Record League Victory: 6-0 v Newport County, Div 3, 3 Sept 1983
Record League Defeat: 0-8 v Everton, League Cup 2nd Round, 29 Aug 1978
Oldest Player in League Match: Dave Donaldson 37 yrs 4 months
Youngest Player in League Match: Kevin Gage 17 yrs 15 days
Most Consecutive Undefeated League Matches: 22 1983
Longest Run of Undefeated Home League Matches: 21 1983
Longest Run Without Home League Win: 7 1980
Most Consecutive League Wins: 7 1983
Most Consecutive League Defeats: 4 1982

League Matches Without a Win: 14 1980
Away League Matches: 12 1982-83
Away League Win: 10 1981
Home League Wins: 8 1978, 1983
Away League Wins: 3 1978-79, 1984

Club Statistician for the Directory: S King

VIMBLEDON

ᴿERS NAME Wt Birthdate	Honours	Birthplace Transfers	Clubs	League	Milk Cup	FA Cup	Other Comps	League	Milk Cup	FA Cup	Other Comps
ᴬLKEEPERS											
ʳd Beasant 13.0 20.3.59		Willesden	Edgware Town Wimbledon	258	15	12	1				
on Tracey 12.0 9.12.67		Woolwich	Wimbledon								
ᴱNDERS											
ʳn Gage 11.2 21.4.64	EY, Div. 4, 83	London	Wimbledon (A)	110+28	5+1	7+3		12	1	1	
ʳn Gayle 12.7 6.3.65		London	Wimbledon (A)	13	2			1			
ʳn Kay 11.6 29.1.64		Sunderland	Arsenal (A) Wimbledon Middlesbrough (L)	13+1 47 8	 3	 1	 1				
id Martin 10.11 25.4.63	FAYC 79	East Ham £35,000	Millwall (A) Wimbledon	131+9 30+5	10+2 2	7 1+1	4	6 3	3	1	
k Morris 11.0 26.9.62	Div. 4, 83	Morden	Wimbledon	147	12	11		9			
k Smith ½ 11.9 28.10.58	Div. 4, 83	Sunderland £12,500	Lincoln City Wimbledon Aldershot (L)	20+5 197+2 7	2 9	 14		 14		2	
ᴵy Thorn 11.5 12.11.66		Carshalton	Wimbledon	27+1	2						
ᵉl Winterburn 10.7 11.12.63	EU21 (1)	Nuneaton F F	Birmingham City (A) Oxford United Wimbledon	 122+1	 11	 18	 1	 1	 2		
ᴵFIELD											
y Downes 10.11 9.6.61	Div. 4, 83	London	Wimbledon (A)	179+12	15+3	9+3					
ᵉ Galliers 9.7 21.8.57	Div. 4, 83	Fulwood £1,500 £70,000 £15,000	Chorley Wimbledon Crystal Palace Wimbledon	 148+7 8+5 130+1	 17+1 12	 13+1 10	 10 5	 2 2			
ᴴolloway 9.12 12.3.63		Kingswood £35,000	Bristol Rovers (A) Wimbledon	104+7 19	10 3	8 1	5	14 2		2	
ʳie Sanchez 12.0 22.10.59	Div. 4, 79	Lambeth F £20,000	Thatcham Town Reading Wimbledon	 249+13 62	 20+1 2	 19	 1	 28 14			
nis Wise 9.5 16.12.66		London	Southampton (A) Wimbledon	 1+4							
WARDS											
ᵉ Cork 12.0 8.10.59		Derby F	Derby County Lincoln City (L) Wimbledon	 5 260+6	 24	 22		 117	 10	 6	
ton Fairweather 11.0 22.9.61		London	Tooting & Mitcham Wimbledon	 25+8		 2		 13			
ᵗ Fashanu 11.12 18.9.62		Kensington	Cambridge United (NC) Norwich City Crystal Palace (L) Lincoln City Millwall Wimbledon	 6+1 1 31+5 50 8+1	 2 4	 2 1 5	 2	 1 11 10 4	 2	 2	 1
ᵉ Fishenden 10.12 2.8.63		Hillingdon	Wimbledon Fulham (L)	57+18 3	1+1	5+1	1	24		4	
ᵗn Gordon 12.12 17.1.63		Stourbridge £80,000	Swindon Town Wimbledon	70+2	6	2	3	34			
ᵃ Hodges 12.3 30.4.63	W (2), U21 (1), Y	Streatham	Wimbledon (A)	168+27	10+1	8+2	0+1	40	3		
y Sayer 10.12 6.6.66		Brent	Wimbledon (A)	21+6		1	1	8			

ᴬITIONAL CONTRACT PROFESSIONALS
y Clement, Gary Fiore, John Gannon (1Lge), Ian Hazel

ᴿRENTICES
ghan Ryan

ᴶ-CONTRACT PLAYERS

Record Attendance: 18,000 v H.M.S. Victory, F.A. Amateur Cup Round 3, 1934-5

Record Receipts: £41,124 v West Ham United, F.A. Cup Round 5 1984-85

Season Tickets: £125, £150, £170, £185

Executive Box Season Tickets: None

Cost of Stand Tickets: Varying from £7 to £13 according to fixture; Ground: varying from £3 to £4 (OAP/Juveniles £2 and £2.50)

Match and Ticket Information: Available 21 days prior to matches

Car Parking: On ground and in streets quarter mile from ground

Nearest Railway Station: Haydons Road (Southern Region), Wimbledon Park (District Line)

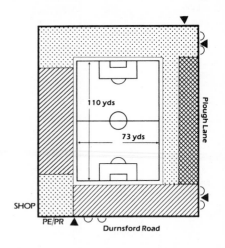

How to get to the ground

From North and West: Use A205 South Circular Road to Wandsworth, forward around one way system then follow signs Earlsfield A217 into Garratt Lane. In 1.6m turn right into Summerstown leading into Plough Lane for Wimbledon F.C.

From South: Use A24 to South Wimbledon Station then in 0.2m turn left into Haydons Road A218. In 0.8m turn right into Plough Lane for Wimbledon F.C.

From East: Use South Circular Road A205 then A24 S.P. Wimbledon to Clapham South Station then turn right B237 into Nightingale Lane. In 2m at T road turn left A217 then shortly turn right into Summerstown leading into Plough Lane for Wimbledon F.C.

Price of 1986-7 Programme: 50p
Number of Pages: 24
Subscriptions: Home matches weekly per season £22.00 (postage included). Home and away matches weekly per season £33.00 (postage included)

Local Newspapers: Wimbledon Guardian, Surrey Comet, Wimbledon News, South London Press

Local Radio Stations: Capital Radio, L.B.C.

President
Sir Jack Hayward

Chairman
Richard Homden

Directors
D Hope
R J Hipkiss
(Joint Vice-Chairmen)
M A Bhatti
J A Harris

Secretary
Keith Pearson ACIS (0902 712181)

Commercial Manager
Vacant

Acting Manager
Brian Little

Reserve & Youth Team Manager
Greg Fellows

Chief Scout
B Hayward

Physiotherapist
E Edwards

Groundsman
Bill Pilbeam

Wolverhampton Wanderers are on a downward spiral and short of extinction, or the present owners selling the club, it is difficult to see where it will end.

Wolves became only the second club in history (Bristol City were the first) to go from the First to the Fourth Division in three consecutive seasons. In fact, but for winning their last match of the season at Lincoln, they would have finished bottom of the Division in each of those seasons.

They were at or near the bottom for the whole of the season and only in March were hopes of avoiding Division Four raised slightly when four matches produced eight points but more defeats quickly followed and the team was sunk.

The usual problems were encountered throughout the season including lack of finance and managerial changes. Sammy Chapman started and finished the season and Bill McGarry was in charge for two months before resigning in despair. All the playing staff are now available for transfer which invariably means that the better players will go, and even worse, the famous Molineux ground is for sale amidst rumours that Wolves will be playing at another venue next year if they survive.

It seems incredible that the club which only six years ago finished sixth in the First Division, won the League Cup and paid out a record British transfer fee for Andy Gray will next season be in the Fourth Division, but that is what faces Wolves, and at the moment the future holds out no hope of better days ahead.

Back Row L to R: Keith Lockhart, Neil Edwards, Scott Barrett, Dean Edwards, Vince Bartram, Russell Turley, Andy Mutch, Steve Stoutt. **Middle Row:** Geoff Palmer, Matt Hellin, David Barnes, Darren Oldroyd, Peter Zelem, Nick Clarke, Roger Eli, Micky Holmes, Floyd Streete, Derek Ryan, Eddie Edwards (Physio). **Front Row:** Henry Wright, John Purdie, Paul Dougherty, Brian Little (Acting Manager), David Heywood, Richard Wood, Matt Forman.

WOLVERHAMPTON WANDERERS

DIVISION THREE: 23rd   **FA CUP:** 1st ROUND   **MILK CUP:** 1st ROUND

MATCH	DATE		COMPE-TITION	VENUE	OPPONENTS	RESULT	HALF TIME	L'GUE POS'N	GOALSCORERS/GOAL TIMES	ATTEN-DANCE
1	A	17	CL	A	Brentford	L	1-2	0-0		Edwards 67	(5,57
2		20	MC1/1	A	Walsall	D	1-1	0-1		Purdie 81	(11,33
3		24	CL	H	Newport County	L	1-2	0-1	20	Clarke 69	6,0
4		26	CL	A	Derby County	L	2-4	1-2		Edwards 45, Purdie 70	(13,15
5		31	CL	H	York City	W	3-2	2-1	20	Coady 34, King (pen) 38, Edwards 55	4,4C
6	S	3	MC1/2	H	Walsall	L	0-1	0-0			11,3
7		7	CL	A	Bolton Wanderers	L	1-4	0-0		Morrissey 86	(4,98
8		14	CL	H	Swansea City	L	1-5	0-4	24	King 85	4,06
9		17	CL	H	Bristol Rovers	L	3-4	2-1		Edwards 3, King 20, (pen) 88	3,24
10		21	CL	A	Plymouth Argyle	L	1-3	0-1	24	Edwards 49	(5,24
11		28	CL	H	Lincoln City	D	1-1	1-0	24	King (pen) 3	3,3
12	O	1	CL	A	Bury	L	1-3	1-0	24	King 28	(3,22
13		5	CL	A	Rotherham United	W	2-1	1-1	23	Edwards 10, 69	(4,01
14		12	CL	H	Doncaster Rovers	L	1-2	1-0	23	King 35	4,3
15		19	CL	H	Walsall	D	0-0	0-0	23		7,5
16		23	CL	A	Reading	D	2-2	1-0	23	Ryan 5, 81	(11,50
17		26	CL	A	Bristol City	L	0-3	0-1	23		(7,13
18	N	2	CL	H	Darlington	W	2-1	0-0	22	Ryan 55, Purdie 71	3,8
19		5	CL	H	Blackpool	W	2-1	1-1	22	Crainie 4, Purdie 52	3,69
20		9	CL	A	A.F.C Bournemouth	L	2-3	1-2	22	King 15, Barnes 63	(4,12
21		16	FAC1	A	Rotherham United	L	0-6	0-2			(3,50
22		23	CL	H	Gillingham	L	1-3	0-0	22	King 80	3,54
23		30	CL	H	Cardiff City	D	1-1	0-1	22	King 61	(2,45
24	D	14	CL	H	Wigan Athletic	D	2-2	1-1	23	Ryan 36, Holmes 68	2,98
25		21	CL	A	Newport County	L	1-3	1-0	24	Purdie 34	(2,22
26		26	CL	A	Notts County	L	0-4	0-1	24		(5,26
27		28	CL	H	Derby County	L	0-4	0-1	24		(9,16
28	J	1	CL	H	Chesterfield	W	1-0	1-0	23	Purdie 43	3,22
29		11	CL	A	York City	L	1-2	0-2	24	Rosario 65	(4,29
30		14	FRT	A	Exeter City	D	1-1	1-0		Edwards 4	(1,27
31		18	CL	H	Brentford	L	1-4	0-3	24	Edwards 81	3,42
32		22	FRT	H	Torquay United	D	1-1	0-1		Cartwright 50	1,61
33		25	CL	A	Swansea City	W	2-0	1-0	24	Streete 3, Cartwright 83	(4,96
34	F	1	CL	H	Bolton Wanderers	L	0-2	0-1	24		3,11
35		9	CL	A	Walsall	D	1-1	1-1	24	Holmes 10	(10,48
36	M	8	CL	H	Rotherham United	D	0-0	0-0	24		2,83
37		11	CL	H	Plymouth Argyle	L	0-3	0-2	24		2,36
38		15	CL	A	Doncaster Rovers	W	1-0	0-0	24	Chapman 75	(2,65
39		18	CL	H	Bury	D	1-1	0-0	24	Chapman 68	2,20
40		22	CL	H	Bristol City	W	2-1	0-0	24	Mutch 68, Edwards 89	3,69
41		25	CL	A	Bristol Rovers	D	1-1	1-1	24	Mutch 5	(3,37
42		29	CL	A	Chesterfield	L	0-3	0-0	24		(2,50
43		31	CL	H	Notts County	D	2-2	2-2	24	Mutch 5, Edwards 39	3,77
44	A	2	CL	A	Darlington	L	1-2	0-0	24	Mutch 53	(3,88
45		5	CL	A	Blackpool	W	1-0	1-0	23	Edwards 18	(4,56
46		8	CL	H	Reading	L	2-3	1-0	24	Edwards 25, Lockhart 48	4,46
47		12	CL	A	Bournemouth	L	0-3	0-1	24		3,38
48		19	CL	A	Gillingham	L	0-2	0-0	24		(3,68
49		26	CL	H	Cardiff City	W	3-1	2-0	24	Lockhart 15, Mutch 18, Holmes 55	3,3
50	M	3	CL	A	Wigan Athletic	L	3-5	1-3	24	Dougherty 4, Mutch 56, Edwards 59	4,02
51		5	CL	A	Lincoln City	W	3-2	2-1	23	Mutch 33, Purdie 44, Edwards 67	(2,17

Best Home League Attendance: 7,522 v Walsall 19/10   **Smallest:** 2,205 v Bury 18/3   **Av Home Att:** 4,00(

Goal Scorers: **Compared with 84-85: −3,64**

League (57):	Edwards 14, King 10 (4 pen), Mutch 7, Purdie 6, Ryan 4, Holmes 3, Chapman 2, Lockhart 2, Barnes 1, Cartwright 1, Clarke 1, Crainie 1, Coady 1, Dougherty 1, Morrissey 1, Rosario 1, Streete 1
Milk Cup (1):	Purdie 1
FA CUP (Nil):	
FRT (2):	Cartwright 1, Edwards 1

548

1985-86

Herbert	Barnes	Zelem	Clarke	Chapman	Morrissey	Edwards	Purdie	King	Crainie	Stoutt	Ryan	Holmes	Flowers	Coady	Dougherty	Ainscow	Cartwright	Raynes	Palmer	Streete	Lomax (L)	Eli	Mutch	Lockhart	Referee	
2*	3	4	5	6	7	8	9	10	11	12															D Axcell	1
	3	4	5	6	7*	8	9	10	11	2	12														N Glover	2
	3	4	5	6	7*	8	9	10	11	2															D Allinson	3
	3	4	5	6	7	8	9	10	11	2															T Mills	4
	3*		5		12	8	9	10	11	2				1		4	6	7							R Gifford	5
	3	4	5	7		8	9	10	11	2*				1			12	6							K Walmsley	6
	3		5	6*	12	8	9	10	11	2				1		4		7							D Phillips	7
	3		5		12	8	9*	10	11	2				1		4	7	6							R Trussell	8
	3	4		7	9			10	11	2	12			1			6	8							D Shaw	9
	3		5		12	9		10	11	4				1		7*	8	6							K Cooper	10
2	3		5	7		9		10*	11	4	12			1			8	6							I Hendrick	11
2	3		5	12	9	7*		10	11	4				1			8	6							C Seel	12
2	3		5		9	7		10	11								8	6		4					N Wilson	13
2	3		5		9	7		10	11*	12							8	6		4					R Bridges	14
2	3			12	9*	7		10	11	5	6						8			4					D Hedges	15
2	3		5*	12		7		10		6	8						9			4					M James	16
2	3		5	12		7		10		6	8						9			4					A Buksh	17
	3		9			7		10	11	5	6						8		2	4					J Deakin	18
	3	12	9			7		10	11	5	6						8		2	4*					B Hill	19
12	3	4*	9			7		10	11	5	6						8		2						R Hamer	20
5	3	4†	10			7			11	2	8				6	9									A Robinson	21
5	3		9*			12	7	10	11			8		1			6		2						R Nixon	22
5	3		11			7	10			9	6	1			8				2						C Downey	23
5	3		11*			10			8	9	6	1	2	12				7							R Milford	24
5	3		10			8		11	2	9	6	1	4	12			7*								N Butler	25
5	3		10			8*		11		9	6	1	4	12			7	2							T Fitzharris	26
5	3		10*			12		11	6	9	8	1	4				7	2							J Worrall	27
5	3*	4				12	10	11		9	8	1				6	7	2							H Taylor	28
5		4				10		11		7*		1	2			6	12	3							M Peck	29
12		5				10		11		7		1				2	8	3	4						R Groves	30
		5				10	12	11				1				2	8*	3	4		7				K Breen	31
		5	3			10	11				12	1				6		2	4		7				B Hill	32
3		5		12		10	11*			9	8	1				6		2	4		7				R Hamer	33
3		5				10	11			9	8	1				6		2	4		7				B Stevens	34
3		5				11	10	9				8						2	4		7				M Reed	35
	3	5				11	10	6				8						2	4		7	9			Alan Robinson	36
	3	5				11	10	6			12	8						2	4		7	9*			D Hutchinson	37
	3	5				11	10	6				8			12			2	4		7	9*			J Lovatt	38
	3	5				11	10	6				8			12			2	4		7*	9			D Vickers	39
	3	5				11	10	6				8						2	4			9	7		P Willis	40
		5				11	10	6				8				3		4	2		9		7		Alan Robinson	41
	3	5				11	10	6				8				12		4	2*		9		7		D Scott	42
	3	5				11	10	6				8						2	4		9		7		F Roberts	43
	3					11	10	6	5			8						2	4		9		7		G Aplin	44
	3					11	10	6	5			8	1					2	4		9		7		R Nixon	45
	3					11	10	6	5			8	1					2		4	9		7		J Key	46
	3	12				11*	10	6	5			8	1					2		4	9		7		H King	47
	3†					11	10	9	5		12	8	1					2	4		6*		7		G Napthine	48
	3	5					10	11*	2			8	1			12		4		6	9		7		T Simpson	49
		5	3				10	7	2			8	1			6		4			9		11		K Hackett	50
		5	7				10	11	2			8	1			6		4			9		3		J McAulay	51
19	38	14	21	29	5	33	41	20	23	26	15	26	25	8	5	16	13	6	20	25	5	14	15	12	League Appearances	
1			2	4	5	3	1			2	4			6			1	1							Substitute Appearances	
	2	2	2	2	1	2	2	2	2	2	0-1		1		0-1	1									Milk Cup Appearances	
1	1		1	1		1		1	1	1				1		1	1								FA Cup Appearances	
0-1		1	2			2	1		1		1	0-1	2			2	1	2	2		1				FR Trophy Appearances	

o Played: Position(Game): Smith 12(3), Hazell 5(9), Wright 2(10), Wassell (NC) 11(16, 17), North 4(22, 23, 24), Rosario 9(29, 30*, 31, 32) Whitehead 8(29, 32) 6(30, 31)

yers on Loan: Hazell (Leicester), Lomax (Man City), North (Luton), Rosario (Norwich)

partures: Morrissey (Tranmere R), Hankin (NL), Flowers (Southampton), Ainscow (Blackburn R), King (Aldershot)

549

'THE WOLVES'

Formed: 1877
Turned Professional: 1888 **Ltd Co:** 1892

Previous Names: In 1880, St Luke's, Blakenall combined with The Wanderers to become Wolverhampton Wanderers (1923) Ltd until 1982 when a new company was formed
Previous Managers: 1927-44 Major Frank Buckley 1944-8 Ted Vizard 1948-64 Stan Cullis 1964-5 Andy Beattie 1965-8 Ronnie Allen 1968-76 Bill McGarry 1976-8 Sammy Chung 1978-82 John Barnwell 1982 Ian Greaves 1982-4 Graham Hawkins 1984-85 Tommy Docherty 1985 Bill McGarry
Honours: Champions Div 1, 1953-5, 1957-8, 1958-9 Champions Div 2, 1931-2, 1976-7, Champions Div 3 (N) 1923-4 FA Cup Winners 1893, 1908, 1949, 1960 Football League Cup Winners 1973-4, 1979-80 Texaco Cup Winners 1970-1
League Career: Founder Members of Football League 1888 Relegated to Div 2 1905-6 Relegated to Div 3 (N) 1922-3 Promoted to Div 2 1923-4 Promoted to Div 1 1931-2 Relegated to Div 2 1964-5 Promoted to Div 1 1966-7 Relegated to Div 2 1975-6 Promoted to Div 1 1976-7 Relegated to Div 2 1981-2 Promoted to Div 1 1982-3 Relegated to Div 2 1983-4 Relegated to Div 3 1984-5 Relegated to Div 4 1985-6
Colours: Old gold shirts with black trim, black shorts, old gold stockings
Change Colours: All white
Reserves League: Central Div 2 **'A' Team:** Midland Intermediate

CLUB RECORDS

Most Appearances for Club: Derek Parkin: Football League 500 + 1 + FA Cup 45 + 1 + League Cup 35 + European Cu' 15 **Total 595 + 2 subs**
Most Capped Player: Billy Wright, 105, England
Record Goalscorer in a Match: Jack Brodie, 5 v Stoke City, 22.2.1890 Tom Phillipson, 5 v Bradford City, (H, 7-2), Div 25.12.26 Billy Harthill, 5 v Notts County, (H, 5-1), Div 2, 12.10.29 and v Aston Villa, (H, 5-2), Div 1 03.09.34
Record League Goalscorer in a Season: Dennis Westcott, 37, Div 1, 1946-7 **In All Competitions:** Dennis Westcott, 4 (League 32 + FA Cup 11), 1938-9
Record League Goalscorer in a Career: Bill Harthill, 164, 1928-35 **In All Competitions:** John Richards, 190 (League 144 + FA Cup 24 + League Cup 18 + European Competitions 4) 1969-83
Record Transfer Fee Received: £1,000,000 from Manchester City for Steve Daley, Sept 1979
Record Transfer Fee Paid: £1,175,000 to Aston Villa for Andy Gray, Sept 1980
Best Performances: League: Champions Div 1 (3) **FA Cup:** Winners (4) **League/Milk Cup:** Winners (2) **European Cup:** Quarter Final **European Cup Winners Cup:** Semi-Final **UEFA Cup:** Runners-up
Most League Points: 75, Div 2, 1982-3 **Most League Goals:** 115, Div 2, 1931-2
Record League Victory and Most Goals Scored in a League Match: 10-1 v Leicester City, Div 1, 15 April 1938
Most Goals Scored in a Cup Tie: 14-0 v Crosswells Brewery, 2nd Round FA Cup, 13 Nov 1886
Record League Defeat: 1-10 v Newton Heath, Div 1, 15 Oct 1892
European Competitions Entered: European Cup 1958-9, 1959-60 European Cup Winners Cup 1960-1 UEFA Cup 1971-2, 1973-4, 1974-5, 1980-1
Oldest Player in League Match:
Youngest Player in League Match: David Wintergill, 16
Most Consecutive Undefeated League Matches: 20 1923-24   **League Matches Without a Win:** 19 1984-8
Longest Run of Undefeated Home League Matches: 27 1923-24, 1937-38   **Away League Matches:** 11 1953-54
Longest Run Without Home League Win: 13 1984-85   **Away League Win:** 32 1922-23
Most Consecutive League Wins: 8 1915, 1967   **Home League Wins:** 14 1953
Most Consecutive League Defeats: 8 1981-82   **Away League Wins:** 5 1938, 1962, 1980

Club Statistician for the Directory: Les Smith

				APPEARANCES				GOALS			
ERS NAME **Wt Birthdate**	**Honours**	**Birthplace** **Transfers**	**Clubs**	League	Milk Cup	FA Cup	Other Comps	League	Milk Cup	FA Cup	Other Comps
LKEEPERS											
t Barrett 12.11 2.4.63		Alverston	Wolverhampton W.	21	1	1					
ent Bartram 12.13 7.8.68		Birmingham	Wolverhampton W.								
ENDERS											
d Barnes 11.4 16.11.61	EY	London £35,000	Coventry City (A) Ipswich Town Wolverhampton W.	9 16+1 60	5	4 3	2				
Clarke 11.10 20.8.67		Walsall	Wolverhampton W.	21+2	2	1	2	1			
d Heywood 11.0 25.7.67		Wolverhampton	Wolverhampton W.	7		1					
ff Palmer 12.5 11.7.54	EU23 (2), Div. 2, 77, Lg Cup 74, 80	Cannock	Wolverhampton W. (A) Burnley Wolverhampton W.	389+5 34	32 2	38+1 3	6 4	13	2		
e Stoutt 11.10 5.4.64		Halifax	Huddersfield (NC) Wolverhampton W.	3 29+3	1 2	2	1				
d Streete 14.8 5.5.59		Jamaica	Derby County Wolverhampton W.	36 25	4	1	1 2				
r Zelem 12.5 13.2.62		Manchester	Chester City (A) Wolverhampton W.	124+5 28	8 2	5	2	15	2	1	
FIELD											
Dougherty 9.5 12.5.66		Leamington	Wolverhampton W. Torquay United (L)	10+6 5	1+1	2	1 1	2			1
er Eli 11.4 11.9.65		Bradford	Leeds United Wolverhampton W.	1+2 14		1					
nael Holmes 10.8 9.9.65		Blackpool	Bradford City Wolverhampton W.	0+5 26			3+1 0+1	3			
h Lockhart 11.2 19.7.64		Wallsend	Cambridge United (A) Wolverhampton W.	55+13 12	15	1	2	8 2			
sell Turley 11.10 28.8.67		Walsall	Nottingham Forest (A) Wolverhampton W.								
WARDS											
n Edwards 10.7 25.2.62		Wolverhampton	Shrewsbury Town Wolverhampton W.	7+6 33+3	2		2	1 14			1
Edwards 11.5 14.3.66		Wall Heath	Olswinford Wolverhampton W.								
y Mutch 11.3 28.12.63		Liverpool	Southport Wolverhampton W.	15				7			
n Purdie 12.1 22.2.67		Corby	Wolverhampton W.	41+1	2	1	1	6	1		
ek Ryan 10.4 4.1.67		Dublin	Wolverhampton W.	31+19	2+1	1	1	5			
DITIONAL CONTRACT PROFESSIONALS											
PRENTICES											
N-CONTRACT PLAYERS											
hard Wood											

Record Attendance: 61,315 v Liverpool, FA Cup Round 5, 11 Feb 1939

Smallest Home Attendance for a First Class Match:

Record Receipts: £80,839 v Swindon Town, League Cup Semi-Final, 12 Feb 1980

Season Tickets: Stand: £70.00; Ground: £50.00 (adults) £35.00 (juveniles/OAPs)

Executive Box Season Tickets: £5,000 per annum

Cost of Stand Tickets: £4.00; **Terraces:** £3.00 (juveniles/OAPs £2 terraces only)

Match and Ticket Information: Seats available by post with payment & SAE one month before each match

Car Parking: Available around 'The West Park', in side streets and at the rear of the North Bank

Nearest Railway Station: Wolverhampton (0902 595451)

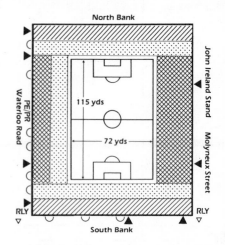

How to get to the ground

From North: Use Motorway M6 until junction 12, leave motorway and follow signs Wolverhampton A5 then A449 and at roundabout take 2nd exit into Waterloo Road then turn left into Molineux Street for Wolverhampton Wanderers FC

From East: Use Motorway M6 until junction 10, leave Motorway and follow signs Wolverhampton A454. Then at crossroads turn right into Stratford Street. In 0.2m turn left into Ring Road. Then at next crossroads turn right into Waterloo Road and shortly turn right into Molineux Street for Wolverhampton Wanderers FC

From South: Use Motorway M5 until junction 2, leave motorway and follow signs Wolverhampton A4123 turn right then shortly turn left into Ring Road. In 1m turn left into Waterloo Road and shortly turn right into Molineux Street for Wolverhampton Wanderers FC

From West: Use A454 S.P. Wolverhampton and at roundabout turn left into Ring Road, then turn left into Waterloo Road and shortly turn right into Molineux Street for Wolverhampton FC

Price of 1986-7 Programme: 40p
Number of Pages: 16
Subscriptions: Please consult club

Local Newspapers: Express and Star, Sports Argus

Local Radio Stations: Beacon Radio, BRMB

WREXHAM

Division 4

President
F Wellum

Chairman
W Pryce Griffiths

Vice-Chairman
G Mytton

Directors
C Griffiths
F J Tomlinson
F Wellum
N Dickens
G Dickens
J Scott
D Rhodes

Company Secretary/Gen. Man.
A E Rance (0978 262129)

Assistant Secretary
Miss M Pike

Manager
'Dixie' McNeil

Assistant Manager/Physiotherapist
George Showell

Commercial Manager
S R Slater (0978 352536)

ack Row L to R: Darren Wright, Frank
ones, Paul Emson, Steve Massey, Nick
encher. **Middle Row:** Dixie McNeil
Manager), Steve Emery, Jim Steel,
hris Pearce, Mike Williams, Paul
omstive, George Showell (Assistant
lanager/Physio). **Front Row:** Roger
reece, Steve Buxton, Steve Charles,
oe Cooke, Barry Horne, Neil Salathiel,
haun Cunnington, Mike Conroy.

As was the case in the two previous seasons Wrexham were involved in the re-election struggle right up to the end of the season. Although they eventually finished in 13th place.

Once again inconsistency was the name of the game and indeed the only thing that Wrexham Football Club are consistent in at the moment is their inconsistency!

The club started off 1985/86 in quite good fashion and the loyal Racecourse fans had every right to believe that better things could be on the way under Dixie McNeil. Unfortunately two long term injuries to Steve Emery and Mike Williams put paid to that. Also the early season sale of goalkeeper Mike Hooper to Liverpool was crucial, as after he left, the Robins had no regular experienced custodian for League matches for the rest of the season. A number were used, loan and part-time keepers included out-of-retirement Dai Davies for Welsh Cup ties who had also assisted Bangor City in their Cup Winners Cup exploits earlier in the season. Cash must be found by the directors to buy a good experienced goalkeeper as the team may have fared a good deal better last season with one.

The number of suspensions to players was far too high and manager McNeil will no doubt feel something must be done about discipline in the side.

The manager had asked striker Jim Steel for 20 goals and the big Scot duly obliged with two in the last home league match with Stockport to bring up that total.

At times the side played some splendid football but so many of the side did not play up to standard on too many occasions. Often the attitude of the players was in question.

Barry Horne is a promising young player and has been included in Mike England's Welsh squad. Paul Comstive has looked a good player in the midfield role as has leading goalscorer Steve Charles.

Mike William's, although out of the side through injury for much of the season, is a fine young defender and won The Player of the Year Award.

Jim Steel is a very good front man as a goalscorer, and a player who skillfully holds up the ball very well. It was his two goals which won Wrexham the Welsh Cup for the first time since 1977/78 in a replay with Kidderminster Harriers (who had earlier knocked out Newport, Swansea, Hereford and Shrewsbury to reach the Final) to ensure another crack at Europe in 86/87. "More glory I wonder?". If and it is an if with little cash available the manager can bring in some quality players to augment those already in the side, there maybe a "chance" of promotion in 86/87, but this seems to be quoted in every Review of the Season.

Anyway we will cross our North Wales fingers.
Gareth M Davies

WREXHAM

DIVISION FOUR: 13th   **FA CUP:** 2nd ROUND   **MILK CUP:** 2nd ROUND

MATCH	DATE	COMPE-TITION	VENUE	OPPONENTS	RESULT	HALF TIME	L'GUE POS'N	GOALSCORERS/GOAL TIMES	ATTEN DANC
1	A 17	CL	A	Swindon Town	W 1-0	0-0		Charles 73	(4,1!
2	20	MC1/1	H	Rochdale	W 4-0	3-0		Gregory 3 (20, 26, 36), Horne 87	1,7
3	24	CL	H	Colchester United	W 2-1	0-1	3	Bowen (og) 57, Steel 62	2,2
4	26	CL	A	Scunthorpe United	D 1-1	0-1	3	Charles 75	(2,0!
5	31	CL	H	Crewe Alexandra	W 2-1	0-0	3	Horne 62, Charles 71	3,0
6	S 3	MC1/2	A	Rochdale	L 1-2	0-1		Steel 67	(1,2!
7	7	CL	H	Mansfield Town	D 1-1	0-0	3	Charles 65	(3,0!
8	14	CL	H	Exeter City	D 1-1	0-1	5	Charles (pen) 74	2,4
9	17	CL	H	Tranmere Rovers	D 1-1	0-1	7	Hencher 88	2,8
10	20	CL	A	Southend United	L 0-3	0-1	9		(4,9!
11	24	MC2/1	H	Stoke City	L 0-1	0-0			5,2
12	28	CL	H	Orient	L 1-3	1-1	10	Gregory 39	1,8
13	O 1	CL	A	Northampton Town	W 2-1	1-0	8	Steel 25, Charles 61	(2,2:
14	5	CL	A	Port Vale	L 0-4	0-1	11		(3,3!
15	9	MC2/2	A	Stoke City	L 0-1	0-0			(6,7!
16	12	CL	H	Halifax Town	W 2-1	2-1	10	Charles 10, Cunnington 45	1,6
17	15	CL	H	Cambridge United	W 6-2	3-0	8	Steel 39, Edwards 3 (43, 45, 52), Hencher 58, Charles 87	1,6
18	19	CL	A	Aldershot	L 0-6	0-2	8		(1,1!
19	26	CL	H	Chester City	D 1-1	0-1	8	Charles 58	3,5
20	N 2	CL	A	Rochdale	L 2-3	0-1	11	Charles (pen) 57, Heaton (og) 58	(1,6!
21	6	CL	A	Peterborough United	D 1-1	0-1	11	Slack (og) 49	(1,9!
22	9	CL	H	Hereford United	L 0-1	0-0	13		2,1
23	16	FAC1	H	Bolton Wanderers	W 3-1	2-0		Keay 12, Hencher 35, Cunnington 87	2,7
24	23	CL	A	Torquay United	W 3-1	1-0	14	Salathiel 31, Steel 75, Edwards 86	(1,1!
25	D 7	FAC2	A	Notts County	D 2-2	0-0		Gregory 61, Horne 90	(4,5!
26	10	FAC2R	H	Notts County	L 0-3	0-1			2,6
27	13	CL	A	Stockport County	L 0-2	0-1	17		(2,4!
28	20	CL	A	Colchester United	L 2-5	0-2	18	Cunnington 55, Gregory 89	(1,6!
29	26	CL	H	Preston North End	D 1-1	1-0	17	Charles 13	2,2
30	J 1	CL	A	Burnley	L 2-5	2-2	17	Brignull 7, Mooney 21	(4,0:
31	11	CL	A	Crewe Alexandra	L 2-3	0-0	18	Charles (pen) 50, 70	(1,6!
32	18	CL	H	Swindon Town	L 0-1	0-1	18		1,7
33	21	FRT	H	Port Vale	D 1-1	1-0		Steel 30	9
34	23	FRT	A	Blackpool	D 2-2	0-0		Charles 55, 62	1,6
35	25	CL	A	Exeter City	W 1-0	1-0	18	Mooney 31	(2,3!
36	F 1	CL	H	Mansfield Town	L 1-2	0-2	18	Hencher 76	1,3
37	4	CL	A	Cambridge United	L 3-4	1-3	18	Hencher 23, Charles (pen) 52, 86	(1,5!
38	15	CL	S	Tranmere Rovers	W 3-1	1-0	16	Comstive 15, Charles 47, Steel 80	(1,7!
39	25	CL	H	Hartlepool United	W 1-0	0-0	15	Steel 86	9
40	M 1	CL	A	Orient	W 3-1	0-0	15	Gregory 46, Charles 48, Comstive 64	(2,1!
41	4	CL	A	Northampton Town	W 1-0	1-0	14	Steel 4	1,4
42	8	CL	A	Port Vale	L 1-3	1-1	14	Edwards 17	2,6
43	11	CL	H	Rochdale	W 2-0	0-0	10	Buxton 61, 86	1,3
44	14	CL	A	Halifax Town	L 2-5	2-3	11	Charles 35, Steel 44	(1,2!
45	22	CL	A	Chester City	L 1-2	1-1	14	Edwards 17	(4,7!
46	25	CL	H	Aldershot	W 4-1	1-0		Edwards 1, 57, Steel 79, Buxton 82	1,0
47	29	CL	H	Burnley	L 0-1	0-1	12		2,0
48	31	CL	A	Preston North End	L 0-1	0-0	15		(5,1!
49	A 5	CL	H	Peterborough United	L 0-1	0-1	16		1,1
50	8	CL	H	Southend United	D 0-0	0-0	16		1,0
51	12	CL	A	Hereford United	L 1-3	1-2	16	Horne 28	(2,5!
52	19	CL	H	Torquay United	W 3-2	1-1	15	Steel 37, Horne 88, Edwards 89	1,0
53	26	CL	A	Hartlepool United	D 3-3	0-1	17	Charles pen 47, pen 73, Steel 49	(1,5:
54	29	CL	H	Scunthorpe United	W 1-0	0-0	16	Steel 84	1,0
55	3	CL	H	Stockport County	W 3-0	1-0	13	Steel 39, 54, Comstive 85	1,3

Best Home League Attendance: 3,500 v Chester 26/10   **Smallest:** 957 v Hartlepool 25/2   **Av Home Att:** 1,82

Goal Scorers: Compared with 84-85: +22

League (68):	Charles 20 (6 pen), Steel 14, Edwards 9, Hencher 4, Buxton 3, Comstive 3, Gregory 3, Horne 3, Cunnington 2, Mooney 2, Brignull 1, Horne 1, Salathiel 1, Opponents 3
Milk Cup (5):	Gregory 4, Steel 1
FA CUP (5):	Cunnington 1, Gregory 1, Hencher 1, Horne 1, Keay 1
FRT (3):	Charles 2, Steel 1

Hooper	Salathiel	Cunnington	Williams	Keay	Emery	Muldoon	Horne	Steel	Charles	Gregory	Hencher (NC)	Edwards	Comstive	Jones	Vaughan (L)	Buxton (NC)	Keen (NC)	McNeil	Mooney (L)	Brignull (L)	Ferguson (NC)	Morriss (NC)	Scott (NC)	Chadwick	Stanton (L)	Referee	
1	2	3	4	5	6	7	8	9	10	11																I Hemley	1
1	2	3	4	5	6	7	8	9	10	11*	12															P Vanes	2
1	2	3	4	5	6	7*	8	9	10	11		12														M Reid	3
1	2	3	4	5	6	12	8	9	10	11		7*														D Hutchinson	4
1	2	3	4	5	6		8	9	10	11		7														N Glover	5
1	2	3	4	5	6		8	9	10†	11		7*	12													M Peck	6
1	2	7	4	5	6		8	9	10	11			3													R Dilkes	7
1	2	7	4	5	6*	12	8	9	10	11			3													T Jones	8
1		6	4	5	2	7*	8	9		11		10	12	3												P Tyldesley	9
1		6	4	5	2	7	8	9*		11		10	12	3												D Reeves	10
1		6	2	5			8		10	11	9	7	3	4												I Hendrick	11
1	2	6		5			8	9*	10	11	12	7	3	4												K Baker	12
1	2	6		5		7	8	9	10	11	12		3	4												E Scales	13
1	2	6		5		7	8	9	10	11			3	4												T Simpson	14
1	2	6	4	5			8		10	11		7	9	3												A Banks	15
1	2*	6	4	5		12	8		10	11		7	9	3												G Ashby	16
1	2			5			8	9	10	11		7	6	3	4											A Robinson	17
1	2			5		12	8	9*	10	11		7	6	3	4											T Ward	18
	2	6		5			8*	9	10	11	12	7	3	4	1											N Midgley	19
	2	6		5			8	9	10	11		7	3	4	1											K Lupton	20
	2	6		5			8	9	10	11		7	3	4	1											D Hedges	21
	2	6		5			8	9	10	11*		7	3	4	1		12									D Scott	22
	2	6		5			8	9	10	11		7	3	4		1										K Breen	23
	2	6		5			8	9	10*	11	12	7	3	4		1										M Cotton	24
	2	6		5		12	8	9*		11		7	3	4		1	10									N Midgley	25
	2	6		5			8	9*		11	12	7	3	4		1	10	1	12							N Midgley	26
	2	6		5			8		10	11		7	3	4		1			9	4						N Wilson	27
	2	6		5			8		10	11		7	3			1			9	4						Allan Robinson	28
	2			5			8	9	10	11			6	3		1			7	4						V Callow	29
	2			5			8	9	10*	11		12	6	3†		1			7	4						G Courtney	30
	2	3		5			8	9		11*		12	6						7	4	1					J Ashworth	31
	2	3		5			8	9*		11		12	6						7	4	1					D Allison	32
	2	3		5			8	9	10				4						7		1					P Tyldesley	33
	2	3		5			8	9	10	11			6	4					7		1					C Seel	34
	2	3	5*				8	9	10	11			6	4					7			1	12			G Ashby	35
	2	3					8	9	10	11			6	4					7			1	5			T Jones	36
	2	3		5			8	9	10	11			6						7			1	4			K Miller	37
	2	3		5			8	9	10	11	12	7*	6	4							1					N Ashley	38
	2	3	12	5			8	9	10	11		7*	6	4							1					N Midgley	39
	2	3	12	5*			8	9	10	11		7	6	4							1					J Bray	40
	2	3		5			8	9	10	11*		7	6	4							1					N Wilson	41
	2	3		5			8	9	10			7	6	4							1			12		T Mills	42
	2	3		5			8	9	10			7	6	4							1			11*		M Scott	43
	2	3		5		12	8	9	10			7	6	4							1					K Redfern	44
	2		6	5			8*	9	10	11	12		3	4							1				7	I Hendrick	45
	2	3	4	5			8	9	10	11		6*					12				1				7	N Glover	46
	2	3*	4	5			8	9	10	11		6					12				1				7	D Shaw	47
	2		4	5			8	9	10	11		6*	3				12				1				7	T Simpson	48
	2	6	4	5			8	9	10	11	12		3*								1				7	L Robinson	49
	2	3	4	5			8	9		11			6					10			1				7	M Heath	50
	2	3	4	5			8	9*	10	11		12	6								1				7	M Dimblebee	51
	2	3	4	5			8	9	12	11			6					10			1				7*	A Robinson	52
	2	3	4	5			8	9	10	11			6								1				7	M Peck	53
	2	3	4	5			8	9	10	11	12	6*									1				7	R Guy	54
	2	3	4	5†			8	9	10*	11	12		6								1				7	J Ball	55
4	42	42	25	40	8	6	46	43	39	34	23	24	34	27	4	1	5		9	5	20	3	2	1	8	League Appearances	
			2		1	5			1	3	3	9	1	1		3							1	1		Substitute Appearances	
3	4	4	4	2	2	4	2	4	4	2·1	2	2·1	1													Milk Cup Appearances	
3	3	3		1·1	3	2	1	3	2	2	3	3		1	3	0·1										FA Cup Appearances	
2	2		2			2	2	2	1	1	1	2							2	2						FR Trophy Appearances	

Also Played: Position(Game): Weetman (NC) 11*(44)

Players on Loan: Vaughan (West Ham), Brinull (Bournemouth), Mooney (Liverpool), Stanton (Huddersfield)

Departures: Hooper (Liverpool), Keay (F), Gregory (F), Muldoon (F), Edwards (F)

'THE ROBINS'

Formed: 1873
Turned Professional: 1912   **Ltd Co:** 1912

Previous Managers: 1921-9 Charles Hewitt   1929-31 Jack Baynes   1932-6 Captain Logan
1936-8 Ernest Blackburn   1938-40 Tommy Morgan   1940-9 Tom W Williams
1949-50 Leslie J McDowall   1951-4 Peter Jackson   1954-7 Clifford Lloyd   1957-9 John Love
1960-1 Billy Morris   1961-5 Ken Barnes   1965-6 Billy Morris   1966-7 Jack Rowley   1967 Cliff Lloyd
1967-8 Alvan Williams   1968-77 John Neal   1977-81 Arfon Griffiths   1981-2 Mel Sutton
1982-Bobby Roberts
Honours: Div 3 Champions, Welsh Cup Winners (22)
League Career: Original members of Div 3 (N) 1921   Transferred to Div 3 1958
Relegated to Div 4 1959-60   Promoted to Div 3 1961-2   Relegated to Div 4 1963-4
Promoted to Div 3 1969-70   Promoted to Div 2 1977-8   Relegated to Div 3 1981-2
Relegated to Div 4 1982-3
Colours: Red shirts with white trim, white shorts with red trim red stockings
Change Colours: Sky blue shirts, blue shorts, sky blue stockings
Reserves League: Welsh National League (Premier Division)

CLUB RECORDS

Most Appearances for Club: Arfon Griffiths: **Total 586 + 6 subs** (not including Cup Ties)
Most Capped Player: Joey Jones (Wales) 29   **For England:** None
Record Goalscorer in a Match: T Bamford, 6 v New Brighton, (H) 11-1, Div 3 (N), 1933-34   T H Lewis 5 v Crewe Alexandra (H) 7-0, Div 3 (N), 20 Sept 1930   T Bamford 5 v Carlisle United (H) 8-1, Div 3 (N), 17 Mar 1934
Record League Goalscorer in a Season: Tommy Bamford, 44, Div 3 (N), 1934-5
Record League Goalscorer in a Career: Tommy Bamford 175, 1929-35
Record Transfer Fee Received: £300,000 from Manchester United for Mickey Thomas, Nov 1978   £300,000 from Manchester City for Bobby Shinton, July 1979
Record Transfer Fee Paid: £210,000 to Liverpool for Joey Jones, Oct 1978
Best Performances: League: 15th Div 2 1978-9   **FA Cup:** 6th Round 1973-4, 1977-8   **League/Milk Cup:** 5th Round 1961, 1978   **Welsh Cup:** Winners (22), Runners-up (19) This is a record number of victories and appearances in the Final   **European Cup Winners Cup:** Quarter Final 1975-6
Most League Points: 61, Div 4, 1969-70, 1977-8   **Most League Goals:** 106, Div 3 (N), 1932-3
Record League Victory and Most Goals Scored in a League Match: 10-1 v Hartlepool, Div 4, 3 March 1962
Most Goals Scored in a First Class Match: 11-1 v New Brighton, (H), Div 3 (N) Cup, 1933-34
Record League Defeat: 0-9 v Brentford, Div 3, 15 Oct 1963
European Competitions Entered: European Cup Winners Cup: 1972-3, 1975-6, 1978-9, 1979-80, 1984-85
Oldest Player in League Match: Bobby Roberts 44 yrs
Youngest Player in League Match: Mark Morris, 16 yrs
Most Consecutive Undefeated League Matches: 16 1966

Longest Run of Undefeated Home League Matches: 38 1969-70
Longest Run Without Home League Win: 10 1980-81
Most Consecutive League Wins: 7 1961, 1978
Most Consecutive League Defeats: 9 1963

League Matches Without a Win: 14 1923-24, 1950
Away League Matches: 8 1961, 1966
Away League Win: 31 1982-83
Home League Wins: 13 1932-3
Away League Wins: 7 1961

Club Statistician for the Directory: Gareth Davies

WREXHAM

PLAYERS NAME / Wt Birthdate	Honours	Birthplace / Transfers	Clubs	League	Milk Cup	FA Cup	Other Comps	League	Milk Cup	FA Cup	Other Comps
GOALKEEPERS											
s Pearce	WYS	Newport	Wolverhampton W. (A)								
11.4 7.8.61		F	Blackburn Rovers								
		F	Rochdale	41	6	1					
		F	Port Vale	47	3	2	3				
		F	Wrexham								
DEFENDERS											
Cooke		Dominica, WI	Bradford City (A)	184+20	10+1	15		62	5	4	
12.7 15.2.55		£40,000	Peterborough United	18				5			
		£50,000	Oxford United	71+1	5	2		13			
		£25,000	Exeter City	17	3	1		3			
		£10,000	Bradford City	61+1	6	4		6	2	4	
		F	Rochdale	74	4	5	2	4	1		
		F	Wrexham								
un Connington		Bourne	Wrexham	126+3	7	5	7	8		1	
11.0 4.1.66											
Comstive		Southport	Blackburn Rovers	3+3							
12.7 25.11.61			Rochdale (L)	4		1	1	2			
		F	Wigan Athletic	37	9	4	1	2			
		F	Wrexham	61+2	2+1	3	3	6			
ik Jones		Llandudno	Wrexham	29+1	1	3	2				
11.0 3.10.60											
Salathiel	WYS	Wrexham	Wrexham	4							
10.0 19.11.62		F	Crewe Alexandra	64+1	4	3					
		F	Wrexham	107	4	4	2	1			
hael Williams†	WY	Mancot	Chester City	38+3				3			1
11.0 6.2.65		F	Wrexham			2					1
MIDFIELD											
ve Charles	Div. 4, 82	Sheffield	Sheffield United	112+11	12	9+1	3	10	1	1	3
10.7 10.5.60			Wrexham	71+1	4	2	2+2	27			
e Conroy	SPD 81, 82, Sc 80	Glasgow	Celtic	58+9	8+5	5+1	2	9	3	1	
½ 11.2 31.7.57		F	Hibernian	31+1	6	1		2	2		
		F	Blackpool	66	6	1	1	1			
			Wrexham								
ve Emery	Div. 3, 76	Ledbury	Hereford United (A)	203+1	17	11		10	1		
11.10 7.2.56		£100,000	Derby County	73+2	2	3		4			
		F	Newport County								
		F	Hereford United	72+3	3	5	3	1	1		
		F	Wrexham	8+1	2						
l Emson	Lincoln	Bridgtown									
11.3 22.10.58		£5,000	Derby County	112+15	4+3	1+3		13			
			Grimsby Town	89+7	12	3+1		15	1	1	
		F	Wrexham								
k Hencher		Lex	Wrexham	23+3	2+1	2	1	4	1		
12.0 24.8.61											
ry Horne		St. Asaph	Liverpool								
12.3 18.5.63			Rhyl								
			Wrexham	90	16	4	4	7		1	
ger Preece		Much Wenlock	Coventry City								
½ 10.0 9.6.69			Wrexham								
ren Wright		West Bromwich	Wolverhampton W.	1							
11.4 14.3.68			Wrexham								
FORWARDS											
ve Buxton		Birmingham	Wrexham	93+16	3+2	4	2	21			
9.8 13.3.60		F	Stockport County	12+6	2+1		0+1		1		
			Altrincham								
			Wrexham	1+3		1		3			
ve Massey		Denton	Stockport County (A)	87+14	8	5		20	3	1	
11.5 28.3.58		F	Bournemouth	85+12	5	3+1		19	1	2	
		F	Peterborough United	13+5		1+1		2			
		F	Northampton Town	60	4	5		26	3	1	
		F	Hull City	62+11	4+2	3+1	4+2	21	1	1	
		F	Wrexham								
Steel		Dumfries	Oldham Athletic (A)	101+7	8+1	6		24	1		
11.6 4.12.59			Wigan Athletic (L)	2				2			
			Wrexham (L)	9				6			
		£5,000	Port Vale	27+1	1+1	0+1		6	1		
		£10,000	Wrexham	109	4	3	8	28	1		1

ADDITIONAL CONTRACT PROFESSIONALS

rk Jones, Michael Keen, Craig Morgan, Mark Morris, Paul Nelson, Gary Pugh, Stepehn Scot, Carl Thomas, Darren Westman, Brian Williams

APPRENTICES

NON-CONTRACT PLAYERS

Davies, Ian Haigh, Nick Hencher, Tom Morgan, Mark Morris

THE RACECOURSE GROUND Mold Road, Wrexham Capacity: 28,5

Record Attendance: 34,445 v Manchester
United, FA Cup Round 4, 26 Jan 1957

**Smallest Home Attendance for a First Class
Match:** 912 v Southend, 8 April 1986

Record Receipts: £49,761.50 v Roma,
European Cup-Winners Cup Round 2, 2nd Leg, 7
Nov 1984

Executive Box Season Tickets: None

Cost of Stand Tickets: see note

Match and Ticket Information: Tickets not
bookable in advance

Car Parking: Parking ground at St. Marks,
Bodlyfryd Square, Eagles Meadows, Old Guild
Hall, Hill Street, Holt Street and Town Hall (Hill
Street)

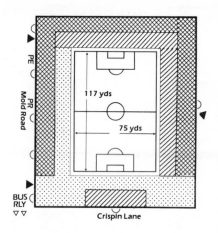

How to get to the ground

From North and West: Use A483 and
Wrexham bypass until junction with A541 then
branch left and at roundabout follow signs
Wrexham into Mold Road for Wrexham FC
From East and South: Follow signs into
Wrexham on A534 or A525 then follow signs
A541 into Mold Road for Wrexham FC

Price of 1986-7 Programme: 50p
Number of Pages: 20
Subscriptions: Available from club

Local Newspapers: Wrexham Evening Leaders,
Daily Post, Shropshire Star, Wrexham Express

Local Radio Stations: Radio City, Marcher
Sound, Radio Clwyd

Y ORK CITY

Chairman
M D B Sinclair

Directors
D M Craig
, BSC, FICE, FIMun E, FCI, ARB, M Cons E
B A Houghton
R B Strachan, MA LLB, FCIS
C Webb
E B Swallow
J A Quickfall

Club Secretary
Tom Hughes (0904 24447)

Medical Officer
Dr A I MacLeod

Manager
Denis Smith

Club Coach
Viv Busby

Physiotherapist
Gerry Delahunt

Sales Executive
Bob Baldwin (0904 24447)

Groundsman
Bryan Foster

Honorary Orthopaedic Surgeon
B J Brotherton FRCS

A lthough completing their 5th successive climb up the League since finishing bottom of Division 4 in 1981 — ending one place higher and 2 points better off than a year ago — it was a slightly disappointing season for 'The Minstermen'. Promotion hopes were high at the beginning of the campaign and at the end of November they were 2nd behind runaway leaders Reading. A bad spell in midterm, however, yielded just ten points out of a possible 39 and only a good finale — unbeaten in the last nine games — enabled them to finish 7th. Without doubt poor away performances cost City dear for whilst their form at Bootham Crescent was excellent with 16 wins and 49 goals they only recorded 4 victories on their travels the last being way back in November. Although average home League attendances fell to 4,111 this figure has only been bettered twice since the 2nd Division days in 1976.

For the 2nd successive season City were knocked out of the FA Cup in a 5th Round replay at Anfield. There was to be no repeat of the seven goal beating of a year ago, however, and the eventual Cup and League winners needed extra-time to extinguish City's dreams. In reaching the last 16 the club had the unique experience of being drawn at home to non-League opposition in four successive rounds. Second Division Grimsby Town ended City's Milk Cup hopes in Round 2 whilst the side failed to qualify for the knock out stages of the Freight Rover Trophy.

Andy Leaning and Tony Canham, both of whom had been playing in Northern Counties East League football the previous year, established themselves in the first team, whilst teenager Marco Gabbiadini showed much promise. During the season 'veteran' Gary Ford became only the 10th player to complete 300 League games for the club and Keith Walwyn reached his century of goals. He is now the 4th highest scorer in City's history — a fine achievement in 5 seasons. Ex-Sheffield Wednesday player Simon Mills did well in his first season at Bootham Crescent and was elected 'Clubman of the Year'. Players to leave during the campaign were Chris Evans and Mick Astbury to Darlington and Keith Houchen — the hero of the FA Cup win over Arsenal in January 1985 — to Scunthorpe.   David Batters

Back Row L to R: Alan Pearce, Simon Mills, Marco Gabbiadini, Derek Hood, Dale Banton, Tony Canham. **Middle Row:** Gerry Delahunt (Physio), Mike Pickering, Keith Walwyn, Neil Smallwood, Andy Leaning, David McAughtrie, Stuart McKenzie, Malcolm Crosby (Reserve Player/Coach). **Front Row:** Viv Busby (First Team Coach), Sean Haselgrave, Steve Senior, Ricky Sbragia, Martin Butler, Gary Ford, Denis Smith (Manager).

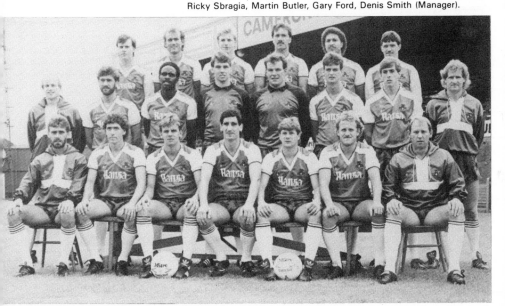

YORK CITY

DIVISION THREE: 7th   FA CUP: 5th ROUND   MILK CUP: 2nd ROUND

MATCH	DATE		COMPE-TITION	VENUE	OPPONENTS	RESULT		HALF TIME	L'GUE POS'N	GOALSCORERS/GOAL TIMES	ATTEN-DANCE
1	A	17	CL	H	Plymouth Argyle	W	3-1	2-0		Canham 11, Walwyn 45, Gabbiadini 57	4,246
2		20	MC1/1	H	Lincoln City	W	2-1	1-1		Walwyn 40, McAughtrie 85	3,636
3		24	CL	A	Bury	L	2-4	0-2	12	MacPhail (pen) 54, Walwyn 61	(2,782
4		26	CL	H	Wigan Athletic	W	4-1	2-0	4	Walwyn 6, 15, Ford 67, 82	4,067
5		31	CL	A	Wolverhampton W.	L	2-3	1-2	12	MacPhail (pen) 6, Walwyn 65	(4,400
6	S	4	MC1/2	A	Lincoln City	W	2-1	1-1		MacPhail (pen) 15, Walwyn 61	(2,257
7		7	CL	H	Cardiff City	D	1-1	1-0	11	Evans 39	3,760
8		14	CL	A	Blackpool	W	2-0	0-0	5	Walwyn 67, Canham 77	4,053
9		17	CL	A	Notts County	L	1-3	0-3	11	Walwyn 71	(3,708
10		21	CL	H	Bristol City	D	1-1	1-0	11	MacPhail (pen) 44	3,904
11		24	MC2/1	A	Grimsby Town	D	1-1	1-1		Walwyn 30	(2,908
12		28	CL	A	Gillingham	W	2-1	1-1	7	Banton 12, McAughtrie 87	(3,509
13	O	1	CL	H	Bolton Wanderers	W	3-0	1-0	5	Houchen 9, 50, Banton 70	4,680
14		5	CL	H	Darlington	W	7-0	2-0	3	Canham 3 (14, 63 (pen) 75), Walwyn 17, 66, Senior 80, Houchen 84	5,039
15		8	MC2/2	H	Grimsby Town	L	2-3	1-2		Houchen (pen) 15, Banton 46	5,030
16		12	CL	A	Chesterfield	L	0-1	0-1	4		(3,723
17		19	CL	A	Derby County	L	1-2	0-1	8	Houchen (pen) 67	(11,157
18		22	CL	H	A.F.C. Bournemouth	W	2-1	1-1	5	Walwyn 14, Ford 81	4,194
19		26	CL	H	Rotherham United	W	2-1	1-1	3	Banton 15, Pickering (og) 52	4,444
20	N	2	CL	A	Bristol Rovers	W	1-0	1-0	3	Banton 35	(4,274
21		6	CL	A	Newport County	D	1-1	0-1	4	Mills 76	(1,529
22		9	CL	H	Reading	L	0-1	0-1	5		6,045
23		16	FAC1	H	Morecambe	D	0-0	0-0			3,692
24		19	FAC1R	A*	Morecambe	W	2-0	2-0		Sbragia 2, Walwyn 10	(1,305
25		24	CL	A	Lincoln City	W	4-3	1-2	5	Banton 29, 81, Senior 47, Walwyn 62	(2,295
26		30	CL	A	Brentford	W	1-0	0-0	2	Walwyn 75	3,674
27	D	7	FAC2	H	Whitby Town	W	3-1	1-0		Ford 7, Walwyn 74, Pearce 79	6,225
28		14	CL	A	Swansea City	L	0-1	0-0	3		(2,779
29		20	CL	H	Bury	D	0-0	0-0	6		3,645
30		26	CL	A	Doncaster Rovers	L	0-1	0-1	7		5,320
31	J	1	CL	A	Walsall	L	1-3	0-2	11	MacPhail 65	(5,643
32		4	FAC3	H	Wycombe Wanderers	W	2-0	1-0		Walwyn 41, 61	5,532
33		11	CL	H	Wolverhampton W.	W	2-1	2-0	10	Houchen 12, Banton 44	4,296
34		14	FRT	H	Rotherham United	D	0-0	0-0			2,122
35		18	CL	A	Plymouth Argyle	D	2-2	1-1	11	Walwyn 31, 48	(5,942
36		25	FAC4	H	Altrincham	W	2-0	0-0		Banton 67, Ford 80	8,834
37		28	FRT	A	Hartlepool United	L	2-3	0-2		Houchen (pen) 53, Butler 71	(1,080
38		31	CL	A	Cardiff City	L	1-2	1-0		Walwyn 8	(2,051
39	F	4	CL	H	AFC Bournemouth	L	0-2	0-2	12		(2,476
40		8	CL	H	Derby County	L	1-3	0-3	12	Houchen (pen) 64	5,994
41		15	FAC5	H	Liverpool	D	1-1	0-0		Ford 60	12,443
42		18	FAC5R	A	Liverpool	L	1-3	1-1		Canham 43	(19,326
43		22	CL	A	Bristol City	D	2-2	1-1	12	MacPhail 45, Canham 90	(6,409
44	M	1	CL	H	Gillingham	W	2-0	0-0	12	Cochrane og 83, Hinnigan og 89	4,351
45		4	CL	A	Bolton Wanderers	D	1-1	1-0	12	Walwyn 32	(3,589
46		9	CL	A	Darlington	L	0-1	0-1	11		(4,255
47		12	CL	H	Bristol Rovers	W	4-0	1-0	9	Canham 7, 72, Walwyn 70, Gabbiadini 77	2,857
48		15	CL	H	Chesterfield	W	2-0	1-0	8	Hood 35, Gabbiadini 73	3,580
49		18	CL	A	Wigan Athletic	L	0-1	0-0	9		(4,307
50		22	CL	A	Rotherham United	L	1-4	0-3	11	Gabbiadini 50	(3,240
51		29	CL	A	Walsall	W	1-0	1-0	10	Walwyn 35	3,695
52		31	CL	A	Doncaster Rovers	D	1-1	1-0	10	Hay 9	(3,319
53	A	5	CL	A	Newport County	W	3-1	0-0	8	Walwyn 16, 66, Canham 80	3,038
54		12	CL	A	Reading	D	0-0	0-0	8		(6,133
55		19	CL	H	Lincoln City	W	2-1	0-0	7	Canham 59, MacPhail (pen) 78	3,874
56		22	CL	H	Notts County	D	2-2	2-1	7	Walwyn 34, MacPhail (pen) 44	3,211
57		26	CL	A	Brentford	D	3-3	0-1	7	Banton (pen) 50, Mills 66, Senior 81	(2,864)
58	M	3	CL	H	Swansea City	W	3-1	2-0	7	Walwyn 28, Banton 32, Canham 76	3,132
59		6	CL	H	Blackpool	W	3-0	1-0	7	Canham 27, 82, Banton 78	3,370

Best Home League Attendance: 6,045 v Reading 9/11	Smallest: 2,857 v Bristol Rovers	Av Home Att: 4,111

Goal Scorers:

Compared with 84-85: −1,439

League (77): Walwyn 22 (1 pen), Canham 13 (1 pen), Banton 10 (1 pen), MacPhail 7 (5 pen), Houchen 6 (2 pen), Gabbiadini 4, Ford 3, Senior 3, Mills 2, Evans 1, Hay 1, Hood 1, McAughtrie 1, Opponents 3

Milk Cup (7): Walwyn 3, Banton 1, Houchen 1 (pen), McAughtrie 1, MacPhail 1 (pen)

FA CUP (11): Walwyn 4, Ford 3, Banton 1, Canham 1, Pearce 1, Sbragia 1

FRT (2): Butler 1, Houchen 1 (pen)

[?]	Hood	Evans	McAughtrie	MacPhail	Haslegrave	Ford	Gabbiadini	Walwyn	Houchen	Canham	Mills	Banton	Senior	Hay	Leaning	Sbragia	Pearce	Murphy	McKenzie (NC)	Butler	Referee	
	2	3	4	5	6	7	8*	9	10	11	12										J Worrall	1
	2	3	4	5	6	7	12	9	10	11		8									**K Redfern**	2
	2	5	3	4	7	6		11	8*	9		10	12								D Shaw	3
	2	3	4*	5	6	7	12	9		11	10	8									C Seel	4
	2	3	4	5	6	7		9	12	11*	10	8									R Gifford	5
	2	3	4	5	6	7		9		11	10	8									**M Heath**	6
	2	3	4	5	6*	7		9	12	11	10	8									A Robinson	7
	2	3	4	5	6	7		9		11	10	8									J Lloyd	8
	2	3	4	5	6*	7		9	12	11	10	8									C Downey	9
			4	5	6	7	12	9	10	11		8	2*	3							J Hough	10
	12		4	5	6	7*		9	10	11		8	2	3							**M Scott**	11
			4	5	6	7		9	10	11		8	2	3							I Hemley	12
			4	5	6	7		9	10	11		8	2	3							K Lupton	13
	12		4*	5	6	7		9	10	11		8	2	3							R Banks	14
			4	5	6	7		9	10	11		8	2	3							**L Dilkes**	15
			4	5	6	7		9	10	11		8	2	3							R Nixon	16
			4	5	6	7		9	10	11		8	2	3							P Tyldesley	17
			4	5	6	7	12	9		11	10*	8	2	3							N Glover	18
			4	5	6	7		9		11	10*	8	2	3							A Saunders	19
			4	5	6	7		9	12	11	10*	8	2	3							D Reeves	20
			4	5	6	7		9		11	10	8	2	3	1						R Groves	21
				5	6	7		9	12	11*	10	8	2	3	1	4					K Breen	22
				5	6	7		9	12	11*	10	8	2	3	1	4					**K Lupton**	23
				5		7		9	10		6	8	2	3	1	4	11				K Lupton	24
	12			5		7		9*	10		6	8	2	3	1	4	11				K Barratt	25
				5		7		9	10		6	8	2	3	1	4	11				N Midgley	26
	2		4	5		7		9	10		6	8		3	1		11				**G Aplin**	27
			4	5		7		9	10		6	8		3	1		11				V Callow	28
	2		4	5		7	12	9	10		6	8		3	1		11*				G Courtney	29
			4	5		7	12	9	10		6	8	2	3	1		11*				N Wilson	30
	3		4	5	6	7	12	9	10	11		8*	2		1						L Dilkes	31
	3		4	5	6	7		9	10	11		8	2		1						**D Allison**	32
	3		4	5	12	7		9*	10	11	6	8	2		1						M Peck	33
	3		4	5	12	7		9*	10*	11	6	8	2	12	1						**A Robinson**	34
	3		4	5		7		9	10	11	6	8	2		1						R Milford	35
	3		4	5		7		9	10	11	6	8	2		1						**G Tyson**	36
			4			7		9*	10	11	6	8	2	3	1			5*	12	12	**M Peck**	37
	3		4	5		7		9	10	11*	6	8	2		1						K Baker	38
	3		4	5	12	7		9	10	11*	6	8	2		1						L Shapter	39
	3		4	5	11	7		9	10	12	6	8*	2		1						K Breen	40
	3		4	5	10	7		9		11	6	8	2		1						**H Taylor**	41
	3		4	5	10*	7	12	9		11	6	8	2		1						**H Taylor**	42
	3		4	5	10	7		9		11	6	8*	2		1						J Deakin	43
	3		4	5	10	7	12	9		11	6		2		1				8*		H Taylor	44
	3		4		10	7	12	9		11	6		2	5	1				8*		R Bridges	45
	3		4		10	7	12	9	8	11	6		2*	5	1						T Fitzharris	46
	3		4	5	10*	7	8	9		11	6				1			2		12	C Trussell	47
	3		4	5	10	7	8	9		11	6				1			2			N Glover	48
	3		4	5	10	7	8*	9		11	6				1			2		12	T Holbrook	49
	3		4	5†	10	7	8	9		11*	6				1			2		12	R Guy	50
	3*		4	5	10	7	8	9		11	6		2		1					12	G Tyson	51
			4	5	10	7	8	9		11*	6†		2	3	1					12	K Lupton	52
	2		4		10		8	9		11	6		12	3	1	5				7*	J Lloyd	53
			4	5	10	7	8*	9		11	6	12	2	3	1						D Reeves	54
	3		4	5	10	12		9		11		8*	2		1		6			7	J Ball	55
	3			5	10	12		9		11		8	2		1	4	6*			7	K Redfern	56
	3			5	10			9		11	6	8	2		1	4				7	V Callow	57
	3			5	10	12		9		11	6*	8	2		1	4				7	J Heath	58
	3		4	5	6		8	9		11	10		2		1					7	T Jones	59
16	29	7	41	42	37	40	10	46	20	40	35	33	33	21	30	7	7		4	8	League Appearances	
	2	2					12		5		1	1	2	1			1			6	Substitute Appearances	
2·1	2		4	4	4	4	0·1	4	3	4	2	3	2	2							Milk Cup Appearances	
5	5		7	4	7	7	4·2	5	6	7	6	3	7	2	2						FA Cup Appearances	
1	2		1	0·1	2	2		2	2	2	2	2	1·1	2				1	0·1	0·1	FR Trophy Appearances	

Players on Loan:

Departures: Evans (Darlington), Houchen (Scunthorpe Utd), Astbury (Darlington), MacPhail (Bristol City)

YORK CITY FC

'THE MINSTER MEN'

Formed: 1922
Turned Professional: 1922   **Ltd Co:** 192

Previous Managers: 1929-36 John Collier   1936-50 Tom Mitchell   1950-2 Dick Duckworth
1952-3 Charlie Spencer   1953-4 Jim McCormick   1956-60 Sam Bartram   1960-7 Tom Lockie
1967-8 Joe Shaw   1968-75 Tom Johnston   1975-7 Wilf McGuinness   1977-80 Charlie Wright
1980-1 Barry Lyons
Honours: Champions Div 4, 1983-4
League Career: Elected to Div 3 (N) 1929   Transferred to Div 4 1958
Promoted to Div 3 1958-9   Relegated to Div 4 1959-60   Promoted to Div 3 1964-5
Relegated to Div 4 1965-6   Promoted to Div 3 1970-1   Promoted to Div 2 1973-4
Relegated to Div 3 1975-6   Relegated to Div 4 1976-7   Promoted to Div 3 1983-4
Colours: Red shirts with white flash, navy blue shorts, white stockings
Change Colours: All sky blue
Reserves League: **'A' Team:**

CLUB RECORDS

Most Appearances for Club: Barry Jackson: Football League 481 + FA Cup 35 + League Cup 22 **Total 538**
Most Capped Player: Peter Scott, 7, Northern Ireland   **For England:** None
Record Goalscorer in a Match: Alf Patrick, 5 v Rotherham United, 6-1, Div 3, 20.11.1948
Record League Goalscorer in a Season: Bill Fenton, 31, Div 3 (N), 1951-2   Arthur Bottom, 1954-5 and 1955-6 Div 3 (N)
Record League Goalscorer in a Career: Norman Wilkinson, 125, 1954-66
Record Transfer Fee Received: £120,000 from Carlisle United for Gordon Staniforth, Oct 1979
Record Transfer Fee Paid: £50,000 to Aldershot for Dave Banton, Nov 1984
Best Performances: League: 15th Div 2 1974-5   **FA Cup:** Semi-Final Replay 1954-5 (as a Third Division
club)   **League/Milk Cup:** 5th Round 1961-2
Most League Points: 101, Div 4, 1983-4   **Most League Goals:** 96, Div 4, 1983-4
Record League Victory and Most Goals Scored in a League Match: 9-1 v Southport, Div 3 (N), 2 Feb 1957
Most Goals Scored in a Cup Tie: 7-1 v Horsforth (h), Prelim Round FA Cup, 1925-5   7-1 v Stockton Malleable (h), FA Cup
3rd Qualifying Round 1927-8   7-1 v Stockton (h), FA Cup 1st Qualifying Round, 1928-9, 6-0 v South Shields (a), FA Cup,
1st Round 1968-9
Record League Defeat: 0-12 v Chester, Div 3 (N), 1 Feb 1936
Oldest Player in League Match:
Youngest Player in League Match:
Most Consecutive Undefeated League Matches: 21 1973-74   **League Matches Without a Win:** 14 1967,
1972

Longest Run of Undefeated Home League Matches: 32 1970-71   **Away League Matches:** 10 1973-74
Longest Run Without Home League Win: 12 1981-82   **Away League Win:** 23 1966-67
Most Consecutive League Wins: 7 1964   **Home League Wins:** 14 1964-65
Most Consecutive League Defeats: 6 1966   **Away League Wins:** 5 1983, 1984

Club Statistician for the Directory: David Batters

YORK CITY

PLAYERS NAME Ht Wt Birthdate	Honours	Birthplace Transfers	Clubs	APPEARANCES League	Milk Cup	FA Cup	Other Comps	GOALS League	Milk Cup	FA Cup	Other Comps
GOALKEEPERS											
Andrew Leaning 6.1 13.7 18.5.63		York	Rowntree Mackintosh York City	30		7	2				
Neil Smallwood 6.2 13.0 3.12.66	·	York									
DEFENDERS											
David McAughtrie 6.1 12.3 30.1.63	SY	Cumnock F £8,000	Stoke City (A) Carlisle United York City	47+3 28 41	6 1 4	1 2 5	2	1 1 1	1		
Stuart MacKenzie 5.11 11.0 9.9.67		Hull	York City	4		0+1					
Mike Pickering 5.11 12.8 29.9.56		Huddersfield	Barnsley Southampton Sheffield Wednesday Norwich City (L) Bradford City (L) Barnsley Rotherham United York City	100 44 106+4 0+1 4 3 102	6 3 8+2 7	3 4 9 2 5	3	1 1 1			
Ricky Sbragia 6.0 11.0 26.5.56	Div. 4, 84	Lennox Town £15,000 £35,000 F	Birmingham City (A) Walsall Blackpool York City	14+1 77 24+2 123	 2 1 7	 5 15	7	 4 1 7	1		
Steve Senior 5.8½ 11.4 15.5.63	Div. 4, 84	Sheffield	York City (A) Darlington (L)	121+10 5	4+1	12 5	3 4	6			
MIDFIELD											
Tony Canham 5.9 11.8 8.6.60		Leeds	Harrogate RI York City	43+1	4	6+1	2	1			
Malcolm Crosby 5.9 11.3 4.7.54	Div. 4, 84	South Shields Player exch.	Aldershot (A) York City Wrexham (L)	272+22 99+4 5+1	11 2	18+1 11	1	36 4	2	3	
Gary Ford 5.8 11.10 8.2.61	Div. 4, 84	York	York City (A)	314+7	20	33	6	48	4	7	
Sean Hazelgrave 5.8 10.7 7.6.51	Div. 4, 84	Stoke £35,000 £20,000 F F	Stoke City Nottingham Forest Preston North End Crewe Alexandra York City	106+7 5+2 111+2 78+4 103+4	9+2 4 4 9+1	7+1 5 3 10	2+2	5 1 2 1	1	1 1	
Derek Hood 5.11 12.8 17.12.58	Div. 4, 84, FAYC 76	Washington F F	WBA (A) Hull City York City	20+4 239+5	3 8+3	4 19+1	4	25			
Simon Mills* 5.8 11.4 16.8.62	EY	Sheffield	Sheffield Wednesday York City	118 35+1	2	6	2	2			
Alan Pearce 5.8 11.6 25.10.60		Middlesbrough	York City	47+1		7	0+1	9		1	
FORWARDS											
Dale Banton 5.10 10.5 15.5.61		Kensington F £50,000	West Ham United (A) Aldershot York City	2+3 105+1 62+3	1 6 3	5 7	1 6	47 22	7 1	4 1	1
Martin Butler 5.8½ 11.9 3.3.66		Hull	York City Aldershot (L)	18+14		4	4+1	3			3
Marco Gabbiadini 5.10 12.4 20.1.68		Nottingham	York City (A)	10+13	0+1		2	4			
Keith Walwyn 6.1 13.2 17.2.56	Div. 4, 84	Jamaica £4,000	Winterton Rovers Chesterfield York City	3 203	0+1 14	1+1 21	0+1 1	2 100	5	8	

ADDITIONAL CONTRACT PROFESSIONALS

APPRENTICES

NON-CONTRACT PLAYERS

Vivian Busby

BOOTHAM CRESCENT York

Capacity: 13,500

Record Attendance: 28,123 v Huddersfield Town, FA Cup Round 6, 5 Mar 1938

Smallest Home Attendance for a First Class Match: 1,981 v Northampton Town, Div 4, 5 May 1981

Record Receipts: £32,000 v Liverpool, FA Cup 5th Round, 15 Feb 1986

Season Tickets: Stand, Main: £126.00; Popular: £84 (£52.50 junior/OAP); Enclosure £73.50 (£42.00 junior/OAP); Ground £63 (£31.50 junior/OAP)

Hospitality Box Season Tickets: Negotiable

Cost of Stand Tickets: Main £6.00 (£4.00 juniors/OAP); Popular £4.00 (£2.50 juniors/OAP); Enclosure £3.50 (£2.50 juniors/OAP); Ground £3.00 (£1.50 juniors/OAP). All include programme with admission

Match and Ticket Information: On sale 14 days before each match (Main stand reduction for OAPs)

Car Parking: Ample parking in side streets

Nearest Railway Station: York (0904 642155)

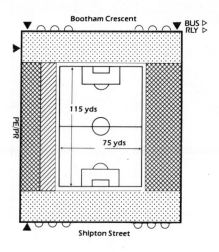

Bootham Crescent

BUS ▷
RLY ▷

PE/PR

115 yds

75 yds

Shipton Street

How to get to the ground

From North: Use A1 then A59 S.P. York. Cross railway bridge and in 1.9m turn left into Water End. At end turn right A19 (S.P. City Centre). In 0.4m turn left into Bootham Crescent for York City FC

From East: Use A1079 into York city centre and follow signs Thirsk A19 into Bootham. Cross railway bridge and then take 2nd turning on right into Bootham Crescent for York City FC

From South: Use A64 S.P. York into city centre and follow signs Thirsk A19 into Bootham. Cross railway bridge and then take 2nd turning on right into Bootham Crescent for York City FC

From West: Use B1224 S.P. York into city centre and follow signs Thirsk A19 into Bootham. Cross railway bridge and then take 2nd turning on right into Bootham Crescent for York City FC

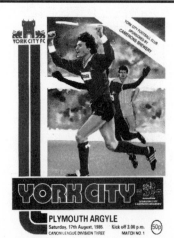

Price of 1986-7 Programme: 50p
Number of Pages: 20
(Included in gate money)

Local Newspaper: Yorkshire Evening Post

Local Radio Station: BBC Radio York

Player	European	Domestic	Representative
...uce Grobbelaar	European Cup 84	Div 1 82, 83, 84, 86. Milk Cup 82, 83, 84. FA Cup 86	
...n Beglin		Div 1 86. FA Cup 86	Eire (11)
...ry Gillespie		Div 1 86	Scotland U-21 (8)
...an Hansen (...cottish honour ...th Partick ...istle)	European Cup 78, 81, 84	Div 1, 79, 80, 82, 83, 84, 86. League Cup 81. Milk Cup 83, 84. Scottish Div 1 (1). FA Cup 86	Scotland (23) Scotland U-23 (3)
...ark Lawrenson	European Cup 84	Div 1-82, 83, 84, 86. Milk Cup 82, 83, 84. FA Cup 86	Eire (35)
...vin McDonald		Div 1 86. FA Cup 86	
...eve McMahon		Div 1 86. FAC 86	England 'B' (1) U-21 (6)
...n Molby		Div 1 86. FA Cup 86	Denmark
...aig Johnston	European Cup 84	Div 1-82, 83, 84, 86. Milk Cup 83, 84. FA Cup 86	England U-21 (2)

Player	European	Domestic	Representative
Steve Nicol	European Cup 84	Div 1-84, 86. FA Cup 86	Scotland (11) U-21 (14)
Ronnie Whelan	European Cup 84	Div 1-82, 83, 84, 86. Milk Cup 82, 83, 84. FA Cup 86	Eire (15), Eire U-21 (1)
John Wark (with Ipswich Town)	UEFA Cup 81	FA Cup 78. FA Youth Cup 75	Scotland (29) Scotland U-21 (9)
Kenny Dalglish (Scottish honours with Celtic)	European Cup 78, 81, 84. European Super Cup 77	Div 1-79, 80, 82, 83, 84, 86. League Cup 81. Milk Cup 82, 83, 84. Scottish Premier (1). Scottish Div 1 (5). Scottish Cup (4), Scottish League Cup (1). FA Cup 86	Scotland (100) Scotland U-23 (4), Scotland Youth (8)
Ian Rush	European Cup 84	Div 1-82, 83, 84, 86. League Cup 81. Milk Cup 82, 83, 84. FA Cup 86	Wales (28) Wales U-21 (2), Wales Schools
Paul Walsh (with Luton Town)		Div 1 86	England (5), England U-21 (7) England Youth

LIVERPOOL victorious Liverpool celebrate their completion of the double

Victorious Liverpool celebrate their completion of the double

LIVERPOOL'S CUP SEASON

P 21 W 15 D 5 L 1 F 49 A 15

HOME P 11 W 9 D 2 L 0 F 29 A 6   AWAY P 8 W 4 D 3 L 1 F 15 A 8   NEUTRAL P 2 W 2 D 0 L 0 F 5 A

Top Cup Goalscorer: Ian Rush 11   Most Cup Appearances: Bruce Grobbelar 21 (Max)

DATE	COMPE-TITION	VENUE	OPPONENTS	RESULT		HALF TIME	GOALSCORERS/GOAL TIMES	ATTEN-DANC
S 17	SC	H	Southampton	W	2-1	2-1	Molby 6, Dalglish 29	16,18
24	MC 2	H	Oldham Athletic	W	3-0	2-0	McMahon 25, 76, Rush 33	16,15
O 9	MC 2	A	Oldham Athletic	W	5-2	2-0	Whelan 5, 48, Wark 25, Rush 65, MacDonald 72	(7,71
22	SC	A	Southampton	D	1-1	0-0	Walsh 81	(10,50.
29	MC 3	H	Brighton & H.A.	W	4-0	1-0	Walsh 3 11, 71, 72, Dalglish 80	15,29
N 26	MC 4	H	Manchester United	W	2-1	0-1	Molby 55 (pen) 57	41,29
D 3	SC	H	Tottenham Hotspur	W	2-0	2-0	MacDonald 19, Walsh 34	14,85
J 4	FAC 3	H	Norwich City	W	5-0	2-0	MacDonald 23, Walsh 33, McMahon 73, Whelan 78, Wark 81	29,08
14	SC	A	Tottenham Hotspur	W	3-0	0-0	Rush 49, 61, Lawrenson 55	(10,07
21	MC 5	H	Ipswich Town	W	3-0	2-0	Walsh 17, Whelan 27, Rush 65	19,76
26	FAC 4	A	Chelsea	W	2-1	1-0	Rush 45, Lawrenson 47	(33,62
F 5	SC SF 1	A	Norwich City	D	1-1	0-0	Dalglish 79	(15,31
12	MC SF 1	A	Q.P.R.	L	0-1	0-1		(15,05
15	FAC 5	A	York City	D	1-1	0-0	Molby (pen) 64	(12,44
18	FAC 5 R	H	York City	W	3-1†	1-1	Wark 19, Molby 94, Dalglish 98	19,32
M 5	MC SF 2	H	Q.P.R.	D	2-2	1-0	McMahon 42, Johnston 69	23,86
11	FAC 6	H	Watford	D	0-0	0-0		36,77
17	FAC 6 R	A	Watford	W	2-1†	0-0	Molby (pen) 80, Rush 107	(28,097
A 5	FAC SF	N	Southampton	W	2-0†	0-0	Rush 100, 105	(44,605
M 6	SC SF 2	H	Norwich City	W	3-1	0-1	MacDonald 56, Molby (pen) 72, Johnston 78	26,69
10	FAC F	A	Everton	W	3-1	0-1	Rush 57, 84, Johnston 63	(98,00

Cup Goalscorers (49):

FA Cup (18):   Rush 6, Molby 3 (2 pen), Wark 2, Dalglish 1, Johnston 1, Lawrenson 1, MacDonald 1, McMahon 1, Walsh 1, Whelan 1
Milk Cup (19):   Walsh 4, McMahon 3, Rush 3, Whelan 3, Molby 2 (1 pen), Dalglish 1, Johnston 1, MacDonald 1, Wark 1
Super Cup (12):   Dalglish 2, MacDonald 2, Molby 2 (1 pen), Rush 2, Walsh 2, Johnston 1, Lawrenson 1   †After extra tir

EVERTON'S CUP SEASON

P 18 W 12 D 3 L 3 F 33 A 19

HOME P 8 W 7 D 0 L 1 F 14 A 6   AWAY P 8 W 4 D 3 L 1 F 16 A 9   NEUTRAL P 2 W 1 D 0 L 1 F 3 A

Top Cup Goalscorer: Gary Lineker 10   Most Cup Appearances: Van Den Hauwe 17 + 1

DATE	COMPE-TITION	VENUE	OPPONENTS	RESULT		HALF TIME	GOALSCORERS/GOAL TIMES	ATTEN-DANCE
S 18	SC	A	Manchester United	W	4-2	2-1	Sheedy 24, 53, Lineker 44, Sharp 79	(33,859
25	MC2/1	H	Bournemouth	W	3-2	2-2	Lineker 22, Marshall 35, Heffernan (og) 54	13,930
O 2	SC	H	Norwich City	W	1-0	0-0	Lineker 70	10,329
7	MC2/2	A	Bournemouth	W	2-0	1-0	Lineker 43, Richardson 64	(8,081
23	SC	A	Norwich City	L	0-1	0-0		(12,26
29	MC3	A	Shrewsbury Town	W	4-1	1-0	Sharp 22, Hughes (og) 47, Sheedy 55, Heath 89	(10,246
N 26	MC4	A	Chelsea	D	2-2	2-2	Sheedy 3, Bracewell 13	(27,544
D 4	SC	H	Manchester United	W	1-0	0-0	Stapleton (og) 84	20,542
10	MC4R	H	Chelsea	L	1-2	1-1	Lineker 8	26,376
J 5	FAC3	H	Exeter City	W	1-0	0-0	Stevens 80	22,726
25	FAC4	H	Blackburn Rovers	W	3-1	2-0	Van Den Hauwe 13, Lineker 39, 82	41,831
F 5	SC SF 1	A	Tottenham Hotspur	D	0-0	0-0		(7,548
M 4	FAC5	A	Tottenham Hotspur	W	2-1	0-0	Heath 51, Lineker 65	(23,338
8	FAC6	A	Luton Town	D	2-2	0-1	Donaghy (og) 65, Heath 77	(15,529
12	FAC6R	H	Luton Town	W	1-0	1-0	Lineker 16	44,264
19	SC SF 2	H	Tottenham Hotspur	W	3-1†	1-0	Heath 76, Mountfield 91, Sharp 112	12,008
A 5	FAC SF	N	Sheffield Wednesday	W	2-1†	0-0	Harper 48, Sharp 97	47,711
M 10	FAC Final	N	Liverpool	L	1-3	1-0	Lineker 28	98,000

Cup Goalscorers (33):

FA Cup (12):   Lineker 5, Heath 2, Harper 1, Opponent 1, Sharp 1, Stevens 1, Van Den Hauwe 1
Milk Cup (12):   Lineker 3, Opponent 2, Sheedy 2, Bracewell 1, Heath 1, Marshall 1, Richardson 1, Sharp 1
Super Cup (9):   Lineker 2, Sharp 2, Sheedy 2, Heath 1, Mountfield 1, Opponent 1   †After extra tim

Grobbelaar	Neal	Kennedy	Lawrenson	Whelan	Hansen	Dalglish	Nicol	Rush	Molby	Beglin	Walsh	Johnston	Lee	McMahon	MacDonald	Wark	Gillespie	Seagraves	Referees
1			4		6	7	2		10	3	9	5	8	11					M Scott
1	2		4	5	6			9		3	7	10	8	11*	12				K Walmsley
1	2		4	5	6*	7		9		3		8		11	12	10			D Allison
1	2		4	5	6		7		8*	3	9	10		11	12				R Lewis
1			4	5	6	7	2		10	3	9	8		11					K Barratt
1			4	5	6		2	9	10	3	7	8		11					D Shaw
1			4	5	6		2	9	10*	3	7	8				11	12		G Aplin
1			4	5	6		2	9	10		7*	8		11	3	12			D Hutchinson
1			4	5	6		2*	9	10		7		8	11*	3	13	12		J Martin
1			4	5	6		2	9	10	3	7	8				12	11*		J Deakin
1			4	5	6		2	9	10	3	7	8				11			Alan Robinson
1			4	5		9	2		10	3	7	8	6			11			J Moules
1			4	5	6			9	10	3		8	2			7		11	G Courtney
1			4		6	7		9	10	3		8	2			5		11	H Taylor
1			4	5	6	7		9	10	3		12	2			8*	11		H Taylor
1			4	5	6			9	10	3		8	2	11		7			D Hutchinson
1			4	5	6	7		9	10	3		12	2*	11		8			R Milford
1			4	5	6	7		9	10	3		8		11		2			R Milford
1				5	6	7	4	9	10	3		8		11*		12	2		A Saunders
1			6	5*			4		12	3	7	8	10	9	11		2		A Seville
1			2	5	6	7	4	9	10	3		8			11				Alan Robinson
8		7	7	8	6	4	8	8	7	2	6·2	3	4	2	2·2	5	1		FA Cup Appearances
7	2	7	7	7	2	3	6	5	7	4	7	3	5	0·2	2·1	2	1		Milk Cup Appearances
6	1	6	5	4	2	6	2	5·1	5	6	5	4	4	3·1	0·2	2·1			Super Cup Appearances
21	3		20	19	19	10	13	16	18·1	19	12	18·2	10	13	5·3	4·5	9·1	2	Total

Southall	Stevens	Van Den Hauwe	Ratcliffe	Mountfield	Reid	Steven	Lineker	Sharp	Bracewell	Sheedy	Heath	Harper	Bailey	Richardson	Wilkinson	Mimms	Pointon	Coyle	Billing	Marshall	Referees
1	2	3	4			7	8*	9	10	11	12	6								5	J Key
1	2	3	4			7	8	9	10	11		6								5	M Heath
1	2	3	4			7	8	9	10	11		6								5	J Hough
1	2	3	4			7	8	9	10	11			3	6							E Butler
1	2	3	4			7	8*	9*	10	11	6	5		12	13						T Ward
1	2	5	4			7	8	9	10	11	6	3									H Taylor
1	5	3	4			7	8	9	10	11†	6	2									D Hedges
1	5	3	4			7	8		10		6	2*		11	9		12				K Walmsley
1	5	3*	4			7	8	9	10		6	2		11						12	K Hackett
1	2	5	4				8	9			6	7		10	11		3				R Milford
1	2	5			6	7	8	9	10	11*		12		11	8		3	8	10	4	A Saunders
1		5	4*		6	7	8	9	10		12	2		11			3				J Martin
1	2	5			6	7	8	9	10		12	4		11			3*				K Hackett
1	2	5			6	7	8	9	10	11*	12	4		11			3				K Hackett
1		12		5				13		11	8	7		6	9*		3	10	2*	4	R Milford
	2	3	4	5	6	7*		9	10		8	12		11		1					B Hill
	2*	3	4	5	6	7	8	9	10	11	12					1					Alan Robinson
5	6	7	5	2	5	6	6	7	6	3	2·4	4·2		5	1	2	5				FA Cup Appearances
5	5	5	5			5	5	5	5	4	3	4	1	2					1·1		Milk Cup Appearances
6	5	5·1	4	1	1	5	4	3·1	4	4	3·1	5		3·1	3·1		2·1	2	2	4	Super Cup Appearances
16	16	17·1	14	3	6	16	15	15·1	15	11	8·5	13·2	1	10·1	4·1	2	7·1	2	2	5·1	Total

FINAL LEAGUE TABLES 1985-86

CANON LEAGUE – DIV 1

		HOME					AWAY				
	P	W	D	L	F	A	W	D	L	F	A	Pts
Liverpool	42	16	4	1	58	14	10	6	5	31	23	88
Everton	42	16	3	2	54	18	10	5	6	33	23	86
West Ham	42	17	2	2	48	16	9	4	8	26	24	84
Man Utd	42	12	5	4	35	12	10	5	6	35	24	76
Sheff Wed	42	13	6	2	36	23	8	4	9	27	31	73
Chelsea	42	12	4	5	32	27	8	7	6	25	29	71
Arsenal	42	13	5	3	29	15	7	4	10	20	32	69
Nottm Forest	42	11	5	5	38	25	8	6	7	31	28	68
Luton Town	42	12	6	3	37	15	6	6	9	24	39	66
Tottenham	42	12	2	7	47	25	7	6	8	27	27	65
Newcastle Utd	42	12	5	4	46	31	5	7	9	21	41	63
Watford	42	11	6	4	40	22	5	5	11	29	40	59
QPR	42	12	3	6	33	20	3	4	14	20	44	52
Southampton	42	10	6	5	32	18	2	4	15	19	44	46
Man City	42	7	7	7	25	26	4	5	12	18	31	45
Aston Villa	42	7	6	8	27	28	3	8	10	24	39	44
Coventry C	42	6	5	10	31	35	5	5	11	17	36	43
Oxford Utd	42	7	7	7	34	27	3	5	13	28	53	42
Leicester City	42	7	8	6	35	35	3	4	14	19	41	42
Ipswich Town	42	8	5	8	20	24	3	3	15	12	31	41
Birmingham C	42	5	2	14	13	25	3	3	15	17	48	29
West Brom	42	3	8	10	21	36	1	4	16	14	53	24

CANON LEAGUE – DIV 2

		HOME					AWAY				
	P	W	D	L	F	A	W	D	L	F	A	Pts
Norwich City	42	16	4	1	51	17	9	5	7	33	22	84
Charlton Ath	42	14	5	2	44	15	8	6	7	34	30	77
Wimbledon	42	13	6	2	38	16	8	7	6	20	21	76
Portsmouth	42	13	4	4	43	17	9	3	9	26	24	73
C Palace	42	12	3	6	29	22	7	6	8	28	30	66
Hull	42	11	7	3	39	19	6	6	9	26	36	64
Sheff Utd	42	10	7	4	36	24	7	4	10	28	39	62
Oldham Ath	42	13	4	4	40	28	4	5	12	22	33	60
Millwall	42	12	3	6	39	24	5	5	11	25	41	59
Stoke City	42	8	11	2	29	16	6	4	11	19	34	57
Brighton H A	42	10	5	6	42	30	6	3	12	22	34	56
Barnsley	42	9	6	6	29	26	5	8	8	18	24	56
Bradford City	42	14	1	6	36	24	2	5	14	15	39	54
Leeds Utd	42	9	7	5	30	22	6	1	14	28	50	53
Grimsby	42	11	4	6	35	24	3	6	12	23	38	52
Huddersfield	42	10	6	5	30	23	4	4	13	21	44	52
Shrewsbury T	42	11	5	5	29	20	3	4	14	23	44	51
Sunderland	42	10	5	6	33	29	3	6	12	14	32	50
Blackburn R	42	10	4	7	30	20	2	9	10	23	42	49
Carlisle Utd	42	10	2	9	30	28	3	5	13	17	43	46
Middlesbro	42	8	6	7	26	23	4	3	14	18	30	45
Fulham	42	8	3	10	29	32	2	3	16	16	37	36

CANON LEAGUE – DIV 3

		HOME					AWAY				
	P	W	D	L	F	A	W	D	L	F	A	Pts
Reading	46	16	3	4	39	22	13	4	6	28	29	94
Plymouth	46	17	3	3	56	20	9	6	8	32	33	87
Derby Co	46	13	7	3	45	20	10	8	5	35	21	84
Wigan Ath	46	17	4	2	54	17	6	10	7	28	31	83
Gillingham	46	14	5	4	48	17	8	8	7	33	37	79
Walsall	46	15	7	1	59	23	7	2	14	31	41	75
York City	46	16	4	3	49	17	4	7	12	28	41	71
Notts Co	46	12	6	5	42	26	7	8	8	29	34	71
Bristol City	46	14	5	4	43	19	4	9	10	26	41	68
Brentford	46	8	8	7	29	29	10	4	9	29	32	66
Doncaster R	46	7	10	6	20	21	9	6	8	25	31	64
Blackpool	46	11	6	6	38	19	6	6	11	28	36	63
Darlington	46	10	7	6	39	33	5	6	12	22	45	58
Rotherham Utd	46	13	5	5	44	18	2	7	14	17	41	57
Bournemouth	46	9	6	8	41	31	6	3	14	24	41	54
Bristol R	46	9	8	6	27	21	5	4	14	24	54	54
Chesterfield	46	10	6	7	41	30	3	8	12	20	34	53
Bolton W	46	10	4	9	35	30	5	4	14	19	38	53
Newport Co	46	7	8	8	35	33	4	10	9	17	32	51
Bury	46	11	7	5	46	26	1	6	16	17	41	49
Lincoln City	46	7	9	7	33	34	3	7	13	22	43	46
Cardiff City	46	7	5	11	22	29	5	4	14	31	54	45
Wolves	46	6	6	11	29	47	5	4	14	28	51	43
Swansea City	46	9	6	8	27	27	2	4	17	16	60	43

CANON LEAGUE – DIV 4

		HOME					AWAY				
	P	W	D	L	F	A	W	D	L	F	A	Pts
Swindon	46	20	2	1	52	19	12	4	7	30	24	102
Chester City	46	15	5	3	44	16	8	10	5	39	34	84
Mansfield T	46	13	8	2	43	17	10	4	9	31	30	81
Port Vale	46	13	9	1	42	11	8	7	8	25	26	79
Orient	46	11	6	6	39	21	9	6	8	40	43	72
Colchester	46	12	6	5	51	22	7	7	9	37	41	70
Hartlepool	46	15	6	2	41	20	5	4	14	27	47	70
Northampton	46	9	7	7	44	29	9	3	11	35	29	64
Southend Utd	46	13	4	6	43	27	5	6	12	26	40	64
Hereford Utd	46	15	6	2	55	30	3	4	16	19	43	64
Stockport Co	46	9	9	5	35	28	8	4	11	28	43	64
Crewe Alex	46	10	6	7	35	26	8	3	12	19	35	63
Wrexham	46	11	5	7	34	24	6	4	13	34	56	60
Burnley	46	11	3	9	35	30	5	8	10	25	35	59
Scunthorpe Utd	46	11	7	5	33	23	4	7	12	17	32	59
Aldershot	46	12	5	6	45	25	5	2	16	21	49	58
Peterborough	46	9	11	3	31	19	4	6	13	21	45	56
Rochdale	46	12	7	4	41	29	2	6	15	16	48	55
Tranmere R	46	9	1	13	46	41	6	8	9	28	32	54
Halifax Town	46	10	8	5	35	27	4	4	15	25	44	54
Exeter City	46	10	4	9	26	25	3	11	9	21	34	54
Cambridge C	46	12	2	9	45	38	3	7	13	20	42	54
Preston N E	46	7	4	12	32	41	4	6	13	22	48	43
Torquay Utd	46	8	5	10	29	32	1	5	17	14	56	37

CENTRAL LEAGUE (3 pts for win)

DIVISION 1

	P	W	D	L	F	A	Pts
Derby County	34	21	3	10	81	35	66
Manchester United	34	19	5	10	55	32	62
Liverpool	34	19	4	11	85	53	61
Nottingham Forest	34	17	5	12	76	54	56
Manchester City	34	16	8	10	58	40	56
Sheffield Wed	34	16	4	14	55	47	52
Leeds United	34	16	3	15	63	70	51
Hull City	34	15	4	15	52	53	49
Aston Villa	34	15	3	16	55	67	48
Blackburn Rovers	34	14	4	16	57	49	46
Leicester City	34	12	10	12	60	58	46
Newcastle United	34	13	7	14	52	61	46
Everton	34	12	6	16	36	44	42
Sheffield United	34	12	5	17	44	76	41
Barnsley	34	12	4	18	44	60	40
West Bromwich A	34	9	10	15	41	65	37
Huddersfield Town	34	8	11	15	51	68	35
Wigan Athletic	34	11	2	21	44	77	35

DIVISION 2

	P	W	D	L	F	A	Pts
Oldham Athletic	34	22	7	5	71	35	73
Sunderland	34	22	6	6	83	46	72
Coventry City	34	21	4	9	76	34	67
Middlesbrough	34	19	5	10	78	50	62
Blackpool	34	15	14	5	68	46	59
Notts County	34	18	3	13	82	58	57
Grimsby Town	34	18	2	14	58	59	56
York City	34	16	6	12	53	46	54
Bolton Wanderers	34	16	5	13	56	48	53
Bradford City	34	14	8	12	66	53	50
Scunthorpe United	34	11	8	15	49	63	41
Rotherham United	34	12	4	18	57	65	40
Wolverhampton W	34	12	2	20	53	77	38
Port Vale	34	8	11	15	39	57	35
Stoke City	34	9	5	20	51	85	32
Doncaster Rovers	34	7	10	17	45	71	31
Burnley	34	6	6	22	36	74	24
Preston North End	34	4	6	24	42	96	18

FOOTBALL COMBINATION
(2 pts for win)

	P	W	D	L	F	A	Pts
West Ham United	42	31	5	6	141	60	67
Arsenal	41	26	10	5	124	41	62
Norwich City	42	27	7	8	93	36	61
Chelsea	42	26	5	11	107	40	57
Watford	42	23	10	9	98	44	56
Tottenham Hotspur	42	23	7	12	105	65	53
Luton Town	42	23	7	12	74	49	53
Ipswich Town	42	21	8	13	87	58	50
Oxford United	42	21	7	14	104	62	49
Queens Park R	42	21	7	14	91	69	49
Millwall	42	22	3	17	75	72	47
Southampton	42	19	8	15	88	80	46
Charlton Athletic	42	18	4	20	76	83	40
Crystal Palace	42	13	10	19	67	104	36
Birmingham City	42	14	5	23	57	96	33
Bristol Rovers	42	12	6	24	64	110	30
Brighton & H A	42	9	9	24	40	93	27
Swindon Town	41	10	5	26	74	120	25
Portsmouth	42	9	8	25	45	73	24*
Fulham	42	8	5	29	51	102	21
Reading	42	8	4	30	46	133	20
Swansea City	42	6	2	34	37	154	14

(* Two points deducted for fielding ineligible player)
Arsenal v Swindon—not played as Swindon unable to field a team on
the scheduled date and, with the heavy fixture commitments of
Arsenal the match could not be re-arranged.

F.A. Charity Shield   16-8-86   Wembley Stadium
EVERTON 1 v LIVERPOOL 1
Liverpool defender Barry Venison holds off Everton
striker Graeme Sharp.

READER'S STATISTICAL FEATURES

In last year's Directory we asked readers to submit their own statistical features and we received some ver
enjoyable and very varied contributions. We are including a few of these which cover vastly differen
aspects of the game and we hope you find them enjoyable.

BRADFORD CITY'S "HOME" RECORD 1985/86

The cruel tragedy that marred Bradford City's Championship season 1984/85 meant that they had to
play all their "home" games in their first season back in the 2nd Division away from Valley Parade. This
being so their final league position of 13th was truly remarkable. A full breakdown of their results at the
three venues is as follows:

Leeds Road, Huddersfield

	P	W	D	L	F	A
Pre-season	1	1	0	0	3	1
Milk Cup	1	0	1	0	2	2
League	5	5	0	0	13	5

Elland Road, Leeds

	P	W	D	L	F	A
League	4	2	0	2	5	6
FA Cup	1	0	0	1	0	1

Odsal Stadium, Bradford

	P	W	D	L	F	A
Milk Cup	1	0	0	1	0	2
League	12	7	1	4	18	13

These results do not include away wins at Halifax Town, Huddersfield and Leeds United which enabled
them to win and retain the West Riding Senior Cup.

It can clearly be seen that their best results were obtained at Leeds Road, Huddersfield which most
resembled their own compact ground.

This season (1986/87) it is planned to play the first half of the season at Odsal Stadium and hopefully
returning to a new Valley Parade on Boxing Day.   **A M Biggins**

The theme of the second feature is 'Birthplace of players' and gives a list of towns or cities mentioned at
least twice on the players pages in 1986. The list shows up the fact that the total number of players listed
account for only some 30% leaving the rest of the registered players as either small town, country boys or
even overseas players.

London	74	Swansea	13	Coventry	6
Liverpool	60	Middlesbrough	12	Portsmouth	6
Birmingham	44	Bradford	11	Preston	5
Manchester	44	Oldham	10	Watford	5
Glasgow	38	Salford	10	Southampton	5
Sheffield	34	Leicester	10	Aberdeen	5
Newcastle	24	Luton	9	Derby	5
Nottingham	23	Edinburgh	9	Bolton	5
Dublin	19	Warrington	7	Northampton	4
Sunderland	18	Gateshead	7	Dundee	4
Leeds	17	Huddersfield	7	St Helens	
Bristol	17	Walsall	7	Blackpool	
Hull	16	York	6	South Shields	
Stoke	15	Birkenhead	6	Warley	2
Belfast	14	Ipswich	6	Brighton	
Wolverhampton	13	Cardiff	6	Oxford	

Alan Patton

THE ALL TIME FOOTBALL HONOURS LIST

The aim of this table is to put the present sucesses of teams in the League into an overall perspective
with successful teams in the past. The use of the gold, silver and bronze system, as the results of the
Olympics are presented, seemed to be the best way to do this. The gold obviously represents a team
winning one of the four trophies indicated. Silver represents a second placed team in the league
column or a losing finalist in the three cup competitions, whilst the bronze represents a third placing in

e league column or a losing semi-finalist in the three cup competitions. The list includes all the resent League teams that have won a major honour in English football since the four competitions egan. The final totals column is a combination of all the other columns and gives rise to the final acings.

Guy Oliver

	LEAGUE			FA CUP			L/GE CUP			EUROPE			TOTAL		
	G	S	B	G	S	B	G	S	B	G	S	B	G	S	B
LIVERPOOL	16	7	2	3	4	8	4	2	2	6	2	1	29	15	13
ASTON VILLA	7	8	2	7	2	8	3	2	3	1	0	0	18	12	13
MANCHESTER UTD	7	8	3	6	4	7	0	1	3	1	0	6	14	13	19
ARSENAL	8	3	4	5	6	5	0	2	2	1	1	0	14	12	11
TOTTENHAM H	2	4	7	7	0	4	2	1	3	3	1	3	14	6	17
EVERTON	8	7	7	4	6	11	0	2	0	1	0	0	13	15	18
NEWCASTLE UTD	4	0	2	6	5	2	0	1	0	1	0	0	11	6	4
WOLVERHAMPTON W	3	5	6	4	4	5	2	0	1	0	1	1	9	10	13
MANCHESTER CITY	2	3	3	4	4	2	2	1	2	1	0	1	9	8	8
SUNDERLAND	6	5	8	2	1	7	0	1	1	0	0	0	8	7	16
BLACKBURN R	2	0	3	6	2	8	0	0	1	0	0	0	8	2	12
WEST BROMWICH	1	2	1	5	5	9	1	2	1	0	0	0	7	9	11
SHEFFIELD WED	4	1	6	3	2	10	0	0	0	0	0	0	7	3	16
NOTT'M FOREST	1	2	1	2	0	7	2	1	0	2	0	1	7	3	9
LEEDS UTD	2	5	1	1	3	3	1	0	2	2	3	2	6	11	8
SHEFFIELD UTD	1	2	0	4	2	4	0	0	0	0	0	0	5	4	4
PRESTON N E	2	6	2	2	5	3	0	0	0	0	0	0	4	11	5
HUDDERSFIELD T	3	3	3	1	4	2	0	0	1	0	0	0	4	7	6
WEST HAM UTD	0	0	1	3	1	1	0	2	3	1	1	1	4	4	6
CHELSEA	1	0	3	1	2	7	1	1	2	1	0	1	4	3	13

PROGRAMME SURVEYS

ootball Club programmes have improved by the season until we have now reached the time when most ubs actually produce very enjoyable 'match day' magazines.

In this feature we record three separate programme surveys which should be of interest to all collectors.

THE FOOTBALL LEAGUE EXECUTIVE STAFFS ASSOCIATION
PROGRAMME OF THE YEAR AWARDS
(Organised by F.L.E.S.A. and sponsored by Match Weekly)

DIVISION 1	DIVISION 2	DIVISION 3	DIVISION 4
1) EVERTON	1) BRIGHTON	1) DERBY CO.	1) SCUNTHORPE
2) ASTON VILLA	2) SHEFF UTD	2) BRENTFORD	2) COLCHESTER
3) WEST HAM	3) SUNDERLAND	3) NOTTS CO $=$	4) PETERBORO
		DONCASTER	

TOP TWENTY

1. EVERTON	Pts	178	8. SHEFF WED	98	15. SHEFF UTD	47
2. ASTON VILLA		151	9. DERBY CO	89	16. SUNDERLAND	45
3. WEST HAM		127	10. SOUTHAMPTON	87	17. PORTSMOUTH	39
4. ARSENAL		123	11. TOTTENHAM H	73	18. NORWICH C	31
5. WATFORD		122	12. BRIGHTON H A	71	19. C PALACE	30
6. MAN CITY		115	13. LEICESTER C	64	20. BARNSLEY	23
7. CHELSEA		114	14. WEST BROM	53		

DIVISION 1	DIVISION 2	DIVISION 3	DIVISION 4
1) SOTON	1) SUNDERLAND	1) NOTTS CO. $=$	1) SCUNTHORPE
2) EVERTON	2) BARNSLEY	WALSALL	2) TRANMERE
3) ASTON VILLA	3) LEEDS	3) DONCASTER	4) WREXHAM $=$
			COLCHESTER

WIRRAL PROGRAMME CLUB 15th PROGRAMME OF THE YEAR SURVEY

Marks were awarded on the following sections: Cover design and details 10; Size (length by breadth) 10, Team layout and position within the programme 10; Results 10; League Tables 10; Pictures 20; Price 10; Printing and paper quality 20; Contents (included were visitor's details, club news, reserve and junior news, away match details, letters, supporter's news, match officials, historical articles, meet-the-player type article, competitions etc) 80; and Value for money 20. In the latter the ratio of adverts to articles, the club's division, size of crowds etc is taken into account.

DIVISION 1	DIVISION 2	DIVISION 3	DIVISION 4
1) EVERTON	1) SUNDERLAND	1) DERBY CO.	1) SWINDON
2) WATFORD	2) BRIGHTON	2) DONCASTER	2) COLCHESTER
3) SOTON	3) HUDDERS'FLD	3) BRISTOL C	4) SCUNTHORPE

NATIONAL TOP TWENTY: 158 to 129 marks. 1. Everton 158; 2. Sunderland 155; 3. Watford, Brighton 149; 5. Southampton, WBA 144; 7. Arsenal, Tottenham H 142; 9. Manchester Utd, Huddersfield, Derby Co. 139; 12. Birmingham C, Leicester C, Oxford Utd, Sheffield Utd 138; 16. Aston Villa, Chelsea, West Ham Utd, Barnsley 137; 20. Sheffield Wed; C Palace 136.

PROGRAMME MONTHLY MAGAZINE 'PROGRAMME OF THE YEAR AWARDS'

Over the past few seasons, "Progamme Monthly" has steered clear of statistical analyses of English League clubs' programmes, preferring at the at the end of the season to award Merit Awards based on value judgements. This season, however, it was decided to adopt a condensed version of the popular and authoritative Scottish awards system, to depend more upon mathematics and less upon opinion. The 92 League club programmes were judged over 12 categories, totalling 100 marks, as follows:
(1) Cover — 5 marks for design, change of cover every week and change from last season.   (2) Size — 10 marks, for number and size of pages in relation to price.   (3) Advertising content — 10 marks, advert pages as a percentage of total pages, with a lower percentage gaining higher marks.   (4) Statistics — 5 marks inclusion of statistical coverage of the home team. (5) Visitors' Coverage — 5 marks, for number of pages allotted, photographic coverage and narrative.   (6) Colour — 10 marks, one for each full colour page.   (7. Reading Material — 10 marks, pages of script as a percentage of the number of pages (the higher the percentage, the higher the mark).   (8) Improvement from Previous Season — 5 marks.   (9) Worth — 10 marks, measured by non-advert pages per pence charged (the higher the ratio, the more marks awarded).   (10) Price Increase from Previous Season — 5 marks, in relation to any improvement shown.   (11) Design and Presentation — 10 marks, for paper quality, placement of team selections, type styles and design techniques used.   (12) Standard and Mixture of Articles and Features — 15 marks, to take into account the quality and balance of articles, such as historical features, club and player news, and general non-club football articles.

FINAL MARKS 1985/86

	1	2	3	4	5	6	7	8	9	10	11	12	To
1. Southampton	4	6	7	5	5	10	6	4	10	5	8	11	8?
2. Everton	3	6	9	5	5	10	6	4	10	5	9	8	8C
3. Sunderland	3	5	10	5	5	8	6	5	10	4	8	8	7?
4. Aston Villa	4	4	9	5	4	9	5	3	8	5	8	12	76
5. Oxford	4	6	5	5	4	10	4	5	8	5	9	10	75
6. West Brom	4	3	9	5	4	6	6	4	8	3	9	13	7?
7. Tottenham H	5	4	6	5	5	10	3	4	7	3	10	11	7?
8. Barnsley	4	5	6	5	5	7	5	4	9	3	9	10	7?
9. Watford	4	5	6	5	4	10	5	3	6	5	9	9	7?
10. Man Utd	4	6	6	5	5	10	4	3	8	2	10	7	7C
=. Arsenal	4	4	10	5	5	5	6	2	8	5	8	8	7C
=. Newcastle Utd	4	5	6	5	5	6	9	4	7	3	8	8	7C
13. Leeds Utd	5	6	5	3	4	10	2	3	8	5	10	7	6?
14. Sheffield Utd	4	4	5	3	4	10	5	4	6	5	9	7	6?
=. Ipswich Town	5	4	7	5	4	5	3	3	7	5	9	9	6?
16. Chelsea	3	3	8	5	4	6	5	3	7	5	9	7	6?
=. Man City	3	3	8	5	3	4	9	3	7	5	7	8	6?
=. Birmingham	4	3	6	5	5	4	5	5	7	4	8	9	6?
=. Middlesbrough	3	9	4	4	3	0	8	5	10	5	7	7	6?
=. Portsmouth	4	3	8	5	4	1	8	3	7	5	9	8	6?

SCORERS OF 30 LEAGUE GOALS IN A SEASON

This very interesting feature by F R Roberts was first published in The Association of Football Statisticians Report No 49 in July.

1. **Middlesbrough 15.** B Clough 43, 40, 39, 37, 34; G Camsell 59, 33, 31, 31; G Elliott 32, 31; J McClelland 32; M Fenton 34, A Peacock 31; A Wilson 31.

2. **Grimsby Town 14.** E Glover 42, 34, 31, 30; J Carmichael 37, 34; J Robson 31, 30; T Briggs 35; E Coleman 35; R Crowbie 35; R Rafferty 34; R Hunt 33; W Cairns 32.

3. **Leicester City 14.** A Rowley 44, 39, 38, 30; A Chandler 34, 34, 33, 32; E Hine 32, 31; W Gardiner 34; J Bowers 33; F Shinton 31; J Duncan 30.

4. **Blackpool 11.** J Hampson 45, 40, 31, 31; H Bedford 34, 32; R Finan 34; J Mudie 32; R Charnley 30; S Mortensen 30; W Tremelling 30.

5. **Everton 10.** W Dean 60, 44, 39, 32; B Freeman 38; T Lawton 35; R Parker 35; J Parker 31; R Latchford 30; A Young 30.

6. **Sunderland 10.** D Halliday 43, 38, 36, 36; J Campbell 32, 31; R Gurney 30, 30; C Buchan 30; H Carter 31.

7. **Liverpool 8.** R Hunt 41, 31, 30; G Hodgson 36, 30; I Rush 32; S Raybould 31; W Liddell 30.

8. **Sheffield United 8.** J Dunne 41, 36, 33; K Edwards 35, 33; H Johnson 33, 33; E Dodds 34.

9. **Sheffield Wednesday 8.** J Trotter 37, 37; J Allen 34, 33; D Dooley 46; J Ball 33; R Shiner 33; D McLean 30.

10. **Stockport County 8.** J Connor 31, 30, 30; F Newton 36, 34; A Lythgoe 46; J Smith 38; H Burgess 30.

11. **Tottenham Hotspur 8.** J Greaves 37, 35; R Smith 36, 32; G Hunt 32, 32; E Harper 36; H Bliss 31.

12. **Arsenal 7.** E Drake 42; J Lambert 38; J Brain 34, 30; C Bastin 33; R Cooke 33; D Jack 31.

13. **Blackburn Rovers 7.** T Briggs 33, 32, 31, 31; E Harper 43, 35; M McEvoy 32.

14. **Luton Town 7.** G Turner 33, 32, 30; J Payne 55; A Rennie 43; J O'Rourke 32; J Ball 30.

15. **Queens Park Rangers 7.** G Goddard 37, 36; N Bedford 36, 33; T Cheetham 35; L Allen 32; R Marsh 30.

16. **Wolverhampton Wanderers 7.** W Hartill 34, 33, 30; D Westcott 37, 32; Phillipson 36, 31.

17. **Bolton Wanderers 6.** H Blackmore 30, 30; J Smith 38; N Lofthouse 32; Milsom 31; R Westwood 30.

18. **A F C Bournemouth 6.** E MacDougall 42, 35; C Eyre 31, 30; D McGibbon 30; S Newsham 30.

19. **Carlisle United 6.** J McConnell 43, 37; H McIlmoyle 39; A Ackerman 35; S Hunt 32; J Slinger 31.

20. **Derby County 6.** J Bowers 37, 35, 35; R Straw 37; A Bentley 31; H Bedford 30.

21. **Doncaster Rovers 6.** T Keetley 40, 36, 34; C Jordan 41; A Jeffrey 36; C Booth 32.

22. **Manchester City 6.** T Johnston 38; F Lee 33, T Browell 31; F Roberts 31; P Doherty 30; D Kevan 30.

23. **Southampton 6.** D Reeves 39, 31; R Davies 37, G O'Brien 32; C Wayman 32; M Chivers 30.

24. **Tranmere Rovers 6.** R Bell 35, 33; J Kennedy 34; R Moore 34; J Clayton 31; E Dixon 31.

25. **Walsall 6.** G Alsop 40, 40; M Lane 36; A Richards 36; A Buckley 34; C Taylor 32.

26. **West Bromwich Albion 6.** J Cookson 38, 32; W G Richardson 39; F Morris 37; D Kevan 33; R Allen 32.

27. **Brentford 5.** J Holliday 36; W Lane 33; S Phillips 32; E Towers 32; D McCulloch 31.

28. **Crystal Palace 5.** P Simpson 46, 36; A Dawes 38; P Cherrett 32; J Byrne 30.

29. **Ipswich Town 5.** E Phillips 42, 30; R Crawford 40, 33; T Parker 30.

30. **Northampton Town 5.** E Bowen 36; C Holton 36; A Worn 34; A Dawes 32; J English 30.

31. **Reading 5.** R Blackman 39, 35; T Senior 36; M McPhee 31; A Wheeler 31.

32. **Wrexham 5.** T Bamford 44, 34, 31, 31; A Mays 32.

33. **Accrington Stanley 4.** G Stewart 35, 31. G Hudson 36; R Mortimer 32.

34. **Aston Villa 4.** T Waring 49; S Brown 38; L Capewell 32; W Houghton 30.

35. **Burnley 4.** G Beel 35, 30; B Freeman 32, 31.

36. **Chelsea 4.** J Greaves 41, 31; R Tambling 35; R Whittington 30.

37. **Chester City 4.** R Yates 36; J Mantle 34; F Wrightson 32; T Jennings 31.

38. **Chesterfield 4.** J Cookson 44, 42; W Sowden 32; J Bulloch 30.

39. **Darlington 4.** D Brown 39; M Wellock 34; W Tulip 32; J Best 30.

40. **Fulham 4.** B Jezzard 38, 34; F Newton 41; H Hammond 32.

41. **Huddersfield Town 4.** G Brown 35; S Taylor 35; D Magnall 33; J Glazzard 30.

42. **Hull City 4.** J Smith 32, 30; W McNaughton 41; W Bradbury 30.

43. **Lincoln City 4.** A Hall 42; J Campbell 36; A Graver 36; J Hutchinson 32.

44. **Mansfield Town 4.** E Harston 55; K Wagstaff 34; H Johnson 31; R Chapman 30.

45. **Plymouth Argyle 4.** J Cock 32, 31; F Richardson 31; T Tynan 31.

47. **Rotherham United 4.** W Ardron 38; J Shaw 37; R Burke 32; A Bramham 30.

48. **Watford 4.** C Holton 42, 32; F McPherson 33; F Pagnam 30.

49. **Bradford City 3.** K McDonald 43, 31; K Hector 44.

50. **Bristol City 3.** D Clark 36; T Walsh 34; L Townsend 31.

51. **Colchester United 3.** R Hunt 37; M King 31; K McCurley 30.

52. **Leeds United 3.** J Charles 42, 38; T Jennings 35.

53. **Manchester United 3.** D Viollet 32; D Law 30; J Rowley 30.

54. **Millwall 3.** R Parker 37; F Burridge 36; J Landells 3.

55. **Newcastle United 3.** H Gallacher 36; G Robledo 33; C Wayman 30.

56. **Preston North End 3.** E Harper 37; T Thompson 34; A Dawson 31.

57. **Shrewsbury 3.** A Rowley 38, 32; A Wood 35

58. **Swindon Town 3.** D Morris 47, 38, 35.

59. **Torquay United 3.** R Collins 40, 30; R Stubbs 31.

60. **York City 3.** A Bottom 31, 30; W Fenton 31.

61. **Barnsley 2.** C McCormack 33; A Blight 31.

62. **Barrow 2.** J Shankly 39; W Miller 30.

63. **Brighton & H A 2.** P Ward 32; H Vallance 30.

64. **Bury 2.** C Madden 35; N Bullock 31

65. **Coventry City 2.** C Bourton 49, 40.

66. **Crewe Alexandra 2.** T Harkin 34; F Lord 31.

67. **Gillingham 2.** F Morgan 31; B Yeo 31.

68. **Halifax Town 2.** A Valentine 34; W Chambers 30.

69. **Hereford United 2.** R McNeil 35, 31.

70. **New Brighton 2.** J Wilcox 35; H Williams 33.

71. **Notts County 2.** T Keetley 39; T Lawton 31.

72. **Peterborough United 2.** T Bly 52, 30.

73. **Portsmouth 2.** W Haines 40; R Saunders 33.

74. **Port Vale 2.** W Kirkham 38, 35.

75. **Rochdale 2.** A Whitehurst 44, 32.

76. **Southend United 2.** S McCrory 31; J Shankly 31.

77. **Stoke City 2.** F Steele 33; C Wilson 31.

78. **West Ham United 2.** V Watson 42, 34.

79. **Birmingham City (Small Heath) 1.** W Abbott 33.

80. **Bradford City 1.** D Layne 34.

81. **Bristol Rovers 1.** G Bradford 32.

82. **Cardiff City 1.** S Richards 31.

83. **Charlton Athletic 1.** R Allen 32.

84. **Exeter City 1.** F Whitlow 34.

85. **Newport County 1.** T Martin 34.

86. **Norwich City 1.** R Hunt 31.

87. **Nottingham Forest 1.** W Ardron 36.

88. **Orient 1.** T Johnston 35.

89. **Oxford United 1.** J Aldridge 30.

90. **Scunthorpe United 1.** B Thomas 31.

91. **Southport 1.** A Watterston 31.

92. **Swansea City 1.** C Pearce 35.

BEST & WORST RECORDS FOR EACH POSITION

These two league tables show the best and worst record for each position in the 1st Division. The Statistics were supplied by Frank Grande who also sent us the players non-league clubs and FA Cup appearances for the competition proper.

BEST RECORD FOR EACH POSITION

			P	W	D	L	F	A	Pts	difference
1.	LIVERPOOL	(78/79)	42	30	8	4	85	16	68	+ 69
2.	LEEDS UTD	(70/71)	42	27	10	5	72	30	64	+ 42
3.	W.B.A.	(78/79)	42	24	11	7	72	35	59	+ 37
4.	MAN CITY	(71/72)	42	23	11	8	77	45	57	+ 32
5.	EVERTON	(67/68)	42	23	6	13	67	40	52	+ 27
6.	TOTTENHAM H	(71/72)	42	19	13	10	63	42	51	+ 21
7.	NOTTS FOREST	(80/81)	42	19	12	11	62	44	50	+ 18
8.	NOTTS FOREST	(85/86)	42	19	11	12	69	53	49	+ 16
9.	LUTON TOWN	(85/86)	42	18	12	12	61	44	48	+ 17
10.	TOTTENHAM H	(85/86)	42	19	8	15	74	52	46	+ 22
11.	NEWCASTLE	(85/86)	42	17	12	13	67	72	46	− 5
12.	WATFORD	(85/86)	42	16	11	15	69	62	43	+ 7
13.	WEST HAM UTD	(24/25)	42	15	12	15	62	60	42	+ 2
14.	DERBY CO	(46/47)	42	18	5	19	73	79	41	− 6
15.	WOLVES	(35/36)	42	15	10	17	77	76	40	+ 1
	CHARLTON ATH	(54/55)	42	15	10	17	76	75	40	+ 1
16.	TOTTENHAM H	(54/55)	42	16	8	18	72	73	40	− 1
17.	W.B.A.	(54/55)	42	16	8	18	76	96	40	− 20
18.	BOLTON W	(54/55)	42	13	13	16	62	69	39	− 7
19.	BURNLEY	(27/28)	41	16	7	19	82	98	39	− 16
20.	PORTSMOUTH	(27/28)	42	16	7	19	66	90	39	− 24
21.	TOTTENHAM H	(27/28)	42	15	8	19	74	86	38	− 12
22.	MIDDLESBROUGH	(27/28)	42	11	15	16	81	88	37	− 7

The above records are taken from 1919/20, when the League Div 1 was extended to 22 teams.

All three point wins have been converted to two point wins, to bring them in line with previous seasons. Where two clubs were level on points GOAL DIFFERENCE was used to separate them, even though the club may have achieved their position on goal average.

Where two clubs have the same points and goal difference, they have both been included.

POOREST RECORD FOR EACH POSITION

			P	W	D	L	F	A	Pts	difference
1.	SHEFFIELD WED	(28/29)	42	21	10	11	86	62	52	+ 24
	CHELSEA	(54/55)	42	20	12	10	81	57	52	+ 24
2.	DERBY CO	(35/36)	42	18	12	12	61	52	48	+ 9
3.	MAN CITY	(29/30)	42	19	9	14	91	81	47	+ 10
4.	DERBY CO	(27/28)	42	17	10	15	96	83	44	+ 13
5.	BURY	(27/28)	42	20	4	18	80	80	44	
6.	CARDIFF C	(27/28)	42	17	10	15	70	80	44	− 10
7.	WEST HAM UTD	(29/30)	42	19	5	18	86	79	43	+ 7
8.	SUNDERLAND	(48/49)	42	13	17	12	49	58	43	− 9
9.	CHARLTON ATH	(48/49)	42	15	12	15	63	67	42	− 4
10.	NEWCASTLE UTD	(67/68)	42	13	15	14	54	67	41	− 13
11.	NOTTS FOREST	(67/68)	42	14	11	17	52	64	39	− 12
12.	CHELSEA	(60/61)	42	15	7	20	98	100	37	− 2
13.	MAN CITY	(60/61)	42	13	11	18	79	90	37	− 11
14.	SOUTHAMPTON	(85/86)	42	12	10	20	51	62	34	− 11
15.	MAN CITY	(85/86)	42	11	12	19	43	57	34	− 14
16.	ASTON VILLA	(85/86)	42	10	14	18	51	67	34	− 16
17.	COVENTRY CITY	(85/86)	42	11	10	21	48	71	32	− 23
18.	IPSWICH TOWN	(69/70)	42	10	11	21	40	63	31	− 23
19.	SOUTHAMPTON	(69/70)	42	6	17	19	46	67	29	− 21
20.	Q.P.R.	(78/79)	42	6	13	23	45	73	25	− 28
21.	BIRMINGHAM C	(85/86)	42	8	5	29	30	73	21	− 43
22.	STOKE CITY	(84/85)	42	3	8	31	24	91	14	− 66

FOOTBALL LEAGUE FIXTURES 1986/87

DIVISION 1

	ARSENAL	ASTON VILLA	CHARLTON	CHELSEA	COVENTRY	EVERTON	LEICESTER	LIVERPOOL	LUTON	MAN CITY	MAN UTD	NEWCASTLE	NORWICH	NOTT'M FOREST	OXFORD	QPR	SHEFF WED	SOUTHAMPTON	TOTTENHAM	WATFORD	WEST HAM	WIMBLEDON
ARSENAL	.	02.05	11.04	25.10	17.01	28.03	20.04	07.02	20.12	22.11	23.08	14.03	09.05	21.02	20.09	06.12	02.09	27.12	06.09	11.10	08.11	01.01
ASTON VILLA	29.11	.	26.12	15.11	28.03	18.04	01.11	21.02	03.09	04.04	13.12	25.10	20.09	03.01	06.09	07.02	04.05	11.10	23.08	14.03	25.04	17.01
CHARLTON	01.11	20.04	.	28.03	20.09	11.10	18.10	20.12	02.05	28.12	07.02	06.12	06.09	17.01	21.02	09.05	23.08	22.11	01.01	04.04	07.03	02.09
CHELSEA	07.03	27.12	04.10	.	02.09	04.04	02.05	09.05	06.09	18.10	21.02	22.11	23.08	20.09	17.01	01.01	07.02	20.04	20.12	01.11	21.03	06.12
COVENTRY	26.08	04.10	28.02	14.02	.	30.08	06.12	05.01	01.01	21.12	11.04	13.09	22.11	08.11	22.03	20.04	07.03	09.05	27.12	27.09	24.01	19.10
EVERTON	04.10	01.01	21.03	08.11	07.02	.	28.12	22.11	09.05	02.05	20.09	20.04	06.12	23.08	02.09	06.09	17.01	14.03	25.10	11.04	03.01	28.03
LEICESTER	26.12	11.04	14.03	29.11	04.05	15.11	.	03.09	23.08	28.03	06.09	08.11	17.01	11.10	14.12	21.02	03.01	25.10	20.09	25.04	18.04	07.02
LIVERPOOL	30.08	27.09	13.09	13.12	29.11	25.04	14.02	.	07.03	25.08	26.12	24.01	01.11	18.04	18.10	04.04	15.11	28.02	11.10	04.05	03.01	28.03
LUTON	13.09	14.02	29.11	03.01	18.04	13.12	24.01	25.10	.	27.09	14.03	30.08	11.10	15.11	05.05	01.11	25.04	26.08	28.03	26.12	28.02	04.04
MAN CITY	25.04	08.11	15.11	14.03	06.09	29.11	04.10	17.01	21.02	.	25.10	21.03	03.09	04.05	03.01	20.09	26.12	11.04	07.02	18.04	13.12	23.08
MAN UTD	24.01	09.05	30.08	27.09	01.11	28.02	20.12	20.04	18.10	07.03	.	01.01	21.12	28.03	04.04	22.11	11.10	13.09	06.12	14.02	25.08	02.05
NEWCASTLE	18.10	07.03	04.05	25.04	03.01	26.12	04.04	23.08	07.02	11.10	18.04	.	21.02	13.12	01.11	03.09	06.09	28.03	17.01	15.11	29.11	20.09
NORWICH	13.12	28.02	03.01	24.01	25.04	04.05	25.08	11.04	21.03	14.02	15.11	27.09	.	26.12	29.11	04.10	18.04	30.08	08.11	13.09	18.10	07.03
NOTT'M FOREST	27.09	13.09	27.08	27.02	04.04	24.01	22.03	01.01	28.12	06.12	04.10	09.05	20.04	.	07.03	18.10	01.11	20.12	02.05	30.08	14.02	22.11
OXFORD	28.02	20.12	27.09	25.08	11.10	14.02	09.05	14.03	06.12	13.09	08.11	11.04	02.05	25.10	.	27.12	28.03	01.01	22.11	24.01	30.08	20.04
QPR	04.05	30.08	13.12	18.04	26.12	03.01	27.09	08.11	11.04	28.02	25.04	14.02	28.03	14.03	15.11	.	29.11	24.01	25.10	26.08	13.09	11.10
SHEFF WED	14.02	06.12	24.01	30.08	25.10	25.08	13.09	27.12	22.11	20.04	21.03	21.12	01.01	11.04	04.10	02.05	.	08.11	14.03	28.02	27.09	09.05
SOUTHAMPTON	15.11	21.03	25.04	26.12	13.12	18.10	07.03	20.09	17.01	01.11	03.01	04.10	07.02	06.09	18.04	23.08	04.04	.	02.09	29.11	04.05	21.02
TOTTENHAM	03.01	24.01	18.04	13.09	15.11	27.09	28.02	21.03	04.10	30.08	04.05	25.08	04.04	29.11	25.04	07.03	18.10	14.02	.	13.12	26.12	01.11
WATFORD	21.03	18.10	08.11	11.04	21.02	07.03	22.11	06.12	21.04	01.01	16.09	27.12	20.12	07.02	23.08	17.01	20.09	02.05	09.05	.	04.10	06.09
WEST HAM	04.04	22.11	25.10	11.10	23.08	01.11	01.01	06.09	20.09	09.05	17.01	02.05	14.03	02.09	07.02	20.12	21.02	06.12	20.04	28.03	.	27.12
WIMBLEDON	18.04	26.08	15.02	05.05	15.03	13.09	30.08	04.10	08.11	24.01	29.11	28.02	25.10	25.04	26.12	21.03	13.12	27.09	11.04	03.01	15.11	.

DIVISION 2

	BARNSLEY	BIRMINGHAM	BLACKBURN	BRADFORD	BRIGHTON	C PALACE	DERBY	GRIMSBY	HUDDERSFIELD	HULL	IPSWICH	LEEDS	MILLWALL	OLDHAM	PLYMOUTH	PORTSMOUTH	READING	SHEFF UTD	SHREWSBURY	STOKE	SUNDERLAND	WEST BROM
BARNSLEY	.	28.03	01.11	11.10	14.03	23.08	15.11	21.02	04.05	18.04	25.04	02.09	07.02	03.01	20.09	06.09	04.04	25.10	17.01	26.12	13.12	29.11
BIRMINGHAM	04.10	.	06.12	25.08	14.02	18.10	30.08	02.05	13.09	28.02	27.09	22.11	27.12	08.11	01.01	21.03	20.04	20.12	09.05	24.01	07.03	11.04
BLACKBURN	11.04	05.05	.	25.10	25.04	20.09	17.04	17.01	26.12	15.11	29.11	23.08	21.02	13.12	30.09	03.01	28.03	08.11	07.02	14.03	06.09	11.10
BRADFORD	21.03	03.01	07.03	.	04.05	03.09	26.12	07.02	15.11	25.04	18.10	20.09	17.01	06.09	23.08	04.04	01.11	04.10	21.02	29.11	18.04	12.12
BRIGHTON	18.10	03.09	22.11	06.12	.	20.04	07.03	06.09	03.04	01.11	21.03	09.05	01.01	21.02	17.01	23.08	27.12	02.05	21.12	04.10	07.02	20.09
C PALACE	24.01	14.03	28.02	14.02	26.12	.	03.01	08.11	09.09	13.12	11.03	21.03	04.10	25.04	11.04	04.05	27.09	13.09	25.10	30.08	29.11	18.04
DERBY	27.12	07.02	01.01	20.04	25.10	06.09	.	20.12	28.03	11.10	08.11	02.05	20.09	23.08	09.05	17.01	06.12	22.11	14.03	11.04	01.10	21.02
GRIMSBY	27.09	29.11	14.10	30.08	03.01	04.04	13.09	.	18.04	05.05	24.01	25.10	01.11	26.12	11.10	25.04	14.02	28.02	28.03	13.12	15.11	14.03
HUDDERSFIELD	06.12	17.01	20.04	27.12	08.11	20.12	04.10	01.01	.	25.10	11.04	06.09	09.05	20.09	22.11	21.02	02.05	14.03	14.10	21.03	23.08	07.02
HULL	01.01	20.09	27.12	22.11	11.04	09.05	21.03	06.12	07.03	.	04.10	22.02	20.02	07.02	06.09	09.09	18.10	20.04	02.05	08.11	17.01	23.08
IPSWICH	22.11	21.02	02.05	14.03	11.10	17.12	04.04	23.08	01.11	28.03	.	01.01	21.04	02.09	19.12	07.02	09.05	06.09	25.10	20.09	11.04	23.08
LEEDS	14.02	25.04	24.01	28.02	13.12	11.10	29.11	07.03	03.01	27.09	18.04	.	04.04	15.11	28.03	18.10	13.09	30.08	01.11	25.08	26.12	04.05
MILLWALL	30.08	15.11	27.09	13.09	18.04	28.03	28.02	11.04	13.12	26.08	26.12	08.11	.	14.03	25.10	29.11	24.01	14.02	11.10	03.01	04.05	25.04
OLDHAM	25.08	04.04	09.05	21.12	27.09	22.11	24.01	20.04	28.02	30.08	14.02	27.12	17.10	.	02.05	01.11	06.03	01.01	06.12	13.09	11.10	28.03
PLYMOUTH	28.02	18.04	14.02	24.01	13.09	01.11	13.12	21.03	25.04	03.01	09.09	04.10	07.03	29.11	.	26.12	30.08	27.09	04.04	04.05	18.10	15.11
PORTSMOUTH	20.12	11.10	13.09	08.11	21.04	06.12	25.08	22.11	27.09	14.02	30.08	14.03	02.05	11.04	20.04	.	01.01	09.05	29.12	28.02	28.03	25.10
READING	08.11	26.12	04.10	11.04	15.11	21.02	04.05	01.10	29.11	14.03	13.12	17.01	23.08	25.10	07.02	18.04	.	21.03	20.09	25.04	03.01	06.09
SHEFF UTD	07.03	06.09	04.04	28.03	29.11	17.01	25.04	20.09	18.10	26.12	04.05	07.02	02.09	18.04	21.02	13.12	11.10	.	23.08	15.11	01.11	03.01
SHREWSBURY	13.09	13.12	30.08	27.09	16.09	07.03	18.10	04.10	14.02	29.11	03.01	11.04	21.03	05.05	08.11	15.11	28.02	24.01	.	18.04	25.04	26.12
STOKE	20.04	23.08	18.10	02.05	28.03	07.02	01.01	09.05	11.10	04.04	07.03	21.12	06.09	17.01	06.12	20.09	22.11	27.12	01.01	.	21.02	02.09
SUNDERLAND	09.05	25.10	21.12	01.01	30.08	02.05	14.02	27.12	24.01	13.09	28.02	20.04	06.12	21.03	14.03	04.10	21.10	11.04	22.11	27.09	.	08.11
WEST BROM	02.05	01.11	21.03	09.05	28.02	01.01	27.09	18.10	30.08	24.01	13.09	06.12	22.11	04.10	27.12	07.03	20.12	25.08	20.04	14.02	04.04	.

DIVISION 3

	BLACKPOOL	BOLTON	BOURNEMOUTH	BRENTFORD	BRISTOL C	BRISTOL R	BURY	CARLISLE	CHESTER	CHESTERFIELD	DARLINGTON	DONCASTER	FULHAM	GILLINGHAM	MANSFIELD	MIDDLESBRO'	NEWPORT	NOTTS CO	PORT VALE	ROTHERHAM	SWINDON	WALSALL	WIGAN	YORK
BLACKPOOL	.	17.03	25.04	03.01	01.11	21.02	13.12	06.09	04.05	23.08	18.04	31.01	17.01	11.04	07.03	21.03	29.11	18.10	30.09	08.11	07.02	04.10	20.09	26.12
BOLTON	21.10	.	31.01	03.03	25.04	17.01	26.12	18.04	25.10	29.09	06.09	04.05	07.02	13.12	03.01	11.04	08.11	04.10	20.09	14.03	23.08	21.03	21.02	29.11
BOURNEMOUTH	20.12	13.09	.	10.01	27.09	20.04	14.03	08.11	16.09	22.11	28.03	21.10	27.12	11.10	14.02	03.03	30.08	24.01	02.05	09.05	01.01	11.04	25.10	28.02
BRENTFORD	22.11	01.11	23.08	.	17.03	27.12	30.09	07.02	04.04	01.01	20.09	17.01	31.01	21.02	21.03	20.12	04.10	04.11	06.09	02.05	20.04	07.03	09.05	18.10
BRISTOL C	03.03	20.12	21.02	21.10	.	01.01	23.08	20.09	28.03	31.01	30.09	07.02	04.04	17.01	04.11	25.10	14.03	02.05	20.04	22.11	09.05	27.12	06.09	11.10
BRISTOL R	27.09	30.08	26.12	04.05	18.04	.	08.11	07.03	03.01	04.10	01.11	29.11	18.03	25.04	13.09	17.09	13.12	28.02	18.10	14.02	11.04	10.01	21.03	24.01
BURY	09.05	20.04	18.10	28.02	10.01	04.04	.	17.03	30.08	02.05	04.11	11.10	07.03	28.03	16.09	24.01	27.09	27.12	01.11	13.09	22.11	20.12	01.01	14.02
CARLISLE	24.01	01.01	04.04	16.09	14.02	25.10	21.10	.	10.01	09.05	11.10	28.03	22.11	14.03	27.09	20.04	28.02	20.12	04.11	27.12	02.05	13.09	03.03	13.08
CHESTER	27.12	07.03	07.02	08.11	04.10	22.11	17.01	23.08	.	20.12	21.02	01.10	06.09	20.09	18.10	02.05	21.03	01.01	09.05	11.04	31.01	01.11	20.04	18.03
CHESTERFIELD	10.01	28.02	03.01	18.04	13.09	28.03	29.11	13.12	25.04	.	04.05	26.12	04.11	03.03	24.01	04.02	25.10	27.09	11.10	16.09	14.03	30.08	21.10	04.04
DARLINGTON	01.01	24.01	04.10	14.02	28.02	03.03	11.04	21.03	27.09	27.12	.	14.03	02.05	21.10	30.08	08.11	16.09	13.09	20.12	20.04	25.10	09.05	22.11	10.01
DONCASTER	13.09	27.12	17.03	30.08	16.09	02.05	21.03	04.10	28.02	20.04	18.10	.	01.11	08.11	10.01	09.05	14.02	07.03	22.11	01.01	20.12	24.01	11.04	27.09
FULHAM	30.08	16.09	04.05	13.09	08.11	21.10	25.10	03.01	24.01	11.04	29.11	03.03	.	26.12	13.12	27.09	18.04	14.02	28.03	10.01	11.10	28.02	14.03	25.04
GILLINGHAM	04.11	09.05	21.03	27.09	30.08	20.12	04.10	18.10	14.02	01.11	17.03	04.04	20.04	.	28.02	13.09	10.01	22.11	07.03	24.01	27.12	01.01	02.05	16.09
MANSFIELD	25.10	22.11	20.09	11.10	11.04	31.01	07.02	21.02	14.03	06.09	17.01	23.08	09.05	30.09	.	27.12	21.10	20.04	01.01	03.03	08.11	11.10	20.12	28.03
MIDDLESBRO'	11.10	04.11	01.11	25.04	07.03	07.02	06.09	26.12	29.11	20.09	04.04	13.12	21.02	31.01	04.05	.	03.01	17.03	23.08	28.03	29.09	18.10	17.01	18.04
NEWPORT	02.05	04.04	17.01	28.03	18.10	09.05	21.02	29.09	11.10	07.03	07.02	20.09	01.01	23.08	17.03	22.11	.	01.11	27.12	20.12	06.09	20.04	31.01	04.11
NOTTS CO	14.03	28.03	06.09	11.04	29.11	30.09	04.05	25.04	18.04	21.02	31.01	25.10	20.09	03.01	26.12	21.10	03.03	.	07.02	11.10	17.01	08.11	23.08	13.12
PORT VALE	28.02	14.02	29.11	24.01	26.12	14.03	03.03	11.04	13.12	21.03	25.04	03.01	04.10	25.10	18.04	10.01	04.05	16.09	.	30.08	21.10	27.09	08.11	13.09
ROTHERHAM	04.04	18.10	13.12	29.11	03.01	20.09	31.01	04.05	04.11	07.02	26.12	18.04	23.08	06.09	01.11	04.10	25.04	21.03	17.01	.	21.02	17.03	29.09	07.03
SWINDON	16.09	10.01	18.04	26.12	13.12	04.11	01.01	29.11	13.09	18.10	07.03	25.04	04.05	04.04	28.02	24.01	30.08	17.03	27.09		.	14.02	04.10	01.11
WALSALL	28.03	11.10	04.11	25.10	04.05	23.08	25.04	31.01	03.03	17.01	13.12	06.09	29.09	18.04	29.11	14.03	26.12	04.04	21.02	21.10	20.09	.	07.02	03.01
WIGAN	14.02	27.09	07.03	13.12	24.01	11.10	18.04	01.11	26.12	17.03	03.01	04.11	18.10	29.11	25.04	30.08	13.09	10.01	04.04	28.02	28.03	16.09	.	04.05
YORK	20.04	02.05	30.09	14.03	21.03	06.09	20.09	17.01	21.10	08.11	23.08	21.02	20.12	07.02	04.10	01.01	11.04	09.05	31.01	25.10	03.03	22.11	27.12	.

DIVISION 4

	ALDERSHOT	BURNLEY	CAMBRIDGE	CARDIFF	COLCHESTER	CREWE	EXETER	HALIFAX	HARTLEPOOL	HEREFORD	LINCOLN	NORTHAMPTON	ORIENT	PETERBOROUGH	PRESTON	ROCHDALE	SCUNTHORPE	SOUTHEND	STOCKPORT	SWANSEA	TORQUAY	TRANMERE	WOLVES	WREXHAM
ALDERSHOT	.	11.10	21.10	09.05	27.12	20.12	02.05	10.01	26.10	03.03	13.09	28.03	20.04	24.01	14.03	22.11	16.09	01.01	09.11	28.02	14.02	27.09	30.08	11.0
BURNLEY	21.03	.	04.04	20.12	04.11	27.12	07.03	27.09	13.09	24.01	22.11	17.03	09.05	01.11	04.10	01.01	30.08	02.05	18.10	16.09	10.01	28.02	14.02	20.0
CAMBRIDGE	17.03	08.11	.	01.05	21.04	31.10	13.09	30.08	24.01	09.05	27.09	17.10	01.01	22.11	21.03	20.12	28.02	28.12	03.10	11.04	16.09	14.02	10.01	07.0
CARDIFF	13.12	25.04	29.11	.	14.03	04.10	14.02	03.03	10.01	27.09	16.09	04.05	21.10	28.02	11.04	30.08	25.10	08.11	03.01	26.12	18.04	13.09	24.01	21.0
COLCHESTER	04.05	10.04	26.12	17.10	.	17.03	29.08	28.11	16.09	27.02	10.01	11.04	27.09	13.12	13.02	03.01	20.03	06.03	24.04	12.09	23.01	31.10	03.1	
CREWE	25.04	04.05	03.03	28.03	21.10	.	16.09	25.10	28.02	30.08	11.04	28.11	10.10	14.02	26.12	12.01	24.01	13.03	17.04	27.09	13.12	03.01	13.09	08.1
EXETER	29.11	25.10	31.01	20.09	17.01	07.02	.	11.04	22.10	14.03	11.10	03.01	23.08	08.11	04.03	28.03	25.04	01.10	06.09	18.04	26.12	13.12	04.05	21.0
HALIFAX	23.08	21.02	17.01	31.10	01.05	07.03	04.11	.	20.04	19.12	01.01	30.09	21.11	09.05	07.02	27.12	03.04	05.09	19.09	04.10	21.03	17.10	17.03	31.0
HARTLEPOOL	07.03	31.01	06.09	23.08	06.02	01.10	18.03	26.12	.	10.10	29.03	01.11	20.02	18.10	04.05	04.04	17.04	17.01	28.11	03.01	04.11	24.04	13.12	21.0
HEREFORD	01.11	06.09	13.12	21.02	01.10	01.11	07.02	18.04	26.12	.	08.11	07.02	20.09	04.10	31.01	13.09	11.01	07.04	14.01	04.05	03.01	18.04	26.12	23.0
LINCOLN	31.01	03.01	22.02	07.02	23.08	04.11	21.03	18.04	05.10	04.04	.	26.04	30.09	08.03	06.09	18.10	04.05	20.09	26.12	13.12	17.03	01.11	29.11	17.0
NORTHAMPTON	04.10	22.10	14.03	27.12	01.01	29.04	22.11	28.02	04.03	25.10	21.12	.	11.04	14.09	08.11	24.01	01.01	20.04	21.03	14.02	31.08	17.09	27.09	13.1
ORIENT	26.12	13.12	18.04	17.03	03.04	21.03	10.01	03.01	27.09	14.02	28.02	04.11	.	30.08	25.04	16.09	13.09	04.10	31.10	24.01	04.05	29.11	07.03	18.1
PETERBOROUGH	06.09	04.03	04.01	01.10	21.01	20.09	04.04	13.12	14.03	28.03	26.10	01.02	17.01	.	29.11	11.10	26.12	23.08	04.05	22.10	25.04	05.11	18.04	07.0
PRESTON	18.10	28.03	11.10	04.11	09.05	20.04	01.11	16.09	27.12	13.09	24.01	03.04	20.12	02.05	.	07.03	13.12	17.03	30.08	27.09	10.01	28.02	02.01	
ROCHDALE	03.01	18.04	25.04	17.01	20.09	23.08	04.10	04.05	08.11	21.10	14.03	06.09	07.02	21.03	25.10	.	13.12	21.02	31.01	03.03	29.11	26.12	11.04	24.0
SCUNTHORPE	07.02	16.01	30.09	07.03	21.11	07.09	19.12	09.11	01.01	01.05	27.12	23.08	31.01	20.04	19.09	09.05	.	11.04	21.02	21.03	17.10	17.03	05.10	01.
SOUTHEND	18.04	28.11	04.05	03.04	10.10	18.10	27.02	23.01	29.08	16.09	14.02	26.12	27.03	10.01	03.01	26.09	04.11	.	13.12	12.09	31.10	06.03	24.04	17.0
STOCKPORT	05.04	13.03	27.03	22.11	24.10	01.01	23.01	14.02	01.05	03.11	20.04	11.10	02.03	27.12	20.10	12.09	26.09	08.05	.	09.01	27.02	29.08	15.09	19.
SWANSEA	30.09	06.02	04.11	20.04	20.12	21.02	01.01	28.03	22.11	27.12	09.05	20.09	06.09	17.03	16.01	01.11	11.10	31.01	23.08	.	06.03	04.04	18.10	02.0
TORQUAY	20.09	23.08	07.02	01.01	31.01	09.05	20.04	11.10	11.04	21.11	21.10	07.12	14.02	21.02	20.12	14.03	03.03	39.09	25.10		.	28.03	08.11	06.0
TRANMERE	21.02	30.09	20.09	30.01	05.09	22.11	08.05	13.03	19.12	01.01	03.03	06.02	01.05	11.04	23.08	20.04	21.10	24.10	16.01	08.11	03.10	.	21.03	17.
WOLVES	17.01	20.09	23.08	06.09	03.03	31.01	27.12	21.10	09.05	20.04	02.05	21.02	25.10	01.01	30.09	04.11	28.03	20.12	07.02	14.03	04.04	11.10	.	22.
WREXHAM	04.11	26.12	25.10	11.10	28.03	04.04	27.09	12.09	14.02	10.01	30.08	09.05	14.03	14.10	18.04	28.02	03.03	21.10	25.04	29.11	24.01	04.05	03.01	.